A GUIDE TO REVIEWING

HISTORY OF THE WORLD

HISTORY OF THE WORLD enables students to unlock the past so they can better understand the present. The textbook's lively prose and clear organization help students make the connections that transform facts into an exciting, comprehensive story.

Critical Thinking Connections

* **Primary Source** features give students practice in reading historical sources. (p. 138)
* **Section Reviews** ask students to think critically about important ideas. (p. 21)
* **Chapter Reviews** allow students to apply critical thinking skills to a variety of activities. (p. 468)
* **Cause and Effect** charts challenge students to think about history as a tapestry of interconnected events. (p. 604)
* **Skill Review** provides students with skills required for reading and thinking critically about history. (p. 866)

Geography Connections

* **Geography Review** and **Geographic Themes** give students the means to apply geography skills to the study of history. (pp. GR1 and GR11)
* **Maps** and **Map Skill Practice** exercises establish the setting of historical periods and events. (p. 578)
* **Geography Connection** features focus on the close connection between geography and history. (p. 190)

Social and Cultural Connections

* **Linking Past and Present** features reveal to students how historical events directly affect the modern world. (p. 232)
* **Meanwhile** features give new perspectives on historical events by tying them to other events from the same time period. (p. 218)
* Special features—**Daily Life** (p. 220), **The Arts** (p. 292), **Biography** (p. 397), and **Historic Places** (p. 762)—spark students' interest by making strong connections between history and specific societies, cultures, people, and places.

Plus

* Vivid **timelines** and **timetables** firmly ground students in chronology of historical periods. (pp. 550, 752, 773, 860)
* **World History Checklists** ask students to self-check their knowledge of key people, places, and terms in each unit. (p. 409)
* **Portfolio of World Art Masterpieces** presents a collection of fine art through the ages, with explanatory captions. (pp. 937–984)

For a fuller description of the program, see the introductory pages of this Teacher's Edition, beginning on page Tvi.

Teacher's Annotated Edition

HISTORY OF THE WORLD

Perry
Scholl
Davis
Harris
Von Laue

Houghton Mifflin Company • BOSTON

Atlanta • Dallas • Geneva, Illinois • Palo Alto • Princeton • Toronto

Printed in the U.S.A.   123456789-VH-96 95 94 93 92

Teacher's Annotated Edition ISBN: 0-395-63219-6

HISTORY OF THE WORLD

Contents: Teacher's Edition

(Note: See pages v–xix for a complete *Table of Contents*
for the student edition of **HISTORY OF THE WORLD**.)

Previewing HISTORY OF THE WORLD

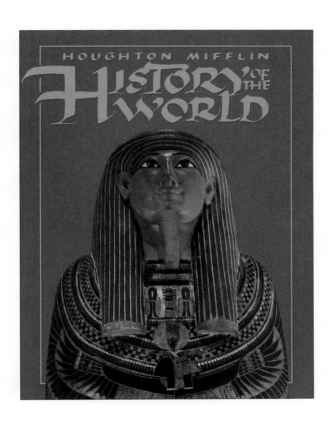

The following overview of **HISTORY OF THE WORLD** (1) highlights important features of the textbook—organization, geography, critical thinking, and important connections with people, places, events, and ideas; (2) points out the features of the Teacher's Annotated Edition and their value to teachers; (3) suggests alternative ways of structuring a year-long course based on the textbook; and (4) describes other materials in the program that provide teachers with valuable support.

Please turn to the back of the book to preview the Portfolio of World Art Masterpieces—captioned illustrations of over 50 artworks ranging through world history from ancient times to the twentieth century and representing masterpieces of both Western and non-Western cultures. These illustrations are also available as a set of overhead transparencies entitled *World Art Transparencies*.

Organized for successful learning

Establishes the setting, provides a purpose for reading, and offers a logically structured text to aid comprehension.

1 **Unit timelines** set the stage with highlighted key events.

2 **Chapter openers** offer motivating introduction and picture, locator map, date span, and chapter outline.

3 Sections set goals with **Focus Questions** and list **Terms to Know.**

4 **Headings** guide students through the text.

5 **Vocabulary** printed in red and defined in context.

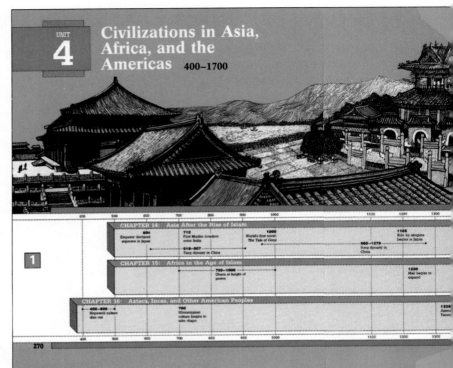

UNIT
4
Civilizations in Asia, Africa, and the Americas 400–1700

1

CHAPTER 14: Asia After the Rise of Islam

CHAPTER 15: Africa in the Age of Islam

CHAPTER 16: Aztecs, Incas, and Other American Peoples

270

2

CHAPTER
35
Europe Before and After the Cold War 1945–Present

See chapter timeline, p. 731.

Before You Read This Chapter

Suppose you have a set of blank world maps. Your job is to color the two or three most powerful countries at certain times in history. Think back over what you have read. What countries were world powers in the 1700's and 1800's? One was certainly Great Britain. By the late 1800's, Germany was powerful as well. As you read this chapter, notice what has happened to Europe's power. After 1945, what two countries were the world's leading powers? What effects did their rivalry have? What countries will be world leaders in years to come?

The Geographic Setting

The Chapter Outline

1. Cold War Tensions
2. Western Europe
3. The Soviet Bloc and Its Collapse

A war-blasted church in Berlin, Germany, was left standing as a reminder of World War II. A new, memorial church stands alongside the old building.

710

1 Cold War Tensions

Focus Questions

3

■ Why did the wartime alliance between the West and the Soviet Union collapse? *(pages 711–715)*
■ What were the main issues in Soviet-American relations during the 1940's and 1950's? *(pages 715–718)*

Terms to Know

cold war   nonaligned
bloc   NATO
Truman Doctrine   Warsaw Pact
containment   deterrence
Marshall Plan   Cuban Missile Crisis

Allied cooperation had made it possible to defeat the Axis countries. Hoping to build a lasting peace, Allied leaders planned to go on working together after the war. Yet relations between the Soviet Union and the Western Allies soon turned sour, and a new era of world tensions began.

4

The United Nations

At their wartime meeting at Yalta (page 703), the leaders of the United States, Britain, and the Soviet Union had agreed to create the United Nations. In April 1945, delegates from 50 countries gathered in San Francisco. They drew up and signed the Charter of the United Nations. According to the Charter, the UN's main purpose was to "save succeeding generations from war." The UN would also promote national self-determination and respect for individual human rights, and it would

help nations work together to solve their problems.

By the fall of 1945, the Charter had been approved by a majority of the members. The UN soon established its headquarters in New York City.

The Charter set up six main bodies within the UN. The most important are the General Assembly and the Security Council. Every UN member nation has one vote in the General Assembly. The Assembly has the power to discuss any matter within the scope of the UN Charter and to suggest solutions. Also, the Assembly chooses the people or nations that serve in other bodies of the UN, and it votes on bringing in new members.

The Security Council deals with international conflicts. To stop aggressive acts by any one country, the Security Council may bar trade with that country or even send troops to keep the peace.

The victorious Allies of World War II—the United States, France, Britain, China, and the Soviet Union—are permanent members of the Security Council. Ten other members are elected by the General Assembly for two-year terms. Security Council actions must be approved by all permanent members. Each permanent member has veto power to block actions that it opposes.

The Division of Europe

The new superpowers. When World War II ended, the center of world power was no longer Western Europe. The United States and the Soviet Union had become the world's two strongest nations. In spite of their alliance against Hitler, relations between the two governments had been cool during the war. In the years afterward, the relationship worsened. The atmosphere of hostility between the superpowers in the postwar period is known as the cold war

711

5

changed the solid rounded arch of the Romans to a delicate "horseshoe" arch held up by narrow columns. Domed roofs in the Byzantine style gave an airy, open feeling to building interiors. Mosaics of light and dark stones or glazed tiles formed graceful patterns. There were no statues or paintings of religious figures in mosques, because Muslim tradition discouraged the representation of living things. Passages from the Koran were written in decorative Arabic script on both the inside and outside walls.

Muslim artisans developed great skill. Weavers made beautiful Persian carpets to decorate the floors and walls of palaces and tents. Metalworkers in Syria and Spain produced such fine swords that "Damascus blades" and "Toledo steel" were admired the world over. Artisans in Cordova became famous for gold, silver, and leatherwork.

Persian artists excelled in delicate miniature paintings. Scenes showing historical figures, lovers, hunters, or warriors often were used as book illustrations or painted on pottery. Some details in these miniatures were so small that they had to be painted with a single hair instead of a brush.

Section Review

6

1. **Define:** mosque, minaret.
2. How did the status of women change under Islamic law?
3. What were some specific Muslim accomplishments in mathematics and the sciences?
4. Why did educated Muslims in other countries learn Arabic?
5. **Critical thinking:** How did Islam's tolerance of other religions contribute to the richness of Islamic culture?

Chapter 10   Summary and Timeline

7

1. The religion of Islam was founded by Mohammed in Arabia in the seventh century. An empire based on Islam spread the new faith through the Middle East, Africa, and Asia. Less than a century after its creation, the Muslim empire had grown to cover lands from Spain to India. In time, the empire was weakened by invasions of Turks and Christians. The Mongols' takeover of the city of Baghdad in 1258 completed the fall of the Muslim empire.

2. Muslim society was based on the Koran. Muslim culture reflected the influences of other peoples, especially the Greeks. Muslim achievements in science, medicine, and philosophy were remarkably advanced.

570
Mohammed born

622
Mohammed leads Hegira

661
Islam splits

661–750
Umayyads rule Muslim Empire

750–1258
Abbasids rule Muslim Empire

1258
Mongols storm Baghdad

550   650   750   850   950   1050   1150   1250

20?

1900   1500

1368–1644
Ming dynasty in China

1520–1566
Suleiman I rules Ottoman Empire

1590
Songhai Empire collapses

1438–1532
Inca Empire expands

1600   1900

---

6 **Section Reviews** check for knowledge of key terms and important information.

7 **Chapter summary and timeline** provide aids for summarizing chapter learning.

8 **Chapter Reviews** check understanding of vocabulary and information and call for application of higher-order thinking.

9 **Surveys** for all units allow flexibility and extra review.

CHAPTER 26 REVIEW

8

Vocabulary Review

Use the following terms to complete the sentences below: *Franco-Prussian War, kaiser, Pan-Slavism, realpolitik, Red Shirts, Risorgimento, tariff.*

1. The ___?___ led by Giuseppe Garibaldi, freed Sicily and Naples in 1860.
2. Russia supported ___?___, the unity of all Slavic peoples.
3. A tax on imported goods is called a ___?___.
4. Napoleon III was taken prisoner during ___?___.
5. ___?___, or resurgence, was a movement for Italian unity.
6. ...hy's emperor was known as the ___?___.
7. ...on Bismarck practiced ___?___, a tough-minded approach to Prus...itics.

2. By 1913 the ___?___ states of Greece, Serbia, Albania, Bulgaria, and Rumania had become independent.
3. Bismarck, as the leader of ___?___, took charge of the drive to unify Germany.

Recalling the Facts

1. How did Mazzini and Cavour differ in their approaches to unifying Italy?
2. Why did Napoleon III sign a truce with Austria and break his promise to Cavour?
3. What event marked the completion of Italian unification?
4. How did the Zollverein encourage German unity?
5. What did Bismarck believe was the only way to unite Germany? Why did Prussia win the Seven Weeks' War?
6. Who held real power in Germany's Second Reich?
7. How did Western influence encourage the growth of nationalism in Eastern Europe?
8. What problem did Serbia present for the leaders of the Dual Monarchy?
9. What were the causes of the Crimean War? What was its outcome?
10. Why was Alexander II of Russia known as the czar-liberator?
11. How did repression in Russia worsen under Alexander III?

...to Identify

...e following people and tell why ...important.
...s Joseph
...s I
...Emmanuel II
...m I
...m II

...to Know

...ollowing place names to complete ...ces below and in the next column:
...russia, Sardinia.
...ngdom of ___?___, led by Camillo ...vour, played a leading role in the ...ent for Italian unification.

Critical Thinking Skills

1. **Recognizing points of view.** All people have points of view on certain subjects. A good historian (and a good student) will be able to recognize when someone's point of

---

S U R V E Y

THE HERITAGE OF THE ANCIENT WORLD
Prehistory–A.D. 950

9

Survey Outline

UNIT 1: The Rise of Civilization
CHAPTER 1: The Birth of Civilization
CHAPTER 2: The Ancient Middle East
CHAPTER 3: Ancient India and China

UNIT 2: Classical Civilizations
CHAPTER 4: The Ancient Greeks
CHAPTER 5: The Roman Republic and Empire

CHAPTER 6: The Legacy of Rome
CHAPTER 7: Great Empires in India and China
CHAPTER 8: Ancient Africa and America

UNIT 1: The Rise of Civilization (Prehistory–450 B.C.)

Chapter 1:
The Birth of Civilization

Some of the most impressive achievements in history took place before people kept written records. This span of time is called prehistory. Our knowledge of prehistory comes from unwritten evidence, such as fossils and artifacts, that scientists have studied.

The Old Stone Age. Most of the objects remaining from the prehistoric period are stone tools and weapons. For this reason, archeologists have named the period the Stone Age. The earliest and longest part of this period, which began more than two million years ago, is called the Old Stone Age or Paleolithic Age.

Old Stone Age people were nomads who moved from place to place hunting wild animals, catching fish, and gathering food from plants that grew wild. They made a variety of tools and weapons—spearpoints, hand axes, choppers, and scrapers. Eventually Old Stone Age people learned to control fire. They developed spoken language and were then able to pass knowledge from one generation to the next. Archeologists have found evidence that some Stone Age peoples held religious beliefs. Some created works of art.

The New Stone Age. The later stage of prehistory began about 10,000 years ago, after the last Ice Age had ended. Because people of this time shaped their stone tools more carefully, the period is called the New Stone Age or Neolithic Age.

A number of significant advances made in this period had far-reaching effects on the way people lived. In the Middle East, Mexico, and other parts of the world, people learned to plant food crops and to domesticate wild animals. Farming people began to build permanent settlements near their crops.

166

Tvii

Emphasizes geography

Interweaves geography with accounts of historical developments. Students learn place names and locations, build map skills, and learn how geographic factors play a part in history.

1 **Geography Review** (GR1–GR10) covers basic terms, concepts, and skills. **Geographic Themes** (GR11–GR14) builds understanding of importance of geography in history.

2 **World locator** on each chapter opener page identifies the area to be studied.

3 **Maps**—over 100—show where and how historical developments took place. Each text map is captioned with questions to guide student understanding.

4 **Regional locators** orient students as they use text maps.

5 **Map Skill Practice** exercises give students practice in map skills, ranging from comprehension to interpretation.

6 **Geography Connection** features help students relate geographic learning and historical developments.

7 **Atlas maps** enable students to compare geographic areas throughout history.

Promotes critical thinking

Emphasizes comprehension through critical thinking—for *all* students.

1 **Primary Source** features ask students to read critically.

2 **Section Reviews** conclude with critical thinking questions.

3 **Chapter Review** activities call for higher-level comprehension, analysis, application, synthesis, evaluation.

4 **Skill Review** provides instruction in critical thinking.

1

PRIMARY SOURCE

The English Bill of Rights

In 1689 Parliament drew up and presented to William and Mary the English Bill of Rights, "an act declaring the rights and liberties" of their subjects, that is, the English people. Adapted b[...] of the rights listed in this d[...] that they aim at preven[...] from abusing their power. **99**

1. The suspending o[...] execution of laws by reg[...] without consent of Parli[...] legal.

4. Levying money [ta[...] the use of the Crown w[...] of Parliament is illegal.

5. It is the right of th[...] petition the king, and a[...] prosecutions for such p[...] are illegal.

6. The raising or kee[...] standing army within th[...] in time of peace, unles[...] consent of Parliament, i[...] law.

7. Subjects who are [...] may have arms for their[...] allowed by law. . . .

9. Freedom of speech[...] bates or proceedings in[...] ought not to be question[...] court or place out of Pa[...]

1. How does the Bill of R[...] monarch's power to r[...] tax subjects?
2. How does the Bill of [...] freedom of speech and p[...] to petition the king?
3. **Critical thinking:** Why[...] were William and Mary[...] a document that limite[...] as monarchs?

400

The Glorious Revolution

James II became king in 1685. He lacked his brother's charm and his policies angered many people. The English made allowances, however, because they thought that James's Protestant daughter Mary would succeed

---

American bankers and manufacturers realized that they would probably lose their money if the Allies lost the war.

American entry into war. Early in 1917, a threatening incident provoked Americans further. In a secret telegram in code, a German diplomat named Arthur Zimmermann tried to make an alliance with Mexico. He promised that if Mexico helped Germany win the war, Germany would help Mexico regain Texas and other parts of the American Southwest. The British broke the German code and reported the message to the United States. Although Mexico remained neutral and did not join Germany, the "Zimmermann telegram" enraged Americans.

In April 1917 the United States declared war on Germany. The American aim, President Wilson said, was to "make the world safe for democracy." Germany now tried to end the war quickly, before large numbers of American troops could be trained for combat and sent to France.

Russia's withdrawal from the war in the spring of 1918 released German troops from the eastern front. Rushed west to France, they joined other German soldiers in a massive march toward Paris. British and French soldiers could not hold back the German advance. A major German victory seemed at hand.

By early summer, however, American troops began to arrive in France. Under the command of General John J. Pershing, they joined with Allied forces. In June 1918 the Allies halted the German offensive at Château-Thierry (shah-TOH-tyeh-REE), on the Marne River. America's entry into the war proved to be a decisive factor, turning the tide in favor of the Allies.

The Armistice

Germany had thrown all its resources into this last, but unsuccessful, attack. Now it faced severe shortages of food, medicine, oil, and weapons. Allied troops swept eastward in a massive counterattack. It became clear to the German generals that the war was lost. In

634

late September they urged their government to ask for an armistice—a halt to the fighting. Germany's position worsened steadily. In October and November 1918, the Ottoman Empire and Austria-Hungary surrendered, and rebellions in Germany forced the kaiser to give up the throne. The government of the newly established German republic quickly agreed to the armistice terms.

On November 11, 1918, the armistice was signed. Soldiers on both sides came out of the trenches and cheered. Enemies embraced in the midst of no man's land, rejoicing that the fighting was over. A newspaper correspondent with the British army in France wrote:

66 Last night for the first time since August in the first year of the war, there was no light of gunfire in the sky, no spreading glow above black trees where for four years of nights human beings were smashed to death. The fires of hell had been put out. **99**

Section Review

1. **Define or identify:** Allies, Central Powers, stalemate, propaganda, U-boat, armistice.
2. What was the German military plan at the beginning of the war? Why did German plans for a quick victory fail on both fronts?
3. In what ways did the war involve parts of Asia, the Pacific, and Africa?
4. Why did the United States have trouble maintaining neutrality?
5. What caused Germany to ask the Allies for an armistice?
6. **Critical thinking:** For what different reasons did Japan, Italy, and the United States enter the war? Why might these differences have made a peace agreement more difficult to reach?

2

3

7. How did the Pax Romana contribute to the growth of Christianity?
8. Why did Roman authorities oppose Christianity? How did Christianity eventually become established in the Empire?

Critical Thinking Skills

1. **Preparing a report.** Research and prepare a report about one of the following topics: the Baths of Caracalla in Rome; Christian painting in the catacombs of Rome; the Battle of Chalons; Attila.

2. **Making recommendations.** Imagine that you are an adviser to the emperor Diocletian. Your task is to suggest ways to improve economic and political life within the Empire. Tell how each of your recommendations will help improve conditions.

3. **Examining cause and effect.** Review the reasons for the decline of the Roman Empire (pages 123–124). Rank these causes, beginning with the one you think was the most important. Tell why you ranked them as you did. Do you think the Empire's decline could have been reversed? If so, at what point? If not, why?

4. **Writing a letter.** Imagine that you are a poor farmer, a merchant, a soldier, or a Roman official living during the final days of the Roman Empire. Write a letter to a friend describing your present troubles and what you expect life in the future to be like for you and your family.

5. **Supporting an opinion.** In your opinion, which of Rome's contributions to the modern world is the most important? Why?

Thinking About Geography

1. **Comparing maps.** Compare the map on page 121 with the Atlas maps at the back of this book. What nations now exist in what was once the Western Roman Empire? The Eastern Roman Empire?

2. **Researching places.** Many of Europe's great cities began as outposts on the frontier

of the Roman Empire. For example, after Julius Caesar conquered Gaul, the Romans built the town of *Lutetia Parisiorum* on the Seine River. Today the city of Paris exists in the same location. Use an encyclopedia to research the origins of Vienna, Austria; Cologne, Germany; and London, England.

Enrichment: Primary Sources

In A.D. 98 the historian Tacitus wrote a description of the early Germanic tribes with whom the Roman troops had been fighting. This passage adapted from his account describes the Germanic soldiers.

66 Only a few of them use swords or large lances; they carry spears with short and narrow blades, but so sharp and easy to handle that they can be used, as required, either at close quarters or in long-range fighting. Their horsemen are content with a shield and a spear; but the foot-soldiers also rain javelins on their foes: each of them carries several, and they hurl them to immense distances. Their horses are not remarkable for either beauty or speed, and are not trained to execute various turns as ours are. The Germans' strength lies in infantry rather than cavalry. Foot-soldiers accompany the cavalry into action, their speed of foot being such that they can easily keep up with the charging horsemen.

1. What was the Germanic soldier's most important weapon? Why was it useful?

2. What was the strongest part of the Germanic army?

3. **Critical thinking:** Do you think Tacitus respected the strength of the Germans? Explain your answer.

131

4

events have occurred. Historians may find after studying an event that several causes led to an effect or that one cause was responsible for multiple effects. Look at this diagram:

Multiple Causes

Cause \
Cause — → Effect
Cause /

Multiple Effects

Cause — → Effect, Effect, Effect

Make it a habit to notice the various effects of certain causes, which of these effects became causes, and whether multiple causes or multiple effects were involved.

Distinguishing among facts, opinions, and values. **Facts** are those things that are known to be true or to have happened. Facts are based on information that can be checked for accuracy. **Opinions** express how people feel about something, what their beliefs are, and what attitudes they take. **Values** are opinions that often involve standards of right and wrong. All values are opinions, but not all opinions are values. You may express an opinion on a subject you know little about. You may also express an opinion about what you think will happen in a certain situation. In either example your opinion may prove to be fact. Values are never facts. They may be so much a part of the creed you live by that they seem like facts. If they cannot be proven to be true, however, they are not facts.

It is important that you distinguish among facts, opinions, and values. Even though opinions are not always based on fact and values cannot be proven to be true, you can still learn from them. You can learn how people felt at a certain time, what they considered important, and what they thought about. You cannot always learn what really happened or what the facts were.

Certain words give clues that opinions are being presented: "It is my belief" or "in my view" are clues to what somebody thinks. Not all opinions are easily recognized. You need to read carefully to identify what you read as fact or opinion.

Read the passage from the primary source document for Chapter 26, page 529,

876

taken from a speech by Giuseppe Garibaldi. What can you identify as fact? What can you identify as opinion? Do you recognize any value statements? When people write facts, they use little emotional language. When people express opinions and values, however, they may become emotional in their choice of words.

Recognizing points of view. A **point of view** reflects an individual's opinion, attitude, belief, or feeling. When you study history, you should try to recognize a point of view for what it is.

Favorable points of view are generally written in positive language, such as "this will benefit all people." Negative points of view take an opposite approach, such as "the election of this candidate will lead to mass unemployment."

Detecting bias. Look carefully for bias—personal preference—on the part of the person whose views are being presented. For a viewpoint to be effective in persuading people to act, the language used may appeal to people's emotions. Many famous historical figures had strong opinions that show up in their writings and speeches. Examine these views carefully. Just because a person is famous or highly regarded does not mean you must agree with his or her opinions. A good student will detect bias and opinion when examining historical documents or reading newspapers and magazine articles.

Interpreting political cartoons. An effective way to express opinions and points of view is through political cartoons.

Political cartoons often use symbols to represent certain things. The United States, for example, is often depicted as Uncle Sam, while the Soviet Union is frequently shown as a bear. Knowing what the various symbols stand for is critical to understanding a political cartoon. How are the countries Japan, China, and Germany symbolized in the cartoon on page 576?

Cartoons in daily newspapers usually deal with contemporary people or events. The events and people depicted in the car-

SKILL REVIEW

Tx

Makes important connections with people, places, events, ideas

Highlights connections between past and present and makes clear the importance of those connections—connections between cultures, societies, nations; connections between geography and history; connections between the people of the past and the people of today.

1 **Chapter openers** set the stage for learning with visual aids and short introductions ("Before You Read This Chapter") that help students relate prior knowledge to important new ideas.

2 **Linking Past and Present** features point out noteworthy connections between then and now.

3 **Meanwhile** features make comparisons between different societies or nations or identify parallel developments around the world.

4 **World History Checklists** provide students the opportunity to self-check their knowledge of key names and terms at the end of each unit.

5 Special features—**The Arts, Biography, Daily Life, Historic Places**—broaden the scope of instruction and stimulate interest.

Using the Program

Teacher's Annotated Edition

The two parts of the Teacher's Annotated Edition of HISTORY OF THE WORLD are: (1) Chapter Planner pages, conveniently presented at the beginning of each chapter; and (2) the complete textbook, with on-page teacher annotations.

Chapter Planners

At the beginning of each chapter, four blue-banded Chapter Planner pages provide background material and teaching ideas. Following a **Chapter Preview,** a short **Bibliography** suggests books for background. The **Section Lesson Plans** then provide (1) objectives for each section and (2) teaching strategies. These strategies are of three kinds:

(1) **Introducing the Lesson.** The introductory activities introduce the central theme or concept of the section and raise questions that allow students to apply their own knowledge or experience to a key idea.

(2) **Developing the Lesson.** These strategies support the section objectives. In most chapters, two strategies are provided, with the aim of maximizing flexibility.

(3) **Closing the Lesson.** These strategies provide for various means of closure—summarizing, forming a generalization or a hypothesis, or evaluating individuals or periods.

All teaching strategies are labeled to identify the higher-level thinking skills, as classified in the Bloom taxonomy of cognitive skills (page Txiii).

The Chapter Planner pages also provide suggested answers to **Map Skill Practice** exercises and to **Chapter Review** questions.

On-Page Annotations

Annotations printed in blue throughout the textbook offer additional teaching ideas and background.

For each lesson objective (based on Focus Questions at beginnings of sections), strategies for **reteaching, reinforcement,** and **enrichment** are provided in the annotations.

Each strategy is labeled to give two kinds of information: (1) the appropriate level of thinking in the Bloom taxonomy is identified in parentheses and italicized (*Comprehension, Application, Analysis, Synthesis,* or *Evaluation*). (2) A specific skill identification—for example, **Drawing Conclusions** or **Comparing Historical Developments**—appears in italicized boldface letters.

Reteaching. A reteaching exercise suggests a strategy to use with students who need extra help in mastering an objective. These sharply focused, short-term activities can be used for either individual or group work and require no teacher preparation. They are practical either as classroom or homework assignments.

Reinforcement. The reinforcement exercises provide follow-through to ensure comprehension by the majority of students. Again, activities are practical for both classroom use and homework assignments.

Enrichment. The enrichment activities offer extension opportunities. These are generally longer strategies that may require students to do some independent work.

Background information. In addition to strategies, the on-page annotations offer teachers interesting background material at the most convenient point for use in class.

Map skills. With each **Map Skill Practice** exercise, an annotation identifies specific map skills the student will use in answering the questions (see example, page 450). (Answers to questions appear in Chapter Planner pages.)

Section Review answers. The on-page annotations also indicate location of answers for **Section Reviews.** For each critical thinking question in the Section Review, a model answer is provided in an annotation on the page (see example, page 188).

On-page annotations also supply answers for map-caption questions and Primary Source feature questions (examples, pages 278, 583).

The Bloom Taxonomy

History is an ideal subject for developing critical thinking skills. Beginning with a body of factual knowledge, students can steadily proceed from the level at which knowledge is gained to the higher-level processing of information.

In HISTORY OF THE WORLD, questions calling for higher-level critical thinking skills are not reserved for the ablest students. Instead, the Teacher's Edition supplies—for each objective—teaching strategies that give all students practice in higher-level thinking processes. Frequent opportunities are provided for students to move beyond the recalling of facts and gain experience in interpreting, applying, analyzing, synthesizing, predicting, and evaluating.

Throughout the program, teaching strategies (both in the Chapter Planner pages and in the on-page annotations) are labeled to indicate the appropriate level of thinking, based on the taxonomy of educational objectives developed by Benjamin Bloom.* The categories of the taxonomy are cumulative; in other words, each successive level includes all lower types of thinking. A question or activity is classified at its highest level.

The levels of the Bloom taxonomy are listed below, together with a brief definition and explanation of how each is implemented in HISTORY OF THE WORLD:

Knowledge is defined as the simple recall of precise information—facts, names, and dates, for example.

Comprehension is the skill most often emphasized in the classroom. Questions require students both to understand information and to make use of it. Examples include restating a principle or problem in the student's own words, translating information from one form to another, and drawing conclusions.

Application questions apply previously acquired student knowledge and skills to new situations. They include independent acquisition of information (reports, for example) and applying social science generalizations to actual problems.

Analysis emphasizes the organization and logic of communication. Questions involve analysis of a point of view, identification of persuasive techniques, or recognition of bias in information.

Synthesis encourages students to compare divergent information, draw conclusions, or solve problems that call for creative input. Synthesis questions have no single correct answer. Some examples include formulating a hypothesis, examining a question and offering a personal conclusion, and participating in a debate or panel discussion.

Evaluation requires students to formulate judgments based on their own standards and values. Questions may involve judging the relative merits of an aspect of social organization or government policy.

It should be noted that in the labeling of questions and exercises in the Teacher's Edition of HISTORY OF THE WORLD, only the levels *beyond* the "Knowledge" level are labeled. It is assumed that the basic knowledge objectives apply throughout.

Bloom taxonomy labels are also applied to critical thinking questions and exercises in each Chapter Review. (See the parenthetical abbreviations following selected questions and exercises, as on page 131.)

As a resource for students, a section titled **Skill Review** is offered in the Reference Section at the back of the book. The first part of the **Skill Review** deals with study skills. The second part helps students understand and develop critical-thinking ability. As teachers assign critical-thinking questions in the section or chapter reviews, students can use the **Skill Review** to check on their understanding of how to carry out such assignments. Finally, participation skills are explained in the third part of the **Skill Review.**

*See *Taxonomy of Educational Objectives*, ed. Benjamin S. Bloom and others, Copyright 1956, David McKay Company, Inc.

Course Planning

To assist teachers in meeting their curricular needs, HISTORY OF THE WORLD offers flexible teaching plans. The Course Plan Chart on

COURSE PLAN CHART

School Year	Course A (average)*	Course B (basic)	Course C (Western Civilization)	Course D (World Cultures/ Area Studies)
First six weeks	Geography Review. Chapters 1–6.	Geography Review. Chapters 2–3. Chapters 4–6 *or* 7–8.	Chapters 1–2, 4–6.	Chapters 1–3
Second six weeks	Geographic Themes. Chapters 7–13.	Survey: The Heritage of the Ancient World Chapters 10–13 *or* 14–16	Chapters 9, 11–13.	Chapters 7–10.
Third six weeks	Chapters 14–20.	Chapters 17, 19–20.	Chapters 17–21.	Chapters 14–16.
Fourth six weeks	Chapters 21–27.	Chapters 21–22, 24–26.	Chapters 22–27.	Chapters 29–30.
Fifth six weeks	Chapters 28–34.	Chapter 28. Survey: The Shaping of the Modern World. Chapters 31–34.	Chapters 28–32.	Chapters 32–33, 36.
Sixth six weeks	Chapters 35–40.	*Options:* (1) choose 2 or 3 chapters from final unit; (2) divide class into teams, give each team a chapter; (3) assign *Survey: The Twentieth Century.* Follow each option by assigning selected topics from Chapter 40 for full class study.	Chapters 33–35, 39–40.	Chapters 37–38, 40.

*The plan for the average course maintains content coverage at a steady pace; the basic course offers a selected content and additional time for review. An enriched course plan, including suggested use of enrichment materials in the ancillary program, can be found in the *Daily Assignment Guide,* located in the *Teacher's Management and Planning Guide.*

Suggested One-Semester Course Plan for HISTORY OF THE WORLD
A suggested plan for a one-semester world history course includes the following:

First six weeks   Geography Review, Chapters 2–5, 11–12

Second six weeks   Chapters 15–19, Geographic Themes, Chapters 22, 25

Third six weeks   Chapters 31–34, 35–38

page Txiv shows possible ways of structuring a year-long course, based on six six-week periods of instruction. Course A is designed for students who can complete reading assignments of average length. Course B is for students who need shorter assignments.

Many modifications are possible in the structures suggested in the Course Plan Chart. The plans offered here are examples only. Teachers wishing to use the textbook with a Western Civilization focus or with a world cultures/area studies focus will find it readily adaptable. Course C and Course D in the Course Plan Chart offer plans for these alternative content approaches.

These course plans assume an annual schedule of 36 weeks. Teachers may want to combine units or chapters across these models in ways that will meet specific instructional objectives of the district or state.

Note that the four Surveys (pages 166–177, 323-1 to 323-12, 610–621, and 836–849) add to flexibility, making possible alternative entry points and allowing teachers to select the coverage and emphasis best suited to their classroom needs. The Surveys can also be used for closure and review.

Ancillary Program

The ancillary program for HISTORY OF THE WORLD gives teachers thorough support.

Teacher's Management and Planning Guide

This valuable management aid supplements the Teacher's Annotated Edition, providing teachers with detailed lesson plans, correlations, a bibliography, audiovisual listings, guidelines for evaluating student writing, and additional blackline-master resources.

Teacher's Resources

A major part of the ancillary program consists of five Teacher's Resource booklets, offering a wealth of worksheet material for reteaching, reinforcement, and enrichment. The five booklets are as follows:

Teacher's Resources: Reteaching. Reteaching worksheets are designed to help students who need extra assistance in mastering content. A worksheet is supplied for each section of each textbook chapter.

Teacher's Resources: Reinforcement. Reinforcement worksheets provide review opportunities—study guide and skill practice exercises and unit activities.

Teacher's Resources: Enrichment and Extension. These worksheets include skill exercises, primary source readings with questions, and selections from classic or modern literary works with questions that help students see connections between literature and history. They also include simulations—classroom dramas that involve students in historic events and meetings—and exercises that show connections between developments of the past and students' role as United States citizens.

Teacher's Resources: Geography. The geography worksheets consist of place-name drill-sheets and more challenging map worksheets; outline maps are included.

Teacher's Resources: Tests. Provided are tests (two forms) for chapters and units as well as for both semesters of full-year courses. Essay questions are included.

Additional Materials

Other supplementary publications include (1) the **Workbook** (with answers provided in an overprinted teacher's edition); (2) **Teaching Transparencies**—content outlines, timetables, diagrams, maps, and pictures, all aimed at supplementing classroom lecture and discussion; and (3) **World Art Transparencies**—reproductions of the artworks in the textbook fine-art portfolio pages.

HISTORY OF THE WORLD

HISTORY OF THE WORLD

Marvin Perry
Allan H. Scholl
Daniel F. Davis
Jeannette G. Harris
Theodore H. Von Laue

Houghton Mifflin Company • BOSTON

Atlanta • Dallas • Geneva, Illinois • Palo Alto • Princeton • Toronto

The Authors

Marvin Perry, senior author and general editor, is a member of the history department of the Bernard M. Baruch College of the City University of New York. He has also taught at Walton and Washington Irving High Schools in New York City. Among Dr. Perry's books is *Western Civilization: Ideas, Politics and Society.*

Allan H. Scholl is an educational consultant in curriculum and instruction. He has taught history at the secondary and college levels for many years, has served on numerous state and national committees, and was formerly secondary social studies specialist in the Office of Instruction of the Los Angeles Unified School District.

Daniel F. Davis is Director of Secondary Social Studies for the Stoughton (Mass.) public schools. He was Associate Director of the Service Center for Teachers of Asian Studies, Ohio State University.

Jeannette G. Harris is Educational Specialist for the Department of Education of the Commonwealth of Massachusetts. Dr. Harris chaired the social studies department, Classical High School, Springfield, Massachusetts.

Theodore H. Von Laue, an authority on Russian history, is the Jacob and Francis Hiatt Professor of History at Clark University. Dr. Von Laue is the author of *Sergei Witte and the Industrialization of Russia.*

Consulting Editor

David Depew is Social Studies Consultant for the Ector County Independent School District, Odessa, Texas.

Special Curriculum Adviser

Ann Cotton teaches world history at O.D. Wyatt High School, Fort Worth, Texas.

Cover: Mummy case of the Egyptian priest Nespanetjer-enpere, fourth prophet of Amon. Constructed about 980–960 B.C. from cartonnage—a material similar to papier-mâché—this mummy case is painted and inlaid with lapis lazuli and glass.

Frontispiece: Greek vase from the sixth century B.C.

Historian Advisers

For assistance with specialized subject areas, the authors and publisher are indebted to the following:

Africa—**David Northrup,** Professor of History, Boston College.

East Asia—**Norman Birnbaum,** Professor of History, Shippensburg University.

Europe—**John Marshall Carter,** Professor of Pedagogical Studies and Supervision, University of North Carolina, Greensboro; **Kathleen Dunlop,** Professor of History, East Carolina University.

India—**Frank F. Conlon,** Professor of History, University of Washington.

Latin America—**Carlos Gil,** Associate Professor of History, University of Washington.

The Middle East—**John Ruedy,** Chairman of the Program of Arab Studies, Center for Contemporary Arab Studies, Georgetown University.

Readers/Classroom Consultants

Diana Beasley, Largo High School, Upper Marlboro, Maryland

Norman Bigham, Osborne High School, Marietta, Georgia

Betty Dean, Bellaire High School, Houston, Texas

Joseph K. Hills, Lake Braddock Secondary, Fairfax County Public Schools, Burke, Virginia

Joseph Lawecki, South Bend Community Schools, South Bend, Indiana

Ron Marinucci, Milford High School, Milford, Michigan

Linda Massey, Seagoville High School, Dallas, Texas

Darrel J. Ochoa, Edgewood Independent School District, San Antonio, Texas

Irene Ramnarine, Brevard County Schools, Rockledge, Florida

Paul Rivera, Baltimore County Public Schools, Towson, Maryland

Roger Shutack, Voorhees High School, Glen Gardner, New Jersey

Jim Witucki, East High School, Salt Lake City, Utah

Please see page 907 for acknowledgments of permissions to reprint copyrighted material.

123456789-VH-96 95 94 93 92

ISBN: 0-395-63218-8

Printed in the U.S.A.

CONTENTS

► The arrow symbol identifies chapters appropriate for courses emphasizing Western Civilization.

Unit 1 See following pages for critical-thinking questions: 16, 21, 25, 27, 33, 34, 42, 49, 51, 59, 64, 65–66.

Use the **Geography Review** to help students review or reinforce basic geography skills and ideas. To help students grasp the importance of the relationships between geography and history, see **Geographic Themes**, pages GR11–GR14, following the survey of medieval history, and preceding page 324.

v

► The arrow symbol identifies chapters appropriate for courses emphasizing Western Civilization.

Unit 2   See following pages for critical-thinking questions: 75, 83, 89, 90, 93, 95, 105, 108, 115, 117, 124, 129, 131, 135, 138, 139, 145, 147, 155, 162, 163–164.
Unit 3   See following pages for critical-thinking questions: 188, 193, 195, 203, 207, 209, 213, 217, 225, 226–227, 234, 242, 245, 251, 253.

Unit 4   See following pages for critical-thinking questions: 276, 280, 285, 293, 295, 303, 307, 309, 315, 320, 322.

viii

► The arrow symbol identifies chapters appropriate for courses emphasizing
  Western Civilization.

Unit 5   See following pages for critical-thinking questions: 331, 337, 343,
         345, 354, 357, 363, 365, 372, 376, 381, 383, 389, 392, 395, 400, 401,
         406, 408.
Unit 6   See following pages for critical-thinking questions: 418, 423, 430,
         431, 433, 438, 440, 445, 453, 455, 461, 467, 469, 476, 479, 484,
         486.

ix

Unit 7 See following pages for critical-thinking questions: 497, 501, 509, 510–511, 516, 518, 521, 527, 528–529, 534, 539, 543, 546, 548.

▶ The arrow symbol identifies chapters appropriate for courses emphasizing Western Civilization.

Unit 8 See following pages for critical-thinking questions: 558, 565, 567, 572, 581, 583, 587, 589, 595, 601, 606, 608.
Unit 9 See following pages for critical-thinking questions: 627, 634, 641, 643, 649, 654, 659, 661, 670, 675, 681, 683, 688, 692, 697, 700, 704, 706.

Unit 10 See following pages for critical-thinking questions: 718, 724,
729, 731, 733, 739, 744, 748, 755, 757, 764, 773, 775, 781, 786, 791,
793, 803, 809, 813, 815, 822, 827, 833–834.

SKILL PRACTICE AND INSTRUCTION

(continued)

The decision-making process. Asking questions. Analyzing.

Determining cause-and-effect relationships. Distinguishing among facts, opinions, and values. Recognizing points of view. Detecting bias. Interpreting political cartoons. Making and supporting generalizations. Inferring. Evaluating historical sources.

Forming hypotheses. Synthesizing. Predicting events.

CAUSE AND EFFECT

PRIMARY SOURCES

SPECIAL FEATURES

MAPS

(continued)

xvii

Note: The map of the Western Pacific Rim is found in the "Geographic Themes" section, preceding page 324.

(continued)

CHARTS/GRAPHS/TABLES

WHY STUDY WORLD HISTORY?

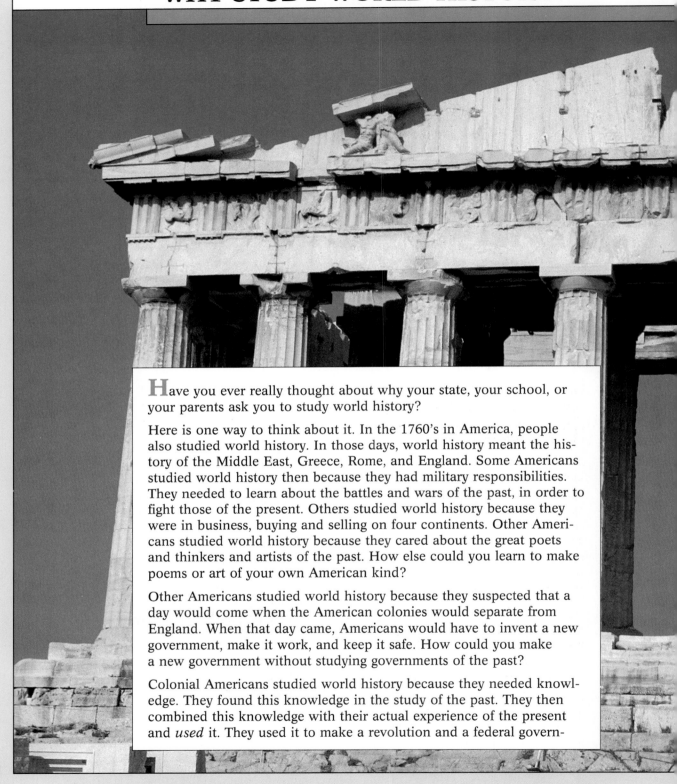

Have you ever really thought about why your state, your school, or your parents ask you to study world history?

Here is one way to think about it. In the 1760's in America, people also studied world history. In those days, world history meant the history of the Middle East, Greece, Rome, and England. Some Americans studied world history then because they had military responsibilities. They needed to learn about the battles and wars of the past, in order to fight those of the present. Others studied world history because they were in business, buying and selling on four continents. Other Americans studied world history because they cared about the great poets and thinkers and artists of the past. How else could you learn to make poems or art of your own American kind?

Other Americans studied world history because they suspected that a day would come when the American colonies would separate from England. When that day came, Americans would have to invent a new government, make it work, and keep it safe. How could you make a new government without studying governments of the past?

Colonial Americans studied world history because they needed knowledge. They found this knowledge in the study of the past. They then combined this knowledge with their actual experience of the present and *used* it. They used it to make a revolution and a federal govern-

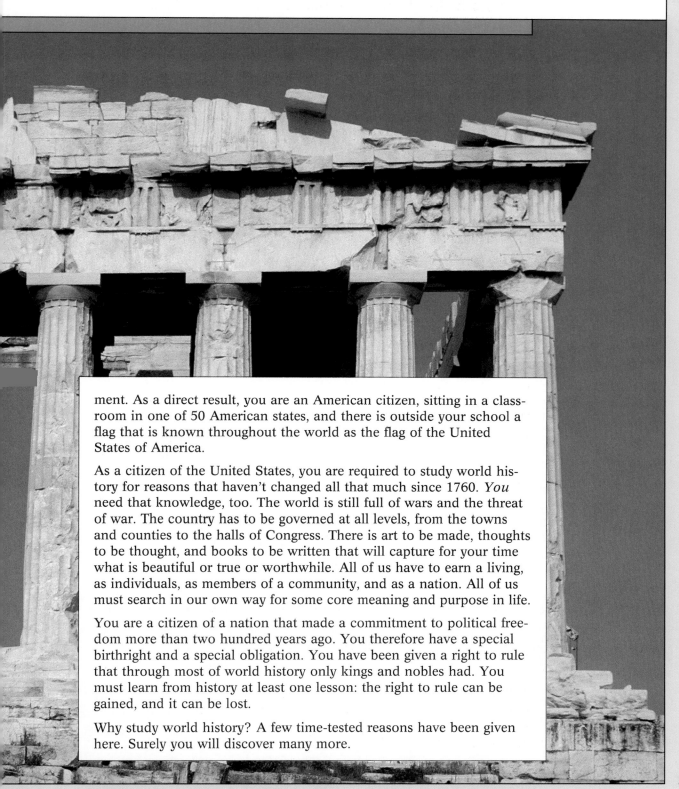

ment. As a direct result, you are an American citizen, sitting in a class-room in one of 50 American states, and there is outside your school a flag that is known throughout the world as the flag of the United States of America.

As a citizen of the United States, you are required to study world history for reasons that haven't changed all that much since 1760. *You* need that knowledge, too. The world is still full of wars and the threat of war. The country has to be governed at all levels, from the towns and counties to the halls of Congress. There is art to be made, thoughts to be thought, and books to be written that will capture for your time what is beautiful or true or worthwhile. All of us have to earn a living, as individuals, as members of a community, and as a nation. All of us must search in our own way for some core meaning and purpose in life.

You are a citizen of a nation that made a commitment to political free-dom more than two hundred years ago. You therefore have a special birthright and a special obligation. You have been given a right to rule that through most of world history only kings and nobles had. You must learn from history at least one lesson: the right to rule can be gained, and it can be lost.

Why study world history? A few time-tested reasons have been given here. Surely you will discover many more.

HOW THIS BOOK HELPS YOU LEARN

Many features in *History of the World* will help you learn and enjoy world history.

Unit and Chapter Introductions

A dramatic picture and timeline introduces each unit. A preview, a brief outline, and focus questions help you establish a purpose for reading each chapter, locate information quickly, and review for exams.

Section Organization

Each chapter is divided into sections. Within each section there are major and minor headings. The section titles, combined with the headings, form an outline of the chapter that will help you organize the information.

Section and Chapter Reviews

Each section ends with questions to help you review vocabulary, recall information, and think about what you have read. At the end of the chapter, a summary and timeline and a variety of review exercises help you recall and apply what you have learned. The Chapter Review also provides practice in using specific study skills, geography skills, and critical-thinking skills.

Primary Sources

Throughout the book, firsthand accounts of the people and events of the past give you a true sense of history in the making. Also included are excerpts from documents that have profoundly shaped people's thoughts and actions. Each Chapter Review contains an exercise that teaches you how to interpret primary sources.

Links Across Time and Space

Understanding how the past connects with the present is a valuable lesson of history. Another important lesson is understanding that history is being made in different parts of the world at the same time. *Linking Past and Present* and *Meanwhile* features encourage these understandings. These links across time and space give you a real sense of history.

xxii

After reading about the many special features included in *History of the World,* students might refer to the Contents listing in this book to find examples of the features.

Pictures

The illustrations in this book have been chosen to broaden your knowledge of people, places, and events. Captions provide background information and relate the pictures to the text.

Special Features

Every chapter contains a lively feature that explores one of the following topics: *Biography, Historic Places, Daily Life,* or *The Arts.* These features give you an inside look at some of the people, places, life-styles, and cultures presented in the book.

Maps, Graphs, and Tables

Numerous maps appear throughout the book. Special suggestions for using maps are given in the *Geography Review* on pages GR7-GR8. *Geography Connection* features make clear the close relationship between geography and history, while *Map Skill Practice* lessons help you apply your map-reading skills. The graphs and tables in the book provide a way for you to organize and interpret historical developments.

Reference Section

Look for the four surveys, located at different points of the book; they will be especially helpful when you want to review. At the back of the book a special reference section provides useful aids to learning—atlas maps, a table of nations, a time chart, a skill review, a glossary, a dictionary of ancient places, a biographical dictionary, and an index.

See the *Teacher's Management and Planning Guide* for Textbook Preview Worksheets, which will be useful in acquainting students with HISTORY OF THE WORLD.

GEOGRAPHY REVIEW

Geography and History: The Connection

At first glance, you might think geography has little or nothing to do with history. History is the study of the human past; written history is a record of events and developments from the past and usually includes a historian's explanation of those happenings and why people acted as they did. Geography may seem to deal only with the earth's physical features and natural resources. Actually, however, geography and history are closely related, since the people and events of history have been strongly affected by the physical environment.

Why, for example, did an early farming people settle in a river valley rather than in a mountainous region? This history question can be answered by considering geography. The valley was a better physical environment for growing crops and the river provided a natural resource—water.

Clearly a study of geography involves not just places but also human interaction with places. The connection between geography and history, then, is people.

Have students read this review of basic geography concepts and terms and then check their skills with the questions on page GR8.

Using Geography to Study History

Historians must study geography because people are strongly affected by the place, or environment, in which they live. Historians must also explore how people adapt to and change their environment.

As you read history, you will begin to understand how a small settlement in a fertile river valley could eventually become a large civilization. You will learn how the climate and vegetation—plant life—of an area could help determine the kinds of houses the human inhabitants built and the kinds of clothes they wore. You might even use the geography of an area to explain why a people's legends, music, and art reflect a certain view of the natural world—one firmly rooted in their environment.

Maps, the tools of geography, can help you understand how a society developed. For example, settlement of the United States turned prairies into farmlands and forests into lumber products. Maps of climate, vegetation, and agricultural products help explain such human interaction with the land.

To consider another example, much of Africa belonged to different European powers during the nineteenth century and the first half of the twentieth century. Historical maps show how the political boundaries of these territorial holdings were established and changed. Such maps are useful aids in learning about the actions of nations, explorers, and settlers.

The examples are endless, but the conclusion is obvious. Studying the effects of geography on human actions will enrich your understanding of the development of history.

GR1

Teacher's note: Geographers have identified five themes central to geographic education. A discussion of these themes is provided in the special geography section on pages GR11–GR14, between the survey of medieval history and the beginning of Unit 5 on page 324.

Continents and Oceans

Picturing the Earth

You have probably heard the saying that a picture is worth a thousand words. A map is a picture. If a map shows just physical features, such as mountains and rivers, it is a picture of only the natural environment. If a map shows roads, airports, national boundaries, battle sites, or the area of an empire, the map is also a picture of the human imprint on the natural environment. To help you better understand the relationship between geography and history, here is a brief review of maps and their special purposes.

Globes and maps. Because the earth is round, the best way to show its surface is on a globe. In fact, globes are the only fully accurate way to represent the earth's surface. A globe accurately shows relative distance, direction, shape, and size of landmasses and oceans. A map is a flat representation of the earth or a part of the earth. Because it is flat, a map cannot show the earth's surface as accurately as a globe. A map, however, can show more detail and is much more convenient to use than a globe, especially for explorers or other travelers.

Continents. When you look at a globe or a world map, you will see that most of the earth is covered with water. In fact, only 30 percent of the earth's surface is land. Geographers divide these landmasses into seven **continents:** North America, South America, Europe, Asia, Africa, Australia, and Antarctica. Europe and Asia are really one large landmass, Eurasia. But geographers have traditionally split it into two continents, using the natural boundary of the Ural Mountains as the dividing line.

Map projections. Look at the world maps on the next page. Notice how the same continents and oceans differ in size and shape from one map to another. These four maps represent four different **map projections.** A map projection is a particular way of drawing a flat picture of the earth's curved surface.

It is impossible to represent accurately the curved surface of the earth on a flat piece of paper. When the earth's surface is shown flattened out to make a map, the appearance

GR2

Map Projections

Mercator Projection. This projection shows direction accurately, but it distorts size, especially away from the equator. Landmasses near the North and South poles appear to be much larger than they really are. Sailors favor the Mercator projection because determining direction is the most important part of plotting a ship's course.

Polar Projection (equidistant). This projection is drawn from above either the North Pole or the South Pole. Size and shape are fairly true near the center of the map but become distorted the farther a landmass is from the pole. However, the distance from the pole to any point on the map is accurate. For this reason and because many of the shortest flying routes go over the pole, airplane pilots prefer this projection.

Robinson Projection. This projection shows accurately how the continents compare with each other in size. Because the oceans are not interrupted, their relative sizes are also shown clearly. There is some distortion of shape, however, near the edges of the map. Most of the maps in this textbook use the Robinson projection.

Goode's Interrupted Projection (equal-area). This projection cuts the world into sections. As a result, it shows sizes and shapes of continents better than other projections. Distances across water areas, however, are generally inaccurate. (An equal-area projection accurately shows the relative sizes of land and water areas.)

of the continents and oceans becomes distorted. In other words, their size and shape are made inaccurate. Distance and direction may also be distorted.

Each projection you see distorts the earth in a different way. Therefore, map users **GR3** with different needs will choose maps with different projections. For some map users, the distance between points on the map must be precise. For others, the size of each landmass must be accurate. Two different projections might suit these two different purposes.

Read each caption and then study the map projection to note its distortions.

p. 851

The grid system. Turn to the world map in the Atlas at the back of the book, and note the numbered lines that run up and down (north-south) and from side to side (west-east). These lines are part of an imaginary grid that geographers and mapmakers place on the earth's surface in order to plot exact locations on a map or globe.

The intersecting lines that make up the grid are known as lines of **latitude** and **longitude.** Lines of latitude are also called parallels because they run parallel to the equator, the imaginary line that runs around the middle of the earth. Lines of longitude are also called meridians. Each longitude line runs from the North Pole to the South Pole.

Both latitude and longitude are measured in degrees. Lines of latitude measure distance north and south of the equator, which is at 0° (zero degrees) latitude. Distance above the equator is measured as north latitude, and distance below the equator is measured as south latitude.

Lines of longitude measure distance east or west of the **prime meridian.** The prime meridian is an imaginary line running from the North Pole to the South Pole and passing through Greenwich, England. It is at 0° longitude. Other lines of longitude are measured from the prime meridian east or west to 180°, which is the meridian halfway around the world from Greenwich.

Every place in the world has one and only one grid location—where the line of latitude for the place intersects with its line of longitude. For example, the latitude of Rome, Italy, is 41°N. Its longitude is 12°E. Therefore, Rome's grid location is 41°N, 12°E (41 degrees north, 12 degrees east). This grid location will never change, no matter what map you use.

Latitude and climate. All around the earth, places at the same latitude have similar climates. Latitude can therefore be used in a general way to describe the climate of an area.

The high latitudes—the areas near the North and South poles—generally have a cold climate throughout the year. The low latitudes—the areas near the equator—generally have a hot climate. These areas are known as the tropics. The middle latitudes—the areas between the tropics and the polar regions—generally have a temperate climate. This means that temperatures there change from hot to cold with the seasons.

Other factors besides latitude, however, also help determine climate. Wind, ocean currents, and elevation—height above sea level—all affect climate. For example, the North Atlantic Drift, the current that carries warm water from the Gulf Stream, flows past Western Europe and warms Great Britain. London, which shares the same latitude as Montreal, Canada, has mild, rainy winters that are much warmer than Montreal's cold, snowy ones. Another striking example is Mount Kilimanjaro. This mountain in East Africa is on the equator; yet it has snow-capped peaks.

GR4

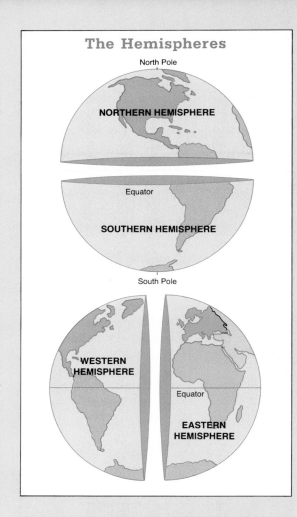

The Hemispheres

North Pole

NORTHERN HEMISPHERE

Equator

SOUTHERN HEMISPHERE

South Pole

WESTERN HEMISPHERE

EASTERN HEMISPHERE

Equator

Hemispheres. In addition to dividing the earth's landmasses into continents, geographers divide the entire earth into **hemispheres.** The word *hemisphere* means "half a sphere" and refers to one half of the earth.

The equator is the dividing line between the Northern Hemisphere and the Southern Hemisphere. From the diagram on this page, you can see that most of South America is in the Southern Hemisphere. All of North America is in the Northern Hemisphere.

The earth can also be divided into Eastern and Western hemispheres. Everything from the prime meridian east to 180° longitude is in the Eastern Hemisphere. Everything from the prime meridian west to 180° longitude is in the Western Hemisphere.

Different Kinds of Maps

Look at the physical map of the world on pages GR9–GR10. A physical map shows the earth's physical features, such as landforms and bodies of water. Study the physical features shown on this map, and use the key to determine the general types of vegetation found on each continent. What is the mountain range in southern Asia? See (1) below.

Now compare this physical map with the world political map in the Atlas. A political map focuses mainly on political units, such as cities, states, and nations. Are there any mountain ranges shown on this map? See (2) below.

Another kind of map is a special-purpose map. It presents one particular kind of information, such as population, cultural, or climate data. Study the two special-purpose maps on page GR6.

The world population map gives the range of population for each country of the world. Find the countries with the highest populations. On what continent are these countries located? According to the map, how many people live in these countries? Can you tell from the map what the exact population of these countries is? Explain. See (3) below.

The average precipitation map gives climate information. (Precipitation is rain and snow.) According to the map, is the climate of Australia basically wet or dry? Does Australia get more or less precipitation than South America? Now compare Australia with South America, using the physical map on pages GR9–GR10. Does Australia have more or less plant life than South America? What general statement can you make about the connection between rainfall and plant life? See (4) below.

These two maps, as well as the political and physical maps you just looked at, show information about the modern world. Another kind of map, however, deals with historical subjects. A historical map shows political boundaries or battle sites or trade routes from earlier periods in history. Most of the maps in this textbook are historical maps.

(1) The mountain range in southern Asia is the Himalayas.
(2) There are no mountain ranges on the world political map.

(3) The most populous countries (China and India) are in Asia. The map shows that at least 500 million people live in each of those countries, but you can not tell the exact population of either because the map shows only ranges of population. (You may want to tell students that population figures for all countries can be found in the Table of Nations at the back of this book.)
(4) Australia has a dry climate. It gets less precipitation and has less plant life than South America. Generally, the less rainfall a place receives, the less plant life it will have.

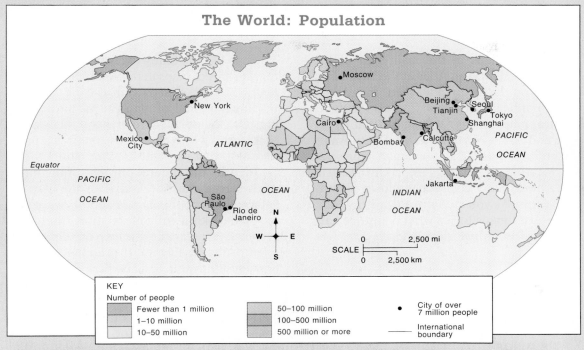

The World: Population

See (1) below.

This special-purpose map shows each country's population, within a range. Do you think this information could be better presented on a chart? Why or why not?

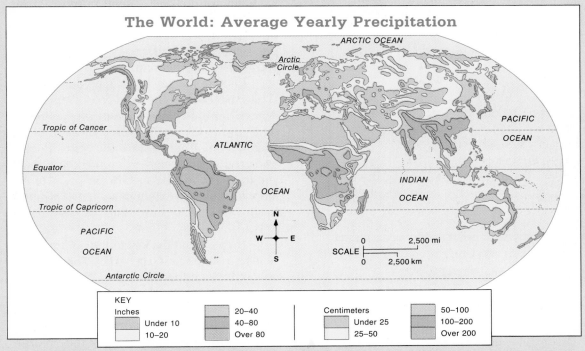

The World: Average Yearly Precipitation

See (2) below.

The purpose of this map is to show how precipitation varies throughout the world. What kinds of comparisons could you make using this map?

GR6

The maps on this page are offered as examples of special-purpose maps. The places and terms that appear on these maps may not yet be familiar to many students. You might, therefore, plan to return to these maps when students have enough information to study them more fully.

(1) Generally, such information is much easier to understand when it appears on a map. Some students may note, however, that more specific information could be included on a chart.

(2) Comparisons could be made of levels of precipitation on different continents, from country to country, and at different latitudes.

Using the Atlas Maps

Besides the maps in the main part of this book, you will find an Atlas at the back of the book. You have already seen the Atlas's world political map. The Atlas also includes political maps of Africa, Eurasia (that is, Europe and Asia), North America, South America, and Australia. The world map shows you the location of all modern countries. The other atlas maps give you a closer view of continents. As you study world history, refer to the Atlas maps to see what countries have developed from historical lands.

KEY

▢ Egypt

▨ Controlled by Egypt

─── Trade routes

SCALE

0 — 300 mi
0 — 300 km

GR7

Ancient Egypt

The Nile River flows north. Into what sea does it empty? With what islands did Egyptians trade? Was Lower Egypt north or south of Upper Egypt?

(See map answers on p. 35.)

Building Map Skills

You can use the following five steps for reading all types of maps in this textbook or in any textbook. These steps can also be used for reading any kind of map you might need to consult, including a road map. Remember that learning to read and use maps is a practical skill that you will use your entire life.

(1) Identify the general purpose of the map. Always read the title and scan the map to determine what the map is about. Ask yourself what kind of information the map presents. For example, the map on this page is titled "Ancient Egypt." It presents information about Egypt in an early period of history. This is a historical map.

Notice that the important areas of the map are shown in strong colors, and the other areas are in a neutral color. Color is used in this way with all the maps presented in this textbook.

(2) Study the symbols on the map. Once you have determined the general purpose of the map, look at the map's key (sometimes called the legend). The key explains the meaning of the symbols, abbreviations, or any special colors used on the map.

Look at the key to the map on this page. What does each of the solid colors represent? What does the colored line in the key represent? Study the area covered by each of the solid colors. Then follow the path of each trade route. You can see that the key allowed you to determine the specific purposes of this map: to show the extent of ancient Egypt and to show the trade routes that passed through Egypt.

Now look at the key to the political map of North America in the Atlas. The dot symbol (•) marks important cities. What does the star symbol (★) represent?

Another symbol, the compass rose, helps you find direction on any map. On the map of North America, follow the "North" arrow of the compass rose along its line of longitude. Where does the line end?

(3) Examine the map scale. The scale of a map helps you determine the distance, in miles or kilometers, between points shown on the map. On the map of Africa in the Atlas, the top line of the scale represents 900 miles on the map. How could you use the scale to find the distance between Capetown, South Africa, and Cairo, Egypt?

Notice that the historical map on page GR7 also has a scale. With it, you can determine the extent of ancient Egypt and the length of each trade route.

(4) Look for inset maps and locator maps. An inset map is a smaller map inside the border of a larger one. An inset map usually shows only a piece of the larger one but shows it in greater detail. It "blows up" an area that is particularly important or that may be difficult to see clearly on the larger map. Look at the inset map on page 361. Why might the mapmaker have decided to present this information on an inset map?

The purpose of a locator map is to show where one area of the world is located within a larger area. Look at the world locator map on page 296. The chapter is about Africa, so this locator map shows the part of the world in which Africa is located. You will find similar locator maps at the beginning of every chapter in this textbook. A *global* locator appears with certain maps in this book, including the map on page GR7. The purpose of a global locator is the same as that of a locator map. It can show where in the world a certain mapped area is located.

(5) Analyze and draw conclusions from the map. After you have determined what information the map presents, consider how that information relates to the chapter content. Does the map show a number of countries in one geographic area? What is the relationship among those countries? Does the map show an event, such as a battle or an invasion? What physical features, such as rivers, mountains, and plains, might have influenced this event? Look again at the map of ancient Egypt. How can you explain the close connection between trade routes and rivers?

See below.

Rivers provided natural highways for the transportation of trade goods. Ask students to look through their books to see the variety of historical maps they will be using. Have them choose one map and describe its purpose and any symbols or other features on the map.

Check Your Skills

Answer the following questions to check your map skills. (See answers below.)

1. A map that shows goods produced by every country in Asia is (a) a political map, (b) a physical map, (c) a special-purpose map.

2. Two different map projections may show North America in two different (a) places, (b) shapes, (c) centuries.

3. The prime meridian runs (a) from pole to pole, (b) on the same line as the equator, (c) through Rome.

4. According to the population map on page GR6, the two countries with the highest populations are (a) north of the equator, (b) south of the equator, (c) on the Atlantic Ocean.

5. According to the climate map on page GR6, average yearly precipitation is greatest near (a) the Arctic Circle, (b) the Antarctic Circle, (c) the equator.

6. One of the trade routes that is shown on the map of ancient Egypt extends from Egypt to (a) the Black Sea, (b) the Caspian Sea, (c) the Persian Gulf.

7. The Atlas map titled "South America" shows that the capital of Brazil is (a) Brasília, (b) São Paulo, (c) La Paz.

8. The Atlas map titled "Africa" shows that the distance between the capitals of Zimbabwe and Tanzania is (a) about 500 miles, (b) about 900 miles, (c) about 1,300 miles.

9. According to the world physical map on the next two pages, there is a river in Asia called (a) the Indus, (b) the Danube, (c) the Congo.

10. According to the world physical map, the body of water that borders both Europe and Africa is (a) the Caspian Sea, (b) the North Sea, (c) the Mediterranean Sea.

GR8

1. c; **2.** b; **3.** a; **4.** a; **5.** c; **6.** c; **7.** a; **8.** b; **9.** a; **10.** c.

The World: A Physical Map

KEY

FOREST

Area where the dominant plant life is trees, the type of tree varying with the climate.

GRASSLAND

Area where grasses dominate.

ARID LAND

Dry land, including deserts and areas of thinly scattered plants.

TUNDRA

Treeless grassland where the layer of earth below the surface soil is permanently frozen.

ICE

Region of permanent ice and snow and subfreezing temperatures, where no plant life exists.

MOUNTAINS

The highest lands on earth, where poor soils and harsh climate often limit plant life.

—— International boundary

GREENLAND

ARCTIC OCEAN

Arctic Circle

NORTH SEA

EUROPE

ALPS

Volga R.

URAL MTS.

Danube R.

R.

ATLAS MTS.

MEDITERRANEAN SEA

CASPIAN SEA

ASIA

BERING SEA

Yellow R.

EAST CHINA SEA

Tropic of Cancer

ARABIAN SEA

HIMALAYAS

Indus R.

AFRICA

Nile R.

Prime Meridian

SOUTH CHINA SEA

PACIFIC OCEAN

Congo R.

Equator

INDIAN OCEAN

ATLANTIC

OCEAN

MADAGASCAR

Tropic of Capricorn

AUSTRALIA

N
W — E
S

SCALE

0   2,000 mi

0   2,000 km

Antarctic Circle

ANTARCTICA

Robinson Projection

The Rise of Civilization

Prehistory–450 B.C.

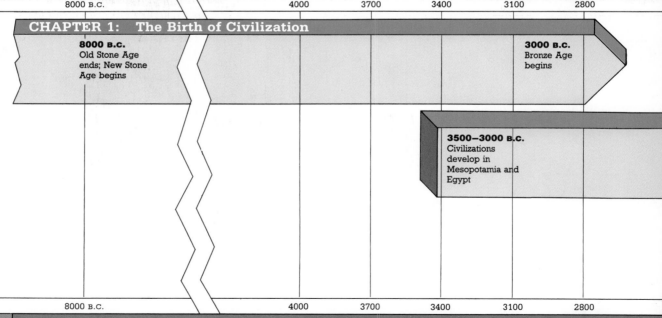

8000 B.C.		4000	3700	3400	3100	2800

CHAPTER 1: The Birth of Civilization

8000 B.C.
Old Stone Age
ends; New Stone
Age begins

3000 B.C.
Bronze Age
begins

3500–3000 B.C.
Civilizations
develop in
Mesopotamia and
Egypt

8000 B.C.		4000	3700	3400	3100	2800

FOCUS STRATEGY. Tell students that the illustration is an artist's conception of a scene from ancient Egypt. Then ask: **(a) What in the picture might be recognizable to many people?** (Students might suggest the pyramids and the Great Sphinx.) **(b) What does the illustration suggest about the climate of ancient Egypt?** (The picture shows laborers wearing little clothing, and the land looks dry, indicating a hot climate with little rainfall.) **(c) What does the picture suggest as the way most ancient Egyptians obtained their food?** (Farming.)

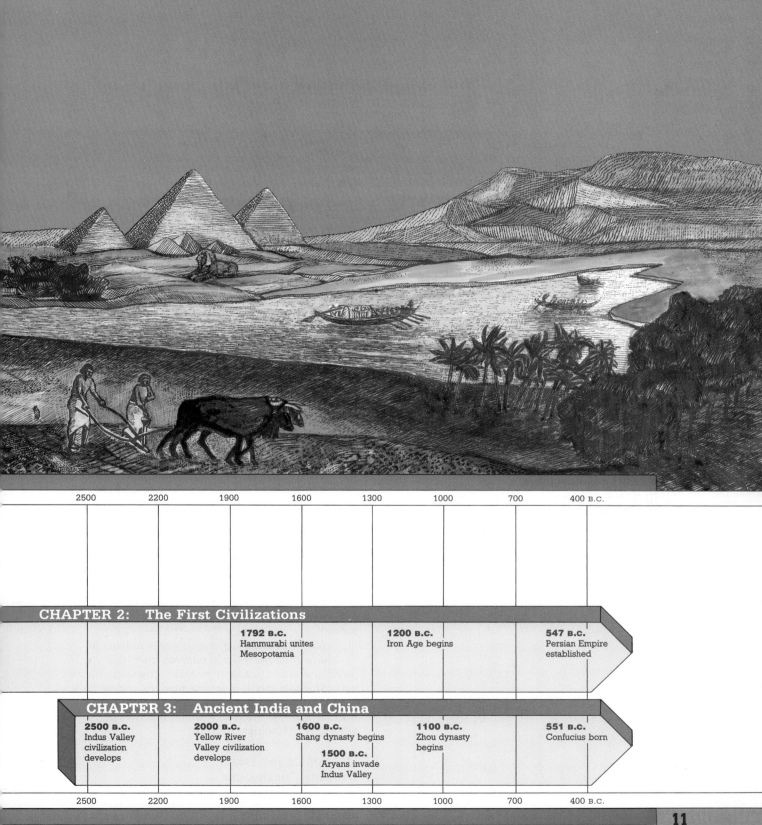

	2500	2200	1900	1600	1300	1000	700	400 B.C.

CHAPTER 2: The First Civilizations

1792 B.C.
Hammurabi unites
Mesopotamia

1200 B.C.
Iron Age begins

547 B.C.
Persian Empire
established

CHAPTER 3: Ancient India and China

2500 B.C.
Indus Valley
civilization
develops

2000 B.C.
Yellow River
Valley civilization
develops

1600 B.C.
Shang dynasty begins

1500 B.C.
Aryans invade
Indus Valley

1100 B.C.
Zhou dynasty
begins

551 B.C.
Confucius born

	2500	2200	1900	1600	1300	1000	700	400 B.C.

Have students refer to the unit timeline to answer the following questions: (a) How much history is covered in this unit? (About 7500
years.) (b) What might account for the apparent absence of historical information between 8000 and 3000 B.C.? (Students may
suggest that written records were not kept during this period.)

The Birth of Civilization   Prehistory-3000 B.C.
(pp. 12–27)

Chapter Preview

Section 1 distinguishes between history and prehistory and examines techniques used by anthropologists and other scientists to study the achievements made before written records were kept. Section 2 describes the advances of the Paleolithic and the Neolithic periods and the revolutionary changes set in motion by the development of farming and herding. Section 3 identifies the river valleys where civilizations first emerged, discusses the relationship between river valleys and the rise of civilization, and examines the general characteristics of civilization.

Bibliography

See the *Teacher's Management and Planning Guide* for additional listings. Starred titles are for both students and teachers.

Farb, Peter. *Humankind.* Houghton Mifflin. Links biology, culture, and human behavior from ancient to modern times.

Glob, P. V. *The Bog People: Iron-Age Man Preserved.* Cornell University Press. A 2000-year-old body found preserved in Denmark.

Leakey, Richard E. and Roger Lewin. *Origins.* E.P. Dutton. Stresses the importance of cooperation among early humans.

*Lewin, Roger. *In the Age of Mankind: A Smithsonian Book of Human Evolution.* Smithsonian Books. Recent anthropological discoveries.

Section Lesson Plans

SECTION 1   (pp. 13–16)
The Old Stone Age

Objectives

After completing this section, students will be able to:
1. Explain how scientists study life in the distant past.
2. Describe what life was like during the Old Stone Age.

Introducing the Lesson

Remind students that in our age of rapidly changing technology, it is often difficult to appreciate the accomplishments of prehistoric peoples. Compared with modern life, the ways of people who lived during prehistory might seem backward to some.

Then ask: *(a) What are some ideas that people today have about early human life?* (Answers will vary. Many think that prehistoric people were not human or were unintelligent.)

(b) What might lead people to view prehistoric humans in this way? (Answers will vary. Some portrayals of early human beings make them seem incapable of thought and ingenuity. Sometimes people compare modern and prehistoric people and their times without considering the technological advantages enjoyed by societies today.)

(c) What evidence might lead scientists to conclude that prehistoric peoples were just as intelligent as present-day people? (Answers will vary. Students might note that modern society is founded on earlier advances. Early human beings learned how to survive without the benefit of advanced technology or skills.)

Developing the Lesson:
Drawing Conclusions

Ask: *(a) How do artifacts reveal information about the prehistoric way of life?* (Weapons and tools provide information about how early human beings got food and made clothing and shelter; pottery and jewelry reveal the level of craftsmanship; decorations on objects can shed light on activities and values.)

(b) Why might scientists consider it important to learn about prehistoric ways of life? (Answers will vary. Knowledge of the extraordinary advances made by peoples of past ages makes us more appreciative of the accomplishments of our ancestors. Knowledge of prehistoric peoples links modern societies with their ancestors. Many people find satisfaction in learning about the lives of people of the distant past.)

(c) What kinds of artifacts might future historians find, and what might the objects reveal about our way of life? (Answers will vary.) *(Application)*

Developing the Lesson: Debating an Issue

Have students work in groups to debate the following: *Some of the most important developments in human history occurred during the Old Stone Age.* Students should support or refute the idea that discoveries made by Stone Age people are as significant as those made in today's advanced technological environment. Have students support their views with examples of inventions or discoveries. *(Synthesis)*

Closing the Lesson: Expressing Point of View

Have students write an essay explaining which Old Stone Age discovery or invention might be considered most significant and why. Students might choose from the following: mastery of fire; invention of tools; development of language; development of religion; or creation of cave paintings. *(Evaluation)*

See *Section Review* questions, p. 16.

SECTION 2 (pp. 17–21)
The New Stone Age

Objectives

After completing this section, students will be able to:
1. Explain why people in the New Stone Age began to farm and build villages.
2. Describe how village life promoted trade and technology.

Introducing the Lesson

Remind students that agriculture and permanent settlements developed during the period known as the New Stone Age. These advances had far-reaching effects on human society.

Then ask: *(a) What is the relationship between agriculture and permanent settlements?* (Farmers tend to stay in one location to guard their crops and to reap them.)

(b) How does settled farm life differ from nomadic life? (Nomads move when the food supply is exhausted; farmers grow their food and can plan for a steady supply.)

(c) How might the lives of people who move frequently differ from the lives of people who settle in one place? (A group that moves frequently would probably have a small population, a simple social organization, and few possessions. A settled community would probably be larger, have a more complex social organization, and a tendency to acquire possessions.)

(d) Which way of life would you prefer, one in a settled community or that of a nomad? Why? (Answers will vary.)

Developing the Lesson: Understanding Point of View

Have students work in groups to present a conversation that might have occurred among a New Stone Age farmer, herder, and artisan. Discussions should describe each lifestyle and why each representative views his or her lifestyle as the most productive and satisfying. *(Application)*

Developing the Lesson: Illustrating History

Have students make art displays illustrating the inventions and achievements of the New Stone Age people. Students might draw posters, make scrapbooks, create cartoons, or decorate a bulletin board. *(Application)*

Closing the Lesson: Discussing History

Ask: *(a) When did farming first develop?* (Between 9000 B.C. and 6000 B.C.)

(b) Where did farming first develop? (It developed in a number of places at the same time—including the Middle East, Mexico, and Thailand.)

(c) Why did some people who domesticated animals become herders? (In some areas poor soil or an unfavorable climate made farming impractical.)

(d) What factors might account for economic and social developments which occurred during the New Stone Age? (Answers will vary, but students might suggest that changes which occurred in climate and geography resulted in social and economic changes at the end of the Ice Age.) (Comprehension)

See *Section Review* questions, p. 21.

SECTION 3 (pp. 21–25)
River Valley Civilizations

Objectives

After completing this section, students will be able to:
1. Explain why the first civilizations developed in river valleys.
2. Describe how the growth of cities changed society.

Introducing the Lesson

Remind students that geography is one of the most influential factors in the development and growth of civilization. While modern technology has made it easier to control environmental factors, in earlier times people were more vulnerable to geographic conditions.

Then ask: (a) What must a geographic region provide for people to survive? (Water, food, materials for shelter.)

(b) Why might river valleys have been the sites of early permanent settlements? (Rivers provided water for drinking, irrigation, and fishing, and were also a means of transportation.)

(c) In what ways does modern technology provide more control over geographic factors? (Answers will vary. Water can be transported hundreds of miles by underground pipe systems; fertilizers improve poor soil; large dams and reservoirs make water control possible; food and other raw materials can be imported from distant places. Modern heating and air conditioning permit temperature control.)

Developing the Lesson: Identifying Causes

Have students make a chart with two columns labeled *Development* and *Cause*. In the first column students should list the characteristics of civilizations that developed in river valleys. In the second column students should identify the causes, sources, or background of those developments. (*Organized government:* planning and direction of large projects needed leadership; growing cities needed laws, defense, tax collectors, and judges. *Organized religion:* people believed they had to win the approval and help of gods who controlled the forces of nature. *Division of labor:* permanent settlements made it possible for some people to specialize in skills. *Class structure:* certain types of work or service acquired more value and status than others. *System of writing:* as government, religion, and the economy grew more complex, people saw a need to organize and keep records. Soon writing acquired other uses, such as the preservation of myths, legends, and history.) (*Comprehension*)

Developing the Lesson: Drawing Conclusions

Ask: (a) What might account for the development of social classes? (Answers will vary. Occupation defined social class and some occupations were probably considered more vital to society than others.)

(b) Do you think social classes are necessary for a civilization? Why or why not? (Answers will vary.) (Synthesis)

Closing the Lesson: Summarizing Information

Have students write an essay titled *How The Growth of Cities Changed Society.* Essays should describe New Stone Age society before and after the development of cities (pp. 17–25). (Before cities, societies had small agricultural or herding populations. Only small, permanent settlements existed. Governments and religions were simple and writing systems were not needed. After cities developed, populations increased, division of labor developed, governmental systems became more complex, and religious rituals became more elaborate.) (*Comprehension*)

See *Section Review* questions, p. 25.

Chapter 1 Review Answers
(pp. 26–27)

Vocabulary Review

1. (a) domesticate (b) barter (c) theocracy (d) artisan (e) nomad (f) technology (g) prehistory (h) artifact (i) migrate (j) ritual

2. (a) Fossil—remains of ancient plant or animal life preserved in rock; carbon-14 dating—technique used by scientists to determine the age of once-living material. (b) Ice Age—one of four periods that occurred over millions of years, during which the earth's climate grew much cooler; glacier—huge, slow-moving sheet of ice. (c) Old Stone Age—earliest and longest part of the Stone Age, which began more than two million years ago when people lived by hunting animals and gathering wild foods; New Stone Age—part of the Stone Age that began about 10,000 years ago when people learned to farm and started to live in permanent settlements. (d) Culture—unique way of life; civilization—advanced level of culture characterized by organized government and religion, division of labor, class structure, and a system of writing.

Places to Know

1. G 2. D 3. B 4. I 5. C 6. H 7. A 8. E 9. F

Recalling the Facts

1. They find fossils, bones, and artifacts such as ancient tools, pottery, jewelry, and weapons. Scientists can learn what ancient peoples looked like, how long they lived, how they dressed, what work they did, how they worshiped, and what kinds of plants and animals were available.
2. Mastery of fire provided warmth and light, kept wild animals away at night, and helped in hunting and food preparation. The invention of tools made survival easier, freeing people to perform other tasks. Spoken language helped people cooperate and allowed them to pass ideas from one generation to the next.
3. They used fire, built sturdier shelters, and made heavy clothing from animal furs to keep warm. They also found new sources of food.
4. People began to farm.
5. Farming was safer, it provided a steadier source of food, and extra grain could be stored.
6. Farmers made permanent settlements, which grew into villages, to protect their crops. People began to practice division of labor, trade, and develop new technology.
7. Because bronze weapons and tools were harder and sharper than copper, they were in great demand.
8. Organized government, organized religion, division of labor, class structure, and a writing system.

9. They developed in Mesopotamia between the Tigris and Euphrates rivers, in Egypt on the banks of the Nile, in India in the Indus River Valley, and in China along the Yellow River.
10. Division of labor led to a system of social classes with priests and nobles at the top. Below them were merchants, traders, and government officials; next were artisans and small shopkeepers, followed by unskilled laborers and farmers. Slaves were at the bottom of the social structure.

Critical Thinking Skills

1. Answers will vary.
2. Government developed because the building of drainage and irrigation systems required planning, leadership, cooperation, and the labor of many people. In addition, the growing population in cities made government necessary. Laws were made to keep order among people and leaders assumed control of building projects, food distribution, and defense. Writing systems developed because complex societies needed a means of keeping records.
3. Answers will vary, but students might suggest that priests' high status was due to their supposed influence over the gods. In a world where natural events seemed unpredictable and unexplainable, power to influence the gods was highly valued.
4. The Old Stone Age tool is on the left. The New Stone Age tool on the right is sharper and less roughly made.

Thinking About Geography

Advantages—rivers provide food, water, irrigation, fertile soil, and transportation. Disadvantages—floods can destroy crops and kill people. Answers will vary, but students may mention dams and levees, which protect against flooding and provide hydroelectric power, improved irrigation, and reservoirs.

Enrichment: Primary Sources

1. It had a varied food supply, good water supply, and spacious meadowlands.
2. Competition may have forced specialization; people may have been trying to establish social order through specialization.
3. Answers will vary, but students may suggest that different tools and food remains were found.

The Birth of Civilization

Prehistory–3000 B.C.

See chapter timeline, p. 25.

Before You Read This Chapter

What do you think is the most amazing invention of all time? The printing press? The computer chip? The airplane? Television? Some of the most remarkable discoveries ever were made by people who lived tens of thousands of years ago. In this chapter you will learn about those notable achievements of our earliest ancestors. As you read, think about how far we have come since ancient times—and how much we still have in common with people of the distant past.

The Geographic Setting

The Chapter Outline

1. The Old Stone Age
2. The New Stone Age
3. River Valley Civilizations

These prehistoric paintings of wild horses and bison come from deep in a cave in France. What do they tell us about the artists who drew them? (See answer below.)

12

Caption Answer: These paintings suggest that the artists were intelligent and talented individuals, and that horses and bison were important to them.

1 The Old Stone Age

Objectives

Focus Questions

★ ■ How do scientists study life in the distant past? *(pages 13–14)*

● ■ What was life like during the Old Stone Age? *(pages 14–16)*

Terms to Know

prehistory	carbon-14 dating
Stone Age	nomad
Old Stone Age	ritual
New Stone Age	Ice Age
artifact	glacier
culture	migrate
fossil	

★ Note strategies for first objective on this page and p. 14.

Much of what we know about the past comes from written records. Over the centuries, people have recorded information about their beliefs, their way of life, and events they considered important. They have made these records in many forms—on clay, stone, wood, bone, paper, and computer tape. Yet systems of writing are only about 6,000 years old, while human beings have existed for hundreds of thousands of years. The period before people began to keep written records is called **prehistory**.

The Stone Age

Early human beings used stone for their tools and weapons. For this reason, the prehistoric period is known as the **Stone Age**. The earliest and longest part of the Stone Age, which began more than two million years ago, is called the **Old Stone Age** or Paleolithic Age.

During this period, people lived by hunting animals and gathering wild foods, such as nuts and berries.

About 10,000 years ago, a new way of life began to take shape. People learned to farm and began to live in permanent settlements. The development of farming marked the beginning of the **New Stone Age** or Neolithic Age.

Some of the most dramatic events in human history—the invention of tools, the taming of fire, the development of language—took place during the Stone Age. We will never know the exact dates of these achievements or the persons responsible, yet we know many other things about this period. In the following part of the chapter, you will read about several ways of searching for clues about the distant past.

The Study of Prehistory

Archeological digs. One of the richest sources of clues to the prehistoric way of life is a "dig"—a site where archeologists (ar-kee-AHL-uh-jists) work to uncover traces of early settlements. By sifting through the dirt in a small plot of land, they may come upon ancient tools, pottery, jewelry, or weapons. Sometimes such **artifacts**—objects made by people—are in pieces. Experts study the fragments carefully and make drawings to show what the object may have looked like before it was broken.

How do archeologists know where to look for this "buried treasure"? Often they study photographs of the land taken from airplanes. These pictures can show bumps or ridges that suggest likely sites. Sometimes a dig is made where artifacts have been found by accident. A farmer plowing a field may turn up stone arrowheads, or a bulldozer operator may uncover the ruins of an ancient building.

13

★ **RETEACHING. Have students make a chart listing differences between the Old Stone Age and New Stone Age.** (Old Stone Age: began more than two million years ago; people were hunters and gatherers. New Stone Age: began around 10,000 years ago; people developed farming and settlements; invented tools, used fire and language.) *(Comprehension)* **Sequencing Information**
Check for Understanding. Ask: Why is the prehistoric period called the "Stone Age"? (People used stone to make weapons and tools.)

★ **REINFORCEMENT. Have students use the following words to describe the study of prehistory:** *"dig"; archeologist; artifacts; anthropologist; culture; geologist; fossils; carbon-14 dating.* **Students might define each word and explain how it relates to the study of prehistory or use the words in an essay about the study of prehistory.** *(Application)* **Developing Vocabulary**

Clues to the past. Specially trained scientists work like detectives to piece together the story of prehistoric peoples. Anthropologists (an-thruh-PAHL-uh-jists) examine the remains of early villages, houses, and gravesites. From ancient bones they can tell what the people looked like, how tall they were, and how long they lived. From artifacts, anthropologists learn a great deal about the **culture**—unique way of life—of Stone Age peoples. A piece of carved ivory or a stone hatchet can reveal a wealth of information— how people dressed, what work they did, or how they worshiped.

★ See below.

Other scientists also help unlock the mysteries of the past. Geologists work to identify the stones and metals that early peoples used to make tools and ornaments. Geologists also analyze **fossils**—traces of ancient animal and plant life preserved in rock. By studying fossils and other evidence, scientists can tell what kinds of plants and animals were used by prehistoric peoples.

Sec. Rev. ques. 2

Scientists use a number of methods to determine the age of objects they find. The most important of these methods was discovered in 1948 by an American chemist named Willard Libby. His technique, called **carbon-14 dating**, depends on the fact that all living organisms contain a certain amount of a radioactive material called carbon 14. When a plant or animal dies, the carbon 14 begins to decrease at a fixed rate. By analyzing how much carbon 14 is left in a piece of wood or bone or other once-living material, scientists can tell its approximate age.

With the findings from all these different kinds of research, scientists have developed theories about how human beings lived in prehistoric times. Yet there are still many unanswered questions and many issues on which experts disagree.

Prehistoric Peoples

● Note strategies for second objective on this page and p. 15.

Early human beings. Many scientists believe that human-like creatures lived in Africa several million years ago. About 250,000 years ago, the first true human beings ap-

14

peared. The brains of these early human beings were only two thirds the size of the modern human brain. Yet these people are called *Homo sapiens* (which means "thinking man") because they were far more intelligent than their ancestors.

By about 100,000 years ago the Neanderthals (nee-AN-dur-thahlz) had appeared. The Neanderthals lived in Africa, Asia, and Europe. They had brains as large as those of modern humans, but they were shorter in height and their skulls were shaped differently. The Neanderthals died out about 35,000 years ago, for unknown reasons.

Ancient human skulls are studied at a museum in Nairobi, Kenya. These fossil remains, dating from millions of years ago, were uncovered by the British anthropologists Louis and Mary Leakey and their son Richard.

Another group, the Cro-Magnons (kroh-MAG-nunz), were the first human beings to have all the physical characteristics of modern people. Remains of Cro-Magnon people have been found in Africa, Asia, and Europe. For many years scientists thought that Cro-Magnons were later descendants of Neanderthals. Recent discoveries suggest that they lived about the same time as Neanderthals.

Hunters and gatherers. The men and women of the Old Stone Age were **nomads**— people who wander from place to place rather than making permanent settlements. These people lived in caves or in tents made of branches and animal skins. Small hunting bands, usually 20 to 30 people, followed herds of wild animals, which they killed for meat. They also gathered fruit, nuts, seeds, honey, roots, and grains. When sources of food ran short, the people moved on.

Sec. Rev. ques. 3

Achievements of the Old Stone Age

Mastery of fire. It was during the Old Stone Age that people developed the basic traits that marked their superiority over animals. The earliest humans, for example, were terrified of fire just as animals are. Yet people had the intelligence to recognize that they could use fire for a variety of purposes.

Fire provided warmth and light and kept wild animals away at night. Fire was useful in hunting, too. Hunters with torches could drive a herd of animals over the edge of a cliff. People also learned that they could cook food with fire and preserve meat with smoke.

The invention of tools. The people of the Old Stone Age also used their intelligence to make tools that helped them perform difficult tasks. Archeologists have found Old Stone Age tools all over the world. The most common are daggers and spearpoints for hunting, hand axes and choppers to cut up meat, and scrapers for cleaning animal hides. Other tools were used to dig up roots, peel the bark off wood, and remove the skins from animals.

Not all Stone Age tools were made of stone. Sharpened wooden sticks were used as spears. Later, splinters of bone were used as needles and fishhooks. Tools such as these made the work of survival easier, freeing people to perform other tasks.

Language. The greatest achievement of the Old Stone Age was the development of language. Language gave people the ability to plan their hunts and cooperate in other tasks. Human beings could now communicate thoughts and experiences and pass ideas from one generation to the next.

Some scientists believe that this leap forward took place in Africa, where human life began. Scholars have been tracing the origins of modern languages by comparing basic word roots and structures of speech. They have even reconstructed ancient languages, long extinct, and identified them as the probable sources of languages spoken today. Some scholars have theorized that the first human language was spoken by people living in Africa close to 100,000 years ago.

As human beings migrated out of Africa and populated the other continents, they took the art of speech with them. This process spread over many thousands of years, and in its course speech changed and developed differently in different regions. As people invented new words and changed pronunciation of old words, new languages evolved. Yet each language carried within it the roots of that first African language (page 23).

Religion. Archeologists have also found evidence that Old Stone Age people developed religion. They apparently performed **rituals**—ceremonies—that they believed would help to bring success in hunting. They also had burial rituals that involved placing tools, ornaments, food, and flowers in the graves of their dead. These practices seem clearly to show that Old Stone Age people believed in life after death.

Sec. Rev. ques. 4

Old Stone Age art. Prehistoric people created many kinds of artwork, including jewelry, sculpture, and music. Their most famous works of art, however, are the stunning paintings found on the walls of caves in Europe.

● See below.

15

● REINFORCEMENT. Have students make a diagram identifying the effects of specific environmental changes late in the Old Stone Age. (Cooling temperatures caused the Arctic ice cap to spread. Glaciers formed; ocean level dropped; people migrated to the Americas. Many kinds of animals died out; humans adapted to environment.) *(Comprehension)* **Identifying Cause and Effect**

● ENRICHMENT. Have students work in groups to present a panel discussion titled *Achievements of Old Stone Age People.* Students might research and draw conclusions about how the use of fire, tools and language; religious beliefs; and the creation of art distinguished human beings from animals, or show examples of Stone Age art, religious rituals, or tools. *(Synthesis)* **Drawing Conclusions**

The first cave art was discovered almost by accident. In 1875 a Spanish nobleman began to look for fossils and artifacts in a cave on his estate. One day in 1879 his 12-year-old daughter came with him, took her lantern, and began to explore a part of the cave in which her father could not stand upright. Looking up, she saw that the ceiling was covered with paintings of animals. There were bison, deer, horses, and other animals painted in red, brown, yellow, and black.

The cave, named Altamira (ahl-tuh-MEER-uh), soon became widely known. Since then, several other caves with paintings have been found in northern Spain and southwestern France. The most famous was found in 1940, when four young boys in Lascaux (lahs-KOH), France, went looking for their lost dog, which had fallen down a hole. The Lascaux cave contains dozens of colorful animal paintings made between 12,000 and 30,000 years ago (picture, page 12).

Cave paintings have told scientists much about life in the Old Stone Age. In addition, the paintings are true works of art. They show that even many thousands of years ago, people had creativity and a sense of beauty.

Environmental Changes

Late in the Old Stone Age, for reasons that are still a mystery, the earth's climate grew much cooler. This was the last of four long cold periods, called Ice Ages, that occurred over millions of years.

The most recent Ice Age is thought to have reached its height about 20,000 years ago. As the weather steadily cooled, the Arctic ice cap thickened and spread. Huge, slow-moving sheets of ice called glaciers formed in mountain ranges. The sheets of ice spread to cover much of the Northern Hemisphere. In North America they reached southward to the present-day Ohio Valley. Northern parts of Europe and Asia also lay buried under ice.

Because so much of the earth's water was frozen in the glaciers, the water level in

16

the oceans dropped by several hundred feet. Land that today is deep under water was exposed, forming land bridges between islands or continents. Scientists believe that people first migrated—moved—to the Americas during this period, crossing over a land bridge from Asia. (You will read about the settlement of the Americas in Chapter 8.)

Many kinds of animals became extinct during the Ice Ages because they were unable to keep warm and find food. Other species were killed off by hunters. Humans, however, used their superior intelligence to adapt their way of life to the changing environment. They used fire and built sturdier shelters to keep warm. They learned to make heavy clothing from animal furs. They managed to find new sources of food when old ones disappeared.

Sec. Rev ques. 5

About 10,000 years ago, at the end of the last Ice Age, the weather grew warmer. The glaciers melted and the climate in many places became hotter and drier. Once again people were forced to adjust to a new environment. This time, however, the changes they made led to an entirely new way of life.

See Sec. 1 *Closing the Lesson,* p. T11B.

Section Review

Answers to Section Review questions are in brackets on pages indicated.

1. **Define or identify:** prehistory, Stone Age, Old Stone Age, New Stone Age, artifact, culture, fossil, carbon-14 dating, nomad, ritual, Ice Age, glacier, migrate. (pp. 13, 14, 15, 16)
2. What kinds of evidence do scientists use to find out how prehistoric people lived? (p. 14)
3. Describe how men and women lived during the Old Stone Age. Discuss food, shelter, tools, and the use of fire. (p. 15)
4. What evidence is there that Stone Age people held religious beliefs? (p. 15)
5. How did Stone Age people adapt to changes during the Ice Ages? (p. 16)
6. **Critical thinking:** How would the use of language have helped people survive in prehistoric times? (See answer below.)

Cultural History Prehistoric peoples painted on rock, modeled in clay, and engraved antlers, bones, and ivory. Early artists used four basic colors: black from charcoal; white from clay and lime mud; and red and yellow from animal blood, red clay, and ground-up iron compounds.

Check for Understanding. Ask: How did human beings survive the Ice Age? (Humans used their superior intelligence to adapt to the changing environment. They used fire, built sturdier shelters, made heavy clothing from animal furs, and found new sources of food.)

6. Answers will vary. Students might suggest that language would have helped people cooperate in carrying out vital tasks. Language would also have supported the survival of the species by enabling humans to pass on ideas, experiences, and methods from one generation to the next.

See lesson plans, pp. T11A–T11C.

2 The New Stone Age

Objectives

Focus Questions

★ ■ Why did people begin to farm and build villages? *(pages 17–18)*

● ■ How did village life promote trade and technology? *(pages 18–21)*

Terms to Know

domesticate   excavate
division of labor   technology
artisan   Bronze Age
barter

★ Note strategies for first objective on this page and p. 18.

For more than a million years, until the end of the last Ice Age, human beings all over the world lived as hunters and gatherers. Then, about 10,000 years ago, enormous changes began to happen. First, people began to use new ways of shaping and polishing their stone tools. For this reason, as you have read, the period is called the New Stone Age.

The most important change that occurred during this period, however, was that people began to farm. From farming came other achievements. Villages slowly grew and trade developed. People became skilled in new crafts that improved the quality of their lives. These changes did not happen quickly, nor did they occur everywhere at the same time. They developed over thousands of years in different places.

The Agricultural Revolution

The start of farming. At the end of the last Ice Age, many of the large game animals died out. Some could not adapt to the changing climate; others fell victim to human hunt-

ers. As a result, food became scarcer. When hunters did make a kill, the meat spoiled quickly because of the warmer weather. For these reasons, Stone Age people began to rely more heavily on plant foods for their survival.

Probably many prehistoric peoples had known how to plant seeds for thousands of years before they began to farm systematically. People in the Old Stone Age often sowed the seeds of wild plants to add to their food supply. However, they did not stay in one place to tend their crops. Instead, they moved in search of game. As hunting became less reliable as a source of food, some people

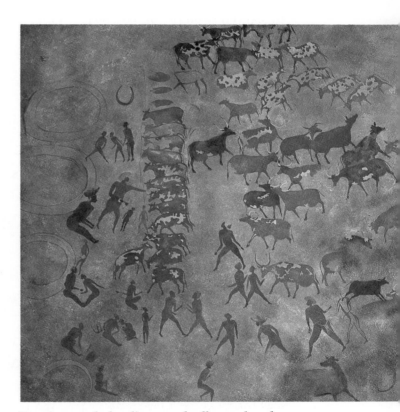

Farming and herding gradually replaced hunting as a way of getting food. This cliff painting in the Sahara, made by African artists of the New Stone Age, shows cattle and nearby corrals.

17

★ RETEACHING. Have students review "The start of farming" and "Domestication of animals" (pp. 17–18) and outline the causes and effects of the development of farming and animal domestication. (The last Ice Age resulted in the death of many animals and a food shortage. People relied more on plants for food and discovered that farming provided a more stable food supply. Raising animals also provided a more secure food source than hunting.) *(Comprehension) Identifying Cause and Effect*

★ REINFORCEMENT. Have students explain why the development of agriculture is considered a significant advance in human history. Students might compare ways of life before and after the development of farming. (Farming provided people with more control over the food supply, greater variety of foods, the possibility of storing foods, and more safety than hunting.) *(Comprehension) Drawing Conclusions* began to plant more seeds and live in permanent settlements to protect their crops.

No one group can be credited with introducing farming. People in the Middle East (the area from Egypt to present-day Iraq) first began to farm between 9000 and 6000 B.C.* Elsewhere at this same time, in places as far apart as Mexico and Thailand, other people were also developing agriculture.

★ See below.

Those who took up farming soon realized its advantages. Unlike hunting, farming provided a steady source of food. People planted such crops as corn, wheat, peppers, and tomatoes, then enjoyed these foods for many months to come. Grain was easier to store than meat, so it was possible to keep large quantities of food in reserve for the future. In addition, hunters were often killed or wounded by the animals they stalked and in the fires and traps they set to catch their prey. Farming was a far safer way to get food.

Sec. Rev. ques. 2

Domestication of animals. Another alternative to hunting was **domestication**—taming—of wild animals, such as sheep, goats, and pigs. People probably began domesticating animals at the same time that they began farming. Farmers living in settled communities saw that they could ensure a steady food supply by keeping herds of animals and slaughtering them as needed.

In areas where poor soil or an unfavorable climate made farming impractical, herding became the chief way of life. Unlike farmers, herders remained nomadic, moving to find pasture for their animals. Both farmers and herders gained a steady source of meat, milk, cheese, furs, and skins by domesticating animals.

The Growth of Villages

● Note strategies for second objective on this page and p. 19.

In time the settlements that farmers made near their fields grew into villages. Village walls and clusters of buildings provided protection from animals and from unfriendly outsiders. The emergence of villages also led to changes in the way people lived.

Artisans. One of the biggest changes was that people began to practice **division of labor.** In other words, people specialized in particular skills rather than splitting their time among different activities. One group of villagers, concentrating on farming, could produce enough food for the whole village. This gave other villagers time to spend on nonfarming tasks. Some people made tools and weapons. Others made shelters or clothing or learned to weave reeds into baskets.

Sec. Rev. ques. 3

* The calendar used today in most Western countries divides time into two periods: before the birth of Christ (B.C.) and since then (A.D.). For a fuller explanation, see the Skill Review section at the back of this book.

p 872

Ⓕ See below.

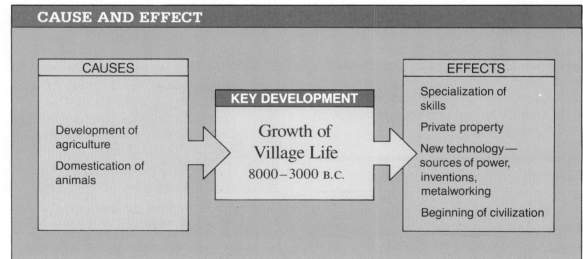

CAUSE AND EFFECT

CAUSES	KEY DEVELOPMENT	EFFECTS
Development of agriculture Domestication of animals	Growth of Village Life 8000–3000 B.C.	Specialization of skills Private property New technology— sources of power, inventions, metalworking Beginning of civilization

★ ENRICHMENT. Have students research the development of agriculture and then draw a map showing the regions of the world where agriculture first developed. (Application) *Relating Geography and History*

Ⓕ CAUSE AND EFFECT CHART ACTIVITY. Ask: How many years ago was 8000 B.C., when village life emerged? (About 10,000 years ago.) Then have students explain how each effect of the growth of village life might be an advance and identify problems that might have resulted from the growth of village life. (Evaluation) *Making Judgments*

● RETEACHING. Have students review "The Growth of Villages" (pp. 18–20) and summarize why permanent settlements were important for Stone Age people. (Permanent settlements led to division of labor, specialization of skills, increased productivity, growth of trade, and acquisition of goods.) (Comprehension) *Observing for Detail*

Ⓕ FEATURE ACTIVITY. Have students develop a hypothesis suggesting why England's early hunters and farmers may have built

Stonehenge (Synthesis) Forming a Hypothesis

Ⓕ See above.

Historic Places

Stonehenge

On a bare, windswept plain in southern England, great chunks of stone lie in a rough circle. Some form arches and doorways. Others have toppled over. This is Stonehenge, one of the most impressive and mysterious monuments left from prehistoric times.

Stonehenge was built and rebuilt many times, beginning about 2800 B.C. Its largest stones weigh more than 50 tons. Somehow the builders hauled these stones from quarries 20 miles away, hewed them into shape with 60-pound hammers, and heaved them upright.

Why did England's early hunters and farmers devote so much work to building this monument? Some archeologists believe that Stonehenge was an important religious center. Other scientists have linked Stonehenge with ancient astronomers. They say that special stones are positioned to "point" to where the sun and moon rise and set on the longest and shortest days of the year. Prehistoric people may have used Stonehenge to keep track of dates for religious festivals. The complete story of Stonehenge, however, remains a mystery.

Still others made pottery containers for cooking and for storing food and water. All these workers became artisans—people with skills in specific crafts.

Trade and property. The demand for the products of expert artisans led to trade. A toolmaker might trade with a farmer, exchanging a stone hoe or ax for grain or a sheep. A potter might trade clay pots for animal skins. This kind of trade, in which one good is exchanged for another, is known as **barter**.

Trade and village living encouraged people to acquire more possessions. Through trade, people were able to obtain a wider variety of goods. Village living made owning things more practical. Hunters and herders, who moved from place to place, needed to travel light. Farmers and artisans, on the other hand, could own more because they lived in permanent settlements.

Çatal Hüyük. In the Middle East, many villages existed by 6000 B.C. Çatal Hüyük (chuh-TUL hoo-YOOK), in what is now Turkey, was built about that time. The site was **excavated**—dug up—from 1961 to 1965, and archeologists have studied its remains thoroughly.

● See below.

19

● REINFORCEMENT. Have students make a chart listing technological advances made during the New Stone Age and then explain how these developments improved the way of life. (Technological advances include the following: plows; wheel and sail; permanent houses; spinning and weaving; potter's wheel; grinding tools; use of bronze.) *Identifying Cause and Effect (Comprehension)*

● ENRICHMENT. Have students analyze the information provided about Çatal Hüyük, and explain why the settlement is representative of Stone Age achievements. Students might make a chart, draw posters, or present an oral report identifying Stone Age advances and giving examples from Çatal Hüyük. (Comprehension) *Analyzing History*

At its height, Çatal Hüyük was home to between 3,000 and 6,000 people. The villagers grew wheat and barley and raised sheep and cattle. They also hunted wild animals. Some villagers were artisans who made finely woven clothing of wool and linen. Traders from other regions brought marble to exchange for obsidian, a volcanic rock that looks like glass. Artisans used obsidian for making jewelry, mirrors, and knives.

The people of Çatal Hüyük built flat-roofed houses made of oak and dried mud bricks. Probably to provide protection and make construction easier, they built the walls of the houses against one another. Houses could be entered only through the roof and down a ladder.

Sec. Rev. ques. 4

Colorful decorations covered the buildings in the village. Walls were painted with pictures of all kinds—flowers, designs, playful leopards, dancers, and hunting scenes. Benches and pillars were studded with cattle horns. Archeologists believe that much of the art had religious meaning. Some buildings were probably shrines, decorated with plaster carvings and statues of clay, marble, or limestone. The people of Çatal Hüyük believed in many gods. The main one was a mother goddess who was believed to control the harvest.

Anthropologists estimate that the average person in Çatal Hüyük lived about 30 years. The dead were buried in their homes, and food was put into their graves. Graves also contained tools, jewelry, mirrors, and weapons.

Meanwhile . . .

IN THE AMERICAS

While artisans in much of the ancient world were working with bronze, in America most cultures still fashioned tools and weapons out of stone. People in the Great Lakes area had begun to use copper, but this technology did not spread to other cultures.

20

New Technology

As New Stone Age people began to specialize in certain useful crafts, they also began to develop new technology. In other words, they invented new methods and tools to meet their needs.

Sources of power. The most valuable advances were those that enabled people to harness the powers of animals and nature. Plows, for example, allowed farmers to use oxen or horses to turn the soil. With the wheel and the sail, people could transport themselves and their goods faster and farther than ever before. For the first time, human beings did not have to rely solely on the strength of their own hands, legs, and backs. They were beginning to learn that animals and machines could do a good part of the work for them.

Domestic inventions. Other advances made life easier and more comfortable for New Stone Age people than it had been for their ancestors. Permanent houses of brick, skins, and wood were warmer and drier than the temporary shelters of the Old Stone Age. The invention of spinning and weaving allowed people to make clothing out of cotton, linen, and wool, which were much more comfortable than animals' skins in warm weather.

New technology made many tasks simpler than before. By turning clay on a flat disk called a potter's wheel, artisans could shape plates, jugs, and bowls. They developed new methods for baking both pottery and mud bricks to make them longer-lasting. Artisans also learned to polish stone tools by grinding them against other stones. Their tools were sharper, more durable, and more efficient than the rough ones made by people in the Old Stone Age.

Metalworking. Late in the New Stone Age, artisans in the Middle East learned to work with metal to make tools and weapons. The knowledge of metalworking spread from the Middle East and was also learned independently by people in other parts of the world.

Science Note that obsidian is formed by lava that cools quickly as it flows onto the earth's surface. Obsidian is usually black or black with red bands.

Copper was probably the first metal used, since it can be separated easily from the rock in which it is found. Copper tools and weapons were sharper than those made of stone, and they could be reshaped if broken.

The Bronze Age. Soon toolmakers discovered how to combine copper with a small amount of tin to make bronze. Bronze was harder than copper. It made weapons and tools with a sharper cutting edge. The demand for bronze objects and for tin led to a great increase in trade.

The term Bronze Age is used to describe the period when bronze replaced copper and stone as the main material used in tools and weapons. This period began in different parts of Asia and Europe at widely separated times and lasted for thousands of years in some regions. The knowledge of bronzeworking was discovered first in southwestern Asia about 5,000 years ago.

See lesson plans, pp. T11A–T11C.

Section Review

Answers to Section Review questions are in brackets on pages indicated.

1. **Define or identify:** domesticate, division of labor, artisan, barter, excavate, technology, Bronze Age. (pp. 18, 19, 20, 21)
2. What advantages did farming and herding have over hunting and gathering as a way of life? (p. 18)
3. How did farming encourage the development of village life, new crafts, and trade? (pp. 18, 20)
4. What do the discoveries made at Çatal Hüyük reveal about life in the New Stone Age? (p. 20)
5. **Critical thinking:** Which of the inventions of the New Stone Age, in your opinion, was the most important? Why? (See answer below.)

5. Answers should reflect students' understanding of how the inventions altered living conditions, tools, and weapons for people of the New Stone Age.

3 River Valley Civilizations

Objectives

Focus Questions

★ ■ Why did the first civilizations develop in river valleys? *(pages 21–22)*
● ■ How did the growth of cities change society? *(pages 22–25)*

Terms to Know

civilization
theocracy

★ Note strategies for first objective on this page and p. 22.

Because of the achievements of the New Stone Age, people's food supply became more reliable, population increased, and trade expanded. Settlements became larger, and some grew into cities. The growth of cit-

ies was the beginning of civilization—an advanced level of culture. Civilizations generally have the following features: (1) organized government, (2) organized religion, (3) division of labor, (4) a class structure, and (5) a system of writing.

MONUMENTAL ARCHITECTURE

Birthplaces of Civilization

The first civilizations developed in four great river valleys in Asia and Africa (map, page 22). The earliest of all was in Mesopotamia (mes-uh-puh TAY-mee-uh). By 3500 B.C. a number of cities had begun to develop in the region between the Tigris (TY-gris) and Euphrates (yoo-FRAY-teez) rivers. Egypt was another early center of civilization; it developed on the Nile River in Africa. Civilization in India emerged in the Indus Valley, and Chinese civilization grew up along the Yellow River, also called the Huang (WAHNG).* **21**

★ **RETEACHING. Have students draw a map showing the locations of the Tigris and Euphrates, Nile, Indus, and Yellow (Huang) rivers.** (Comprehension) *Relating Geography and History*
★ **REINFORCEMENT. Have students summarize the advantages and disadvantages of living in a river valley civilization.** (Advantages: water available for drinking, irrigation, and transportation. Disadvantages: floods could destroy crops and other property, and take lives.) (Comprehension) *Summarizing Information*

Check for Understanding. Ask: What are the characteristics of civilization? (Organized government; organized religion; division of labor; a class structure; a system of writing.)

You will read about each of these civilizations in Chapters 2 and 3.

There are several reasons why civilizations first arose in river valleys. Rivers provided food and fresh water for both people
and animals. Rivers also supplied water to
irrigate nearby fields. In addition, some rivers
flooded each year and deposited fertile soil
on the fields. Finally, because travel by water
was easier than travel by foot, rivers encouraged trade.

All of these factors made river valleys
attractive places to settle. Yet living near a
river meant problems, too. The floods that
brought fertile soil to fields also filled irriga-

tion canals with silt that had to be cleaned
out. Even worse, flood waters destroyed
crops and often killed many people.

Government

● Note strategies for second objective on this page and p. 24.

The building and upkeep of irrigation systems
required planning, leadership, cooperation,
and the labor of many people. The need to
plan and direct such large projects was probably one reason why governments were first
organized.

The growing populations of cities also
made government necessary. Laws were
made to keep order among the people. Leaders took charge of building projects, food
distribution, and defense against enemies.
Tax collectors and judges were also needed.

---

* Most Chinese names in this book are spelled according to the Pinyin system, which has been the official
system used in China since 1979. Both Pinyin and traditional spellings appear in the Index of this book.

Map Answers: (1) Nile—Africa. Tigris-Euphrates, Indus, and Yellow—all in Asia. (2) Coasts of Mexico,
peninsula extending into the Caribbean, and northern Pacific coast of South America. (3) Africa.

Early Civilizations

Find the four river valley civilizations shown on this map. On what continent was each civilization located? Where were early civilizations in the
Americas located? On what continent were the earliest known remains of
human beings found?

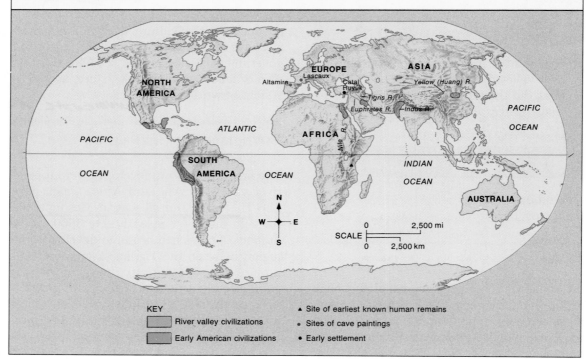

★ **ENRICHMENT.** Have students research and compare the development of civilizations in the Tigris and Euphrates, Nile, Indus, and
Yellow River valleys. Students should find information on the
dates of the civilizations and their achievements. *(Synthesis) Locating Information*

● **RETEACHING.** Have students review "Government" and "Religion"
(pp. 22; 24) and answer the following: **(a) Why did government
develop in the river valley civilizations?** (The building of irrigation
systems required planning, leadership, cooperation, and the labor of
many people. The growing population required laws to keep order.) **(b)
Why did religious ritual develop in river valley civilizations?** (People believed this would help them win the approval and help of nature
gods. *(Comprehension) Observing for Details*

Ⓕ See below.

The Geography Connection

The Origin and Spread of Language

Some scientists believe that Africa was not only the home of the first human beings but also the birthplace of human speech. They theorize that the people who migrated out of Africa carried with them the ancestor of all the world's languages.

Linguists—scientists who study language—have no written evidence of humankind's earliest languages. Just as archeologists piece together the history of early civilizations from surviving artifacts, however, linguists can study the history of languages through careful analysis of different kinds of evidence.

Linguists trace the development of language by comparing the words and structures of different languages, often with the help of computers. They have reconstructed what they call proto-languages—ancient languages that were the ancestors of all modern languages. Some linguists have also concluded that these proto-languages all stemmed from a single parent language that developed in Africa about 100,000 years ago. They have reconstructed more than 150 words that were part of the first human language, which they call "proto-World."

Strong evidence for this theory lies in the similarities among words in the various proto-languages. For instance, linguists know that the word for tooth was *gin* in China and Siberia, *nigi* in the Congo in Africa, *nigi* or *gini* in India and Europe, and *gini* in Southeast Asia. Such closely related words must have derived from a single source.

The study of world migration adds weight to the theory of a single parent language. Using fossil evidence, archeologists have sketched the migratory paths of early human beings; these paths seem to parallel the paths of world language development (see the map). Evidence from the study of human genes also supports the theory. Genetic evidence suggests that the people of southern Africa who speak a language called Khoisan (KOY-san) were probably the first group to split off from the original *Homo sapiens* group that arose in Africa 250,000 years ago. The Khoisan languages are likewise believed to have been the first to split off from the ancient parent language.

Making the connection. How do linguists uncover the history of human language? What evidence do they have that all languages may be related?

The Spread of Ancient Languages

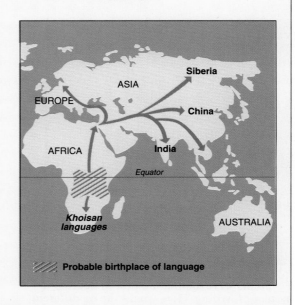

23

Ⓕ **GEOGRAPHY CONNECTION.** Point out to students that the map on this page shows the Eastern Hemisphere only. Ask them what continents are in the Western Hemisphere (Americas). Ask them to suggest geographic factors that acted as a barrier to the spread of proto-languages to the Western Hemisphere (oceans).

Background Research on proto-World has been reported in *The Sciences,* the journal of the New York Academy of Science.

Religion

As early as the Old Stone Age, people had religious beliefs involving nature, animal spirits, and some form of life after death. In the New Stone Age, farming peoples believed in many gods who controlled the sun, the rain, the wind, and other natural forces. The people of the river valley civilizations built on these beliefs. They developed elaborate religious rituals to win the gods' help and approval. They also paid heavy taxes to support huge temples where priests lived, studied, and taught younger priests.

Priests were not only religious leaders but powerful government leaders as well. All four of the great river valley civilizations were theocracies (thee-AHK-ruh-seez) ruled by priest-kings. A theocracy is a form of government in which the ruler is seen either as a god or as the chosen representative of the gods. Laws, under this system, are believed to be the commands of the gods.

Sec. Rev. ques. 3

Egyptians were among the first to develop a system of writing. How would life be different without written language? (See answer below.)

24

The Formation of Classes

As you have read, the development of permanent farming settlements led to a division of labor. Some members of a community developed special skills, such as weaving, metalworking, and brick-making. As cities grew, more specialized occupations appeared. People became merchants, priests, traders, and government officials.

Division of labor affected society in two important ways. First, it helped artisans become more accomplished. People who worked full time at their crafts could perfect their skills and share ideas with other artisans. Traders from other cities and towns also brought new ideas and materials.

A second effect of division of labor was that a system of social classes took shape. At the top of this system was the ruler. Below the ruler came a class of priests and nobles. Priests were respected because they were believed to have special influence with the gods. Nobles, who often were skilled warriors, owned large estates and sometimes served as high government officials.

Sec. Rev. ques. 4

Below the nobles were merchants, traders, and lower government officials. Next were the artisans and small shopkeepers. The largest social class was made up of unskilled laborers and farmers. At the bottom of society were the slaves. Some slaves were foreign captives; others had lost their freedom by committing crimes or going into debt.

In general, people in ancient cities did not move from one class to another. Membership in the noble class was hereditary. Most people followed their parents' way of life and married persons of the same class.

Systems of Writing

As government, religion, and the economy became more complex and organized, people saw the need to keep records. Government officials, for example, needed to remember what taxes were owed, what laws had been passed, and how much grain was stored in a

● See below.

Sec. Rev. ques. 5

● REINFORCEMENT. Have students analyze the class structure that developed in the river valley civilizations. Students should explain the organization of the class system and analyze why each class might have been given its respective rank. (Priests were believed to have special influence over the gods. Nobles were wealthy estate owners and often government officials or warriors.) *(Comprehension)* **Analyzing History**

● ENRICHMENT. Have students write a paper comparing government, religion, class structure, and writing systems in the river valley civilizations with those in present-day society. *(Synthesis)* **Linking Past and Present**

Caption Answer: Without written language, humans could not reliably pass on knowledge and tradition to later generations.

warehouse. Priests had to keep track of the passage of time and the positions of the sun and moon, which were important in religious rituals. Merchants needed to keep records of what they bought and sold. As a result, almost every ancient civilization developed some form of writing.

People soon began to use writing for much more than just record-keeping. They wrote down the myths, legends, and poems that had been passed orally from generation to generation. They preserved their knowledge of nature and mathematics. They wrote down their thoughts about religion. They also wrote about great events in the lives of their cities, such as wars, floods, and the deaths of kings. For this reason, the beginning of civilization also marked the beginning of written history.

Section Review

Answers to Section Review questions are in brackets on pages indicated.

1. **Define:** civilization, theocracy. (pp. 21, 22)
2. How did geographic conditions in river valleys encourage the development of civilizations? (p. 22)
3. What role did religion play in the governments of river valley civilizations? (p. 24)
4. What social classes existed in river valley civilizations? (p. 24)
5. Why did writing systems come into use? (p. 24)
6. **Critical thinking:** Cooperation is considered a necessary ingredient for civilization. Do you agree? Explain your answer. (See answer below.)

6. Answers will vary. Students might cite the five characteristics of civilization in explaining the need for cooperation.

Chapter 1   Summary and Timeline

1. The people of the Old Stone Age lived by hunting and gathering their food. They also made some remarkable advances—making tools, controlling and using fire, and developing spoken language.

2. The New Stone Age began about 10,000 years ago, at about the same time that the last Ice Age ended. People in different parts of the world began to plant crops, domesticate animals, and establish villages. Late in the New Stone Age, artisans in the Middle East learned to work with metals.

3. In four river valleys in Africa and Asia, farming villages gradually grew into cities. As cities developed, so did organized government and religion, a division of labor, social classes, and systems of writing. In this way, the first civilizations were born.

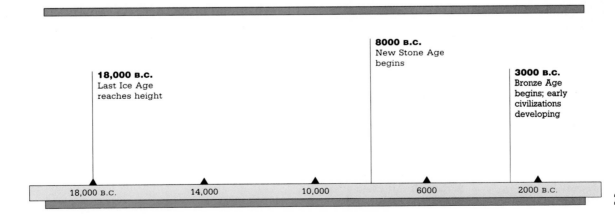

18,000 B.C. Last Ice Age reaches height

8000 B.C. New Stone Age begins

3000 B.C. Bronze Age begins; early civilizations developing

18,000 B.C.   14,000   10,000   6000   2000 B.C.

25

CHAPTER 1 REVIEW

See p. T11C for answers to Chapter Review.

Vocabulary Review

1. Match each of the following terms with its correct definition: *artifact, artisan, barter, domesticate, migrate, nomad, prehistory, ritual, technology, theocracy.*
   a. tame
   b. exchange one good for another
   c. form of government in which the ruler is seen either as a god or as the chosen representative of the gods
   d. person who is skilled in a specialized craft
   e. person who wanders from place to place rather than making a permanent home
   f. methods and tools used by humans to meet their needs
   g. period of time before people began to keep written records
   h. object made by a person
   i. move from one region and settle in another
   j. ceremony
2. Define the terms in each of the following pairs.
   a. fossil; carbon-14 dating
   b. Ice Age; glacier
   c. Old Stone Age; New Stone Age
   d. culture; civilization

Places to Know

Match the letters on this map of the world with the continents and oceans listed below. You may want to refer to the map on page 22.
1. Africa
2. Asia
3. Atlantic Ocean
4. Australia
5. Europe
6. Indian Ocean
7. North America
8. Pacific Ocean
9. South America

Recalling the Facts

1. What types of evidence about the past do archeologists obtain from digs? What can scientists learn from the archeologists' findings?
2. What were the most important achievements of the Old Stone Age, and how did they affect the people who lived during this period?
3. How did Stone Age people adapt to the changes in climate during the last Ice Age?
4. What was the most important change that took place at the beginning of the New Stone Age?
5. Why was farming a more satisfactory way of getting food than hunting?
6. Why did farming lead to the development of villages? What changes did the growth of villages bring to the lives of New Stone Age people?
7. Why did the discovery of techniques for making bronze lead to a great increase in trade?
8. What are the five characteristic features of civilization?
9. Where did the four earliest civilizations develop?
10. What kind of social structure developed in early civilizations?

26

1. Building vocabulary. *Neolithic* comes from the Greek words *neos*, meaning "new," and *lithos*, meaning "stone." Use a dictionary to find and define five other words that have the prefix *neo-*. *(App.)*

2. Identifying causes and effects. What are the factors or causes that led to the development of organized government in the first river valley civilizations? Why did systems of writing develop? *(Comp.)*

✔ **3. Inferring.** Priests held the highest positions in the system of social classes that developed in early river valley civilizations. *(Syn.)* Why might this group have ranked at the top?

✔ **4. Comparing.** One of the tools pictured here dates from the Old Stone Age. The other was made in the New Stone Age. Which do you think is which? Why? *(Syn.)*

✔ **Interpreting.** As you have read, the first civilizations developed in river valleys. What are the advantages and disadvantages of settling in a river valley? What developments have helped people use rivers more efficiently today? *(Syn.)*

✔ A checkmark identifies questions and exercises calling for the three higher-order levels of thinking at the top of the Bloom taxonomy: Analysis, Synthesis, and Evaluation.

Archeological digs have helped us learn about the cultures of Stone Age peoples. The following passage describes a community of Cro-Magnon people who lived 17,000 years ago in Kom Ombo. This was a fertile region along the Nile River, about 400 miles southeast of present-day Cairo, Egypt.

Not suprisingly, Kom Ombo's varied food supply, its streams, and its spacious meadowlands attracted many people to the area. Archeologists think that the plain may have supported as many as 150 to 200 people at a time. At nearly one person per square mile, that would have amounted in Stone Age terms to crowding. And it seems to have produced some interesting results. Clustered in enclaves along the banks of the many streams, each group of people—numbering perhaps about 25 or 30—developed its own distinctive style of living. Sometimes the communal "trademark" was a particular kind of tool, sometimes it was a particular technique for food-gathering. Competition may have driven the groups into some of these forms of specialization, but in a world suddenly grown populous, perhaps men were seeking to establish some sort of social order, a sense of group identity.

1. Why was Kom Ombo a good place for Stone Age people to settle?

2. The passage suggests two reasons why specialization might have taken place among the Kom Ombo people. What were they?

3. Critical thinking: What kind of evidence might archeologists have used to draw conclusions about specialization in Kom Ombo? *(App.)*

T27A

The First Civilizations   3200–450 B.C.
(pp. 28–51)

Chapter Preview

Section 1 describes the emergence of civilization in the Sumerian city-states and explains how the development of writing, government, and religion influenced later Mesopotamian cultures. In Section 2, students learn about the major periods of Egyptian history, including Egyptian religious beliefs and the political, social, and economic organization of ancient Egyptian life. Section 3 discusses the contributions to civilization of the Hittites, Lydians, and Phoenicians, the history and religious beliefs of the Hebrews and their legacy to Western religions, and the establishment of the Persian Empire.

Bibliography

See the *Teacher's Management and Planning Guide* for additional listings. Starred titles are for both students and teachers.

*Coolidge, Olivia. *Egyptian Adventures.* Houghton Mifflin.

*Cottrell, Leonard. *Horizon Book of Lost Worlds.* American Heritage. Explores Hittites, Sumerians, Egyptians and others.

Keller, Werner. *The Bible as History,* 2nd edition. Bantam. Updated version of a classic study.

Lesko, B. *The Remarkable Women of Ancient Egypt.* Scribe Publications. Women's roles in ancient Egyptian society.

*Macaulay, David. *Pyramid.* Houghton Mifflin. Details the conception and construction of the pharaohs' burial places.

Section Lesson Plans

SECTION 1   (pp. 29–34)
Mesopotamian Civilization

Objectives

After completing this section, students will be able to:
1. Describe life in Sumerian city-states.
2. Explain how the Sumerians influenced later Mesopotamian civilizations.

Introducing the Lesson

 No!

Remind students that the Fertile Crescent—the land between the Tigris and Euphrates Rivers—was home to the earliest civilizations in history. Groups of nomads settled in this area of the ancient Middle East and developed agricultural communities. Over time, complex political, social, and economic systems gave rise to important civilizations.

Then ask: *(a) Why might an agricultural way of life encourage the development of civilization more than a nomadic way of life?* (People who stay in one place are more likely to develop complicated social systems. As society becomes more complex, civilization emerges.)

(b) Why might civilizations be greater sources of technological and social change than other forms of human organization? (Civilizations involve populations larger than those in other kinds of societies and are more interdependent and organized. New ways to meet evolving human needs are more easily developed.)

(c) What might future historians cite as the important technological and social inventions of our civilization? (Answers will vary.)

Developing the Lesson:
Relating Geography and History

Have students explain how the geography of the region contributed to the rise of the Mesopotamian civilization. (The Tigris and Euphrates rivers brought rich soil, supplied water for irrigation, and provided a transportation system. The location of Mesopotamia between two rivers helped to promote trade and the exchange of ideas.) *(Comprehension)*

Developing the Lesson: Analyzing Information

Have students refer to the definition of civilization on p. 21 and then identify the achievements of the Mesopotamians that indicate the growth of civilization. (Mesopotamians learned to deal with geographic factors, established farming communities, developed city-states, organized religious practices, developed a system of writing, and wrote a code of laws.) (*Comprehension*)

Closing the Lesson: Drawing Conclusions

Have students work in groups to compile a list of items that Mesopotamians might have put in a time capsule to represent their achievements, values, and concerns. Have each group explain their list of items to the class. (Answers will vary.) (*Comprehension*)

See *Section Review* questions, p. 34.

SECTION 2 (pp. 34–42)
Egyptian Civilization

Objectives

After completing this section, students will be able to:
1. Explain how the Nile affected Egyptian society.
2. Discuss what religious beliefs and form of government the Egyptians had.
3. Describe the Egyptian way of life.

Introducing the Lesson

Remind students that they read on page 14 that the world's first human beings lived in Africa. Have them find Africa and the Nile River on the physical map of the world on page GR10 and then find the Nile on the map on page 35. Mention that less than 4 percent of Egypt's total area is farmland, along the banks of the Nile, and that most of the rest of Egypt's land is desert.

Then ask: (a) *How might Egypt's geography have affected its population?* (Answers might suggest (1) that most people would live in the farmland areas rather than in the desert and (2) that the Nile probably made it possible for Egypt to have contacts with other peoples of Africa living to the south.)

(b) *How might Egypt's geography have affected its political organization?* (Students might mention the difficulties of governing a land that spread for hundreds of miles along the Nile. Others might say the Nile probably served as a unifying factor.)

Developing the Lesson: Supporting Generalizations

Have students find information to support the following: *The Nile River influenced Egypt's political, religious and economic systems.* (*Political:* united villages. *Religious:* floods believed to have been sent by gods; the Nile considered a god. *Economic:* provided a means of transportation; encouraged trade; supplied water for irrigation.) (*Comprehension*)

Developing the Lesson: Organizing Ideas in Written Form

Have students write an essay explaining the importance of religion in ancient Egypt. Essays should indicate the relationship between religion, government, and economics. (The pharaoh was considered a god and ruled as a divinity. Egyptians believed that their agriculture depended on the gods.) (*Comprehension*)

Closing the Lesson: Writing a Documentary

Have students work in groups to write a documentary titled *Life in Ancient Egypt*. The documentary should include reports on the following: the role of the Nile; religion; social classes; writing; and political history. Have students present their reports in class. (*Application*)

See *Section Review* questions, p. 42.

SECTION 3 (pp. 43–49)
Other Peoples of the Ancient Middle East

Objectives

After completing this section, students will be able to:
1. List the contributions various Middle Eastern groups made to civilization.
2. Describe how the Persians united all the peoples of the ancient Middle East.

Introducing the Lesson

Remind students that ancient peoples with different histories, languages, beliefs, and governments influenced one another in many ways. Even though ancient civilizations did not have modern transportation and communications systems, different cultures came into contact through trade, wars, and migration.

Then ask: *(a) What are some ways that different groups influence each other?* (Answers will vary. People are influenced by different ideas, languages, and technology.)

(b) Why might cultural exchange in the ancient world have been slower and more difficult than today? (Answers will vary. Modern technology such as air travel, faster land and sea transportation, telephones, radios, and television all make the exchange of ideas and products faster.)

(c) What are some other ways in which people today exchange culture? (Answers will vary, but might include international businesses and other organizations, Peace Corps programs, United Nations agencies, and student exchange programs.)

Developing the Lesson: Organizing Information

Have students work in groups to prepare a chart of the major contributions to civilization made by the following peoples: Hittites, Lydians, Phoenicians, Hebrews, Assyrians, Persians. Then have students evaluate their achievements, rank them in order of importance, and explain their ranking in class. *(Evaluation)*

Developing the Lesson: Summarizing Ideas

Have students summarize the difference between Hebrew monotheism and Mesopotamian polytheism. (*Hebrew monotheism:* worshiped one God; believed God set standards of right and wrong behavior; believed God was eternal, ageless, supreme, and the creator of all. *Mesopotamian polytheism:* worshiped many gods; believed gods had human characteristics and human weaknesses.) *(Comprehension)*

Answers to *Map Skill Practice,* p. 47.

1. Parts of Macedonia and Thrace, Lydia, Palestine, Phoenicia, Syria, Media, Persia, Egypt.
2. Europe, Asia, Africa.
3. About 475 miles north.
4. Caucasus.
5. Answers might mention the need for good communication in governing a huge empire.

Closing the Lesson: Evaluating History

Have students evaluate the importance of the following: Hittites' use of iron; Lydian development of money economy; Hebrews' monotheism. Evaluations should consider the impact of each on the ancient world and its lasting influence on world history. (Answers will vary.) *(Synthesis)*

See *Section Review* questions, p. 49.

Chapter 2 Review Answers (pp. 50–51)

Vocabulary Review

1. (a) tribute (b) Exodus (c) Code of Hammurabi (d) city-state (e) Iron Age (f) pharaoh (g) empire (h) dynasty
2. (a) Behistun Rock—key to understanding cuneiform writing; Rosetta Stone—tablet used to decipher hieroglyphics. (b) Cuneiform—wedge-shaped writing on clay tablets; hieroglyphics—Egyptian system of writing. (c) Judaism—Hebrew religion based on belief in one God; Zoroastrianism—religion based on belief that life is a struggle between good and evil. (d) Monotheism—belief in one god; polytheism—belief in many gods. (e) Ten Commandments—set of moral laws handed down by Moses from God to the Hebrew people; Torah—first five books of the Bible containing Hebrew law.

People to Identify

1. Akhenaton was an Egyptian pharaoh of the New Kingdom who tried to replace traditional religion with the worship of a single god, Aton.
2. Ashurbanipal, who built a library at Nineveh, ruled the Assyrian Empire at its height.
3. Cyrus the Great was the Persian ruler whose conquests created the Persian Empire.
4. Hatshepsut was the first great woman ruler, who reigned as Egypt's pharaoh after the death of her husband in the 1400's B.C.
5. Menes united Upper and Lower Egypt and established the first dynasty.

6. Moses led the Hebrew people out of Egypt, united them in the worship of one God, and received the Ten Commandments.

7. Nebuchadnezzar, the greatest Chaldean king, rebuilt the city of Babylon.

8. Rameses II, one of the last pharaohs of the New Kingdom, fought against the Hittites, achieved peace, and built many temples and statues.

9. Sargon the Great, the ruler of Akkad, brought the Sumerian city-states under his control around 2350 B.C., creating the world's first empire.

10. Solomon, king of Israel at the height of its power, built the temple in Jerusalem.

Places to Know

1. A 2. E 3. D 4. C 5. H 6. F 7. I
8. G 9. B

Recalling the Facts

1. The ziggurat was the religious, social, and economic center. The bazaar was the marketplace where people gathered to exchange goods.

2. They needed a record-keeping system for business and other transactions.

3. Answers may include the following: cuneiform writing; religious beliefs; technology; art; written laws; literature.

4. The Nile provided water and rich soil, which encouraged farming. It also provided a transportation route for trade with other regions and helped unite the villages along the river.

5. People were embalmed and buried with the possessions they might need for the afterlife.

6. Keeping the irrigation works in order, directing the army, keeping peace, making laws, controlling trade and the economy, and feeding the people in times of famine.

7. The New Kingdom pharaohs built an empire by conquering neighboring lands in Mesopotamia and Africa.

8. Peasants worked in the fields, raised cattle, worked on the irrigation system, and helped build temples and tombs for the pharaohs. Slaves became household servants or were appointed to government jobs. Many slaves worked in the mines or on the pharaoh's ships.

9. Hittites—ironworking; Phoenicians—writing system based on an alphabet; Hebrews—monotheism; Lydians—use of coins in trade.

10. They improved and extended roads; created a uniform system of weights, measures, and coins; used one language for official business; set up the first efficient postal system; gave local people positions as governors and inspector-spies.

Critical Thinking Skills

1. Answers will vary.

2. Both peoples believed in many gods that could control nature. While Sumerian rulers were believed to be chosen by the gods, Egyptian pharaohs were seen as gods themselves. Both peoples believed in an afterlife, though the Sumerians pictured a gloomy underworld while the Egyptians believed that good people would be rewarded in the Other World with everything they had enjoyed in life.

3–4. Answers will vary.

Thinking About Geography

1. Fertile Crescent—all of Kuwait, Israel, Lebanon. Palestine—parts of Iraq, Turkey, Syria, Jordan. Most of Asia Minor is present-day Turkey.

2. Answers will vary, but it is unlikely that one of the earliest civilizations would have developed there. Without the Nile, this dry area could not support a large population.

Enrichment: Primary Sources

1. The embalmers used a sharp Ethiopian stone, spices, sewing tools, chemical preservatives, linen bandages, and gum.

2. In the first paragraph, the phrase "having concluded their bargain" suggests payments, as does the reference in the last paragraph to the "costly way of embalming."

3. Answers should suggest that only the wealthy could afford to be embalmed.

The First Civilizations

3200–450 B.C.

See chapter timeline, p. 49.

Before You Read This Chapter

Imagine, for a moment, what life would be like without the wheel, without coins, without writing. How would people travel to distant places or transport heavy loads? How would they pay for goods they needed or keep business records? For centuries during the Stone Age, people did without wheels and coins and writing. Then, about 5,000 years ago, these inventions were developed in certain regions of Africa and Asia. In this chapter you will read more about the peoples of ancient Egypt and Mesopotamia and of other ancient societies that contributed to modern civilization.

The Geographic Setting

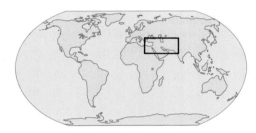

The Chapter Outline

1. Mesopotamian Civilization
2. Egyptian Civilization
3. Other Peoples of the Ancient Middle East

King Tut's golden throne is one of the treasures that survives from ancient Egypt, Africa's first great civilization.

1 Mesopotamian Civilization

Objectives

Focus Questions

★ ■ What was life like in Sumerian city-states? *(pages 29–31)*

● ■ How did the Sumerians influence later Mesopotamian civilizations? *(pages 31–33)*

Terms to Know

city-state	empire
ziggurat	polytheism
bazaar	Code of Hammurabi
scribe	Behistun Rock
cuneiform	

★ Note strategies for first objective on this page and p. 30.

The earliest of the river valley civilizations developed in southern Mesopotamia (present-day Iraq). The people of this land built communities, farmed, and wrote down laws.

The Geography of Mesopotamia

The Greeks called the area between the Tigris and the Euphrates rivers *Mesopotamia*, meaning "land between rivers." Mesopotamia was part of the Fertile Crescent, a great arc of rich land stretching from the Persian Gulf to the eastern shore of the Mediterranean Sea (map, page 30).

Mesopotamia is a flat plain with a hot, dry climate. Its land is fertile only because of the rivers that flow through it. The Tigris River, which is about 1,200 miles long, and the Euphrates River, which is more than 1,700 miles long, bring water and rich soil to the region.

These two rivers lose speed as they move from their mountain sources into the plain. The soil settles to the riverbeds, making the rivers shallower and causing frequent floods. Also, the slower current is not strong enough to keep the water inside the riverbanks. The rivers sometimes wander off course. In fact, in ancient times they flowed separately to the Persian Gulf. Because of floods and silt deposits, they now meet to form a single river more than 100 miles from the gulf.

[handwritten margin note: OR 150 MI. INLAND.]

Sumerian City-States

During the New Stone Age, about 6,000 years ago, nomadic herders settled in the southern part of Mesopotamia. They learned to deal with the flooding of the rivers and gradually changed to the farming way of life. The people drained the swamps so that they could farm the rich land. They built dams and dikes to keep the rivers from flooding their fields. In the drier northern areas they built irrigation canals. These canals could carry water from the rivers to the fields when there was little rain.

Into this farming area, about 3200 B.C., came Sumerian nomads from the mountains to the northeast. The Sumerians mixed with the farming people, and southern Mesopotamia became known as Sumer. It was here that the world's first advanced civilization arose. The farming villages along the Tigris and Euphrates rivers gradually grew into 12 separate **city-states**. A city-state was an independent, self-governing community that included a city and the surrounding farmlands.

Although Mesopotamia had rich soil for farming, it lacked resources such as timber and stone. To meet their building needs, the Sumerians used what was plentiful: clay from the rivers. To construct homes, palaces, and temples, the Sumerians shaped clay into **29**

★ RETEACHING. Have students review "Sumerian City-States" and "Transportation and Trade" (pp. 29–30) and summarize how early Mesopotamians became farmers and why transportation and trade developed. (They drained swamps, built dams and irrigation canals. The wheel and the sail made transportation and trade easier.) *(Comprehension)* **Understanding Causes**

★ REINFORCEMENT. Have students draw a diagram of a Sumerian city-state, illustrating the elements discussed in "Sumerian City-States" (pp. 29–30). *(Comprehension)* **Translating Information into Another Form**
Geography The Fertile Crescent passes through present-day Israel, Jordan, northern Syria, southern Turkey, northern Iraq, and western Iran.

Mesopotamia About 1700 B.C.

Find the Fertile Crescent on the map. What rivers flowed through it? Into what body of water did they flow? Name the cities that grew up along these rivers.

Map Answers: (1) Tigris, Euphrates. (2) Persian Gulf. (3) Babylon, Ur.

bricks and dried it in the sun. Bricks for important buildings were baked, which made them last much longer. Most houses and temples were windowless, with rooms built around a central court.

Sec. Rev. ques. 2

In each city-state, people built a large brick temple called a **ziggurat** (ZIG-uh-rat), to provide a home for their gods. Shaped like a pyramid, the ziggurat had several levels, each smaller than the one below it. Stairways connected the different levels and led to a shrine at the top.

The ziggurat, which towered over the plain around it, was more than a religious center. It was also the heart of social and economic life. Around the base of the ziggurat were homes for the priests and shops for artisans. Most potters, weavers, metalworkers, and other artisans worked either for the temple or for the royal court.

★ See below.

30

Transportation and Trade

Between 5,000 and 6,000 years ago, transportation improved enormously with the invention of the wheel and the sail. The wheel, first used in Sumer, made it easy to transport large loads of goods by land. The sail helped people take advantage of rivers, lakes, and oceans in carrying on trade with distant peoples.

In each Mesopotamian city, people gathered to exchange goods at the bazaar—marketplace. Merchants also set up trading posts in foreign lands. Copper came from the area around the Persian Gulf, precious metals from central Asia, and ivory from Africa and the west coast of India. Cedar and cypress woods and oils were shipped from lands around the Mediterranean Sea. In exchange, Mesopotamian merchants exported wool and woven cloth, handicrafts, grain, and hides.

Cuneiform Writing

Writing on clay. Sumerian scribes—record-keepers—devised a system of writing that used baked clay. With a sharply pointed stick called a stylus, a scribe cut pictures representing ideas or sounds into a square tablet of damp clay. This form of writing is called cuneiform (kyoo-NEE-uh-form), meaning "wedge-shaped," because of the marks the stylus left (as shown in sample above). If scribes made mistakes, they could smooth out the clay and start fresh. The completed tablet was dried or baked and then stored in a library.

Cuneiform tablets are an invaluable record of the history of the Sumerians and later peoples in Mesopotamia. Each tablet ended with the complete date (day, month, and year) and the name of the city where the record was made. The tablets recording business transactions were also marked with the signature seals of the buyers, sellers, and

 Sec. Rev. ques. 3

Religion The word *ziggurat* is Mesopotamian for "to be high" or "pointed." Sumerians believed that ziggurats reduced the distance between the people and their gods.

★ **ENRICHMENT. Have students research and report on Mesopotamian architecture and crafts. Students might discuss materials used, styles of art and architecture, and use of art objects. *(Application) Locating Information***

Technology The first wheels were made from three planks of wood that were clamped together with copper or wooden braces and then cut to form a circle.

Vocabulary The word *cuneiform* is derived from the Latin *cuneus*, meaning "wedge." Cuneiform strokes, made with a sharp, pointed tool (stylus), are broad at one end and pointed at the other.

witnesses. Signature seals, made in the shape of cylinders, were carved in stone and worn on a cord around the owner's neck. The pictures on seals often showed scenes of life in Mesopotamia—a farmer plowing, a priest receiving offerings, a woman weaving. When the seal was rolled across the damp clay of a tablet, it left the owner's personal symbol.

Schools for writers. Only a few people knew how to write in cuneiform. The Sumerians had schools that trained boys in this art. Students were mostly the sons of upper-class professionals—priests, temple and palace officials, army officers, and other scribes. The poor could not afford the schools' fees, and girls were not enrolled.

Learning to write in cuneiform demanded years of study and practice. To help their pupils, teachers prepared "textbooks" of word lists and mathematical problems. Students who mastered the art could work as scribes for the priests, the royal court, or wealthy merchants.

Later Peoples of Mesopotamia

● Note strategies for second objective on this page and p. 32.

The Sumerians did not form a strong or united government. Wars over land and water rights were common among the city-states. About 2350 B.C. Sargon the Great, the ruler of the neighboring kingdom of Akkad (AK-ad), conquered the city-states. He brought them under his control as part of the world's first **empire**—a state in which one ruler controls several kingdoms or territories. Sargon's empire stretched from the Persian Gulf to the Mediterranean Sea.

In time, other neighboring peoples invaded and conquered the Tigris-Euphrates Valley. One of the Sumerian city-states, Ur, regained power about 2100 B.C. and ruled both Sumer and Akkad. Invasions continued, however, and another city, Babylon, rose to power. About 1792 B.C. a Babylonian ruler named Hammurabi (hah-muh-RAH-bee) conquered and united Mesopotamia.

The ziggurat of Ur was a massive temple dedicated to the moon god Nanna. Built of baked mud bricks and mortar, the layered platforms are thought to represent steps leading toward the heavens.

31

● RETEACHING. Have students review "Many gods" (p. 32) and list the facts that support the following statement: Religion was important in the daily life of Mesopotamians. (Each city-state was considered the property of one of the gods. Gods and goddesses were believed to be everywhere and to cause natural disasters.) *(Comprehension)* **Supporting Generalizations**

● REINFORCEMENT. Have students summarize the legal and scientific contributions of Mesopotamian civilization. (Written codified laws; 360-degree circle; 60-minute hour; multiplication and division tables; first written astronomical records; 12-month lunar calendar.) *(Comprehension)* **Observing for Detail**
Geography The ruins of Ur lie 187 miles southeast of present-day Baghdad, Iraq, and about 9 miles southwest of the Euphrates River.

Soldiers march to war in this panel found in the Sumerian city of Ur. The wheels of their wagons were formed from half-circles of wood.

Although the Sumerians would never rise again, they had a profound impact on later peoples. All the conquerors of Mesopotamia adopted the Sumerians' achievements. The Akkadians and the Babylonians both spoke languages unlike Sumerian, but they borrowed cuneiform writing. Sumerian religious beliefs, technology, art, written laws, and literature became the foundation for later civilizations in Mesopotamia.

Mesopotamian Religion and Law

Many gods. The Sumerians, like most other ancient peoples, believed in many gods. This belief is called **polytheism**. Each city-state considered itself the property of one of the gods. It was thought that this god chose the ruler and protected the city.

Sec. Rev. ques. 4

Polytheism continued among later Mesopotamians. These people believed in many major gods and goddesses and in thousands of lesser spirits and demons. They believed that these supernatural beings were found

32

everywhere—in the sky, in rivers, in wind and fire and storms.

Prayers and rituals written on clay tablets show that the Mesopotamians greatly feared the gods and demons. They were thought to cause natural disasters such as floods, famines, and sandstorms—all of which happened at times in Mesopotamia. To protect themselves, people wore charms and carried out rituals. Rulers consulted the gods before making decisions. Priests studied dreams and the stars and looked for signs that would show what the gods wanted.

The Mesopotamians believed that the dead descended to a gloomy underworld. In the *Epic of Gilgamesh*, one of the world's earliest literary works, an unknown Babylonian poet described the underworld. He called it a huge dark cave "where they sit in darkness, where dust is their food and clay their meat; they are clothed like birds with wings for garments; over bolt and door lie dust and silence."

Strict laws. Rulers in Mesopotamia were expected to carry out the gods' wishes in making and enforcing laws. Hammurabi, the ruler of Babylon from 1792 to 1750 B.C., had the laws of the kingdom collected and carved onto a block of stone eight feet high. This made the **Code of Hammurabi** visible to all the people and provided a lasting record. Copies of the laws were made on clay tablets and sent to all the lands ruled by Babylon. (Some of these laws appear on page 33.)

Sec. Rev. ques. 4

Much of Hammurabi's Code seems harsh today. For example, if a house fell in and killed its owner, the builder could be put to death. The laws also show inequalities in Babylonian society. Nobles and priests were punished less severely than common people.

● See below.

Women and the law. Women had fewer legal rights than men, but some ran shops and inns and owned property. Women were allowed to testify in court even if they were slaves. Laws protected Mesopotamian wives from abuse and neglect and made sure they received some payment if they were divorced. On the other hand, a wife might be forced into slavery for three years to pay back a debt her husband owed.

Cultural History The first illustration in the Portfolio of World Art Masterpieces at the back of the book shows another part of the Ur panel pictured above.

● ENRICHMENT. Have students find more information on the *Code of Hammurabi* or the *Epic of Gilgamesh*, and report on the legal or religious values of the Mesopotamians. *(Application)* **Locating Information**

Advances in Mathematics and Astronomy

The Mesopotamians also made important advances in mathematics and astronomy. They drew up multiplication and division tables and made calculations using geometry. The Mesopotamians' number system used a base of 60. From this came the system of dividing a circle into 360 degrees and an hour into 60 minutes.

Sec. Rev. ques. 5

The first written records in astronomy were made by the Mesopotamians. The clear dry air made it possible to observe the stars regularly. Astronomers also kept records of the changing positions of the planets and the different phases of the moon. From this information, the Mesopotamians developed a 12-month calendar based on the cycles of the moon.

Behistun: The Key to Mesopotamian History

Thousands of cuneiform tablets have been found in the Middle East, dating back to the time of the Sumerian city-states. They include trade contracts, lists of rulers, maps, poems, legends, prayers, and laws. Until the nineteenth century, however, they could not be read.

In the 1840's a British officer named Henry Rawlinson found the key to cuneiform writing. He identified three types of writing on a huge cliff, known as the **Behistun Rock** (bay-his-TOON), in what is now western Iran. Rawlinson climbed the sheer face of the cliff and made copies of the writings. One inscription was in Babylonian cuneiform; the other two were in ancient languages that scholars knew how to read. Rawlinson guessed that the three inscriptions said the same thing. After many years of studying and comparing the scripts, he succeeded in translating most of the cuneiform message. The Behistun Rock has helped scholars translate the Mesopotamians' own records of their history, thoughts, and achievements.

Science The Behistun Rock includes eyewitness accounts of a battle and a list of provinces in the empire. ✳

PRIMARY SOURCE

The Code of Hammurabi

Hammurabi's laws dealt with everything that affected the community, including religion, family relations, business, and crime. The following statements are adapted from Hammurabi's Code.

❝ If a man stole an ox, a sheep, a pig, or a goat that belonged to the state, he shall repay thirty times its cost. If it belonged to a private citizen, he shall repay ten times its cost. If the thief does not have sufficient means to make repayment, he shall be put to death. . . .

If a man was too lazy to make the dike of his field strong and a break has opened up in his dike and he has accordingly let the water ravage the farmland, the man in whose dike the break was opened shall make good the grain that he let get destroyed. . . .

If a son has struck his father, they shall cut off his hand.

If a man has destroyed the eye of a member of the aristocracy, they shall destroy his eye. . . .

If a man has knocked out a tooth of a man of his own rank, they shall knock out his tooth. ❞

1. Which was punished more severely—theft from a private citizen or theft from the state?
2. How did the law make sure that irrigation works would be kept sound?
3. What punishments were provided for personal injuries?
4. **Critical thinking:** In your opinion, were Hammurabi's punishments fair or were they too harsh? Explain.

Ⓕ See answers below.

33

Ⓕ **Primary Source Answers 1.** Theft from the state. **2.** A man who allowed the dike on his land to break had to pay for what was destroyed as a result of the break. **3.** A person who injured someone was punished by having the same injury inflicted on him. **4.** Answers will vary. Students may think some were fair and some were very harsh.

Section Review

Answers to Section Review questions are in brackets on pages indicated.

1. **Define or identify:** city-state, ziggurat, bazaar, scribe, cuneiform, empire, polytheism, Code of Hammurabi, Behistun Rock. (pp. 30, 31, 32, 33)
2. How were Sumerian cities typically laid out? (p. 30)
3. How did the Sumerians keep written records? (p. 30)

4. What part did Mesopotamian religious beliefs play in government and law? (p. 32)
5. What advances did the Mesopotamians make in mathematics and science? (p. 33)
6. **Critical thinking:** Why might Hammurabi have wanted the laws carved in stone for all to see? Would a ruler ever want to keep the laws secret? Explain. (See answer below.)

6. Answers will vary. Written laws provide a public record that asserts the ruler's authority and holds the ruler responsible to uphold established law. A ruler who ignored or changed laws might not want a written record.

See lesson plans, pp. T27A–T27C.

2 Egyptian Civilization

Objectives

Focus Questions

★ ■ How did the Nile affect Egyptian society? *(pages 34–35)*
● ■ What religious beliefs and form of government did the Egyptians have? *(pages 35–40)*
▲ ■ What was the Egyptian way of life like? *(pages 40–42)*

Terms to Know

dynasty   papyrus
pharaoh   Rosetta Stone
tribute   surplus
hieroglyphics

★ Note strategies for first objective on this page.

The Sumerians owed their prosperity to the fertile farmland that lay between the Tigris and Euphrates rivers. Southwest of Mesopotamia, in the valley of the Nile River in Egypt, the first great African civilization was built. Egyptian civilization lasted much longer than that of Sumer. In fact, it endured for several **34** thousand years.

Geography and People of Egypt

The Greek historian Herodotus (hih-RAHD-ih-tus) once called Egypt "the gift of the Nile." This river, the longest in the world, flows north from central Africa and empties into the Mediterranean Sea more than 4,000 miles away.

Without the water provided by the Nile, all Egypt would be desert, for it receives little rainfall. In ancient times, heavy spring and summer rains at the source of the Nile caused the river to overflow. These floods, which occurred regularly, gave the soil its moisture. They also made it more fertile. The Nile carried silt from central Africa to Egypt and deposited it there during the floods. Silt gradually built up a marshy delta at the mouth of the Nile. This rich land provided a home for many birds and wild animals.

Sec. Rev. ques. 2

By about 5000 B.C. human settlement became possible on the land that emerged from the marshes, and people migrated there to cultivate the rich soil. Egypt's location made it a natural meeting ground for migrants from neighboring regions. The first settlers of Egypt were probably peoples from African lands to the south and east and from the Fertile Crescent. Surviving paintings and sculp-

★ RETEACHING. Have students make a diagram illustrating how the Nile River made agriculture possible in Egypt. *(Application) Translating Information into Another Form*
★ REINFORCEMENT. Have students write a paragraph explaining how the Nile River affected agricultural and technological advances in ancient Egypt. (Reservoirs and canals built; new technology developed for large irrigation projects; methods of predicting time.) *(Comprehension) Explaining Cause and Effect*

★ ENRICHMENT. Have students analyze Herodotus's statement that Egypt is "the gift of the Nile" above. Analyses should include an explanation of what Herodotus meant and examples that he might have given to support the statement. *(Analysis) Analyzing a Statement*
Linking with Art Students might want to compare appearances of Egyptians in illustrations on pp. 28, 41, 42, 148, and second and third pages of Portfolio of Art Masterpieces at the back of the book.

ture show that the ancient Egyptians were a people of racial diversity.

To ensure water for their crops each year, the ancient Egyptians built reservoirs and used canals to carry water to the fields. Digging canals and reservoirs required the labor of many workers. People invented new technology and carefully planned and organized large irrigation projects. They also devised a calendar to use in predicting when floods would come. The year was made up of three seasons: the time of flood, the time when the river returned to its banks, and the rainless time before the next flood.

Besides encouraging farming, the Nile was an excellent transportation route. It provided access to the Mediterranean, allowing Egypt to trade with other regions, including lands farther south in Africa. It also helped unite the villages along the river. Vast deserts to the east and west of the Nile protected Egypt from attack, allowing the villages to enjoy long periods of peace and prosperity.

Sec. Rev. ques. 2

Religion in Ancient Egypt

● Note strategies for second objective on this page and p. 36.

Polytheism. Like other farming peoples in ancient times, the Egyptians believed that many gods controlled nature, sent the yearly floods, and made the crops grow. The sun, the stars, and the Nile itself were seen as gods or as the dwelling places of gods. Chief among the gods was Amon-Re (AH-mun-RAY). Originally Amon and Re had been two distinct sun gods, but the Egyptians merged

Sec. Rev. ques. 3

Linking Past and Present

The completion of the Aswan High Dam in 1970 ended the flooding of the Nile. Today the dam provides both irrigation water and low-cost hydroelectric power to Egypt's people. The dam has led to problems, however—soil erosion along the Mediterranean coast and an explosion in the population of tiny disease-causing worms.

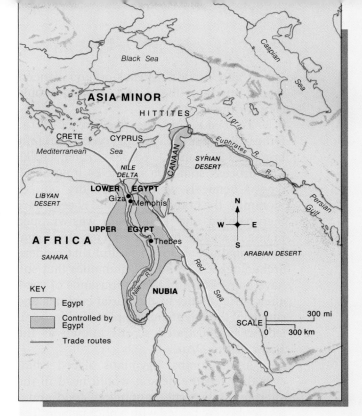

Egypt About 1450 B.C.

The Nile River flows north. Into what sea does it empty? With what islands did Egyptians trade? Was Lower Egypt north or south of Upper Egypt?

Map Answers: (1) Mediterranean. (2) Crete, Cyprus. (3) North.

them and worshiped Amon-Re as the king of gods. Besides Amon-Re, Egyptian polytheism included the worship of such animals as cats and crocodiles.

Life after death. An important feature of Egyptian religion was the belief in life after death. The Egyptians connected their beliefs about birth and death with the rising and setting sun and with the yearly floods of the Nile. They worshiped Osiris (oh-SY-ris) as the god of the Nile and rich harvests. It was believed that he died each year and was brought back to life by his wife Isis (EYE-sis). Egyptians believed that when they died, their souls would be weighed against a feather symbolizing the law. Those who had lived good lives would journey to the Other World, ruled by Osiris.

In the Other World, people would do all the things they liked most in life. They would hunt, fish, picnic, and enjoy the company of **35**

Geography The climate change that turned the Sahara from a fertile area into a desert took place over the period 5000–2000 B.C. African peoples who had hunted, fished, and raised cattle in the once-fertile area migrated both north and south, with some making their way into Egypt.

● **RETEACHING.** Have students review pp. 35–36 and summarize Egyptian beliefs about life after death. (Individuals were judged at death; those who lived good lives went to the Other World, where life was pleasant.) *(Comprehension) Observing for Details*
● **REINFORCEMENT.** Have students review the material on Old, Middle, and New Kingdoms (pp. 36–38) and make a chart identifying the achievements of each period. *(Comprehension) Comparing Information*

family and friends. Musicians and dancers would entertain them, and servants would care for their needs.

To make sure the dead reached the Other World safely, the Egyptians carefully preserved human bodies before their burial. The process sometimes took as long as 70 days. Chemicals were used to dry out, or mummify, the body. The lips and cheeks were then painted, and the mummy was wrapped in fine linen and adorned with jewelry. Egyptian embalmers were so skillful that modern archeologists have found mummies that still have hair, skin, and teeth thousands of years after burial. Many of the burial customs and rituals of the Egyptians are recorded in a collection of illustrated scrolls known as the *Book of the Dead*.

In the tombs, Egyptians placed whatever they felt the person would need in the afterlife. Only some handfuls of food and a few tools were buried with a poor person. The tombs of the wealthy, however, were filled with clothing, food, furniture, games, perfumes, cosmetics, jewels—everything that might be needed for a pleasant life in the Other World.

Uniting Upper and Lower Egypt

The farming villages along the Nile gradually were united into two kingdoms—Upper Egypt and Lower Egypt. About 3100 B.C. a ruler of Upper Egypt known as Menes (MEE-neez) conquered Lower Egypt and brought all of Egypt under his rule. Where the two kingdoms met, he built the city of Memphis as his capital. A double crown became his symbol.

Menes' rule began the first dynasty—family of rulers—in Egypt. There were at least 30 dynasties in Egypt's history. Each held power until it was overthrown or there were no heirs to rule. Strong dynasties helped keep the country united as one kingdom. There were, however, also times of unrest, when weak dynasties controlled only part of Egypt.

Scholars divide the early history of **36** Egypt according to the three periods when strong dynasties united the country. They call these periods the Old Kingdom (about 2686–2181 B.C.), the Middle Kingdom (about 2040–1786 B.C.), and the New Kingdom (about 1570–1090 B.C.).

Old Kingdom Rulers

About 400 years after Menes united Egypt, its rulers established a central government in which they held supreme power. This marked the beginning of the Old Kingdom.

To the people of Egypt, the ruler, later called **pharaoh** (FAYR-oh), was more than a king. He was also considered a god and was believed to possess the secrets of heaven and earth. Most pharaohs thought of themselves as the protectors of the people and so tried to rule fairly. One pharaoh advised his son, "Do right so long as thou live on the earth. Calm the weeper, threaten no widow, expel no man from the possessions of his father. Take heed lest thou punish wrongfully."

The pharaoh's power. The pharaoh was responsible for all aspects of life in Egypt. These included keeping the irrigation works in order, directing the army, keeping peace, and making laws. He also controlled trade and the economy. Egyptian peasants paid most of their taxes in grain, which was stored in the royal warehouses. If a famine occurred, feeding the people became the responsibility of the pharaoh.

Taxes and payments from other countries were used to maintain public buildings, irrigation works, and ports. The pharaoh owned Egypt's mines and quarries and the trading fleets that sailed to foreign lands. Foreign merchants had to deal with royal officials, not with the merchants of Egypt.

Many officials were appointed to watch over the details of government. The most important official was the chief overseer. He presided over the royal court, acted as a diplomat, and was in charge of tax collection and public works. Other officials helped the chief overseer carry out the details of running the Egyptian government. In time, powerful officials became an upper class of nobles.

Cultural History To see how an Egyptian artist visualized life in the Other World, students can turn to the Egyptian tomb painting on the second page of the Portfolio of World Art Masterpieces at the back of the book.

Check for Understanding. Ask: What was the ancient Egyptian concept of the afterlife? (At death, souls that had lived a good life journeyed to the Other World, where they enjoyed a life of pleasures.)
● **ENRICHMENT.** Have students evaluate the importance of pharaohs in ancient Egyptian society. Evaluations should include the political, social, religious, and economic responsibilities of the pharaoh. *(Evaluation)* **Evaluating Historical Roles**

The enduring pyramids of Giza are monuments not only to the rulers buried within them but also to the skill of their builders. The diagram shows the interior of the Great Pyramid of Khufu. The Grand Gallery measures 29 feet from floor to ceiling.

The pyramids. Pharaohs of the Old Kingdom had immense pyramids built to serve as their tombs. These demanded the greatest skills of Egypt's architects and engineers and also the labor of thousands of workers. Except for passages leading to burial chambers, the pyramids were built of solid stone. Huge limestone blocks were built up in layers and then covered with a smooth facing of white limestone. Because so many of these tombs were built during the Old Kingdom, this period is often called the Pyramid Age.

The Great Pyramid is one of three that still stand in the desert on the west bank of the Nile near Giza (GHEE-zuh). It was built about 2600 B.C. for the pharaoh Khufu (KOO-foo). Standing 450 feet high, the Great Pyramid is made of more than two million stone blocks, each weighing about two and a half tons. It took some 20 years to build this impressive tomb. Using logs as rollers and levers, teams of Egyptian workers dragged huge blocks of stone up ramps. The blocks were fitted with such precision that a knife blade could not be slipped between them.

Royal power reached its height with the age of pyramid-building. Then nobles who ruled in distant parts of Egypt challenged the supreme rule of the pharaoh. As a result, Egypt was torn by civil war for nearly 200 years. An ancient Egyptian poet described the hardships of wartime: "The wrongdoer is everywhere. Plunderers are everywhere. Nile is in flood, yet none plow. Laughter has perished and is no longer made. It is grief that walks through the land."

The Middle Kingdom

About 2040 B.C. Egypt again came under the control of a strong dynasty, which ruled from the city of Thebes. Culture and trade flourished for more than 250 years during the **37**

Middle Kingdom. The pharaohs sent expeditions south into the neighboring territory of Nubia to bring back gold. Traders also traveled to Palestine, Syria, and the island of Crete in the Mediterranean. Eventually the power of nobles and priests grew again and weakened the pharaoh's rule.

As the Middle Kingdom's power declined in the 1700's B.C., invaders from Asia moved into the delta region. The newcomers were called Hyksos (HIK-sahs), meaning "Princes from Foreign Lands." They had horses and war chariots, bronze swords and daggers, and heavy bows. These superior weapons helped the Hyksos rule Egypt for about 100 years. Then the Egyptians learned to use the Hyksos' weapons and regained their independence.

The New Kingdom

After overthrowing the Hyksos about 1570 B.C., a new dynasty established the New Kingdom and began a time of expansion for Egypt. The pharaohs built an empire, conquering land eastward to the Euphrates River in Mesopotamia and southward in Africa. The period of the New Kingdom is sometimes called the Empire Age.

The pharaohs demanded that the conquered peoples of the empire pay **tribute** to Egypt. This tribute included slaves, food products, and treasure such as gold, jewels, or ivory. The payment of tribute was a way of showing that the conquered people recognized the supremacy of Egypt.

Several strong leaders ruled Egypt during the 500 years of the New Kingdom. Among them was Queen Hatshepsut (hat-SHEP-soot), who took the throne after her husband's death about 1504 B.C. Hatshepsut was the first great woman ruler in history. She sent large trading expeditions to other lands and began a major building program at home. The temples she ordered built at Thebes are among the outstanding achievements of Egyptian architecture.

38 Hatshepsut's stepson, Thutmose III (thoot-MOH-suh), was one of the greatest

pharaohs of Egypt. When he came to power around 1490 B.C., he set Egypt on a course of military expansion. His armies conquered Syria and Palestine (map, page 47), bringing the empire to its greatest size.

A New Religion

Even strong pharaohs were sometimes challenged by powerful priests and nobles. In the 1300's B.C. a pharaoh named Amenhotep IV (ah-mun-HOH-tep) tried to reduce the power of the priests in Egyptian government. He wanted to change the Egyptians' worship of many gods to the worship of a single supreme god, Aton, who was represented by the sun.

Amenhotep took the name Akhenaton (ah-kuh-NAH-tun), which means "It is well with Aton." He spoke of Aton as the creator of the universe and the god of love, justice, and peace. By believing in one god instead of many, Akhenaton tried to give a new direction to Egyptian religious thought. At the same time, however, he insisted on being worshiped as a god himself.

The Egyptian priests opposed Akhenaton's religion, and it gained few followers. Shortly after Akhenaton died, about 1360 B.C., his nine-year-old son-in-law Tutankhamon (too-tahng-KAH-mun) became pharaoh. During the reign of the young King Tut, the monuments to Aton were destroyed and the new religion soon died.

The Decline of Egyptian Power

Rameses II. One of the last effective rulers of the New Kingdom was Rameses II (RAM-ih-seez), who ruled from 1304 B.C. to 1237 B.C. When he came to the throne, Hittite warriors (page 43) were invading the eastern parts of Egypt's empire. Rameses fought nearly 20 years against the Hittites before peace was made. His marriage to the daughter of the Hittite king helped to keep peace for the rest of his long reign. Rameses had many temples built and huge statues made of himself and his family.

Cultural History Students can see a fresco portrait of an Egyptian queen from the period of the New Kingdom on the third page of the Portfolio of World Art Masterpieces at the back of the book. She was Queen Nefertari of the twentieth dynasty.

Tutankhamon

F See below, right.

Golden chariots, golden beds, a golden throne—gold everywhere! That is what English archeologist Howard Carter saw in 1922 as he peered through the doorway of Tutankhamon's tomb.

Carter had been searching the rocky, barren Valley of the Kings in Egypt for years, hoping to find this tomb. Archeologists had found nearly a dozen other royal tombs in the valley. In each case, however, robbers had looted the treasures centuries earlier. Robbers had also broken into Tutankhamon's tomb, but they must have been caught or frightened off, for Tutankhamon's burial gifts remained in his grave. There they lay for more than 3,000 years, until Carter opened the ancient door.

22 CARAT

Tutankhamon was buried in a solid gold coffin (shown here), which weighed nearly 2,500 pounds. This coffin was the innermost of a "nest" of three coffins that protected Tutankhamon's remains. The lid of the gold coffin pictures the calm and youthful king. The golden rays on the headdress identify him with the sun, and the staff he holds symbolizes the god of death and the afterlife.

Little is known about Tutankhamon himself. Nine

years old when he came to the throne about 1360 B.C., he was only eighteen when he died. Yet because of the artifacts found in his tomb, King Tut is as famous today as any other Egyptian ruler.

Like all child kings, he must have felt himself pushed and pulled by the powerful adults around him. For example, his name was originally Tutankha*ton*, in honor of the god Aton. Within a few years, however, the priests of Amon regained the power they had lost during the reign of Akhenaton. The young pharaoh was forced to change his name to Tutankha*mon*.

The paintings and carvings in Tutankhamon's tomb often show him with his young wife, Ankhesenamon (picture, page 28). She was the daughter of Akhenaton and closely related to Tutankhamon. (After all, a pharaoh could not marry a mere commoner. A queen had to be of royal blood herself.) In the pictures, the young couple sit side by side, touch hands, share food. When Carter uncovered Tutankhamon's coffin, a withered wreath of flowers lay on its lid, perhaps a last gift from Ankhesenamon.

Cultural History In May 1988, King Tutankhamon's funeral wreath was "rediscovered" at the Royal Botanic Gardens in London. Removed from the tomb in 1922 by archeologist Howard Carter, the wreath, along with samples of millet, barley, black cumin seeds, coriander, and watermelon seeds, had apparently been stored in cardboard boxes and forgotten.

F **FEATURE ACTIVITY.** Have students write an entry to a royal journal that Tutankhamon might have written when he was ruler of Egypt. The entry should reflect the young pharaoh's concerns about his rule and his ability to meet his responsibilities. *(Application) Understanding Point of View*

Invasions. The pharaohs' power at home again began to weaken. This time outside invasions also threatened the existence of the empire. By about 1200 B.C. Egyptian civilization had passed its time of greatness. Libyans from the desert to the west invaded the fertile valley of the Nile. The "Sea Peoples"—raiders from Asia Minor and islands in the Mediterranean and Aegean (ih-JEE-un) seas—attacked the coast. Egypt had to abandon its empire. In later centuries Egypt came under the rule of many different peoples, including Libyans and Nubians. Egyptian dynasties often came back into power, however. Not until the conquests of Alexander the Great (page 91) in the 300's B.C. did native rule in Egypt finally end.

For 3,000 years, Egyptian civilization had remained stable. Dynasties changed, but the way of life continued.

Egyptian Writing

A new kind of writing. Early in the Old Kingdom the pharaohs began to keep written records of their reigns. As in Mesopotamia, these records provide much of our knowledge of ancient Egypt. The Egyptian writing system was a form of picture writing called **hieroglyphics** (hy-ur-uh-GLIF-iks). The term comes from Greek and means "sacred carving." Greek travelers in Egypt probably used this term because they first saw the writing carved on the walls of Egyptian temples. The Egyptians also wrote on paper scrolls, which they made from a reedlike plant called **papyrus** (puh-PY-rus).

As in Sumerian cuneiform writing, in the simplest form of hieroglyphics a picture stood for one idea. For instance, a picture of a woman indicated the *idea* of a woman; a picture of a bird indicated the *idea* of a bird. In time, the system changed so that pictures stood for sounds as well as ideas. The owl, for example, stood for an *m* sound. Hieroglyphics could be used almost like letters of the alphabet.

It took years of training to learn to write in hieroglyphics. Schooling for scribes began at about age five and lasted for about 12 years. Students could look forward to comfortable lives at the end of their studies, for trained scribes were in great demand. One father advised his son, "Learn to write, for this will be of greater advantage to you than all the other trades."

The Rosetta Stone. As Egypt declined, most of the knowledge of reading hieroglyphics disappeared. For centuries scholars puzzled over their meaning. Then, in A.D. 1799, French engineers working in the Nile delta dug up a stone tablet. The tablet, now known as the **Rosetta Stone**, had been carved in 196 B.C. It contained inscriptions in three kinds of writing—hieroglyphics, a more recent Egyptian script, and Greek.

The Rosetta Stone provided the key that enabled scholars to translate thousands of ancient inscriptions. Above is a sample of hieroglyphics from the upper part of the stone.

40

In this three-thousand-year-old wall painting an Egyptian peasant couple harvests wheat with a sickle. Water from the Nile irrigated their field.

Like the Behistun Rock (page 33), the Rosetta Stone provided a key to deciphering ancient writing. A French scholar named Jean François Champollion (shahm-poh-lee-AWN) guessed correctly that all the inscriptions said the same thing. By comparing them, he deciphered the hieroglyphics, thus enabling us to learn more about ancient Egyptian life. *How — Via Cartouche*

Social Classes in Ancient Egypt

▲ Note strategies for third objective on this page and p. 42.

Nobles and priests. The families of those who held high government positions made up part of the upper class in ancient Egypt. These nobles lived in spacious houses built around courtyards with beautiful gardens. They had many servants and often entertained guests with lavish feasts. Priests made up the rest of the upper class and were the nobles' equals in Egyptian society. They advised the pharaoh and directed the religious ceremonies.

Sec. Rev. ques. 5

Scribes. The scribes who wrote hieroglyphics were a special social class. Scribes kept the records that made government orderly and efficient. They recorded lists of imports and exports, taxes, workers, tribute payments, calculations for surveying land, and supplies for the army. Scribes also worked in the temples. They wrote down hymns and poems to the gods and instructions for religious ceremonies.

Artisans. Artisans also held a special place in Egyptian society. They produced a great variety of goods—furniture, cloth, glassware, baskets, and jewelry. Some of these products were used in trade. Others went to decorate the homes and the tombs of the wealthy. The more skilled the artisans were, the more they were paid.

Peasants and slaves. Life in Egypt depended on the labor of the thousands of peasants. Peasant men and women lived in mud huts and spent their days working in the fields. They grew wheat, barley, and fruit and raised herds of cattle, sheep, and goats. They also grew cotton and flax, which was used to make linen cloth. The peasants produced the food for Egypt's cities and the **surplus**—extra supply—on which the pharaoh's trade depended. In addition, peasants often had to work on the irrigation system or build temples and tombs for the pharaohs.

The labor of slaves also helped to maintain Egyptian society. Most slaves were prisoners captured in war. Slaves performed a variety of tasks. Some became the household servants of nobles and priests. A few who showed special ability were appointed to important government jobs. Many slaves, however, were forced to work in the pharaoh's mines or to pull the oars on the pharaoh's ships. Chained, often whipped, unable to rest, denied adequate food, and always suffering from the heat, such slaves usually lived short and miserable lives.

41

▲ RETEACHING. Have students work in groups to prepare a dialogue that might have occurred between different Egyptian social classes. Dialogues might include a description of social responsibilities and ways of life. *(Application) Understanding Points of View*

Check for Understanding. Ask: How did scribes help increase government efficiency? (Kept official records of trade, taxes, tribute, and army supplies.)

▲ REINFORCEMENT. Have students draw a chart identifying the class structure of ancient Egypt. The chart should list the classes in their order of importance in ancient Egypt and define the role of each social class. *(Comprehension) Translating Information into Another Form*

Wealthy Egyptians were entertained by musicians like this woman harp player.

The Status of Women

Although an upper-class Egyptian woman was expected to obey her father and her husband, she did have some rights. She could inherit and own property and sell it if she wanted to. She could also run a business and testify in court. An Egyptian wife and mother was shown great respect. While divorce was permitted, it was not common. Sometimes the wives and mothers of pharaohs became the real power in government, though they usually ruled from behind the scenes. Only one woman, Hatshepsut (page 38), ever ruled as pharaoh in her own right.

Medicine, Astronomy, and Engineering

Papyrus scrolls provide evidence of the Egyptians' knowledge of medicine. One of the first **42** medical textbooks was an Egyptian work written on the diagnosis and treatment of injuries. The scroll shows that the Egyptians understood the structure of the body, set broken bones, and treated wounds. They also used a variety of medicines to cure sickness. The skills of Egyptian doctors were well-known, even outside of Egypt.

Egyptian priests studied astronomy. Their observations of the sun and stars were important both in farming and in conducting religious rituals. Noting that the Nile flooded each year soon after the star Sirius was seen in the sky, the Egyptians developed a calendar to predict the time of the flood. This calendar was based on the sun and had 365 days. More accurate than the Sumerians' moon-based calendar, it was the best calendar created in ancient times.

Egyptian engineers and architects used their skills in building the temples, palaces, and tombs of the pharaohs. Engineers used geometry to survey the land, plan buildings, and develop irrigation works. Egyptian architects were the first to use stone columns in homes, temples, and palaces. The surviving temples and tombs of ancient Egypt remind us of the strengths of that civilization.

See Sec. 2 *Closing the Lesson,* p. T27B.

Sec. Rev. ques. 6

▲ See below, left.

Section Review

Answers to Section Review questions are in brackets on pages indicated.

1. **Define or identify:** dynasty, pharaoh, tribute, hieroglyphics, papyrus, Rosetta Stone, surplus. (pp. 36, 38, 40, 41)
2. In what ways was the Nile River important to early peoples in Egypt? (p. 34)
3. What religious beliefs did the Egyptians hold? (p. 35)
4. What role did pharaohs play in ancient Egypt? (p. 36)
5. How was Egypt's society structured? (p. 41)
6. What advances did the Egyptians make in the fields of medicine, astronomy, and engineering? (p. 42)
7. **Critical thinking:** What were the advantages and disadvantages of rule by dynasties? (See answer below.)

---

7. Answers will vary. Advantages might include the unity, stability, and advances that often result from strong, consistent government. Disadvantages might include harsh dynastic policies not easily changed and disruption that often follows the decline of dynastic rule.

3 Other Peoples of the Ancient Middle East

Objectives

Focus Questions

★ ■ What contributions did various Middle Eastern groups make to civilization? *(pages 43–46)*

● ■ How did the Persians unite all the peoples of the ancient Middle East? *(pages 46–48)*

Terms to Know

Iron Age	Torah
Exodus	prophet
Ten Commandments	money economy
monotheism	Zoroastrianism
Judaism	

★ Note strategies for first objective on this page and p. 46.

At the eastern end of the Mediterranean Sea, Europe and Asia meet at the peninsula of Asia Minor (map, page 47). Since ancient times this peninsula and the coast south of it have been a crossroads for traders, nomadic herders, and invading armies.

Many different peoples migrated to this region, and some settled there. This region was later conquered by expanding empires. Eventually the entire Middle East came under one rule.

The Hittites

About 2000 B.C. people known as Aryans (AYR-ee-unz) began to migrate from their homeland, somewhere northeast of the Black Sea. Some headed south; others traveled west. As they moved into new areas, the Aryans took with them a distinctive language. Today this language is usually called Indo-European, because it became the ancestor of nearly all the languages now spoken in Europe and India. One group of Aryans settled in the mountains of western Asia Minor. They became known as the Hittites.

Hoping to gain control of trade routes, the Hittites invaded northern Mesopotamia about 1600 B.C. They raided Babylon, Syria, and Palestine and challenged Egypt's power. By about 1450 B.C. the Hittite Empire included Asia Minor and northern Syria.

While neighboring peoples were still using bronze, Hittite artisans had discovered how to make iron spears and other weapons. They realized that iron tools and weapons were stronger and sharper than those made of bronze. The Hittites kept the secret of ironworking until the fall of their empire, about 1200 B.C. Within the next 200 years, however, knowledge of ironworking spread throughout the ancient Middle East. The Bronze Age thus gave way to the **Iron Age**, which continues to the present day.

Sec. Rev. ques. 2

The Phoenicians

Southeast of Asia Minor, where Lebanon now lies along the eastern shore of the Mediterranean, was the land of Phoenicia (fih-NISH-uh). Many Phoenicians turned to the sea to make their living, becoming sailors, shipbuilders, and merchants.

Trade flourished in the busy ports of Tyre and Sidon. Timber from tall cedar trees, used in shipbuilding, was exported to Egypt as early as the Old Kingdom. In addition to the cedar wood, Phoenicia was famous for cloth dyed a deep purple. The dye was obtained from seashells and cost so much to produce that only the wealthy could afford garments dyed with "royal purple." The Phoenicians were also known for being the first to make objects of clear glass.

MUREX

Adventurous Phoenician sailors explored the Mediterranean Sea. After about **43**

★ **RETEACHING.** Have students make a time chart of the major military and political achievements of the following: Hittites; Phoenicians; Assyrians; Babylonians. *(Comprehension) Sequencing Events*

★ **REINFORCEMENT.** Have students make a timeline of the important events in the history of the Hebrew people. *(Comprehension) Understanding Chronology*

Geography Asia Minor lies between the Black Sea and the Mediterranean Sea; it is present-day Turkey.
Background Note that the Iron Age in Asia Minor began between 1500 and 1000 B.C.

Phoenicia and the Israelite Kingdoms About 900 B.C.

Into what two kingdoms had the Hebrew kingdom been divided by 900 B.C.? What land lay to the north? What modern states exist in this region today? (See the Atlas maps at the back of this book.)

Map Answers: (1) Judah, Israel. (2) Phoenicia. (3) Israel, Lebanon, Syria.

1200 B.C. they began to settle colonies as far away as northern Africa and southern Spain (map, page 74). Sailing out into the Atlantic Ocean, the Phoenician traders may even have reached Britain and southern Africa. Because they spread the ideas of the ancient Middle East as well as its products, the Phoenicians are called "carriers of civilization."

Sec. Rev. ques. 3

The Phoenicians used a writing system based on an early alphabet. Each letter-symbol stood for a sound, which meant that any word could be written by combining letters. Though the alphabet had no vowels, the letter-symbols were far easier to learn than the thousands of picture symbols needed to write hieroglyphics. Phoenician traders carried the alphabet wherever they traded. About 800 B.C. the Greeks adopted this system and added vowels, creating the alphabet **44** on which our own is based.

Check for Understanding. Ask: Why were Phoenician traders called "carriers of civilization"? (They spread the ideas and products of the ancient Middle East.)
Check for Understanding. Ask: How did the Phoenician writing system differ from Egyptian hieroglyphics? (The Phoenician system was based on an alphabet in which each letter-symbol stood for a sound, so any word could be written by combining letters. Hieroglyphics used pictures for ideas.)

The Hebrews

South of Phoenicia, in a fertile valley, lay a land called Canaan (KAY-nun). About 1900 B.C. a group of people called Israelites, or Hebrews, entered Canaan from the east. The Hebrews were a small group, yet their influence in world history was great.

The flight from Egypt. The first books of the Bible are the source for much of early Hebrew history. Originally herders from Mesopotamia, the Hebrews traveled into Canaan with their leader Abraham. Because of a famine, some Hebrews then moved to Egypt, and many settled there as farmers and herders. Later, however, the pharaohs began to enslave the Hebrews in Egypt.

About 1290 B.C., during the rule of Rameses II (page 38), the Hebrews of Egypt fled across the Sinai (SY-ny) Peninsula back to Canaan. Their flight, known as the **Exodus**, was led by Moses, a Hebrew who had been raised at the pharaoh's court.

A strong leader, Moses kept the people united during their long journey. Moses also came to be regarded as the Hebrew people's chief lawgiver. According to the Bible, while they were in the Sinai desert, Moses handed down a set of moral laws that became known as the **Ten Commandments**. The Hebrews believed these laws came from God.

The Hebrew kingdom. Eventually the Hebrews returned to the land of Canaan, which they believed God had promised them. They arrived at about the same time that another people, the Philistines, were entering the area. About 1200 B.C. the Philistines migrated to the western part of Canaan. From their name the land became known as Palestine. The Hebrews fought with the Canaanites and the Philistines. About 1020 B.C. they established the kingdom of Israel.

One of Israel's earliest kings was David, who ruled from about 1000 to 972 B.C. After defeating the Philistines, he made Jerusalem the royal capital. David's trade treaty with the city-state of Tyre gave the Hebrews a share in the rich Phoenician trade. The Hebrew kingdom reached its greatest height of power and prosperity under David's son Solomon, who ruled from about 972 to 922 B.C. In Jerusalem, Solomon built a palace and a magnificent temple for God.

After Solomon died, the Hebrew kingdom broke in two. The northern part, called Israel, was conquered in 722 B.C. by the Assyrians, a people from the northeast who enslaved many Hebrews. The southern part, called Judah, was conquered in 586 B.C. by Nebuchadnezzar (neb-uh-kud-NEZ-ur), the ruler of Babylon (page 46). Nebuchadnezzar destroyed Solomon's Temple, captured several thousand Hebrews, and sent them to Babylon. When the Persians conquered Babylon in 538 B.C., they allowed the exiles, now called Jews, to return home. (The word *Jew* comes from the name of the southern king-dom of Judah.) Palestine was under Persian rule at that time and continued to be held by other conquerors for centuries.

The belief in one God. The Hebrews had a lasting influence on world religions. They believed in one God, a belief called **monotheism** This made the Hebrew religion, now called **Judaism**, profoundly different from the Mesopotamian and Egyptian belief in a great number of gods.

Sec. Rev. ques. 4

Other Middle Eastern peoples believed that their gods had human characteristics and weaknesses. The gods needed food, drink, and sleep; they sometimes misbehaved and were punished; they grew old and died. To the Hebrews, God was eternal, ageless, and supreme. He had created the universe and all within it.

Hebrew law. The Hebrews believed that God set forth standards of right and wrong behavior. They also believed, however, that each individual was responsible for observing those standards. Hebrew law, based mainly on the Ten Commandments, was recorded in the **Torah**—the first five books of the Bible. Hebrew law stressed fairness and justice and set up strict rules for behavior and religious observances.

Prophets. Throughout Hebrew history, many men and several women became known as **prophets**—messengers of God. The prophets preached obedience to God's law, warned of the dangers of breaking this law, and urged the Hebrews to remain firm in their faith. The wise sayings and teachings of such prophets as Elijah, Isaiah, Deborah, and Micah are recorded in the early books of the Bible, along with the laws, history, and literature of the Hebrews.

The Assyrian Empire

The Assyrians lived in the upper Tigris valley, a region often invaded by people from the nearby mountains. The Assyrians became skilled and ruthless warriors. Their well-trained army used iron weapons and horse-drawn war chariots. With battering rams, they knocked down the walls of enemy cities. **45**

Sec. Rev. ques. 5

Moses, leader and lawgiver of the Hebrews, appears with the Ten Commandments in this powerful sculpture by Michelangelo.
See below.

Background The horns coming from the top of Moses' head are the result of a faulty translation. Michelangelo based his sculpture on a description taken from an ancient Hebrew text. Scholars, however, had mistranslated the phrase "rays of light" as "horns."

Social History The Assyrians scattered the leaders of the Israelite kingdom throughout the Assyrian territories. This dispersed group became known as the "ten lost tribes of Israel."

Check for Understanding. Ask: What are three characteristics of Hebrew law? (Based on the belief that God established standards of right and wrong; viewed individuals as responsible for meeting these standards; stressed fairness and justice.)

Early Assyrian rulers invaded other lands mainly for plunder. They deliberately used terror in the lands they invaded. One conqueror boasted in this way:

> 66 I crushed the corpses of their warriors in battle. I made their blood to flow. I cut off their heads and piled them up at the walls of their cities like heaps of grain. I carried off their goods and their property. Their troops who had thrown themselves at my feet, I took away as prisoners and added to the people of my country. 99

By about the 700's B.C. the Assyrians had developed efficient methods to govern the people they conquered. Appointed officials collected taxes, kept law and order, and built roads. Messengers carried news from place to place. Assyrian rulers, however, still used terror to control conquered subjects.

The Assyrian Empire reached its height about 660 B.C., during the reign of Ashurbanipal (ah-shur-BAH-nee-pahl). By this time the lands from Egypt to the Persian Gulf were under Assyrian control. The Assyrians adopted the religion, art, and literature of Mesopotamia. In the capital city of Nineveh (NIN-uh-vuh) Ashurbanipal built a library that held thousands of cuneiform tablets.

The Rulers of Babylon

Conquered peoples often rebelled against harsh Assyrian rule. In 612 B.C. the Chaldeans (kal-DEE-unz) of Babylon joined forces with the Medes (MEEDZ) of Persia. Together they overthrew the Assyrians and destroyed the city of Nineveh.

The Chaldeans remained powerful for several decades. Their greatest king was Nebuchadnezzar, who ruled from 605 to 562 B.C. Nebuchadnezzar conquered much of the Fertile Crescent. He also rebuilt Babylon into a magnificent city. Huge gates in the city walls were decorated with colorful glazed bricks in animal designs. The ziggurat of the Babylonian god Marduk was rebuilt. Most impres-

46

Biography Cyrus the Great pursued a policy of religious toleration. His generosity toward conquered peoples became standard Persian practice.

sive, however, was a series of terraces planted with trees and flowers and watered by streams. Supposedly built for Nebuchadnezzar's wife, these became famous as the beautiful Hanging Gardens of Babylon. ✳

The Lydians

For centuries Middle Eastern merchants had carried on trade by bartering one kind of goods for another. The Lydians (LID-ee-unz) of northern Asia Minor began the use of coins in trade. Gold, silver, or a mixture of both metals was formed into disks of equal weight. Stamped into the metal of the coin were its value and a symbol that showed government authority and approval. Official Lydian government coinage came into use by about 560 B.C. during the reign of Croesus (KREE-sus), the last king of Lydia. People still use the phrase "rich as Croesus" to refer to someone with great wealth.

Sec. Rev. ques. 6

The newly invented coins made trade much easier. Suppose, for example, a shepherd wanted some pottery, and his only wealth was sheep. In a barter system, he would have to find a potter who wanted some wool or a sheep. After coins came into use, the shepherd could sell a sheep to anyone who had the coins to buy it. With the coins, he could buy the pottery he wanted. Peoples in all parts of the ancient Middle East soon recognized the usefulness of coins and accepted them as payment. Thus a **money economy**—an economic system based on the use of money—began.

★ See below, left.

The Persian Empire

● Note strategies for second objective on this page and p. 48.

More than two centuries before the reign of Croesus, the Persians, one of several Aryan peoples, had settled in the area east of Mesopotamia. About 547 B.C. the Persians, led by Cyrus the Great, began to build the largest empire that had yet existed in the ancient Middle East. Cyrus conquered his neighbors, the Medes and the Chaldeans, and released

★ ENRICHMENT. Have students research Phoenician shipbuilding, Lydian coins, Assyrian military skills, or the Hanging Gardens of Babylon. (Application) Locating Information
● RETEACHING. Have students review "The Persian Empire" (pp. 46–48) and outline the ways Persian rulers united their empire. (Roads, postal system, money system, official language, provinces established, local people chosen as officials.) (Comprehension) Organizing Ideas in Written Form

● REINFORCEMENT. Have students compare the Assyrian and Persian empires in the following areas: territories, important dates, methods of rule, achievements. (Assyrian: Upper Tigris Valley, Egypt to Persian Gulf; 660 B.C.; skilled ruthless warriors who used terror. Persia: Mesopotamia, Fertile Crescent, Asia Minor, Egypt, northern India; 547 B.C.) (Comprehension) Comparing Information

Map skills: locating places, using the key, estimating distance, using direction.

Map Skill Practice

See p. T27C for answers to *Map Skill Practice*.

Persian Empire About 500 B.C.

1. Using the map below, identify lands that were part of the Persian Empire in 500 B.C.
2. What three continents did the empire span?
3. How many miles and in what direction would a trader have to sail to transport goods from the island of Crete to Macedonia?

4. What mountains formed the boundary of the empire between the Caspian and Black seas?
5. **Drawing conclusions.** The Royal Road was the main highway in a network of roads built by the Persians. Why were these roads important in the administration of the empire? In your answer, use what you read about the Persian Empire on this page and the next.

the Hebrews from their captivity in Babylon (page 45). He then took over the rest of the Fertile Crescent and Asia Minor. His son, who followed him as ruler in 530 B.C., soon brought Egypt into the empire.

The next ruler, Darius (duh-RY-us) the Great, extended the Persian conquests into northern India. Darius's only military failure was his invasion of Greece in 490 B.C. His son Xerxes (ZURK-seez) also failed to conquer Greece. Although stopped in their move

westward, the Persians united all the Middle Eastern peoples—Egyptians, Babylonians, Assyrians, Jews, Phoenicians, Hittites, and Lydians—under one rule.

Governing the empire. Persian rulers looked for ways to tie the vast empire together. They improved and extended the Assyrians' roads in order to link distant cities and speed travel by soldiers, merchants, and messengers. Everywhere in the empire people used the same coins and the same system of **47**

Biography Darius I was an excellent soldier and empire-builder, but he saw himself primarily as an organizer and lawgiver. His empire covered over one million square miles.

Timetable

Major Peoples of the Ancient Middle East

Region	People/Period	Accomplishments
Mesopotamia	Sumerian (3200–2350 B.C.)	Use of wheel; cuneiform.
	Babylonian (1792–1600 B.C.)	Code of Hammurabi.
	Assyrian (1000–612 B.C.)	Library at Nineveh.
	Chaldean (626–539 B.C.)	Hanging Gardens of Babylon.
Egypt	Old Kingdom (2686–2181 B.C.)	Pyramids; hieroglyphics; papyrus.
	Middle Kingdom (2040–1786 B.C.)	Extensive trade.
	New Kingdom (1570–1090 B.C.)	Expansion of empire.
Asia Minor/	Hittite (1600–1200 B.C.)	Ironworking.
Eastern	Phoenician (1200–850 B.C.)	Alphabet; seafaring.
Mediterranean	Hebrew (1020–586 B.C.)	Judaism.
	Lydian (690–547 B.C.)	Coinage.
Persia	Persian (547–331 B.C.)	Efficient government; Zoroastrianism.

(Most dates are approximate.)

weights and measures. Government officials and merchants all spoke the same language, Aramaic (ayr-uh-MAY-ik), in official business. Cyrus the Great set up the first efficient postal system. It used relays of mounted messengers, much like the Pony Express of the American West some 2,400 years later. The 1,200-mile-long Royal Road from Sardis to Susa had more than 80 stations where the riders could change horses.

To govern the empire, Darius divided it into 20 provinces and appointed governors to supervise them. Through inspector-spies, known as "Eyes and Ears of the King," the ruler kept track of these governors. Officials were often chosen from the local people, another practice that helped hold the empire together. The Persians allowed the different peoples in their empire to keep their local customs, beliefs, and traditions. They had only to pay their taxes and provide recruits for the army.

Zoroaster's religion. Most ancient Middle Eastern peoples believed in many gods who helped or rewarded people in

● See below.

48

exchange for sacrifices. About 600 B.C. a Persian religious teacher named Zoroaster (zor-oh-AS-tur) began to teach that human beings had a choice between doing good and doing evil. He saw the world as a struggle between these forces. Ahura Mazda (AH-hoo-ruh MAZ-duh), the Wise Lord, was seen as the supreme god, standing for truth, goodness, and light. Ahriman (AH-rih-mun) was the Evil Spirit, representing darkness.

According to Zoroaster, Ahura Mazda and the forces of good would triumph at the end of the world, when the earth would be destroyed by fire. Those who had chosen to follow the way of truth and goodness would, he said, enter a realm of eternal light and goodness. Others would be punished.

Zoroaster's followers considered him to be the first of several great prophets as well as the author of their sacred book, called the *Zend-Avesta*. The Persian kings adopted Zoroastrianism as the official religion of the empire, and it spread widely in the ancient Middle East. The religion is still practiced in a few scattered places.

● ENRICHMENT. Have students make two maps to compare the geographic boundaries of the Assyrian and Persian empires. Maps should include important cities. (Application) *Relating Geography and History*

Biography The name *Zoroaster* is the Greek form of the Persian *Zarathustra.* Zoroaster left home at the age of 20 to find religious truth. He wandered and lived alone for 10 years.

Check for Understanding. Ask: What is Zoroastrianism? (Persian religion that started in the sixth century B.C. It teaches that the world is a struggle between good and evil forces and that human beings have a choice between the two.)

Religion Followers of Zoroaster's religion in India, called Parsis, are descendants of Persians who fled to India in the tenth century to escape Muslim persecution.

Section Review

Answers to Section Review questions are in brackets on pages indicated.

1. **Define or identify:** Iron Age, Exodus, Ten Commandments, monotheism, Judaism, Torah, prophet, money economy, Zoroastrianism. (pp. 43, 44, 45, 46, 48)
2. What was the Hittites' main contribution to civilization? (p. 43)
3. What system of writing did the Phoenicians use? (p. 44)
4. How did the Hebrews' ideas about religion differ from those of other peoples in the ancient Middle East? (p. 45)
5. How did the Assyrians gain power in the ancient Middle East? (p. 45)
6. What did the Lydians do that made trade easier? (p. 46)
7. **Critical thinking:** Why might the Persians have allowed defeated peoples to keep their local customs? (See answer below.)

Chapter 2   Summary and Timeline

1. One of the world's first civilizations arose in Sumer, on the Tigris and Euphrates rivers in Mesopotamia. The Sumerians developed irrigation systems, kept records written in cuneiform, made advances in technology, mathematics, and astronomy, and drew up codes of law. Sumerian traditions were adopted by later peoples of Mesopotamia.

2. The civilization that developed along the Nile River in Africa lasted 3,000 years, sustained by strong traditions. The Egyptians were ruled by pharaohs. Pharaohs of the Old Kingdom built pyramids as tombs. Trade flourished during the Middle Kingdom, and New Kingdom pharaohs built an empire. High-ranking officials ran Egypt's complex government and economy. Scribes and artisans held an important place in Egypt, but the majority of Egyptians were peasants. Egyptians made advances in medicine, created a sun-based calendar, and showed a talent for engineering. Their belief in a life after death influenced many customs.

3. Other peoples of the ancient Middle East also made advances. The Phoenicians spread the use of an alphabet, and the Hittites discovered how to work with iron. The Hebrews introduced laws for moral behavior and the belief in one God. The Lydians introduced the use of coins. The Assyrians' efficient methods of governing were later adopted by the Persians. By about 500 B.C. the Persian Empire had united all the different peoples of the ancient Middle East.

3200–3000 B.C. Civilizations develop in Mesopotamia and Egypt

2686–2181 B.C. Old Kingdom of Egypt

2040–1786 B.C. Middle Kingdom of Egypt

1792 B.C. Hammurabi unites Mesopotamia

1570–1090 B.C. New Kingdom of Egypt

1290 B.C. Hebrew Exodus from Egypt

1200 B.C. Iron Age begins

547 B.C. Persian Empire established

3200 B.C. — 2800 — 2400 — 2000 — 1600 — 1200 — 800 — 400 B.C.

49

7. Answers will vary. The Persians might have thought they could avoid resistance from conquered peoples if they did not force new ways on them. It probably was easier to gain cooperation from local people if they were allowed to continue their own customs.

See p. T27C for answers to Chapter Review.

Vocabulary Review

1. Match each of the following terms with its correct definition: *city-state, Code of Hammurabi, dynasty, empire, Exodus, Iron Age, pharaoh, tribute.*
   a. payment demanded from a conquered people
   b. flight of the Hebrews from Egypt
   c. written collection of Babylonian laws
   d. independent, self-governing community that includes a city and surrounding territory
   e. period that began in the 1200's B.C. with the Hittites
   f. ruler of ancient Egypt
   g. state in which one ruler controls several territories
   h. family of rulers
2. Define the terms in the following pairs.
   a. Behistun Rock; Rosetta Stone
   b. cuneiform; hieroglyphics
   c. Judaism; Zoroastrianism
   d. monotheism; polytheism
   e. Ten Commandments; Torah

People to Identify

Identify the following people and tell why each was important.
   1. Akhenaton
   2. Ashurbanipal
   3. Cyrus the Great
   4. Hatshepsut
   5. Menes
   6. Moses
   7. Nebuchadnezzar
   8. Rameses II
   9. Sargon the Great
   10. Solomon

Places to Know

Match the letters on this map of the ancient Middle East with the places listed below. You may want to refer to the map on page 30.
   1. Asia Minor
   2. Egypt
   3. Euphrates River
   4. Mediterranean Sea
   5. Mesopotamia
   6. Nile River
   7. Persian Gulf
   8. Sinai Peninsula
   9. Tigris River

Recalling the Facts

1. What role did the ziggurat and the bazaar play in a Sumerian city-state?
2. Why did the Sumerians create a system of writing?
3. Name three Sumerian achievements that later had an influence on Mesopotamian civilizations.
4. How did the Nile River help the ancient Egyptians?
5. What custom expressed the Egyptian belief in life after death?
6. What were the responsibilities of the pharaohs of the Old Kingdom?

7. Why is the New Kingdom sometimes called the Empire Age?
8. What tasks did the peasants and slaves of ancient Egypt perform?
9. For what are the Hittites best known? The Phoenicians? The Hebrews? The Lydians?
10. How did Persian rulers unite the many peoples in their empire?

Critical Thinking Skills

1. **Paraphrasing.** To paraphrase is to rewrite something in your own words. Reread the laws from the Code of Hammurabi on page 33, and then paraphrase two or three of the laws. *(Comp.)*

2. **Comparing and contrasting.** How were the religions of the Sumerians and the ancient Egyptians similar? How were these religions different? *(Syn.)*

3. **Preparing a report.** Research and prepare a report about one of the following topics related to ancient Egypt: how the pyramids were built; the Sphinx; Tutankhamon's tomb; the rock temples of Abu Simbel; the pharaoh Rameses II; Nefertiti, the wife of Akhenaton. *(App.)*

4. **Making a chart.** Make a chart to show some basic information about the Hittites, Phoenicians, Assyrians, and Lydians. Use the following headings: *People, Location, Dates, Achievements*. *(Comp.)*

Thinking About Geography

1. **Comparing maps.** Compare the maps in this chapter with the modern political maps in the Atlas at the back of this book. What nations now exist in what was once known as the Fertile Crescent? What nations now exist in what was once Palestine? What present-day nation occupies most of Asia Minor? *(Comp.)*

2. **Critical thinking.** The Nile was a valuable resource for the Egyptian people. How might Egypt's early history have been different if this river had not existed? *(Syn.)*

A checkmark identifies questions and exercises calling for the three higher-order levels of thinking at the top of the Bloom taxonomy: Analysis, Synthesis, and Evaluation.

Enrichment: Primary Sources

In the 400's B.C. the Greek historian Herodotus traveled to Egypt, where he observed embalmers at work. This passage is adapted from his account of the trip.

66 There are men in Egypt who practice the art of embalming. These persons, when a body is brought to them, show the bearers various models of corpses, made in wood, and painted so as to be lifelike. The embalmers then ask in which way it is wished that the corpse should be prepared. The bearers tell them, and having concluded their bargain, take their departure, while the embalmers proceed to their task.

They make a cut along the flank with a sharp Ethiopian stone and take out the whole contents of the abdomen. After this they fill the cavity with every sort of spicery and sew up the opening. Then the body is placed in [a chemical preservative] for seventy days and covered. At the end of that time, which must not be exceeded, the body is washed and wrapped round, from head to foot, with bandages of fine linen cloth, smeared over with gum and in this state it is given back to the relations, who enclose it in a wooden case shaped into the figure of a man. Such is the most costly way of embalming the dead. 99

1. What tools and materials were used in the embalming process?
2. Which phrases in the account suggest that the embalmers were paid for their services?
3. **Critical thinking:** Do you think everyone in Egypt was embalmed in this way? Explain your answer.
   (Comp.)

Ancient India and China   2500–500 B.C.
(pp. 52–66)

Chapter Preview

Section 1 describes Mohenjo-Daro and Harappa, the central cities of the ancient Indus Valley civilization. The Aryan invasion of India is discussed, as well as changes that occurred during the Vedic Age, and the influence of Hinduism and its traditions. In Section 2, the development of Chinese civilization is traced from the legendary foundations of the Xia dynasty, around 2000 B.C., through the Shang and Zhou dynasties. Advances in culture and technology made by the Chinese and the impact of Confucianism on government and social life are discussed.

Bibliography

See the *Teacher's Management and Planning Guide* for additional listings. Starred titles are for both students and teachers.

Basham, A. L. *The Wonder That Was India.* Taplinger. Classic account of ancient Indian history and culture.

*Seeger, Elizabeth. *Eastern Religions.* Crowell. Survey of such Eastern religions as Hinduism, Buddhism, Taoism, Shinto.

Wheeler, Mortimer. *Civilizations of the Indus Valley and Beyond.* McGraw-Hill. Authoritative, well-illustrated account of archeology in northern India and Pakistan.

Section Lesson Plans

SECTION 1   (pp. 53–59)
The Roots of Civilization in India

Objectives

After completing this section, students will be able to:
1. Describe what life was like among early Indus Valley people.
2. List ways in which the Aryan conquest changed ways of life in India.
3. Explain how religion affected daily life.

Introducing the Lesson

Tell students that the civilization that emerged in India in 1500 B.C. developed a social structure that remains influential today. Although India has experienced foreign control—Muslim rule and British colonization—and is governed by a constitutional democracy, the fundamental organization of Hindu society remains unchanged.

Then ask: (a) *What do you think the term "social structure" means?* (Answers will vary. Social structure is the way a group of people with common values organizes its economic and social relationships.)

(b) *How important is social structure?* (Answers will vary. Social structure is important because of its influence on individual opportunity and the order and unity of a society.)

(c) *What might account for the endurance of a social structure over hundreds of years, as in India?* (Answers will vary, but might include the following: its success in organizing a society; unwillingness of a society to change; inability of new influences to produce change; the strong belief of the people in the established social order.)

Developing the Lesson: Drawing Conclusions

Have students consider the following discoveries about the Harappan society and draw conclusions about the Indus Valley political and economic life, literacy, and level of civilization:

(a) *Carefully planned cities; orderly, planned streets.* (Indicates some form of centralized government that regulated or supervised city construction.)

(b) A huge, central fortress with rooms for storing grain. (Indicates centralized government and an organized economic system.)

(c) Indoor baths with sewer systems for drainage. (Shows engineering capability and importance of hygiene.)

(d) Stamp seals. (Indicates existence of a written language.)

(e) Harappan stamp seals found in Sumer. (Points to trade with that region.)

(f) Toys representing carts and animals. (Indicates domestication of animals and the use of the wheel.) *(Application)*

Developing the Lesson:
Organizing Information

Have students make a chart on *Traditional Hindu Families*. The chart should include information on family organization, individual roles, and underlying beliefs about family. (*Family Organization:* everyone directly related to the father lived near one another. *Individual Roles:* women ran households, cared for children, obeyed husbands; men gave wives whatever luxuries they could afford. *Underlying Beliefs About Family:* close family ties provided a deep sense of security; obedience to elders; respect for ancient customs.) *(Comprehension)*

Closing the Lesson:
Tracing Cause and Effect

Have students trace the effects of Aryan settlement in the Indus River Valley. Students should consider how Indus River culture and Aryan culture blended to form Hindu civilization. (Aryan social classes developed into the Hindu caste system; Harappan society's belief in many gods evident in Hinduism; Aryan definition of male and female roles visible in Hindu system; conquered Indian peoples became the lowest caste in the social system.) *(Comprehension)*

See *Section Review* questions, p. 59.

SECTION 2 (pp. 59–64)
The Start of Lasting Traditions in China

Objectives

After completing this section, students will be able to:
1. Describe how the Shang and Zhou dynasties ruled their territories.
2. Explain how Confucius influenced Chinese thought.

Introducing the Lesson

Tell students that a complex social structure was one of the most important developments in ancient China. Emphasizing peace and harmony at all levels of their society, the Chinese established a system of social rules and behavior that united the people for centuries.

Then ask: *(a) What might lead a people to establish social rules of conduct?* (Answers will vary. People often establish rules of conduct to promote particular values or a certain way of life.)

(b) Why do societies usually accept certain types of behavior and forbid others? (Answers will vary. Societies usually accept behavior that is viewed as beneficial to people.)

(c) How does American society establish rules of conduct? (By its laws and its system of justice.)

(d) What are some examples of acceptable and unacceptable behavior in American society? (Answers will vary. Respect for the law, political participation, and donations to charitable causes are examples of acceptable behavior; theft, murder, perjury, and vandalism are examples of unacceptable behavior.)

Developing the Lesson:
Relating Geography and History

Have students study the map of China on p. 60 and answer the following questions:

(a) *What geographic features border China?* (The Himalayas; the Kunlun, Tian Shan, and Altai mountains; the Gobi Desert; the Yellow Sea, East China Sea, South China Sea.)

(b) *How might these geographic features have contributed to China's belief that they were the world's only civilized people?* (Answers will vary. Geographic factors isolated China from other cultures. This might have resulted in a sense of self-sufficiency and superiority.)

(c) *What are some of the advantages and disadvantages of geographic isolation?* (Answers will vary. Geographic isolation might protect a country from invasions, but it often limits a country's access to other cultures.) *(Comprehension)*

Developing the Lesson:
Understanding Point of View

Have students work in groups to present a skit on the social structure of ancient China. Skits might include speeches by rulers, dialogues between parents and children, or narratives by the elders of a community. (Students should emphasize the following: respect for and worship of superiors, the good example of superiors, Confucian virtues, and filial piety.) *(Application)*

Closing the Lesson:
Comparing Information

Have students make a chart comparing China's social structure with that of ancient India. Charts should compare the five basic relationships with the caste system and the responsibilities of groups in both systems. (*Five Basic Relationships:* ruler-subject, father-son, husband-wife, older brother-younger brother, members of a community. *Caste System:* Brahmin, Kshatriya, Vaisya, Sudra.) *(Comprehension)*

See *Section Review* questions, p. 64.

Chapter 3 Review Answers
(pp. 65–66)

Vocabulary Review

1. (a) reincarnation (b) bureaucrat (c) filial piety (d) epic (e) caste
2. (a) karma; dharma (b) An extended family (c) feudalism (d) Vedas (e) subcontinent

Places to Know

1. F 2. G 3. D 4. C 5. B 6. E 7. A

Recalling the Facts

1. They have given archeologists much information about the lives of the early Indus Valley people.
2. The loose class structure grew into a complex caste system.
3. By performing the appropriate dharma, Hindus could build good karma. Because Hindus wanted to build good karma so they could reach the goal of being absorbed into the universal spirit, they respected the caste system and lived according to its rules. Thus, the ideas of dharma and karma reinforced the caste system and the structure of Hindu society.
4. To maintain their government, the Shang collected tribute from neighboring peoples. To keep control over the region, the Shang often fought with peoples who would not pay tribute.
5. The Zhou found that the territory they had conquered was too large to be ruled by the royal family alone. As people began to accept the lords' rule, the lords' power increased and the power of the Zhou kings declined.
6. The relationships are between ruler and subjects, father and son, husband and wife, older and younger brothers, and members of a community. The superior person was expected to set a good example of moral behavior.
7. The family was the foundation of Chinese society. Order in the family was the key to a peaceful society and a well-run government.

Critical Thinking Skills

1–2. Answers will vary.
3. 2500–500 B.C. The development of Indus Valley civilization. The birth of Confucius. The Shang dynasty. 500 years.
4–5. Answers will vary.

Thinking About Geography

1. Students should locate the following information: Indus—Himalayas in Tibet; 1,800 miles; northwest coast of the Indian subcontinent in what today is Pakistan; Arabian Sea. Ganges—Alaknanda in the Himalayas; 1,557 miles; Calcutta, on the northeast coast of India; Bay of Bengal. Brahmaputra—glacier in the Kailas Range of the Himalayas; 1,800 miles; enters the Ganges-Brahmaputra delta and becomes the Jamuna River; Bay of Bengal.
2. Maps should show summer winds blowing northeast and winter winds blowing southwest.
3. Answers will vary.

Enrichment: Primary Sources

1. To be brave in battle, protect his people, and honor the Brahmins.
2. By fighting with all his strength and not turning back.
3. He would receive all of his master's sins (bad karma) and lose all his merit (good karma) to his master.
4. The part that describes the punishment for fleeing from battle.
5. Both a Kshatriya king and a weeder have an obligation to remove the bad in order for the good to survive.

Ancient India and China

2500–500 B.C.

See chapter timeline, p. 64.

Before You Read This Chapter

If you were to list the cultural traditions that Americans grow up with, what would you put down? Baseball, apple pie, and Superman? Belief in the "American dream"? The Pledge of Allegiance and "The Star-Spangled Banner"? Every society has its own values, traditions, and folklore. This chapter discusses some of the basic beliefs that shaped early civilizations in India and China. As you read, remember that these ideas outlasted empires and endured for centuries.

The Geographic Setting

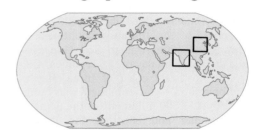

The Chapter Outline

1. The Roots of Civilization in India
2. The Start of Lasting Traditions in China

The largest river in China and the fourth largest in the world, the Yangtze provided early settlers with water, food, rich soil, and transportation.

1 The Roots of Civilization in India

Objectives

Focus Questions

★ ■ What was life like among early Indus Valley people? *(pages 53–55)*
● ■ How did the Aryan conquest change ways of life in India? *(pages 55–56)*
▲ ■ How did religion affect daily life? *(pages 57–59)*

Terms to Know

subcontinent	caste
monsoon	Hinduism
Vedas	reincarnation
rajah	karma
dharma	epic

★ Note strategies for first objective on this page.

Today India is only one of several countries on the peninsula of South Asia. Historically, however, the whole peninsula was home to the Indian people.

The Geography of India

The huge triangular peninsula of South Asia is so distinct from the rest of Asia that it is often called the Indian **subcontinent**. As you can see from the map on page 54, a mountain range to the north separates the subcontinent from other parts of Asia.

India is made up of three basic regions: (1) the Himalayas, (2) the northern plains, and (3) the Deccan (DEK-un), or southern plateau. The Himalayas, the world's highest mountains, stretch across India's northern border. This is the only region of India where temperatures drop below freezing. Because of the rugged climate and terrain, few people live in the Himalayas.

Immediately south of the Himalayas lies a wide stretch of plains. It includes the valleys of India's two largest rivers, the Indus and the Ganges (GAN-jeez). Most of India's people have always lived in this region because of its fertile soil and abundant water supply.

South of the plains lies the region known as the Deccan, which forms most of India's peninsula. The Deccan is an enormous plateau surrounded by hills. Its climate tends to be dry, and farmers in this region depend on the **monsoons** for water. The monsoons are seasonal winds that cross southern Asia. In winter, the monsoons blow hot dry air from the northeast. In summer, cooler wet winds come from the southeast, picking up moisture from the Indian Ocean and bringing heavy rains.

Each year farmers await the monsoons with a mix of hope and fear. Too much rain—or too little—can mean ruined crops and terrible famine.

Indus Valley Civilization

Early cities. The cities of the Indus Valley are the most recently discovered of all the early centers of civilization. In the 1920's, archeologists found the remains of two great cities on the Indus River and one of its tributaries. They named the cities Mohenjo-Daro (moh-HEN-joh-DAH-roh) and Harappa (huh-RUP-uh).

These cities developed about 2500 B.C., when civilization was already flourishing in Sumer (page 29). The territory of the Indus Valley civilization was much larger than ancient Egypt or Mesopotamia. It included much of the northwest corner of the subcontinent, which is now the nation of Pakistan.

Harappa and Mohenjo-Daro were carefully planned cities, each about a square mile in area. Wide streets were laid out in an orderly pattern. Buildings were square, with **53**

★ RETEACHING. Have students review "Indus Valley Civilization" (pp. 53–55) and then answer the following: (a) What kinds of buildings made up Indus Valley cities? (Square buildings with windowless brick walls facing the street; large homes, with indoor bathrooms.) (b) What foods did the Indus people grow? (Grain and fruit.) (c) What was Indus writing like? (Picture-like symbols.) (Comprehension) *Observing for Detail*

★ REINFORCEMENT. Have students make a chart comparing the government, religious, economic, and social systems found in the Indus Valley and Sumerian civilizations (pp. 29–33). (Application) *Comparing History*

★ ENRICHMENT. Have students find information on the religious significance Hindus place on the Ganges River. Students might explain the river's relationship to rituals and reincarnation. (Synthesis) *Locating Information*

Indian Subcontinent

What mountain ranges divide the Indian subcontinent from the rest of Asia? How were Aryan invaders able to enter the subcontinent? What three major rivers are shown on the map? Along which river did an early civilization develop?

windowless brick walls facing the street. A huge central fortress contained rooms for storing grain, an assembly hall, and public baths. Most homes were large; some stood two stories high. They had indoor bathrooms, with the earliest known sewer systems for drainage.

Indus Valley life. Archeological digs have given us much information about the lives of the early Indus people. We know, for example, that the people of Harappa and Mohenjo-Daro believed in many gods. They had a deep respect for nature, and they tended their land carefully. Farmers grew grain and fruit and they were among the earliest peoples to grow cotton and make cotton cloth. They also domesticated many animals, including elephants, sheep, goats, cats, and dogs.

The Indus people had a system of weights and measures for weighing grain and gold. Artisans worked with copper, bronze,

Sec. Rev. ques. 2

54

and gold. On the edge of the city, people baked bricks and pottery in large ovens. They also used clay to make children's toys—whistles, small carts, and animals.

As in many early civilizations, merchants used stone or clay seals to mark goods and sign contracts. Seals from the Indus Valley were flat, used like modern rubber stamps. They combined carved animal designs and a few picture-like symbols that probably stood for the merchant's name. These are the only surviving examples of Indus Valley writing. So far, no one has found out their exact meaning.

The Indus people built ports on the Arabian Sea. Traders sailed along the coast and into the Persian Gulf, dealing in cotton cloth, grain, turquoise, and probably timber and ivory. Some Harappan seals have been found in Sumer, showing that the two cities traded with each other as early as 2300 B.C.

The decline of Indus Valley civilization. After about 1,000 years of prosperity, the Indus Valley civilization began to collapse. Cities were abandoned, trade slowed, and law and order broke down. The reasons for this decline are a mystery. Some historians think that the Indus people fled their cities after they were attacked by Aryans. Others believe that environmental problems, such as floods, changes in the course of rivers, and soil exhaustion, had already driven away many valley dwellers even before the Aryans came. Whether or not the Aryans caused the downfall of the Indus Valley civilization, their arrival around 1500 B.C. marked a turning point in Indian history.

The Arrival of the Aryans

● Note strategies for second objective on this page and p. 56.
The Aryans probably came from the plains of Central Asia, west of the Hindu Kush—a mountain range bordering India on the northwest. From there, the Aryans crossed into South Asia by way of mountain passes. They were taller and lighter-skinned than the Indus Valley people. They spoke a different language, too—what we now call Indo-European (page 43).

Indra was chief among the Aryan or Vedic gods. Hinduism later transformed him from a storm god to a king mounted on an elephant.

The conquest of the Indus Valley. The Aryans built no cities in Central Asia and had no art, architecture, or written language. They were warlike nomads who measured their wealth in livestock. They came to northern India in search of land and animals.

The peaceful people of the Indus Valley were no match for the fierce Aryans, who fought with bronze axes and horse-drawn war chariots. Many of the valley dwellers became slaves of the conquerors.

From the fall of the Indus Valley civilization, about 1500 B.C., until the third century B.C., people in India kept no written records. The information we have about that period comes from archeological studies or from reports written by foreign travelers.

The Vedas. Nearly all that is known about the first thousand years of the Aryans' dominance in northern and northwest India comes from the four sacred texts known as the Vedas (VAY-duz). The Vedas are a collection of hymns, prayers, explanations of religious rituals, and wise sayings. These texts **55**

Economics In addition to trading with Sumer, the Indus people imported gold from southern India; silver, copper, and lapis lazuli (a gemstone) from Afghanistan; and turquoise from Iran.
● **RETEACHING. Have students identify the following: Aryan** (Nomads from Central Asia who settled in the Indus Valley around 1500 B.C.) **Rig-Veda** (Oldest of the Aryan religious texts.) **Brahmin** (Member of the priestly caste.) **Dharma** (Code of conduct for each class.) *(Comprehension) Identifying Information*

● REINFORCEMENT. Have students make a diagram illustrating the caste system that developed after the Aryan invasion of the Indus Valley. Diagrams should include a brief description of each group. (Groups include Brahmins, Kshatriya, Vaisya, Sudra, and untouchables.) *(Application)* *Translating Information Into Another Form*

Meanwhile . . .

IN MESOPOTAMIA

About the same time that the Aryans invaded the Indus Valley, the Hittites—another Aryan people—were invading Mesopotamia (page 43). Both of these peoples were successful conquerors. Unlike the Aryans in India, however, the Hittites produced fine examples of architecture, sculpture, and pottery.

show how Aryan life changed between 1500 and 500 B.C., the period called the Vedic Age. Before the Vedas were written down, they were carefully memorized and passed orally from generation to generation.

Oldest and most important of the Vedas is the Rig-Veda. It contains more than 1,000 hymns, prayers, and songs. These show that the early Aryans were proud people who enjoyed fighting, singing, and chariot racing. The Rig-Veda also reveals that the Aryans worshiped natural forces, such as the sun.

● See
below.

Aryan Society

The early Aryans lived in tribes. Within each tribe, the Aryans had a class system with three levels: warrior-nobles, priests, and the common people. One of the warriors was chosen to be the chief, or **rajah**.

The class system was fairly flexible, and people could move between classes. Male and female roles, though, were clearly defined. Men made war and tended cattle; women raised crops, wove cloth, ground grain, and tended their homes and children.

Sec. Rev.
ques. 3

Stricter class divisions. After the Aryans conquered the Indus Valley, their simple, nomadic way of life changed. Each rajah claimed land and set up his own kingdom made up of small villages. There he ruled as a hereditary king, not simply a chosen leader.

56

The loose class structure of early Aryan times slowly gave way to a more rigid system with four main groups. At the top were priests known as Brahmins. Next came the warrior-nobles, the Kshatriya (kuh-SHAT-ree-uh). The Vaisya (VY-shuh), the common people, were traders, artisans, farmers, and herders.

Far below these three classes was the laboring class, the Sudra (SHOO-drah). The Sudra included the conquered Indian peoples as well as the descendants of Aryans who had married non-Aryans. They were looked down upon by all other groups.

The rise of a caste system. Aryans believed that both human beings and gods were part of a universal order. Class distinctions soon came to be seen as an important and unchangeable part of this order. Each class had its own **dharma** (DAR-muh)—a code of conduct for its members, spelling out their rights and duties. As these rules grew more and more strict, the four main classes of Aryan society became **castes**—fixed social groupings.

Over thousands of years, the caste system became more complex. Hundreds of subcastes formed within castes, and each had tiny differences in customs. What people ate, what jobs they did, whom they could marry—all depended on their caste. One of the most important rules forbade associating with someone of a lower caste. Such contact was thought to bring spiritual "pollution" or uncleanliness. Though people of different castes had everyday business dealings, they avoided each other on ritual occasions.

Outcastes. One large group of people was not even part of the caste system. These were the outcastes, also known as untouchables. This group was probably made up of the most recent arrivals in Aryan society. People who committed serious crimes or broke the dharma for their caste also became outcastes.

Most Indians thought of outcastes as the lowest of all human beings and would have nothing to do with them. Outcastes thus lived on the fringe of society. They did jobs that caste members would not dream of doing, such as sweeping streets and cremating the dead.

Religion The most popular god in the Rig-Veda was Indra, pictured on page 55. Indra personified the qualities of a warrior; he threw thunderbolts, ate bulls, and rode his chariot across the sky.
● ENRICHMENT. Have students research the Vedas. Reports might explain the history of the four Vedas, how they differ from one another, their purposes and uses, and their relevance to modern India. *(Synthesis)* **Using Primary Sources**

Social History In the 1920's, Mohandas Gandhi rejected the traditional name "untouchables" and called outcastes *Harijans,* or "children of God."
Critical Thinking. Ask: What is the difference between *caste* and *class?* (Class is a flexible social division usually determined by occupation. Castes are fixed social groupings, each with a code of conduct and specific rights and duties.)

Hinduism and Hindu Society

▲ Note strategies for third objective on this page and p. 58.

Religious beliefs and customs were the major force in everyday life in India. The religions of the early Indus Valley people and the Aryans gradually melted together into the religion called **Hinduism**. Hinduism drew on many traditions as it evolved, but it stayed flexible enough to be the faith of most Indian people. This religion guided them in practical matters of daily life as well as in spiritual matters.

The Upanishads. For hundreds of years, priests memorized and passed on the hymns and poems of the Vedas (page 55). Religious thinkers wrote down their ideas about these hymns. One famous collection of writings is the Upanishads (oo-PAN-uh-shadz), which date from about 800 B.C. to 300 B.C. They discuss basic ideas about right and wrong, the universal order, and human destiny.

Reincarnation. The Upanishads describe a "world spirit" or "supreme principle," called Brahman. Hindus believe that this spirit is present in every living creature and that, at the same time, everything is a part of the world spirit. The goal of a Hindu is to return to Brahman and be absorbed back into the universal spirit. Hindus believe that to reach this goal, the human soul must progress and become purer. They do not expect to accomplish this in one lifetime. They believe in **reincarnation**—rebirth of the soul over and over in different bodies until it is purified. How quickly or slowly this happens depends on one's karma.

Karma can be understood most simply as all of the good and bad acts of one's previous lives. Hindus believe that good karma assures a person of being reborn into a better life. The caste system reflected the Hindu belief that people are born at different levels of purity. The Brahmins, with their knowledge of the Vedas, were believed to be the purest social group.

Sec. Rev. ques. 4

Hindu ideas about caste, dharma, and karma are closely related. Performing the correct dharma for one's class and status is essential to achieving good karma.

This picture from a Hindu epic shows the god Krishna and his wife Radha. They represent some of the qualities—bravery, loyalty, devotion—prized in Indian culture.

Hindu families. Life in Hindu villages revolved around the family. Parents, children, wives of married sons, grandchildren, and others who were directly related to the father all lived with or near each other. These close family ties provided people with a deep sense of security.

The traditional Hindu family stressed obedience to elders and respect for ancient customs. Married Hindu women were supposed to run their households smoothly, look after their children, and obey their husbands without question. In return, a husband would give his wife as many luxuries as he could afford—jewelry, rich foods, fine clothing.

Sec. Rev. ques. 5

In families that followed strict Hindu custom, a woman faced a bleak future after her husband died. A widow, particularly in an upper-class family, could not remarry. She had to live with her in-laws, spending her time in prayer. She could no longer wear bright clothes or perfume, attend festivals, or **57**

▲ RETEACHING. Have students write one paragraph summarizing how religion affected life in the Indus Valley. (Religion was the major force in everyday life; it guided both practical and religious matters.) (Comprehension) *Organizing Ideas*
Check for Understanding. Ask: What is the difference between *Brahmin* and *Brahman*? (Brahmins are priests; Brahman is seen as the world spirit.)

▲ REINFORCEMENT. Have students explain how the following are related: reincarnation; Brahman; karma. (Brahman was believed to be the world spirit of which all is part. Individual souls return to Brahman after reincarnation, which is determined by a person's karma.) (Comprehension) *Identifying Relationships*
Check for Understanding. Ask: What is the difference between *karma* and *dharma*? (Karma is all of the good and bad acts of one's previous lives. Dharma is a code of conduct for each of the classes.)

The Arts

Hindu Art

(F) See below

Like Hindu society, Hindu art showed a blending of several influences. Many works of art celebrated the gods of the Aryan Vedas and the heroes of the *Ramayana* and the *Mahabharata.* However, the influence of the early Indus Valley civilization also survived, especially in the statues and carvings of animals. Unlike artists of the ancient Middle East, who showed fierce hunting scenes, Hindu artists usually portrayed animals as noble, peaceful, and wise. The bull, the lion, the elephant, and the horse all became important religious and royal symbols.

Hindus believe that gods can take many forms. Here the god Shiva is shown in a creative form, as lord of the dance. Yet Shiva is also known as the lord of destruction. How can two such different personalities be represented by the same god? The fiery ring that surrounds the bronze statue may suggest an answer. It represents the cycle of birth, death, and rebirth—an idea basic to Hinduism. Birth, Hindus believe, could not exist without death, nor could creation exist without destruction. Shiva's opposing personalities accurately reflect this view of the world.

Sec. Rev. ques. 5 cont.

enjoy such foods as honey and meat. Rather than lead such a grim life, some women chose suicide by burning themselves on their husband's funeral pyre (the cremation fire). This practice, known as suttee, was believed to purify the sins of the husband's family.

Although Hindu women had little real independence, they did have some rights. They could own personal property, such as jewelry, which their daughters could inherit. A few women owned business property, though they were restricted in business dealings with men. Most upper-class women received some education, especially in the arts, music, and dance.

58

Gods and heroes. Hindus believe in many different gods and goddesses, but all are considered to be symbols and expressions of Brahman. Although each deity can appear in many forms, each form is part of the universal spirit. The most important gods are Brahma the creator, Shiva (SHEE-vuh) the destroyer, and Vishnu the preserver.

Within the basic beliefs of Hinduism, followers can worship in many different ways. People in different regions, villages, or families may honor separate gods or goddesses and may follow different rituals, practices, and customs. All still worship Brahman, however.

▲ See below.

(F) FEATURE ACTIVITY. Have students write an essay describing how acceptance of the Hindu concept of birth, death, and rebirth—represented by the god Shiva—might affect an individual's beliefs about life and death. *(Synthesis)* **Making Judgments**

Check for Understanding. Ask: What characteristic do all Hindu gods and goddesses share? (They are symbols of Brahman. Each of the gods' and goddesses' many forms are part of the universal spirit.)

Religion The god Vishnu is thought to have come down to earth at times as a human to save the world from impending disaster. One of those times was as Krishna in the *Mahabharata;* another was as Rama in the *Ramayana.*

▲ ENRICHMENT. Have students find information about one of the Hindu gods or goddesses. Research should include information on the personality of the god and forms of worship. *(Application)* **Locating Information**

Vocabulary Note that *Mahabharata* means "the Great Story." *Ramayana* translates as "Rama's Way."

See Sec. 1 *Closing the Lesson*, p. T51B.

Hindu tradition rests not only on religious writings but also on **epics**. An epic is a long poem that tells the adventures of heroes. Two great epics that came from the Vedic Age, the *Mahabharata* (muh-hah-BUR-uh-tuh) and the *Ramayana* (rah-MAH-yah-nuh), are still well known in India. These tales reveal the virtues and ideals that are important in Hindu life.

The *Mahabharata* tells of a great war in which people and gods fight side by side to control a kingdom. It is thought to be based on a real war fought about 1000 B.C. The other great epic, the *Ramayana*, teaches moral lessons as it follows the adventures of Prince Rama and Princess Sita. These two characters represent the ideal Hindu couple. Rama is a strong hero; Sita is his devoted and obedient wife.

See lesson plans, pp. T51A–T51C.

Section Review

Answers to Section Review questions are in brackets on pages indicated.

1. **Define:** subcontinent, monsoon, Vedas, rajah, dharma, caste, Hinduism, reincarnation, karma, epic. (pp. 53, 55, 56, 57, 59)
2. By what activities did early Indus Valley people make a living? (pp. 54–55)
3. How did Aryan life change after the conquest of the Indus Valley? (p. 56)
4. How was the caste system related to Hindu beliefs? (p. 57)
5. What rights and responsibilities did Hindu women have? (pp. 57–58)
6. **Critical thinking:** Why might class divisions be more rigid in a settled community than among nomads?

(See answer below.)

6. Answers will vary. Students might suggest that private ownership of land and accumulation of wealth are more readily achieved in settled communities. As wealth increases among certain segments of a society, social gaps and changing values make class divisions more rigid.

2 The Start of Lasting Traditions in China

Objectives

Focus Questions

★ ■ How did the Shang and Zhou dynasties rule their territories? *(pages 59–63)*

● ■ How did Confucius influence Chinese thought? *(pages 63–64)*

Terms to Know

Mandate of Heaven   extended family
feudalism   filial piety
bureaucrat

★ Note strategies for first objective on this page and p. 61.

East of India lies China. Though the two countries share a border hundreds of miles long, the ancient Chinese had little contact with Indian civilization. Mountains to the south and west, the Gobi (GOH-bee) Desert to the north, and the Yellow Sea to the northeast cut China off from the rest of Asia.

Believing themselves to be at the center of the world, the Chinese came to call their land *Zhung-Guo* (JUNG-GWAH),* which means "the Middle Kingdom."

The Geography of China

China's first civilization, like those in the ancient Middle East and India, developed along a great river. The Yellow River, known to the Chinese as the Huang, begins in the mountains of western China. It then forms a huge loop as it flows nearly 3,000 miles to the Yellow Sea. Over thousands of years the river has changed course many times. Gradually it created a broad valley known as the North China Plain.

This flat plain, watered and fertilized by the river that runs through it, has some of the

---

* As noted on page 22, most of the Chinese names in this book are spelled according to the Pinyin system. Both Pinyin and traditional spellings appear in the Index.

59

China, 1100–800 B.C.

What great rivers flowed through Zhou territory in China? How had Zhou territory changed by 800 B.C.? How does the extent of ancient China compare with China's present-day boundaries? (See answers below, left.)

richest farmland in China. The Yellow River, however, can be as dangerous as it is helpful. Like the Tigris and Euphrates rivers (page 29), the Yellow River deposits soil along its bed. These deposits raise the river and give it a tendency to flood. The many floods, which cause great destruction, have earned the river the nickname "China's Sorrow."

The Shang Dynasty

It was in the Yellow River Valley that Chinese people first settled. Legend has it that China's first dynasty, the Xia (SHEE-uh), was founded about 2000 B.C. by a prince named Yu. Yu is said to have tamed the waters of the river so that farmers could live in the valley.

Ancient stories claim that the Xia rulers who followed Yu were terribly cruel. They **60** were overthrown around 1600 or 1500 B.C.

by another noble family, the Shang (SHAHNG). For many years, scholars doubted that the Shang people had really existed. In the 1920's, however, archeologists found the ruins of a great Shang city at Anyang (AHN-YAHNG), on the North China Plain (map, this page). The excavations at Anyang produced much information about the culture of the Shang.

An unusual Bronze Age people. Shang artisans are famous for their fine bronzework. Yet bronze was scarce. Most items made of bronze were either weapons or religious artifacts that only members of the upper class could afford.

Unlike other Bronze Age peoples, the Shang made most tools and weapons of stone, bone, and wood. They also worked with jade, ivory, and marble. Artisans often inlaid the costly objects they created with turquoise and mother-of-pearl.

Geography The Yellow River is named after yellow silt picked up by the river from mountains in Mongolia.

Map Answers: (1) Yellow (Huang), Wei, Yangtze (Chang). (2) It had expanded to the south and east. (3) Ancient China covered a fraction of present-day China.

Background Anyang was excavated from 1928 to 1937, and again after 1950. It is the chief site of the Shang civilization and includes several palaces, royal graves, and deposits of dragon bones (p. 61).

Check for Understanding. Ask: How were the Bronze Age people of the Shang dynasty different from other Bronze Age peoples? (They made most of their tools and weapons from stone, bone, and wood. Bronze was reserved for weapons and religious articles belonging to the wealthy.)

Warfare. The Shang had a powerful army with as many as 30,000 soldiers. Mounted on war chariots, nobles led groups of 3,000 to 5,000 men into battle. Nobles were armed with spears and protected by bronze shields and helmets. Foot soldiers were armed with bows and arrows.

Sec. Rev. ques. 2

The Shang rulers needed such an impressive army. They controlled a fairly small state near the Yellow River, but they demanded tribute from neighboring peoples. This tribute kept the Shang government running. The Shang rulers were often at war with their neighbors and with sheep-herding nomads who trespassed on Shang farmlands.

Social structure. Under the Shang dynasty, Chinese society was dominated by a small upper class. The king, who headed this class, was not a warrior but a high priest. The nobles, who made up the rest of the upper class, were either warriors who protected the dynasty's interests or priests who helped the king perform religious rituals.

The lower class—farmers, artisans, and slaves—made up most of the population. The farmers, along with slaves, grew millet and other foods. They also raised silkworms, whose threads were woven into fine cloth.

The writing system. The first known writing system in China appeared during the Shang dynasty. Writing was probably developed for a religious use. Priests wrote questions on bones or tortoise shells, called dragon bones. They then touched a red-hot needle to the object until it cracked. The

ORACLE BONES

priest studied the shape and position of the crack to understand the gods' answer. Writing helped the Chinese keep records of such events as wars and changes of rulers.

The Zhou Dynasty

Around 1100 B.C. the Shang dynasty was conquered by the Zhou (JOH) people. The Zhou had long lived in a small kingdom on the western frontier of the Shang empire. Tired of paying tribute to the Shang, the Zhou royal family decided to take over the empire. The Zhou justified this move by claiming they had been given the **Mandate of Heaven**—the approval of the gods to rule. The Shang, they said, had lost the Mandate of Heaven because they governed poorly.

The Zhou reigned nearly 900 years, longer than any other dynasty in Chinese history. Although the Zhou rulers themselves gradually lost all real power, the period named for them was a time of far-reaching changes.

The development of feudalism. At first the Zhou governed from their western homeland along the Wei (WAY) River. They soon found, however, that the territory they had conquered was too large to be ruled effectively by the royal family. They tried to solve the problem by setting up a system of **feudalism**. Feudalism is a political system in which nobles, or lords, are granted the use of lands that legally belong to the king. In return, the nobles owe loyalty and military service to the king and protection to the people who live on their estates.

Sec. Rev. ques. 3

★ See below.

The king divided up the Shang lands among members of the royal family and military leaders whom he especially trusted. Each of the men named to rule over one of the Shang domains took an oath of loyalty to the king. In return, the king gave the land as a gift for the use of the new lord. The king and the feudal lord promised to aid each other.

At first the local lords lived in small, walled towns that were surrounded by hostile peoples. The lords depended on the king's armies to defend them. Over time, however, the towns grew into cities and expanded into **61**

Shang artists produced some of the world's finest works of bronze. This rhinoceros held ceremonial foods.

Religion It was believed the Shang king could communicate with the spirit of his ancestors, who were thought to be powerful guardians. The people sought the spirits' protection through offerings.

Religion The Shang king was believed to be a descendant of the supreme god, Shang Ti, founder and ancestor of the Shang people. When a king died, it was believed he joined his great ancestor in heaven and gave to his eldest son the role of chief worshiper in the ancestor cult.

Cultural History Chinese writing consisted of over 2,000 characters, some of which are still used. Some characters were pictures of actual objects, some represented ideas, and others indicated pronunciation.

★ ENRICHMENT. Have students identify the following statements as either a Cause or Effect and then write an essay explaining their answers. (a) The Zhou grew tired of paying tribute. (b) The Zhou established a feudal system. (Analysis) Identifying Cause and Effect

Horses became important in Chinese life, as shown by these bronze statues found in a general's tomb.

the surrounding territory. Peoples who had once been hostile toward the lords now accepted their rule and adopted Zhou ways. The result was that the lords no longer had to depend on the king. More and more, they fought among themselves and with neighboring peoples outside the empire for wealth and territory. As their power grew, that of the Zhou kings declined.

In 771 B.C. the nobles led a successful rebellion against the Zhou king. The royal family fled 300 miles east along the Wei River to a new capital at Luoyang (luh-WOH-yahng). There the Zhou rulers were little more than figureheads. Real power was in the hands of the great local lords.

Improvements in technology, trade, and transportation. The Zhou dynasty continued until 256 B.C. Though war and disunity marked their reign, this was also a time of important developments in Chinese society. Metalworkers of the Zhou period learned to make sturdy plows and sharp weapons of iron. Workers dug canals for shipping grain, and farmers developed irrigation systems to water their crops.

As new trading centers sprang up, many people became merchants. The invention of coined money to replace the barter system greatly boosted trade. Although merchants were the lowest social class, they became wealthy and influential members of their communities.

Some new ideas, such as the knowledge of ironworking, probably came into north China from western and Central Asia. The nomadic herding peoples there also had learned to domesticate and ride horses. These mounted horsemen raided border areas and posed a danger to farmers, but they introduced horseback riding to the Chinese. This skill brought many changes. Soldiers learned to ride horseback rather than drive war chariots. Mounted messengers carried news much faster than runners could, and the improvement in communication helped rulers control their distant territories.

Government by bureaucrats. New states grew up around the old central states of the North China Plain. Chinese culture spread over an area from the borders of Mongolia south to the Yangtze (YANG-see) River, called the Chang by the Chinese (map, page 60). This area included many people whom the inhabitants of the Middle Kingdom considered barbarians.

Local lords knew they needed efficient forms of government to organize such large projects as flood control and defense. Therefore, the rulers of the outlying states began to centralize their rule. They established tax systems, military organizations, and codes of

62

Politics Warfare among Chinese lords and against invaders reduced the number of feudal states from about 200 in the eighth century B.C. to less than 20 by 500 B.C.

Check for Understanding. Ask: How did the feudal system established by the Zhou eventually threaten their leadership? (Feudal towns grew into large cities, the lords' rule was accepted, and the lords no longer depended on the king. As the power of the nobles grew, royal power decreased.)

law. Some took control of the trade in salt and iron, which brought their states a good income. States in north China began to build frontier walls to keep out invaders.

To run the government, there grew up a new class of trained public officials and administrators, or **bureaucrats** (BYOO-ruh-kratz). Most bureaucrats were not high-ranking nobles but scholars and teachers. They traveled from state to state advising different rulers on correct behavior and political matters. Some also attracted students and set up schools. Their writings became guides for later Chinese society.

Sec. Rev. ques. 4

The Teachings of Confucius

● Note strategies for second objective on this page and p. 64.

One of the traveling bureaucrats was K'ung Fu-tzu ("Master Kung"), whom we know by the name Confucius (kun-FYOO-shus). He is regarded as China's greatest thinker and teacher. Confucius (551–479 B.C.) did not concern himself with the soul, the afterlife, or the worship of gods. He was most interested in questions of morality. He tried to define ways in which people should live and behave in their everyday dealings with others.

Confucius outlined five basic social relationships: between ruler and subjects, father and son, husband and wife, older and younger brothers, and members of a community. In the first four relationships, one person was viewed as superior and worthy of respect and obedience. In turn, this superior person was expected to set a good example of moral behavior. According to Confucius, evil rulers were responsible for the evil actions of their officials and subjects. Similarly, a father was responsible for his children's good or bad behavior.

Sec. R. ques. 5

Confucius cared deeply about government and tried to teach his students to develop the qualities that would make them good public officials. The Confucian virtues included integrity, loyalty, generosity, and politeness. Confucian ideals became a part of Chinese culture. Like Hinduism in India, they united the people even during periods of political unrest.

The Family in Chinese Society

The family was the foundation of Chinese society. It was considered more important than the individual or the state. Confucius believed that order in the family was the key to a peaceful society and a well-run government. A Chinese family typically included parents, children, and grandparents all living under one roof. Such a household is called an **extended family**.

The roles of men and women. Within the family, according to Chinese beliefs, men were superior to women. The birth of a son was a joyous event that brought honor to a family. Girls held a less favored position because they would eventually marry out of the family. A daughter had to obey her father until she married; then she owed obedience

The teachings of Confucius formed the basis of Chinese education for 2,000 years, making this philosopher one of the most influential figures in history.

63

● RETEACHING. Have students summarize the ways in which Confucius influenced Chinese society. Summaries should include an explanation of the five basic relationships and Confucian virtues. (Relationships: Ruler and subject; father and son; husband and wife; older brother and younger brother; members of a community. Virtues: Integrity, loyalty, generosity, and politeness.) (Comprehension) **Summarizing Information**

● REINFORCEMENT. Have students analyze how Confucian principles, the Chinese view of the family, the roles of men and women, and the concept of filial piety supported each other. (Answers will vary. Confucius's structure of society was reinforced by acceptance of male superiority and filial piety.) (Analysis) **Analyzing Ideas** to her husband. She could own nothing except the property she brought with her when she married. Still, many husbands honored their wives and asked their advice on family and business matters.

Filial piety. The Chinese had a high regard for the wisdom of the elderly. Both men and women looked forward to old age, for it brought them respect and leisure time. Every child was taught to show **filial piety** (FIL-ee-ul PY-ih-tee)—respect for one's parents and for the family ancestors. Filial piety required the eldest son to provide a good life for his aging parents. There were few sins in ancient China greater than treating a parent with disrespect. The belief in filial piety, still strong in China today, is an example of Chinese traditions that have lasted thousands of years.

● See below, right.

See Sec. 2 *Closing the Lesson,* p. T51C.

Section Review

Answers to Section Review questions are in brackets on pages indicated.

1. **Define or identify:** Mandate of Heaven, feudalism, bureaucrat, extended family, filial piety. (pp. 61, 63, 64)
2. How did the Shang rulers control their territory? (p. 61)
3. What system did the Zhou set up to govern their territory? (p. 61)
4. Why did scholars become important in Chinese society? (p. 63)
5. What qualities did Confucius urge his followers to develop? (p. 63)
6. **Critical thinking:** Compare Chinese and Indian ideas about the family (pages 57–58, 63–64). (See answer below.)

6. Answers will vary, but students should note that in both Chinese and Indian cultures, the family was the basis of society. Family relationships were valued above all others, and filial piety was an essential part of family life.

Chapter 3   Summary and Timeline

1. The Indian subcontinent was the site of one of the great early river valley civilizations, in the Indus Valley. After about 1,000 years, the highly organized Indus culture declined. At the same time, Aryans from Central Asia took control of the Indus Valley. They gradually developed a rigid caste system with strict codes of conduct for each social group. Aryan beliefs also shaped the religion of Hinduism, which provided both spiritual and practical rules for Indian society.

2. The first Chinese cultures grew up about 2000 B.C. along the Yellow River in north China. During China's Bronze Age, the Shang dynasty ruled with the help of a powerful army. Around 1100 B.C. the Zhou conquered the Shang empire and developed a feudal system to control the large territory. In 771 B.C. the nobles, who had been given power to rule under the Zhou, rebelled against the Zhou dynasty. Local lords created a highly organized government run by public officials who were trained scholars. Confucian teachings about government and family life became an important part of Chinese thought.

2500 B.C.
Indus Valley civilization develops

2000 B.C.
Yellow River Valley civilization develops

1600 B.C.
Shang dynasty begins

1500 B.C.
Aryans invade Indus Valley

1100 B.C.
Zhou dynasty begins

551 B.C.
Confucius born

2500 B.C.   2000   1500   1000   500 B.C.

64

Religion Filial piety grew out of the Chinese belief in ancestor worship. Ancestors, who were believed to influence the fate of living descendants, could be assured honor only by those trained to respect elders. Filial piety reinforced the reverence due ancestors.

Check for Understanding. Ask: (a) What was the most important set of relationships in Chinese society? (Family.) **(b) What was the principle of respect for the elderly called?** (Filial piety.)

● ENRICHMENT. **Have students research the Confucian social system. Students should find information on how individuals were expected to honor the five relationships and the consequences for those who failed to respect social roles.** (Application) *Locating Information*

See p. T51C for answers to Chapter Review.

Vocabulary Review

1. Match each of the following terms with its correct definition: *bureaucrat, caste, epic, filial piety, reincarnation.*
   a. rebirth of the soul
   b. trained public official
   c. respect for one's parents and ancestors
   d. long poem that tells the adventures of heroes
   e. fixed social grouping
2. Choose the term that best completes each sentence. Write your answers on a separate sheet of paper.
   a. Hindus believe they can achieve good [karma/dharma] by following the [karma/dharma] for their caste.
   b. [An extended family/A rajah] includes parents, children, and grandparents all living together under one roof.
   c. The system the Zhou set up to govern their large territory is called [feudalism/Hinduism].
   d. The Aryan sacred books that contain hymns, prayers, religious rituals, and wise sayings are called the [Mandate of Heaven/Vedas].
   e. India is such a distinct geographical area that it is often called a [monsoon/subcontinent].

Places to Know

Match the letters on this map of Asia with the places listed below. You may want to refer to the maps on pages 54 and 60.
1. Deccan
2. Ganges River
3. Himalayas
4. Indus River
5. North China Plain
6. Yangtze River
7. Yellow River

Recalling the Facts

1. Why are the digs at Harappa and Mohenjo-Daro important?
2. How did social classes in Aryan society change after the conquest of the Indus Valley?
3. How did the ideas of karma and dharma influence Hindu life?
4. Why did the Shang need a powerful army?
5. Why did the Zhou rulers decide to rely on the feudal system? How did this system lead to a decline in the power of the Zhou rulers?
6. According to Confucius, what were the five basic social relationships? How was the superior person in these relationships expected to act?
7. Why did Confucius think the family was important?

Critical Thinking Skills

1. **Interpreting.** Consider the statement ✔ "Hinduism was more than a religion, it was a way of life." In what respects is this true? *(Syn.)*

65

✔ A checkmark identifies questions and exercises calling for the three higher-order levels of thinking at the top of the Bloom taxonomy: Analysis, Synthesis, and Evaluation.

2. Researching a topic. Consult the *National Geographic Index* or the *Readers' Guide* to find articles on the excavations at Anyang and more recent archeological discoveries in China. Describe the artifacts found and what archeologists have learned about ancient Chinese life. *(App.)*

3. Using a timeline. A good way to organize events in chronological order is to put them on a timeline. Timelines are used in this book at the beginning of every unit and at the end of every chapter. Look at the timeline on page 64. What is the time span shown? What is the first event on the timeline? What is the last event? Which came first, the Zhou dynasty or the Shang dynasty? How many years apart did these dynasties begin? *(Comp.)*

4. Preparing an oral report. Research and prepare an oral report on one of the following topics: the *Ramayana* or the *Mahabharata;* the status of outcastes, known today as Harijans; Hindu gods; Chinese writing. *(App.)*

5. Making a value judgment. On page 63, you read about the qualities Confucius believed a public official should have. Do you think Confucius was right in believing those qualities would help a ruler govern? Are these the qualities you would want to see in a political leader today? Are there other qualities you would look for? *(Eval.)*

Thinking About Geography

1. Researching. The three great river systems of India are the Indus, the Ganges, and the Brahmaputra. Find the following information about each river: its source; its length; the location of its mouth; the body of water into which it flows. *(App.)*

2. Drawing a map. Find maps and information about the effects of the monsoons on India. Draw a map of India and use arrows to show where the seasonal winds blow. *(App.)*

3. Synthesizing. Looking at the map on page 60, you can see that China is cut off from the rest of the world by mountains, desert, and sea. Do you think China's isolation helped or hurt its early development? *(Syn.)*

66

Enrichment: Primary Sources

As you have read, each Hindu caste followed its own rules of dharma. About 2,000 years ago many of these rules were written down in a work known as the *Laws of Manu*. The adapted passage below describes the duties of the Kshatriyas (warrior-nobles).

> ❝ A Kshatriya king who, while protecting his people, is defied by enemies, should not shrink from battle but should remember the duty of a Kshatriya not to turn back in battle, to protect his people, and to honor the Brahmins.
>
> Those who fight with all their strength and do not turn back go to heaven.
>
> But the Kshatriya who has agreed to fight for another and is killed while fleeing from battle takes upon himself all the sins of his master, and whatever merit he may have gained for the next world is taken by his master.
>
> As the weeder pulls up weeds and leaves the corn to grow, even so must the king protect his kingdom and destroy his enemies. ❞

1. What, according to this passage, were the duties of Kshatriyas?
2. How could a Kshatriya win a place in heaven?
3. What punishment was said to await a Kshatriya who was killed while running away from battle?
4. Which part of this passage has to do with the Hindu belief in karma?
5. **Critical thinking:** In the last paragraph, a king is compared to a weeder of a corn field. Explain this comparison. Why was "weeding" an important duty of the king? *(Anal.)*

A checkmark identifies questions and exercises calling for the three higher-order levels of thinking at the top of the Bloom taxonomy: Analysis, Synthesis, and Evaluation.

WORLD HISTORY Checklist

UNIT 1

Try to identify the following key people, groups and dynasties, places, and terms from the unit. If you need help, refer to the pages listed.

Key People

Sargon the Great *(31)*
Hammurabi *(31)*
Menes *(36)*
Hatshepsut *(38)*
Akhenaton *(38)*
Rameses II *(38)*
Moses *(44)*
Ashurbanipal *(46)*
Nebuchadnezzar *(46)*
Cyrus the Great *(46)*
Confucius *(63)*

Key Groups and Dynasties

Sumerians *(29)*
Hittites *(43)*
Phoenicians *(43)*
Hebrews *(44)*
Assyrians *(45)*
Lydians *(46)*
Persians *(46)*
Aryans *(55)*
Shang dynasty *(60)*
Zhou dynasty *(61)*

Key Places

Altamira *(16)*
Lascaux *(16)*
Çatal Hüyük *(19)*
Mesopotamia *(29)*
Fertile Crescent *(29)*
Tigris River *(29)*
Euphrates River *(29)*
Egypt *(34)*
Nile River *(34)*
Asia Minor *(43)*
Canaan *(44)*
Jerusalem *(45)*
Babylon *(46)*

Himalayas *(53)*
Indus River *(53)*
Ganges River *(53)*
Deccan *(53)*
Harappa *(53)*
Mohenjo-Daro *(53)*
Yellow River *(59)*
North China Plain *(59)*
Yangtze River *(62)*

Key Terms

Old Stone Age *(13)*
New Stone Age *(13)*
culture *(14)*
Ice Age *(16)*
Bronze Age *(21)*
civilization *(21)*
theocracy *(24)*
polytheism *(32)*
Code of Hammurabi *(32)*
Behistun Rock *(33)*
Old Kingdom *(36)*
Middle Kingdom *(37)*
New Kingdom *(38)*
Rosetta Stone *(40)*
Iron Age *(43)*
Exodus *(44)*
Ten Commandments *(44)*
monotheism *(45)*
Judaism *(45)*
Torah *(45)*
Zoroastrianism *(48)*
Vedas *(55)*
caste *(56)*
Hinduism *(57)*
Upanishads *(57)*
Mandate of Heaven *(61)*
feudalism *(61)*

An Old Stone Age spearhead and a Lascaux cave painting.

REVIEW ACTIVITIES. *Key People:* For each person listed, identify the world region with which he or she is associated and name the person's most significant accomplishment or action. *Key Groups and Dynasties:* Identify the time period during which each group or dynasty developed and declined. *Key Places:* Show on a world outline map the location of each place. (See pages 74 and 162 of *Teacher's Resources: Geography* for world outline maps that can be copied.) *Key Terms:* Define or identify each term listed.

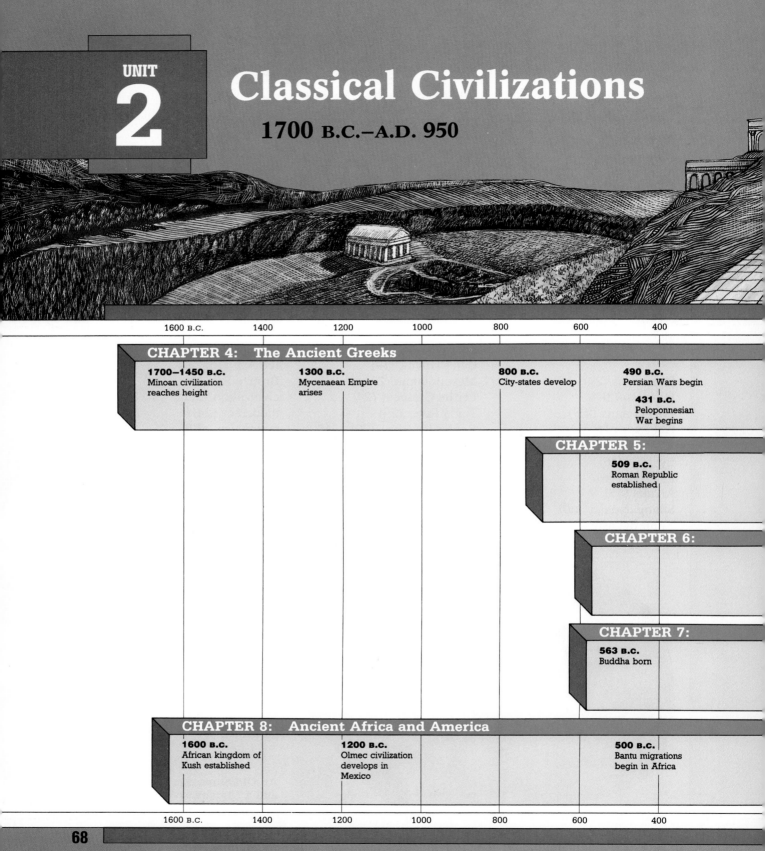

UNIT 2

Classical Civilizations

1700 B.C.–A.D. 950

1600 B.C.	1400	1200	1000	800	600	400

CHAPTER 4:   The Ancient Greeks

1700–1450 B.C.
Minoan civilization
reaches height

1300 B.C.
Mycenaean Empire
arises

800 B.C.
City-states develop

490 B.C.
Persian Wars begin

431 B.C.
Peloponnesian
War begins

CHAPTER 5:

509 B.C.
Roman Republic
established

CHAPTER 6:

CHAPTER 7:

563 B.C.
Buddha born

CHAPTER 8:   Ancient Africa and America

1600 B.C.
African kingdom of
Kush established

1200 B.C.
Olmec civilization
develops in
Mexico

500 B.C.
Bantu migrations
begin in Africa

1600 B.C.	1400	1200	1000	800	600	400

68

| 200 | B.C. A.D. | 200 | 400 | 600 | 800 | A.D. 1000 |

336 B.C.
Alexander the
Great comes to
power

The Roman Republic and Empire

264 B.C.
Punic Wars begin

31 B.C.
Roman Empire
established

A.D. 180
Pax Romana ends

The Legacy of Rome

A.D. 29
Jesus crucified

A.D. 312
Constantine converts
to Christianity

A.D. 476
Fall of Western
Roman Empire

Great Empires in India and China

221 B.C.
Qin dynasty
begins
in China

202 B.C.
Han dynasty
begins in
China

A.D. 320
India's Gupta
Empire begins

A.D. 220–589
Age of Disunity
in China

A.D. 300–700
Maya civilization
flourishes in
Central America

A.D. 350
Aksum conquers
Kush

| 200 | B.C. A.D. | 200 | 400 | 600 | 800 | A.D. 1000 |

69

Have students refer to the unit timeline to answer the following questions: **(a) What is the oldest civilization shown on the timeline?** (The
Minoan civilization developed before 1700 B.C.) **(b) What is the earliest African civilization shown on the timeline?** (The kingdom of
Kush.) **What is the earliest Mexican civilization?** (The Olmec civilization.)

The Ancient Greeks   1700–300 B.C.
(pp. 70–95)

Chapter Preview

Section 1 examines the early Minoan and Mycenaean civilizations and the rise of city-states during the Hellenic Age. In Section 2 life in the Greek city-states, differences between Sparta and Athens, and changes in Greek life after victory in the Persian Wars are described. The evolution of Greek drama, art, and literature is traced in Section 3, and achievements in science and philosophy made by Greece are identified. Section 4 explains how Alexander the Great spread Greek culture.

Bibliography

See the *Teacher's Management and Planning Guide* for additional listings. Starred titles are for both students and teachers.

Boardman, John, *et al.*, editors. *The Oxford History of the Classical World.* Oxford University Press. Articles on classical civilization by distinguished scholars.

Browning, Robert. *The Greek World: Classical, Byzantine, and Modern.* Thames and Hudson. Valuable for its striking photographs and fine text on key topics.

*Coolidge, Olivia. *Greek Myths.* Houghton Mifflin. Based on original sources. Heroes, simple folk, and visitors from Olympus.

*Coolidge, Olivia. *The Trojan War.* Houghton Mifflin. Retold from original sources.

Stone, I. F. *The Trial of Socrates.* Little, Brown. Controversial view of Athens' most infamous act.

Wood, Michael. *In Search of the Trojan War.* Facts on File. An attempt to discover the historical core of the legendary and poetic accounts.

Section Lesson Plans

SECTION 1   (pp. 71–75)
The Beginnings of Greek Civilization

Objectives

After completing this section, students will be able to:
1. Describe how Aegean peoples laid the foundation for Greek civilization.
2. Explain how Homer's poetry expressed Greek ideals.

Introducing the Lesson

Remind students that Western ideas about society and government have their foundation in ancient Greece. The Greeks in turn, were influenced by other Mediterranean cultures.

Then ask: *(a) How do people from different lands and cultures influence one another?* (Through trade, travel, and military conflict.)

(b) Why is cooperation between people with different cultural experiences important? (Answers will vary.)

(c) How has cooperation between cultures influenced American society? (Answers will vary but should reflect awareness that the United States is a nation of people from many cultures.)

Developing the Lesson: Understanding Chronology

Have students refer to pp. 71–73 in their text and make a timeline of important events in the Minoan, Mycenaean, and early Greek civilizations. (Timelines should include information for the following dates: 2600, 1900, 1700–1450, 1300–1200, 1100–800, 800–750. Note that all dates are B.C.) *(Comprehension)*

Developing the Lesson: Organizing Information

Have students organize the information on Greek gods in a chart. Charts should list the gods in order of importance and indicate the relationships between them. (Charts should include information on Zeus, Hera, Poseidon, Hades, Ares, Apollo, and Athena.) *(Comprehension)*

Closing the Lesson:
Relating Geography and History

Have students refer to "The Geography of Greece" (p. 71) to answer the following questions:

(a) How has Greece's proximity to the sea affected its historical development? (Good harbors encouraged fishing and trading; trade increased contact with other cultures.)

(b) In what ways did mountains influence the history of Greece? (Mountains limited communication among the city-states, slowed the spread of ideas and technology, and resulted in cultural differences between city-states.)

(c) How did poor soil contribute to the development of the Greek culture? (Many Greeks turned to the sea for a living. Their seagoing expertise put them in contact with other Mediterranean peoples from whom they borrowed ideas and knowledge.) *(Comprehension)*

See *Section Review* **questions, p. 75.**

SECTION 2 (pp. 76–83)
Greek City-States

Objectives

After completing this section, students will be able to:
1. Explain how Sparta and Athens differed.
2. Describe how Greek life changed after the Persian Wars.

Introducing the Lesson

Remind students that democracy is a form of government in which free people govern themselves. Democratic institutions, first organized in ancient Greece, were very different from our own.

Then ask: *(a) What are some of the essential elements of American democracy?* (The right to vote, representative institutions, constitutional guarantees of basic rights and freedoms.)

(b) Why might many people view democracy as the best system of government? (Answers will vary.)

(c) What characteristics of American democracy would you expect to have been absent in ancient Greek democracy? (Answers will vary.)

Developing the Lesson:
Comparing Social Values

Have students write an essay titled *Athenian and Spartan Ideals* comparing the ideals of Athens and Sparta. Students should conclude their essays

by choosing the Greek city-state in which they would have preferred to live and explain why. *(Evaluation)*

Developing the Lesson:
Observing for Detail

Ask: *(a) How did the defeat of the Persians lead to the golden age of Greece?* (Greeks gained freedom to develop political and artistic ideas.)

(b) What democratic reforms were made by Pericles? (Government jobs opened to all classes; salaries paid to officials; direct democracy adopted; officials chosen by lot.)

(c) What type of education were boys given? (Reading, arithmetic, music, literature, and physical education.)

(d) What role did slavery play in Athenian society during the "golden age" of Greece? (Slaves were one fourth of the total Athenian population. Although most were household servants or teachers, slaves could buy their freedom.) *(Comprehension)*

Closing the Lesson:
Evaluating Information

Have students make a time chart showing the development of democracy in ancient Greece. Then have students choose which step they consider most important to the overall development of democracy and explain why. (All dates are B.C. *800—archons* chosen to represent upper class. *621—*Draco writes down Athenian laws. *594—*Solon's reforms. *510—*Cleisthenes' democratic reforms. *460–429—*Pericles' democratic reforms.) *(Comprehension)*

See *Section Review* **questions, p. 83.**

SECTION 3 (pp. 84–89)
The Flowering of Greek Culture

Objectives

After completing this section, students will be able to:
1. Explain how the literature and art of Greece reflected Greek values.
2. Name Greek achievements in science and philosophy.

Introducing the Lesson

Remind students that classical Greek culture manifested a deep appreciation for art, literature, architecture, and the development of the intellect.

Then write the following quotation by Thucydides, Greek historian, on the board: "We are lovers of beauty without extravagance, and lovers of wisdom without unmanliness. Wealth to us is not mere material for vainglory but an opportunity for achievement; and poverty we think it no disgrace to acknowledge but a real degradation to make no effort to overcome."

Then ask: *(a) How would you paraphrase this quotation?* (Answers will vary.)

(b) What values of ancient Greece does the statement express? (Simplicity, order, beauty, strength, achievement, effort.)

(c) Do you think this quote represents the values of present-day American society? Why or why not? (Answers will vary.)

Developing the Lesson: Understanding Historical Developments

Have students trace the development of drama from its roots in Greek religious festivals to the writing of tragedy and comedy. Students might make a chart or a diagram showing the progression of drama, outline "Drama" (pp. 85–86), or write a summary of the emergence of drama. (Poetry recitals at religious festivals were chanted by the chorus and gradually developed into plays. Early tragedies were based on stories of gods and heroes. Comedies dealt with politics and current events.) *(Comprehension)*

Developing the Lesson: Analyzing Ideas

Have students review "Science and Philosophy" (pp. 86–88) and analyze the differences between ancient Mesopotamian and Egyptian scientific thinking (p. 42) and that of the Greeks of the Hellenic Age. (Mesopotamians and Egyptians believed that gods and demons caused natural events. Greeks of the Hellenic Age gradually accepted the idea of natural law and believed that the use of reason, rather than magic, would reveal the sources of events.) *(Analysis)*

Closing the Lesson: Forming a Hypothesis

Have students develop a hypothesis stating why and how the classical Greek civilization emerged at the time and place it did. When forming their hypotheses, students might consider the following: geographic factors; the Persian Wars; the development of democracy; the concept of natural law. *(Synthesis)*

See *Section Review* questions, p. 89.

SECTION 4　　(pp. 89–93)
The Legacy of Greece

Objectives

After completing this section, students will be able to:
1. Explain the significance of the Peloponnesian War.
2. Describe how Alexander's conquest of Greece caused Greek culture to spread.

Introducing the Lesson

Remind students that ancient Greek civilization was the source of many Western traditions. Despite their achievements, however, the Greeks were not able to overcome weaknesses caused by years of rivalry and war.

Then ask: *(a) What factors contribute to the peace and unity of a state?* (Cooperation; basic agreement on values, goals, and institutions; respect for differences; a willingness to compromise; unity against foreign threats.)

(b) What factors weaken a state? (Divisive differences and unwillingness to compromise; rivalry among groups; inability to agree on fundamental values and goals; foreign threats.)

(c) Why are foreign threats more likely to succeed when a state is torn by internal conflict? (Internal conflict weakens the ability of a state to present a united front against outside threats.)

Developing the Lesson: Relating Geography and History

Have students compare the map of Alexander's empire (p. 91) with the map of the Persian Empire (p. 47) and answer the following questions:

(a) Which empire included all of Asia Minor? (Persian)

(b) Which empire included Athens? (Alexander's)

(c) Which Greek city-state was not included in Alexander's empire? (Sparta) *(Comprehension)*

Developing the Lesson: Evaluating Ideas

Have students evaluate the Hellenistic philosophies *Epicureanism* and *Stoicism* and explain how they represented the classical Greek values of moderation, simplicity, order, honor, and scholarship. (Both philosophies emphasized moderation, order, and harmony and focused on individuality.) *(Comprehension)*

Closing the Lesson: Making Judgments

Have students evaluate which event or development of the Peloponnesian War, the rise of Macedonia, or the Hellenistic Age might be viewed as the most significant and explain why. *(Peloponnesian War:* led to the defeat of Athens. *Rise of Macedonia:* Philip conquered Greece; Alexander expanded the empire throughout the ancient Middle East. *Hellenistic Age:* Greek ideas spread throughout Alexander's empire.) *(Synthesis)*

See *Section Review* questions, p. 93.

Chapter 4 Review Answers
(pp. 94–95)

Vocabulary Review

1. (a) Sophists (b) colonies (c) Parthenon; classical (d) natural laws (e) Socratic method (f) agora (g) tyrant
2. (a) Acropolis—high ground on which a polis's fort stood; polis—Greek city-state. (b) Hellenic Age—great age of Greek civilization; Hellenistic Age—time when Greek culture spread through lands conquered by Alexander. (c) Democracy—government in which free citizens rule themselves; direct democracy—government in which all citizens can participate first-hand. (d) Epicureanism—Hellenistic philosophy based on belief that happiness comes from enjoying simple pleasures; Stoicism—Hellenistic philosophy based on belief that people should accept what life brings and try to exercise self-control and reason.

People to Identify

1. Pericles 2. Herodotus 3. Euclid 4. Socrates; Plato 5. Sophocles 6. Aristotle

Places to Know

1. B 2. E 3. I 4. C 5. A 6. H 7. F 8. D 9. G

Recalling the Facts

1. Knowledge about navigation, pottery making, and metalworking.
2. Children recited these works and learned to value the qualities of Homer's heroes.
3. An ideal Spartan was strong-bodied, fearless, disciplined, and obedient to authority. Athenians believed that people should develop all their talents, not just their bodies.
4. It gave the Greeks freedom to develop the political and artistic ideas that still influence Western civilization.
5. Dramatists expressed the idea that people should be wise and humble; artists showed people in calm and dignified poses. Architects aimed for harmony and balance.
6. It caused widespread death and destruction. Fighting broke out in many city-states and democracy declined. In addition, the city-states could not unite in time to stop the Macedonian invasion, which cost the Greeks their independence.
7. He conquered lands from Egypt to India, including Macedonia, Asia Minor, Phoenicia, Mesopotamia, and Persia.
8. Both used reason to explain human conduct, but Hellenic thinkers were concerned with community, while Hellenistic philosophers were more concerned with individuals.

Critical Thinking Skills

1. Autocracy—government by one person having unlimited power; gerontocracy—government based on rule by elders; plutocracy—government by the wealthy.
2. Answers will vary.

Thinking About Geography

1. (a) Irregular coastline provided natural harbors, encouraging trade and fishing. (b) Mountainous terrain slowed the spread of ideas and technology and caused each city-state to develop a distinctive character. (c) Poor soil encouraged the Greeks to fish and trade.
2. All or parts of Albania, Bulgaria, Rumania, Yugoslavia, Greece, Libya, Egypt, Israel, Lebanon, Jordan, Syria, Turkey, Iraq, Iran, Afghanistan, Pakistan, Kuwait, and the Soviet Union.
3. The Hellespont joins the Aegean Sea and the Sea of Marmara. The Bosporus joins the Sea of Marmara and the Black Sea. These straits offered the only water route from the Greek peninsula and islands in the Aegean Sea to the Greek colonies along the coast of the Black Sea.

Enrichment: Primary Sources

1. Either he was present at the events described or he cross-checked the reports of eyewitnesses.
2. Different eyewitnesses gave different accounts of the same events.
3. He probably felt his account would be more objective and accurate if he did not rely on his own general impressions.

The Ancient Greeks

1700–300 B.C.

See chapter timeline, p. 93.

Before You Read This Chapter

American citizens gain the right to vote when they turn 18. Think for a minute about casting your ballot to elect a President, a senator, or a governor. No Egyptian pharaoh or Sumerian king was ever chosen in this way. How did this right become part of our heritage? The idea of government *by* the people began many centuries ago in Greece. As you read this chapter about ancient Greek civilization, look for the steps by which self-government developed.

The Geographic Setting

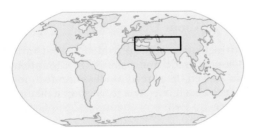

The Chapter Outline

1. The Beginnings of Greek Civilization
2. Greek City-States
3. The Flowering of Greek Culture
4. The Legacy of Greece

This dramatic sculpture, *Winged Victory*, displays the Greek ideals of strength, purity, and beauty.

Cultural History *Winged Victory*, also known as *Nike of Samothrace*, commemorates a Greek naval victory in the second century B.C. The sculpture is now housed in the Louvre in Paris.

1 The Beginnings of Greek Civilization

Objectives

Focus Questions

★ ■ How did Aegean peoples lay the foundation for Greek civilization? *(pages 71–74)*

● ■ How did Homer's poetry express Greek ideals? *(page 75)*

Terms to Know

Hellenic Age   *Iliad*
colony   *Odyssey*
oracle

★ Note strategies for first objective on this page and p. 74.

The earliest civilizations that grew up on the Greek islands developed a unique culture. Although these people were conquered by foreign invaders, many of their traditions endured. Greek ideas would come to have a powerful influence on the politics, thought, and art of Europe and the Western Hemisphere. For this reason, Greece is known as the "cradle of Western civilization."

The Geography of Greece

Greece is a land dominated by the sea. Its mainland is a peninsula in southeastern Europe that extends into the eastern Mediterranean. The coastline of the peninsula is very irregular, providing excellent natural harbors. In addition to the mainland, Greece includes dozens of offshore islands in the Aegean Sea, as the map on page 72 shows.

The terrain of Greece is rugged and mountainous. The mountains limited communication among the city-states that developed. This slowed the spread of ideas and technology, but it also brought benefits. The isolation caused by natural barriers led each city-state to form a distinctive character that contributed to the richness of the culture.

Greece's climate is mild, but its soil is not good for farming. Only about one quarter of its land is suitable for growing crops. To add to their food supply, the Greeks learned to harvest fish from the sea. In time they became expert sailors, and their voyages led them into contact with other Mediterranean peoples. Such contact allowed the Greeks to combine their achievements and borrow ideas from other civilizations.

Minoan Civilization

Centuries before civilization developed in Greece itself, a civilization grew up on the island of Crete, to the southeast. It is usually called the Minoan (mih-NOH-un) civilization, after a legendary king named Minos (MY-nus). As early as 2600 B.C., people on Crete were working with bronze and gold and developing a system of writing. Their civilization reached its height between 1700 and 1450 B.C. During this period Crete dominated the Aegean area.

The Minoans were seafaring traders, exporting wine, honey, and olive oil to Egypt, Asia Minor, Syria, and Greece. At home, they built magnificent palaces for their royal families, priests, and government officials. The palace at Knossos (NAW-sus) was like a small city. It had more than 800 rooms, including bathrooms and kitchens with sewer systems and running water. The palace walls were painted with lively scenes showing religious ceremonies and the activities of daily life. In the palace workshops, artisans made fine pottery, bronze daggers, and tools.

Minoan civilization began to decline about 1450 B.C., perhaps because of an earthquake or volcanic eruption. Soon afterward, Greeks from the mainland invaded Crete.

71

★ RETEACHING. Have students scan pp. 72–73 for information supporting these statements: **(a) The Mycenaeans borrowed much from Minoan civilization.** (Mycenaeans used Minoan designs on their pottery and jewelry; borrowed Minoan writing.) **(b) The Greeks inherited much from their Mycenaean ancestors.** (Greeks learned Mycenaean skills of navigation, pottery-making, and metalworking, some of their religious practices, and myths and legends.) *(Comprehension)* *Supporting Generalizations*

★ REINFORCEMENT. Have students make a chart titled *Facts About Early Greek Civilization* and write these statements in a column labeled *Cause:* (a) Greece's mountainous terrain limited communication among city-states. (b) Greece's soil was not productive. (c) Greeks became expert sailors. (d) Frequent warfare occurred among Mycenaean kingdoms. Have students write the effects of each cause in a second column labeled *Effects.* *(Comprehension) Identifying Effects*

Ancient Greek World

Along the shores of what seas did the Greeks settle? Find Mycenae, Olympia, Sparta, and Athens on the map. About how far from Athens was Troy? What was the name of the large island south of the Greek mainland?

(See answers below.)

Mycenaean Civilization

The invaders of Crete were Greek-speaking tribes who had moved into the Greek peninsula about 1900 B.C. They mixed with the local people and settled throughout the peninsula. Warrior-kings ruled cities built around palaces at Mycenae (my-SEE-nee), Thebes (THEEBZ), and other places in southern Greece. Their civilization is usually called Mycenaean (my-suh-NEE-un), after the palace at Mycenae, the richest and most important city.

The Mycenaeans borrowed much from Minoan civilization. Mycenaean pottery and

72

jewelry were decorated with designs in the Minoan style. Mycenaean scribes kept their records in a kind of writing that had been borrowed from Crete. The Mycenaeans also took over the Minoans' sea trade, sending ships to Egypt, Phoenicia, Sicily, and southern Italy.

Rival Mycenaean kingdoms often went to war with one another. About 1300 B.C., the king of Mycenae brought several kingdoms together in an empire that controlled the Aegean region. Writers of the time refer to the people of these kingdoms as the Achaeans (uh-KEE-unz).

Frequent warfare among the kingdoms caused a decline in Mycenaean civilization after 1200 B.C. Mycenaean palaces were destroyed, and many of the people moved to other areas. With the collapse of this civilization about 1100 B.C., Greece entered a "dark age" that lasted until about 800 B.C. Wars became common, disrupting trade, farming, and the arts. During the dark age, a tribe of Greeks called Dorians moved into the southern part of the peninsula. Though the Dorians spoke Greek, they could not read or write, and the art of writing was forgotten.

Hellenic Civilization

Not all the accomplishments of Aegean civilization were lost during the dark age, especially among the Greeks who had moved to Asia Minor and central Greece. By about 800 B.C., the great age of Greek civilization began to take shape. It is known as the **Hellenic Age** (heh-LEN-ik), from *Hellas,* the Greeks' name for their country. From their Minoan and Mycenaean ancestors, the Hellenic Greeks had learned skills such as navigation, pottery-making, and metalworking. Some of their religious practices and many of their myths and legends were the same.

Sec. Rev. ques. 2

Working on land and at sea. Most Greeks were farmers who grew wheat, barley, olives, and grapes. On the dry slopes of the mountainous land they raised sheep and goats. Greek artisans produced fine woolen cloth, pottery, and metal tools and weapons.

Other Greeks made a living by fishing or trading. They shipped wool, wine, olive oil, marble, and pottery all over the Mediterranean. In exchange, they imported goods from other lands. Trade also brought new ideas. The Greeks adopted the Phoenician alphabet for writing their own language. They learned the Lydian practice of using coins, and they gained knowledge of geometry from the Egyptians.

Greek colonies. Between about 800 and 750 B.C. the Greeks began to establish colonies—settlements in other lands. These colonies were independent of Greece, but they kept close ties with the Greek homeland through their trade and culture. Over a 200-year period the Greeks set up colonies in Asia Minor and North Africa, on the islands of the Aegean Sea, in Sicily and southern Europe, and along the coast of the Black Sea (map, page 74). The settlers carried Greek traditions and ways of living to their new homes.

Sec. Rev. ques. 3

Religious beliefs. Ancient Greeks, like the farming peoples of the ancient Middle East, looked to religion to explain changes in nature. They hoped, too, that by following religious practices they would gain good fortune. For advice the Greeks some-

A gold death mask from a king's tomb at Mycenae provides evidence of the great wealth this Bronze Age culture possessed.

73

Social History Archeological evidence suggests that the Dorians originated in present-day Albania and in the region of Macedonia.
Cultural History Note that the Greeks believed that *Hellas* had no physical boundaries but existed wherever Greek ideas could be found.
Check for Understanding. Ask: What were two ways that the Mycenaean civilization influenced Hellenic civilization? (Hellenic civilization was influenced by Mycenaean navigation, pottery-making, and metalworking.)

Check for Understanding. Ask: What ideas did the Greeks adopt from other Mediterranean peoples? (Phoenician alphabet; Lydian use of coins; Egyptian knowledge of geometry.)
Check for Understanding. Ask: What did many Greeks hope to gain from their religious practices? (Explanations of changes in nature; good fortune.)

Greek and Phoenician Colonies About 550 B.C.

In what parts of the Mediterranean world did the Greeks start colonies? About how far from Athens was Byzantium? Where did the Phoenicians establish colonies?

Map Answers: (1) On the coasts of southern Spain, Gaul (France), Italy, and Sicily; on Corsica and Sardinia; along the North African coast near Egypt; along Asia Minor and the coast of Europe near Asia Minor. (2) About 350 miles. (3) Coastal North Africa and Spain, northwest tip of Sicily.

times turned to oracles—priests and priestesses who predicted the future. The most famous of these oracles was the one at the temple at Delphi (DEL-fy).

ANTHROPOMORPHIC gods

Sec. Rev. ques. 4

The Greeks believed in many gods, who were said to live on Mount Olympus in northern Greece. Myths show that the Greeks did not view these gods as terrifying or all-powerful. Rather, the Greeks thought of the gods as a family whose members experienced joy and sorrow just as human beings did.

Linking Past and Present

An earthquake buried the stadium at Olympia in the 500's. The discovery of the ruins in 1875 gave Baron Pierre de Coubertin, a French educator, the idea of reviving the Olympics. De Coubertin's organizational skills and determination to succeed led to the first modern Olympic Games, which were held in 1896 in Athens.

74

Myths about the gods were told and retold in poems and plays.

The king of the Greek gods was Zeus (ZOOS). His wife was Hera (HEER-uh), the goddess of marriage. Other important gods were Zeus's brothers Poseidon (poh-SY-dun), the god of the sea, and Hades (HAY-deez), the god of the underworld. Zeus's children included Ares (AYR-eez), the god of war; Apollo (uh-PAHL-oh), the god of music, prophecy, medicine, and rational thinking; and Athena (uh-THEE-nuh), the goddess of wisdom and handicrafts.

The Greeks built temples to the gods and honored them with festivals. Musicians and poets presented their best songs, and athletes tried to give their best performances. The most famous athletic games were held every four years at Olympia to honor Zeus, whose temple was there. The best athletes from all Greece competed in foot racing, jumping, throwing the discus and javelin, wrestling, boxing, and other contests. The winners were crowned with a wreath of olive leaves.

★ See below.

Geography Mt. Olympus, the highest mountain in Greece, is on the border between the regions of Macedonia and Thessaly in southeastern Europe.

Religion Greeks believed that Mt. Olympus was the center of the earth. Because it seemed to touch the clouds, many believed it was the home of the gods.

Religion Ares was held in awe by many Greeks as a symbol of war, but was not honored by them.

Cultural History The Olympic games were first held in 776 B.C. Although Greek city-states frequently fought among themselves, they observed a sacred truce during the Olympic games.

★ **ENRICHMENT.** Have students research and write a report on the Minoans, Mycenaeans, Greek mythology, or Olympic games. (Application) **Locating Information**

The Epics of Homer

● Note strategies for second objective on this page.

One of the most important influences on Greek religion and thought was the poet Homer, who probably lived during the eighth century B.C. Nothing is known of Homer's life. According to legend, he was a blind man who lived in what is now the country of Turkey. His two great epics were the **Iliad** (IL-ee-ud) and the **Odyssey** (AHD-uh-see).

The stories told in Homer's epics take place in the 1100's B.C., near the end of the Trojan War. This was a legendary struggle between the Mycenaean Greeks and warriors from the city of Troy in Asia Minor. According to Homer, the war broke out when a Trojan prince named Paris kidnaped Helen, the beautiful wife of the Greek king. After 10 years of fighting, the Greeks won the war by capturing Troy. They built a huge, hollow wooden horse and hid their army inside. The Trojans, thinking the horse was a peace offering, brought it into the city. After nightfall, the Greeks crept out of the Trojan Horse and took the city by storm.

The *Iliad* tells of a tragic quarrel between two heroes of the Trojan War. Today historians believe that many incidents in the *Iliad* are based on a real war that was fought about 1300 B.C. The *Odyssey* relates the adventures of the hero Odysseus (oh-DIS-ee-us) on his way home to Greece after the Trojan War.

The *Iliad* and the *Odyssey* describe the ways of life and the values of the early

Homer wove ancient tales of gods and heroes into epic poetry. No portraits were made of the blind storyteller during his lifetime; this is how a second-century Roman sculptor imagined he might have looked.

Greeks. To Homer, a hero combined courage with intelligence. Homer spoke of the deeds of noble warriors who were not only brave and skillful in battle, but also concerned about their honor and pride. For centuries Greek children grew up reciting Homer's works and learning about the Greek outlook and character through the deeds of legendary figures. Developing the qualities of Homer's heroes became the goal of Greek education.

Sec. Rev. ques. 5

See Sec. 1 *Closing the Lesson*, p. T69B.

Section Review

Answers to Section Review questions are in brackets on pages indicated.

1. **Define or identify:** Hellenic Age, colony, oracle, *Iliad*, *Odyssey*. (pp. 73, 74, 75)
2. What did the Minoans and the Mycenaeans contribute to Hellenic culture? (p. 73)
3. How did Greek civilization spread? (p. 73)
4. What image did the Greeks have of their gods? (p. 74)
5. What ideals did Homer's epics teach? (p. 75)
6. **Critical thinking:** In ancient Greece, young people learned the ideals of their culture from Homer's poetry. What are some of the sources from which young people in the modern world learn ideals and values?

(See answer below.)

75

● **RETEACHING.** Have students review "The Epics of Homer" (above) and identify the topics of the two epics. (*Iliad*: quarrel between two heroes of the Trojan War. *Odyssey*: adventures of Odysseus.) (*Comprehension*) *Observing for Details*

● **REINFORCEMENT.** Have students write an essay on *Themes in Homer's Poetry*. Students should summarize the themes and discuss the relevance of those themes today. (*Synthesis*) *Making Judgments*

● **ENRICHMENT.** Have students work in groups to present a reading from the *Iliad* or the *Odyssey*. Presentations might include a dramatization, posters, or other art illustrating a scene from one of the epics. (*Application*) *Relating Literature and History*

6. Answers will vary. Students might suggest that young people today learn ideals and values from family, community, school, religious instruction, literature, and the media.

2 Greek City-States

Objectives

Focus Questions

★ ■ How did Sparta and Athens differ? *(pages 76–78)*
● ■ How did Greek life change after the Persian Wars? *(pages 78–83)*

Terms to Know

polis	archon
acropolis	tyrant
agora	ostracism
helot	Persian Wars
democracy	direct democracy

★ Note strategies for first objective on this page and p. 78.

As the Hellenic Age began, independent city-states developed in Greece. These grew out of earlier villages that had been built in the rugged mountains and on scattered islands. The two leading city-states, Sparta and Athens, developed in very different ways.

The Polis

During the Hellenic period, wars broke out frequently and the Greeks built forts on hills or mountaintops for protection. A city-state often grew up around such a fort. The Greek word for city-state is **polis** (POH-lis).

The high ground on which the fort stood was called the acropolis (uh-KRAHP-uh-lis), meaning "high city." In case of enemy attack, the people of the city would go there for protection. As the polis grew, the acropolis also became a religious center with temples, altars, and public monuments. The other main part of the polis was the marketplace, or **agora** (AG-uh-ruh). The agora was usually a large square surrounded by shops and government buildings.

76

Sparta

The polis of Sparta (map, page 72) was founded by the Dorians who occupied the Peloponnesus (pel-oh-puh-NEE-sus), the southern peninsula of Greece. In the eighth century B.C., the Spartans conquered nearby regions and forced many of the people to work as farm laborers, or helots (HEL-uts). The helots were virtual slaves who worked for the polis, not for individual owners. They outnumbered the Spartans by as many as ten to one. Because the Spartans always feared that the helots would revolt, they set up a military government to keep order.

The Spartan aim was to produce strong-bodied, fearless men and women. Every aspect of a Spartan's life was planned to meet this aim. Sickly babies were left on the hilltops to die. At the age of seven a Spartan boy moved into a military barracks. There he lived for 23 years, toughening his body, learning discipline, and training for war. Winter and summer he went barefoot and wore only a short tunic (a kind of robe). He learned to be brave and to endure pain in silence. Only when he reached the age of 30 did he leave the barracks and become a full-fledged citizen.

Although Spartan women could not become citizens, they too were trained in gymnastics and physical endurance. It was believed that strong women would give birth to strong sons, Sparta's future soldiers. When one mother sent her son off to battle, she told him to win or to die trying: "Come home *with* your shield or *on* it."

In all of Greece there were no braver warriors than the Spartans. Yet while other Greeks admired the Spartans' courage and obedience to authority, they also criticized the one-sidedness of Spartan life. Northeast of Sparta, in the city-state of Athens, people followed a very different ideal.

TRAINING

Sec. Rev. ques. 2

★ RETEACHING. Have students complete the following sentence and then find three examples in the text to support their statement: *The main difference between Sparta and Athens was . . .* (Answers will vary, but might suggest the Spartan focus on physical and military strength and the Athenian emphasis on political and intellectual development.) *(Comprehension) Supporting a Generalization*

★ REINFORCEMENT. Have students make a chart with two columns labeled *Sparta* and *Athens*. Then have students write each of the following statements in the column whose city-state is described: **(a)** Citizens proud of political freedom. (Athens) **(b)** Set up military governments. (Sparta) **(c)** Valued strong, fearless warriors. (Sparta) **(d)** Valued using mind and developing all talents. (Athens) *(Comprehension) Observing for Detail*

Athens

Athens became the shining center of Greek culture. The Athenians came to look upon themselves as the teachers of all Greece. They were proud of their political freedom and their artists, playwrights, poets, and thinkers. Unlike the Spartans, the Athenians believed that people led empty lives if they failed to use their minds and develop all their talents.

The beginnings of democracy. The Greeks were the first people in history to establish a democracy—a government in which free citizens rule themselves. Athens was not the only polis where this idea took hold. The people of Athens, however, led in the creation of democracy.

It took several centuries for Athens to develop a democratic government. Like the other city-states, Athens was at first ruled by a king. About 800 B.C. the aristocrats—wealthy land-holding nobles—gained more power. They chose a group of officials from within their own ranks to rule the city-state. These officials, known as archons (AHR-kahnz), tended to favor the upper class.

Written laws. Over time the merchants, artisans, and farmers of Athens began to protest against the unfairness of the archons' rule. To prevent an uprising by the poor, in 621 B.C. the aristocrats asked a man named Draco (DRAY-koh) to write down the city's laws. Greek laws were harsh, and Draco's code did not change them. Nevertheless, as in the case of Hammurabi's Code (page 32), the writing of the laws made society more just. Leaders were less free to interpret the laws as they pleased.

Still, discontent in Athens continued. Many poor Athenians were forced to sell themselves and their families into slavery to repay debts. Other Athenians demanded a greater share of political power.

Solon's reforms. Next the aristocrats turned to a statesman and poet named Solon (SOH-lahn), who had a reputation for being wise and fair. About 594 B.C. Solon was given full power to deal with the unrest in Athens. He canceled the debts of the poor and made slavery for debt illegal. He also created a legal system in which all citizens—all free adult men born to Athenian parents—could serve as jurors.

Solon then made political reforms that increased the power of the middle and lower classes. Finally, he began new economic programs to boost foreign trade and make life more secure for the poor. These reforms solved some immediate problems and strengthened Athens's economy. Yet Solon's actions displeased the aristocrats. They felt that the lower classes had been given too much power.

Sec. Rev. ques. 3

Greek battleships such as this one protected merchant vessels in the eastern Mediterranean and guarded trade routes to the Black Sea.

77

Empire of Athens About 450 B.C.

This map shows battles of the Persian Wars. Locate Marathon, Thermopylae, and Salamis. Why was control of the Hellespont important to both the Persians and the Greeks? What sea did Athens dominate when it formed an empire after the Persian Wars?

(See answers above.)

The tyrant Pisistratus. In 546 B.C. a politician named Pisistratus (py-SIS-trah-tus) seized power in Athens. In ancient Greece, a ruler who took power by force was known as a tyrant. Since many tyrants used harsh measures, the word later came to mean "a person who rules harshly."

Many nobles, including the aged Solon, objected to rule by a tyrant. Pisistratus, however, had support among both city dwellers and farmers. He gave more land to the farmers and granted them loans. In the city of Athens, Pisistratus improved the water supply and built a number of splendid temples and fountains.

78

Pisistratus also took an interest in Athenian cultural life. He supported sculptors and painters and sponsored drama festivals. His promotion of the arts helped Athens become the brightest center of Greek culture.

Cleisthenes' democratic reforms. Since the time of Solon, Athens had been moving toward a more democratic government. About 510 B.C. a statesman named Cleisthenes (KLYS-thuh-neez) reformed the political system. Cleisthenes divided Athens into 10 districts. Fifty men from each district served on an advisory council, which proposed laws to the Assembly—the lawmaking body. For the first time, all citizens could vote in the Assembly, whether they owned land or not.

To safeguard the new democratic government, Cleisthenes started a new practice. Once a year citizens were given the opportunity to point out anyone they believed was a threat to Athens. If 6,000 votes were cast against a particular person, he or she was forced to leave Athens for 10 years. Because votes were written on a piece of broken pottery called an *ostrakon*, the practice of expelling people became known as ostracism (AHS-truh-siz-um). Few people actually were ostracized, but the custom gave the citizens more power.

Sec. Rev. ques. 3, cont.

★ See below, left.

The Persian Wars

● Note strategies for second objective on this page and p. 83.

Although democratic Athens and military Sparta had developed in very different ways, the people of the Greek city-states had many things in common. They spoke the same language, believed in the same gods, read and recited the epics of Homer, and competed in the same athletic contests. The Greek people considered themselves superior to all non-Greeks. In fact, they referred to non-Greeks as "barbarians."

Threat from the Persians. Despite these bonds, the Greeks had never been politically united. They were intensely loyal to their own city-states, and war between one polis and another was common. Only the threat of conquest by the Persian Empire

★ ENRICHMENT. Have students work in groups to dramatize a meeting that might have occurred between Spartan and Athenian government officials. Presentations should include a discussion of government, military service, and social responsibilities. (Synthesis) Translating Information into Another Form

● RETEACHING. Have students explain the significance of: (a) Persian Wars (United the Greeks; led to "golden age.") (b) Delian League (Led to Athenian empire.) (e) Age of Pericles (Height of Greek culture and democracy.) (Comprehension) Observing for Detail

● REINFORCEMENT. Have students write an essay summarizing the development of democracy in ancient Greece and evaluating Greek influence on modern democratic systems. (Evaluation) Linking Past and Present made the Greeks set aside their differences. From 490 to 479 B.C., the city-states joined together to fight a long string of battles known as the **Persian Wars**.

Early in the struggle, the Persians succeeded in taking over Greek settlements in Asia Minor. The Greek colonists lived under Persian rule for nearly 50 years. Then, in 499 B.C., some colonists rebelled against the Persian king, Darius (duh-RY-us). Athens sent ships to help the Greek rebels, but eventually they were defeated. To punish Athens for its part in the revolt, Darius invaded Greece.

The Battle of Marathon. In 490 B.C. the Persians landed at Marathon, about 25 miles from Athens. There a small Athenian army easily defeated the invaders. Wanting the news of the victory to reach Athens as quickly as possible, the Greeks sent a messenger. Their swiftest runner, Phidippides (fy-

This vase painting of two Greek warriors shows weapons and armor similar to those used by the Greeks in the Persian Wars.

DIP-ih-deez), had just returned from a trip to Sparta, 150 miles away. According to legend, he set off immediately for Athens. Reaching the city, Phidippides cried out the message "Rejoice, we are victorious!" and then collapsed and died. The modern marathon, a race of about 26 miles, is named in memory of Phidippides' run from Marathon.

The Battle of Thermopylae. The Persians would not accept defeat. Ten years after the battle at Marathon, Darius's son Xerxes (ZURK-seez) set out with a large army to conquer all of Greece. The invading Persians crossed the waters of the Hellespont (a narrow channel, now called the Dardanelles, between the Sea of Marmara and the Aegean Sea). The Persians then made their way through mountainous northern Greece. At the narrow mountain pass of Thermopylae (thur-MAHP-uh-lee), they clashed with the Greek army.

Led by the king of Sparta, 300 Spartans and about 700 other Greeks refused to retreat. The small Greek force held off the much larger Persian army for three days. Then a traitor showed the Persians a path around the pass. The Greek historian Herodotus described how bravely the Greeks met their death:

> 66 Here they resisted to the last, with their swords if they had them, and if not, with their hands and teeth, until the Persians, coming on from the front over the ruins of the wall and closing in from behind, finally overwhelmed them. 99

The end of the wars. After Thermopylae fell in 480 B.C., the Persians had an open route to Athens. The terrified Athenians fled to the nearby island of Salamis (SAL-ah-mis) and watched as the Persians burned the city. The Athenians had no intention of giving up, however. At the Battle of Salamis, they outwitted the Persians and scored a key victory (see feature, next page). The next year (479 B.C.), the Spartans defeated the Persians at Plataea (pluh-TEE-uh) and forced the invaders out of Greece.

Sec. Rev. ques. 4

79

ⒻSee
below.

The Geography Connection

The Greek Victory at Salamis

Throughout history, people have used the local geography as an aid in defending against invaders. In the fifth century B.C., for example, the Greeks used their knowledge of the physical characteristics of their own land to plan a strategy against the invading Persians.

In 480 B.C. the Persian army under Xerxes marched through Greece toward Athens. The Athenians abandoned their city to the Persians and fled with their allies to the nearby island of Salamis. There the Greek commander, Themistocles (thuh-MIS-tuh-kleez), made a plan. The Greeks would lure the Persian fleet into the narrow strait between Salamis and the mainland.

Themistocles organized a defending navy of about 400 vessels. Against this force, Xerxes sent his fleet of 800 huge warships. Xerxes himself sat on a throne by the edge of the water to watch the battle.

The Persians boldly entered the narrow strait, believing the Greeks would not dare to stand and fight. They were wrong. The Greeks struck in waves, ramming enemy hulls and shearing off enemy oars. In the narrow waters, the large Persian vessels had great difficulty maneuvering. Many of the warships crashed into each other as they tried to defend themselves.

The smaller Greek ships attacked relentlessly, and soon the wreckage of Persian ships filled the strait. Xerxes watched in horror as his hopes for conquest sank to the bottom of the sea.

Making the connection. Why did the Greeks want to meet the Persian ships in a narrow strait and not in the open sea?

The Delian League

Even after the defeat of Persia, the Greeks did not feel safe. The Persian Empire was still a mighty power. Furthermore, old rivalries among the city-states broke out again. To protect themselves, both Sparta and Athens made alliances with other city-states.

In 478 B.C. the Athenians formed an alliance with more than 150 other city-states of Asia Minor and the Aegean islands. This alliance was called the Delian (DEE-lee-un) League, since it met on the island of Delos. Each city-state contributed ships, soldiers, and money.

Athens, because it had the strongest fleet and the most wealth, soon came to dominate the League. When some city-states tried to leave the alliance, Athens forced them to remain. The Delian League had turned into **80** an Athenian empire.

The Golden Age of Athenian Democracy

The Persian Wars were a crucial period in history. The defeat of the Persians kept them from expanding their empire into Europe. It therefore gave the Greeks the freedom to develop political and artistic ideas that still influence Western civilization. The birthplace of these developments was Athens. There Greek democracy and culture reached their height in a "golden age" during the 50 years after Persia's defeat.

The Age of Pericles. Under the leadership of Pericles (PEHR-uh-kleez), between about 460 and 429 B.C., Athens became the political and cultural center of the eastern Mediterranean. Pericles had the city rebuilt and strengthened. His leadership of Athens was so remarkable that the period is often called the Age of Pericles.

Ⓕ **GEOGRAPHY CONNECTION. Have students describe the factors that helped the Greeks win the Battle of Salamis.** (The following factors gave the Greek navy an advantage over the Persian fleet: the Persian expectation of an easy victory; the narrow waters of the battle site; the maneuverability of the Greek ships; and tactical problems caused by the size of the Persian ships.) *(Comprehension)* **Observing for Detail**

Background Sparta was not a member of the Delian League. In 454 B.C. the treasury of the League was transferred from Delos to Athens; from then on, other city-states were actually paying tribute to Athens.

Battle of Salamis

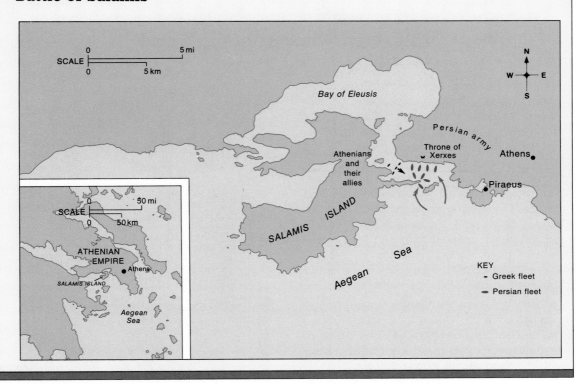

Democratic reforms. Pericles expanded Athenian democracy. He opened government jobs to all classes and paid salaries to government officials. Even poor citizens could thus seek such positions. The government of Athens, said Pericles, "is in the hands of the many and not of the few."

Athenian democracy was, however, limited by strict citizenship requirements. Citizenship was considered a great privilege. As in earlier times, it was restricted to free men whose parents had both been Athenians. Only about 10 percent of the population—between 30,000 and 45,000 people—fell into this category. Their numbers were small enough to set up a **direct democracy**—a form of government in which all citizens can participate first-hand. Thus the Athenians did not elect representatives as most modern democracies do. About 40 times a year all citizens met in the Assembly. There they debated, voted, and made the laws.

Athens had no professional government officials or judges, and no professional soldiers. The duties of government were performed by ordinary people. They took care of the public buildings, kept the waterfront safe for ships, and watched over the city's food supply. They served in the army and rowed ships in the navy. The Athenians believed every citizen should take part in government. A man who would not vote, hold government office, or serve on juries was thought of as useless. Rather than being elected, officials were chosen by lot—a process similar to picking names out of a hat. They held office for one year and could not hold the same position again.

The most active politicians and military leaders came from noble families. These men were educated, had free time, and felt a responsibility to serve their city. In time, wealthy merchants also took an important role in government.

Citizenship. Ask: How does a democratic system give its citizens more power than other forms of government? (Democracy allows citizens to share in political power by making decisions that are implemented by the government.)

Sec. Rev. ques. 5

81

Ⓕ See
below.

Historic Places

The Seven Wonders of the World

Travel was slow and difficult in ancient times. Nevertheless, the Greeks were enthusiastic travelers. Like tourists today, they wanted to see the most famous sights of their times. About 200 B.C., a Greek writer listed "seven wonders of the world"—the seven most impressive works human beings had built. (The writer knew little or nothing about India and China, so his "world" included only places near the Mediterranean Sea.)

Just two of the wonders had existed before the rise of Greek civilization:

- The **Egyptian Pyramids** were already more than 2,000 years old in 200 B.C.
- The **Hanging Gardens of Babylon** were lush terraces of greenery built by King Nebuchadnezzar about 600 B.C.

The other wonders on the list were all works of Greek artists and builders:

- The **Mausoleum at Halicarnassus** was a massive tomb designed for a Persian ruler by Greek architects.
- The **Temple of Artemis at Ephesus** was renowned for its size and beauty. Artemis was goddess of the hunt.
- The **Colossus of Rhodes** was a bronze statue that towered 120 feet over the harbor of the island of Rhodes.
- The **Lighthouse at Alexandria,** as tall as a 30-story building, stood for 1,500 years until an earthquake shattered its foundation in the fourteenth century.

- The **Statue of Zeus at Olympia,** made of gleaming gold and ivory, stood over three stories high. (See statue above.)

Only one of these wonders survives for modern travelers to marvel at—the pyramids, oldest of all.

The Athenians appreciated freedom of speech and thought. Citizens could criticize political leaders without being punished. In the Assembly every citizen was free to say what he thought. The poorest shoemaker had as much right to speak and vote as the richest landowner.

82

Education. The Athenians considered education necessary for good citizenship. Boys were sent to private schools or taught at home by tutors, most of whom were educated slaves. They learned reading, arithmetic, music, and the works of Homer and other great poets. Young men studied public

Ⓕ **FEATURE ACTIVITY. Have students work in groups to develop a list of Modern Wonders of the World.** After the class agrees on a time frame for consideration, have each group name and explain its choices for **Seven Modern Wonders.** *(Synthesis) Making Decisions*

Citizenship. Ask: How does freedom of speech strengthen democratic institutions? (Free exchange of ideas increases knowledge and understanding and allows for consideration of alternative solutions to problems.)

speaking, geometry, astronomy, and poetry. They were encouraged to discuss art, politics, and questions of right and wrong. Athletics were also part of a young man's education.

At the age of 18, young Athenian men began two years of military training and service. They then could become citizens and take part in government.

The status of women. In ancient Athens, as in most early civilizations, women were considered inferior to men. They were denied citizenship and could not take part in public affairs. Moreover, they could not own property and they received no formal education. Their lives revolved entirely around the running of their households and the raising of their children.

According to the Athenian ideal, a woman was to live a quiet life, seeing no men but her relatives. This was possible, however, only for women who did not have to work. Poor women led freer lives than wealthy ones. They worked in the fields along with men or sold goods in the agora, where they had contact with all classes of people.

Girls received whatever education their parents thought proper for them at home. Although some learned to read and write, most were taught only the skills they would need to run a household. Between the ages of 14 and 16, girls were married to men chosen by their parents.

Slaves. Slaves made up about one quarter of Athens's population. Some were Greeks who had been captured in wars with other city-states. Most were foreign prisoners of war. Slaves who worked in the mines led short, harsh lives. Most Athenian slaves, however, were household servants. Others served as teachers or as skilled workers. These slaves led fairly comfortable lives and were allowed, by law, to buy their freedom. Even if they gained freedom, however, they could not become citizens of Athens.

Daily life. Most Athenians earned their living by farming. They lived inside the city but went outside its walls each day to work in the fields. They were helped by family members, hired labor, and slaves. Most farmers needed all they produced to feed their families. Any surplus was exchanged for goods, such as pottery and tools, that could not be made at home.

The Athenians' public buildings were very grand, but their houses were plain. Made from mud bricks, each house was built around a central courtyard. The two central living areas were the dining room, in which the men alone ate, and the women's room, which was set up primarily for weaving wool into cloth. Other rooms included bedrooms, a bathroom, and a kitchen.

Because of the mild climate, Athenians spent most of their time outside. The courtyard of the average house contained a well, an altar for worship, a washbasin, and whatever domestic animals the family kept.

Even the wealthiest Athenians lived modestly by modern standards. Their houses were simple, their diets plain, and their possessions few. Yet out of this way of life came some of the most brilliant artists, writers, and thinkers who have ever lived. What Pericles said of Athens 2,400 years ago remains true: "Future ages will wonder at us as the present age wonders now."

● See below.

See Sec. 2 *Closing the Lesson,* p. T69B.

Section Review

Answers to Section Review questions are in brackets on pages indicated.

1. **Define or identify:** polis, acropolis, agora, helot, democracy, archon, tyrant, ostracism, Persian Wars, direct democracy. (p. 76, 77, 78, 79, 81)
2. **What was the aim of education in Sparta?** (p. 76)
3. **How did Solon and Cleisthenes contribute to the growth of democracy?** (p. 77–78)
4. **How did the Greeks finally defeat the Persians?** (p. 79)
5. **What part were the citizens of Athens expected to play in government?** (p. 81)
6. **Critical thinking:** According to Pericles, government in Athens was "in the hands of the many and not of the few." How true was this statement? Explain your answer. (See answer below.)

83

3 The Flowering of Greek Culture

Objectives

Focus Questions

★ ■ How did the literature and art of Greece reflect Greek values? *(pages 84–86)*

● ■ What did the Greeks achieve in science and philosophy? *(pages 86–88)*

Terms to Know

classical   Sophist
Parthenon   Socratic method
natural laws

★ Note strategies for first objective on this page and p. 86.

The ideas of democratic government that developed in Athens are one important part of our heritage from ancient Greece. Western traditions in art, architecture, and literature also began with the brilliant achievements made during the golden age of Greece.

The Value of Moderation

The Greeks held themselves to high standards. They believed that every person should live a well-rounded life. At the same time, they believed that anything worth doing was worth doing well. While they aimed for excellence in all their pursuits, they also believed in a balance between extremes—a life of moderation. In the Greek view, moderate people did not eat, drink, work, play, or even sleep too much. More important, they did not devote their lives entirely to the pursuit of one thing, such as pleasure or wealth. They used reason to protect themselves from excesses of any kind.

Greek society in the 400's and 300's B.C. is considered to be the first example of a classical civilization. The word *classical* describes a style of art and thought that emphasizes order and simplicity.

Sec. Rev. ques. 2

84

Art and Architecture

Like Greek literature, Greek art and architecture provided models that are still followed today. Greek painters and sculptors showed human beings as beautiful and unflawed, rarely expressing extremes of emotion. The human figures in Greek art stood or sat in calm and dignified poses.

Greek architects also strove for harmony and balance. They applied mathematical laws of proportion to their temples and theaters and tried to make buildings fit in with the natural surroundings. One remarkable example of this harmony is the group of temples on the Acropolis of Athens. They were part of Pericles' rebuilding program (page 80).

The largest in the group is the **Parthenon**, the temple of Athena. Begun in 447 B.C., the temple took 15 years to finish. Built of white marble, it is simple but perfectly proportioned. The Parthenon may be the greatest remaining example of the classic simplicity of Greek architecture. The influence of this magnificent temple can be seen in public buildings throughout the Western world.

Literature

History. One important form of Greek literature was written history. Greek historians were the first to examine the past with a critical eye. They investigated events, checked facts, and tried to understand people's actions and motives.

Herodotus, traditionally called the "father of history," was born about 484 B.C. His

★ RETEACHING. Have students write a one-sentence summary of Greek contributions in each of the following areas: *poetry; drama; history; art and architecture. (Comprehension) Summarizing Information*

Critical Thinking. Ask: How did Greek art and architecture reflect Hellenic social values? (Art depicted unflawed, beautiful humans and rarely expressed emotional extremes; architects strove for harmony and balance.)

★ REINFORCEMENT. Ask: (a) What ideals characterized the Greek classical civilization? (Well-rounded life; moderation; order, simplicity; courage; honor.) (b) How did Greek literature reflect these ideals? (Greek poetry described people striving to live up to high standards; Greek drama explored human choices.) (c) How did Greek historians influence written history? (First to investigate, check facts, and try to understand human motives and actions.) *(Comprehension) Observing for Detail*

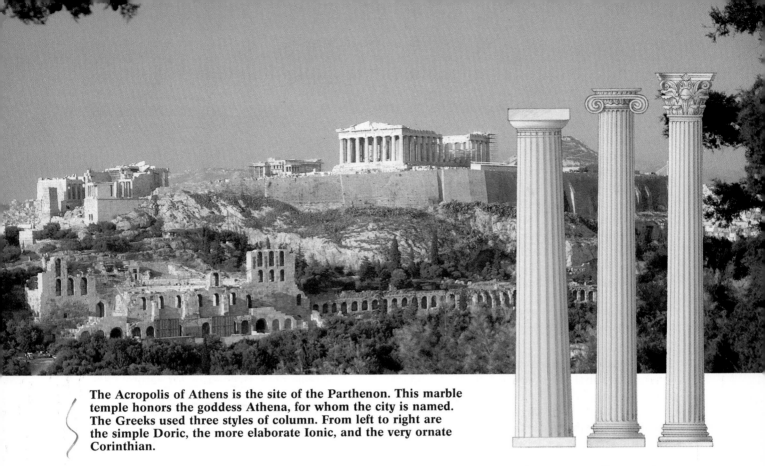

The Acropolis of Athens is the site of the Parthenon. This marble temple honors the goddess Athena, for whom the city is named. The Greeks used three styles of column. From left to right are the simple Doric, the more elaborate Ionic, and the very ornate Corinthian.

vivid account of the Persian Wars set a new standard for reporting (page 78). Herodotus often included ancient stories and legends in his accounts, but he also made his own investigations of recent events.

Thucydides (thoo-SID-uh-deez), another historian, is famous for his account of the Peloponnesian War (page 89). Thucydides' history, unlike Herodotus's, contained no myths, legends, or supernatural explanations for events. Thucydides believed that the historian must search for factual truth and human motives. The skill with which he analyzed politics and events made his work a model for later historians.

Poetry. Poetry played an important part in expressing the Greek view of life. Homer's epics were a basic part of a Greek's upbringing (page 75). These poems described people striving to live up to high standards of courage and honor.

The Greeks also wrote poems to honor the winners of athletic games and heroes killed in battle. One of the most famous writers of such poems was Pindar, who lived in the 400's B.C. Another outstanding early Greek poet was Sappho (SAF-oh), who was born about 600 B.C. Many of her poems celebrated friendship and love.

Drama. Poetry recitals were an important part of Greek religious festivals. Dancers and singers participated, and poems were chanted by a group of performers called the chorus. These performances gradually developed into plays. In the 500's B.C., an actor named Thespis began to speak lines as an individual. Soon a second and then a third actor took major roles and spoke back and forth with the chorus. In time this new kind of performance, called drama, became the central feature of important festivals.

The early Greek dramas were tragedies based on old stories of gods and heroes. Playwrights used these stories to explore human problems. Greek dramatists believed that people had freedom to make decisions that might bring them greatness. If they chose unwisely, or were too proud of their success, however, they would bring disaster upon themselves and others.

Sec. Rev. ques. 3

Sec. Rev. ques. 3, cont.

85

Biography Herodotus did not judge other peoples against Greek standards. An objective observer, he believed that all cultures were parts of a whole.

Check for Understanding. Ask: How did Herodotus and Thucydides differ in their historical explanations? (Herodotus made use of myths, legends, and supernatural explanations; Thucydides did not.)

Cultural History Note that comedy festivals were held in January and February, and tragedy festivals were held in March and April. During drama festivals in Athens, all business was suspended, law courts were closed, and prisoners were released. Women, prohibited from attending most public events, were welcome at the theater.

NOT COMEDIES

This theme was used by the three greatest writers of Greek tragedy: Aeschylus (ES-kih-lus), Sophocles (SOF-uh-kleez), and Euripides (yoo-RIP-ih-deez). All lived in Athens during the golden age. Some of the best-known works of these writers—particularly Sophocles' *Antigone* and *Oedipus Rex*—are still read and performed today.

Greek playwrights could also be lighthearted and witty. Greek comedies were mostly about politics and current events. Aristophanes (ayr-is-TAHF-uh-neez) made fun of Athenian politicians, generals, philosophers, and other playwrights.

★ See below.

Science and Philosophy

● Note strategies for second objective on this page and p. 88.

The Mesopotamians and Egyptians had taken the first steps toward the creation of science (pages 33, 42). They were not true scientific thinkers, however, because they saw gods and demons as the causes of natural events. The Greeks began to search for different ways to explain the natural world.

Sec. Rev. ques. 4

Our word *philosophy*, meaning "the study of basic truths," comes from the Greek words for "love of wisdom." Ancient Greek philosophers sought two kinds of knowledge: knowledge about the natural world and knowledge about human beings' place in that world. The Greeks believed that nature follows general rules called **natural laws**, which could be discovered by using reason.

Thales. Probably the earliest scientist and philosopher was Thales (THAY-leez), who came from one of the Greek city-states in Asia Minor. Thales observed that all living things required water. He concluded, therefore, that water was the basic element of nature. Thales also looked for a natural cause for earthquakes. Myths had said that the god Poseidon shook the earth when he was angry. Thales suggested instead that the earth floated on water and was sometimes rocked by great waves. Although many of Thales' ideas were wrong, other thinkers followed his way of reasoning. By looking for natural laws and causes, they laid the foundations for modern science.

Pythagoras. Pythagoras (pih-THAG-ur-us), who lived in the 500's B.C., believed that the universe was arranged according to mathematical laws. He studied music, astronomy, and mathematics to find these laws or principles. Students today still learn Pythagoras's theorem about the relationship between the sides of a right triangle.

Democritus. In the late fifth century B.C., Democritus (dih-MOK-ruh-tus) taught that nature was made up of tiny atoms, particles that could not be divided. Although modern science has found even smaller particles, Democritus's idea was the first atomic theory.

Hippocrates. The physician Hippocrates (hih-PAHK-ruh-teez) taught other doctors to find the causes of disease by using reason, rather than blaming illness on the anger of the gods. The doctors trained by Hippocrates took notes on the appearance and behavior of their patients and carefully recorded the medicines and methods they used in treating sick people. In this way, Greek doctors began to separate medicine from magic. Many doctors today swear to uphold the high standards set by Hippocrates when they take the Hippocratic Oath.

Greek drama was a religious performance whose theme was the relationship between gods and humans. Theaters like this one, carved into a hillside in Athens, were designed to amplify the actors' words.

86

★ ENRICHMENT. Have students read selections by Homer, Aeschylus, Sophocles, or Euripides and write an essay explaining how the poem or drama reflects Greek values. *(Synthesis) Relating History and Literature*
Biography Pythagoras believed that a universal life-spirit was present in all living things. He taught that the human soul was immortal and destined to undergo a cycle of rebirth until it achieved freedom through the purity of its life, a belief similar to one held by followers of Hinduism (p. 57).

● RETEACHING. Have students write one paragraph explaining how the Greek concept of natural law laid the foundations of modern science. (The Greeks believed that nature followed natural laws. Using reason, human beings could discover and study these laws.) *(Comprehension) Synthesizing Information*
● REINFORCEMENT. Have students review pp. 86–88 and outline the contributions of Greek scientists and philosophers. *(Comprehension) Organizing Ideas in Written Form*

Timetable

Important Greeks of Ancient Times

Poets and Dramatists
Homer (700's B.C.)   Epics (*Iliad; Odyssey*).
Sophocles (496–406 B.C.)   Tragedies (*Oedipus Rex; Antigone*).

Leaders
Solon (638–559 B.C.)   Political reforms.
Pericles (495–429 B.C.)   Expansion of democracy.
Alexander (356–323 B.C.)   Spread of Greek culture.

Historians
Herodotus (484–425 B.C.)   "Father of history."
Thucydides (471–400 B.C.)   Search for factual truth and human motives.

Scientists
Pythagoras (580–497 B.C.)   Geometry theorem.
Hippocrates (460–377 B.C.)   Training of physicians.

Philosophers
Socrates (470–399 B.C.)   Socratic method.
Plato (427–347 B.C.)   Dialogues (*The Republic*).
Aristotle (384–322 B.C.)   Science of biology; *Politics*.

The Sophists. In the decades after the Persian Wars, teachers known as **Sophists** (SAHF-ists) traveled from city to city teaching speech, grammar, poetry, gymnastics, mathematics, and music. The Sophists claimed they could teach people how to make good laws, speak well, and win debates in the Assembly. Their teaching attracted many politically ambitious young men.

In Athens, the Sophists angered many citizens by arguing that the gods did not exist. Clever leaders, the Sophists said, used fear of the gods to force people to follow customs and obey laws. Sophists also argued that Athenian laws were not based on principles of justice but represented only the wishes of the most powerful group in the city. Some Sophists attacked traditional ideals of moderation and self-discipline. Many Athenians decided that the Sophists were a bad influence on young people.

Socrates. Another criticism of the Sophists was made by Socrates (SAHK-ruh-teez), one of the most extraordinary thinkers in history. Socrates said that the Sophists failed to help young people consider the question that really mattered—not "How can I succeed in politics?" but "How should I live my life?" Socrates devoted his life to gaining self-knowledge. He encouraged his fellow Athenians to do the same, telling them, "Know thyself."

To help people think about how they lived their lives, Socrates drew them into conversation. By asking a series of questions, he would lead them to see that they held many opinions that contradicted each other. This question-and-answer approach, known as the **Socratic method**, helped people recognize that they did not know the answers to many questions. Socrates taught them that the first step toward wisdom is to become aware of "what one thinks one knows but does not."

Many leading Athenians disapproved of Socrates. His questioning, like that of the Sophists, appeared to challenge the authority of the gods, of parents, and of the city's laws. **87**

Biography Note that Hippocrates, called the "father of medicine," wrote a collection of 70 works that are the oldest surviving medical books.
Linking Past and Present The Hippocratic Oath, named for Hippocrates, established high standards of conduct for the medical profession. Among its requirements are that physicians pass on their art to others and treat patients with respect.

Check for Understanding. Ask: Which Athenian traditions did the Sophists challenge? (Existence of the gods; laws based on just principles; moderation; and self-discipline.)
Biography Note that Socrates claimed that "the unexamined life is not worth living."
Critical Thinking. Ask: What might Socrates have meant when he said that the first step toward wisdom is to become aware of "what one thinks one knows but does not"?

"The Death of Socrates," painted in France in 1787, depicts the Greek philosopher as noble and upright in the face of death.

In 399 B.C. Socrates was officially accused of not believing in the gods and corrupting the young. Although he could have avoided prosecution by going into exile, he chose to stand trial. In court, he refused to pretend to be sorry for what he had done or to beg for the jurors' mercy (a common practice in ancient Athens). When given a death sentence, Socrates calmly drank poison and talked with his friends until it took effect.

Plato. Socrates never wrote down his ideas. His teachings were recorded by his most famous student, Plato (427–347 B.C.). All of Plato's writings are dialogues—conversations between two or more characters. In almost all of the dialogues, one of the characters is Socrates. The dialogues deal with a wide range of questions: What is the best form of government? What is the best way of life? What is love? Why should people behave morally?

Sec. Rev. ques. 5

Plato's most famous work, *The Republic,* is a discussion of the ideal polis—the form of government that would bring all its people the greatest happiness. Pointing out that ruling groups tend to put their own needs first, Plato suggested a new kind of ruler. "There will be no end to the troubles of the states," he said, "or indeed, . . . of humanity itself, till philosophers become kings in this world."

Unlike other rulers, Plato argued, the philosopher-kings would be both wise and unselfish. They would be chosen at an early age and spend years getting the education and experience that would enable them to

88

rule well. When they came to power, they would do only what was best for society as a whole. The rest of the people would have no say in the government of the city. They would not object, however, because they would understand that the philosopher-kings acted for the good of all.

● See below.

Aristotle. Plato's most brilliant student was Aristotle (ar-ih-STAHT-uhl), who lived from 384 to 322 B.C. The son of a doctor, Aristotle studied plants, animals, astronomy, and physics, keeping careful records of his observations. In science, Aristotle taught that a theory should be accepted only if it agreed with the facts that could be observed. Many later scientists followed his methods, and he is considered the founder of the science of biology.

Aristotle tried to discover and organize the basic ideas in many fields of knowledge. In his *Poetics,* he examined what made plays good or bad. His *Rhetoric* (RET-ur-ik) outlined the ways in which a speaker should organize a speech. Aristotle also wrote about logic, ethics, and government.

Sec. Rev. ques. 5, cont.

In his book *Politics,* Aristotle discussed how different forms of government worked and what benefits and responsibilities citizens had under these governments. He emphasized the importance of able leaders and respect for the law. "Political society," he wrote, "exists for the sake of noble actions."

With Aristotle, Greek philosophy reached its height. He influenced not only his own students but also philosophers and scientists for centuries to come.

Background Note that Aristotle established his own school, the Lyceum, which emphasized the study of nature.

● **ENRICHMENT.** Have students write a paper evaluating Plato's concept of the philosopher-king. Students might point out the possible advantages and disadvantages of a government with a philosopher-king, discuss the likelihood of its being a fair government, and then state an opinion about Plato's idea. *(Evaluation) Making Judgments*

Section Review

Answers to Section Review questions are in brackets on pages indicated.

1. **Define or identify:** classical, Parthenon, natural laws, Sophist, Socratic method. (p. 84, 86, 87)
2. Describe the Greek belief in a life of moderation. (p. 84)
3. How did Greek poetry and drama express the Greek view of life during the golden age of Greece? (p. 85)
4. How did the Greeks differ from the

Egyptians and the Mesopotamians in the ways in which they explained natural events? (p. 86)
5. What contributions to human knowledge did Plato and Aristotle make? (p. 88)
6. **Critical thinking:** After being accused of crimes, Socrates refused to take actions that could have saved his life. What reasons might he have had?

(See answer below.)

6. Answers will vary. Students might suggest that Socrates would have had to abandon his principles to save his life. He may have preferred death to exile.

See lesson plans, pp. T69A–T69C.

4 The Legacy of Greece

Objectives

Focus Questions

★ ■ What was the significance of the Peloponnesian War? *(pages 89–90)*
● ■ How did Alexander's conquest of Greece cause Greek culture to spread? *(pages 90–92)*

Terms to Know

Peloponnesian War
Hellenistic Age
Epicureanism
Stoicism
stoa

★ Note strategies for first objective on this page and p. 90.

The 50 years of peace that followed the defeat of the Persians allowed Greek civilization to flourish. However, without a common enemy (such as the Persians), the Greeks did not stay united. A war between the city-states so weakened them that they fell victim to a conqueror from the north.

The Peloponnesian War

Sparta feared Athens's power and its domination of the Delian League (page 80). To protect itself against the might of Athens and its allies, Sparta found its own allies. It joined with other city-states on the Peloponnesus (page 76) to form the Peloponnesian League.

In 431 B.C. Sparta invaded the countryside near Athens. This was the beginning of what was called the **Peloponnesian War**. Knowing the Spartans were better fighters on land, Pericles brought the Athenians inside the walls of the city. He then sent the Athenian navy to attack Sparta by sea. Disaster struck Athens as disease swept through the crowded city, claiming thousands of lives. One of the victims was Pericles himself, who died in 429 B.C.

The men who led Athens after Pericles' death made a number of unwise decisions. The most famous of these leaders was Alcibiades (al-sih-BY-uh-deez). Shortly after Alcibiades took command of the Athenian army, his enemies accused him of acting against the religion of the city. To avoid trial, he fled to Sparta, where he worked against his own people.

89

★ RETEACHING. Have students identify three causes of the Peloponnesian War. (Sparta feared Athens' power and its domination of the Delian League; Sparta and its allies formed the Peloponnesian League; Sparta invaded Athenian territory in 431 B.C.) *(Comprehension)* **Identifying Causes**

★ REINFORCEMENT. Have students evaluate the factors which led to the defeat of Athens by Sparta. Evaluations should identify the factors and discuss their effects. (Disease claimed thousands of lives in Athens; Pericles died; conflict developed among the leaders who followed Pericles; Alcibiades betrayed Athens and helped Sparta; after his return, Alcibiades was unable to defeat Sparta.) *(Analysis)* **Making Judgments**

Pericles' Funeral Oration

During the golden age, Athens benefited from the leadership of Pericles (495–429 B.C.), a statesman who held the democratic ideal in the highest regard. After war broke out with Sparta and the Peloponnesian League, Pericles gave a formal speech honoring the Athenian soldiers who had died in the fighting. Part of what he said about the government of Athens is adapted below.

66 Our form of government is called a democracy because power is in the hands not of a minority but of the whole people. When it is a question of settling private disputes, everyone is equal before the law. When it is a question of putting one person before another in positions of public responsibility, what counts is not membership in a particular class, but the actual ability which the man possesses.

Here each individual is interested not only in his own affairs but in the affairs of the state as well. We do not say that a man who takes no interest in politics is a man who minds his own business; we say that he has no business here at all. 99

1. What, in Pericles' opinion, made Athens a democracy?
2. Which counted more in Athens—nobility or ability?
3. What did Pericles say about the responsibilities of citizens?
4. **Critical thinking:** Later in the oration, Pericles praised the men who had fallen in battle. Why, do you think, did Pericles first talk about the importance of the government?

Ⓕ See answers below.

90

Athens forgave Alcibiades when he promised to help defeat the Spartans. Once again, he was placed in charge of all military operations. Although he managed to win some stunning victories for Athens, Alcibiades could not change the tide of the war. Sparta won more battles and finally forced Athens to surrender in 404 B.C. That same year, the Spartans took their revenge on Alcibiades by having him murdered.

The 27-year Peloponnesian War was a great tragedy for all of Greece. It caused widespread death and destruction. In many city-states fighting broke out between those who wanted democratic government and those who wanted aristocrats to rule. Democracy declined even in Athens, where a small group of nobles ran the city.

Sec. Rev. ques. 2

★ See below, left

The Rise of Macedonia

● Note strategies for second objective on this page and p. 91.
Greeks who worried about foreign invasion thought the danger was still the Persian Empire. A new kingdom, however, was arising in Macedonia (mas-ih-DOH-nee-uh), in the northern part of the Greek peninsula.

Philip. In 359 B.C. a young ruler named Philip became king of Macedonia. Philip built a strong army and won the support of some city-states that opposed Athens. A great Athenian statesman and public speaker, Demosthenes (dih-MAHS-thuh-neez), warned of this new threat, but the quarrelsome city-states could not unite soon enough to stop the invaders. In 338 B.C., at Chaeronea (kehr-uh-NEE-uh), Philip's forces crushed the Greek alliance. The Greeks lost what they loved most—their independence.

Alexander the Great. Philip was assassinated in 336 B.C., and his 20-year-old son Alexander became ruler. He is known to history as Alexander the Great. From his father Alexander had learned military skill, leadership ability, and a deep desire to conquer the Persian Empire. Alexander had also studied under Aristotle (page 88), developing scientific curiosity and a love for Greek culture. He knew Homer's epics well, and he

Ⓕ **Primary Source Answers** 1. Power was in the hands of all people rather than a minority. 2. Ability. 3. Citizens have a responsibility to take an interest in government. 4. Answers will vary. Students may suggest that in Athens government was more important than the individual.

★ **ENRICHMENT.** Have students work in groups to research and develop a time chart of significant events leading to the rise and fall of Classical Greece. *(Application)* **Sequencing Historical Information**

● **RETEACHING.** Have students review "The Rise of Macedonia" (pp. 90–91) and make a timeline of the events that led to Alexander's control of the ancient Middle East. *(Comprehension)* **Understanding Chronology**

● **REINFORCEMENT.** Have students review "The Hellenistic Age" (pp. 91–92) and outline the characteristics of the Hellenistic period. *(Comprehension)* **Organizing and Expressing Information in Written Form**

Alexander's Empire by 323 B.C.

Into what three continents did Alexander's Empire extend? Use the scale to estimate the distance of the empire from its eastern limit to its farthest western point.

Map Answers: (1) Europe, Asia, and Africa. (2) About 3,060 miles.

SEE OTHER READING

dreamed of matching the deeds of the heroes of the *Iliad* and *Odyssey*.

Daring and intelligent, Alexander became one of the greatest military leaders in history. In 334 B.C. he crossed the Hellespont and took over the Greek colonies held by the Persians in Asia Minor. Phoenicia was next to fall, and then Egypt. In 331 B.C. Mesopotamia came under Alexander's rule. After defeating the king of Persia in battle, Alexander sped on to northwestern India. Between 334 and 326 B.C. Alexander's armies conquered the lands from Egypt to India without losing a battle.

In Babylon in 323 B.C. Alexander died of a fever. He was not quite 33 years old. His death ended the brief period of unity that had brought together Greece and the ancient Middle East. None of Alexander's generals was able to control the vast empire, and it broke into three separate kingdoms.

The Hellenistic Age

Sec. Rev. ques. 3

Although Alexander's empire split apart, his conquests had a lasting effect. He had en- couraged Greek soldiers, merchants, and government officials to settle in the conquered lands. The increased contacts between the Greeks and the peoples of the ancient Middle East helped to spread Greek culture. The Greek language became widely used in the cities of the Mediterranean world. Upper-class people throughout the ancient Middle East learned about Greek literature, ideas, and customs.

The spread of Greek culture through the lands Alexander had conquered marked the opening of a new stage of civilization. In this new age, called the **Hellenistic Age**, the distinction between Greek and non-Greek lessened. For over 200 years, Hellenistic culture dominated the entire Mediterranean world.

The city of Alexandria in Egypt (map, page 91) was founded by Alexander in 332 B.C. After his death, Egypt came under the rule of one of his generals, Ptolemy (TAHL-uh-mee). By 304 B.C. Ptolemy had established a new dynasty, centered in Alexandria, whose rulers encouraged scholarship. They set up the greatest library and research center

● See below.

91

● ENRICHMENT. Have students find information on the effects of Greek art on Egyptian art and architecture during the Hellenistic Age. Students' reports might include pictures or slides showing Egyptian art before and after the Hellenistic period and identify the differences. Have students present reports in class. *(Application) Locating Information*

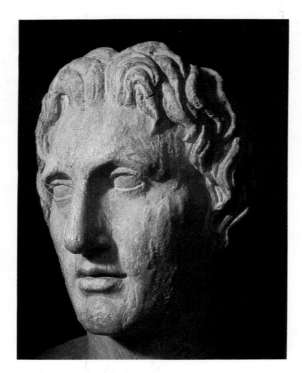

Alexander the Great's military conquests spread Hellenism eastward as far as India.

the ancient world had known. The library contained about 500,000 books written on papyrus scrolls.

Science. Besides gathering knowledge, the scientists at Alexandria also made new discoveries. A mathematician named Euclid (YOO-klid) organized existing knowledge of geometry into a logical system. Students in geometry courses today still study Euclid's proofs. Eratosthenes (ehr-uh-TAHS-thuh-neez) was both a scholar and the head librarian at Alexandria. Using geometry, he estimated the distance around the earth.

Sec. Rev. ques. 4
Aristarchus (ar-ih-STAR-kus) was a mathematician and astronomer. He argued that the planets revolve around the sun—an idea too startling for other Greek scientists to accept. People continued to believe in an earth-centered universe for 1,700 years.

Archimedes (ahr-kuh-MEE-deez), a physicist and mathematician, discovered the principles of the lever and the pulley as well as the natural laws for calculating the weight of an object in water. Archimedes also won **92** fame for his inventions, especially weapons such as the catapult, which hurled huge stones at an enemy.

Philosophy. Both Hellenic and Hellenistic philosophers used reason to explain human conduct. However, while Hellenic thinkers had focused on human beings as members of a community, Hellenistic thinkers wrote of people as individuals.

Two important Hellenistic schools of philosophy developed in Athens about 200 B.C. One was **Epicureanism** (ep-ih-KYOOR-ee-uh-niz-um) named after Epicurus, a writer and teacher. Epicurus said that a happy life was one that held the least pain and anxiety. He criticized attempts to gain wealth, power, or fame, since such attempts increase anxiety. He also said that wise people should not give in to strong emotions. He recommended the enjoyment of simple pleasures such as talking with good friends or lying "on soft grass by a running stream."

Some later followers of Epicurus stressed pleasure rather than simplicity, which was the opposite of Epicurus's aim. The modern meaning of the word *epicure*—a person who is fond of luxury—comes from these followers.

Stoicism (STOH-ih-siz-um), the other Hellenistic philosophy, had the most lasting influence. It was founded about 300 B.C. by Zeno, a Phoenician thinker and teacher who met with his students on a **stoa** (STOH-uh)— open porch—in the marketplace of Athens. The Stoics emphasized dignity, self-control, and reason. The individual, said Zeno, should accept what life brings and try to live virtuously. Because the Stoics urged people above all to remain calm, *stoic* has come to mean one who is indifferent to both pain and pleasure.

The Stoics were the first philosophers to emphasize the unity of all people. "Our lives should not be based on cities or peoples, each with its own view of right and wrong," declared a Stoic, "but we should regard all men as our fellow countrymen and fellow citizens." This belief in the bonds among all people was an important influence on the Romans, who would soon dominate the Mediterranean. See Sec. 4 *Closing the Lesson*, p. T69D.

Social History Note that the Stoics advocated an end to slavery. They believed that using another human being was corrupting to the owner.

Section Review

Answers to Section Review questions are in brackets on pages indicated.

1. **Identify:** Peloponnesian War, Hellenistic Age, Epicureanism, Stoicism, stoa. (pp. 89, 91, 92)
2. How did the Peloponnesian War weaken Greece? (p. 90)
3. How did Alexander's conquests help Greek culture spread? (p. 91)
4. What were some of the important ideas of Hellenistic scientists? (p. 92)
5. **Critical thinking:** Were the ideas of Epicurus and Zeno in keeping with the Greek ideal of moderation? Explain your answer. (See answer below.)

5. Students might point out the philosophers' focus on avoiding strong emotions as a means of attaining an ideal life.

Chapter 4   Summary and Timeline

1. About 2600 B.C. Minoans on the island of Crete developed a civilization with close ties to the sea. Mycenaeans from the Greek peninsula later invaded Crete and took control of Minoan trade. With the fall of Mycenae about 1100 B.C., Greece entered a dark age. In the Hellenic Age that followed, Greeks made intelligence and bravery part of the Greek ideal.

2. During the Hellenic Age, city-states developed in Greece. Sparta had the best-trained warriors. Athens, where the idea of democracy was born, was famous for its statesmen, thinkers, writers, and artists. When the Persian Empire attacked Greece in the early fifth century B.C., the city-states united to preserve their freedom. Their victory brought on a golden age.

3. Besides developing democratic government, the Greeks made outstanding achievements in literature, art, architecture, science, and philosophy. The ideal of the Greeks, developed in the Hellenic Age, was a balanced life in which both excellence and moderation were goals to be attained.

4. When Athens built an empire in the fifth century B.C., Sparta's challenge brought on the Peloponnesian War. Divided and weakened, the Greek city-states were easily conquered by Macedonia in 338 B.C. Alexander the Great made Greece part of a huge empire. He encouraged contacts between Greeks and non-Greeks. During the Hellenistic Age, after Alexander's death, Greek ideas continued to develop and spread to the lands of the ancient Middle East.

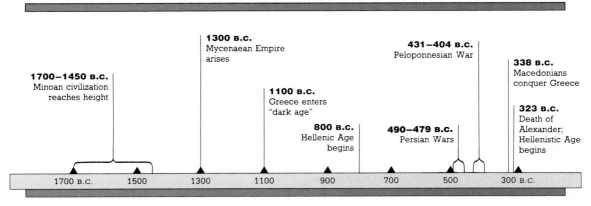

1700–1450 B.C.
Minoan civilization reaches height

1300 B.C.
Mycenaean Empire arises

1100 B.C.
Greece enters "dark age"

800 B.C.
Hellenic Age begins

490–479 B.C.
Persian Wars

431–404 B.C.
Peloponnesian War

338 B.C.
Macedonians conquer Greece

323 B.C.
Death of Alexander; Hellenistic Age begins

1700 B.C.   1500   1300   1100   900   700   500   300 B.C.

See p. T69D for answers to Chapter Review.

Vocabulary Review

1. Use the following terms to complete the sentences below: *agora, classical, colonies, natural laws, Parthenon, Socratic method, Sophists, tyrant.*
   a. Traveling teachers called __?__ challenged Athenian religious beliefs, laws, and ideals.
   b. The early Greeks set up __?__ in other lands.
   c. The __?__, atop the Acropolis in Athens, is a fine example of __?__ Greek architecture.
   d. Greek philosophers believed that __?__ could be discovered by using reason.
   e. The __?__ is a question-and-answer approach to teaching.
   f. Greek citizens met in the __?__ to discuss business and politics.
   g. The __?__ Pisistratus seized power in Athens and helped the city become the center of Greek culture.
2. Define the terms in each of the following pairs.
   a. acropolis; polis
   b. Hellenic Age; Hellenistic Age
   c. democracy; direct democracy
   d. Epicureanism; Stoicism

People to Identify

Choose the name that best completes each sentence. Write your answers on a separate sheet of paper.
1. Cleisthenes, Solon, and [Ptolemy/Pericles] all contributed to the growth of democracy in Athens.
2. The historian [Herodotus/Draco] is called the "father of history."

3. [Euclid/Hippocrates] organized geometry into a logical system.
4. We know the ideas of the philosopher [Zeno/Socrates] through the writings of his student [Plato/Epicurus].
5. [Pythagoras/Sophocles] wrote *Oedipus Rex* and other tragedies.
6. The philosopher [Aristotle/Homer] wrote about science, government, and many other fields of learning.

Places to Know

Match the letters on this map of the Athenian Empire with the places listed below. You may want to refer to the map on page 72.
1. Aegean Sea
2. Athens
3. Crete
4. Hellespont
5. Macedonia
6. Mediterranean Sea
7. Peloponnesus
8. Persian Empire
9. Sparta

94

Recalling the Facts

1. What did Hellenic civilization gain from the Minoans and Mycenaeans?
2. How did the *Iliad* and the *Odyssey* influence Greek education?
3. What were the qualities of an ideal Spartan? Why did Athenians criticize that ideal?
4. What was the long-term effect of the Greek victory in the Persian Wars?
5. How did classical Greek writers, artists, and architects express the Greek value of moderation?
6. Why was the Peloponnesian War a tragedy for all of Greece?
7. What lands did Alexander the Great conquer?
8. How were the ideas of Hellenic and Hellenistic philosophers similar? How were they different?

Critical Thinking Skills

1. **Researching words.** The word *democracy* comes from the Greek words *demos,* meaning "the people," and *-kratia,* meaning "government." The following words all end in the English suffix *-cracy,* meaning "government": *autocracy, gerontocracy, plutocracy.* Use a dictionary to find out the full meaning of each word. *(App.)*

2. **Defending a viewpoint.** Plato said that the people of Athens would be happier under the rule of a philosopher-king than they were under democratic government. List arguments supporting this position, and then list arguments opposing it. *(Anal.)*

Thinking About Geography

1. **Analyzing.** Explain how each of the following geographic features influenced the development of Greece: (a) irregular coastline, (b) mountainous land, (c) poor soil. *(Comp.)*

2. **Comparing maps.** Compare the map of Alexander's empire on page 91 with the world map in the Atlas at the back of this book. What nations now exist in the lands once ruled by Alexander the Great? *(Comp.)*

3. **Drawing conclusions.** A strait is a narrow passage of water that joins two larger bodies of water. The Hellespont and Bosporus (map, page 72) are examples. What bodies of water are joined by each of these straits? Why were these straits important for Greek trade? *(Comp.)*

Enrichment: Primary Sources

As you have read, Thucydides is famous for his account of the Peloponnesian War. In the adapted passage below, Thucydides describes his efforts to learn the truth about what happened.

 With regard to my factual reporting of the events of the war, I have made it a principle not to write down the first story that came my way, and not even to be guided by my own general impressions. Either I was present myself at the events which I have described or else I have heard of them from eyewitnesses whose reports I have checked with as much thoroughness as possible. Even so, the truth was not easy to discover; different eyewitnesses give different accounts of the same events, speak out of favor for one side or the other, or else from imperfect memories.

My Story

1. In what two ways did Thucydides get his information?
2. What problems did he experience with the reports of eyewitnesses?
3. **Critical thinking:** Why, do you think, would he have decided not to be guided in his reporting by his own "general impressions"? *(Syn.)*

95

 A checkmark identifies questions and exercises calling for the three higher-order levels of thinking at the top of the Bloom taxonomy: Analysis, Synthesis, and Evaluation.

The Roman Republic and Empire   700 B.C.–A.D. 180
(pp. 96–117)

Chapter Preview

In Section 1 the rise, expansion, and decline of the Roman Republic are described. Section 2 discusses the Pax Romana and the expansion of the Roman Empire. Section 3 explores the social classes and culture of imperial Rome and describes how Roman and Greek culture blended.

Bibliography

See the *Teacher's Management and Planning Guide* for additional listings. Starred titles are for both students and teachers.

Balsdon, John. *Roman Women.* Greenwood Press. A highly praised introduction to women's roles in Roman society.

*Cercopino, Jerome. *Daily Life in Ancient Rome.* Yale University Press. A good basic survey.

Cornell, Tim, and John Matthews. *The Atlas of the Roman World.* Facts on File. Thirteen hundred years of Roman history, including many maps and illustrations.

Grant, Michael. *The Twelve Caesars.* Scribner's. Readable biographies of the rulers who set the pattern for the Roman Empire.

*Macaulay, David. *City.* Houghton Mifflin. Construction of an ancient Roman city.

Section Lesson Plans

SECTION 1   (pp. 97–105)
The Roman Republic

Objectives

After completing this section, students will be able to:
1. Describe how Rome established a republic that expanded through the Mediterranean.
2. Explain what problems brought an end to the Republic.

Introducing the Lesson

Remind students that Rome established a representative government that provided for the election of officials. The Roman Republic, however, was very different from the democratic system of some cities of ancient Greece.

Then ask: *(a) What is the difference between representative government and direct democracy* (p. 81)? (In a representative government, some individuals are chosen to stand up for the interests and values of others. In a direct democracy, those actually affected by political decisions directly participate in making them.)

(b) What are the advantages of each type of government? (Answers will vary. Direct democracy gives individuals an opportunity to speak for themselves. Representative government is effective when the nation or state has a large population or covers an extensive territory.)

Developing the Lesson:
Organizing Information

Have students make a diagram illustrating the structure of Rome's republican government. (Diagrams should include information on consuls, the senate, the assembly, and tribunes.) *(Comprehension)*

Developing the Lesson:
Understanding Chronology

Have students make a time chart showing the important political and military developments of the Roman Republic. (Timelines should include information for the following dates: 509, 451, 287, 225, 264–241, 218–202, 146, 196, 133. Note that all dates are B.C.) *(Comprehension)*

Closing the Lesson: Identifying Causes

Have students work in groups to identify the causes of the rise and decline of the Roman Republic. Have students organize the information in a chart and present the chart to the class. (Answers will vary, but might include the following: *Rise:* one-year term for consuls prevented the abuse of power; the veto guaranteed a check on power; a strong army; discipline and organization of the army. *Decline:* crisis in agriculture; unemployment; failure of reform; social and political disorder; slave revolts; rise of military dictators.) *(Comprehension)*

Answers to *Map Skill Practice*, p. 102.

1. Caesar's invasion of Britain.
2. The capital, Rome.
3. Gaul; more land along the eastern Adriatic; larger areas in Macedonia and Asia Minor; Syria and Palestine; Egypt and more land elsewhere in North Africa.
4. The Empire now extended around all shores of the Mediterranean.

See *Section Review* questions, p. 105.

SECTION 2   (pp. 105–108)
The Rise of the Roman Empire

Objectives

After completing this section, students will be able to:
1. Name the accomplishments of Augustus and later emperors.
2. Explain how the Pax Romana benefited people throughout the Empire.

Introducing the Lesson

Remind students that the reign of Augustus began a long period of political stability in Rome. Strong leadership, a disciplined military, and able administration led to a time of peace and prosperity that lasted for over 200 years.

Then ask: *(a) What is the relationship between a period of peace and the growth of economic prosperity?* (Answers will vary. When a state's resources are not needed for military programs, they can be used for other purposes.)

? JAPAN

(b) How might prosperous times reinforce peace? (Answers will vary. If members of a society can meet their basic needs, or if opportunities for economic growth exist, there is less likelihood of civil unrest.)

(c) What is the relationship between strong leaders, a disciplined military, able administration, and times of peace and prosperity? (A government that provides security and order is likely to be supported by society. Strong leaders are able to provide the confidence and leadership necessary to provide services needed by society.)

Developing the Lesson: Making Judgments

Have students write an essay explaining the difference between an effective leader and a poor leader. Students should support their evaluations of leadership with examples from Roman history. (Answers will vary, but might include the following: *Effective*—Augustus, Claudius, Vespasian, Nerva, Trajan, Hadrian, Marcus Aurelius. *Poor*—Caligula, Nero, military emperors [except Vespasian].) *(Evaluation)*

Developing the Lesson: Expressing Point of View

Ask: *(a) If you had lived in the time of the Pax Romana, which of the emperors would you have preferred? Why?* (Answers will vary.)

(b) What do you think was the greatest achievement of the Pax Romana? (Answers will vary.)

(c) Why might Nerva and the "Good Emperors" have chosen the adoptive system for selecting successors? (Earlier events indicated that some legitimate procedure was needed; perhaps the only acceptable way of choosing one's successor was to make the person a member of the family.) *(Evaluation)*

Closing the Lesson: Analyzing Historical Evidence

Have students analyze the information in this section and answer the following question: *What values in political life seemed to be most important to the Romans?* When answering the question, students should note the goals and policies of the emperors, the policies that received greatest support from the people, and the consequences for emperors who ruled badly. (Answers will vary, but should include some of the following: political representation; order; a disciplined and loyal army; an empire secure from invasion; effective authority; patriotism; care for the poor; peace; prosperity; respect for government; military expansion.) *(Comprehension)*

See *Section Review* questions, p. 108.

SECTION 3　　　　　(pp. 109–115)
Roman Society and Culture

Objectives

After completing this section, students will be able to:
1. Describe Roman society.
2. Discuss how the Romans blended Greek culture with their own.

Introducing the Lesson

Remind students that the Pax Romana created a time of prosperity for the Roman Empire. The increased wealth affected the entire Roman class structure and multiplied the economic and political opportunities of plebeians and others.

Then ask: *(a) How might increased wealth affect an empire's social structure?* (If more money is available to more people, poorer classes would have greater opportunities to improve their economic status.)

*(b) Under what circumstances might an empire's increased wealth **not** affect the social structure?* (If one class monopolized the wealth, other classes would not benefit from increased wealth.)

(c) How might added prosperity affect political organization? (Answers will vary. When members of a social class experience a rise in economic status, they may also seek to increase their political participation and power.)

Developing the Lesson:
Analyzing Statements

Have students paraphrase the two statements by writer and orator Cicero, quoted on p. 114.

Then ask: *(a) How can law be "bent by influence"?* (Answers will vary. Important individuals may be able to influence the application of law.)

(b) How can law be "broken by power"? (Answers will vary. Individuals with military influence or political power may at times seek to override the rule of law.)

(c) How can law be "spoiled by wealth"? (Answers will vary. Sometimes wealthy individuals may try to use their money to "buy" a favorable legal settlement.)

(d) How can being "servants of the law" help individuals be free? (Answers will vary. Governments create laws in order to build a just society; individuals who observe and respect the laws help to protect and maintain freedom and justice.) *(Analysis)*

Developing the Lesson:
Understanding Point of View

Have students write a letter that might have been written by a senator, a rural peasant, a poor city-dweller, or a slave who lived in the Roman Empire. The letter should describe a typical day in the life of a family in that social group, and might include a description of housing, meals, clothing, occupation, education, religious practices, or recreation. *(Application)*

Closing the Lesson: Illustrating Ideas

Have students work in groups to illustrate the contributions of Roman civilization to the heritage of the Western world. Students might make posters, a scrapbook, or a bulletin board showing examples of Roman literature, art, engineering, and architecture, as well as portraits of important political leaders. Samples of Roman law and of languages that developed from Latin might also be included. *(Comprehension)*

See *Section Review* questions, p. 115.

Chapter 5 Review Answers
(pp. 116–117)

Vocabulary Review

1. (a) republic (b) dictator (c) aqueduct (d) law of succession (e) veto (f) Pax Romana (g) gladiators (h) Punic Wars
2. (a) Patricians—members of the class of wealthy landowners; plebeians—the common people. (b) Law of Nations—a legal code applied throughout the Roman Empire; Twelve Tables—code of laws written during the Republic to protect plebeians from unfair patrician officials. (c) First Triumvirate—three military heroes (Pompey, Crassus, Julius Caesar) who joined together in 60 B.C. to oppose the Senate; Second Triumvirate—three of Caesar's supporters (Mark Antony, Lepidus, Octavian) who joined together to defeat his murderers. (d) Circus Maximus—Rome's oldest public outdoor arena, built to house games and parades, held more than 300,000 spectators; Colosseum—another arena that held about 50,000 people.

People to Identify

1. Known as Octavian until 27 B.C., when the Senate gave him power to rule and the Roman Empire began.
2. Greek scientist whose theories dominated Roman medicine.
3. "Good Emperor" who concentrated on protecting the Empire; built Hadrian's Wall in Britain.
4. General who led the forces of Carthage in the Second Punic War.
5. General who was made dictator because of his popularity as a military leader. Fear that he would end republican government led to his assassination in 44 B.C.
6. Author of *History of Rome.*
7. Last of the "Good Emperors" chosen by the adoptive system; his death in A.D. 180 marked the end of the Pax Romana.
8. Scientist who compiled the *Almagest,* a summary of the ancient world's knowledge of astronomy and geography.
9. Leader of an unsuccessful slave revolt in 73 B.C.
10. First emperor appointed under the adoptive system.
11. One of the greatest Roman poets and author of the *Aeneid.*

Places to Know

1. B   2. E   3. A   4. H   5. G   6. D   7. F   8. C

Recalling the Facts

1. A strong army and help from allies.
2. They faced a sharp decline in farmers' incomes, growing unemployment, bitter conflicts between the rich and the poor, selfish patrician leaders, and slave revolts. The unemployed and landless joined the armies of military leaders who promised them money and loot from conquered peoples.
3. He took control of the army and gained the loyalty of his soldiers by giving large bonuses and land to veterans. He granted citizenship and rights to more people in the provinces, supervised the actions of provincial governors, and took direct control of potentially troublesome provinces. He passed laws encouraging people to marry and raise families.
4. Trade flourished, citizenship was granted generously, and Roman law and a common language unified the people.
5. They were based on wealth.
6. They could not be forced to marry; they could also own property, keep their own money or property if divorced, make business arrangements, and write their own wills.

7. The Romans valued the Greeks' devotion to excellence and the use of reason. The Romans added organizational ability, skill in engineering, and talent for government and law.

Critical Thinking Skills

1. c–509 B.C.; b–264 B.C.; g–146 B.C.; d–31 B.C.; f–A.D. 14; e–A.D. 98; a–A.D. 180.
2–3. Answers will vary.
4. (a) The Twelve Tables protected plebeians from unfair legal decisions; enslavement for debt was outlawed; plebeians gained the right to marry patricians, serve as consuls, and become Senate members; the plebeians' assembly gained broader lawmaking powers; by 287 B.C. plebeians and patricians had equal legal rights. (b) Roman soldiers were loyal and strong; they used battle formations instead of fighting like a mob; they were organized in tightly knit legions, which strengthened the determination and confidence of the soldiers.

Thinking About Geography

1. Answers will vary.
2. To reach Italy, Caesar had to cross a river—the Rubicon—that was part of the boundary between Italy and Gaul. Today the phrase means making an irrevocable decision.

Enrichment: Primary Sources

1. Whether something was done by accident or on purpose, and the age and inexperience of the guilty person.
2. "No one is compelled to defend a cause against his will." "No one suffers a penalty for what he thinks."
3. The law put the burden of proof on the accuser, not the accused.
4. No. Students should recognize that freedom of *thought* does not necessarily imply these other freedoms; a person might be free, for example, to disagree with government policies, but not free to speak or write about the disagreement.

The Roman Republic and Empire 700 B.C.–A.D. 180

See chapter timeline, p. 115.

Before You Read This Chapter

What city do you think is the most important one in the United States today? New York is the largest. Washington, D.C., is the center of government. Cities in the South and West are growing rapidly. To the people of the Roman Empire, there was no question. Rome was the greatest city—the ruler of all the world they knew. Even today, we still use proverbs that show how important Rome was: *All roads lead to Rome. When in Rome, do as the Romans do. Rome wasn't built in a day.* As you read, think about what it was that made Rome great.

The Geographic Setting

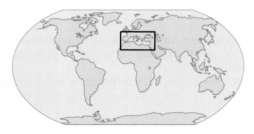

The Chapter Outline

1. The Roman Republic
2. The Rise of the Roman Empire
3. Roman Society and Culture

The might of its army made Rome the most powerful empire of the ancient world. These soldiers were the emperor's personal guards.

Background The original home of the Latins was *Latium*, a region in the lower valley of the Tiber River.

1 The Roman Republic

Objectives

Focus Questions

★ ■ How did Rome establish a republic that expanded through the Mediterranean? *(pages 97–101)*

● ■ What problems brought an end to the Republic? *(pages 101–104)*

Terms to Know

republic   Punic Wars
patrician   dictator
veto   First Triumvirate
plebeian   Second Triumvirate
Twelve Tables

★ Note strategies for first objective on this page and p. 98.

In its early days, Rome was influenced by the Greeks and other peoples. Yet the Romans achieved something unique in history. They became a great power not only by conquering other lands but also by bringing the conquered peoples into their system.

The Geography of Italy

The geography of Italy has much in common with that of Greece. Like Greece, Italy occupies a peninsula that extends from southern Europe into the Mediterranean Sea. The peninsula is shaped like a high-heeled boot. Italy also includes a number of islands, the largest of which is Sicily.

Most of Italy's land is hilly or mountainous. In the north, the Alps separate Italy from the rest of Europe. The Apennine (AP-uhnyn) Mountains run the length of the peninsula. In ancient times, as in Greece, the mountains encouraged the development of

many independent city-states. However, Italy had better farmland than Greece, and its fertile plains supported a large population.

Rome, which became the center of a new civilization in Italy, lies about halfway up the front of the boot. The city was built on seven hills along the Tiber River, an excellent location. The river supplied food, fresh water, transportation, and an outlet to the sea 15 miles to the west. The surrounding hills protected the early Romans from floods as well as from enemy attacks.

Early Rome

Among the first people to settle in Italy were the Latins, farmers and herders from the north. By 700 B.C. they had built several small villages on the hills of Rome. To the south and in Sicily, Greek colonists had established city-states. The early Romans adopted the ✳ Greeks' military systems and styles of literature, art, and architecture.

To the north and west of Rome, a people called the Etruscans (ih-TRUS-kunz) lived in prosperous trading cities. The Etruscans had military power and ambitious kings. By 600 B.C. they had extended their influence throughout the northern half of Italy, including Rome. From the Etruscans the Romans adopted an alphabet (which the Etruscans, in turn, had borrowed from the Greeks). The Romans also learned practical skills in road-building, architecture, pottery-making, and sanitation. Etruscan kings ruled Rome for more than 100 years. During their reign, Rome grew into a great city.

The Roman Republic

In 509 B.C., according to ancient reports, the *TARQUIN* Romans drove out their Etruscan ruler and established a **republic**—a government with- **97**

★ RETEACHING. Have students compare the economic, political, and social differences between the patricians and the plebeians. (Patricians: landowners; government leaders; elected consuls and senators; controlled finances. Plebeians: common people; restricted political and social rights; elected an assembly and tribunes.) *(Comprehension) Observing for Detail*

★ REINFORCEMENT. Have students make a timeline of events resulting in Rome's control over the Mediterranean. (Punic Wars—264–241 B.C., 218–202 B.C., 146 B.C.; victories over Macedonians and in Greece and Asia Minor—196–133 B.C.) *(Comprehension) Understanding Chronology*

Cultural History The legendary founders of Rome were twins, Romulus and Remus, who supposedly were raised by a female wolf. When the twins reached adulthood, they built a city on the Tiber.

Ancient Italy

Rome was located in the central part of Italy. What mountains stretched through much of the Italian peninsula? About how far was Rome from the mouth of the Arno River?

Map Answers: (1) Apennines. (2) About 170 miles.

out a king or queen. In a republic, supreme power rests with the citizens, who have the right to elect their leaders. The Roman Republic was not, however, a democracy like Athens. Its leaders were aristocrats. All came from the class of wealthy landowners, called **patricians** (puh-TRISH-uns).

Two patricians called consuls ran the government and led the army. Since consuls held office for only a year, there was little risk that they would gain too much power. The consuls could also keep each other in check by using the power to **veto**, or reject, proposals and acts. (The word *veto* means "I forbid" in Latin, the Roman language.)

98

Politics The Twelve Tables included laws dealing with court actions, family law, wills, property rights, and public behavior of citizens.

The Senate. A 300-member council of patricians, the Senate, was the most powerful part of the government of the Republic. In the Senate, Rome's most influential citizens debated and decided such important issues as Rome's finances and foreign affairs. Most senators had held other high government positions. They believed that they honored themselves and their families by serving Rome.

The plebeians. The common people, or **plebeians** (plih-BEE-unz), had little say in the government. Although plebeians were citizens, Roman laws kept them from holding high government positions or marrying patricians. The plebeians' struggle to gain equality went on for 200 years.

Early in the Republic, the plebeians threatened to stop serving in the army and paying taxes unless they were given a voice in the government. Since Rome was often at war with its neighbors in Italy, this threat was a serious danger to the Republic. To avoid civil war, the patricians allowed the plebeians to form their own assembly. The assembly had the power to pass laws for the common people. It also elected ten officials called tribunes, who could veto the actions of the consuls or the Senate.

In 451 B.C. the patricians agreed to plebeian demands that Roman laws be collected and written down. These laws, known as the **Twelve Tables**, gave the common people some protection against unfair decisions by patrician judges.

Over the next two centuries, the plebeians' position continued to improve. Enslavement for debt was outlawed. Plebeians also gained the right to marry patricians and hold the office of consul. Their assembly gained the power to make laws for the patricians as well as the plebeians. Eventually plebeians won the right to become members of the Roman Senate.

By 287 B.C., plebeians and patricians had equal legal rights. Nevertheless, real political power remained in the hands of the patricians, who made up the nobility. Men from this class held the highest offices in the Republic and dominated the Senate.

Sec. Rev. ques. 2

★ See below.

Roman Expansion

During the long struggle between patricians and plebeians, Rome continued to expand. The Romans showed a toughness of character and a genius for warfare and diplomacy. They knew how to win battles and how to gain allies through lenient treatment of defeated enemies. By the middle of the third century B.C., Rome ruled most of Italy.

The army.   The army had been important throughout Rome's history. At first only patricians fought for Rome. By 390 B.C., however, plebeians served as well. The sturdy Roman farmer made an excellent soldier. He was loyal to his city and strong enough to march 30 miles a day carrying 60 pounds of armor, weapons, and supplies.

The strength of the Roman army lay in its superior discipline and organization. Roman troops used the same weapons as their enemies—swords, spears, daggers, bows and arrows, and stones. Yet while their opponents often fought like a mob, the Romans adopted and improved upon the Greek phalanx—a close battle formation. The basic unit of the Roman army was the legion. A legion was made up of 3,000 to 6,000 foot soldiers and 100 or more cavalry—troops on horseback. This tight organization strengthened the determination and confidence of the Roman soldiers.

Allies.   Despite the strength of its army, Rome could not have conquered Italy without the help of neighboring peoples. Rome made allies of some former enemies by giving them protection and, in some cases, Roman citizenship and self-government. In return, Rome gained new foreign soldiers for its armed forces. By 225 B.C. more than half of the Roman army was made up of allies. The Romans' conquests in Italy gave them the soldiers they needed to expand further.

The Punic Wars

In 264 B.C. Rome went to war with the North African city-state of Carthage. Founded by the Phoenicians (page 43), Carthage had become a strong sea power. It controlled large areas in the western Mediterranean, including parts of Spain, North Africa, and the island of Sicily. Rome considered Carthage a threat to its allies in southern Italy and to the supply of grain from Sicily. The three wars that Rome fought with Carthage are called the **Punic Wars.** *Punic* (PYOO-nik) comes from the Latin word for "Phoenician."

Rome began the First Punic War with a stronger army, but the Carthaginians had a

Sec. Rev. ques. 3

The phalanx, as shown here, was a close battle formation that gave the Roman army flexibility against the massed armies of their opponents.

99

Geography Note that Carthage was founded about 814 B.C. in the territory of present-day Tunisia.

Background Note that the Romans found an abandoned Carthaginian warship and used its design to construct a fleet of 100 ships in 60 days.

Background The Romans perfected the technique of boarding enemy ships by using a *corvus*, a movable bridge.

better navy. The Romans quickly built their own fleet and won battles both at sea and in Sicily. Carthage was forced to make peace in 241 B.C. and to give up Sicily to Rome. Sicily became the first Roman province—the first territory outside the Italian peninsula to be ruled by Rome. (See map below.)

Hannibal's invasion of Italy. Because the Carthaginians continued to expand in Spain, Rome planned to attack them there. In 218 B.C., however, the Carthaginian general Hannibal decided to strike at Rome by invading Italy from the north. This marked the start of the Second Punic War.

With his entire army and a number of elephants, Hannibal marched northeast through Spain and what is now southern France. Then, after crossing the steep and icy mountain passes of the Alps, the Carthaginians moved southward through Italy. Hannibal showed his military genius at the Battle of Cannae (KAN-ee) in 216 B.C. When the Romans attacked, Hannibal pulled back the

forces in the middle of his battle line. To the Romans, it looked like the start of a retreat. Falling for the trick, the whole Roman army surged quickly forward. Hannibal's cavalry, which was waiting at both ends of the line, swung around behind the Romans and attacked. As many as 50,000 Roman soldiers were killed or captured.

This staggering defeat shocked the people of Rome. "The streets were loud with the wailing and weeping of women," wrote the historian Livy (LIV-ee). The Romans feared that Hannibal would now march on Rome itself. These were the Republic's worst days.

Scipio's invasion of North Africa. Though Hannibal continued to win battles in Italy, he lacked the military strength to capture Rome. Moreover, the Roman allies near the city remained loyal. An army led by the Roman general Scipio (SKIP-ee-oh) attacked the Carthaginians in Spain, preventing them from sending help to Hannibal. In 204 B.C. the Romans also invaded North Africa. To

SCHLIEFFEN IN W.W.I.

Growth of Roman Power, 264–133 B.C. (See answer below.)

During the Punic Wars, Rome gained land outside Italy. What gains had Rome made by 201 B.C.? After that date, what lands did Rome take over?

Biography Hannibal, who was forced by his father at the age of nine to swear eternal hatred of Rome, was described by the Roman historian Livy as a brave leader who shared all hardships with his troops.

Map Answers: (1) Italy, Sicily, Corsica, Sardinia, southern coast of Spain, Balearic Islands. (2) Most of Spain, region north of Italy, Macedonia, Greece, coastal area northwest of Macedonia, western Asia Minor, Carthage and surrounding area.

NEW TACTICS

protect his homeland, Hannibal returned to Carthage. He was defeated by Scipio in the Battle of Zama in 202 B.C. This defeat brought an end to the Second Punic War and gave Rome even more Carthaginian land (map, page 100).

TERMS

The destruction of Carthage. In 146 B.C. Rome triumphed over Carthage in a third war. Although Carthage had become too weak to threaten Rome, many Romans wanted to crush their enemy permanently. Driven by old hatreds and the memory of Hannibal's victories, the Romans burned Carthage to the ground and sold its survivors into slavery. They poisoned the ground with salt so that nothing could grow in it. As they left, the Romans cursed the site of the ruined city, saying that people would never return there.

Roman Conquest of the Mediterranean

The defeat of Carthage in the Second Punic War gave Rome control of the western Mediterranean Sea. Yet the lands of the eastern Mediterranean still belonged to cities and Hellenistic kingdoms that had arisen after the breakup of Alexander's empire. Shortly after defeating Hannibal, Rome went to war against his ally, the king of Macedonia. By 196 B.C. Rome had defeated the Macedonians and taken over as the "protector" of the Greek city-states in Asia Minor. Other victories followed in Greece and Asia Minor. By 133 B.C. Rome had extended its rule over the entire Mediterranean (map, page 100).

The Decline of the Republic

● Note strategies for second objective on this page and p. 102.

While Rome's wars were bringing it new lands and power, economic and political problems surfaced at home. Some leaders tried to solve these problems, but the Republic began to grow unstable.

Sec. Rev. ques. 4

Farm debts. The decline of the Republic began with a crisis in agriculture that brought disaster to thousands of small farm-

ILLEGAL!

Linking Past and Present

People did eventually return to Carthage, which became a Roman colony under Julius Caesar. By the second century A.D., Carthage was an important center of learning and Christianity. Later, however, the city was permanently destroyed by Arab conquerors. Today the modern city of Tunis stands not far from the ruins of Carthage.

ers. Hannibal's invasion of Italy had destroyed farms and farmland. Other farms had gone untended while their owners were away fighting. The shipments of large amounts of grain and other farm products to Rome from conquered lands created a surplus. Prices in Italy fell and so did the farmers' incomes.

Sinking ever deeper into poverty and debt, many farmers sold out to Romans who had grown rich during the war. These wealthy Romans, eager to invest in land, created huge estates. They found workers for their farms among the thousands of slaves taken prisoner during the Punic Wars.

Unemployment. Many of the small farmers who had neither land nor jobs moved to the Roman cities to look for work. Few were able to find jobs there. They became part of the huge class of unemployed and resentful urban poor.

Attempts at reform. The Gracchus (GRAH-kus) family of Rome were wealthy plebeians who were active in politics. Tiberius Gracchus, elected tribune in 133 B.C., promised to help the farmers. He called for the state to limit the size of large estates and give land to the poor, even if it meant taking some land from the wealthy. Many landholding senators, however, saw this idea as a threat. They also feared that Tiberius would use his support among the poor to gain political power for himself. When Tiberius sought re-election as tribune, violence broke out. Tiberius and 300 of his followers were killed in the rioting.

PROBLEMS SOLVED BY VIOLENCE

101

● **RETEACHING.** Have students scan "The Decline of the Republic" (pp. 101–103) and answer the following: **(a)** What were two economic problems that led to unrest in Rome during the first century B.C.? (Farm debts and unemployment.) **(b)** How did generals gain power? (They recruited private armies from the landless city dwellers, who felt loyalty to the generals.) **(c)** Why did the government remain unstable? (Competition among military leaders.) *(Comprehension) Observing for Detail*

● **REINFORCEMENT.** Have students review pp. 101–103 to find statements that support or refute this statement: *Conflict between classes contributed to the decline of the Republic.* Then have students evaluate the accuracy of the statement. *(Evaluation) Making Generalizations*

Map Skill Practice

See p. T95B for answers to *Map Skill Practice*.

Growth of Roman Power by 44 B.C.

1. On the map below, what does the arrow above Julius Caesar's name represent?
2. What does the star in southern Europe represent?
3. Compare this map with the map "Growth of Roman Power, 264–133 B.C." on page 100. What areas were added to the Empire between 133 and 44 B.C.?
4. **Drawing conclusions.** By 44 B.C. the Mediterranean could be called a "Roman lake." Using the information on this map, explain why that description was accurate.

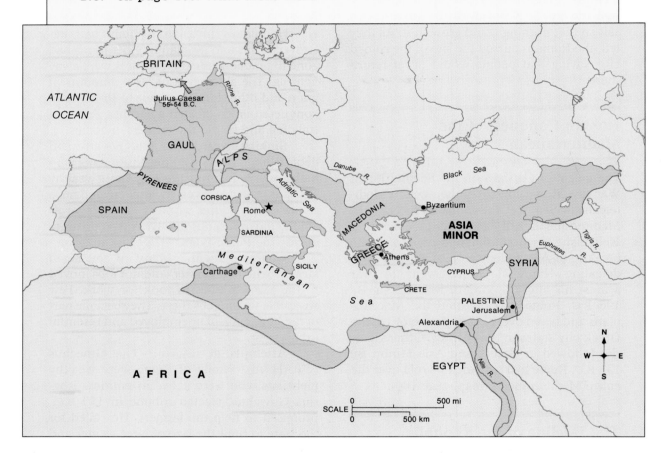

Gaius (GY-us) Gracchus, a younger brother of Tiberius, became tribune 10 years later and urged more reforms. He gave grain to the poor, opened up more land for the farmers, and won more rights for the middle class. In 121 B.C. fighting broke out between Gaius's supporters and opponents. Gaius and several thousand others were killed.

● See below.

Social and political disorder. The Roman Republic in the second century B.C. was very different from the Rome that had defeated Carthage. Fear of Carthage had united Romans in the past. Now bitter conflicts divided the rich and the poor, and violence often erupted. The Senate provided little leadership in these troubled times. Many

102

● ENRICHMENT. Have students work in groups to prepare a debate that might have occurred between plebeians supporting the Gracchus land reforms and Roman senators who opposed the reforms. Debates should include an explanation of the program and its advantages and disadvantages for plebeians and senators. *(Synthesis) Debating an Issue* patricians became more concerned with keeping their power and wealth than with promoting the welfare of Rome. The common people, including thousands of landless farmers and unemployed urban poor, were ready to follow leaders who promised them food and entertainment.

Slave revolts. Another cause of unrest in the Republic was fear of the thousands of slaves in the population. In 73 B.C. the slave Spartacus proclaimed a war to free slaves in Italy. Some 90,000 slaves ran away to join his revolt. For two years the slave army outfought Roman forces and devastated southern Italy. The revolt ended when Spartacus was killed in battle and 6,000 of his followers were put to death. *—CRUCIFIED ON ROUTE TO ROME*

The Rise of Military Dictators

During this period of unrest, it was easy for powerful and ambitious military leaders to gain support. About 108 B.C. Gaius Marius, a popular general, began to recruit soldiers from the jobless poor of the cities. Before this time, only men who owned property could be Roman soldiers. They had served in the army out of loyalty to Rome. Landless city dwellers, on the other hand, volunteered for service because Marius had promised them money, loot from conquered peoples, and land when the fighting was over. These soldiers felt loyalty to Marius rather than to the government.

Other ambitious commanders followed Marius's example by creating their own private armies. Marius's greatest rival was Lucius Cornelius Sulla. The bloody wars between the supporters of these two generals finally ended with Sulla's capture of Rome. In 82 B.C. Sulla was given the title of **dictator**—absolute ruler—of Rome. This position was supposed to be limited to a term of six months. Actually Sulla remained dictator for two years. During that time he used his power to have many opponents murdered.

The First Triumvirate. The ambitions of army leaders continued to threaten the Republic. In 60 B.C. three military heroes joined together to form the **First Triumvirate**

This statue of Julius Caesar, like many ancient statues, was originally painted to appear more lifelike.

(try-UM-vih-rut). The three were Gnaeus (NY-us) Pompey, Marcus Licinius Crassus, and Julius Caesar (SEE-zur). These men had few aims in common except their opposition to the Senate. Each was jealous of the other's power, but they at first cooperated to have Caesar made consul.

Julius Caesar

Caesar knew that he needed the support of an army to succeed in politics. He quickly took command of the Roman legions in Gaul (present-day France). Over the next 10 years Caesar showed a genius for leadership and military strategy. He brought all of Gaul under Rome's control and briefly invaded Britain.

In Rome, meanwhile, Pompey was gaining favor in the Senate. In 49 B.C. he persuaded the Senate to order Julius Caesar to return home without his army. To obey would have left Caesar without power. Instead, Caesar led his troops into Italy. Civil war began again. Caesar defeated Pompey's armies in Italy, Greece, Egypt, Asia Minor, Africa, and Spain. Returning to Rome in 46

Sec. Rev. ques. 5

against LAW!

103

Politics Note that the slave war led by Spartacus was *not* a revolt of the lower classes against the wealthy. Spartacus received little support from the Italian population, which remained loyal to Rome.

Biography Although an aristocrat, Gaius Marius remarked that "men are born equal and alike; nobility is achieved by bravery."

Check for Understanding. Ask: Why did military dictators enjoy popularity in first century B.C. Rome? (They recruited landless poor with the promise of money and land.)

Politics Note that the First Triumvirate combined the strengths of Pompey's wealth and military might, Crassus's wealth and political connections, and Caesar's position as consul and his political astuteness.

Biography After his victory in Asia Minor (present-day Turkey) in 47 B.C., Caesar evaluated his success with the famous claim, *"Veni, vidi, vici,"* or "I came, I saw, I conquered."

? CLEOPATRA INFO

B.C. as the Republic's greatest hero, he took over the government. He became the sole ruler, with the titles of dictator and consul.

Caesar wasted no time in making popular reforms. He reorganized the government and lowered taxes in the provinces. To aid the poor in Rome, he moved 100,000 army veterans and others to new colonies and gave them land to farm. He granted citizenship to more people outside Italy. Caesar also put into effect a new and accurate calendar called the Julian calendar. In 44 B.C. he was named dictator for life.

Caesar's power, success, and popularity alarmed many nobles and senators. They feared that he would destroy the Senate and become a king, thereby ending the Republic. To prevent this, a group of nobles led by Marcus Brutus and Gaius Cassius (GY-us KAS-ee-us) plotted to kill him. They stabbed Caesar to death in the Senate on the Ides of March (March 15) in 44 B.C. (Under the Julian calendar, the Ides was a date in the middle of each month that was supposed to correspond to the full moon.)

KING? *

The End of the Republic

Caesar's death plunged Rome into a new struggle for power. Three of Caesar's supporters—Mark Antony, Lepidus, and Caesar's adopted son Octavian—joined forces against his murderers. This Second Triumvirate defeated the armies of Brutus and Cassius, but Antony and Octavian then became enemies. Each wanted to rule Rome.

Antony's wife, Queen Cleopatra of Egypt, shared his ambition. She dreamed of making Egypt great once more, and not just a province in the Roman Empire. Many Romans, however, turned against Antony because of his union with Cleopatra. In 31 B.C., in a naval battle off the coast of Greece, Octavian's fleet crushed the combined navies of Antony and Cleopatra.

Octavian's victory made him the unchallenged ruler of Rome. Yet the years of turmoil had destroyed the Republic. A new kind of government would be necessary to maintain order.

One of Caesar's reforms created many new farmers. Here a Roman farmer taking his goods to town passes by a shrine to the gods. Farmers sold olive oil, grain, vegetables, fruits, meat, and herbs in nearby markets.

104

History and Literature The assassination of Julius Caesar was dramatized in a play by William Shakespeare, who portrayed Brutus as the "noblest Roman of them all." Brutus insisted that action be taken only against Caesar and believed that the death of the dictator would restore liberty and republican government.

Biography After his defeat by Octavian, Mark Antony committed suicide and died in the arms of his wife, Cleopatra. Poisoned by the venom of a snake, Cleopatra died in 30 B.C. and was buried next to Antony.

Section Review

Answers to Section Review questions are in brackets on pages indicated.

1. **Define or identify:** republic, patrician, veto, plebeian, Twelve Tables, Punic Wars, dictator, First Triumvi- (pp. 97, rate, Second Triumvirate. 98, 99, 103, 104)
2. Why did plebeians and patricians come into conflict during the early Republic? (p. 98)
3. What factors helped Rome become a military power? (p. 99)

4. How did the problems of Roman farmers and poor people in the cities create unrest? (p. 101)
5. What events marked the career of Julius Caesar? (p. 103)
6. **Critical thinking:** In what ways did Rome's military successes lead to the decline of the Republic?
(See answer below.)

6. Students might suggest that Roman rulers concentrated on expansion at the expense of the Roman people. Rome was in domestic turmoil fueled by class conflict, and wars destroyed farmland, hurting an already fragile economy.

See lesson plans, pp. T95A–T95C.

2 The Rise of the Roman Empire

Objectives

Focus Questions

★ ■ What did Augustus and later emperors accomplish? *(pages 105–108)*
● ■ How did the Pax Romana benefit people throughout the Empire? *(page 108)*

Terms to Know

Pax Romana
law of succession

★ Note strategies for first objective on this page and p. 106.

When Octavian came to power in 31 B.C., he planned to restore the Republic. Yet he, like Caesar, saw that Rome's empire was too large and its government too weak and corrupt for that to be possible. In place of the Republic, Octavian established the Roman Empire.

As the first emperor, Octavian kept all real power for himself. Yet he won the support of the Senate by asking its advice, permitting it to run some of the provinces, and letting it have its own treasury. In 27 B.C. the

senators gave Octavian a title that was also used for the gods. They called him Augustus, meaning "honored and majestic." This became the name by which he was known.

The Age of Augustus

Augustus was not a power-hungry tyrant but a creative and responsible statesman. He used his authority to bring order and good government to Rome and its provinces.

Reforms in the army and government. Ambitious military leaders with their own troops had often caused trouble for the Republic. To solve this problem, Augustus took complete control of the army. He gained the loyalty of his soldiers by giving large bonuses and land to veterans. He was then able to use the army to keep order and guard the frontiers of the Empire.

To strengthen the unity of the Empire, Augustus granted citizenship to more people in the provinces. In addition, Augustus tried to improve government in those regions. He supervised the actions of provincial governors and took direct control of provinces that might cause trouble, leaving the Senate to watch over regions that were peaceful.

Sec. Rev. ques. 2

105

★ **RETEACHING. Have students review "The Age of Augustus" (pp. 105–106) and make a list of facts that support the following statement:** *Octavian was a good ruler.* (Octavian won support of the Senate by letting it keep some power and was a creative and responsible statesman who used authority to bring order and good government. He gained the loyalty of soldiers, expanded citizenship, emphasized traditional values, and provided food for the poor.) *(Comprehension)* **Supporting Generalizations**

★ **REINFORCEMENT. Have students review "Augustus's successors" (p. 106) and outline the information on the four members of Augustus's family who ruled Rome.** (Emperors include Tiberius, Caligula, Claudius, and Nero.) *(Comprehension)* **Organizing Ideas in Written Form**

Check for Understanding. Ask: How did Augustus reform the army? (He took complete control and gained the loyalty of the troops by offering bonuses.)

Traditional values. Augustus also tried to restore the values that had made the Romans a great people—patriotism, close family ties, hard work, discipline, and simple living. He passed laws encouraging people to marry and raise families. Augustus sponsored the building of roads, water systems, and other projects that improved people's lives and provided jobs. The government also gave free or low-cost grain to poor people in need.

★ See below.

Caesar Augustus, Rome's first emperor, said that he "found Rome bricks and left it marble." Like Alexander the Great and the Egyptian kings before him, Augustus claimed to be a divine ruler.

106

Rulers of the Pax Romana

Augustus died in A.D. 14. His rule had begun the period known as Pax Romana (PAHKS roh-MAH-nuh)—"the Roman Peace." For more than 200 years, from 27 B.C. to A.D. 180, people throughout the Mediterranean world enjoyed the peace and prosperity that Roman power and Roman law had made possible. Never before had the world experienced such a long period of stability.

Augustus's successors. The Empire had no law of succession—no rule stating how the next emperor would be chosen. Most rulers handed down power to members of their family. The first four emperors after Augustus were related to him or to his second wife, Livia. Although none of these rulers was as able as Augustus, they followed many of his policies.

Sec. Rev. ques. 3

During the rule of Augustus's stepson, Tiberius (A.D. 14–37), plots and violence again became common in Roman politics. Tiberius ran the Empire well, however. The next emperor, Caligula (kah-LIG-yoo-lah), was incompetent and cruel. To show his contempt for the Senate, he appointed his horse consul. After four years Caligula was assassinated by members of the royal guard. These soldiers then chose a scholar named Claudius to be emperor. Claudius restored order during his reign (A.D. 41–54) and sponsored a military expedition that made Britain part of the Empire.

The last of Augustus's family to rule was the emperor Nero, Claudius's stepson. Nero began his reign well but soon turned to bloodthirsty violence. He was suspected of starting the fire that destroyed Rome in A.D. 64. Four years later the army rebelled against him, and Nero committed suicide.

Military emperors. In the year following Nero's death, lawlessness swept Rome as military commanders battled for the throne. After the assassination of two emperors and the suicide of another within a year, the army chose Vespasian (ves-PAY-zhun) as emperor. During his 10-year reign (A.D. 69–79), Vespasian restored discipline in the army

★ ENRICHMENT. Have students develop a hypothesis explaining why Rome's transition from republic to empire was acceptable to most Romans. (Synthesis) Forming a Hypothesis

Biography Caligula, whose real name was Gaius, was raised among the soldiers of his father's command. Caligula's mother dressed him in the uniform of a Roman legionnaire when he was a child; he was nicknamed "Caligula" or "little boots" by the soldiers.
Biography Claudius suffered from a physical handicap that affected his ability to walk, and he had a speech defect that caused him to stutter. He was one of the few Romans who could read the language of the Etruscans (p. 97).

Trade in the Roman Empire, A.D. 117

People in the Empire traded widely with one another and with other lands. Which country grew grain for Rome's bakeries? Where were the mines that supplied Rome with metals? What products came from North Africa? From Asia?

Map Answers: (1) Egypt. (2) Britain, Spain. (3) Grain, gold, ivory, wild animals. (4) Cotton, medicines, pearls and jewelry, perfume, silks and other textiles, spices, leather, timber, olive oil, carpets.

and in the administration of the Empire. He also put down uprisings in the provinces of Gaul and Judaea (joo-DEE-uh).

Judaea (now southern Israel and southwestern Jordan) was home to many Jews who wanted to re-establish their ancient kingdom. In A.D. 66, they had begun a revolt against Rome. Though Roman soldiers captured Jerusalem in A.D. 70, about 1,000 Jews escaped to the mountaintop fortress of Masada (muh-SAH-duh). For nearly two years they resisted the Roman siege. The fortress finally fell to the Romans in A.D. 73. Rather than surrender to their enemies, the defenders of Masada burned their possessions, and then nearly all committed suicide.

The "Good Emperors." Between A.D. 79 and 98, three more emperors followed Vespasian. Two were his sons, and the third, Nerva, was chosen by the Senate. Nerva took a new approach to naming a successor. He adopted as his son a man of proven ability—Trajan (TRAY-jun), the Spanish-born military governor of the region north of Italy. This way of choosing the new ruler—the adoptive system—was followed by later emperors until A.D. 180. It provided a series of competent rulers who are sometimes called the "Good Emperors."

The Roman Empire reached its greatest size under Trajan, who ruled from A.D. 98 to 117. He conquered Mesopotamia and lands

Sec. Rev. ques. 3, cont.

Sec. Rev. ques. 4

107

Background Note that Trajan was the first Roman emperor born outside of Italy.

Politics The revolt was caused by Hadrian's decision to build a temple to the Roman god Jupiter on the site of the Jewish Temple in Jerusalem.

Critical Thinking. Ask: Why do you think Roman citizenship was a source of pride? (Answers will vary.)

north of the Danube (DAN-yoob) River and east of the Black Sea. A wise and popular ruler, Trajan also lowered taxes in the provinces, gave aid to the poor, and had many buildings constructed in Rome.

Trajan's successor, Hadrian (HAY-dree-un), devoted his reign (A.D. 117–138) to protecting the Empire rather than expanding it. He encouraged people in the provinces to join the armies that guarded their borders. In the province of Britain, he had a wall built along the northern frontier. Parts of Hadrian's Wall, which stretched for 73 miles and rose 20 feet high, still stand today.

In A.D. 132–133, Hadrian defeated a second Jewish revolt in Judaea and harshly punished the rebels. The Romans renamed the province Syria Palestina (or Palestine), and encouraged non-Jews to settle there. Jews were allowed to enter Jerusalem only once a year. Most of the Jews who survived fled to other lands or were sold into slavery.

The last of the "Good Emperors" was Marcus Aurelius (aw-REE-lee-us). He was a scholarly man, influenced by the Stoics (page 92). He would have preferred a life devoted to his books, but he was forced to concentrate on border wars with Germanic peoples from the north. After Marcus Aurelius's death in A.D. 180, the adoptive system broke down and the Pax Romana ended.

Achievements of the Pax Romana

• Note strategies for second objective on this page.

The 200 years of the Pax Romana were the years of the Empire's greatest glory. Roman armies extended the borders of the Empire in Asia Minor, secured the frontiers in Europe at the Rhine and Danube rivers, and conquered most of Britain. These troops guarded against civil wars within the cities and prevented warfare between cities. This extended period of peace made possible several improvements in people's lives.

Sec. Rev. ques. 5

1. Order. The Pax Romana was generally a time of order and good government. The Romans demonstrated a great talent for organizing and ruling. Roman governors, assisted by capable officials, enforced the law

108

and settled disputes in the provinces. At first, almost all government officials were upper-class Romans, but in time many talented people in the provinces became administrators.

2. Prosperity. Roman rule brought prosperity as well as peace. The Romans built roads, improved harbors, cleared forests, drained swamps, irrigated deserts, and turned undeveloped land into thriving farms. Hundreds of new cities were built in the Empire, and old cities grew larger and wealthier. Trade flourished, too. Products from all over the Empire flowed into Rome over roads built by Roman engineers and protected by Roman soldiers. Rome also imported goods from foreign lands as far away as China.

SILK ROAD

3. Unity. From Britain to Arabia and from the Danube River to the North African desert, some 70 million people, speaking different languages and following different customs, were united under Roman rule and Roman law. Citizenship was granted generously, and by A.D. 212 almost all free people in the Empire became Roman citizens. Peoples from different lands learned to speak Latin. They used one system of weights and measures, obeyed one set of laws, and served one emperor. People throughout the Empire were proud to say, *"Civis Romanus sum"*— "I am a citizen of Rome."

See Sec. 2 *Closing the Lesson,* p. T95B.

Section Review

Answers to Section Review questions are in brackets on pages indicated.

1. **Define or identify:** Pax Romana, law of succession. (p. 106)
2. How did Augustus restore order in the Empire? (p. 105)
3. By what different methods were emperors selected during the Pax Romana? (p. 106)
4. Who were the "Good Emperors"? (p. 107)
5. What benefits did Roman rule bring to the people of the Empire? (p. 108)
6. **Critical thinking:** Which groups of people within the Empire might have preferred not to be citizens of Rome? Explain. (See answer below.)

• **RETEACHING.** Have students review "Achievements of the Pax Romana," list three characteristics of that period, and cite two examples of each. *(Comprehension) Observing for Detail*

• **REINFORCEMENT.** Have students write an essay supporting this statement: *Much progress is possible during peaceful times.* Students should cite examples from the Pax Romana period. *(Comprehension) Supporting Generalizations*

6. Answers will vary. Any of the peoples conquered by Rome might have preferred to remain independent, especially people whose political or religious beliefs conflicted with those of the Romans.

• **ENRICHMENT.** Have students work in groups to prepare a dialogue that might have occurred between one of the emperor's officials and a representative of a region dominated by Rome. *(Synthesis) Understanding Point of View*

3 Roman Society and Culture

Objectives

Focus Questions

★ ■ What was Roman society like? *(pages 109–112)*

● ■ How did the Romans blend Greek culture with their own? *(pages 112–115)*

Terms to Know

Circus Maximus   Greco-Roman culture
Colosseum   aqueduct
gladiator   Law of Nations
oratory

★ Note strategies for first objective on this page and p. 110.

Through its conquests, Rome remade the Mediterranean world. Yet Rome itself was transformed as well. Its growth from a small town to an imperial capital produced great wealth and cultural achievement.

Class Divisions

There were great contrasts between rich and poor in Rome and, to a lesser extent, in the provinces. The class divisions between Romans were based mainly on wealth.

The well-to-do. Prominent among upper-class Romans were wealthy landowners. Merchants, doctors, lawyers, and government officials were also members of the upper class, as were some scholars, writers, and artists. The most distinguished Romans came from old senatorial families. They had wealth, social position, and power.

Wealthy Romans lived in luxurious town houses or large country houses with swimming pools and courtyards. They dressed in fine silk and wore gold and jewels. At a traditional Roman banquet, guests lounged on couches while slaves waited on them and dancers, acrobats, and musicians provided entertainment. Roman nobles dined far into the night on such unusual dishes as

Sec. Rev. ques. 2

Roman houses were designed to be open and cool in the warm Mediterranean climate. Bedrooms, the dining room (triclinium), and reception-room (tablinium) surrounded the central courtyard (atrium). A hole in the roof (compluvium) let in light and air, as well as rain, which was stored in the pool below.

| 1 atrium |
| 2 tablinium |
| 3 triclinium |
| 4 compluvium |
| 5 kitchen |

109

★ **RETEACHING.** Have students review "Class Divisions" (pp. 109–110) and list four social classes in Roman society and their distinguishing characteristics. (Wealthy: landowners, merchants, and professionals. Poor: little political power or economic security; depended on free food given by government. Farmers: majority of population. Slaves: harsh and brutal lives; freed slaves became citizens.) *(Comprehension)* **Observing for Detail**

★ **REINFORCEMENT.** Have students review "Family Life" (pp. 110–111) and find information that supports the following statement: *During the time of the Roman Empire, family life changed and religious tradition declined in importance.* (Family Life: parents became overindulgent; women gained freedom; boys were educated at school rather than at home. Religious belief: many Romans were dissatisfied with their traditional religion and turned to new beliefs.) *(Comprehension)* **Supporting Generalizations**

This Roman mosaic shows lightly armed gladiators in deadly combat with wild animals. Thousands died in such spectacles.

Popular Entertainment

The Roman people, both rich and poor, loved violent sports and games. Roman politicians paid for such spectacles to win the voters' approval and to pacify the unemployed. They built huge amphitheaters—outdoor arenas— to house these events. The **Circus Maximus**, Rome's oldest arena, could seat more than 300,000 people. The smaller **Colosseum**, which held about 50,000, was sometimes flooded for mock naval battles.

The most popular form of entertainment was chariot racing. The drivers in chariot races might be trained slaves or daring Roman nobles. Many people came to see their favorite teams compete.

Roman crowds also loved contests between **gladiators**. These were fighters—usually slaves or condemned criminals—armed with swords or spears. If no one was killed in the fight, the crowd might choose either death or freedom for the loser. Even more brutal were the contests with animals. Tigers fought elephants, or people were sent into the arena with lions or wild bulls. In one such spectacle, 5,000 wild animals were killed. Much of Rome's trade with Africa was devoted to buying animals for these shows.

★ See below.

boiled ostrich, roast parrot, flamingo boiled with dates, and larks' tongues.

The poor. The poor people in the cities and the countryside had little share in politics and little economic security. Since slaves did so much of the work, many Romans had no jobs. Public building projects provided some jobs for the poor, but probably half of Rome's one million people depended on free food given them by the government.

Farmers. Rome depended heavily on agriculture. Farmers made up the majority of the Empire's population. They worked long hours to provide cheap food for the people in the cities.

Slaves. Slavery was common in Rome. In the early days of the Republic, most slaves were Italian farmers who had lost their freedom because they could not pay their debts. Once Rome began to expand, the number of foreign slaves increased enormously. By the time of Augustus, slaves may have accounted for one quarter of Italy's population.

Life was harsh and brutal for most slaves. They spent their lives rowing the ships of the Roman navy, working on farming estates, or cutting stone in the quarries. Household slaves, however, and those who worked as artisans usually received better treatment.

Several emperors passed laws protecting slaves from cruel masters. In time Roman law provided for the freeing of slaves under certain conditions. Freed slaves became citizens with most of the rights and privileges of other Roman citizens.

Family Life

In the early days of the Republic the male head of the family had complete authority over every person in his household. By the second century A.D., however, family discipline was much less harsh. Some parents became overly permissive with their children. Old-fashioned Romans complained that children were spoiled and poorly disciplined.

Women. The change in family authority brought Roman women more freedom. Formerly, fathers had often arranged for their daughters to marry by the age of 12 or 13. A Roman woman thus went from obeying her father's commands to obeying her husband's. By the time of the Empire, however, a father could no longer force his daughter to marry

110

against her will. A woman could own property and keep her own money or property if divorced. She could also make business arrangements and write a will without her husband's approval.

Roman women enjoyed greater freedom and respect than did upper-class women in Greece. Girls from noble Roman families had opportunities for education that were denied to the daughters of Greek nobles. Some women of prominent senatorial families acquired great political influence. Livia, the dynamic wife of the emperor Augustus, often advised him on decisions. She continued to influence policy during the reign of her son Tiberius. Still, no Roman woman could hold public office or vote.

Education. Many of the important Roman values and attitudes were learned at home. That was where girls might be taught Greek and Latin literature as well as skills in music and dance. A formal system of schooling for Roman boys developed, however, during the Republic. Young boys were taught reading, writing, and arithmetic by special teachers. Older boys studied music, geometry, astronomy, literature, and oratory—public speaking. As in Greece, public speaking and debating were essential skills in Roman political life.

The 50,000-seat Colosseum in Rome was built by prisoners from the Jewish wars. At the opening performance in A.D. 80 the arena was flooded and a complete naval battle with over 3,000 participants was reenacted.

111

Religion

The Roman gods. The Romans, like the Greeks, traditionally worshiped many gods and goddesses. Like the Chinese, they also practiced a form of ancestor worship. In each Roman house was a shrine to Vesta, the goddess of the hearth and the keeper of fire. The family made daily offerings to Vesta, calling on her to protect their homes and guard the spirits of their ancestors.

Besides Vesta, the most important gods were Jupiter, the god of the sky, and Mars, the god of war. As they came into contact with other cultures, the Romans accepted new gods. From other Italian peoples, for example, they adopted the worship of Diana, the goddess of the moon. As they became more familiar with the culture of Greece, educated Romans began to identify their gods with those of the Greeks (page 74). They identified Jupiter with Zeus, Mars with Ares, and Juno with Hera. The Romans also borrowed much of Greek mythology and many entirely new gods from the Greeks.

Beliefs and practices. Morality was not a central concern of Roman religion. The Romans did not think that what they believed or how they behaved toward others was of interest to the gods. They believed that the gods' only demand was to be properly respected. Accordingly, they performed complex ceremonies to earn the gods' favor.

The Romans often viewed changes in nature as signs from the gods. To determine the gods' will, priests carefully studied the flights of birds, the sound of thunder, and the livers of sacrificed animals. No general would begin a battle, nor would any bride marry, unless the signs showed the gods' approval.

The decline of religion. By the time of the Empire, many Romans felt dissatisfied with their traditional religion. It offered no moral code, no emotional warmth, and no promise of an afterlife. As you will read in Chapter 6, they turned to new beliefs that were spreading gradually to Rome from different parts of the Empire.

Sec. Rev. ques. 3

112

Greek Influence on Roman Culture

● Note strategies for second objective on this page and p. 114.

From the Greek cities in southern Italy and Sicily, the Roman Republic had borrowed some elements of Greek civilization. After the Romans conquered the eastern Mediterranean in the second century B.C., they adopted even more from the Greeks. Roman generals shipped libraries and works of art from Greek cities to Rome. Greek teachers, poets, and philosophers came to work in Roman households. Some Romans even sent their sons to Athens to study. Greek and Roman influences blended together, producing what is now called Greco-Roman culture.

Roman intellectuals preserved and spread the Greeks' devotion to excellence and their use of reason. The Romans, however, added their own practical strengths—organizational ability, skill in engineering, and a talent for government and law. Greco-Roman culture spread throughout the Empire during the Pax Romana, and people in the Roman cities enjoyed its benefits.

Sec. Rev. ques. 4

Literature

The time of the emperor Augustus was a golden age in Greco-Roman literature. At Augustus's request, the poet Virgil (70–19 B.C.) wrote the *Aeneid* (ih-NEE-id), an epic poem praising the Roman talent for governing. Like Homer's *Iliad* and *Odyssey* (page 75), the *Aeneid* is a masterpiece. It tells the legend of Aeneas, whose descendants were said to have founded Rome.

The historian Livy (59 B.C.–A.D. 17) also wrote about Aeneas. Livy's classic work, *History of Rome*, described key figures from Rome's past in an uncritical, colorful style.

Another great writer of Augustus's time was the poet Horace (65–8 B.C.). The son of a freed slave, Horace became a friend of Virgil and Augustus. Like them, he had grown up under the Republic and remembered its civil wars. Horace wrote that human greed had caused these conflicts, and he criticized the

Religion Birdwatching became an important way of trying to interpret signs from the gods. During the first Punic War, the commander of the Roman fleet, Pulcher, took a flock of chickens to sea with him, hoping to read good or bad omens from the way the chickens pecked at their food. Annoyed when the chickens refused to eat, Pulcher threw them overboard exclaiming, "Then drink if you won't eat." The Romans attributed Pulcher's personal defeat by the Carthaginians to his irreligious behavior and fined him.

● **RETEACHING. Have students write one-sentence identifications for each of the following: Greco-Roman** (Greek and Roman influences blended together) **Aeneid** (An epic written by Virgil that tells the legend of Rome's founders) **aqueducts** (Channels for carrying water to distant places) **Ptolemy** (Mathematician, geographer, and astronomer who worked in Alexandria) **Cicero** (Roman writer and orator). *(Comprehension)* **Developing Vocabulary**

(F) See below.

Daily Life

Life in Pompeii

On a hot August day in A.D. 79, the volcano Vesuvius in southwestern Italy erupted with little warning. Deadly fumes and tons of poisonous ash filled the air, quickly burying the prosperous town of Pompeii (pom-PAY). Its 20,000 terrified inhabitants fled with whatever belongings they could carry. About 2,000 of them died with their city.

Time stopped for Pompeii. For nearly 1,700 years it lay under 12 feet of hardened ash and mud. When archeologists began to explore Pompeii in the mid-1700's, they found perfectly preserved scenes of first-century Roman life. Loaves of bread sat on the shelves of a bakery; cups lay on tables in an inn. Signs on walls identified shops or advertised rooms for rent.

Pompeii offered many amusements—three public baths, two theaters, and an amphitheater big enough to hold all the people of the city. Aristocrats and wealthy merchants lived in large homes, their walls colorfully painted with landscapes, scenes from myth, and designs of animals, fruits, and flowers. Their libraries held hundreds of books and scrolls. Statues and fountains graced their gardens. Archeologists could only wonder at the private life of Pompeii—tragically stopped in a few hours of terror.

113

(F) FEATURE ACTIVITY. Ask: (a) Why might the exploration of Pompeii have been viewed as a significant archeological event? (Answers will vary. The town of Pompeii was well-preserved and offered many artifacts of ancient Roman life.) (b) If you could question a citizen of ancient Pompeii about the destruction of the city, what would you ask? (Answers will vary.) (Synthesis) *Drawing Conclusions* luxurious lives of many wealthy Romans. It would be better, he said, if Romans followed the Greek ideal of moderation.

While Virgil and Horace celebrated the simple life of the countryside, the poet Ovid (AH-vid) spoke for the upper-class people of the Empire's cities. Ovid lived from 43 B.C. to A.D. 18. He wrote of wealth, fashion, romance, and other pleasures. He also retold Greek and Roman myths in his own verses.

Art and Architecture

Along with literature, art and architecture flowered during the Empire. Roman artisans used bronze and precious stones to craft jewelry and decorative objects. Roman sculptors tried to show the unique qualities of an individual. Unlike Greek artists, who had presented perfect human beauty, the Romans carved every detail—even wrinkles and tan-

Multilayered Roman roads were built to last. Some are even still in use. Ditches and sloping sides provided efficient drainage. Roads (such as the one pictured here) helped expand Rome's commerce and military influence throughout the Mediterranean world.

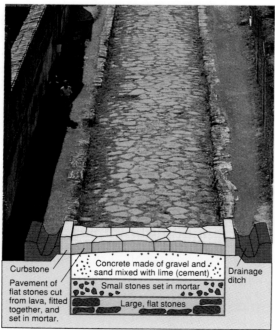

Curbstone

Pavement of flat stones cut from lava, fitted together, and set in mortar.

Concrete made of gravel and sand mixed with lime (cement)

Small stones set in mortar

Large, flat stones

Drainage ditch

114

gled hair—realistically. Another popular form of art in Rome was the wall painting. Wealthy Romans decorated the walls of their homes with richly colored portraits, ocean views, or scenes from mythology.

Roman architects were skilled engineers. They designed amphitheaters, public baths, and temples with graceful columns, arches, and domes. They also excelled at building roads, bridges, and **aqueducts** (AK-wih-dukts)—channels and bridgelike structures that carried water to distant places. The remains of many such structures can be seen today in the lands once ruled by the Empire. Some are still in use.

● See below.

Science

The two most important scientists of the Greco-Roman age were Ptolemy (TAHL-uh-mee) and Galen (GAY-lun). Both lived during the second century A.D. Ptolemy was a mathematician, geographer, and astronomer who worked in Alexandria, Egypt, about A.D. 150. His 13-volume *Almagest* (a Greek-Arabic word meaning "the greatest") summarized the ancient world's knowledge of astronomy and geography. Ptolemy believed that the earth stood in the center of the universe while the sun, moon, and planets moved about it in circles or combinations of circles. Although Ptolemy's idea turned out to be wrong, it seemed to account for most of the changes that could be seen in the skies. It was accepted until the sixteenth century.

Galen was a Greek, but his theories dominated Roman medicine. To study the workings of the body, Galen dissected animals. Although Galen's work contained many errors, it was the basis of Western medical knowledge for centuries.

Roman Law

A system of law and justice was perhaps Rome's greatest contribution to Western civilization. The law codes of present-day Italy, Spain, France, and Latin America are based

● REINFORCEMENT. Ask: (a) What Greek and Roman influences blended to form Greco-Roman culture? (Greek devotion to excellence and use of reason and Roman organizational ability, engineering skill, and talent for government and law.) (b) What Greek ideal did the poet Horace admire? (Moderation) (Comprehension) Observing for Detail

● ENRICHMENT. Have students work in groups to compare the art and architecture of the Greeks and Romans. Students might research how differences in Greek and Roman society and culture influenced their contributions to the arts, and then give illustrations of Greek and Roman art, architecture, and literature. (Synthesis) Relating History and Art

Sec. Rev.
ques. 5

on Roman law. The Romans believed that law should be based on principles of reason and justice and should protect citizens and their property.

The Roman writer and orator Cicero (SIS-uh-roh), who lived from 106 to 43 B.C., said that the law should not be "bent by influence or broken by power or spoiled by money." Cicero thought obedience to law was one of the requirements of civilized life. "We are servants of the law in order that we may be free," he said.

One branch of Roman law, called the **Law of Nations,** was applied to citizens in all provinces of the Empire. Under this law a citizen was not a Briton, a Spaniard, an Italian, or a Greek, but a Roman. The idea that law could be based on fair and logical principles and could apply to all peoples regardless of their nationality was a major contribution to civilization.

See Sec. 3 *Closing the Lesson,*
p. T95C.

6. Answers will vary. Cicero might have meant that, when observed consistently and applied equally among citizens, the law acted as a stabilizing influence on society and allowed people to have more freedom of action.

Chapter 5   Summary and Timeline

1. Ruled at first by Etruscan kings, the Romans in 509 B.C. set up a republic. The Roman Republic became a great military power, conquering the entire Mediterranean world. Social and political conflict eventually brought the Republic to an end. In 27 B.C. Octavian, later called Augustus, became the first Roman emperor.

2. Augustus's rule marked the beginning of the Pax Romana. For 200 years the Roman Empire brought order, prosperity, and unity to its many people.

3. Class divisions among the people of the Empire were based mainly on wealth. The Roman conquest of Greece led to widespread Greek influence in Roman culture. The result was a Greco-Roman culture that combined the achievements of both peoples.

700 B.C. Latins settle Rome	**509 B.C.** Roman Republic established	**451 B.C.** Laws written down in Twelve Tables	**264 B.C.** Punic Wars begin	**146 B.C.** Rome destroys Carthage	**44 B.C.** Caesar assassinated / **31 B.C.** Roman Empire established	**A.D. 180** Pax Romana ends	
750 B.C.	600	450	300	150	B.C. A.D.	150	A.D. 300

See p. T95C for answers to Chapter Review.

Vocabulary Review

1. Match each of the following terms with its correct definition: *aqueduct, dictator, gladiators, law of succession, Pax Romana, Punic Wars, republic, veto.*
   a. government in which supreme power rests with citizens, who elect their leaders
   b. ruler with absolute power
   c. structure for carrying water to distant places
   d. rule that states how a leader is to be chosen
   e. reject
   f. 200-year period of peace and prosperity in the Roman Empire
   g. slaves or condemned criminals who fought as entertainment for Romans
   h. wars between Rome and Carthage
2. Define the terms in the following pairs.
   a. patricians; plebeians
   b. Law of Nations; Twelve Tables
   c. First Triumvirate; Second Triumvirate
   d. Circus Maximus; Colosseum

People to Identify

Identify the following people and tell why each was important.
1. Augustus
2. Galen
3. Hadrian
4. Hannibal
5. Julius Caesar
6. Livy
7. Marcus Aurelius
8. Ptolemy
9. Spartacus
10. Trajan
11. Virgil

Places to Know

Match the letters on this map with the places listed below. You may want to refer to the maps on pages 98 and 102.
1. Alps
2. Carthage
3. Gaul
4. Greece
5. Mediterranean Sea
6. Rome
7. Sicily
8. Tiber River

Recalling the Facts

1. What factors helped Rome expand in the 300's and 200's B.C.?
2. What problems did Romans face at home while they were conquering other lands? How did these problems lead to the rise of military dictators?
3. What major changes did Augustus make?
4. How did the people of the Empire benefit from the Pax Romana?
5. What were class divisions based on in the Roman Empire?
6. What rights did Roman women have?
7. What Greek ideals did the Romans value? What skills did the Romans add to those ideals to form the basis for Greco-Roman culture?

1. **Sequencing.** On a separate sheet of paper, list the following events in chronological order, giving the date for each entry. *(Comp.)*
   a. Pax Romana ends.
   b. Punic Wars begin.
   c. Roman Republic founded.
   d. Roman Empire begins.
   e. First of the "Good Emperors" comes to power.
   f. Augustus dies.
   g. Rome destroys Carthage.

2. **Writing a summary.** A summary is a restatement in brief form of the main ideas of a speech or a piece of writing. Reread pages 99–101 and write a one-page summary of the events of the Punic Wars. *(Comp.)*

✔ 3. **Exploring the arts.** With some classmates, choose one or two scenes from William Shakespeare's play *Julius Caesar* to perform for your class. Before your presentation, explain what the scenes are about and why they are important to the history that you have studied in this chapter. *(Syn.)*

4. **Supporting generalizations.** Generalizations are conclusions that are based on facts. Find the facts in Section 1 of this chapter that support these generalizations: (a) "Between 451 B.C. and 287 B.C. the plebeians' position improved." (b) "The strength of the Roman army lay in its superior discipline and efficient organization." *(Comp.)*

Thinking About Geography

1. **Relating geography and history.** Geography and the ability to adapt to it played a big role in Hannibal's military successes and failures. Use the library to research and describe some of these geographic factors and how they affected Hannibal and his troops. *(App.)*

2. **Researching.** When the Senate ordered Caesar to return to Rome, he ignored the order. Instead of giving up his power, Caesar led his troops into Italy. Research this event to explain the background and modern meaning of the phrase "cross the Rubicon." *(App.)*

Enrichment: Primary Sources

During the early Republic, Roman officials began to publish lists of laws they planned to enforce. From these simple beginnings Roman law evolved into a set of legal principles that applied to peoples throughout the Empire. Some of these principles are quoted below.

❝ In the case of major offenses, it makes a difference whether something is committed purposely or accidentally.

In setting penalties, the age and inexperience of the guilty party must be taken into account.

The principles of law are these: to live uprightly, not to injure another man, to give every man his due.

No one is compelled to defend a cause against his will.

No one suffers a penalty for what he thinks.

The burden of proof is upon the party accusing, not on the party denying.

The credibility of witnesses should be carefully weighed in judging their testimony. One should take into account whether a witness is honorable or is branded with public disgrace. ❞

1. What factors were considered in determining guilt and in sentencing people?
2. Which of these principles protected the liberties of individuals?
3. How did the law protect persons accused of crimes?
4. **Critical thinking:** The Constitution of the United States guarantees citizens freedom of speech. Do any of these Roman legal principles indicate that the citizens of Rome enjoyed this freedom? Explain your answer. *(Anal.)* ✔

✔ A checkmark identifies questions and exercises calling for the three higher-order levels of thinking at the top of the Bloom taxonomy: Analysis, Synthesis, and Evaluation.

The Legacy of Rome   509 B.C.–A.D. 476
(pp. 118–131)

Chapter Preview

Section 1 examines the crises that weakened the Roman Empire in the third century. Efforts by Diocletian and Constantine to halt the Empire's decline are described, along with the fourth-century Germanic invasions that ended the Roman Empire in the West. Section 2 describes the life and teachings of Jesus and traces the spread of Christianity through the efforts of Paul and other missionaries.

Bibliography

See the *Teacher's Management and Planning Guide* for additional listings. Starred titles are for both students and teachers.

Cochrane, C. M. *Christianity and Classical Culture.* Oxford University Press. Early Christianity's place in Roman society.

Fox, Robin L. *Pagans and Christians.* Knopf. The formative years of Christianity from the second to the fourth centuries.

Gibbon, Edward. *The Decline and Fall of the Roman Empire.* Penguin. Abridgement.

*Payne, Robert. *The Horizon Book of Ancient Rome.* American Heritage.

Section Lesson Plans

SECTION 1   (pp. 119–124)
The Fall of the Empire

Objectives

After completing this section, students will be able to:
1. Explain what steps the government took to save the Empire.
2. Describe how barbarian invasions and internal problems led to Rome's fall.

Introducing the Lesson

Remind students that the strengths of the Roman Empire included efficient government, a disciplined and loyal army, strong and able leadership, a well-developed road system, thriving trade, and expanded citizenship.

Then ask: *(a) What factors might contribute to the disintegration of an empire as successful as Rome's?* (Answers will vary. An empire as large as Rome's might be challenged by groups within. The expense of maintaining a large empire might grow unmanageable. Factors outside the control of government—disease, poor crops, invasions—might weaken an empire.)

(b) Does the history of other civilizations already studied (Sumerian, Egyptian, Harappan, Greek) suggest a pattern of rise and decline? (Answers will vary. All appear to have experienced periods of slow development, great achievement, and then gradual decline. Sometimes the decline resulted from civil unrest or foreign threats.)

(c) If you were an adviser to a present-day leader of a powerful nation, how would you maintain the strength and endurance of your nation? (Answers will vary.)

Developing the Lesson: Making Decisions

Have students work in groups to dramatize a policy-making session that might have occurred during the rule of Diocletian. Students should represent leading Roman farmers, townspeople, artisans, merchants, and government officials who meet to discuss the problems facing the Empire and formulate policies to save it. Have students present their policies to the class as they might have presented them to Emperor Diocletian. (Students should base their discussions on information in the text and should be encouraged to develop original approaches to Rome's problems.) *(Synthesis)*

Developing the Lesson: Observing for Detail

Ask: *(a) Which crisis posed the most serious threat to Rome's empire? Why?* (Answers will vary.)

(b) Why was the Roman army no longer the disciplined, loyal force it had once been? (Fewer citizens volunteered for military service; the government recruited soldiers who cared little about Roman ideals.)

(c) How might the emperor have solved the crisis with the army? (Answers will vary.)

(d) How did policies designed to control Rome's declining economy weaken the Empire? (Trade and use of Roman money declined; taxes were raised, goods were seized, people were forced to work for the state, food was scarce—these factors increased bitterness toward the government.) *(Comprehension)*

Answers to *Map Skill Practice*, p. 121.

1. Adrianople.
2. Rome, Constantinople. Approximately 1,250 miles.
3. From the east.
4. Rhine, Danube.
5. Franks, Vandals, Burgundians, Lombards, Ostrogoths, Visigoths, Huns.
6. The Huns so terrified the Visigoths that they asked the Roman Empire for refuge, which was granted. The Visigoths then turned against the Romans and Roman border defenses collapsed. Germanic tribes began pouring into the Empire.

Closing the Lesson: Evaluating History

Have students write a letter that a Roman historian during the rule of Diocletian might have written to present-day national leaders. Letters should include the Roman historian's opinion about the Empire's crises and advice to future leaders about their governments. (Answers will vary.) *(Synthesis)*

See *Section Review* questions, p. 124.

SECTION 2   (pp. 125–129)
The Spread of Christianity

Objectives

After completing this section, students will be able to:
1. Describe how the Christian faith arose.
2. Explain how Christianity spread through the Roman Empire.

Introducing the Lesson

Tell students that Jesus began to preach his message during the early days of Roman decline. Roman officials saw the growing strength of Christianity as a threat and began to persecute the religion's followers.

Then ask: *(a) Why might the religious beliefs of citizens be a matter of concern to government officials?* (Religious beliefs affect people's attitudes and behavior as citizens. In some governments, officials may see religion as a threat to political and social order.)

(b) How might religious beliefs conflict with the interests of the state? (Answers will vary. Military policy, social legislation, or educational standards may at times be inconsistent with the religious beliefs of some groups.)

(c) How are conflicts between religious beliefs and government interests dealt with in today's world? (Answers will vary. Some governments—such as those in Communist nations—restrict the expression of religion. Governments may restrict or outlaw certain religious practices, for example, polygamy. Note that the First Amendment to the United States Constitution guarantees freedom of religion and forbids the establishment of a state religion.)

Developing the Lesson: Relating Geography and History

Have students compare the map "Journeys of Paul, A.D. 45–65" (p. 128) with the world map in the Atlas at the back of the book to determine what present-day nations exist in the lands through which Paul traveled. (Present-day nations include Italy, Greece, Turkey, Syria, Lebanon, Israel.) *(Application)*

Developing the Lesson: Organizing Information

Have students make a chart tracing the development of the Christian religion and the response of the Roman Empire. Charts should include information from the time of Jesus to the establishment of Christianity as the state religion. (Jesus preaches and gains a following, is rejected by Jewish and Roman leaders, and is crucified. Belief in Jesus' teachings grows and Christianity becomes a separate religion. Paul journeys throughout the Roman Empire and establishes Christian communities. Roman authorities, at first tolerant, increasingly see the religion as a threat, and persecution begins during the rule of Nero. Acceptance of Christianity grows and persecution ends as invasions increase. Constantine converts; Christianity becomes the official religion of the Roman Empire.) *(Comprehension)*

Closing the Lesson: Comparing History

Have students compare the ancient Roman religion (p. 112) with the principles of Christianity. (*Roman religion:* gods not interested in human behavior, only in proper respect; complex ceremonies; changes in nature were signs from the gods; no moral code; no emotional warmth; no promise of afterlife. *Christianity:* emphasized love, compassion, and a personal relationship with God; Christians believe that Jesus is the Son of God and that he rose from the dead and ascended to heaven.) *(Comprehension)*

See *Section Review* questions, p. 129.

Chapter 6 Review Answers (pp. 130–131)

Vocabulary Review

1. Christianity 2. Messiah 3. martyr 4. spoils 5. Gospels 6. persecutions 7. disciples

People to Identify

1. Diocletian 2. Pontius Pilate 3. Constantine 4. Paul 5. Attila 6. Augustine 7. Nero

Places to Know

1. C 2. E 3. D 4. B 5. A

Recalling the Facts

1. They forced farmers, government workers, and artisans to keep their jobs for life and they raised taxes to support the army, the royal court, and government officials. Citizens lost many liberties; many were ruined financially, and their loss of faith in the economy led to further decline.
2. To make it easier to govern. The Western Empire was further weakened, since it could no longer depend on financial and military help from the wealthier eastern regions.
3. Visigoths, Huns, Vandals.
4. Germanic soldiers overthrew the Western Roman emperor and declared a German, Odoacer, king of Italy.
5. Weakened army, smaller population, oppressive government, declining farms and cities, stagnant economy, and loss of confidence in the Empire.
6. He traveled as a missionary throughout the Roman Empire and set up Christian communities.
7. The peace and unity of the Pax Romana made it easier for Christian missionaries to spread their message throughout the Empire.
8. They viewed Christianity as a threat to the government because Christians refused to worship the emperor as a god. More Romans converted in the third century, the emperor Constantine became a strong supporter of the Church, and after Theodosius outlawed worship of the old gods in 380, Christianity became the official religion.

Critical Thinking Skills

1–5. Answers will vary.

Thinking About Geography

1. *Western Roman Empire*—England, Portugal, Spain, France, Italy, Switzerland, Austria, Luxembourg, Belgium, the Netherlands, West Germany, Hungary, Yugoslavia, Libya, Tunisia, Algeria, Morocco; *Eastern Roman Empire*—Greece, Cyprus, Albania, Yugoslavia, Bulgaria, Rumania, Turkey, Syria, Israel, Lebanon, Jordan, Saudi Arabia, Egypt, Libya.

2. Vienna, Austria—*Vindobona* was an important Roman center on the Danube River; Cologne, Germany—the emperor Claudius founded *Colonia Agrippina,* named after his wife, in A.D. 50; London, England—Roman life in Britain was centered on the fort of *Londinium.*

Enrichment: Primary Sources

1. The spear. Because it was sharp and easy to handle.
2. The infantry.
3. Answers will vary.

The Legacy of Rome

509 B.C.–A.D. 476

See chapter timeline, p. 129.

Before You Read This Chapter

What do you think are the most serious problems facing the United States today? Military threats from other countries? Economic troubles? Crime or drug abuse? This chapter describes some of the problems that beset the Roman Empire after A.D. 180. As you read, think back to the strengths that helped Rome build its vast Empire. What changes weakened Rome? How did the Romans try to solve their problems? Which of these solutions worked well for a time, and which did not work at all?

The Geographic Setting

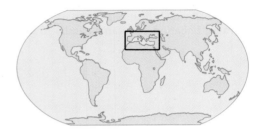

The Chapter Outline

1. The Fall of the Empire
2. The Spread of Christianity

Roman aqueducts still stand as reminders of the Empire's technological achievements. This massive bridge carried water to a colony in France.

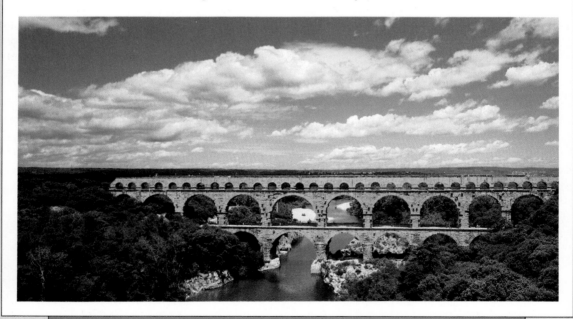

MULTIPLE CAUSATION

1 The Fall of the Empire

Objectives

Focus Questions

★ ■ What steps did the government take to save the Empire? *(pages 119–120)*

● ■ How did barbarian invasions and internal problems lead to Rome's fall? *(pages 120–124)*

Terms to Know

spoils
imperial

★ Note strategies for first objective on this page and p. 120.

The Pax Romana (page 106) had brought the ancient world 200 years of peace, rule by law, and civilized life. The Roman system of government had lasted during the reigns of both able and incompetent rulers. By late in the second century A.D., however, the Empire had begun to collapse.

Troubled Times

The third century A.D. found the Roman Empire facing crises without the strong leadership it needed to overcome them. The discipline and loyalty of the army had broken down. Men enlisted simply to gain weapons and **spoils**—goods taken in war. Soldiers were loyal to their commanders rather than to Rome, and military leaders fought one another for the throne. Between A.D. 235 and 285, twenty-six emperors held power. Some held the throne for less than a year, and all but one were assassinated.

Sec. Rev. ques. 2

Weakened defenses. Rome's worries over these internal rivalries blinded it to foreign threats. Troops needed for border defense were instead called back to Rome to fight for the ambitions of their leaders. Those who remained to guard the borders were unable to hold back invasions. Germanic tribes from northern Europe crossed the Roman frontier along the Rhine and Danube rivers. They invaded Greece, Italy, and Spain and raided coastal cities in Asia Minor, terrorizing the local people. At the same time, the Persians seized Roman lands in the Middle East. The Romans referred to all these peoples as barbarians because they spoke neither Greek nor Latin.

Internal problems. Signs of decay were everywhere. Plagues spread from town to town. Crimes went unpunished. Frequent wars drained the **imperial** treasury—the Empire's treasury. An attempt to save money by lowering the value of coins backfired: people lost confidence in Roman money and turned to barter. Deteriorating roads slowed travel, which slowed trade. During this period of disorder, revolts broke out in the provinces. These outbreaks of violence forced the government to maintain a large and costly army. To pay for the army, emperors raised taxes and seized goods from citizens. They even forced people to work for the state. Both peasants and townspeople became bitter and resentful.

Faced with all of these problems, the cities of the Mediterranean world—the centers of Greco-Roman civilization—began to decay. Food supplies were short and food prices high. Many city people fled to the countryside in search of food.

Diocletian and Constantine

In A.D. 284 the army made Diocletian (dy-uh-KLEE-shun) emperor. He and his successor Constantine (who reigned from 306 to 337) tried to save the Empire by imposing strong one-man rule. They made drastic

Sec. Rev. ques. 3

119

★ RETEACHING. Have students review "Troubled Times" (above) and outline the following problems faced by the Roman Empire in the third century A.D.: Leadership and military problems (No strong leaders; breakdown of army discipline and loyalty; rivalry among leadership.) Weakened defenses (Border troops recalled to Rome.) Internal problems (Plagues, crime, wars, and loss of confidence.) (Comprehension) Organizing Ideas in Written Form

★ REINFORCEMENT. Have students make a chart with three columns labeled *Problems, Solutions,* and *Long-term Effects.* Students should list the problems faced by Diocletian and Constantine, the efforts of the emperors to solve these problems, and the long-term effects of each policy. (Problems: food shortages; weakened army; government disorganization.) (Comprehension) *Understanding Cause and Effect*

Geography Note that Constantinople is the present-day city of Istanbul, Turkey.

The Roman emperor Constantine transformed Christianity from a persecuted minority sect to the Empire's official religion.

changes that took away more liberties from the people. These changes hurt farmers and townspeople alike.

To keep food supplies high, the imperial government ordered farmers to stay on their land. Government agents hunted down those who tried to leave their farms. Government workers and artisans also had to keep their jobs for life, and children were forced to follow their father's occupation.

To support the army, the royal court, and the officials of the imperial government, Diocletian raised taxes to a crippling level. If town officials could not collect all the money the state demanded, they had to pay the difference out of their own pockets. Many artisans and merchants, as well as city officials, were ruined financially. Those who still had some money never knew when tax collectors or army officers might simply seize their goods. The Romans' loss of faith in the economy caused a further decline in city life.

120

Division of the Empire

To make the Empire easier to govern, Diocletian appointed a loyal general as co-ruler in the western regions. In A.D. 285 he moved the imperial court to Asia Minor and ruled from there. Rome was no longer the center of the Empire. The split between the two parts of the Empire grew wider, and rival rulers fought for power. In 330 the emperor Constantine built a new imperial capital at Constantinople (kahn-stan-tuh-NOH-pul), overlooking the waterway where Europe and Asia meet (map, page 121). The division of the Empire soon became accepted fact.

Sec. Rev. ques. 2, cont.

The shift of power to the East had serious consequences. The Western Empire was already weak economically. Yet it had to pay for troops and border defenses to keep out invaders. With the split of the Empire, the West could no longer depend on financial and military help from the wealthier eastern regions.

Like the increase in government regulation, the division of the Empire restored order, but at a heavy cost. Rome's collapse had been delayed, not prevented.

★ See below, left.

Barbarian Invasions

● Note strategies for second objective on this page and p. 124.

The Germanic peoples who lived in the forests and marshes of northern Europe posed a continuing threat to the Romans. The warmer climate, rich farmlands, and plentiful resources of the Roman lands attracted the Germanic tribes. They settled along the Rhine and Danube rivers, and only the troops along the frontier kept them from crossing into Roman territory.

The Visigoths. About A.D. 370 the Danube plain was invaded by Huns, a fierce nomadic people from Central Asia. Terrified of the Huns, a Germanic tribe called Visigoths (meaning "West Goths") asked for refuge within the Roman Empire. In 376 the Roman emperor reluctantly allowed the Visigoths to cross the Danube River into what is now Rumania.

Cultural History Diocletian had observed that rulers who kept themselves secluded from their people seemed less vulnerable to insurrection. He therefore made fewer public appearances.
★ **ENRICHMENT.** Have students work in groups to debate this assertion: *If Diocletian and Constantine had not imposed such oppressive reforms, Rome could have survived its crises.* Students should give factual evidence to support their positions. *(Synthesis)* **Making Judgments**

● **RETEACHING.** Have students review "Barbarian Invasions" and "The Fall of Rome" and answer the following: **(a) Why were some Germanic tribes able to defeat the Roman Empire?** (The borders of the Empire were undefended or weakened.) **(b) What Roman policy weakened the army?** (The hiring of Germanic soldiers to fight in the Roman army.) **(c) How did the Germanic soldiers turn against the Romans?** (They overthrew the Western emperor and declared a German to be king of Italy.) *(Comprehension)* **Observing for Detail**

Ⓕ See below.

Map Skill Practice

See p. T117B for answers to *Map Skill Practice.*

Invasions of the Roman Empire About A.D. 400

1. What important battle is shown on the map?
2. What were the two capitals of the divided Roman Empire? How far would a person have had to travel by land to get from one of these cities to the other?
3. From what general direction did the Huns first invade the Western Roman Empire?
4. What two rivers formed the boundary of the Western Roman Empire?
5. What barbarian tribes crossed this boundary?
6. **Analyzing cause and effect.** What part did the Huns play in the fall of the Western Roman Empire?

KEY

- Western Roman Empire
- Eastern Roman Empire
- → Germanic Invasions
- → Huns
- ✕ Battle

SCALE 0 — 500 mi / 0 — 500 km

121

Ⓕ **Feature Note** The Visigoths had occupied a vast area north of the lower Danube River and the Black Sea. They were allowed to enter Roman territory to form a frontier force to oppose possible invasions by the Huns. The Visigoths revolted against the Romans because of ill-treatment.

Two years later Rome went to war with its unwelcome guests. In the Battle of Adrianople (ay-dree-uh-NOH-pul), the Visigoth cavalry slaughtered thousands of Roman troops. This defeat, Rome's worst since the days of Hannibal some 600 years before (page 100), was a clear sign that Rome could no longer defend its borders.

As more soldiers were called home to defend Italy, the border defenses collapsed. Germanic tribes began pouring into the Empire. Some moved into Gaul, others into Spain. The Visigoth leader Alaric (AL-uh-rik) led his troops into Italy, demanding land and a generalship in the Roman army. When his demands were refused, the Visigoths attacked and looted the city of Rome in 410. To make peace, Rome allowed them to set up a kingdom in Spain and Gaul.

Sec. Rev. ques. 4

The Huns. The next threat to the Western Roman Empire came from the Huns. Their king, Attila (uh-TIL-uh), had conquered lands from the Black Sea to the Rhine River. A Roman historian described the terror these ruthless warriors caused: "A race of men suddenly descended like a whirlwind from the lofty mountains destroying everything in their way." In 451 Attila led his forces into Gaul. An alliance of Germanic tribes and what was left of the Roman army defeated Attila. A year later, the Huns invaded northern Italy, but hunger and disease forced them to withdraw. The death of Attila in 453 ended the Hun threat, but the Germanic invasions continued.

The Fall of Rome

One Roman province after another fell to invading Germanic tribes. In 455 the city of Rome was again looted, this time by the Vandals, a Germanic tribe that had established a kingdom in North Africa. The Vandals carried off even more of Rome's wealth than the Visigoths had.

Sec. Rev. ques. 4, cont.

By the time of the Vandal attack, the Romans had hired many Germanic soldiers to fight in the Roman army. In A.D. 476 some of these Germanic officers revolted against the Roman commanders and overthrew the Western emperor, who was only a child. They declared a fellow German, Odoacer (oh-doh-AY-sur), king of Italy. Because Odoacer replaced the last native Roman ruler, this event is usually regarded as the end of the Western Roman Empire.

Some Roman traditions, such as law, art forms, and language, continued in the Western Empire after 476, but it was ruled by Germanic kings. Odoacer was killed in 493 by Theodoric (thee-AH-dur-ik), king of the Ostrogoths, or East Goths. Theodoric restored peace and prosperity in Italy. He reigned until 526, supported by the Eastern Roman Empire, which survived the fall of Rome. The Eastern Roman Empire later became known as the Byzantine Empire, as you will read in Chapter 9.

This helmet found in the tomb of an Anglo-Saxon king combines the design of Roman helmets with Germanic decoration.

122

Cultural History The Huns were nomads and herders who knew little about agriculture. Hun invasions were the result of their search for pastureland and water.

Check for Understanding. Ask: What event signaled the end of the Western Roman Empire? (In 476, Germanic officers overthrew the Western emperor and declared Odoacer to be king of Italy.)

Background The Ostrogoths were attacked and overrun by the Huns about A.D. 370. Forced to join the Hun army, the Ostrogoths did not regain their freedom until after the death of Attila in 453. They were admitted into the army of the Roman Empire, but grew rebellious.

Politics Note that Theodoric maintained the Roman legal and administrative systems. Official documents state that Theodoric believed the Goths were in Italy only to protect and save Roman civilization, by force if necessary.

Linking Past and Present

The Vandals destroyed many precious works of art when they sacked Rome. Today the word *vandal* refers to anyone who purposely destroys something beautiful or useful.

Reasons for the Decline of the Empire

In the second century A.D. the Roman Empire seemed indestructible. Yet by the end of the fifth century it had collapsed. This collapse was not sudden but the result of a long slow decline. Historians continue to debate the reasons for Rome's fall. Certainly, outside invasions played a part. Yet internal problems were perhaps even more important.

1. Weakened army. By the fourth century, the quality of the army had dropped sharply. The strength of Rome had always depended on its soldier-citizens. As time went on, however, fewer Roman citizens volunteered for military service. The government recruited men from the less developed parts of the Empire and also from the Germanic tribes. Soon most of the soldiers and officers of the Roman army were Germanic. These soldiers cared little about Rome's goal of preserving order and spreading peace.

2. Smaller population. A combination of warfare, famine, a declining birthrate, and plagues cut deeply into the population of the Empire. From about 70 million people during the Pax Romana, the population fell to about 50 million by the late fourth century. Population loss meant fewer soldiers for the army, fewer taxpayers for the government, and fewer farmers to feed Rome's people.

3. Oppressive government. Military and economic pressures led the government to become extremely harsh in its rule. The threat of Germanic invasion forced emperors to spend more and more money on defense. To pay for the food, weapons, and armor needed by soldiers, the state raised taxes and seized grain and property from citizens. Officials also forced people to repair roads and bridges and do other work. These demands created resentment among both townspeople and farmers. Many came to hate and fear government officials more than they did the Germanic invaders.

4. Declining farms and cities. The heavy hand of the government, along with

⒡ See below.

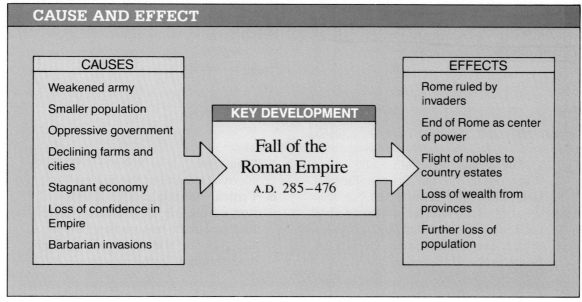

CAUSE AND EFFECT

CAUSES	KEY DEVELOPMENT	EFFECTS
Weakened army		Rome ruled by invaders
Smaller population		End of Rome as center of power
Oppressive government	**Fall of the Roman Empire** A.D. 285–476	Flight of nobles to country estates
Declining farms and cities		Loss of wealth from provinces
Stagnant economy		Further loss of population
Loss of confidence in Empire		
Barbarian invasions		

123

⒡ **CAUSE AND EFFECT CHART ACTIVITY.** Have students work in groups to evaluate the causes of the fall of the Roman Empire and decide which were the result of decisions made by rulers and which were the result of circumstances beyond their control. Then have students suggest ways that some of the causes might have been avoided. *(Synthesis) Making Judgments*

Check for Understanding. Ask: How did a smaller population contribute to the decline of Rome? (There were fewer soldiers, fewer taxpayers, and fewer farmers.)

Check for Understanding. Ask: In what ways did the Roman government become more oppressive? (It raised taxes, seized grain and property, and forced citizens to work for the government.)

barbarian attacks, drove many small farmers out of business. When they abandoned their farms, powerful nobles snatched up these lands. More and more nobles now retreated to the country to live behind the fortified walls of their enormous estates. The flight of the nobles left Roman cities without strong leadership.

5. Stagnant economy. As small farms disappeared and cities decayed, Rome's economy began to collapse. The widespread use of slave labor meant that common people and landless farmers had trouble finding jobs. With little income, they could not possibly pay steep prices for goods, and business activity slowed.

Fighting in the provinces only worsened the situation. It disrupted trade and made tax collecting nearly impossible. In addition, after the division of the Empire, Rome could no longer count on aid from the wealthier eastern provinces. Another source of wealth, spoils from newly conquered lands, dried up when the Empire stopped expanding.

6. Loss of confidence. The patriotism and dedication of Rome's citizens had made possible Rome's spectacular growth from a small town to a mighty empire. The government's inability to deal with the problems it faced, however, shook many Romans' faith in their civilization. They began to think only of their own needs and security, neglecting their responsibility to serve the Empire. For many people, Rome was simply not worth defending any longer.

● See below, right.

The Roman Heritage

In spite of its collapse, Rome left a heritage that has profoundly affected Western civilization ever since. Rome kept alive the arts and learning of ancient Greece, added its own contributions, and spread Greco-Roman culture throughout Western Europe. Rome also united many different peoples, bringing benefits to all parts of its empire.

Cultural contributions. Rome's influence is especially obvious in the areas of language and law. Latin, the language of the Romans, became the common language of educated people in Europe, allowing greater communication across cultural boundaries. In addition, Latin served as the basis of many European languages. Thousands of English words—from *aquarium* to *zebra*—can be traced to Latin.

The legal codes of nations in Europe and the Americas are just as firmly rooted in Roman tradition. Many beliefs that are common today, such as the idea that a person is innocent until proven guilty, come from Roman law.

Unity. The unity provided by Roman rule long outlived the Empire. Not only did Roman language and law continue to influence former Roman provinces, but the idea of a united Europe continued to inspire leaders. As you will read, Rome also contributed to European unity by nourishing the growth of a new religion.

See Sec. 1 *Closing the Lesson*, p. T117B.

Sec. Rev. ques. 5

Section Review

Answers to Section Review questions are in brackets on pages indicated.

1. **Define:** spoils, imperial. (p. 119)
2. What crises did the Roman Empire face in the third century A.D.? (p. 119)
3. What steps did Diocletian take to save the Empire from collapsing? (p. 119–120)
4. Which two tribes looted the city of Rome in the fifth century? (p. 122)
5. What elements of Roman civilization survived the fall of the Empire? (p. 124)
6. **Critical thinking:** The reasons for Rome's decline were closely related. Pick two of the reasons listed on pages 123–124 and show how one problem made another problem worse. (See answer below.)

124

● **REINFORCEMENT.** Have students review "Reasons for the Decline of the Empire" (pp. 123–124) and identify six causes of Rome's decline. For each cause have students write a one-sentence explanation. (Weakened army, smaller population, oppressive government, decline of farms and cities, stagnant economy, loss of confidence in Rome.) *(Comprehension) Identifying Cause and Effect*

6. Students should demonstrate an understanding of how each condition listed exacerbated other problems.

● **ENRICHMENT.** Have students work in groups to present skits about the decline of the Roman Empire. Presentations might include narratives, dialogues, or dramatizations and should represent members of various groups affected by the decline of Rome's power. Have students give their presentations in class. *(Application) Dramatizing History*

See lesson plans, pp. T117A–T117C.

2 The Spread of Christianity

Objectives

Focus Questions

★ ■ How did the Christian faith arise?
   (pages 125–126)
● ■ How did Christianity spread through the
   Roman Empire? *(pages 126–129)*

Terms to Know

Christianity   disciple
Messiah   persecution
Gospels   martyr
crucify

★ Note strategies for first objective on this page and p. 126.

Even before the Roman Empire began to decline, Romans were turning away from their traditional, polytheistic religion (page 112). Many people were attracted by the ideas of a new religious leader, a man named Jesus. By the time the Empire came to an end, **Christianity**—the religion based on Jesus' teachings—had become the official faith throughout the Mediterranean world.

Religious Toleration

Sec. Rev. ques. 2

While the Romans brought their laws and government to all parts of the Empire, they allowed local peoples to keep many of their own religious customs. Romans followed a number of different religions and tolerated local beliefs in the provinces.

In the Roman province of Judaea (Palestine) and other parts of the Empire, the Hebrews, or Jews, had considerable religious freedom. Other conquered peoples were required to show their loyalty to Rome through rituals honoring the emperor. Because of

their belief in one God, Jews did not have to take part in these rituals. The Romans established a line of Jewish kings named Herod (HEHR-ud) on the throne of Judaea, though Roman officials and soldiers also occupied the country.

Many Jews hoped to regain their independence. Some hoped for the coming of the **Messiah** (muh-SY-ah), or savior, which had been promised by Jewish prophets. The Messiah, they believed, would restore their kingdom's ancient greatness and would bring an age of prosperity and peace.

The Good Shepherd appears often in early Christian art. The Bible quotes Jesus as saying "I am the good shepherd; the good shepherd gives his life for the sheep." This marble sculpture is from third-century Rome.

125

★ RETEACHING. Have students review "Religious Toleration" (above) and identify the cause and effect of Roman religious policy toward the Jews. (The Romans tolerated local beliefs. Jews were not required to honor the emperor through rituals.) *(Comprehension)* **Identifying Cause and Effect**
Cultural Background Roman tolerance of Jewish beliefs dated back to 47 B.C. Jews were allowed to worship in their synagogues throughout the Empire and did not have to attend court on their Sabbath.

★ REINFORCEMENT. Ask: (a) What was the Jewish concept of Messiah? (A savior who would restore Jewish greatness and establish a time of peace and prosperity.) (b) What ideals did Jesus teach? (Love, compassion, a personal relationship with God.) (c) Why was Jesus crucified? (Jewish leaders did not accept him as the Messiah; Roman authorities feared he might lead a rebellion.) *(Comprehension) Observing for Detail*

F See above.

The Arts

Early Christian Art

During the years when they were persecuted by Roman officials, Christians worshiped secretly. Sometimes they met in the catacombs—underground burial chambers and passageways that ran beneath the city of Rome. Christian artists decorated the walls and ceilings of the catacombs with paintings of scenes from the Bible.

After Constantine declared Christianity the official religion of the Empire, Christians were free to meet openly. Churches sprang up in many cities. Constantine and later emperors spent lavishly to make these churches beautiful. Religious art flourished.

Some churches were still decorated with paintings, but many used a more costly form of art, the mosaic. Mosaics are pictures created from many small colored tiles. Romans had long made mosaics with pieces of marble. Christian artists began using bits of colored glass. Glass gave artists a wider choice of colors, as well as much brighter colors. Each tiny piece reflected the light, so that the walls of the churches glittered with jewel-like brilliance.

The Teachings of Jesus

Early in the first century A.D. a teacher named Jesus gained a following among the people of Judaea. The account of Jesus' preaching appears in the Gospels, the first four books of the New Testament in the Christian Bible.* Jesus himself left no writings. His teachings and the events of his life were preserved by word of mouth and then recorded by four writers—Matthew, Mark, Luke, and John.

★ See below.

According to the Gospels, Jesus was born in the town of Bethlehem during the rule of Augustus. The Gospel of Luke says that even as a young boy, Jesus had a great interest in religious questions and amazed Jewish scholars with his knowledge. Some years later, according to all the Gospels, he began to preach and gather followers.

The accounts in the Gospels indicate that Jesus accepted the Jewish laws and traditions of the Old Testament, but he put a new emphasis on love, compassion, and a personal relationship with God. The Gospel writers report that he attracted enthusiastic crowds and worked miracles of healing. About A.D. 29 Jesus traveled to the city of Jerusalem to celebrate the Jewish holiday of Passover. Crowds there welcomed him as "king of the Jews" and "Messiah." Because the Greek word for the Messiah was *Christos,* Jesus' followers became known as Christians.

Sec. Rev. ques. 3

Jesus' popularity appeared threatening both to traditional Jewish leaders, who did not accept him as the Messiah, and to the Roman authorities, who feared he might lead a rebellion against the Empire. Jesus was arrested and brought before the Roman governor, Pontius Pilate (PAHN-shus PY-lut), who ordered his death. Following Roman custom, Jesus was crucified—nailed to a cross and left to die.

The Growth of Christianity

● Note strategies for second objective on this page and p. 129.

At the time of the Crucifixion, the disciples—followers—of Jesus made up only a small Jewish sect. They believed that Jesus was the

126

* The Christian Bible is made up of the Old Testament (the Hebrew Scriptures) and the New Testament.

★ ENRICHMENT. Have students find information on the authors of the Gospels. Students might research the lives of Matthew, Mark, Luke, or John; or find information on the writing of the Gospels. (Application) Locating Information

Social History Note that crucifixion was a common method of capital punishment among the Persians, Jews, Carthaginians, and Romans. It was thought to be a suitable punishment for political or religious agitators, pirates, slaves, or those who had no civil rights.

● RETEACHING. Have students review "The Growth of Christianity" (pp. 126–127) and identify the importance of the following in the spread of Christianity: Paul of Tarsus (Distinguished the ideas of Christianity from Judaism; spread Christianity throughout the Roman Empire.) Peace and unity of Pax Romana (Made it easier for Christianity's message to be carried.) Roman roads (Made travel by land easy.) A common language (Facilitated communication.) (Comprehension) Understanding Cause and Effect

ROMAN CITIZEN

This fifth-century mosaic illustrates the Bible story of the loaves and fishes.

Son of God and that he had risen from the dead and been taken to heaven. The disciples believed they had the responsibility to spread Jesus' teachings to other people. At first the disciples taught and preached mainly to other Jews in the Middle East. As the new beliefs attracted more followers, Christianity became a religion independent of Judaism, with followers throughout the Mediterranean world.

A major reason for Christianity's development into a world religion was the work of a Greek-speaking Jew named Saul, from the city of Tarsus in Asia Minor. According to the Bible, Saul was working actively against the disciples and their followers when he was suddenly converted to a belief in Jesus' teachings. Changing his name to Paul, he devoted his life to Christianity.

Sec. Rev. ques. 4

The role of Paul. Paul set forth many of the ideas that form the basis of Christianity and separate it from Judaism. Paul taught that although all human beings are born sinful, Jesus was sent by God to redeem humanity from their sins. By dying on the cross, said Paul, Jesus had made it possible for human beings to gain salvation and enter the kingdom of heaven.

Paul made another great contribution to Christianity by spreading these ideas. He traveled to many parts of the Roman Empire, setting up Christian communities (see map, page 128). He also wrote letters to these communities to reinforce their faith. Many of these letters, called the Epistles (ih-PIS-ulz), appear in the New Testament.

Sec. Rev. ques. 4, cont.

Paul's missionary work lasted from A.D. 45 to 65. He was eventually arrested in Jerusalem by Roman authorities and, as a Roman citizen, was sent to Rome for trial. Accounts differ as to whether he was released or was executed by the emperor Nero.

Sources of unity. Besides the work of Paul, other factors helped the spread of Christianity. One was the peace and unity of the Pax Romana, which made it easier for missionaries to carry the message of Christianity throughout the Empire. Excellent Roman roads made passage by land easy; the Roman navy protected ships in the Mediterranean from pirates. Latin was spoken throughout Europe, and Greek was the common language in most of the eastern Mediterranean.

The first Christian communities were small groups of followers scattered throughout the eastern Mediterranean. As the new faith spread, an organized Christian Church developed, helping unite Christians in different lands. By welcoming people of all backgrounds and calling its members brothers and sisters, the Church gave people a sense of community and fellowship.

From Persecution to Acceptance

Roman authorities, generally tolerant of different religions, did not at first interfere with Christianity. As more and more people turned to Christianity, however, Roman officials began to see it as a threat to their rule. The Christians did not accept the Roman gods or celebrate their festivals. Although they obeyed Roman law, they refused to worship the emperor as a god. That was seen as an act of disloyalty to Rome. Moreover, the Romans found some Christian ways strange. **127**

Biography Paul was studying to be a rabbi and had acquired an outstanding reputation as a defender of Judaism. For this reason he had been authorized by Jewish officials to prosecute members of the Christian sect.

Check for Understanding. Ask: What were Paul's Christian teachings? (Human beings are born sinful, but are redeemed by Christ's death on the cross.)

Religion Note that the Church gained such popularity in cities that Christians started to use the word *paganus*, meaning "rustic," to describe non-Christians. From this originated the Christian practice of calling all non-Christians *pagans*.

Check for Understanding. Ask: What factors led to Roman persecution of Christians? (Christians did not accept Roman gods and refused to worship the emperor; the growing popularity of the religion threatened Roman authority.)

Christians stayed away from the gladiatorial contests and at times refused to serve in the army.

When fire swept through Rome in A.D. 64, the emperor Nero blamed the Christians. He began the first official **persecutions**—systematic mistreatment. Though persecution never became widespread, several later emperors followed Nero's example. Christians lost their property and were imprisoned, executed, or sent to face wild beasts in the arena. Yet such measures failed to stop the spread of Christianity. Many Romans were impressed by the heroism and devotion of those willing to die for their faith. The dedication of these **martyrs**—people who suffer or die for a cause—led many Romans to convert to Christianity.

The invasions and unrest of the third century A.D. (page 119) brought more converts and new strength to the Christian Church. The persecutions ended, and Christianity became one of the many religions allowed in the Empire. In A.D. 312 the Roman emperor Constantine converted to Christianity, becoming the first Christian emperor. He strongly supported the Church and allowed Christians to practice their religion freely. In 380 the Emperor Theodosius I (thee-uh-DOH-shus) declared worship of the old gods to be illegal. Christianity soon became the official religion of the Empire.

The Ideas of Augustine

As the Christian Church grew, many writers and thinkers explained its beliefs and set forth principles for following Christianity. These early Christian thinkers are usually called "Fathers of the Church." One of the earliest and greatest Church Fathers was Augustine (354–430). Born in North Africa, Augustine studied Latin literature and Greek

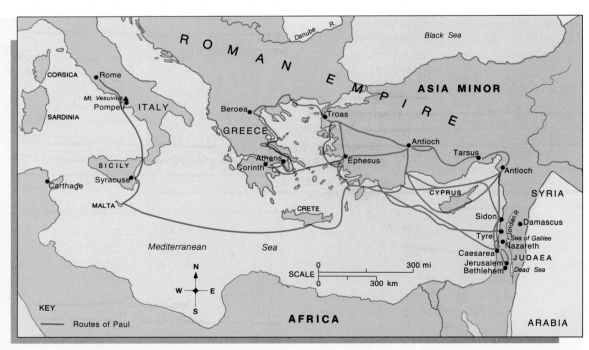

Journeys of Paul, A.D. 45–65

In his missionary effort, Paul traveled to many parts of the Empire. In what direction from Rome did he mainly travel? What cities did he visit in Judaea? In Asia Minor? In Greece?

128

Map Answers: (1) East. (2) Sidon, Tyre, Caesarea, Nazareth, Jerusalem, Bethlehem. (3) Antioch, Tarsus, Ephesus, Troas. (4) Athens, Corinth, Beroea.

Religion Tertullian, a convert and defender of Christianity during the time of Roman persecutions, claimed that Christians "multiply every time we are mowed down" by Romans.

Biography Constantine claimed to have seen a cross of light across the sun with the message *in hoc signo vinces* ("in this sign you shall conquer"). Constantine had his troops inscribe a cross, the symbol of Christ, on their shields, and he attributed his success in battle to protection by the Christian God.

Cultural History Note that the Church was exempted from taxation and the sign of the cross was added to coins.

Cultural History As the Church and the state worked more closely together, the old public buildings of Rome (basilicas) were turned into churches and church and civil courts exchanged cases.

philosophy in Carthage before becoming a Christian.

The Germanic invasions of Rome in the early 400's brought terror to Italy. Some non-Christians blamed Christianity, claiming that the ancient gods were punishing Rome. Christians, on the other hand, wondered why good people should have to suffer. In response, Augustine wrote a book called *The City of God*.

The true Christian, said Augustine, was a citizen of a heavenly city that could never be destroyed by ungodly barbarians. The cities and empires of earth did not matter, he said, only the individual's salvation. Nevertheless, Augustine declared, Christians should try to run their earthly city according to Christian principles and teachings. Augustine believed that the aim of life was the fulfillment of God's will. His contrast of the earthly sinful city and the perfect City of God remained an important idea for later Christian thinkers.

The ideas of thinkers like Paul and Augustine helped Christianity spread. So too did

the strength of the early Christians' faith. In only three centuries, Christianity gained followers throughout the Roman world.

See Sec. 2 Closing the Lesson, p. T117C.

See Sec. 2 Closing the Lesson, p. T117C.

Section Review

Answers to Section Review questions are in brackets on pages indicated.

1. **Define or identify:** Christianity, Messiah, Gospels, crucify, disciple, persecution, martyr. (p. 125, 126, 128)
2. What was Roman policy toward religion in the Empire? (p. 125)
3. What were the main elements of Jesus' teachings? (p. 126)
4. How did Paul contribute to the spread of Christianity? (p. 127)
5. How did Christianity come to be accepted in the Empire? (p. 128)
6. **Critical thinking:** Which events leading to the fall of Rome would Augustine have used as proof that Rome was a sinful city? (See answer below.)

6. Answers will vary and might include: civil war, onset of plagues, increased religious persecution, the sacking of Rome by the Visigoths and Vandals, the invasion by the Huns.

Chapter 6   Summary and Timeline

1. A combination of internal weakness and invasion destroyed the Roman Empire. The Empire was divided into two parts to make it easier to govern. Rome, the capital of the Western Empire, fell to Germanic tribes. The Eastern Empire, whose capital was Constantinople, survived.

2. The religion of Christianity, based on the teachings of Jesus, began in Judaea. Despite persecution of its followers, Christianity soon spread throughout the Mediterranean. Christianity was eventually accepted, and it became the official religion of the Roman Empire in the late 300's.

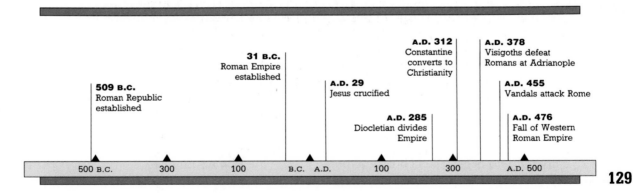

509 B.C. Roman Republic established

31 B.C. Roman Empire established

A.D. 29 Jesus crucified

A.D. 285 Diocletian divides Empire

A.D. 312 Constantine converts to Christianity

A.D. 378 Visigoths defeat Romans at Adrianople

A.D. 455 Vandals attack Rome

A.D. 476 Fall of Western Roman Empire

500 B.C.   300   100   B.C. A.D.   100   300   A.D. 500

129

• REINFORCEMENT. Have students write an essay explaining how the ideas Augustine discussed in *The City of God* might have helped early Christians explain the suffering brought on by the Germanic invasions. *(Synthesis) Synthesizing Information*

• ENRICHMENT. Have students work in groups to present a panel discussion on the growth of Christianity. Students might research early Christian practices, Roman persecutions, Christian martyrs, Constantine and Christianity, or Christianity as Rome's official religion. *(Synthesis) Locating Information*

See p. T117C for answers to Chapter Review.

Vocabulary Review

Use the following terms to complete the sentences below: *Christianity, disciples, Gospels, martyr, Messiah, persecutions, spoils.*

1. ___?___ is the religion based on the teachings of Jesus.
2. Another word for "savior" is ___?___.
3. A ___?___ is a person willing to suffer or die for a cause.
4. Goods taken in war are called ___?___.
5. The first four books of the New Testament, the ___?___, contain an account of Jesus' preaching.
6. Even though several emperors used ___?___ to try to discourage Christianity, the religion spread.
7. Jesus' ___?___ spread his teachings and attracted new followers.

People to Identify

Match each of the following people with the correct description: *Attila, Augustine, Constantine, Diocletian, Nero, Paul, Pontius Pilate.*

1. emperor who appointed a co-ruler and moved the imperial court to Asia Minor
2. Roman governor who ordered the execution of Jesus
3. first Christian emperor, who built the new capital at Constantinople
4. missionary who brought Jesus' teachings to much of the Roman Empire
5. king of the Huns who threatened the Western Roman Empire with invasions of Gaul and northern Italy
6. Church Father who taught that the aim of life was to fulfill God's will
7. emperor who began the first official persecutions against Christians

130

Places to Know

Match the letters on this map of the Roman Empire with the places listed below. You may want to refer to the maps on pages 121 and 128.

1. Adrianople
2. Bethlehem
3. Constantinople
4. Eastern Roman Empire
5. Western Roman Empire

Recalling the Facts

1. What steps did Diocletian and Constantine take to gain greater control over the Empire? How did these actions hurt Roman citizens?
2. Why did Diocletian divide the Empire? What were the negative effects of this division?
3. What barbarian groups invaded the Empire in the fourth and fifth centuries?
4. What event marked the end of the Western Roman Empire?
5. What internal problems led to the fall of the Roman Empire?
6. How did Paul help spread Christianity?

7. How did the Pax Romana contribute to the growth of Christianity?

8. Why did Roman authorities oppose Christianity? How did Christianity eventually become established in the Empire?

Critical Thinking Skills

1. **Preparing a report.** Research and prepare a report about one of the following topics: the Baths of Caracalla in Rome; Christian painting in the catacombs of Rome; the Battle of Chalons; Attila. *(App.)*

✔ 2. **Making recommendations.** Imagine that you are an adviser to the emperor Diocletian. Your task is to suggest ways to improve economic and political life within the Empire. Tell how each of your recommendations will help improve conditions. *(Syn.)*

✔ 3. **Examining cause and effect.** Review the reasons for the decline of the Roman Empire (pages 123–124). Rank these causes, beginning with the one you think was the most important. Tell why you ranked them as you did. Do you think the Empire's decline could have been reversed? If so, at what point? If not, why? *(Syn.)*

4. **Writing a letter.** Imagine that you are a poor farmer, a merchant, a soldier, or a Roman official living during the final days of the Roman Empire. Write a letter to a friend describing your present troubles and what you expect life in the future to be like for you and your family. *(App.)*

✔ 5. **Supporting an opinion.** In your opinion, which of Rome's contributions to the modern world is the most important? Why? *(Eval.)*

Thinking About Geography

1. **Comparing maps.** Compare the map on page 121 with the Atlas maps at the back of this book. What nations now exist in what was once the Western Roman Empire? The Eastern Roman Empire? *(Comp.)*

2. **Researching places.** Many of Europe's great cities began as outposts on the frontier of the Roman Empire. For example, after Julius Caesar conquered Gaul, the Romans built the town of *Lutetia Parisiorum* on the Seine River. Today the city of Paris exists in the same location. Use an encyclopedia to research the origins of Vienna, Austria; Cologne, Germany; and London, England. *(App.)*

Enrichment: Primary Sources

In A.D. 98 the historian Tacitus wrote a description of the early Germanic tribes with whom the Roman troops had been fighting. This passage adapted from his account describes the Germanic soldiers.

66 Only a few of them use swords or large lances: they carry spears with short and narrow blades, but so sharp and easy to handle that they can be used, as required, either at close quarters or in long-range fighting. Their horsemen are content with a shield and a spear; but the foot-soldiers also rain javelins on their foes: each of them carries several, and they hurl them to immense distances. Their horses are not remarkable for either beauty or speed, and are not trained to execute various turns as ours are. The Germans' strength lies in infantry rather than cavalry. Foot-soldiers accompany the cavalry into action, their speed of foot being such that they can easily keep up with the charging horsemen. 99

1. What was the Germanic soldier's most important weapon? Why was it useful?

2. What was the strongest part of the Germanic army?

3. **Critical thinking:** Do you think Tacitus respected the strength of the Germans? Explain your answer. *(Anal.)* ✔

131

✔ A checkmark identifies questions and exercises calling for the three higher-order levels of thinking at the top of the Bloom taxonomy: Analysis, Synthesis, and Evaluation.

Great Empires in India and China   565 B.C.–A.D. 589
(pp. 132–147)

Chapter Preview

Section 1 traces the development of Buddhism, its early influence on Indian government and society, and its spread to other Asian lands. In Section 2, the emergence of the Mauryan and Gupta empires in northern India and the distinguishing characteristics of the Tamil culture in southern India are described. Advances in culture and technology made by the Chinese, particularly the establishment of the examination system for government officials, are discussed in Section 3, and the impact of Confucianism and Legalism on the Qin and Han dynasties is described.

Bibliography

See the *Teacher's Management and Planning Guide* for additional listings. Starred titles are for both students and teachers.

De Bary, William Theodore. *Sources of Indian Tradition.* Columbia University Press. Outstanding collection of source readings. Can be used for critical thinking studies.

Fairbank, John K., Edwin O. Reischauer, and Albert M. Craig. *East Asia: Tradition and Transformation.* Houghton Mifflin. A revised edition of a classic text.

*Loewe, M. *Everyday Life in Early Imperial China.* B. T. Batsford. Makes the Chinese past come alive.

*Luo Zewen, Dick Wilson, J. P. Drege, and H. Delahaye. *The Great Wall.* McGraw-Hill. The effects of the Great Wall on China's history. Lavishly illustrated.

*Pan, K. *Courtier and Commoner in Ancient China: Selections from the History of the Former Han.* Columbia Press. A collection of short biographies depicting people from many different walks of life.

Section Lesson Plans

SECTION 1   (pp. 133–135)
The Development of Buddhism

Objectives

After completing this section, students will be able to:
1. Discuss the main ideas of Buddhism.
2. Describe how Buddhism spread through India and beyond.

Introducing the Lesson

Tell students that Buddhism, an important world religion, developed in India in the sixth century B.C. Followers of Buddhism believed that individuals could escape life's sorrow and suffering without repeating cycles of death and rebirth.

Then ask: *(a) Why do you think new religions develop?* (Answers will vary. Sometimes religious leaders teach new ideas or historical developments lead to new interpretations of older principles.)

(b) Why might people abandon one religion and adopt another? (Answers will vary. People might believe that a new religion holds greater truth than a more traditional religion. Sometimes a new religion appears to answer difficult questions or to address unmet needs.)

(c) How might the introduction of a new religion affect a society? (Answers will vary.)

Developing the Lesson:
Comparing Ideas

Have students compare the Buddhist belief in nirvana with the Hindu belief in karma and explain how both are concerned with human experience and behavior. (The Hindu concept of karma teaches that good karma assures rebirth into a better life, but because individual happiness is related to caste, there is no religious practice that can remove suffering. Nirvana, the Buddhist state of enlightenment, can be achieved by following the "middle way." Nirvana is possible for people of all classes and castes, and does not depend on the accumulation of good acts through a series of rebirths.) *(Analysis)*

Developing the Lesson:
Making Judgments

Have students explain how the Buddha's Four Noble Truths answered the questions that started his search—Why is there sorrow in the world? What hope is there for the poor? (Sorrow and suffering are part of life because people try to get things they cannot have. The poor have the same opportunities that everyone else has to overcome desires and follow a middle way, and to achieve nirvana.) *(Comprehension)*

Closing the Lesson:
Understanding Point of View

Have students work in groups to present a skit on Buddhism. Students might write narratives, dialogues, or short dramas; or draw posters to describe one of the following: the principles of Buddhism; how Buddhism differed from Hinduism; the life of a Buddhist monk or nun; the disagreements that caused the split within the Buddhist community. *(Application)*

See *Section Review* questions, p. 135.

SECTION 2   (pp. 136–139)
A Golden Age for India

Objectives

After completing this section, students will be able to:
1. Describe how the Mauryan Empire ruled northern India.
2. Explain what made the Dravidian culture distinctive.
3. Discuss why the Gupta period is considered India's Classical Age.

Introducing the Lesson

Tell students that religion has been one of the most important influences on the course of history. Religious convictions have often motivated armies, guided leaders, and fueled conflict or cooperation among communities.

Then ask: *(a) How might religion affect a political leader's decisions?* (Answers will vary. Sometimes people are free to believe what they want, but government policies reflect the leader's faith.)

(b) What problems might develop if the leader of a state tried to impose one religion on all citizens? (Answers will vary. People may be forced to support a religion in which they do not believe. Individuals may be forbidden to express their personal beliefs. Civil unrest, disunity, and resentment of the government may develop.)

Developing the Lesson:
Organizing Information

Have students organize information about the Persian, Mauryan, and Gupta empires in a chart with columns labeled *Rulers, Important Events,* and *Territory.* (*Persia:* Cyrus the Great and Darius I; established centers of culture; Indus Valley and Punjab. *Maurya:* Chandragupta and Asoka; strengthened central government, Asoka based his rule on Buddhism; northern India and part of present-day Afghanistan. *Gupta:* Chandra Gupta; India's Classical Age, flowering of literature, science, mathematics; northern India, centered at Magadha.) *(Comprehension)*

Developing the Lesson:
Identifying Effects

Have students summarize the effects of the Persian conquest and Alexander the Great's incursion into India. (*Persia:* conquered the Indus Valley and the Punjab. Courts and cities of the Persians became centers of culture. *Alexander the Great:* ended Persian power in India; established some Greek forts and settlements; his death in 323 B.C. left northwest India without effective leadership.) *(Comprehension)*

Closing the Lesson:
Forming a Hypothesis

Have students form a hypothesis about why Dravidian culture developed differently from north India. (Answers will vary, but students should consider the following: Dravidian culture, like that of north India, began in the Indus Valley, but the Dravidians migrated south to avoid the Aryan invasion. Unlike the people in north India, the Dravidians escaped the invasions of the Persians and Alexander the Great.) *(Synthesis)*

See *Section Review* questions, p. 139.

SECTION 3   (pp. 139–145)
China Under the Qin and Han Dynasties

Objectives

After completing this section, students will be able to:
1. Describe new philosophies that developed in China after Confucius.
2. Explain how the Qin dynasty established the Chinese Empire.
3. Discuss how the Han dynasty strengthened China.

Introducing the Lesson

Tell students that during the third century B.C., Confucian principles (p. 63) and a new philosophy, Legalism, influenced the thinking of Chinese rulers. These two ways of thinking were vastly different from each other: Confucianism taught that individuals are naturally good while Legalism was based on the assumption that human beings are evil and selfish.

Then ask: *(a) How might a ruler's ideas about human nature influence government policy?* (Answers will vary, but should consider that the ruler's beliefs about human nature will probably be reflected in government policies).

(b) How might the policies of a Legalist have differed from those of a supporter of Confucian principles? (Answers will vary. A Legalist might have adopted policies to control what he or she considered to be the evil, selfish actions of individuals. A supporter of Confucian principles might have formed policies to guide, rather than control, the behavior of others.)

(c) How influential do you think a ruler's philosophy should be in the formation of policies and laws? (Answers will vary.)

Developing the Lesson:
Understanding Point of View

Have students work in groups to prepare a dialogue that might have occurred between scholars who supported the Confucian, Taoist, and Legalist points of view. Representatives of these viewpoints might explain their beliefs and the differences in government that would result if each had an opportunity to rule. *(Application)*

Developing the Lesson:
Understanding Cause and Effect

Have students write an essay explaining how the Legalist policies of the Qin caused both the rise and the decline of the Chinese Empire. (The strong central government unified the Chinese states, protected them against nomadic invasions, and censored ideas that did not support the Legalist policies of the Qin. The oppressive nature of Qin rule caused the best-trained public officials to be banished or executed and turned many people against Legalist policies. Soldiers and peasants rebelled.) *(Comprehension)*

Closing the Lesson:
Identifying Information

Draw a two-column chart on the chalkboard and label one side *Qin Dynasty* and the other *Han Dynasty*. Have student volunteers identify the following as characteristics of the Qin or Han dynasty and write the statement in the appropriate column.
(a) First Chinese empire. (Qin)
(b) The Great Wall. (Qin)
(c) Lasted 400 years. (Han)
(d) Simplified written language. (Qin)
(e) Extended empire to include parts of Southeast Asia, Korea, and Manchuria. (Han)
(f) Called "Serica" by the Romans. (Han)
(g) Book burning. (Qin)
(h) Established written examinations for public officials. (Han)
(i) Banished or executed its best-trained public officials. (Qin)
(j) Manufactured paper and fine porcelain or "china." (Han) *(Comprehension)*

See *Section Review* questions, p. 145.

Chapter 7 Review Answers
(pp. 146–147)

Vocabulary Review

1. ahimsa 2. dynastic cycle 3. Age of Disunity 4. Buddhism; nirvana 5. Sanskrit

People to Identify

1. Kalidasa 2. Mencius 3. Siddhartha Gautama 4. Wu Di 5. Laozi 6. Li Si 7. Shihuangdi 8. Gao Zu 9. Chandra Gupta

Places to Know

1. Magadha 2. Chang'an 3. Silk Road 4. Indus River

Recalling the Facts

1. First, sorrow and suffering are part of life. Second, people suffer because they are constantly trying to get things they cannot have. Third, the way to escape suffering is to overcome desire. Fourth, to reach enlightenment, people should follow a "middle way" and avoid too much or too little pleasure.
2. Buddhism placed more importance on how one lived than on one's caste and saw little value in the Brahmins' complex rituals. It also taught that people could gain enlightenment in one lifetime and so escape Hinduism's cycle of rebirth.
3. Missionaries and travelers carried Buddhism beyond India.
4. He had a strong central government over which, as emperor, he had supreme power. To make it easier to govern his large territory, he divided it into districts and provinces and used a strong army and spies to control them.
5. He had the laws of the empire written down, supported ahimsa, urged respect for human and animal life, called for tolerance of all beliefs, and promoted the spread of Indian culture.
6. Because it remained free from foreign domination, there was little or no mixing with other cultures.
7. Fables, folk tales, plays, and poetry were written. Mathematicians established the decimal system, the idea of zero, and the beginnings of algebra. Indian astronomers and physicians were also ahead of those in the rest of the world. Universities with large libraries developed.
8. Taoism advocated less-strict rules of behavior than Confucianism. Legalism taught that people were basically evil and selfish and could live well only under strict laws. It did not have the moral or spiritual appeal of Confucianism or Taoism.
9. They built roads and canals to improve communication and simplified the written language. The government lost its best-trained public officials when it banished or executed Confucian scholars. Such harsh policies also sparked rebellions by soldiers and peasants.
10. They set up a civil service system with written examinations to find educated and competent government officials. Internal rivalries, rebellions among the peasants, and deterioration of the examination system all contributed to the fall of the dynasty.

Critical Thinking Skills

1. Possible entries for *Applies Only to Buddhism:* Four Noble Truths; rejection of caste system; possibility of enlightenment in one lifetime. Possible entries for *Applies Only to Hinduism:* belief in caste system and complex rituals; impossibility of returning to universal spirit in one lifetime. Possible entries for *Applies to Both:* belief in reincarnation; idea of Brahman; belief in karma and dharma; polytheism.
2. Legalism provided a justification for the Qin to take full power and ruthlessly crush opponents. In the long run, Legalist policies caused the loss of well-trained public officials and aroused discontent among the people.
3. (a) second (b) second (c) third (d) first (e) first (f) third (g) second

Thinking About Geography

The northern border and part of the western border were protected. Answers will vary, but students may suggest that mountains and bodies of water acted as barriers to invasion from other directions or that the Chinese had friendly relations with people living to the south of China.

Enrichment: Primary Sources

1. Without humanity, an emperor could not protect his empire, a feudal lord could not protect his land or crops, and an individual's life was not safe.
2. Water flowing downward and beasts taking to wilderness are natural occurrences. Similarly, according to Mencius, it is natural for people to respect and follow a humane ruler.
3. Because using violence to conquer people would not win their hearts and they would not be loyal to the ruler.

Great Empires in India and China   565 B.C.–A.D. 589

See chapter timeline, p. 145.

Before You Read This Chapter

Imagine that you are the ruler of an empire surrounded by enemies. How could you protect your lands? In Chapter 5 you read how Hadrian built a wall to protect the Roman province of Britain. In this chapter you will learn that empires in India and China also faced threats from outsiders. Like the Romans, the Chinese hoped a wall would keep them safe. However, no empire has ever successfully walled out change. As you read this chapter, look for the part that invaders, traders, and newcomers played in bringing change to India and China.

The Geographic Setting

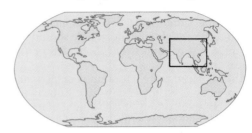

The Chapter Outline

1. The Development of Buddhism
2. A Golden Age for India
3. China Under the Qin and Han Dynasties

The Great Wall of China stretches over some 1,500 miles of mountainous countryside. The largest construction project in history, the Great Wall was built to keep out invaders from the north.

1 The Development of Buddhism

Objectives

Focus Questions

★ ■ What are the main ideas of Buddhism? *(page 133)*

● ■ How did Buddhism spread through India and beyond? *(pages 134–135)*

Terms to Know

Buddhism
Four Noble Truths
nirvana

★ Note strategies for first objective on this page and p. 134.

By the sixth century B.C., the Hindu religion and the caste system had become a way of life in India. For Hindus, the only way to gain salvation was by obeying caste rules and following complex rituals performed by Brahmin priests. These rules and rituals, however, did not meet the needs of the common people. As a result, some Hindus began to listen to the message of a new religious teacher.

Siddhartha Gautama

Sec. Rev. ques. 2

The founder of the new religion of **Buddhism** (BOO-diz-um) was Siddhartha Gautama (GAW-tuh-muh), an Indian prince born about 563 B.C. His father, a wealthy Kshatriya noble, tried to protect him from the realities of the world. Shielded from any knowledge of sorrow or hardship, the young man had everything a prince could want. Yet inwardly he was unhappy.

One day when he was almost 30, Gautama saw first a dying old man, then a sick man in great pain, then a dead man, and finally a wandering religious beggar. These encounters came as a shock to the prince. Why, he asked, was there such sorrow in the world? Why was there no hope for the poor? Gautama decided to give up his life of luxury to seek understanding.

For several years Gautama followed the Hindu way of self-denial and meditation. Still he felt troubled. Finally, at the age of 35, he sat down under a sacred fig tree and vowed never to leave the spot until he found answers. On the forty-ninth day, he suddenly saw the reason for life's sufferings and a way to overcome them. From that time on, he was known as the Buddha, the "Enlightened One."

The Buddha's Teachings

The Four Noble Truths. Many of the important ideas of Buddhism were presented in a sermon that the Buddha gave shortly after this experience. He spoke of **Four Noble Truths**. First, sorrow and suffering are part of life. Second, people suffer because they constantly try to get things they cannot have. Third, the way to escape suffering is to overcome these frustrating desires and reach a state of "not wanting." Fourth, to reach this state of enlightenment, called **nirvana**, people should follow a "middle way." They should have neither too much nor too little pleasure.

Challenge to Hinduism. Many of the Buddha's teachings were consistent with Hindu beliefs. However, some sharp differences existed. For example, Buddhism placed more importance on how one lived than on one's caste. In addition, Buddhists saw little value in the Brahmins' complex rituals. Also, while the Buddha believed in reincarnation, he did not believe it was necessary for becoming pure. He taught that a person could gain enlightenment in one lifetime and so escape Hinduism's cycle of rebirth.

Sec. Rev. ques. 3

133

★ RETEACHING. Have students write an essay evaluating the Buddha's Four Noble Truths. Students should summarize the teachings of the Buddha and then evaluate the Buddha's conclusions about the causes of sorrow and suffering and how they can be overcome. (The Four Noble Truths state that sorrow and suffering are part of life and result from desire. Pain can be avoided by overcoming desire and following the middle way.) *(Evaluation)* **Making Judgments**

★ REINFORCEMENT. Ask: How did the two schools of Buddhism (p. 134) differ in their view of Buddha? (Theravada: Buddha was a teacher. Mahayana: Buddha was a god.) *(Comprehension)* **Observing for Detail**

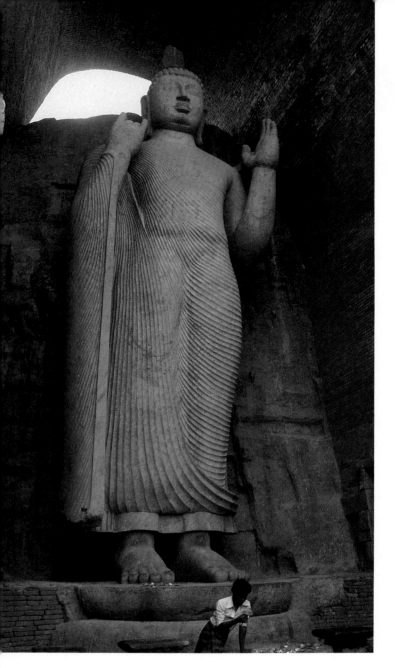

Religion Note that as the Buddha came to be seen as a god, nirvana was viewed as a kind of heaven.

This huge standing Buddha from the island of Sri Lanka was carved around 1,000 years after the Buddha lived.

The Growth of Buddhism

For the next 40 years, the Buddha and his followers traveled widely, doing missionary work. The Buddha's teachings had a strong appeal. People from any caste could, and did, join Buddhist communities.

Monasteries. The Buddha had established a community of monks and, at the **134** request of his aunt, a community of nuns.

Buddhist monks and nuns followed a strict discipline. They wore yellow robes, lived simply, owned little, and usually begged their food from followers.

Rulers and nobles supported Buddhist communities with gifts of land and money. Some of these communities grew quite large. Shrines, teaching halls, and rest houses for pilgrims were built alongside the monastery or convent.

Buddhist monks and nuns studied medicine and looked after the sick and aged. They also opened their doors to scholars from all parts of Asia. Buddhist monasteries quickly became centers of teaching and learning in India.

A split within Buddhism. As Buddhism spread, disagreements grew up about some of its teachings and beliefs. Originally the Buddha had presented a set of guidelines for living. His followers saw him only as a teacher. The Theravada (thehr-uh-VAH-duh) school of Buddhism remained close to these original teachings. Another group of Buddhists, however, came to look upon the Buddha as a god ruling over other gods. They developed a complex religion with temples, saints, and statues of the Buddha. This was the Mahayana (mah-huh-YAH-nuh) school of Buddhism. ● Note strategies for second objective on this page and p. 135.

★ See below, left.

The spread of Buddhism. In the centuries after the death of the Buddha, Buddhism spread through India. Buddhists and Hindus had many things in common, and Hinduism gradually absorbed a number of important Buddhist teachings and attitudes. Eventually, Buddhism began to disappear as a separate faith in India.

While Buddhism was declining in India, however, missionaries and travelers were carrying its message to nearby lands. In other parts of Asia, it eventually became the dominant religion. Mahayana Buddhism spread into China, Japan, and Korea. Theravada Buddhism took hold in Ceylon (present-day Sri Lanka), Burma, and Southeast Asia.

Sec. Rev. ques. 4

See Sec. 1 *Closing the Lesson,* p. T131B.

SCALE
0   500 mi
0   500 km

MONGOLIA
TURKESTAN
ASIA
KOREA
JAPAN
AFGHANISTAN
East
China
Sea
CHINA
TIBET
•Lhasa
NEPAL
Kapilavastu
(birthplace of Buddha)
INDIA
PACIFIC
OCEAN
Arabian
Sea
BURMA
PHILIPPINES
Bay
of
Bengal
SOUTHEAST
ASIA
Sea
China
South
CEYLON
N
W—E
S
MALAYA
BORNEO
INDIAN   OCEAN
KEY
SUMATRA
Hindu-Buddhist influence
Buddhism
JAVA
Spread of Indian influence

Spread of Hinduism and Buddhism by About A.D. 750

• See
below.

The religions of Hinduism and Buddhism both spread from India to other
lands. Where outside of India were followers of both religions found? In
what lands did Buddhism become the major religion?

Map Answers: (1) Ceylon, Nepal, Burma, Southeast Asia, Malaya, Java, part of Sumatra and
Borneo. (2) Tibet, China, Mongolia, Korea, Japan, part of Afghanistan.

Section Review

Answers to Section Review questions are in brackets on pages indicated.

1. **Define or identify:** Buddhism, Four
   Noble Truths, nirvana. (p. 133)
2. **How and when was the Buddhist religion founded?** (p. 133)
3. **In what ways did Buddhism differ from Hinduism?** (p. 133)

4. **Where did Buddhism spread?** (p. 134)
5. **Critical thinking:** Compare the Buddha's teachings with those of the Stoics and the Epicureans (page 92).
   (See answer below.)

● ENRICHMENT. Have students make a chart comparing the spread
of Buddhism with the spread of Christianity (pp. 126–127). Charts
should include information on the time period concerned, the geographic area where each religion began, the methods by which
each religion was spread, and the regions to which the faiths
spread. (Application) *Translating Information into Another Form*

5. Students might point out that each philosophy taught acceptance of
what life brings. In teaching how to escape suffering, however, Epicureans advised avoiding all cause for pain, Stoics counseled indifference to
pain and pleasure, and Buddhists sought a state of nirvana.

2 A Golden Age for India

Objectives

Focus Questions

★ ■ How did the Mauryan Empire rule northern India? *(pages 136–137)*

● ■ What made the Dravidian culture distinctive? *(pages 137–138)*

▲ ■ Why is the Gupta period considered India's Classical Age? *(pages 138–139)*

Terms to Know

ahimsa
Sanskrit

★ Note strategies for first objective on this page.

By about the sixth century B.C.—the time of the Buddha—several kingdoms existed in northeast India, on the great plain of the Ganges River.

The Kingdom of Magadha

The kingdom of Magadha (MAH-guh-duh) was the most stable and prosperous. Through marriages and conquests, the kings of Magadha steadily gained more and more land. By the 400's B.C., Magadha ruled the entire plain of the Ganges and all of northern India as far as the Punjab. (The Punjab is the region through which the Indus and its five main tributaries flow.)

Foreign Powers in India

Persian conquests. At the same time that Magadha was expanding, Cyrus the Great of Persia (page 47) led an army across the mountains into northwest India. By about **136** 518 B.C., Darius I, Cyrus's successor, had conquered the Indus Valley and the Punjab. This part of India remained under Persian rule for almost 200 years. The courts and cities of the Persians became centers of culture.

Alexander the Great. Persian power in India ended as Alexander the Great moved steadily across the ancient Middle East, extending his vast empire (map, page 91). He defeated the Persians in several battles, then moved into India in 327 B.C. Though the Persians and Indians fought fiercely, Alexander's army crossed the Indus River. By then, however, his troops felt they had gone too far into unknown hostile territory, and they threatened to mutiny. Alexander moved his army out of India, but some Greek forts and settlements remained near the northwest frontier. Alexander's death in 323 B.C. left northwest India without an effective ruler.

Sec. Rev. ques. 2

The Rise of the Mauryan Empire

Soon after the death of Alexander, a young adventurer named Chandragupta Maurya (MAWR-yah) seized power in the kingdom of Magadha. Then he moved into the territory Alexander had abandoned. His empire now included all of northern India and part of what is today Afghanistan.

The Mauryan Empire had a strong central government in which the emperor was the supreme authority. To make it easier to govern, the empire was divided into districts and provinces. Chandragupta depended on a powerful army and a wide-ranging network of spies to control the many local governments and officials in his huge empire.

According to legend, Chandragupta gave up the throne after 24 years and adopted the strict life of a monk. His son added more territory in the south to the empire. About 269 B.C. the Mauryan Empire passed to Chandragupta's grandson Asoka (ah-SHOH-kuh).

★ RETEACHING. Have students review "Asoka's Reign" (p. 137) and summarize the principles by which Asoka ruled. *(Comprehension) Observing for Detail*

★ REINFORCEMENT. Write this quotation of Asoka on the board: "This is the root, to reverence one's own faith and never to revile that of others. Whoever acts differently injures his own religion while he wrongs another's." Ask: How did Asoka live this precept? *(Evaluation) Making Judgments*

★ ENRICHMENT. Have students research and write a biographical sketch of the emperor Asoka. Students might find information on Asoka's conquest of Kalinga, his conversion to Buddhism, and his government policies. Have students present their biographies in class. *(Application) Locating Information*

Biography Chandragupta was constantly fearful for his life. To guard against assassination he had all his food tested for poison, slept in a different room every night, and filled his palace with spies.

Cultural History Asoka banned most animal sacrifices, restricted the slaughter of animals for food, and forbade the killing of certain species.

Politics Note that Asoka hoped to set an example of enlightened government and to convince others to adopt his policies.

Asoka's Reign

Asoka began his career with the fierce conquest of the coastal province of Kalinga in 261 B.C. Some 100,000 people were killed in battle. Horrified by this slaughter, Asoka converted to Buddhism and decided never again to use war and violence.

The teachings of Buddhism set the tone for the remaining 30 years of Asoka's rule. His proclamations were written in stone and carried throughout his empire. One of the most famous called for "security, self-control, justice, and happiness for all beings." Asoka supported the ideal of **ahimsa** (uh-HIM-sah), or nonviolence, urging respect for both human and animal life. He also called for tolerance of all beliefs.

Sec. Rev. ques. 3

In addition to his efforts to improve the spiritual and practical lives of his own people, Asoka promoted the peaceful spread of Indian culture. Under his rule, Buddhist missionaries traveled throughout Southeast Asia. As they went, they won not only converts to Buddhism, but admiration for India.

The Breakup of the Mauryan Empire

Asoka has been judged one of the world's greatest rulers. His death in 232 B.C. left a great void in leadership. The next emperor could not hold the huge empire together. Over the next 500 years, northern and central India splintered into many small kingdoms and states. Invaders crossed through the mountain passes into northwest India. Greeks from the former colonies of Alexander's empire, wandering tribes from Central Asia, and adventurers from Persia all set up states in northern India. However, none of them reached the land south of the Deccan.

The Dravidians of South India

● Note strategies for second objective on this page.

Sec. Rev. ques. 4

South India developed quite separately from the north. Settled by the Dravidians (drah-VID-ee-unz), a dark-skinned people from the

Meanwhile . . .

IN ROME

When Asoka became emperor, Rome—far to the west of India—had just begun its empire-building. In 264 B.C. Rome went to war with its enemy Carthage. Rome's victory in that war (in 241 B.C.) gave it Sicily as its first overseas province (page 100).

Indus Valley who had fled southward from the Aryan invaders (page 55), south India remained free from foreign domination.

Culture and language. Over time, the Dravidians absorbed Hindu teachings and some other influences from northern India. Yet the people of the south kept a distinctive

Asoka's Empire About 260 B.C.

Asoka's empire included most of the subcontinent of India. What part of India was not under his rule?

Map Answer: The southernmost part (and Ceylon).

137

● RETEACHING. Have students make a chart with two columns labeled *North India* and *South India*. Students should list the physical characteristics of the people, the historical occurrences, and cultural differences that distinguish the two regions from each other. (North India: Aryan settlers; influenced by Persian and Macedonian invaders; Indo-Aryan language. South India: dark-skinned people from Indus Valley; free from foreign invasions; Dravidian language.) *(Comprehension) Organizing Ideas in Written Form*

● REINFORCEMENT. Have students review "The Geography of India" (p. 53) and find information that supports this statement: *The geography of India helped the Dravidian culture remain distinct from that of north India.* (The Deccan separated north and south India.) *(Comprehension) Relating Geography and History*

● ENRICHMENT. Have students research the Tamils' move for independence in present-day India and Sri Lanka. *(Synthesis) Linking Past and Present*

PRIMARY SOURCE

The Edicts of Asoka

Curly-maned lions sat atop the monuments on which Asoka had his proclamations inscribed. These inscriptions instructed his subjects on matters of morality and compassion. The following statements are adapted from some of Asoka's edicts.

66 One should obey one's father and mother. One should respect the supreme value and sacredness of life. One should speak the truth.

In the same way, pupils should honor their teachers, and in families one should behave with fitting courtesy to relatives. . . .

The faiths of others all deserve to be honored. By honoring them, one glorifies one's own faith and at the same time performs a service to the faith of others. In this way, men may learn and respect the values accepted by others.

Envy, anger, cruelty, impatience, and laziness interfere with the attainment of the middle path. Therefore, each of you should try to make sure that you are not possessed by these passions. 99

1. What values did Asoka want people to live by?
2. According to Asoka, why should people honor each other's religions?
3. What emotions did Asoka say people should avoid? Why?
4. **Critical thinking:** How did Asoka's edicts reflect his belief in Buddhism? (See pages 133–134.)
  Ⓕ See answers below.

138

culture. The Dravidian languages, still spoken today in India and Sri Lanka, are not Indo-European. In fact, they are unrelated to any other language in the world. The main Dravidian language is Tamil (TAM-ul).

Trade. Dravidian merchants took full advantage of India's location between the huge markets of the Mediterranean and China. The prosperity of both areas during the first century B.C. and the first century A.D. helped south Indian trade grow by leaps and bounds. Indian traders sold spices, jewels, perfumes, and exotic animals to Arab merchants who stopped at Indian ports. The Arab ships then headed west, eventually selling most of their rich cargoes to Rome. From ports on India's east coast, merchants sailed to China, exchanging Indian goods for cloth and porcelain.

The Gupta Empire

▲ Note strategies for third objective on this page and p. 139.

About A.D. 320, after centuries of invasions and turmoil, northern India was again united under one ruler. Like the earlier Mauryan Empire, this new empire was centered at Magadha. The first emperor even took the name Chandra Gupta in honor of the ruler of the old Mauryan Empire.

The Gupta Empire was the last great Hindu empire in India. While it held power (the fourth and fifth centuries A.D.), peace settled over India and culture blossomed. During this time, the Indian people established forms in art, literature, and philosophy that served as models for centuries to come. The period of the Gupta Empire is thus often called India's Classical Age.

Literature. Gupta literature showed the importance of Hinduism in everyday Indian life. Many fables and folk tales from this period (such as the tale of Sinbad the Sailor) were translated and read in Persia and then in Europe. Gupta writers produced plays and poetry in **Sanskrit**, the Indian language of literature. India's greatest poet and playwright was Kalidasa (kah-lih-DAH-suh). His play *Shakuntala*, based on an idea from one of the Hindu epics, is still performed in India.

Ⓕ **Primary Source Answers** 1. People should obey their parents and teachers, respect all living things, and be courteous and truthful. 2. Through tolerance people learn about and respect each other's beliefs. 3. Envy, anger, cruelty, impatience, and laziness. These get in the way of attaining the middle path, which leads to enlightenment according to Buddhist principles. 4. Answers will vary. Asoka advocates the Buddhist belief in following the middle way, or path.

▲ **RETEACHING.** Have students explain why the Gupta period is called India's Classical Age. (Northern India was united under one ruler; peace was established over India; culture blossomed.) *(Comprehension) Observing for Detail*

▲ **REINFORCEMENT.** Have students make a chart of the accomplishments of India's Classical Age. Columns should be labeled *Literature* and *Mathematics. (Comprehension) Translating Information into Another Form*

Science and mathematics. Astronomers, mathematicians, and physicians in Gupta India were far ahead of those in western Europe and the rest of the world. Probably the most impressive achievements were made in the field of mathematics. Gupta mathematicians established the decimal system, the idea of zero, and the beginnings of algebra. Europeans later gave the Arabs credit for so-called Arabic numerals (that is, *1, 2, 3,* and so on), but the Arabs called mathematics "the Indian art."

Although the Gupta kings were Hindus, Buddhism still influenced much Indian scholarship. Some monasteries had developed into universities with large libraries. Buddhist scholars flocked there from China and other countries to which Buddhism had spread.

The fall of the Gupta Empire. The two centuries of the Gupta Empire were the high point of Indian culture. Prospering while Rome declined, India was the most advanced civilization in the world during this period.

About the middle of the fifth century, however, the Huns (page 122) began to raid the borders of the Gupta Empire. These attacks weakened the central government, and power passed to the local leaders. By about A.D. 500 the northern part of India was once again a checkerboard of states and kingdoms.

▲ See below, left.

See Sec. 2 *Closing the Lesson*, p. T131B.

Section Review

Answers to Section Review questions are in brackets on pages indicated.

1. **Define or identify:** ahimsa, Sanskrit. (pp. 137, 138)
2. What ended Persian power in India? (p. 136)
3. What contributions did Asoka make to India? (p. 137)
4. Who were the Dravidians? (p. 137)
5. **Critical thinking:** Compare the fall of the Gupta Empire with the fall of the Mauryan Empire. (See answer below.)

5. Answers will vary. Students should note that both empires declined after invasions led to the splintering off of smaller states and weakening of the central government.

See lesson plans, pp. T131A–T131C.

3 China Under the Qin and Han Dynasties

Objectives

★ Note strategies for first objective on this page and p. 141.

Focus Questions

- ★ ■ What new philosophies developed in China after Confucius? *(pages 139–141)*
- ● ■ How did the Qin dynasty establish the Chinese Empire? *(pages 141–142)*
- ▲ ■ How did the Han dynasty strengthen China? *(pages 142–145)*

Terms to Know

Taoism	dynastic cycle
Legalism	Silk Road
Great Wall	Age of Disunity

When the Gupta Empire broke apart in India in the fifth century, disorder followed. Much the same thing had happened in China in the third century B.C., when the Zhou dynasty collapsed. The unrest and confusion that marked the end of Zhou rule led many Chinese to search for order. The new ideas that resulted helped the Chinese build an empire that lasted many centuries.

New Philosophies

As you learned in Chapter 3, the teachings of Confucius became a central feature of Chinese culture during the late Zhou dynasty. However, Confucius was just one of many scholars who offered new philosophies. **139**

▲ ENRICHMENT. Have students compare the effects of the Hun invasions on both the Gupta and Roman empires (p. 122). Students might research how Indian and Roman strength compared with that of the Huns, draw a map illustrating Indian and Roman territory invaded and seized by the Huns, and draw conclusions about why the Huns were so effective against established empires. *(Synthesis) Synthesizing Information*

★ RETEACHING. Have students identify each of the following statements as a characteristic of Mencius's views, Taoism, or Legalism: (a) Individuals are naturally good. (Mencius) (b) The "way" had to be sensed or felt. (Taoism) (c) The welfare of the people should be a ruler's main concern. (Mencius) (d) A ruler needed complete control and should weed out anything that stood in the way. (Legalism) *(Comprehension) Observing for Detail*

Some scholars welcomed his ideas and built on them, but others flatly rejected them.

Mencius. The philosopher known to the West as Mencius (MEN-shee-us) lived about 200 years after Confucius, from 372 to 289 B.C. Mencius said that individuals are naturally good and that this goodness can be developed into the Confucian virtues. He also taught that the welfare of the people should be a ruler's main concern. A ruler who did not protect and help his people, Mencius argued, lost the Mandate of Heaven (page 61) and should be overthrown.

Taoism. While Confucian philosophers set up strict rules for people's behavior within society, a different group of thinkers believed in less structure. During the 300's and 200's B.C., they developed a philosophy and religion called **Taoism** (DOW-iz-um). Their aim was to discover the *Tao*, or "way," of the universe and to live simply and in harmony with nature.

Sec. Rev. ques. 2

The first great teacher of Taoism is said to have been the wise man Laozi (LOW-dzuh). Legend has it that Laozi, whose name is sometimes spelled Lao-tse, set down his

Qin Empire, 221–206 B.C.

By 221 B.C. the rulers of the Qin state had expanded their power and created an empire in China. What river flowed through the northern part of the empire? What protected the empire's northern boundary? What seaport in the south did the Qin control?

Map Answers: (1) Yellow. (2) Great Wall. (3) Canton (Guangzhou).

ideas at the age of 80. He may, however, have been only a mythical figure.

In about the third century B.C., Taoist teachings were collected in a book called the *Tao Te Ching*, which means "The Classic of the Way and Its Power." Taoist thinkers agreed, though, that the *Tao* could not really be explained in words. It had to be sensed or felt, and this could only occur after the mind had been emptied of all other thought and emotion.

Sec. Rev. ques. 2, cont.

Taoists found special meaning in such symbols as raw silk, an uncarved block of wood, and a newborn child. All of these were in their natural state, unchanged by society. To find the way of the natural universe, some Taoists became hermits. Their mystical philosophy served as an alternative to the practical rules of Confucianism. Both ways of thinking lasted in China until modern times.

Legalism. Besides Confucianism and Taoism, another influential Chinese philosophy was **Legalism**. Developed in the third century B.C., Legalism taught that people were basically evil and selfish and could live well only under strict laws. Legalists argued that to make the state wealthy and powerful, a ruler needed complete control. Any people, ideas, or institutions that stood in the ruler's way should be weeded out.

Sec. Rev. ques. 3

The harsh philosophy of the Legalists had none of the moral or spiritual appeal of Confucian or Taoist thought. It did have great practical value for those willing to use it. Legalist ideas were put into practice by Qin (CHIN) rulers during the third century B.C.

★ See below.

The Qin Dynasty

● Note strategies for second objective on this page and p. 142.
The ruler of the powerful state of Qin, sometimes spelled *Ch'in*, overthrew the last of the Zhou rulers in 256 B.C. In 221, after putting down resistance, the Qin established their own dynasty. It lasted fewer than 15 years, but it laid the basis for an empire that endured into the twentieth century.

Legalist rule. The Qin ruler called himself *Shihuangdi* (SHIR-HWAHNG-DEE), meaning "First Emperor." His most trusted

In 1979, peasants in the Yellow River Valley unearthed the enormous tomb of the First Emperor while digging a well. The figure at the lower right is one of six thousand life-size clay soldiers that guard the tomb.

adviser was Li Si (LEE SEE), one of the founders of Legalism. They began to apply Legalist thinking to all of China, crushing the local lords and strengthening defenses against nomadic tribes.

Qin achievements. Earlier, rulers of states on China's northwest border had built high walls to protect their lands. Shihuangdi ordered that these walls be linked to form one **Great Wall** (map, page 140). About one million laborers were forced to work on the Great Wall. When finished, it stretched from the Yellow Sea to China's western frontier, a distance of about 1,500 miles (roughly the distance between Denver and Boston). Soldiers stood atop this mighty barricade to guard China's frontier. More than a military success, the Great Wall was also a monument to the emperor's power.

Sec. Rev. ques. 4

141

★ REINFORCEMENT. Have students write an essay explaining which philosophy they would have preferred their ruler to follow had they lived in China during the third century B.C., and why. (Synthesis) *Expressing Point of View*

★ ENRICHMENT. Have students explain how the following excerpt from the *Tao Te Ching* exemplifies the concepts of Taoism. "The way that can be told is not the way." (Application) *Interpreting a Primary Source*

● RETEACHING. Have students review "The Qin Dynasty" (pp. 141–142) and categorize each action of the Qin leaders as one that *Strengthened* or one that *Weakened the dynasty*. (Comprehension) *Making Judgments*

Biography Known as the "Tiger of Qin," Shihuangdi was described by one of his officials as "a man with a high-bridged nose, long narrow eyes, the chest of a bird of prey, the voice of a jackal, and the mind of a tiger."

To help unify the country, the Qin government built roads and canals, making communication quicker and safer. Li Si made the written language simpler so that more people could learn to read and write. Conquests by Qin armies also extended the emperor's rule into southern China.

Censorship. As followers of Legalism, the Qin officials felt that other ways of thinking were dangerous to the state. In 213 B.C. Li Si began a policy of book-burning. The court library kept copies of early histories and the classics, but privately owned books were ordered destroyed. Scholars who discussed earlier times, criticized the government, or objected to the control of ideas were executed or banished.

Decline of the Qin. These actions of the Qin authorities weakened the dynasty. The banished Confucian scholars had been the best-trained public officials. Without them, the government ran poorly. In addition, many people did not support the rigid Legalist policies. Soldiers and peasants rebelled, and the dynasty collapsed only a few years after the death of the First Emperor.

● See below.

The Dynastic Cycle in China

The fall of the Qin dynasty showed some of the basic problems faced by Chinese dynasties: rebellions by local lords and peasants, barbarian invasions, and natural disasters. These problems caused the rise and fall of dynasties in a regular pattern. Many historians call this pattern the dynastic cycle.

The dynastic cycle generally began with the rise of a new dynasty and a period of peace and prosperity. Believing that the ruler held the Mandate of Heaven, people were loyal to him. Population rose steadily. The government spent money on public works—walls, canals, and roads.

As the dynasty continued, less able rulers came to power. Court officials and bureaucrats became corrupt and greedy. More funds also went to defend newly won lands or hold off invaders. Even though the peasants were taxed more heavily, the gov-

142

ernment did not keep things in repair. Dams and walls, weakened by neglect, failed to hold back floods and invasions. Crops were destroyed, and famine sometimes resulted.

Peasant rebellions broke out as people complained that the ruling dynasty had lost the Mandate of Heaven. Nobles began to seize power. Tax collections grew smaller. Finally the old dynasty fell. The new dynasty started by restoring peace and prosperity, and the cycle began again.

The Han Dynasty

▲ Note strategies for third objective on this page and p. 145.

For several years after the fall of the Qin, rival leaders struggled for power. In 202 B.C., a military leader declared himself emperor and established the Han (HAHN) dynasty. This leader took the title *Gao Zu* (KOW DZOO), meaning "Great Ancestral Father."

"The Han people." Gao Zu and his successors drew on Qin patterns of governing but avoided the extremes of that rigid rule. This enabled the Han dynasty to last until A.D. 220. The 400 years of Han rule were so remarkable that the Chinese still call themselves "the Han people." The Han capital at Chang'an in the Wei River valley became a model city. Today the city of Xi'an (SHEE-AHN) stands on the site of Chang'an.

Sec. Rev. ques. 5

Expansion. The Han dynasty's greatest growth in land and power came about during the long reign of Wu Di (WOO DEE), who ruled from 141 to 87 B.C. Han armies conquered many non-Chinese peoples along the southern coast and in Southeast Asia. To the north and east, the empire expanded far beyond the Great Wall to include large parts of Korea and Manchuria.

Wu Di also launched a campaign against the Huns. After his death, the Chinese conquered most of the barren mountains and plains of Central Asia. By about the first century B.C., the borders of China reached as far west as northern India.

Trade. Since ancient times the Chinese had known how to raise silkworms and weave silk cloth from the fibers spun by the worms. Since no other people knew this se-

Han Empire About A.D. 100

Under Han rule, the Chinese Empire stretched from the Pacific coast far to the west. Describe the routes followed by merchants who carried goods between southern China and the Roman Empire. (See answer below.)

cret, Chinese silk was valuable for trade. With bundles of silk heaped high on their camels, merchants headed westward through China on what became known as the **Silk Road**. They traveled to India, Persia, and even Roman provinces along the Mediterranean, a journey of some 4,000 miles.

Trade provided a way for ideas as well as goods to travel between cultures. In trading with Rome, the Chinese had contact, for the first time in their history, with a civilization they considered as rich as their own. To

Han dynasty prince Liu Sheng expected this burial suit, made from 3,000 pieces of sewn jade, to preserve his body for eternal life.

143

Map Answer: Went south around Southeast Asia, west to India, and then either overland through Persia, by sea to Egypt, or by sea and land to Antioch and Arabia.

The Arts

Making Silk

Making silk cloth took weeks of work. When the tiny caterpillars, or silkworms, hatched, they were spread on trays and carefully tended. Workers had to pick and chop *tons* of leaves to feed just one pound of the silkworms.

Eventually, each caterpillar spun a single silk thread into a cocoon. The cocoons were dropped into boiling water so that the thread could be unwound and wrapped on a reel. Dyers dipped the thread into vats of colors. Weavers then wove the threads into dazzling patterns. Sometimes the threads were pounded, as shown in this painting of ladies in the imperial court.

Each bolt of precious cloth that made its way along the Silk Road represented thousands of hours of work. But people in distant lands were willing to pay dearly for this wondrous fabric.

ⓕ See above.

show their admiration, they called the Roman Empire "Great Qin." The Romans called China *Serica*, "the silk country."

Educated government officials. Han rulers realized that the growing empire needed well-educated officials if it was to run properly. To find qualified candidates, Han rulers set up a civil service system with written examinations. Anyone wanting a government job was tested on Confucian ideas about government.

Soon scholar-officials replaced men of noble birth as the leading class in Han society. Scholar-officials were most likely to be the sons of landowners. Merchants, no matter how well educated, were barred from government posts because the Han rulers despised moneymaking. In theory, farmers or peasants had a chance to rise in society through their own efforts, but this rarely happened. They could not afford the years of study needed to pass the tests.

Scientific and technological achievements. The Han period produced some remarkable advances in science and technology. The Chinese had been recording information about the stars and planets since ancient times. Comets, sunspots, and eclipses were thought to be messages from heaven. In Han times, Chinese astronomers devised an accurate calendar, water clocks, sundials, star maps, and several astronomical instruments. Chinese scientists also discovered the principle of the magnetic compass and made an instrument to record earthquakes. Other scientists made discoveries in medicine.

About the first century A.D., the Chinese learned to make paper. Like silk-weaving, this remained a uniquely Chinese skill for centuries. Another of China's famous crafts—the making of fine porcelain or "china"—also began during the Han dynasty. Han potters invented glazes that gave plates and bowls a smooth, clean surface.

144

Cultural History The Chinese guarded the secret of the silkworm for 3,000 years. Disgrace and death faced anyone who revealed the origin of silk to the outside world. Around A.D. 500, the Byzantine emperor Justinian sent two monks to China as spies. They smuggled out silkworm eggs in hollow bamboo canes and ended the Chinese monopoly of silk production.

Social History A civil service candidate started preparation for the exams as a teenager by studying the Confucian classics. At about age 23, the candidate began the examination process. Exams lasted from one to nine days. The final exam, sometimes administered to as many as 3,500 candidates, eliminated all but 10 percent of those seeking public office.

The Age of Disunity

By early in the second century A.D., the Han rulers were facing ruin. There were rivalries at court as well as rebellions among the peasants. Even the examination system no longer worked well. Officials were more likely to be chosen on the basis of political influence than knowledge.

In A.D. 220, the Han Empire split into three kingdoms. Constant warfare caused great hardship. This time of trouble came to be called the Age of Disunity. It continued until the year 589.

▲ See below.

The collapse of the Han dynasty plunged China into disorder. However, Han achievements in philosophy, politics, and culture would continue to benefit China.

See Sec. 3 *Closing the Lesson*, p. T131C.

Section Review

Answers to Section Review questions are in brackets on pages indicated.

1. **Define or identify:** Taoism, Legalism, Great Wall, dynastic cycle, Silk Road, Age of Disunity. (pp. 140, 141, 142, 143, 145)
2. What were the main ideas and teachings of the Taoists? (p. 140, 141)
3. What did the Legalists teach? (p. 141)
4. What were some of the achievements of the Qin dynasty? What caused its downfall? (p. 141–142)
5. Why do the Chinese call themselves "the Han people"? (p. 142)
6. **Critical thinking:** How did both the Qin and the Han dynasties contribute to Chinese unity? (See answer below.)

6. Answers will vary. Students should cite examples of improved communication and transportation, territorial expansion, increased trade, and changes in government.

Chapter 7   Summary and Timeline

1. The religion of Buddhism was founded in India by Siddhartha Gautama in the sixth century B.C. It was similar in many ways to Hinduism but had wider appeal. Buddhism took root outside India, while within India it was absorbed into Hinduism.

2. India was never united politically. In the north, the Mauryan Empire reached its height under the emperor Asoka in the third century B.C. After Asoka's death, northern India broke into many small kingdoms. It was not until 320 A.D. that another great Indian

empire arose—the Gupta. Meanwhile, the Dravidian people in the south developed their own culture and a busy trade with Rome and China.

3. After the death of Confucius, Chinese thinkers developed new philosophies. One of these philosophies, Legalism, became the basis of the Qin dynasty, which ruled briefly during the third century B.C. After the fall of the Qin, the Han dynasty ruled for four centuries. Han rulers gave China strength and prosperity.

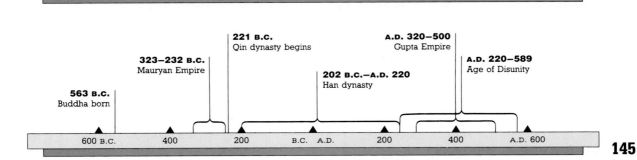

221 B.C. Qin dynasty begins

A.D. 320–500 Gupta Empire

323–232 B.C. Mauryan Empire

A.D. 220–589 Age of Disunity

202 B.C.–A.D. 220 Han dynasty

563 B.C. Buddha born

600 B.C.   400   200   B.C. A.D.   200   400   A.D. 600

145

▲ REINFORCEMENT. Ask: (a) How long did the Han Dynasty last? (400 years.) (b) What was the Silk Road? (The road west through China traveled by silk merchants.) (c) Which culture in the West did the Chinese consider to be as rich as their own? (Roman civilization.) (d) What did the Romans call China? (Serica, or "the silk country.") (e) What might have been some advantages of the examination system for government officials? (Answers will vary.) *(Comprehension) Observing for Detail*

▲ ENRICHMENT. Have students apply the dynastic-cycle theory (p. 142) to the rise and decline of the Han dynasty. Students might make a chart or a diagram listing the stages of the dynastic cycle and then correlate the pattern to the Han dynasty. *(Application) Applying a Theory*

CHAPTER 7 REVIEW

See p. T131C for answers to Chapter Review.

Vocabulary Review

Use the following terms to complete the sentences below: *Age of Disunity, ahimsa, Buddhism, dynastic cycle, nirvana, Sanskrit.*

1. The Buddhist and Hindu belief in nonviolence is called ___?___.
2. The pattern of the rise and fall of ruling families is known as the ___?___.
3. The ___?___ was the period of troubles that followed the collapse of the Han dynasty.
4. The followers of ___?___ believe it is possible to reach a state of ___?___ in one lifetime.
5. ___?___ is the language used in the literature of India.

People to Identify

Match each of the following people with the correct description: *Chandra Gupta, Gao Zu, Kalidasa, Laozi, Li Si, Mencius, Shihuangdi, Siddhartha Gautama, Wu Di.*

1. India's greatest poet and playwright
2. philosopher who added to Confucian principles and taught that the people's welfare should be a ruler's main concern
3. the Buddha's name before he became the "Enlightened One"
4. Han leader who expanded the empire to its greatest size
5. first (and possibly mythical) teacher of Taoism
6. Legalist thinker who simplified the Chinese written language
7. Qin ruler whose name translates as "First Emperor"
8. first ruler of the Han Dynasty
9. first ruler of the Gupta Empire

Places to Know

Use the following place names to complete the sentences below: *Chang'an, Magadha, Indus River, Silk Road.*

1. The Mauryan Empire and the Gupta Empire were both centered at ___?___.
2. The Han capital of ___?___ was a model city, with great parks, palaces, and public buildings.
3. Chinese traders traveled along the ___?___ to India, Persia, and the Roman Empire.
4. Alexander's army crossed the ___?___ during its invasion of India.

Recalling the Facts

1. What are the Four Noble Truths of Buddhism?
2. In what ways did the teachings of Buddhism challenge Hinduism?
3. How did Buddhism spread beyond India?
4. What kind of government did Chandragupta Maurya set up?
5. What were some of Asoka's policies as ruler of the Mauryan Empire?
6. Why did south India develop a culture that was quite different from that of north India?
7. What achievements were made during India's Classical Age?
8. How did Taoism differ from Confucianism? How did Legalism differ from other Chinese philosophies?
9. How did the Qin rulers unify China? Why did the dynasty decline?
10. How did the Han rulers make sure their growing empire was governed well? Why did the dynasty decline?

1. **Classifying.** Buddhism and Hinduism are two of the major religions of Asia. List their beliefs in a chart, classifying them under the following headings: *Applies Only to Buddhism, Applies Only to Hinduism; Applies to Both.* For a discussion of Buddhism, you may want to look at Section 1 of this chapter. Hinduism is discussed on pages 57–58 of Chapter 3. *(Comp.)*

2. **Making judgments.** In what ways was Legalism useful for the Qin dynasty? How can it be argued that, in the long run, Legalism hurt the dynasty? *(Syn.)*

3. **Interpreting a diagram.** The diagram below shows three key phases of the dynastic cycle. Read each of the following statements and tell whether the event would occur after the first, second, or third phase. *(Comp.)*

    a. Peasants are heavily taxed.
    b. Government officials become corrupt.
    c. Old dynasty falls.
    d. Funds are spent to improve public works.
    e. Population rises.
    f. Nobles begin to seize power from the ruler.
    g. Public works deteriorate, leading to floods, invasions, and famine.

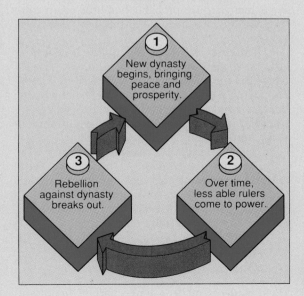

1. New dynasty begins, bringing peace and prosperity.
2. Over time, less able rulers come to power.
3. Rebellion against dynasty breaks out.

Analyzing a map. On the map of China on page 140, locate the Great Wall. Which of the Qin Empire's borders were protected by the wall? Why, do you think, was the wall built along these frontiers rather than along the empire's other borders? *(Comp.)*

Enrichment: Primary Sources

During the third century B.C., when disorder plagued China, the philosopher Mencius tried to convince warring rulers to be fair and kind. In the adapted passage below, Mencius presents some of his ideas.

“ It was because of their humanity that earlier rulers won the empire. Without humanity, the emperor would be unable to safeguard the four seas, a feudal lord would be unable to safeguard the land and grain, and the individual would be unable to safeguard his four limbs.

Here is the way to win the empire: win the people. Here is the way to win the people: win their hearts. Here is the way to win their hearts: give them and share with them what they like, and do not do to them what they do not like. The people turn to a humane ruler as water flows downward or beasts take to wilderness. ”

1. According to Mencius, why was it important for rulers to act humanely?
2. How does Mencius make comparisons with nature in giving his advice?
3. **Critical thinking:** Why, do you think, would Mencius say that violence is not an effective way to win an empire? *(Anal.)*

147

Ancient Africa and America   1600 B.C.–A.D. 950

(pp. 148–164)

Chapter Preview

Section 1 describes the geography of Africa and then traces the rise and decline of kingdoms and trading empires in eastern Africa and the Sudan. Students will read about the extensive migrations of Bantu-speaking peoples and some of the states established in central and southern Africa. Section 2 focuses on the migration of hunting peoples from Asia to the Americas and the rise of the Olmec, Teotihuacán, and Maya civilizations.

Bibliography

See the *Teacher's Management and Planning Guide* for additional listings. Starred titles are for both students and teachers.

Coe, Michael. *The Jaguar's Children*. Museum of Primitive Art. A survey of Olmec culture.

Davidson, Basil. *The Lost Cities of Africa*. Little, Brown. Sketches of many cultures.

Gallencamp, Charles. *Maya: The Riddle and Rediscovery of a Lost Civilization*. Penguin. Newly updated.

*Karen, Ruth. *Feathered Serpent: The Rise and Fall of the Aztecs*. Scholastic, Inc.

Section Lesson Plans

SECTION 1   (pp. 149–155)
Africa's Early Civilizations

Objectives

After completing this section, students will be able to:
1. Explain how geography shaped Africa's early history.
2. Describe how migrations helped spread ideas and customs.
3. Discuss the African trading kingdoms.

Introducing the Lesson

Remind students that Africa is a vast continent with many variations in climate and geography. Differences in rainfall, temperature, and terrain help explain the development of diverse cultures.

Then refer students to the map of African landforms and vegetation (p. 151) and ask:

(a) How might the size of the African continent have affected the development of cultures? (Answers will vary. Because Africa is so large, many groups probably had little or no contact with one another, making cultural exchange slow.)

(b) How might the geographic location of African societies have affected cultural change? (Answers will vary. Societies that lived in coastal regions or along rivers would more likely have contact with others; this access to a means of transportation would increase the opportunity to share knowledge.)

(c) Why might African and European societies have been so different? (Answers will vary. Africans and Europeans had infrequent contact except in North Africa and Egypt. With little opportunity for cultural exchange, European and African development took different paths.)

Developing the Lesson:
Understanding Chronology

Have students make a time chart of important developments on the African continent. Students should include geographic, political, technological, and economic developments. (Time chart should include information for the following: New Stone Age; formation of the Sahara; spread of agriculture; migrations; kingdom of Kush; Egyptian dominance; revival of Kush; Assyrian invasions; use of iron; Kush attacked by Aksum; introduction of Christianity.) *(Comprehension)*

Developing the Lesson: Comparing Information

Have students write three paragraphs comparing the Nok, Kushite, and Aksum peoples (pp. 150–154). Each paragraph should include information that identifies the group and distinguishes it from the other two. (*Nok:* culture arose about 500 B.C. in central Nigeria; made pottery; knew weaving and metalworking; were farmers and herders. *Kushites:* traded with Egyptians; people lived along the Nile; founded kingdom of Kush in 1600's B.C.; capital at Meroë became one of ancient world's major ironworking centers. *Aksum:* located in northern highlands of present-day Ethiopia; farmers and traders; developed a form of writing; first sub-Saharan kingdom to make coins; built stone palaces and monuments; Christianity introduced in A.D. 350.) *(Comprehension)*

Closing the Lesson: Summarizing Information

Ask: *(a) What were the important economic activities of early Africans?* (Hunting and gathering; herding; farming; trade; metalworking.)

(b) How did geography influence the occupations of early Africans? (Climate and terrain determined the success of herding and farming; it also influenced settlements.)

(c) In which part of Africa would you have preferred to live? Why? (Answers will vary.) *(Comprehension)*

See **Section Review** questions, p. 155.

SECTION 2   (pp. 156–162)
Civilizations in the Americas

Objectives

After completing this section, students will be able to:
1. Explain how people first came to the Americas.
2. Describe the kinds of civilizations built by the Olmecs, Teotihuacános, and Mayas.

Introducing the Lesson

Tell students that the earliest Americans were probably migrants who crossed the Bering Strait from Asia. Groups of these hunters gradually worked their way through North, Central, and South America over a period of hundreds of years.

Then ask: *(a) What might have motivated early Americans to travel across the Bering Strait?* (Answers will vary. The early Americans were hunters and were probably following roaming herds of animals.)

(b) What are some reasons why people today might move from one region to another? (Answers will vary. Some people may move because their jobs require it, or to find employment. Some people might move for adventure or a change of scene.)

Developing the Lesson: Summarizing Information

Ask: *(a) Why did ancient peoples in the Americas have no way to learn from the achievements of other civilizations?* (The land bridge from Asia disappeared and societies in the Americas were cut off from other parts of the world.)

(b) What evidence is there that the Olmecs had contact with other Central American peoples? (Olmec carvings have been found all over Central America and sculptures showing Olmec influence appear in western Mexico and southern Guatemala. Later peoples in Mexico and Central America adopted or improved on the Olmec system of writing, number system, calendar, style of architecture.)

(c) Why can't archeologists fully explain the advances of the Olmecs and their influence on others? (Olmec writing has not yet been deciphered.) *(Comprehension)*

Answers to *Map Skill Practice,* p. 157.

1. The land bridge in the area of what is today the Bering Strait.
2. From Asia.
3. By route lines.
4. To Cape Horn.
5. The extensive ice cover.
6. The Plains area east of the Rockies would have been much easier for travel.

Developing the Lesson:
Analyzing Information

Have students use the definition of *civilization* (p. 21) to analyze the Olmec, Teotihuacán, and Maya societies. Students might make a chart to organize the information about each group and then decide if the characteristics of each describe a civilization. (Civilization includes an organized government, organized religion, division of labor, class structure, and system of writing.) *(Analysis)*

Closing the Lesson:
Understanding Point of View

Have students work in groups to prepare a dialogue that might have occurred between representatives of the first Americans and ancient Africans. The dialogue might include a discussion of both groups' homelands, their economic systems and social organizations, and their cultural achievements. Have students present their dialogues in class. *(Application)*

See *Section Review* questions, p. 162.

Chapter 8 Review Answers
(pp. 163–164)

Vocabulary Review

1. pilgrimage 2. savanna 3. silent barter 4. isthmus

Places to Know

1. F 2. G 3. H 4. C 5. E 6. B 7. A 8. D

Recalling the Facts

1. The weather in the Sahara became extremely dry, turning the land into desert. Disease killed off large animals in the Congo Basin and on the Guinea Coast.

2. Iron tools made farming easier and iron weapons were more effective against enemies.
3. Meroë was located on major trade routes between sub-Saharan Africa and Egypt. Nomadic desert peoples raided Kush, trade and farm production dropped, and the kingdom was conquered by Aksum about A.D. 350.
4. States of the Middle East, India, Egypt, China, and other parts of Asia.
5. They taxed the trade on salt and gold.
6. Asia. They were hunters looking for food.
7. Olmec carvings and sculptures that show Olmec influence have been found all over Central America. Later peoples adopted or improved on the Olmec system of writing, number system, calendar, style of architecture, and ritual ball game.
8. It was not just a religious center visited by pilgrims but a city where all classes of people lived and worked.
9. Priests helped rule Maya city-states, kept track of time, and decided when ceremonies should be held and ventures undertaken. Nobles helped run the government by collecting taxes, keeping records of work that was done, and watching over the road system. Warriors led troops in wars between city-states. Peasants farmed the land. Men also worked on building projects and served as soldiers, while women gathered honey, wove cloth, made pottery, and cared for their households.

Critical Thinking Skills

1. (a) An employee not worth his salt is not worth his salary; something not worth its salt is not valuable. This phrase has the same Latin root, *sal*, as the word *salary* and takes its meaning from the days when Roman salaries were paid partially in salt. (b) "The salt of the earth" was first used in Matthew 5:13 and refers to the most admirable people. (c) To take something with a grain of salt is to be skeptical about it. As you would not find much salt in your food, so you would find little truth in a statement that was made.
2–5. Answers will vary.

Thinking about Geography

1. Kush—Egypt; Aksum—Ethiopia; Bantu lands—Cameroon, Central African Republic, Equatorial Guinea, Gabon, Congo, Angola, Zaire, Rwanda, Burundi, Tanzania, Zambia, Malawi, Mozambique, Uganda, Kenya.

2. At the end of the last Ice Age, the disappearance of the land bridge that connected the continents of Asia and the Americas caused peoples in the Americas to be cut off from the civilizations in other parts of the world. As the glaciers melted and the climate in some areas grew hotter and drier, many animals died out and food became scarce. Hunters learned to cultivate wild foods, realizing that this provided a steadier source of food than hunting and gathering.

Enrichment: Primary Sources

1. The population was too great for the food supply, which was dwindling.

2. Answers should include two of the following: the soldiers' declining power may have left the Mayas unable to defend themselves against invasion. The disappearance of the priests, who kept the calendar, may have led to a decline in education and traditional practices. Attacks by enemies from the north and west drove the Mayas out of their homes and villages. The fighting among chiefs may have caused political unrest and violence.

3. The gods were saddened by the situation and their failure to protect the people.

4. The civilization was slowly dying.

Ancient Africa and America 1600 B.C.–A.D. 950

See chapter timeline, p. 162.

Before You Read This Chapter

Why do people travel? You probably make short trips every day—to get to school, to visit friends. Do you make longer trips at special holidays? Do you know anyone who has moved to take a new job? This chapter describes how people lived and worked in ancient civilizations on three vast continents. Often these people overcame great geographic barriers to travel, trade, or settle in new lands. As you read, look for the motives that led these people to travel within their own lands or beyond their borders. What were they seeking? How were their motives similar to ours today?

The Geographic Setting

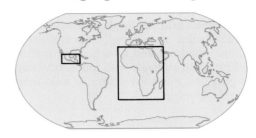

The Chapter Outline

1. Africa's Early Civilizations
2. Civilizations in the Americas

An Egyptian wall painting records a group of nobles from the African kingdom of Kush attending the funeral of a pharaoh in 1290 B.C.

148

1 Africa's Early Civilizations

Objectives

Focus Questions

★ ■ How did geography shape Africa's early history? *(pages 149–150)*
● ■ How did migrations help spread ideas and customs? *(pages 150, 152)*
▲ ■ What trading kingdoms arose in Africa? *(pages 152–155)*

Terms to Know

savanna
silent barter

★ Note strategies for first objective on this page and p. 150.

Geography strongly influenced how and where people lived in ancient Africa. Over thousands of years people learned the skills needed to live in the continent's different climates. When the climate changed or the population increased, people moved to find land that would better meet their needs. Differences in language, customs, and appearance resulted from migrations and from the adaptation to new environments.

Geography also influenced when and where important civilizations arose. The oldest and most influential of the ancient African civilizations was Egypt, which took shape in the fertile Nile Valley (Chapter 2). Egypt's political, economic, and cultural life influenced other early kingdoms along the Nile. Later, city-states based on trade grew up along the coast of eastern Africa and the southern edge of the Sahara.

The Geography of Africa

Most of the African continent has a very warm climate all year round, but differences in rainfall have produced five vegetation zones (map, page 151). The wettest regions are in the Congo River Basin and along the Guinea (GHIN-ee) Coast. Heavy rainfall in these areas produces a lush tropical rain forest. On the plateaus south of the Congo Basin and in the highlands to the northeast, dry forests grow.

Savannas—open grasslands with scattered shrubs or trees—cover large stretches of land on both sides of the equator. North and south of the savannas lie deserts, the vast Sahara across the north and the Namib (NAH-mib) and Kalahari (kah-luh-HAR-ee) deserts in the south. At the northern and southern edges of Africa are narrow coastal strips with seasonal rains. These areas have a temperate climate like that of Mediterranean Europe.

Sec. Rev. ques. 2

The First Africans

As you read in Chapter 1, scientists believe that human life began in Africa. Early humans lived in the savannas, where they hunted the plentiful game and gathered wild foods. Over many hundreds of thousands of years, small groups of people spread throughout Africa. As their numbers increased, some groups became more settled. By the New Stone Age, which began about 10,000 years ago, permanent fishing communities existed along many of Africa's lakes and major rivers.

During the New Stone Age, food production gradually became more important than food gathering. Africans began to keep herds of domesticated animals and to grow their own plants for food. Settlements of farmers and cattle herders took form along the Nile Valley. Another early farming center developed in the Ethiopian highlands.

Cattle once grazed in the area that is now the Sahara. Until about 5000 B.C. this land was covered by forests and grasses. Then the weather turned extremely dry. Between **149**

★ RETEACHING. Have students review "The First Africans" (pp. 149–150) and find facts that support the following statement: *Geography influenced where people lived in ancient Africa.* (Savannas provided plentiful game and wild foods; fishing communities were established along lakes and rivers; farmers and herders settled in the Nile Valley; farming centered in Ethiopian highlands.) *(Comprehension)* **Supporting Generalizations**

★ REINFORCEMENT. Have students identify the regions and geographic features of Africa. (North Africa: narrow coastal strips with seasonal rain; temperate climate. Sahara: desert. West Africa: lush tropical rain forest (Guinea Coast), savanna. East Africa: dry woodland, highlands. Central Africa: tropical rain forest (Congo Basin), savanna. Southern Africa: desert, southern coastal strip with seasonal rains and temperate climate.) *(Comprehension)* **Observing for Detail**

5000 and 2000 B.C., more and more land turned to desert. Eventually the Sahara stretched entirely across Africa. The cattle-keeping people there were forced to migrate to better-watered areas.

The Spread of Agriculture

While the Sahara was expanding, agriculture was spreading through Africa. During the centuries after 3000 B.C., farming became more important than herding in the wetter parts of the western Sudan (soo-DAN), the grassland region north of the equator. Because disease killed off large animals, the rain forests of the Congo Basin and the Guinea Coast could not support herding. Yet the dense vegetation and heavy rains made it impossible to grow millet, rice, and other savanna-type crops there. Over many centuries the people of Guinea domesticated new root crops such as yams.

★ See below.

Growth of villages. The spread of farming produced major changes in Africa, as it did in all regions. Food gatherers (except for fishing peoples) had to move almost constantly to find new wild foods. Herders, too, had to move fairly often to find grass for their animals. Farmers, however, tilled the same land for several years. As a result, permanent villages grew up. When farm families raised more food than they needed to feed themselves, some people in these villages had time to specialize in crafts, such as weaving, pottery-making, and toolmaking. The abundance of food also led to more rapid population growth.

Nok culture. As communities grew larger and artisans became more skilled, people started to develop distinctive cultures. One of these, which archeologists call the Nok culture, arose about 500 B.C. in the grasslands of what is now central Nigeria.

The people of the Nok culture lived by farming and herding. They were also skilled metalworkers who made tools and jewelry from iron, gold, and tin. From clay, they fashioned beautiful, nearly life-sized figurines. Clothing on the human figurines shows that

150

the Nok people knew how to weave cloth. The artwork of other West African peoples seems to have been influenced by the Nok.

Bantu Peoples

● Note strategies for second objective on this page and p. 152.

The people who lived in sub-Saharan Africa (Africa south of the Sahara) did not have a single name for themselves or a common language. Hundreds of different languages and cultures developed. One group of languages and cultures is called the Bantu.

Bantu languages. The many Bantu languages, spoken throughout the southern half of the continent, are among the younger languages of Africa. The Bantu languages trace their roots to an older language group in the area of the Nok culture. The new languages developed as people migrated to other areas. The earliest migrations are thought to have begun about 2,500 years ago. Over the next thousand years, waves of people spread over about a third of the continent to the east and south. Smaller movements continued until the nineteenth century.

Sec. Rev. ques. 3

Bantu migrations. In their homeland, at the edge of the forest and savanna, the original Bantu-speakers lived by fishing, farming, and herding goats and sheep. As they moved to new areas, the Bantu peoples came into contact with other African groups and learned to live in a variety of environments.

Some Bantu-speaking peoples moved east across the savannas. In the open grasslands they learned to cultivate grains. Others moved southward along rivers. Some local peoples were absorbed into the Bantu culture, while others fled deeper into the forest. Farther south, hunters and gatherers sought refuge by moving into desert regions.

Migrating Bantu peoples also moved eastward into the Great Rift Valley. There they came into contact with cattle herders from the northeast, who were migrating southward. Some Bantu began to herd cattle themselves. Others settled as farmers. They planted new food crops—bananas and a starchy root called taro—that grew well in the warm, moist climate. These crops had

ATLANTIC

OCEAN

Strait of Gibraltar

Mediterranean Sea

Atlas Mts.

ARABIAN PENINSULA

Canary Islands

SAHARA

LIBYAN DESERT

Ahaggar Mts.

Tibesti Mts.

Nile R.

Red Sea

Cape Verde

Senegal R.

Niger R.

Lake Chad

SUDAN

Volta R.

Benue R.

Blue Nile

White Nile

Ethiopian Highlands

Gulf of Aden

Somali Peninsula

Gulf of Guinea

Nile

Lake Rudolph

African Landforms

SCALE

0   1,000 mi
0   1,000 km

N
W   E
S

Congo R.

Congo Basin

Lake Victoria

Mt. Kenya

Kilimanjaro

GREAT RIFT VALLEY

Lake Tanganyika

Zanzibar

Lake Malawi

African Vegetation

Zambezi R.

INDIAN OCEAN

NAMIB DESERT

KALAHARI DESERT

MADAGASCAR

Limpopo R.

SAHARA

SUDAN

Orange R.

Drakensberg Mts.

GUINEA COAST

Equator

Congo Basin

LAKE REGION

NAMIB DESERT

Cape of Good Hope

KEY

Rain forest

Dry woodland

Mediterranean vegetation

Savanna

Desert shrub

No vegetation

KALAHARI DESERT

SCALE

0   700 mi
0   700 km

African Landforms and Vegetation

These maps show the landforms and vegetation zones of Africa. Locate the Sudan, the
Sahara, the Congo Basin, and the Lake Region.
What kinds of vegetation are found in each
of these areas? Where are deserts located?

151

Map Answers: (1) Sudan—savanna. Sahara—desert
shrub or no vegetation. Congo Basin—rain forest. Lake
Region—dry woodland and savanna. (2) Deserts found in
north and south and along Somali coast.

culture, the earliest Bantu pioneers had no knowledge of ironworking. At some point in their migrations they learned how to smelt iron. Later waves of Bantu speakers carried this knowledge with them. Iron tools made the cultivation of the savannas and forests easier and more productive. Iron weapons were more effective against enemies.

The Kingdom of Kush

▲ Note strategies for third objective on this page and p. 154.

Along the great bend of the middle Nile River is the region called Nubia. Ancient Egyptians traded with Nubia for ivory and a very hard black wood called ebony. The Nubians obtained these items from Africans farther south. Around 1600 B.C. the Nubians established the kingdom of Kush, which would last for 2,000 years. The ancient kings of Kush built an impressive capital at Kerma with a castle and royal tombs. The state's wealth depended on its control of the gold trade with Egypt.

Egypt conquered Kush about 1525 B.C. Over several centuries of Egyptian rule, the influence of Egyptian culture increased. Kushites adopted Egyptian religious practices and dress. Egypt also undertook enormous building projects in Nubia, including the vast temple of Abu Simbel, which was carved in solid rock. Between about 800 and 750 B.C., as Egypt went into a period of decline, the Kushites proclaimed their independence and began the conquest of Egyptian lands. By 715 B.C. a Kushite king ruled all of Egypt.

Sec. Rev. ques. 4

A new Kushite capital. Kushite rule in Egypt lasted nearly a century. Then, beginning in 671 B.C., Assyrian invasions gradually drove the Kushites back to their own lands. About 590 B.C. the Kushites moved their capital south along the Nile to Meroë (MEHR-oh-ay).

The new location had two advantages. First, the greater rainfall of the area around Meroë, along with the Nile's annual flooding, made farming and cattle-herding easier. Second, Meroë was located on major trade routes between sub-Saharan Africa and Egypt. Gold, ebony, ivory, leopard skins, and

Ancient Africa

This map shows empires and kingdoms, Bantu migrations, and major trade routes of ancient Africa. Why might Meroë have been a valuable center of Kushite trade? What were the general directions of the routes of Bantu migrations?

Map Answers: (1) Meroë was on a major trade route that followed the Nile. (2) South and east.

been brought into eastern Africa from Southeast Asia, probably by Asian sailors or traders. Bananas and taro soon became staple foods for the peoples of Eastern Africa.

For generations, farmers and herders lived side by side in the Great Rift Valley. Sometimes they fought over land; sometimes they cooperated for their mutual benefit. Farmers, for example, might let herd animals graze on their harvested fields, because the animal droppings made land more fertile. Farmers also traded their crops for milk and meat from the herders.

●See below.

Knowledge of ironworking. Although they first came from near the Nok

152

ostrich feathers flowed through Meroë to Egypt and the Middle East. An eastern trade route led into the Ethiopian hills and down to ports on the Red Sea. Traders also carried goods south and west into central Africa.

About 500 B.C. Meroë's artisans began to smelt iron from local mines. The Kushites had probably learned the art of smelting and forging iron from the Assyrian invaders. Since there was timber for fuel, Meroë became one of the major ironworking centers of the ancient world. From iron the Kushites made fine weapons and farming tools.

The peak of Kushite power. Kush reached the height of its political and economic power about 200 B.C. The Romans attacked Kush in 23 B.C. but did not conquer it. Kush's negotiations with Rome were led by a woman the Romans called Candace (KAN-duh-kay). *Candace* was not a name, however, but the title given to the mothers of ruling kings. These women played an important part in governing Kush.

Kush was famous for being a major gold producer. Meroë had many skilled artisans, including jewelers, furniture makers, artists, and architects. Its pottery was known for high quality and original design, decorated with

Meanwhile . . .

IN ROME

At the height of Kushite power, about 200 B.C., the Romans had just defeated Hannibal, though they had not yet destroyed Carthage. When the Romans attacked Kush in 23 B.C., Augustus ruled the Roman Empire.

drawings of plants and animals. Egyptian customs continued to have a strong influence on Meroë's temple architecture, and all of the city's kings were buried under pyramids. The people of Meroë inscribed tombstones and altars with Egyptian hieroglyphics, but they kept trade records in a language of their own. Unfortunately, modern scholars have not been able to translate these records.

Over time, nomadic peoples from the desert began to raid Kush. The kingdom's trade and farm production fell sharply. About A.D. 350 Kush was invaded and conquered by the rival state of Aksum (AHK-soom).

Sec. Rev. ques. 4, cont.

These pyramids and the temple carving of a Nubian god are from Meroë. What do they suggest about the influence of Egypt on the kingdom of Kush? (See answer below.)

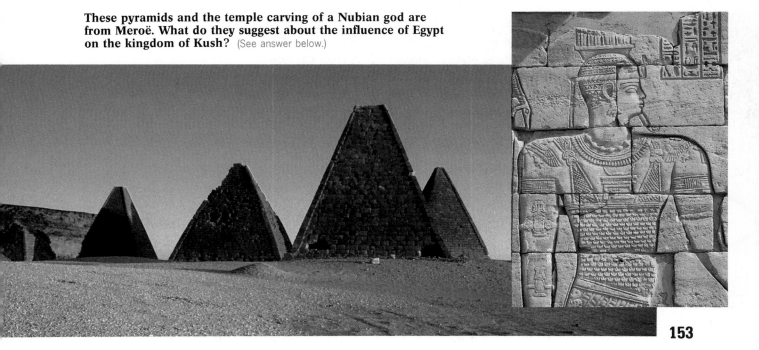

153

Caption Answer: The pyramids and temple suggest that architects and artists of Meroë were influenced by Egyptian ideas.

Cultural History *Aethiopia* was the name given by the Greeks to territory that is present-day Ethiopia. The word means "burnt faces."

Background There is disagreement among scholars as to whether silent barter actually existed.

The Kingdom of Aksum

Aksum was an impressive kingdom in the northern highlands of present-day Ethiopia. The early inhabitants were a mixture of local Africans and immigrants from southern Arabia. Gradually they built a strong agricultural economy and a thriving trade on the Red Sea.

Aksum's wealth and culture. By about A.D. 100, Aksum controlled a sizable territory (map, page 152) and traded widely. African elephants, ivory, gold, rhinoceros horns, slaves, and spices from inland Africa were shipped from the port city of Adulis (AD-yoo-lis) to ports on the Mediterranean Sea and the Indian Ocean. Aksum's culture combined Arabic and African influences with many of its own distinctive features. The kingdom developed a form of writing and was the first African kingdom south of the Sahara to make its own coins. Its cities had grand stone palaces and towering monuments.

The arrival of Christianity. Christianity was brought to Aksum by two Syrian youths who were shipwrecked along its coast. About A.D. 350 they converted King Azana, the conqueror of Meroë, to the new religion. Azana made it the official religion of his kingdom. Two hundred years later, Christianity became the official religion of an important new kingdom in Nubia. From there it spread south into central Africa, where many churches were built. Centuries later Christianity was wiped out in Nubia as the new religion of Islam expanded (page 200), but it survived in Ethiopia, the successor of Aksum.

Trading States in East Africa

Sec. Rev. ques. 5

From early times the civilizations of the Middle East and India had sought to trade with the African peoples south of the Somali Peninsula (map, page 151). The Bible mentions that in the tenth century B.C. King Solomon of Israel (page 45) sent fleets to a land called Ophir (OH-fur) to trade for gold, silver, sandalwood, and gems. Ophir was probably on the Somali Peninsula.

154

Trade with Egypt. Egypt, too, was eager to promote trade with Africa. As early as 600 B.C. the Egyptian pharaoh Necho (NEE-koh) commissioned a fleet to sail down the Red Sea and around Africa in search of new trading partners. Later, Egyptians and Arabs began doing business with a series of independent port cities in Azania (eastern Africa).

The Egyptians and Arabs traded specially made goods for African gold, tortoise shells (used in jewelry), rhinoceros horns, spices, and slaves. During the centuries after 500 A.D. the trade on Africa's east coast grew in importance. Goods and slaves were shipped as far as India and China.

Trade in West Africa

Not all African trade was centered in East Africa. According to the Greek historian Herodotus, North African merchants from the wealthy city of Carthage traded for gold along the west coast of the continent.

Silent barter. Because the West Africans mistrusted outsiders, they used a method of trade called **silent barter**. The Carthaginians brought their goods to a prearranged place, used smoke to signal their desire to trade, and withdrew to their boats. West African gold miners then came to the spot, placed what they considered an equal value of gold beside the goods, and left. The Carthaginians then returned and, if they agreed to the bargain, took the gold. If they wanted more gold, however, they went away again and waited for the miners to make a better offer. According to Herodotus, both sides acted with "perfect honesty."

▲ See below.

Herodotus also mentioned that merchants from North Africa crossed the Sahara to cities south of the desert. They wanted gold and slaves in return for salt and other goods. Salt was very precious to the people of sub-Saharan Africa. In their warm, tropical climate, they lost a great deal of salt from perspiration. To stay healthy, they added salt to their diet.

Some of the North Africans who ventured to the Sudan must have used chariots,

▲ REINFORCEMENT. Ask: (a) What trade advantage did Meroë have? (It was located on major trade routes between sub-Saharan Africa and Egypt.) **(b) How might Aksum's development of writing and a coin system have helped its trade?** (Writing helped record-keeping; a coin system simplified trading and enabled traders to purchase goods rather than barter.) *(Comprehension) Discussing History*

Religion Ethiopian Orthodox Christianity is the major religion in Ethiopia today. Although the Marxist government claims that freedom of religion is guaranteed by the constitution, government harassment and intimidation of worshipers occurs.
▲ ENRICHMENT. **Have students work in groups to dramatize silent barter. Students might portray silent barter between Carthaginians and West African gold miners or between other African groups.** *(Application) Dramatizing History*

since local artists carved pictures of chariots into the rocks along the way. The people of Nok probably learned the secret of how to smelt iron from their contact with the North Africans.

"Ships of the desert." The trade across the Sahara grew rapidly from the first century A.D., when camels began to be used to cross the desert. Able to carry heavy loads for days without water, camels became known as "ships of the desert."

Camel caravans brought more visitors from North Africa, and the growth of trade encouraged some of the people of the desert and the Sudan to become full-time traders. North Africans called Berbers pushed deeper and deeper into the desert to control this trade, driving other Africans farther south. Among those driven away were the Soninke (soh-NEEN-kay), who were farmers, traders, and metalworkers living north of the upper Niger (NY-jur) River. The Soninke profited by taxing the trade between the salt mines in the desert and the gold fields farther south and west.

As you will read in Chapter 15, this trade expanded enormously after A.D. 500, stimulating the growth of a great Soninke empire, Ghana. Ghana came to control the trade of the southern Sahara and the western Sudan. Meanwhile, on the other side of the Atlantic Ocean, peoples of the Americas had been building their own civilization.

See Sec. 1 *Closing the Lesson,* p. T147B.

Section Review

Answers to Section Review questions are in brackets on pages indicated.

1. **Define:** savanna, silent barter. (pp. 149, 154)
2. What are the main vegetation zones of Africa? (p. 149)
3. Who were the Bantu-speaking peoples and how did migrations affect their culture? (p. 150)
4. How were the Kushites influenced by the Egyptians? How was Egypt influenced by Kush? (p. 152)
5. With whom did the peoples of East Africa trade? What products did they trade? (p. 154)
6. **Critical thinking:** How did African peoples adapt to the continent's different environments? (See answer below.)

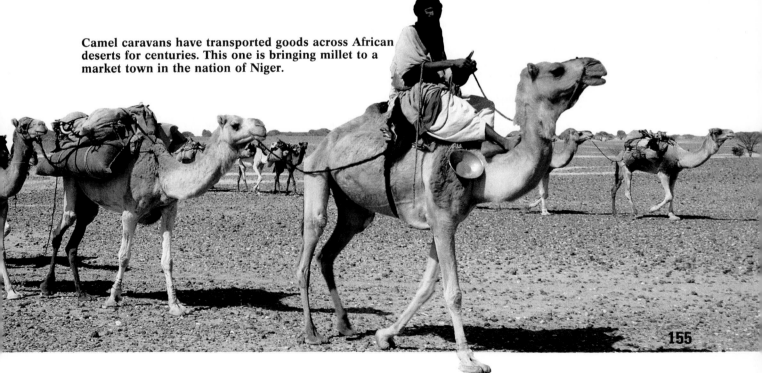

Camel caravans have transported goods across African deserts for centuries. This one is bringing millet to a market town in the nation of Niger.

155

Background Camels may drink about five gallons of water a day, but can go without water for up to five days. Camels lose little body moisture through sweating, and their body temperature may change as much as 11 degrees without harm. Camels may live for 50 years.

Check for Understanding. Ask: How did the introduction of camels affect the economy of Africa? (Because camels can travel great distances without water, the camel caravan increased trade between western and northern Africa.)

6. Answers will vary, but students might suggest that migrations, cultivation of various crops, and the use of camels to cross deserts are examples of early African peoples' methods of adapting to different environments.

2 Civilizations in the Americas

Objectives

Focus Questions

★ ■ How did people first come to the Americas? *(pages 156–158)*
● ■ What kind of civilizations did the Olmecs, Teotihuacános, and Mayas build? *(pages 158–161)*

Terms to Know

isthmus
pilgrimage

★ Note strategies for first objective on this page and p. 157.

Scientists believe that thousands of years ago many bands of hunting peoples migrated from Asia into North America. Gradually they moved south and east until scattered groups were living throughout North and South America. About 1200 B.C. the earliest civilization in the Americas developed among the Olmec people in what is now Mexico. Other early American peoples followed the pattern set by the Olmecs.

The Geography of the Americas

North and South America are vast continents with many different climates and kinds of terrain. North America stretches from what is now Canada southward through the region of Central America (the area from present-day Guatemala to Panama). South America includes the world's largest tropical rain forest—the Amazon Basin—and the world's driest desert—the Atacama. The two continents are joined by a narrow strip of land called an **isthmus**, now the country of Panama.

Both continents have certain common features. The most striking is the rugged mountain chain that runs from Alaska to the southern tip of South America. These mountains are known as the Rockies in most of North America, the Sierra Madre (see-AYR-uh MAH-dray) in Mexico, and the Andes throughout South America. Both continents also have large areas of fertile grasslands that are good for farming and ranching, and both are rich in natural resources.

The First Americans

As you read in Chapter 1, people first came to the Americas during the Ice Ages. A land bridge across what is now the Bering Strait connected the Americas to Asia.

Hunters from Asia. The first Americans, hunters following herds of animals, probably came from many different parts of Asia. They did not come in large groups, nor did they all come at one time. One theory is that people migrated from Asia over a period of several thousand years.

Though glaciers covered all of what is now Canada and the northern United States, there were ice-free river valleys. Some of the hunters traveled south and east along these natural paths (map, page 157). South of the ice sheets they found thick forests, sparkling lakes and rivers, and plenty of wild animals to hunt. Huge mammoths, elk, bison, camels, wolves, and tigers roamed the land. Some hunters moved farther and farther south. After many centuries, the Americas' first settlers had spread throughout the continents, from the arctic areas of the north to the southern tip of South America, 11,000 miles away.

New languages. As these migrant hunters made widely scattered settlements in the Americas, they became very different from one another. Each group developed its

Sec. Rev.
ques. 2

156

Geography The name *Andes* is believed to have come from *anti*, the Incan word for copper. The mountain range stretches for 4,500 miles along the entire west coast of South America.
Geography Note that the Bering Strait is 55 miles wide and is the shortest distance between North America and Asia.
Check for Understanding. Ask: Why did the first Americans cross what is now the Bering Strait and come to North America? (They were hunters tracking animals.)

Map Skill Practice

See page T147B for answers to *Map Skill Practice.*

Migrations in the Americas

1. Using the map at the right, describe where the first Americans probably crossed into the Americas.
2. From what continent did these early peoples apparently come?
3. How are the migration routes of the early Americans shown on this map?
4. How far south in the American continents did groups spread?
5. What probably slowed down the settlement of the northern part of North America?
6. **Drawing conclusions.** Find the Rocky Mountains on this map and on the world map on pages GR9–10 at the front of the book. Why would the migrating peoples have avoided traveling through these mountains?

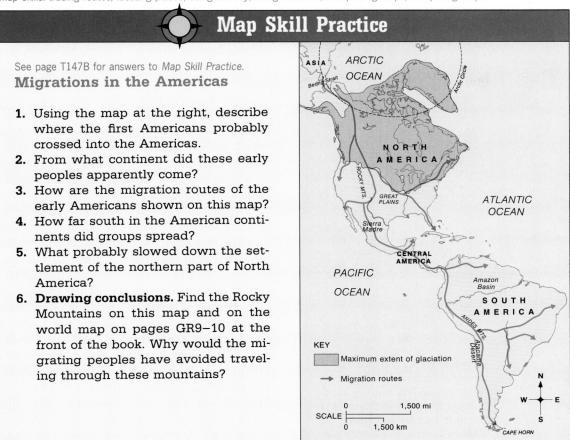

KEY

▨ Maximum extent of glaciation

→ Migration routes

SCALE
0   1,500 mi
0   1,500 km

own language and its own way of doing things. Eventually hundreds of different languages were spoken by the peoples of North and South America.

New technologies. After the glaciers melted and the land bridge from Asia disappeared, the people of the Americas were cut off from the civilizations developing in other parts of the world. This helps to explain why the technology developed by early peoples in the Americas was different from that of other early civilizations. Although some groups worked with metals such as gold, silver, and copper, they did not learn to make bronze or work with iron. Metals were used mainly for ornaments. People continued to make their tools and weapons of stone, wood, or bone. Though they knew about the wheel, they did not use it for transportation.

From hunting to farming. The climate in North America changed as the glaciers melted. Some areas became hotter and drier. Many of the great herds of animals vanished, and food became scarcer. Some time between 9000 and 6000 B.C., some hunters learned to cultivate grains and other plants that they found growing wild. Realizing that farming could provide a more stable supply of food than hunting and gathering, people eventually settled in villages and tended their crops.

The first farming settlements were located in Mexico and in Central America. In the fertile Valley of Mexico, people were growing corn and other crops as early as 3500 B.C. By 1500 B.C. many small farming villages had been built. People raised squash, beans, and cotton as well as corn. They added

★ See below.

157

Early Civilizations in Mexico and the Yucatan

In what valley did the Teotihuacán culture develop? On what peninsula did the Maya people live? What continents were linked by the land shown in this map? (See map, page 157.)

Map Answers: (1) Valley of Mexico. (2) Yucatan Peninsula. (3) North and South America.

to their food supply by hunting wild animals and fishing. From these small farm settlements, several civilizations developed.

The Olmecs

● Note strategies for second objective on this page and p. 160.

By about 1200 B.C., while the Egyptians were ruling the kingdom of Kush, a people we call the Olmecs had settled on the coast of the Gulf of Mexico (see map above). We do not know what these people called themselves or whether they were newcomers to this region. The name we use means "rubber people," because the Olmecs were the first people to tap rubber trees for sap. Most archeologists believe that Olmec culture set the pattern for

158 civilization in Mexico and Central America.

Writing and mathematics. The Olmecs, like the ancient Egyptians, had a hieroglyphic form of writing. No one, however, has yet found a way to read either the Olmec writing or the similar writing systems of later peoples of this region.

The Olmecs also worked with mathematical ideas. Their number system was based on combinations of only three symbols—a dot (standing for "one"), a bar (for "five"), and zero. Centuries before mathematicians in India discovered the idea of the zero (page 139), Olmec priests were using it to make remarkably precise calculations. The Olmecs observed, recorded, and accurately predicted eclipses and the orbits of planets. They developed two calendars—one for everyday use and one for use by the priests.

Olmec religion. Religious ritual was an important part of Olmec life. The Olmecs had a ceremonial ball game (later called *pok-a-tok*) that was something like basketball. The players could not touch the hard rubber ball with their hands. Instead they had to use their elbows and hips in trying to send the ball through a small stone ring set sideways in a high wall. Archeologists believe that some players were sacrificed to the gods at the end of the game.

Besides such rituals, the Olmecs also expressed their religious beliefs by constructing huge temples and monuments. The Olmecs built cone-shaped mounds of earth shaped like the nearby volcanoes. On the tops of these mounds they built temples. Unlike Egyptian pyramids, which were built as tombs (page 37), Olmec temple-pyramids were primarily places of worship. Steep flights of stairs led to a temple on the flat summit. The temple-pyramids drew the worshipers' eyes upward toward the skies, where, it was believed, the gods looked down from the stars.

At the oldest known center of Olmec culture, San Lorenzo in present-day Mexico, archeologists have unearthed the ruins of what they call the "colossal heads." The heads were carved from huge blocks of volcanic rock. They weighed as much as 18 tons

● RETEACHING. Have students review "The Olmecs" (pp. 158–159) and "Maya Civilization" (pp. 160–161) and find statements that support this generalization: *Both the Olmecs and the Mayas developed advanced civilizations.* Students should find at least three statements for each of the societies. *(Comprehension) Supporting Generalizations*

● REINFORCEMENT. Have students work in groups to make a chart comparing the locations and achievements of the Olmec, Teotihuacán, and Maya civilizations. (Olmec: first to use rubber; hieroglyphic writing; mathematical ideas. Teotihuacán: earliest city in Americas; Pyramid of the Sun; highly organized society. Maya: calendar; astronomy; trade; cities; great pyramids.) *(Comprehension) Organizing Information in Written Form* each and stood as high as 14 feet. The Olmecs did not use the wheel and had no animals to carry heavy loads. Yet they moved these blocks of stone more than 60 miles through swamps and rain forest. They probably used logs as rollers, moving the huge blocks to rivers and floating them to the religious centers on rafts. The Olmecs must have had a highly organized society to accomplish this labor and to maintain the religious centers. Priests probably directed the hundreds of laborers needed to carry out the work.

Olmec influence. By about the first century B.C., Olmec culture had vanished. Olmec sculptures lay broken and buried, and the religious centers were swallowed up by the fast-growing vines and trees of the rain forest. The ruins of Olmec civilization were not discovered until the twentieth century. The reasons for the disappearance of the Olmecs remain a mystery to historians.

Colossal stone heads were distinctive Olmec cultural achievements.

Archeologists have found much evidence that the Olmecs influenced other peoples. Small Olmec carvings, many made from highly prized jade, have been found all over Central America. Sculptures that show Olmec influence appear in places as far apart as western Mexico and southern Guatemala. Later Mexican and Central American peoples adopted or improved on the Olmec system of writing, number system, calendar, style of architecture, and ritual ball game. Because of this, Olmec culture is considered the "parent culture" of this region.

Sec. Rev. ques. 3

Teotihuacán

Around the time of Jesus' birth, the first true city in the Americas, Teotihuacán (tay-oh-tee-wah-KAHN), arose in the Valley of Mexico. While the Olmec religious centers had been strictly places of worship that people visited on **pilgrimages**—trips with a special religious purpose—Teotihuacán was different. All classes of people lived and worked there. It was the largest city in the Americas until the arrival of the Spanish 1,500 years later. At one time it covered eight square miles and was home to as many as 200,000 people.

Sec. Rev. ques. 4

Most Teotihuacános lived on the outskirts of the city, where they farmed the land. Closer in were the homes of officials, artisans, and merchants. The city center was dominated by temples and public buildings. The grandest of these was the massive Pyramid of the Sun—larger than any pyramid made in Egypt.

The Teotihuacános' most important god was Quetzalcóatl (ket-sahl-KOH-ah-tul), the Feathered Serpent god. Teotihuacános believed that he had given them all the good things of civilization: a knowledge of farming, the ability to write, the calendar, arts, crafts, and laws. Quetzalcóatl was thought of as a gentle god of peace and humility. The people of Teotihuacán appear to have followed his example, living peacefully as farmers and traders.

159

Check for Understanding. Ask: What evidence suggests that the Olmecs had a highly organized society? (Huge statues carved out of blocks of volcanic rock could have been completed only by an organized society.)

Cultural History The name *Teotihuacán* means "place of the gods" and originates from a myth about a meeting of the gods after the death of the sun. One by one the gods threw themselves into a fire to ensure that the sun would rise again and light the world.

Cultural History The Pyramid of the Sun is 700 square feet at the base and stands as tall as a 20-story building.

The Teotihuacános also were skilled in arts and crafts. Artisans made life-size masks of highly polished stone. The walls of homes in Teotihuacán were covered with scenes of dancing gods, jaguars, birds, and priests. Beautifully painted pottery reproduced the wall paintings in miniature. Traders from Teotihuacán carried goods from their city hundreds of miles to other parts of Central America. In time the Teotihuacános built the largest trade empire in the area.

About A.D. 600, wandering tribes from the north attacked and burned Teotihuacán. Its people fled, but their skills and learning influenced people of other cultures.

Maya Civilization

At about the same time that Teotihuacán was expanding, people known as the Mayas (MY-uz) were building religious centers on the Yucatan Peninsula, where modern Mexico and Guatemala meet. Though hampered by dense forests and a lack of metal, the Mayas managed some extraordinary achievements. Between about A.D. 300 and 700, Central American civilization reached its height among the Mayas.

Government and trade. Maya civilization, like that of the Olmecs, grew up around large religious centers. These centers eventually became city-states where thousands of people lived. At the head of each city-state was an absolute ruler known as the "true man." Maya paintings show that the city-states often went to war. They fought in

order to add to their territory and to take prisoners. Prisoners of war were either enslaved or sacrificed to the gods.

Wide, paved roads and sea routes linked the Maya city-states. Merchants carried on an active trade in corn, salt, smoked meat, dried fish, honey, wood products, and animal skins. They also traded in luxury items, including jade, carved shells, fine pottery, and textiles.

Preoccupation with time. Although the priests were not the sole rulers of the city-states, they played an important role in the everyday lives of the Mayas. The priests' chief concern was time, for apparently it was believed that the gods would destroy the world if ceremonies were not held on exactly the right days. The priests also taught that the date of a person's birth influenced his or her future. They decided which days were lucky or unlucky for couples to marry, for crops to be planted, for trading ventures to begin, for battles to be fought, or for new temples to be started.

To obtain their measurements of time, Maya priests observed the stars and planets, kept records of the seasons, and accurately predicted eclipses. Their calendar was one of the most accurate ever developed. The Maya year had 365 days, the last five of which were considered unlucky.

Maya society. The Mayas had a strict social order. Priests, nobles, and warriors made up the upper classes of Maya society. Warriors led troops in the frequent wars between city-states. Maya nobles helped run the government. They collected taxes, kept records of work that was done, and watched over the road system.

● See below.

Most of the Maya people were peasants. Each peasant family had to set aside part of its corn crop for taxes. Men also had to work on building projects and serve as soldiers. Farmers spent their spare time gathering forest products and making tools, ornaments, and household goods for sale.

Sec. Rev. ques. 5

Farm women gathered honey, wove cloth, and made pottery. Their fine weaving and pottery were much in demand. Maya women also cared for their households and

---

Linking Past and Present

The Maya language is still alive in Central America, especially in Guatemala. Though the official language of Guatemala is Spanish, more than 40 percent of the people are Indians who speak some form of the ancient Maya tongue.

160

Background Note that the tribes from the north were the Chichimecs, nomads who had mastered agriculture and developed farming settlements that sustained large populations.

● ENRICHMENT. Have students make a chart or poster comparing the Olmec, Teotihuacán, Maya, Egyptian (pp. 35–36), and Hindu (pp. 57–59) religions. Charts or posters should distinguish each culture's beliefs about gods; describe the monuments or temples; and show how the religion of each culture affected daily life. (Synthesis) *Comparing Cultures*

Historic Places

Palenque

Of all the ruined Maya cities that have been found, Palenque (puh-LENG-kay) may be the most beautiful. It stands in a wooded, hilly area overlooking a river valley in southern Mexico. Begun about A.D. 600, Palenque was one of the last Maya cities to be built.

Like other Maya cities, Palenque had many temples, broad open spaces within the city, and a ball court used for ceremonial games. Thousands of people probably lived within walking distance of the city center, their homes set in small clusters separated by stretches of open land.

At the center of the city stood the royal palace, topped by a four-story tower (at the right in the picture). Palen-

que's priests and rulers may have climbed this tower to observe the stars for their sacred calendar calculations. An aqueduct carried running water to the palace from a river that ran through the city.

Close to the palace stood the Temple of the Inscriptions (at the left in the picture). Under the temple floor is the burial chamber of the great Lord Pacal. Pacal ruled Palenque from 615 to 683, when the city was at the height of its wealth and power. Pacal probably supervised the construction of the tomb and may have specified the unusual picture on the lid of his coffin. The picture shows Pacal at the moment of death, cheerfully dropping into the underworld.

worked in the fields. They could not hold public office, and they were not allowed even to enter the temples.

Decline of the Mayas. The emphasis in Maya society was on respect for tradition, and the civilization apparently changed little for about 600 years. Then, between about

A.D. 850 and 950, the great Maya centers were abandoned one by one. The Mayas did not move away—their descendants still live in the same area—yet their civilization collapsed. No one is sure why. Central American civilization never again reached the heights it had under the Mayas.

161

See Sec. 2 *Closing the Lesson,* p. T147C.

�F **FEATURE ACTIVITY. Ask: In addition to the Mayas, what other cultures have you studied that used the pyramid as an architectural form?** (Sumerian culture in Mesopotamia, p. 31; Egyptian culture in northern Africa, p. 37; and the Kush in northeast Africa, p. 153.) *(Comprehension) Observing for Detail*

Section Review

Answers to Section Review questions are in brackets on pages indicated.

1. **Define:** isthmus, pilgrimage. (pp. 156, 159)
2. According to scientists, how were the Americas first settled? (p. 156)
3. In what ways was the Olmec culture the "parent culture" of Mexico and Central America? (p. 159)
4. How did Teotihuacán differ from the Olmec religious centers? (p. 159)
5. What roles did different classes play in Maya society? (p. 160)
6. **Critical thinking:** Like the Mayas, the Egyptians (Chapter 2) and the Greeks (Chapter 4) were deeply interested in astronomy. What were their different reasons for studying the sky?

(See answer below.)

6. Students should note that Maya priests studied astronomy to determine exact times for rituals; Greek scientists investigated ways to explain the natural world; and Egyptian priests' studies in astronomy were used in farming and in religious rituals.

Chapter 8   Summary and Timeline

1. Africa's many climates have shaped the civilizations that have existed on this continent. Early peoples moved often in search of food. Later peoples turned to farming and built permanent communities. The kingdoms of Kush and Aksum grew out of such communities. Like the cities along Africa's east coast and in the western Sudan, these kingdoms traded widely.

2. The first people to live in the Americas were wandering hunters from Asia who probably crossed into North America during the Ice Ages. These peoples gradually settled throughout the two American continents. Some of the nomadic hunters began to farm, settling in villages. The Olmec people established patterns that became the "parent culture" for Mexican and Central American civilization. This civilization reached its height with the Mayas, who built remarkable religious centers between the years A.D. 300 and 700.

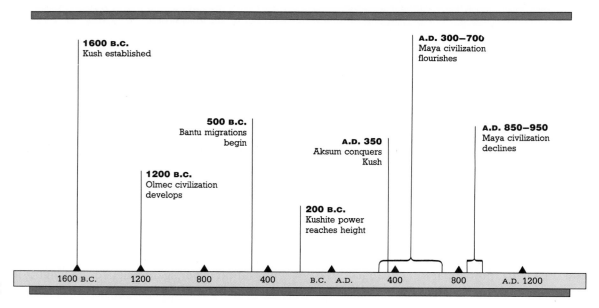

1600 B.C.
Kush established

1200 B.C.
Olmec civilization develops

500 B.C.
Bantu migrations begin

200 B.C.
Kushite power reaches height

A.D. 350
Aksum conquers Kush

A.D. 300–700
Maya civilization flourishes

A.D. 850–950
Maya civilization declines

1600 B.C.   1200   800   400   B.C.   A.D.   400   800   A.D. 1200

CHAPTER **8** REVIEW

See p. T147C for answers to Chapter Review.

Vocabulary Review

Use the following terms to complete the sentences below: *isthmus, pilgrimage, savanna, silent barter.*

1. A ___?___ is a journey with a religious purpose.
2. A ___?___ is an area of open grasslands with scattered trees or shrubs.
3. Africans sometimes traded gold for other goods using the method of ___?___.
4. A narrow strip of land connecting two large landmasses is called an ___?___.

Places to Know

Match the letters on this map of Africa with the places listed below. You may want to refer to the maps on pages 151 and 152.

1. Aksum
2. Atlantic Ocean
3. Congo River
4. Indian Ocean
5. Kush
6. Nile River
7. Sahara
8. Sudan

Recalling the Facts

1. What made the Sahara, the Congo Basin, and the Guinea Coast unsuitable for herding?
2. Why was knowledge of ironworking important to the Bantu-speaking peoples of Africa?
3. What helped Meroë become a major trading center? How did the kingdom of Kush fall?
4. Who were the trading partners for cities on the east coast of Africa?
5. How did the Soninke benefit from the trade across the Sahara?
6. Where did the first Americans come from? What brought them to the American continents?
7. What evidence suggests that the Olmecs influenced the cultures of other peoples in the Americas?
8. What made Teotihuacán the first true city in the Americas?
9. What part did each of the following groups play in Maya society? Priests? Nobles? Warriors? Peasants?

Critical Thinking Skills

1. **Building vocabulary.** As you have read, one of the most valuable products traded by Africans was salt. Several words and phrases in use today reflect salt's importance in the ancient world. For example, the word *salary* comes from the Latin word *salarium,* which means "money given to Roman soldiers to buy salt."

Find the origin and meaning of the following phrases, all connected with salt: (a) "not worth one's salt"; (b) "the salt of the earth"; (c) "take with a grain of salt." *(App.)*

163

2. Making a bulletin board. Make a bulletin board display featuring archeological studies on human cultural development. Indicate how discoveries of artifacts or of remains have given clues about how early people lived. *(App.)*

3. Preparing a report. Research and prepare a report about one of the following topics: findings of prehistoric life in the Olduvai Gorge in Africa; the rock paintings of the Sahara; Nok pottery and jewelry; the Maya calendar; the Olmec number system; legends of Quetzalcóatl. *(App.)*

✔ **4. Making a hypothesis.** A hypothesis is an educated guess about the reasons for an unexplained event. Hypotheses are based on all available information about the event and on prior knowledge and experience. The disappearances of the Olmec and the Maya civilizations are two examples of mysterious or unexplained developments. Develop a hypothesis about why these two ancient cultures disappeared. Then explain what types of evidence would be needed to prove your hypothesis. *(Syn.)*

5. Identifying main ideas. The main ideas in a reading passage are those key points that you must grasp in order to understand the author's purpose. Reread Section 2 of this chapter, identifying at least four of the main ideas. For each main idea, list two supporting details. *(App.)*

Thinking About Geography

1. Comparing maps. Compare the maps of Africa in this chapter with the Atlas map of present-day Africa at the back of this book. What nations now exist in what were once known as the kingdoms of Kush and Aksum? What nations now exist in the lands once settled by the Bantu? *(Comp.)*

2. Recognizing cause and effect. What geographic factors help explain why peoples living in the Americas developed different forms of technology from peoples living in other parts of the world? What conditions help explain why farming replaced hunting and gathering? *(Comp.)*

164

Enrichment: Primary Sources

Myths, ceremonies, and prophecies of the ancient Mayas were recorded by their descendants centuries after their civilization declined. The following passage adapted from these writings suggests problems that may have led to the decline of Maya civilization.

66 The vegetation was fast disappearing. Too many mouths in our houses; too many mouths for the number of squash.

The strength of many great warriors declines. There is no one left on whom to lean. There is no one left with sufficient understanding to set the calendar in order. There will be no great abundance of water.

There came enemies from the north and west. In great distress we were scattered among the forests and in the mountains.

For months there was discord among the chiefs, and all men suffered deeply.

The gods bind up their faces in pain because men swelter in toil and hunger is their burden, and because of their bad conscience about protecting the people.

One by one the stars fall. 99

1. Why did the Mayas not have enough food?
2. Identify two more of the Mayas' other problems and tell how each might have contributed to the collapse of Maya civilization.
3. According to the passage, how did the gods feel about the Mayas' plight?
4. **Critical thinking:** What do you think is meant by the last sentence of the quoted passage? *(Anal.)* ✔

WORLD HISTORY
Checklist

UNIT 2

Try to identify the following key people, groups and dynasties, places, and terms from the unit. If you need help, refer to the pages listed.

Key People

Homer *(75)*
Pericles *(80)*
Herodotus *(84)*
Thucydides *(85)*
Sophocles *(86)*
Socrates *(87)*
Plato *(88)*
Aristotle *(88)*
Alexander the Great *(90)*
Ptolemy *(91)*
Hannibal *(100)*
Julius Caesar *(103)*
Cleopatra *(104)*
Augustus *(105)*
Virgil *(112)*
Diocletian *(119)*
Constantine *(119)*
Attila *(122)*
Jesus *(126)*
Paul *(127)*
Augustine *(128)*
Buddha *(133)*
Chandragupta Maurya *(137)*
Asoka *(136)*
Mencius *(140)*
Laozi *(140)*
Li Si *(141)*

Key Groups and Dynasties

Minoans *(71)*
Mycenaeans *(72)*
Visigoths *(120)*
Huns *(122)*
Vandals *(122)*
Qin dynasty *(141)*
Han dynasty *(142)*
Bantu *(150)*
Soninke *(155)*
Olmecs *(158)*
Mayas *(160)*

Key Places

Sparta *(76)*
Athens *(77)*
Macedonia *(90)*
Rome *(97)*
Tiber River *(97)*
Carthage *(99)*
Constantinople *(120)*
Western Roman Empire *(120, 122)*
Eastern Roman Empire *(122)*
Bethlehem *(126)*
Magadha *(136)*
Mauryan Empire *(136)*
Gupta Empire *(138)*
Chang'an *(142)*
Sahara *(149)*
Kush *(152)*
Meroë *(152)*
Aksum *(154)*
Teotihuacán *(159)*

Key Terms

Hellenic Age *(73)*
Iliad (75)
Odyssey (75)
democracy *(77)*
Persian Wars *(79)*
classical *(84)*
Parthenon *(84)*

Sophist *(87)*
Socratic method *(87)*
Peloponnesian War *(89)*
Hellenistic Age *(91)*
Epicureanism *(92)*
Stoicism *(92)*
republic *(97)*
Twelve Tables *(98)*
Punic Wars *(99)*
First Triumvirate *(103)*
Second Triumvirate *(104)*
Pax Romana *(106)*
Circus Maximus *(110)*
Colosseum *(110)*
Greco-Roman culture *(112)*
Law of Nations *(115)*
Messiah *(125)*
Gospels *(126)*
Christianity *(125)*
Buddhism *(133)*
Four Noble Truths *(133)*
Sanskrit *(138)*
Taoism *(140)*
Legalism *(141)*
Great Wall *(141)*
dynastic cycle *(142)*
Silk Road *(143)*
Age of Disunity *(145)*

The Colosseum in Rome.

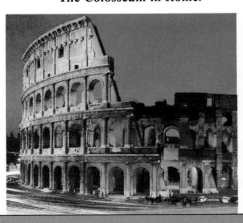

165

REVIEW ACTIVITIES: *Key People:* For each person listed, identify the civilization with which he or she is associated and name the person's most significant accomplishment or action. *Key Groups and Dynasties:* Identify the impact each group or dynasty had on its region. *Key Places:* Show on a world outline map the location of each place. (See pages 74 and 162 of *Teacher's Resources: Geography* for world outline maps that can be copied.) *Key Terms:* Define or identify each term listed.

THE HERITAGE OF THE ANCIENT WORLD
Prehistory–A.D. 950

UNIT 1: The Rise of Civilization (Prehistory–450 B.C.)

Chapter 1: The Birth of Civilization

Some of the most impressive achievements in history took place before people kept written records. This span of time is called prehistory. Our knowledge of prehistory comes from unwritten evidence, such as fossils and artifacts, that scientists have studied.

The Old Stone Age. Most of the objects remaining from the prehistoric period are stone tools and weapons. For this reason, archeologists have named the period the Stone Age. The earliest and longest part of this period, which began more than two million years ago, is called the Old Stone Age or Paleolithic Age.

Old Stone Age people were nomads who moved from place to place hunting wild animals, catching fish, and gathering food from plants that grew wild. They made a variety of tools and weapons—spearpoints, hand axes, choppers, and scrapers. Eventually Old Stone Age people learned to control fire. They developed spoken language and were then able to pass knowledge from one generation to the next. Archeologists have found evidence that some Stone Age peoples held religious beliefs. Some created works of art.

The New Stone Age. The later stage of prehistory began about 10,000 years ago, after the last Ice Age had ended. Because people of this time shaped their stone tools more carefully, the period is called the New Stone Age or Neolithic Age.

A number of significant advances made in this period had far-reaching effects on the way people lived. In the Middle East, Mexico, and other parts of the world, people learned to plant food crops and to domesticate wild animals. Farming people began to build permanent settlements near their crops.

166

Because they now had a steady source of food, some people of the New Stone Age turned to nonfarming crafts—making tools, building shelters, and producing cloth or pottery. The demand for such products led to trade, or barter. In time, trade brought contacts between villages.

Stone Age craftworkers, or artisans, created new technology. Their invention of the wheel and the sail made transportation easier and encouraged trade. Among their other inventions were the plow and the potter's wheel.

Late in the New Stone Age, some artisans in the Middle East learned to work with copper. As knowledge of metalworking spread, improved tools and weapons were made. Gradually people began to work with bronze, a mixture of metals that is harder than copper. The term

A Stone Age artisan at work.

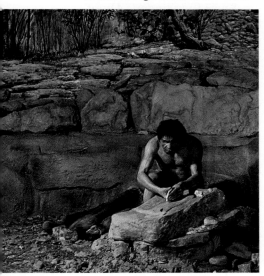

Bronze Age describes the period when bronze became the main material used for tools and weapons.

River valley civilizations. Because of the achievements made during the New Stone Age, people had a steadier food supply, population increased, and trade expanded. Settlements grew larger, and some villages developed into cities.

The first civilizations emerged in the four great river valleys of Mesopotamia, Egypt, India, and China (map, page 22). The rivers provided food and fresh water for humans and animals, as well as a means of trade and travel. The rivers also supplied water for irrigation systems.

The people of the river valley civilizations developed the beginnings of organized government and religion, a division of labor, a class structure, and a system of writing. These five developments are all characteristics of early civilizations. Because almost every ancient civilization developed some form of writing, the beginning of civilization also marked the beginning of written history.

Chapter 2:
The Ancient Middle East

Several of the earliest civilizations developed in the ancient Middle East—in Mesopotamia, Egypt, and other

lands at the eastern end of the Mediterranean. Metalworking probably began in this area, and there people also made advances in writing, engineering, mathematics, and astronomy.

Mesopotamian civilization. Sumer, the home of the earliest civilization, lay between the Tigris and Euphrates rivers in the region called Mesopotamia. It was at one end of the Fertile Crescent, an arc of rich farmland between the Persian Gulf and the Mediterranean Sea (map, page 30).

In time, farming villages along the two rivers grew into 12 independent city-states. Each included a city and the farmlands around it. The Sumerians were polytheists—believers in many gods. These gods were thought to protect the cities and to choose their rulers.

Because Mesopotamia lacked a number of resources, trade was very important. To keep records of their dealings, Sumerians developed cuneiform, a system of writing on clay tablets. Sumerian cuneiform tablets are the oldest written records in the world.

Sumer was conquered about 2350 B.C. by Sargon, the ruler of Akkad, who built the world's first empire. In time, other city-states rose to power in the region. These civilizations all built on the knowledge of the Sumerians.

The Mesopotamians drew up multiplication and

division tables, made calculations using geometry, and kept written records of their observations in astronomy. About 1792 B.C. Mesopotamia was united under the rulers of Babylon. One ruler, Hammurabi, had the laws of Babylon collected and recorded in cuneiform. Known as the Code of Hammurabi, these were the world's first written laws.

King Sargon of Akkad ruled the world's first empire.

Egyptian civilization. Another early center of civilization was in the Nile River valley, southwest of Mesopotamia. Farming villages sprang up there because of the rich soil deposited by the Nile's yearly floods. These villages gradually were united into two kingdoms—Upper Egypt and Lower Egypt (map, page 35). About 3100 B.C. the ruler Menes brought both kingdoms under his control. Thus he established Egypt's first dynasty, or family of rulers.

168

Egyptian civilization continued for at least 30 dynasties. After Menes, there were three periods during which strong dynasties united Egypt. The Old Kingdom (about 2686–2181 B.C.) is often called the Pyramid Age because of the great tombs built for its pharaohs. The Middle Kingdom (about 2040–1786 B.C.) brought flourishing trade with Palestine, Syria, and the island of Crete. The New Kingdom (about 1570–1090 B.C.) saw the establishment of an empire stretching as far east as the Euphrates River and south into Africa.

While rulers changed, the society and culture of Egypt remained stable for more than 3,000 years. Religion influenced much of life. Egyptians were polytheists, and believed that the pharaoh was one of many gods who controlled nature's forces.

The ancient Egyptians invented hieroglyphics, a writing system on papyrus scrolls. They developed a calendar more accurate than that of the Sumerians. Egyptian engineers used geometry to map the land and to plan irrigation works. Their architects were the first to use stone columns. The remains of their structures show the wealth and power of Egyptian civilization. By about 1200 B.C., however, Egypt had passed its peak and other peoples were coming to power.

The Egyptian pyramids.

Other peoples of the ancient Middle East. Among those who challenged Egypt were the Hittites. They built an empire that included Asia Minor and northern Syria. Hittite artisans discovered how to make iron, which is stronger and sharper than bronze. As knowledge of ironworking spread, the Bronze Age gave way to the Iron Age.

While the Hittites built an empire by conquest, Phoenicia built a trading empire. Phoenician merchants kept records with a writing system that used an alphabet. They carried this system with them wherever they traded. About 800 B.C. the Greeks adopted it and created the alphabet on which our own is based.

The Hebrews, or Israelites, were a nomadic people who settled in Canaan, south of Phoenicia, about 1900 B.C. They were the first monotheists—people who believe in one God. The Hebrews considered God eternal and all-powerful. They believed that God set standards of right and wrong behavior for humans, and that each person was responsible for observing those standards. Hebrew law is recorded in the Torah, the first five books of the Bible.

By 660 B.C. the Assyrians had built an empire stretching from Egypt to the Persian Gulf. Assyrian rulers developed harsh but efficient methods of government, building roads to link the parts of the empire. They were overthrown in 612 B.C. by the Chaldeans of Babylon and the Medes of Persia.

In northern Asia Minor another people, the Lydians, held power. To make trade easier, they began to use coins. Sometime after 560 B.C., coins were accepted as payment throughout the Middle East.

About 547 B.C. the Persians began to build a huge empire (map, page 47). They united all the Middle Eastern people under one rule with a single official language. Local customs and traditions were respected, but the empire was unified by a road network, a postal service, and a standard system of coinage. A new religion, Zoroastrianism, spread widely in Persian lands.

Chapter 3:
Ancient India and China

Of the four great river valley civilizations that began to develop about 5,000 years ago,

two were in Asia—in the valleys of the Indus River in India and the Yellow River in China.

The roots of civilization in India. Evidence of the first civilization on the Indian subcontinent has been found at Harappa and Mohenjo-Daro. Both were carefully planned cities, and both carried on extensive trade. Around 1500 B.C., as Indus Valley culture was declining, Aryans from Central Asia invaded the subcontinent and took control (map, page 54).

Because the Aryans had no written language, what is known about these people comes from artifacts, accounts of travelers, and the

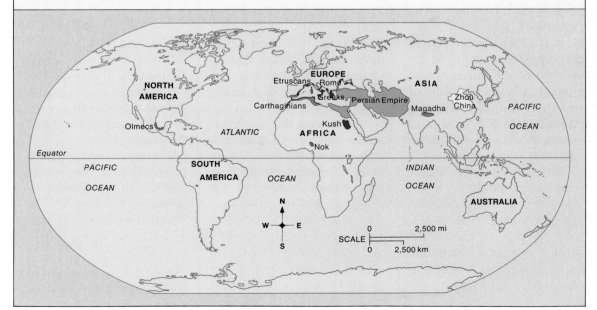

Major States and Empires About 500 B.C. (Persian. Nok, Kush. Olmec.)

What Asian empire had reached into Europe by 500 B.C.? What centers of culture had developed in Africa? In the Americas?

Vedas, a collection of hymns, rituals, sayings, chants, and tales.

According to the Vedas, the early Aryans had a class society of three levels, with flexibility for people to move from class to class. After the Aryans settled in the Indus Valley, the class system evolved into a more rigid caste system.

At first there were four main castes: (1) priests, (2) warrior-nobles, (3) common people such as merchants and farmers, and (4) laborers. Each group had its own dharma, or code of conduct, that described its place in society. Over time the rules became stricter and hundreds of subcastes formed. One large group of people, known as outcastes or untouchables, was not even included in the caste system.

Religious beliefs and customs were the major force in everyday life in India. The traditional religions of the early Indus Valley people and the Aryans gradually developed into Hinduism. The Upanishads, a collection of writings, discuss the basic Hindu ideas of right and wrong, the universal order, and human destiny.

Hindus believe that a world spirit called Brahman is present in every creature and, at the same time, everything is part of the world spirit. The goal of a Hindu is to be taken back into the spirit world by purifying the soul.

Hindus do not expect to do this in one lifetime but through reincarnation over and over. How quickly or slowly the soul is purified depends on one's karma—the sum total of one's good and bad acts in previous lives. Hindu ideas about caste, dharma, and karma are closely related. Performing the correct dharma for one's caste is essential to achieving good karma.

The start of lasting traditions in China. About 1600 or 1500 B.C., the Shang dynasty came to power in northern China. The Shang ruled from a small state near the Yellow River. With the help of a powerful army, they demanded tribute from neighboring peoples. The Shang are noted for their fine bronzework and for the development of China's first known writing system.

About 1100 B.C. the Zhou conquered the Shang (map, page 60). To rule their vast lands, the Zhou rulers developed a feudal system. Gradually, local nobles became more powerful than the king.

Although this was a turbulent time in Chinese history, many advances were made. China entered the Iron Age, canals were dug for shipping, and irrigation systems were built. New towns grew up as trading centers, and coins replaced barter.

More states rose in the North China Plain, and rulers began to centralize their governments. A new class of trained public officials and administrators known as bureaucrats advised these Chinese rulers.

The great teacher Confucius was one of these bureaucrats. His interest in questions of morality led him to describe five basic social relationships: between ruler and subjects, father and son, husband and wife, older and younger brothers, and members of a community.

In the first four relationships, one person was viewed as superior and worthy of respect and obedience. In turn, this superior person was expected to set a good example of moral behavior. These ideas influenced both family life and government in China.

Review Questions

1. What achievements did prehistoric people make?

2. Why did the first civilizations begin in river valleys?

3. Describe the religious beliefs and the writing systems of the Sumerians and of the Egyptians.

4. Name at least three other peoples of the ancient Middle East and describe their accomplishments.

5. How was the caste system in India connected to Hindu beliefs?

6. How did Confucius influence Chinese society?

170 Answers to Review Questions
  1. Making tools and weapons, controlling fire, developing spoken language and art, farming, domesticating animals, developing crafts and new technology.
  2. Rivers provided food, fresh water, a means of trade and travel, and a means of irrigation.

  3. The Sumerians believed in many gods and developed cuneiform—a system of writing on clay tablets. The Egyptians were also polytheists and worshiped the pharaoh as a god. They developed hieroglyphics—a system of writing on papyrus scrolls.
  4. Answers should include three of the following: The Hittites discovered how to make iron. The Phoenicians

UNIT 2: Classical Civilizations (1700 B.C.–A.D. 950)

Chapter 4:
The Ancient Greeks

Western civilization began in the eastern Mediterranean, on the Greek peninsula and neighboring islands.

The beginnings of Greek civilization. In the Aegean region the earliest civilization was that of the Minoan people on the island of Crete. Minoan civilization reached its height between 1700 and 1450 B.C. Somewhat later, about 1300 B.C., Mycenean civilization spread throughout southern Greece. Minoan and Mycenean arts, crafts, and legends became part of the Hellenic civilization that developed about 800 B.C.

One of the most important influences on the thought of the Hellenic Greeks was the poet Homer. His epic poems, the *Iliad* and the *Odyssey,* described heroes who were brave, intelligent, and proud. Developing these qualities became the goal of Greek education. Hellenic ideas spread through the peninsula and to Greek colonies along the Mediterranean and Black seas (map, page 74).

The Greek city-states. Greece developed as a land of independent city-states, each with its own character. Sparta emphasized military skills, discipline, and service to the polis—the city-state. Athens became the cultural center of Greece and originated the idea of democracy.

The Parthenon in Athens—a model of elegance and harmony.

Although the Greeks shared the same language, religious beliefs, and Homeric traditions, they had never united. People felt intensely loyal to their own polis, and city-states often fought with one another. About 500 B.C., however, the threat of conquest by the Persian Empire forced the Greeks to unite. In battles at Marathon in 490 B.C. and at Salamis in 480 B.C. (map, page 78), they defeated the Persians.

After the Persian Wars, Athens became a direct democracy under the leadership of Pericles. All citizens—free adult men whose parents had both been Athenians—met in the Assembly to debate, vote, and make laws. The Athenians believed that every citizen should participate in government. Women, slaves, and foreigners, however, were denied citizenship and thus had no part in ruling Athens.

The flowering of Greek culture. The Greeks believed that every person should live a well-rounded life and aim for excellence in all pursuits. These ideals were best served by a life of moderation—a balance between extremes. Greeks expressed these ideals in the arts as well as in science and philosophy.

The Greek playwrights, such as Aeschylus, Sophocles, and Euripides, wrote tragedies that used stories of gods and goddesses to explore human problems. In another important form of Greek literature, historians such as Herodotus and Thucydides examined the past with a critical eye.

Greek sculptors and painters showed human beings as beautiful and unflawed, only rarely expressing extremes of emotion. Architects tried to bring proportion, balance, and grace to their designs.

Ancient Greek philosophers searched for two kinds of knowledge: knowledge about the natural world and knowledge about human beings' place in that world. The Greeks believed that nature follows general rules called natural laws, which can be discovered by reason.

171

developed the alphabet on which our own is based. The Hebrews were the first monotheists. The Assyrians developed efficient methods of government and built an extensive road network. The Lydians introduced coins to the Middle East. The Persians united all the people of the Middle East under one rule with a single official language, a road network, a postal service, and a standard coinage system.

5. The caste system divided Indian society into separate groups with distinct codes of conduct. According to Hindu beliefs, these codes must be followed in order to purify one's soul.

6. His teachings about the five basic social relationships influenced family life and government.

Among those who made contributions in science and mathematics were Thales, Pythagoras, Democritus, and Hippocrates. Two major philosophers were Socrates and his student Plato. Socrates used a question-and-answer approach, which became known as the Socratic method. It required people to think critically and logically. Plato expressed his ideas about government in the *Republic*, a description of the ideal state.

Aristotle, one of Plato's students, was an exceptionally brilliant thinker. He tried to discover and organize basic ideas in many fields of knowledge. In science, he taught that theory should be accepted only if it agreed with observed facts.

The legacy of Greece. In 431 B.C. the city-states of the Peloponnesus, led by Sparta, went to war against Athens, which had built an empire in the lands around the Aegean Sea. Pericles died early in the war. Thus deprived of wise leadership, Athens was finally forced to surrender in 404 B.C.

The 27-year Peloponnesian War had caused widespread death and destruction. When invaders under Philip of Macedon later attacked Greece, the weakened city-states were unable to resist. The Macedonians crushed the Greek forces in 338 B.C., and the city-states lost their independence.

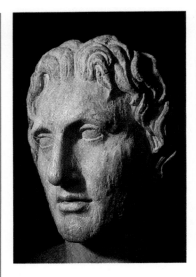

Alexander the Great.

After Philip was assassinated, his 20-year-old son Alexander became ruler. Known as Alexander the Great, he was one of the greatest military leaders in history. Between 334 and 326 B.C., his armies conquered the lands from Egypt to India without losing a single battle (map, page 91).

After Alexander's death in 323 B.C., his empire broke apart. However, Greek culture continued to spread and soon dominated the Mediterranean world. A new stage of civilization—the Hellenistic Age—had begun.

Hellenistic scholars included Euclid, whose work in geometry is still studied, and Archimedes, an inventor and scientist. Studies in philosophy also continued. Unlike the Hellenic thinkers, who wrote about people as members of a community, Hellenistic philosophers were concerned with people as individuals. Epicureanism, named after Epicurus, urged people to live untroubled lives and not to seek wealth, political power, or fame. Stoicism, founded by Zeno, emphasized dignity, reason, and self-control.

Chapter 5: The Roman Republic and Empire

While Hellenic civilization was at its height, a small town in Italy was growing into a major power.

The Roman Republic. In 509 B.C., according to ancient accounts, the Romans established a republic. Unlike Athenian democracy, Rome's government was led by wealthy landowners called patricians. The common people, or plebeians, had little political influence.

A 300-member council of patricians, the Senate, was the most powerful part of the government. By 287 B.C., ordinary plebeians had gained equal legal rights, but the patricians held the real political power.

During this time, the Roman Republic expanded. By the middle of the third century B.C., it ruled most of the Italian peninsula. In 264 B.C. Rome went to war with the North African city-state of Carthage. In the three Punic Wars, Rome defeated Carthage and gained prov-

172

inces outside Italy. Rome controlled the western Mediterranean by 146 B.C. and the eastern Mediterranean—the center of Hellenistic culture—by 133 B.C. (map, page 100).

The Punic Wars were costly for Rome, however. Many farmers whose farms had been destroyed in the fighting sold out to wealthy landowners. They lost both their lands and their livelihoods and joined the huge class of the unemployed poor in the cities.

Attempts at reform failed because many patricians were more concerned with keeping their power and wealth than with Rome's welfare. Ambitious military leaders took advantage of the unrest by recruiting soldiers from the jobless poor. Promising them wealth and land, these generals built private armies. Bloody wars broke out between the supporters of rival generals.

In 46 B.C. Rome came under the control of Julius Caesar, a general who had conquered Gaul. Caesar reorganized the government in the provinces, helped the poor, and granted citizenship to more people outside Italy. Caesar was named dictator and consul for life, a development which many nobles saw as a threat to the Republic. In 44 B.C. a group of nobles stabbed Caesar to death. Instead of saving the Republic, the act plunged Rome back into civil war.

The rise of the Roman Empire. Eventually Caesar's adopted son Octavian defeated his opponents and became the unchallenged leader of Rome. He won the support of the Senate, and was given the title Augustus. His rise to power in 31 B.C. marked the end of the Republic and the beginning of the Roman Empire.

Augustus's rule introduced a 200-year period of peace known as the Pax Romana. Roman armies extended the borders of the Empire in Asia, secured the frontiers in Europe at the Rhine and Danube rivers, and conquered most of Britain. It was generally a time of order, good government, and prosperity.

The Romans built roads, improved harbors, cleared forests, drained swamps, irrigated deserts, and turned undeveloped land into thriving farms. Hundreds of new cities were built and old cities grew larger and wealthier. Trade flourished (map, page 107). Throughout the Empire, some 70 million people were united under Roman rule and Roman law.

Roman society and culture. During the Pax Romana, Roman society was marked by sharp class divisions. The small, wealthy upper class lived far more comfortably than did the unemployed poor, farmers (who were the largest group), or slaves.

Discipline within the family gradually grew more lax. At the same time, many Romans were becoming dissatisfied with their traditional religion. Some turned to new beliefs spreading to Rome from other parts of the Empire.

Outside influences were shaping not only the Roman religion but other aspects of life as well. The strongest influence came from Greece, creating a culture that is often called Greco-Roman. One of the greatest Greco-Roman literary works was the *Aeneid*, written by the poet Virgil. It glorified the Roman talent for governing.

Notable achievements were also made in art and architecture. While Greek artists had tried to present perfect human beauty, Roman sculptors carved every detail realistically. Roman

One of Rome's soldiers—the force behind the Empire.

173

architects and engineers used domes, columns, and arches in their buildings. They built aqueducts, bridges, and roads that lasted for many centuries.

Rome's system of law and justice was perhaps its greatest contribution to Western civilization. Within the Empire, people were united under the Law of Nations. Roman law applied to all citizens, regardless of nationality.

Chapter 6: The Legacy of Rome

The Roman system of government had lasted through both good and bad emperors.

By the second century A.D., however, the Empire had begun to collapse from within and without.

The fall of the Empire. Military leaders began to battle for the throne again. As troops were called back from the frontier to fight for the ambitions of their leaders, the Empire's border defenses broke down. Germanic tribes invaded the Empire and terrorized the people.

In an attempt to end the unrest and restore order, the emperors Diocletian and Constantine imposed strong one-man rule. To make the Empire easier to govern, Diocletian appointed a loyal general as co-ruler in the West and moved his court to Asia

Minor. Diocletian's and Constantine's reforms restored order but did not solve Rome's problems.

About the year 370, Germanic invasions increased (map, page 121). The Visigoths defeated the Roman army at the Battle of Adrianople. As it became clear that Rome could no longer defend its frontiers, Germanic tribes poured into the Empire.

In 476, Germanic officers who had been hired to fight in the Roman army overthrew the Western emperor and declared a fellow German, Odoacer, king of Italy. This event marked the end of the Roman Empire in the West. Several factors con-

---

Major States and Empires About A.D. 200 (Rome. Han. Teotihuacán, Mayas, pre-Incas.)

What empire controlled the Mediterranean? What dynasty ruled China at the same time? What peoples had developed in the Americas?

tributed to the end of the Empire: a weakened army, a smaller population, oppressive government, the decline of farms and cities, a collapsing economy, and a loss of confidence in the Empire itself.

The spread of Christianity. Even before the Empire began to decline, Christianity was gaining followers. The new religion had its beginnings early in the first century A.D., when Jesus preached among the people of Judaea. Many believed he was the Messiah. Jewish and Roman authorities, however, saw Jesus as a threat, and about A.D. 29 he was arrested and crucified.

After the Crucifixion, Jesus' followers—including Paul—spread Christianity throughout the Mediterranean (map, page 128). Roman officials, regarding the new faith as dangerous, began to persecute Christians. The religion nevertheless continued to grow. In 312 the emperor Constantine converted to Christianity, and soon after 380 Christianity became the official religion of the Roman Empire.

Chapter 7: Great Empires in India and China

Between the sixth and third centuries B.C., new ideas and new empires arose in India and China.

The Hindu god Krishna and his wife, Radha.

The development of Buddhism. Over the years, Hinduism had become so complex that it no longer met the needs of the common people. As a result, some Hindus began to listen to a new teacher, the Buddha.

Buddhist teachings are expressed in the Four Noble Truths. First, sorrow and suffering are part of life. Second, people suffer because they try to get things they cannot have. Third, the way to escape suffering is to overcome these desires and reach a state of "not wanting," or nirvana. Fourth, to reach this state, people should follow a "middle way," having neither too much nor too little pleasure.

As Buddhism spread, disagreements grew up and its followers split into two groups: Theravada and Ma-

hayana. The former spread into China, Japan, and Korea, and the latter into Sri Lanka, Burma, and Southeast Asia (map, page 135). In India, Buddhism merged into Hinduism and began to disappear as a separate faith.

A golden age for India. The Mauryan Empire in northern India was founded by Chandragupta Maurya sometime after 323 B.C. A powerful army and a network of spies helped the emperor control local governments. In 269 B.C. rule passed to Asoka, one of the world's great leaders.

Asoka worked to improve the spiritual and practical lives of his people. He also promoted the peaceful spread of both Indian culture and Buddhism. After his death, invaders split up his empire.

Meanwhile, in southern India, the Dravidians established a flourishing trade empire. Merchants went as far as Rome to the west and China to the east.

Northern India remained splintered until about A.D. 320, when the Gupta Empire was established. Thus began a period known as India's Classical Age. Artists, writers, and philosophers developed new forms that served as models for centuries. Mathematicians made remarkable advances: they worked out the decimal system, the idea of zero, and the beginnings of algebra.

175

About the middle of the fifth century, the Huns began to invade the Gupta Empire. By 500, northern India was again a checkerboard of states and kingdoms.

China under the Qin and Han dynasties. Among the philosophies that developed in China after Confucius were Taoism and Legalism. Taoism aimed at understanding the universe and living simply and harmoniously with nature. Legalism taught that people were basically selfish and could live good lives only under strict laws. To make the state wealthy and powerful, a ruler needed complete control.

Legalism was put into practice under the Qin, who had overthrown the Zhou in 256 B.C. The Qin rulers applied Legalist thinking to all of China, crushing local lords and building the Great Wall to keep out nomadic tribes. Other harsh measures, such as banishing Confucian scholars, caused the dynasty's downfall.

The decline of the Qin shows some of the basic problems faced by Chinese dynasties: rebellions by local lords and peasants, invasions, and natural disasters. These problems caused the rise and fall of dynasties in a regular pattern known as the dynastic cycle.

In 202 B.C. the Han took power. Their empire traded along the Silk Road as far as the Mediterranean. Han astronomers and scientists devised an accurate calendar, sundials, and water clocks. Artisans learned to make paper and porcelain known as "china." Han rulers set up a civil service system. In A.D. 220 the Han Empire split into three kingdoms. Warfare raged for the next 300 years.

Chapter 8:
Ancient Africa and America

Migrations and trade played an important role in the development of civilizations in Africa and the Americas.

Africa's early civilizations. Over thousands of years Africans learned the skills necessary to live in Africa's different climate and vegetation zones. When the climate changed (as it did with the drying up of the Sahara), people moved to find land that would better meet their needs.

Of the hundreds of cultures that developed in sub-Saharan Africa, the prominent group is called Bantu. In their homeland, at the edge of the forest and savanna, the Bantu-speakers lived by fishing, farming, and herding. As they began to move to new areas about 2,500 years ago, the Bantu learned to live in a variety of environments.

Some of the Bantu moved east across the savanna and learned to cultivate grains. Others moved to the tropical forests near the equator. Some local peoples were absorbed into Bantu culture, while others fled.

Migrating Bantu also moved east into the Great Rift Valley. There they came into contact with cattle herders, and some adopted this way of life. Others settled as farmers and learned to grow bananas and taro—crops brought into Africa from Southeast Asia. During their migrations, the Bantu learned how to smelt iron.

Other peoples in sub-Saharan Africa developed

The Great Wall of China.

Answers to Review Questions
1. Sparta was strong militarily; Athens was a cultural center and the birthplace of democracy.
2. Writers produced great tragedies and histories; artists and architects created works of beauty and grace; other Greeks made contributions to science, mathematics, and philosophy.
3. A 200-year period of peace, expansion, and prosperity for the Roman Empire.
4. Its system of law and justice.
5. A weakened army, a smaller population, oppressive government, the decline of farms and cities, a collapsing economy, and a loss of confidence in the Empire.

trading kingdoms (map, page 152). About 1600 B.C., Nubians founded the kingdom of Kush to control the gold trade with Egypt. By building a new capital at Meroë, located on important trade routes, Kush increased the scope of its power. In A.D. 350, however, after suffering a decline in trade and farm production, Kush was conquered by Aksum.

In the highlands of Ethiopia, Aksum had a strong agricultural economy and a thriving trade along the Red Sea. Goods were shipped to ports on the Mediterranean Sea and the Indian Ocean.

From early times, Egypt and the civilizations of the Middle East traded with the east coast of Africa. After A.D. 500 this trade grew in importance. Goods and slaves were shipped as far away as India and China.

Trade across the Sahara also grew rapidly from the first century A.D. Merchants from North Africa crossed the Sahara seeking gold and slaves in return for salt and other goods.

Civilizations in the Americas. People first came to the Americas during the Ice Ages, crossing over a land bridge that connected North America to Asia. The first Americans, hunters following herds, probably came from different parts of Asia in small groups over several thousand years. After many centuries, they had spread throughout North and South America.

Each group developed its own language and ways of doing things. As in other parts of the world, these early peoples went through several stages of development.

By about 1200 B.C. people called Olmecs had settled along the Gulf Coast of Mexico (map, page 158). Like the Egyptians, they had a hieroglyphic writing system. They also developed a number system, the idea of zero, and a calendar. As part of their religion, they built huge pyramid-temples and played a ritual ball game.

By about the first century B.C., Olmec culture had vanished. However, it so influenced later cultures that it is considered the "parent culture" of Central America and Mexico.

About the time that the Olmecs disappeared, the first true city in the Americas arose at Teotihuacán in Mexico. The people of Teotihuacán farmed, crafted beautiful masks and pottery, and built a large trading empire. About A.D. 600, however, the city was burned down by invaders from the north.

Between about A.D. 300 and 700, Central American civilization reached its height with the Mayas. The Mayas built religious centers on the Yucatan Peninsula (map, page 158). The Maya centers grew into rich city-states that often fought with one another. Trade flourished, nevertheless.

Between 850 and 950, Maya centers were abandoned one by one. No one knows why Maya civilization collapsed.

Review Questions

1. What characteristics of Sparta and Athens made them great city-states?

2. Identify some of the cultural achievements of the Greeks.

3. What was the Pax Romana?

4. What do many people believe is Rome's greatest contribution to Western civilization?

5. What factors contributed to the end of the Roman Empire?

6. How did Christianity begin? How did it become established in the Roman Empire?

7. What are the Four Noble Truths of Buddhism?

8. How did the Qin and Han systems of government differ?

9. What did Kush, Aksum, and the cities of Africa's east coast have in common?

10. Why is the Olmec culture considered to be a "parent culture"?

6. Christianity began early in the first century A.D. when Jesus preached among the people of Judaea. Christianity was spread by Jesus' followers and adopted by Constantine in 312. It became the Empire's official religion soon after 380.

7. Sorrow and suffering are part of life; people suffer because they try to get things they cannot have; the way to escape suffering is to overcome desires; to reach nirvana, people should follow a "middle way."

8. Following Legalist ideas, the Qin ruled harshly, crushing local lords and banishing Confucian scholars. The Han governed with the help of a civil service system that tested public officials on Confucian ideas.

9. All developed a thriving trade.

10. The Olmecs influenced later cultures in Mexico and Central America.

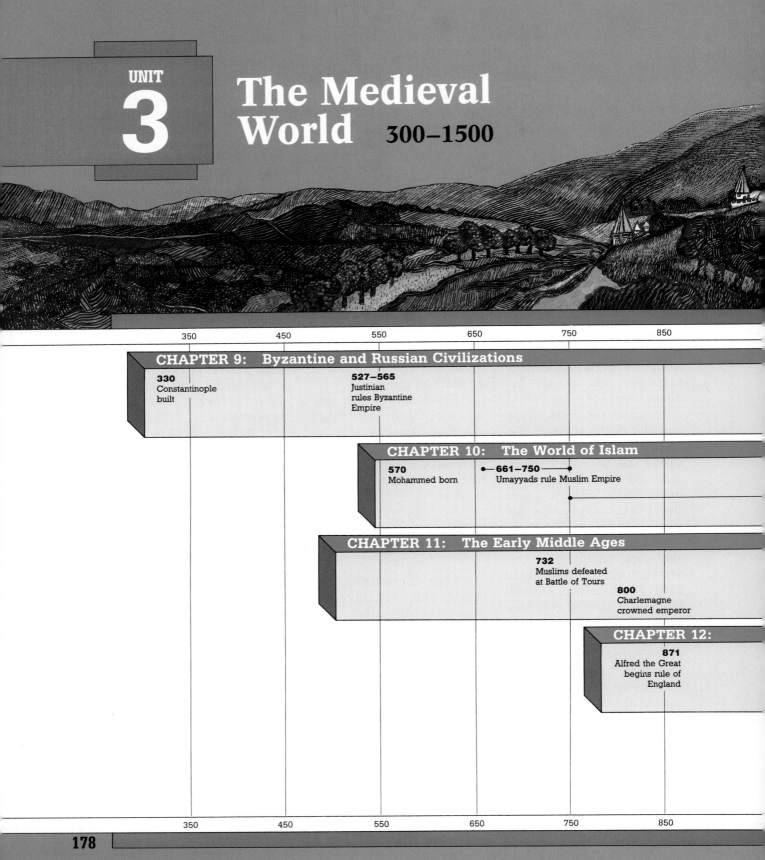

UNIT 3 — The Medieval World 300–1500

	350	450	550	650	750	850

CHAPTER 9:   Byzantine and Russian Civilizations

330
Constantinople
built

527–565
Justinian
rules Byzantine
Empire

CHAPTER 10:   The World of Islam

570
Mohammed born

661–750
Umayyads rule Muslim Empire

CHAPTER 11:   The Early Middle Ages

732
Muslims defeated
at Battle of Tours

800
Charlemagne
crowned emperor

CHAPTER 12:

871
Alfred the Great
begins rule of
England

	350	450	550	650	750	850

FOCUS STRATEGY. Tell students that the illustration shows a European walled city and the surrounding countryside as they might have looked in the Middle Ages. Then ask: (a) How do the buildings in this medieval town compare with architectural styles today? (Answers will vary. Similarities include multi-storied buildings and steepled churches.) (b) Why, do you think, did medieval people build their towns behind high walls? (Students might suggest that walls were a way of defending against attacks and invasions.)

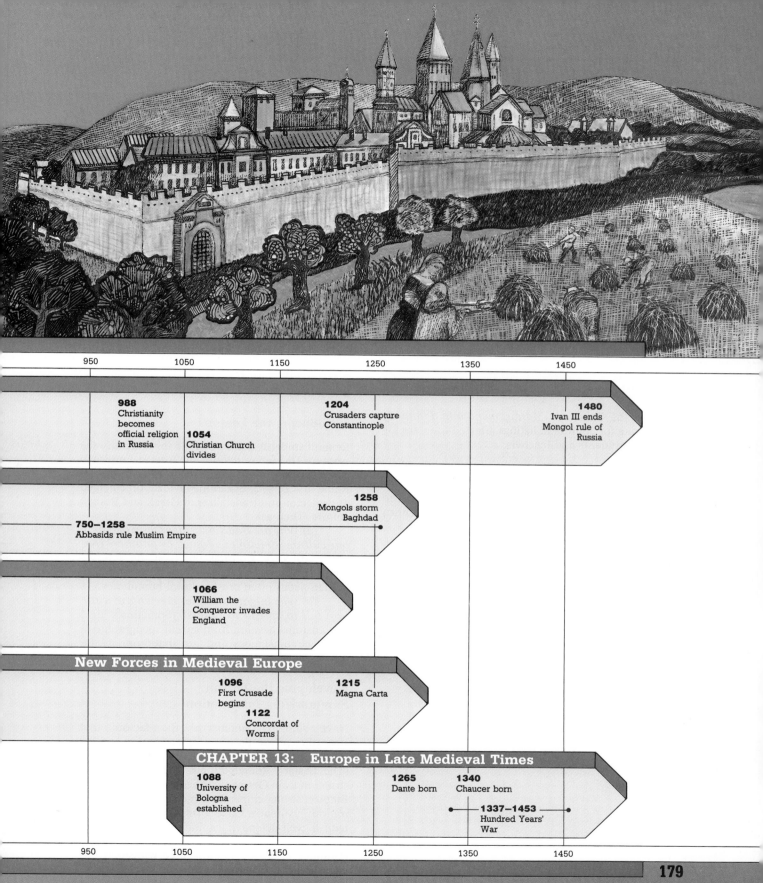

950   1050   1150   1250   1350   1450

988
Christianity
becomes
official religion
in Russia

1054
Christian Church
divides

1204
Crusaders capture
Constantinople

1480
Ivan III ends
Mongol rule of
Russia

1258
Mongols storm
Baghdad

750–1258
Abbasids rule Muslim Empire

1066
William the
Conqueror invades
England

New Forces in Medieval Europe

1096
First Crusade
begins

1122
Concordat of
Worms

1215
Magna Carta

CHAPTER 13:   Europe in Late Medieval Times

1088
University of
Bologna
established

1265
Dante born

1340
Chaucer born

1337–1453
Hundred Years'
War

950   1050   1150   1250   1350   1450

Have students refer to the unit timeline to answer the following question: **What evidence is there in the timeline that religion was a
significant factor in medieval life?** (Students may mention the following events: Christianity becomes the official religion in Russia [988];
the Christian church divides [1504]; Mohammed is born [570].)

Byzantine and Russian Civilizations   300–1500

(pp. 180–195)

Chapter Preview

Section 1 focuses on the rise of the Byzantine civilization in the eastern Mediterranean and western Asian regions. The Byzantine Empire and its cultural influences are examined, and the effects of invasions by the Seljuk Turks, the Ottoman Turks, and the Crusaders are then reviewed. Section 2 traces the growth of the Russian state from its beginning as Slav and Viking settlements through the Mongol invasions.

Bibliography

See the *Teacher's Management and Planning Guide* for additional listings. Starred titles are for both students and teachers.

Billington, James. *The Icon and the Axe*. Random House. Early Russian culture.

*Chambers, James. *The Devil's Horsemen: The Mongol Invasion of Europe*. Atheneum. A short, lively account.

Fennell, J. L. *Ivan the Great of Moscow*. St. Martin's Press. Ivan's role in the founding of the Russian state.

*Grabar, A., ed. *Byzantine Painting*. Skira. Introduces students to Byzantine art.

Runciman, Steven. *Byzantine Style and Civilization*. Penguin. Account by a leading scholar.

Section Lesson Plans

SECTION 1   (pp. 181–188)
Byzantine Civilization

Objectives

After completing this section, students will be able to:
1. Describe how the Byzantines built on Greco-Roman accomplishments.
2. Discuss the invasions that destroyed the Byzantine Empire.

Introducing the Lesson

Remind students that late in the third century the emperor Diocletian divided the Roman Empire to make it easier to govern (p. 120). After the fall of Rome in A.D. 476, Byzantine civilization emerged as protector and transmitter of Greek and Roman culture. Then ask:

(a) *Why are traditions, ideas, and beliefs of one culture sometimes adopted by another?* (Answers will vary. Cultures build on the achievements of others, and ideas and customs that meet human needs often cross cultural boundaries.)

(b) *Why might particular elements of a culture fail to spread to others?* (Sometimes ideas and customs develop from specific geographic or social circumstances and are inappropriate for other groups.)

Developing the Lesson:
Summarizing Information

Have students summarize the factors that strengthened the Eastern Roman Empire and led to the establishment of the Byzantine Empire. (The Eastern Roman Empire did not suffer destruction from Germanic tribes as did the Western Empire; strong emperors forged an able administration; Justinian's Code formalized the legal system; a well-defended capital discouraged invasions; the lands of the Roman Empire were reunified; a superb military force withstood foreign threats.) *(Comprehension)*

Developing the Lesson:
Observing for Detail

Have students identify differences between the Byzantine and Western European cultures and explain how those differences affected the Byzantine religion. (Differences in language, rituals, and church organization resulted in the split between the Byzantine Church and the Western Church.) *(Comprehension)*

Answers to *Map Skill Practice*, p. 185.

1. Islands in the Mediterranean (including Sicily and Crete but not Cyprus), coastal areas in western and southern Italy, Greece, Bulgaria, and Asia Minor.
2. About 2,100 miles.
3. Lombards, Avars, Slavs, Bulgars.
4. If the Byzantines had not held Constantinople, the Arabs could have taken southeastern Europe and moved along the Danube into the heart of Europe.

Closing the Lesson:
Comparing Historical Developments

Have students compare the role of foreign invasions in the decline of the Byzantine and Roman empires (pp. 187–188; 120). (*Byzantine Empire:* Seljuk Turks destroyed the Byzantine army on the eastern frontier; European Crusaders took Constantinople; Ottoman Turks occupied much of Asia Minor and the Balkans. *Roman Empire:* Visigoths attacked Rome and established a kingdom in Spain and Gaul; Vandals attacked Rome.) *(Comprehension)*

See *Section Review* questions, p. 188.

SECTION 2   (pp. 188–193)
The Rise of Russia

Objectives

After completing this section, students will be able to:
1. Describe how Russian culture blended Slavic, Viking, and Byzantine traditions.
2. Explain how a common faith and a common conqueror helped unify Russia.

Introducing the Lesson

Remind students that invading warriors played a significant role in the decline of the Egyptian, Indus Valley, Greek, Roman, and Byzantine civilizations. The Kievan state, seized by Mongols in the middle of the thirteenth century, suffered economically but grew stronger in other ways.

Then ask: *(a) What might account for the devastating effects of invasions on many states?* (Answers will vary. The defending state may find it difficult or impossible to mobilize sufficient military, economic, and political resources to defeat the invaders.)

(b) Why are states with internal problems often more vulnerable to invaders? (Sometimes a state with economic or civil problems must use military resources to suppress internal unrest. Public morale may be so low that a state cannot sustain support for a military effort.)

(c) How might a state be strengthened by the impact of invasion? (Answers will vary. Sometimes the task of repelling a common threat unites a people.)

Developing the Lesson:
Comparing Effects

Have students compare the effects of invasions on the Byzantine Empire with the effects of Mongol invasions on the Kievan state. (The Byzantine Empire lost territory but survived invasions during the seventh and eighth centuries. Although the Lombards, Bulgars, and Visigoths captured Byzantine lands, the empire did not fall. The Arab Muslim invasions were not successful. Seljuk Turks, marauding Crusaders, and Ottoman Turks brought down the empire by 1300. In the Kievan state, the Mongols took full control by 1240, but were only interested in tribute. Because Mongols allowed Russians to keep their religion, customs, and local rulers, the conquered state grew in political and religious unity, but suffered economically.) *(Comprehension)*

Developing the Lesson:
Evaluating History

Have students write an essay evaluating the political and religious factors that contributed to the development of a strong Russian state. (*Political:* acting as Mongol agents, Russian princes acquired power and exercised more control over the people. *Religious:* Christianity helped to unify the Russian people, promoted a stronger alliance with the Byzantine Empire, and reduced Western European influence.) *(Synthesis)*

Closing the Lesson:
Analyzing a Statement

Have students analyze the statement, "Two Romes have fallen, the third Rome will be Moscow and a fourth is not to be" (p. 193). Analyses should answer the following questions:

(a) *What are the "two Romes" to which the statement refers?* (Rome and Constantinople.)

(b) *How might Moscow have become the third Rome?* (With the fall of Constantinople, Russia became the strongest Christian state.)

(c) *What might have been meant by the claim that "a fourth is not to be"?* (The claim probably referred to the belief that Russia's strength would endure.) *(Analysis)*

See *Section Review* questions, p. 193.

Chapter 9 Review Answers
(pp. 194–195)

Vocabulary Review

1. Justinian's Code 2. Crusades 3. czar 4. icon 5. Eastern Orthodox Church; Roman Catholic Church 6. Golden Horde 7. boyars 8. diplomacy 9. Hagia Sophia

People to Identify

1. One of the Byzantine missionaries who created the Cyrillic alphabet, which enabled Slavic languages to be written for the first time.
2. Leader who united the Mongols of Central Asia and took control of the Kievan state in 1240.
3. Founder of unified Russia and the first ruler to take the title of czar.
4. Emperor who ruled the Byzantine Empire from 527 to 565 and developed a code of laws.
5. Viking chieftain who became the leader of Kiev in 860.
6. Influential wife of Justinian.
7. Prince of Kiev who chose the Byzantine form of Christianity as the religion for Russia.

Places to Know

1. B　2. D　3. C　4. A

Recalling the Facts

1. Its language and traditions were Greek, and its art was influenced by the Greeks. Its legal system was Roman and its military organization followed Roman traditions. Its religion was Christian and its art was influenced by Christian sources.
2. The wars were long and costly and led the government to neglect the defense of its lands in the Middle East and the Balkan Peninsula.
3. Disagreements over whether Byzantine emperors had authority over the entire Church and disputes about Church practices.
4. They captured Constantinople in the 1200's, sacking the city and seizing control of important trade routes.
5. Constantinople fell in 1453 to the Turks.
6. Slavic, Viking, Byzantine.

7. He admired the splendor of Byzantine churches; the people of Kiev were familiar with the Byzantine form of Christianity; adopting this religion was likely to build stronger ties between Kiev and the Byzantine Empire.

8. He stopped paying tribute to the Mongols and brought other Russian cities under his control.

Critical Thinking Skills

1. The leaders of the Byzantine Church believed their religion was the correct form of Christianity. Dictionary look-up—answers will vary.

2. Answers will vary.

3. In Russia, Vladimir made Christianity the official religion and imposed it upon the people; in the Roman Empire, the faith spread gradually through the work of missionaries.

4. e–330; a–527; d–988; b–1054; c–1204; f–1462.

Thinking About Geography

1. Answers will vary. Its location made it the key to controlling trade routes and to invading Western Europe.

2. Kiev is on the Dnieper River. The Dnieper flows into the Black Sea. Students should note that Kiev's location on a river made trade and travel easier.

Enrichment: Primary Sources

1. Administering financial and political affairs in his absence.

2. The powers to increase salaries and to exempt people from paying taxes.

3. He respected her and trusted her judgment.

Byzantine and Russian Civilizations 300–1500

See chapter timeline, p. 193.

Before You Read This Chapter

You have already learned that the Roman Empire collapsed in A.D. 476. What might it mean, then, to speak of a "second Rome" or a "third Rome"? In this chapter, you will read of two cities that claimed to match the greatness of ancient Rome. One was Constantinople, the capital of the Byzantine Empire from the 400's to the 1400's. The other was Moscow, which became the leading city in Russia during the 1300's. As you read about the Byzantine world and about early Russian civilization, look for the factors that linked each with the Roman Empire. Consider, too, the differences that set them apart from Rome.

The Geographic Setting

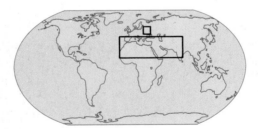

The Chapter Outline

1. Byzantine Civilization
2. The Rise of Russia

This ivory sculpture of the Archangel Michael is an early example of Byzantine religious art.

1 Byzantine Civilization

Objectives

Focus Questions

★ ■ How did the Byzantines build on Greco-Roman accomplishments? *(pages 181–182)*

● ■ What invasions destroyed the Byzantine Empire? *(pages 182–188)*

Terms to Know

patriarch
Justinian's Code
Roman Catholic
  Church
Eastern Orthodox
  Church

icon
Hagia Sophia
diplomacy
Crusades

★ Note strategies for first objective on this page and p. 182.

Late in the third century A.D. the Roman Empire had divided into eastern and western regions (map, page 121). While the western regions were weakened by attacks of Germanic tribes, the eastern provinces thrived. Gradually the center of power in the Empire shifted from Rome to the eastern Mediterranean. Even before the West fell to invaders in A.D. 476 (page 122), there were, in effect, two empires. The new civilization that took shape in the east was called Byzantine (BIZ-unteen) civilization.

A New Empire in the East

Constantinople. As you read in Chapter 6, when the emperor Diocletian divided the Roman Empire, he moved his court to Asia Minor. A co-emperor continued to rule in Italy, but Rome was no longer the center of the Empire. In A.D. 330 the emperor Constantine had a new capital city built for

the Empire. Called Constantinople, it was located on the site of the ancient Greek city of Byzantium (bih-ZAN-shee-um). The map on page 185 shows that the city was on a peninsula in the Bosporus Strait.

The new capital was a fortress city, perfectly located to resist attack from land or sea. The three seaward sides of the peninsula were protected by the sea and a wall. On the land side were a wide moat and three massive walls. For centuries, invaders tried in vain to break through Constantinople's defenses.

Culture and politics. Constantinople became the center of the new Byzantine Empire that developed out of the Eastern Roman Empire. Byzantine culture was a blending of several influences. Its language and traditions were Greek, and its legal system was Roman. ⎤ Sec. Rev. ques. 2

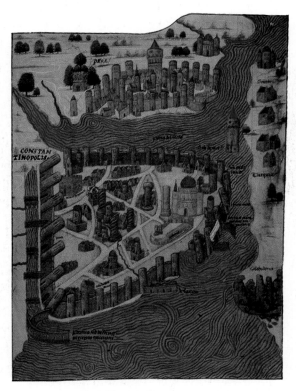

An ancient map shows how Constantinople's location—nearly surrounded by water—helped shield the city from attack.

181

★ RETEACHING. Have students review "Constantinople" (p. 181) to find the following information: (a) Why was the center of the Roman Empire moved? (Diocletian divided the Empire and moved his court to Asia Minor.) (b) What was the name and location of the Empire's capital after A.D. 330? (Constantinople, located on the site of the ancient Greek city Byzantium.) *(Comprehension) Observing for Detail*

★ REINFORCEMENT. Ask: (a) What were the Greek, Roman, and early Christian influences on Byzantine culture? (Greek: language and traditions. Roman: legal system. Early Christian: beliefs and practices.) (b) Why were there frequent and violent power struggles in Constantinople? (There was no law of succession for emperors.) (c) How did Justinian reunite the Roman Empire? (Byzantine forces seized North Africa, Sicily, southern Spain, and Italy.) *(Comprehension) Observing for Detail*

★ See
below.

Its religion followed the beliefs and practices of the early Christian communities in the eastern Mediterranean. Byzantine artists were influenced by Greek, Asian, and Christian sources.

Byzantine emperors considered themselves the successors of the Roman emperors. They claimed, therefore, all the lands that had once been part of the Roman Empire. There was no law of succession in Constantinople, however. Struggles for power were frequent, and many emperors died violently.

Byzantine emperors were all-powerful leaders who declared that God had chosen them to rule. The emperors made and unmade the laws, took charge of foreign affairs, commanded the army and navy, and supervised trade and industry. They also claimed the right to appoint the patriarch (PAY-tree-ahrk), the head of the Church in Constantinople. In this way, the emperors were able to influence Church policy.

The Reign of Justinian and Theodora

Justinian's Code.   The first great Byzantine ruler was Justinian (jus-TIN-ee-un), who reigned for nearly 40 years, from 527 to 565. Justinian's most lasting achievement was in the field of law. With the decline of Rome, the Roman laws and legal system were in danger of being lost. Justinian appointed a group of scholars to collect and organize the ancient laws of Rome. The result of their work

Sec. Rev.
ques. 3

Linking Past and Present

Justinian's Code made Roman law more consistent throughout the Empire—and thus more fair. The value of this code, or system of laws, lived on long after the Roman Empire had collapsed. Today most European countries can trace the roots of their legal system to this code.

182

was a set of laws that in time became known as Justinian's Code.

An influential empress.   Justinian often relied on the advice of his wife, Theodora. Theodora's background was unusual for an empress. She was not an aristocrat but a former actress and the daughter of a bear trainer in the circus. However, Theodora showed great political skill. Until her death in 548, she had much influence in lawmaking and choosing officials. In a number of crises, this strong-willed and intelligent woman gave Justinian the courage to act decisively. In 532, for instance, rioting crowds burned parts of Constantinople and tried to place another emperor on the throne. Some officials urged Justinian to flee, but Theodora persuaded him to face the crowds and restore order.

Regaining Roman territory.   Justinian dreamed of winning back the Roman lands in the western Mediterranean that the Germanic tribes had conquered. Early in his reign, Byzantine forces retook North Africa, Sicily, and southern Spain from the Goths and Vandals. Later they recaptured all of Italy, establishing a western capital at Ravenna (ruh-VEN-uh) about 585.

The Byzantine victories were due to the superb organization of the army, which followed the Roman tradition. Byzantine generals were skilled in military strategy and understood the importance of efficient supply lines and well-built roads and bridges.

The backbone of the Byzantine army was its cavalry. Cavalry soldiers wore steel helmets and suits of armor. They carried an array of weapons—sword, dagger, lance, and bow and arrow. Stirrups, first used by the Byzantines in the sixth century, helped the riders stay astride their horses and left their hands free to use their lances or swords.

The Byzantine Empire Besieged

● Note strategies for second objective on this page and p. 186.
Although Justinian's conquests regained much Roman territory, the Byzantine Empire paid a high price for these victories. The wars were long and costly. Short of money, the government neglected the defense of its lands

★ ENRICHMENT. Have students work in groups to prepare a documentary on how Byzantine culture synthesized elements of Greek, Roman, and Asian art. Students might find information on classic Greek, Roman, and Asian styles of art and architecture that were adopted by Byzantine artists and then display photographs or drawings that illustrate these stylistic influences. *(Synthesis)* *Understanding Cultural Synthesis*

● RETEACHING. Have students review "The Byzantine Empire Besieged" (pp. 182–184) and then draw a map illustrating European, Arab, and Asian invasions of the Byzantine Empire. Maps should indicate the territories and dates of the invasions. *(Comprehension)* *Translating Information into Another Form*

Background The Byzantine cavalry's battle plans had two phases: first, mounted archers harassed the enemy and broke its ranks; then a line of armored lancers engaged in closer combat.

in the Middle East and the Balkan Peninsula. (The Balkan Peninsula lies in southeastern Europe, between the Black and the Adriatic seas.) The rulers who followed Justinian were less able and could not control the army.

European and Asian invaders. Early in the 600's, the Balkans were invaded from the north, first by Slavs, a people from Central Europe, and then by Avars, a people originally from Central Asia. The Avars and Slavs laid siege to Constantinople in 626 but could not break through the city's thick walls. From the east, the Persians attacked Syria, Palestine, and Egypt, all of which were part of the empire.

The Byzantine Empire steadily lost territory throughout the seventh century. The Germanic Lombards conquered Byzantine lands in Italy, and by 631 the Visigoths had recaptured all of Spain. The Bulgars from Central Asia conquered the Slavic tribes in the Balkans and became a constant threat.

Arab invaders. The greatest threat to the Byzantines came from the Arab Muslims, who followed the new religion of Islam (page 198). By 642, these Arabs had taken Egypt, Syria, and Palestine from Byzantium. Beginning in 673, they regularly attacked Constantinople by land and sea. By this time, however, the Byzantines had discovered a new chemical weapon called "Greek fire." An explosive liquid shot from tubes, it set enemy ships afire and made blazing pools of flame on the surface of the water. Armed with

Empress Theodora and her attendants carry an offering to the Church in this sixth-century mosaic from Ravenna. The coin at the right portrays the Emperor Justinian.

183

Background The Avars were paid by Emperor Justinian to conquer the Slavs and the Huns. By 600 the Avars were a powerful group in Europe, but were destroyed in 805 by Charlemagne.

Science Note that Greek fire is thought to have been a mixture of naphtha, sulphur, and saltpeter. The formula for Greek fire was a state secret and was never written down.

"Greek fire" shot from ancient flame throwers helped the Byzantines win naval battles.

this frightening weapon, the light Byzantine ships held off the better-built Arab ships.

In 717–718, an Arab naval attack on Constantinople failed. This defeat ended for a time the Muslim advances in the eastern Mediterranean and marked a crucial point in the history of Europe. If Constantinople had fallen, the Muslims could have overrun the Balkans and sailed up the Danube River into the heart of Europe. After this defeat, however, and another in 732 (page 215), the Arab invaders made no further conquests in Europe.

The Split Between East and West

Europe survived the threat from Islam, but its unity had begun to crumble. Religious and economic differences separated the Byzantine Empire from Western Europe.

A division in Christianity. Over the years, Christians in the Byzantine Empire and in Western Europe had developed different beliefs and ways of practicing their faith. For example, Greek was the language used in Byzantine churches; Western European churches held services in Latin. Disagreements also arose over ceremonies, holy days, the display of religious images, and the right of the clergy to marry.

Another key difference concerned relations between the Church and political authorities. In Western Europe, the Church and the Pope held great political power as well as spiritual power. In the Byzantine Empire, the Church had to answer to the emperor.

184

A bitter dispute over control of the Church gradually developed between Rome and Constantinople. Byzantine emperors claimed that because they were the successors to the Roman emperors, they had authority over the entire Church, in Italy as well as in the Byzantine Empire. They refused to accept the authority of the Pope.

The final break between East and West came in 1054. The Christian Church split into the Roman Catholic Church, ruled from Rome, and the Eastern Orthodox Church, ruled from Constantinople.

Byzantine prosperity. There were other contrasts between the Byzantine world and Western Europe. In the West, trade, town life, and learning declined after the fall of Rome. The Byzantine Empire, on the other hand, remained a center of wealth and culture. Constantinople grew into a magnificent city of more than half a million people. The city's location at the crossroads of Asia and Europe helped make it a center of trade and industry. Into its markets came carpets from Persia, jewels from India, and slaves, ivory, and gold from Africa. Down the rivers of Eastern Europe came Scandinavian merchants with furs, fish, and Slavic slaves.

Byzantine artisans contributed to the empire's prosperity. After traders smuggled silkworms out of China, the Byzantines developed a thriving silk industry. From captive Arabs brought to Constantinople, the Byzantines learned the carefully guarded secret of making paper from rags. Taxes on the prospering industries and trade provided the money needed to run the government and pay for the defense of the Byzantine Empire.

The Influence of Byzantium

Preservation of Greco-Roman culture. At a time when learning was declining in Europe, Byzantine scholars were studying the literature, philosophy, science, mathematics, law, and arts of ancient Greece and Rome. The Byzantines made few original contributions, but they kept much ancient knowledge from being lost. Their work also stimulated

Sec. Rev. ques. 4

Check for Understanding. Ask: Why was the Byzantine defeat of the Arab Muslims in 717–718 important for Europe? (If Constantinople had fallen, the Muslims would have moved into the heart of Europe.)

Religion The Eastern Orthodox Church accepts married men as priests, but bishops and monks may not marry. The adoration of Mary, mother of Jesus, is central to Orthodox worship.

Check for Understanding. Ask: On what matters did Christians in the Byzantine Empire and Western Europe disagree? (Language, ceremonies, holy days, religious images, the right of clergy to marry, and the relationship between Church and political authorities.)

Check for Understanding. Ask: How did Constantinople's geographic location help it grow into a magnificent city? (It was at the crossroads of Asia and Europe, making it a center of trade and industry and the heart of the empire.)

Map Skill Practice

See p. T179B for answers to *Map Skill Practice*.

Byzantine Empire, A.D. 565–700

1. According to the map below, what areas were within the Byzantine Empire in 700?

2. Using the scale, estimate the farthest east-west distance of the empire in 700.

3. What groups attacked the Byzantine Empire in Europe?

4. **Analyzing cause and effect.** Why was it important that the Byzantines defend Constantinople from the Arab naval attack in 717–718 (page 184)?

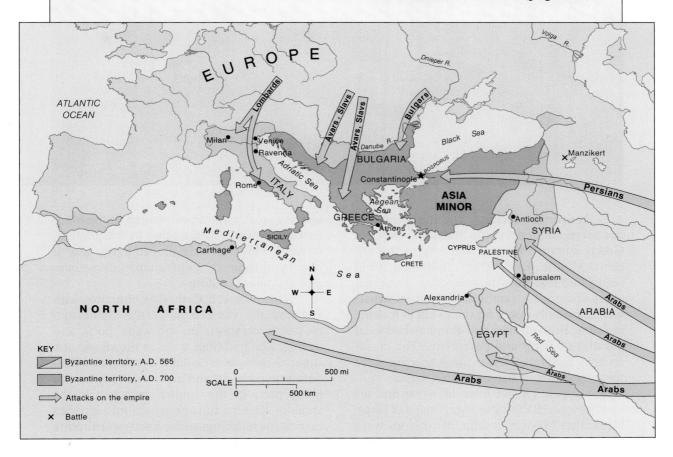

KEY

- ▨ Byzantine territory, A.D. 565
- ▨ Byzantine territory, A.D. 700
- ⇨ Attacks on the empire
- ✕ Battle

SCALE
0 — 500 mi
0 — 500 km

scholarship in the Muslim world and helped bring about a revival of learning in Western Europe.

Protection and expansion of Christianity. Byzantium was the eastern stronghold of Christianity, protecting Europe from invading Islamic armies for centuries. In addition, Eastern Orthodox missionaries carried Eastern Christianity and Byzantine culture to many Slavic peoples in southern and eastern Europe.

In order to enable the Slavs to read the Bible, two Byzantine missionaries, Cyril and Methodius, invented an alphabet that made it possible to write in the Slavic language. A form of this Cyrillic (suh-RIL-ik) alphabet is still used in Russian and other Slavic languages of today.

185

Background Note that Hagia Sophia was used as a mosque after the Turks conquered the city and has served as a museum since 1935.

Religion The Greek cross, also called the Tau cross, was named for the Greek letter *T*.

Historic Places

Hagia Sophia

Artistic creativity. The Byzantine artists were influenced by both the classical Greco-Roman style and the arts of the ancient Middle East. They combined vivid colors and elaborate designs, often using religious themes or symbols. Byzantine artists were especially noted for their skill in making mosaics. Both Greeks and Romans had used mosaics on walls and pavements. The mosaics that decorated Byzantine churches were the most brilliant use of this art form.

Another typical form of Byzantine art was the icon (EYE-kahn)—an image of Jesus, his mother Mary, or a saint. Most icons were painted on wood. Regarded as holy, they were kept both in homes and in Eastern Orthodox churches.

Architectural innovations. Byzantine architecture was distinctive. After riots and fire destroyed much of Constantinople in 532 (page 182), Justinian started a vast program to build fortresses, monasteries, and churches.

The city's new cathedral, finished in five years, was Hagia Sophia (HAH-jah soh-FEE-ah), the "Church of Holy Wisdom." It

186

was the most magnificent church in the Mediterranean world at the time. In designing it, Byzantine architects developed a new way of placing a rounded, onion-shaped dome over a rectangular building.

Later Eastern Orthodox churches usually had the same high central dome and mosaic decorations on the walls, floor, and ceiling. The buildings were in the shape of a squared cross, also called a Greek cross. Byzantine styles in art and architecture spread to many parts of the empire, particularly the areas of Eastern Europe where missionaries carried the teachings of the Eastern Orthodox Church. Richly decorated Greek-cross churches became common in Greece, the Balkans, and Russia.

● See below.

The Decline of the Byzantine Empire

The Byzantine Empire remained fairly stable and prosperous for several hundred years despite continuing invasions. To protect their lands, Byzantine emperors relied on well-

● REINFORCEMENT. Have students evaluate the factors that led to the decline of the Byzantine Empire and then explain which was most harmful to the empire's strength. (Factors include invasions by the Seljuk and Ottoman Turks; the Crusades; seizure of trade routes by Venetians; high taxes; decrease in farm production; loss of territory.) (Evaluation) **Making Judgments**

● ENRICHMENT. Have students work in groups to present a panel discussion on the achievements of the Byzantine Empire. Students might find information on the Justinian Code, the reunification of the empire, Byzantine art and architecture, and the Eastern Orthodox Church. (Synthesis) **Presenting a Panel Discussion**

Religion Eastern Orthodox Christians believe that icons—images of Jesus, Mary, and the saints—are visible witnesses to Orthodox belief that Jesus was God born as man.

When riots swept through Constantinople in 532 and nearly drove Justinian from his throne, much of the city was destroyed by fire. Among the churches that burned was Hagia Sophia, built in the time of Constantine. Justinian resolved to rebuild this church and make it the most splendid in the world.

Many cathedrals in Europe took more than a generation to build. The new Hagia Sophia, however, took only five years (532–537). The work went quickly because the emperor poured money into the project—enough to hire as many as 10,000 laborers.

From the outside, Hagia Sophia was impressive. A cluster of arched roofs rose up to the mighty central dome, which stood 180 feet above the city. By sheer height and mass, the cathedral dominated Constantinople. Yet its true beauty could be seen only from the inside. The huge dome, built with tons of marble and concrete, looked almost weightless from within the church. It seemed to float on a halo of sunlight from the circle of windows around its base. One historian wrote that the dome looked as if it were "suspended by a golden chain from heaven."

The columns and walls gleamed with many-colored marble and polished stone. Glittering mosaics reflected the light of a thousand lamps and candles. The scent of incense filled the air. Overwhelmed by all this beauty, some visiting nobles from Russia were sure they saw angels hovering in the lofty dome.

Ⓕ See below, left.

trained armies and shrewd **diplomacy**—the art of working out political agreements. Emperors were experts at making alliances, arranging political marriages, and using bribes to gain friends. They kept their enemies divided by stirring up hatred among them. Nevertheless, attacks from a number of directions nibbled away at Byzantine territory.

The Seljuk Turks. In the early eleventh century a new enemy appeared in the east. The Seljuk (SEL-jook) Turks, originally from Central Asia, had converted to Islam. Moving steadily westward, in 1071 they destroyed the Byzantine army at the town of Manzikert on the empire's eastern frontier (map, page 185). The Seljuks now seemed ready to overrun Asia Minor.

Sec. Rev. ques. 5

The Crusades. The Byzantines turned to European Christians for help resisting the Turks. Angered by the Turkish conquest of Christian holy places in the Middle East, European Christians began a series of military campaigns against the Turks. These expeditions are known as the **Crusades** (page 247).

European Crusaders had little interest in restoring lands to the Byzantines. They set up their own kingdoms in territories they captured in the Middle East. In 1204, Western European Crusaders and Venetian merchants decided to capture the rich city of Constantinople for themselves rather than fight the Turks. The Crusaders wanted the city's wealth, while the Venetians sought control over the rich Byzantine trade.

The Crusaders devastated Constantinople. They destroyed sacred books, vandalized churches, and carried gold, jewels, and works of art back to Western Europe. The Venetians seized islands along Constantinople's major trade routes. Not until 1261 was Constantinople restored to the Byzantines.

The capture of Constantinople greatly weakened the empire. The Byzantines also faced problems of crushing taxes, falling agricultural production, declining trade, and loss of territory.

The Ottoman Turks. The deathblow to the Byzantine Empire was dealt by another group of Turks. The Ottoman Turks (page 277) were followers of Islam who considered their battles with Byzantine Christians a holy war. During the 1200s and 1300s, they **187**

Ⓕ **FEATURE ACTIVITY. Have students compare the picture of the Hagia Sophia (facing page) with the picture of the Blue Mosque on page 196. Then ask: What architectural features do the buildings share?** (Rounded domes over rectangular buildings, tall towers, and rounded arches.) *(Comprehension)* **Observing for Detail**

Vocabulary Note that the word *Ottoman* comes from *Osman* or *Othman*, the founder and first ruler of the Ottoman Empire.

defeated the Byzantines and the earlier Turk-ish conquerors and occupied much of Asia Minor and the Balkans. By the early 1400's, the Byzantine "empire" consisted of only the city of Constantinople and two small territories in Greece.

Sec. Rev. ques. 5, cont.

The fall of Constantinople. In 1453 the Turks attacked Constantinople itself, out-numbering the Byzantines by more than ten to one. For over a month the Turks bom-barded Constantinople's great walls with cannon balls that weighed as much as 1,000 pounds. This massive attack finally over-whelmed the fierce resistance of the city's defenders. Three days of looting and slaugh-ter followed.

The fall of Constantinople marked the end of the thousand-year reign of the Byzan-tine Empire. Yet the Byzantines left a lasting imprint on European and Russian history. They had preserved Greco-Roman culture, protected Western Europe from Muslim in-vaders, and spread their own culture into Eastern Europe and Russia.

See Sec. 1 *Closing the Lesson*, p. T179B.

See lesson plans, pp. T179A–179C

(pp. 182, 184, 186, 187)

Section Review

Answers to Section Review questions are in brackets on pages indicated.

1. **Define or identify:** patriarch, Justin-ian's Code, Roman Catholic Church, Eastern Orthodox Church, icon, Hagia Sophia, diplomacy, Crusades.
2. What different cultural traditions con-tributed to the development of Byzan-tine civilization? (pp. 181–182)
3. What was Justinian's greatest achieve-ment as emperor? (p. 182)
4. How did the Byzantines influence other peoples? (pp. 184–185)
5. What foreign invasions destroyed the Byzantine Empire? (pp. 187–188)
6. **Critical thinking:** Consider the state-ment: "The Greeks were the thinkers, the Romans were the builders, and the Byzantines were the preservers." Do you agree or disagree with this state-ment? Explain your answer. (See answer below.)

6. Answers will vary. The Byzantine Empire was a blend of Greek philosophy, language, and traditions, and Roman lands and legal systems.

2 The Rise of Russia

Objectives

Focus Questions

★ ■ How did Russian culture blend Slavic, Viking, and Byzantine traditions? *(pages 188–191)*

● ■ How did a common faith and a common conqueror help unify Russia? *(pages 191–193)*

Terms to Know

| steppe | Golden Horde |
| boyar | czar |

188

★ Note strategies for first objective on this page and p. 191.

Though the Turks overran the Byzantine Empire, they ignored the easternmost part of Europe. This area had been settled by Slavs after the fall of the Roman Empire. The cul-ture the Slavs developed was a blend of Slavic, Viking, and Byzantine traditions.

The Geography of Russia

The region of Russia lies on a vast plain in the easternmost part of Europe. Over the north-ern part of Russia stretch immense forests. South of the forests are the **steppes**—prairie grasslands similar to the plains region of the United States. Both the forest and the steppes have fertile soil. Because the steppes were

★ RETEACHING. Have students review p. 191 and make a chart iden-tifying the causes and effects of Prince Vladimir's choice of Christianity as the state religion. (Causes: rejection of Judaic dietary laws, Islam, and Western Christianity; familiarity with Byzantine culture; desire to strengthen alliance with Byzantines. Effects: Cyrillic alphabet created; churches became centers of learning and art; Russians became united.) (Comprehension) **Identifying Cause and Effect** often too dry for farming, however, people settled mostly in the northern forests, living in log cabins. The climate was warm in the summer, cold and snowy in the winter.

Rivers that flowed into the Black, Caspian, and Baltic seas provided the settlers with ways to make contact with other peoples. Russia's lack of mountains also aided trade and transportation. At the same time, the absence of natural barriers made it easy for outsiders to invade Russia.

Slavic Russia

The Slavs were an Indo-European people who had lived in Central Europe for many centuries. During the 400's, some of them began to move north and east into Russia.

Sec. Rev. ques. 2
Like the Germans, the Slavs lived in tribal groups. They had no written language and their religion was a form of polytheism (a belief in many gods). They lived by farming, hunting, and fishing. Although the tribes were often conquered and ruled by invaders, their culture was not much affected by these outside contacts.

The Vikings

During the ninth century, a new group of invaders ruled the Slavs. Unlike earlier invaders, they left a deep imprint on the Slavic people. The Vikings, who came from Scandinavia, were mainly interested in trade. They
Sec. Rev. ques. 3
entered Slavic lands by means of rivers. From the Slavs they obtained slaves and other trade goods. They then continued their river journey south to the Black Sea, where they exchanged these goods for Byzantine silk and Persian spices.

The Vikings built forts at strategic points along the trade routes. From these forts they raided Slavic settlements, demanding payments of valuable goods as tribute. Over time, the forts grew into cities ruled by princes. The two most important cities were Novgorod (NAHV-guh-rahd) in the north and Kiev (kee-EV) in the south.

Cultural History Note that the word *slav* is the root of the word *slave* in many European languages because the Vikings took slaves from areas where Slavs lived.

The Kievan State

The city of Kiev became the center of the first state in Russia. (The term *Russia* comes from *Rus*, a name for the Vikings who settled in Kiev.) To strengthen their hold on the riches of Russia, the Vikings forced the Slavs to accept their rule. According to legend, the first Great Prince of Kiev was Rurik, a Viking chieftain. (The Great Prince was the supreme leader of the state, with more power than the local princes.) Rurik established his dynasty about 860. From the capital at Kiev, his successors ruled over a loosely organized group of Slavic cities. The Vikings intermarried with the Slavs, and their ways of life blended to form a new society that would become the basis of Russian culture.

Conversion to Christianity. An important part of the emerging culture was

A Russian icon from the late 1300's shows St. George slaying a dragon. St. George was the patron saint of Russian peasants.

189

ⓕ See
below.

The Geography Connection

River Routes in Early Russia

Much of Russia's territory lies in the cold latitudes, where the climate is severe. However, the country has one great natural asset—a magnificent network of easily navigable rivers. These rivers formed important trade routes during the Middle Ages and laid the foundation for the first Russian state in the mid-800's.

To the Vikings, Russia was a land that promised access to the riches of Constantinople and Persia. Viking raiders and merchants sailed from Scandinavia across the Baltic Sea and entered Russia by way of rivers. From Lake Ladoga in northern Russia, the Vikings followed two main routes. One route headed south through Novgorod and Kiev to the Black Sea and Constantinople (see map). The other route headed southeast along the Volga River to the Caspian Sea and Persia.

The Viking merchants obtained furs, honey, and beeswax from Russia's northern forests and amber from the shores of the Baltic. They traded these products and others for wines, silk, and art objects in Constantinople and for spices and precious stones in Persia.

Eventually the Vikings established open trade routes between the Baltic Sea and the Caspian and Black seas. Merchants from Poland, Germany, and England used these routes to reach Constantinople and areas to the south.

The great rivers of Russia encouraged exploration by the Vikings and led to the development of important trade routes between East and West. The wealth and power that resulted from this trade enabled the Vikings to establish order among Russia's Slavic tribes and to unify the country.

Making the connection. How did Russia's rivers affect its early history?

Russia About 900

ⓕ GEOGRAPHY CONNECTION. Have students refer to "The Geography of Russia" (pp. 188–189) and "The Vikings" (p. 189) and then list the economic and cultural advantages and disadvantages of Russia's geography. (Synthesis) *Drawing Conclusions*

Biography Vladimir was baptized a Christian in 988, and married the sister of Byzantine emperor Basil II.

Vocabulary The Mongol army was called the "Golden Horde" because yellow was the imperial color.

This icon of Mary and the infant Jesus decorated an Orthodox church in Russia. The clothing and the thoughtful expressions suggest the influence of Byzantine painting styles.

neither Viking nor Slavic but Byzantine. The Vikings and Slavs had traditionally practiced a polytheistic nature worship. In 988, according to legend, Great Prince Vladimir decided to adopt instead a monotheistic religion. He sent 10 men out of the country to observe the religious practices of Jews, Muslims, Christians in the West, and Christians in the Byzantine Empire. His men reported that both Jews and Muslims were forbidden to eat certain foods, so Vladimir rejected those faiths. He also disliked the fact that Western Christians were required to fast (do without food) on certain days. When his men described the splendor of the Byzantine churches and the beauty of their ceremonies, Vladimir decided to adopt the Christianity practiced in Constantinople.

Actually, there were more substantial reasons for Vladimir's choice. First, the people of Kiev were familiar with the new faith because of their trade with the Byzantines and their admiration for Byzantine culture. Second, adopting the religion of the Byzantines was likely to promote a stronger alliance between Kiev and its powerful neighbor to the south.

Vladimir ordered all the people of Kiev to follow the new faith. Although many continued to worship their traditional gods in secret, all were required by law to be baptized as Christians. The holy places of the old faiths were destroyed, and magnificent churches were built in the Byzantine style.

Effects of the conversion. Vladimir's choice affected the lives of the Kievan people in a number of ways. First, Byzantine clergy came to Kiev, building schools and monasteries. They also created the Cyrillic alphabet (page 185) so that the Slavic language could be written for the first time. Second, the establishment of a common faith helped to unite the Russians as a people, thus paving the way for a strong, unified state. Third, Kiev's close ties with the Byzantines reduced Western European influence on Russian culture. Russia's independence of the West had important consequences for later Russian history.

Sec. Rev. ques. 4

★ See below, left.

Power struggles. The Kievan state, like Rome, was hurt by its lack of a law of succession. There were no fixed rules that said who would come to power when the reigning Great Prince died. During the late 1100's and early 1200's, the Kievan state was increasingly torn by civil war among the boyars—Russia's powerful nobles. Order was restored not by a great leader like Augustus but by a brutal conqueror from the East.

The Mongol Invasion

● Note strategies for second objective on this page and p. 192.

Genghis Khan. One of the most feared warriors of all time was Genghis Khan (JENG-gis kahn). During the 1200's he built an enormous empire in Asia. His people, the Mongols, were fierce nomads from Central Asia. The Mongol army—called the Golden Horde—conquered all of China (page 283). Riding fast ponies, the Mongols swept across the steppes of Asia and on into Europe. Their ruthless killing and burning earned them a reputation for savagery that has rarely been equaled.

191

★ REINFORCEMENT. Have students write an essay explaining how the Byzantine Church had a stronger unifying effect on the people of Kiev than did their traditional polytheistic nature worship. (Synthesis) Drawing Inferences
★ ENRICHMENT. Have students research Viking, Slavic, and Byzantine influences on the Soviet Union's language, art, and religion. (Application) Locating Information

● RETEACHING. Have students review "Demands for tribute" and "Consequences of Mongol rule" (p. 192) and evaluate how Mongol demand for tribute affected Russian society. (Impossible for Russians to rebuild after Mongol conquest; renewed interest in agriculture; foreign trade and travel almost disappeared; power of local princes increased because they collected taxes for Mongols.) (Comprehension) Making Judgments

Genghis Khan led his army of ferocious nomadic horsemen against the settled societies of Asia and created one of the largest land empires in history.

By 1240 the Mongols were in full control of the Kievan state. The city of Kiev itself was demolished. A Roman Catholic bishop who traveled through the remains of the city five years later wrote:

66 The Mongols went against Russia and carried out a great massacre. They besieged Kiev, which had been the capital of Russia, and after a long siege they took it and killed the inhabitants of the city. When we passed through that land, we found lying in the field countless heads and bones of dead people. This city had been extremely large and very populous; now it has been reduced to nothing. 99

Demands for tribute. The Mongols had no interest in changing the Russian way of life. They allowed the Russians to keep their religion and customs and even to be ruled by their own princes, who were subject to Mongol approval. The only demand they made was for enormous amounts of tribute.

192

The princes of Russia thus became the agents and tax collectors of the conquerors, and the peasants, who paid the taxes, suffered greatly.

Consequences of Mongol rule. Although the Mongols did not try to change Russian society, the 250 years of their rule had important effects on Russia. First, by destroying so much property during their conquest, the Mongols dealt a crippling blow to the Russian economy. Recovery was made impossible because the Russians had to pay so much tribute. Instead of trying to rebuild industry, which had begun to develop under the Kievan state, Russians turned back to the land. As a result, agriculture became the foundation of the Russian economy.

Sec. Rev. ques. 5

Second, as commerce and industry disappeared, foreign trade and travel slowed to a near halt. The city of Novgorod kept its contacts with other lands, but most of Russia became cut off from Western Europe and the Byzantine Empire.

Third, Mongol rule strengthened the authority of both the Church and the Russian princes. Respecting the clergy as scholars, the Mongols did not require the Church to pay taxes. Thus the Church grew stronger. In addition, local princes had to build up their power to collect the taxes demanded by the Mongols. They kept this power after Mongol rule ended, and the Russian people came to accept greater control of their lives by the government.

The Rise of Moscow and Ivan the Great

The princes of Moscow profited under Mongol rule. Because they were loyal to the Mongols they gained special privileges. The Mongols allowed them to use the title of Great Prince, which was made hereditary. As Moscow grew in importance, the Eastern Orthodox Church moved its headquarters there from Kiev in 1328. Later, when internal conflicts weakened the Mongol empire, Moscow led the fight to free Russia from Mongol rule.

● See below.

Ivan III (known as Ivan the Great), the founder of unified Russia, ruled from 1462 to

● REINFORCEMENT. Have students write the script for a conversation that might have occurred among a Russian peasant, a prince, and a member of the clergy during Mongol rule. The conversation should include each participant's views on the advantages and disadvantages of Mongol rule. *(Synthesis) Understanding Point of View*

● ENRICHMENT. Have students consider the following question which might have faced a Russian prince after the Mongol invasions: *Should I defend Russian peasants against Mongol demands for tribute, or should I cooperate with the Mongols and increase my political and economic strength?* Students should evaluate the advantages and disadvantages of each position and then be prepared to explain their choice in class. *(Synthesis) Problem Solving*

1505. In 1480 he formally announced Russia's independence by declaring that he would pay no further tribute to the Mongols. Ivan then used bribes and force to bring the other Russian cities under his control.

By this time, the Byzantine Empire had fallen to Muslim invaders (page 188). As the only Eastern Orthodox ruler in Europe, Ivan regarded himself as the heir to the emperors of Rome and Constantinople. To strengthen his claim, he married the niece of the last Byzantine emperor. Taking the title of **czar**—the Russian word for *Caesar*—Ivan established himself as the sole ruler of Russia.

From its creation, the state of Russia was extremely proud and ambitious. One Russian boasted: "Two Romes have fallen, the third Rome will be Moscow and a fourth is not to be." Later czars would attempt to make that prediction a reality.

See Sec. 2 *Closing the Lesson*, p. T179C.

Section Review

Answers to Section Review questions are in brackets on pages indicated.

1. **Define or identify:** steppe, boyar, Golden Horde, czar. (pp. 188, 191, 193)
2. Describe the culture of the Slavs who first settled Russia. (p. 189)
3. How and why did the Vikings come to Russia? (p. 189)
4. What were the consequences of Prince Vladimir's conversion to Orthodox Christianity? (p. 191)
5. What long-term effects did the Mongols have on Russia? (p. 192)
6. **Critical thinking:** What evidence could Ivan the Great have used to prove that he was heir to the Roman and Byzantine emperors?

(See answer below.)

Chapter 9   Summary and Timeline

1. Byzantine civilization took shape in the 300's A.D. in the eastern half of the Roman Empire. The Byzantine Empire recaptured much Roman territory and protected Christian Europe from Muslim invasion. The empire was gradually weakened by a series of invasions, finally falling to the Ottoman Turks in 1453. The Byzantines preserved many elements of Greco-Roman civilization.

2. From the combination of Slavic, Viking, and Byzantine traditions, a distinctive Russian culture emerged. Established in the mid-ninth century, the first Russian state adopted Christianity from the Byzantine Empire. Mongol invaders then occupied Russia from the 1200's until the mid-1400's. The city of Moscow led the fight to defeat the Mongols and became the center of a unified Russia.

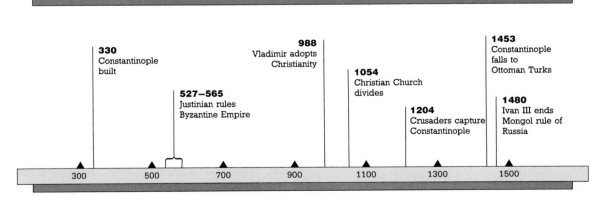

| 330 Constantinople built | 527–565 Justinian rules Byzantine Empire | 988 Vladimir adopts Christianity | 1054 Christian Church divides | 1204 Crusaders capture Constantinople | 1453 Constantinople falls to Ottoman Turks | 1480 Ivan III ends Mongol rule of Russia |

300   500   700   900   1100   1300   1500

193

6. Answers will vary. Ivan was the only Eastern Orthodox ruler in Europe and therefore heir to the emperors of Constantinople and to their forerunners the Roman Caesars. He also married the niece of the last Byzantine emperor and thus created a tie of kinship to the throne.

See p. T179C for answers to Chapter Review.

Vocabulary Review

Use the following terms to complete the sentences below: *boyars, Crusades, czar, diplomacy, Eastern Orthodox Church, Golden Horde, Hagia Sophia, icon, Justinian's Code, Roman Catholic Church.*

1. The ancient laws of Rome were collected and organized into ___?___.
2. European Christian military campaigns against the Turks were known as the ___?___.
3. Ivan the Great was the first ___?___ of Russia.
4. An ___?___ is a religious image, often painted on wood.
5. The Christian Church split into the ___?___, ruled from Constantinople, and the ___?___, ruled from Rome.
6. The Mongol army, known as the ___?___, conquered China in less than five years.
7. Russia's powerful nobles were known as ___?___.
8. The Byzantine emperors used clever ___?___ to protect their lands.
9. ___?___ was Constantinople's most magnificent cathedral.

People to Identify

Identify the following people and tell why each was important.
1. Cyril
2. Genghis Khan
3. Ivan the Great
4. Justinian
5. Rurik
6. Theodora
7. Vladimir

Places to Know

Match the letters on this map of the Kievan state with the places listed below.
1. Black Sea
2. Constantinople
3. Kiev
4. Novgorod

Recalling the Facts

1. In what ways was the developing Byzantine Empire influenced by Greek, Roman, and Christian traditions?
2. How did Justinian's military conquests hurt the Byzantines in the long run?
3. What issues led the Christian Church to split into eastern and western branches?
4. How did Crusaders and Venetian merchants weaken the Byzantine Empire?
5. When did Constantinople finally fall, and who was responsible?
6. What three cultures helped to shape early Russian civilization?
7. Why did Vladimir I decide to adopt the Christianity of Constantinople?
8. How did Ivan the Great help to unify Russia?

194

1. **Building vocabulary.** As you learned, the Church in Constantinople became known as the Eastern Orthodox Church. *Orthodox* comes from the Greek works *orthos*, meaning "straight" or "correct," and *doxa*, meaning "opinion." Why was the Byzantine Church called orthodox? Use a dictionary to find at least two other words with the prefix *ortho* and explain what they mean. *(App.)*

2. **Preparing a report.** Research and write a report about one of the following topics: Byzantine architecture; Russian icons; the various branches of the Eastern Orthodox Church today; Genghis Khan. *(App.)*

3. **Making comparisons.** How was the introduction of Christianity into Russia different from its introduction into the Roman Empire (Chapter 6)? *(Comp.)*

4. **Sequencing.** On a separate sheet of paper, list the following events in chronological order, giving the date for each entry.
   a. Justinian begins his rule of the Byzantine Empire.
   b. Christian Church splits into eastern and western branches.
   c. Crusaders capture Constantinople.
   d. Christianity becomes the official religion in Kiev.
   e. Constantine builds a new capital at Constantinople.
   f. Ivan III begins his rule of Russia.

   (Comp.)

Thinking About Geography

1. **Analyzing.** Reread the discussion of Constantinople on page 181 and refer to the map on page 185. What made Constantinople easy to defend? Why did invaders from the east keep trying to capture the city? *(Anal.)*

2. **Studying a map.** Find Kiev on the map on page 190. On what river is the city located? Into what body of water does this river flow? What geographic advantages helped make Kiev an early center of the Russian state? *(Comp.)*

Enrichment: Primary Sources

Alexius I ruled the Byzantine Empire from 1081 to 1118. Soon after becoming emperor, he left the capital at Constantinople to fight invaders. The passage below is adapted from Alexius's decree announcing that his mother will rule during his absence.

66 Now I, your ruler, am preparing for a campaign against our enemies, and with great care am collecting and organizing an army. Yet I judge the administration of financial and political affairs a matter of supreme importance. And certainly I have found a way to continue good government, that is, that the whole administration should be entrusted to my most deeply honored mother.

I, your ruler, therefore decree that whatever orders she shall give shall be considered as coming from my hand. My holy mother shall have power to do whatsoever shall seem good to her. With regard to increase of salaries and exemption from taxes, these my mother shall settle absolutely. For her words and her commands shall be considered as given by me. Not one of those commands shall be canceled, but shall remain valid and in force for the coming years. 99

1. What was the major concern of Alexius at the time the decree was made?
2. What two powers did Alexius specifically grant his mother?
3. **Critical thinking:** What can you conclude about Alexius's feelings toward his mother? *(Anal.)*

The World of Islam
(pp. 196–209)

Chapter Preview

Section 1 outlines the rise of Islam and its expansion to the Middle East, Africa, and Europe; describes Mohammed's life and the major beliefs of Islam; and then traces the conquests of later Muslim rulers. The empire-building of the Seljuk Turks and the Mongols is discussed, as is the effect of the Crusades on the Muslim world. Section 2 describes the influence of Islamic culture and Muslim achievements in the arts and sciences.

Bibliography

See the *Teacher's Management and Planning Guide* for additional listings. Starred titles are for both students and teachers.

Arberry, Arthur J. *Aspects of Islamic Civilization As Depicted in the Original Texts.* Barnes. Good primary sources.

Arnold, T. W., ed. *The Legacy of Islam.* Gordon Press. How Islam affected Europe.

Lewis, Bernard. *Arabs in History.* Harper & Row. Pre-Islam to post-World War I.

*Rogers, Michael. *The Spread of Islam.* Phaidon. Islamic history and art.

Section Lesson Plans

SECTION 1   (pp. 197–203)
The Spread of Islam

Objectives

After completing this section, students will be able to:
1. Explain how the religion of Islam arose.
2. Describe how Islam spread to other parts of Asia, Africa, and Europe.
3. Identify the causes of the breakup of the Muslim empire.

Introducing the Lesson

Remind students that Islam is a major world religion that was founded by Mohammed in the seventh century. Islam became a source of unity for many Arab tribes in the Middle East and remains a significant regional influence in religious and political matters today.

Then ask: *(a) How might religion be a source of political unity?* (A common faith and value system can sometimes result in a willingness to work for shared goals.)

(b) How does religion spread from one region to another? (Answers will vary. Trade, migration, territorial expansion, or missionary activity might lead to the spread of a religion.)

(c) Why might members of a religion seek to convert nonbelievers? (Answers will vary. Sometimes believers feel a duty to convert others.)

Developing the Lesson:
Comparing Historical Events

Have students compare the lives of Mohammed and the Buddha (p. 133). Students might describe the lives of Mohammed and the Buddha, the circumstances surrounding the establishment of their religions, and the popularity of their teachings. (Buddha was a prince who had been shielded from hardship. When confronted by suffering, he left home to discover the truth about human experience and was enlightened while sitting under a tree. Mohammed was an honest and successful businessman. While meditating, he became convinced that he saw a vision and that he was chosen to serve as a prophet and bring the Arabs a new faith.) *(Comprehension)*

Developing the Lesson: Understanding Vocabulary

Have students define or identify the following terms: *Islam* (Arabic for "surrender to Allah"); *Allah* (Arabic for God); *Muslim* (means "those who submit to God's will"); *Koran* (Holy Book of Islam); *Five Pillars of Islam* (religious duties); *Hegira* (Mohammed's flight from enemies in Mecca to Medina; means "the breaking of former ties"); *jihad* (holy war); *caliph* (Muslim leader). *(Comprehension)*

Closing the Lesson: Understanding Chronology

Have students make a timeline showing events that led to the rise and decline of the Muslim empire. (*570*—Birth of Mohammed. *610*—Mohammed believes he had a vision and was chosen to serve as the prophet of a new faith. *622*—the Hegira. *630*—Mecca surrenders to Muslims. *632*—death of Mohammed. *632–661*—first four caliphs rule. *661*—Umayyad family claims rule, split between Sunnis and Shiites occurs. *732*—Muslims turned back in what is now France. *750*—Abbasids establish power. *756*—Umayyad ruler controls most of what is now Spain and Portugal. *1071*—Seljuk Turks extend Islam into the Byzantine Empire. *Eleventh and twelfth centuries*—the Crusaders combat supporters of Islam. *1258*—Mongols storm Baghdad, Muslim empire collapses.) *(Comprehension)*

See *Section Review* questions, p. 203.

SECTION 2   (pp. 203–207)
Islamic Culture

Objectives

After completing this section, students will be able to:
1. Explain how the Koran influenced Islamic society.
2. Describe the achievements that distinguished Islamic culture.

Introducing the Lesson

Remind students that Islam had a profound influence on the social customs, art and architecture, and philosophy of the Muslim world. As Muslims expanded their empire, the cultures of Asia, Africa, and Europe came to reflect the world of Islam.

Then ask: *(a) How might religion influence social customs?* (Social customs express values and standards that are often founded on religious principles.)

(b) How might religion influence art and architecture? (Artists and architects often use religious themes. In earlier times, places of worship were important architectural structures, and art objects were designed for worship or to represent gods or holy men and women.)

(c) Do you think that religion influences customs, values, and art as much today as in earlier times? Explain your answer. (Answers will vary.)

Developing the Lesson: Understanding Point of View

Have students write a narrative that might have been written by a woman who lived in Mecca during the height of the Muslim civilization. Narratives should describe the rights enjoyed by Muslim women and the restrictions placed on them. *(Comprehension)*

Developing the Lesson: Organizing Information

Have students make a chart listing Asian, African, and European influences on the Muslim world. (Muslim scholars translated the works of Greek philosophers and borrowed the idea of zero and "Arabic" numbers from India. Muslim astronomers tested and corrected observations made by Ptolemy. Physicians used Greek medical knowledge. Architects modified the rounded Roman arch to a "horseshoe" arch and used the Byzantine dome.) *(Comprehension)*

Closing the Lesson: Discussing History

Ask: *(a) How did Islamic culture influence other peoples?* (People who followed religions other than Judaism, Christianity, and Islam were forced to convert to Islam; Christian and Jewish scholars attended Muslim universities; Muslims introduced Arabian horses, new foods, and the Arabic language to Western Europe.)

(b) What do you think was the greatest contribution Muslims made to other cultures? (Answers will vary.) *(Synthesis)*

See *Section Review* questions, p. 207.

Chapter 10 Review Answers
(pp. 208–209)

Vocabulary Review

1. (a) oasis (b) Bedouin (c) Five Pillars of Islam (d) Hegira (e) jihad (f) Koran

2. (a) Shiite—sect within Islam that broke away from Umayyad rule, claiming that only a direct descendant of the Prophet should rule; Sunni—majority group within Islam that continued to support the Umayyad caliphate. (b) Sultan—political leader of a Muslim state; caliph—both a religious and a political leader of a Muslim state. A caliph was regarded as the Defender of the Faith, whose authority was God-given. (c) Mosque—Muslim house of worship; minaret—tower on a mosque from which the prayer leader calls Muslims to prayer. (d) Islam—religion founded by Mohammed; Muslim—a follower of Islam.

People to Identify

1. Chief judge of Cordova and Muslim scholar who influenced later Christian philosophers.
2. Muslim thinker and doctor whose *Canon of Medicine* was widely used by physicians in both Muslim and Christian lands.
3. Caliph who corresponded with other rulers to learn about their cultures.
4. Founder of Islam.
5. Muslim mathematician, astronomer, and author of the *Rubaiyat*.
6. Persian doctor who headed the hospital of Baghdad in the ninth century and whose works on medicine were consulted by doctors in Europe.

Places to Know

1. B   2. A   3. D   4. C   5. E

Recalling the Facts

1. Islam's belief in one God upset those who believed in many tribal gods. Mohammed also made enemies by speaking out against greedy merchants and moneylenders.
2. Mohammed began a jihad against nonbelievers.
3. Palestine, Syria, Egypt, and most of Persia.
4. They made widespread conquests. Areas they conquered included part of the Byzantine Empire, North Africa, and much of Spain.
5. The Seljuks, the Crusaders, and the Mongols. The Seljuks moved into Muslim lands and took political power. Crusaders from Western Europe seized Muslim territories along the eastern shore of the Mediterranean, retook large parts of Spain, and seized the island of Sicily. Mongols sacked Baghdad in 1258 and killed the last Abbasid caliph.
6. Jews and Christians were allowed to practice their religions and customs and have their own communities; people who followed other religions were forced to convert to Islam. Slaves were treated more kindly and permitted to own property. Arab women gained some legal rights, such as a share in family inheritance and the right to own property, but over time their lives became more restricted. Women lived in separate quarters called harems and wore heavy veils when they went out of their homes.
7. Some caliphs set up libraries and classrooms in their palaces. Universities were established in many parts of the Muslim world. Scholars translated ancient Greek works into Arabic.
8. It gave them access to the works of earlier thinkers in many lands. Mathematicians did original work in algebra, geometry, and trigonometry. Scientists discovered some basic chemical formulas and made new compounds. Astronomers tested and corrected observations of the stars and planets. Doctors made medical advances.
9. Muslim mosques and other buildings had horseshoe arches, domed roofs, and mosaics decorating the walls, roofs, and courtyards.

Critical Thinking Skills

1. Arithmetic using symbols to represent numbers; annual publication containing useful information; symbol denoting zero; lowest point; highest point.
2. Answers will vary.
3. The Umayyads ruled 89 years. The division among Muslims happened first. 222 years.
4. Answers will vary.

Thinking About Geography

1. The harsh desert environment forced the Bedouin to develop a nomadic lifestyle, traveling from one oasis to another to find pasture and water for their animals. They valued loyalty to the tribe, bravery in combat, kindness towards guests, and personal honor. The Bedouin's strong sense of loyalty strengthened Islam; bravery in combat supported jihad against nonbelievers.

2. *Africa:* Gambia, Chad, Egypt, Malawi, Niger, Senegal, Sudan, Algeria, Libya, Mauritania, Morocco, Somalia, Tunisia, Mali. *Middle East:* Bahrain, Kuwait, Oman, Qatar, Saudi Arabia, United Arab Emirates, Yemen, People's Democratic Republic of Yemen, Turkey, Syria, Iraq, Iran, Jordan. *Others:* Albania, Bangladesh, Afghanistan, Indonesia, Pakistan.

Enrichment: Primary Sources

1. To help cure the sultan's illness.
2. He allowed Avicenna to read the books in his library.
3. Books on medicine, language, poetry, and works of the ancient Greeks.
4. Students should suggest that learning is a life-long process.

The World of Islam

570–1258

See chapter timeline, p. 207.

Before You Read This Chapter

Do you know what people mean when they speak of the Holy Land? They are referring to Palestine—the birthplace of Judaism and Christianity. Southeast of Palestine lies another "holy land"—Arabia, the birthplace of Islam. Almost from its start, Islam became a powerful force in the Middle East. In little more than a century, the followers of the new religion won control of lands as far west as North Africa and Spain and as far east as India. As you read, think about how the teachings of Islam helped its believers build such a vast empire. Look, too, for reasons why Islamic culture survived even after the empire broke apart.

The Geographic Setting

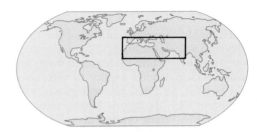

The Chapter Outline

1. The Spread of Islam
2. Islamic Culture

The Blue Mosque is one of several Islamic religious centers in the city of Istanbul (formerly Constantinople).

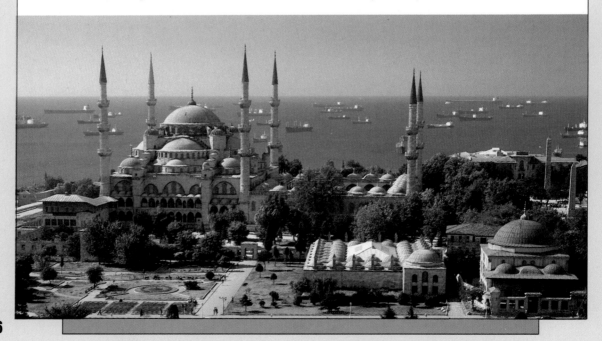

Vocabulary Note that the word *Bedouin* comes from the Arabic *badawi,* or "desert dweller."

1 The Spread of Islam

Objectives

Focus Questions

- ★ ■ How did the religion of Islam arise? *(pages 197–199)*
- ● ■ How did Islam spread to other parts of Asia, Africa, and Europe? *(pages 199–201)*
- ▲ ■ What caused the breakup of the Muslim empire? *(pages 202–203)*

Terms to Know

oasis	Hegira
Bedouin	jihad
Islam	caliph
Muslim	Sunni
Koran	Shiite
Five Pillars of Islam	sultan

★ Note strategies for first objective on this page and p. 199.

In the early 600's, an inspiring leader by the name of Mohammed began to preach a new faith. His ideas united many different peoples, giving them a common sense of purpose. This new religion got its start in Arabia, but soon spread throughout the Middle East and beyond.

The Geography of Arabia

Arabia is the world's largest peninsula—about 22 times the size of Florida. It makes up most of the Middle East and extends into the Arabian Sea, which is part of the Indian Ocean. On the peninsula's west coast, the Red Sea separates it from Africa. On its east coast, the waters of the Persian Gulf separate it from Iran (ancient Persia).

The land of Arabia is extremely dry. In the south lies an enormous desert that the Arabs call the "Empty Quarter." Most of the rest of the land is hilly, hot, and only slightly less dry than the desert. Farming is possible only where there is an oasis (oh-AY-sis)—a small fertile area fed by a water source like a spring or well. (The plural form of *oasis* is *oases.*)

The People of Arabia

In early times, most of the Arabian people were nomads called Bedouin (BED-oo-in). They lived in tribes, moving their tents from one oasis to another to find pasture and water for their herds of camels, goats, and sheep. The Bedouin traded with the villages that grew up around the oases and along the coast. They provided camels and served as guides for the caravan trade that traveled across the peninsula.

Sec. Rev. ques. 2

Tribal society. Living in a harsh desert environment meant that people had to work together to survive. The Bedouin valued loyalty to the tribe, bravery in combat, kindness toward guests, and personal honor. Because there was no written law, individuals depended on the tribe for protection. Bedouin tribes fought over scarce resources. They regularly raided the camps of other tribes, merchant caravans, and villages located in the oases.

Religious beliefs. The trading town of Mecca, on Arabia's west coast, had long been thought of as a holy city. Many Arabs traveled to Mecca to worship at a holy well and at a shrine called the Kaaba (KAH-ah-bah). The shrine contained more than 300 statues of gods, as well as a black stone (probably a meteorite) believed to be sacred.

Most Arabs who lived in the desert worshiped tribal gods that they believed lived in stones, sand, and the sun and stars. In the **197**

★ **RETEACHING. Have students review "Mohammed's Teachings" (pp. 198–199) and summarize Muslim belief about the Koran and God.** (In Muslim belief, the Koran contains the word of God and should not be questioned or challenged. Muslims view God as the creator and ruler of heaven and earth; he is all-powerful, merciful, and just.) *(Comprehension)* **Observing for Detail**
Check for Understanding. Ask: What values were important to Bedouin society? (Loyalty, bravery, kindness, and personal honor.)

Religion According to legend, the Kaaba was originally white and was given to Adam when he sinned and lost Paradise. The stone blackened as it absorbed the sins of pilgrims who touched and kissed it.
★ **REINFORCEMENT. Have students make a chart comparing Islam with Judaism (pp. 44–45).** (Islam: belief in one God; strict moral code; Five Pillars of Islam. Judaism: belief in one God; individual responsibility for individual actions; Ten Commandments.) *(Comprehension)* **Comparing Ideas**

towns and trading centers, however, many Arabs had learned of the beliefs of Judaism and Christianity.

The Beginnings of Islam

The man who was to change forever the lives of the Arabs, Mohammed, was born in Mecca about the year 570. As a young man, he took part in the caravan trade, becoming known for his honesty and good business sense. Mohammed married Khadija (kah-DEE-jah), a widow who ran her own business, and became a successful trader.

According to legend, Mohammed often meditated in a cave in the hills outside Mecca. When he was about 40, he believed he saw the angel Gabriel, who ordered him, "Recite in the name of thy Lord!" Mohammed was convinced he had been chosen to serve as a prophet and bring the Arabs a new faith.

Mohammed rejected the many gods of the tribal religions. The new faith he offered the Arabs was monotheistic, like Judaism and Christianity. It is called **Islam**, which in Arabic means "surrender to Allah." (*Allah* is the Arabic word for God.) The followers of Islam are called **Muslims**, "those who submit to God's will."

A halo of flame surrounds Mohammed's head in this miniature painting. The Prophet wears a veil because Islam disapproves of portraits showing the face of a holy person.

Mohammed's Teachings

The **Koran** (koh-RAHN) is the holy book of Islam. Muslims believe it contains the word of God as revealed to Mohammed. They believe the Koran should not be questioned or changed. Even translations from Arabic are discouraged.

A monotheistic religion. Like Jews and Christians, Muslims view God as the creator and ruler of heaven and earth. He is, in their eyes, all-powerful, merciful, and just. Because Muslims believe they can communicate directly with God through prayer, they have no priests.

Muslims believe that Islam completes the teachings of Judaism and Christianity. They regard Jesus and the Hebrew prophets as messengers of God, but they believe that Mohammed was the last and greatest of the prophets. They do not, however, worship Mohammed as a god.

Moral code. Mohammed taught that to gain salvation, people must follow a strict moral code. The Koran forbids Muslims to gamble, drink alcohol, or eat certain foods. Greed and dishonesty in business are condemned. Marrying nonbelievers is also frowned upon.

Every Muslim has five religious duties, called the **Five Pillars of Islam**. (1) Muslims must accept and repeat the statement of faith: "There is no God but Allah, and Mohammed is his Prophet." (2) At least five times a day, believers must face the holy city of Mecca and pray. (3) Muslims have a duty to be generous

198

to the poor. (4) During the holy month of Ramadan (ram-uh-DAHN), the ninth month in the Muslim calendar, believers may not eat or drink between sunrise and sunset. (5) Muslims who are physically and financially able to do so must make at least one pilgrimage to the holy city of Mecca.

According to the Koran, on the Day of Judgment, nonbelievers and the wicked will be dragged into a fearful place of "scorching winds and seething water. . . . Sinners shall eat bitter fruit and drink boiling water." Faithful Muslims who have led good lives are promised a garden of pleasure called Paradise. There they will dress in silks, eat delicious foods, and experience happiness in beautiful surroundings.

The Establishment of a Muslim Community

Mohammed's teachings stirred up great hostility in Mecca. Islam's belief in one God upset those who believed in the tribal gods. Mohammed also spoke out against greedy merchants and against moneylenders who charged high interest. To escape his enemies, Mohammed and a small band of followers left Mecca in 622 for Medina (muh-DEE-nuh), a town about 280 miles away. Their flight is known as the **Hegira** (hih-JY-ruh)—"the breaking of former ties." The year 622 became Year One of the Muslim calendar.

Mohammed in Medina. Many men and women in Medina welcomed Mohammed warmly. He met with people of all classes and races, for all believers in Islam are considered equal. He gained political power and respect as a judge, making decisions on family relations, property inheritance, and punishment for crimes. Mohammed rejected tribal law as a way of settling disputes. The law of Islam was to be the final authority.

★ See below.

Not all the people of Medina accepted Mohammed's leadership. The city's Jews in particular did not view Mohammed as a prophet. Although Mohammed had adopted some Jewish customs, he began to persecute Arabian Jews, seizing their farmlands.

Vocabulary Note that the word caliph is a title that means "successor of the Prophet."

Unification of Arabia. Mohammed then preached a holy war, or **jihad** (jih-HAHD), against nonbelievers. With help from Bedouin tribes that had accepted Islam, his followers raided trading caravans from Mecca and conquered unfriendly tribes.

In 630 Mecca surrendered to a Muslim army without a fight. Bedouin tribes all over Arabia converted to Islam and accepted the authority of the Prophet, as Mohammed came to be called. By the time he died, in 632, Mohammed had united the Arabian tribes into a powerful force dedicated to Islam.

After Mohammed's death his friend Abu Bakr became the leader. He held the office of **caliph** (KAY-lif)—political and religious head of a Muslim state. The caliph's authority was said to be God-given. He governed according to the laws set forth in the Koran and took the role of Defender of the Faith.

The Growth of Islam

● Note strategies for second objective on this page and p. 200.

Islam gave the many Arab tribes the unity, discipline, and dedication needed to conquer other peoples. The Persian and Byzantine empires, weakened by warfare and internal problems, were no match for the armies of Islam. Under the first four caliphs, who ruled from 632 to 661, Muslim armies swept over Palestine, Syria, Egypt, and most of Persia. Arab warriors went into battle with swords and an unshakable faith. Theirs was a holy mission to spread Islam to nonbelievers. According to the Koran, those who died in a jihad could be sure of a place in Paradise.

Sec. Rev. ques. 3

Linking Past and Present

Each year about two million Muslims make the trip to Mecca to fulfill their religious duty. Many still make the pilgrimage on foot or by ship, but thousands now come by jet plane on special flights from all over the world.

199

★ ENRICHMENT. Have students compare present-day Islamic ideas and practices with those of seventh-century Islam. Students might compare the importance of the Koran, the practice of the Five Pillars of Islam, and the relationship between Islam and government. *(Synthesis)* **Synthesizing Information**

Religion Muslims may fulfill their duty of jihad in one of the following ways: spiritual purification by avoiding evil; supporting what is "right" and correcting "evil"; or fighting unbelievers.

● RETEACHING. Have students compare the map on p. 200 with the Atlas map "Nations of the World" and identify the present-day states in the territory controlled by the Muslims in 750. (Saudi Arabia, Yemen, Yemen P.D.R., Oman, Jordan, Iraq, Syria, Lebanon, Israel, Cyprus, Kuwait, Qatar, United Arab Emirates, Iran, Afghanistan, Pakistan, Portugal, Tunisia, and parts of Spain, Turkey, Libya, Egypt, Algeria, and Morocco.) *(Comprehension)* **Relating Geography and History**

The split within Islam. When the fourth caliph, Ali, was murdered in 661, a member of the powerful Umayyad (oo-MY-yad) family claimed the right to rule. This move divided Muslims into two rival camps. Some people, who became known as **Sunni** (SOON-ee), supported the Umayyads. A smaller number of Muslims, called **Shiites** (SHEE-eytz), would accept only a direct descendant of the Prophet as caliph. They repeatedly tried to challenge the Umayyads and, in time, developed other beliefs and traditions that set them apart from the Sunni.

● See below, right.

The Umayyads. With the support of the Muslim majority, the Umayyads ruled from 661 to 750. They were hugely successful conquerors who built an empire even larger than the Roman Empire at its height (map, page 107). Islamic territory in the east reached into India and to the borders of China. Muslim armies advanced into Asia Minor, too. Though they failed to capture Constantinople, they did gain some land at the eastern edge of the Byzantine Empire. To the west, Muslims took North Africa from the Byzantines and most of Spain from the Visi-

Expansion of Islam, 632–750

This map shows the lands ruled by the Muslims at the time of Mohammed's death in 632 and the territory that was added to Muslim rule by 750. Find the lands added to Muslim territory by the first four caliphs. On what continents were those lands located?

200

Map Answer: Asia, Africa, Europe.

● **REINFORCEMENT. Have students identify the factors that led to the expansion of Islam. Students might make a chart or a poster, or outline the religious, political, and economic causes of the spread of Islam.** (Religious: Islam provided unity, discipline, and dedication. Arab warriors believed they had a holy mission to spread Islam. Political: Persian and Byzantine empires were weak from war and internal problems. Economic: Muslim conquests increased travel and trade.) *(Comprehension) Identifying Causes*

Cultural History Shiite Muslims stress the spiritual function of the Prophet's successor, the *imam*, who is believed to be divinely protected against sin and error, to possess an infallible understanding of the Koran, and to have a supernatural knowledge of future events.
● **ENRICHMENT. Have students research differences between present-day Sunni and Shiite Muslims.** *(Synthesis) Linking Past and Present*

goths. The Muslims then continued their march north. In 732, however, their advance was halted at the Battle of Tours (TOOR) in what is now France (page 215).

Early in their rule, the Umayyads moved the Muslim capital from Medina to Damascus, Syria. Arabs, however, still held the most important positions in the government, the army, and society. This caused resentment among Persians, Syrians, Egyptians, and other non-Arabs who had become Muslims. In 750, several discontented groups, both Arabs and non-Arabs, rebelled against the Umayyad rulers. They succeeded in putting a new ruling family, the Abbasids (uh-BAS-idz), in power.

Sec. Rev. ques. 4

The Abbasids. The new dynasty lasted for some 500 years, until 1258. Though they too were Arabs, the Abbasids had a wider outlook than the Umayyads. They chose their officials from many peoples, not just Arabs. Moving the capital to Baghdad (BAG-dad)—now the capital of Iraq—they established a brilliant court where Islamic culture reached its greatest glory. Under Abbasid rule, Persian, Arab, and other influences combined to create a distinctive Muslim culture.

Spain Under Muslim Rule

When the Umayyad rulers were overthrown, one member of the family fled to Muslim Spain. By 756 he ruled most of what is now Spain and Portugal. The Muslims brought prosperity to Spain at a time when the rest of Europe faced hardship. Farming, industry, and trade flourished in Spain. By the tenth century the Spanish capital of Cordova (KOR-duh-vah) had blossomed into a center of the arts and learning. Cordova rivaled even the court at Baghdad.

The Christian kingdoms in Spain never accepted Muslim rule. Again and again, over hundreds of years, they tried to regain power (page 246). In spite of this conflict, Muslim and Christian cultures in Spain existed side by side for centuries and greatly influenced one another.

An old man makes his way across the courtyard of the Umayyad Mosque in Damascus. The mosque, begun in 705, is one of Islam's oldest and holiest shrines.

Expansion of Trade

Muslim conquests gave a sharp boost to trade and travel. Because many different peoples from Spain to lands east of Persia learned Arabic, communication became easier. Merchants and travelers crossed Central Asia by caravan. Adventurous Arabs reached Ceylon (sih-LAHN) and Malaya (muh-LAY-uh) by sea and even started a colony in China.

By the thirteenth century, Muslim merchants were trading heavily with the peoples of Malaya, Indonesia, and the southern Philippines. As a result, Islam spread through Southeast Asia.

The Muslims dominated trade with eastern Asia until the 1400's. Arab traders brought spices from Asia and sold them to Italian merchants. Through Baghdad, at the heart of the Muslim world, passed Chinese porcelain, African gold, and Egyptian grain. **201**

Check for Understanding. Ask: What Umayyad policy created resentment among non-Arab Muslims? (Restricting important government positions to Arabs.)

Economics Note that Muslim traders used checks and receipts, and formed trade associations and joint-stock companies (p. 368).

Mongol Empire, 1294

The Mongols built one of the world's largest empires. About how many miles separated Kiev, in the western part of the empire, and Guangzhou (Canton), on the Pacific coast? What three large bodies of water bordered the Mongol Empire to the west? What lands did the Mongols attack but fail to conquer?

Map Answers: (1) About 4,500 miles. (2) Black Sea, Persian Gulf, Arabian Sea. (3) Poland, Hungary, the area controlled by the Seljuk Turks, India, Southeast Asia, and Japan.

The Fall of the Muslim Empire

▲ Note strategies for third objective on this page and p. 203.

Disunity in the Islamic world. From India to Spain, Muslims shared a common language (Arabic) and a common faith. Yet Muslim lands were not politically united. Almost from the start of Abbasid rule, different parts of the empire (such as Spain and North Africa) had broken away to form separate states. By the middle of the 800's, the caliph in Baghdad had lost nearly all his power.

The invasion of the Seljuks further weakened Abbasid rule. Though the Abbasid caliphs still acted as religious leaders, Seljuk

Sec. Rev.
ques. 5

202

rulers called **sultans** held political power. In 1071 the Seljuks extended the boundaries of Islam by advancing into the Byzantine Empire. Yet rivalry among sultans kept the Islamic world divided.

The Crusades. The steady spread of Islam alarmed Christians in Western Europe. In the eleventh and twelfth centuries, they launched attacks against the Muslims. The largest of these attacks, as you read in Chapter 9, were the Crusades. Crusaders seized Muslim lands along the eastern shore of the Mediterranean (map, page 248). During this same period, large parts of Spain were retaken by the Christian kingdoms, and the

▲ RETEACHING. Have students review "The Fall of the Muslim Empire" (pp. 202–203) and identify the effects of invasions by the Seljuk Turks, the Crusaders, and the Mongols on the Muslim Empire. (Seljuk Turks: conquered Muslim lands in Persia, Syria, and Palestine; extended boundaries of Islam. Crusaders: seized Muslim lands along the eastern Mediterranean and Sicily. Mongols: completed the collapse of the Muslim Empire.) (Comprehension) Identifying Effects

▲ REINFORCEMENT. Have students write an essay explaining why Islam survived the breakup of the empire. (Synthesis) Making Judgments

Muslims who held the island of Sicily lost it to Christian soldiers.

The Mongols. In the thirteenth century Muslim lands, like Russia, became a target for the dreaded Mongols. Mongol warriors poured across Asia into Persia. Storming Baghdad in 1258, they burned, robbed, and killed, as they had in Kiev (page 192) and other lands. The Mongols tore apart the palaces, libraries, and schools that had made Baghdad the glory of the Islamic world. Among the 50,000 people slaughtered in the city was the last Abbasid caliph. His murder completed the collapse of the Muslim empire.

Islam, however, survived the breakup of the empire. Embedded in the lives of the peoples of the Near East, North Africa, and Southeast Asia, Islamic culture continued to shape the development of these areas.

▲ See below.

See lesson plans, pp. T195A–T195C.

See Sec. 1 *Closing the Lesson,* p. T195B.

Section Review

Answers to Section Review questions are in brackets on pages indicated.

1. **Define or identify:** oasis, Bedouin, Islam, Muslim, Koran, Five Pillars of Islam, Hegira, jihad, caliph, Sunni, Shiite, sultan. (pp. 197, 198, 199, 200, 202)
2. How did Arabia's geography affect life among the Bedouin? (p. 197)
3. Why did Islam spread so rapidly? (p. 199)
4. How did Abbasid rule differ from Umayyad rule? (p. 201)
5. What factors led to the downfall of the Muslim empire? (pp. 202–203)
6. **Critical thinking:** Why did Islamic culture survive after the destruction of the Muslim empire? (See answer below.)

6. Students might suggest that Islam inspired a fierce dedication among its followers and united them with cultural bonds independent of the government in power.

2 Islamic Culture

Objectives

Focus Questions

★ ■ How did the Koran influence Islamic society? *(pages 203–204)*
● ■ What achievements distinguished Islamic culture? *(pages 204–207)*

Terms to Know

mosque   minaret

★ Note strategies for first objective on this page and p. 204.

In founding Islam, Mohammed had planted the seeds of a new society as well as a new religion. Islamic beliefs influenced government, the arts, social customs, and business dealings. The Islamic faith and the Arabic language helped unite people from many different backgrounds.

Islamic Society

Religious tolerance. In the lands they conquered, Muslims allowed other believers in one God to practice their religions and customs and have their own communities. Jews and Christians, called "People of the Book," only had to obey Muslim laws and pay a special tax. People who followed other religions, however, were forced to convert to Islam.

Treatment of slaves. Under Muslim rule the lives of slaves improved, for the Koran said slaves should be treated kindly and allowed to own property. Most slaves in the Muslim world were household servants and helpers in workshops. Some were well educated and became government officials, entertainers, or soldiers.

The status of women. Although they did not have equality with men, Arab women gained some rights under Islamic law. For example, the Koran outlawed the Bedouin custom of killing unwanted baby girls. It also

Sec. Rev. ques. 2

203

▲ **ENRICHMENT.** Have students research the relationship between Islam and the Black Muslim religion in America, or how Islam influences governments in the Middle East or in other areas. *(Synthesis)* *Linking Past and Present*

★ **RETEACHING.** Have students review "The status of women" (pp. 203–204) and make a chart on the rights and restrictions of women in Islamic society. *(Comprehension)* *Translating Information into Another Form*

Religion Mohammed taught that all Muslims were equal; members of many races mingled with one another in mosques and marketplaces.
Religion Muslims believed that Jews and Christians worshiped the God of Islam but in different ways. For this reason, Jews and Christians were permitted to practice their religion.
★ **REINFORCEMENT.** Have students describe how Islam affected the lives of conquered people, slaves, and women. *(Comprehension)* *Observing for Detail*

gave women a share in family inheritances and the right to own property. A divorced wife could keep part of her dowry (the property her family gave her when she married). She was entitled to support from her former husband and could marry again. Some Muslim women, especially in the caliph's court and the upper classes, were well educated.

However, the Koran also said that "men have authority over women because God has made the one superior to the other." A Muslim man could have as many as four wives if he could provide equally for all of them, but a woman could have only one husband. It was nearly impossible for an unhappy wife to get a divorce. A man, on the other hand, could divorce his wife simply by saying three times, "Thou art dismissed."

The lives of Muslim women gradually became more restricted, particularly in towns and among the upper classes. It became customary for a woman to wear a heavy veil whenever she went out in public. At home— whether in a palace or a tent—women lived in an area called the harem. No men except family members could enter this area.

★ See below.

This panel of Persian tiles shows a servant waiting on a Muslim noblewoman. Women wore veils in public but went unveiled inside their homes.

204

Cultural Achievements

● Note strategies for second objective on this page and p. 207.

Scholarship. Learning was highly prized in the Muslim world. Mohammed encouraged education, saying that "the seeking of knowledge is a duty of every Muslim, man or woman." In order to learn about other cultures, a caliph named Harun al-Rashid (hah-ROON al-rah-SHEED) corresponded with other rulers, including Charlemagne and the emperor of China. Some caliphs set up libraries and study rooms in their palaces where scholars could hold classes. Great universities developed in many parts of the Muslim world, from Cordova in Spain to Timbuktu in the African kingdom of Mali. The university at Cordova attracted brilliant scholars, Christian and Jewish as well as Muslim. Ancient works in Greek were translated into Arabic, which became the language of learning and literature throughout the empire.

Philosophy. At a time when learning was neglected in Europe, Muslim scholars translated and studied the works of Greek philosophers. These scholars played an important role in the later revival of learning in Western Europe (Chapter 13).

The most famous Muslim thinker was Avicenna (ah-vih-SEN-ah), whose name in Arabic was ibn-Sina. Born in Afghanistan in 980, Avicenna was a poet, doctor, scientist, and philosopher. He wrote about every field of knowledge, relying heavily on Aristotle (page 88).

Another important Muslim scholar was Averroës (ah-VEHR-oh-eez). Born in Spain in 1126, Averroës became chief judge in Cordova. His commentaries on Aristotle's writings had a great impact on later Christian philosophers.

Mathematics and science. With the spread of Islam, Muslim mathematicians and scientists gained access to the works of earlier thinkers in many lands. From India they borrowed the idea of zero and "Arabic" numerals, passing these ideas on to the West. A ninth-century Arab mathematician wrote the first work on algebra. Others worked out new ideas in geometry and trigonometry. Arab sci-

Sec. Rev. ques. 3

Biography

Harun al-Rashid

According to the *Thousand and One Nights* (page 206), the caliph Harun al-Rashid liked to roam the streets of Baghdad in disguise, seeking adventure. Harun was the fifth caliph of the Abbasid dynasty, and he ruled the Islamic empire from 786 to 809. In literature and in legend, his reign came to stand for Islam's golden age.

When Harun came to the throne, the city of Baghdad was only 24 years old, having been founded by his grandfather in 762. Yet it was already one of the largest cities in the world, rivaling Constantinople.

At the center of the city stood the caliph's palace, where Harun and his court lived amid fabulous wealth. (See picture, at right, of Harun on his throne.) Hundreds of officials, clerks, guards, cooks, singers, dancers, and visitors thronged around the caliph. Slaves carried his meals to him on dishes of gold and silver. Thousands of exquisite Persian rugs covered the palace floors, and thousands of silken tapestries embroidered with gold hung on the walls.

Although poets praised Harun extravagantly, he was neither a great con-queror nor a great lawgiver. He was, however, a great patron of the arts. One poet who pleased him received 5,000 gold pieces, 10 slaves, and a fine warhorse. Harun was equally generous to scholars in law, religion, medicine, science, and mathematics. Thus his court drew musicians, dancers, poets, and scholars from all over the Islamic empire.

entists discovered some basic chemical formulas and made new compounds.

Muslim astronomers tested and corrected the observations made by ancient astronomers, particularly the Greek scientist Ptolemy (page 91). Observatories were built in the great Muslim centers at Cordova, Toledo, Baghdad, and Cairo. There astronomers studied the movements of stars and planets. The Persian poet Omar Khayyam (ky-YAHM), who is best known for the poems called the *Rubaiyat*, was also a mathematician and astronomer.

Technology and farming. When Islamic civilization was at its height, people in the cities and royal courts of the Muslim world lived more comfortably than people in Christian areas of Europe. Cordova had paved streets that were lighted at night. In many cities, pipes carried water to the baths and courtyard fountains of private homes. Muslim agriculture and irrigation were far more efficient than the farming methods used in Western Europe. The Muslims had already learned how to keep the soil fertile by planting different crops in different years. They **205**

ⒻFEATURE ACTIVITY. Ask: (a) Why do you think Harun al-Rashid was considered a great leader by his contemporaries? (Harun al-Rashid was a great patron of the arts.) (b) Why might a leader who contributes to cultural achievements be viewed as a great leader? (A culture's artistic legacy often lasts for centuries while other achievements may be judged differently or forgotten.) *(Synthesis) Drawing Conclusions*

Cultural History Note that by the eleventh century, Cordova had approximately 80,000 shops and 3,000 mosques.

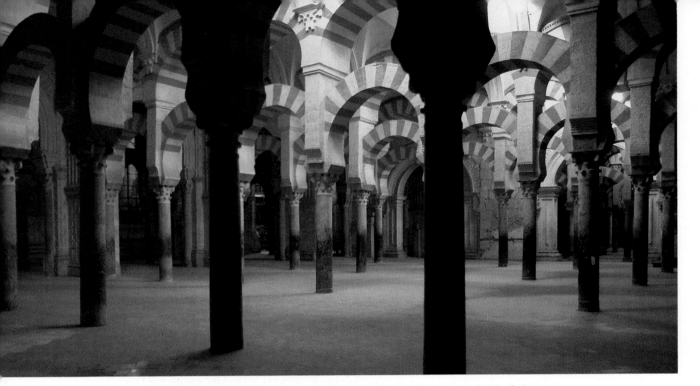

The horseshoe arches that both support and decorate the prayer hall of the Cordova Mosque are typical of Muslim architecture in Spain. The mosque was converted into a cathedral after Christians reconquered Spain in the 1400's.

introduced Arabian horses to Europe, as well as many new foods, including oranges, lemons, and melons.

Medicine. Using the medical knowledge of the ancient Greeks, physicians in Muslim lands became the best-trained and most skillful doctors of their time. Surgeons performed amputations and removed cancerous growths. Muslim advances in chemistry led to new medicines and anesthetics that were used in performing operations.

The Persian al-Razi, or Rhazes (RAY-zeez), headed the hospital in Baghdad in the ninth century. In his writings he discussed measles, kidney stones, smallpox, poisons, skin diseases, and ways of staying in good health. He carefully noted the symptoms of various illnesses. The works of Rhazes, along with Avicenna's *Canon of Medicine*, were widely consulted by doctors in Europe.

Sec. Rev. ques. 4

Literature. Because translations of the Koran were not allowed, educated people throughout the Muslim world learned Arabic. The Koran set the style for other Islamic literature, which included histories, geographies, philosophical and scientific works, and,

206

above all, poetry. Folk tales, fantasies, and legends were also popular.

The caliphs, many of whom were skilled poets, encouraged writers. After the court moved to Baghdad, much literature came to be written in the Persian language, using Arabic script. The world-famous *Thousand and One Nights* (sometimes called *The Arabian Nights*) is set in Baghdad, but it is a collection of stories from India, Persia, Arabia, and other lands. Among the well-known tales are those about Aladdin and his wonderful lamp and Sinbad the Sailor.

Architecture and art. Religion had a strong influence on Muslim architecture. In any Muslim city or village, the mosque (MAHSK)—the Muslim place of worship— stood out from all other buildings. The mosque was a constant reminder of the Islamic faith. Its slender minaret, or tower, was the town's tallest structure. From it, a prayer leader called the faithful to prayer five times a day.

In building mosques, tombs, palaces, and private homes, Muslim architects adapted features from other styles. They

Science Note that Muslim doctors developed a method of vaccination against smallpox.
Check for Understanding. Ask: **Why did the Arabic language spread throughout the Muslim world?** (Translations of the Koran were not allowed.)

changed the solid rounded arch of the Romans to a delicate "horseshoe" arch held up by narrow columns. Domed roofs in the Byzantine style gave an airy, open feeling to building interiors. Mosaics of light and dark stones or glazed tiles formed graceful patterns. There were no statues or paintings of religious figures in mosques, because Muslim tradition discouraged the representation of living things. Passages from the Koran were written in decorative Arabic script on both the inside and outside walls.

● See below.

Muslim artisans developed great skill. Weavers made beautiful Persian carpets to decorate the floors and walls of palaces and tents. Metalworkers in Syria and Spain produced such fine swords that "Damascus blades" and "Toledo steel" were admired the world over. Artisans in Cordova became famous for gold, silver, and leatherwork.

Persian artists excelled in delicate miniature paintings. Scenes showing historical figures, lovers, hunters, or warriors often were used as book illustrations or painted on pottery. Some details in these miniatures were so small that they had to be painted with a single hair instead of a brush.

See Sec. 2 *Closing the Lesson,* p. T195B.

Section Review

Answers to Section Review questions are in brackets on pages indicated.

1. **Define:** mosque, minaret. (p. 206)
2. How did the status of women change under Islamic law? (pp. 203–204)
3. What were some specific Muslim accomplishments in mathematics and the sciences? (pp. 204–205)
4. Why did educated Muslims in other countries learn Arabic? (p. 206)
5. **Critical thinking:** How did Islam's tolerance of other religions contribute to the richness of Islamic culture?

(See answer below.)

Chapter 10   Summary and Timeline

1. The religion of Islam was founded by Mohammed in Arabia in the seventh century. An empire based on Islam spread the new faith through the Middle East, Africa, and Asia. Less than a century after its creation, the Muslim empire had grown to cover lands from Spain to India. In time, the empire was weakened by invasions of Turks and Christians. The Mongols' takeover of the city of Baghdad in 1258 completed the fall of the Muslim empire.

2. Muslim society was based on the Koran. Muslim culture reflected the influences of other peoples, especially the Greeks. Muslim achievements in science, medicine, and philosophy were remarkably advanced.

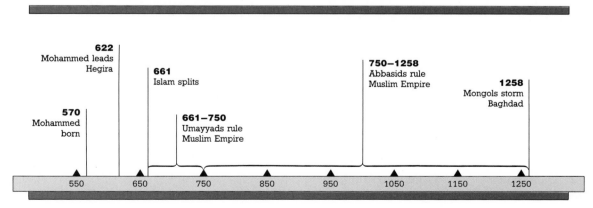

570 Mohammed born

622 Mohammed leads Hegira

661 Islam splits

661–750 Umayyads rule Muslim Empire

750–1258 Abbasids rule Muslim Empire

1258 Mongols storm Baghdad

550   650   750   850   950   1050   1150   1250

207

● **REINFORCEMENT.** Have students evaluate Islamic culture and explain which aspect might be considered the most significant. *(Evaluation) Making Judgments*

● **ENRICHMENT.** Have students compare Islamic and Byzantine (pp. 184–186) achievements in their development of Greek ideas, education, art, and architecture. *(Application) Comparing Historical Developments*

5. Answers will vary. Other religious traditions influenced Islamic culture, and the scientific, literary, artistic, and architectural achievements of Jews and Christians were studied by Muslim scholars.

See p. T195C for answers to Chapter Review.

Vocabulary Review

1. Match each of the following terms with its correct definition: *Bedouin, Five Pillars of Islam, Hegira, jihad, Koran, oasis.*
   a. small fertile area surrounding a water source like a spring or well
   b. nomadic Arab
   c. most important religious duties of a Muslim
   d. Mohammed's flight from Mecca
   e. Arab term meaning "holy war"
   f. holy book of Islam
2. Define or identify the terms in the following pairs.
   a. Shiite; Sunni
   b. sultan; caliph
   c. mosque; minaret
   d. Islam; Muslim

People to Identify

Identify the following people and tell why each was important.
   1. Averroës
   2. Avicenna
   3. Harun al-Rashid
   4. Mohammed
   5. Omar Khayyam
   6. Rhazes

Places to Know

Match the letters on this map of the Middle East with the places listed below. You may want to refer to the map on page 200.
   1. Baghdad   4. Medina
   2. Damascus   5. Persian Gulf
   3. Mecca

Recalling the Facts

1. Why did many of the people of Mecca react at first with hostility to Mohammed's teachings?
2. How did the religion of Islam spread throughout Arabia?
3. Which countries were conquered by the armies of Islam in the period between 632 and 661?
4. What conquests did the Umayyads make in building their empire?
5. What groups helped bring about the downfall of the Muslim empire? How did they do so?
6. How were non-Muslims treated by their Muslim rulers? How did the position of slaves and women change in areas that came under Muslim rule?
7. What evidence shows that the leaders of the Muslim world considered learning important?
8. How did Muslim mathematicians benefit from the spread of Islam? What original contributions did Muslims make to mathematics and the sciences?
9. What features characterized Islamic architecture?

1. Building vocabulary. Many English words have Arabic origins and have come to us through Spanish, French, or Latin. Use a dictionary to find the meaning of each of the following words: *algebra, almanac, cipher, nadir, zenith.* (App.)

2. Preparing a report. Research and write a report about one of the following topics: the Islamic calendar; Toledo steel; the Sufis; the position of women in present-day Islamic countries; the Alhambra in Spain; Persian miniatures. (App.)

3. Comparing timelines. Refer to the timelines for this chapter and Chapter 9 (page 193) to answer the following questions: How many years did the Umayyads rule? Which happened first, the split within the Christian Church or the division of the Muslims into Shiites and Sunni? How many years passed between the Mongols' attack on Baghdad and the end of their rule in Russia? (Comp.)

4. Making a bulletin board. Make a bulletin board display featuring Islamic architecture. Label each illustration with the location and purpose of the building shown, the approximate date of its construction, and a description of its special features. (App.)

Thinking About Geography

✔ **1. Analyzing.** How did the climate and physical environment of the Arabian Peninsula influence the life of the Bedouin? What values did the Bedouin hold as a result of living in a harsh, desert environment? How might these same values have helped the Muslim empire expand after the Bedouin converted to Islam? (Syn.)

2. Making a map. Make a map showing the countries of the modern Muslim world. Include all countries in which a majority of the population are followers of Islam. (Use an almanac to find this information.) Compare your map with the map of the Muslim empire on page 200. (App.)

✔ A checkmark identifies questions and exercises calling for the three higher-order levels of thinking at the top of the Bloom taxonomy: Analysis, Synthesis, and Evaluation.

Enrichment: Primary Sources

As you have read, Avicenna was a famous Muslim doctor, scientist, poet, and philosopher. In the following passage, adapted from his autobiography, Avicenna describes his early education.

66 It happened that the sultan fell sick of an illness which baffled all the physicians. My name was famous among them and they begged the sultan to summon me. I attended the sick-room and worked with them in treating the royal patient. So I came to be enrolled in his service. One day I asked his permission to enter the library, to examine the contents and read the books on medicine. I entered a mansion with many chambers. In one were books on language and poetry, in another law, and so on. I glanced through the catalogue of the works of the ancient Greeks. I saw books whose very names are as yet unknown to many—works which I had never seen before and have not seen since. I read these books, taking notes on their content.

By the time I reached my eighteenth year I had finished learning all these sciences. My memory for learning was at that period of my life better than it is now, but my knowledge is exactly the same, nothing further having been added to my mind since then. 99

1. Why did the sultan hire Avicenna?
2. What did the sultan let Avicenna do?
3. On what works did Avicenna base his early education?
4. **Critical thinking:** Why might someone doubt Avicenna's claim that he'd learned no more since the age of 18? (Anal.)

The Early Middle Ages   500–1200
(pp. 210–227)

Chapter Preview

Section 1 describes developments in Europe after the fall of Rome. Roman and Germanic political practices are contrasted, and the Christian Church is identified as the focal point of the newly emerging medieval civilization. Events that led to the formation of the kingdom of the Franks are also identified. In Section 2, students learn about the development of feudalism, life on a feudal manor, and the economic system of the early Middle Ages.

Bibliography

See the *Teacher's Management and Planning Guide* for additional listings. Starred titles are for both students and teachers.

Cantor, Norman F. *Medieval History: The Life and Death of a Civilization.* Macmillan. Medieval Europe as a culture in its own right.

Holmes, George, ed. *The Oxford Illustrated History of Medieval Europe.* Oxford University Press. Six scholars present a survey of medieval civilization.

*Power, Eileen. *Medieval People.* Harper & Row. Accounts of the lives of six people of the Middle Ages.

Scherman, Katherine. *The Birth of France: Warriors, Bishops, and Long-Haired Kings.* Random House. A colorful account of France's first dynasty—the Merovingians.

Section Lesson Plans

SECTION 1   (pp. 211–217)
The Birth of Medieval Europe

Objectives

After completing this section, students will be able to:
1. Explain why the fall of Rome created disorder in Europe.
2. Describe how the Christian Church brought unity to Europe in the early Middle Ages.
3. Discuss how Charlemagne created an empire that blended several traditions.

Introducing the Lesson

After the fall of the Roman Empire, European government, law, and economy disintegrated. With no central government to provide order and security, the Christian Church emerged as a source of unity during the Middle Ages.

Then ask: *(a) What characteristics of the Christian Church might account for its unifying role during the early Middle Ages?* (The Church offered its many members a single faith and social organization.)

(b) How might the Church have been affected by its new role? (Answers will vary. The Christian Church acquired political power.)

(c) Why do you think people accepted the Church's assumption of responsibilities once fulfilled by the Roman government? (Answers will vary. Society seems to need a source of organization and structure. The Church was the only institution after the fall of Rome capable of providing order and unity.)

Developing the Lesson: Summarizing Information

Have students summarize the effects of the fall of the Roman Empire and explain why the Christian Church acted as a source of unity and power. (*Effects:* Strong government vanished, economic life was in turmoil, law and order broke down, towns and cities were abandoned, the level of learning declined. *Christian Church:* Christian peoples shared a bond of faith and accepted the Church as a way to salvation; monks and nuns taught skills and set up hospitals and centers of learning.) (*Comprehension*)

Developing the Lesson: Synthesizing Information

Ask: *(a) Why did the Church acquire so much power during medieval times?* (Systems of government and law and order had disintegrated and Christian peoples viewed the Church as the guardian and interpreter of religious truth.)

(b) How did the Church combine religious and political power? (Because of its strong organization and its acceptance by Christians as the only way to salvation, the Church gradually assumed duties and power usually given only to governments.) (*Comprehension*)

Closing the Lesson: Making Decisions

Have students work in groups to dramatize a policy-making session that might have occurred between Charlemagne and Pope Leo III. Students should consider the problems facing Europe and suggest ways in which Charlemagne and the Christian Church might have worked together to improve order, the economy, and education. (Answers will vary. Students might consider Charlemagne's support of the Church, his military strength, his commitment to education and the preservation of Greco-Roman culture, as well as the organization of the Church and its acceptance by the people.) (*Synthesis*)

See *Section Review* questions, p. 217.

SECTION 2   (pp. 217–225)
Life in Feudal Europe

Objectives

After completing this section, students will be able to:
1. Explain how invasions destroyed central authority in Europe.
2. Describe what life was like in medieval times.

Introducing the Lesson

Remind students that government in medieval Europe was characterized by local authorities whose power was derived from the ownership of land. Unlike the extensive and centralized administration of the Roman Empire, the feudal system placed power in the hands of local lords who owned large estates.

Then ask: *(a) What might account for the increased power of local lords?* (When the central government weakened, local rulers acquired wealth and power once controlled by the state.)

(b) Why might land ownership have been a factor in the increased power of lords? (With the disruption of trade and the decline of cities caused by invasions, more people moved to rural areas. As agriculture became increasingly important, land was a significant source of power.)

(c) How might the increased power of local authorities have affected society? (Answers will vary.)

Developing the Lesson: Interpreting History

Have students work in groups to develop two charters that might have been written in feudal times. One charter should describe a land grant from a lord to a vassal and list the lord's responsibilities. The second charter should explain the duties of the vassal. Students might dramatize the signing and exchange of these charters in a class presentation. (*Comprehension*)

Developing the Lesson: Outlining Information

Have students outline the information on the manorial system and serfdom. Outlines should include the following information: *Elements of the manorial system* (Lord's estate; set of rights and obligations between the lord and serfs). *How the manor worked* (The manor was a self-sufficient community that produced a variety of goods and services). *Duties of serfs* (Farmed lord's land and performed other services). *Rights of serfs* (Protected by custom; could live in their cottages and farm their land). *Serfs' living conditions* (Small crowded cottages; simple diets; backbreaking labor). *(Comprehension)*

Closing the Lesson: Organizing Information

Have students draw a diagram illustrating the relationship between the feudal and manorial systems. Diagrams should identify the relationships between lords, vassals, knights, and serfs and explain the differences in the levels of authority and power. (The manor system was the basis of medieval economy; feudalism was the system of alliances between lords and vassals and formed the political system. Lords were the most powerful group, followed by vassals, who could also be lords. The least powerful group in the system was the serfs.) *(Comprehension)*

See *Section Review* questions, p. 225.

Chapter 11 Review Answers
(pp. 226–227)

Vocabulary Review

1. (a) manor (b) sacrament (c) manorial system (d) papacy (e) knight (f) fief (g) chivalry
2. (a) vassal—noble who pledged his services to another noble in exchange for a grant of land and serfs; serf—peasant who was legally bound to the estate of a lord. (b) clergy—Church officials; order—community of monks or nuns. (c) medieval—describes the civilization of the Middle Ages; Middle Ages—period from A.D. 500 to 1500.

People to Identify

1. Charlemagne 2. Venerable Bede 3. Clovis 4. Saint Benedict 5. Gregory I 6. Pepin the Short 7. Saint Patrick 8. Eleanor of Aquitaine

Places to Know

1. Rome 2. Monte Cassino 3. Papal States 4. Aachen

Recalling the Facts

1. Political life—Germanic peoples had loyalty to their tribe and its chieftain, rather than to a country. The kingdom was viewed as the personal property of its ruler. Urban life—Germanic peoples were basically rural, so old cities were not revived nor were new ones built. Legal systems—Germanic peoples had no written laws that applied to all the tribes and they used trial by ordeal instead of trial in court to determine guilt.
2. The Pope led the Church and had the powers and duties of a political leader. Priests administered sacraments, gave advice, taught people the rules of right and wrong, and tried to help the sick and needy. Monks and nuns taught skills to the peasants who worked their lands, established hospitals and shelters for travelers, and set up centers of learning in their monasteries and convents.
3. He spread Christianity, encouraged learning, and reunited Western Europe for the first time since the Roman Empire.
4. They stopped trade, hurt agriculture, and destroyed villages and monasteries. They also undermined the power of central rulers, leading people to turn instead to local lords who had their own armies.
5. The lord promised protection and land to his vassal; the vassal helped his lord in battle, gave his lord certain payments, and served in the lord's law court.
6. They were to be brave, loyal, gentlemanly, and obedient to the Church.
7. Obligations—serfs farmed the lord's land, did other work on the manor, and paid him for the use of his oven, mill, and winepress. Rights—serfs' children could not be taken from them and sold; serfs could live in their cottages and farm their strips of land as long as they carried out their duties to their lords.

Critical Thinking Skills

1. Answers will vary.
2. The chart shows a king, greater lords, lesser lords, and knights. It does not show serfs or clergy. The king was chief ruler. The same knight could be a vassal to more than one lord, and the same lord could be a vassal to more than one greater lord.
3. Serfs might not have imagined that any better life was possible. Also, fear of the unknown may have kept them from rebelling and leaving the manor. The Church encouraged serfs to accept their lot by teaching that God determined everyone's place in society.
4. Answers will vary.

Thinking About Geography

1. The best site for a castle or fortress was thought to be a rocky hill or the bend of a river, with no buildings nearby. This terrain gave defenders a better view of the surrounding territory and made it easier to defend the castle. Lords also had trees and bushes cut down and a moat dug around the castle walls.
2. France, Belgium, Luxembourg, the Netherlands, Switzerland, and parts of Austria, West Germany, Spain, Italy, East Germany, and Yugoslavia.

Enrichment: Primary Sources

1. The serf's best ox and all of his pigs, goats, horses, bees, flax and woolen cloth, gold, and silver.
2. The lord had to divide the rest of the animals with the serf's family. The lord took one animal, the wife one, and the children one. If there were no children, the animals were divided equally between the lord and the serf's wife.
3. Most students will suggest that the lord set the price, because he had all the authority on the manor.

The Early Middle Ages

500–1200

See chapter timeline, p. 225.

Before You Read This Chapter

What does loyalty mean to you, and to whom do you owe loyalty? Your family and friends? Your school? A religious group? Your town and your country? The citizens of ancient Rome were expected to be loyal to the emperor. When the Roman Empire collapsed, however, new loyalties arose.

As you read this chapter, you will discover how different groups in the Middle Ages were bound together by different sets of loyalties.

The Geographic Setting

The Chapter Outline

1. The Birth of Medieval Europe
2. Life in Feudal Europe

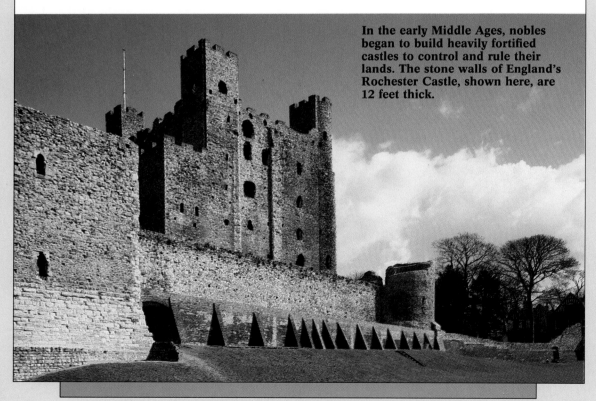

In the early Middle Ages, nobles began to build heavily fortified castles to control and rule their lands. The stone walls of England's Rochester Castle, shown here, are 12 feet thick.

1 The Birth of Medieval Europe

Objectives

Focus Questions

★ ■ Why did the fall of Rome create disorder in Europe? *(pages 211–212)*

● ■ How did the Christian Church bring unity to Europe in the early Middle Ages? *(pages 212–215)*

▲ ■ How did Charlemagne create an empire that blended several traditions? *(pages 215–216)*

Terms to Know

Middle Ages	illuminated
trial by ordeal	manuscript
medieval	sacrament
clergy	papacy
order	

★ Note strategies for first objective on this page and p. 212.

After the fall of Rome, the Byzantine and Islamic empires developed in the eastern regions of the old Roman Empire. In Western and Central Europe, the decline of Roman authority led to the rise of a new way of life. This was the dawn of the **Middle Ages**—the period from about A.D. 500 to 1500.

A Time of Change

The gradual decline of the Roman Empire in the West left Western and Central Europe in confusion. Strong government had vanished and economic life was in turmoil. The system of law and order developed by the Romans broke down. Bands of armed men roamed the countryside, killing and robbing. Although Germanic kingdoms formed, it was mainly the Christian Church that gave Europeans a feeling of unity.

The spread of Germanic customs. By the fifth century, Germanic peoples had established kingdoms in North Africa, Italy, Spain, Gaul, and England—lands formerly belonging to Rome. Germanic political life was very different from that of the Roman Empire. The Germanic peoples were divided into tribes, and their loyalties were to their own tribe and its chieftain. There was no idea of loyalty to a country that included many different peoples. A Germanic kingdom was viewed as the personal property of its ruler. By custom, Germanic kings divided up their lands and willed them to their sons—a practice that resulted in frequent civil wars.

Sec. Rev. ques. 2

There were other differences between the Germanic peoples and the Romans. At its height the Roman Empire had been a world of cities with a rich culture. By the end of the Empire, many towns were abandoned as people fled to country estates. Since the Germanic invaders were rural people, they did not try to revive the cities or build new ones.

After Rome fell, Germanic tribes settled in the western Mediterranean area. This mosaic of a Vandal landowner is from North Africa.

211

★ RETEACHING. Have students review "A Time of Change" (pp. 211–212) and identify three sources of disunity in Europe after the decline of the Roman Empire. (Strong government had vanished; economic life was in turmoil; law and order had broken down.) (Comprehension) Identifying Causes

Cultural History Note that a tribe is a group of people who share common values, customs, language, and territory. Members of tribes believe they share a real or mythical ancestor.

★ REINFORCEMENT. Have students outline the differences between the Germanic peoples and the Romans. (Germanic peoples: a rural people who lived in tribes; had unwritten laws; their system of justice used trial by ordeal. Romans: citizens of a large empire that included many peoples and cities. Roman law was a written code and the system of justice used evidence and proof.) (Comprehension) Organizing Information in Written Form longer the major language spoken in the former Roman provinces. Knowledge of Greek was almost lost, and few people could read Greek works of literature, science, or philosophy. Though the Germanic tribes had a rich oral tradition of songs and legends, there was no written literature.

★ See below, left.

Compared with the time of the Pax Romana (pages 106–108), the sixth to eighth centuries seemed to be a "dark age." Yet learning did not completely vanish in Europe. Christian scholars worked to preserve Greco-Roman knowledge.

The Ostrogoth king Theodoric (page 122) ruled Italy from 493 to 526. He admired Roman culture and encouraged scholarship at his court. Boethius (boh-EE-thee-us), a Roman in Theodoric's service, translated some of Aristotle's writings from Greek into Latin. Boethius also wrote about Greek music and mathematics. Cassiodorus (kas-ee-uh-DAWR-us), another Roman at Theodoric's court, collected, copied, and translated ancient manuscripts. He did much of this work after retiring to a monastery, setting an example that other monks would follow. Without Cassiodorus's labors, some of the great literary treasures of classical Greece might have been lost.

Churchmen in other parts of Europe also helped to preserve learning. In 731 an English monk known as the Venerable Bede completed a history of the Church in England. Written in Latin, Bede's work is considered one of the finest pieces of scholarship of the Middle Ages.

The Church in the Middle Ages

● Note strategies for second objective on this page and p. 214.

During the early part of the Middle Ages, people in Europe were struggling to recover from the destruction and turmoil caused by the breakup of the Roman Empire. Yet it was also a time of growth. Germanic, Christian, and Roman traditions were being woven together into what is called **medieval** civilization. (*Medieval* comes from the Latin words meaning "middle ages.")

Christianity in Europe About 1000

This map shows the parts of Europe where people had become Christian by the year 1000. What two forms of Christianity were found in Europe at this time? What was the main religion of southern Spain?

Map Answers: (1) Latin Church (Roman Catholic) and Eastern Orthodox. (2) Islam.

Another difference between Germanic peoples and Romans was the nature of their legal systems. Roman law was written law. It applied to each citizen of the Empire, regardless of place of birth. At the time of the invasions, the different Germanic tribes had their own unwritten laws. Though some Germanic rulers later had tribal laws written down, no one law applied to all the tribes.

The Germanic system of justice was also less advanced than the Roman court system. In Roman courts, judges studied evidence and demanded proof. Germanic judges used **trial by ordeal** to determine guilt. In a typical ordeal, a person accused of a crime was tied up and thrown into a river. A person who sank was considered innocent. Floating was seen as proof of guilt.

The decline of learning. After the fall of Rome, the level of learning dropped sharply in Europe. The old Roman schools disappeared. Few people except Church officials learned to read or write. Latin was no

212

★ ENRICHMENT. Have students work in groups to list possible consequences of the decline of learning in Europe. Students might summarize the reasons for this decline and then list how European society might have changed as a result of the lowered level of learning. (Comprehension) Drawing Inferences
Biography In 510 Boethius was given a high political office by Theodoric, the Ostrogoth king. Theodoric grew to suspect Boethius of treason, however, and had him executed around 525.

● RETEACHING. Have students review "Church Organization" (pp. 213–215) and make a chart showing Church organization. (Comprehension) Organizing Information
● REINFORCEMENT. Ask: How did the Church influence medieval civilization? (It gave form and unity to the new civilization and expressed a bond shared by all Christian peoples; monks and nuns taught skills, set up hospitals and shelters, and preserved ancient manuscripts.) (Comprehension) Observing for Detail

Vocabulary Note that the term *Christendom* was given to the Christian world and came to signify lands in which Christians lived.

A guiding force in this new civilization was Christianity. Many Germanic peoples converted to Christianity during the late Roman Empire. Christian missionaries carried on the work of conversion after the fall of Rome.

Sec. Rev. ques. 3

The Christian Church gave form and unity to the new civilization arising in Europe. Centered in Rome, the Church was the leading power in medieval society. It was a bond shared by all Christian peoples.

Nearly everyone in medieval Europe saw the Church as the guardian and interpreter of religious truth. Medieval people believed that the way to heaven was through the Church. Only by following Christian teachings, they believed, could they hope to gain salvation.

Church Organization

The Christian Church had begun as small communities of people who met to worship together. By the late years of the Roman Empire, the Church had built a strong organization made up of different levels of officials, called **clergy** (KLUR-jee).

Sec. Rev. ques. 4

Monks and nuns. Some men and women chose to serve the Church by joining religious **orders**—communities of monks or nuns. Living apart from society in monasteries or convents, they devoted their lives to prayer and good works. The earliest order was established by Saint Benedict, an Italian monk. The Benedictine monastery at Monte Cassino in Italy, built in 529, became the most famous monastery of medieval times.

Monks and nuns made valuable contributions to medieval society. They taught skills such as carpentry and weaving to the peasants who worked on Church lands. Convents and monasteries also set up hospitals and gave shelter to travelers. They were centers of learning as well. Monks kept classical learning alive by reading and writing Latin, studying ancient manuscripts, and copying them by hand. Some monks added beautiful pictures and designs to the manuscripts in

PRIMARY SOURCE

The Rules of Saint Benedict

Saint Benedict set forth guidelines to a Christian life for his order, the Benedictines. These guidelines became a model for many other religious orders. According to the rules, monks' lives were to consist mainly of hard work and prayer; they could own nothing and could not marry. The following statements are adapted from his rules.

    ❝ In the first place to love the Lord God with all one's heart, all one's soul, and all one's strength.

Then to love one's neighbor as oneself.

Then not to kill.

Not to steal. . . .

To honor all men.

Not to do to another what one would not have done to oneself.

Not to seek soft living.

To relieve the poor.

To love one's enemies.

Not to be proud. . . .

Not to yield to anger. . . .

Not to swear. . . .

To utter truth from heart and mouth.

To do no wrong to anyone and to bear patiently wrongs done to oneself. ❞

1. What guideline did Saint Benedict put above all others?
2. What kinds of behavior did he advise against? What qualities did he recommend?
3. **Critical thinking:** The sixth statement is known as the "golden rule." Restate this rule in your own words, or give an example to explain its meaning.

Ⓕ See answers below.

213

Vocabulary Note that the word *church* comes from the Greek *kuriaké*, meaning "belonging to the Lord."

Vocabulary The word *nun* is from the Latin *nonna*, meaning "monk," and originally was a title given to elderly persons. The word *monk* is from a Greek word meaning "alone."

Biography Saint Benedict said he wanted "to erect a school for beginners in the service of the Lord."

Cultural History In the Middle Ages, monasteries were economically self-sufficient and included farmland, a well, and buildings. Monastic meals were simple, consisting of bread, wine, vegetables, fish, and sometimes chicken. Bathing, considered a luxury, was discouraged.

Ⓕ Primary Source Answers 1. To love God. 2. He advised against killing, stealing, doing wrong to others, living easily, being proud, yielding to anger, and swearing. He recommended loving God, loving and honoring all others, helping the poor, and being honest. 3. Answers will vary.

An illustration from a medieval Bible shows monks preparing an illuminated manuscript. Monks were among the few in medieval society who were able to read and write.

gold and silver. These hand-produced books, called **illuminated manuscripts**, are works of art.

The monasteries of England and Ireland played an especially important role in preserving learning. Saint Patrick had converted the Irish to Christianity in the early fifth century. In Ireland, the Latin language, which seemed in danger of being lost, became the language of the Church and of scholars. Greek survived in Ireland long after it had almost completely disappeared elsewhere in Western Europe.

In addition to teaching and helping the community, monks and nuns also served as missionaries. During the early Middle Ages, they converted many Germans to Christianity. The people of medieval Europe looked upon monks and nuns as unselfish, devoted servants of God.

● See below.

Priests. For most people, the local priest was their connection with the Church and with God. The priest administered the **sacraments**. These were special religious ceremonies such as baptism, communion, and marriage. The priest gave advice, taught peo-

214

ple the rules of right and wrong, and tried to help the sick and needy. Since few people could read, the priest was their source of Church teachings. The local churches were centers of village life.

Bishops. Archbishops and bishops were important clergy. The most influential bishops were those in large cities or the oldest and largest Christian communities, such as Rome, Constantinople, and Jerusalem. Bishops supervised the priests in their districts and settled disputes over Church teachings and religious practices. Archbishops, in turn, supervised the bishops.

The Pope. The leader of the Church in Rome, later called the Pope, came to be considered the overall head of the Church. Popes believed they inherited from Peter, one of Jesus's original followers and the first Pope, the responsibility for the souls of all Christians. Popes felt they had a duty to lead Christians on the path marked out by God.

An important early Pope was Gregory I, also called Gregory the Great. He held the **papacy**—the office of Pope—from 590 to 604. Under Gregory, the Church did more

The Pierpont Morgan Library, New York M.240 f.8 detail.

Biography Note that Clovis was fifteen years old when he became king and united the Franks in 481.

Cultural History Gaul was called "France" after the Franks; Clovis is considered by the French to be their first king.

than watch over Christians' spiritual lives. It also had powers and duties usually held only by governments. For centuries to come, the Church played a part in European politics.

Frankish Kingdoms

▲ Note strategies for third objective on this page and p. 216.

With the decline of Roman rule, a new style of government appeared in the kingdom of the Franks. A Germanic people, the Franks had migrated westward from the valley of the Rhine River. As Rome's border defenses weakened in the fourth and fifth centuries, Frankish tribes settled in Roman territory.

Clovis. About 481 a Frankish ruler named Clovis (KLOH-vis) united the Franks and conquered the Romans and Germanic peoples in northern Gaul. A few years later he captured part of the Visigoths' kingdom in southern Gaul.

After Clovis died in 511, his sons divided up the Frankish lands. The rulers of these lands gradually lost much of their power to nobles who held large estates. In each Frankish kingdom real power fell into the hands of the king's chief officer, who held the title "Mayor of the Palace."

Reuniting Frankish lands. One Mayor of the Palace, Pepin II, triumphed over the mayors of rival kingdoms and reunited the Frankish lands. From 687 to 714 Pepin ruled all the Franks. Then Pepin's son, Charles Martel (which means "Charles the Hammer"), inherited the title and the lands. From 717 to 741 he ruled over most of Gaul as Mayor of the Palace. In 732 Charles's forces defeated a Muslim army at the Battle of Tours. This victory halted the Muslim advance into Western Europe (page 201).

Pepin the Short. In 751 Pepin the Short, son of Charles Martel, was given the title "King of the Franks" instead of "Mayor of the Palace." The Pope in Rome and the Frankish nobles approved the change. Setting a tradition for later rulers, the Pope crowned Pepin as king "by the grace of God." Thus began the rule of the Carolingian (kar-uh-LIN-jin) dynasty, which lasted into the 900's.

The Pope supported Pepin in hopes that the Franks would protect the Church from the Lombards, another Germanic people. The Lombards had conquered much of northern Italy in the sixth century, and they now threatened the Church's lands around Rome. Pepin invaded Italy, defeated the Lombards, and gave the Pope the territory between Rome and Ravenna. This region became known as the Papal States.

The Empire of Charlemagne

In 768 Pepin's son Charlemagne (SHAHR-luh-mayn), also known as Charles the Great, became king of the Franks. Called by some

Charlemagne's Empire, 814

Charlemagne ruled western and central Europe from his capital city, Aachen. What lands did he add to the Frankish kingdom? How does the map show the division of the empire after Charlemagne's death? (See answers below.) **215**

Map Answers: (1) Land between Gaul and Spain, Saxon lands to the northeast, Bavaria, Lombard land in northern Italy, Papal States, Corsica. (2) With dashed lines.

▲ RETEACHING. Have students make a time chart of events leading to the creation of Charlemagne's empire. Time charts should include the date and a brief summary of each event. (Charts should include information for the following dates: 481; 687–714; 717–741; 751; 768.) (Comprehension) Sequencing Information
Critical Thinking. Ask: What was the significance of changing Pepin the Short's title to "King of the Franks"? (It indicated an extension of Pepin's rule to include all Franks.)

▲ REINFORCEMENT. Have students explain why Charlemagne is called by some the "father of Europe." Students might consider his cultural and political achievements. (He spread Christianity, encouraged preservation of classical culture, and reunited Europe.) (Comprehension) Synthesizing Information the "father of Europe," Charlemagne was an extraordinary figure in medieval history. At six feet four inches he towered over the people of his time, and he had energy and determination to match.

Charlemagne was a devoted Christian and a strong supporter of the Church. Through military conquests he spread the faith; he also played an active role in Church affairs. He had a beautiful church built at Aachen (AH-kun), his capital, and attended services there regularly.

Charlemagne was an admirer of the cultures of ancient Greece and Rome. Though he never learned to write, he greatly encouraged learning in Europe. Charlemagne brought some of Europe's finest scholars to his palace school at Aachen. Under the direction of the English monk Alcuin (AL-kwin), they collected books and read the works of the ancient Romans. The palace scholars also wrote new poems, histories, and religious works, copying the style of Roman literature. In this way they helped to keep interest in classical writings alive.

Charlemagne devoted much of his reign to expanding his empire. He defeated the Lombard kingdom in Italy and took part of northern Spain from the Muslims. He also seized parts of what is now Germany. After terrible wars there, he forced the people to submit to his rule and convert to Christianity. These conquests reunited Western Europe for the first time since the height of the Roman Empire.

On Christmas Day in the year 800, Pope Leo III crowned Charlemagne "Emperor of the Romans." Charlemagne was not trying to revive the Roman Empire, however. Instead, Charlemagne's empire represented a new kind of civilization, one that blended Germanic customs, Christianity, and Greco-Roman culture. This combination came to characterize Europe in the Middle Ages.

Sec. Rev. ques. 5

▲ See below.

See Sec. 1 *Closing the Lesson*, p. T209B.

This illuminated manuscript shows Pope Leo III crowning Charlemagne emperor. The event marked the coming together of Germanic power, the Christian Church, and the heritage of imperial Rome.

216

Background Aachen, called Aix-la-Chapelle by the French, lies 44 miles southwest of Cologne in present-day West Germany. Twenty-eight Holy Roman Emperors were crowned there.

Biography Einhard (Charlemagne's secretary and biographer) claimed that the king went to St. Peter's to attend Christmas service and "would not have entered the Church" had he known about Pope Leo's decision to crown him emperor at this time. According to Einhard, Charlemagne had his own plans about when and where to assume imperial command.

▲ ENRICHMENT. Have students compare the achievements of the Byzantine emperor Justinian (p. 182), with those of Charlemagne, and evaluate who was the more successful leader. Students should cite evidence to support their opinions. *(Evaluation) Making Judgments*

Answers to Section Review questions are in brackets on pages indicated.

1. **Define or identify:** Middle Ages, trial by ordeal, medieval, clergy, order, illuminated manuscript, sacrament, papacy. (pp. 211, 212, 213, 214)
2. How did Germanic government, laws, and traditions differ from those of the Roman world? (pp. 211–212)
3. How did the Christian Church eventually come to unite the peoples of Europe? (p. 213)
4. How was the Christian Church organized in the early Middle Ages? (pp. 213–215)
5. In what way was Charlemagne's empire the sign of something new in Europe? (p. 216)
6. **Critical thinking:** It was the Pope who crowned Charlemagne emperor of the Romans. What does this suggest about the role of the Church in medieval European society? (See answer below.)

6. Students might suggest that the Church was the highest authority in medieval society.

See lesson plans, pp. T209A–T209C.

2 Life in Feudal Europe

Objectives

Focus Questions

★ ■ How did invasions destroy central authority in Europe? *(pages 217–218)*
● ■ What was life like in medieval times? *(pages 218–225)*

Terms to Know

fief	manor
vassal	manorial system
knight	self-sufficient
chivalry	fallow
serf	

★ Note strategies for first objective on this page and p. 218.

Through the sheer strength of his personality, Charlemagne held together his great empire for nearly 50 years. After Charlemagne's death in 814, local landowners and nobles once more came into power. Charlemagne's empire split into a patchwork of small kingdoms. Invasions weakened central authority even further.

The Decline of Central Authority

Division of Charlemagne's empire. Charlemagne's son Louis inherited the throne from his father and tried to preserve the empire. He succeeded, but only temporarily. After Louis died in 840, three of his sons agreed to divide the empire. In the Treaty of Verdun in 843, each claimed part of the kingdom (map, page 215). Disputes among the sons soon broke up the empire even more.

Viking raiders. As Charlemagne's empire was collapsing, invaders attacked Europe from several directions. The most frightening invaders were the Vikings, or Northmen—the ancestors of the Norwegians, Swedes, and Danes of today. The Vikings were adventurous seafarers and ferocious warriors. Sailing in open boats powered by sails and oars, some Vikings traveled to Iceland and Greenland. They made settlements there between the years 850 and 1000. The Vikings also explored the northeast coast of North America, which they called Vinland. Their explorations came 500 years before Christopher Columbus reached the Americas (Chapter 18).

Sec. Rev. ques. 2

217

★ RETEACHING. Have students review "The Decline of Central Authority" (pp. 217–218) and explain what might have been meant by this statement about the Vikings: *"God deliver us from the fury of the Northmen."* (Northmen were invaders from the region that forms present-day Norway, Sweden, and Denmark. They were ferocious warriors who looted and burned, and enslaved or killed the local people.) *(Comprehension) Drawing Conclusions*

★ REINFORCEMENT. Have students analyze why central authority declined and what replaced it. (The empire was divided. Invasions interrupted economic life and people turned to local lords for protection.) *(Analysis) Analyzing Information*

Background Note that the divisions of Charlemagne's empire roughly coincided with later national boundaries: Charles II received most of present-day France, Louis the German took present-day Germany, and Lothair I inherited what is present-day Italy.

Cultural History The Vikings were masterful military strategists and excellent boatbuilders and navigators.

Vocabulary The word *feudalism* is from the Latin *feudum* (fief), a grant of land by a superior to a lesser lord in return for homage and service.

Meanwhile . . .

IN RUSSIA

While bands of Vikings were terrorizing Western Europe, their cousins in Russia were settling down to become traders and nation builders. Earlier Viking invasions of Russia had led to the establishment of the first Russian state in the mid-800's (page 189).

Sec. Rev. ques. 2, cont.

During the ninth century, Viking bands raided the coastal areas of Western Europe and pushed inland along the rivers. Wherever they landed, the Vikings looted settlements, killed people, and burned homes.

In time, most Vikings became Christians and turned from raiding to trade. Some settled on the coasts in Britain, France, and southern Europe. In the 800's and 900's, however, they were so feared that people prayed: "God deliver us from the fury of the Northmen."

Other invaders.   The Vikings were not the only invaders of Europe in the early Middle Ages. The Magyars (MAG-yahrz) were originally nomads from Central Asia. Superb horseback riders, they swept across the broad Danube River plain in the late 800's and invaded northern Italy and southern Germany. Along the Mediterranean, there were still other raids. From bases in Spain and North Africa, Muslim pirates attacked coastal regions and captured islands.

These invasions, which went on until early in the 900's, had terrible consequences for Western Europe. Like the earlier Germanic invasions, they stopped trade, hurt agriculture, and left villages and monasteries in ruins. People no longer looked to a central ruler for security. Living in an age of warfare and disaster, they turned instead to the local lords, who had their own armies. Western Europe had entered an age in which lords, not kings, held the political power.

★ See below.

218

A New Social Order

● Note strategies for second objective on this page and p. 221.

Rule by lords.   The lack of strong rulers led to a new system of government and landholding—feudalism. The feudal system of medieval Europe, like that of China under the Zhou dynasty (page 61), placed power in the hands of strong local lords with large estates. These lords, trying to increase their power and influence, sought allies among their fellow nobles.

The basis for these alliances was land. In exchange for military assistance and other services, one lord granted land, called a **fief** (FEEF), to another, less rich, noble. The noble who received the land was called a **vassal**. This relationship was made official in a solemn ceremony in which the vassal pledged loyalty to the lord.

Mutual obligations.   Besides promising loyalty, the vassal agreed to perform certain duties for the lord. It was a two-sided bargain, however, for the lord promised protection and land to his vassals.

The most important duty of a vassal was to help his lord in battle. When the lord went to war or when an enemy attacked the lord's land, the faithful vassal rushed to help. Usually the vassal had to give military service for 40 days each year.

Sec. Rev. ques. 3

The vassal also had to make certain payments to his lord. If a lord were captured by an enemy, it was the vassal's duty to help pay the ransom. When a lord gave his eldest daughter in marriage, he demanded and expected a contribution from his vassals.

Finally, court service was required of each vassal. In feudal days each lord had his own law court. There the vassals would meet to settle disputes among themselves or with the lord. Usually a lord would not punish one of his vassals unless he had the approval of the court.

Relationships between the lords and vassals were complex. The same noble might be a vassal to a number of different lords. If two of these lords clashed, the vassal would have to decide which of the lords to support.

★ ENRICHMENT. Have students compare events that led to the decline of the Roman Empire (pp. 119–124), the Byzantine Empire (pp. 186–188), and Charlemagne's empire and then develop a hypothesis about why empires fall. (Synthesis) *Forming a Hypothesis*
Check for Understanding. Ask: What effect did the invasions have on Western Europe? (They stopped trade, hurt agriculture, and left villages and monasteries in ruins.)

● RETEACHING. Have students review "A New Social Order" (pp. 218–219) and write a paragraph describing the characteristics of feudalism. (Feudalism was a new system of government based on landholding. Political power was in the hands of local lords who owned large estates. Alliances were based on loyalty, military service, and land grants.) (Comprehension) *Observing for Detail*

This Viking helmet was intended to terrify enemies as well as protect the wearer.

Moreover, a vassal might grant land to other nobles and in this way become a lord himself. For example, William of Normandy, holder of a fief from the king of France, conquered England in 1066. The English nobles became his vassals. Yet William himself was still a vassal of the French king.

Peoples of Europe, 800–1000

The period after 800 was marked by invasions and migrations throughout Europe. What groups invaded Europe from the east? Which of the groups shown here swept over the largest area?

219

Map Answers: (1) Slavs and Magyars. (2) Vikings.

Ⓕ See below, right.

Daily Life

Castle Life

The castles of medieval Europe were not palaces. Palaces were designed for luxurious living. Castles, on the other hand, were designed mainly as fortresses that could be defended against enemy armies. For this reason, they were not very comfortable places in which to live.

A castle's outer walls had no real windows—only narrow slits through which archers could shoot. Most castle rooms, therefore, were dark even at midday. Stone walls were strong defenses, it is true, but they did not keep out the winter cold.

Keeping a castle stocked with food was a major problem. Meat was scarce because most farm animals had to be kept alive to give milk, lay eggs, grow wool, or pull a plow. Kitchen gardens within the castle grounds supplied much-needed vegetables and herbs.

Water and sanitation posed problems, too. To withstand a siege, a castle had to have its own water supply—usually a well near the center of the castle. Drawing enough water for bathing or laundry was a time-consuming process, so baths and clean clothes were rare.

Castles were a necessity in medieval warfare. In the 1400's, however, when cannons began to replace bows and arrows, castles provided little protection. At the same time, kings were forming national armies. No longer did each local lord have to defend his own land. Most lords and ladies willingly gave up their old-fashioned castles to move into comfortable, elegant palaces or country houses.

Knighthood and Chivalry

In an age when warfare was common, the feudal lord had to be a skilled fighter. Through combat, lords protected their estates, snatched up new lands, and added to their wealth. A young noble was trained to be a **knight**—a mounted warrior. He learned how to wear armor, ride a war-horse, and fight with sword and lance. When the youth had proven his ability and courage, he was knighted in an impressive ceremony.

Knights longed for glory and the respect of their fellow nobles. They wanted minstrels to sing of their heroic deeds and ladies to admire their bravery. To keep up their skills, knights spent time each day practicing with their weapons. Lords sometimes held fighting tournaments in which knights competed with each other to win prizes and honor. For the audiences, tournaments provided entertainment. For the knights, they were a challenge in times of peace.

By the 1100's the feudal nobility had a code of behavior called **chivalry** (SHIV-ul-

220

Sec. Rev. ques. 4

ree). A true knight was expected to fight bravely, be loyal to his lord, and treat other knights with respect and courtesy. He also protected women, children, and the weak. A priest blessed the knight's weapons and prayed that the knight would always "defend the just and right." A knight was expected to be a Christian gentleman who honored Church laws and defended the Church against its enemies.

The Church recognized that the warfare among lords contributed to disorder. In the eleventh century it tried to impose the "Peace of God" and the "Truce of God." These were rules that limited feudal warfare to certain days of the week and certain times of the year. Such restrictions were not always respected, however.

Feudal Castles

Because they lived in violent times, feudal lords built homes that could withstand attack. The first castles, built in the 900's, were simple wooden structures. By the 1100's, however, castles were usually built of stone and encircled by massive walls and guard towers.

The lord's castle stood high on a rocky hill or by the bend of a river. There were no buildings near it. Trees and bushes were cut down so that lookouts could easily see an approaching enemy. Around the castle was a moat—a wide ditch filled with water. When an enemy force drew near, the drawbridge across the moat was raised, and the knights defending the castle took positions high on the castle walls.

Attacking forces laid careful plans to capture a castle. First, they filled part of the moat with logs and earth so they could cross it. Once they had a road across the moat, the attackers tried to go under, over, or through the castle walls. As the attackers raised ladders against the castle walls, its defenders hurled boiling water, hot oil, melted lead, and huge stones at the enemy. Some attackers tried to climb the wall. Others tried to break it down with battering rams or catapults that

hurled huge stones against the wall until a section crumbled.

Sometimes the attackers used a movable tower that reached as high as the castle wall. Built of heavy timber, the tower was pushed on wheels or rollers close to the castle. After a drawbridge was lowered from the tower to the castle wall, the attacking soldiers rushed across the bridge and fought hand-to-hand with the castle's defenders.

Another method of attack was to tunnel under the castle walls. The attackers used timbers to support the roof of their tunnel. After the tunnel reached a point well under the castle wall, the timbers were set on fire. When the wood burned through, the castle wall above it collapsed.

The castle was also a home. In it lived the lord and lady, members of their family, knights and other men-at-arms, and servants. The castle had bedrooms, a kitchen, storerooms, and a chapel where the lord and his family attended religious services. The most important room in the castle was the great hall. Here the lord and lady ate, gave orders to servants, and received guests.

● See below.

Tournaments between knights were fierce and bloody competitions. Defeated knights were often forced to pay large ransoms to the victors. **221**

● REINFORCEMENT. Have students work in groups to dramatize the roles of lords, vassals, knights, noblewomen, and serfs during the feudal period. Students might prepare narratives, a skit, or draw posters to illustrate how the values of chivalry, the system of alliances between lords and vassals, and the manor system affected the lives of the people of that time. *(Comprehension) Translating Information into Another Form*

Social History The Peace of God called on lords to abstain from attacking priests, churches, peasants' livestock, mills, vines, merchants, and people on their way to Church. The Truce of God banned all fighting from nine o'clock on Saturday to daybreak on Monday.

● ENRICHMENT. Have students illustrate the architecture of a castle. Students might make a model or sketch of the defensive elements and living quarters of a castle. Have students present the illustrations in class. *(Application) Illustrating History*

After dinner, which was often a feast, traveling entertainers performed for the family and guests. Clowns called jesters amused the diners with clever remarks and foolish actions. Jugglers, acrobats, magicians, and animal trainers also performed. Minstrels played harps, guitars, or flutes and sang about the deeds of brave knights.

The Lives of Noblewomen

People in the Middle Ages believed that women should be subordinate to men. Nevertheless, the Church taught that both men and women were children of God, and it regarded marriage as a sacred rite. A noble's daughter was usually married by the age of 14, often to a man who was much older. The marriage was arranged by her father.

The lady of a medieval castle supervised the household. She looked after the preparation of food and kept a garden where she grew herbs for cooking and for making medicine. She also taught young girls in her household how to sew, spin, and weave, and she tended the sick and wounded. When the lord was away from the castle, the lady took charge. She gave orders to the servants and made financial decisions. If the lord were taken prisoner in war, she raised the ransom to pay for his release. Sometimes she put on armor and went to war herself.

For amusement noblewomen enjoyed chess and other board games or played musical instruments. They embroidered tapestries to cover the bare castle walls and keep the rooms warmer. A lady might also join her husband on the hunt, a favorite sport of the medieval nobility.

In some parts of Europe, women could inherit lands and the power that went with them. In England, Matilda, the daughter of King Henry I, raised an army and went to war in 1135, trying to establish her claim to the English throne. In the early 1200's, Blanche of Castile ruled France while her son King Louis was away. She did much to bring peace and unity among the various regions.

Eleanor of Aquitaine, a twelfth-century noblewoman, inherited her father's rich lands in southern France. A ruler in her own right, Eleanor also married King Louis VII of France and, later, King Henry II of England. She played an important role in the politics of both countries.

The Manorial System

The wealth of feudal lords came from the labor of the peasants who lived on their land. In the last years of the Roman Empire, many peasant farmers had begun to work for landowners because they could not afford farms themselves. By the early Middle Ages few peasants owned the land they worked.

Serfdom. The overwhelming majority of people in medieval Europe were peasants. Most peasants were serfs—people who did not have the freedom to leave the land where they were born. When a lord acquired a new fief, he acquired the serfs as well. Serfs lived in a small village on the manor—the lord's estate.

While feudalism was the basic political arrangement during the Middle Ages, the manorial system was the basic economic arrangement. The manorial system rested on a set of rights and obligations between a lord and his serfs. The lord gave the serfs housing, land to farm, and protection from bandits. In return, serfs tended the lord's land, looked after his animals, and did other work on the estate.

Each lord owned at least one manor. The richest lords owned many. The Church also held many manors. Since neither the nobility nor the clergy did work that produced goods, it was the toil of the peasants that made the manorial system work.

A self-sufficient community. Between 15 and 30 families usually lived in the village on a manor. Besides the serfs' cottages, the village included the lord's castle or manor house, a church, and workshops. Surrounding the village were fields, pastures, and forests.

Sec. Rev. ques. 5

222

Social History Note that manors included farmland ranging in size from 900 to 3,000 acres.

Check for Understanding. Ask: What was the difference between feudalism and the manorial system? (Feudalism was a political system based on the relationships between lords and vassals; the manorial system was an economic system based on the rights and obligations of lords and serfs.)

A wide variety of goods and services were produced on the manor. The serfs raised grain and other crops in the lord's fields and orchards. Carpenters and stonemasons did the building and repairing, and blacksmiths made weapons for knights and tools for household use. Women spun wool into thread and wove the thread into fabric for clothing. A priest tended to the religious needs of the people. While goods such as salt and iron had to come from the outside, trade was very limited. For the most part, the manor was self-sufficient—able to produce almost everything it needed.

Farming methods. Medieval farmers understood that soil loses its fertility if the same crops are planted year after year. They used compost and manure to enrich the soil, but there was never enough fertilizer. To keep the soil from losing its fertility, farmers used a three-field system. A third of the land was planted in autumn with winter wheat. Another third was planted the following spring with oats and vegetables. The last third of the land was left fallow—unplanted. Each year the fields were switched.

Each field was divided into strips. Many of these strips belonged to the lord, but some were set aside for the serfs. Because the fields were not all equally fertile, each serf was given strips in several different fields.

A single farmer could not plow and harvest without help. The plow was heavy, the oxen were small, and the harness was poor. Since eight oxen might be needed to pull a plow, serfs shared their oxen and worked together to get the land plowed. Each family received the produce from its own strips, but the plowing and harvesting were done by all the families together.

Medieval manors were self-contained communities. This diagram shows the arrangement of a typical manor. Why, do you think, was the manor located near a stream? (See answer below.)

A MEDIEVAL MANOR

Caption Answer: The stream probably provided water for drinking, washing, transportation, fishing, and irrigation.

Cultural History Note that, in England, serfs had their own class distinctions. They were divided into *cotters*, who were given three or four acres to farm and owed service to the manor households, and *villeins* (from *villa* for farm), who had the use of forty acres of manorial land.

The Lives of Serfs

Duties. Serfs owed many obligations to their lords. They farmed the land set aside for the lord and turned over all its crops to him. They had to bake their bread in the lord's oven, grind their wheat in the lord's mill, and press their grapes in his winepress. They paid for these services by giving the lord of the manor part of the crops they grew on their own strips of land. Serfs also dug ditches, gathered firewood, built fences, and repaired roads and buildings. Besides helping in the fields, women made clothing for the lord's family. Each serf worked about three days a week for the lord.

Sec. Rev. ques. 5, cont.

Serfs could not leave the manor without the lord's permission. The lord could even decide whom a serf would marry. (Serfs who did not want to marry the persons chosen for them could pay a fine instead.)

This picture shows peasants on a manor beating flax to loosen its fibers. Behind them, a woman spins the fibers into linen thread for clothing.

The Pierpont Morgan Library, New York M.399 f.12

224

Rights. Although serfs were not free, neither were they slaves. Their rights were protected by custom. Their children could not be taken from them and sold. As long as serfs carried out their duties to their lord, they could live in their cottages and continue to farm their strips of land. If a lord tried to take away these rights, serfs might resist by refusing to work.

Living conditions. Serfs lived in crowded cottages that had only one or two rooms. The roofs were made of thatch, and the walls were mud-plastered logs. The floors were often hard-pounded dirt. In winter the open windows were closed with wooden shutters or stuffed with straw. There was no chimney. Smoke from the hearth seeped out through the thatched roof. Rough benches, a table, beds, and perhaps a storage chest were the only furniture. The serfs might share their homes with chickens and pigs.

Unlike the lord, serfs almost never sat down to a feast. They ate a simple diet—vegetables, coarse brown bread, grain, cheese, and soup. Honey from beehives sweetened their food. Fresh meat, milk, and butter were luxuries. The wild animals in the forests belonged to the lord, and serfs were forbidden to hunt them. When crops failed, the peasants faced starvation.

The life of a serf was hard and tiring. Men and women worked in the fields from sunrise to sunset. This backbreaking labor left them exhausted and they aged very quickly. Disease often crippled and killed their children. Warring lords might destroy the serfs' homes, steal their animals, and ruin their crops.

Although serfs had rough lives, they did have some simple pleasures. Traveling minstrels and entertainers—acrobats, bear-trainers, and actors—visited the manors. Wrestling and soccer were other forms of amusement. On religious holidays, serfs gathered in front of the village church to sing and dance.

Open rebellion by serfs was rare before the 1300's, partly because serfs knew so little about the world beyond the manor. Serfs rarely left the manor where they lived. Thick forests separated one manor from another. Poor roads made travel difficult; thieves and warring knights made it dangerous. Serfs lived, worked, and died on the lord's estate and were buried in the village churchyard.

An unquestioned order. Serfs accepted their lot because they, like all Christians in medieval times, believed that God determined a person's place in society. A few people, they thought, were meant to be nobles; the majority were meant to be serfs.

Men of lowly birth sometimes joined the clergy and a few even became bishops. Sometimes a lord granted knighthood to a peasant who distinguished himself in battle. Most serfs, however, lived almost exactly as their parents and grandparents had. Though they lacked freedom and opportunity, they did have security and a sense of belonging.

See Sec. 2 *Closing the Lesson*, p. T209C.

Section Review

Answers to Section Review questions are in brackets on pages indicated.

1. **Define:** fief, vassal, knight, chivalry, serf, manor, manorial system, self-sufficient, fallow. (pp. 218, 220, 222, 223)
2. What invading peoples caused turmoil in Europe in the 800's? (pp. 217–218)
3. What duties did lords and vassals owe each other? (p. 218)
4. What qualities did the code of chivalry demand of knights? (p. 221)
5. What duties did lords and serfs owe each other? (pp. 222–224)
6. **Critical thinking:** What were the positive and negative effects of rule by feudal lords? (See answer below.)

6. Rule by feudal lords brought order to a society lacking a central government. Because feudalism was based on land ownership, rivalry between lords for more land often led to war.

Chapter 11   Summary and Timeline

1. The fall of Rome created confusion in Western and Central Europe, and political authority broke down. During the early Middle Ages, Christianity blended with Germanic traditions and Greco-Roman culture to form medieval civilization. The Church organization, along with the empire of Charlemagne, restored a sense of unity to Europe.

2. Charlemagne's heirs could not hold the empire together. Raids by Vikings, Magyars, and Muslims caused widespread disorder. Feudalism, which was based on relationships between lords and their vassals, developed as central authority declined. Along with feudalism came the manorial system. Serfs—peasants who could not leave the manor—worked the lord's land in exchange for protection. The manor was largely self-sufficient and the basic economic unit of the Middle Ages.

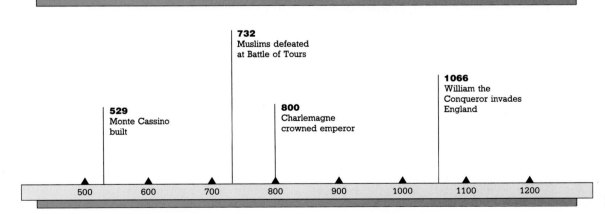

500	600	700	800	900	1000	1100	1200

529 Monte Cassino built

732 Muslims defeated at Battle of Tours

800 Charlemagne crowned emperor

1066 William the Conqueror invades England

See p. T209C for answers to Chapter Review.

Vocabulary Review

1. Match each of the following terms with its definition: *chivalry, fief, knight, manor, manorial system, papacy, sacrament.*
   a. lord's estate
   b. special religious ceremony
   c. Europe's economic system during Middle Ages
   d. office of Pope
   e. mounted warrior
   f. land granted by one noble to another in exchange for military aid and other services
   g. feudal code of behavior for nobles
2. Define the terms in the following pairs.
   a. vassal; serf
   b. clergy; order
   c. medieval; Middle Ages

People to Identify

Match each with the correct description: *Charlemagne, Clovis, Eleanor of Aquitaine, Gregory I, Pepin the Short, Saint Benedict, Saint Patrick, Venerable Bede.*

1. Frankish ruler who was crowned "Emperor of the Romans" by the Pope
2. English monk who wrote a history of the Church in England
3. ruler who united the Franks in 481 and conquered much of Gaul
4. Italian who established an order of monks
5. important early Pope
6. first Mayor of the Palace to be crowned Frankish king
7. missionary who converted the Irish to Christianity in the early 400's
8. French noblewoman who influenced politics in France and England

Places to Know

Use the following place names to complete the sentences below: *Aachen, Monte Cassino, Papal States, Rome.*

1. The Pope headed the Church in the city of ___?___ .
2. The most famous medieval monastery was at ___?___ in Italy.
3. The Church ruled the ___?___, the lands between Rome and Ravenna.
4. Charlemagne built a beautiful church at his capital at ___?___ .

Recalling the Facts

1. What changes took place in political life, urban life, and legal systems after Germanic kingdoms replaced the Roman Empire?
2. What role did the Pope play in medieval life? Priests? Monks and nuns?
3. What were Charlemagne's most notable achievements?
4. How did the Vikings, Magyars, and other invaders affect medieval Europe?
5. Describe the mutual obligations between lord and vassal.
6. Under the code of chivalry, how were knights expected to act?
7. What obligations did serfs owe to their lords? What rights did serfs have?

Critical Thinking Skills

1. **Preparing an oral report.** Research one of the following topics for an oral report: the life of St. Patrick; the armor and weapons of medieval knights; songs and poems describing acts of chivalry; medieval tournaments.

(App.)

2. Analyzing a chart. The chart below shows the relationship between four groups in feudal society. What groups are shown? What important groups in medieval society are not shown? Who was the chief ruler? Notice that some knights are connected to more than one lesser lord, and a lesser lord is connected to more than one greater lord. What does this indicate? *(Comp.)*

King

Greater lords

Lesser lords

Knights

✔ **3. Explaining cause and effect.** Serfs knew little about the world outside the manor on which they lived. Why would this make open rebellion rare? How did Church teachings also discourage rebellions? *(Syn.)*

✔ **4. Creative writing.** If you had lived in medieval society, would you prefer to have been a knight, a monk or nun, a serf, a minstrel, a noble, or someone else? Explain your choice, and write a fictional account describing a typical day in your life. *(Syn.)*

Thinking About Geography

1. Analyzing. The term *terrain* refers to land features. What type of terrain did feudal lords prefer for building castles and fortresses? What changes did they make in the surrounding land to further strengthen their defenses? *(Comp.)*

2. Comparing maps. Study the map on page 215 and the map of present-day Europe in the Atlas at the back of this book. What nations now exist in the area ruled by Charlemagne in 814? *(Comp.)*

Enrichment: Primary Sources

Historians can gain valuable insight into a society by examining its laws. The excerpt below is adapted from the laws of a medieval English manor called Dernale.

❝ When a serf dies, the lord shall have all the pigs of the deceased, all his goats, all his mares at grass and his horse also, all his bees, all his cloth of wool and flax, and whatsoever can be found of gold and silver.

Also, the lord shall have the best ox and the Holy Church shall have another.

After this, the rest of the animals ought to be divided in this way: if the deceased has children, one animal for the lord, one for the wife, one for the children; and if he leaves no children, the animals shall be divided into two parts, one for the lord and one for the wife of the deceased equally.

Also, if the lord wishes to buy corn or oats, or anything else, and the serfs have such things to sell, it shall not be lawful for them to sell elsewhere if the lord is willing to pay them a reasonable price. ❞

1. According to this document, which of a serf's possessions automatically became the property of the lord when the serf died?
2. Which possessions did the lord have to divide with the serf's family? How were they divided?
3. **Critical thinking:** The last paragraph says that serfs could sell their extra crops only to the lord, provided he paid them a "reasonable price." Who do you think decided what was "reasonable"? Explain your answer.
   (Comp.)

✔ A checkmark identifies questions and exercises calling for the three higher-order levels of thinking at the top of the Bloom taxonomy: Analysis, Synthesis, and Evaluation.

New Forces in Medieval Europe   800–1270

(pp. 228–253)

Chapter Preview

Section 1 explains how agricultural advances and the cultivation of new lands contributed to the revival of trade and the growth of towns. New business practices, the growth of guilds, and the development of a middle class are also described. Section 2 traces changes that led to political unity and the growth of royal power in France and England, and to continued division among the territories of Italy and Germany. In Section 3 the growth of papal power and the Church's efforts to stamp out heresy are described. Section 4 examines the Christian Reconquest of Spain, the Crusades and their effects, and the German conquest and colonization of the Baltic Sea area.

Bibliography

See the *Teacher's Management and Planning Guide* for additional listings. Starred titles are for both students and teachers.

Finucane, Ronald C. *Soldiers of the Faith: Crusaders and Moslems at War.* St. Martin's. A short, illustrated survey.

Hallam, Elizabeth, ed. *The Plantagenet Chronicles.* Weidenfeld. A broad collection of original sources—both literary and artistic—on England's colorful medieval rulers.

*Kelly, Amy. *Eleanor of Aquitaine and the Four Kings.* Harvard University Press. The dramatic events in the life of Eleanor of Aquitaine reveal the international sphere of a medieval ruler.

*Turnbull, Stephen. *The Book of the Medieval Knight.* Crown. Lavishly illustrated study of knights, armor, chivalry, and warfare.

Section Lesson Plans

SECTION 1   (pp. 229–234)
New Economic Developments

Objectives

After completing this section, students will be able to:
1. Explain how changes in agriculture affected European life.
2. Describe how the growth of trade led to new ways of doing business.
3. Discuss how the revival of towns gave many people more freedom.

Introducing the Lesson

Remind students that agricultural and business developments during the Middle Ages set the stage for the emergence of the middle class. In time, this new social class dominated medieval towns.

    Then ask: *(a) What might account for the development of a new social class?* (Answers will vary. Economic changes might result in the emergence of a new social class.)

    (b) How might a social class cause change? (A social class can affect change through economic strength or political power.)

Developing the Lesson:
Analyzing Historical Relationships

Have students make a chart illustrating the relationships between the following economic and social developments: *Increase in food production; increase in population; decline in serfdom; greater demand for goods; revival of trade and town life; greater employment opportunities for women. (Comprehension)*

Developing the Lesson:
Linking Past and Present

Have students identify economic and social developments of the Middle Ages that are also characteristics of modern societies. (Answers might include the following developments: technological advances; more individual freedom; growth of the population, middle class, and towns; expansion of trade; business partnerships; banking; trade groups.) *(Synthesis)*

Closing the Lesson:
Evaluating Historical Developments

Have students evaluate economic and social developments of the Middle Ages and explain which were the most important. (Answers will vary.) *(Evaluation)*

See *Section Review* questions, p. 234.

SECTION 2   (pp. 235–242)
The Rise of European States

Objectives

After completing this section, students will be able to:
1. Describe how England came to be united under a king with limited power.
2. Explain how French kings expanded their power.
3. Discuss what kept Germany and Italy divided.

Introducing the Lesson

Remind students that the feudal system was based on the power of local lords and their relationships with their vassals. In time economic and political factors increased the power of monarchs and led to the rise of European national states.

Then ask: *(a) How do you think a national state might differ from a feudal state?* (Answers will vary. In feudal states, individual contracts between lords and vassals were the basis of loyalty. In a national state, the people form one society and their loyalty is usually to the state.)

(b) What developments during the Middle Ages might account for the rise of national states? (Feudal society was rural. With the growth of towns and an independent middle class, new political forms emerged.)

Developing the Lesson:
Analyzing Historical Developments

Have students work in groups to present a panel discussion explaining how English kings sought to unify England and strengthen the monarchy and how their efforts led to a limited monarchy. *(Synthesis)*

Developing the Lesson:
Observing for Detail

Ask: *(a) What prevented centralized rule in France?* (English control of French territory.)

(b) What unifying measures did English and French monarchies adopt? (Common law, a court system, and a system of taxation.)

(c) How were the English and French monarchies different? (Limited monarchy developed in England and absolute monarchy developed in France.)

(d) What was the main reason absolute monarchy developed in France? (The French Estates-General had no economic power over the king.) *(Comprehension)*

Closing the Lesson:
Linking Past and Present

Have students write an essay explaining how the following principles, important to many present-day governments, originated in the English legal system and the Magna Carta: *Equality under the law, rule by law, and government by consent of the governed. (Synthesis)*

See *Section Review* questions, p. 242.

SECTION 3   (pp. 242–245)
The Growth of Church Authority

Objectives

After completing this section, students will be able to:
1. Discuss the internal problems and political struggles the Church faced.
2. Describe how the Church responded to its opponents.

Introducing the Lesson

Remind students that after the fall of Charlemagne's empire, the Church emerged as the only institution with the power to unify Europe. In time, the Church's religious role was clouded by political involvements and challenges to Church authority.

Then ask: *(a) What might account for the Church's acquisition of political power during the Middle Ages?* (Answers will vary. During feudal times, the Church was the institution that united most Europeans.)

(b) Why might the Church and political authorities have worked together at first? (Answers will vary. Political authorities might have felt they could benefit from cooperation with the Church. The Church might have cooperated with local rulers because they had the most direct control over people.)

(c) What might account for the growth of conflict between political authorities and Church leadership? (Answers will vary. If either one viewed the other as a threat, conflict would develop. If the strength of political leaders grew, they might challenge the right of the Church to fulfill government functions.)

Developing the Lesson:
Making Decisions

Have students dramatize a meeting between the Holy Roman Emperor Henry IV and his advisers about Henry's excommunication by Pope Gregory VII. Participants in the meeting might consider the following issues: specific conflicts between Henry and the Pope; why Henry could not ignore the decree of excommunication; alternative solutions for Henry; why the journey to Canossa was necessary; advantages and disadvantages of the journey to Canossa. *(Application)*

Developing the Lesson:
Linking Past and Present

Have students compare the medieval view of the Church and religious authority with the modern idea of freedom of religion. Comparisons might include a definition of both points of view and a discussion of why each is characteristic of its time. (The Church was the sole representative of Christianity during the Middle Ages and therefore accepted as the interpreter and protector of God's word; it was a source of unity during feudal times and acquired authority. Today, many religious institutions claim authority; governments that are committed to the protection of individual freedom and rights have guaranteed separation of religion and politics.) *(Synthesis)*

Closing the Lesson:
Forming a Hypothesis

Have students develop a hypothesis about why the Church used excommunication and the Inquisition against those who challenged Church authority and beliefs. Students might consider the following: What might have happened if the Church had ignored challenges? How else might the Church have dealt with challenges to its authority?) *(Synthesis)*

See *Section Review* questions, p. 245.

SECTION 4   (pp. 246–251)
The Expansion of Christian Europe

Objectives

After completing this section, students will be able to:
1. Explain how Christians recaptured European lands from the Muslims.
2. Discuss why the Crusades failed to keep Palestine under Christian control.
3. Describe how German culture expanded eastward.

Introducing the Lesson

Remind students that Christian Europe expanded mainly in three ways: the reconquest of Spain, religious Crusades to the Holy Land, and the German conquest of lands on the Baltic Sea.

Then ask: *(a) Why might it be important to a religious group to expand its influence?* (Answers will vary. Some groups might want to increase their political and territorial control; some might want to spread their message.)

(b) Do you think religious beliefs influence political and military actions today as they did in the past? Why or why not? (Answers will vary.)

Developing the Lesson:
Comparing Historical Developments

Have students compare the motives of Crusaders with the motives for a jihad (p. 199). (The Crusaders engaged in war against Muslims to reclaim land that was important to their traditions. Muslims engaged in jihad to convert nonbelievers.) *(Synthesis)*

Developing the Lesson:
Organizing Information

Have students make a chart organizing the results of the Peasant Crusade and the First, Second, Third, and Fourth Crusades. (*Peasant Crusade:* thousands massacred Jews. Most participants were killed by Muslims in Asia Minor. *First Crusade:* created four Christian states in the Middle East. *Second Crusade:* Jerusalem lost to the Muslims. *Third Crusade:* doomed by rivalry between the English and French kings. *Fourth Crusade:* last of the recaptured lands fell to Muslims.) *(Comprehension)*

Closing the Lesson:
Understanding Point of View

Have students work in groups to present a panel discussion that might have occurred among participants in the Crusade. Students might present the viewpoints of peasants, lords, knights, merchants, religious and political leaders, and the Seljuk Turks. *(Application)*

See *Section Review* questions, p. 251.

Chapter 12 Review Answers
(pp. 252–253)

Vocabulary Review

1. Answers will vary, but should reflect students' understanding of the terms.
2. (a) trial jury (b) absolute monarchy (c) apprentice (d) Battle of Hastings (e) cardinal (f) Inquisition; heresy (g) Hanseatic League

People to Identify

1. Saint Dominic 2. William the Conqueror 3. Gregory VII 4. John 5. Peter the Hermit

Places to Know

1. Spain 2. Holy Roman Empire 3. England 4. France

Recalling the Facts

1. Europeans cleared more land and invented new farming tools that increased productivity.
2. Partnerships made it possible for merchants to expand their businesses and increase profits. Letters of credit allowed merchants to do business without having to carry heavy gold and silver coins that might be lost or stolen. Banks encouraged the growth of business by financing projects in trade and industry.
3. Some serfs gained their freedom by running away to towns; others earned money to buy their freedom by selling extra crops in town.
4. Henry I began to establish a common legal system for all of England by sending royal judges throughout the kingdom to try cases. Henry II had cases tried in royal courts instead of in the courts of the Church or feudal lords, established the basis for common law by having the decisions of royal judges written down and used as guides for future decisions, and introduced the jury system.
5. The English monarch could not set taxes without the people's approval, he could not punish a freeman without a trial, and he had to govern according to law. Parliament limited royal power mainly through control of money matters, especially taxation.
6. French kings did not need its help to raise money, so they tended to ignore it.
7. Germany was divided into duchies, which were ruled by powerful dukes independent of the emperor's rule. Italy was divided into kingdoms and city-states that maintained their independence.
8. The papacy was fought for, like a political office; the Church lost the power to appoint bishops; and spiritual values among the clergy declined.
9. An agreement between the Holy Roman Emperor and the Pope that gave the Church supreme authority in spiritual matters but did not settle the question of who had supreme political authority.
10. It used persuasion, excommunication, and the Inquisition.
11. The freeing of the Holy Land from the Seljuk Turks, the return of Jerusalem to the Christians, and an end to the fighting among knights and lords.
12. German nobles hoped to carve out new estates, peasants wanted land of their own and freedom from manor life, missionaries were looking for converts, and merchants desired new trade opportunities. The expansion led to the growth of towns, the spread of Christianity and German culture, and the growth of trade.

Critical Thinking Skills

1. Communicate—to share information; community—a group having a common locality or set of interests; commonwealth—a nation or state.
2. Farming. Serfs or peasant class. Horsepower, windpower, and human power. A harness and a windmill. Descriptions will vary.
3. Students should note that the common law meant more uniformity and consistency in court rulings.

Thinking About Geography

Medieval towns were most likely to develop where merchants gathered: on seacoasts (Naples, Marseilles), along riverbanks (Lyons, Hamburg, Buda, Pest), and at crossroads of major trade routes (Novgorod, Augsburg, Vienna).

Enrichment: Primary Sources

1. He was suspended from the guild until he paid a fine and took the guild oath again.
2. People who were not guild members could not buy anything to sell again in the same city or form partnerships with guild members.
3. Some of these functions would be performed by labor unions, others by government agencies.

New Forces in Medieval Europe 800–1270

See chapter timeline, p. 251.

Before You Read This Chapter

Have you ever gone to a home show, car show, or computer show where companies display their latest products? Afterward, you probably wanted things that you never knew existed before. In the Middle Ages, as long as people remained on the manor, they did not want Byzantine silks, rare perfumes, or exotic spices, because they had never seen such goods. When merchants began to hold great fairs, however, people discovered all those items and more. As you read this chapter, look for other changes that came about as more and more Europeans left their manors.

The Geographic Setting

The Chapter Outline

1. New Economic Developments
2. The Rise of European States
3. The Growth of Church Authority
4. The Expansion of Christian Europe

Knights of the Middle Ages, such as this one from Italy, were trained from boyhood to fight the enemies of their lords.

Background Note that England's population rose from about 1,100,000 in 1086 to about 3,700,000 in 1346.

1 New Economic Developments

Objectives

Focus Questions

★ ■ How did changes in agriculture affect European life? *(page 229)*

● ■ How did the growth of trade lead to new ways of doing business? *(pages 229–232)*

▲ ■ Why did the revival of towns give many people more freedom? *(pages 233–234)*

Terms to Know

moneychanger	journeyman
guild	charter
apprentice	middle class

★ Note strategies for first objective on this page.

By the middle of the eleventh century, Western Europe had entered a period of growing prosperity. Important changes in agriculture were taking place. Trade and commerce began to flourish. Along with these changes came the rebirth of towns and the rise of a prosperous middle class.

Changes in Agriculture

In the eleventh and twelfth centuries, large areas of land in many parts of Europe were cleared and settled. Peasants drained swamps, cut down forests, and started new villages. Vast stretches of the continent were farmed for the first time. Lords encouraged the farming of new lands because the extra crops brought in more money.

Sec. Rev. ques. 2

New inventions. The water mill and the windmill, two inventions that made it easier to grind grain, allowed farmers to take advantage of the larger harvests. New farming tools also helped farmers boost their production. Heavier plows, sometimes mounted on wheels, were able to cut deeply into the soil. With the new plows, farmers could work on moist, rich land that the older plows could not break up.

New inventions also made it possible to use farm horses more efficiently. Horses moved faster and had greater stamina than oxen. This made them more useful for farm work. Yet the old-fashioned yoke harness, which worked well with oxen, tended to choke horses. The new collar harness shifted the strain of pulling from the horse's neck to its shoulders. With the new harness, horses could be used both for plowing and for pulling loads. Horseshoes were another important invention. The metal shoes protected horses' hoofs and made it easier for the animals to work on rocky land.

Decline in serfdom. The settlement of new lands helped bring about a decline in serfdom. Most serfs were reluctant at first to move to new parts of the lord's estate. To give them a reason to move, the lord promised them more freedom. Serfs who did settle on these lands were often allowed to pay the lord rent instead of working his lands. In time they came to regard the land they farmed as their own. They were making the shift from serfdom to freedom.

Population growth. The changes in agriculture altered the conditions of life in Europe. With greater food production, fewer people died from starvation and malnutrition, and the population climbed steadily. In addition, more people were free to work at nonfarming tasks, such as crafts.

The Growth of Trade

● Note strategies for second objective on pages 230 and 231.

The rapid growth of population also increased the demand for goods. Trade expanded to meet this new demand.

Sec. Rev. ques. 3

229

★ RETEACHING. Have students identify the effects of the following agricultural advances: Improved plow (Farmers could work on moist, rich land that earlier plows could not break up.) Harnesses and horseshoes (Horses could be used for plowing and pulling loads and could work on rocky land.) *(Comprehension)* *Identifying Effects*

★ REINFORCEMENT. Have students explain why there was a decline in serfdom during the Middle Ages. *(Comprehension)* *Identifying Causes*

★ ENRICHMENT. Have students develop a hypothesis about how technological improvements during the eleventh and twelfth centuries and the decline in serfdom might have affected medieval society. *(Synthesis)* *Forming a Hypothesis*

Science and Technology Note that the first windmills were used for irrigation in Persia (present-day Iran) around the fifth century A.D. and were widely used in Europe by 1100. Water wheels turned the grindstones of corn mills.

Medieval Trade Routes

The revival of trade encouraged contacts among people all over Europe.
What route might a merchant ship have followed from London to Naples?
Why was Constantinople a key city for European trade?

Map Answers: (1) South along the coasts of France and Spain, then east across the Mediterranean.
(2) It linked trade routes from China, India, and Syria with routes to central and southern Europe.

Major trade routes. During the early Middle Ages, Italian towns had kept a weak trade link with the Byzantine lands in the eastern Mediterranean. In the eleventh century, the Italians defeated the Muslim pirates who had been raiding the coasts. Once they were able to protect their lands and ships from Muslim raiders, the Italians could increase their trade with the Byzantine Empire and North Africa.

The growing population in Western Europe provided a market for silks, sugar, spices, and dyes from Asia. Italian merchants were quick to fill this demand. By the 1300's the Italian city-states of Venice, Genoa, Milan, and Pisa controlled the profitable Mediterranean trade.

Other trade routes opened up between Scandinavia and the Atlantic coast; between England, northern France, and Flanders (now Belgium); and along the rivers between the Baltic Sea in the north and the Black Sea and Constantinople to the south. The fine woolen cloth made in Flanders was in great demand. In exchange for this cloth, Scandinavian merchants offered hunting hawks and

● RETEACHING. Have students summarize the advantages of the following: Partnerships (Large amounts of money could be raised and businesses could expand and increase profits with reduced financial risk.) Moneychanging (Money was left with moneychangers for safekeeping; "letters of credit" prevented theft, allowing merchants to do business without carrying coins.) Banking (Encouraged business growth; financed trade and industry; lent money to kings and the Church.) (Comprehension) *Observing for Detail*

● REINFORCEMENT. Have students work in groups to analyze the advantages and disadvantages of guilds. (Advantages: established standards for products, set prices, and protected artisans from competition. Disadvantages: craftsworkers could be penalized for not fulfilling guild requirements; profits were regulated; little motivation for individual initiative; merchants were forced to pay a set price and accept certain goods.) (Comprehension) *Analyzing Information* furs. The English offered raw wool, and the Germans offered iron and timber.

Trade fairs. As trade picked up, fairs began to be held regularly along the main trade routes. At these fairs, merchants and craftsworkers from many places set up booths to show their goods. They laid out shiny swords and leather saddles, household tools and beautiful rugs. Buyers could also find shoes, silks, spices, furs, metalwork, and fine furniture. Each fair lasted a few weeks. Then the merchants moved on. To protect traders from robbers, lords provided guards for merchants traveling to and from the fairs.

New Business Practices

The increase in trade also led to changes in ways of doing business.

1. Partnerships. Merchants who wanted to raise large amounts of money formed partnerships. This made it possible for them to expand their business and increase profits. Partnerships also reduced risk, because no single merchant had to provide all the money. The development of insurance to cover loss or damage to shipments of goods also helped to limit risk.

Sec. Rev. ques. 4

2. Moneychanging. Another new business practice was developed by people called **moneychangers**. Moneychangers exchanged coins from one region for those of another, much as banks today exchange money from one country for money from another. Moneychangers kept their coins in strongboxes, and people found it convenient to leave money with them for safekeeping. After the moneychangers set aside the funds needed for each day's business, they could lend the rest and charge interest.

Moreover, a merchant traveling to another city could carry a moneychanger's "letter of credit," which other moneychangers would accept as cash. This service allowed merchants to do business without having to carry heavy gold and silver coins that might be lost or stolen.

3. Banking. Eventually the moneychangers came to be called bankers. Their services encouraged the growth of business, and they used their profits to finance projects in trade and industry. They also lent money to kings and to the Church.

● See below.

Trade fairs were an important meeting ground for peoples and products of different lands. What are some of the foods and other goods displayed here? (See answer above.)

231

Background Among the most famous medieval trade fairs were those held annually in towns of the French region of Champagne. These included a twelve-day cloth fair, an eight-day leather, hide, and fur fair, and fairs for other products.

Vocabulary Note that moneychangers displayed their coins on benches called "banks." Eventually, people who engaged in the lending, exchanging, or safekeeping of money were called *bankers*.

● ENRICHMENT. Have students work in groups to present a trade fair that might have occurred in medieval times. Students might research different crafts and guilds of the period, display representative products, and reenact exchanges among moneychangers, bankers, and business partners. Students might wear costumes or assemble props to make the trade fair appear authentic. *(Application) Dramatizing History*

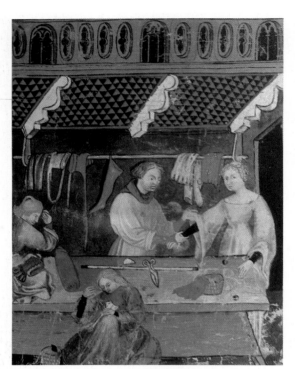
In this tailor's shop the master serves a customer while his apprentices sew garments and stock the shelves.

The Formation of Guilds

Still another economic development of the Middle Ages was the appearance of **guilds**. These were organizations formed by merchants and master craftsworkers. Craft guilds were made up of people who practiced the same trade—for example, shoemaking, glass-blowing, carpentry, or weaving.

Rules for members. At first guilds were simply a form of fellowship, giving people with similar interests a chance to meet and talk. Soon guilds began to set regulations and protect their members.

Merchant guilds prevented outside traders from doing business in a town. A crafts-worker who opened a shop without having been accepted by the guild would not stay in business long. The guild members would close the shop and burn the goods. They would also lock the artisan for several hours in the town pillory, wooden boards in which a person's head and hands were clamped.

The pillory was set up in an open place in the middle of town, so that prisoners had to face the jeers of the townspeople as well as physical discomfort.

The guilds also discouraged competition among their members. They set strict rules to prevent any member from making much more money than the others. All members of the shoemakers' guild, for example, had to keep their shops open the same number of hours, pay their employees the same wages, produce shoes of equal quality, and charge customers a fair price. Guild rules were strictly enforced. Violators could be fined, thrown out of the guild, or even physically punished.

Apprenticeship. To become a member of a craft guild, a young person first had to serve as an **apprentice**—trainee—to a master artisan. An apprenticeship lasted from two to seven years, depending upon the craft. The young apprentice lived in the master's house, helped in the shop, and learned the trade. During this time the apprentice received little or no pay.

After completing the apprenticeship, the youth became a **journeyman**—a day laborer who worked for a master for a daily wage. Most journeymen hoped to become masters themselves. To do so, they had to prove their skill by presenting a fine work sample (called a masterpiece) to the guild's governors. For example, a journeyman wishing to become a master baker might bake a cake for the guild. If the guild members liked the cake, the new master was admitted to the guild and was free to open a shop.

Linking Past and Present

Craft guilds eventually became associations of wage earners—people who worked for others, not for themselves. This form of guild was the forerunner of today's labor union. Its main purpose was to obtain decent wages and working conditions for its members.

Social History Craft guilds owned property; maintained their own chapels inside churches; and cared for destitute members, widows, and orphans. Even thieves and beggars formed trade associations in imitation of guilds.
Religion Note that each guild had its own patron saint.

Vocabulary Note that the word *apprentice* is from a French word meaning "to apprehend" or "to understand."
Social History Note that journeymen did not travel from place to place; the title is from the French word that means "day." Journeymen were laborers who worked for a daily wage.
Check for Understanding. Ask: What was the purpose of guilds? (To support members, protect them from competition, and maintain the quality of products.)

The Revival of Towns

▲ Note strategies for third objective on this page and p. 234.

As you read in Chapter 11, most Europeans lived on manors during the early Middle Ages. Towns had almost disappeared except in Italy. Even the Italian towns suffered a decline in trade and population. In the eleventh century, towns sprang up again throughout Europe. By the next century they had become active centers of commercial life.

Reasons for growth. The expansion of trade and of the food supply encouraged the growth of towns. Towns often arose at locations that were natural places for merchants to gather—on seacoasts and riverbanks, at crossroads, and near castles and monasteries. Greater farm production provided food for the urban population of artisans, merchants, students, and laborers.

Self-government. Many of the new towns were on lands held by a feudal lord. If a lord tried to treat the townspeople like serfs, the townspeople resisted. They wanted to make their own laws and settle disputes in their own courts. They expected to marry whom they pleased and to do as they wished with their property. By paying feudal lords money—and sometimes by fighting them— townspeople could gain a **charter**. This was a document in which a lord gave the people of a town the right to set up their own laws and their own system of taxes. Through their charters, European towns became self-governing city-states, the first since Greco-Roman times.

Town Life

Most medieval towns had small populations. The largest—Florence, Ghent, Bruges (BROOZH), and Paris—had between 50,000 and 100,000 inhabitants. High thick walls, towers, and drawbridges protected the towns from outside attack.

A medieval town was usually crowded, and garbage littered the narrow, crooked streets. At street level were the shops of merchants and artisans, many of whom lived

above their businesses. During the day the streets were filled with merchants, peddlers, beggars, women shopping and selling goods, men transporting produce and other merchandise, and children playing.

Occasional religious processions and executions of criminals drew large crowds. Townspeople also gathered to watch street musicians and traveling entertainers. At night, however, few people ventured into the unlighted streets. The elderly watchmen were no match for the thieves who lay in wait for passers-by.

Opportunities for women. Women had many more opportunities in the towns than in the country. On the manor, women Sec. Rev. ques. 5

In this painting the citizens of a Flemish town have gathered to receive a charter that freed them from obligations to a feudal lord. The growth of self-governing towns marked a turning point in medieval society.

233

▲ RETEACHING. Have students review "Reasons for growth" and "Self-government" (above) and identify the causes and effects of the growth of medieval towns. (Causes: expansion of trade and the food supply. Effects: charters granted by feudal lords; self-governing city-states formed.) (Comprehension) Identifying Causes and Effects

▲ REINFORCEMENT. Have students compare life in a medieval town with life on a manor (pp. 222–225). Then ask: If you had lived during the Middle Ages, would you have preferred to live in a town or on a manor? Have students explain their answers. (Synthesis) Making Judgments

Social History Medieval streets were unsanitary and littered with the remains of butchered animals, unsold fish, and water dumped from dyers' vats.

Social History Note that guild records indicate that women received lower wages than men because women were thought to require less income.

Check for Understanding. Ask: What groups of people formed the middle class? (Master artisans and merchants and their families.)

Ⓕ See below.

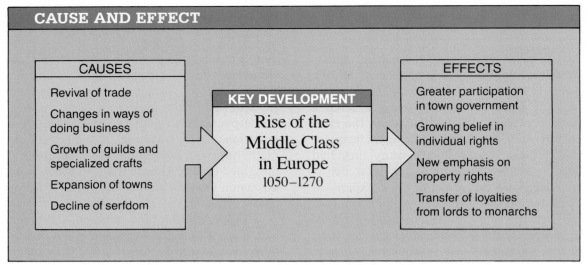

CAUSE AND EFFECT

CAUSES
Revival of trade
Changes in ways of doing business
Growth of guilds and specialized crafts
Expansion of towns
Decline of serfdom

KEY DEVELOPMENT

Rise of the Middle Class in Europe 1050–1270

EFFECTS
Greater participation in town government
Growing belief in individual rights
New emphasis on property rights
Transfer of loyalties from lords to monarchs

worked in the fields, made clothing, and did household chores. In towns, women spun, wove, and dyed cloth. Some worked as shoe-makers, tailors, bakers, glove-makers, or barbers. Women also brewed beer and ale, made charcoal, sold fish and poultry, and ran inns and food stalls. In Paris and London, women dominated the silk-making industry.

In many towns the wives and widows of master craftsmen were admitted to guilds. These guildswomen had all the privileges that a master had, including the right to train apprentices.

Freedom for serfs. Towns also contributed to the decline of serfdom. "City air makes a man free," went a medieval saying. Many serfs fled from the manors with the hope of hiding in a crowded town. After remaining in the town for a year and a day, serfs could legally claim their freedom and their lord could not force them to return. Even the serfs who stayed on the manor benefited from towns, for they could sell their extra crops to townspeople. In this way, some serfs were able to earn enough money to buy their freedom.

Rise of the middle class. Towns brought about the rise of a new social class— the **middle class**, made up of master artisans, merchants, and their families. The life of people in the middle class was very different from **234** that of the clergy and nobles. Their world was

the market rather than the Church or the manor. Members of the middle class owed nothing to a lord. Their prosperity came from industry and trade. They believed people could use their skills to improve their position in life. Middle-class townspeople took part in local government, and their business activities brought wealth to the town. In the centuries to come, the middle class would bring about great economic, political, and intellectual changes in European life.

▲ See below.

See Sec. 1 *Closing the Lesson,* p. T227B.

Section Review

Answers to Section Review questions are in brackets on pages indicated.

1. **Define:** moneychanger, guild, apprentice, journeyman, charter, middle class. (pp. 231, 232, 233, 234)
2. What were the results of changes in agriculture during the Middle Ages? (p. 229)
3. What brought about a revival of trade in Western Europe? (p. 229)
4. What new business practices developed along with the growth of trade? (p. 231)
5. Which groups benefited from the growth of towns? (pp. 233–234)
6. **Critical thinking:** How were trade and town life linked to developments in agriculture? (See answer below.)

Ⓕ **CAUSE AND EFFECT CHART ACTIVITY.** Have students develop a hypothesis to answer the following questions: (a) How did economic developments play a role in the rise of the middle class? (b) What political changes resulted from the rise of the middle class? *(Synthesis) Forming a Hypothesis*

▲ **ENRICHMENT.** Have students develop a hypothesis about how the changes caused by the growth of medieval towns might have affected the development of European society. *(Synthesis) Forming a Hypothesis*

6. Increased food production encouraged population growth, which in turn led to a greater demand for goods. Trade expanded to meet this demand. As trade and the food supply expanded, towns—centers of commercial life—re-emerged.

See lesson plans, pp. T227A–T227C.

2 The Rise of European States

Objectives

★ Note strategies for first objective on this page and p. 238.

Focus Questions

★ ■ How did England come to be united under a king with limited power? *(pages 235–239)*

● ■ How did French kings expand their power? *(pages 239–240)*

▲ ■ What kept Germany and Italy divided? *(pages 241–242)*

Terms to Know

Battle of Hastings	Magna Carta
baron	parliament
common law	limited monarchy
grand jury	absolute monarchy
trial jury	duchy

The revival of trade and the reappearance of towns were signs of growth in Western Europe. Another sign of vitality was the development of national states. England and France became more unified during the Middle Ages. Conflicts within Germany and Italy, however, kept those regions divided into a number of separate territories.

The Changing Role of Kings

Limited authority. As the feudal system developed in medieval Europe, power came into the hands of noble lords who owned vast lands and kept their own armies. Kings still held court in some parts of Europe, but they had little power. Often a king was simply regarded as the chief feudal lord, to whom the nobles of the region owed loyalty as vassals. Some kings in early medieval times actually had less wealth and power than many of the nobles who were their vassals.

The feudal lords did not want kings to grow stronger. They feared that a strong monarch would reduce their power and take away their land. Late in the Middle Ages, this began to happen in France and England. Kings expanded their territories and created strong central governments. In return for the protection that a strong central government could provide, people were willing to pay taxes to royal officials. Gradually people transferred their loyalty from the local lord to the monarch.

Towns and monarchs. The growth of towns helped to strengthen royal power. By taxing the townspeople, kings raised money to hire soldiers. This meant that kings no longer had to depend on the lords to supply them with fighting men. Because professional soldiers were loyal to the ruler who hired them, the king could count on them to fight lords who resisted royal rule. The king could also hire educated townspeople to serve as tax collectors, judges, and administrators. These government officials contributed to the growth of royal power.

Sec. Rev. ques. 2

Early England

The early history of England is a story of many invasions. In the year A.D. 43, armies of the Roman emperor Claudius had conquered much of the island of Britain, which was then inhabited by Celtic (KEL-tik) peoples. The Romans built roads and towns, and areas under their rule prospered. Many Roman soldiers and merchants settled there.

Anglo-Saxons. When the Roman Empire began to collapse in the fifth century, however, the Roman legions abandoned Britain. The island was soon invaded by three Germanic tribes—Jutes, Angles, and Saxons—who crossed from the continent.

235

★ RETEACHING. Have students review "The Changing Role of Kings" (above) and explain why the growth of towns changed the role of monarchs. (Townspeople were willing to pay taxes to the king to gain the protection of a strong central government. Kings could afford to hire soldiers and educated government officials.) *(Comprehension) Observing for Detail*

★ REINFORCEMENT. Have students summarize the political values that support a limited monarchy. (Limited monarchy represents the idea that government must share power with those governed.) *(Comprehension)* **Summarizing Information**

Check for Understanding. Ask: How did the growth of towns help strengthen royal power? (Kings raised money to hire soldiers by taxing townspeople, and they no longer had to depend on lords to supply fighting men.)

KEY

Anglo-Saxon lands (England)

Celtic lands

SCOTLAND

NORTHUMBRIA

IRELAND

Irish Sea

North Sea

EAST ANGLIA

WALES

MERCIA

ESSEX

London

Canterbury

Thames R.

KENT

Winchester

WESSEX

SUSSEX

Hastings

WEST WALES

ATLANTIC OCEAN

English Channel

FRANCE

SCALE

0   100 mi

0   100 km

N
W   E
S

British Isles About 870

In the ninth century the Anglo-Saxons and Celts were the main peoples living in the British Isles. In what parts of the island did the Celts live? What Anglo-Saxon kingdoms existed by 870? What body of water divided the British Isles from France?

Map Answers: (1) Scotland, Ireland, Wales, West Wales. (2) Northumbria, East Anglia, Essex, Mercia, Kent, Sussex, Wessex. (3) English Channel.

Roman culture died out, and the southern part of the island became known as Angleland, and then England. Eventually the invaders, who became known as Anglo-Saxons, set up seven kingdoms in England.

Alfred the Great. In the early 800's, Danish Vikings invaded England. Alfred the Great, the ruler of the kingdom of Wessex (the West Saxons), took the lead in resisting the Danes. Alfred's forces defeated the invaders in 886 and forced them to agree to peace.

Ruler of England from 871 to 899, Alfred was a cultural leader as well as a warrior. **236** He set up a school at his court and translated

Latin works into the Anglo-Saxon language. He also had his scholars begin writing *The Anglo-Saxon Chronicle*, a record of events in England. English scholar-monks kept up this record long after Alfred's death.

The Norman Conquest of England

A landmark victory. In 1066, Normans from northern France invaded England near the seacoast village of Hastings. Though French-speaking, they were descendants of the Vikings who had first raided France and then settled there. Led by William, the duke of Normandy, the Normans defeated the Saxon king at the historic **Battle of Hastings**. Quickly the Normans pressed on to London. There William the Conqueror, as the Norman leader was called, took a new title: King of England.

While armed resistance to Norman rule soon ended in England, it took much longer for the defeated Saxons to accept the language and culture of their conquerors. For some time, the ruling class spoke Norman French and followed French customs, while the common people and the old Saxon nobles kept their own traditions. Slowly, however, Norman and Anglo-Saxon speech blended together into what became the English language.

William's strong rule. William the Conqueror was determined to establish effective control over his new kingdom. He kept a sixth of the land for himself and divided the rest among the Norman **barons**—feudal lords. These barons pledged their loyalty to William and promised to send him soldiers when needed.

William also strengthened royal authority in England by setting up an efficient administration. The Anglo-Saxon rulers had divided their kingdoms into counties, which were run by royal officials. By continuing this practice, William gained control over local government.

To find out what he could collect in taxes from the English, William had his officials make a detailed list of people and their

Biography Alfred the Great felt it was his responsibility to "worthily and fittingly steer and rule the dominion that was entrusted" to him. He organized his army so that some people were always ready for battle while others remained on the farm. He also earned the title of founder of the English navy. Alfred the Great's legal system reflected his desire to protect both nobles and commoners from violence and wrongdoing.

Cultural History Note that the Normans transported approximately 5,000 knights, bowmen, and supporting infantry and horses in open boats across the English Channel to fight the Battle of Hastings.

Politics William the Conqueror insisted on his right to control the Church in England, to approve papal actions, and to approve the issue of decrees and excommunication by bishops.

property. Royal officials traveled around England and counted the number of people on every farm and in every village. They also noted cattle, sheep, pigs, farm equipment, and other kinds of property. This record, the first English census, became known as the *Domesday* (DOOMZ-day) *Book*. It was used as a basis for setting taxes for many years.

Reform of English Law

Sec. Rev. ques. 3

The kings who followed William strengthened unity in England by making changes in the legal system. Several different systems had existed before. There had been the old Anglo-Saxon law, the French feudal law introduced by the Normans, the Church law, and business laws that had developed in the new towns. William's youngest son, Henry I, who ruled from 1100 to 1135, began to establish a common legal system for all England. He sent royal judges to different parts of the kingdom to try court cases.

Common law. Henry I's grandson, Henry II, expanded the legal system. During his reign (1154–1189), he tried to bring as many cases as possible into the royal courts instead of into the courts of the Church or the feudal lords. The decisions of the royal judges were written down and used as guides for future cases, replacing older, unwritten laws. Because these decisions were common to all of England, they later became known as **common law**. Common law helped to provide a fairer system of justice and became the foundation of the English legal system.

Jury system. A jury system also began to take shape during the reign of Henry II. In each district a number of citizens—later called a **grand jury**—were brought together to report to visiting royal judges. Taking an oath to tell the truth, these people gave the judges the names of persons suspected of crimes. Grand juries are still used in many countries today to decide whether cases should go to trial. Later another type of jury, called a **trial jury**, developed. Trial juries had the power to settle disputes.

The Magna Carta

The power of the English monarch grew steadily after the Norman conquest in 1066. It began to weaken late in the reign of Henry II, whose sons quarreled with him and with each other over who should be the next king. The

The history of the Norman conquest is recorded on the Bayeux (bah-YOO) Tapestry. This scene from the tapestry shows French warriors and their horses landing in England on their way to do battle with the Saxons.

237

Background Note that *Domesday* is taken from the Anglo-Saxon word *doom*, meaning "judgment." Today the *Domesday Book* is displayed at the Public Record Office in London.

Check for Understanding. Ask: How did common law develop? (Decisions of royal judges were written down and used as guides for future cases.)

Politics Note that a *grand jury* determines whether or not there is "probable cause" to believe that a crime has been committed; a *trial jury* determines guilt "beyond reasonable doubt."

Ⓕ FEATURE ACTIVITY. Ask: What features of the Tower of London would have served as security measures against attacks? (Its hill-

top location; the thick, stone wall; and towers.) (Analysis) Drawing Conclusions

Ⓕ See above.

Historic Places

The Tower of London

When Duke William of Normandy conquered England in 1066, his first goal was to keep the English people under control. At key points all over the country, he built strong castles and filled them with Norman soldiers. Because London, the most important city, was said to have a "vast and fierce populace," William built his greatest fortress there.

William chose the site for this London castle carefully. It stood on a hill near the wooden bridge across the Thames (TEMZ) River. Legend said that Julius Caesar had chosen this very spot for a Roman fort more than a thousand years earlier. William, in a hurry to secure London, had his first castle built of wood. A few years afterward, he ordered the wooden tower pulled down and replaced with one of stone. The stone tower was completed in 1078. Later kings enlarged the Tower of London many times, adding gates, walls, halls, and courtyards.

In the centuries that followed, the Tower of London served many purposes—royal residence, fortress, prison, zoo, and treasure house. It was the scene of banquets, battles, riots, robberies, public executions, secret murders, and terrorist bombings.

Today, tourists throng to the Tower to see its collection of armor and its display of Britain's crown jewels—priceless gems and gold ornaments. They also come to see the building that has played a part in English history for 900 years.

first to inherit the throne, Richard I, was an adventurer known as Richard the Lion-Hearted. He spent little of his reign in England, and the English had to pay heavy taxes to support his foreign journeys.

Richard's brother John, who ruled from 1199 to 1216, was a much-disliked king. His demands for high taxes and his other oppressive actions finally led the angry barons to rebel. In 1215 the barons forced John to set his seal to the Magna Carta, which means "Great Charter." In this document the king agreed to recognize the barons' rights and privileges, including that of fair trial.

Historians regard the Magna Carta as one of the foundations of modern British and American liberties. Originally meant to protect the nobles' rights, three principles stated in the Magna Carta came to be applied to other groups as well.

1. Taxation only with representation. The Magna Carta stated that no unusual taxes "shall be imposed in our kingdom except by the common council of our kingdom." Over the years this came to mean that the English monarch had to have the approval of the people's representatives to impose taxes.

2. Right to trial. The Magna Carta provided that "no freeman [can] be taken or imprisoned or dispossessed or banished or in any way destroyed . . . except by the lawful judgment of his peers [social equals] or by the law of the land." The barons who drew up the document had intended this to mean that those accused of crimes must be tried by their fellow barons. In time this idea was expanded into the principle that any accused person had a right to trial by jury and could not be imprisoned unless found guilty in court.

3. Limits to power. Implied in the Magna Carta was the idea that royal power had limits. In other words, monarchs had no right to rule in any way they pleased but rather had to govern according to law.

Sec. Rev. ques. 4

238

★ See below.

Biography Richard the Lionhearted did not want to live in England and was there only twice during his life: once at the time of his coronation as king and once to raise money. He said, "I would sell London if I could find a bidder."

Biography Note that King John was nicknamed "Lackland" because his father, Henry II, assigned no provincial territory to his youngest son.

Politics The Magna Carta was drawn and sealed on June 15, 1215 at Runnymede, a meadow on the Thames River in Surrey, southern England.

★ **ENRICHMENT. Have students research the topic of English common law to find examples of laws that became precedents, or the Magna Carta to find how the document protected the rights of English barons.** (Analysis) Locating Information the House of Commons were lesser landowners (the knights) and townspeople.

Control of finances. Over the years the power of Parliament grew, mainly because it had control of money matters. Monarchs had to have the approval of Parliament before they could raise money through taxes. They could not build roads, increase the salaries of their officials, or pay the expenses of keeping an army without the funds collected through taxes. Frequently in need of money, the English rulers had to turn to Parliament for help. On such occasions Parliament was in a position to demand additional powers from the monarch.

Limited monarchy. Thus during the Middle Ages England came to have a strong king, a centralized government, and a unified state. The rights of the people were protected by basic principles made clear in common law, the Magna Carta, and the rise of Parliament. These principles were: (1) English subjects had certain liberties; (2) the king could not violate those liberties; and (3) the power to govern was held not by the king alone but by king and Parliament together. The foundations had been laid for **limited monarchy**—a government in which limits are set on the ruler's powers.

The Foundations of Limited Monarchy

Other limits on royal power grew out of the development of the English Parliament. Parliament had its roots in Anglo-Saxon traditions. Before making decisions, the Anglo-Saxon rulers had asked the advice of powerful leaders. William the Conqueror continued to seek the advice of important officials, landowners, and nobles. These advisers to the monarch met in the Great Council. During the late 1200's the council came to include lesser landowners and townspeople. It developed into a **parliament**—an official group of representatives.

Parliament's two houses. In time the members of Parliament split into two groups, each called a "house." The House of Lords was made up of bishops and great nobles. In

The Unification of France

● Note strategies for second objective on this page and p. 240.

Early disunity. In France the road to national unity was rockier than in England. France had been the western part of Charlemagne's empire. By the late 900's it was a patchwork of territories ruled by feudal lords. France did have a king, but he had little control over the feudal lords. His power was mainly confined to his own lands, which were smaller than those of some of the great lords in France.

It took hundreds of years for the French kings to build a unified state. They used many different methods to get more land. When a lord died without heirs, the king might take over his estate. Kings made alliances with landholding families and sometimes married the daughters of great lords. They worked to **239**

Politics Parliament evolved into a lawmaking body when it adopted a policy called *redress of grievances*. Members of Parliament drew up statements of demands called *bills* and refused to grant money to the king until he agreed to correct what Parliament viewed as inequities.
● **RETEACHING. Have students review "Early disunity" and "English claims on France" (pp. 239–240) and identify sources of disunity in France.** (Powerful feudal lords and English claims on French land.) *(Comprehension) Observing for Detail*

● **REINFORCEMENT. Have students identify four strategies that led to greater unity in France during the thirteenth century.** (Philip II regained some French land from King John of England; Louis IX drew up laws that applied throughout France; Louis outlawed private warfare; Louis established royal courts.) *(Comprehension) Identifying Causes* gain the support of townspeople, who provided the kings with soldiers, the services of skilled administrators, and money raised from taxes. When all else failed, French kings simply went to war and took the nobles' lands by force.

English claims on France. Perhaps the greatest obstacle to French unity was that English kings claimed large parts of France. Because William the Conqueror had been duke of Normandy before becoming king of England, his successors in England saw themselves as rulers of Normandy as well as England.

English control over French lands increased in 1152 when Henry II married Eleanor, duchess of Aquitaine (page 222), who ruled much of southern France. With this marriage, the English king came to rule more land in France than the French king. Regaining these English holdings became an important goal of the kings of France.

Building unity. The French monarch who laid the basis for a unified state was Philip II, known as Philip Augustus. In 1202 Philip went to war with King John of England and stripped the English ruler of most of his territories in northern France. This tripled the size of Philip's kingdom and made him stronger than any French lord.

Philip's successors continued to add to the royal lands. Louis IX, who ruled from 1226 to 1270, made changes in the legal system to strengthen royal power. He drew up the first laws that applied throughout the kingdom. Louis also outlawed private warfare and established royal courts to replace the courts of feudal lords. By the end of the Middle Ages, France was a unified state, although regional and local loyalties remained strong.

The movement toward absolute monarchy. Government in France differed from the English government in several ways. In England, where Parliament served as a check on the ruler, the basis for limited monarchy had been laid. In France, there were no such checks on the king's power.

French kings sometimes called meetings of nobles and clergy in various parts of the country. Eventually these meetings developed into the Estates-General, an assembly for all of France. Yet the Estates-General never became an important political body. French kings tended to ignore it since they could set taxes and thus raise money without its help. The assembly therefore had little chance to restrict royal power. In contrast to the limited monarchy in England, France was moving toward **absolute monarchy**—a government in which the ruler has complete power.

● See below.

France, 1270

By 1270 most French towns had gained independence from feudal lords and were ruled directly by the king. In which regions did nobles still control large areas?

240

Map Answer: Flanders, Champagne, Burgundy, Brittany.

Background Louis IX carried a staff with the image of an open hand on it to symbolize his belief in fair dealing. He abolished trial by combat and insisted that guilt be proven by evidence alone. To control private wars among nobles, Louis IX imposed a forty-day "cooling-off" period before any action could be taken on conflicts between individuals.

● **ENRICHMENT.** Have students research and compare the growth of trade, towns, and the middle class in France and England during medieval times. Then have students evaluate the economic and political reasons that might account for England's development of a limited monarchy and France's move toward absolute monarchy. *(Synthesis)* ***Comparing Historical Developments***

The France, 1270 map:

ENGLAND
Calais
FLANDERS
HOLY ROMAN EMPIRE
English Channel
Seine R.
CHAMPAGNE
NORMANDY
Paris
BRITTANY
Troyes
ANJOU
Loire R.
BURGUNDY
POITOU
Bay of Biscay
Rhône R.
AQUITAINE
N W E S
GASCONY
Avignon
Toulouse
Mediterranean Sea

KEY
Land held by king of France
Lands held by French nobles
French land held by England

SCALE
0   100 mi
0   100 km

Below, sainted French king Louis IX (with halo) reads a book as his mother, Blanche of Castile, looks on. At right, he judges feudal lords responsible for hanging three youths.

Divided Germany and Italy

▲ Note strategies for third objective on this page and p. 242.

German duchies. The German lands had formed the eastern part of Charlemagne's empire (page 215). When the empire collapsed, the German lands broke into large **duchies** (DUTCH-eez)—lands ruled by dukes. Following an ancient Germanic practice, the dukes elected a fellow noble as king. The German king, however, had little authority outside his own lands; the other duchies were largely independent of his rule.

Otto the Great, who became the German king in 936, began expanding royal power. He defeated some of the German dukes in war and formed alliances with others. He also made the Church in Germany an ally in his disputes with other nobles. By this action, Otto set the stage for a long struggle for power between the German kings and the Pope.

The Holy Roman Empire. In 962 Otto persuaded the Pope to crown him "Emperor of the Romans." Like Charlemagne, Otto thought this title showed that he now possessed the greatness of the ancient Romans as well as the backing of the Church. Later German kings also claimed the title, and the lands they ruled came to be called the Holy Roman Empire (map, page 244).

Sec. Rev.
ques. 5

241

▲ RETEACHING. Have students review "German duchies" and "The Holy Roman Empire" (pp. 241–242) and summarize the factors contributing to German disunity. (German lands were divided; the king had no real power; many resisted Holy Roman emperors.) *(Comprehension)* **Summarizing Information**

Background Note that the land ruled by the German kings was called "holy" because it was consecrated by the Pope and "Roman" because it recalled the time when Europe was unified under Rome.

▲ REINFORCEMENT. Ask: (a) How did Otto the Great try to expand royal power? (He defeated some dukes in wars and formed alliances with others; he made the Church in Germany an ally in his disputes with other nobles.) (b) How was Italy divided in the 1300's? (South: kingdoms of Naples and Sicily. North: rich and independent city-states. Central: Papal states.) *(Comprehension)* **Discussing History**

Otto the Great and later Holy Roman emperors worked hard to preserve and extend their control over Italy. Independent northern Italian cities, however, had no wish to be part of the Holy Roman Empire. Many of the German dukes also refused to submit to rule by the Holy Roman emperors. Weakened by their struggles with the Italian cities, the Holy Roman emperors never fully established control over the German dukes.

Italy. Like the German lands, Italy remained divided during the Middle Ages. By the 1300's Italy was broken into several regions. In the south were the kingdoms of Naples and Sicily, sometimes known as the Kingdom of the Two Sicilies. Northern Italy was split into many rich and independent city-states that were often at war with each other. In central Italy, the Pope ruled the ▲ See Papal States (page 215). See Sec. 2 *Closing the Lesson,* below. p. T227B.

See lesson plans, pp. T227A–T227C.

Section Review

Answers to Section Review questions are in brackets on pages indicated.

1. **Define or identify:** Battle of Hastings, baron, common law, grand jury, trial jury, Magna Carta, parliament, limited monarchy, absolute monarchy, duchy. (pp. 236, 237, 238, 239, 241)
2. How did the power of kings change during the Middle Ages? Why? (p. 235)
3. How was the English monarchy made stronger by changes in English law? (p. 237)
4. What three basic principles did the Magna Carta establish? (p. 238)
5. Why did neither Germany nor Italy become united during the Middle Ages? (pp. 241–242)
6. **Critical thinking:** How were French monarchs able to gain more power than English monarchs? (See answer below, left.)

3 The Growth of Church Authority

Objectives

Focus Questions

★ ■ What internal problems and political struggles did the Church face? *(pages 242–244)*

• ■ How did the Church respond to its opponents? *(pages 244–245)*

Terms to Know

cardinal	heresy
depose	Inquisition
excommunicate	friar
Concordat of Worms	layman

★ Note strategies for first objective on this page and p. 244.

In the 1100's and 1200's, the European economy prospered and governments provided more order and stability. The period

242 was also marked by a growing religious vital-

ity. Some Church officials called for greater devotion among the clergy. Popes tried to prevent lords and kings from interfering with Church affairs. They also tried to make sure that Christians obeyed Church teachings.

The Need for Church Reform

In the early 900's the Church faced many problems. Some leading families in Italy saw the papacy as a political prize. They plotted and even committed murder to get relatives named as Pope. Such activities weakened the prestige and moral authority of the Pope.

The Church's problems extended far beyond Rome. The Church had lost control over the appointment of bishops, who now were chosen by kings and lords. Bishops were often selected for political reasons and not for devotion to Church duties. In this way, rulers controlled the churches and monasteries in their territories.

Sec. Rev. ques. 2

▲ **ENRICHMENT.** Have students make a chart comparing the political systems of England, France, Germany, and Italy during medieval times. *(Application) Translating Information into Another Form*

6. Answers will vary. Students should note that French monarchs set taxes and thus raised money without the help of Estates-General. The monarchs ruled without limits on their power. In England, Parliament checked the monarch's power.

★ **RETEACHING.** Have students review "The Need for Church Reform" (pp. 242–243) and identify three problems that weakened the Church. (Some fought to control the papacy; the Church lost control over the appointment of bishops; the spirituality of some clergy declined.) *(Comprehension) Identifying Causes*

★ **REINFORCEMENT.** Have students work in groups to dramatize the conflict between Pope Gregory VII and Holy Roman Emperor Henry IV. *(Application) Understanding Point of View*

Another problem for the Church was a decline in spiritual values among the clergy. Many priests and monks showed more interest in wealth and pleasures than in the Church's work.

Devoted members of the clergy began calling for reform. The monks of the French abbey of Cluny, founded in 910, demanded that clergymen live strict and holy lives. The monks of Cluny opposed the buying of Church offices as well as political control over monasteries.

In the middle of the eleventh century a Church council tried to end political involvement in the appointment of Popes. The council named a group of leading clergymen, called **cardinals**, to be responsible for choosing the Pope.

Conflict Between Pope and Emperor

The most determined supporter of reform was a Benedictine monk who became Pope Gregory VII in 1073. Gregory believed that the Pope's mission was to build a Christian society on earth. He declared that emperors had a solemn duty to obey the Pope, the spiritual leader of the Christian world. This led to a struggle between Gregory and Henry IV, the Holy Roman Emperor from 1056 to 1106.

The trouble began over the appointment of bishops. Pope Gregory insisted that only the Church had the power to name bishops. Henry did not agree. The German bishops were his most important allies. If he could not appoint them, he would lose their support.

Sec. Rev. ques. 3

Struggle over authority. Gregory claimed that he, as Pope, could **depose** the emperor—that is, remove him from the throne. Henry would not hear of such a thing. He fired off a letter saying that Gregory was "now not Pope, but false monk." Pope Gregory, in turn, decided to **excommunicate** Henry—in other words, to expel him from the Church. The decree of excommunication, filed in 1076, read, "I declare Henry deprived of his kingdom in Germany and Italy because he has rebelled against the Church."

This decree in effect also freed the German nobles from their feudal loyalty to Henry. The conflict over the appointment of bishops had grown into a struggle over who had supreme authority—the Holy Roman Emperor or the Pope.

The German bishops hesitated to support Henry, fearing they might also be excommunicated. The German nobles seized the opportunity to strike at Henry's power, and civil war swept through Germany. Matters grew worse when the nobles invited Pope Gregory to travel to Germany to crown a new emperor.

Journey to Canossa. To stop the Pope, Henry went to Italy in January 1077. He hoped to persuade Gregory to lift the ban of excommunication. This action would deprive the German lords of their legal grounds for rebellion.

Henry arrived at Canossa (kuh-NAHS-uh), where Gregory was a guest of Matilda of Tuscany, who ruled much of central Italy and was one of the Pope's strongest supporters.

Pope Gregory VII (at left) and Emperor Henry IV (kneeling) negotiate for power at Canossa as Countess Matilda of Tuscany mediates.

243

Holy Roman Empire About 1200

The Holy Roman Empire, located in Central Europe, included many small states. How did its boundaries compare with those of Charlemagne's empire (map, page 215)? What city was the capital of the papal lands?

Map Answers: (1) The Holy Roman Empire did not include Gaul (France) but did include Sardinia and more of Eastern Europe. (2) Rome.

For three days the German emperor stood barefoot in the snow outside the castle walls until Pope Gregory agreed to forgive him. The image of the emperor begging for forgiveness increased the prestige of the papacy. The journey to Canossa was a victory for Henry too, because Gregory gave up his plan to support the rebellious German lords and crown a new emperor.

244

Vocabulary Note that a *concordat* is a formal agreement between the Church and a sovereign state.

The Concordat of Worms. Years later, in 1122, the Church and a new Holy Roman Emperor, Henry V, reached a compromise at the city of Worms (VORMZ) in Germany. In this agreement, called the **Concordat of Worms**, Henry gave up the right to appoint bishops. Bishops were to be chosen only by the Church. In return, Henry kept the right to grant lands and political powers to bishops.

Renewed conflict. The Concordat of Worms recognized the Church as the supreme authority in *spiritual* matters. It did not settle the question of who held supreme *political* power. Popes continued to claim that kings and emperors should answer to the papacy. The Holy Roman Emperors rejected these claims. They also tried to get control of the prosperous northern Italian city-states.

Between 1154 and 1186, Holy Roman Emperor Frederick I (known as Frederick Barbarossa, or "Red Beard") made six military expeditions to Italy. The Italian city-states, aided by the Pope, managed to resist the attacks. Yet Frederick's expeditions, like Henry IV's conflict with Pope Gregory VII, weakened the emperor's authority.

Papal power reached its high point under Pope Innocent III (1198–1216), who stated that the Pope, "lower than God but higher than man, judges all and is judged by no one." Innocent made the papacy the center of European political life. He claimed that the Pope had the right to intervene in the affairs of any kingdom. For example, when King John of England (page 238) ignored the Pope's wishes, Innocent excommunicated John and took steps to close the churches in England. Eventually John backed down and became a vassal of the Pope.

★ See below, left.

The Battle Against Heresy

● Note strategies for second objective on this page and p. 245.

Popes believed that they had a sacred mission to show people the way to salvation. For this reason, they fought monarchs who challenged papal authority. For the same reason, they opposed **heresy** (HEHR-uh-see)—the holding of beliefs that the Church considered

Religion The Dominican Order was the first major religious order to emphasize intellectual work rather than manual labor.

Biography Francis of Assisi dedicated his life to poverty. He claimed to have married "the fairest of all brides, the Lady Poverty."

wrong. (People accused of heresy were called heretics.)

Freedom of religion is a modern idea that had no place in the medieval outlook. The clergy taught that people had to obey God's rules exactly as taught by the one true Church. Heresy was the greatest crime in the Middle Ages. The Church held that heretics had committed treason against God.

The Church tried to persuade heretics to give up their beliefs. If that failed, it threatened them with excommunication. An excommunicated person was expelled from the Church and denied the sacraments. This unfortunate person lived without friends, died without the comfort of a priest, and was denied hope of salvation.

Challenges to Church beliefs. In the 1100's and 1200's several groups challenged the teachings of the Church. One such group was the Albigensians (al-buh-JEN-see-unz), who were especially strong in southern France. They taught that anything physical or material was evil, and they insisted that Jesus never took a human form. When the Albigensians refused to give up their beliefs, Pope Innocent III in 1209 called on kings and lords to destroy them. A merciless war to crush the Albigensians went on for more than 20 years.

The Inquisition. In 1232 Pope Gregory IX set up the Inquisition—a Church court that searched for suspected heretics and put them on trial. The accused people were urged to confess their crime and to ask forgiveness. Sometimes torture was used to make people admit to heresy. If they confessed, they were given minor punishments and welcomed back into the Church. If they did not confess, or if they held to their beliefs, they were turned over to the government for punishment. Heretics might face the loss of their property, exile, or imprisonment. Some were even burned at the stake.

New Religious Orders

Sec. Rev. ques. 4 [Religious zeal also led to the establishment of two orders of friars. Friars were monks who did not live in monasteries but wandered

among the people, preaching and doing good works.

The Dominican order was started by Saint Dominic (1170–1221), a Spanish nobleman. Known as the Preaching Friars, the Dominicans included some of the leading teachers of religion in medieval universities. They also served as missionaries and worked actively in the Inquisition and in other efforts to stamp out heresy.

A second order of friars, the Franciscans, took their name from their founder, Saint Francis of Assisi (1182–1226). Born into a wealthy Italian merchant family, Francis had an intense religious experience when he was in his mid-20's. This experience caused him to give up his possessions and devote himself to trying to live as Jesus had.

Francis went into villages and towns preaching, healing, and befriending people. He soon gathered a band of followers who adopted his way of life. The Franciscans grew from a movement of inspired laymen—people outside the clergy—into an organized religious order that carried out the policies of the Popes. The Franciscans served the Church as teachers and eventually as missionaries in Eastern Europe, North Africa, the Middle East, and China.

● See below, left.

See Sec. 3 *Closing the Lesson*, p. T227C.

Section Review

Answers to Section Review questions are in brackets on pages indicated.

1. **Define or identify:** cardinal, depose, excommunicate, Concordat of Worms, heresy, Inquisition, friar, layman. (pp. 243, 244, 245)
2. What problems troubled the Church in the tenth century? (pp. 242–243)
3. Why did Pope Gregory VII and Henry IV come into conflict with each other? What was the result? (pp. 243–244)
4. In what ways did the religious orders formed in the late 1100's seek to serve the Church? (p. 245)
5. **Critical thinking:** Which was a greater threat to the Church, a heretic or a monarch who opposed the Church's role in politics? Why? (See answer below.)

245

● ENRICHMENT. Have students find information on Albigensianism and other medieval heresies; St. Francis of Assisi; or St. Dominic. Students might explain why heresies developed and how they differed from Church teachings; or report on the lives of St. Francis or St. Dominic, and describe how their families, friends, and the Church responded to the establishment of their orders. *(Synthesis)* *Locating Information*

Religion People who confessed to crimes during the Inquisition were given penances like flogging, fasting, making a pilgrimage, or paying a fine. Some were forced to wear a yellow "cross of infamy" and suffer social ostracism. Since the Church was not permitted to shed blood, heretics sentenced to death were turned over to the civil government.

5. Some students might argue that by widely influencing others' beliefs, heretics could threaten the Church's existence. Others might argue that monarchs constantly challenged the Church's political powers.

4 The Expansion of Christian Europe

Objectives

Focus Questions

★ ■ How did Christians recapture European lands from the Muslims?
   (page 246)
● ■ Why did the Crusades fail to keep Palestine under Christian control?
   (pages 247–250)
▲ ■ How did German culture expand eastward? *(page 250)*

Terms to Know

Reconquest
Hanseatic League

★ Note strategies for first objective on this page.

As you read in Chapter 10, invading Muslims had threatened Christian Europe in the early Middle Ages. By the eleventh century, however, the kings and great lords of Western and Central Europe had grown powerful enough to take the offensive against the Muslims.

The Recapture of European Lands

Around 1015 the Italian city-states of Genoa and Pisa drove the Muslims from the island of Sardinia. By the end of the century Norman knights had retaken Sicily from the Muslims. Italian and Norman ships began to patrol the western Mediterranean, preventing the Muslims from attacking Christian ships. This gave the Italian city-states an open route to the rich markets of the eastern Mediterranean lands.

246 Christians also waged war against the Muslims in Spain. In the middle of the eighth

century, Muslims controlled most of present-day Spain and Portugal. Only some small kingdoms in the northern part of that peninsula remained in Christian hands. These Christian kingdoms, determined to recover the rest of Spain, began a 500-year struggle known as the **Reconquest**. From the eleventh century on, the Christian rulers of Castile (kas-TEEL) led the war against the Muslims in Spain, regaining considerable territory (see map below). As a result of the Reconquest, by the thirteenth century, only the kingdom of Granada was still held by the Muslims.

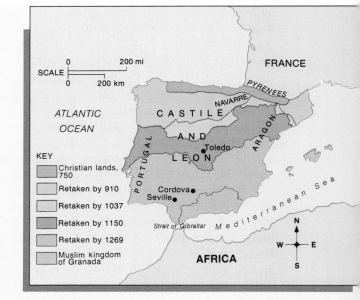

KEY
- Christian lands, 750
- Retaken by 910
- Retaken by 1037
- Retaken by 1150
- Retaken by 1269
- Muslim kingdom of Granada

Christian Reconquest of Spain, 750–1269

After Muslims conquered most of Spain, the remaining Christian kingdoms began the struggle to regain control. By what year was most of Spain again under Christian rule?

Map Answer: 1269

Christians and Muslims clashed frequently during the period of the Crusades. In these battles, the swift, lightly armored Turkish horsemen (shown at left) often held a tactical advantage over the heavily armored Christians.

The Crusades

● Note strategies for second objective on this page and p. 249.

The call to arms. Meanwhile, at the end of the eleventh century, Europeans decided to carry the struggle against Islam to Palestine, which they called the Holy Land. In 1095 Pope Urban II appealed to the lords and knights of Europe to free the Holy Land from the Seljuk Turks (page 202). The Pope wanted Jerusalem to be in Christian hands. He hoped, too, that the knights and lords would stop fighting among themselves and come together for a Christian cause—the recovery of the Holy Land.

Sec. Rev. ques. 2

Pope Urban's appeal created great excitement. Lords and knights, eager for glory, adventure, and wealth, began to organize armies. They saw themselves as armed pilgrims who would rescue Christian holy places from the Muslims. "God wills it!" people cried with spirit. Thus, the Crusades began. The word *crusade* comes from the Latin word *crux,* meaning "cross." The Crusaders—those who took part in these religious wars—sewed the symbol of the cross on their outer garments.

The Peasant Crusade. The spirit of the Crusades quickly spread through Western Europe. Some preachers wandered from village to village, urging the common people to join in the Crusades. The most remarkable of these preachers was Peter the Hermit. Small and thin, with a long gray beard, Peter rode a **247**

The Four Major Crusades, 1096–1204

What was the general direction of the Crusades? What four states were established by the Crusaders? Which Crusades passed through Vienna? Which Crusade ended at Constantinople? Compare this map with the world map in the Atlas at the back of this book. What countries now exist in the area where the Crusaders carved out Christian states?

Map Answers: (1) East. (2) Edessa, Antioch, Tripoli, Kingdom of Jerusalem. (3) First, second, and third. (4) Fourth. (5) Syria, Iraq, Jordan, Lebanon, Israel.

donkey through the French countryside, calling the peasants to march with him. Similarly, a knight called Walter the Penniless roused German peasants.

Thousands of poor people left their villages and joined the Peasant Crusade. These simple folk, who knew little of the world outside their villages, expected to find Jerusalem just beyond the horizon. Some thought that they were heading straight to heaven.

The Peasant Crusade quickly got out of hand. Regarding all non-Christians as enemies of the faith, the peasants began massacring Jews, despite the objections of bishops. Few of the peasants ever reached Jerusalem. Most were trapped in Asia Minor by Muslim forces and then wiped out.

The First Crusade. The first major Crusade was more carefully planned than the peasant marches. In 1096, lords and knights

248

Biography Peter the Hermit promised his followers that God would guide them to Jerusalem. His preaching was so effective that entire families decided to follow him. Many of Peter's listeners, convinced that he was immortal, plucked the hairs from his donkey's tail for souvenirs.

gathered together armies that met in Constantinople the following year. From there the knights crossed to Asia Minor. A Crusader described the hardships they faced:

66 Hunger and thirst attacked us everywhere and we had hardly anything left to eat except thorns. Such was the food on which we wretchedly lived. Most of our horses died, so that many of our knights had to go on foot; we used goats, sheep, and dogs to carry our baggage. 99

The Christian army arrived at Antioch and captured it from the Turks after a long siege. In June 1099, more than two years after leaving their homes, the Crusaders stood outside the walls of Jerusalem. Five weeks later the Christians captured the city.

In what became known as the First Crusade, the knights of Europe had won a victory. They had captured Jerusalem and carved out four Christian states in the Middle East (map, page 248). Yet these Christian states were like islands in a Muslim sea. They had little chance of surviving.

The Second Crusade. After the Muslims retook Edessa, one of the Christian states, in 1144, a Second Crusade was organized. King Louis VII of France and the Holy Roman Emperor, Conrad III, raised large forces. These armies suffered terrible losses to the Turks; only a small number of the Crusaders even reached the Holy Land.

Under Saladin (SAL-uh-din), sultan of Egypt, the Muslims fought back against the Christian invaders. Famous for his bravery and honor, Saladin was admired even by the Christian knights. Saladin united both Egyptian and Syrian Muslims under his command. In 1187 he invaded Palestine and recaptured several cities, including Jerusalem.

The Third Crusade. Shocked by the loss of Jerusalem, the leading rulers in Europe took up the cross in the Third Crusade (1189–1192). These rulers were Richard I of England, Philip Augustus of France, and Holy Roman Emperor Frederick I. Rivalry between the English and French kings doomed this expedition. Furthermore, the Crusaders were no match for Saladin's able army.

The Fourth Crusade. As leader of Christian Europe, Pope Innocent III called for a Fourth Crusade. In 1202 about 10,000 Crusaders gathered in Venice, Italy, ready to depart for the Holy Land. Only a few ever reached the Middle East to fight the Muslims. Instead, the bulk of the army attacked Constantinople in 1204. They looted churches and massacred the Byzantine defenders. The Pope was enraged, for the Fourth Crusade did much to tarnish the image of the crusading movement.

Sec. Rev. ques. 3

The Muslims, meanwhile, continued to retake the lands that had been conquered by the Christian Crusaders. In 1291, almost 200 years after Pope Urban's speech, the last of the Christian outposts in Palestine fell to the Muslims.

Results of the Crusades

1. Loss of papal prestige. In the beginning, the Crusades had strengthened the power of the papacy. It was the Pope who had inspired the crusading armies and acted as their spiritual leader. Later Popes, however, called for crusades against heretics and rulers who resisted papal commands. Many Christians came to believe that the papacy was using religious zeal merely to boost the Church's political power. As these criticisms grew, the prestige of the papacy fell.

2. Decline in the power of nobles. The Crusades proved disastrous for many of the nobles who took part. Some were killed in battle; others lost their fortunes paying for weapons and the long voyage to the Holy Land. Monarchs took advantage of their weakened opponents to strengthen royal power. Thus, feudalism was weakened.

3. Increase in trade. Another result of the Crusades was an increase in trade. Europeans who went on the Crusades came to know and value the products of the East—

● See below.

249

Biography During a battle between the forces of Richard and Saladin, the sultan learned that Richard's horse had been killed in the fighting. Saladin immediately sent two horses for Richard's use. A man of enormous courage and a proven military leader, Saladin was also a patient statesman and a chivalrous warrior. He once urged his followers to "abstain from the shedding of blood, for blood that is spilt never slumbers."

Check for Understanding. Ask: How did the Crusades result in the loss of papal prestige? (Many Christians believed that the Pope used religious zeal to increase the Church's political power.)
● **ENRICHMENT.** Have students work in groups to debate the following: *Despite the eventual loss of all lands captured from the Turks, the Crusades benefited Europe.* **Students might consider both the costs and the results of the Crusades.** (Evaluation) *Making Judgments*

Bruges, one of medieval Europe's most important commercial cities, traded with cities of the Hanseatic League. Pictured here is the Town Hall of Bruges, built in the 1300's.

sugar, rice, fruits, spices, silk, cotton, cosmetics, pistachio nuts, mirrors, dyes, perfumes, and many other goods. The demand for these goods led to greater trade between East and West, and the Italian cities benefited. Italian merchants bought products from the East, which they sold at large profits to eager buyers in Western Europe.

German Expansion Eastward

▲ Note strategies for third objective on this page.

The enthusiasm for the Crusades and the success of the Reconquest reflected the growing strength of Christian Europe during the 1100's and 1200's. A third sign was the German conquest and colonization of areas south of the Baltic Sea.

Several factors led to this German expansion. Lords hoped to carve out new estates, while peasants wanted land of their own and freedom from life in the manors. Missionaries wished to convert the people of these new lands to Christianity. Merchants were looking for new opportunities for trade.

The Germans did succeed in conquering some Slavic peoples and converting them

250

to Christianity. During the 1200's they also won victories over the Prussians, a people living along the Baltic Sea.

The German expansion eastward had important consequences. Thousands of German settlers, merchants, and missionaries moved into the Baltic Sea region. Towns were started in places where city life had been unknown. Using the new heavy plows (page 229), the German colonists cleared vast plots of land for farming. This expansion increased German territory by a third, while spreading Christianity and the German language and culture into a large area.

Sec. Rev. ques. 4

Colonization of the new lands also encouraged trade. In the late 1200's, cities along the Baltic Sea joined with the older German cities in a trade league. Through this alliance the cities hoped to expand their trade, to protect shipping from pirates, and to defend themselves from rivals such as Denmark. In the middle 1300's the trade union became known as the **Hanseatic League** (han-see-AT-ik). The member cities controlled much of the trade of northern Europe, from the eastern end of the Baltic Sea to the western end of the North Sea (map, page 230).

See Sec. 4 *Closing the Lesson*, p. T227D.

Answers to Section Review questions are in brackets on pages indicated.

1. **Define or identify:** Reconquest, Hanseatic League. (pp. 246, 250)
2. Why did Pope Urban II command Christians to win the Holy Land from the Muslims? (p. 247)
3. How did the Fourth Crusade discredit the Church? (p. 249)

4. Why was the expansion of the Germans into Eastern Europe important? (p. 250)
5. **Critical thinking:** Describe the religious, political, and economic effects of the Crusades. (See answer below.)

5. Answers will vary, but students should note the following: loss of papal prestige, weakening of feudalism, and increased trade.

Chapter 12   Summary and Timeline

1. The 1100's and 1200's were a period of vitality for Western Europe. Changes in agriculture increased food production and led to population growth. Trade revived, banking practices developed, and merchants and artisans formed guilds. The growth of towns contributed to the decline of serfdom and led to the rise of the middle class.

2. Powerful rulers laid the foundations of national states in Europe. England was unified soon after the Norman conquest in 1066, but it took French kings centuries to create a unified state. The development of Parliament and the Magna Carta limited the power of the English monarch. There were no similar checks on the French king.

3. The Church used its strength and organization to punish its opponents. Church demands for a role in European politics created disputes with the Holy Roman Emperor and other monarchs. These quarrels prevented the development of unified states in Germany and Italy. The Church campaign against heresy led to the Inquisition and the formation of two important orders. These orders performed missionary work as well.

4. The Church also tried to expand the area of Christian influence by retaking Muslim lands in Spain. The Crusades, an attempt by Europeans to take control of the Holy Land from the Muslim Turks, ended in failure, weakening both the Church and the nobles. Nevertheless, the Crusades did stimulate trade between Europe and the East. Meanwhile, Germans made conversions for Christianity along the Baltic coast.

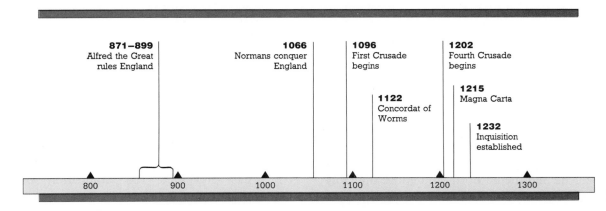

| 871–899 Alfred the Great rules England | 1066 Normans conquer England | 1096 First Crusade begins | 1122 Concordat of Worms | 1202 Fourth Crusade begins | 1215 Magna Carta | 1232 Inquisition established |

800   900   1000   1100   1200   1300

See p. T227D for answers to Chapter Review.

Vocabulary Review

1. Use each of the following terms in a sentence: *baron, charter, common law, excommunicate, guild, limited monarchy, middle class, parliament.*
2. Use the following terms to complete the sentences below: *absolute monarchy, apprentice, Battle of Hastings, cardinal, Hanseatic League, heresy, Inquisition, trial jury.*
   a. A ___?___ has the power to settle disputes in court.
   b. Partly because the Estates-General was a weak political body, France moved toward ___?___.
   c. Before becoming a member of a craft guild, a young person first served as an ___?___.
   d. In 1066, invading Normans defeated the Saxon king at the ___?___.
   e. A ___?___ was a leading clergyman, responsible for helping to choose the Pope.
   f. The ___?___ was set up to search for and try people suspected of ___?___.
   g. German cities formed a trade union known as the ___?___.

People to Identify

Choose the name that best completes each sentence.
1. [Saint Dominic/Saint Francis] founded an order known as the Preaching Friars.
2. The Norman ruler who invaded England in 1066 was [William the Conqueror/Philip Augustus].
3. [Gregory VII/Innocent III] claimed that he had the authority to depose the Holy Roman Emperor.
4. English barons forced [John/Alfred the Great] to agree to the Magna Carta.
5. [Henry IV/Peter the Hermit] recruited French peasants to fight in the Crusades.

Places to Know

Use the following place names to complete the sentences below: *England, France, Holy Roman Empire, Spain.*
1. The Reconquest was a struggle to recover the rest of ___?___.
2. The ___?___ included many German duchies.
3. In ___?___, Norman and Anglo-Saxon speech combined to form a new language.
4. One obstacle to unity in ___?___ was that England controlled much of that country's territory.

Recalling the Facts

1. What developments increased food production in the 1100's and 1200's?
2. How did partnerships, letters of credit, and banks each contribute to the growth of trade?
3. How did towns contribute to the decline of serfdom?
4. What changes did Henry I and Henry II make in the English legal system?
5. What limits did the Magna Carta put on the powers of the king? How did the growth of Parliament affect royal power?
6. Why did the Estates-General have little power in France?
7. What prevented the unification of Germany and Italy?

252

8. What problems did the Church face in the tenth century?

9. What was the Concordat of Worms?

10. What steps did the Church take to respond to heresy?

11. What did Pope Urban II hope the Crusades would accomplish?

12. Why did the Germans decide to expand eastward? What were the results?

1. **Researching words.** The common law in England is the law that applies to all citizens. *Common* comes from the Latin *communis*. Using a dictionary, find the meaning of the following words with the same root: *communicate, community, commonwealth.* (App.)

2. **Translating visual information to written form.** What are the people doing in the picture below? To what social class do these people probably belong? What three sources of power do you see? What two medieval inventions are shown? Write a description of a typical day in the lives of these people. (App.)

The Pierpont Morgan Library, New York M.399 f.8 v

3. **Critical thinking.** Compare common law to the legal system that existed in England before the reign of Henry I. Why was the common law considered a fairer system of justice? (Syn.)

Thinking About Geography

Analyzing. For trading purposes, where were towns in medieval Europe most likely to develop? In answering, consider access to land and water trade routes. Support your conclusions with specific examples from the map on page 230. (Comp.)

Enrichment: Primary Sources

Along with the growth of medieval towns came the formation of merchant and craft guilds. The following adapted passage lists some of the rules of a merchant guild in Southampton, England.

❝ If any guildsman strikes another with his fist and is convicted thereof, he shall lose membership in the guild until he shall have paid ten shillings and taken the oath of the guild again like a new member.

No one of the city of Southampton shall buy anything to sell again in the same city, unless he is of the guild.

No one of the guild ought to be partner in any business with anyone who is not of the guild.

If any guildsman falls into poverty and has not the means to live and is not able to work or to provide for himself, he shall receive aid from the guild. ❞

1. According to the guild rules, what was the punishment for a person who struck another guild member?

2. What rules of the guild concerned people who were not members?

3. **Critical thinking:** Today, who would perform the kind of function mentioned in the last paragraph? (Syn.)

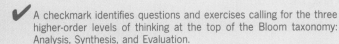

A checkmark identifies questions and exercises calling for the three higher-order levels of thinking at the top of the Bloom taxonomy: Analysis, Synthesis, and Evaluation.

Europe in Late Medieval Times   1050–1485

(pp. 254–268)

Chapter Preview

This chapter examines the revival of learning that took place in the Middle Ages, with special emphasis on the rise of universities and on the beliefs of medieval scholars. In Section 1, medieval achievements in literature and architecture are discussed and the influences of medieval civilization on modern thought are analyzed. Section 2 explains the reasons for the decline of medieval civilization in the fourteenth century, how the French and English monarchies became stronger, and why the Church's political power weakened.

Bibliography

See the *Teacher's Management and Planning Guide* for additional listings. Starred titles are for both students and teachers.

Herlihy, David. *Medieval Households*. Harvard University Press. Medieval family as a moral and emotional unit.

*Labarge, Margaret Wade. *A Small Sound of the Trumpet: Women in Medieval Life*. Beacon Press. The roles of medieval women at all social levels.

Matthew, Donald. *The Atlas of the Medieval World*. Facts on File. Rich in illustrations as well as maps.

Thompson, M. W. *The Decline of the Castle*. Cambridge University Press. The role of castles in medieval life and why they disappeared.

*Tuchman, Barbara W. *A Distant Mirror: The Calamitous Fourteenth Century*. Ballantine. The collapse of the medieval order.

Section Lesson Plans

SECTION 1   (pp. 255–261)
A Revival of Learning and Culture

Objectives

After completing this section, students will be able to:
1. Describe how learning advanced in medieval times.
2. Explain what new forms of literature, art, and architecture developed.

Introducing the Lesson

Remind students that culture is a unique way of life developed by a society. Although people express culture in many ways, language, literature, and art are three of the most important.

Then ask: *(a) What might account for the development of culture?* (Answers will vary. Human societies develop characteristics that distinguish them from others. These characteristics are influenced by particular geographic and historical factors.)

(b) How might language express the uniqueness of a culture group? (A language acquires words and phrases that express the particular historical experiences, philosophy, and beliefs of a people.)

(c) What information might a society's level of learning provide? (Answers will vary. An educational system often reflects the level of technological advancement and social organization.)

Developing the Lesson:
Understanding Point of View

Have students explain the viewpoint of someone who might have supported or opposed the following medieval religious concern: *Faith and reason are incompatible ideas.* Students might present the views of a medieval thinker who was concerned that reliance on reason could lead a person away from God or might represent the views of a Scholastic. Have students present their ideas in class. *(Application)*

Developing the Lesson:
Synthesizing Information

Have students write a character sketch of the medieval hero as described in the literature of the Middle Ages. Students should consider the characters described in medieval drama, poetry, epics, and songs. (The medieval hero was a devout Christian, usually a knight or a warrior, who was brave, loyal, and chivalrous. He honored and respected women and pledged his loyalty and devotion to his lady.) *(Comprehension)*

Closing the Lesson:
Organizing Information

Have students make a chart organizing the text information on medieval architecture. Students should list the distinguishing characteristics of Romanesque and Gothic architecture. (Romanesque architecture had rounded arches, massive walls, small windows, little color decoration, and dark interiors. Gothic architecture had pointed arches, flying buttresses, taller and less massive walls, stained-glass windows, and interiors filled with light.) *(Comprehension)*

See *Section Review* questions, p. 261.

SECTION 2　　　　　　　　(pp. 261–266)
The End of the Middle Ages

Objectives

After completing this section, students will be able to:
1. Describe the problems that troubled Europe in the late Middle Ages.
2. Explain how the English and French monarchies grew stronger.
3. Discuss why the prestige of the Church declined.

Introducing the Lesson

Remind students that the focus of political power shifted from the Church to stronger monarchies at the end of the Middle Ages. After centuries of political influence, the authority of the Church was challenged by the actions of kings.

Then ask: *(a) What might account for the shift of political power from one institution to another?* (Answers will vary. Political power is a result of factors such as popular support, wealth, type of government, and social and economic conditions. If these factors change, then the power of institutions may be affected.)
(b) What factors might indicate a loss of political power? (Answers will vary. Difficulty in enforcing decisions, a decrease in popular support, or an increase in the importance of a rival might indicate a loss of power.)
(c) What do you think are the most powerful institutions today? Why? (Answers will vary.)

Developing the Lesson:
Comparing Historical Developments

Have students make a chart comparing the social, political, and economic characteristics of medieval Europe at its height with changes that occurred at the end of the Middle Ages. (The end of the Middle Ages saw a decline in agricultural production, a decreasing population, increased warfare, stronger monarchies, a weakening of the noble class, and the decline of Church authority.) *(Comprehension)*

Developing the Lesson:
Understanding Cause and Effect

Have students write an essay explaining why the feudal system declined and Church power weakened at the end of the Middle Ages. (At the end of the Middle Ages, strong monarchies offered security and order at a time when the power of the nobles was weakening. As kings increased their political power, the Popes lost authority and influence, the Church was no longer the only unified institution, and state government rivaled the authority of the Church.) *(Comprehension)*

Closing the Lesson: Evaluating History

On the chalkboard draw a chart titled *The Importance of the Middle Ages for Western History* and include columns labeled *Economic, Social, Political, and Cultural Achievements.* Then have students work in groups to list the advances made in each area during the Middle Ages. Have each group compare its list with those of others. (*Economic:* agricultural improvements; new business practices; increased trade. *Social:* revival of towns; expansion of individual freedom; rise of the middle class. *Political:* limited monarchy; Magna Carta; rise of European states. *Cultural:* revival of universities; new forms of literature and art.) (*Evaluation*)

See *Section Review* questions, p. 261.

Chapter 13 Review Answers
(pp. 267–268)

Vocabulary Review

1. (a) curriculum (b) troubadour (c) vernacular (d) morality play
2. (a) Astrology—the attempt to predict events by studying the stars and planets; alchemy—the search for magic formulas or substances that would turn lead into gold. (b) Romanesque—style of architecture characterized by massive walls, rounded arches, and small windows; Gothic—style of architecture characterized by pointed arches, soaring heights, and huge windows. (c) Hundred Years' War—a war (1337–1453) between France and England; Wars of the Roses—a civil war (1455–1485) between two branches of the English royal family for control of the monarchy. (d) Babylonian Captivity—period from 1309 to 1377 when all the Popes were French and ruled from Avignon, not Rome; Great Schism—period from 1378 to 1417 when there were two Popes, one in Avignon and one in Rome.

People to Identify

1. Henry VII 2. Roger Bacon 3. Joan of Arc
4. Geoffrey Chaucer 5. John Ball 6. Dante
7. Thomas Aquinas 8. John Wycliffe; John Huss

Places to Know

1. A   2. B   3. C   4. D

Recalling the Facts

1. The growth of towns, the rise of the middle class, and increased contact with the civilizations of the Byzantine Empire and the Muslim world.
2. Some Christian thinkers thought the logic of the Greeks would lead people away from God. Scholastics believed reason could be used to explain Christian teachings.
3. Scientific investigations were mixed with ideas based on magic, superstition, and folk legends. Medieval scholars also continued to believe many mistaken theories of earlier Greek and Muslim thinkers.
4. Dante, Chaucer, and other poets wrote in vernacular languages, and troubadours composed songs in the vernacular.
5. Soil in heavily farmed areas became unproductive, cold weather reduced food supplies by shortening the growing season, and many farm workers died from the Black Death.
6. They rebelled against new taxes and social inequality.
7. Philip defied church laws and even had the Pope arrested.

Critical Thinking Skills

1. Answers will vary.
2. a–1348; d–1378; f–1382; c–1429; e–1430; b–1453.
3. The war increased royal power. For England, the war meant the loss of French lands and an unpopular peace settlement, soon followed by civil war. The growing power of monarchs caused Popes to lose authority and political clout.
4. Students should be able to use what they have read about medieval art, religion, and education to dispute this view.

Thinking About Geography

1. It hurt their ability to produce food. Future armies would use this tactic to achieve the same result.

2. Answers will vary. Soldiers might have spread it as they conquered other peoples, merchants might have spread it as they traded with different regions, and colonists might have spread it as they established new homes in other parts of the Empire.

Enrichment: Primary Sources

1. That the plague was caused by the influence of the stars and planets or by God as punishment for human sins.

2. It could be caught through contact with the sick or with anything a sick person had touched.

3. Citizens and even family members avoided each other and refused to tend each other.

4. Many people believed that God was responsible for every happening on earth. People were also very superstitious.

Europe in Late Medieval Times   **1050–1485**

See chapter timeline, p. 266.

Before You Read This Chapter

Suppose you wanted to explain contemporary American culture to a stranger. What achievements in science and learning would you point out? What books, movies, or television shows would you mention? What kinds of buildings are typical of modern architecture? As you read this chapter, look for the cultural achievements made in medieval times. What features of medieval civilization have survived to become part of our culture today?

The Geographic Setting

The Chapter Outline

1. A Revival of Learning and Culture
2. The End of the Middle Ages

A colorful panel of stained glass from a fifteenth-century cathedral shows the architect and stonemasons who built the cathedral.

Vocabulary Note that the word *university* is from the Latin word, *universitas*, meaning "corporation" or "guild."

1 A Revival of Learning and Culture

Objectives

Focus Questions

★ ■ How did learning advance in medieval times? *(pages 255–257)*
● ■ What new forms of literature, art, and architecture developed? *(pages 258–261)*

Terms to Know

curriculum   vernacular
Scholastics   troubadour
astrology   Romanesque
alchemy   Gothic
morality play

★ Note strategies for first objective on this page and p. 256.

The height of the Middle Ages—the 1100's and 1200's—was a time of cultural richness in Europe. As towns sprouted and trade expanded, interest in learning revived too. Signs of this interest included the rise of universities and a rebirth of scientific studies.

The Revival of Learning

During the Middle Ages, trade brought Western Europeans into contact with the civilizations of the Byzantine Empire and the Muslim world. Scholars in these civilizations had continued to value and study ancient Greek works of literature, philosophy, and science. They had translated many of these writings into Arabic.

Sec. Rev. ques. 2

In Europe, Spain and Sicily became the main centers where ancient works were translated into Latin, the language of European scholars. A famous school of translation grew up at the university of Toledo in Muslim Spain. There Christian, Jewish, and Muslim scholars collected and translated Greek and Arabic manuscripts into Latin. Scholars from the Byzantine Empire and the Muslim lands in the Mediterranean also flocked to the court at Sicily.

The growth of European towns and the rise of the middle class encouraged the revival of learning. Townspeople had the money to pay for schools. Moreover, as a town's population grew, so did the need for educated people.

The First Universities

To gain an education, young people went to study with scholars (often monks or priests) who were famous for their learning. Over time, these meetings of students and teachers developed into universities. One of the first universities was established in 1088 at Bologna (boh-LOH-nyah) in Italy. By about 1200 there were also universities at Paris, at Oxford in England, and at Salerno in Italy.

The curriculum. Universities at first were organized somewhat like guilds (page 232). They set standards for courses and regulated students and teachers. To receive a degree of "master" and enter the teachers' guild, students had to pass examinations and write a scholarly paper.

The basic **curriculum**—the course of study—included seven subjects. These were grammar (Latin language and literature), rhetoric (composition and speech), logic (the art of reasoning), arithmetic, geometry, astronomy, and music. More advanced courses included studies in religion, law, and medicine. Lectures and examinations were given in Latin. Students read Latin translations of ancient texts, especially the works of Aristotle (page 88) and other Greek thinkers.

University life. The medieval student's day was long and hard. Students rose before five o'clock in the morning, were in church until six, and attended class until ten **255**

★ RETEACHING. Have students review "The Revival of Learning" and "The First Universities" (pp. 255–256) and then answer the following: (a) How did the growth of towns and the rise of the middle class encourage the revival of learning in Europe? (Townspeople had the money to pay for schools; the need for educated people increased.) (b) How were medieval universities like guilds? (They set standards and regulations.) (Comprehension) *Observing for Detail*

★ REINFORCEMENT. Have students write a letter that might have been written by a medieval student to friends back home. Letters should describe the course of study and life at the university. *(Application) Understanding Point of View*

Cultural History The university in Bologna, a student guild, differed from other schools that were professors' guilds. Students at Bologna controlled the university, hired and fired their professors, and fined them for unexcused absences and lateness, or for avoiding difficult questions.

o'clock. After a simple midday meal of soup or stew, they went back to classes until five in the afternoon.

Living conditions were often uncomfortable. Students sat on hard benches or on straw scattered on the floor. In winter, classrooms might be cold and damp. Candles provided the only light for studying at night. Books were costly and rare, for they had to be copied by hand on parchment, or sheepskin. Usually the teacher read aloud from a book while the students took notes on slates. Not until the 1400's did printed books come into use. Students relied on their memories to learn their assignments.

In some ways, medieval students were much like modern ones. Letters to students from their parents still sound familiar. One father wrote his son, "I have learned that you do not study in your room or act in the schools as a good student should, but play and wander about, disobedient to your master and indulging in sport." Another father complained that he had sent his son to college to study, but the boy preferred "play to work and strumming a guitar while the others are at their studies."

Students' letters home also brought up problems common today:

66 Well-beloved father, I have not a penny, nor can I get any except through you, for all things at the University are so expensive; nor can I study in my lawbooks, for they are all tattered. Moreover, I owe ten crowns in dues to the Provost [head of school], and can find no man to lend them to me. Well-beloved father, to ease my debts at the baker's, with the doctor, and to pay the laundress and the barber, I send you word of greetings and of money. 99

★ See below, right.

Scholarship Guided by Faith

The best minds of the Middle Ages studied the Bible and the writings of important clergy. When scholars wanted an answer to a question, they turned to the Bible and to Church

256

authorities. They saw Christian teachings as a guide to life and as the basis of knowledge. Medieval thinkers held that politics, economic life, law, and views of nature must be based on the Bible. To understand nature and society, they said, one first needed to understand God's plans for humanity.

The Scholastics. As the writings of ancient Greek philosophers and scientists began to be known in Western Europe, medieval thinkers faced a problem. Greek philosophy seemed to conflict with Christian teachings. Some Christian thinkers distrusted scholars who studied Greek philosophy. They thought that the logic of the Greeks would lead people away from God.

Medieval philosophers who were known as **Scholastics** disagreed. They argued that reason could be used to explain Christian teachings. The Scholastics did not challenge or reject Christian beliefs. They never doubted the existence of God, nor did they question the teachings of the Bible. "I would not be a philosopher if this were to separate me from Christ," wrote one Scholastic.

Sec. Rev. ques. 3

Aquinas. Probably the most brilliant Scholastic was Thomas Aquinas (uh-KWY-nus), a member of the Dominican order of monks in the 1200's. According to Aquinas, both reason and Christian teachings came from God. Therefore, he taught, reason and faith went hand in hand. Aquinas's book, *Summa Theologica,* used Aristotle's methods of logic to explain certain points in Church teachings. The *Summa* had an important influence on later Christian thinkers.

A New Interest in Science

Aquinas and many other medieval thinkers also took an interest in studying the natural world. Many ancient scientific works were translated into Latin during the Middle Ages. They were brought into Western Europe along with translations of the works of Muslim scholars. These writings, which had been unknown in Europe during the early Middle Ages, sparked a new interest in observing nature.

Cultural History The standard method of teaching at a medieval university was lecture. Examinations were given only after three, four, or five years of study. The tests were oral, very difficult, and designed to test the student's ability to think quickly and to express thoughts effectively.

Check for Understanding. Ask: Who were the Scholastics? (Medieval philosophers who argued that the study of Greek philosophy and the use of reason did not contradict Christian beliefs. They taught that reason could be used to explain Christian teachings.)

Cultural History Note that thirteenth-century Scholastics published collections of information on various subjects. These publications, called summa, were used as reference books.

★ ENRICHMENT. Have students compare the basic curriculum of the medieval university with a typical course of studies at a present-day college or university. Students might consult a college catalogue or arrange an interview with a university recruiter for information. (Application) Linking Past and Present

Bacon's ideas. One of the greatest medieval scientists was Roger Bacon (1214–1294). An English monk and philosopher, Bacon warned that too many thinkers neglected science. He himself studied Muslim writings on light rays, did experiments in optics, and observed that light traveled faster than sound. In his writings Bacon gave an accurate description of the eye and discussed the causes of tides and the appearance of rainbows.

Bacon felt sure that science would bring great changes in people's lives. He predicted that one day ships would move

     66 without rowers, . . . cars without animals to pull them. Also flying machines can be built so that a man sits in the midst of the machine turning some engine by which artificial wings are made to beat the air like a flying bird. Also

machines can be made for walking in the sea and rivers, even to the bottom without danger. 99

Bacon's ideas were so mystifying to some people that they thought he was using witchcraft.

The limitations of medieval science. Although medieval scholars made important experiments and observations of nature, their work also rested partly on magic, superstition, and folk legends. Some scholars pursued **astrology**—the attempt to predict events on earth by looking at the movements of stars and planets. Other scholars practiced **alchemy** (AL-kuh-mee)—the search for magic formulas that would turn lead into gold. (Alchemy eventually grew into modern chemistry.) Medieval scholars also continued to believe many mistaken theories of earlier Greek and Muslim scientific thinkers.

Sec. Rev. ques. 4

Cold, bare medieval classrooms made concentration difficult at times, but most university students willingly endured discomfort for the opportunities an education provided.

257

Science Many alchemists were educated people who felt that they could learn to perfect other elements if they could first make gold from lesser metals. Another aim of the alchemists was to discover the *elixir of life,* a substance believed to cure disease and lengthen life.

Check for Understanding. Ask: What were some of the limitations of medieval scientific study? (Much scientific work relied on magic, superstition, and folk legends and scholars relied on mistaken Greek and Muslim theories.)

Ⓕ FEATURE ACTIVITY. Have students write an epitaph that would have been appropriate for Chaucer's tombstone. *(Comprehension)*   *Translating Information Into Another Form.*

Ⓕ See above.

Biography

Geoffrey Chaucer

Poet, courtier, soldier, prisoner of war, royal valet, lawyer, civil servant, diplomat, justice of the peace—Geoffrey Chaucer was all of these. He led an eventful life in an eventful age. Between Chaucer's birth about 1340 and his death in 1400, England experienced a horrible plague, an international war, and a violent peasants' revolt.

The son of a London winemaker, Chaucer grew up among the small shopkeepers and the great merchants of the city. At the age of 15, he was employed as a personal attendant in a noble household. As he grew older, Chaucer learned the ways of high society and talked easily with dukes and princes. Eventually he became a trusted representative of the king himself. He served three kings of England: Edward III, Richard II, and Henry IV. Chaucer's broad experience made him a skilled observer of life at all levels of society.

Today, however, Chaucer is remembered not for his role in government but for his poetry. In the 1300's, French and Latin were the languages of literature in England. Serious literary works rarely appeared in English, which was the everyday language. Yet Chaucer chose to write in English. His most famous work, *The Canterbury Tales,* is rich in fascinating characters, worldly wisdom, and humor. By writing in English, Chaucer inspired other poets in his country to do the same. For this reason, Geoffrey Chaucer is honored as the father of English poetry.

Literature and Language

● Note strategies for second objective on this page and p. 261.

Medieval drama. Despite the revival of learning, most people in the Middle Ages still could not read or write. The spoken word—in hymns, songs, and dramas—was important in bringing Church teachings to a wide audience. Stories from the Bible and the lives of the saints were told in verse in religious pageants, or plays.

A later development in religious drama was the **morality play.** Characters represented human virtues and vices, such as Good Deeds or Greed. They acted out conflicts between good and evil, often in a comic way.

Vernacular languages. Since Roman times, Latin had been the language of the Church and of scholars. By the Middle Ages, however, Latin was no longer used in everyday speech, even in Italy. Instead, people spoke such languages as French, Spanish, Italian, and Portuguese. Because these languages all grew out of Latin, the language of the Romans, they are called Romance languages. Another group of languages, the Germanic languages, developed in northern Europe. All these **vernacular** (vur-NAK-yoo-lur)—local—languages began to be used

258

● RETEACHING. Have students review "Medieval drama" and "Vernacular languages" (above) and then explain how both might have affected society. (Medieval drama brought Church teachings to a wider audience. Vernacular languages might have unified people who shared a particular language.) *(Comprehension)* *Observing for Detail*
Check for Understanding. Ask: What was the purpose of medieval drama? (To spread Christian teachings.)

● REINFORCEMENT. Have students explain how medieval literature, art, and architecture expressed the values of the Middle Ages. (Drama was based on religious themes and stressed the importance of the Church; epics described heroic deeds of knights and warriors, and poems often reflected a knight's bravery, loyalty, and respect for noblewomen. Most medieval art and architecture focused on religion.) *(Comprehension)* *Interpreting Information* throughout Europe in written literature as well as in everyday speech.

Epic poetry. Old legends that had been told or sung were now written down in the vernacular. Some took the form of epic poetry, describing the heroic deeds of knights and warriors. Most medieval epics came from northern Europe. The oldest great literary work in a vernacular language is *Beowulf* (BAY-uh-wolf). Based on Danish legend, it was first written down in the early 700's in Anglo-Saxon, one of the languages of England. The poem tells the story of the hero Beowulf, who chased and killed the monster Grendel before becoming king of his people.

Epics also retold stories that had grown up around heroes of the early Middle Ages. In France, *The Song of Roland* was based on tales of the warriors of Charlemagne's court. In England, the tales were of the legendary King Arthur, his court at Camelot, and the knights of the Round Table. Arthur and his knights stood as shining examples of the medieval ideals of courage, faith, and chivalry. Other epics in Germany and Spain told tales of the heroes Siegfried and El Cid.

Poems and songs of love. Vernacular languages were also used by troubadours (TROO-bah-dorz)—poet-musicians at the castles and courts in Europe. Troubadours wrote short verses and songs about the pleasures of life and love. They addressed their poems to noblewomen, praising their beauty and promising them devotion. Unlike minstrels, who were professional entertainers, troubadours were usually nobles. The troubadour pledged to honor and serve his lady as loyally as he would his lord.

The troubadours' songs reflected an almost worshipful attitude toward women, at least in the upper classes. To prove worthy of his lady, a knight had to be brave, loyal, and charming. While courtly love reversed old ideas about men's superiority to women, it also created an artificial image of women. In the poets' eyes, noblewomen were always beautiful and pure.

Dante. The greatest poet of the Middle Ages was Dante (DAHN-tay) of Florence, Italy. In the tradition of the troubadours, Dante (1265–1321) wrote love poems to his beloved Beatrice. His masterpiece, however, was the *Divine Comedy*, a description of a journey through hell, purgatory (where sinners seek forgiveness), and finally paradise. Within this framework, Dante also painted a vivid picture of the people and places of medieval Italy. The poem was written in medieval Italian and helped establish the vernacular as a literary language.

One of the most famous parts of the *Divine Comedy* is the description of the entrance gate to hell. On this gate, wrote Dante, were the words:

> 66 Through me you go into the city of grief,
> Through me you go into the pain that is eternal,
> Through me you go among people lost. . . .
> Abandon every hope, you who enter here. 99

Chaucer. Late in the 1300's an English poet, Geoffrey Chaucer, wrote *The Canterbury Tales*, a long story in verse. This masterpiece of English literature tells of a group of pilgrims on their way to the cathedral at Canterbury. Chaucer's descriptions of the pilgrims show humor, charm, and a keen understanding of human nature.

Like Dante, Chaucer encouraged the use of the vernacular in literature. He wrote in the dialect spoken by the people of medieval London. *The Canterbury Tales* was so widely read that this dialect strongly influenced the development of modern English.

Sec. Rev. ques. 5

Sec. Rev. ques. 5, cont.

Meanwhile . . .

IN THE MIDDLE EAST

While *The Canterbury Tales* were amusing English readers, Persian storytellers were delighting listeners with tales from the *Thousand and One Nights* (page 206).

259

History and Literature *The Song of Roland* is a 4,000-line epic poem and was written about A.D. 1100. The poem describes a conflict between Roland and Oliver, who represent valor and honor, and illustrates a disagreement about concepts of feudal loyalty and honor.

History and Literature *El Cid* describes the adventures of an eleventh-century Spanish warrior, Rodrigo Diaz de Vivar, exiled by his king because of the jealousy of other nobles. Despite the exile, el Cid (the lord) always remained loyal to his king.

Biography Dante saw Beatrice only twice, in 1274 and in 1283. Although Beatrice and Dante were never married to each other, Dante remained spiritually devoted to her all his life and modeled his poetic savior in the *Divine Comedy* after her.

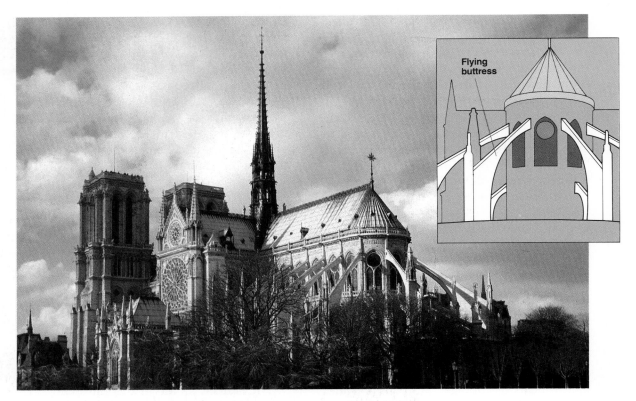

Flying buttress

Notre Dame in Paris is one of the largest and best-known Gothic cathedrals. Architects used flying buttresses to push the walls of Gothic cathedrals higher to create an impression of greater majesty (see diagram).

Art and Architecture

Religious art.   Nearly all the artists of the Middle Ages created works to show their religious faith and devotion. The people of a medieval town took great pride in the beauty of their church. To decorate it, artists and artisans created paintings, carvings, tapestries, and stained-glass windows. These showed scenes in the lives of Jesus and the saints. Because many people could not read, these works of art helped them learn Bible stories and Church teachings.

Romanesque architecture.   Two important styles of architecture developed during the Middle Ages. The earlier style, called **Romanesque** (roh-mun-ESK), was used most commonly from about the ninth through the twelfth century. The most typical feature of Romanesque buildings was the rounded arch. This style of building was adapted from Roman architecture.

Romanesque structures usually had massive walls and small windows, making the interiors dark. There was little color or use of ornament, though doorways and walls were often decorated with religious sculptures. Churches, castles, and monasteries in the Romanesque style were built throughout Europe.

Gothic architecture.   The walls of Romanesque buildings were massive because they had to support the weight of the roof. In the late 1100's, stonemasons began to construct buildings that were higher and more graceful. Instead of using rounded arches to support the roofs, they designed pointed arches. To handle the weight of the roof, the walls were supported from the outside by leaning arches called flying buttresses. The walls could, therefore, be made taller and less

260

Religion Note that early Christians did not have special buildings for worship, but usually met in private homes. As the Christian community grew and the worship service developed, assembly rooms became larger and included an altar and a *cathedra,* or armchair, for the bishop.

Religion and Culture A medieval monk, explaining the value of religious art to his pupil, wrote that artists "have adorned the House of God with beauty and have, in some measure, shown the paradise of God, glowing with flowers, green with herbs and foliage. They have given people cause to praise the Creator and proclaim Him wonderful in all His works."

Religion and Culture During the building of the Chartres cathedral, citizens harnessed themselves to carts and hauled stones to the site.

Cultural History It is estimated that 80 cathedrals and 500 large churches were built in France between 1050 and 1350.

massive, and much of the wall space could be used for stained-glass windows.

The new style of architecture came to be called **Gothic**. The high-arched ceilings and tall windows made Gothic buildings lighter and more spacious than Romanesque structures. Gothic architecture was used for castles, college buildings, and town halls. Its first and most impressive use, however, was in the soaring, graceful Gothic cathedral.

One of the finest Gothic cathedrals is at Chartres (SHAHR-truh) in France. The building of such a masterpiece often took 200 or 300 years. Raising a cathedral was an act of religious devotion in which an entire town took part. The wealthy gave their money, the poor their labor, and the artisans their skills to make these buildings beautiful works of art. Many Gothic cathedrals still stand today. They show the skill of medieval artisans, and they remind us of the importance of religion in medieval times.

● See below.

See Sec. 1 *Closing the Lesson*, p. T253B.

See lesson plans, pp. T253A–T253C.

Section Review

Answers to Section Review questions are in brackets on pages indicated.

1. **Define or identify:** curriculum, Scholastics, astrology, alchemy, morality play, vernacular, troubadour, Romanesque, Gothic. (pp. 255, 256, 257, 258, 259, 260, 261)
2. How was the revival of learning in Western Europe aided by contact with Muslim and Byzantine civilizations? (p. 255)
3. What two things did the Scholastics try to combine? (p. 256)
4. What were the strengths and weaknesses of medieval scientists? (p. 257)
5. What effect did Dante's *Divine Comedy* and Chaucer's *Canterbury Tales* have on Italian and English? (p. 259)
6. **Critical thinking:** What was the symbolic importance of Gothic cathedrals in medieval towns? (See answer below.)

6. Building a cathedral was an act of devotion in which an entire town participated: the wealthy gave money, the poor gave labor, and artisans used their skills to make cathedrals works of art.

2 The End of the Middle Ages

Objectives

Focus Questions

★ ■ What problems troubled Europe in the late Middle Ages? *(pages 261–264)*
● ■ How did the English and French monarchies grow stronger? *(page 264)*
▲ ■ Why did the prestige of the Church decline? *(pages 264–266)*

Terms to Know

Black Death	Babylonian
Hundred Years' War	Captivity
Wars of the Roses	Great Schism

★ Note strategies for first objective on this page and p. 262.

The 1100's and 1200's were the high point of medieval civilization. In the 1300's Western Europe went through great changes. Economic distress, a decreasing population, devastating warfare, and a weakening of the power of the Church were signs of these difficult times. They were also signs that the medieval period was drawing to an end.

A Decline in Population

Famine. In the late Middle Ages, Western Europe faced many economic problems. The earlier increases in agricultural output (page 229) did not continue. Farmers did not know much about how to keep soil fertile. As a result, the soil in heavily farmed

Sec. Rev. ques. 2

261

● ENRICHMENT. Have students compare examples of Romanesque and Gothic architecture. Students might study the Romanesque Abbey of Cluny in France; Durham Cathedral in England; or the Cathedral of Pisa, Italy, and compare them with the Gothic cathedral of Notre Dame or Chartres in France. Have students display sketches or diagrams or show slides to illustrate differences. *(Application) Locating Information*

★ RETEACHING. Have students outline the effects of famine, the Black Death, and peasant rebellions on European society in the late Middle Ages. (Famine: frequent starvation. Black Death: perhaps one third to one half of Europe's population died. Peasant rebellions: uprisings were put down by force.) *(Comprehension) Identifying Effects* areas wore out and became unproductive. Unusually cold weather in the 1300's further reduced food supplies by shortening the growing season. People had too little to eat, and there were periods of severe famine.

The Black Death. The greatest blow to fourteenth-century Europe was the bubonic plague, perhaps the worst natural disaster in human history. Known as the Black Death, the bubonic plague was a disease carried by fleas on rats. It probably struck first in Asia in 1331 and moved west across Russia. Italian ships returning from Black Sea ports carried the plague to Sicily. In 1348 it began to spread through Europe with incredible speed. Perhaps 20 million people—one third to one half of the European population—died from the plague.

Even those who did not fall sick were seized by panic. Some believed the plague to be a punishment from God. They tried to make up for their sins by beating themselves and each other with sticks and whips. Other people turned to magic and witchcraft. Frightened mobs slaughtered Jews in the belief that they had caused the plague.

Peasant Rebellions

The millions of deaths among farm workers and artisans left farmlands and workshops idle. Fewer crops and goods were produced, and prices rose. Badly in need of money, nobles demanded more taxes from peasants. In 1381 John Ball and Wat Tyler led English peasants in a revolt against new taxes. Ball stirred up strong feelings by attacking the inequality between the poor and the rich:

> 66 Are we not all descended from the same parents, Adam and Eve? and what can they show, or what reasons give, why they should be more the masters than ourselves? They are clothed in velvets and rich fabrics, ornamented with ermine and other furs, while we are forced to wear poor cloth. They have handsome houses and manors, when we must brave the wind and rain in our labors in the field; but it is from our labor they support their pomp. 99

Sec. Rev. ques. 2, cont.

★ See below.

This illuminated manuscript shows survivors struggling to bury plague victims. Later, the dead became too numerous for coffins and had to be buried in mass graves.

Science The bubonic plague produced hemorrhages—dark patches of clotted blood that eventually covered the whole body—and the tongue turned black. Swellings and carbuncles appeared under the arms and in the groin (the term *bubonic* plague comes from the *buboes,* or carbuncles, that form). Although some people infected by the disease survived, most died within three days.

★ REINFORCEMENT. Have students make a cause-and-effect chart illustrating the relationships between famine, the Black Death, and peasant rebellions in the late Middle Ages. Students should indicate how some problems caused others. *(Application)* **Understanding Cause and Effect**

★ ENRICHMENT. Have students analyze the primary source above. Students might paraphrase or explain the ideas expressed. *(Analysis)* *Analyzing a Primary Source*

Background The battle of Crécy crippled French power for nearly a century and led to England's dominance in world affairs.

Background Note that approximately 1,542 French lords and knights, almost half of the French force, were killed at the Battle of Crécy.

The peasants' revolt in England, like similar revolts in France and Flanders, was put down by the king's soldiers.

Social unrest occurred in the towns as well as the countryside. The wage earners of Florence (1378), the weavers of Ghent in Flanders (1382), and the poor of Paris (1382) revolted against the upper class in those cities. Like the peasant uprisings, the rebellions of the urban poor were put down by force.

The Hundred Years' War

● Note strategies for second objective on this page.

More trouble came because of the long-standing quarrel between the English and French kings. As you have read, rivalries over land created bitterness between the English and the French (page 240). Other conflicts arose over control of the profitable wool trade. Matters worsened in 1328, when the French king died without leaving a direct heir. Edward III of England, a nephew of the French king, decided to claim the French throne in 1337. Thus began a series of destructive conflicts known as the **Hundred Years' War** (1337–1453).

Sec. Rev. ques. 3

Importance of the longbow. In two early battles, at Crécy (kray-SEE) in 1346 and Poitiers (pwah-TYAY) in 1356 (map, page 265), the English overwhelmed the French. English archers used longbows, a weapon that greatly changed medieval warfare. It allowed archers to shoot arrows farther and faster than did the traditional crossbow. With their longbows, English foot soldiers cut down wave after wave of charging French cavalry. Once knocked to the ground by English arrows, French knights were helpless. They could barely move because of the heavy armor they wore.

English victories. The Hundred Years' War continued on and off during the 1300's and early 1400's. Fought almost entirely on French land, the war caused great suffering for French peasants and townspeople. Many were killed, and vast amounts of crops were destroyed by wandering bands of soldiers. At the battle of Agincourt (ah-zhan-KOOR) in 1415, the archers of the English

At the battle of Crécy, English archers (shown at right) used their longbows to devastate the French cavalry. Longbows shot arrows 400 yards at a rate five times faster than the crossbow. In order to show both armies in detail, a medieval artist pictured the archers much closer to the center of the battle than they actually were.

king, Henry V, again defeated the French. This victory gave England control of most of northern France. By a treaty signed in 1420, Henry married the French king's daughter Catherine and became heir to the throne. It appeared that England would soon join the two lands under one crown.

Joan of Arc. At this critical point a 17-year-old peasant named Joan of Arc came to the rescue of France. The French king's son, called the Dauphin (DAW-fin), had been denied the throne by the peace treaty. Joan went to him and persuaded him to give her an army. She believed that God had chosen her to drive the English out of France.

Dressed in armor and carrying a religious banner, Joan rallied the French soldiers and led them to victory at Orléans (or-lay-AHN) in 1429. The Dauphin was then crowned king of France as Charles VII. Other victories followed, but in 1430 Joan was captured by opponents of the French king and **263**

● RETEACHING. Have students summarize the results of the Hundred Years' War. (Comprehension) Summarizing Information

● REINFORCEMENT. Have students compare the processes by which the French and English monarchies were strengthened. (French: monarchs built a strong army; reduced nobles' power; brought French lands under control. English: the Tudor dynasty resulted from a civil war.) (Application) Comparing Historical Developments

● ENRICHMENT. Have students write an essay evaluating how advances in military technology affect relationships between nations. Students might refer to the discussion of the longbow or consider how nuclear arms have affected modern international relations. (Synthesis) Drawing Conclusions

Background At the Battle of Agincourt, 13,000 English soldiers armed with longbows defeated a force of 50,000 French.

Joan of Arc's inspired leadership helped free France from English domination and created a new spirit of devotion to country in France.

turned over to the English. A Church court condemned her as a heretic and a witch, and Joan was burned at the stake. (In 1920 the Catholic Church made Joan of Arc a saint.)

Joan had set an example that inspired the French people and strengthened their devotion to France. They fought the English with new courage. By 1453 the English had lost all their lands in France except the northern port city of Calais (kah-LAY).

A Stronger Monarchy in France

Besides giving the French people a sense of unity, the Hundred Years' War increased the power of the French monarchs. During the war French kings introduced new taxes that added greatly to the royal income. Kings were then able to hire soldiers who were loyal to the monarchy. The French rulers no longer had to rely on the uncertain loyalty of troops supplied by feudal vassals.

After Charles VII's death in 1461, Louis **264** XI became king. Louis was a shrewd ruler

who took advantage of every opportunity to trim the power of the feudal lords. Using bribery, diplomacy, and force, Louis brought many French lands under royal control. His success contributed to the development of absolute monarchy in France.

The Struggle for the English Throne

The Hundred Years' War had different results in England. The loss of French lands and an unpopular peace settlement with France caused widespread discontent. Moreover, the English royal family was split into two rival branches. Civil war began between these two branches in 1455. The struggles for the throne later came to be called the **Wars of the Roses** because of the two sides' symbols—a red rose for one, a white rose for the other.

In 30 years of fighting, four kings came to the English throne and each was overthrown, murdered, or killed in battle. Hundreds of noblemen from England's most powerful families died in the Wars of the Roses. These losses seriously weakened the English nobility.

The wars came to an end in 1485, when Henry Tudor became king as Henry VII. Henry devoted his reign (1485–1509) to unifying England. He married a member of the opposing side and began the Tudor dynasty of monarchs. Members of this family ruled England until 1603. England, like France, now had a strong monarchy.

The Crisis in the Papacy

▲ Note strategies for third objective on this page and p. 265.

Loss of political power. As the power of monarchs grew in the late Middle Ages, the Popes lost authority and political clout. This shift in power became clear when Pope Boniface VIII came into conflict with King Philip IV of France in 1296. To raise money, Philip demanded taxes from the French churches. Next he put on trial and then imprisoned a French bishop. Both of Philip's actions violated Church law. In 1302 Boniface declared that the Pope had supreme authority over all

Sec. Rev. ques. 4

Social History Besides witchcraft and heresy, Joan of Arc was charged with impurity, wearing men's clothes, and rebellion against the Church. At Joan's execution, a secretary of the English king said, "We are all lost, for we have burned a good and holy person." Two years later Joan's case was reopened and she was declared innocent of all charges.
Cultural History The Wars of the Roses were between the House of York, whose symbol was a white rose, and the House of Lancaster, whose symbol was the red rose. The House of Lancaster won.

▲ RETEACHING. Have students review "Loss of political power" (above) and explain how Philip IV's actions indicated a loss of papal power. (Philip demanded taxes from the Church and imprisoned a bishop, violating Church law. He also arrested the Pope for declaring that the Pope had supreme authority.) (Comprehension) Interpreting Information rulers. Philip, outraged, sent soldiers to arrest him. Boniface was soon released, but the elderly Pope died a month later.

The Babylonian Captivity. Clement V, a French archbishop and friend of Philip IV, was elected Pope in 1305. Rather than move to Rome, Clement set up the papal court in Avignon (ah-vee-NYAWN) in southeastern France. From 1309 to 1377, all the Popes were French and ruled from Avignon, not Rome. Under the influence of the French king, they often had to support policies favorable to France. Romans called this period of the papacy the **Babylonian Captivity**, a comparison with the time the Hebrews were in exile in Babylon (page 45).

The Great Schism. The papacy returned to Rome in 1377, but conflicts went on. In 1378 the Romans insisted on the election of an Italian Pope, Urban VI. Urban, however, soon clashed with the cardinals who had chosen him. The cardinals, most of them French, left Rome and elected Clement VII to be Pope at Avignon. To the dismay of devout Christians, there were now two Popes, neither of whom would step down. Thus began the **Great Schism** (SIZ-um)—a division within the Church that lasted 40 years. In 1417 both sides agreed on a new Pope who would rule from Rome.

Demands for reform. The Church still had other troubles. Many Christians felt that certain Popes behaved more like political leaders than spiritual leaders. They believed that the Church should deal only with religious matters and not interfere with the way monarchs ruled their lands.

Reformers also attacked the Church for its wealth and argued that the clergy should have to obey the laws of the state. One such reformer was John Wycliffe (WIK-lif), a scholar at Oxford University in England. In the late 1300's Wycliffe questioned the teaching that a person could gain salvation only through the Church. He said Christians should regard the Bible, not the Church, as the supreme source of authority. So that people could read the Bible for themselves, Wycliffe and his followers made the first complete translation of the work into English.

▲ See below.

One of those influenced by Wycliffe was John Huss, head of the University of Prague (PRAHG) in what is now Czechoslovakia. Like Wycliffe, Huss challenged the Pope's authority and criticized the Church's wealth. In 1410 he was excommunicated, and in 1415 he was burned at the stake for heresy. Wycliffe, too, was condemned as a heretic. Nevertheless, reformers continued to criticize the Church. As you will read in Chapter 17, discontent eventually led some Christians to split away from the Catholic Church.

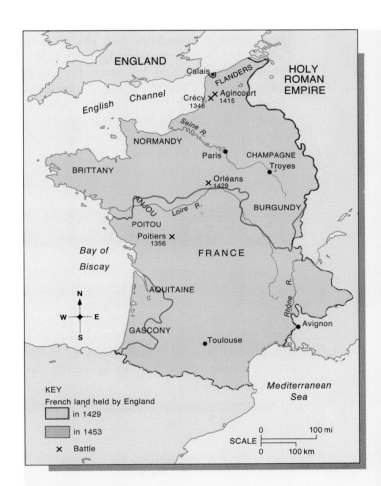

France, 1453

By 1453 England had lost control of all its territory in France except Calais. What was the farthest north-south distance of the area England controlled in 1429? What important battle in the Hundred Years' War was fought along the Loire River?

Map Answers: (1) About 375 miles.
(2) The battle at Orléans.

AVS4

A Time of Transformation

It was once common to view the Middle Ages as the "dark ages," a period of cultural decline that contrasted with the glory of Greco-Roman civilization. Studies of the period have changed that view. People now appreciate the richness of medieval civilization.

People recognize, too, that important changes took place in the Middle Ages: (1) By the 1400's, England and France were strong, unified states. Rulers had great power, but people had begun to gain a voice in government through assemblies like the English Parliament. (2) The new middle class in the towns had wealth and influence. (3) Christianity and the Church remained important forces in people's lives, but the political power of the Church was lessening. These changes were all signs that the medieval period was coming to an end.

See Sec. 2 *Closing the Lesson*, p. T253C.

Section Review

Answers to Section Review questions are in brackets on pages indicated.
1. **Identify:** Black Death, Hundred Years' War, Wars of the Roses, Babylonian Captivity, Great Schism.
2. What factors caused Europe's population to decline in the late Middle Ages? How were peasant revolts a result of this decline? (pp. 261, 262)
3. What was the basic cause of the Hundred Years' War? (p. 263)
4. What controversies weakened the papacy in the late Middle Ages? What reforms were suggested? (pp. 264, 265)
5. **Critical thinking:** Compare the conflict between Pope Boniface VIII and Philip IV with the earlier conflict between Pope Gregory VII and Henry IV (page 243). (See answer below.)

(pp. 262, 263, 264, 265)

Chapter 13   Summary and Timeline

1. Europe's prosperity in the 1100's and 1200's was accompanied by a cultural flowering. The first universities developed, and contacts with Muslim and Byzantine cultures made the knowledge of ancient Greece and Rome available in Western Europe. A rich literature began to be written in vernacular languages. Architecture moved from the massive Romanesque style to the graceful Gothic.

2. The famine, disease, and warfare of the 1300's greatly changed Europe. The power of kings increased and the political power of Popes declined. These changes would bring the Middle Ages to an end.

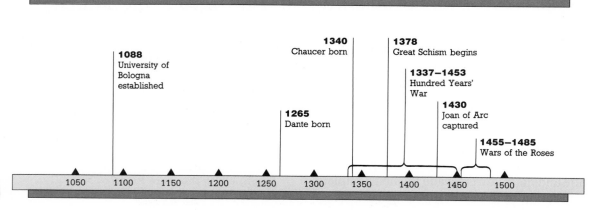

1088 University of Bologna established

1265 Dante born

1340 Chaucer born

1378 Great Schism begins

1337–1453 Hundred Years' War

1430 Joan of Arc captured

1455–1485 Wars of the Roses

1050 1100 1150 1200 1250 1300 1350 1400 1450 1500

5. Answers will vary. In both cases a smaller controversy escalated into a contest for supremacy in Europe. Henry IV and Gregory VII argued over who had the right to appoint bishops; Philip IV and Boniface VIII argued over Philip's violation of Church policy.

See p. T253C for answers to the Chapter Review.

Vocabulary Review

1. Match each of the following terms with its correct definition: *curriculum, morality play, troubadour, vernacular.*
   a. course of study
   b. medieval poet-musician
   c. local language
   d. religious drama
2. Define or identify the terms in the following pairs.
   a. astrology; alchemy
   b. Romanesque; Gothic
   c. Hundred Years' War; Wars of the Roses
   d. Babylonian Captivity; Great Schism

People to Identify

Use the following names to complete the sentences below: *Thomas Aquinas, Roger Bacon, John Ball, Geoffrey Chaucer, Dante, Henry VII, John Huss, Joan of Arc, John Wycliffe.*

1. The English king who started the Tudor dynasty was ___?___.
2. ___?___ was an English monk and thinker who was noted for his scientific experiments.
3. ___?___ led French troops to victory at Orléans in 1429.
4. The author of *The Canterbury Tales* was ___?___.
5. ___?___ led a peasant revolt in England against new taxes.
6. ___?___ was the Italian poet who wrote the *Divine Comedy.*
7. *Summa Theologica* was written by ___?___.
8. ___?___ and ___?___ urged Church reforms in the late 1300's.

Places to Know

Match the letters on this map of France with the places listed below. (See map, page 265.)

1. Paris   3. Orléans
2. Agincourt   4. Avignon

Recalling the Facts

1. What encouraged the revival of learning in Europe?
2. Why did some Christian thinkers oppose the study of Greek philosophy? How did the Scholastics answer their criticisms?
3. What were some of the weaknesses of medieval science?
4. How did poets help to popularize the use of vernacular languages?
5. What factors led to a drop in food production in the late Middle Ages?
6. Why did peasants rebel in the 1300's?
7. How did Philip IV contribute to the Church's loss of authority?

267

1. **Preparing a report.** Research and write a report about one of the following topics: the English peasants' revolt in 1381; the life of Joan of Arc; medieval clothing; a Gothic cathedral in England or France; the Dance of Death (a reaction to the bubonic plague); the method of electing Popes. *(App.)*

2. **Sequencing.** On a separate sheet of paper, list the following events in chronological order, giving the date for each entry. *(Comp.)*

   a. Black Death begins to spread in Europe.
   b. Hundred Years' War ends.
   c. Battle of Orléans is fought.
   d. Great Schism begins.
   e. Joan of Arc is captured.
   f. Weavers of Ghent rebel.

3. **Relating cause and effect.** What was the effect of the Hundred Years' War on the French monarchy? What effect did the war have on England? How did the growing power of monarchs in the late Middle Ages affect the papacy? *(Comp.)*

✔ 4. **Writing a rebuttal.** Earlier scholars once thought of the Middle Ages as the "Dark Ages," because of a supposed decline in learning during the period. What arguments could be used to rebut—challenge or disprove—this view? Write your rebuttal in essay form. *(Syn.)*

Thinking About Geography

✔ 1. **Analyzing.** In the Hundred Years' War, English soldiers destroyed vast amounts of French crops. Why did this hurt the French war effort? Why would future armies continue to use this tactic? *(Syn.)*

2. **Hypothesizing.** Romance languages grew out of the Latin spoken by the common people of Rome. As this common Latin spread throughout the Roman Empire, it mixed with other European languages, eventually resulting in the different Romance languages. In what ways might common Latin have spread to other parts of the Empire? *(Comp.)*

268

Enrichment: Primary Sources

Giovanni Boccaccio (buh-KAH-chee-oh) was in Florence when the bubonic plague broke out. In this adapted account, he describes the destruction the Black Death caused.

❝ In the year 1348 that most beautiful of Italian cities, noble Florence, was attacked by deadly plague. It started in the East either through the influence of the heavenly bodies or because God's anger with our wicked deeds sent it as a punishment to mortal men; and in a few years it killed about two-thirds of the population of the city.

The violence of this disease was such that the sick communicated it to the healthy who came near them. To speak to or go near the sick brought infection and death. To touch the clothes or anything else the sick had touched or worn gave the disease to the person touching.

One citizen avoided another. Such terror was struck into the hearts of men and women by this calamity that brother abandoned brother, and very often the wife abandoned her husband. What is worse and nearly incredible is that fathers and mothers refused to see and tend their children, as if they had not been theirs. ❞

1. What possible explanations did Boccaccio give for the plague's origins?
2. According to Boccaccio, how did the disease spread?
3. What effect did the plague have on relationships between people?
4. **Critical thinking:** Why might many medieval people have accepted a nonscientific explanation of the plague? *(Syn.)*

✔ A checkmark identifies questions and exercises calling for the three higher-order levels of thinking at the top of the Bloom taxonomy: Analysis, Synthesis, and Evaluation.

WORLD HISTORY
Checklist

UNIT 3

Try to identify the following key people, groups and dynasties, places, and terms from the unit. If you need help, refer to the pages listed.

Key People

Justinian *(182)*
Theodora *(182)*
Vladimir *(191)*
Ivan III, "the Great" *(192)*
Mohammed *(198)*
Avicenna *(204)*
Venerable Bede *(212)*
Saint Benedict *(213)*
Saint Patrick *(214)*
Clovis *(215)*
Charlemagne *(215)*
Eleanor of Aquitaine *(222)*
Alfred the Great *(236)*
William the Conqueror *(236)*
King John *(238)*
Philip Augustus *(240)*
Pope Gregory VII *(243)*
Henry IV *(243)*
Pope Innocent III *(244)*
Saint Dominic *(245)*
Saint Francis of Assisi *(245)*
Thomas Aquinas *(256)*
Roger Bacon *(257)*
Dante *(259)*
Geoffrey Chaucer *(259)*
Joan of Arc *(263)*
Henry VII *(264)*
John Wycliffe *(265)*
John Huss *(265)*

Key Groups and Dynasties

Slavs *(189)*
Vikings *(189)*
Mongols *(191)*
Umayyads *(200)*
Abbasids *(201)*
Magyars *(218)*
Normans *(236)*
Tudor dynasty *(264)*

Key Places

Constantinople *(181)*
Byzantine Empire *(181)*
Kiev *(189)*
Novgorod *(192)*
Moscow *(192)*
Arabia *(197)*
Mecca *(197)*
Medina *(199)*
Baghdad *(201)*
Papal States *(215)*
Aachen *(216)*
Holy Roman Empire *(241)*
Orléans *(263)*
Avignon *(265)*

Key Terms

Justinian's Code *(182)*
Roman Catholic Church *(184)*
Eastern Orthodox Church *(184)*
Hagia Sophia *(186)*
Crusades *(187)*
Golden Horde *(191)*
Bedouin *(197)*
Islam *(198)*
Muslim *(198)*
Koran *(198)*
Five Pillars of Islam *(198)*
Hegira *(199)*
jihad *(199)*
Sunni *(200)*
Shiite *(200)*
Middle Ages *(211)*
feudalism *(218)*
manorial system *(222)*
middle class *(234)*
Battle of Hastings *(236)*
common law *(237)*
Magna Carta *(238)*
parliament *(239)*
limited monarchy *(239)*
absolute monarchy *(240)*
Concordat of Worms *(244)*
heresy *(244)*
Inquisition *(245)*
Reconquest *(246)*
Hanseatic League *(250)*
Scholastics *(256)*
Romanesque *(260)*
Gothic *(261)*
Black Death *(262)*
Hundred Years' War *(263)*
Wars of the Roses *(264)*
Babylonian Captivity *(265)*
Great Schism *(265)*

Byzantine empress Theodora and two of her attendants.

269

REVIEW ACTIVITIES: *Key People:* Make a chart identifying the key people as political or military rulers, religious leaders, scientific thinkers, or literary artists. Then list each person's most important contribution. *Key Groups and Dynasties:* Identify the world region influenced by each group or dynasty. *Key Places:* Show on a world outline map the location of each place. (See pages 74 and 162 of *Teacher's Resources: Geography* for world outline maps that can be copied.) *Key Terms:* Define or identify each term listed.

UNIT 4

Civilizations in Asia, Africa, and the Americas 400–1700

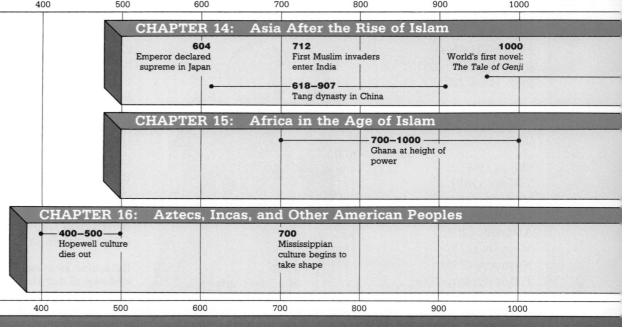

| 400 | 500 | 600 | 700 | 800 | 900 | 1000 |

CHAPTER 14:   Asia After the Rise of Islam

604
Emperor declared
supreme in Japan

712
First Muslim invaders
enter India

1000
World's first novel:
The Tale of Genji

618–907
Tang dynasty in China

CHAPTER 15:   Africa in the Age of Islam

700–1000
Ghana at height of
power

CHAPTER 16:   Aztecs, Incas, and Other American Peoples

400–500
Hopewell culture
dies out

700
Mississippian
culture begins to
take shape

| 400 | 500 | 600 | 700 | 800 | 900 | 1000 |

FOCUS STRATEGY. Tell students that the illustration shows a scene
from China's Forbidden City as it might have looked in the 1500's.
Then ask: (a) How does the architecture shown here differ from
Western styles? (Answers may mention upturned roofs and large, decorative gateways.) (b) What characteristics of Chinese architecture
do you find most striking? Explain your answer.   (Answers will
vary.)

	1100	1200	1300	1400	1500	1600	1700

1185
Rule by shoguns
begins in Japan

1368–1644
Ming dynasty in
China

960–1279
Song dynasty in
China

1520–1566
Suleiman I rules
Ottoman Empire

1230
Mali begins to
expand

1590
Songhai Empire
collapses

1325
Aztecs build
Tenochtitlán

1438–1532
Inca Empire
expands

	1100	1200	1300	1400	1500	1600	1700

271

Have students refer to the unit timeline to answer the following question: Which of these dynasties ruled China longer than the
others—the Tang, the Song, or the Ming? (The Song dynasty ruled
China for 319 years, 30 years longer than the Tang dynasty and 43 years
longer than the Ming dynasty.)

T271A

Asia After the Rise of Islam 500–1700
(pp. 272–295)

Section 1 describes the expansion of the Muslim empire in India and the effect of Islam on the Hindu world. The growth of the Ottoman Empire and the establishment of the Safavid Empire in Persia are discussed in Section 2. Section 3 describes the power and prosperity of China during early dynastic rule, Mongol control of China, and how the Ming dynasty emphasized traditional Chinese ways. In Section 4, early Japanese society and the development of feudalism in Japan are described.

Bibliography

See the *Teacher's Management and Planning Guide* for additional listings. Starred titles are for both students and teachers.

Benedict, Ruth. *The Chrysanthemum and the Sword: Patterns of Japanese Culture.* New American Library. Classic account by a well-known anthropologist.

*Gernet, Jacques. *Daily Life in China on the Eve of the Mongol Invasion, 1250–1276.* Stanford U. Pr. Society during the late Sung dynasty.

*Morris, Ivan. *World of the Shining Prince.* Penguin. The elaborate etiquette and cultivated arts of Heian Japan.

Schafer, Edward H. *The Golden Peaches of Samarkand.* University of California Press. Social life and culture at the height of the Tang golden age.

Spear, Percival. *India: A Modern History.* University of Michigan Press. A clearly written survey.

Section Lesson Plans

SECTION 1 (pp. 273–276)
India Under Muslim Rule

Objectives

After completing this section, students will be able to:
1. Describe how a series of Muslim invaders conquered India.
2. Explain what weakened the Mogul Empire.

Introducing the Lesson

Remind students that although Hinduism absorbed India's earlier invaders, the Muslim and Hindu traditions never merged. Basic differences in Islamic and Hindu principles fortified their separate identities.

Then ask: *(a) How might the existence of two strong religious traditions affect a society?* (Answers will vary. Some people might broaden their understanding and acceptance of differences; others might feel threatened by different ideas and customs.)

(b) How might people with different religious and social customs learn to cooperate? (Answers will vary.)

Developing the Lesson:
Understanding Chronology

Have students make a time chart showing the dates and the social and cultural effects of Muslim invasions in India. (Charts should include information for the following dates: *712; 1398; 1526; 1556; 1658.) (Comprehension)*

Developing the Lesson:
Understanding Point of View

Have students work in groups to discuss the advantages and disadvantages of Akbar's and Aurangzeb's methods of government. The debates should explain each ruler's ideas about government, strategies and results of each ruler's reign. *(Synthesis)*

Closing the Lesson:
Evaluating Historical Developments

Have students evaluate the strengths and weaknesses of Mogul rule in India and identify reasons for its decline. (*Strengths:* strong leadership that encouraged cooperation between Muslims and Hindus; support of art and architecture. *Weaknesses:* Aurangzeb's rule began a period of religious intolerance, war, and neglect of government.) (*Comprehension*)

See *Section Review* questions, p. 276.

SECTION 2   (pp. 277–280)
The Ottoman and Safavid Empires

Objectives

After completing this section, students will be able to:
1. Describe how the Ottoman Empire became powerful.
2. Explain how the Safavids unified Persia.

Introducing the Lesson

Remind students that the Ottoman and Safavid empires were Muslim kingdoms that owed their success to organization and leadership. The Ottoman Empire lasted for six centuries and the Safavid Empire for two centuries.

     Then ask: *(a) How might political organization affect a government's strength?* (A strong organization can often sustain a government during crisis and improve performance during peaceful times.)

     (b) How important to the strength of a government is good leadership? (Answers will vary. Good leadership may be critical during times of war or economic hardship.)

Developing the Lesson:
Analyzing Information

On the chalkboard draw a chart titled *Advantages and Disadvantages of the Millet System.* Then have students suggest possible advantages and disadvantages of the millet system for both Ottoman officials and local people. (*Comprehension*)

Developing the Lesson:
Forming a Hypothesis

Have students develop a hypothesis about why the Ottoman and the Safavid empires recruited non-Muslims to form the elite corps of their armies, and why these groups were more trusted than those who were born Muslims. (Answers will vary.) (*Synthesis*)

Closing the Lesson:
Comparing Historical Developments

Have students compare the leadership styles of Suleiman and Abbas I, and then draw conclusions about why they were effective rulers. (*Suleiman:* reformed the educational and legal systems; expanded his empire. *Abbas I:* reunited his country; expelled foreigners; reformed the military; made Persia the Islamic cultural center, built Isfahan.) (*Comprehension*)

See *Section Review* questions, p. 280.

SECTION 3   (pp. 281–285)
Imperial China

Objectives

After completing this section, students will be able to:
1. Explain how the Sui, Tang, and Song dynasties helped China prosper.
2. Discuss how China became part of the Mongol Empire.
3. Describe how the Ming dynasty tried to return China to traditional ways.

Introducing the Lesson

Remind students that after a 300-year period of disunity, three successive dynasties arose to reunite China.

     Then ask: *(a) What factors might account for the reunification of a people after a time of disunity?* (Answers will vary, but might include a shared culture, the rise of strong leaders, a common threat, or technological advances.)

(b) Why might a society that is politically united have more opportunities for growth than one that is politically divided? (Answers will vary. Unified societies are usually more secure against military threats and have greater opportunities for economic and technological growth.)

Developing the Lesson:
Evaluating Historical Developments

Have students evaluate the achievements made in China during the Sui, Tang, and Song dynastic rules; during Mongol rule; and during the Ming dynasty, and decide which period resulted in the greatest growth for Chinese society. Students should support their decisions with examples from the text. *(Evaluation)*

Developing the Lesson:
Understanding Cause and Effect

Have students write an essay tracing the causes and effects of China's periodic rejection of foreign influence. (A fear of Buddhist influence resulted in persecution of Buddhists and destruction of monasteries. Later, Ming rulers stopped expeditions and trade, possibly because of the cost of the expeditions and a fear of foreign influence.) *(Comprehension)*

Closing the Lesson:
Analyzing Information

Have students explain why some societies are able to survive foreign invasion and control and others are not. Students should consider the survival of Chinese traditions through years of Mongol role as an example. (Answers might mention that the Mongols isolated themselves from their subjects.) *(Synthesis)*

See *Section Review* questions, p. 285.

SECTION 4   (pp. 286–293)
The Development of Japanese Society

Objectives

After completing this section, students will be able to:
1. Explain how early Japanese society combined Japanese and Chinese traditions.
2. Describe how a feudal system developed in Japan.
3. Discuss how Japanese rulers unified the country and cut it off from the West.

Introducing the Lesson

Remind students that Japan's geography has had many advantages and disadvantages for the Japanese people. Have students refer to the map on p. 290 to answer the following questions:

(a) What might have been some advantages of Japan's geography? (Answers will vary. Japan has the natural defense of being surrounded by water. The ocean provided a steady source of food and an excellent means of transportation.)

(b) What might have been disadvantages of Japan's geography? (Answers will vary. Living on an island might isolate a people from other cultures; limited land area might restrict agricultural and economic opportunities.)

Developing the Lesson:
Interpreting Ideas

Have students work in groups to prepare a dialogue that might have occurred between a Japanese shogun, a samurai, a European feudal lord, and a knight. The dialogue might include a discussion of feudalism in Japan and Europe, the role of the shogun and the feudal lord, and the qualities considered important for the samurai and the knight. *(Application)*

Developing the Lesson:
Forming a Hypothesis

Have students develop a hypothesis about possible disadvantages of the Tokugawa policy of isolation. Students should consider why isolation was chosen as a foreign policy and how it was enforced. *(Synthesis)*

Closing the Lesson:
Illustrating Historical Processes

Have students work in groups to make a chart comparing the political leadership of the Mogul, Ottoman, Safavid, Chinese, and Japanese empires. Charts should include the names and dates of important rulers, achievements, and reasons for decline. *(Comprehension)*

See *Section Review* questions, p. 293.

Chapter 14 Review Answers
(pp. 294–295)

Vocabulary Review

1. (a) Shinto (b) Taj Mahal (c) deity (d) archipelago (e) Bushido (f) shogun (g) shah (h) daimyo (i) Janissary Corps
2. (a) Zen Buddhism (b) samurai (c) sultanate (d) classics

People to Identify

1. Great Mogul ruler who expanded the empire and supported the arts.
2. Mogul ruler whose religious intolerance and neglect of the government hurt the empire.
3. "Great Khan" of the Mongol Empire who established a new dynasty in China.
4. Venetian trader who wrote of his travels in China in the 1200's.
5. Japanese author who wrote *The Tale of Genji.*
6. Ottoman sultan who promoted culture.
7. Leader of the Minamoto clan who established the Kamakura shogunate.
8. Tang empress who became her country's only woman emperor.
9. Chinese admiral who led sailing expeditions during the Ming dynasty.

Places to Know

1. B   2. C   3. D   4. A

Recalling the Facts

1. Muslims believed in one God and were offended by Hindu belief in many deities. Muslims believed in the equality of all people, while Hindus saw class divisions as divinely ordered.
2. Akbar gained the support of the northwestern kings by giving them important positions. He also allowed all Hindus religious freedom and canceled the special taxes on non-Muslims.
3. Weak provincial government and army, poor leadership, and economic problems.
4. He made peace with the Ottomans, reorganized Persia's military forces, and won back lost territory.
5. The Chinese exported silk and porcelain, and Tang culture spread to other countries. Tea, new ideas in mathematics and astronomy, and foreign religions were introduced into China.
6. They developed the wheelbarrow, the abacus, gunpowder, paper money, and a method of block printing.

7. They used an examination system that stressed traditional ideas. Scholars restored the classics, and the government cut foreign trade.
8. The system of scholar-officials, the design of their capital city of Nara, and Buddhism.
9. When the power of the central government declined, large landowners in the countryside set up private armies. Strong warlords became powerful and a feudal system developed.
10. The Tokugawa shoguns restricted the power of the daimyo and limited foreign influence in Japan.

Critical Thinking Skills

1–2. Answers will vary.
3. Similarities include the emphasis on military skills, personal bravery, and loyalty to the lord. Differences include the emphasis on courteous treatment of women and Christian values in the code of chivalry and the emphasis on a life of discipline, duty, and self-control in the samurai code; also, the samurai concept of ritual suicide, or *seppuku,* was unique to Bushido.
4. Answers will vary, but students may argue that some parts of the dynastic cycle apply to all three empires. All began with dynamic leaders, but all fell into decline. The Ottoman Empire was troubled by poor leadership, economic problems, and rebellious peasants. The Sui dynasty began a rebuilding program that led to peasant rebellions. The Fujiwara family lost control of the government because court families grew more interested in their fortunes than in governing.

Thinking About Geography

1. The canal helped to facilitate trade and transportation between north and south. This would have increased contact and communication between peoples, making unification easier.
2. Japan's many mountains made political unification difficult. The sea was useful as a source of food, a means of transportation, and a protective barrier against foreign invasions. Proximity to the Asian mainland allowed the Japanese to borrow from the Chinese and Koreans.

Enrichment: Primary Sources

1. An envious person could always find reasons to envy others.
2. During the summer months, people were busy farming.
3. Important decisions should be made through discussion with other people.
4. Answers should suggest government leaders, because they would be in a position to employ the people in forced labor and they would be called on to make "decisions on important matters."

Asia After the Rise of Islam   500–1700

See chapter timeline, p. 293.

Before You Read This Chapter

If someone asked you to explain what makes a winning sports team, you might suggest several things—solid defense, strong offense, individual stars, good coaching. Could any of these same elements help build a strong empire? This chapter covers many empires in Asia over a broad span of time. As you read, try to decide for yourself what makes a successful empire. What part does political organization play? What about great leaders? The army? A sound economy? Religious unity? Cultural achievements?

The Geographic Setting

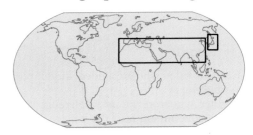

The Chapter Outline

1. India Under Muslim Rule
2. The Ottoman and Safavid Empires
3. Imperial China
4. The Development of Japanese Society

The palaces inside Beijing's Forbidden City housed China's emperors for more than 500 years. Entrance was forbidden to all except members of the emperor's household.

1 India Under Muslim Rule

Objectives

Focus Questions

★ ■ How did a series of Muslim invaders conquer India? *(pages 273–274)*
● ■ What weakened the Mogul Empire? *(pages 275–276)*

Terms to Know

deity   shah
sultanate   Taj Mahal

★ Note strategies for first objective on this page and p. 275.

Soon after the rise of Islam, the followers of this new religion set about conquering neighboring peoples (Chapter 10). From the 700's to the 1500's, four different groups of Muslims invaded India. Eventually most of the Indian peninsula was united under Muslim rule. Although the majority of Indian people remained Hindu, Muslim rulers left a lasting mark on Indian society and culture.

The Conflict Between Islam and Hinduism

All of India's earlier invaders had gradually been absorbed into Hindu culture and society. The beliefs of Islam and Hinduism, however, differed in their most basic principles. The Muslims believed in one God, while the Hindus accepted many **deities**—gods and goddesses. Conquering Muslims had been tolerant toward other monotheistic religions (Christianity and Judaism), but Hinduism's many gods offended them. Also, Muslims believed in the equality of all people, while Hindus saw class divisions as part of the divine order. The two faiths could not mix.

Sec. Rev. ques. 2

Muslim Invasions of India

As you read in Chapter 10, Muslim rulers in the 600's and 700's began to expand their empire. In 712 the first Muslim invaders crossed the mountains from Persia and moved into India. They could not advance beyond the Indus Valley and the mountains on the northwest frontier, but they claimed that region for the Muslim empire.

The next invasion of India was launched by Turkish Muslims from present-day Afghanistan. During the eleventh century these Muslims led 17 quick, merciless raids on India, killing Buddhist and Hindu monks and priests and carrying off slaves and booty. About 1175 another group of Turks moved in. They eventually occupied all of India north of the Deccan. The Indian territories then became a separate Muslim kingdom, or **sultanate**, with its capital at Delhi (DEL-ee).

Sec. Rev. ques. 3

The Delhi Sultanate

The rulers of Delhi were named sultans of India by the caliph of Baghdad, and they stayed in power for more than 300 years. At its greatest extent, the sultanate included the entire northern plain, much of the Deccan, and even parts of the south.

Extravagance and unsteady rule. The Delhi sultans lived in great luxury, taxing non-Muslims heavily to pay their bills. To guard against being absorbed into the Indian culture, they brought in Turks and Persians to work for them. Persian styles in art and architecture spread into Indian society.

The Delhi sultanate was never stable. Plots, revolts, and assassinations brought about the downfall of many sultans. The sultans also found it hard to rule the distant provinces. Local princes and governors often rebelled and declared their independence.

273

★ RETEACHING. Have students make a chart comparing the effects of the Muslim invasions of India. (Persians: could not advance beyond the Indus Valley but claimed it for the Muslim Empire. Turks: occupied India as far south as the Deccan. Mongols: destroyed Delhi; established Mogul empire.) *(Comprehension)* **Understanding Effects**

★ REINFORCEMENT. Have students review "The Mogul Empire" (pp. 274–275) and find information supporting the following generalization: *Early Mogul policies contributed to peace and prosperity in India.* (Akbar saw political and religious compromise as a way to promote unity; Jahangir and Shah Jahan continued these policies.) *(Comprehension)* **Supporting Generalizations**

Cultural History Persian architectural elements included onion-shaped domes, cupolas, and intricate lattices.

The descendants of the Mongol conqueror Tamerlane (on a throne at right) founded India's Mogul dynasty. Mogul paintings like the one of a prince riding an elephant (above) were influenced by Muslim art from Safavid Persia.

Mongol raids. In the early 1200's, as you have read (page 191), Genghis Khan led the Golden Horde across Asia. These fierce Mongol warriors swarmed first over China and then turned west into Persia. There they raided many of the great cultural centers of the Muslim empire.

During this same period, the Mongols also overran northern India in search of plunder. For Muslims in the areas under Mongol attack, the Delhi sultanate was an island of safety. Scholars, scientists, artists, and thousands of others fled into India from Baghdad and other Middle Eastern cities. The sultanate became a center of Muslim learning and culture.

Sec. Rev. ques. 4

Mongol raids on northern India continued throughout the next century. In the late 1300's, the conqueror Tamerlane, who claimed descent from Genghis Khan, led his Mongol armies through Central and Western Asia. Although he was a devout Muslim himself, Tamerlane laid waste to the great Muslim cities of Asia. In 1398 his forces sacked Delhi and killed or enslaved all of its people. The Mongols soon moved on to other lands, and the Delhi sultanate survived for another hundred years. It had been severely weakened, however.

274

The Mogul Empire

In the early 1500's Babur, a descendant of Genghis Khan and Tamerlane, led his army into India. In 1526 the Delhi sultanate fell. Though Babur died shortly after the conquest, he succeeded in establishing a new empire in India, called the Mogul Empire. (*Mogul* comes from the Persian word for "Mongol.")

The reign of Akbar. Babur's grandson Akbar was only 13 years old when he inherited the throne in 1556. He soon gained absolute power and became a wise and skillful ruler. During Akbar's 49-year reign, the Mogul Empire grew to include all of northern India and much of the south (map, page 275).

Akbar understood the value of compromise in bringing together the many different peoples and religions within the empire. He

Sec. Rev. ques. 5

Biography The name *Tamerlane* is a form of the Persian, "Timur-il-Lang," or Timur the Lame. The massacres committed during Tamerlane's military campaigns were recorded by his own historian. After a battle in what is now Afghanistan, Tamerlane ordered the construction of a tower made of living men cemented together with bricks and mortar. It is estimated that Tamerlane's troops slaughtered approximately 100,000 Hindu people in Delhi.

Biography Babur's first impressions of India were not favorable: he was annoyed by the absence of grapes, muskmelons, ice, and cold water. Babur was pleased, however, with the abundance of gold and silver and the presence of artisans in many different trades.

Politics Akbar divided his empire into twelve provinces, each ruled by an appointed administrator. Government officials were selected on the basis of merit from all classes and ethnic groups and were paid high salaries to discourage corruption.

gained the support of kings in the northwest by giving them important positions in the court and the army. Akbar allowed all Hindus religious freedom and canceled the special taxes that non-Muslims had to pay in most other Muslim lands. His marriage to a Hindu princess also helped lessen conflict between Hindus and Muslims.

Akbar's successors. The two rulers who followed Akbar never achieved his greatness or wisdom. For the most part, however, they continued his policies of fairness, tolerance, efficiency, and compromise. They expanded the empire still more and took care to keep on good terms with their Hindu allies.

Akbar's son and grandson both supported the arts, as Akbar had before them. A new style—neither Hindu nor Persian, but distinctively Mogul—flourished in art, music, poetry, and architecture. Akbar's son Jahangir (1569–1627) married a clever and beautiful Persian woman. She and her family helped shape politics and change ways of living in the empire. Persian influence increased at court and among the upper classes. Nobles spoke Persian, while a new language called Urdu gradually formed from a blend of Indian languages and Persian.

Jahangir's son, Jahan, led a rebellion against his father. In 1628 he gained the Mogul throne. Taking the title of **shah**—king— he spent enormous amounts of money to construct mosques, forts, and other public buildings. Although he made many conquests, Shah Jahan is best remembered for the tomb he had built for his wife, Mumtaz Mahal. The **Taj Mahal**, in the city of Agra, is one of the architectural wonders of the world. After the beautiful white marble building was completed, Shah Jahan supposedly ordered the blinding of the builders. He wanted to make sure they would never produce another such masterpiece. ● Note strategies on this page and p. 276.

★ See below.

The Mogul Empire under Aurangzeb. The first three Mogul emperors held together their empire through policies of compromise and tolerance. This changed when Shah Jahan's son Aurangzeb (AWR-ung-zeb), imprisoned his father and seized the throne in 1658.

A stricter Muslim than the earlier emperors, Aurangzeb tried to force the Hindu population to follow the laws and practices of Islam. He brought back the special tax on non-Muslims and took away the rights of many Hindu nobles. These actions, and his refusal to bend on any points, also led to disagreements with allies of the Mogul Empire.

Aurangzeb cut support for the arts and poured all the empire's treasure into efforts to conquer southern India. While he concentrated on war, he neglected the government, and it became weak and corrupt. By the time of Aurangzeb's death in 1707, the Mogul Empire had gained vast amounts of territory but had lost its strength.

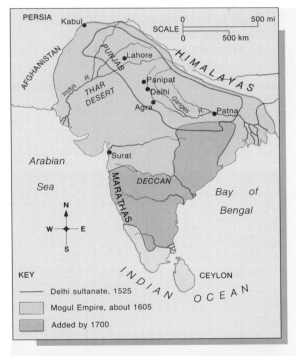

PERSIA · Kabul · AFGHANISTAN · PUNJAB · Lahore · HIMALAYAS · Indus R. · THAR DESERT · Panipat · Delhi · Agra · Ganges R. · Patna · Arabian Sea · MARATHAS · DECCAN · Bay of Bengal · Surat · N W E S · CEYLON · INDIAN OCEAN

SCALE 0 500 mi / 0 500 km

KEY
— Delhi sultanate, 1525
▢ Mogul Empire, about 1605
▢ Added by 1700

Mogul Empire, 1605–1700

Locate Ghazni, Delhi, Agra, Patna, and Surat. Which of these cities had been part of the Delhi sultanate in 1525? What landform marked the empire's border on the northeast? What part of India never came under Mogul control?

(See answers below.)

275

★ **ENRICHMENT.** Have students study examples of Mogul art and architecture and describe their Persian and Hindu influences. Students might research the Taj Mahal or Mogul miniature painting. *(Analysis) Relating Art and History*

Biography Grief-stricken when his wife, Mumtaz Mahal, died in childbirth, Shah Jahan decided to build a tomb "as beautiful as she was beautiful." Mumtaz Mahal had been the shah's constant companion through 19 years of marriage. Her name means "Chosen of the Palace."

● **RETEACHING.** Have students review "The Mogul Empire under Aurangzeb" (above) and then describe how Aurangzeb's rule was different from those of his predecessors. (Akbar, Jahangir, and Shah Jahan emphasized compromise and cooperation with Hindus; Aurangzeb reversed those policies and tried to force Islam on the Hindus.) *(Comprehension) Evaluating Information*

Map Answers: (1) Delhi, Agra, Patna. (2) Himalayas. (3) The southern tip of India.

New Threats to Mogul Rule

The Hindu kings of the northwest were among the allies who turned against Aurangzeb. Another people who held firm against Mogul power were the Sikhs (SEEKS), followers of a new religion established about the time of the first Muslim conquest. The Sikhs, neither Hindu nor Muslim, had their own customs and formed a small, self-sufficient society. Their center of power lay in the Punjab (map, page 275).

Aurangzeb's tactics also created a new, powerful enemy in the Deccan. The Marathas (mah-RAH-tahz), a Hindu people living along the western coast, set up a small, independent empire within the Mogul Empire. The Marathas remained a threat to Mogul rule for more than 100 years.

● See below.

See Sec. 1 *Closing the Lesson*, p. T271B.

Section Review

Answers to Section Review questions are in brackets on pages indicated.

1. **Define or identify:** deity, sultanate, shah, Taj Mahal. (pp. 273, 275)
2. Why were Hindu and Muslim beliefs unable to mix? (p. 273)
3. From which areas did Muslims invade India? (p. 273)
4. What effect did Mongol raids have on the Delhi sultanate? (p. 274)
5. How did Akbar unite different peoples within the Mogul Empire? (pp. 274–275)
6. **Critical thinking:** Why was Akbar a more successful ruler than Aurangzeb? (See answer below.)

6. Answers will vary. Aurangzeb reversed Akbar's policies of compromise and religious tolerance, refused to compromise with important allies, and neglected government and the arts.

The Taj Mahal is the most famous work of Mogul architecture. Its domes and minarets reveal the influence of Islam on Indian art.

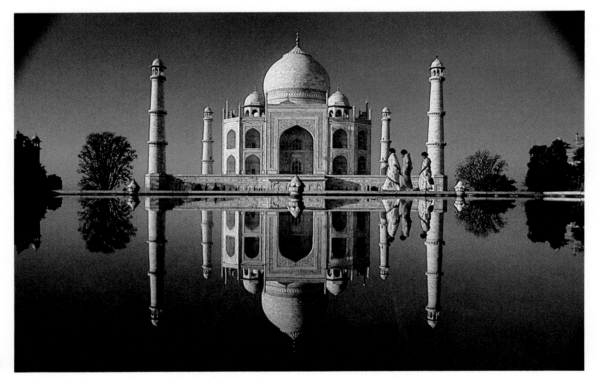

● REINFORCEMENT. Have students identify the following: (a) Followers of a religion that was neither Hindu nor Muslim, but formed a self-sufficient society. (Sikhs) (b) A Hindu people that formed an independent empire within the Mogul Empire. (Marathas) *(Comprehension) Observing for Detail*

Religion The Sikh religion, founded by Guru Nanak, combined Hindu and Muslim beliefs and taught "the unity of God, brotherhood of man, rejection of caste, and the futility of idol worship."

● ENRICHMENT. Have students find information on present-day conflict between the Sikh community and the Indian government. Students might write a report on the sources and consequences of the conflict or present an oral report describing the Sikh community, its disagreement with the Indian government, and the government's response. *(Application) Linking Past and Present*

2 The Ottoman and Safavid Empires

Objectives

Focus Questions

★ ■ How did the Ottoman Empire become powerful? *(pages 277–278)*
● ■ How did the Safavids unify Persia? *(pages 279–280)*

Terms to Know

Janissary Corps
millet

★ Note strategies for first objective on this page and p. 278.

Islam, which had its beginnings in the deserts of Arabia, spread rapidly. It became a strong force not only in the Middle East but also in India, Southeast Asia, Africa, and Europe. During the 1500's and 1600's, while the Mogul Empire dominated India, two other great Muslim empires—the Ottoman and the Safavid (sah-fah-VID)—flourished.

Ottoman Rule

The Ottoman Empire lasted for six centuries and was, at its peak, the most powerful empire in the world. The founder of the Ottoman dynasty, Osman I, established a small but strong state in present-day Turkey in the late 1200's. He and the rulers who followed him set about expanding their territory.

The Ottoman Turks first attacked Byzantine lands in western Asia Minor and southeastern Europe. They then conquered the rest of Asia Minor, which was populated by other Turks. In 1453 the Ottomans captured the city of Constantinople. They made it their own capital, changing its name to Istanbul. Over the next 250 years, they extended their rule over all of Asia Minor,

Sec. Rev. ques. 2

North Africa, and much of the Middle East. They also moved into Europe as far north as modern Czechoslovakia (map, page 278).

Government organization. The key to the long survival of the Ottoman Empire lay in the strength of its organization. Power was divided between the central government and the provinces, with neither able to overwhelm the other. This balance allowed the Ottoman Empire to last for many centuries.

Four key groups shared power in the Ottoman Empire. (1) At the head of the government was the sultan. He and his council made the important decisions. (2) The bureaucracy collected and spent tax money and handled the daily affairs of the government. (3) The religious leaders won converts to Islam and interpreted and enforced Islamic law. They also had almost complete control over education. (4) The army expanded the empire, defended it against outside threats, and kept the peace.

A key part of the army was the **Janissary Corps**—an elite fighting unit. Many of its soldiers had been non-Muslims, taken as slaves when they were between the ages of 12 and 20. Forced to convert to Islam and forbidden to marry, these troops became the fiercest and most loyal of all the sultan's soldiers.

The Ottoman sultans recruited non-Muslims for positions in the bureaucracy, too. Many upper-class Christians, who were allowed to keep their own religion, were given high government jobs. By drawing on people of talent—Muslim or not—the Ottomans strengthened their government.

The millet system. The sultan did not attempt to control every aspect of his subjects' lives. Local matters were handled by local religious leaders. Jews and Christians lived in separate communities, called **millets**. Within each millet, a religious leader chosen by the sultan acted as representative of that community to the sultan. He also made sure that people paid their taxes.

277

★ RETEACHING. Have students make a diagram of the structure of the Ottoman government and include a brief description of each level of organization. (The empire was divided into central and provincial governments and included four levels: sultan, bureaucracy, religious leaders, army.) (Comprehension) Translating Information into Another Form

Background Note that Constantinople's name was not officially changed to "Istanbul" until 1930.

★ REINFORCEMENT. Have students work in groups to stage a debate that might have occurred among members of the Ottoman government. Groups should represent those who support a balance of power between the central and provincial governments and those who support absolute control by the central government. (Evaluation) Making Decisions

Vocabulary Note that the word millet comes from the Arabic word millah, meaning "religion."

Ottoman Empire, 1350–1683

What three continents did the Ottoman Empire span? In what direction did the Ottomans advance in their siege of Vienna? Compare this empire with that ruled by earlier Muslims (map, page 200). Which Ottoman lands were not part of the earlier empire?

Map Answers: (1) Europe, Asia, Africa. (2) Northwest. (3) Balkan Peninsula (including Serbia), Hungary, part of Russia north of the Black Sea, Asia Minor.

Suleiman the Magnificent

The Ottoman Empire reached the peak of its wealth and power in the sixteenth century, under Suleiman I (SOO-lay-mahn). This sultan ruled from 1520 to 1566. Europeans called him "Suleiman the Magnificent" because of the splendor of his court. He was known to his subjects, however, as the "Lawgiver" because of his legal reforms.

Military expansion. Suleiman devoted much of his reign to a series of campaigns against the Hapsburgs, whose European possessions were located north of the Ottoman Empire. Ottoman troops invaded the kingdom of Hungary, which separated the Hapsburgs from the Ottomans. Having destroyed the Hungarian army at the **278** Battle of Mohács (MOH-hahtch), the Ottomans pressed on. In 1529 they besieged Vienna, the last remaining barrier to Muslim conquest of Europe. The Viennese, however, held off the Ottoman advance.

Ottoman culture. Throughout his reign, Suleiman promoted Ottoman culture. He encouraged a flowering of Turkish literature, learning, and fine craftswork. Ottoman artisans became especially skilled in carpet-weaving and ceramics. Yet it was in the field of architecture that Suleiman had the greatest impact. Under his direction, the decaying city of Istanbul was restored to splendor.

The Decline of the Ottoman Empire

Immediately after the death of Suleiman, the empire began a long, slow decline. There were several reasons. ★ See below.

★ ENRICHMENT. Have students write an editorial that might have appeared in a daily newspaper published during the decline of the Ottoman Empire. Editorials should analyze the problems facing the Ottoman Empire, compare them with the problems of the Roman Empire, and suggest ways that the empire might be saved. (Application) *Synthesizing Information*

Suleiman the Magnificent directs the siege of Budapest in this sixteenth-century miniature. His military campaigns greatly expanded the Ottoman Empire.

Sec. Rev. ques. 3

1. Weakening of the provinces. As time went by, government officials from the provinces realized that more money and more power could be gained by joining the central bureaucracy. Many left their homes in the country to take positions in the central government, thus upsetting the balance of power between Istanbul and the provinces.

2. Poor leadership. In Istanbul, the bureaucrats began more and more to serve their own interests instead of serving the sultan. As their power grew, they saw to it that only weak sultans came to the throne or stayed in power.

3. Economic problems. The greed and corruption of government leaders harmed the Ottoman economy. Many lands that had once been sources of wealth for the empire fell into private hands and farm production dropped. Officials responded by placing heavier taxes on the already-suffering peasants. Whole villages were abandoned as people fled to the cities. Other peasants joined rebel bands and took what they could from those who stayed in the countryside.

4. Military weakness. The strength of the Ottoman army had always been its cavalry. As guns came into widespread use, however, the Ottoman horsemen found themselves at a disadvantage. Unable to shoot well while riding, they were no match for armed foot soldiers. This fact, along with internal problems, made it hard for the empire to fight off enemies. During the late 1500's and early 1600's, the Ottomans continued to face threats from Europe. They also had a new enemy to the east.

The Safavid Empire

● Note strategies for second objective on this page and p. 280.

As the Ottoman Empire was prospering, another Muslim empire was being built in Persia. In 1500 a 14-year-old Muslim warrior named Ismail (is-mah-EEL) overthrew the Turkish rulers of Tabriz, in northwestern Persia. Over the next 10 years, his army conquered much of the rest of Persia and parts of present-day Iraq. Ismail belonged to the Shiite branch of Islam (page 200). Although most of his subjects were Sunnis, Ismail made Shiism the state religion. The dynasty begun by Ismail is called the Safavid dynasty after one of Ismail's ancestors.

Abbas the Great. The Safavid shahs who followed Ismail lost much of their land to their Sunni enemies, the Ottomans and the Uzbek (OOZ-bek) Turks. A ruler named Abbas I, however, turned things around.

Abbas was only 16 years old when he took the Safavid throne in 1588. Nonetheless, he acted decisively to reunite his country and drive its enemies from Persian soil. His first step was to buy time by making a peace treaty with the Ottomans.

Abbas then set about reorganizing the country's military forces. With the aid of an English adviser, he created the Safavid dynasty's first professional army. Like the Ottoman army, this force was made up of foreigners who had been forced to convert to Islam. Abbas had the utmost confidence in these troops. The soldiers were trained

Sec. Rev. ques. 4

279

● RETEACHING. Have students write a paragraph explaining their answer to this question: *In which empire do you think Jews and Christians would have preferred to have lived, the Ottoman or the Safavid?* (The Ottoman Empire, because Jews and Christians were undisturbed as long as they paid taxes. In the Safavid Empire, Islam was the state religion.) *(Comprehension) Drawing Conclusions*

● REINFORCEMENT. Have students summarize the actions of Ismail and Abbas I that led to the establishment of the Safavid Empire. (Ismail took control of Tabriz, conquered the rest of Persia, and imposed Shiism as the state religion. Abbas made peace with the Ottomans, created a standing army, won back the territory lost by former shahs, and made Persia the cultural center of the Islamic world.) *(Comprehension) Observing for Detail*

Safavid Empire in 1629

Until the Safavid dynasty, native Persians had not ruled Persia for hundreds of years. What was the Safavid capital? How far was the city of Tabriz from the capital? Into what body of water does the Amu Darya flow?

Map Answers: (1) Isfahan. (2) About 480 miles. (3) Aral Sea.

according to European standards, and the best of them were promoted to the highest positions in the government. With his new army, Abbas won back the territory earlier shahs had lost.

Cultural prosperity. Persia under Abbas was the cultural center of the Islamic world. Abbas built the city of Isfahan and made it Persia's capital. Its splendid streets, gardens, public baths, religious schools, and mosques had a graceful style that was widely copied in other Muslim lands.

Abbas also encouraged the arts. Carpet-weaving became a major industry. Persian carpets and fine textiles were exported not only within the Muslim world but to the trading centers of Europe as well. Painting, poetry, bookbinding, and manuscript illumination reached new heights during this period.

The legacy of the Safavids. The Safavid dynasty lasted for another hundred years after Abbas's death in 1629, but decline set in. Abbas's successors, like Suleiman's, were poor leaders. The Safavids left an impor-

280

tant legacy to their people, however. Their creation of a Persian state, united by the Shiite religion, set Persia off from the rest of the Muslim world. Today the people of Iran, as Persia is now known, still have a strong sense of identity.

See Sec. 2 *Closing the Lesson,* p. T271B.

● See below.

Section Review

Answers to Section Review questions are in brackets on pages indicated.

1. **Define or identify:** Janissary Corps, millet. (p. 277)
2. What lands did the Ottomans rule when their empire was at its peak? (p. 277)
3. Why did the Ottoman Empire decline after Suleiman? (p. 279)
4. How did Abbas I strengthen the Safavid Empire? (pp. 279–280)
5. **Critical thinking:** How did the Safavid dynasty create a strong sense of identity for Persians and their descendants? (See answer below.)

Background Note that during the reign of Abbas I, Isfahan included 162 mosques, 48 Muslim schools, 1800 caravansaries (overnight inns for caravans), and 273 public baths. Isfahan's population grew to about one million people.

● **ENRICHMENT. Have students find information on present-day Iran and explain what distinguishes it from the rest of the Muslim world.** *(Synthesis)* **Locating Information**

5. Answers will vary. The Safavid dynasty regained Persia's territory and further unified Persia through Shiism. Persia's cultural and political unity, along with its distinctive artistic styles, set it apart from other Muslim nations for generations.

See lesson plans, pp. T271A–T271C.

3 Imperial China

Objectives

Focus Questions

★ ■ How did the Sui, Tang, and Song dynasties help China prosper?
(pages 281–283)

● ■ How did China become part of the Mongol Empire? *(pages 283–284)*

▲ ■ How did the Ming dynasty try to return China to traditional ways?
(pages 284–285)

Terms to Know

calligraphy
classics

★ Note strategies for first objective on this page and p. 282.

The Chinese Empire, torn by constant warfare from the early 200's on, was reunited in the sixth century by the Sui (SWAY) dynasty. For a time it was the greatest empire in the world. Under later dynasties, imperial China surpassed Europe in culture and technology, and Chinese civilization became a model for all of eastern Asia.

The Sui and Tang Dynasties

Near the end of the Age of Disunity (page 145), a military leader in northern China conquered the south and declared himself the first emperor of the Sui dynasty. Only one Sui emperor followed the first, and their dynasty lasted from 589 to 618.

Sec. Rev. ques. 2

The two Sui emperors rebuilt the Great Wall, reconquered part of Central Asia, and reclaimed part of Southeast Asia. They also began an ambitious program of canal-building. Because China's great rivers all flow west to east, canals were important for north-south transportation and for trade between northern cities and the rice-producing provinces of the Yangtze delta.

Tired of being sent to war and forced to work on the canals and the Great Wall, the people soon rebelled against Sui rule. In a struggle for power, a former Sui official and his son took control of the throne in 618. Thus began a new dynasty, the Tang (TAHNG), which lasted until 907. This dynasty created another age of great achievement in China.

Wu Hou's leadership. Early Tang rulers wanted to expand the Chinese Empire. Chinese armies made conquests in Central Asia and Tibet. By 668 China had extended its influence over all of Korea as well. The leader of the campaign in Korea was the empress Wu Hou (WOO HOH). From about 660 on, she held the real power while weak emperors were on the throne. She became

A golden lion, symbol of majesty and strength, guards the entrance to an imperial palace inside the Forbidden City.

281

★ RETEACHING. Have students identify how the Sui, Tang, and Song dynasties unified the Chinese people. (Sui began program of canal-building. Tang expanded the Chinese bureaucracy. Song encouraged growth of trade between north and south China.) *(Comprehension)* *Observing for Detail*

★ REINFORCEMENT. Have students outline the achievements of the Sui, Tang, and Song dynasties. (Sui rebuilt the Great Wall; reconquered parts of Central Asia and Southeast Asia; began canal-building. Tang acquired land in Central Asia and Tibet; extended influence over Korea; expanded trade and travel. Song increased foreign trade; developed urban life; encouraged art and literature.) *(Comprehension)* *Comparing Historical Development*

Tang Empire About 750

During the Tang dynasty, goods and ideas flowed between China and other Asian countries. By what routes could trade goods reach Chang'an (Xi'an) from the Pacific coast? Besides the Tang Empire, what other empires and kingdoms does the map show?

Map Answers: (1) By the Grand Canal or along the Yangtze River and overland. (2) Muslim Empire, Byzantine Empire, Frankish kingdom.

emperor in her own right in 690, the only woman ever to hold that title in China. Brilliant and ruthless, Wu Hou stayed in power for 45 years.

Sec. Rev. ques. 3

Prosperity and foreign contacts. As the center of the greatest empire in the world at the time, the Tang capital at Chang'an drew both Chinese and foreign visitors. They admired its broad streets, elegant houses, temples, palaces, and landscaped parks.

China's central position encouraged

282 trade and communication with other Asian

lands. There was great demand in both Europe and Asia for Chinese silk and porcelain. Through trade and travel, Tang culture spread to other Asian countries such as Japan, Korea, and Tibet. The exchange of goods and ideas was two-way. Tea was introduced into China from Southeast Asia, and new ideas in mathematics and astronomy developed from contact with India. Foreign religions, including Buddhism, Islam, and some Eastern sects of Christianity, also spread into China and won followers there.

★ See below.

★ ENRICHMENT. Have students research present-day Chinese influence on the Korean, Southeast Asian, and Tibetan cultures. Students might report on evidence of the Chinese language, social customs, or art and architecture in the lands conquered by China during the Sui, Tang, and Song dynasties. *(Analysis) Linking Past and Present*

Buddhism in China. Buddhism had probably first reached China from India in the first century A.D. Traders, missionaries, and Chinese converts carried Buddhist ideas between India, China, and Korea.

Buddhist monasteries in China, like those in India, became centers of learning, places of pilgrimage, and hospitals. As they acquired gifts of land and money, the Buddhist monasteries also gained political power. Buddhism was encouraged and protected by early Tang rulers, particularly Wu Hou.

In time, however, Confucian scholars and Tang rulers began to fear the monasteries' influence. Some Buddhist ideas seemed to go against the Confucian rules for proper conduct and family responsibility. During the mid-800's a Tang ruler ordered the destruction of thousands of Buddhist monasteries and temples. This ended the period of Buddhism's greatest influence in China.

Decline of the Tang. From the 700's on, the imperial government was steadily weakened by attacks on China's borders. In 907, military leaders in the provinces rebelled and drove the last Tang emperor from the throne. More than 50 years of disorder passed before a new dynasty, the Song (SOONG), reunited China under one ruler.

The Song Dynasty

When the Song dynasty was established in 960, nomadic peoples controlled much of northern China. Repeated invasions finally forced the Song to leave the north in 1126. The period that followed, called the dynasty of the Southern Song (1127–1279), was one of growth and prosperity.

People in the south traded with other Chinese in the north, with the nomads of Central Asia, and with people of Asia and Europe. In earlier times, camels had carried goods to distant markets. Now ocean-going trade became important. The Chinese learned to use the compass, and they began building large ships. The ships were soon piled high with rice, tea, and silk from the rich farmlands of the Yangtze Valley.

Sec. Rev. ques. 3, cont.

Chinese Culture

Daily life. While dynasties rose and fell in China, daily life changed little for most people. Peasants still worked the land, planting every spring and harvesting every fall. More people, however, moved to cities during the Song dynasty. City streets were crowded with shops selling rice, noodles, paper fans, silk robes, bamboo birdcages, pearl necklaces, and many other goods.

The arts. The culture of the Chinese Empire under Tang and Song rulers was remarkable. Painting and poetry were favorite pastimes of the upper classes. Tang and Song artisans produced beautiful porcelain and silks. The Chinese also became masters of **calligraphy** (kuh-LIG-ruh-fee)—the art of fine handwriting.

By Song times, Chinese painting showed the influence of Taoist attitudes toward nature (page 140). Artists emphasized the beauty of natural landscapes and objects such as a single branch or flower.

Advances in technology. The Chinese developed such useful items as the wheelbarrow and gunpowder. They also invented a calculating machine called the abacus (AB-uh-kus), and they were the first to use paper money. The Chinese had invented paper about the first century A.D., and they later developed a method of printing. They pressed large sheets of paper against carved wooden blocks covered with ink. When the sheets were folded, they became the pages in a book. By about the eleventh century, **classics**—great literary works—from Taoism, Buddhism, and Confucianism were printed by this method.

Mongol Rule of China

● Note strategies for second objective on this page and p. 284.

In the early 1200's the Mongol leader Genghis Khan began his conquest of Asia with the invasion of northern China (page 191). By 1215 the Mongol archers and horsemen had defeated the northern rulers and gone on to conquests in Central Asia. After Genghis **283**

Khan's death in 1227, his grandson Kublai Khan (KOO-bly KAHN) completed the conquest of the Southern Song. In 1260 Kublai became "Great Khan" of the Mongol Empire in East Asia and ruled for 34 years. From his capital at Beijing (bay-JING), the Khan established a new dynasty. The Mongols gradually wiped out the ships and soldiers of the last Song rulers, making China part of the largest empire in history (map, page 202).

For the first time in China's long and brilliant history, foreign "barbarians" ruled the entire country. The Mongols were very different from the Chinese in language, culture, and customs. They kept their separate identity as one way of controlling their Chinese subjects, whom they did not trust. Mongols lived apart from the Chinese and obeyed different laws. The Mongol rulers even restricted the Chinese to low-ranking government posts.

Sec. Rev. ques. 4

The Mongol Empire's control of the vast central plains of Asia and Eastern Europe made it safe to travel overland from Europe to China. Many European travelers, including Christian missionaries, reached China. Ideas and inventions also began to move more freely between China and Europe and between China and Muslim Asia. Some of China's notable inventions, including printing, gunpowder, and the compass, were taken back to Europe by travelers and traders.

The most famous of the European travelers was a young Venetian trader, Marco Polo. With his father and uncle, he traveled by caravan on the Silk Road across Central Asia, arriving in China in 1275. Marco had learned several Asian languages in his travels, and the Khan sent him to various Chinese cities on government missions. Marco marveled to find splendid palaces, fine silks and carpets, all sorts of spices, and something he had never seen before—coal.

● See below.

The Polos returned to Venice in 1292 with a large fortune. Marco Polo's colorful account of his travels in China was widely read in medieval Europe. Western Europeans were amazed that a society so rich and advanced as China had never before come to their attention.

284

The Ming Dynasty

▲ Note strategies for third objective on this page and p. 285.

The death of Kublai Khan in 1294 weakened Mongol rule, and rebellions broke out in many parts of China. In 1368 a Buddhist monk led a successful revolt against the Mongols. He declared himself emperor and founder of a new dynasty—the Ming.

Return to Chinese ways. After years of Mongol rule, the Ming emperors wanted to return to a purely Chinese state. Once again the examination system became important. The version of the system used by the Ming lasted into the twentieth century. Stressing traditional ideas, the Ming rulers tested only knowledge of the Confucian classics. Originality was frowned upon. The test, therefore, helped create a government bureaucracy that was unlikely either to produce or to welcome new ideas.

Sec. Rev. ques. 5

Scholars restored the classics and collected China's ancient knowledge into an encyclopedia. Novels were also widely read. The most famous was *All Men Are Brothers*, an adventure story about a band of outlaws led by a hero like Robin Hood.

Exploration by sea. Trade by sea with other parts of Asia

Ming dynasty artists produced beautiful porcelain jars like the one at the right. The water buffalo below is carved from jade, a favorite stone of Chinese sculptors.

● ENRICHMENT. Have students work in groups to stage a meeting that might have occurred between Marco Polo and the Great Khan. Students might find information on gifts given to the Khan by Marco Polo, on the Khan's reception of the Polos, and on how they viewed each other. *(Application)* *Dramatizing History* (
Cultural History Marco Polo called China "Cathay," which sounded to him like the name of the Khitans, a people ruled by the Mongols. Marco Polo described the Great Khan as wise, tolerant, and forceful.

▲ RETEACHING. Have students explain how the Ming dynasty tried to return to traditional ways. (It reinstated the examination system, and tested only knowledge of Confucian classics.) *(Comprehension) Observing for Detail* (
▲ REINFORCEMENT. Have students develop a hypothesis about possible advantages and disadvantages of China's policy of isolation during the Ming dynasty. *(Synthesis)* *Forming a Hypothesis* (

had grown under the Mongols, and the Ming boosted trade further. In 1405 the Ming rulers sent a great admiral named Zheng He (JUNG HUH) on the first of seven expeditions to India, Arabia, and the east coast of Africa. These were the most ambitious sea voyages of the time. On the first trip, Zheng He sailed with more than 300 ships and nearly 28,000 merchants and crew. This huge fleet amazed people in every port. To honor the superiority of the Chinese emperor, the rulers of "inferior" countries sent him tribute.

Decline of the Ming dynasty. In 1433 the Ming rulers suddenly stopped sponsoring expeditions and encouraging trade. The high cost of these expeditions, as well as a fear of foreign influence on China, may have led the Ming rulers to choose isolation. China soon became cut off from the rest of the world. In the 1590's the Ming rulers had to fend off a Japanese invasion of Korea. The fighting drained the government's resources. Internal disorder and rebellion brought the dynasty to an end in 1644.

By this time, however, the traditional Chinese culture was so well established that it lasted through the reign of another foreign dynasty, the Manchu (1644–1912). China's ▲ See below. stability depended on keeping its traditional values and remaining apart from the changes taking place in the rest of the world.

See Sec. 3, Closing the Lesson, p. T271C.

(AVS3)

Section Review

Answers to Section Review questions are in brackets on pages indicated.

1. **Define:** calligraphy, classics. (p. 283)
2. What were the contributions of the two Sui emperors? (p. 281)
3. What were some of the achievements that were made during the Tang and Song dynasties? (pp. 282–283)
4. What changes did Mongol rule bring to China? (p. 284)
5. How did Ming rulers encourage a return to traditional Chinese ways?
6. **Critical thinking:** How did extensive sea voyages both help and hurt the Ming? (See answer below.)

A Chinese View of Government

Wang Fuzhi (1619–1692), a scholar who lived during the decline of the Ming dynasty and the rise of the Manchu dynasty, gave much thought to what made a good government. Adapted below are his ideas about the need for a government to be flexible.

❝ The ancient laws were designed to govern the ancient world and cannot be applied to the present day. One uses what is right for today to govern the world of today, but this does not mean that it will be right for a later day. Therefore the wise man does not try to hand down laws to posterity [future generations]. . . .

Times change; conditions are different. How then can a government adjust to these changes? There are crises of the moment to be met in each age, but the way to solve them is not to establish a whole new theory of government. When it comes to questions of particular incidents and laws, one must follow the times and try to determine what is fitting in each case. Every age has its different points of strictness. Every situation has its special circumstances. It is better, therefore, not to have inflexible rules. ❞

1. According to Wang Fuzhi, why does a wise ruler not try to hand down laws to posterity?
2. How, in his opinion, should a government react to change?
3. **Critical thinking:** What might Wang Fuzhi have thought about the Ming policy of reviving the old examination system?

Ⓕ See answers below.

▲ **ENRICHMENT.** Have students research the Ming examination system and compare it with the earlier system. Students might trace use of the Ming system into this century and evaluate its cultural impact. *(Synthesis) Locating Information*

6. Students might note that the expeditions expanded trade and drew praise from other nations. They were costly, however, and made China susceptible to foreign influences.

Ⓕ **Primary Source Answers** 1. Laws that are right for one time are not always right for a future time. 2. It should make laws according to what is accepted at the time. 3. Answers will vary. Students may suggest that he might have opposed the policy because it was created in an earlier time and might not take current circumstances into account.

4 The Development of Japanese Society

Objectives

Focus Questions

★ ■ How did early Japanese society borrow from Chinese traditions? *(pages 286–288)*

● ■ How did a feudal system develop in Japan? *(pages 288–290)*

▲ ■ How did Japanese leaders unify the country and cut it off from the West? *(pages 290–292)*

Terms to Know

archipelago	samurai
clan	Bushido
Shinto	daimyo
shogun	Zen Buddhism

★ Note strategies for first objective on this page.

Located off the coast of Asia, Japan has, from ancient times, borrowed ideas, institutions, and culture from the Chinese people. Yet Japan is far enough from the Asian mainland to have kept its independence and uniqueness.

The Geography of Japan

Japan is an **archipelago** (ar-kuh-PEL-uh-goh)—a large group of islands. The four biggest islands are Hokkaido (hoh-KY-doh), Honshu (HAHN-shoo), Shikoku (SHEE-kaw-koo), and Kyushu (kee-OO-shoo). There are thousands of smaller islands too.

Mountains cover about 85 percent of the land, and there have been at least 40 active volcanoes since record-keeping began. Still, Japan has a mild, wet climate. The northern islands have moderately cold winters and cool summers. Farther south in the archipelago, temperatures never drop below freezing.

Because of Japan's many mountains, only a small part of the land is suitable for farming. The farming areas are located mostly in small river valleys. Plentiful rainfall throughout the country allows the growing of rice, the staple crop of the Japanese.

Geography influenced the history of early Japan in much the same way that it influenced the history of early Greece. The mountains made political unification difficult. The sea was useful, both as a source of food and as a means of transportation, and it provided protection from foreign invasion.

Early Japan

By about the second or third century B.C., people in Japan were growing rice in irrigated fields. They were also working with both bronze and iron. Their technology and farming methods had probably come from China and Korea.

Early Japanese lived in hundreds of **clans**—small tribal communities—that were often at war with one another. The clans' rulers were also religious leaders.

Shinto. The most ancient beliefs of the Japanese were based on respect for the forces of nature. These were seen as spirits, called *kami*. Out of such beliefs grew the religion called **Shinto**, meaning "the way of the gods." This religion had no complex rituals or philosophy. Instead, believers in Shinto found beauty and wonder in nature.

The chief deity of Shinto was Amaterasu, the sun goddess. Her shrines were built in places where they could catch the first rays of the rising sun. Amaterasu was believed to be the protector of the Japanese nation. To this day, Japan is known as the Land of the Rising Sun, and its flag—a red circle on a white background—represents that image.

Sec. Rev. ques. 2

286

★ RETEACHING. Have students review "Chinese Influence on Japan" (p. 287) and identify several areas of influence. (Buddhism; system of scholar-officials; capital city design; style of Buddhist temples and pagodas; written language.) *(Comprehension)* **Identifying Effects**

Geography The Japanese islands cover approximately 150,000 square miles, an area slightly smaller than the state of California.

★ REINFORCEMENT. Have students explain how the Taika Reforms strengthened the central government. (Improved control of economy, increased revenue, linked villages, divided empire into manageable units.) *(Comprehension)* **Observing for Detail**

★ ENRICHMENT. Have students research Shinto and compare its ideas and rituals with those of the Chinese religion Taoism (p. 140). *(Synthesis)* **Comparing Ideas**

The imperial family. The first known line of Japanese rulers were the Yamato kings of the fifth century A.D. Because they claimed to descend from the sun goddess, the Yamato acquired a special authority. Although many of its later rulers lacked real power, the imperial family in Japan was never overthrown. It has reigned without interruption into the twentieth century.

Chinese Influence on Japan

About the sixth century A.D., the Japanese began deliberately choosing things to borrow from the Chinese and the Koreans.

Government reforms. In 592 Prince Shotoku, a great admirer of Chinese civilization, became the power behind the throne in Japan. Shotoku began making changes to strengthen the central government and weaken the clans. In 604 he made his ideas official in the Seventeen-Article Constitution. It declared the supremacy of the emperor. It also took away the inherited offices held by members of clans. Instead Japan began to use a Chinese-style system of scholar-officials.

The Taika (TY-kah) Reforms of the mid-600's carried Prince Shotoku's ideas even farther. All land in Japan was declared the property of the imperial government. A new tax system was begun, a network of roads was built, and the country was reorganized into provinces whose governors were named by the imperial rulers.

As part of the move toward a stronger central government, the Japanese built a capital city at Nara in 710. Nara was modeled after Chang'an, the Chinese capital. It was the only real city in Japan at the time. Its broad streets were lined with the houses of noble families, along with tile-roofed Buddhist temples and pagodas in the Chinese style.

Buddhism. About the mid-500's, the Japanese imperial court had officially brought Buddhism to Japan. At first there were some objections from powerful clans who were strong Shintoists. Buddhism soon became popular and fashionable, however. Nara's monasteries and temples grew rich from the gifts donated to them, and the Buddhist clergy began interfering in the imperial government. Mainly to escape the influence of the Buddhist monasteries, the imperial court moved to a new capital in 784.

The Heian Court

The new capital was given the name Heian (HAY-AHN), meaning "the capital of peace and tranquility." Later renamed Kyoto (kee-OH-toh), the city remained the Japanese capital until the nineteenth century.

In this painting of the creation story, the sun goddess looks on as drops of water from the sea god's spear form the islands of Japan.

287

Politics The Seventeen-Article Constitution, Japan's first written set of laws, included a collection of moral sayings about social behavior, many of which were derived from Confucian writings. The constitution declared the importance of *wa*, or concord and harmony, asserted the supremacy of the imperial throne, and authorized the use of forced labor only at "seasonable times."

Background The Taika ("great change") Reforms directly attacked the Japanese clan system by ending clan landholding and strengthening the emperor's power.

Check for Understanding. Ask: Why did the imperial court move in 784? (To escape the influence of the Buddhist monasteries.)

Politics The title "shogun" was traditionally granted by the emperor during times of barbarian threat and abolished when the crisis was over.

Background Note that the emperor could not be deposed because he was considered a direct descendant of the sun goddess.

Because the Chinese developed a written language before the Japanese, many Japanese learned to write in Chinese. Some Japanese men continued to write in Chinese even after a written Japanese language had been devised. The women of the Heian court, however, did all their writing in Japanese. They wrote diaries, poems, letters, and novels describing the elegant life of the court. The most famous court novel is *The Tale of Genji*. This romance is about Prince Genji, a hero who appears as the perfect Japanese court gentleman. Written about A.D. 1000 by the Lady Murasaki Shikibu, it is often said to be the first novel in world literature.

Japanese Feudalism

● Note strategies for second objective on this page.

Decline of central authority. For most of the Heian period, the rich Fujiwara family held the real power in Japan. Members of this family held many influential posts. By about the middle of the eleventh century, however, the power of the central government (and the Fujiwaras) began to slip. Court families grew more interested in luxury and personal fortunes than in governing.

Large landowners living away from the capital set up private armies, and the countryside became lawless and dangerous. Farmers and small landowners traded parts of their land to strong warlords in exchange for protection. With more land, the lords gained more power. This marked the beginning of a feudal system like that of medieval Europe.

Meanwhile . . .

IN EUROPE

While samurai provided military support for Japanese shoguns, knights in Europe did battle for their feudal lords. Both groups of warriors rode horses, wore armor, and knew how to handle a sword. Both also followed a strict code of loyalty and bravery.

288

Military dictatorship. For about 30 years two powerful warrior families struggled for power. In 1180 full-scale war broke out between them. Five years later the Minamoto family and its navy triumphed after a great battle on the Inland Sea.

The Minamoto leader, Yoritomo, set up his government in the town of Kamakura, where it could be independent of the imperial court. Yoritomo gained the title of **shogun**, which means "barbarian-defeating general." In theory, the shogun ruled over military matters in the name of the Japanese emperor. In practice, the shogun was the real ruler, and his descendants inherited his title.

Sec. Rev. ques. 3

With the establishment of the Kamakura shogunate (government by the shogun), Japan had, in effect, become a military dictatorship. While emperors continued to sit on the throne, military leaders kept control of Japan's government into modern times.

"The way of the warrior." The **samurai** (SAH-moo-ry)—a class of warriors or knights—dominated society in feudal Japan. A samurai spent a lifetime perfecting military skills. Bravery and loyalty to his lord outweighed loyalty to friends, family, or the emperor. The samurai code came to be called **Bushido** (BUSH-ih-doh), or "the way of the warrior." Bushido called for a life of discipline, duty, and self-control, both on and off the battlefield.

Sec. Rev. ques. 4

Honor was supremely important to a samurai. If he was dishonored in any way, he was supposed to commit seppuku (SEP-oo-koo), or ritual suicide. This also was true for women of the samurai class. (Seppuku is popularly called hara-kiri, which means "belly-slitting.")

Mongol Invasion

By the late 1200's Japan's neighbor, China, had become part of the growing Mongol Empire. The Mongol ruler, Kublai Khan (page 284), demanded that Japan also accept his rule. When the Japanese refused, Kublai Khan sent a fleet to invade the country in 1274. The samurai fought off the Mongol

● RETEACHING. Have students outline the characteristics of Japanese feudalism. (Large landowners with private armies, exchange of land for protection, samurai, Bushido code, seppuku.) (Comprehension) *Organizing Information in Written Form*

● REINFORCEMENT. Have students compare Japanese and European feudalism. (Both resulted from the decline of central authority and were characterized by powerful landowners, a class of warriors, and an exchange of services or property for protection.) (Comprehension) *Comparing Historical Developments*

● ENRICHMENT. Have students compare the shogunate with the military dictatorships of the Roman Republic (p. 103). (Comprehension) *Comparing Historical Developments*

This picture of a legendary Japanese warrior empress shows her wearing the armor of Japan's warrior class, the samurai.

horsemen, helped by a fierce storm that forced the ships to withdraw.

Seven years later, a Mongol force of about 140,000 men again attacked Japan. Again, a storm swept out of the Pacific. The raging winds and towering waves of the typhoon wrecked many Mongol ships. Believing that the typhoon had been sent by the *kami* to protect them, the Japanese named the storm *kamikaze* (kah-mih-KAH-zee), which means "divine wind."

The victory over the Mongols proved to be expensive for the Kamakura shogunate. Shoguns had kept the loyalty of their soldiers by giving them captured lands and riches. Because the Japanese seized few goods from the Mongols, the shogun had no way to reward the samurai. Discontented samurai and nobles switched their loyalty to an ambitious emperor who wanted to regain power

from the shogun. Civil war broke out, and the Kamakura shogunate ended in 1333 with the suicide of the last shogun.

An Age of Change

The 1400's and 1500's in Japan are sometimes called the Age of the Country at War. The central government had almost collapsed, and neither the shogun nor the emperor was in control. Local lords, called **daimyo** (DY-mee-oh), had the loyalty of the samurai and held absolute rule over the people of their territories. Their samurai were almost constantly at war and the countryside was once again lawless and dangerous.

The breakdown of class lines. War destroyed old distinctions between classes. The lower classes became more important in Japanese society, as the daimyo recruited peasants and commoners to serve in their armies. Many old noble families of the court lost their estates to the daimyo and so had no income. For a time in the early 1500's, an emperor could not be officially enthroned because the court was too poor to pay for the ceremony. One emperor earned a living by writing poems and selling them on the street.

The spread of Zen Buddhism. Buddhism had at first appealed mainly to the court aristocrats in Japan. During the feudal period, however, new Buddhist sects gained followers among the common people.

The most important of these sects, **Zen Buddhism**, was brought from China by Japanese monks around the year 1200. Zen emphasized enlightenment through meditation and included some elements of Taoism (page 140). Its stress on simplicity and discipline was popular with the samurai and helped them develop qualities needed to follow their code of bravery and loyalty.

The shoguns and most samurai followed Zen Buddhism, and Zen monasteries influenced politics, trade, and the arts. Certain arts are typical of the Zen style: the tea ceremony, the simple arrangements of Japanese gardens, and landscape paintings done with a few brush strokes.

289

Background The people who lived on a daimyo's land were completely subject to his will. The rule of a daimyo was so harsh that an entire family might be killed if one of its members criticized the landowner.

Check for Understanding. Ask: Why are the fifteenth and sixteenth centuries in Japan sometimes called the "Age of the Country at War"? (The central government had almost collapsed, neither the emperor nor the shogun was in control, and the samurai were almost constantly at war.)

Religion The word *zen* comes from a Sanskrit word that means "meditation." Zen Buddhism taught that enlightenment could come only through sudden and direct intuitive perception.

KEY
☐ Lands held by Tokugawa and allies
☐ Lands not allied with Tokugawa
☐ Small landholders
✕ Battle

Sea of Japan

HOKKAIDO

KOREA

Sekigahara ✕

HONSHU

Edo (Tokyo) ★

Kyoto ★
Osaka ●
Inland Sea

KYUSHU   SHIKOKU

PACIFIC OCEAN

Nagasaki ●

SCALE
0   200 mi
0   200 km

Tokugawa Japan, 1600–1868

The Tokugawa shoguns tightened their power by awarding land near Edo to lords who were loyal allies. Who else held large areas of land near Edo? How is the landholding pattern shown on the map?

Map Answers: (1) Small landholders. (2) Different colors indicate who held the lands.

The growth of trade and towns. The changes taking place in Japanese society during the 1400's and 1500's encouraged trade and crafts despite the disorder and warfare. Some merchants grew rich by supplying food and equipment to the armies. Peasants also became more prosperous because of new farming techniques. Farmers, artisans, and merchants met on market day to trade goods, crafts, and food. Some merchants and artisans formed groups that were like the guilds of medieval Europe (page 232).

290

As in medieval Europe, the increase in trade and the rise of markets led to the growth of towns. People settled near marketplaces, monasteries, and seaports, or around the fortified castles of the daimyo. Although the old feudal system was breaking down, the Japanese economy and arts continued to thrive.

The Unification of Japan

▲ Note strategies for third objective on this page and p. 292.

During the late sixteenth century a military leader named Hideyoshi (hid-ee-YOH-shee) unified Japan by force. He crushed the daimyo's armies and destroyed their fortresses. When Hideyoshi died in 1598, he was followed by his long-time supporter, Tokugawa Ieyasu (ee-eh-YAH-soo). Ieyasu established the Tokugawa shogunate, which was the last to rule Japan. This shogunate brought Japan a 250-year period of peace and order.

Restrictions on the daimyo. While they did not destroy the feudal system, the Tokugawa shoguns reformed it to protect their own power. In dealing with the daimyo, the Tokugawa shoguns followed a policy of "divide and conquer." For various reasons they might change, take away, or reduce the size of a lord's landholdings. Fearing rebellion, the shoguns kept the daimyo from forming alliances. Marriages between daimyo families, visits to another lord's lands, and all legal contracts had to be approved by the shogun. The daimyo had to spend every other year in Edo, the shogun's capital. The emperor himself never left the capital at Kyoto.

Sec. Rev. ques. 5

Japan's choice of isolation. Another way in which Tokugawa shoguns protected their power was by limiting foreign influence in Japan. The Japanese had been trading with China, Korea, and Southeast Asia for years. In the mid-1500's, contact began with the West as well. About 1542 a Portuguese ship had landed near Kyushu, and soon many Portuguese traders were visiting Japan regularly. In 1549 a Jesuit missionary, Francis Xavier (ZAY-vee-ur), began a campaign to make Japan the first Christian country in Asia. Other Jesuits soon followed. By 1600 about 300,000 Japanese had become Christians.

At first the Tokugawa rulers admired the missionaries' discipline and learning. They soon grew worried, however, that Japanese Christians would turn their loyalties from the shoguns to the Pope. The Tokugawa feared, too, that European armies might follow the missionaries.

Afraid of foreign influence, the Tokugawa shoguns strictly limited all foreign contacts. Laws issued in the 1630's forbade the Japanese to travel abroad or to return home if they had already left the country. Christian missionaries and many of their converts were forced to leave, and remaining Japanese Christians were harshly treated. The Dutch, who made no attempt to send missionaries, were the only European traders allowed in Japan. Along with Chinese traders, they were restricted to the area around the port of Nagasaki.

Tokugawa Society

The growth of Edo. Tokugawa policies of national unification helped the Japanese expand their own economy. Edo, home of the shogun and the daimyo, became an important business center. A network of major roads linked the daimyo's lands with Edo. Towns, inns, and busy markets served the travelers. Merchants and artisans thrived.

Some family businesses grew into large companies, and merchants and bankers came to control much of the country's wealth.

Though some peasant farmers became poorer because of heavy taxes, many lived well by selling their crops to townspeople. Edo soon became Japan's largest and wealthiest city. By 1800 it had a million people.

Problems for the daimyo and samurai. Although many merchants and peasants prospered under the Tokugawa, the daimyo and samurai rapidly fell into financial trouble. Their incomes came mostly from agriculture, especially rice, which was heavily taxed. They did not benefit from the increased trade and prosperity in the towns, though they had to pay the resulting higher prices.

Trained only as professional soldiers, the samurai found themselves out of work during the peace of the Tokugawa period. Although it was against the law and also meant giving up their social rank, some samurai became farmers or merchants. Most preferred to remain proud but poor. Like the daimyo, they went deep into debt.

Popular arts. Life in the fast-growing cities was busy and exciting for the merchants, businesspeople, and samurai who lived there. Two new forms of theater drew enthusiastic crowds. In Kabuki (kuh-BOO-kee) theater, the actors dressed in colorful costumes, wore heavy makeup, and used

Ⓕ See below.

CAUSE AND EFFECT

CAUSES	KEY DEVELOPMENT	EFFECTS
Rise to power of Tokugawa shogunate Expansion of Edo as commercial and political center	Unification of Japan 1598–1700	Reduction of power of daimyo Strict limitation of foreign contacts Loss of status of samurai Long period of peace and prosperity

291

Ⓕ CAUSE AND EFFECT CHART ACTIVITY. Have students list the causes and effects of the unification of Japan in the order of their occurrence. Then have students explain which effect might have been the most significant in unifying Japan. *(Synthesis) Sequencing Causes and Effects*

F See
below.

The Arts

Kabuki Theater

While real political power was in the hands of the Tokugawa shoguns, Japan's emperor and his court devoted themselves to the arts. At the isolated and peaceful court in Kyoto, the nobility spent hours watching traditional stage plays, which were almost like rituals. The beauty of these plays sprang from the elegant costumes and slow, graceful gestures of the actors.

Although refined drama suited the tastes of the imperial court, it did not appeal to the common people. In the late 1500's a woman named Okuni began staging lively performances that mixed music, dance, and humor. Together with a troupe of women actors and dancers, she developed an art form that became known as Kabuki theater. Kabuki was an immediate success among the merchants and artisans of Edo. Large audiences flocked to see this new and different kind of entertainment.

The Tokugawa shoguns, however, were shocked. They thought much of the humor in the new plays was improper. In 1629 the shoguns banned women's Kabuki. Male actors quickly took over the women's roles on stage, and the new form of theater continued to grow in popularity.

Gradually, Kabuki theater became more serious. The plays told melodramatic stories of revenge, suicide, or ill-fated romance. However, elaborate costumes, bizarre make-up, and exaggerated acting turned these serious plays into colorful spectacles. Today Kabuki theater is still popular in Japan.

exaggerated movements. In Bunraku (bun-RAH-koo) theater, large wooden puppets acted out historical dramas or realistic plays.

A new type of poetry, the haiku (HY-koo), also became popular with all classes of people. A haiku is very short—three lines totaling seventeen syllables (in Japanese)—and gives the reader an instant image or picture. The following is the English version of the work of a haiku poet named Onitsura:

▲ See
below,
right.

> 66 A trout leaps high—
> below him, in the river bottom,
> clouds flow by. 99

292

Isolation and change. The Tokugawa policies of isolation cut off the people of Japan from Western ideas for about 200 years. Japan's strict class structure kept peace and brought prosperity. Yet Japan did not stand still during its isolation. Social change continued. People of the merchant and peasant classes gained the education, freedom, and respect that once only the samurai had enjoyed. Artisans perfected their skills. Banking and commerce grew steadily. Unlike China, which resisted change, Japan moved forward even during its isolation, though it moved in different ways than did the West.

See Sec. 4 *Closing the Lesson*, p. T271C.

F FEATURE ACTIVITY. Ask: (a) Why might the common people have found Kabuki more appealing than traditional Japanese drama? (Kabuki included a lively mix of music, dance, and humor; traditional plays were long, ritual-like performances.) (b) Why, do you think, were women banned from Kabuki theater? (In many medieval societies, women were not allowed to assume public roles.) *(Synthesis) Drawing Conclusions*

▲ ENRICHMENT. Have students find information on Kabuki, Bunraku, or the haiku, and then prepare a class presentation on one of the three art forms. Students might dramatize Kabuki theater using makeup and props, make puppets for Bunraku theater, or write haiku poetry and read or display their poems in class. *(Application) Relating Literature and History*

Section Review

Answers to Section Review questions are in brackets on pages indicated.

1. **Define or identify:** archipelago, clan, Shinto, shogun, samurai, Bushido, daimyo, Zen Buddhism. (pp. 286, 288, 289)
2. What beliefs did Shintoists hold? (p. 286)
3. How did a shogun replace the emperor as the actual ruler of Japan? (p. 288)
4. Describe the samurai way of life. (p. 288)

5. What were the steps that Tokugawa shoguns took to prevent rebellions by the daimyo? (p. 290)
6. **Critical thinking:** Why might the Japanese have welcomed Buddhism in the 1200's but rejected Christian influences in the 1600's? (See answer below.)

6. Answers will vary. Students might suggest that the Japanese rulers resented Western influence in Japan. Outside influences were perceived as threats to domestic peace and a stable political order. Students might argue that Buddhism was more easily adapted to traditional Japanese culture.

Chapter 14   Summary and Timeline

1. From the 700's to the 1500's, various Muslim groups invaded India. The Muslims did not adopt Hindu customs, but they did set up the Mogul Empire in India. The Mogul Empire reached its height in the 1500's and 1600's. Corruption and intolerance led to its later decline.

2. The Ottoman Turks captured Constantinople from the Byzantines in 1453 and built an empire that included the Middle East, North Africa, and parts of Europe. After its peak in the 1500's, the Ottoman Empire weakened. Meanwhile, Safavid rulers built an empire in Persia. Though it prospered for only a short time, it left the legacy of a united Persian state.

3. China's Age of Disunity was ended in the sixth century by the Sui dynasty. During the Tang and Song dynasties, which

followed the Sui, the arts flourished and new technology was developed. In the 1200's Mongol invaders crushed the Song and took control of China. The Ming dynasty arose when Mongol rule weakened. It attempted to return China to traditional ways, partly by isolating China from the outside world.

4. Japan borrowed many elements of culture from China but developed its own civilization. By the late 1100's, real governing power had passed from the Japanese emperor to military leaders called shoguns. Feudalism developed, putting power in the hands of landowning lords (daimyo) and warriors (samurai). In the late 1500's Japan became a strong national state. Foreign trade flourished for a time, but in the mid-1600's the Tokugawa shoguns adopted a policy of isolation from the rest of the world.

618–907
Tang dynasty in China

1000
The Tale of Genji written

960–1279
Song dynasty in China

1368–1644
Ming dynasty in China

1520
Suleiman I begins rule of Ottoman Empire

1556
Akbar inherits Mogul throne

1598
Tokugawa shogunate begins in Japan

500   650   800   950   1100   1250   1400   1550   1700

See p. T271D for answers to Chapter Review.

Vocabulary Review

1. Match each of the following terms with its correct definition: *archipelago, Bushido, daimyo, deity, Janissary Corps, shah, Shinto, shogun, Taj Mahal.*
   a. ancient Japanese religion
   b. tomb for Shah Jahan's wife
   c. god or goddess
   d. large group of islands
   e. code of Japanese warriors
   f. military ruler in Japan
   g. Muslim king
   h. local lord in Japanese feudal society
   i. elite unit of the Ottoman army

2. Use the following terms to complete the sentences below: *classics, samurai, sultanate, Zen Buddhism.*
   a. Monks brought ___?___ to Japan from China.
   b. Japanese warriors and knights were called ___?___.
   c. The rulers of the Delhi ___?___ stayed in power for more than 300 years.
   d. ___?___ are great literary works.

Places to Know

Match the letters on this map of Japan with the places listed below. You may want to refer to the map on page 290.
1. Edo 2. Osaka 3. Kyoto 4. Honshu

People to Identify

Identify the following people and tell why each was important.
1. Akbar
2. Aurangzeb
3. Kublai Khan
4. Marco Polo
5. Lady Murasaki Shikibu
6. Suleiman I
7. Yoritomo
8. Wu Hou
9. Zheng He

Recalling the Facts

1. What differences prevented Hinduism and Islam from blending in India?
2. How did Akbar use compromise to unify the Mogul Empire?
3. What factors caused the Ottoman Empire to decline?
4. What steps did Abbas I take to rid Persia of foreign rulers?
5. What two-way exchange of goods and ideas took place between China under the Tang dynasty and other Asian lands?

6. What technological advances did the Chinese make?
7. How did the Ming rulers return China to traditional ways?
8. What ideas did early Japanese rulers borrow from China?
9. How did a feudal system develop in Japan?
10. In what ways did the Tokugawa shoguns protect their power?

Critical Thinking Skills

1. **Preparing a report.** Research and write a report on one of the following topics: the Delhi sultanate; the Taj Mahal; Persian carpet-weaving; the Grand Canal of China; Chang'an, imperial capital of the Tang dynasty; pottery of the Ming and Song dynasties; Shinto; the practice of Zen Buddhism today. *(App.)*

2. **Exploring the arts.** Under the Tang and Song dynasties, China experienced a golden age in the arts, especially poetry. The greatest poets of this period were Li Po, Po Chu-i, and Tu Fu. Read several poems by one of these writers. Then select one poem and write a short essay explaining its meaning. *(Anal.)*

3. **Comparing.** Make a list of similarities and differences between the code of chivalry followed by medieval European knights and the samurai code. *(Comp.)*

4. **Applying theories.** Review the explanation of the dynastic cycle on page 142 of Chapter 7. Is this concept a useful way of explaining the rise and fall of the Ottoman Empire, the Sui dynasty in China, and the Fujiwara family in Japan? Why or why not? *(Eval.)*

Thinking About Geography

1. **Analyzing.** How might the Grand Canal have played a part in unifying the Chinese Empire? *(Comp.)*

2. **Relating geography and history.** How did geography influence the early history of Japan? *(Syn.)*

Enrichment: Primary Sources

In A.D. 604 Japan's Prince Shotoku completed his Seventeen-Article Constitution. The following adapted passage lists some of the rules of behavior that the prince wanted people to follow.

66 Harmony should be valued and quarrels should be avoided. Everyone has his opinions and few men are far-sighted.

Do not be envious! For if we envy others, then they in turn will envy us. The evils of envy know no limit. If others surpass us in intelligence, we are not pleased; if they are more able, we are envious. But if we do not find wise men and sages, how shall the realm be governed?

Employ the people in forced labor at seasonable times. Employ them in the winter months when they are at leisure, but not from spring to autumn, when they are busy with agriculture.

Decisions on important matters should not be made by one person alone. They should be discussed with many people. One should consult with others so as to arrive at the right conclusion. 99

1. What did Shotoku mean when he said that "evils of envy know no limit"?
2. Why did Shotoku say that people should be employed in forced labor only during the winter months?
3. How did Shotoku advise people to go about making important decisions?
4. **Critical thinking:** To what group in society was this constitution probably addressed? Explain your answer. *(Anal.)*

A checkmark identifies questions and exercises calling for the three higher-order levels of thinking at the top of the Bloom taxonomy: Analysis, Synthesis, and Evaluation.

Africa in the Age of Islam   500–1600
(pp. 296–309)

Chapter Preview

This chapter explains how Arab conquest of North Africa affected trade in the western Sudan and describes the trading empires of Ghana, Mali, and Songhai. Section 1 also discusses the growth and achievements of new kingdoms in eastern and central Africa. In Section 2 the impact of Islam on African cultures is described. The chapter concludes with an explanation of the expansion of the slave trade.

Bibliography

See the *Teacher's Management and Planning Guide* for additional listings. Starred titles are for both students and teachers.

Mazrui, Ali. *The Africans: Triple Heritage*. Little, Brown. Africa's indigenous traditions, Islamic culture, and Western influences.

Osae, T. A., et. al. *A Short History of West Africa, A.D. 1000 to the Present*. Hill and Wang.

*Shinnie, Margaret. *Ancient African Kingdoms*. Mentor.

Vansina, Jan. *Kingdoms of the Savanna*. University of Wisconsin Press. Authoritative work by a well-known scholar.

Section Lesson Plans

SECTION 1   (pp. 297–303)
African Kingdoms and Trading Empires

Objectives

After completing this section, students will be able to:
1. Describe how a series of trading empires developed in the western Sudan.
2. Identify the new kingdoms that emerged in eastern and central Africa.

Introducing the Lesson

Remind students that the continent of Africa has long been a source of exotic and valuable goods desired by many people. As trade with the Arabs increased, African societies experienced many economic and political changes.

Then ask: *(a) Why might trade relationships be a source of social change?* (People with different backgrounds have the opportunity to learn new languages, new ways of thinking, and new ways of behavior.)

(b) In what ways might Arab traders have influenced African societies? (Answers will vary. Africans who had contact with Arabs probably learned the Arabic language; Arabs probably converted many people to Islam.)

(c) How might African peoples have influenced Arab traders? (Answers will vary. Arab traders probably learned African languages and became familiar with African customs.)

(d) Do you think people today are influenced by international trade as much as in the past? Why or why not? (Answers will vary.)

Developing the Lesson:
Relating Geography and History

Have students draw a chart with four columns labeled *West Africa, East Africa, Central Africa, and Southern Africa* and then identify the locations of African states discussed in this lesson. *(Comprehension)*

Developing the Lesson:
Drawing Inferences

Have students write a paragraph to explain the meaning of the following excerpt about empires in western Africa: "Their large, diverse empires were held together by tribute and strong personal rule rather than by any sense of loyalty to the state. This lack of state loyalty might have helped cause the decline of the empires of the western Sudan" (p. 298). *(Comprehension)*

Answers to *Map Skill Practice*, p. 298.

1. Ghana, Mali, Songhai.
2. About 1,700 miles.
3. Kongo, Lunda, Luba, Katanga (Shaba).
4. Zaire.
5. Off the east coast of southern Africa in the Indian Ocean.
6. About 750 miles.
7. Timbuktu was the point where trade routes out of the Sahara intersected with the Niger River.

Closing the Lesson:
Understanding Chronology

Have students make two timelines comparing political and economic developments in the western Sudan with those of eastern and central Africa. *(Comprehension)*

See *Section Review* questions, p. 303.

SECTION 2   (pp. 303–307)
African Cultures

Objectives

After completing this section, students will be able to:
1. Describe how the growth of trade and the spread of Islam affected African cultures.
2. Name the changes that took place in African society and in the slave trade.

Introducing the Lesson

Remind students that African traditions were centuries old by the time Arab traders brought their social customs and religion to the continent. The introduction of the Islamic faith and the Arab culture brought both advantages and disadvantages to Africa.

Then ask: *(a) What advantages might Africans have enjoyed from changes brought by Arab influence?* (Answers will vary. New technology, added wealth from trade, and greater access to Arab products.)

(b) What disadvantages might have resulted from Arab influence? (Answers will vary. Some people might have been forced to change their ways; African traditions and customs might not have prepared people to address challenges arising from new ideas and goods.)

Developing the Lesson:
Comparing Ideas and Beliefs

Have students compare traditional African religions with Islam (pp. 198–199) and then answer the following:

(a) How did African and Muslim ideas about God differ? (Traditional African religions and Islam believed in a Supreme Being who created the world, but Africans also believed that lesser spirits lived in nature.)

(b) How did traditional African ideas about prophets compare with those of Islam? (Many Africans believed that *diviners* were prophets who could read signs from the spirit world and foretell the future. Muslims believed that Mohammed was the last and the greatest of Allah's prophets.)

(c) How did African and Muslim ideas about the afterlife differ? (Africans believed that ancestors were part of the spirit world and could protect the living; Muslims believed that after death, nonbelievers and the wicked went to a fearful place, and faithful Muslims went to Paradise.) *(Comprehension)*

Developing the Lesson:
Making Inferences

Have students explain what might have made the following a true statement: "Islam gained an especially strong foothold among the trading cities of the Swahili coast and West Africa. In these places Islam became the religion of the ruling and the trading classes, but not of the masses of the people" (p. 305). (Rulers and traders are those who would have had the most contact with Muslim traders and more to gain by converting to Islam. The masses would have had less contact with Islam and less reason to change their beliefs.) *(Comprehension)*

Closing the Lesson:
Analyzing Cause and Effect

Have students explain how the Islamic religion affected African culture. (Schools were started to teach the Koran; mosques and shrines were built; men adopted the clothing of Arab Muslims.) *(Comprehension)*

See *Section Review* questions, p. 307.

Chapter 15 Review Answers
(pp. 308–309)

Vocabulary Review

1. literacy 2. dhow 3. terra cotta 4. *ghana* 5. diviner

People to Identify

1. Mwene Mutapa 2. Abu Bakari 3. Sunni Ali 4. Mansa Musa 5. Askia Mohammed 6. Lalibela

Places to Know

1. A   2. E   3. C   4. D   5. B

Recalling the Facts

1. The Arab conquest of North Africa stimulated trade with sub-Saharan Africa.
2. Ghana's wealth came from control of the gold and salt trade.
3. Ghana was weakened by the lack of loyalty among its people and by a Muslim attack in 1076. Mali was raided by desert nomads, weakened by internal rebellions, and conquered by the Songhai people in 1468. Songhai was destroyed by internal disorder and by a Moroccan invasion in 1590.
4. The trade routes across the Sahara shifted to the east in order to avoid unrest in the western Sudan. Trade also expanded south along the Atlantic Coast and along the Niger River.
5. The king, a descendant of the kingdom's founder, passed down authority to provinces, then to chiefdoms, and finally to villages.
6. They farmed, fished, and traded. They traded ivory, slaves, leopard skins, gold, and the shells of sea tortoises.
7. People had to communicate in order to trade.
8. Many Africans learned to read, write, and speak Arabic; schools were opened to teach Islamic texts; many Africans converted to Islam, and clothing styles changed.
9. Wealthy people in Africa and other lands wanted black slaves as servants, laborers, soldiers, and administrators.

Critical Thinking Skills

1–4. Answers will vary.
5. They would have to rely more heavily on artifacts and other physical evidence, and they would have to consider carefully the reliability and accuracy of information passed down orally.

Thinking About Geography

1. Mauritania, Gambia, Senegal, Mali, Burkina Faso, Niger, Nigeria, Guinea-Bissau, Sierra Leone, Ivory Coast, Benin.

2. (a) Ghana, Mali, and Songhai were all located on the southern edge of the Sahara. Their location enabled them to take control of the trade routes from North Africa as well as those to the south and west. (b) The Hausa city-states and Bornu took advantage of increased trade with North Africa after trade routes shifted east following the decline of the Songhai Empire. (c) These cities on the east coast of Africa near the Indian Ocean became ports for trading ships from Arabia, Persia, and India.

Enrichment: Primary Sources

1. He was shown honor and entertained.
2. They had clothes made of Egyptian fabric.
3. His mother's brothers.
4. He says the state of affairs is "extraordinary." He remarks on the beauty of the women, the unusual system of inheritance, the fairness of the people, the absence of crime.

Africa in the Age of Islam

500–1600

See chapter timeline, p. 307.

Before You Read This Chapter

Where do the foods you eat and the goods you use come from? Your local supermarket probably sells fish from Canada, coffee from Kenya, beef from Argentina. At a department store you could buy Japanese radios and cameras, Swiss watches, French perfume. On the street you probably see cars made in Germany, Japan, and Italy. How did all these goods reach the United States? Trade has been important throughout history, and it is an important theme in this chapter. As you read, think about how trade leads to the exchange of ideas as well as goods. Consider, too, how long-distance trade and cultural exchanges have become easier in modern times.

The Geographic Setting

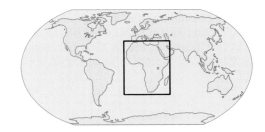

The Chapter Outline

1. African Kingdoms and Trading Empires
2. African Cultures

This aerial view shows the stone ruins of Great Zimbabwe, an ancient religious and trading center in southern Africa.

1 African Kingdoms and Trading Empires

Objectives

Focus Questions

★ ■ How did a series of trading empires develop in the western Sudan? *(pages 297–300)*

● ■ What new kingdoms emerged in eastern and central Africa? *(pages 301–302)*

Terms to Know

ghana
terra cotta

★ Note strategies for first objective on this page and p. 299.

Sec. Rev. ques. 2

The Arab conquest of North Africa in the seventh century A.D. stimulated trade across the Sahara. To satisfy the growing demands of wealthy Arabs for luxuries, more camel caravans followed the ancient routes across the desert. They were seeking West Africa's gold, slaves, and other valuable items.

The African peoples who lived on the broad savannas (open grasslands) south of the desert responded enthusiastically to these new trading opportunities. To control the markets and guarantee safety to the visiting traders from the north, they created impressive new empires. For a thousand years, stability was provided by the empires of Ghana, Mali, and Songhai in the western Sudan.

The Kingdom of Ghana

As you read in Chapter 8, the Soninke people lived at the southern edge of the Sahara. For many centuries they had been exchanging gold from lands to the south and west for salt and other goods brought across the desert by Berber traders (page 155). Sometime after A.D. 500 they put together a large new empire

that controlled this trade. Its powerful ruler was called the *ghana* (GAH-nah). Foreign visitors gave his kingdom the name Ghana, too, and called it "the land of the gold."

A growing empire. Protecting the trade routes from the gold-producing regions was one of the main functions of the new empire. To ensure a fair price from North African traders, the *ghana* set careful limits on how much gold could be sold. The state also taxed the salt and gold that passed over its borders. These taxes supported an army that kept peace within Ghana and protected the empire from outside attacks.

The empire's wealth allowed the *ghana* to live in a lavish style that impressed visitors from the Islamic world. The royal revenues also enabled the king to pay government officials to oversee the trade and provide protection for traders. From about 700 to 1000, Ghana was at the height of its power. The rulers of a number of smaller states paid tribute to the king in taxes and in goods.

Two capitals. Ghana's capital city, Kumbi, was in fact "twin" towns located only a few miles apart and linked by road. The business capital became a Muslim town, where traders brought fruit, wheat, and cloth from northern Africa and Spain. The Muslims also brought their religion with them, and Islam spread quickly.

The second town, where the king lived, was a center of traditional Soninke culture. Here Islam was not accepted. Though the kings of Ghana recognized that their wealth depended on Muslim traders, they did not want Muslim ways to influence their subjects. After all, this would weaken their own role as the spiritual leaders of the people.

A model for other empires. The great empires in western Africa all followed a pattern of development and decline much like Ghana's. Their wealth came from gold and from the control of trade. They also conquered neighboring states and demanded **297**

★ **RETEACHING.** Have students review pp. 297–299 and then explain why new trading empires developed in the western Sudan. (Trade was stimulated by an increased demand for goods. Larger camel caravans made more frequent trading journeys across ancient trade routes. To control markets and protect traders, new empires arose.) *(Comprehension) Summarizing Facts*
Background In Africa, salt was as important a trade commodity as gold. It was found primarily in the Sahara and traded in southern Africa.

★ **REINFORCEMENT.** Have students evaluate the information on the kingdoms of Ghana, Mali, and Songhai and explain the following: the most significant achievement of each empire; which empire contributed most to political and economic stability in the western Sudan. *(Synthesis) Making Judgments*
Cultural History One of the kings of ancient Ghana was reported to have owned 1,000 horses, each with its own mattress and three servants.

Map Skill Practice

See p. T295B for answers to *Map Skill Practice*.

Africa, 500–1500

1. According to this map, what empires developed in the western Sudan—the grassland region south of the Sahara?
2. What was the longest east-west distance of Songhai?
3. What states grew up in central Africa south of the Congo River?
4. Compare this map with the modern political map of Africa in the Atlas at the back of this book. What country now exists in the region that contained Luba, Lunda, and the Kongo?
5. Where was Madagascar located?
6. About how long was the trade route between Kilwa and Mogadishu?
7. **Making inferences.** Why might Timbuktu have been called the "meeting place of camel and canoe"?

tribute from these conquered peoples. Kings had absolute power and ruled with the help of family members and appointed officials. Their empires were held together by tribute and strong personal rule rather than by any sense of loyalty to the state. This lack of loyalty eventually helped cause the decline of the empires of the western Sudan.

In the case of Ghana, the death blow came when invaders struck from the north. Fierce Muslims swept across the Sahara and captured the capital in 1076, severely weakening the empire. Ghana never regained its former glory.

Sec. Rev. ques. 3

The Rise of Mali and Songhai

Mali. Ghana's place at the crossroads of the north-south caravan routes was taken **298** by the Malinke (mah-LING-kay) people of

Mali (MAH-lee), who were distant kin of the Soninke. Mali had begun as a small kingdom. In the eleventh century its rulers converted to Islam. A ruler named Sundiata (soon-JAH-tah), who became king about 1230, greatly expanded the kingdom and built a new capital city. Mali soon gained control of the caravan routes and the profits from trade.

Abu Bakari II, ruler of Mali in the early 1300's, dreamed of reaching the sea and exploring the world beyond it. He ordered 200 ships and 200 supply boats to be built and outfitted for a two-year voyage.

The fleet set sail with orders not to turn back until the ships had reached the end of the ocean or run out of food. Only one ship finally returned, and its captain reported that all the other ships had been lost. Abu Bakari then prepared for a second expedition, this time leading the fleet himself. The ships headed west and were never heard from again.

Check for Understanding. Ask: How was Ghana representative of other African empires? (Ghana's wealth came from gold and trade; conquered states paid tribute; kings had absolute power.)

Abu Bakari II was succeeded by his brother, Mansa Musa, Mali's most famous king (picture, page 304). In Arabic, *Mansa* means "emperor" and *Musa* means "Moses." An Arab scholar of the time, comparing the king with other West African rulers, said he was "the most powerful, the richest, the most fortunate, the most feared by his enemies, and the most able to do good to those around him."

In 1324 Mansa Musa, a devout Muslim, made a pilgrimage to Mecca in Arabia. Riding on horseback across the hot Sahara sands, he covered nearly 4,000 miles. Along the way he dazzled people with his show of wealth. Amazed witnesses reported that Mansa Musa traveled with 12,000 slaves dressed in rich silks. He took with him 50,000 ounces of gold to give to the poor and to the leaders of other lands.

Mali reached the peak of its power during Mansa Musa's reign (1312–1332). The empire stretched from the Atlantic coast inland to the cities of Timbuktu and Gao (map, page 298). Timbuktu was known far and wide for its great mosque and royal palace. Its university was an important center of Muslim scholarship.

Songhai. Like Ghana, Mali was weakened by the raids of nomadic desert peoples. Rebellions also broke out among states under Malinke rule, including Songhai (SONG-hy). Led by a powerful king named Sunni Ali, the Songhai people captured Timbuktu in 1468 and went on to conquer much of the middle and upper Niger River valley.

Sec. Rev. ques. 3, cont.

After the death of Sunni Ali in 1492, one of his generals, Askia Mohammed, seized the throne. Askia Mohammed ruled from 1493 to 1528. A devout Muslim, he tried to unite his territories into an Islamic empire by launching a series of wars. His religious zeal also drew scholars back to Timbuktu, which once again became famous as a center of Muslim studies and culture. Larger than either Ghana or Mali, Songhai at its height covered an area about the size of Western Europe.

★ See below, left.

An outside attack and internal disorder destroyed Songhai. In 1590 the sultan of Morocco sent an invasion force against the empire. Five months of desert travel to Songhai cost the Moroccans many soldiers. Nevertheless, with the advantage of firearms, the Moroccans were able to defeat a much larger army. The Songhai Empire never recovered, and no new power replaced it.

The Muslim kings of Mali built this mosque at Timbuktu, the administrative and academic center of the great medieval African empire.

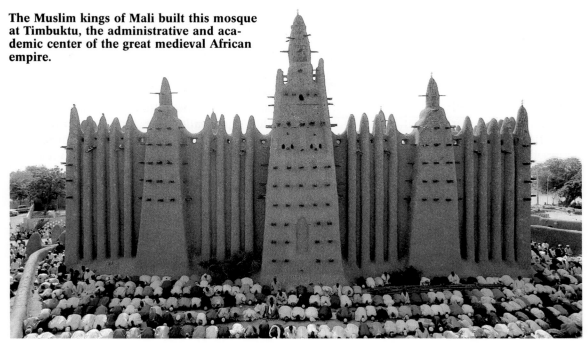

299

★ ENRICHMENT. Have students find information on the importance of Timbuktu to the Mali and Songhai empires and compare the imperial city with present-day Timbuktu in what is now the nation of Mali. *(Synthesis)* *Linking Past and Present*

Biography Sunni Ali was a very successful ruler who created provinces, appointed their governors, created a bureaucratic administration, and established a professional army.

ⒻSee
below.

The Geography Connection

Katanga Copper

The availability of natural resources in a region is an important factor in the development of the region's people. One such resource, copper, has influenced strongly the cultures of central Africa.

Copper was prized in ancient times for its beauty and for its special qualities. The metal was easy to shape, either hot or cold, and it could be bent bent into unusual shapes. African artisans made elaborate jewelry, religious articles, lidded pots, and children's toys out of pure copper. They also combined copper with other metals to make stronger and heavier metals called alloys. The most important copper alloys were bronze and brass. Artists of the African Bronze Age poured molten metals into clay molds to cast lifelike portraits, plaques, and sculptures, such as the bronze head at left.

The richest sources of copper lay in the Katanga region of central Africa (map, page 298). For hundreds of years the Bantu-speaking people of the region mined and traded copper. Trade routes led into Katanga from both the east and the west—from West Africa by way of the Congo River and from Arab trading posts on the East African coast. The copper trade brought these people wealth and eventually led to the establishment of a network of Bantu kingdoms.

The Katanga region, which is today a part of Zaire known as the Shaba region, still yields copper. In fact, Zaire ranks among the world's leading copper-producing nations. The metal that once served Bronze Age artists and Bantu kings is now used in color television sets, refrigerators, and electronic guidance systems for spacecraft.

Making the connection. How did the people of the Katanga region make use of a natural resource? What effects did this have on the people?

New African Trade Routes

With the decline of Songhai, the trade routes across the Sahara shifted to the east. Caravans tried to avoid the unrest in the western Sudan by traveling to the central Sudan instead. There they were met by the traders of the Hausa (HOW-sah) city-states and the empire of Bornu (BOHR-noo). These states profited from the increase in trade that came their way.

Trade was also expanding south of the western Sudan. In the early 1400's, the Malinke had opened important new trade routes leading to the gold fields near the Atlantic

coast. Later that century the first Portuguese explorers reaching this area built a fort on what they called the Gold Coast. African miners now could transport their gold in two directions. They could take it east to the central Sudan or south to the Atlantic coast.

The Portuguese also started an important trade near the Niger River. From the kingdom of Benin (beh-NEEN) they bought pepper, cotton cloth, ivory, and slaves. Benin was an old kingdom that had expanded widely in the fifteenth century. It was known for beautiful art made of bronze, ivory, and terra cotta—hard ceramic clay. The broad, straight avenues of its capital city greatly impressed early European visitors.

ⒻGEOGRAPHY CONNECTION. Have students compare the economic and political benefits that copper brought to Katanga with those enjoyed by Ghana as a result of its gold trade. Then ask: (a) Why are natural resources important to the strength of a society? (b) Are natural resources as important to nations today as in the past? Why or why not? (Synthesis) Drawing Conclusions

Politics Each of the Hausa city-states had as its center a walled village, or birni, and was governed by a council. The Hausa city-states formed a loose confederation and sometimes competed for trade.
Economics Between the fifteenth and eighteenth centuries pepper from the malaguetta plant was so important an export in western Africa that the coast of present-day Liberia was called the Malaguetta Coast.

Bantu Kingdoms

● Note strategies for second objective on this page and p. 302.

After about A.D. 1000, new kingdoms began to appear among the Bantu-speaking peoples of eastern and central Africa. Along the Indian Ocean and on the plateau south of the Zambezi River, trade was an important factor in the rise of the new states.

Sec. Rev. ques. 4

The well-watered lands along the lakes of eastern Africa (map, page 298) had become the home of many African farmers and cattle herders. As their numbers grew, they set up hundreds of small states. In the fifteenth and sixteenth centuries, many of these small states were absorbed into larger kingdoms.

East Africa. In what is now Uganda, the kingdoms of Bunyoro (boon-YOHR-oh) and Buganda (boo-GAHN-dah) took shape. Other kingdoms were developing to the south in Rwanda (roo-AHN-dah) and Burundi (boo-ROON-dee). These were the most densely populated kingdoms in Africa during this period. They are also among the few African kingdoms of that time to survive as modern nations.

The states of Luba and Lunda. By A.D. 1000 the ancestors of the Luba, a Bantu-speaking people in central Africa, had established a strong agricultural economy. Copper-mining and long-distance trade added to the wealth of the Luba. By the 1400's a series of powerful warrior-kings had organized a Luba state. The Luba king was always a descendant of the kingdom's founder. Authority was passed down to provinces, then to chiefdoms, and finally to villages made up of family groups. Such a political organization became common in Africa.

Some time before 1500, the neighboring empire of Lunda was founded. According to legend, this happened when the queen of several small Lunda kingdoms married the nephew of the Luba king. He then broke all ties with the Luba. Other members of the royal family also set up separate states, and the Lunda Empire developed as a series of loosely associated kingdoms. In this way, the Luba royal family influenced the formation of

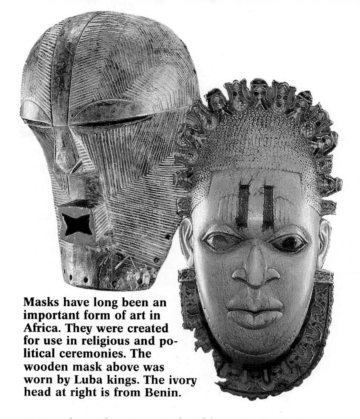

Masks have long been an important form of art in Africa. They were created for use in religious and political ceremonies. The wooden mask above was worn by Luba kings. The ivory head at right is from Benin.

states throughout central Africa. Trade in copper and salt was another important factor holding these states together.

The Kongo kingdom. Near the mouth of the Congo River lay the Kongo kingdom, established in the 1300's. The Kongo state grew and prospered, extending south along the Atlantic coast. Its people were known for their skill in pottery-making, weaving, ironworking, and sculpture. They traded heavily with neighboring states and, beginning in the 1480's, with the Portuguese.

Great Zimbabwe. By A.D. 1000, Bantu farmers and herders lived on the fertile plateau between the Zambezi and Limpopo rivers in southeast Africa. The area became a major producer of gold, which was mined locally and exported out of Sofala on the coast. Imports included cotton and spices.

From the late 1100's, a wealthy kingdom was expanding its control over the plateau. Many of the settlements built during this period included stone buildings. Of these the most impressive was Great Zimbabwe (zim-BAHB-way), the king's residence. The word *Zimbabwe* comes from a Bantu phrase meaning either "dwelling of the chief" or "stone enclosure."

Sec. Rev. ques. 5

301

● RETEACHING. Have students review "Bantu Kingdoms" (pp. 301–302) and then arrange the following in the order in which they occurred: people in the Kongo state traded with the Portuguese (third); ancestors of the Luba established a strong agricultural economy (first); Lunda Empire founded (fifth); Luba state organized (second); kingdom of Kongo established (fourth). *(Comprehension) Sequencing Information*

● REINFORCEMENT. Have students write a summary of economic activity in eastern and central Africa after A.D. 1000. (Africans traded gold, jewelry, ivory, slaves, leopard skins, and tortoise shells. They also farmed, raised cattle, fished, and mined gold and copper.) *(Comprehension) Observing for Detail*

Linking Past and Present Today, Burundi is one of Africa's smallest and most heavily populated countries. About as large as Maryland, Burundi has a population density of about 386 people per square mile.

Background It has been estimated that the wall surrounding Great Zimbabwe contained approximately 15,000 tons of cut stone.

Vocabulary Note that the word *Swahili* means "coast people."

The extraordinary remains of Great Zimbabwe are encircled by two massive oval walls built of stone. These walls are 32 feet high and more than 800 feet around. A long, narrow passage between the walls led visitors inside the ancient city. There they saw a great cone-shaped tower and several walled chambers. This was where the king lived and held royal audiences.

On a rocky hilltop overlooking the royal residence are similar stone ruins and a series of passages. These were probably part of an important religious shrine. The structures all had curved walls, and they were built of granite blocks skillfully fitted together without mortar.

By the early 1400's the buildings at Great Zimbabwe were complete and the state was at the peak of its power. Its ruler was called the Mwene Mutapa (MWAY-nay moo-TAH-pah), meaning "great plunderer." The wealth of the empire came from its gold mines. The gold was used to make jewelry or was traded to the coast for imported beads and pottery. Through this trade the empire of the Mwene Mutapa had access to the Indian Ocean trade.

The Swahili City-States

Much of the gold from the Mwene Mutapa's empire passed through the city-states of Kilwa and Sofala. These trading cities were located on the Swahili (swah-HEE-lee) coast. The Swahili were a Bantu-speaking people who farmed the coastal lands, fished in the ocean waters, and traded with foreign visitors. For many centuries, trading ships from Arabia, Persia, and India had been sailing to this coast on the monsoon winds that blew across the Indian Ocean.

The Swahili sold these traders ivory, slaves, and leopard skins, as well as gold. They obtained these products from Africans farther inland. The Swahili also caught sea tortoises. The shells were then sold overseas, where they were made into combs.

The Swahili city-states developed a sophisticated urban culture. Merchants from Arabia and Persia settled in these coastal African cities. As the cities grew larger and more prosperous, their residents imported more luxuries, including large quantities of Chinese porcelain and Indian glass beads.

See Sec. 1 *Closing the Lesson*, p. T295B.

● See below.

Timetable

Major African Trading Empires

Empire	Location	Peak of Power	Source of Power
Ghana	western Africa	700–1000	Gold and salt trade; control of trans-Saharan caravan routes through the western Sudan.
Mali	western Africa	early 1300's	Control of gold-trade routes after Ghana's decline.
Songhai	western Africa	late 1400's	Military might; religious zeal.
Luba and Lunda	central Africa	late 1500's	Strong agricultural economy; copper mining; copper and salt trade.
Kongo	central Africa	1500's	Trade.
Mwene Mutapa	southeast Africa	early 1400's	Gold mining; gold trade.

Cultural History The Mwene Mutapa was believed to be semi-divine, and the welfare of the kingdom was linked to his health. If the king became ill, it was considered his duty to commit suicide so that a healthy king could replace him and keep the country strong.

● ENRICHMENT. Have students draw a map of present-day Africa and indicate the locations of Bantu kingdoms discussed in the text. Students might refer to the map on p. 298. *(Application) Linking Past and Present*

1. **Define:** *ghana*, terra cotta. (pp. 297, 300)
2. How did the Arab conquest of North Africa help boost trade across the Sahara Desert? (p. 297)
3. What factors led to the decline of the empires of the western Sudan? (pp. 298–299)
4. How did trade help stimulate the growth of Bantu kingdoms? (p. 301)

5. What was Great Zimbabwe? When was it built? (p. 301)
6. **Critical thinking:** Which would have been hurt more by a decline in trading activity, the western Sudan empires or the Bantu kingdoms? Give reasons for your answer. (See answer below.)

6. Students might point out how a strong economic base in agriculture and diversity in products and trading partners put Bantu-speaking peoples in good standing. The Sudan empires had traded fewer items and depended on trade revenues to fund the military.

See lesson plans, pp. T295A–T295C.

2 African Cultures

Objectives

Focus Questions

★ ■ How did the growth of trade and the spread of Islam affect African cultures? *(pages 303–305)*

● ■ What changes took place in African society and in the slave trade? *(pages 306–307)*

Terms to Know

literacy
diviner
dhow

★ Note strategies for first objective on this page and p. 304.

Between A.D. 500 and 1600 many parts of Africa experienced far-reaching cultural changes. Some of these changes resulted from internal developments, such as the growth of cities and states. Other changes were due to outside forces, such as growing contacts with the Islamic world. African society was greatly enriched by these changes, but suffered from new problems as well.

Improving Communications

The spread of trade and the growth of states made it necessary for people in distant parts of Africa to understand each other. This was not easy, because the many groups in Africa, like the many nationalities in Europe, were quite different from one another. Each had its own history and identity, and many different African languages had evolved when peoples and villages were more isolated.

Trading languages. To overcome the communication problem, people began using some languages over much wider areas. Local traders learned the language of the long-distance traders who passed through their villages and towns. In the western Sudan the Mandinka language came to be a major trading language. In the central Sudan the Hausa language dominated.

The Swahili language began to spread inland along the trade routes in eastern Africa. It soon became an important trading language and borrowed many Arabic terms as a result. Swahili also developed a strong oral and literary tradition in its coastal homelands. Swahili speakers excelled at reciting stories and poetry. Today Swahili is spoken by some 30 million Africans.

303

★ RETEACHING. Have students identify the causes of the following: Trading languages developed (People used the same language over wider areas, and local traders learned the languages of long-distance traders.) **Knowledge of the Arabic language grew** (Schools were opened to teach the Koran and other Islamic texts in Arabic.) *(Comprehension) Identifying Causes*

★ REINFORCEMENT. Have students list the ways that Islam affected African cultures, evaluate which effect was most significant, and explain why. *(Evaluation) Evaluating Effects*
Check for Understanding. Ask: Why was it so difficult for the many groups in Africa to understand one another? (The groups were very different from one another: each had its own history and identity and many different African languages had evolved.)

Oral traditions. In many places the spread of spoken languages was accompanied by growing literacy—the ability to read and write. While some African peoples, such as the Kushites and Ethiopians, had long used written languages, most African societies had relied on oral traditions. These societies often had specialists who recited or sang the great stories and histories of their people.

One famous oral epic of this era celebrated the deeds of Sundiata, an early king of Mali (page 298). Other legends told of the founding heroes of the new Bantu kingdoms. Writing was not necessary for preserving stories, since they were memorized by each generation. However, the writing down of these traditions during the past two centuries has preserved many of them for all time.

Arabic literacy. In parts of Africa the Arabic language became widely used. Many Africans in contact with the Muslim traders learned to read, write, and speak it. Today Arabic is the official language of all North African countries, as well as the Republic of the Sudan, and is widely known in Muslim areas of sub-Saharan Africa.

Sec. Rev. ques. 2

As Islam spread, schools were opened to teach the Koran (page 198) and other Islamic texts in Arabic. Students who mastered these texts might go on to read other works in Arabic. In this way they became familiar with the learning of Islam and the ancient Mediterranean world.

After the Mali ruler Mansa Musa returned from his pilgrimage in the fourteenth century (page 299), he spent large sums of money to promote higher learning among his people. Many schools grew up in Timbuktu along the desert edge. As you have read, Timbuktu became a famous center of learning.

Old and New Religions

Traditional beliefs. African religions varied widely, but all groups traced the origin of the world to a Supreme Being. They believed, too, in lesser spirits that lived in nature—in the sky, the trees, thunder, and rain. African peoples also had great respect for their ancestors. It was believed that ancestors were a part of the spirit world and could help protect the living.

Africans honored their ancestors and the spirits with prayers, offerings, and rituals. Dance, song, and drum music usually played a part in these ceremonies. For special favors from the gods, some African groups turned to diviners. Diviners were prophets who read signs from the spirit world and foretold the future. Some relied on dreams and trances; others interpreted the patterns made by throwing special nuts or shells on the ground.

★ See below.

Expansion of Islam and Christianity. In northeastern Africa the Islamic and Christian religions both expanded after 1000. In parts of East Africa, Islam gained followers by persuasion and by force, especially among the Somali. Islam spread among other people of the Ethiopian highlands in the 1100's and 1200's. Christianity also took hold in this region as the Ethiopian kingdom expanded southward from its ancient base at Aksum.

This is the first European map of northwest Africa, made in 1375. It pictures Mansa Musa on his throne holding a nugget of gold. An Arab merchant on a camel is coming to trade with him.

304

Critical Thinking. Ask: Why might literacy have accompanied the spread of Islam? (The religious teachings of the Koran, Islam's holy book, were the most important elements of the Islamic faith; to study the Koran, Muslims had to know how to read Arabic.)

Religion In Africa, nature spirits were worshiped as local gods. Ancestors were important because they had established the community and decided its religious, moral, and social rules. It was believed that ancestors could become dangerous enemies if they were neglected.

★ ENRICHMENT. Have students find examples of African legends and myths and report to the class on the characteristics of the heroes and gods that are described in the literature. Students might compare African legends with those of Greek or Roman origin. (Application) *Relating Literature and History*

Yet some people saw these foreign religions as unwelcome influences. They continued to follow traditional beliefs and practices.

Islam gained an especially strong foothold among the trading cities of the Swahili coast and West Africa. In these places Islam became the religion of the ruling and the trading classes, but not of the masses of the people.

As states grew larger, they became more difficult to govern. Some rulers (such as those of Ghana) hired Muslim advisers to teach them about the laws and government of the great Islamic empires. As you read earlier in this chapter, the rulers of Mali and Songhai became Muslims themselves.

Sec. Rev. ques. 3
African rulers who converted to Islam had to be careful not to anger subjects who still held to the old religious beliefs. To avoid conflict, many African Muslim rulers found it wise to follow both Muslim and traditional practices. For example, they often had dancers perform at Muslim celebrations.

A Building Boom

The growth of great towns and empires and the spread of new religions led to important building programs. Wealthy African rulers and traders erected impressive homes and palaces for themselves. New churches, mosques, and shrines were built.

In much of western Africa, stone suitable for building was extremely rare. The great mosque at Timbuktu in Mali was therefore made of wood and clay, with elaborate towers. In eastern Africa, however, stone was more common. By the eleventh and twelfth centuries the leading Swahili merchants lived in elegant houses of coral stone, with as many as four stories. To serve the growing Muslim population of the towns, beautiful stone mosques were built to replace older wooden ones.

Among the marvels of this period are 11 large churches built in Ethiopia. On the orders of King Lalibela (LAH-lih-bel-uh), who ruled from 1200 to 1230, these churches were carved out of solid rock.

Historic Places

F See below, left.

The Churches of Lalibela

When the armies of Islam swept across northern Africa in the 600's, they failed to conquer the kingdom of Ethiopia. Ethiopia's rulers had been Christian since A.D. 350 (page 154), and later rulers built impressive churches for their people. Ethiopia's most famed church builder was King Lalibela, who built 11 churches in his capital city, Roha.

Roha stood in rugged highlands, where solid rock lay under a thin layer of soil. To begin a church, Lalibela's workers cut a deep, rectangular trench in this bedrock. When the trench was done, a huge block of solid stone stood in the center, its top surface at ground level. From this block, the stoneworkers cut and carved and hollowed the church.

The problems facing the builders were enormous. If they made a mistake in carving, they could not simply replace the one spoiled stone. They shaped arches, columns, windows, and doors, all out of a single natural mass of solid rock.

King Lalibela's churches became so famous that eventually Roha was renamed Lalibela. Over the years, many thousands of pilgrims visited the town to worship in its unique stone churches.

305

F **FEATURE ACTIVITY. Ask:** Why might a political leader like King Lalibela undertake a monumental church-building program? (Answers will vary. Some leaders might view such a building program as an expression of their power; others might see it as a way to gain spiritual blessing.) *(Synthesis)* ***Drawing Conclusions***

Background The largest of Lalibela's churches is Beit Medhane Alem (The House of the Savior of the World), which measures 35 feet deep, 109 feet long, and 77 feet wide. Lalibela is buried in one of the churches, Beit Giorgis.

Social Changes

● Note strategies for second objective on this page and p. 307.

The changes taking place in African economic and political life affected African society. Some people found their social positions improved, but others lost status.

Sec. Rev. ques. 4

For women, change came more slowly than for men, especially in areas where Islam was spreading. For example, African Muslims did not seclude women, as was common in North Africa and the Middle East. Nor did Africans adopt the custom of having every woman wear a veil across her face. Indeed, men's clothing styles were much more affected by the spread of Islam than were women's. In fourteenth-century Mali, Muslim men wore the long white garments typical of Arab Muslims. However, women still followed the Malinke custom of wearing little or no clothing until they married.

The growth of the slave trade. Inequality began to increase in African society. At the upper end of society, wealth and power became concentrated in the hands of a few families that belonged to the ruling and merchant classes. At the other end of society there was an enormous increase in slavery.

Since ancient times, Africa's exports to the outside world had included slaves. The wealthy classes in many lands wanted African slaves as servants and laborers. Every year thousands of blacks were taken from sub-Saharan Africa. Lined up in columns, they marched barefoot across the Sahara behind the camel caravans. Many did not survive these long journeys. All who made it safely to North Africa had to be fed well for several weeks before they looked healthy enough to be sold in the slave markets.

The Arabian **dhows** (DOWZ)—sailing ships—that left from East Africa carried slaves to the Muslim lands of the Middle East and India. Some found themselves in China, where black doorkeepers were a prized possession. In what is now southern Iraq, a work force of East African slaves was used to drain swamps for planting sugarcane. However, in A.D. 869, these slaves rose in revolt. The uprising was not completely crushed until 14 years later. This revolt led to a sharp drop in the use of African slaves as laborers in the Middle East, but the slave trade continued to provide men for Muslim armies.

The lives of slaves. Slaves also became more common within Africa, especially in the Sudan. The rulers of Mali and Songhai, for example, used male slaves as soldiers, servants, administrators, and farm laborers. Female slaves worked as servants or entered the harems of powerful men. Slaves usually

Arabian dhows sailed the Indian Ocean for centuries by taking advantage of monsoon winds. Today they are still used for trade.

306

● RETEACHING. Have students draw a diagram illustrating the steps of the African slave trade. (Blacks were taken from sub-Saharan Africa, marched across the Sahara, prepared for slave markets in North Africa, and then shipped to the Middle East and India.) *(Comprehension) Translating Information into Another Form*

● REINFORCEMENT. Ask: (a) How did the work of male slaves differ from that of female slaves? (Males were used as soldiers, servants, administrators, and farm laborers; females were used as servants or placed in harems.) (b) How were slaves obtained? (They were taken as prisoners in wars and in raids against weaker people.) *(Comprehension) Observing for Detail* worked harder and had less to eat than free persons. Yet a few slaves were actually better off than many free persons. For example, some slaves were able to become high officials in the governments and armies of the Sudanic empires.

Slaves for export and domestic use were obtained as prisoners in wars and raids launched against weaker peoples. Sometimes the strong also found themselves enslaved. Slave dealers became much more common as the market for slaves expanded. European slave traders were already beginning to make their presence felt on Africa's west coast. As you will read in Chapter 19, the slave trade remained an important part of the African economy until the 1800's.

● See below.

See Sec. 2 *Closing the Lesson*, p. T295C.

Section Review

Answers to Section Review questions are in brackets on pages indicated.

1. **Define:** literacy, diviner, dhow. (pp. 304, 306)
2. How did the Arabic language help spur higher learning in Africa? (p. 304)
3. Why did African rulers who were Muslims still follow traditional religious practices? (p. 305)
4. What changes took place in African society between A.D. 500 and 1500? (pp. 306–307)
5. **Critical thinking:** How could it be argued that African society was hurt as well as helped by the increase in contact with Islamic civilization? (See answer below.)

5. Answers will vary. Students should note that Islam overshadowed traditional African languages and culture, and that Muslim demand for slaves encouraged the slave trade.

Chapter 15   Summary and Timeline

1. New empires arose in the western Sudan as a result of increased contact with Islamic civilizations to the north. The empires of Ghana, Mali, and Songhai helped provide stability for a thousand years. After these empires declined, trade routes across the Sahara shifted east. Farther south, new Bantu kingdoms based on traditional African culture were appearing. Swahili city-states arose that were heavily influenced by Muslim traders from Arabia, Persia, and India.

2. African culture was deeply affected by its increasing exposure to Islamic civilization. Two examples were the growth of the Swahili language, which borrowed many Arabic terms, and the growth of Arabic literacy. Islam especially gained many converts in the trading cities. The spread of religion and trade also led to a tremendous increase in the construction of new buildings. Meanwhile, class divisions grew sharper and the slave trade increased.

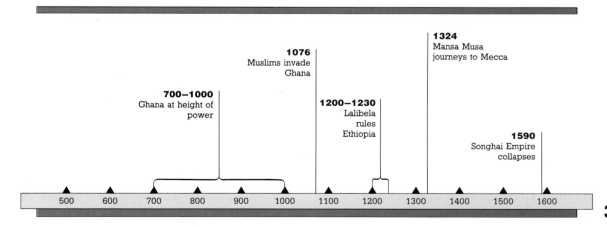

1324
Mansa Musa journeys to Mecca

1076
Muslims invade Ghana

700–1000
Ghana at height of power

1200–1230
Lalibela rules Ethiopia

1590
Songhai Empire collapses

500   600   700   800   900   1000   1100   1200   1300   1400   1500   1600

● ENRICHMENT. Have students find information on the importance of Islam in present-day Africa. Students might compare the area in which Islam is practiced today with that of the period between 500 and 1600, or they might describe the impact of Islam on the daily life of African people. Students might refer to the world religions map in Chapter 40. *(Synthesis) Locating Information*

See p. T295C for answers to Chapter Review.

Vocabulary Review

Use the following terms to complete the sentences below: *dhow, diviner, ghana, literacy, terra cotta.*

1. The spread of spoken languages was often accompanied by growing ___?___.
2. A ___?___ was an Arabian sailing ship.
3. The kingdom of Benin was known for beautiful art made of ___?___.
4. The ___?___ was a powerful ruler who controlled trade routes in the western Sudan.
5. A ___?___ was believed to read signs from the spirit world and foretell the future.

People to Identify

Match each of the following people with the correct description: *Sunni Ali, Abu Bakari, Lalibela, Askia Mohammed, Mansa Musa, Mwene Mutapa.*

1. ruler of Great Zimbabwe in the early 1400's
2. ruler of Mali who never returned from an Atlantic sailing expedition
3. Songhai king who captured Timbuktu
4. wealthy king of Mali who made a famous pilgrimage to Mecca
5. Songhai ruler who tried to build an Islamic empire
6. Ethiopian king who ordered the building of 11 rock churches

Places to Know

Match the letters on the map of Africa with the five places listed at the top of the next column. You may want to refer to the map on page 298.

308

1. Kumbi
2. Great Zimbabwe
3. Benin
4. Kongo
5. Timbuktu

Recalling the Facts

1. What development in the seventh century created new trading opportunities for African peoples south of the Sahara?
2. Where did the wealth of the Ghana Empire come from?
3. What caused the decline of Ghana? Mali? Songhai?
4. How did trading patterns change after the fall of the Songhai Empire?
5. What was the political structure of the Luba kingdom and many other African kingdoms?
6. How did the Swahili earn their living? What did they trade?
7. Why did the Mandinka, Hausa, and Swahili languages become widely spoken in Africa?

8. How did Muslim traders and the spread of Islam affect African culture?

9. Why were African slaves in demand?

Critical Thinking Skills

1. Writing a report. Research and write a report comparing the development of government, religion, trade, or culture in Africa between 1000 and 1600 with that in Asia during the same period. You may want to refer to Chapter 14 for information about Asia. *(Syn.)*

2. Taking notes. Rwanda and Burundi are among the few African kingdoms that have survived as modern nations. Using encyclopedias or library books, take notes on how these nations developed from the eleventh century to the present. *(App.)*

3. Organizing information. Make a time chart to compare events in Africa with events elsewhere in the world between 500 and 1600. *(Comp.)*

4. Exploring the arts. Choose one of the African kingdoms discussed in this chapter and research one of its art forms—its dance, sculpture, literature, or music. Then share what you have learned in a presentation to the class. *(App.)*

5. Inferring. As you have read, most early African peoples did not use written languages. How would this fact affect the work of historians studying Africa? *(Comp.)*

Thinking About Geography

1. Comparing maps. Using the map on page 298 and the map of Africa in the Atlas at the back of this book, determine what nations now exist in the area once occupied by the empires of the western Sudan. *(Comp.)*

2. Analyzing. Trading relationships were very important in the development of many African kingdoms and cities. Explain how location helped the following places become centers of trade: (a) Ghana, Mali, and Songhai; (b) the Hausa city-states and the empire of Bornu; (c) Kilwa and Sofala. *(Comp.)*

Enrichment: Primary Sources

The writings of the famous Muslim traveler Ibn Battuta are a major source of knowledge about fourteenth-century Africa. The following passage is adapted from Ibn Battuta's account of his visit to the kingdom of Mali.

> 66 My stay at Mali lasted about fifty days; and I was shown honor and entertained by its inhabitants. It is an excessively hot place, and boasts a few small date palms, in the shade of which they sow melons. The garments of its inhabitants are of fine Egyptian fabrics. Their women are of surpassing beauty, and are shown more respect than the men.
>
> The state of affairs among these people is indeed extraordinary. No one claims descent from his father, but on the contrary from his mother's brother. A person's heirs are his sister's sons, not his own sons. The people are seldom unjust, and have a greater hatred of injustice than any other people. There is complete security in their country. Neither traveler nor inhabitant has anything to fear from robbers. 99

1. What does Ibn Battuta say about the treatment he received from the people of Mali?

2. What suggests that the people of Mali traded with other civilizations?

3. From whom did a man in Mali inherit property?

4. Critical thinking: What opinion does Ibn Battuta express about conditions in Mali? In what way does he support this opinion? *(Anal.)*

 A checkmark identifies questions and exercises calling for the three higher-order levels of thinking at the top of the Bloom taxonomy: Analysis, Synthesis, and Evaluation.

Aztecs, Incas, and Other American Peoples   400–1600

(pp. 310–322)

Chapter Preview

The empires established by the Aztecs and Incas and the cultures of Indians who lived north of Mexico are discussed in this chapter. Section 1 traces the growth of the Aztec Empire and describes the political and social systems developed by the Aztecs in land that is present-day Mexico. The Inca Empire is described next, and the authoritarian nature of its government is explained. In Section 2, Indian cultures north of Mexico and their differences from societies to the south are described.

Bibliography

See the *Teacher's Management and Planning Guide* for additional listings. Starred titles are for both students and teachers.

Anton, F. *Women in Pre-Columbian America.* Abner Schram. A general treatment; richly illustrated.

Coe, Michael. *Mexico.* Thames and Hudson. Covers the period from 7000 B.C. to Cortés.

Davies, Nigel. *The Aztecs: A History.* University of Oklahoma Press.

*Von Hagen, Victor W. *The Aztec, Man and Tribe.* Mentor. Authoritative and readable.

*Von Hagen, Victor W. *Realm of the Incas.* Mentor.

Section Lesson Plans

SECTION 1   (pp. 311–315)
The Aztec and Inca Empires

Objectives

After completing this section, students will be able to:
1. Describe how the Aztecs built a great empire.
2. Explain what life was like in the Inca Empire.

Introducing the Lesson

Remind students that the first Americans were hunters who traveled from Asia during the last Ice Age. Gradually, communities arose in both North and South America. Although Indian societies developed sophisticated social, political, and economic institutions, technological development was slower than in Europe and in Asia.

Then ask: *(a) Why do groups of people develop social, political, and economic systems?* (Answers will vary. For people to survive they must develop some way to get food; if a group is to survive, its members must develop a social structure that allows them to live together peaceably.)

(b) What might have accounted for slower technological development in the Americas than in Europe and Asia? (Answers will vary. Trade and conquests spread new forms of technology in Europe and Asia. Because people in the Americas had little or no contact with other societies, advances in technology could not have been shared.)

Developing the Lesson: Comparing Cultural Development

Have students work in groups to develop a chart comparing the Aztec and the Inca empires in the following areas: *dates and location; economic activity; technological developments; government; religion.* (*Aztecs:* 1325–1519 in Mexico; people farmed and traded; they built aqueducts, sewers, dams, and irrigation systems; the emperor had absolute power; people worshiped many gods, but sun god was most important. *Incas:* 1438–early 1500's in the Andes; people farmed; they built system of roads, swinging bridges, tunnels; emperor had absolute power; people worshiped the sun.) *(Comprehension)*

Developing the Lesson: Translating Information into Another Form

Have students write the script for a dialogue that might have occurred between members of the Aztec and Inca societies. Dialogues might include a discussion of how the government of each society affected its members, how the Incas and Aztecs viewed each other's religion, and the differences between their educational and social systems. *(Synthesis)*

Closing the Lesson: Making Judgments

Have students write an essay explaining whether they would prefer to have lived in the Aztec Empire or the Inca Empire. Students should explain their choice and describe what aspects of both the Aztec and Inca empires they find appealing or unappealing. Have students read their essays in class. *(Evaluation)*

See *Section Review* questions on p. 315.

SECTION 2   (pp. 316–320)
Cultures North of Mexico

Objectives

After completing this section, students will be able to:
1. Describe how a variety of Indian cultures developed north of Mexico.
2. Identify the features that characterized North American Indian communities.

Introducing the Lesson

Remind students that many people have learned about American Indians largely from movies and television, sources that generally portray Indian ways of life after the arrival of Europeans. Indian groups north of Mexico were different both from modern media descriptions and from the Aztecs and Incas.

Then ask: *(a) Why might there be differences among Indian cultures in North, Central, and South America?* (Answers will vary. The geography and climate of the regions were different; an important factor in the development of culture is a society's adaptation to its environment.)

(b) How have movies and television generally portrayed Indians who lived north of Mexico? (Answers will vary. Usually Indians have been portrayed as warlike people who were nearly always in conflict with European settlers.)

(c) What might have influenced the ways of life developed by the various Indian cultures north of Mexico? (Answers will vary. Ways of life would have depended on where specific groups lived, the availability of resources, and contact with others.)

Developing the Lesson: Organizing Information in Written Form

Have students make a chart listing the locations, economic activities, and distinguishing characteristics of the North American Indian groups. (*Hopewell:* Ohio River valley, farming and trading, Mound Builders; *Anasazi:* the Southwest, farming and trading, pueblos; *Mississippian Culture:* the Southeast, farming and trading, pyramids; *Northwest Coast Culture:* Pacific coast (present-day California to Alaska), fishing, hunting, and gathering, carved totems and valued wealth.) *(Comprehension)*

Developing the Lesson:
Making Judgments

Have students identify what they consider to be the most significant aspect of each North American group discussed and explain their choices. *(Synthesis)*

Closing the Lesson:
Observing for Detail

Ask: *(a) Why were the Hopewell Indians called "Mound Builders"?* (They constructed large earthworks that were used as burial or ceremonial mounds.)

(b) Where did the name "Anasazi" originate? (*Anasazi* is a Navajo word meaning "strange ancient ones.")

(c) What were pueblos? (Large multi-storied buildings constructed by the Anasazi and used as houses.)

(d) Which North American culture had a strict social class system and an absolute ruler as did some Mexican and Central American societies? (The Mississippian culture.)

(e) Which North American culture remained almost unchanged until modern times? (The Eskimos.) *(Comprehension)*

See *Section Review* questions, p. 320.

Chapter 16 Review Answers
(pp. 321–322)

Vocabulary Review

1. terrace-farming 2. *quipu* 3. kiva 4. pueblo
5. *chinampa* 6. Adobe 7. totem 8. confederacy

Places to Know

1. A　2. C　3. E　4. D　5. B

Recalling the Facts

1. Causeways, aqueducts, sewers, dams, irrigation systems, open plazas, large marketplaces.
2. They forced conquered peoples to pay tribute.
3. They worshiped many gods, saw changes in nature as signs and omens, and believed that the sun god demanded offerings of flowers, food, and human hearts.
4. Like the Aztecs, the Incas grew powerful through conquest, and they worshiped the sun. From earlier cultures they learned techniques of weaving, pottery-making, and working with gold and silver.
5. The Incas ruled directly over the peoples they conquered, forcing them to accept the Inca religion, language, and style of clothing. Rebellious peoples were resettled in the midst of loyal groups, and village leaders were closely supervised.
6. Some were burial mounds, others were ceremonial mounds.
7. They waged war only when necessary, and returning warriors ritually cleansed themselves of the hatred aroused by war.
8. Farming and trade.
9. Northwest Coast Indians lived by fishing, gathering berries, and hunting wild animals rather than by farming. They had no apparent ties with Mexico or Central America, and they greatly valued wealth and possessions.
10. Villages and tribes were organized fairly democratically and governed by a council of respected elders and warriors rather than by a king. Most groups had a strong sense of community and did not believe in private ownership of land.

Critical Thinking Skills

1. Moist, warm wind; soft leather slipper; cooked mixture of corn, lima beans, and tomatoes; long, runnerless sled.
2–5. Answers will vary.

Thinking About Geography

1. Aztec Empire—about 1,000 miles; Inca Empire—about 3,000 miles. The Andes.
2. (a) Paragraphs should mention the building of causeways, aqueducts, sewers, dams, irrigation systems, and *chinampas*. (b) Paragraphs should mention the Eskimos' use of native animals for food, weapons, tools, clothing, and fuel; their use of ice and snow for building homes.

Enrichment: Primary Sources

1. They took about 6,000 or 7,000 families from a conquered province and resettled them in another province.
2. To maintain Inca rule and keep conquered peoples in submission.
3. They became soldiers.
4. Giving them privileges would encourage their loyalty, and ordering them to obey all commands would turn them into a disciplined force.

Aztecs, Incas, and Other American Peoples 400–1600

See chapter timeline, p. 320.

Before You Read This Chapter

Today when we hear the word *environment* in the news, it is often because of some crisis—an oil spill, toxic chemicals, or acid rain. Yet our environment surrounds us all the time. We use it, we change it, we take it for granted, we *need* it. The peoples described in this chapter lived in a wide range of environments covering two continents. As you read, notice how each group adapted to its natural surroundings. What resources did people use? What difficulties did they overcome? How did the environment affect food supplies? City-building? Religion? What changes did people make in their environment?

The Geographic Setting

The Chapter Outline

1. The Aztec and Inca Empires
2. Cultures North of Mexico

This double-headed serpent, a mosaic made of turquoise and shells, was a symbol of life in Aztec culture.

1 The Aztec and Inca Empires

Objectives

Focus Questions

★ ■ How did the Aztecs build a great empire? *(pages 311–313)*

● ■ What was life like in the Inca Empire? *(pages 313–315)*

Terms to Know

chinampa   *quipu*
terrace-farming

★ Note strategies for first objective on this page and p. 313.

In the fifteenth century, a new kind of state developed both in Mexico and on the Pacific coast of South America. Through conquest, small tribes gained control of great amounts of land and wealth. Two major warrior-states were formed: one by the Aztecs in Mexico and the other by the Incas in South America. Although there were similarities in their cultures, the Aztecs and Incas governed their huge states differently.

The Toltecs

In Chapter 8 you read about the Mexican city of Teotihuacán, the first city in the Americas. In about A.D. 600 this great city fell to invaders and was burned to the ground (page 160). The invaders were nomadic tribes from the north whose culture was much less advanced than that of the Teotihuacános.

Like the Germanic tribes that overran the Roman Empire, the invaders of Teotihuacán were heavily influenced by the civilization they had defeated. They admired many aspects of Teotihuacán culture and intermarried with its people.

For several hundred years, various tribes fought among themselves for control of the region. By the year 1000, the Toltec tribe had defeated its rivals and had created a new empire with its capital at Tula (TOO-luh). The Toltecs ruled over all of central Mexico for two centuries until they, in turn, were conquered by a new group of invaders.

The Rise of the Aztec Empire

Following the conquest of the Toltecs, a nomadic tribe called the Aztecs came to Mexico from the dry lands to the north. Aztec legend claims that a god led the Aztecs to the Valley of Mexico, where they saw an eagle perched on a cactus and holding a snake. The Aztecs regarded this as a sign that they should settle on that spot.

The imperial capital. In 1325 the Aztecs built the village of Tenochtitlán (teh-NAWCH-teet-lahn) on an island in a lake, where Mexico City stands today. Tenochtitlán soon became the showcase of Aztec achievement. Causeways, or raised roadways, linked the island city with the mainland. Aztec engineers dug aqueducts to bring fresh water from the mainland. They built sewers to carry away waste. Dams protected the city from floods, and irrigation systems carried water to crops during the dry season.

Sec. Rev. ques. 2

Tenochtitlán grew into a great city with broad, open plazas and large marketplaces. The homes of the wealthy were built around courtyards with fountains, and many had colorful roof gardens. By the mid-1400's Tenochtitlán had an estimated population of about 300,000, greater than that of any European city at the time.

Resourceful farmers. The Aztecs found an unusual way to increase the amount of land available for growing food in Tenochtitlán. In the shallow lake that surrounded the city, Aztec farmers built up many small **311**

★ RETEACHING. Have students review "The Rise of the Aztec Empire" (pp. 311–312) and draw conclusions about why the Aztec Empire might be considered an organized and complex system. (The building of an island-city, causeways, aqueducts, sewers, dams, an irrigation system, and *chinampas* required a high degree of organization.) *(Comprehension) Drawing Conclusions*
Vocabulary The word *Tenochtitlán* means "stone rising in the water" and was taken from the name *Tenoch,* a legendary Aztec leader.

★ REINFORCEMENT. Have students work in groups to compare the achievements of the Aztecs with those of the people who built Great Zimbabwe (p. 301). Then have students state an opinion about which of the two represented the greater achievement and explain why. *(Evaluation) Evaluating Information*
Technology The Aztec aqueduct had double channels so that the sides could be alternately cleaned without disrupting the flow of water.

This map of the island city of Tenochtitlán shows its causeways and canals. The walled central area contained temples and a pyramid.

islands made of layers of dirt, vegetation, and mud. These gardens, called *chinampas*, were fertilized naturally by the decaying animal and plant material in the islands. Using *chinampas*, the Aztecs harvested crops as many as three times a year. Their staple food was corn, but they also grew beans, squash, tomatoes, and peppers.

Expansion. By the 1400's the Aztecs had conquered most other groups in central Mexico. As the empire expanded, the Aztecs borrowed ideas and skills from other peoples. Aztec architecture had its roots in Teotihuacán. From the Toltecs came the Aztec calendar and writing system. The Aztecs' social system, their religion, and many of their arts and crafts also came from earlier American cultures.

312

Aztec Society

Government. The government of the Aztec Empire was headed by an emperor with absolute power. Some rulers took control by force, but most were elected by the priests and warriors of the Aztecs. The emperor was head of state, military commander, and chief priest. His word was law, and he expected his commands to be obeyed without question. The greatest nobles and priests fell on their faces when the Aztec emperor appeared. Even to look on his face might be punished by death.

The Aztecs did not rule directly over the peoples they conquered. Instead they demanded tribute from the conquered lands. Tribute payments included food, clothing, woven blankets, precious stones, furs, feathers, fine woods, and slaves or captives. Trade and tribute, not political organization, held the Aztec Empire together. Products from every part of the empire poured into the great marketplace of Tenochtitlán.

Sec. Rev. ques. 3

Religion. The Aztecs worshiped many gods. Priests kept a complex religious calendar that they consulted to decide when to honor each god. Religious ceremonies were performed daily before large audiences in Tenochtitlán. Aztec priests, like those of ancient Rome, also predicted the future, interpreting changes in nature as signs and omens.

Like the Toltecs, the Aztecs apparently believed that the sun would stop shining if they did not make offerings to the sun god. Usually they offered flowers and food. It was believed, however, that on special occasions and in times of crisis the sun had to be given human hearts. The Aztecs used prisoners of war and slaves for these sacrifices. Many were obtained from conquered peoples as part of their payment of tribute to the emperor.

In earlier American cultures, human sacrifice had been rare; to be chosen for sacrifice to the gods was considered an honor. Under the Aztecs, sacrifices were made frequently. In fact, Aztec priests encouraged warfare for the purpose of gaining prisoners for sacrifice. On one occasion, 20,000 captives were sacrificed at the dedication of a temple in Tenochtitlán. Such ceremonies led other peoples of Mexico and Central America to fear and despise the Aztecs.

Education. Aztec society was organized much like that of the Mayas (page 160), but it was less rigid. Education gave the Aztecs the opportunity to advance socially. All Aztec children were required to go to school, where they learned Aztec history and religion. Girls were taught weaving, while boys learned the skills of warfare and their duties as citizens.

Even greater opportunities existed in special schools where the brightest young people were trained for religious duties. There both boys and girls could learn how to read and write, interpret the calendar, use medicines, make prophecies, compose poetry, and debate. Education made it possible for a young man from any class to become a high-ranking government official, a military commander, or a priest. Women, regardless of their education, were expected to devote themselves to their homes and families.

★ See below.

The end of an era. The Aztecs ruled the last Indian empire in Mexico and Central America. As you will read in Chapter 18, Spanish conquerors arrived in 1519 and abruptly brought to an end the Aztecs' power.

The Building of the Inca Empire

● Note strategies for second objective on this page and p. 315.

Early Andean cultures. In the valleys of the Andes, which form the mountainous backbone of South America, many different cultures developed. The South American cultures, like those in Mexico and Central America, relied mainly on farming for food. Because people lived on the steep slopes of mountains, they practiced terrace-farming. They cut into the mountain sides and built wide, step-like banks of soil. On these terraces they grew potatoes, squash, beans, peanuts, and cotton. In dry regions they learned how to irrigate the land.

At an early date the Andeans also learned to work with metals and to weave

fine textiles. They raised llamas for their wool and meat. Many families also kept guinea pigs as a source of meat.

Inca conquests. As early as 1000 B.C. some villages in the central Andes became religious centers. Several states conquered their neighbors, but none dominated the

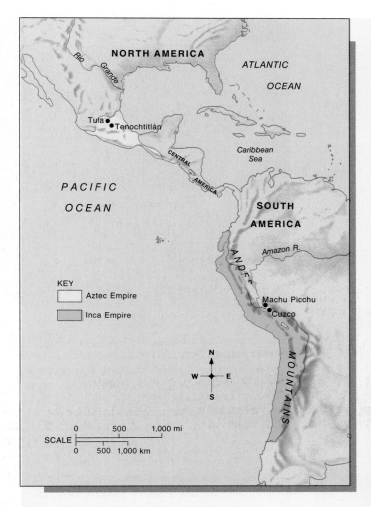

KEY

☐ Aztec Empire

▨ Inca Empire

Aztec and Inca Empires

At its height, the Aztec Empire covered almost half of Mexico. The Inca Empire in South America stretched along the Pacific coast. What city lay near the center of the Inca Empire?

313

Map Answer: Cuzco.

★ ENRICHMENT. Have students work in groups to prepare a panel discussion comparing the Aztec social and educational systems with those of the United States today. Students might examine the roles of men and women and education, and then draw conclusions about the similarities or differences between the two societies. (Synthesis) Linking Past and Present

Check for Understanding. Ask: What is terrace-farming? (A way of creating land for crops by cutting into mountain slopes.)

● RETEACHING. Have students review "Government" (p. 315) and identify strategies used by Inca rulers to maintain control. (Criticism of emperor punished by death; conquered peoples forced to accept Inca culture; rebellious groups relocated.) (Comprehension) Observing for Detail

● REINFORCEMENT. Have students develop a hypothesis about the advantages and disadvantages of a political system like that of the Incas. (Synthesis) Forming a Hypothesis

Ⓕ See
below.

Historic Places

Machu Picchu

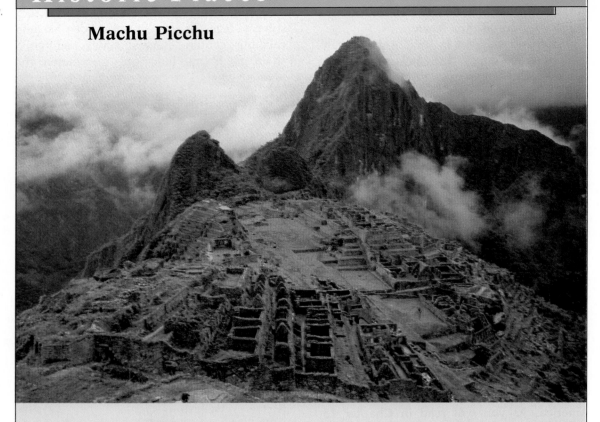

In 1911, long after the Inca Empire had fallen, American archeologist Hiram Bingham struggled up the steep, rocky slopes of the Andes in Peru. Here, about 9,000 feet above sea level, the air was so thin that lowlanders gasped for breath. Yet Bingham was convinced that there had once been a great city nearby.

The first sign that Bingham was close to the lost city came when he saw narrow, terraced fields on the mountainside. He knew that these terraces were the work of the Incas. After another short climb Bingham found himself surrounded by the stairways and roofless houses of an ancient Inca city. Today that city is known as Machu Picchu (MAH-choo PEEK-choo), after a nearby peak.

Although heavy undergrowth covered the buildings when Bingham found them, the prying roots and thrusting trunks had not toppled the Inca stonework. The massive building stones—some weighing several tons—had been shaped and fitted carefully enough to withstand centuries of neglect.

The last Inca rulers retreated to this city after their defeat by the Spanish in the 1500's. From here, Inca war parties harassed their enemy. Spanish rulers heard rumors of the city and searched for it but never found it. The mountains had hid it well.

Sometime in the later 1500's, the Incas finally left their secret stronghold. Why? No one knows for certain. Bingham thought perhaps their source of water had run dry. Abandoned for centuries, Machu Picchu stands today as the best preserved of all the Inca cities.

314

Ⓕ **FEATURE ACTIVITY.** Have students write an essay describing what it may have been like to flee Spanish conquerors and settle in Machu Picchu in the 1500's. Students should consider how the retreat from Spanish conquerors and resettlement in this city on top of a mountain might have affected a young person. *(Application) **Understanding Point of View*** area until the fifteenth century A.D. By 1438 a people called the Incas had conquered a large area around their capital city of Cuzco (KOOS-koh). They gradually expanded their lands until they ruled an empire that stretched 2,000 miles along the Pacific coast. By 1532 the empire included lands that are now part of Peru, Ecuador, Bolivia, Chile, and Argentina. Probably about six million people lived in the Inca Empire.

Influences on the Incas. The Incas had some things in common with the Aztecs. They, too, began as a small tribe that grew powerful through conquest. Like the Aztecs, the Incas worshiped the sun. They also adopted the achievements of earlier cultures. From coastal peoples they learned techniques of weaving and pottery-making. From peoples to the north they learned to work with gold and silver. Gold covered the walls of the great temple in Cuzco, and gold and silver jewelry glittered on Inca nobles.

Inca Society

Sec. Rev. ques. 4

Links within the empire. The Incas were superb engineers. Like the Romans, they built a system of roads to link distant parts of the empire with the capital. These roads, some of which still survive, ran across coastal deserts and over the highest mountains in the Western Hemisphere. Swinging bridges woven of reeds and vines crossed rivers and canyons. Sometimes tunnels were dug through mountains. The roads were traveled by merchants, officials, and messengers carrying royal orders. Inca travelers went on foot, for they had no wheeled vehicles and used their animals only to carry loads. Inns along the roads provided shelter and comfort for travelers.

Government. The Inca emperor, like the Aztec ruler, had absolute power. The Incas believed that the emperor was descended from the sun god. His wife might rule for him when he was away from the capital at Cuzco, but she was expected to be completely obedient when he was home. Criticism of the emperor or of his policies brought death.

The Inca Empire was more tightly organized than the Aztec Empire. The Incas ruled directly over the peoples they conquered, forcing them to accept the Inca religion, language, and style of clothing. To keep rebellious peoples under control, the Incas resettled them in the midst of loyal groups.

Sec. Rev. ques. 5

Every village had a leader who was closely supervised by government officials. These officials enforced royal laws and punished wrongdoers. They kept detailed records of the size of the population and the food supply. Lacking a written language, they used the *quipu* (KEE-poo) to keep numerical records. *Quipus* were made of colored cords of various lengths and were knotted at intervals to indicate different sums.

● See below.

The government kept a tight hold over its people's lives. The poor could not use hard work or education to rise into another class, but anyone in need could draw upon the food and wool in the royal storehouses. Most people had to spend several days each week farming public lands, and they were often forced to work on government building projects. Detailed official records restricted people's privacy. Everyone was required to marry; people who didn't choose a mate were assigned one instead. Travel was rarely permitted. Regulations like these created much discontent within the Inca Empire by the early 1500's.

See Sec. 1 *Closing the Lesson,* p. T309B.

Section Review

Answers to Section Review questions are in brackets on pages indicated.

1. **Define:** *chinampa,* terrace-farming, *quipu.* (pp. 312, 313, 315)
2. In what ways was Tenochtitlán a remarkable city? (p. 311)
3. How did the Aztecs control the peoples they conquered? (p. 312)
4. What kind of communication network did the Incas set up? (p. 315)
5. How did the Incas control the peoples they conquered? (p. 315)
6. **Critical thinking:** Compare and contrast Inca and Aztec societies. (See answer below.)

315

Cultural History According to Inca legend, Cuzco was founded by Manco Capac, the first Inca, about A.D. 1100. Incas believed that the sun god showed Manco Capac fertile land on which to settle.

Background The expansion of the Inca Empire is remarkable in that it occurred primarily over a period of only thirty years, between 1463 and 1493. The Inca Empire was conquered by Francisco Pizarro in 1532 (pp. 355–356).

Background The Inca road system covered approximately 12,000 miles.

● ENRICHMENT. Have students prepare a display of the achievements of the Inca civilization. Students might research Inca architecture, religion, social structure, territorial expansion, or government and then draw diagrams, posters, or charts to illustrate their findings. Have students present their displays in class. (Application) Translating Information into Another Form

6. Answers will vary and might focus on comparisons of government, religion, technology, arts, and society.

2 Cultures North of Mexico

Objectives

Focus Questions

★ ■ How did a variety of Indian cultures develop north of Mexico? *(pages 316–319)*

● ■ What features characterized North American Indian communities? *(pages 319–320)*

Terms to Know

adobe   totem
pueblo   confederacy
kiva

★ Note strategies for first objective on this page and p. 319.

Hundreds of cultures and languages developed among the Indians who settled the North American continent north of Mexico. These different peoples are often grouped by geographical regions where people had similar ways of life (map, page 317). As in Mexico, archeologists have found evidence that distinct cultures had emerged as early as 1000 B.C. Some were influenced by civilizations to the south. Trade, agriculture, and arts flourished, and different forms of political organization arose.

The Hopewell Culture

About the fifth or fourth century B.C., a highly organized farming society developed in the Ohio River valley. This was the Hopewell culture, named for the owner of the land where evidence of the culture was first found. The Hopewell people are also known as "Mound Builders" because of the large earthworks they constructed. Some of these were burial mounds; others, in the shape of animals such as snakes or birds, were ceremonial.

The Mound Builders traded widely along the rivers and lakes, acquiring copper from the northern Great Lakes region, seashells from the Gulf of Mexico, and mica (a shiny mineral) from people to the east. Their artists worked with wood, stone, and copper to make ornaments and household objects. Hopewell culture spread over the central part of the continent from what is now Wisconsin south to the Gulf Coast and as far west as present-day Kansas. The Hopewell way of life lasted for about a thousand years, until A.D. 400 or 500.

The Anasazi

By the first century A.D. another group, the Anasazi (ah-nah-SAH-zee), had created a farming culture in the dry lands of the Southwest—present-day Arizona, New Mexico, Colorado, and Utah. The name Anasazi was given to them by the Navajo (NAV-uh-hoh) Indians, who much later discovered the ruins of their huge, many-storied homes. In the Navajo language *Anasazi* means "strange ancient ones."

Pueblos. The Anasazi built their houses of stone or of sun-baked clay called **adobe** (uh-DOH-bee). As the population rose and communities grew more crowded, people worked together to build huge "apartment houses." These stood several stories high and had hundreds of rooms. People hauled logs long distances to make the framework and roof; they cut blocks of sandstone for the walls. The Spaniards who arrived several hundred years later called these huge buildings **pueblos** (PWEB-lohz), which means "towns" in Spanish.

Many pueblos were built in canyons or high on steep cliffs. One of the largest, Pueblo Bonito in present-day New Mexico, took more than 100 years to build. Completed about A.D. 1085, it had 650 rooms and could

316

★ RETEACHING. Have students identify and explain each of the following: Mound Builders (People of the Hopewell culture who built burial or ceremonial mounds.) Pueblos (Anasazi culture; large "apartment houses" made of stone or sun-baked clay.) Totems (Nootka and Chinook cultures; wooden poles on which were carved symbols of families or clans.) *(Comprehension) Observing for Detail*
Background Note that the earliest mounds date from more than 2,000 years ago.

★ REINFORCEMENT. Have students list the differences between the Northwest Coast Indian culture and the Hopewell, Anasazi, and Mississippian cultures. Then have students explain how geography and climate affected these groups' ways of life. (Northwest Coast people did not depend on farming. The colder environment and the availability of ocean resources might account for differences in ways of life.) *(Comprehension) Comparing Cultures*

Indian Peoples North of Mexico

Indian peoples north of Mexico are often grouped by culture areas—geographic regions that shaped their ways of life. Name the eight culture areas. What Indian peoples lived in the Northern Forest region? Into which culture area did the Rio Grande extend?

Map Answers: (1) Arctic, Northern Forest, Northwest Coast, California, Southwest, Plains, Eastern Woodlands, Southeast. (2) Beaver, Cree, Ojibway, Algonquin. (3) Southwest.

house well over a thousand people. Every great pueblo had a **kiva** (KEE-vah)—a central room used for community ceremonies and religious rituals. Colorful murals decorated the walls of the kiva.

Anasazi culture. The early Anasazi probably learned farming techniques about 1500 B.C. from the peoples of Mexico. Corn, beans, and squash became their staple foods. Because the Anasazi were farmers in a dry land, they depended upon help from nature. They devised a kind of sun clock to track the seasons and the cycles of the sun. Through religious rituals Anasazi men asked the spirits of nature to bring them good hunting and large harvests.

The Anasazi valued peace and moderation. Fearful of disrupting the world's natural harmony, they went to war only when necessary. Returning warriors performed a ritual to cleanse them of the hatred aroused by war.

Like women of other North American cultures, Anasazi women had many responsibilities and rights. They owned all the houses and property and headed family clans. When a woman wanted to divorce her husband, she simply placed all his belongings outside the house.

The Anasazi culture stretched over a huge area in the Southwest. Networks of wide roads linked central pueblos with outlying villages and other centers. The people **317** traded with Mexican Indians for copper and feathers and with Indians of the Great Plains for buffalo meat. Their only farm animals were turkeys, but they kept dogs as pets.

Sec. Rev. ques. 2

In the late 1200's a very long drought struck the central area of Anasazi culture. The Anasazi were forced to abandon their pueblos and search for better lands to farm. They moved away to join neighboring groups, and the first great culture of the Southwest vanished.

The Mississippian Culture

About A.D. 700, as the Anasazi were building adobe houses, another culture was taking shape in the eastern half of North America. By about 1200, people along the lower Mississippi River had built the most advanced culture north of Mexico. Because of its location, this culture is called Mississippian.

Influences from the south. Mississippian society was heavily influenced by ideas from Mexico and Central America. As in Mexico, corn was an important part of the people's diet. In the center of their walled villages, the Mississippians built steep-sided earth pyramids with wooden temples on the flat summits. These temple mounds were similar to ones built in Mexico. (The Mississippians also built burial mounds, like the Hopewell.) Mississippian drawings of a feathered serpent resemble the Teotihuacán god Quetzalcóatl (page 159). Finally, like some Mexican and Central American societies, Mississippian society was divided into strict classes under an absolute ruler.

Sec. Rev. ques. 3

Spread of Mississippian influence. The Mississippian culture prospered from both trade and farming, and its influence spread throughout the Southeast. Fortified villages, located mainly along rivers, grew into city-states with as many as 20,000 residents. Artisans worked in metal and stone, making knives and hoe blades for trade. A trade in salt also developed.

The largest town of this culture was located near the site of present-day St. Louis. Its central temple mound covered 15 acres

318

and rose 100 feet high. The Mississippian way of life lasted among the Natchez people (map, page 317) until French explorers arrived in the Mississippi Valley in the 1600's.

The Northwest Coast Culture

Along the Pacific coast, from present-day northern California to Alaska, a very different culture had taken shape by about 1000 B.C. The people of the Northwest Coast culture area included the Nootka and Chinook. Unlike other Indian peoples who lived to the north of Mexico, the Northwest Coast people did not depend on farming and apparently had no ties with Mexico or Central America.

Northwest Coast Indians lived by fishing the rivers and the ocean, gathering berries, and hunting wild animals for food and furs. The plentiful forests provided cedar wood for making canoes, houses, ceremonial masks, and finely carved boxes. In front of their houses were wooden poles on which they carved totems—symbols of their family or clan. Totems were usually animals, such as bears or owls. A totem pole showed a series of totems and might stand more than 30 feet tall.

Sec. Rev. ques. 4

The Northwest Coast peoples were also unusual among North American Indians because they greatly valued wealth and possessions. Their communities were divided into strict social classes, with a large population of slaves captured in raids.

Linking Past and Present

Today some Eskimos in Alaska, northern Canada, and Greenland still live by hunting. Instead of dogsleds, however, many use snowmobiles to cross the frozen land. They often own motorboats for going fishing and use guns to kill caribou, walrus, and seal. At the end of a big hunt they may even charter a small plane to carry the meat back to their community.

Science Note that growth rings on trees dating back to the Anasazi period indicate that the drought lasted for 23 years.

Background At the end of the seventeenth century the Natchez population was approximately 4,000.

Check for Understanding. Ask: Why did the Northwest Coast Indians carve totems? (To make symbolic representations of their families or clans.)

The Eskimos

The Eskimos, or the Inuit (IN-uh-wut), as they called themselves, settled the northern-most parts of North America. They were probably the last of the immigrants who came from Asia after the last Ice Age. Although they shared some land and some customs with the Indians of the Northwest Coast, they had little in common with other Indians living to the south. They created a way of life uniquely adapted to the Arctic environment.

The Eskimos fished and hunted walrus, whale, seal, and caribou for food. From these animals they made practically everything they needed—harpoons, fishing hooks, knives, needles, warm weatherproof clothing, sleds, kayaks, tents for summer use, and oil for lamps. In their leisure time they carved bone and ivory, mapped their fishing grounds, and made pictures of their daily life. They took advantage of their icy surroundings by storing food in its natural "freezer." Some even used snow and ice to build homes. This way of life met the Eskimos' needs so well that it remained virtually unchanged until modern times.

Sec. Rev. ques. 4, cont.

★ See below.

Indian Communities

● Note strategies for second objective on this page and p. 320.
Indians throughout North America were generally peaceful and uninterested in conquest. Their local villages and tribal groups were organized fairly democratically. The rigid class divisions of the Mississippians and the Northwest Coast peoples were unusual. Government by a king or absolute ruler was also rare. More commonly, respected elders and warriors formed a governing council.

Most Indian peoples had a strong sense of community, shared a feeling of harmony with nature, and did not believe in private ownership of land. In a farming village, families might be assigned particular fields to use, but it was understood that the land really belonged to all.

Communities often welcomed new members who came from a different tribe,

Sec. Rev. ques. 5

Some Indians of the Atlantic coast lived in long houses made of wood and grass. Villages were protected by a wall of wooden stakes.

spoke a different language, or had new skills and ideas. Strangers or captives taken in war were likely to be adopted into the Indian community.

Children were brought up to feel a part of community life. Indian boys and girls grew up sharing in daily work and learning the history and rituals of their people. In their teens they went through special ceremonies to be recognized as adults in the society.

Indian Confederacies

Large kingdoms or empires did not develop among the Indians north of Mexico. Different Indian peoples, however, often joined together in a loose alliance, or confederacy. Villages in an alliance sometimes sent tribute to a central leader, but they continued to govern themselves independently.

Southeastern groups. By the early 1600's, a leader known as Powhatan (pow-uh-TAN) had brought together one of the largest of these confederacies. It included about 200 villages in what is now Virginia. At the same time, about 50 settlements in the Southeast were allied in what the English called the Creek Confederacy. In addition to

319

★ ENRICHMENT. Have students work in groups to prepare a presentation on the Indian cultures of North, Central, and South America. Students might build models of different types of housing, illustrate economic activities, or write a play with characters from the different cultures. (Synthesis) Synthesizing Information

● RETEACHING. Have students review "Indian Communities" (above) and outline the characteristics of North American Indians. (Comprehension) Observing for Detail

● REINFORCEMENT. Have students compare the Indian communities of what is now the United States with the Aztec and Inca cultures (pp. 311–315). (Unlike the Aztecs and Incas, these Indian peoples generally were not interested in territorial expansion and did not establish empires. Whereas the Aztecs and Incas formed large, well-organized political systems, most Indians north of Mexico lived in smaller communities.) (Comprehension) Comparing Historical Developments the Creek Indians, this confederacy included the Choctaw, Chickasaw, and Cherokee. These Indians were prosperous, peaceful farmers and traders living in walled villages.

The Iroquois League. The best-known alliance, and perhaps the longest-lived, was the Iroquois (EER-uh-kwoy) League in what is now New York State. It included the "Five Nations"—five different groups that each spoke an Iroquois language.

The Iroquois League was formed, probably about 1580, to act for the good of all. Though its members never cooperated fully, they did keep peace among themselves. The leading women in each family clan in the Five Nations chose a man to be a member of the League council, which met yearly. Respected warriors, known as the "solitary pine trees," served as advisers. At the time the Europeans arrived in this part of North America, the Iroquois League dominated the Northeast.

● See below, right.

See Sec. 2 *Closing the Lesson,* p. T309C.

Section Review

Answers to Section Review questions are in brackets on pages indicated.

1. **Define:** adobe, pueblo, kiva, totem, confederacy. (pp. 316, 317, 318, 319)
2. Why did Anasazi culture disappear? (p. 318)
3. What kinds of mounds were built by the Hopewell and Mississippian peoples? (p. 318)
4. What were the distinctive features of the Northwest Coast culture? Of the Eskimos? (pp. 318, 319)
5. What features of most Indian societies tended to support a strong sense of community? (p. 319)
6. **Critical thinking:** How did the Indian confederacies north of Mexico differ from the empires of the Aztecs and Incas? (See answer below.)

6. Answers will vary. The Aztecs and Incas developed large empires through conquest. Both groups were governed by emperors with absolute power. Indian peoples north of Mexico tended to coexist peacefully, and their confederacies did not develop into large kingdoms.

Chapter 16   Summary and Timeline

1. In the 1400's, warrior-states became dominant in Mexico and along the Pacific coast of South America. The Aztecs in Mexico built an empire based on conquest and trade from their capital city Tenochtitlán. In South America, Inca conquests created an empire in the Andes.

2. North of Mexico, farming began

about 1500 B.C. The earliest distinctive cultures in what is now the United States were developed by the Anasazi in the Southwest, the Hopewell and Mississippians farther east, and the people of the Northwest Pacific Coast. Trading and political alliances linked many of the different North American peoples, most of whom were peaceful farmers.

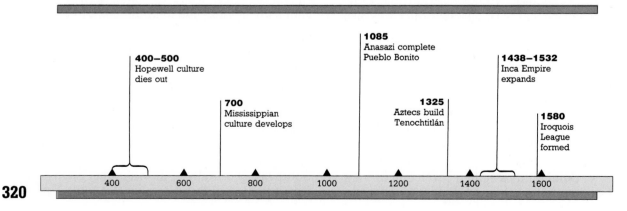

400–500
Hopewell culture
dies out

700
Mississippian
culture develops

1085
Anasazi complete
Pueblo Bonito

1325
Aztecs build
Tenochtitlán

1438–1532
Inca Empire
expands

1580
Iroquois
League
formed

400   600   800   1000   1200   1400   1600

320

Background Note that the title "solitary pine tree" comes from the code of the Iroquois League, which advised the chiefs to "uproot the tallest pine tree and, into the cavity that remains, cast all weapons of war. Into the depths of the earth, deep down into the undercurrents of water flowing to unknown regions, cast all weapons of strife, and then plant the tree again."

● ENRICHMENT. Have students develop a hypothesis explaining why Indians north of Mexico were different from those in Central and South America. Hypotheses should include an explanation of differences in political and social structures. *(Synthesis) Forming a Hypothesis*

CHAPTER 16 REVIEW

See p. T309C for answers to Chapter Review.

Vocabulary Review

Use the following terms to complete the sentences below: *adobe, chinampa, confederacy, kiva, quipu, pueblo, terrace-farming, totem.*

1. South American peoples practiced ___?___, a method of growing food on mountainsides.
2. A colored cord knotted at intervals and used for numerical record-keeping was called a ___?___.
3. A central room used for community ceremonies and religious rituals was called a ___?___.
4. A ___?___ was a building that was several stories high and contained hundreds of rooms.
5. A small island of dirt, vegetation, and mud used by the Aztecs to grow food was called a ___?___.
6. ___?___ is sun-baked clay that was often used for building houses.
7. The symbol of a family or clan, called a ___?___, was carved on a wooden pole by Northwest Coast Indians.
8. A ___?___ was a loose alliance often formed among different Indian peoples north of Mexico.

Places to Know

Match the letters on this map of North America with the location of the Indian cultures listed below. You may want to refer to the map on page 317.
1. Anasazi
2. Hopewell
3. Mississippian
4. Northwest Coast
5. Eskimo

Recalling the Facts

1. What features made Tenochtitlán the showcase of Aztec achievement?
2. How did the Aztecs control conquered lands?
3. What religious beliefs did the Aztecs hold?
4. How were the Incas similar to the Aztecs? How were the Incas influenced by earlier cultures?
5. How did the Incas control the peoples they conquered?
6. What was the purpose of the mounds built by the Hopewell people?
7. What showed that the Anasazi valued peace and moderation?
8. What activities helped the Mississippian culture prosper?
9. How was the Northwest Coast culture different from that of other North American Indian cultures?
10. What was the typical pattern of political organization among North American Indian groups? What attitudes did they have toward the land?

1. **Building vocabulary.** A number of English words have their roots in American Indian languages. Using a dictionary, define each of the following: *chinook, moccasin, succotash, toboggan.* (App.)

✔ 2. **Comparing.** Make a chart comparing Aztec and Inca civilizations. Use the following categories: *Location, Government, Religion, Opportunities for Social Advancement.* In which society would you have pre-
(Syn.) ferred to live? Give reasons for your answer.

3. **Preparing a report.** Research and write a report about one of the following topics: Aztec architecture; the Inca city of Cuzco; the ruins of Machu Picchu in Peru; religious beliefs and practices of North American Indian groups; Indians' games; the Great Serpent Mound in Ohio; varieties of Indian dress; totem poles. (App.)

4. **Writing a summary.** Reread the account of what Aztec civilization was like on pages 311–313. Then write a one-page summary of the main ideas. (Comp.)

5. **Taking notes.** Using at least three sources from your school or local library, take notes on the role women played in the following societies: *Aztec, Eskimo, Inca, Mississippian.* (App.)

Thinking About Geography

1. **Reading maps.** Study the map on page 313. What is the approximate north-south distance of the Aztec Empire? The Inca Empire? What geographical feature made communication and trade difficult within the Inca Empire? (App.)

2. **Supporting a conclusion.** Select one of the following statements and write a paragraph supporting it: (a) The Aztecs found creative ways to overcome the geographic limitations of the site they had chosen for their capital city. (b) The Eskimos created a way of life that was uniquely adapted to the Arctic environment. (Comp.)

322

✔ A checkmark identifies questions and exercises calling for the three higher-order levels of thinking at the top of the Bloom taxonomy: Analysis, Synthesis, and Evaluation.

Enrichment: Primary Sources

Diaries of Spanish missionaries often told of Inca life. In this adapted passage, a priest describes Inca methods of conquest and resettlement.

❝ The first thing that the Inca rulers did after conquering a province was to remove six or seven thousand families and transfer them to the quiet, peaceful provinces, assigning them to different towns. In their place they introduced the same number of people, taken from such other places as seemed convenient.

The Incas introduced these changes in order to maintain their rule with greater ease, quiet, and security. The Incas reasoned that since the city of Cuzco, their capital, was so distant from the conquered provinces in which there were many barbarous and warlike nations, there was no other way to keep conquered peoples in peaceful submission. And since this was the principal purpose of the transfer, they ordered the majority of the people whom they sent to the recently conquered towns to serve as soldiers. As soldiers they received certain privileges to make them appear of nobler rank and they were ordered to obey the slightest commands of their captains. ❞

1. What was the first change Inca rulers made in a conquered area?
2. What was the purpose of resettlement?
3. What job was given to most of the people sent to conquered provinces?
4. **Critical thinking:** Why did the Incas give privileges to soldiers and order them to obey the slightest commands?
(Syn.)

WORLD HISTORY Checklist

UNIT 4

Try to identify the following key people, groups and dynasties, places, and terms from the unit. If you need help, refer to the pages listed.

Key People

Akbar *(274)*
Shah Jahan *(275)*
Aurangzeb *(275)*
Suleiman I *(278)*
Abbas I *(279)*
Wu Hou *(281)*
Kublai Khan *(284)*
Marco Polo *(284)*
Zheng He *(285)*
Shotoku *(287)*
Lady Murasaki Shikibu *(288)*
Yoritomo *(288)*
Tokugawa Ieyasu *(290)*
Abu Bakari II *(298)*
Mansa Musa *(299)*
Sunni Ali *(299)*
Askia Mohammed *(299)*
Mwene Mutapa *(302)*
Lalibela *(305)*

Key Groups and Dynasties

Sui dynasty *(281)*
Tang dynasty *(281)*
Song dynasty *(283)*
Ming dynasty *(284)*
Swahili *(302)*
Toltecs *(311)*
Aztecs *(311)*
Incas *(315)*
Hopewell Indians *(Mound-Builders)* *(316)*
Anasazi *(316)*
Mississippians *(318)*
Northwest Coast Indians *(318)*
Eskimos *(Inuit)* *(319)*

Key Places

Delhi *(273)*
Mogul Empire *(274)*
Ottoman Empire *(277)*
Istanbul *(277)*
Safavid Empire *(279)*
Isfahan *(280)*
Chang'an *(282)*
Beijing *(284)*
Nara *(287)*
Heian *(287)*
Edo *(290)*
Ghana *(297)*
Kumbi *(297)*

The Taj Mahal.

Mali *(298)*
Timbuktu *(299)*
Songhai *(299)*
Benin *(300)*
Luba *(301)*
Lunda *(301)*
Kongo *(301)*
Great Zimbabwe *(301)*
Kilwa *(302)*
Sofala *(302)*
Tenochtitlán *(311)*
Cuzco *(315)*

Key Terms

Taj Mahal *(275)*
Janissary Corps *(277)*
Shinto *(286)*
shogun *(288)*
samurai *(288)*
Bushido *(288)*
Zen Buddhism *(289)*
literacy *(304)*
confederacy *(319)*

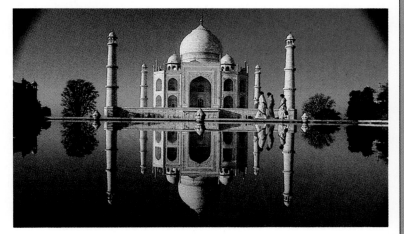

323

REVIEW ACTIVITIES: *Key People:* Explain why each of the people listed is considered a key historical person. *Key Groups and Dynasties:* Show on a world outline map the geographic location of each group or dynasty. (See pages 74 and 162 of *Teacher's Resources: Geography* for world outline maps that can be copied.) *Key Places:* Add the locations of the listed places to the world outline map used for "Key Groups and Dynasties." *Key Terms:* Define or identify each term listed.

THE HERITAGE OF THE MIDDLE AGES
300–1700

Survey Outline

UNIT 3: The Medieval World (300–1500)

Chapter 9: Byzantine and Russian Civilizations

Late in the third century A.D. the Roman Empire had divided into eastern and western regions. By A.D. 476, when the Western Roman Empire fell to Germanic invaders, the center of power in the Empire had shifted from Rome to the eastern Mediterranean. Constantinople, the capital of the Eastern Roman Empire, became the center of the new Byzantine Empire.

Byzantine culture. In A.D. 330 the emperor Constantine ordered the building of a new capital city called Constantinople. It was located on the ruins of the ancient Greek city of Byzantium, a fortress city perfectly located on a peninsula that was protected from attack on all sides. The new civilization that grew up in Constantinople, called Byzantine (BIZ-un-teen) civilization, blended aspects of many cultures. Its legal system was Roman, its language and customs were Greek, and its religion was that of early Christian communities in the eastern Mediterranean. Byzantine art, which was characterized by brilliant colors and intricate designs, was influenced by the classical Greco-Roman style, Christian sources, and the arts of the ancient Middle East.

Byzantine emperors claimed to be the successors of the Roman emperors. They were absolute rulers whose authority was believed to come from God. Their word was law, not only in civil affairs, but also in the Church. By reserving the right to appoint the patriarch (head) of the Church in Constantinople, they exerted great influence over Church policies. Because no law of

323-1

succession was ever established, struggles for power were frequent, and many emperors died violently.

The most famous of the Byzantine emperors was Justinian, who ruled from A.D. 527 to 565. Justinian ordered scholars to collect and organize the laws of Rome, which were in danger of being lost under Germanic rule. Justinian's Code, as this set of laws came to be known, preserved Roman law for future ages. Justinian also sent Byzantine forces to regain Roman lands in the western Mediterranean that had been conquered by Germanic tribes.

Hagia Sophia, built in Constantinople in the 530's, was the most magnificent church in the Mediterranean world.

His superb armies retook vast territories in Europe and North Africa.

The legacy of Byzantium. Christianity developed differently in the Byzantine Empire from that in Western Europe. Byzantine churches used the Greek language, while the Western churches used Latin. Moreover, there were many disagreements between Byzantine churches and Western churches over beliefs and practices. In the eleventh century a dispute over the refusal of the Byzantine emperor to recognize the authority of the Pope in Rome led to a permanent break. Christendom was divided into the Roman Catholic Church, which remained under the authority of the Pope, and the Eastern Orthodox Church, which was un-

der the authority of the Byzantine emperor and the patriarch of Constantinople.

Despite continuing invasions, the Byzantine Empire remained relatively stable for centuries. At a time when learning was declining in Europe, the Byzantines continued to teach and study Greek and Roman philosophy, literature, science, and mathematics. Although Byzantine scholars made few original contributions, their preservation of the ancient texts prevented classical learning from being lost to the world. Byzantine scholarship stimulated learning in the Muslim world, and eventually contributed to a revival of learning in the West. The eastern stronghold of Christianity, Byzantium protected the West from invading Mus-

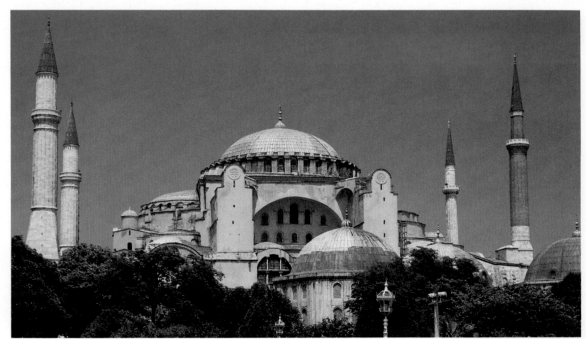

323-2

lim armies for centuries. During this time, Eastern Orthodox missionaries worked to spread Christianity to Slavic peoples in eastern and southern Europe.

The fall of the Byzantine Empire. Warfare with Muslim armies gradually weakened the Byzantines after the eleventh century. The death blow to the Empire came from the Ottoman Turks. In 1453 Constantinople fell to the Turkish army, marking the end of the Byzantine Empire.

Early Russia. For many centuries, Russia was

An icon of Mary and the infant Jesus from an Orthodox church in Russia.

inhabited by Slavic peoples who lived in culture groups and had no written language. Though their geographic location made them the target of many invaders, their culture was little affected. In the ninth century, however, the Vikings not only conquered the Slavs but settled among them and intermarried. The blending of Viking and Slavic ways became the basis of a new Russian culture, and the city of Kiev (kee-EV) became the center of the first state in Russia.

The third important element of Russian culture was

Empress Theodora ruled along with her husband, Justinian.

323-3

added in the tenth century, when a Kievan ruler named Vladimir decided to adopt the form of Christianity practiced by the Byzantines and impose it on his subjects. The Byzantine clergy built schools and monasteries and developed the Cyrillic alphabet with which the Slavic language could be written for the first time. Thus, they brought to Russia the rich culture of Byzantium. The adoption of a common faith helped unite the people of Russia, laying the basis for a national state.

The Mongol invasion. In the thirteenth century, fierce Mongol invaders conquered the Kievan state. For the next 250 years, Russia was isolated from both Western Europe and Byzantium. Mongol rule weakened the Russian economy but strengthened the authority of the Church and the Russian princes, who continued to rule in local affairs.

The rise of Moscow and Ivan the Great. In 1328 the Eastern Orthodox Church moved its headquarters from Kiev to Moscow. This marked a shift of power to Moscow as that city led the fight to free Russia from Mongol rule. During the fifteenth century, the weakening of Mongol rule made it possible for Ivan III (known as Ivan the Great) to declare Russia's independence by refusing to pay further tribute. He then brought the other Russian cities under his con-

trol. Claiming succession from the emperors of Rome and Byzantium, Ivan established himself as the absolute ruler of the first unified Russian state.

Chapter 10: The World of Islam

In the seventh and eighth centuries a new religion, known as Islam, spread from Arabia throughout the Middle East and into Asia, Europe, and North Africa.

The origin and spread of Islam. The religion of Islam was founded by an Arab trader named Mohammed in the early 600's. Mohammed preached a monotheistic religion that he said completed the teachings of Judaism and Christianity. He called on his followers, called Muslims, to reject the many gods of their group religions and follow the strict moral code of the Koran, which is the Muslim holy book.

In order to spread the new religion, Mohammed called for a jihad (jih-HAHD), or holy war, against nonbelievers. In the next century and a half, Muslim warriors conquered all the Middle East and large parts of Spain, North Africa, and western Asia, building an empire larger than that of Rome. Other monotheists in the conquered lands were allowed to practice their own religions, but polytheists were forced to convert to Islam.

Islamic culture. Muslim rule boosted trade and travel in the conquered areas. Many Muslims throughout the empire learned Arabic, which allowed them to communicate with one another. Increased contact and a common religion created a dis-

This panel of Persian tiles shows a servant waiting on a Muslim noblewoman.

323-4

tinctive Muslim culture that was a blending of many traditions. Learning was highly prized in the Muslim world. Muslim scholars made advances in many fields—including science, mathematics, medicine, and philosophy—and helped to preserve the culture of ancient Greece. Muslim artists and architects throughout the empire created lasting treasures.

Chapter 11:
The Early Middle Ages in Europe

After the fall of Rome, Western and Central Europe suffered a decline in trade, town life, and learning. Law and order vanished as the loss of strong government left the region in chaos. During the early Middle Ages (the period from about 500 to about 1500) the Christian Church emerged as the institution that gave Europeans a feeling of unity.

Medieval culture. The new culture that gradually developed in Europe was a blending of Germanic, Christian, and Greco-Roman elements. In the ninth century the Frankish ruler Charlemagne (SHAHR-lah-mayn) united much of Europe under his rule. Charlemagne's empire spread and strengthened the new medieval culture.

Charlemagne's heirs could not hold the empire together. Raids by Vik-

Charlemagne was crowned "Emperor of the Romans" by Pope Leo III in the year 800.

ings, Magyars, and Muslims caused widespread disorder. Trade and agriculture were interrupted and whole villages were destroyed by pillage and plunder. When central governments were unable to provide security, people looked to local lords for protection.

Feudalism and manorialism. The system of government and landholding that developed out of this disorder was known as feudalism. In exchange for military aid, great lords granted land to lesser lords. The noble who received the land was called a vassal. The wealth of feudal lords came from the labor of peasants, or

serfs, who farmed the lords' lands. Serfs agreed to work on the land of the lord's estate, or manor, in exchange for his protection. In return for housing and land to work, serfs owed many services to their lords. Although the conditions of life were harsh, few serfs questioned the feudal system. They accepted their lot because they, like all other Christians in medieval times, believed that God had determined a person's place in society.

The manor was the basic economic unit during the Middle Ages. Because opportunities for trade were very limited, manors were self-sufficient. The serfs produced not only the food but also most of the clothing, furniture, tools, and weapons they needed.

Chapter 12:
New Forces in Medieval Europe

By the middle of the eleventh century, Western Europe had entered a period of growing prosperity. Important changes in agriculture and trade were taking place. Along with these changes came the rebirth of towns and the rise of a middle class.

Economic change. The eleventh and twelfth centuries were a time of change and growth for Europe. New lands were cleared and settled, and new inventions greatly increased agricultural production. The result was a steady population

growth. A larger population led to increased demand for goods and more trade. Towns grew up along trading routes and contributed to the decline of serfdom and the rise of a middle class. This new social class was made up of master artisans, merchants, and their families. These people owed nothing to a lord; their prosperity came from industry and trade. They took part in local government, and their business activities brought wealth to the town. In centuries to come, the middle class would bring about great economic, political, and intellectual changes in European life.

National unification. Economic and social change paved the way for political change. The growth of towns strengthened monarchies at the expense of local lords. England was unified soon after the Norman conquest in

The Pierpont Morgan Library, New York M.399 f.8 v

Medieval farm workers.

1066. There lords remained powerful enough to check the power of the monarch through the Magna Carta and the growing importance of Parliament. In this way, the foundations were laid for limited monarchy—a government in which limits are set on the ruler's powers. In

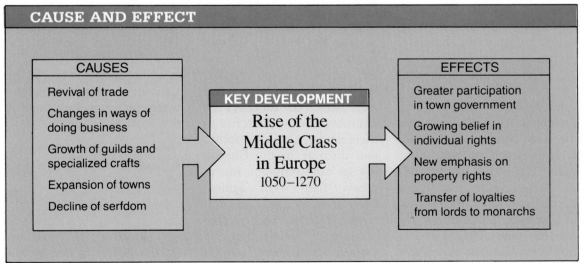

CAUSE AND EFFECT

CAUSES	KEY DEVELOPMENT	EFFECTS
Revival of trade	**Rise of the Middle Class in Europe** 1050–1270	Greater participation in town government
Changes in ways of doing business		Growing belief in individual rights
Growth of guilds and specialized crafts		New emphasis on property rights
Expansion of towns		Transfer of loyalties from lords to monarchs
Decline of serfdom		

Citizens of a Flemish town gather to receive a charter that frees them from obligations to a feudal lord.

France, on the other hand, unification took longer, but no checks on royal power developed. As a result, France moved toward absolute monarchy—government in which the ruler has complete power.

The role of the Church. The demands of the Roman Catholic Church for a role in European politics created disputes between the Pope and the Holy Roman Emperor and other monarchs. These disputes prevented the development of unified states in Germany and Italy. During the late Middle Ages, however, German states ex-panded their power eastward into the Baltic region. This expansion led to the spread of Christianity and Western culture and strengthened trade.

By the 900's the Church faced many problems. It had lost control over the appointment of bishops, and rulers were able to control the churches and monasteries in their lands. Also, corruption and disunity in the Church led to new religious movements that went against Church teachings. The campaign against heresy (the holding of beliefs that the Church considered wrong) led to the establishment of the Inquisition—a Church court that searched for suspected heretics and put them on trial. Religious zeal also led to the establishment of the Franciscan and Dominican religious orders.

The Crusades. In 1095 Pope Urban II appealed to the lords and knights of Europe to go on a crusade to recapture the Holy Land (Palestine) from the Seljuk Turks. He hoped that this campaign would unite the Christians of Europe in a common cause and increase the area of Christian influence. A series of military campaigns, called the Crusades, followed over the next two centuries.

The Crusades ultimately failed since Palestine remained in Muslim hands. Nevertheless, the Crusades had an enormous influence on life in Europe: (1) The Crusades led to a reduction in the prestige of the Popes. (2) They weakened feudalism as many nobles were killed in battle or lost their fortunes. (3) Monarchs took advantage of the weakened nobility to add to their power. (4) The Crusades also stimulated trade between Europe and the East.

Chapter 13: Europe in Late Medieval Times

Revival of learning. At the height of the Middle

Ages, growing trade and town life led to a revival of interest in learning and artistic achievement. Contact with the Byzantine and Muslim civilizations gave Western scholars access to long-lost classical manuscripts. The prosperity of the middle class allowed the opening of schools and universities.

Medieval scholars depended on the Bible and Church doctrine for guidance in their studies. Some looked askance at those who studied Greek philosophy, which seemed to conflict with Christian teachings. The Scholastics, the most famous of which was Thomas Aquinas, believed that reason could be used to explain and defend Christian teachings

Geoffrey Chaucer.

and to reconcile them with the teachings of non-Christian thinkers.

Other medieval thinkers, influenced by Muslim advances in the sciences, took a new interest in studying nature. Medieval science was

limited, however, in that its explanations included elements of superstition and folk legends.

Literature and the arts. During the late Middle Ages, a rich literature began to be written in the vernacular (local) languages. Old legends and tales of heroism were the basis for epic poems such as *Beowulf*. Troubadours in the courts of Europe wrote verse and songs about love. Such writers as Geoffrey Chaucer wrote of ordinary people.

The art of the Middle Ages was almost entirely religious in its themes. One of the main forms of art during this period was the cathedral. During the early Middle Ages, the main style of architecture was Romanesque,

A colorful panel of stained glass from a fifteenth-century cathedral shows the architect and stonemasons who built the structure.

323-8

Joan of Arc helped free France from English domination and created a new spirit of devotion to country.

which was characterized by massive walls and rounded arches. In the late 1100's, cathedrals began to be built in the Gothic style, which included high-arched ceilings, large windows, and soaring steeples.

Fourteenth-century crises. During the fourteenth century famine, plague, political unrest, and prolonged warfare created great changes in Europe. The power of monarchs increased, while the power and prestige of the papacy de-

clined. Reformers called for fundamental changes in Church practices. These changes, combined with the continuing growth of towns and the emergence of the middle class, signaled that medieval times were coming to an end.

Unit Questions

1. What were the Byzantines' greatest contributions to European history?

2. What influences contributed to the Russian culture that emerged in the Kievan state?

3. Who was the founder of Islam and what were his teachings?

4. How was the Islamic empire built?

5. What elements were blended in the making of medieval European culture?

6. Describe the feudal system of medieval Europe and

the economic system that supported it.

7. How did changes in agriculture contribute to the growth of trade and town life?

8. Contrast the development of the monarchy in England with that in France.

9. Describe three changes in European cultural life that occurred in the late Middle Ages.

10. What crises in fourteenth-century Europe brought the Middle Ages to an end?

UNIT 4: Civilizations in Asia, Africa, and the Americas (400–1700)

Chapter 14: Asia After the Rise of Islam

The conquest of the Muslim empire brought changes to much of Asia. Muslims conquered vast territories in the

Middle East, India, and China. Japan alone withstood the invasions.

Muslim rule in India. By the early 700's, Muslim armies, following Mohammed's call for a jihad against nonbelievers, had reached India again and again. Unlike

earlier invaders, the Muslims did not adopt Hindu customs and blend into Indian society. The greatest of the Muslim empires in India was the Mogul Empire, which reached its peak in the 1500's and 1600's, ruling most of the subcontinent. Corruption

323-9

Answers to Unit Questions
1. They preserved classical Greek and Roman culture, contributed to a revival of learning in the West, protected the West from Muslim invasion, and spread Christianity to Slavic peoples.
2. The Slavic and Viking cultures, and the form of Christianity practiced by the Byzantines.
3. Mohammed founded Islam in the early 600's. He taught monotheism and a strict moral code.
4. Mohammed called for a jihad against nonbelievers, and Muslims conquered the Middle East and large parts of Spain, North Africa, and western Asia.
5. Germanic, Christian, and Greco-Roman elements.
6. Feudal lords granted land to vassals in exchange for military aid; serfs exchanged labor on lords' manors for protection.

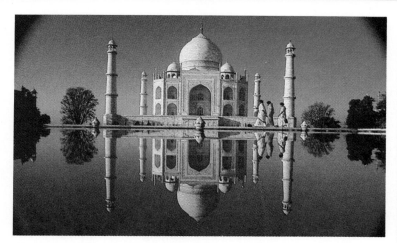

The Taj Mahal, in Agra, India, is the most famous work of Mogul architecture. Its domes and minarets show the influence of Islamic culture.

and religious intolerance led to its decline.

The Ottoman and Safavid empires. At the same time that the Mogul Empire controlled India, two other great Muslim empires dominated other parts of Asia. The Ottoman Turks captured Constantinople from the Byzantines in 1453 and used it as a base for building an empire that eventually included Asia Minor, North Africa, and much of the Middle East. This tightly organized empire was, at its peak, the most powerful empire in the world. Its long, slow decline began in the late 1500's and resulted mainly from poor leadership, economic problems, and the introduction of new types of warfare.

The Safavid (sah-fah-VID) Empire dominated Persia in the 1500's and early 1600's. Although their reign was for a relatively short time, the Safavid rulers left the legacy of a strong national identity to the people of Persia (Iran).

Imperial China. The Age of Disunity, which lasted in China from the third century through most of the sixth century, ended with the establishment of the Sui dynasty (A.D. 589–618). During the Tang and Song dynasties (618–907 and 1127–1279), which followed the Sui, China flourished, and Chinese culture and technology surpassed that of Europe. In

The palaces inside Beijing's Forbidden City housed China's emperors.

323-10

7. Newly settled lands and inventions increased food production and population growth; demand for goods led to the growth of towns along trading routes.
8. In England, unification came soon after the Norman conquest in 1066. Nobles remained powerful enough to limit the monarchy. In France, no checks on royal power developed; France moved toward absolute monarchy.
9. Answers might include the rise of universities, the rediscovery of classical texts, new interest in science, literature written in the vernacular, or the shift from Romanesque to Gothic architecture.
10. Famine, plague, political unrest, prolonged warfare, and demand for Church reform.

the thirteenth century, Mongol invaders led by Genghis Khan and his grandson, Kublai Khan, conquered China and ruled for more than a century. The Ming dynasty, established in 1368, returned China to its ancient ways and isolated that land from the rest of the world. The Ming dynasty came to an end in 1644 and was followed by a foreign dynasty, the Manchu (1644–1912).

Medieval Japan. Japan was heavily influenced by Chinese culture but developed its own language and unique civilization. The centralized Japanese government broke down during the eleventh century, and the Japanese lived under a feudal system. Landowning lords and warriors dominated Japanese politics for the next 400 years. During the 1400's and 1500's, a period known as the Age of the Country at War, Japan was in chaos, with almost constant warfare and lawlessness.

In the late 1500's the country was again brought under centralized control with the establishment of the Tokugawa shogunate, which brought the country a 250-year period of peace and order. Like China, Japan chose a course of isolation from the rest of the world after the mid-1600's.

Chapter 15:
Africa in the Age of Islam

Between A.D. 500 and 1600, many parts of Africa experienced far-reaching changes. Some of these changes resulted from internal developments, such as the growth of cities and states. Other changes came about from increasing contacts with the Islamic world. Africa was deeply affected by its increasing exposure to Islamic empires and civilization. The conquests of Muslim armies brought change even to people who had never been conquered. In African lands south of the Sahara, for example, economic and social change resulted from increased contact with Islamic culture.

African kingdoms and trading empires. The spread of Islam across North Africa had important effects on the rest of the continent. New empires arose in the western Sudan as a result of increased contact with Islamic civilizations to the north. The empires of Ghana, Mali, and Songhai provided stability for a thousand years. Farther south, new Bantu kingdoms appeared. In eastern Africa, Swahili (swah-HEE-lee) city-states arose that were influenced by Muslim traders from Arabia, Persia, and India.

CAUSE AND EFFECT

CAUSES	KEY DEVELOPMENT	EFFECTS
Rise to power of Tokugawa shogunate Expansion of Edo as commercial and political center	Unification of Japan 1598–1700	Reduction of power of daimyo Strict limitation of foreign contacts Loss of status of samurai Long period of peace and prosperity

323-11

An ivory head from the African kingdom of Benin.

African cultures. African cultures were deeply affected by increasing exposure to Islamic civilization. Two examples were the spread of the Swahili language, which borrowed many Arabic terms, and the growth of literacy in Arabic. These developments facilitated trade and allowed different African groups to communicate with one another more extensively. Islam gained many converts in Africa's trading cities, and many Africans adopted Muslim clothing styles. The spread of Islam and of trade led to a tremendous increase in the construction of new buildings in the eleventh and twelfth centuries. During this period the slave trade increased as Arabian sailing ships carried slaves from East Africa to the Muslim lands of the Middle East and India. Meanwhile, African society changed as wealth became concentrated in the hands of a few families.

Chapter 16:
Aztecs, Incas, and Other American Peoples

Because of their geographic isolation, American cultures developed independently of influences from other parts of the world. In Mexico and South America, large warlike empires were established in the fifteenth century. North of Mexico, hundreds of cultures developed. Most were small and peaceful.

The Aztec and Inca empires. In the fifteenth century, two powerful empires developed in different parts of the Americas. These were the Aztec Empire of Mexico and the Inca Empire of South America's Andes region. These empires arose as, through conquest, small, warlike groups gained control of neighboring territories and immense wealth. The rulers of both empires had absolute power, but the Inca Empire was more tightly controlled. Whereas the Aztecs merely demanded tribute from conquered peoples, the Incas forced others to adopt Inca ways.

Cultures north of Mexico. North of Mexico, hundreds of different Indian cultures developed. Because their ways of life were closely tied to the natural environment, there was a great range of cultural differences across the land. Among the major cultural groupings were the peoples of the Southwest, the Plains, California, the Southeast, the Eastern Woodlands, the Northwest Coast, the Northern Forest, and the Arctic. Most Indians lived in peaceful farming cultures governed by councils of elders and warriors. In the Iroquois League, the leading women of the group chose the male members of the League Council. Major characteristics of the Indian communities were strong ties among their members and common ownership of land.

Unit Questions

1. How did Muslim invaders differ from earlier invaders of India?

2. Where and when did the Ottoman and Safavid empires reach their peaks?

3. What development in the seventh century created new trading opportunities for African peoples south of the Sahara?

4. How did Muslim traders affect African culture?

5. What similarities and differences were there between the Aztecs and the Incas?

6. What were some common features of Indian cultures north of Mexico?

conquered peoples only through demands for tribute, while the Incas demanded that conquered peoples adopt Inca ways.

6. Most Indians north of Mexico were peaceful farmers who lived in tightly knit communities ruled by councils of elders and warriors. Their ways of life were closely tied to their natural environments.

GEOGRAPHIC THEMES

Geography and History: The Connection (continued)

In the Geography Review in the early pages of this book, you learned something about the connection between geography and history. You learned, for example, about maps as the way that geographers "picture" the earth, and you learned about the latitude-longitude system for locating places on maps. You also read that geography involves not just places but also the interaction of human beings with places—you found, in other words, that there is a connection between people and the places where they live and work.

As you continue to study the lives and achievements of people of the past, it will be useful for you to look for natural and cultural patterns in history. As a way of doing this, keep in mind five important themes that geographers use in their study of places and people. These themes are location, place, the relationship between people and environment, movement, and regions. Recognizing these themes will help you understand the significance of geography in human affairs.

Location: Position on the Earth

In Unit 4 (Chapters 14-16) you read about a number of places in far-flung parts of the world—including India, China, Mali, Ghana, Mexico, and Peru. You probably had to look at several maps to be sure where on the earth those places were located. Maps showing the locations of the peoples and societies you read about make the study of the world's history much more understandable. It also helps to think of location as being *absolute* and as *relative*.

Absolute location. The absolute location of a place is determined by latitude and longitude (page GR4). If you look at a map, you can find Mexico City at the point where the imaginary line of latitude at 19 degrees north of the equator crosses the imaginary line of longitude at 99 degrees west of the prime meridian. Absolute location is called absolute because there is no disagreement about it. As long as Mexico City exists, it will be found at 19 degrees north latitude and 99 degrees west longitude.

Relative location. Relative location may tell more about a place than absolute location. Relative location is the situation of a place rather than its pinpointed location on earth. In thinking about a place's relative location you might consider its relationship to nearby resources—for example, distance from or nearness to transportation routes. In reading about Russia on page 190 you learned that to the Vikings, Russia was a land that "promised access to the riches of Constantinople and Persia." How did the river routes that flowed north and south make Russia's relative location attractive to the Vikings?

GR11

Note to teachers: The review of basic geographic concepts and terms on pages GR1-GR10 is designed to ensure that students have fundamental skills needed to grasp the relationship between geography and history. This section on the five geographic themes will extend students' understanding of that relationship.

Relative location can also show how places are linked. You read in Chapter 14, for example, that, beginning in the sixth century A.D., Japan began to borrow features of Chinese civilization. Japan's location in relation to China (map, page 282) helps to explain why the Japanese borrowed more from that country rather than, say, from India, a much more distant land.

Place: Characteristics of an Area

Every place on earth has its unique characteristics. These characteristics may be physical or natural features, such as landforms, bodies of water, climate, soil, vegetation, and animal life. They may also be features created by human beings. Cities, roads, pyramids, walls, language, and metalworking are all examples of human endeavors that have shaped the character of places.

In Chapter 15 you read about the two capitals of Ghana, an African kingdom that was at the height of its power from about 700 to 1000 (page 297). The two capitals probably had very similar physical settings, but one of them became a headquarters for Muslim traders. Many people in that town became Muslims, and Islam became its main religion. The second town, where the king lived, remained a center of traditional Soninke culture; there Islam was not accepted. In developing different cultural characteristics, the two towns clearly emerged as two distinct places.

Relation Between People and Environment

Geographers also examine the ways in which people interact with the environment and the consequences of such interaction.

Throughout history people have made use of the natural environment—either adapting to it or changing it in some way that has met their needs. Rice, for example, has been

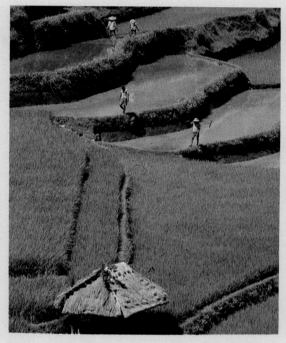

The people of Bali, an island of the Asian nation of Indonesia, build earth banks on the slopes of mountains—creating fields that can be flooded for growing rice.

the staple food for people in many places that are too warm and too wet for the cultivation of other grains. Rice requires a constant supply of water, and farmers plant it in flooded fields or where rainfall is plentiful.

As technology has advanced, people's ability to alter their environment has become enormously greater. You read in Chapter 12 about the Norman conquest of England in 1066. Duke William and his warriors had to sail across the English Channel to carry out their invasion. With the completion of the 24-mile tunnel under the English Channel in the early 1990's people will be able to travel from France to England by train in less than an hour.

In modern history, studying the relationship between people and their environment often involves looking at the impact of industrialization. Many features of modern industrial society, such as cars and factories, have been sources of pollution. Factors such **GR12** as prevailing winds or constant tides may cause the effects of pollution to be felt at places far distant from the source. Studying the interaction of people and their environment is a way of looking for a solution to this problem.

Movement: Human Interaction

The theme of movement concerns the way people in different places interact with one another. Human societies have rarely developed in complete isolation. When people come into contact with the members of a different society or with the ideas of that other society, they are generally changed by the experience.

Human interaction can take many forms. Throughout history large groups of people have sometimes moved from their homeland to another place or region. They may be looking for a better place to live; or they may be members of an invading army, such as the Mongol warriors who swept across Asia under the rule of Genghis Khan (page 191). The buying and selling of goods is another form of human interaction—one that has been part of human life from the earliest days of specialization in skills.

The movement of ideas can be as powerful a force for change as an invading army. Religious beliefs and political philosophies can revolutionize the countries through which they spread. Christianity, for example, began in the Middle East but eventually had a profound impact on Europe and America. Technological inventions, too, may change societies. Think how different European history would be if the use of gunpowder, invented in China, had not spread to Europe in the 1200's.

In modern times, radio, computers, and orbiting satellites are among the many technological developments that make it possible for people to exchange ideas more quickly than ever before.

GR13

Regions: How They Form and Change

The fifth theme in the study of geography is *region*. Regions can be thought of as units that are useful in organizing our knowledge of the world. They are areas that can be defined according to given characteristics. Some regions are governmental units, like the countries of the world or the states within a country. Others are based on landforms and plant life, like the Everglades in Florida. Still other regions are based on the characteristics of the people who live there. The Arab world, for example, is a region distinguished by language, religion, and other cultural features.

Since there are so many different ways of defining regions, a single place can be part of more than one region. Also, regions can change through time. The Ottoman Empire was one of the regions you studied in Chapter 14 (see map, page 278); in the 1500's and 1600's it was a powerful force, both politically and culturally. Yet today the Ottoman Empire no longer exists.

As you continue with your study of world history, keep in mind these five themes and look for patterns they help to explain. With awareness of these themes and remembering how geography influences human affairs, you will gain a better understanding of history.

Check What You Know

In items 1–7, choose the correct answer.

1. Absolute location is determined by (a) polar projection, (b) position on the equator, (c) latitude and longitude.

2. Relative location may show how places are (a) the same, (b) linked, (c) higher or lower in altitude.

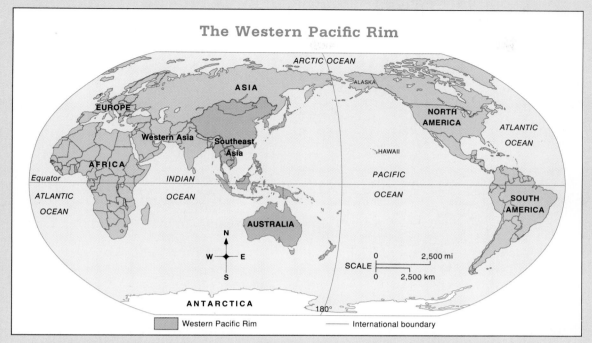

The Western Pacific Rim

In studying world history, you will read about the past and present of different regions of the world. Asia is one very large region. The Western Pacific Rim is a region that includes part of Asia but also the island groups that lie along the western side of the Pacific Ocean. How does this map show the location of the Western Pacific Rim? What continents lie along the *eastern* rim of the Pacific? Where is the United States on this map? To learn the names of the nations that border the Pacific along both eastern and western rims, find the map called "Nations of the World" at the back of this book.

3. Place is defined (a) by the movement of people, (b) by physical and human characteristics, (c) only by type of soil and climate.

4. Settlers who clear forests to create farmland are (a) changing the environment, (b) polluting the environment, (c) increasing industrialization.

5. Interaction between people in different places has been identified as the theme of (a) expansion, (b) migration, (c) movement.

6. Modern technology and communication have (a) increased global interdependence, (b) ended the movement of people, (c) encouraged the movement of armies.

7. Regions, as defined in geography, are (a) based only on landforms and plant life, (b) based only on language and religion, (c) based on a variety of characteristics.

Answer the following questions:

8. How might the relative location of a community affect population and employment? Consider, for example, what happens to a town or city if a large business or industry shuts down.

9. How do ideas—such as philosophies or technological advances—spread from place to place? Compare how that happened in past ages with how it happens today.

GR14

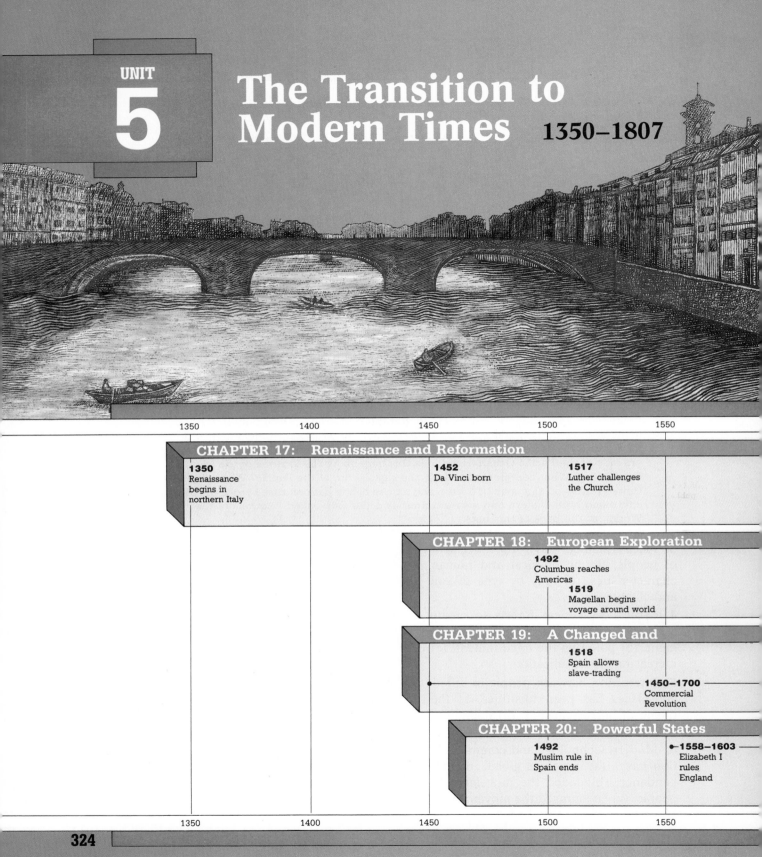

UNIT 5

The Transition to Modern Times   1350–1807

1350	1400	1450	1500	1550

CHAPTER 17:   Renaissance and Reformation

1350
Renaissance begins in northern Italy

1452
Da Vinci born

1517
Luther challenges the Church

CHAPTER 18:   European Exploration

1492
Columbus reaches Americas

1519
Magellan begins voyage around world

CHAPTER 19:   A Changed and

1518
Spain allows slave-trading

1450–1700
Commercial Revolution

CHAPTER 20:   Powerful States

1492
Muslim rule in Spain ends

1558–1603
Elizabeth I rules England

1350	1400	1450	1500	1550

FOCUS STRATEGY. Tell students that the illustration represents a city in Renaissance Italy. Then ask: (a) How does this Renaissance city compare with the drawing of the medieval city shown on page 179? (The Renaissance city looks larger and has more buildings. The medieval city is protected by a wall.) (b) What do you think life in this Renaissance city might have been like? (Answers will vary.)

| 1600 | 1650 | 1700 | 1750 | 1800 |

1605
Cervantes'
Don Quixote
published

and Colonization

1607
English settle
Jamestown

1682
La Salle explores
Mississippi River

1754–1763
French and
Indian War

Changing World

1580
Drake completes
voyage around world

1807
Britain and United
States outlaw
slave-trading

in Europe

1618–1648
Thirty Years' War

1689
English Bill of
Rights

1762–1796
Catherine the
Great rules Russia

1588
Spanish Armada
defeated

1643–1715
Louis XIV rules
France

| 1600 | 1650 | 1700 | 1750 | 1800 |

325

Renaissance and Reformation   1350–1600
(pp. 326–345)

Chapter Preview

Section 1 examines the changes in art, culture, and intellectual outlook that distinguished the Renaissance from the Middle Ages. In Section 2 the ideas and works of the influential thinkers, writers, and painters of the Italian and northern European Renaissance are discussed. Section 3 explains the developments that led to the Reformation, the effects of the spread of Protestantism on the people of Europe, and the response of the Catholic Church to the breakdown of religious unity in Western Europe.

Bibliography

See the *Teacher's Management and Planning Guide* for additional listings. Starred titles are for both students and teachers.

Bainton, Roland H. *Here I Stand: A Life of Martin Luther*. New American Library. Conveys a strong sense of the times.

*Mee, Charles L., Jr. *Lorenzo de Medici and the Renaissance*. American Heritage. Portrays the Florentine ruler who was known as Il Magnifico.

*Read, Conyers. *The Tudors: Personalities and Practical Politics in Sixteenth-Century England*. Norton. Portraits of each Tudor ruler.

Section Lesson Plans

SECTION 1   (pp. 327–331)
The Spirit of the Renaissance

Objectives

After completing this section, students will be able to:
1. Identify the ideas that marked Renaissance thought.
2. Describe how the Renaissance spread beyond Italy.

Introducing the Lesson

Remind students that *renaissance* is a French word that means "rebirth" and is the name given to a time period in Europe marked by significant social, cultural, and scientific changes. People began to view the world and their lives differently as a result of the Renaissance.

Then ask: *(a) Why might a person's view of the world and of life change?* (Answers will vary. People hold certain values and make decisions based on their goals, expectations, and ideas. Sometimes values and expectations change because of experiences and events in life.)

(b) What circumstances might change the way people view the world and their lives? (Answers will vary. Education increases one's knowledge; wealth gives greater access to goods; travel affords contact with different people and places.)

(c) What might be considered significant influences on the way people view themselves and the world today? (Answers will vary.)

Developing the Lesson: Linking Past and Present

Have students describe a person who might have been considered representative of Renaissance ideals. (Educated, witty, charming, artistically creative, practiced in military skills, athletic, trained in the humanities, public-minded.) Then have students write a paragraph about how future historians might describe a person who lived in our times. Students should consider the following: *(a) What kind of person is considered successful today? (b) What programs of study are encouraged in schools? (c) What social skills are valued? (Application)*

Developing the Lesson: Translating Information into Another Form

Have students work in groups to design a government that might have been formed by a supporter of Machiavelli's political views. Students should consider the goals, structure, laws, and participants likely to be found in such a government. *(Synthesis)*

Closing the Lesson: Analyzing Information

Have students explain why wealthy merchants and bankers led the Italian Renaissance. In their analyses, students should consider Renaissance values and the social and political status of merchants and bankers. *(Analysis)*

See *Section Review* questions, p. 331.

SECTION 2   (pp. 332–337)
Renaissance Literature and Art

Objectives

After completing this section, students will be able to:
1. Name some of the great literary works of the Renaissance.
2. Describe new art styles that developed.
3. Identify major artists of the Renaissance.

Introducing the Lesson

Remind students that literature and art are expressions of individuals who reflect the society and time period in which they live.

Then ask: *(a) How can writers help us to understand history?* (Writers describe the relationships, ideals, and goals of their times.)

(b) How can artists help us to understand history? (Artists show us what people valued and believed in, what they wore, how they looked, what their occupations were, and what buildings and transportation were like.)

(c) What are some examples found in art and literature of today that might help people in the future better understand our time? (Answers will vary.)

Developing the Lesson: Analyzing Information

Have students explain how the art of the period reveals the differences between the Renaissance and medieval views of life. (Human figures in medieval art had little individuality and showed people who were stiffly posed. Renaissance artists tried to show each individual's character and personality in a lifelike way. Renaissance art shows ancient Roman and Greek influence, emphasizes natural poses and settings, and portrays rich and elaborate clothing.) *(Application)*

Developing the Lesson: Drawing Conclusions

Have students write a short essay titled *Renaissance Writers and Literature*. Students should refer to the text discussion of Cervantes, Rabelais, and Shakespeare, and draw conclusions about the values and interests of Renaissance writers and literature. (Essays might emphasize humor, ridicule of medieval codes of honor, adventure and interest in nature, human relationships, and human potential.) *(Synthesis)*

Closing the Lesson: Translating Information into Another Form

Have students make a chart organizing the lesson material on Renaissance writers and artists. Charts should identify important artists and writers and their countries, and describe their major works or ideas. *(Comprehension)*

See *Section Review* questions, p. 337.

SECTION 3   (pp. 337–343)
The Reformation

Objectives

After completing this section, students will be able to:
1. Explain why some Christians broke away from the Catholic Church.
2. Name the effects of the Reformation.

Introducing the Lesson

Remind students that the Renaissance replaced an emphasis on religious themes with an interest in worldly ambition and success, confidence in human potential, and a focus on earthly satisfaction rather than the afterlife.

Then ask: *(a) How did Renaissance ideas contrast with the Church's teachings?* (The Church valued spiritual rather than earthly treasures and success. The Church believed that faith in God was more important than confidence in human potential, and that earthly satisfaction and pleasure were unimportant and sometimes sinful.)

(b) How might Renaissance attitudes have resulted in the criticism and questioning of Church authority? (The values and attitudes of the Church had not changed. The Church continued to represent medieval ideas.)

(c) How might Renaissance ideas have caused a change in religious beliefs and practices? (Answers will vary. People who represented Renaissance values might have assumed positions of authority in the Church. To maintain the support of political leaders, religious leaders might accept "earthly" values.)

Developing the Lesson: Organizing Information

Have students make a chart comparing the German and English protests against the Catholic Church. The comparison should include the motives for the protests and the form the protests took. (*German motives:* resentment of Italian control of Church offices, heavy taxes, and the sale of indulgences; desire to return to a time when church leaders were poor, but religious; led by Martin Luther. *Form:* new ideas on salvation, grace, and the Bible; new churches formed. *English motives:* Henry VIII's desire to remove England from the authority of the Pope. *Form:* Parliament broke with the Church in 1534 and created the Church of England with the monarch as its head.) *(Comprehension)*

Answers to *Map Skill Practice*, p. 340.

1. Roman Catholicism.
2. The German States, Norway, Sweden, Denmark, Prussia.
3. With abbreviations of minority religions in the areas where they existed.
4. This map shows less religious unity. Discontent with Church practices sparked the Reformation and rise of new Protestant groups.

Developing the Lesson: Organizing Information in Written Form

In an outline titled *The Counter-Reformation,* have students summarize efforts made by the Church to reform and strengthen Catholicism. Subheads in the outline should include the *Council of Trent, the Inquisition, the Index, and New Religious Orders. (Comprehension)*

Closing the Lesson: Making Judgments

Have students reread the last paragraph in the lesson (p. 342) and then explain how the qualities emphasized by Protestantism continue to be important to the modern world. (Answers will vary.) *(Synthesis)*

See *Section Review* questions, p. 343.

Chapter 17 Review Answers
(pp. 344–345)

Vocabulary Review

1. (a) Renaissance (b) patron (c) humanities (d) perspective (e) indulgence (f) predestination (g) Vatican (h) fresco (i) Calvinism
2. (a) Peace of Augsburg—1555 treaty allowing German princes to decide which religion would be followed in their lands; Act of Supremacy—English law passed in 1534 making the monarch the head of the Church of England. (b) Reformation—sixteenth-century movement to reform the Catholic Church; Counter-Reformation—the Church's efforts to strengthen and spread Catholicism.

People to Identify

1. Machiavelli 2. Cervantes 3. Lorenzo de Medici 4. Isabella d'Este 5. Giotto 6. Petrarch 7. Michelangelo 8. Rembrandt

Places to Know

1. E 2. C 3. F 4. D 5. A 6. B

Recalling the Facts

1. Emphasis on living as fully as possible, appreciation of the individual, ambition, belief in people's ability to achieve great things, belief in the importance of public service.
2. It made books cheaper and more accessible, literacy became more widespread, and scholars had better access to one another's work.
3. He drew on Greek and Roman history for several of his plays, and he explored human behavior and feelings by creating complex, believable characters.
4. Renaissance artists used Greek and Roman themes and ideas, emphasized the uniqueness of each human subject; architects returned to the Romanesque style to make buildings perfectly balanced. Renaissance artists rejected the stiff pose, lack of individuality, and unrealistic proportion characteristic of medieval painting; architects rejected the Gothic style, which seemed to defy laws of balance.
5. They did not all share the Italians' interest in classical themes and styles. Instead, some used religious themes and symbols, while others showed contemporary life in the town and countryside. They also emphasized precise, realistic detail and the use of light and shadow.

6. They disliked heavy taxes and Church corruption. Many Germans also resented Italian control of important Church offices.

7. He opposed the sale of indulgences and reliance on the Pope and the clergy for interpretations of the Bible; he also urged changes in church services, and said that members of the clergy should be allowed to marry. Some people agreed with his ideas about reading the Bible for oneself, others supported his attacks on the Church, and some princes backed him in hopes of acquiring Church property and showing their independence from the Holy Roman Emperor.

8. He believed that the Bible was the supreme authority in matters of faith, that salvation could be achieved through faith alone, that people were predestined for salvation, and that hard work and devotion might be signs of God's grace.

9. Under Henry VIII Parliament passed the Act of Supremacy, which made the monarch head of the Church of England and ended papal authority in England; he also closed English monasteries and convents and seized their land and properties. Mary I, a devout Catholic, persecuted English Protestants who refused to become Catholics again. Elizabeth I turned England back to Protestantism; during her reign, Parliament approved the teachings of the Church of England.

10. The Church banned the sale of indulgences, tightened discipline for the clergy, started seminaries to train the clergy, and encouraged reform of monasteries and convents. In addition, the Inquisition threatened Protestants; Catholics were forbidden to read, own, or sell certain books; and new religious orders were set up to serve the Church and spread its teachings.

11. Religious unity ended in Western and Central Europe as Christians were divided into Catholics and Protestants, which were further divided into groups. The Church's influence in political affairs was weakened as Protestant rulers rejected the authority of the Pope and as Catholic rulers allowed the Church fewer privileges and less say in political matters. The spread of education was encouraged because Protestants urged people to read the Bible, and Catholics set up schools and universities. The middle class was strengthened because Protestantism taught that the qualities already held by the middle class were those that please God.

Critical Thinking Skills

1–2. Answers will vary.

3. Answers will vary, but students might suggest that Henry VIII did follow Machiavelli's advice in doing whatever was necessary to keep power. Henry broke with the Church because the Pope refused to serve Henry's interests.

4. Answers will vary. Communication skills are still valuable assets; an elegant writing style is not as important to a politician as a good speechwriter and a public relations firm; good manners are important, but perhaps less so than in the past. Students might suggest that today's politicians should be honest, decisive, and intelligent.

Thinking About Geography

Country	Principal Rel.	Minority Rel.
Austria	Roman Catholic	Calvinist
Bohemia	Roman Catholic	Calvinist
Denmark	Lutheran	none
England	Anglican	Roman Catholic Calvinist
France	Roman Catholic	Calvinist
German states	Roman Catholic Calvinist Lutheran	Calvinist
Hungary	Roman Catholic	Calvinist
Ireland	Roman Catholic	Anglican
Italian states	Roman Catholic	none
Norway	Lutheran	none
Ottoman Empire	Eastern Orthodox	Muslim
Poland	Roman Catholic	Lutheran Calvinist
Prussia	Lutheran	none
Russia	Eastern Orthodox	none
Scotland	Calvinist	Roman Catholic
Spain	Roman Catholic	none
Spanish Netherlands	Roman Catholic	none
Sweden	Lutheran	none
Swiss Confed.	Roman Catholic Calvinist	none
United Provinces	Calvinist	Roman Catholic

Enrichment: Primary Sources

1. "I would have the courtier endowed . . . not only with . . . beauty of person and feature, but with a certain grace and air that shall make him at first sight pleasing and agreeable to all."

2. Showiness and self-praise, because they "excite hatred and disgust" in others.

3. Answers will vary. Both the Renaissance and the Athenian ideals emphasized a sound mind, a sound body, and moderation. One difference is the Renaissance emphasis on noble birth compared with the Athenian idea of democracy.

Renaissance and Reformation 1350–1600

See chapter timeline, p. 343.

Before You Read This Chapter

When did "modern times" begin? Of course, there is no clear dividing line that marks the beginning of modern history. Yet many historians say that the change-over to the modern world began during the Renaissance. Although ways of living and working during the Renaissance did not differ dramatically from those of the Middle Ages, people began thinking in new ways. As you read this chapter, try to decide which ideas seem "modern" to you. What do you think was the most important change in people's outlook?

The Geographic Setting

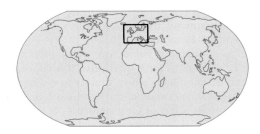

The Chapter Outline

1. The Spirit of the Renaissance
2. Renaissance Literature and Art
3. The Reformation

The great Renaissance artist Michelangelo painted the Biblical scenes that decorate the Sistine Chapel in Vatican City.

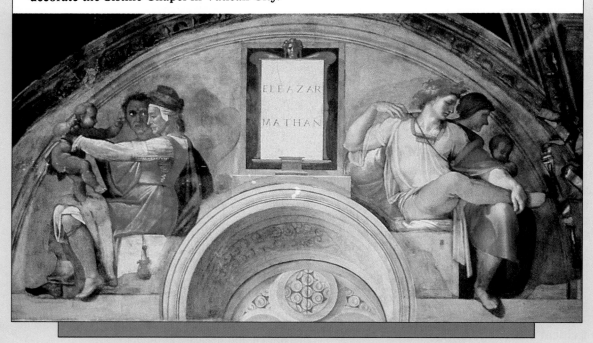

1 The Spirit of the Renaissance

Objectives

Focus Questions

★ ■ What ideas marked Renaissance thought? *(pages 327–330)*

● ■ How did the Renaissance spread beyond Italy? *(pages 330–331)*

Terms to Know

Renaissance
patron
humanities

★ Note strategies for first objective on this page and p. 329.

Late in the Middle Ages, a long period of wars, epidemics, and economic upheaval in Europe came to an end. A new spirit of optimism, confidence, and creativity took hold. These developments led to the start of a remarkable period that has become known as the Renaissance (ren-uh-SAHNS), from the French word for "rebirth." The Renaissance was an explosion of cultural achievement in Europe and lasted from the fourteenth to the sixteenth century.

The Italian City-States

Sec. Rev. ques. 2

The Renaissance began about 1350 in the northern Italian city-states. These cities, profiting from their central location, had long dominated trade routes between Eastern and Western Europe and between Europe and the Middle East. By the 1300's they had become the richest cities in Europe.

Italian merchants and bankers had the wealth to acquire libraries and fine works of art. They admired and encouraged art, literature, and scholarship. Surrounded by reminders of ancient Rome—amphitheaters,

monuments, and sculptures—they took an interest in classical culture and thought.

In Italy the most famous patrons—supporters—of the arts were the members of the Medici (MED-uh-chee) family. The Medici were bankers who had branch offices in cities all over Western Europe. They became active in the politics of Florence in the 1400's and controlled the city for most of the next 300 years.

The best-known member of the family was Lorenzo de Medici (1449–1492), known as "the Magnificent." Lorenzo was a scholar, a skilled architect, and a talented poet. He collected a huge library of classical manuscripts, which he invited other thinkers to use. To give the city's young people an opportunity to study classical literature, he expanded the university at Florence. Lorenzo also hired painters, architects, and sculptors to create works of art not only for his palace but also for the city of Florence. Many of these works still survive, making Florence one of the most beautiful cities in the world.

The Recovery of Classical Culture

Like Lorenzo the Magnificent, many wealthy Italians of the fifteenth century took a keen interest in the ancient Romans. They paid for the restoration of old monuments and works of art. They searched out classical manuscripts in the libraries of European monasteries, often finding them in poor condition and entirely forgotten. Popes, princes, and merchants collected these neglected treasures and stored them in magnificent libraries. There they could be studied by scholars from every corner of Europe.

Sec. Rev. ques. 3

Renaissance scholars' interest in Greek and Roman learning developed into the study of the humanities—subjects concerned with humankind and culture, as opposed to science. The humanities included Latin and

327

★ RETEACHING. Have students write a one-page explanation of the cause-and-effect relationship between the increased economic prosperity of the Italian city-states and the Renaissance. (Wealthy patrons acquired libraries and art; they patronized artists, scholars, and schools.) *(Comprehension) Identifying Cause and Effect*
Citizenship. Ask: What are some ways in which members of society support the arts today? (Answers will vary.)

★ REINFORCEMENT. Have students review "The Recovery of Classical Culture" (pages 327–328) and then write a paragraph summarizing the work of Renaissance scholars. (The study of the humanities developed; Petrarch rediscovered forgotten Roman authors and wrote love poems; Machiavelli wrote *The Prince*; Erasmus wrote *The Praise of Folly*; Sir Thomas More wrote *Utopia*.) *(Comprehension) Observing for Detail*

The city of Florence was the seat of the Italian Renaissance. The large domed building in the center is the cathedral. The fifteenth-century painter of this picture has drawn himself in the lower right-hand corner.

Greek language and literature, composition, history, and philosophy. Music and mathematics were sometimes studied as well. Those who read and wrote about these subjects were called humanists.

Enthusiasm for ancient Greece and Rome spread from scholars to the rest of the Italian upper classes. Many people imitated not only the language but the customs and ways of life of the classical civilizations. Some even tried to trace their ancestry back to ancient Rome.

Petrarch: A Pioneer of Humanism

Francesco Petrarch (PEH-trahrk), an Italian poet born in 1304, led the early development of Renaissance humanism. Regarding ancient Roman times as a much grander period than his own day, he studied Roman literature and philosophy and encouraged others to do the same. A collector of ancient manuscripts, Petrarch rediscovered a number of Roman authors whose work had been forgotten during the Middle Ages.

In his scholarly writings in Latin, Petrarch discussed the ideas of Roman writers and copied their style. He also wrote hundreds of love poems in Italian. Petrarch enjoyed writing so much that he often worked all night long at his desk. When a worried friend urged him to relax, he replied, "Nothing weighs less than a pen, and nothing gives more pleasure." On July 19, 1374, Petrarch was found dead in his library, his head resting on an open book, his pen fallen from his hand.

New Attitudes

Interest in earthly life. Thinkers in the Middle Ages, such as the Scholastics (page 256), had tried to use ideas of the ancient writers to support and clarify Church teachings. In contrast, Petrarch and other Renaissance humanists tried to understand the entire civilization of the ancient world. Medieval thinkers had thought of earthly existence chiefly as preparation for an afterlife. The

Citizenship. Ask: What qualities admired by Renaissance humanists make people effective citizens today? (Answers will vary.)

Politics Machiavelli valued the republican form of government but claimed that the Italy of his day needed a strong political leader.

people of the Renaissance, following the examples of classical Greece and Rome, believed that life on earth should be lived as fully as possible.

Development of individual talents. Another characteristic borrowed from classical times was an intense appreciation of the individual. The people of the Renaissance were interested in the unique qualities that made one person stand out from others. Like the Romans, they were ambitious for fame and worldly success. Like the Greeks, they believed human beings could achieve great things. These attitudes encouraged a spirit of curiosity and adventure.

The men and women of the upper classes benefited most from the new spirit of the times. They had the money and leisure to develop their talents. The Renaissance ideal was a well-rounded person: educated, witty, charming, and artistically creative. In addition, men were expected to practice swordsmanship and other military skills. People of both sexes were expected to develop their athletic abilities.

Public service and politics. Like the ancient Greeks and Romans, upper-class Italians valued public service and praised those who were useful to society. They believed that an education in the humanities was a sound preparation for a rewarding life. The skills admired by the humanists—effective public speaking, polished manners, an elegant writing style—were valuable ones for social and political leaders.

★ See below, right.

The political climate in Renaissance Italy was one of intense rivalry. The Pope, the Holy Roman Emperor, and the rulers of France and Spain all hungered for power. As a guide, they turned to handbooks on how to succeed in politics.

The most famous of these handbooks was written by Niccolo Machiavelli (mak-ee-uh-VEL-ee) of Florence, a diplomat and student of politics. Machiavelli (1469–1527) drew on Roman history to set up guidelines for rulers of his time. Machiavelli argued that a ruler should do whatever was necessary to gain and keep power. In his book *The Prince*, written about 1513, Machiavelli pointed out

that rulers often lied, broke treaties, and killed. In politics, he said, actions must be judged only by their results. Machiavelli's controversial ideas have been debated ever since.

The role of women. While men held center stage in the fields of politics and business, women were expected to make use of their education and talents at home. Well-to-do young ladies studied poetry, languages, and music so that they might entertain graciously and be a credit to their husbands.

One of the most admired women of the Renaissance was Isabella d'Este (DES-tay). She was not only a great patron of the arts and learning but also a skilled diplomat. Few women exercised as much political power as Isabella. Indeed, though women of the Renaissance were better educated than women in medieval times, they had less chance to shape political or economic life.

The Printing Press

The Renaissance was a time of change in technology as well as in culture. The most exciting development was the printing press. In the 1450's Europeans first used movable metal type to print a book. On small pieces of metal they engraved single letters of the alphabet. These could then be arranged and rearranged to form words and sentences. A German, Johann Gutenberg (GOOT-un-burg), is usually credited with printing the first book, a copy of the Bible. By 1500 there were hundreds of printers, in nearly every country in Europe.

Linking Past and Present

As the centuries have passed, Machiavelli has been best remembered for his defense of lies and deception. Today the word *Machiavellian* is used to describe any crafty or deceitful actions used for one's own advantage.

329

Check for Understanding. Ask: How did the Renaissance attitude toward earthly life differ from that of the Middle Ages? (Medieval thinkers viewed earthly existence as preparation for an afterlife. Renaissance thinkers emphasized living earthly life as fully as possible.)

★ ENRICHMENT. Have students make a chart titled *Renaissance Ideas Valued Today.* In one column students should list the ideas still valued and, in a second column, give examples for each idea. (Ideas include appreciation of individual differences and achievements, ambition, belief in human potential, importance of education, and respect for public service.) (Application) Evaluating Information

Ⓕ See above.

BIOGRAPHY

Isabella D'Este

In February 1490 the small Italian city-state of Ferrara was the scene of a magnificent wedding. Fifteen-year-old Isabella D'Este—eldest child of Ferrara's ruling family—married Francesco Gonzaga. The 24-year-old Francesco was a leading noble from the neighboring city-state of Mantua. During the festivities, the youthful couple dined on gold and silver dishes and drank from solid gold goblets. When Isabella set forth by river barge for her new home in Mantua, 13 trunkloads of clothing and linens followed her.

Even as a young bride, Isabella was famous for her intelligence, her beauty, her lovely singing voice, and her brilliant conversation. Later, as wife of the ruler of Mantua, she became a renowned patron of the arts. Her collection of paintings, rare manuscripts, fine books, musical instruments, and sculpture was one of the finest in all Italy.

In 1509 Isabella faced a dangerous situation. Francesco had been captured in a war against Venice. Enemies threatened Mantua's borders. Isabella took command and ordered her soldiers not to open the gates of their forts, even if the Venetians threatened to kill Francesco. She kept Mantua safe and eventually negotiated her husband's release. He thought she had worried too much about Mantua, however, and not enough about him. He was ashamed, he wrote to her, "to have as his wife a woman who is always ruled by her head." Perhaps he was also ashamed of having a wife who was clearly a better politician than he.

After Francesco died in 1519, Isabella increased her power and influence. Until her death in 1539, she remained *la prima donna del mondo*—the first lady of the world—for Renaissance Italy.

The invention of movable type had three main effects. First, bookmaking became much cheaper, which meant that more people could afford to own books. As a result, literacy became more widespread.

Second, bookmaking became faster, so that many more books could be published. The earliest printed books dealt with religious subjects, but the new reading public wanted books on other subjects as well. Many of the new books were published in the vernacular (the language of the common people) rather than in Latin.

A third effect was that scholars had better access to one another's works and to the great books of the ancient and medieval worlds. This leap in communication brought important advances in knowledge.

Sec. Rev. ques. 4

The Northern Renaissance

● Note strategies for second objective on this page and p. 331.
Printing helped carry the spirit and ideas of the Renaissance northward from Italy to France, England, Germany, and the Netherlands.* While sharing the Italians' admiration of classical civilizations and respect for

_____

* The Netherlands is sometimes called Holland, and the people of this country are called the Dutch.

330

● RETEACHING. Have students review "The Northern Renaissance (pages 330–331) and then write a paragraph summarizing the ideas in Erasmus's book, *The Praise of Folly,* and Sir Thomas More's book, *Utopia.* (*The Praise of Folly* criticizes clergy, scholars, scientists, and philosophers of Erasmus's time. *Utopia* describes an ideal, peaceful society.) *(Comprehension) Translating Information into Another Form*

● REINFORCEMENT. Have students contrast the spirit and ideas of the Italian Renaissance with those of the northern Renaissance. (The North shared the Italians' love of the classics and respect for the individual and was concerned with religious matters; the most influential northern Renaissance person was Erasmus, a priest, not a patron or artist.) *(Comprehension) Observing for Detail*
Check for Understanding. Ask: To which areas of Europe did the Renaissance spread? (France, England, Germany, Netherlands.)

A drawing from the 1500's shows how labor was divided in a print shop. At left, workers arrange metal letters according to the manuscript on the wall in front of them. In the center, a man applies ink to type that has been set. At right, a printer uses a press to transfer the print onto paper pages.

individual achievement, northern Europeans were deeply concerned with religious questions as well.

Erasmus. The most respected and influential humanist of the northern Renaissance was Desiderius Erasmus (ih-RAZ-mus), who was born about 1466 in Rotterdam, Holland. Trained as a Catholic priest, Erasmus studied both the humanities and Christian teachings. He argued that the Church had become greedy and corrupt, and he called for a return to the simple faith of early Christianity.

● See below.

In *The Praise of Folly* (1509), Erasmus criticized scholars, scientists, philosophers, and clergy of his time for being narrow-minded. This work had a wide influence, as

did his Latin translation of the New Testament (1516), which was admired for its style and scholarship. The new craft of printing made Erasmus's books available throughout Europe. He was one of the first authors whose writings were read by thousands of people.

Sir Thomas More. Another important scholar of the northern Renaissance was Sir Thomas More, an English statesman. More and Erasmus were close friends. More was a devout Catholic and a student of both Church doctrine and the humanities. His book *Utopia* (Greek for "nowhere"), published in 1516, described an ideal, peaceful society. It also contained criticism of the politics, society, and religion of the times.

See Sec. 1 *Closing the Lesson,* p. T325B.

Section Review

Answers to Section Review questions are in brackets on pages indicated.

1. **Define or identify:** Renaissance, patron, humanities. (p. 327)
2. Why did the Renaissance begin in Italian cities? (p. 327)
3. What aspects of Greek and Roman culture appealed to some people during the Renaissance? (pp. 327–328)

4. What were the effects of the invention of movable type? (p. 330)
5. **Critical thinking:** Why did Sir Thomas More use a word meaning "nowhere" as the title of his book? (See answer below.)

5. Sir Thomas More might have been implying that such an ideal society did not and perhaps could not exist.

331

See lesson plans, pp. T325A–T325C.

2 Renaissance Literature and Art

Objectives

Focus Questions

★ ■ What were some of the great literary works of the Renaissance? *(pages 332–333)*

● ■ What new styles developed in art? *(page 333)*

▲ ■ Who were the major artists of the Renaissance? *(pages 334–336)*

Terms to Know

perspective   fresco
Vatican

★ Note strategies for first objective on this page and p. 333.

The Renaissance spirit and the renewed interest in ancient Greece and Rome were the inspiration for a brilliant creative period in literature and art. With great realism and individuality, writers and artists brought to life the ideals of the Renaissance.

Renaissance Literature

Cervantes. The greatest Spanish writer of the Renaissance was Miguel de Cervantes Saavedra, usually known as Cervantes (sur-VAHN-teez). Cervantes (1547–1616) served as a soldier against the Turks and was imprisoned for five years by pirates in North Africa. He later became a Spanish tax collector.

Cervantes' eventful life gave him a wealth of material for his masterpiece, *Don Quixote* (kee-HOH-tee), first published in 1605. In this book Cervantes mocked medieval codes of chivalry. Don Quixote is a kind, elderly gentleman who spends so much time reading medieval tales that he loses his sense of reality. He decides to become a knight and

Sec. Rev. ques. 2

332

sets out to do heroic deeds. Don Quixote has a series of comic adventures. For example, he sees a herd of sheep as an army and thinks windmills are giants.

Rabelais. François Rabelais (RAHB-uh-lay), who was born in France about 1494, encouraged the Renaissance ideal of living a full, busy life. He himself was a monk, a scholar, and a physician. He also studied plants and Roman archeological sites. Rabelais wrote, "Let nothing in the world be unknown to you." Over a period of about 20 years, Rabelais wrote a five-volume work, *Gargantua and Pantagruel*, that made fun of those who did not take the humanist point of view. The books combined humor, imagination, and adventures with scholarship.

Shakespeare. In England the Renaissance spirit reached its height in the work of

Shakespeare's brilliant imagination, use of language, and understanding of human nature won him recognition as the greatest writer in English. In front of him is a drawing of the Globe Theater, where many of his plays were performed.

★ RETEACHING. Have students outline the section information on Renaissance writers, where they were from, and their masterpieces. (Writers include Cervantes, Spain; Rabelais, France; Shakespeare, England.) *(Comprehension)* **Observing for Detail**

★ REINFORCEMENT. Have students find the definitions, origins, and uses of the following adjectives: *quixotic, Rabelaisian, Gargantuan.* Then have students write two sentences for each word. *(Comprehension)* **Locating Information**

William Shakespeare (1564–1616). Shakespeare was an actor, poet, and playwright, not a classical scholar. A fellow writer said that he had "small Latin and less Greek." However, Shakespeare shared the humanists' interest in other times and places, particularly the ancient world. Several plays—such as *Julius Caesar* and *Antony and Cleopatra*—draw on Greek and Roman history. Others take place in Renaissance Italy and in medieval England, Scotland, and Denmark.

Sec. Rev. ques. 2, cont.

Shakespeare's admiration for humanity also marked him as a man of the Renaissance. In the play *Hamlet* he wrote: "What a piece of work is a man! How noble in reason! . . . In action how like an angel!" Shakespeare's characters were complex, believable people. Few writers in any age have explored human behavior and feelings with such insight.

★ See below.

Features of Renaissance Art

● Note strategies for second objective on this page and p. 335.

Individualism. Like the writers of the Renaissance, the artists of the time looked back to the ancient Greeks and Romans for their themes and ideas. They used ancient works of art as their models in painting a variety of subjects—stories from Greek mythology, scenes from Roman history, incidents in the Bible, and Church history. They also captured on canvas Renaissance politicians, patrons of art, and ordinary people busy with their daily activities.

Medieval artists had used their creativity mainly to serve the Church and express their religious feelings. Their paintings generally showed people who were stiffly posed and whose faces had little individuality. Renaissance art, like classical art, emphasized the uniqueness of each human face and figure. In portraits, Renaissance artists tried to show each individual's character and personality in a lifelike way.

Sec. Rev. ques. 3

Balance and proportion. Renaissance artists and architects saw nature as the standard for balance and proportion. They hoped to achieve these same qualities in their own work so that it would look more realistic. While medieval painters had often drawn people larger than buildings, Renaissance artists tried to show people, trees, buildings, and mountains in their proper sizes.

Renaissance architects scorned the Gothic cathedral, the symbol of the Middle Ages, which soared upward toward heaven and seemed to defy laws of balance. Renaissance architects turned back to the Romanesque style (page 260), adding domes, windows, and balconies to let in light and air. They tried to make all the parts of a building appear perfectly balanced in size and shape.

Use of perspective. Another step toward realism was the discovery of how to achieve **perspective**—the impression of depth and distance on the flat surface of a painting. The Florentine painter Giotto (JAHT-oh) had first used this technique about 1300. Giotto's realistic style seemed odd to medieval eyes, however, and his advances were ignored until the Renaissance.

In the 1400's the Florentine architect Filippo Brunelleschi (broo-nuh-LES-kee) discovered that painters could use mathematical laws in planning their pictures. In this way they could show perspective accurately. Masaccio (mah-ZAHT-choh), a friend of Brunelleschi's, applied these laws in his paintings. (For an example of the use of perspective, see the picture on page 334.)

New materials. Medieval painters had commonly used a kind of paint called tempera. It dried so quickly that painters could not change or correct what they had painted. A new technique, oil painting, was developed by the Flemish painter Jan van Eyck (IKE), who lived from about 1380 to about 1440. ("Flemish" refers to the language or people of Flanders, then a part of the Netherlands.) Oil painting let artists work more slowly, create new colors, and obtain more lifelike effects. For example, they could show realistically the look and texture of different fabrics.

The use of oil-based paints quickly spread from Flanders to other parts of Europe. In Italy, Renaissance artists soon began to use both perspective and oil painting to produce many important works that are now considered masterpieces.

333

★ ENRICHMENT. Have students write an essay titled *Medieval and Renaissance Values.* Students should compare medieval and Renaissance values and explain which ideas appeal to them more. *(Evaluation) Making Judgments*

● RETEACHING. Have students explain the features that distinguish Renaissance art. (*Individualism*—uniqueness; *balance and proportion*—objects in proper sizes; *perspective*—impression of depth and distance.) *(Comprehension) Observing for Detail*

● REINFORCEMENT. Have students write an essay explaining how Renaissance changes in art reflected a new view of the world. (Changes include interest in individual qualities and talents, realism, lifelike images and creativity.) *(Comprehension) Evaluating Information*

Culture The painter Masaccio, whose real name was Tommas Di Giovanni Di Simone Guidi, was so involved in art that he took little care of himself or his appearance. He was nicknamed Masaccio, or "Sloppy Tom."

Raphael recalled the grandeur of the classical age in his painting *The School of Athens*. This fresco shows Plato and Aristotle walking under the central arch. The diagram (inset) shows how Raphael used perspective in his work. Lines within the painting come together at a point in the background, giving the impression of depth and distance.

Three Geniuses of Renaissance Art

While the Renaissance produced many outstanding artists, three of the greatest were Raphael (RAF-ee-ul), Michelangelo (my-kul-AN-juh-loh), and Leonardo da Vinci (duh VIN-chee). All were Italians born in the late 1400's.

Sec. Rev. ques. 4

Raphael. Raphael combined religious art with a Renaissance spirit. He became famous for his madonnas—pictures of Mary, the mother of Jesus. Instead of depicting the angelic, otherworldly Mary shown in medieval paintings, Raphael painted a loving, human woman. Raphael was also a master of design. He used perspective skillfully to create a sense of space and balance in his paintings.

Michelangelo. Most Renaissance artists worked in several areas—painting, sculpture, and architecture. Many were poets or musicians as well. Michelangelo, an immensely skilled painter, poet, and architect, considered himself a sculptor above all. He called sculpture "the first of arts." In this art form, he said, "each act, each limb, each bone is given life and, lo, man's body is raised breathing, alive, in wax or clay or stone."

Michelangelo was a pupil of Donatello, a master who could produce great sculptures from any material. When he was 23, Michel-

334

angelo made the statue called the *Pietà* (pyay-TAH). Carved in marble, it shows Mary holding the body of Jesus after the Crucifixion. This work won the artist instant fame.

In 1508 Pope Julius II, a leading patron of the arts, called for Michelangelo to come to the Vatican, his palace in Rome. He asked Michelangelo to decorate the ceiling of the Sistine Chapel with frescoes—watercolor paintings on fresh plaster. The paintings were to show Biblical events from the Creation to the great flood of Noah's time.

For the next four years Michelangelo worked on the ceiling, stretched out on his back for hours at a time atop a high platform. The sun's heat beat down on him through the roof of the chapel, and paint dripped into his eyes. When darkness came, he worked by candlelight. "I have been here a thousand years," Michelangelo wrote to his father. "I am more exhausted than man ever was." Despite his agony, Michelangelo created a masterpiece. The Sistine Chapel paintings made his reputation as Rome's greatest artist.

Sec. Rev. ques. 4, cont.

Leonardo da Vinci. Less famous in his time than Michelangelo, Leonardo da Vinci is now regarded as a genius. Leonardo, who lived from 1452 to 1519, had great curiosity and energy. Only a few of his paintings remain, but they include such famous works as *The Last Supper* and the *Mona Lisa.*

The proof of Leonardo's brilliance is found in the many notebooks he left. To learn more about the human body, he dissected corpses and made careful drawings of the structure of muscles and bones. Leonardo examined natural objects—a bird's wing, the vein of a leaf, the leg of a horse—with close attention to detail. He tried to find general rules that would apply to the information he gained from his observations. This approach to the study of nature reflected views that eventually became important in the shaping of modern scientific research.

Leonardo was also an engineer, scientist, and inventor who was far ahead of his time. His notebooks recorded designs for inventions such as flying machines, submarines, parachutes, and machine guns.

● See below.

The *Mona Lisa* (above) by Leonardo da Vinci is probably the world's most famous portrait. It is usually remembered for the woman's mysterious smile. Michelangelo's *Pietà* (below) established his reputation as an artist. It adorns St. Peter's Church in Rome, whose dome the multi-talented artist also designed.

335

Technology Leonardo da Vinci designed the bicycle but it remained unknown to the world until "reinvented" three centuries later.

Background In one collection of his works, Leonardo signed his name "Leonardo da Vinci, disciple of experiment."

● **ENRICHMENT.** Have students research and write a report on the background and achievements of one Italian Renaissance artist. *(Application) Locating Information*

Flemish painter Pieter Breughel's winter scene, *Hunters in the Snow*, is one of the world's great landscape paintings.

Artists of the Northern Renaissance

▲ Note strategies for third objective on this page.

Sec. Rev. ques. 5

Painters from northern Europe did not all share the Italians' interest in classical themes and styles. The northern painters emphasized precise, realistic detail and the use of light and shadow. Many used religious themes and symbols. Others showed life in the towns and countryside. The center of the northern Re-

naissance in art was the Netherlands, especially the region of Flanders. It was a Flemish artist, van Eyck (page 333), who was the first master of oil painting.

Brueghel and Rembrandt. Another great painter of realistic scenes was Pieter Brueghel (BROY-gul) the Elder (1525–1569). Using a wealth of detail and often sly humor, he created large, dramatic paintings of farm workers and crowds of townspeople at work and play. Dutch art reached its height in the 1600's with the works of Rembrandt. His paintings are especially remarkable for their use of light and shadow.

Dürer and Holbein. The leading German artist of the Renaissance was Albrecht Dürer (DOO-rur), who was equally skilled in creating paintings, woodcuts, and engravings. Dürer was the court painter to the Holy Roman Emperors from 1512 to 1528.

Another German painter, Hans Holbein (HOHL-byn) the Younger (1497–1543), was the most famous portrait painter of his time. Holbein created portraits that vividly show his subjects' personalities as well as the details of their clothing and the objects around them. Two of Holbein's most famous portraits are of his friends Erasmus and Sir Thomas More. To escape the religious wars in Europe, Holbein moved to England, where he became court painter to King Henry VIII in 1536. See Sec. 2 *Closing the Lesson*, p. T325B.

▲ See below.

Rembrandt's portraits express the inner life and individuality of their subjects. He painted this portrait of himself when he was 23.

336

▲ **RETEACHING.** Have students review "Artists of the Northern Renaissance" and make a chart describing the differences between painters of Northern Europe and Italian artists. (Northern painters: did not all share Italians' interest in classical themes and styles; emphasized precise, realistic detail and light and shadow; used religious themes and symbols.) *(Comprehension) Translating Information Into Another Form*

▲ **REINFORCEMENT.** Have students identify the artists of the Northern Renaissance and their achievements. (Students should mention van Eyck, Brueghel the Elder, Rembrandt, Dürer, Holbein the Younger.) *(Comprehension) Observing for Detail*

▲ **ENRICHMENT.** Have students write a dialogue concerning art and ideals that might have occurred between an Italian Renaissance artist and a northern Renaissance artist. *(Application) Understanding Point of View*

1. **Define or identify:** perspective, Vatican, fresco. (pp. 333, 335)
2. How did Cervantes, Rabelais, and Shakespeare each express the Renaissance spirit? (pp. 332–333)
3. What were the distinctive features of Renaissance art? (p. 333)
4. Why is Raphael famous? Michelangelo? Leonardo da Vinci? (pp. 334–335)
5. What techniques and subjects did northern Renaissance painters emphasize? Where was the center of northern Renaissance art? (p. 336)
6. **Critical thinking:** How does the painting on page 334 reflect the spirit of the Renaissance? (See answer below.)

3 The Reformation

Objectives

Focus Questions

★ ■ Why did some Christians break away from the Catholic Church? *(pages 337–341)*

● ■ What effects did the Reformation have? *(pages 341–342)*

Terms to Know

Protestant	Calvinism
Reformation	predestination
indulgence	Act of Supremacy
Peace of Augsburg	Counter-Reformation

★ Note strategies for first objective on this page and p. 341.

The Renaissance brought to Europe a way of thinking quite different from that of the Middle Ages. Another kind of change from medieval times came as religious thinkers challenged the authority of the Church. Known as **Protestants** for their protests, these thinkers began the **Reformation**—a movement to reform the Church.

The Need for Church Reform

As you read in Chapter 13, in the fourteenth and fifteenth centuries John Wycliffe and John Huss criticized Church practices. Their views grew out of the belief that the Church had grown worldly and corrupt.

By the sixteenth century such discontent had spread, particularly in Germany. Many Germans resented Italian control of the most important offices in the Church. People also disliked the heavy taxes the Church demanded. Such Christians felt that the Church had strayed from its mission. They wanted to return to the days when clergy were poor but deeply religious and when the Church showed more interest in preparing souls for heaven than in adding to its land and riches.

One notable example of Church corruption was the sale of **indulgences**—Church pardons. The Church taught that most sins would be forgiven if a person took certain prescribed steps. A sinner had to confess to a priest, ask forgiveness, and show regret through good works such as fasting or praying. An indulgence took the place of part or all of the good works.

337

Indulgences had at first been given in exchange for special service to the Church, such as going on a crusade. By the 1300's, these pardons could be obtained in return for a money contribution to the Church. Some clergy, who received a cut of the profits from each sale, used indulgences as a way of raising funds for the Church. A few even allowed people to believe that an indulgence guaranteed their entry into heaven.

The Birth of Protestantism

Luther's faith. The man who became the leader of the protest against the Church was a German monk, Martin Luther (1483–1546). Luther taught Biblical studies at the University of Wittenberg. Though he led a strict and pious life, he was troubled by a feeling of sin and feared that he would never enter heaven. After an intense emotional struggle, Luther came to believe that men and women could be saved only by the grace of God. He believed that, while a true Christian would perform good works, these did not bring salvation. Rather, thought Luther, salvation came through faith in God.

Luther's challenge to the Church. Luther's beliefs brought him into open conflict with the Church. On October 31, 1517, Luther nailed a list of 95 theses (arguments) to a church door in Wittenberg. In this document he attacked the sale of indulgences and invited a debate.

Sec. Rev. ques. 2

Although Church officials opposed Luther, many people agreed with his ideas. He soon began to question other Church teachings. Like earlier reformers, Luther said that the Bible provided all the guidance a person needed to live a Christian life. Luther believed that people should read the Bible to find the path to faith. He did not think they had to rely on the interpretations given by the Pope or the clergy. He urged changes in church services and said that members of the clergy should be allowed to marry.

Excommunication. Luther's writing and speeches won him more followers. The **338** Pope ordered Luther to give up his beliefs,

Martin Luther's deeply felt beliefs caused him to lead a revolt against the Church.

but Luther burned the papal order before a crowd of cheering students, professors, and townspeople. Early in 1521 the Pope excommunicated him.

In May 1521, Charles V, the Holy Roman Emperor, called Luther to appear before the imperial assembly, which met in the city of Worms. Luther refused to change his views and go against his conscience, reportedly saying, "Here I stand. I cannot do otherwise." Declared an outlaw by the emperor, Luther fled to the castle of Frederick of Saxony, a German prince. While Luther was in hiding, he translated the New Testament into German, making it possible for more people to read the Bible.

The Spread of Protestantism

Neither Church officials nor the Holy Roman Emperor could keep the reform movement from spreading. People became Lutherans (followers of Luther) for religious and political reasons. Some converts were attracted to Luther's teachings, especially his belief that

Check for Understanding. Ask: In what ways did some clergy abuse the use of Church indulgences? (Indulgences were sold for money or given in exchange for special services. Some clergy let people think that indulgences guaranteed entrance to heaven.)

Religion Luther wrote his 95 theses as the basis for a discussion on indulgences at the University of Wittenberg.

Check for Understanding. Ask: How did Luther's beliefs conflict with the Church's teaching on indulgences? (Luther believed that faith alone could save people and he attacked the sale of indulgences.)

Social History The peasants who rebelled in 1524–1525 also wanted to abolish serfdom and feudal services.

Religion Calvin fled France and moved to Geneva when it appeared that he might be imprisoned for his beliefs.

Sec. Rev. ques. 2, cont.

people should read the Bible for themselves. Others supported Luther because of his attacks on the Church. A number of German princes backed Luther in hopes of gaining property owned by the Church or as a way of showing their independence from the Holy Roman Emperor.

Many peasants, meanwhile, wanted not only reform of the clergy but also lower taxes. In 1524 and 1525, peasants rebelled against the German princes. They expected Luther's encouragement, but he opposed political revolution and instead urged them to stop fighting. When they did not, he called on the nobility to crush the revolt.

Though many peasants felt betrayed by Luther and turned back to Catholicism, some German princes became strong Lutherans. In 1530 the Lutheran princes signed the Augsburg Confession, a written statement of their beliefs. This act of open rebellion against the Church and the Holy Roman Emperor led to a series of wars. Emperor Charles V could not put down the rebellion because he was busy defending Austria and Hungary from an invasion by the Ottoman Turks (page 278). Charles was also opposed by France, which sided with the Protestant princes in order to limit the emperor's power.

Finally, Charles's brother, Ferdinand of Austria, reached a compromise with the princes. In 1555 a treaty called the **Peace of Augsburg** ended the religious wars in Germany. The treaty allowed the German princes to decide which religion would be followed in their lands. Most of the southern German rulers remained Catholic; most of those in the north chose to become Lutheran (map, page 340).

The Reformation quickly spread to other lands where opposition to the Church had been mounting for years. New forms of Protestantism also emerged in Europe.

Calvinism

The Swiss city of Geneva was an important center for Protestant thinking. In 1536 a French religious scholar, John Calvin, joined the reformers in Geneva and developed the form of Protestant belief called **Calvinism**.

Calvin's teachings. Calvin, like Luther, regarded the Bible as the supreme authority in matters of faith. He also attacked abuses by the clergy and believed in salvation through faith alone. Calvin's main idea was **predestination**—the belief that certain people were chosen by God (predestined) for salvation. According to Calvin, those who had not been chosen could never enter heaven, no matter how virtuous they were. Calvinists believed there was no way of telling who had been chosen for salvation. They thought, though, that hard work and devotion might be signs of God's grace.

Calvinism in practice. Calvin and his followers tried to make Geneva a holy city. The government they created supervised people's lives to make sure they lived strictly and solemnly. Laws punished those who gambled, danced, made noise during church services, drank at certain hours, sang "outrageous songs," or did not know their prayers. Those who challenged Calvinist teachings faced persecution or exile from Geneva.

Sec. Rev. ques. 3

Calvinist teachings were carried to other countries by dedicated missionaries. Although the French monarchs remained Catholic, Calvinism appealed to many French people, some of whom were already Protestants. The French Calvinists became known as Huguenots (HYOO-guh-nahts).

A Scottish Protestant, John Knox, carried Calvinist ideas to Scotland in the 1550's. His missionary work laid the foundations for the Presbyterian Church. Calvinism also influenced "reformed" churches in other parts of Europe, including Holland and Hungary.

English Protestantism

Some of the earliest demands for Church reform had been made in England (page 265). The Reformation in England, however, became closely connected with a struggle for political power.

Sec. Rev. ques. 4

Henry VIII. In 1527 the Tudor king Henry VIII, who ruled England from 1509 to

Religion The Peace of Augsburg is viewed by many as the end of the Reformation in Germany.
Check for Understanding. Ask students to identify the following: **indulgences** (Church pardons); **95 theses** (Luther's arguments against Church practices); **Peace of Augsburg** (German treaty that ended the religious wars and allowed the princes to decide what religion would be followed in their lands); **predestination** (belief that certain people are chosen by God for salvation).

Check for Understanding. Ask: How did Calvin's belief in predestination support Luther's belief in faith and grace as the source of salvation? (Both agreed that it was God alone who could grant salvation, and that human actions could not affect salvation.)

Map Skill Practice

See p. T325C for answers to *Map Skill Practice.*

Christian Europe About 1600

1. What was the religion of most countries in Europe in 1600?
2. Which parts of Europe were mainly Lutheran?
3. How does the map show the location of "minority" religions?
4. **Interpreting information.** Compare this map with the map on page 212. What developments account for the changes you see?

1547, wanted to divorce his wife, the Spanish princess Catherine of Aragon. Henry feared that their only surviving child, Mary, would not be accepted as heir to the English throne. Moreover, Henry wanted to marry Anne Boleyn (BUL-in), a lady at his court.

Because the Church prohibited divorce, Henry asked the Pope to annul (cancel) his marriage. When the Pope refused, Henry and his advisers took steps to remove England from the authority of the Pope. Henry named Thomas Cranmer, a churchman who agreed with some Protestant ideas, to be archbishop of Canterbury, the highest church office in England. Cranmer approved the annulment of the marriage with Catherine, and Henry married Anne Boleyn early in 1533.

The Act of Supremacy. The English Parliament next was persuaded to approve a break with the Church in Rome. In 1534 Parliament passed the Act of Supremacy, making the monarch the head of what was now called the Church of England or the Anglican Church. Two years later Henry closed the English monasteries and convents, seizing their rich lands and properties.

Henry VIII himself remained a Catholic. The Reformation in England was carried

340

Check for Understanding. Ask: **What was the result of the Act of Supremacy?** (The English monarch was named head of the Church of England.)

Background Catherine of Aragon was the wife of Henry's brother, who died four months after marrying the Spanish princess.

forward by Cranmer and others. They urged a new English translation of the Bible and began to prepare the Book of Common Prayer—a collection of prayers and services for use in the Church of England.

Henry did insist on using the power given him by the Act of Supremacy. Some English Catholics who supported reform refused to give up their loyalty to the Pope. The most prominent was Sir Thomas More (page 331). Henry had More executed for not accepting the Act of Supremacy.

Henry's successors. Henry VIII married six times, but he had only one son. Edward VI, who was nine years old when Henry died in 1547, had been taught by Protestant tutors, including Cranmer. Protestantism became more established in England during his reign. Edward was in poor health, however. After his death in 1553, the crown went to his half-sister Mary I, the daughter of Catherine of Aragon.

A devout Roman Catholic, Mary ordered the persecution of English Protestants who refused to become Catholics again. Among those burned at the stake during her reign was Thomas Cranmer. Mary's harsh tactics earned her the nickname "Bloody Mary." Her marriage to Philip II, the Catholic king of Spain, also made her unpopular.

When Mary died in 1558, she was succeeded by her half-sister Elizabeth I, the daughter of Anne Boleyn. With a shrewd understanding of the English people, Elizabeth turned England back to Protestantism. In 1571 Parliament gave official approval to the teachings of the Church of England.

Sec. Rev. ques. 4, cont.

★ *See below.*

The Counter-Reformation

EE 4C

● Note strategies for second objective on this page and p. 342.

Alarmed by the spread of Protestantism, the Church began a number of reforms and took other actions to strengthen and spread the Catholic religion. These efforts are called the **Counter-Reformation** or Catholic Reformation.

Sec. Rev. ques. 5

The Council of Trent. In 1545 the Pope called Church leaders to Trent in northern Italy to deal with the problems facing the

Henry VIII broke away from the Pope's authority, and England later became Protestant. This portrait was done by Hans Holbein, Henry's court painter.

Church. The Council of Trent (1545–1563) did not change basic teachings. Catholics were to continue to accept the principles that: (1) only the Church could explain the Bible, (2) both faith and good works were necessary for salvation, and (3) the Pope was the highest and final authority in the Church. Church ritual was to remain an essential part of the Catholic faith, and the clergy were not allowed to marry.

The Council of Trent did, however, recommend important reforms. It banned the sale of indulgences and tightened discipline for the clergy. It insisted that only worthy people should enter the clergy and ordered the establishment of seminaries to train the clergy. It also encouraged reform of monasteries and convents. These actions corrected abuses that had long disturbed many Church members.

Sec. Rev. ques. 5, cont.

Other measures. The Church took additional steps as part of the Counter-Reformation. In Catholic countries the Inquisition (page 245) stepped up its activities,

341

Background Henry VIII's wives were Catherine of Aragon (divorced), Anne Boleyn (executed), Jane Seymour (died), Anne of Cleves (divorced), Catherine Howard (executed), Catherine Parr (survived Henry).

★ ENRICHMENT. Have students organize a panel discussion on *The Relationship Between Religion and Government During the Reformation.* Students should explain how religion and government influenced each other in Europe during the Reformation. *(Synthesis) Synthesizing Information*

● RETEACHING. Have students explain the effects of the Reformation. (Religious unity ended in Europe; the state was strengthened; education spread; the middle class was strengthened.) *(Comprehension) Understanding Cause and Effect*

● REINFORCEMENT. Have students develop a hypothesis about how the Council of Trent might have influenced the Reformation. (Answers will vary. The Council could have stopped further breakup of the Church.) *(Synthesis) Forming a Hypothesis* threatening Protestants with imprisonment or death. The Church also drew up a list of books, called the Index, that Catholics were forbidden to read, own, or sell. In this way the Church hoped to prevent the spread of ideas it regarded as heresy.

New religious orders were set up to serve the Church and spread Catholic teachings. The most important of them was the Society of Jesus, commonly known as the Jesuits (JEZH-oo-its). The society was started by a young Spanish nobleman named Ignatius Loyola and approved by the Pope in 1540.

The Jesuits tried to keep Catholics from leaving the Church, to persuade Protestants to return to the Church, and to win new converts. To achieve these aims, the Jesuits established colleges and seminaries and sent missionaries to many lands. One of the most famous of these missionaries was Francis Xavier, who brought Roman Catholicism to Japan (page 290).

Effects of the Reformation

Sec. Rev. ques. 6
The Reformation had a profound influence on later history. (1) The religious unity that had characterized Western and Central Europe in the Middle Ages vanished as Christians were divided into Catholics and Protestants. Protestants themselves were divided into a number of different groups. These divisions remain in place today, with southern Europe mostly Catholic and northern Europe mostly Protestant.

(2) In both Catholic and Protestant countries, the Reformation strengthened the state at the expense of the churches. Protestant rulers rejected the authority of the Pope, while Catholic rulers allowed the Church fewer privileges and less influence in political matters.

(3) The Reformation and Counter-Reformation both encouraged the spread of education. The Protestants' call for people to read the Bible themselves made literacy more important. As part of the Counter-Reformation, the Jesuits played an important role in education by starting Catholic schools and universities.

(4) The Reformation strengthened the middle class. Protestantism emphasized many of the same virtues—responsibility, hard work, and upright living—that middle-class townspeople were already practicing. In countries where Protestantism became the official religion, the entire population was taught that these qualities pleased God.

See Sec. 3 *Closing the Lesson*, p. T325C.

● See below.

Ⓕ See below.

CAUSE AND EFFECT

CAUSES	KEY DEVELOPMENT	EFFECTS
Discontent over Church policies and practices	The Reformation 1517–1563	End of religious unity in Europe
Luther's challenge to Church authority		Strengthening of state authority over Church authority
Opposition of some German princes to authority of Holy Roman Emperor		Spread of education
Spread of Calvinist ideas		Strengthening of European middle class

342

Religion The Inquisition was a committee of six Church officials with judicial authority over all Catholics and the power to arrest, imprison, and execute people.

Ⓕ **CAUSE AND EFFECT CHART ACTIVITY.** Have students explain what causes of the Reformation reflected the Renaissance. Then have students determine which effects of the Reformation might have had the most impact on European society. *(Comprehension) Evaluating Causes and Effects*

● **ENRICHMENT.** Have students write an essay explaining how the increased power of the state and a strengthened middle class— two effects of the Reformation—remain important factors in political and economic life today. *(Synthesis) Linking Past and Present*

Section Review

Answers to Section Review questions are in brackets on pages indicated.

1. **Define or identify:** Protestant, Reformation, indulgence, Peace of Augsburg, Calvinism, predestination, Act of Supremacy, Counter-Reformation. (pp. 337, 339, 340, 341)
2. What teachings and practices of the Church did Luther challenge? For what different reasons did people support Luther? (pp. 338–339)
3. What part did John Calvin play in the Reformation? (p. 339)
4. How was Protestantism established in England? (pp. 339–341)
5. How did the Roman Catholic Church try to stop the spread of Protestantism? What was the Council of Trent? (pp. 341–342)
6. What were the four main results of the Reformation? (p. 342)
7. **Critical thinking:** How was the Reformation linked to the spirit of the Renaissance? (See answer below.)

7. Answers will vary. Students might point out that the Reformation revived and encouraged intellectual life, thereby advancing the Renaissance spirit.

Chapter 17   Summary and Timeline

1. The 1300's saw the beginning of the Renaissance, a rebirth of interest in ancient Greece and Rome. The Renaissance began in Italy, where wealthy merchants and bankers encouraged the arts and the study of the humanities. Renaissance people placed a high value on varied achievements and individualism. The Renaissance spread from Italy to other parts of Europe in the 1400's and 1500's.

2. The Renaissance marked a period of great creativity in painting, sculpture, and literature. Renaissance literature was characterized by the use of the vernacular and an interest in individuals. New techniques, as well as the genius of men such as Leonardo da Vinci, contributed to the distinctiveness of Renaissance art.

3. Calls for reform in the Church led to major changes in the 1500's. Martin Luther challenged basic Church teachings. Those who protested against Church teachings became known as Protestants; the overall movement for change was called the Reformation. Lutheranism and other forms of Protestantism spread in northern Europe. The Catholic Church launched the Counter-Reformation to strengthen its position. Important results of the Reformation were the end of religious unity in Europe and the strengthening of European states at the expense of Church authority.

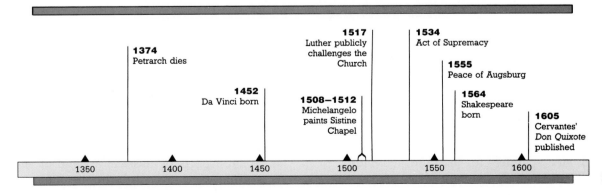

| 1374 Petrarch dies | 1452 Da Vinci born | 1517 Luther publicly challenges the Church | 1508–1512 Michelangelo paints Sistine Chapel | 1534 Act of Supremacy | 1555 Peace of Augsburg | 1564 Shakespeare born | 1605 Cervantes' *Don Quixote* published |

1350   1400   1450   1500   1550   1600

See p. T325C for answers to Chapter Review.

Vocabulary Review

1. Match each of the following terms with its correct definition: *Calvinism, fresco, humanities, indulgence, patron, perspective, predestination, Renaissance, Vatican.*
   a. period of great cultural achievement in Europe from the 1300's to the 1500's
   b. supporter of the arts
   c. subjects concerned with culture
   d. impression of depth and distance on the flat surface of a painting
   e. Church pardon for a sin
   f. idea that certain people were chosen by God for salvation
   g. Pope's residence in Rome
   h. watercolor painting on fresh plaster
   i. strict form of Protestantism
2. Define the terms in the following pairs.
   a. Peace of Augsburg; Act of Supremacy
   b. Reformation; Counter-Reformation

People to Identify

Match each of the following people with the correct description: *Cervantes, Giotto, Isabella d'Este, Machiavelli, Lorenzo de Medici, Michelangelo, Petrarch, Rembrandt.*
1. author of *The Prince,* a handbook on how to succeed in politics
2. greatest Spanish Renaissance writer and author of *Don Quixote*
3. patron of the arts who expanded the university of Florence
4. patron of the arts and diplomat
5. first painter to use the technique of perspective

6. Italian poet who led the early development of Renaissance humanism
7. artist who painted the Sistine Chapel ceiling
8. Dutch artist famous for his use of light and shadow

Places to Know

Match the letters on this map of Europe with the cities of the Renaissance and Reformation listed below. You may want to refer to the map on page 340.

1. Florence   3. Rome   5. Wittenberg
2. Geneva   4. Trent   6. Worms

Recalling the Facts

1. What attitudes about life and the individual did Renaissance thinkers borrow from Greco-Roman culture?
2. In what ways did the invention of the printing press help spread Renaissance ideas?
3. How did Shakespeare reveal Renaissance themes in his works?
4. What aspects of classical art and architecture were revived during the Renais-

344

sance? What aspects of medieval art and architecture were rejected?

5. How did the themes and styles of northern European painters differ from those of Italian artists?

6. Why were people unhappy with the Church in the sixteenth century?

7. What Church teachings and practices did Martin Luther oppose? For what reasons did people support him?

8. What were John Calvin's religious beliefs?

9. What part did Henry VIII, Mary I, and Elizabeth I each play in England's break with the Catholic Church and the establishment of the Church of England?

10. What steps did Roman Catholic officials take to strengthen the Catholic Church and spread Catholicism?

11. How did the Reformation affect religious unity in Europe? The influence of the Church in political affairs? The spread of education? The middle class?

Critical Thinking Skills

1. **Gathering information.** Research and prepare a report about one of the following topics: the method of printing developed by Gutenberg; the inventions of Leonardo da Vinci; the history of Saint Peter's Church in Rome. *(App.)*

✔ 2. **Exploring world literature.** Read an act or a scene from one of Shakespeare's plays. Explain how it reflects the humanist ideals of the Renaissance. *(Anal.)*

✔ 3. **Inferring.** Do you think Henry VIII was following Machiavelli's principles when he broke with the Roman Catholic Church? Explain your answer. *(Syn.)*

✔ 4. **Drawing conclusions.** The humanists of the Renaissance believed that a talent for public speaking, an elegant writing style, and polished manners were valuable for political leaders. Are these skills still considered assets for a politician? Explain your answer. What additional skills or qualities do politicians today need? *(Syn.)*

Thinking About Geography

Translating information from one medium to another. Using the map on page 340, make a chart of religious groups in Europe about 1600. Use these headings: *Nation/Territory, Principal Religion, Minority Religions.* *(Comp.)*

Enrichment: Primary Sources

Baldassare Castiglione (kahs-teel-YOH-nay) was a Renaissance writer and diplomat. In the adapted passage below from *The Book of the Courtier* (1528), Castiglione describes some of the qualities a person needed in order to be successful in court life.

66 Besides his noble birth I would have the courtier endowed by nature not only with talent and beauty of person and feature, but with a certain grace and air that shall make him at first sight pleasing and agreeable to all.

Above all things he must avoid showiness and that shameless self-praise by which men excite hatred and disgust in all who hear them.

It is fitting also to know how to swim, to leap, to run, and to throw stones, for besides the use that may be made of this in war, a man often can win a good name with such skills.

I would have him accomplished in letters, at least in those studies that are called the humanities. 99

1. What words show that Castiglione thought good looks were important?

2. What two qualities did Castiglione advise the courtier to avoid? Why?

3. **Critical thinking:** Compare and contrast the Renaissance ideal of the courtier with the Athenian ideal of the well-rounded citizen (Chapter 4). *(Syn.)*

European Exploration and Colonization　1450–1763
(pp. 346–365)

Chapter Preview

Section 1 of this chapter examines the factors that led to the Age of Exploration. Students will learn about Spanish and Portuguese discoveries and conquests of the fifteenth and sixteenth centuries. In Section 2 the effects of colonial rule on native populations are described. Dutch, English, and French voyages of exploration are also outlined, and the early colonial settlements founded by these nations are discussed in Section 3.

Bibliography

See the *Teacher's Management and Planning Guide* for additional listings. Starred titles are for both students and teachers.

Boorstin, Daniel J. *The Discoverers*. Random. A far-reaching investigation of people's changing views of the world.

Cipolla, Carlo M. *Guns, Sails, and Empires*. Sunflower University Press. The technology and material culture that provided the basis for conquest.

*Morison, Samuel E. *Christopher Columbus, Mariner*. New American Library. A shorter biography by the author of the classic 2-volume life of Columbus.

Parry, J. H. *The Age of Reconnaissance: Discovery, Exploration, and Settlement, 1450–1650*. New American Library. Outstanding survey.

Section Lesson Plans

SECTION 1　　(pp. 347–354)
Voyages of Exploration

Objectives

After completing this section, students will be able to:
1. Name the factors that led European nations to sponsor voyages of exploration.
2. Explain how the Portuguese gained control of trade between Europe and India.
3. List the achievements of Spanish explorers.

Introducing the Lesson

Remind students that in the 1480's, territories and waters far from Europe were as mysterious to Europeans as many of the universe's planets are for us today. During the Renaissance, however, many factors encouraged monarchs and explorers to travel to unfamiliar lands.

Then ask: (a) *What skills might a ship's crew have needed for a successful voyage from Portugal or Spain to Asia?* (Map-reading, astronomy, navigation, carpentry, cooking, caring for the sick and injured.)

(b) *What might have motivated explorers to cross the seas to search for unknown lands?* (Answers will vary. People might have sought new products to sell; some people may have wanted adventure, while others might simply have desired employment.)

(c) *Under what circumstances would you undertake a dangerous journey to an unknown place?* (Answers will vary.)

Developing the Lesson:
Identifying Cause and Effect

Have students make a chart explaining how the following might have affected fifteenth-century European exploration:

(a) *Muslim control of land and sea trade routes from Asia to Europe.* (Europeans desired a water route that would allow them to trade directly with Asia.)

(b) *Italian control of the sale of Asian goods in Europe.* (Other European countries desired some of the profit controlled by the Italians.)

(c) The anti-Muslim spirit that had persisted since the Crusades. (Some Europeans considered it their Christian duty to capture or convert Muslim areas.)

(d) Renaissance values. (Appreciation for individual achievement and adventure, pursuit of glory and fame, and the desire for wealth led to exploration.)

(e) Improved technology. (Long-distance exploration was possible because of improved sailing ships and advances in navigation technology.) *(Comprehension)*

Developing the Lesson: Translating Information into Another Form

Have students draw cartograms showing the power of the Italian city-states and Portugal, Spain, England, France, and the Netherlands before and after the Age of Exploration. The size of each region should be proportionate to the wealth and power it gained or lost as a result of the Age of Exploration. (For instance, the Italian city-states would be large on the "before" map but small on the "after" map. The opposite would be true of Portugal.) *(Comprehension)*

Closing the Lesson: Organizing Ideas in Written Form

Have each student write an essay on the voyage of discovery he or she believes was the most significant. Students should support their views with details drawn from the text. Have students read their essays in class. *(Synthesis)*

See *Section Review* questions, p. 254.

SECTION 2   (pp. 354–357)
Spanish and Portuguese Colonization

Objectives

After completing this section, students will be able to:
1. Describe how Spain defeated the Aztec and Inca empires.
2. Explain how Spain and Portugal set up colonies in the Americas.

Introducing the Lesson

Remind students that European explorers found lands that were new only to the Europeans. It is estimated that when the Spanish arrived, over 25 million people lived in the Western Hemisphere, with most of them in what is now Mexico.

Then ask: *(a) What might explain the ability of a small group of explorers to conquer thousands of Indians?* (Answers will vary, but should include technological advantages.)

(b) Why might the explorers have decided to conquer the Indians, rather than to rely on negotiation to get what they wanted? (Answers will vary. The Spanish may have decided that it was pointless to compromise and that they had a better chance of getting wealth and power by using force.)

Developing the Lesson: Translating Information into Another Form

Have students organize the information in their text about Portuguese and Spanish colonization of the Americas into a table. Table columns should include the following labels: *Location of Colonies, Settlers, Motivations of Settlers, Effects of Colonization.* *(Comprehension)*

Developing the Lesson: Comparing Effects

Have students compare the effects of Spanish rule on the Spanish colonists and on the Indians. Students should answer the following questions: *(a) Which group prospered under colonial rule? (b) Which group suffered the greatest hardships? (c) How were the experiences of the two groups similar? (Comprehension)*

Closing the Lesson: Analyzing Information

Have students analyze the economic, social, religious, and political effects of Spanish and Portuguese rule on the Americas. Reports should include specific examples of changes that occurred in American ways of living as a result of European influence. *(Analysis)*

See *Section Review* questions, p. 357.

T345C

SECTION 3 (pp. 358–363)
Dutch, English, and French Colonies

Objectives

After completing this section, students will be able to:
1. Describe how the Netherlands and England took part in exploration and trade.
2. Explain the roles England and France played in the colonization of North America.

Introducing the Lesson

Remind students that the Dutch, the French, and the English traveled to the Americas for most of the same reasons that the Spanish and the Portuguese did: to find new trade routes and new sources of profit. Many also hoped for greater opportunity for religious and political freedoms.

Then ask: *(a) For what reasons might modern explorers travel to unknown places?* (Answers will vary. Some might seek knowledge, others may be attracted by adventure or the hope of profit.)

(b) What would motivate you to leave the people and environment you know and travel to an unknown place? (Answers will vary.)

Developing the Lesson:
Connecting History and Geography

Have students make a map showing the areas of the world that eventually became part of the Dutch trading empire. Students might use different colors to distinguish between the regions controlled by the Dutch East India Company and the Dutch West India Company. (The Dutch East India Company gained control of most of Asia. The Dutch West India Company controlled the slave trade in the Atlantic and the Caribbean.) *(Comprehension)*

Developing the Lesson:
Observing for Detail

Ask: *(a) What economic advantages did many English colonists find in America?* (Many had the chance to own farms for the first time; they could earn an independent living more easily than in Europe; even colonists without much money could afford land in America.)

(b) What political advantages did American settlement offer the English? (As landowners, many English would acquire the right to vote for the first time. In Europe, where a small group of nobles owned the land, political participation was limited. Colonists could elect local representatives to legislatures that made laws. Colonists also were protected by traditional English liberties.) *(Comprehension)*

Closing the Lesson:
Analyzing Cause and Effect

Have students write an essay analyzing the causes and effects of Dutch, French, and English exploration and settlement during the Age of Exploration. Essays should include a summary of what motivated the countries to explore new territories, and then explain why some attempts at settlement were more successful than others. (The Dutch were primarily interested in economic gain, while the English and French explored and settled for a variety of economic, political, and religious reasons.) *(Synthesis)*

See *Section Review* questions, p. 363.

Chapter 18 Review Answers
(pp. 364–365)

Vocabulary Review

1. privateers; bullion 2. conquistadors 3. *encomiendas;* peons 4. legislatures 5. monopoly 6. Puritans

People to Identify

1. Queen Isabella; Columbus 2. Dias 3. Cartier 4. Montezuma; Cortés 5. Ponce de León 6. Champlain

Places to Know

1. G 2. I 3. F 4. C 5. B 6. A 7. H 8. D 9. E

Recalling the Facts

1. The desire for wealth and power, the desire to spread Christianity, the Renaissance spirit of curiosity and adventure, and technological advances that made long voyages possible.

2. European nations hoped that finding an all-water route would allow them to trade directly with Asia without reliance on the Muslims and Italians.

3. The fortified trading post and the plantation. After Vasco da Gama sailed to India in 1497, the Portuguese found Indian merchants and rulers who were either eager to trade or who responded to threats of force.

4. He brought new lands to Europeans' attention and he established the first European colony in the Americas.

5. It moved the Line of Demarcation farther west, allowing Portugal to claim Brazil and giving the rest of the Americas to Spain.

6. That the Pacific Ocean separated Asia from the Americas and was much larger than suspected, that all the oceans are connected, and that the ocean winds follow a consistent pattern.

7. Montezuma believed that the Europeans might be gods or messengers from the god Quetzalcóatl, Malinche acted as an interpreter and informer to help Cortés make allies and keep track of spies, and disease weakened the Aztecs. Pizarro took advantage of Atahualpa's friendliness, and the Spanish were far better equipped for war than the Incas.

8. They divided their lands into provinces and the king appointed a viceroy to carry out his policies in each province. The colonies existed for the economic benefit of Spain; they provided Spain with gold, silver, raw materials, and a market for finished goods.

9. Spanish missionaries worked to protect Indians from exploitation, convert them to Christianity, and set up schools to teach them new skills. Portuguese missionaries were the first to explore and settle the interior of Brazil, where they started schools and churches for the Indians.

10. The Northwest Passage, a sea route through North America to Asia.

11. Some came to escape religious persecution; others came seeking economic opportunity.

12. With the Treaty of Paris, France lost nearly all of its North American colonies to Britain and Spain.

Critical Thinking Skills

1–3. Answers will vary.

Thinking About Geography

Hispaniola was originally named *La Isla Espanola,* meaning "the Spanish Island," by Columbus because it reminded him of Spain. Jamaica was named *Xaymaca,* meaning "land of springs," by the Arawaks who lived there because the island was full of springs and waterfalls. Jamestown was named for King James I of England. The Mississippi River gets its name from an Indian word meaning "big river." Panama was named from an Indian word meaning "fishermen" or "plenty of fish" because it was an Indian fishing village when the Spaniards found it. Puerto Rico, claimed by Columbus for Spain in 1493, means "rich port" in Spanish. The Saint Lawrence River was so named because Cartier arrived there on the saint's feast day, August 10, 1535. Tierra del Fuego, Spanish for "land of fire," was so named by Magellan because when he sailed by it, he saw many fires on its shore.

Enrichment: Primary Sources

1. He said he was the voice of Christ.
2. He said they were in mortal sin.
3. He was harsh, trying to frighten his listeners.

European Exploration and Colonization 1450–1763

See chapter timeline, p. 363.

Before You Read This Chapter

American astronauts were the first human beings to set foot on the moon. Americans take great pride in that achievement, but people have also raised serious questions about space exploration. What are our goals? Scientific knowledge? Future profits? National prestige? Is exploration worth the expense? The risk to human life? As you read, think how these questions might have applied to exploration in the 1400's and 1500's. Do you think people of that time could have chosen *not* to explore?

The Geographic Setting

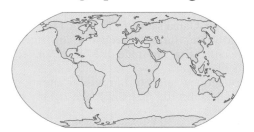

The Chapter Outline

1. Voyages of Exploration
2. Spanish and Portuguese Colonization
3. Dutch, English, and French Colonies

A map of the world from the 1540's reveals how little accurate information explorers possessed about the lands beyond Europe. With the aid of the magnetic compass (inset), they undertook long and dangerous sea voyages in search of wealth and knowledge.

1 Voyages of Exploration

Objectives

Focus Questions

★ ■ What factors led European nations to sponsor voyages of exploration? *(pages 347–348)*

● ■ How did the Portuguese gain control of trade between Europe and India? *(pages 348–349)*

▲ ■ What did Spanish explorers achieve? *(pages 349–354)*

Terms to Know

Age of Exploration   Line of Demarcation
monopoly   circumnavigate
bullion

★ Note strategies for first objective on this page and p. 348.

In the fifteenth and sixteenth centuries, the many changes that had been taking place in Western Europe all came together to bring about an era of worldwide exploration. This period, which began about 1450 and lasted into the 1700's, has since that time been called the Age of Exploration. Several factors help explain why Europeans eagerly set off for distant lands.

Motives Behind Exploration

Sec. Rev. ques. 2

1. The desire for wealth and power. A longing for riches was the first motive that pushed Europeans to make long voyages of exploration. Rulers in many countries saw that trade with Asia could make both them and their countries rich and powerful. Merchants, too, dreamed of the money to be earned by selling Eastern goods to Europeans. Such luxuries as spices, sugar, and silk, rarely seen in Europe before the Crusades, were now much in demand.

For centuries Muslim traders had controlled the rich land and sea trade routes to Asia (page 201). The Muslims sold Asian goods to merchants in the Italian city-states, who then sold them throughout Europe. This system benefited only Muslim traders and Italian merchants. Other Europeans—especially the Portuguese—hoped to find a water route to the East that would allow them to trade directly with Asia.

2. Religious aims. The desire to spread Christianity was another reason for the European voyages to distant parts of the world. Fear and hatred of Muslims continued long after the Crusades had ended. The Spanish and Portuguese in particular felt they had a God-given duty to drive the Muslims out of other lands, just as they had done in the Reconquest of Spain (page 246). They hoped to take Africa from the Muslims and to convert the peoples of Asia.

3. The Renaissance spirit. The restless, individualistic spirit of the Renaissance also helped launch the Age of Exploration. Sea captains who ventured into uncharted oceans, explorers who penetrated unknown lands, soldiers who conquered vast overseas territories—all were driven by curiosity, the desire for adventure, and the hope of fame. Many of them had read exciting accounts of the trips of other adventurers, such as Marco Polo (page 284).

4. Improvements in technology. The motives for the Age of Exploration are often summed up as a search for "glory, God, and gold." The long sea journeys, however, could not have taken place without technological progress. Europeans built sturdy sailing ships that could be handled by smaller crews and make longer voyages than ships propelled by rowers. More accurate maps allowed sea captains to venture far from the sight of land. Ships also began to carry new kinds of **347**

★ RETEACHING. Have students review "Motives Behind Exploration" (above) and take notes on the factors that contributed to the Age of Exploration. (Desire for wealth and power; religious aims; Renaissance spirit; improvements in technology.) *(Comprehension)* **Observing for Detail**

Check for Understanding. Ask: How did European merchants hope to profit from exploration? (Merchants hoped to find a water route to the East that would allow them to trade directly with Asia.)

★ REINFORCEMENT. Have students analyze the phrase "glory, God, and gold" as it relates to European exploration. (Many explorers sought the glory of discovery, were sponsored by monarchs who wanted to spread Christianity, or wanted to profit from trade.) *(Analysis)* **Analyzing Information**

Check for Understanding. Ask: What factors led to the Age of Exploration? (Desire for wealth and power, religious aims, Renaissance spirit, improved technology.)

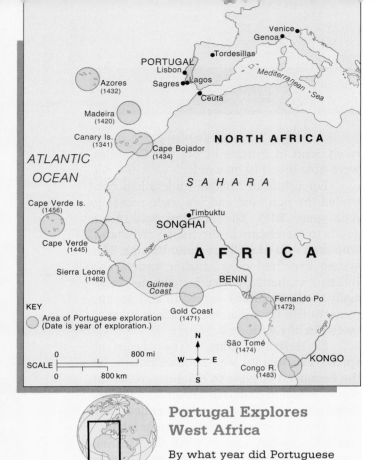

Technology Of Arabic origin, the astrolabe was the earliest instrument for navigation by the stars.

Portugal Explores West Africa

By what year did Portuguese explorers reach the Gold Coast?

Map Answer: 1471.

weaponry—cannons and guns—to protect themselves at sea.

Navigational instruments also were improving. Sea captains used a device called an astrolabe to find their latitude by observing the positions of the sun, moon, and stars. The mariner's compass, a Chinese invention brought to Europe by the Arabs, was made more accurate.

★ See below.

Portuguese Exploration

● Note strategies for second objective on this page and p. 349.

Prince Henry the Navigator. The first European nation to sponsor voyages of exploration was the small seafaring country of Portugal. Spurred by both economic and religious motives, Portugal's Prince Henry (1394–1460) sent ships to explore the West African coast and look for a sea route to the East. His interest in ships and sailing helped Portugal move ahead of wealthier European states in the search for a sea route to India.

Prince Henry spent his own fortune to build a naval station at Sagres (SAH-graysh) on the southwestern tip of Portugal. To Sagres came geographers, mathematicians, astronomers, and experienced sailors. From these experts Prince Henry collected information about the stars, tides, winds, and currents. His mapmakers used the information to draw maps of the African coast. With these maps, which were kept secret by the Portuguese, sea captains could sail with confidence into unfamiliar waters. Although Henry himself made no voyages, his success in advancing knowledge of the sea caused English writers to call him "Prince Henry the Navigator."

Trading posts and plantations. The Portuguese established two profitable institutions in West Africa—the fortified trading post and the plantation. These became the economic base for Portugal's overseas empire. Both were later introduced in Asia, the Americas, and other parts of Africa.

Trading posts, guarded by armed soldiers, were built where rivers emptied into the sea. The posts provided a central point where traders could store goods to sell or barter for African slaves, ivory, gold, and other products. The soldiers and their weapons were also used to force local rulers to give the Portuguese a **monopoly** on trade. A monopoly is complete control over a good or service.

The Portuguese also set up plantations in fertile areas of West Africa. These large farms were run by the Portuguese but worked by Africans, who produced crops for export. The success of Portuguese sugar plantations in West Africa made this type of agriculture common in colonial settlements throughout the world. Plantation agriculture was an important factor in the expansion of the slave trade (pages 306–307).

A route around Africa. Though Portugal grew rich from its dealings with African kingdoms, the Portuguese rulers still dreamed of finding a water route to India. Sailors explored the coast of West Africa for nearly 70 years, venturing farther and farther south. Then in 1488 a South Atlantic gale blew the ships of Bartholomeu Dias (DEE-ahs)

348

---

around the southern tip of the African continent. Days later, the exhausted crew sighted land again, but the sun was rising on their right rather than on their left, and they realized they were now sailing north along the east coast of Africa. Dias called the tip of the continent "Cape of Storms." The Portuguese king, however, was so excited at the news Dias later brought back that he gave the area the name it still holds today—the Cape of Good Hope.

The journey to India. Dias's discovery of a sea route into the Indian Ocean encouraged further Portuguese exploration. In 1497 the king of Portugal sent a navigator named Vasco da Gama on a diplomatic mission to India. Da Gama's fleet of four ships was armed with cannons and loaded with goods to trade.

Sec. Rev. ques. 3

Da Gama rounded the Cape of Good Hope and sailed up the coast of East Africa. Soon he saw the minarets and white plaster houses of the rich Muslim city of Mozambique (moh-zam-BEEK). An Arab pilot guided da Gama's fleet across the Indian Ocean to Calicut, on the west coast of India. Da Gama landed there, saying, "We come in search of Christians and spices."

Control of the spice trade. Da Gama's voyage placed Portugal in a position to dominate trade with India. The Portuguese in India acquired a fortune in spices and dyes to take back to Europe. Some Indian merchants and rulers welcomed the new opportunity for trade. In other cases, the Portuguese resorted to threats, using the ship's cannons to make Indian rulers grant trading rights.

● See below.

Goods that were shipped from Calicut to Europe by sea cost the Portuguese only a fifth of what they cost when brought over land and water by the Arabs and Venetians. Prices for Asian goods were now within the reach of many more Europeans. Trade in both Asian and European cities increased greatly. Europe, however, produced few goods that wealthy Asians wanted to buy. To pay for the expensive Asian goods, Europeans had to use **bullion** (BUL-yun)—bars of gold and silver.

Columbus's Voyages for Spain

▲ Note strategies for third objective on this page and p. 350.

Columbus's plan. The Portuguese ships all followed an eastward route to Asia. In 1484 an Italian navigator, Christopher Columbus, went to King John II of Portugal with a daring new idea. Columbus proposed to find a *westward* route to Asia. Not realizing the true size of the earth, he thought that his voyage would take about two months and cover about 2,500 miles. The Portuguese naval advisers were skeptical of his figures, for they had correctly calculated the westward distance to Asia as about 10,000 miles. No ship, they claimed, could carry the amount of food and water the crew would need for such a long journey. King John, therefore, rejected Columbus's idea.

Sec. Rev. ques. 4

Columbus then took his proposal to the rulers of Spain, King Ferdinand and Queen Isabella. They, too, had doubts about Columbus's plan at first. After several years, however, Isabella agreed to sponsor Columbus's voyage. She provided him with the money to outfit three ships—the *Niña*, the *Pinta*, and the *Santa María*.

Although Columbus always believed he had reached Asia, his voyages actually led the way to European colonization of the Americas.

349

(F) FEATURE ACTIVITY. Have students write an essay explaining why sailors might make a long voyage despite the problems they would have to face. (Application) Understanding Point of View

(F) See above.

Daily Life

Food at Sea

On Vasco da Gama's first voyage to India, more than half his sailors died of scurvy. Scurvy is a disease caused by poor diet, especially the lack of vitamin C. The greatest danger sailors faced on a long sea voyage was not raging storms or enemy cannons but hunger, thirst, and sickness.

Before the 1450's, European sea captains stayed close to shore. They dropped anchor every few days to take on fresh food and water. Once they began to make longer voyages, however, they had to carry supplies to last several months. Most fresh foods spoiled too quickly to be practical.

The main foods in a sailor's diet were salt beef and salt pork. To cut the constant taste of salt, sailors ate hardtack, a kind of biscuit made of flour and water and baked hard as rock. For variety, the ship's cook might also fix a porridge of dried peas.

The food was poor enough when it was loaded on board, and it got worse as time went on. Weevils—a type of beetle—infested the supplies. Experienced sailors knocked their biscuits against the table a few times before eating, so that at least a few of the weevils might run out. Even the water in the ship's barrels turned slimy and bad-smelling after a few weeks.

By 1600, European doctors knew that fresh oranges and lemons could help prevent scurvy. Most ship owners, however, thought these fruits were too expensive for common seamen. Finally, in the late 1700's, the British navy began to issue a little lemon or lime juice to sailors each day. At once, the number of sailors who died at sea dropped sharply.

Columbus's fleet left Spain in August 1492, heading west across the Atlantic Ocean. As weeks passed, the crew became nervous. The weather and winds were good, but no one was sure where they were going—or whether they would ever be able to return home. Columbus offered a prize to the sailor who first spotted land. Early on the morning of October 12, one day before Columbus was planning to give up and return to Spain, a lookout saw white sand gleaming in the moonlight. Joyously he shouted the Spanish word for land: *"Tierra, tierra!"*

Arrival in the Americas. Columbus had landed far short of his goal, on an island in the Caribbean. He, however, was convinced that he had reached the Indies, a group of islands in Southeast Asia. When he was met by the local people, the Arawaks, he called them "Indians." Believing that he had a mission to bring Christianity to these people, he named the island San Salvador ("Holy Saviour" in Spanish). From the Arawaks, Columbus learned of a richer land to the south (probably Cuba). He sailed there expecting to meet the Grand Khan of China, but his hopes were disappointed.

After visiting the island of Hispaniola (today the nations of Haiti and the Dominican Republic), Columbus sailed back to Spain. He took some of the Arawaks with him to "prove" that he had reached Asia. Delighted by the voyage, the queen gave Columbus the title "Admiral of the Ocean Sea."

Columbus returned to the Caribbean three more times. On his second voyage, in 1493, he brought 17 shiploads of settlers to Hispaniola and established the first European colony in the Americas. Columbus proved to be a poor colonial administrator,

Sec. Rev. ques. 4, cont.

▲ See below.

350

▲ REINFORCEMENT. Have students complete an outline titled *Spanish Exploration in the 1400's and 1500's,* and include the names of Spanish explorers, the dates, and outcomes. (Comprehension) Organizing Information
Background Columbus offered a prize of an annual payment equal to $700 to the first person to sight land. Pedro Yzquierdo claimed to be the first to sight land, but Columbus insisted that he himself was the winner. Columbus got the prize and Yzquierdo, in a rage, went to Africa.

▲ ENRICHMENT. Have students research the life of an explorer sponsored by Spain and write a biographical sketch. Reports might focus on the personality, talents, and achievements of the explorer. (Application) Locating Information
Social History The Arawaks were an agricultural people who lived in large villages with up to 3,000 inhabitants. Although most Arawaks died from disease and forced labor after the Spanish arrived, a few tribes moved to territory along the Xingu River in Brazil.

Sailors taking on fresh water and fruit.

The Division of the World

The rulers of Spain had immediately sent news of Columbus's first voyage to Pope Alexander VI. Spain hoped that the Pope would support its claim to newly discovered lands. To prevent disputes between Spain and Portugal over these lands, the Pope established an imaginary **Line of Demarcation** in the Atlantic Ocean. It gave Spain possession of all lands already "discovered and to be discovered" west of Europe. Portugal was to have the lands to the east of the line. King John of Portugal, however, threatened war against Spain, claiming that the Spanish monarchs had been given much too great an advantage.

In 1494 diplomats from the two countries met at Tordesillas (tor-day-SEE-yahs) in Spain. They agreed to move the Line of Demarcation farther west. The Treaty of Tordesillas, like the Pope's order, allowed Spain and Portugal to divide the entire non-Christian world between themselves. The revised treaty line gave Portugal a claim to what is now Brazil; Spain was given the rest of the Americas (map, pages 352–353).

Sec. Rev. ques. 5

however. In 1500 he was arrested by a royal investigator and sent back to Spain.

The importance of Columbus's discovery. Columbus died in 1506, convinced that he had reached Asia. Other Europeans, though, realized that Columbus had stumbled across new lands. They called the Caribbean islands the "West Indies," and renamed the Indies on the other side of the world the "East Indies."

Columbus was not the first European to reach the Americas. Almost 500 years earlier, a Viking named Leif Ericson had explored a land he called Vinland—the eastern coast of North America (page 217). Columbus's voyage, however, came at a time when European nations were able and eager to follow up on discoveries such as his. They were so eager, in fact, that they set out to gain control of these new lands.

Later Spanish Explorers

To follow up Spain's claim, more and more Spanish expeditions headed west across the Atlantic. An Italian sailor, Amerigo Vespucci (ves-POO-chee), made voyages to the Americas for both Spain and Portugal and wrote a colorful account of his travels. In 1507 a German geographer and mapmaker labeled the new southern continent with the Latin form of Vespucci's first name. Other people picked up the practice, and *America* eventually became the name for both continents in the Western Hemisphere.

The colony Columbus had established at Hispaniola became a base for further Spanish exploration of the Caribbean area. In 1508 a colonist named Juan Ponce de León explored the nearby island of Puerto Rico and established a colony there. He later sailed **351**

Background In 1541 the body of Christopher Columbus was transferred from Seville, Spain, to the Catholic cathedral in Santo Domingo, present-day capital of the Dominican Republic.
Geography The Vikings thought that eastern North America, which they called Vinland, was an island. Although most scholars believe that the name refers to an abundance of wine berries found on the land, some think that the name *Vinland* means "grassland" or "pastureland." It is now thought that the Vikings explored present-day Newfoundland.

Check for Understanding. Ask: What factors led to the establishment of the Line of Demarcation? (The Pope wanted to prevent disputes between Portugal and Spain.)
Background Vespucci, a Florentine diplomat, scholar, and businessman, played a major part in the organization of Columbus's second expedition. He was the first to claim that the land found by Columbus was not part of Asia but a continent previously unknown to Europeans.

Age of Exploration, 1492–1682

The routes of major European explorers are shown here. Which voyages did England sponsor? Which explorer led an expedition that sailed around the world? Which country sponsored that expedition? What part of South America lay west of the line drawn by the Treaty of Tordesillas? (See answers below.)

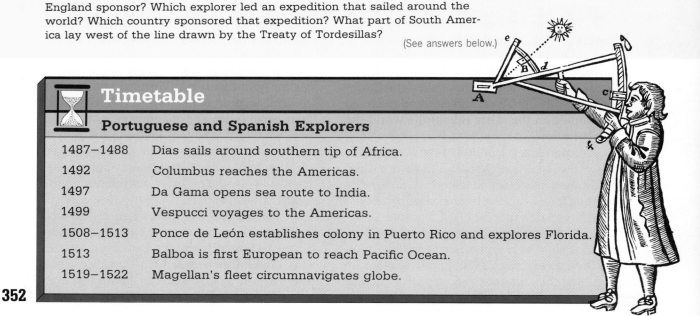

Timetable

Portuguese and Spanish Explorers

1487–1488	Dias sails around southern tip of Africa.
1492	Columbus reaches the Americas.
1497	Da Gama opens sea route to India.
1499	Vespucci voyages to the Americas.
1508–1513	Ponce de León establishes colony in Puerto Rico and explores Florida.
1513	Balboa is first European to reach Pacific Ocean.
1519–1522	Magellan's fleet circumnavigates globe.

352

Map Answers: (1) Cabot's and Hudson's explorations of North America. (2) Magellan. (3) Spain. (4) All of South America except the far eastern part (Brazil).

Check for Understanding. Ask: Which explorers are associated with the following: (a) San Salvador (Columbus); **(b)** circumnavigation of the globe (Magellan); **(c)** the "fountain of youth" (Ponce de León); **(d)** first European sighting of the "Great South Sea" (Balboa).

Magellan's Voyage Around the World

In 1519 a Portuguese navigator, Ferdinand Magellan, persuaded the Spanish king to pay for an expedition to explore the Pacific Ocean. This voyage was by far the boldest undertaking of the Age of Exploration.

In September of that year, Magellan set sail from Spain with five ships and a crew of 265. After the Atlantic crossing, they sailed south along the coast of South America. Grumbling soon began among the cold and weary crew. The fleet, however, pressed on to a spot about 200 miles above the tip of South America, where they spent the winter.

When spring at last came, three of Magellan's ships continued southward. With enormous skill and luck they navigated the raging tides and the twisted passages of the waterway now called the Strait of Magellan. After more than a month of dangerous sailing, the ships emerged into the "Great South Sea." Magellan found it so calm that he called it *Mar Pacifico*—the "peaceful sea."

Crossing the Pacific, however, proved to be a nightmare for Magellan's ships. An Italian on board wrote a journal for the Spanish king, describing the horrors the sailors went through:

❝ We were three months and twenty days without getting any kind of fresh food. We ate biscuit, which was no longer biscuit, but powder of biscuits swarming with worms. We drank yellow water that had been putrid for many days. We also ate some ox hides. Rats were sold for one-half ducado [a gold coin] apiece, and even then we could not get them. But of all misfortunes the following was the worst. The gums of both the lower and upper teeth of some of our men swelled, so that they could not eat under any circumstances and therefore died. We sailed about 12,000 miles during those three months and twenty days through an open stretch in that Pacific Sea. Had not God and His

north, searching for the legendary "fountain of youth." Though he never found this magical spring, Ponce de León discovered a beautiful peninsula on Easter Sunday in the year 1513. He named it *Florida*, Spanish for "full of flowers."

Vasco Núñez de Balboa, another settler in Hispaniola, set out to look for gold on the mainland. He established a settlement in what is now Panama. In 1513 he crossed the Isthmus of Panama—the narrow strip of land connecting Central America with South America—and became the first European to see the "Great South Sea," which is now called the Pacific Ocean.

353

blessed mother given us so good weather we would have all died of hunger in that exceeding vast sea. I believe no such voyage will ever be made again. 🙶

Though many sailors died, two ships at last reached the Philippine Islands, southeast of the Asian mainland. The explorers became involved in a war among the local people, in which Magellan and some of his men were killed. The rest of the crew, led by Juan Sebastián del Cano, found their way back to Spain with a rich cargo of cloves. Magellan's proud fleet had been reduced to one ship with 18 exhausted, hungry men aboard. Yet these sailors made a triumphant return to Europe in 1522, becoming the first people ever to **circumnavigate**—sail around—the globe.

This historic voyage had important lessons for later explorers. First, it showed that the Pacific Ocean separated Asia from the Americas and was much larger than suspected. Second, the voyage demonstrated that all the oceans are connected and that the ocean winds follow a consistent pattern. This

See lesson plans, pp. T345A–T345C.

new knowledge enabled Western Europeans to sail almost anywhere on the face of the planet. See Sec. 1 *Closing the Lesson*, p. T345B.

Section Review

Answers to Section Review questions are in brackets on pages indicated.

1. **Define or identify:** Age of Exploration, monopoly, bullion, Line of Demarcation, circumnavigate. (pp. 347, 348, 349, 351, 354)
2. What factors help explain the Age of Exploration? (pp. 347–348)
3. How did the voyages of Dias and da Gama help Portugal establish trade with Asia? (p. 349)
4. What did Columbus intend to do when he set out from Spain? What was the actual result of the voyage? (pp. 349–350)
5. What was the purpose of the Treaty of Tordesillas? (p. 351)
6. **Critical thinking:** Compare the importance of Columbus's and Magellan's voyages of exploration.

(See answer below.)

6. Answers will vary. Students might argue the relative merits of Columbus's discovery of new lands versus Magellan's expansion of geographic and navigational knowledge.

2 Spanish and Portuguese Colonization

Objectives

★ Note strategies for first objective on this page and p. 355.

Focus Questions

★ ■ How did Spain defeat the Aztec and Inca empires? *(pages 354–356)*

● ■ How did Spain and Portugal set up colonies in the Americas? *(pages 356–357)*

Terms to Know

conquistador
viceroy
encomienda
peon

354

Between 25 and 100 million people were living in the Americas at the time of the first European settlements. As you read in Chapter 16, two American peoples—the Aztecs and the Incas—had built strong empires that controlled large territories (map, page 313). Yet neither of these civilizations was able to turn back the attacks of the Europeans armed with cannons and steel swords.

The Conquest of the Aztecs

The first settlers from Spain stayed primarily on the Caribbean islands. Soon, however, the Spaniards' desire for gold led them to the

★ RETEACHING. Have students review pp. 355–356 and write two paragraphs describing the conquistadors. Students should describe the background, values, and motives of the conquistadors and then explain how these characteristics might have helped the Spanish conquer the Indian people. (Conquistadors wanted fame, gold, land, and adventure. Most conquistadors were daring and ruthless soldiers.) (*Comprehension*) **Drawing Conclusions**

★ REINFORCEMENT. Have each student prepare a dialogue that might have occurred between Cortés and Montezuma or Pizarro and Atahualpa. Dialogues might refer to the demands of the Europeans or to possible compromises between the two parties. (*Application*) **Understanding Point of View**

Geography Named after the Carib Indians, the Caribbean islands are divided into the Greater Antilles (Cuba, Jamaica, Hispaniola, Puerto Rico) and the Lesser Antilles (a group of smaller islands).

Religion Quetzalcóatl, portrayed as a rattlesnake covered with the green feathers of the quetzal bird, represented a wise, benevolent god.

Background Pizarro claimed that the Inca chief was plotting an attack against the Spanish troops.

mainland, where they encountered the rich Aztec and Inca states. Many of the Spanish **conquistadors** (kon-kee-stah-DORZ)—conquerors—were sons of aristocratic families. They came to the Caribbean seeking fame, gold, land, and adventure. Some were motivated by religious reasons as well. Many were very brave and daring; they were also willing to use any means to achieve their ends.

Hernando Cortés was a typical conquistador—courageous, charming, and ruthless. With 11 ships, he sailed from Cuba to the Gulf coast of Mexico in 1519 (map, page 352). Cortés had an army of 508 soldiers, 2 priests, 16 horses, and several small cannons.

News of these fair-skinned, bearded strangers, who rode unfamiliar beasts and had thundering weapons, astonished the Aztecs. Their ruler, Montezuma (mahn-tuh-ZOO-muh), believed the Europeans might be gods or messengers from the god Quetzalcóatl. (Aztec priests had predicted that Quetzalcóatl would return that very year.)

Sec. Rev.
ques. 2 Although his warriors could easily have overcome Cortés's small army, Montezuma sent ambassadors with gifts of gold and featherwork. Unsure of the Spaniards' aims, Montezuma hoped the intruders would take the gifts and leave. The gold, however, only made the Spaniards eager to find its source.

Cortés decided to march inland. To prevent his outnumbered soldiers from turning back, Cortés ordered the ships sunk behind them. Malinche (mah-LEEN-chay), an Aztec noblewoman who had been sold into slavery, aided Cortés in dealing with local leaders. Quick to learn Spanish, she acted as both interpreter and informer. Her knowledge and influence helped Cortés make allies of other Indians and keep track of Aztec spies.

Cortés's army and allies crossed the mountains to Tenochtitlán. There they spent several months as Montezuma's guests. Some of the Aztec nobles, however, suspected the Spaniards of wanting to take over the empire. In a fierce battle, they drove the Spaniards out of the Aztec city, killing or wounding more than half of Cortés's small army.

Undiscouraged, Cortés began a siege of Tenochtitlán. The Aztecs resisted until most

The Inca ruler Atahualpa sits on a golden throne, wearing ornaments of the finest gold.

of their warriors had been killed or captured or had come down with smallpox. Meanwhile, Montezuma had died, probably from being stoned by an angry crowd of Aztecs. The Aztec resistance was now led by Cuauhtémoc (kwah-TAY-mok), nephew of Montezuma. Cuauhtémoc valiantly defended the Aztec city against a three-month Spanish siege, but Tenochtitlán finally fell to Cortés. The Spanish conqueror captured Cuauhtémoc and had him executed. Cortés then took control of the rest of Mexico. Today Cuauhtémoc is honored by all Mexicans as a national hero.

The Conquest of the Incas

The great Inca Empire lay south of the Aztec lands, in what is now Peru. The Spaniards' conquest of the Incas was quicker than the defeat of the Aztecs, but equally dramatic.

Francisco Pizarro gained permission from Spain's ruler, Emperor Charles V, to attempt the conquest of the South American coast. When Pizarro arrived in 1532, the Inca ruler, Atahualpa (at-ah-WAHL-puh), met him cordially but was immediately taken prisoner. In the fighting that followed, the Inca **355**

★ See below.

Check for Understanding. Ask: Why were the Aztecs friendly to Cortés and his warriors? (Their ruler, Montezuma, believed that the Europeans might be gods or messengers of the god Quetzalcóatl.)
Geography Remind students that Tenochtitlán (p. 311) was located on an island in Lake Texcoco. The city was founded about A.D. 1325, and grew to support a population of several hundred thousand. It was destroyed by the Spanish in 1521, and Mexico City was built on its ruins.

★ ENRICHMENT. Have students research and report on the Spanish conquest of the Aztecs or the Incas. Reports might include an explanation of the methods of conquest or focus on one of the Spanish conquistadors. (Application) Locating Information foot soldiers, armed with spears, war clubs, and bows and arrows, were no match for Spanish cannons, steel swords, and mounted soldiers. Not one Spaniard died in the fighting that killed hundreds of the Inca people.

Pizarro promised to set Atahualpa free on the payment of a great ransom—a room full of gold. After the gold had been collected from throughout the empire, though, Pizarro ordered Atahualpa strangled. One fifth of the ransom was sent to the king of Spain. The rest was divided among some 150 conquistadors, who soon began to fight among themselves. Pizarro himself was assassinated. Unrest continued until 1551, when the Spanish king sent a representative called a **viceroy** (VYS-roy) to govern Peru.

Later Spanish Explorers

The Spanish conquests of the Aztec and Inca empires gave Spain control of territory stretching from modern Mexico to Chile. Other Spanish adventurers explored the lands around the great South American rivers, claiming still more of the continent. Rumors of treasure and legends of cities whose streets were paved with gold lured Spaniards north of Mexico as well.

Hernando de Soto, who had been with Pizarro, led an expedition to Florida. He and his party traveled north as far as the Carolinas and then turned westward. They reached the Mississippi River in 1541 and explored the lands nearby.

Francisco de Coronado set out northward from Mexico in 1540 and captured the pueblos of the Zuni Indians there. His expedition then split up. Some members of the group followed the course of the Colorado River inland from the coast. Others traveled north and became the first Europeans to see the Grand Canyon. Another group traveled as far east as present-day Kansas.

Although neither de Soto nor Coronado found gold or rich empires, their travels took them across the entire southern edge of what is now the United States. In 1560 Spain **356** claimed these lands as part of its empire.

Spain's Empire in the Ámericas

● Note strategies for second objective on this page and p. 357.

Centralized government. The Spanish moved quickly to set up a strong, centralized government in the Americas. They divided their lands into provinces, and the king appointed a viceroy to carry out his policies in each province.

The Spanish government believed that the colonies existed for the economic benefit of Spain. The king claimed one fifth of all the gold and silver mined in the Americas. Spain also controlled the trade of the colonies, encouraging the export of raw materials and discouraging the development of manufacturing. In this way, the colonists were forced to buy finished goods from Spain.

Sec. Rev. ques. 3

Indian laborers. The Spanish government gave huge tracts of land in the colonies to the conquistadors and other royal favorites. These settlers believed it was beneath their dignity to work with their hands. From the Spanish government, therefore, settlers received *encomiendas*—grants that entitled them to demand labor and taxes from the Indians who lived on their lands. These Indians, called **peons**, had once worked for the Aztec and Inca nobles. They now worked for the Spanish landowners. In return, the settlers pledged to protect the Indians and pay for the support of village priests.

Although the Spanish government passed laws to make sure that Indian workers would not be mistreated, local officials did not enforce the laws. The *encomienda* system was, in practice, a brutal form of slavery. Thousands of Indians died during the 1500's because of harsh working conditions.

Spanish missionaries. The suffering of the Indians deeply troubled many of the Catholic missionaries who journeyed to the Americas. One such missionary was Bartolomé de Las Casas, who became a priest in Hispaniola. He began a lifelong campaign to protect Indians from colonists who were interested only in the profits to be made from their labor. His appeals to the king resulted in new laws passed in 1542 forbidding the further enslavement of Indians.

Sec. Rev. ques. 4

Geography During Atahualpa's rule, the Inca Empire (pp. 313–315) extended from present-day southern Colombia through Ecuador, Peru, and Bolivia into northwest Argentina and northern Chile.

Vocabulary *Viceroy* is derived from a French word meaning "in place of the king."

Check for Understanding. Ask: Who were two Spanish explorers whose expeditions took them into regions that are now part of the United States? (Hernando de Soto and Francisco de Coronado.)

● **RETEACHING.** Have students explain how each of the following influenced Portuguese colonization of Brazil: **(a)** Pedro Cabral (claimed Brazil); **(b)** wealthy nobles (received land grants, established settlements). *(Comprehension)* **Observing for Detail**

● **REINFORCEMENT.** Have students review "Centralized government" (p. 356) and outline Spain's governmental and economic systems in the Americas. *(Comprehension)* **Translating Information into Another Form**

An Indian artist of the 1500's may have drawn these rock paintings of Spanish soldiers who rode into Arizona's Canyon de Chelly.

In the late 1500's, as part of the missionary effort of the Counter-Reformation (page 342), the Catholic Church sent many of Spain's best-trained friars to the Americas to convert the Indians. In order to preach, the friars learned Indian languages. They wrote accounts of the Indians' customs and set up schools to teach them new skills.

● See below.

Portuguese Colonization of Brazil

Missionary efforts also played an important part in the settlement of Brazil by the Portuguese. In 1500, following the same route as da Gama (page 349), the fleet of Pedro Cabral (kuh-BRAHL) made a wide arc into the western Atlantic and landed on the coast of Brazil. Cabral immediately claimed this territory for Portugal. Eventually the Portuguese claimed the east coast of South America as far south as present-day Uruguay.

Sec. Rev. ques. 5

Most of the settlements in Brazil were started by wealthy nobles who received large grants of land from the Portuguese king. Unlike the Spanish colonies, however, the Portuguese colonies attracted settlers from all classes of society. By the mid-1500's there were about 15 fortified towns on the Brazilian coast. Jesuit missionaries pioneered the exploration of the interior, where they started schools and mission churches for the Indi-

ans. Portuguese settlers followed the missionaries inland. Some were farmers looking for good grazing land. Others were adventurers looking for gold or for Indians to capture and sell as slaves.

Like Spain, Portugal gained power and prestige from its American colonies. Other European monarchs were slow to take advantage of the opportunities for colonization. In the late 1500's and early 1600's, however, they began to enter the competition.

See Sec. 2 *Closing the Lesson*, p. T345B.

357

Vocabulary *Dutch* is a word used by English-speaking peoples to identify people of the Netherlands. The Netherlands is also called *Holland*.

3 Dutch, English, and French Colonies

Objectives

Focus Questions

★ ■ How did the Netherlands and England take part in exploration and trade? *(pages 358–359)*
● ■ What roles did England and France play in the colonization of North America? *(pages 359–363)*

Terms to Know

Northwest Passage   legislature
privateer   French and Indian
Puritan   War

★ Note strategies for first objective on this page and p. 359.

The Netherlands, England, and France played only a small part in the early voyages of exploration, for religious conflicts and civil wars focused their interests at home. By the time these countries were ready to join the search for new lands, both Spain and Portugal had already claimed (under the Treaty of Tordesillas) all undiscovered territories. Ignoring the treaty, the Netherlands, England, and France began their own explorations.

Dutch and English Exploration

The Dutch and English were eager to find sea routes to Asia. Their seafarers sailed northeast into the Arctic Ocean along the coast of Russia. Ice made this route impassable much of the year, however. The Dutch and English next set out across the Atlantic, hoping to find a **Northwest Passage**—a waterway through North America to Asia.

In 1497 the English king, Henry VII, **358** financed the journey of an Italian navigator,

John Cabot, westward to the Americas. Cabot reached Newfoundland and explored its coast (map, page 361). On his return to Europe, he reported rich fishing grounds. However, he also described a cold land quite different from the tropical islands found by Columbus.

About 100 years later, Henry Hudson, an English explorer, made four voyages in search of a Northwest Passage. In 1609, sailing for Dutch merchants, Hudson took his ship *Half Moon* up the Hudson River, claiming the region for the Netherlands. There Dutch settlers established the colony of New Netherland, including what is now New York City (originally called New Amsterdam). Dutch holdings in the Western Hemisphere also included some islands in the Caribbean, the colony of Dutch Guiana (now Suriname), and parts of Brazil.

Sec. Rev. ques. 2

Henry Hudson and his son were set adrift by their angry crew after a harsh winter voyage. They perished in the region of northern Canada now known as Hudson Bay.

★ **RETEACHING. Have students write a summary of efforts to find a Northwest Passage.** (John Cabot of England reached Newfoundland in 1497. In 1609, Henry Hudson of the Netherlands explored the Hudson River.) *(Comprehension) Identifying Cause and Effect*
**Check for Understanding. Ask students to define the concept of Northwest Passage by answering the questions *What? Where?* and *Why?* (The passage was thought to be a waterway through North America to Asia which would shorten the journey from Europe to Asia.)

★ **REINFORCEMENT. Have students make a chart comparing the economic activities of the French and British in North America.** (Most English colonists farmed; in the South, plantations and slavery developed. The French acquired wealth as fur traders.) *(Comprehension) Translating Information into Another Form*

Religion The Puritans called for simpler religious services, more emphasis on reading the Bible, and the election of clergy by Church members.

Religion In England, Quakers were fined and imprisoned because they held their own services and refused to attend the Anglican Church.

The Dutch and English Trading Empires

By the mid-1500's, the Netherlands had come under Spanish control (page 386). When the people of the Netherlands revolted against their Spanish rulers in 1568, their ships could no longer enter either Spanish or Portuguese ports. Undiscouraged, the Dutch decided to take over the Portuguese trade routes and set up their own trade with ports in India and the East Indies.

In 1602 the Netherlands provided a charter establishing the Dutch East India Company. This powerful trading company soon gained control of nearly all the Portuguese ports in Asia. The Netherlands also became the only European country allowed to trade with Japan. By the mid-1600's the Dutch had a near monopoly on the Asian trade.

Similarly, the Dutch West India Company, founded in 1621, soon controlled much of the slave trade and other shipping in the Atlantic and the Caribbean. Unlike the Spaniards and Portuguese, the Dutch (who were Protestant) sent no missionaries to their American colonies. Their main interest was profitable trade.

In the Americas, the Dutch were an important power for only a brief period, but their control of islands in the East Indies lasted for nearly three centuries. The forts and fleets of the Dutch East India Company protected its monopoly in pepper and spices. Later, cotton, silk, tea, and coffee made up the bulk of the Dutch trade.

Like the Netherlands, England concentrated on developing its trade and its strength at sea. To trade in Africa, India, or the Americas, however, the English had to fight both rival traders and pirates from other countries. Traders of the English East India Company, chartered by Queen Elizabeth I in 1600, fought the French to gain trading posts in India (Chapter 29). Privateers—private ships authorized by the government to attack enemy shipping—were used by England to capture Spanish treasure ships and bombard ports in South America.

Sec. Rev. ques. 3

★ See below.

England's American Colonies

● Note strategies for second objective on this page and p. 363.

During the 1600's and 1700's, English settlers established a number of colonies in the Americas. Thirteen of these were on the east coast of what is today the United States. Others were established in Canada and on the islands of the Caribbean.

Reasons for settlement. Many English settlers came to the Americas to escape religious conflicts in their home country. (You will read about these conflicts in Chapter 20.) They wanted to live in a place where they could freely practice their religion. The founders of Massachusetts and Connecticut, for example, were Puritans. Puritans were Protestants who were persecuted because they believed that the Church of England had not gone far enough in reforming (purifying) its doctrines and ceremonies. Pennsylvania was founded by Quakers, another Protestant group that faced discrimination in England. Maryland began as a refuge for Roman Catholics fleeing England.

Other colonies were settled by people who came to the Americas mostly for economic reasons. In 1607 a group of aristocratic Englishmen made a settlement at Jamestown, Virginia, expecting to find a fortune in gold. Their hopes fell flat, and many starved to death their first winter because they had not bothered to store food. Later colonists had

Sec. Rev. ques. 4

Meanwhile . . .

IN SIBERIA

In the 1600's Russians began to settle Siberia, the huge area east of the Ural Mountains. Among the settlers were many Old Believers—Christians who were fleeing Russia. Like the Puritans, the Old Believers were seeking religious freedom. Their traditional religious practices had been outlawed by the Russian state as part of its reform of the Church.

Economics The Dutch East India Company was granted a trade monopoly and authority to raise an army and a navy, erect forts, establish colonies, make war and peace, sign treaties, coin money, and administer justice.

★ ENRICHMENT. Have students research and report on the Dutch East and West India companies. Students might compare their organizations and trade products, and draw a map showing the territories they controlled. (Synthesis) Locating Information

● RETEACHING. Have students review "Conflict over Colonies" (pp. 362–363) and outline the cause and effects of the French and Indian War. (Cause: rivalry over colonial empires. Effects: France lost nearly all its North American colonial possessions.) (Comprehension) Identifying Cause and Effect

● REINFORCEMENT. Have students evaluate the economic opportunities, populations, and freedoms in the English and French colonies in America. (Analysis) Making Judgments more realistic ideas about the kind of wealth to be found in the colonies. For the most part, that wealth was land, which was free for the taking.

The colonial economies. Throughout the English colonies, most people lived on small farms. In the south, however, plantations dominated the economy. To supply the labor needed on their tobacco and rice plantations, planters imported thousands of African slaves (Chapter 19).

A painting by English settler John White shows how Indians fished the abundant waters of North Carolina. Besides nets and spears, Indians used traps made of reeds (at left). The fire inside the canoe was used to smoke the fish. White deliberately emphasized the beauty and bounty of life in America so that more English people would want to settle there.

360

As the colonial population grew and soil became less fertile from overuse, settlers moved to the frontier, where they could carve out new farms. Because this expansion often forced the Indians off their traditional lands, many wars were fought between Indians and settlers.

A land of opportunity. The abundance of land in America gave English colonists a great deal of economic opportunity and political freedom. First, by owning and working their own farms, settlers could earn an independent living much more easily than in Europe. Even colonists who had little money could prosper.

Second, owning land carried with it the right to vote. In Europe small groups of nobles held most of the political power because they held most of the land. In England's American colonies, however, a large number of men owned property and thus had a voice in government. Colonists elected representatives to legislatures—lawmaking bodies. Colonists were also guaranteed English liberties, such as the right to trial by jury and protection from unlawful imprisonment.

The French in North America

Early explorers. Like the English, the French sought territory in the Americas. In the early 1500's, French fishing boats regularly sailed the ocean off Newfoundland. The French king, Francis I, hoped the Northwest Passage would be found in that area, and he sent out several expeditions. In 1535 Jacques Cartier (car-TYAY) reached the St. Lawrence River and claimed for France the land that is now eastern Canada. It became known as New France.

French leaders did not immediately follow up on Cartier's discovery because they were preoccupied with conflicts at home. In 1608, however, Samuel de Champlain (sham-PLAYN) established Quebec, the first permanent French colony in North America. Considered the "Father of New France," Champlain explored the coast of what is now Maine and established other settlements at

Sec. Rev. ques. 5

GREENLAND

ICELAND

NORTH AMERICA

Hudson Bay

NEW FRANCE
Quebec
Montreal
Great Lakes
St. Lawrence R.
Wisconsin R.

NEWFOUNDLAND
CAPE BRETON I.
Louisbourg
NOVA SCOTIA

NEW ENGLAND
Plymouth

VIRGINIA
Jamestown

Grand Canyon
Colorado R.
Ohio R.
Mississippi R.

LOUISIANA

NEW SPAIN
(MEXICO)

FLORIDA

BERMUDA

PACIFIC OCEAN

Gulf of Mexico

Mexico City • • Veracruz

BAHAMAS
CUBA
JAMAICA
WEST INDIES

ST. DOMINGUE
SANTO DOMINGO
PUERTO RICO

Caribbean Sea

KEY

English
French
Dutch
Portuguese
Spanish
Swedish
Danish

DARIEN (PANAMA)

NEW ANDALUSIA (VENEZUELA)

TRINIDAD

Orinoco R.

GUIANA

ATLANTIC OCEAN

Isthmus of Panama

NEW GRANADA (COLOMBIA)

SOUTH AMERICA

Amazon R.

to Portugal, 1654

Colonies in the Americas About 1700

By 1700 seven European nations had claimed lands in the Western Hemisphere. What were those nations? Which ones had colonies near the English settlements along the Atlantic coast? (See inset map.)

NEW CASTILE (PERU)
Lima •
• Cuzco

BRAZIL

• Bahia

São Vincente

Swedish and Dutch Colonies About 1650

N
W — E
S

Fort Orange (Albany)

NEW NETHERLAND

NEW ENGLAND

Hudson R.
Delaware R.

New Amsterdam (New York)

Fort Christina (Wilmington)
NEW SWEDEN

MARYLAND

Delaware Bay

VIRGINIA

ATLANTIC OCEAN

SCALE
0   100 mi
0   100 km

N
W — E
S

NEW ESTREMADURA (CHILE)

LA PLATA

• Buenos Aires

SCALE
0   1,000 mi
0   1,000 km

361

This painting by American artist George Catlin shows the French explorer La Salle meeting with the chiefs of the Taensa Indians in northern Louisiana in 1682. France appointed La Salle Viceroy of North America.

Montreal and in Nova Scotia. He traveled through much of northeastern North America in his efforts to build up the fur trade to support New France.

Later explorers. In the second half of the 1600's, as France's interest in North America grew, new expeditions were organized. Louis Joliet (joh-lee-ET), a fur trapper, and Jacques Marquette (mahr-KET), a priest, traveled together by boat in the Great Lakes and along the Wisconsin and Mississippi rivers in 1672. A French nobleman known as La Salle, who had moved to New France to become a fur trader, explored the lower Mississippi River in 1682. Starting north of the Ohio River, he traveled all the way to the Gulf of Mexico. La Salle claimed the entire Mississippi Valley for France and named it Louisiana in honor of King Louis XIV.

Economic activities. Fur trading was the primary source of wealth for French settlers. At scattered outposts around the Great Lakes and in the Mississippi and Ohio valleys, French traders bought the valuable furs collected in the wilderness by French and Indian trappers.

Attempts at farming were less successful. The king granted large tracts of farmland in the valley of the St. Lawrence River to French lords. Yet there was a shortage of farm labor. The French government refused to let Protestants settle in New France for fear that they would spread Protestantism. Only Catholic peasants could emigrate, and those who did seldom had the opportunity to start farms of their own.

Many French people preferred to settle in French-owned islands in the West Indies. The large sugar plantations on these islands were extremely profitable. France's colony of St. Domingue (doh-MANG), today the nation of Haiti, was at one time regarded as the richest colonial possession in the world.

Conflict over Colonies

Since both England and France wanted to expand their holdings in North America, they soon came into conflict. The struggle for overseas colonies became mixed up with other disputes among European nations. Between 1689 and 1763, while various conflicts were going on in Europe, English and French colonists in North America fought four different wars for control of the continent.

The final showdown between England and France came in the **French and Indian War**, which began in 1754. The two sides, each with Indian allies, clashed over lands around the Great Lakes and the St. Lawrence River. English victories at Quebec in 1759 and Montreal in 1760 spelled doom for New France, and Britain's superiority at sea was a decisive factor in the outcome of the war. In the Treaty of Paris of 1763, France was forced to surrender.

The treaty cost France nearly all of its North American colonial possessions. French lands in Canada went to Britain, while French territory west of the Mississippi River went to Spain. The treaty did allow France to keep its rich sugar colonies in the Caribbean, but French power in the Americas had been broken.

● See below.

See Sec. 3 *Closing the Lesson*, p. T345C.

Chapter 18   Summary and Timeline

1. A thirst for wealth and power, the desire to spread Christianity, the Renaissance spirit of curiosity and adventure, and improvements in technology all paved the way for European exploration and expansion in different parts of the world. The Portuguese took the lead in these voyages and gained control of trade between Europe and India. Spain sponsored Columbus's expeditions to the Americas. Spain also sponsored Magellan's voyage around the world.

2. In the Americas, Spain's explorations led to wars of conquest. The Spanish defeated the Aztecs and Incas and gained an empire that included southwestern North America, Central America, and much of South America. The Portuguese claimed and colonized Brazil. Both Spain and Portugal gained power and prestige from their American colonies.

3. Other European nations began their own explorations. The Netherlands, England, and France established colonies in North America. A series of wars in the 1700's gave England control of most of France's possessions in North America.

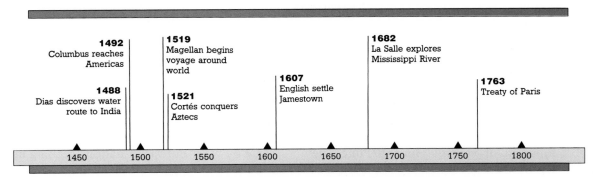

1492 Columbus reaches Americas

1488 Dias discovers water route to India

1519 Magellan begins voyage around world

1521 Cortés conquers Aztecs

1607 English settle Jamestown

1682 La Salle explores Mississippi River

1763 Treaty of Paris

1450   1500   1550   1600   1650   1700   1750   1800

● **ENRICHMENT.** Have students research the conflict between the French and the British in North America and in Europe. Students might compare the causes, strategies, battles, and outcomes of the wars. *(Synthesis) Synthesizing Information*

6. Answers will vary. Students might note that religious persecution in England drove people to seek religious freedom in North America. On the other hand, the French government did not allow Protestants to migrate to New France for fear that they would spread Protestantism.

CHAPTER **18** REVIEW

See p. T345C for answers to Chapter Review.

Vocabulary Review

Use the following terms to complete the sentences below: *bullion, conquistadors, encomiendas, legislatures, monopoly, peons, privateers, Puritans.*

1. English ___?___ attacked Spanish ships in hopes of capturing gold ___?___.
2. The ___?___ were the Spanish conquerors of the Aztecs and Incas.
3. With ___?___, Spanish settlers had the right to demand labor and taxes from the Indian ___?___ who lived on their lands.
4. Through the representatives they elected to ___?___, English colonists had a voice in government.
5. A ___?___ is one group's complete control over a good or service.
6. The founders of Massachusetts and Connecticut were ___?___, Protestants who wanted reforms in the Church of England.

People to Identify

Choose the name that best completes each sentence. Write your answers on a separate sheet of paper.

1. [Queen Isabella/Prince Henry] backed the voyages of [Balboa/Columbus].
2. When his ship was blown around the southern tip of Africa, [Dias/Vespucci] discovered a new route to India.
3. In 1535 [Cartier/Las Casas] reached the St. Lawrence River and claimed the surrounding land for France.
4. [Malinche/Montezuma], the ruler of the Aztecs, believed that [Cortés/Coronado] and his army might be gods.
5. Although he never found the fabled fountain of youth, [Hudson/Ponce de León] did discover and name Florida.

364

6. Known as the "Father of New France," [Champlain/La Salle] established Quebec, the first permanent French colony in North America.

Places to Know

Match the letters on the map with the places listed below. You may want to refer to the maps on pages 352–353 and 361.

1. Brazil
2. Cape of Good Hope
3. Isthmus of Panama
4. Jamestown
5. Mississippi River
6. New France
7. Strait of Magellan
8. Tenochtitlán
9. West Indies

Recalling the Facts

1. What led Europeans to begin voyages of exploration?
2. Why were European nations seeking an all-water route to Asia?

3. What two economic institutions became the basis for Portugal's overseas empire? How did the Portuguese begin trading with India?

4. Why were Columbus's voyages of discovery important?

5. What did the Treaty of Tordesillas do?

6. What did later explorers learn from Magellan's voyage around the world?

7. What factors helped Cortés conquer the Aztecs? What helped Pizarro conquer the Incas?

8. What steps did the Spanish take to establish a strong, centralized government in their colonies? According to the Spanish government, what purpose were their colonies supposed to serve?

9. What contributions did Spanish missionaries make in the Americas? What contributions did Portuguese missionaries make in the Americas?

10. What were Dutch and English explorers searching for?

11. Why did English settlers come to the Americas?

12. What was the result of the French and Indian War?

Critical Thinking Skills

1. **Relating past to present.** Write an essay comparing the first European explorers with the astronauts of today. Consider similarities and differences in motives, the personal qualities needed, and the challenges faced. *(Syn.)*

2. **Making judgments.** Hernando Cortés is described in this chapter as "ruthless." What evidence is given to support this judgment? How might the conquistadors have justified their actions? *(Anal.)*

3. **Creative writing.** Imagine that you are a sailor with Columbus or Magellan on his first voyage of exploration. Write three journal entries for your trip. The first one might be on the day you set sail, the second one after several weeks on the open seas, and the last one when the ship reaches land or returns to its home port. *(App.)*

A checkmark identifies questions and exercises calling for the three higher-order levels of thinking at the top of the Bloom taxonomy: Analysis, Synthesis, and Evaluation.

Thinking About Geography

Researching and locating places. Use an encyclopedia to find the origin of these place names: *Hispaniola, Jamaica, Jamestown, Mississippi River, Panama, Puerto Rico, Saint Lawrence River, Tierra del Fuego.* Then locate and label each place on an outline map of the Americas. *(App.)*

Enrichment: Primary Sources

Like his friend Bartolomé de Las Casas, the missionary Father Antonio Montesino took a strong stand against mistreatment of Indians. In the adapted passage below, Las Casas described one of Montesino's sermons to the Spanish settlers on Hispaniola.

❝ Father Antonio Montesino said: "In order to make your sins known to you I have mounted this pulpit, I who am the voice of Christ; and therefore you should listen to me with all your heart and senses.

"This voice," he said, "declares that you are in mortal sin, by reason of the cruelty that you practice on these innocent people. Tell me, by what right or justice do you hold these Indians in such cruel and horrible slavery? Why do you so greatly burden and fatigue them?

"Are they not men? Do they not have souls? Are you not bound to love them as you love yourselves? Be sure that in your present state you cannot be saved." ❞

1. Why did Montesino say the settlers should listen to him?

2. What judgment does Montesino make about the Spaniards' treatment of the Indians?

3. **Critical thinking:** How did Montesino try to convince his listeners?

(Anal.)

365

T365A

A Changed and Changing World   1450–1807
(pages 366–383)

Chapter Preview

Section 1 of this chapter describes the Commercial Revolution and the changes it brought about in economic life. Emphasis is given to the ways in which the Commercial Revolution contributed to the rise of a capitalistic economy. In Section 2 students will read about European settlement in the Americas and how it affected the Indians who lived there. Finally, the chapter explains the development of the African slave trade to supply labor for the colonies.

Bibliography

See the *Teacher's Management and Planning Guide* for additional listings. Starred titles are for both students and teachers.

Bailyn, Bernard. *The Peopling of British North America: An Introduction*. Knopf. An overview of the great transatlantic migration.

Curtin, Philip D. *The Atlantic Slave Trade: A Census*. University of Wisconsin Press. The impact of the slave trade on Africa.

Gies, Joseph, and Frances Gies. *Merchants and Moneymen: The Commercial Revolution, 1000–1500*. Crowell. Readable account of changing roles of businesspeople.

*Sherry, Frank. *Raiders and Rebels: The Golden Age of Piracy*. Morrow. The period from 1692 to 1725, when piracy flourished.

Section Lesson Plans

SECTION 1   (pp. 367–372)
A Revolution in Economic Life

Objectives

After completing this section, students will be able to:
1. Explain how mercantilism changed trade and business practices.
2. List the changes that occurred in the European economy in the 1500's and 1600's.

Introducing the Lesson

Remind students that, during the Age of Exploration, navigators, monarchs, and conquistadors were motivated by the desire for adventure and profit. The discovery of new routes to Asia, unknown lands, and new products resulted in dramatic economic changes in the world.

Then ask: *(a) How might the discovery of new products affect trade?* (Answers will vary. New products increase the kinds of goods available and the competition among traders.)

(b) How do you think the availability of products affects prices? Why? (Answers will vary. The more there is of an item the less it will cost because it is easier to get. The less there is of an item wanted by many people the more it will cost, because people are willing to pay a higher price to get a scarce item.)

(c) How do you think the discovery of territories might change the way products are bought and sold? (Answers will vary. New territories might mean more places to sell goods, new supplies of raw materials, and greater wealth.)

Developing the Lesson:
Analyzing Information

Have students write a paper analyzing the relationship between the rise of mercantilism and the increased power of European rulers. Students should show how the principles of mercantilism supported the growth of strong governments.

(Mercantilists believed that the power of the state could be increased if rulers accumulated wealth in precious metals and built up colonial trade. Monarchs needed gold and silver to pay for armies, so they sponsored voyages of exploration hoping to profit from new lands and products. Royal wealth increased with expanding exports and trade. The accumulation of wealth made possible larger armies, colonial expansion, and greater profit.) *(Comprehension)*

Developing the Lesson:
Identifying Cause and Effect

Have students make a cause-and-effect chart tracing the development of capitalism. (Italian merchants accumulated large amounts of capital from trade profits and interest on loans. They reinvested this wealth in their own businesses. As the costs of foreign trade increased, merchants pooled their money to form joint-stock companies. Bookkeeping systems were developed to organize and run businesses. Banking and the extension of credit grew.) *(Comprehension)*

Closing the Lesson: Observing for Detail

Have students summarize the factors that expanded Europe's economy from an agricultural to a market economy. (Increased wealth and population caused a greater demand for food. The demand for food led some English landlords to remove their land from community use and hire peasants at low wages, or rent the land. This change in the use of land made agriculture commercial because both land and labor could be bought and sold.) *(Comprehension)*

See *Section Review* questions, p. 372.

SECTION 2 (pp. 372–376)
New Populations in the Americas

Objectives

After completing this section, students will be able to:
1. Explain what groups made up the populations of the Americas.
2. Discuss how peoples in the Americas influenced one another's cultures.

Introducing the Lesson

Remind students that mercantilism and colonization had far-reaching consequences for people who lived in the Western Hemisphere. Indians who had lived in North and South America for hundreds of years were forced to share their land with Europeans. Black African society was disrupted when African slave labor was adopted in the Americas. American Indians, black Africans, and Europeans—populations with different histories, languages, religions, and cultures—were faced with the challenge of living side by side for the first time.

Then ask: *(a) Why do you think groups of people develop different ways of living?* (Answers will vary. Groups have different cultures because their histories, environments, and resources differ.)

(b) Why do people with different ways of life sometimes find cooperation difficult? (Answers will vary. Sometimes people feel threatened by what is unfamiliar, or they do not understand new ways and people and want to force them to change.)

(c) How do you think groups of people who are different from each other can learn to get along? (Answers will vary. Cooperation among different groups and a willingness to respect differences are important.)

Developing the Lesson:
Understanding Cause and Effect

Have students summarize the effects of colonization on American Indians, African slaves, and Europeans in a chart titled *Shifts in World Population*. Students should assign a column to each of the groups and, in brief phrases, list the effects of colonization on each population. (*American Indians:* many lives lost in battle or from forced labor, mistreatment, and disease. *African slaves:* black Africans were shipped to the Americas to work in mines and on plantations. *Europeans:* after 1650, most immigration was from Northern Europe, and included indentured servants and immigrants seeking religious, political, and personal freedoms.) *(Comprehension)*

Developing the Lesson:
Understanding Point of View

Have students work in groups to prepare a dialogue that might have occurred between an American Indian, an African slave, and a European settler. Dialogues might include a discussion about cultural backgrounds and how colonization affected the different groups. (Answers will vary.) *(Application)*

Closing the Lesson:
Drawing Conclusions

Have students draw conclusions about how contact between American Indians, African slaves, and European settlers affected each group. Students might consider the social, political, technological, religious, and economic influences the groups had on each other. (Answers will vary, but students should note that, generally, the Europeans prospered from settlement in the Americas, and the Indians and black Africans suffered from disease, forced labor, and forced migration.) *(Comprehension)*

See *Section Review* questions, p. 376.

SECTION 3   (pp. 376–381)
Africa and the Slave Trade

Objectives

After completing this section, students will be able to:
1. Explain what factors contributed to the growth of the slave trade.
2. Describe how the slave trade affected Africa.

Introducing the Lesson

Remind students that, at its height, the slave trade transported about 88,000 Africans a year in medium-sized ships that carried about 500 slaves. The average loss per voyage to sickness and violence was about fifty people. Then have students study the illustration of a scene below decks on a slave ship (p. 380).

Ask: *(a) How would you describe the area below deck on a slave ship?* (Answers will vary, but should suggest that it was overcrowded and dark.)

(b) What health problems might result from conditions like these? (Answers will vary. Unsanitary, crowded, and airless conditions would result in the easy spread of disease.)

(c) What do you think it was like to travel from Africa to the Americas in these conditions? (Answers will vary.)

Developing the Lesson:
Sequencing Events

Have students draw a diagram illustrating the development of the slave trade. Students should consider African slavery before the arrival of Europeans, European trade with Africa, increased demand for slaves, and the role of African traders. (Diagrams should include the use of slavery in Africa before the arrival of the Europeans; Europe's trade with Africa for gold, pepper, and ivory; the influence of colonial expansion; the growth of plantation agriculture; and the willingness of African rulers to trade slaves for European goods.) *(Comprehension)*

Developing the Lesson:
Summarizing Information

Have students summarize the political and social impact of the slave trade on Africa. (Political: included political unrest and rebellion, wars among African kingdoms, and the expansion of some kingdoms at the expense of others. Social: although Africa as a whole did not suffer long-term population loss, and African culture remained largely unaffected by contact with the Europeans, the greatest impact of slavery was felt by the enslaved individuals who were forced from their homes and families, treated no better than animals, and denied their basic rights.) *(Comprehension)*

Closing the Lesson: Making Judgments

Have students write an essay analyzing the effects slavery might have on countries that trade or acquire slaves. Students should consider the economic, political, social, and cultural effects on both the supplier and the purchaser country. (Answers will vary. Essays should evaluate the stability of economies that sell and use slaves, the political problems that might occur by keeping a slave population, the effects of slavery on social customs and values, and how cultures are affected by slavery.) *(Synthesis)*

See *Section Review* questions, p. 381.

Chapter 19 Review Answers
(pp. 382–383)

Vocabulary Review

1. Mercantilism 2. market economy 3. inflation
4. capital 5. Middle Passage 6. mestizo
7. Abolitionists

People to Identify

1. King of the Kongo from about 1505 to 1545 who protested the slave trade.
2. English sea captain who stole treasure from Spanish ships and circumnavigated the globe.
3. English merchant who defied the Spanish by selling European goods and African slaves to Spanish settlers in the Caribbean.
4. Dutch admiral who captured the Spanish silver fleet in the Caribbean, which helped finance the war against Spanish rule.

Places to Know

1. D   2. C   3. B   4. A

Recalling the Facts

1. Rulers encouraged exports and discouraged imports.
2. They could finance costly trading voyages and reduce the risk to individual investors.
3. They wanted to capture Spanish treasure and weaken Spain's monopoly on trade with the Americas.
4. With increased wealth, people bought more goods and food, depleting supplies and causing prices to rise. With the increased demand for food, landlords saw that they could profit from their farmland by commercializing agriculture, so they raised rents, forced peasants off the land, and hired cheap laborers.
5. Private ownership of capital, the production of goods and services in order to make a profit, and the exchange of goods and services in a free market with open competition.
6. The Indian population declined sharply as a result of forced labor, other forms of mistreatment, and the spread of diseases new to the Americas.
7. The Spanish and Portuguese brought African slaves to work in the colonies.
8. Europeans brought new political and religious institutions, languages, technology, foods, styles of architecture, farming methods, and animals to the Americas, and they came to dominate the culture. Europeans learned about the hammock, the ca-

noe, the tepee, and many food crops from the Indians.
9. Intermarriage between Europeans and Indians produced mestizos, and intermarriage between Europeans and Africans produced mulattos. Both groups grew more quickly than the Indian population because the children who survived infancy tended to be more immune to disease than their Indian parents.
10. The population did not suffer long-term loss and the culture was largely unaffected.
11. Britain in 1807; the United States in 1808.

Critical Thinking Skills

1. Answers will vary.
2. In the Middle Ages, wealth meant land; by the time of the Commercial Revolution successful merchants had come to view wealth as money and goods. Medieval nobles left their money idle or spent it on luxuries, and rulers and landowning nobles looked down on moneymaking and hard work. During the Commercial Revolution, merchants believed that money should be used to make more money and they considered hard work and thrift to be virtues. Without these changes in attitudes, it can be argued that this revolution might not have taken place, since it was the industrious traders in their pursuit of profit who helped launch and sustain the Commercial Revolution.
3. (a) effect; cause (b) effect; cause (c) cause; effect (d) effect; cause
4. Answers will vary. Students may suggest that slavery is never justifiable and that the Africans may not have wanted to change their religion.

Thinking About Geography

Answers will vary. Students may suggest that trading posts were established along the coast and near rivers where they were easy to reach by boat, rather than inland in hard-to-reach areas.

Enrichment: Primary Sources

1. Their country was rich in natural resources, so it was easy to grow or obtain food and the people had few needs.
2. Students might suggest that they produced the goods themselves.
3. The villagers had few goods to sell, and barter was the standard form of trade.
4. Students might suggest that the people did not support the type of slave trading in which people were taken from their villages by force and sold to slave traders. However, they did not oppose slavery altogether, as suggested by their willingness to sell prisoners of war and criminals to the Oye-Ebo.

A Changed and Changing World   1450–1807

See chapter timeline, p. 381.

Before You Read This Chapter

How often do you or your friends eat foods made with chocolate? Tomatoes? Potatoes? Corn? If you had grown up in Europe before 1500, you would never have tasted any of these foods, because they came from the Americas. History affects more than kings or governments— it changes people's everyday lives. The grand colonial empires of the 1500's are gone. The changes in population patterns, daily life, and business methods that began then are still with us. As you read, try to identify the long-lasting effects of the events in this chapter.

The Geographic Setting

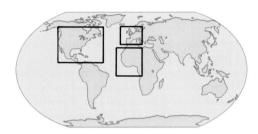

The Chapter Outline

1. A Revolution in Economic Life
2. New Populations in the Americas
3. Africa and the Slave Trade

This painting shows a Dutch fleet returning from a voyage to Brazil. The Dutch relied on overseas trade for much of their wealth.

1 A Revolution in Economic Life

Objectives

Focus Questions

★ ■ How did mercantilism change trade and business practices? *(pages 367–368)*
● ■ What changes occurred in the European economy in the 1500's and 1600's? *(pages 369–372)*

Terms to Know

Commercial
  Revolution
mercantilism
balance of
  trade
joint-stock
  company
inflation

capitalism
capital
free-enterprise
  system
law of supply
  and demand
market economy

★ Note strategies for first objective on this page and p. 368.

The voyages of exploration that began in the 1400's brought European nations vast new lands and new resources. Important changes occurred in ways of carrying on business and trade. Even greater changes took place in the ways that people thought about money and economic life. Thus the developments of the years 1450–1700 are often referred to as the **Commercial Revolution**.

Mercantilism

The manor-centered economy of the early Middle Ages had given way to a town-centered economy in the late medieval period. This, in turn, later gave way to a state-centered economy. During the Age of Exploration, European rulers increased their power enormously. The combination of booming economic growth and expanding royal power gave rise to the theory known as **mercantilism** (MUR-kun-til-iz-um). Mercantilists believed that the power of the state could be greatly increased if economic activities were carried on according to certain basic principles:

1. Accumulation of wealth. One mercantilist principle was that the state should build up wealth in the form of precious metals—gold and silver bullion. In the 1600's a ruler's power was judged by the luxury of the royal court and the size of the armed forces. Since armies were made up mostly of hired soldiers, a ruler short of cash could not afford to build a large navy or recruit a large army. Royal power therefore depended on a plentiful supply of bullion.

To increase the country's supply of bullion, rulers encouraged exports, which brought money into the country. To stop precious metals from leaving the country, they discouraged or outlawed imports. If the country sold more than it bought, it would have a favorable **balance of trade**. The term *balance of trade* means the difference in value between imports and exports.

2. Trade with colonies. Colonies played an important part in mercantilist thinking. Mercantilists saw colonies as a source of profit for the home country. The colony was expected to supply wealth—either gold or silver from its mines or valuable raw materials. For example, spices came from the East Indies, and sugar came from the Americas.

Mercantilists insisted that colonies buy goods from the home country, not from other countries or even other colonies. For instance, even though both Mexico and South America were under Spanish control, goods exchanged between these two areas first had to be shipped to Seville in Spain, then sent back across the Atlantic. Merchants and shipowners in Spain, not the colonies, made most of the profit.

Sec. Rev. ques. 2

367

★ RETEACHING. Have students review "Mercantilism" (above) and define the term *mercantilism* by answering the following questions: What? (The belief that the power of the state could be increased by following certain economic principles.) When? (1450–1700.) Why? (Great economic growth helped expand royal power.) How? (Accumulation of wealth and trade with colonies.) *(Comprehension) Observing for Detail*

★ REINFORCEMENT. Have students make a chart titled *Effects of Mercantilism.* Students should organize the effects of mercantilism in two columns labeled *Positive* and *Negative* and explain who enjoyed the benefits and who suffered the disadvantages of mercantilism. (*Effects:* desire for bullion; increased exports and colonial trade; start of joint-stock companies; increased European rivalry.) *(Comprehension) Making Judgments*

Changing Trade Practices

Joint-stock companies. It took large amounts of money to send ships from Europe to Asia or the Americas. Moreover, while profits could be great, so were the risks. Many ships never completed the long and dangerous ocean voyage. Few individual merchants could afford the high costs of an Asian voyage or the loss of a ship at sea.

To pay for trading voyages, a new type of business arrangement developed. It was called the **joint-stock company**. It ran in much the same way as a modern corporation: investors bought shares of stock that gave them part ownership in the business. This arrangement attracted large amounts of money and at the same time reduced the risk to individual investors.

Two of the most successful joint-stock companies were the English East India Company and the Dutch East India Company. After one very profitable voyage, the English company paid its investors more than twice the sum they had first put into the venture. For centuries the Dutch East India Company paid its stockholders large profits on their investments.

★ See below, right.

Working for wealth. In feudal times, wealth had meant land. To the new class of rich traders, however, wealth was money and goods. Rich middle-class merchants believed that money should be used to make more money. Instead of leaving their savings idle or buying luxuries, they wanted to put their money to work. For the middle class, hard work and thrift were important virtues. This outlook was very different from that of most rulers and aristocrats, who looked down on moneymaking and those who took part in it.

Sec. Rev. ques. 3

Dutch traders were typical of the new class of wealthy merchants—tough-minded, hardworking individuals out to make money. They found ways to lower costs, drove hard bargains to get the maximum profits, and tried to capture more and more of the market from competitors. The Dutch fought to sail their ships everywhere and deal in every type of good.

368

Rivalries at sea. European rulers and states competed fiercely for the new wealth of the colonies throughout the world. In the 1500's the Portuguese grew rich by monopolizing the trade in African slaves and Asian spices. Spain prospered from the treasure its rulers received from the Americas. Monarchs in other European countries realized that one way to weaken Spain was to cut off the flow of American gold and silver.

Both patriotism and the hope of a fortune brought pirates to the Caribbean to attack Spanish treasure ships. Merchant privateers smuggled goods into Spanish colonies, plundered towns along the Caribbean coast, and captured ships loaded with silver, gold, and gems from Spanish colonial mines. Dutch and English joint-stock companies, with royal approval, waged naval war against Spain.

The Spanish monopoly in the Americas began to crack in 1562. A daring English merchant, John Hawkins, defied Spanish trade laws and brought European goods and African slaves to the Spanish settlements in the Caribbean. The colonists of these settlements welcomed Hawkins, and he sold his cargo at a good profit.

In 1577 Hawkins's cousin, Francis Drake, sailed his ship the *Golden Hind* into the Pacific. Along the west coast of South America he attacked Spanish ships, seizing tons of silver and other treasure. Fearing capture if he headed back to England across the Atlantic, Drake sailed westward across the Pacific instead. Three years later he returned home—a hero congratulated by Queen Elizabeth herself. Like Magellan's crew nearly 60 years earlier, Drake and his men had circumnavigated the globe.

Before long, France and the Netherlands also began to prey on Spanish ships, particularly those carrying gold and silver. In 1628 Admiral Piet Heyn (PEET HYN) of the Dutch West India Company captured the Spanish silver fleet in the Caribbean. The treasure included four million gold and silver coins. It helped the Dutch finance their war against Spanish rule and made Heyn a Dutch national hero.

Economics Note that a joint-stock company differed from a modern corporation in that shareholders in joint-stock companies were personally liable for a company's debts.

Check for Understanding. Ask: How did joint-stock companies help finance trading voyages? (The purchase of stock by many investors created large amounts of money that could be used to finance voyages.)

★ **ENRICHMENT. Have students write a report comparing the organization of joint-stock companies and modern corporations.** (Application) *Locating Information*

Check for Understanding. Ask: How did the middle-class attitude toward work and money differ from that of aristocrats? (The middle class valued hard work and thrift; aristocrats looked down on moneymaking and those who took part in it.)

Ⓕ FEATURE ACTIVITY. Ask: How might this painting reflect middle-class life? (The fine room and clothing, and the man's profession as a geographer.) (Comprehension) *Observing for Detail*

Ⓕ See above.

The Arts

Dutch Painting

By the early 1600's, the Dutch were masters of the seas. They prospered from the spice and sugar trade with their colonies in the East and West Indies. As Italian merchants had done during the Renaissance, Dutch merchants spent some of their profits on art.

The Dutch artists of this period worked in a different style from French and Italian painters. Instead of classical scenes, Dutch art focused on the beauty of everyday life—a person reading a letter, a woman weighing pearls, or a man making pancakes.

Merchants and artisans—not kings or nobles—were the primary supporters of Dutch art. A traveler who visited Amsterdam in 1640 reported that even butchers, bakers, blacksmiths, and cobblers hung paintings in their homes and shops. As a result, much of Dutch art reflects middle-class life.

The straightforward realism and the skillful use of light in Jan Vermeer's *The Geographer* (shown here) is typical of Dutch painting. Vermeer's use of geog-

***The Geographer* by Jan Vermeer.**

raphy as a subject is also typical. Geography was, after all, of great interest to those who bought Vermeer's paintings. Dutch merchants owned ships that visited ports around the world. To them, the new geographic knowledge that had begun to appear with the great voyages of the 1400's was vitally important.

Upheavals in the European Economy

● Note strategies for second objective on this page and p. 371.

Inflation. The Americas had been a new and unexpected source of great wealth for Spain and Portugal. Gold poured in from the Inca Empire and the mines of Brazil. Silver flowed from the rich mines of Mexico and Peru (including what is now Bolivia).

This huge supply of precious metals was desirable from a mercantilist point of view, but it also created problems. Rich Europeans used their wealth to buy more goods and

food. As these products became scarce, prices began to rise. At the same time, population throughout Europe was growing, and more people needed more food and other goods. This, too, made prices rise—particularly for basic foods like bread and grain. The result was **inflation**—a sharp, steady rise in prices caused by excess demand.

Inflation affected different groups of people in different ways. Landowning nobles, who received fixed rents from peasants, could no longer buy as much with the same income. City workers found that their wages bought less food as prices continued to increase.

369

● RETEACHING. Have students review "The Foundations of Capitalism" (pp. 371–372) and outline the three major characteristics of capitalism. (Private ownership: capital belongs to individuals who are free to decide how to use it. Profit motive: the law of supply and demand leads producers to supply what is wanted. Market economy: price and quantity decisions are made in a free market.) (Comprehension) *Organizing Information in Written Form*

● REINFORCEMENT. Have students work in groups to present different points of view about the effects of capitalism. Students might present interviews or biographical sketches that show how capitalism may have affected a poor peasant, a merchant, a landowning noble, a city worker, or a banker. (Application) *Understanding Points of View*

World Trade, 1763

European merchant ships of the late 1700's followed the routes shown here. What was the extent of the British colonial empire during this time? Compare this map with the one on page 361. How had France's possessions in North America changed by 1763?

Map Answers: (1) It included much of the eastern half of North America as well as Gibraltar and territory in the Caribbean, West Africa, and India. (2) France lost all possessions in North America except the islands of Miquelon and St. Pierre.

Merchants, on the other hand, often profited by charging higher and higher prices for the goods they sold. Because people were demanding more goods than Europe could produce, foreign trade boomed.

Changes in agriculture. In England the demand for more food led some greedy landlords to snatch up farmland that had been set aside for community use. Landlords also raised rents on farms. As a result, thousands of English men and women had to leave the land their families had farmed for many generations.

The landlords then hired these displaced people to work for low wages, or they rented the land to prosperous independent farmers. Both the landowners and the independent farmers profited from this change in

ASIA

JAPAN
•Nagasaki

CHINA

BENGAL
•Macau

INDIA
Bombay•
Goa•
Madras•
Pondicherry•

CEYLON

SOUTH
CHINA
SEA

PHILIPPINE
ISLANDS

PACIFIC
OCEAN

INDIAN
OCEAN

SUMATRA

BORNEO

MOLUCCAS

E A S T   I N D I E S

CELEBES

NEW GUINEA

JAVA

NEW HOLLAND
(AUSTRALIA)

Arctic Circle

SCALE
0   2,000 mi
0   2,000 km

The Foundations of Capitalism

The busy town life and thriving trade that developed in the late Middle Ages laid the foundation for **capitalism**—an economic system based on the private ownership and use of capital. **Capital** is wealth, in the form of property or money, that is used to make more money. Land, tools and machinery, ships, and shops are all capital.

Capitalism has three major features:

1. Private ownership. In a capitalist system, capital belongs to individuals, who are free to decide what to do with it. They may put money in the bank to draw interest. They may use it to start their own business or invest it in a company of their choosing. Because the owners of capital are free to do with it what they please, capitalism is often called the **free-enterprise system**.

2. Profit motive. In a capitalist system, when the demand for a product is greater than the supply of that product, the price goes up. Conversely, when the supply of a product exceeds the demand, the price goes down. This principle has become known as the **law of supply and demand**.

When enough people want a certain product, producers will supply it because they want to make a profit. The demand for sugar, for example, led to the development of plantations where sugar cane could be grown. A company produces goods and services to make profits for those who have invested in it—that is, its owners. The profit motive—the wish to make a profit—is an essential part of capitalism.

Sec. Rev. ques. 4

3. Market economy. In capitalism a money value is placed on all forms of property. That is, just about everything—land, goods, people's time and labor—can be bought and sold. Buyers and sellers of goods and services are free to exchange these things; prices are determined by supply and demand. Because price and quantity decisions are made in a free market, capitalism is sometimes called the **market economy**.

Development of capitalism. During the late Middle Ages, new business practices **371**

agriculture. The small farmers who had lost their land, however, made up a new group of homeless poor looking for work. Like trade, agriculture had become commercial—farmland and farm labor had become things that were bought and sold. This marked a great change from farming in the Middle Ages, when farm workers were bound to the land on the lords' estates.

● See below.

Check for Understanding. Ask: How did mercantilism change the use of farmland and labor? (Land and labor became goods that were bought and sold.)
● ENRICHMENT. Have students form a hypothesis about how agricultural changes caused by mercantilism might have been different if peasants had owned land and had access to sizable amounts of money. (Synthesis) Forming a Hypothesis

Check for Understanding. Ask: What is capital? (Money and goods that are used to make more money.) What is capitalism? (The economic system based on private ownership and use of capital.)
Check for Understanding. Ask: What is inflation? (A sharp, steady rise in prices caused by excess demand.) What is the law of supply and demand? (The principle that when demand for a product exceeds its availability, prices rise; when the supply exceeds demand, prices fall.)

in Italy spurred the development of capitalism in a number of ways. Profits from trade and interest on loans enabled Italian merchants and bankers to build up large amounts of capital, which they reinvested in their own businesses or in other enterprises. Sometimes merchants also pooled their money and expanded their businesses. As business activity increased, merchants came up with bookkeeping systems to keep track of the flow of money. The development of banking and the use of credit (page 231) also made business dealings easier.

The capitalist practices of the Middle Ages became more widespread during the Commercial Revolution, spurred by the enormous growth in international trade. The mercantile capitalism of the 1600's and 1700's differed from modern capitalism. For example, there were no large industries like those of today. Yet mercantile capitalism helped make modern industrial capitalism possible.

See Sec. 1 *Closing the Lesson*, p. T365B.

See lesson plans, pp. T365A–T365C.

5. Students might note that a free market responds quickly to demand; that competition keeps prices low while encouraging producers to maintain quality; and that capitalists are motivated to reinvest profits.

2 New Populations in the Americas

Objectives

Focus Questions

★ ■ What groups made up the population of the Americas? *(pages 372–374)*
● ■ How did peoples in the Americas influence one another's cultures? *(pages 374–376)*

Terms to Know

indentured servant	mulatto
mestizo	maroon

★ Note strategies for first objective on this page and p. 373.

European colonization of the Americas forever altered the Western Hemisphere. Vast changes occurred as people came into con-

372

tact with one another's ideas, beliefs, and customs. All the way from the tip of South America to the northern regions of North America, diverse societies began to take shape.

Shifts in World Population

The balance of world population shifted after Europeans settled among Africans, American Indians, and Asians. During the centuries of colonial rule, the population of the Americas changed dramatically.

American Indians. The Spanish conquest of the Caribbean islands and much of North and South America took the lives of thousands of Indians. Forced labor and other mistreatment claimed countless more. However, the most deadly result of the European

Sec. Rev. ques. 2

★ RETEACHING. Have students review "Shifts in World Population" (pp. 372–374) and then write a one-sentence summary of what happened to each of the three major population groups in the Americas. (*American Indians:* population reduced by disease, forced labor, and mistreatment. *Africans:* forced to serve as slaves. *Europeans:* gained economic profit; found religious and political freedom.) (*Comprehension*) *Observing for Detail*

★ REINFORCEMENT. Have students write a paragraph comparing the way Europeans treated Indians and Africans in the Americas. (Both Indians and Africans suffered from forced labor and mistreatment, but Indians had not been shipped from another continent. Both groups suffered many deaths from disease. Eventually Indians were protected from slavery.) (*Comprehension*) *Organizing Ideas in Written Form* expansion was the spread of diseases new to the Americas. In the span of a generation, smallpox, measles, flu, and the common cold killed millions of Indians, who had no natural immunities against these diseases. Indian populations on larger Caribbean islands were wiped out altogether. In some parts of the Mexican mainland, the population fell to about one twentieth of what it had been before Europeans arrived.

Sec. Rev. ques. 3

African slaves. The deaths of so many Indians caused a severe labor shortage in the Spanish colonies. The Spanish rulers tried to protect the Indians by forbidding slavery. By the mid-1500's Portuguese settlers in Brazil also needed workers for their newly established sugar plantations. Their solution was to import slaves from Africa.

In 1518 Spain licensed Portuguese slave traders to ship captured Africans directly to

Graph Answer: 1530–1550.

The decline of central Mexico's population resulted from war, slavery, and disease. Which 20-year period showed the steepest decline?

Decline in the Population of Central Mexico, 1532–1608

millions

Estimated population (y-axis: 0, 2, 4, 6, 8, 10, 12, 14, 16, 18, 20)

Year (x-axis: 1530, 1550, 1570, 1590, 1610)

Source: Borah and Cook, *The Aboriginal Population of Central Mexico on the Eve of the Spanish Conquest*

Background By 1550 the Spanish colonies were receiving approximately 4,000 slaves annually.

the Americas. The Spanish Crown justified this new policy by two arguments: (1) Africans were not Christians and had already been enslaved in Africa. Being sent to America would not change their status as slaves, and it would give them the chance to convert to Christianity. (2) Africans were thought to be used to heavy field work in a tropical climate, while the Indians were not. African slaves soon did most of the hard labor on plantations throughout tropical regions of the Americas.

★ See below.

The first shipload of African slaves sailed from western Africa to the West Indies in 1518. Over the next 350 years, the traffic in human beings grew steadily. All through South America, the West Indies, and the English colonies of North America, African slaves toiled in the mines and on plantations. Others worked as servants and artisans. When the trade finally ended in the mid-1800's, between 10 and 12 million young Africans had been shipped across the Atlantic.

From the time the first Africans landed in the Americas until 1800, seven times as many Africans arrived as Europeans. Slaves were brought to the colonies where the demand for plantation labor was heaviest. Before 1650 most slaves were sent to the Portuguese colony of Brazil to work on sugar plantations. A large number also went to Spanish America, especially to Peru, where they mined gold and silver.

After 1650 the different islands of the West Indies became the major destination for slaves. The Dutch had set up sugar plantations there and the English and French quickly did the same. Sugar-growing became hugely successful during the 1700's. Two large islands captured from the Spanish were especially important. Jamaica grew into England's major plantation island; Hispaniola became the location of the French colony of St. Domingue.

The English colonies that eventually became the United States imported few slaves before 1700. At first, slaves were brought mainly to Virginia and the Carolinas to grow tobacco and rice. When the demand for cotton rose in the late 1700's, more and more **373**

Background Remind students that the Treaty of Tordesillas (p. 351) gave Portugal a monopoly of new territory east of the Line of Demarcation. Thus the Spanish had to rely on Portuguese traders to supply African slaves.

Social History In the 1700's sugar became Jamaica's major crop, and the island ranked as the most important slave market in the West. In present-day Jamaica, more than 90 percent of the population have African or African and European ancestry.

★ **ENRICHMENT.** Have students review "African slaves" (pp. 373–374) and evaluate the Spanish Crown's justification of the use of slaves in the Americas. Students should explain why the Spanish monarch believed the enslavement of Africans was legitimate. Then have students write an argument opposing the Spanish Crown's point of view. *(Evaluation)* **Evaluating Information**

Geography Present-day Hispaniola includes the nations of Haiti and the Dominican Republic.

Colonial plantations in the Caribbean used slave laborers to grow sugar cane. Freshly cut cane was crushed at a windmill and then boiled to produce sugar and molasses. This picture shows slaves working at a sugar mill on the Caribbean island of Antigua.

slaves were imported to work in the fields. Plantations using slave labor began spreading westward to the Mississippi River and the lands beyond.

Europeans. European immigration was also very important in repopulating the Americas. The Spanish and Portuguese came first, seeking adventure and riches. After 1600 most immigrants were from Northern Europe. Some were sent as slaves, like the Scots and the Irish taken prisoner by the English in seventeenth-century wars. Other immigrants were **indentured servants**—people who agreed to work a certain number of years for an American employer in exchange for paid passage overseas. Many newcomers arrived in search of religious, political, or personal freedom, like the Puritans in New England. In the 1700's the English colonies in North America had the greatest increase in European settlers.

374

Cultural Exchange in the Americas

● Note strategies for second objective on this page and p. 375.

European influences. European settlers brought new political and religious institutions to the Americas. Royal governors laid down European codes of law as well as systems of private ownership of land. Missionaries spread Christianity.

The settlers also carried with them European languages, technology, foods, and styles of architecture. The Spanish conquerors brought horses and firearms. Later settlers introduced the metal fishhook, the potter's wheel, the plow, and new techniques of weaving and farming. They brought many new food crops (such as wheat) and fruits (such as apples, pears, and oranges). The introduction of new domestic animals—chickens, cattle, pigs, sheep, goats, mules, and donkeys—changed diet and transportation.

Sec. Rev. ques. 4

The Europeans' culture dominated the Americas. Their governments and religions were the only ones officially recognized. Moreover, persons of European descent formed a third of the population of the Americas by 1800. This happened because European immigrants, even those who came as slaves or indentured servants, had better food and housing than the Africans or Indians, and so their numbers grew faster.

Indian influences. In spite of European dominance, Indian culture did not completely disappear. Many Indians lived beyond the frontier of European settlement. There they continued to follow traditional ways of life. Furthermore, European settlers borrowed many things from Indian culture. In tropical America they slept in Indian hammocks; settlers to the north used canoes and tepees. In addition, Europeans quickly adopted the plants grown by American Indians. Potatoes, corn, tomatoes, squash, pumpkins, and chocolate became part of their diet. In time these tastes spread to Europe too.

New population groups. Intermarriage was common between European or African men and Indian women in the colonies. Children of Indians and Europeans were called **mestizos**. The descendants of Europeans and Africans were called **mulattos**. Most of these people spoke Spanish or Portuguese, were baptized Christians, and followed other European ways. In Brazil, where social class lines were not rigid, people from all groups mingled freely, particularly in the towns.

Sec. Rev. ques. 5

This "mixed" population grew more quickly than the Indian population. While many children died before the age of two, those who survived infancy tended to be more immune to disease than their Indian parents. In much of Latin America—the lands of Central and South America where Spanish and Portuguese are spoken—people of mixed ancestry came to make up most of the urban population.

The African slave population. The Africans who were brought to the Americas also strongly influenced life there. Black cultures developed in Brazil, the Caribbean, and North America.

On slave plantations, newly arrived Africans had to learn enough of the European language to follow orders. However, in the slave quarters they used their native languages and kept African traditions of storytelling, dancing, and music alive. Some slaves were required to attend Christian church services, but they secretly followed African religious customs as well. The slaves also held on to other African traditions—basketry, pottery, wood-carving, and styles of clothing—as reminders of their former way of life.

Free Africans. Not all blacks in the Americas remained in slavery. Some earned or were given their freedom. There were also communities of runaway slaves, called **maroons**, who fought hard to defend their freedom. Maroons in Dutch Guiana (now Suriname) and Jamaica, for example, were never conquered. In 1800 free blacks outnumbered black slaves in Spanish America by two to one. A third of all Brazilian blacks were free. However, free blacks were only a small minority in the non-Spanish Caribbean and in North America.

● See below.

Varieties of peoples and cultures. At the end of the 1700's the population of the Americas formed a patchwork of different cultures. European languages—Spanish, Portuguese, French, English, and Dutch—were commonly spoken except among isolated Indian communities. Different racial groups

Linking Past and Present

Colonists in the Americas sent samples of American Indian crops back to their home countries, and the cultivation of these crops gradually spread around the world. Today American Indian corn accounts for about one sixth of all the grain produced in the world. Root crops such as cassava, sweet potatoes, and white potatoes are grown in places as distant from the Americas as China, the Soviet Union, and the nations of Africa.

375

predominated in different places. Europeans dominated in British North America, mestizos in Mexico, blacks in the Caribbean and Brazil, and Indians in much of Central and South America.

Yet out of this diversity some common cultural patterns were emerging. No matter what their language or origins, persons born in the Americas thought of themselves as different from those born elsewhere. Their speech, diet, dress, and tastes were the product of the different populations—European, African, and Indian—that intermixed. These people felt at home in the Americas; they had no memory of a homeland abroad. In the late 1700's and early 1800's, they would organize revolutions to overthrow colonial rule and establish independent states in most of the Americas (Chapter 23).

See Sec. 2 *Closing the Lesson,* p. T365C.

See lesson plans, pp. T365A–T365C.

(pp. 372–373)

Section Review

Answers to Section Review questions are in brackets on pages indicated.

1. **Define:** indentured servant, mestizo, mulatto, maroon. (pp. 374, 375)
2. What happened to American Indians when Europeans began to colonize?
3. Why were Africans first brought to the Americas? (p. 373)
4. In what ways did cultural exchange take place between Europeans and American Indians? (pp. 374–375)
5. How did the mixed population differ from the native Indians? (p. 375)
6. **Critical thinking:** Why did African slaves try to preserve traditions from their homelands? (See answer below.)

6. Students might suggest that Africans sought to maintain their cultural identity. Because Africans were forcibly cut off from their homeland, their religious and social traditions, languages and art helped to sustain a memory of Africa.

3 Africa and the Slave Trade

Objectives

Focus Questions

★ ■ What factors contributed to the growth of the slave trade? *(pages 376–378)*
● ■ How did the slave trade affect Africa? *(pages 378–381)*

Terms to Know

Middle Passage
abolitionist

★ Note strategies for first objective on this page and p. 378.

While the slave trade was changing the population and culture of the Americas, it was also having a great effect on Africa. As you read in Chapter 15, trade was an important cause of the growth of many African states and empires. From ancient times trade had **376** brought new religions, new weapons, and other cultural influences to northern and eastern Africa. The voyages of Europeans along the West African coast promised similar benefits. At first, Africa's mineral and agricultural resources were the main goods offered in trade. Soon, however, trade with Europe involved a very different type of resource—the African people themselves.

The Origins of the Slave Trade

Slavery in African society. In Africa, as in the rest of the world, slavery had existed since ancient times. War captives, criminals, debtors, or the very poor were likely to become slaves. Some slaves served as trusted officials in African states. Other slaves were exported from Africa across the Sahara, the Red Sea, and the Indian Ocean. New markets for slaves in the Americas led to a vast increase in the export of African slaves.

European trade with Africa. As you read in Chapter 18, Portuguese explorers

★ RETEACHING. Have students review "The Origins of the Slave Trade" (pp. 376–377) and draw a map of Africa illustrating the areas discussed in the section. Students should label the areas to show the **kingdoms, rivers, and products involved in European trade.** (Regions include Gold Coast, Niger River, Congo River, Kingdom of Benin, Kingdom of Kongo.) (Comprehension) *Connecting History and Geography*

★ REINFORCEMENT. Have students make a chart organizing the information on the capture of Africans for trade. (Prisoners taken from battles between African states; children and young adults kidnapped; debtors seized; criminals sold as punishment.) (Comprehension) *Translating Information into Another Form* began sailing south along the coast of western Africa during the 1400's. Their main goal was to find a route around Africa to India, but the Portuguese also traded with the coastal kingdoms of Africa.

The people of the Kongo kingdom wanted to trade with the Portuguese, but they had none of the things—gold, pepper, or ivory—that the Portuguese wanted to buy. The king of the Kongo then agreed to sell slaves to the Portuguese. The slaves were brought to Portugal, where they served as house servants.

Increasing demand for slaves. In the 1490's and early 1500's, the Portuguese began growing sugar cane on islands off the African coast. To plant and harvest the crop, they used African slaves. At first the slave trade was small. However, as the sugar plantations expanded, more and more slaves were brought from the Kongo.

Sec. Rev. ques. 2

Alarmed by this growing trade, King Affonso (who ruled the Kongo about 1505–1545) tried to stop it. The king, a Catholic who had been educated in Portugal, urged his "brother"—the king of Portugal—to end the traffic in slaves:

> 66 We cannot reckon how great the damage is, since the slave traders are taking every day our natives, sons of the land and the sons of our noblemen and vassals and our relatives. Our country is being completely depopulated. That is why we beg Your Highness to help and assist us in this matter, because it is our will that in these kingdoms there should not be any trade in slaves nor outlet for them. 99

However, Affonso's appeal and others made to the Pope in Rome failed to stop the trade.

When plantations were set up in Brazil and the West Indies, the demand for slaves soared. Some African rulers, like those in Benin and on the Gold Coast, resisted selling slaves for a time. Others took part willingly in order to get the goods offered in return. By the 1600's the trade in slaves had overtaken the early trade in gold and pepper.

The Triangular Trade

The slave trade was part of a triangular trade that linked Europe, Africa, and the Americas. It began with ships loaded with goods leaving Europe for Africa. These ships then called at many locations along the African coast. At some of these trading posts, Europeans built permanent coastal forts and warehouses. At others, slave traders lived on their ships and only came on shore at the invitation of the African rulers.

The supply of slaves for export came from a number of sources. Perhaps the largest number of slaves were prisoners captured in battles between African kingdoms. In some areas of Africa large numbers of children and young adults were kidnapped and sold in slave markets for export. Sometimes debtors were seized and sold. Other people were enslaved as a punishment for crimes.

Sec. Rev. ques. 3

There was much difficult negotiating with European traders over the goods to be

King Affonso is shown receiving European ambassadors. The Portuguese carried on a slave trade with the Kongo beginning in the 1500's.

377

Check for Understanding. Ask: What groups were Africans likely to enslave? (War captives, children, debtors, and criminals.) What led to Portugal's use of slaves? (Portuguese settlers needed labor for sugar plantations.)
Critical Thinking. Ask: Why might King Affonso have thought that the king of Portugal would fulfill the request to stop the slave trade? (Affonso, who was educated in Portugal and had accepted the Catholic faith, considered the Portuguese king his "brother.")

Check for Understanding. Ask: On what grounds did King Affonso seek the end of the slave trade? (The depopulation of his country.)

Ⓕ See
below,
right.

The Geography Connection

The Triangular Trade

As Europeans traveled to new lands during the Age of Exploration, a remarkable fact emerged—sailing from Europe to North America took twice as long as sailing from North America to Europe. This fact can be explained by the presence of westerly winds and the Gulf Stream.

The Gulf Stream is a strong current that flows north along the coast of North America and then east across the Atlantic Ocean to Europe. This mighty stream is only one part of a vast system of currents that flow through the North Atlantic in a clockwise direction. During the 1600's and 1700's these currents enabled a triangular trade to develop between Europe, Africa, and the Americas.

For trading to be profitable, a ship had to be loaded with goods on each leg of its trip. Triangular trade routes were especially profitable, because ships usually sailed full and they usually sailed fast, aided by the wind and the current.

Over time, merchants formed several triangular trade routes (see map). On one route, ships set out from British ports, such as London or Bristol, loaded with cloth, firearms, and various low-cost goods. Sailing south with the wind and the Canary Current, the ships reached the coast of West Africa, where ship captains exchanged their cargo for slaves.

On the second leg of the voyage, the ships sailed west along the North Equatorial Current to colonies in the West Indies and North America. There the slaves were sold for huge profits and ship captains picked up new cargo consisting of lumber, rice, and other goods produced in the colonies. The ships then sailed back to England, taking advantage of the westerly winds and the Gulf Stream.

The geography of the North Atlantic set the pattern for triangular trade. By shortening the time spent at sea, this pattern helped make the trade profitable.

Making the connection. How did ocean currents and winds affect trade in the North Atlantic?

---

exchanged for each slave. Some of the goods Africans bargained for included cotton cloth, firearms, and Brazilian rum. In general, as the demand for slaves rose, so did the price paid for them, as Africans took advantage of their control over the supply of slaves.

The voyage of the slaves from Africa to the Americas was called the **Middle Passage**. The slave ships were crammed with as many Africans as they could hold. Kept below deck, breathing foul air and eating spoiled food, many people died as a result of disease. Others, overcome with despair, took their own lives. Those who survived the nightmarish voyage were unloaded and sold when the ships docked in the Americas. The ships then

★ See
below.
378

returned to Europe with sugar and other plantation products bought with the profits from the sale of African people.

The Impact of the Slave Trade

● Note strategies for second objective on pages 379 and 381.

Political effects. The effects of the slave trade varied widely from region to region of Africa. Generally, areas near the coast were affected much more than those farther inland, whose trade was mainly with other African kingdoms. Within coastal societies, merchants and the ruling classes profited from slavery, while other classes were harmed.

Sec. Rev.
ques. 4

Background On their voyage to the Americas, Africans were often shackled to one another below deck, in a space no higher than three feet.

★ **ENRICHMENT.** Have students write a short story describing the experience of a young African in the Middle Passage. The story might describe his or her capture and sale, the thoughts and feelings of the young person, and the experience of the voyage across the Atlantic. Have students read their stories in class. *(Application) Understanding Points of View*

Ⓕ **GEOGRAPHY CONNECTION.** Have students explain how triangular trade reflected these principles of mercantilism: (a) Colonies were expected to supply raw materials to the home country. (b) Colonies were expected to buy goods from the home country. *(Comprehension) Analyzing Information*

Triangular Trade Routes

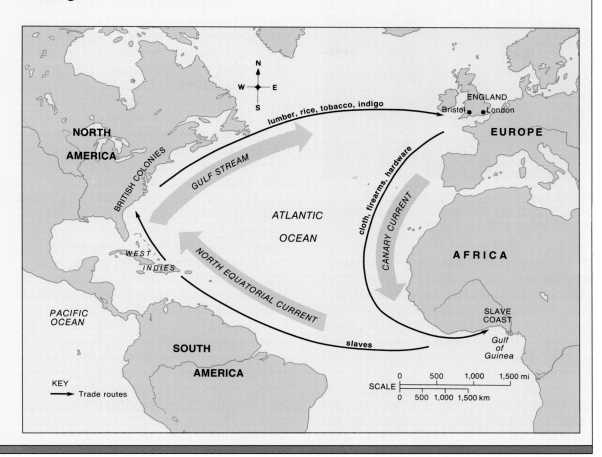

The slave trade played an especially important role in Angola (an-GOH-luh), which lay south of the Congo River. Along the coast of Angola the Portuguese established the main base for trading slaves in Africa. As you have read, the Portuguese demand for slaves weakened the nearby kingdom of the Kongo during the 1500's. In the 1600's the Portuguese encouraged a rebellion by local chiefs against the Kongo government, and later the Portuguese invaded the kingdom. It broke into several parts, each eventually brought under the control of Portugal.

Other kingdoms inland from the Kongo kept the Portuguese from extending their control. These kingdoms traded with the Portuguese for cloth and firearms over routes that reached far into the interior of the continent. The slaves traded for these goods were won in wars with other states.

Another major slave-trading region was West Africa, north of the equator. In the 1500's the western end of the coast, nearest the Americas, was favored by slave traders. At the peak of the trade in the 1700's, most slaves came from the Gulf of Guinea, at the eastern end of the coast (map, this page). One section of the Gulf coastline, the area from the Gold Coast to the Niger delta, became known as the Slave Coast.

The most important state along the Slave Coast was Dahomey (dah-HOH-may), **379**

This drawing, made by a British seaman in 1846, records the inhumane conditions that existed below deck on a slave ship.

Sec. Rev. ques. 4, cont.

which developed in the 1600's. This small state lay between powerful neighbors. From European traders Dahomey obtained firearms, which it used to expand and to defend itself against its neighbors. To pay for these weapons, Dahomey sold captives taken in its wars of expansion. Thus it became a powerful slave-trading center.

Much farther inland and northeast of Dahomey, was an older African kingdom called Oyo. This powerful kingdom of the Yoruba (YOH-roo-bah) people at first traded to the north through other African states that took part in trade across the Sahara. From this trade Oyo received horses, which gave it a powerful cavalry.

Oyo used its cavalry to raid Dahomey in 1730 and to make the Dahomeans pay an annual tribute. Oyo's part in the Atlantic slave trade remained fairly small. However, when the kingdom weakened and was overthrown in 1817 by invaders from the north, the Yoruba area was thrown into chaos. Decades of warfare followed. So many thousands of Yoruba people were sold into the Atlantic slave trade during this period that their language and religion became prominent in Brazil and Cuba.

On the other side of Dahomey and inland was the kingdom of Ashanti (ah-SHAHN-tee). It arose about 1795 in the area

380

just north of the Gold Coast. This state too participated in trade across the Sahara. It had a powerful ruler, whose symbol was a sacred throne called the Golden Stool. When Ashanti began to be raided by the smaller trading states on the Gold Coast, it pushed southward to establish order. This brought it into contact with the Atlantic slave trade.

Social effects. Both Africa's population and its culture managed to survive the slave trade. Some communities did lose many of their citizens to the slave traders. Because the slave trade was spread out over five centuries, however, Africa as a whole did not suffer long-term population loss.

Similarly, African culture remained largely unaffected by contact with Europeans. Regarding Africa as a source of slaves rather than a site for colonization, Europeans made few attempts to reshape African life. In fact, only a handful traveled to the interior of Africa. For most Europeans, Africa remained an unknown continent.

The true impact of slavery was felt by those enslaved. Torn from their homes, taken to strange new lands, and treated no better than animals, these unfortunate people were denied even the most basic rights. Their hardships were the clearest proof of the inhumanity of the slave trade.

The End of the Slave Trade

Three hundred years after the African slave trade began, European abolitionists—reformers who opposed slavery—began to write books and pamphlets describing the evils of slavery. Convinced that slavery was immoral, they worked to end the trade.

Finally, Britain prohibited the slave trade in 1807,* and the United States did likewise in 1808. Other European nations soon followed. Yet, because slavery itself was still legal, many Westerners found it profitable to continue the trade despite these laws and the naval patrols that tried to enforce them. A number of African kingdoms whose

---

* In 1707 England had joined with Scotland and Wales to form Great Britain.

Social History By the time the slave trade ended, approximately one third of all persons of African descent lived outside Africa.
Social History Note that, except for sections of South Africa, European slave traders generally were not interested in settlement but only in acquiring slaves for trade.

economies had grown dependent on profits from the slave trade also cooperated in keeping the trade going.

Increased British efforts against both European and African slave traders gradually choked off the export of slaves from western Africa. As this was happening, however, the slave trade from eastern Africa was undergoing an enormous increase. To escape the British naval patrols along the west coast of Africa, many European slave traders turned to Africa's east coast. The centuries-old slave trade with the Arab lands of the Middle East continued in the nineteenth century. Not until about 1870, after slavery had been abolished nearly everywhere in the Americas, did ● See the Atlantic trade come to an end.
below.

See Sec. 3 *Closing the Lesson,* p. T365C.

Chapter 19   Summary and Timeline

1. Mercantilist policies led European states to build foreign trade, accumulate wealth in the form of gold and silver, and set up colonies as sources of profit. The social and economic changes that took place in Europe and in European colonies changed the nature of the world economy. The new economic outlook emphasized the money value of land and labor, and the investment of capital to make a profit. The Commercial Revolution saw the beginning of the modern market economy.

2. With colonization, the population of the Americas came to include Europeans and Africans as well as native American Indians. As these peoples interacted, their cultures mixed as well. This exchange led to the formation of new and unique cultural patterns.

3. Because the European demand for slave labor increased, Africa's existing slave trade expanded. As a link in the Atlantic slave trade, Africa received European goods in exchange for slaves. The three centuries of slave trade had a long-lasting impact on Africa.

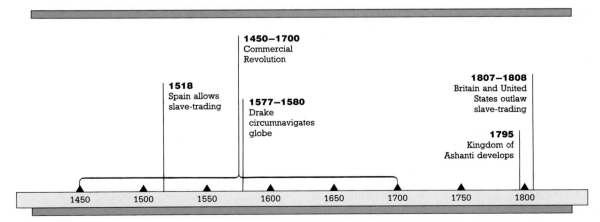

1450–1700 Commercial Revolution

1518 Spain allows slave-trading

1577–1580 Drake circumnavigates globe

1807–1808 Britain and United States outlaw slave-trading

1795 Kingdom of Ashanti develops

1450   1500   1550   1600   1650   1700   1750   1800

381

● ENRICHMENT. Have students work in groups to prepare a documentary titled *The African Slave Trade.* Students might research the following aspects of the slave trade: Europe's role, African rulers' participation, effects on Africa, destinations of slaves, the end of the slave trade. Have students present their documentaries to the class. *(Synthesis) Locating Information*

See p. T365D for answers to Chapter Review.

Vocabulary Review

Choose the term that best completes each sentence. Write your answers on a separate sheet of paper.

1. [Capitalism/Mercantilism] was an economic policy that stressed the accumulation of gold and silver, the establishment of colonies, and profit from foreign trade.
2. In a [market economy/joint-stock company] prices of goods and services are set by supply and demand.
3. Rising prices caused by a scarcity of goods is called [inflation/balance of trade].
4. Money or property that is used to produce more money is called [free-enterprise system/capital].
5. The voyage of slaves from Africa to the Americas was known as the [Commercial Revolution/Middle Passage].
6. A person whose parents were Indian and European was called a [mestizo/mulatto].
7. [Indentured servants/Abolitionists] were reformers who opposed slavery.

People to Identify

Identify the following people and tell why each was important.
1. Affonso
2. Francis Drake
3. John Hawkins
4. Piet Heyn

Places to Know

Match the letters on this map of West Africa during the slave trade with the places listed below. You may want to refer to the maps on pages 370 and 379.
1. Angola
2. Congo River
3. Niger River
4. Slave Coast

382

Recalling the Facts

1. According to the theory of mercantilism, how did rulers accumulate wealth?
2. What were the advantages of joint-stock companies?
3. What did England and other nations hope to gain by attacking Spanish ships?
4. How did increased wealth lead to inflation? To changes in agriculture?
5. What are the three major features of a capitalist economic system?
6. What effect did European expansion have on American Indians?
7. Why were Africans first brought to the Americas?
8. How did Europeans influence culture in the Americas? How did American Indians influence European settlers?
9. What new population groups emerged in the Americas? Why did these groups grow more rapidly than the Indians?
10. What was the effect of the slave trade on the population and culture of Africa?
11. When did Britain and the United States outlaw the slave trade?

1. **Writing a report.** Research and write a report about one of the following topics: Sir Francis Drake and the *Golden Hind;* John Hawkins; the English East India Company; the Dutch East India Company; the history of modern banking. *(App.)*

2. **Drawing conclusions.** What changes in attitudes toward wealth, work, and the uses of money accompanied the Commercial Revolution? Would the Commercial Revolution have been possible without these changes in attitudes? *(Syn.)*

3. **Identifying cause and effect.** In each of the following sets of statements identify which is the cause and which is the effect. *(Comp.)*

    a. Foreign trade increased.
    People demanded more goods than Europe could produce.

    b. The price of a product rises.
    The demand for a product is greater than its supply.

    c. Europeans in the Americas were better fed and housed than the Africans and Indians.
    The European population in the Americas grew more rapidly than either the African or the Indian population did.

    d. European traders exported slaves from Africa's east coast.
    The British worked to prevent the export of slaves from western Africa.

4. **Writing a rebuttal.** Reread the account of the Spanish Crown's justification of the African slave trade policy on page 373. Write a brief response opposing each of the two arguments presented. *(Syn.)*

Thinking About Geography

Using a map. Look at the physical map of Africa on page 151. Consider the role that rivers and other geographic features played in the development of the West African slave trade. Why, do you think, did Europeans establish trading posts where they did? *(App.)*

Enrichment: Primary Sources

Olaudah Equiano was a former slave who became an activist in the British antislavery movement. The passage below was adapted from Equiano's autobiography, which was published in 1789. He describes life in his village, in what is now the Benin province of Nigeria.

“ As we live in a country of great natural resources, our wants are few and easily supplied. Of course, we have few manufactured goods. They consist for the most part of cloths, pottery, ornaments, weapons, and farming tools. But these are not traded. The principal articles of trade are foodstuffs. In such a state money is of little use.

We also have markets. These are sometimes visited by men from the region southwest of us. We call them Oye-Ebo. They always carry slaves through our land, but they must account for their manner of getting the slaves before they are allowed to pass through. Sometimes we have sold slaves to them, but they have been only prisoners of war or such among us as have been convicted of kidnapping or some other crimes which we consider horrible. ”

1. According to Equiano, why was it easy for the people in his village to make a living?
2. How might the villagers have acquired the few manufactured goods they had?
3. Why was money of little use?
4. **Critical thinking:** Judging from this passage, how did the people of Equiano's village feel about slavery? *(Anal.)*

A checkmark identifies questions and exercises calling for the three higher-order levels of thinking at the top of the Bloom taxonomy: Analysis, Synthesis, and Evaluation.

T383A

Powerful States in Europe 1469–1796
(pp. 384–408)

Chapter Preview

Section 1 describes how Spain emerged as the dominant power in Europe and then lost economic and political strength. Section 2 traces the causes and effects of the Thirty Years' War on Europe; the triumph of absolute monarchy under the French king, Louis XIV, is described in Section 3. Changes in England that led to the limiting of the monarch's power by Parliament are explained in Section 4. The final section of the chapter considers the formation of states in Eastern Europe, particularly Poland, Hungary, and Russia.

Bibliography

See the *Teacher's Management and Planning Guide* for additional listings. Starred titles are for both students and teachers.

*Blitzer, Charles. *The Age of Kings*. Time-Life. Seventeenth-century Europe comes to life in this colorful and interesting volume.

Cronin, Vincent. *Catherine, Empress of All the Russians*. Morrow. Covers both the political and the personal aspects of Catherine's life.

Massie, R. K. *Peter the Great: His Life and World*. Knopf. Portrays Peter's unquenchable energy in his struggle to remold Russia in a more modern image.

Mitford, Nancy. *The Sun King*. Harper & Row. The daily life of Louis XIV and his glittering court at Versailles.

*Smith, Lacey Baldwin. *Elizabeth Tudor*. Little, Brown. A readable biography of England's first Queen Elizabeth.

*Wilkinson, Burke. *Cardinal in Armor*. Macmillan. A fascinating biography of France's Cardinal Richelieu.

Section Lesson Plans

SECTION 1   (pp. 385–389)
The Era of Spanish Domination

Objectives

After completing this section, students will be able to:
1. Describe how Spain became a world power.
2. Discuss why Spanish power faded in the 1600's.

Introducing the Lesson

Remind students that Spain was controlled by the Muslims from the 700's (p. 201) until the 1200's. Isabella and Ferdinand and their successors took strong action to reunite and strengthen Spain and to make it a leading power.

    Then ask: (a) *How do you think a country becomes a leading power?* (Answers will vary. Becoming a power might mean that a country develops a stronger economy, controls more territory, or becomes militarily stronger than others.)

    (b) *What actions might rulers have taken during the fifteenth century to make their countries leading powers?* (Answers will vary. Rulers might have taken steps to repress or resolve social unrest, develop foreign trade and exploration, or strengthen the army and navy.)

    (c) *What might a present-day leader do to enhance national power?* (Answers will vary.)

Developing the Lesson: Making Judgments

Have students write an essay to answer the following question: *Is religious intolerance in the best interests of a nation?* When writing their essays, students should review Spain's religious policies in the late 1400's and consider possible motives and results of such a policy. (*Evaluation*)

Closing the Lesson:
Understanding Cause and Effect

Have students explain the following cause-effect relationship: *Some of the efforts made by Spain to increase its strength actually resulted in a loss of power. (Comprehension)*

See *Section Review* questions, p. 389.

SECTION 2 (pp. 389–392)
Religious Wars

Objectives

After completing this section, students will be able to:
1. Describe how French leaders dealt with religious conflicts.
2. Explain the effects of religious conflicts in Germany.

Introducing the Lesson

Remind students that religious repression was employed by leaders for centuries in Europe, the Middle East, and Asia. In the sixteenth century, some European leaders abandoned the idea that a strong state required religious unity.

Then ask: *(a) What might cause political leaders to abandon policies that were once effective?* (Leaders usually abandon policies that no longer produce results.)

(b) What are some examples of political policies today that might be seen as ineffective and that might, therefore, be abandoned in the future? (Answers will vary.)

Developing the Lesson: Observing for Detail

Have students review "Expansion of the war" (p. 390) and "The Reign of Charles V" (p. 386) and then answer the following questions: *(a) What might have explained Catholic France's support of Protestant countries?*

(b) How did France's actions turn the Thirty Years' War into a struggle against Hapsburg ambitions? (Comprehension)

Closing the Lesson: Linking Past and Present

Have students write an essay comparing Cardinal Richelieu's efforts to maintain the balance of power in Europe with efforts of today's leaders to maintain a balance in nuclear weapons. Areas of comparison might include leaders' motives, their methods, and possible consequences of failure. *(Synthesis)*

See *Section Review* questions, p. 392.

SECTION 3 (pp. 392–395)
Absolute Monarchy in France

Objectives

After completing this section, students will be able to:
1. Describe how the reign of Louis XIV marked the height of absolute monarchy in France.
2. Explain the problems that resulted from the policies of Louis XIV.

Introducing the Lesson

Remind students that throughout history many rulers have claimed that their power and right to rule was divine. King Louis XIV of France, called the "Sun King," used this concept of authority to strengthen his monarchy.

Then ask: *(a) How might the idea of divine right strengthen a monarchy?* (People who believe that their monarch is divinely authorized are more likely to accept the leader's decisions.)

(b) Why do you think most leaders of modern nations make no claim to rule by divine authority? (Answers will vary.)

Developing the Lesson: Making Judgments

Have students evaluate the political and economic policies of Louis XIV. *(Comprehension)*

Closing the Lesson: Debating an Issue

Have students work in groups to debate the following issue: *The exercise of absolute power by a ruler is the key to a strong state.* Each group should randomly select a position for or against the issue, and then present their arguments to the class. *(Synthesis)*

See *Section Review* questions, p. 395.

SECTION 4 (pp. 396–401)
The Triumph of Parliament in England

Objectives

After completing this section, students will be able to:
1. Describe how Queen Elizabeth brought prosperity to England.
2. Explain how disagreements between kings and Parliament led to civil war.
3. Discuss the aftermath of the English Civil War.

Introducing the Lesson

Remind students that common law, the jury system, and the Magna Carta limited the power of English monarchs. In the 1600's, conflict between monarchs and Parliament led to a civil war which resulted in the extension of nobles' rights.

Then ask: *(a) What are political rights?* (Political rights are those rights that a person is entitled to as a citizen.)

(b) What are some examples of political rights? (In most democratic societies political rights include representation, freedom of speech, and due process of law.)

(c) Why do you think many countries today have different ideas about the rights of their citizens? (Answers will vary.)

Developing the Lesson: Organizing Information

Have students make a chart of English rulers and their achievements between 1558 and 1688. Students should include the names of the rulers, the dates of their rule, and a brief characterization of the period. *(Comprehension)*

Closing the Lesson: Understanding Chronology

Have students outline the emergence of a strong Parliament in England. Students might draw a timeline identifying significant events or write a summary of how Parliament grew in political power during the sixteenth and seventeenth centuries. *(Comprehension)*

See *Section Review* questions, p. 401.

SECTION 5   (pp. 401–406)
States in Eastern Europe

After completing this section, students will be able to:
1. Describe how Hungary and Poland grew into strong states, and then lost their independence.
2. Explain how Russia became a major European power.

Introducing the Lesson

Remind students that states in Eastern Europe took longer to develop political unity than those in Western Europe.

Then ask: *(a) What might account for significant political differences between people who live relatively close to one another?* (Answers will vary. Geographic barriers can cause neighboring peoples to develop quite differently from one another.)

(b) How might you expect Eastern and Western Europe to differ? (Answers will vary. Western Europe was influenced by the Roman Empire; Eastern Europe was influenced by Byzantine culture. As a result, cultural and political differences developed.)

Developing the Lesson: Organizing Information

Have students make a chart identifying the Russian rulers and his or her contribution to making Russia the strongest state in Eastern Europe. *(Comprehension)*

Closing the Lesson: Analyzing Information

Have students write an essay explaining Poland's failure to develop a strong central government and Russia's emergence as a powerful, unified state. *(Comprehension)*

See *Section Review* questions, p. 406.

Chapter 20 Review Answers
(pp. 407–408)

Vocabulary Review

1. (a) divine right (b) Edict of Nantes (c) Time of Troubles (d) westernize (e) habeas corpus
2. (a) Petition of Right—1628 document limiting the power of the English king; English Bill of Rights—1689 document listing Parliament's complaints against James II and setting rules to limit the power of the Crown and strengthen individual rights. (b) English Civil War—(1642–1651) struggle for power setting Charles I against Parliament; Commonwealth—republican government formed by Cromwell after the execution of Charles I.
(c) Restoration—reign of England's Charles II (1660–1685); Glorious Revolution—accession of Mary and William III to English throne in 1689.

People to Identify

1. Louis XIV 2. Charles I 3. Stephen 4. Philip II 5. Casimir III 6. Richelieu 7. Charles V 8. Ivan IV

Places to Know

1. G 2. C 3. I 4. B 5. F 6. E 7. D 8. H 9. A

Recalling the Facts

1. They reduced the power of nobles, won the support of the Church, completed the Reconquest of Spain, and worked toward religious unity.
2. He forced Protestants to convert or leave Spain, fought Ottoman expansion in the Mediterranean, conquered Portugal, raised taxes in the Netherlands, and passed trade laws there that favored Spain.
3. The Spanish economy was crippled by war expenses, the neglect of trade and industry, a decline in farming, foreign raids on Spanish ships, dwindling supplies of colonial silver, and poor fiscal management.
4. A war between Catholics and Protestants throughout the German states from 1618 to 1648.
5. Hapsburg dominance ended and France became the leading power in Europe.
6. He encouraged the establishment of French colonies and trading companies, improved methods of taxation, supported shipbuilding and a new navy, had canals and roads built, and encouraged new industries. King Louis XIV's extravagance and France's frequent wars drained the treasury, and Louis's persecution of the Huguenots led to the loss of business leaders and artisans.
7. European nations (except France) feared the balance of power in Europe would be upset if a Bourbon prince took power in Spain. The Peace of Utrecht prevented the union of the French and Spanish Crowns.
8. She increased overseas trade, expanded the navy, and sponsored voyages of discovery. She aided the Protestant Dutch in their revolt against Spain, defeated the Spanish Armada, established the Church of England as the country's official church, and put down a challenge for the throne by her Catholic cousin, Mary, Queen of Scots.
9. James I claimed to rule by divine right and resisted Parliament's interference.
10. Charles I and Parliament disagreed about the king's power to tax and his harsh treatment of Puritans. When Parliament tried to weaken Charles's control over the army and called for reforms in the Church of England, the king had parliamentary leaders arrested, causing the people of London to riot and begin a civil war.
11. They disliked military rule and wanted to return to monarchy.
12. The accession of Mary and William III to the throne of England in 1689. William and Mary signed the English Bill of Rights, making monarchs dependent on Parliament.
13. The Hungarians were defeated by the Ottoman Turks in 1526 at the Battle of Mohács.
14. Its parliamentary system kept the central government weak, and a lack of natural barriers made Poland accessible to conquerors. Russia, Prussia, and Austria partitioned Poland.
15. Peter ordered the nobles to wear Western-style clothing, started schools for the children of nobles, modernized the Russian calendar, simplified the alphabet, stopped excluding women from social life, and tried to train bureaucrats in the Western manner. Catherine defeated the Ottoman Turks to win control of the Black Sea's northern shore, gained farmland in the west, and added territory from the partitions of Poland.

Critical Thinking Skills

1. Answers will vary.
2. Answers will vary, but students should note that in 1628 Charles I's need for funds led him to agree to sign the Petition of Right, which limited the power of the king and increased individual rights; in 1640, Charles's need for money led him to agree to further restrictions on the powers of the monarchy during the Long Parliament.
3. Answers will vary. Peter had the courage, determination, and vision to expand Russia and adapt Western ideas to Russian conditions. Catherine made Russia a power in European politics, expanded its boundaries to include a warm-water port, and further developed Russian culture. The peasants and serfs benefited least from the actions of these rulers and would not be likely to consider the rulers "great."

Thinking About Geography

Mountains made many land routes impractical, and ice blocked northern water routes during the winter. The Baltic gave access to northern and western Europe through the North Sea. The Black Sea gave access to southern Europe through the Mediterranean.

Enrichment: Primary Sources

1. Those who for a good cause are not afraid to displease their king.
2. The advice to make all decisions himself, never to allow himself to be ruled, and to be the master.
3. Answers will vary.

Powerful States in Europe

1469–1796

See chapter timeline, p. 406.

Before You Read This Chapter

We see reports nearly every day of fighting or war somewhere in the world. Warfare was just as common in Europe during the years covered in this chapter. As you read, list some of the reasons for these wars—not the specific events, but the broad causes. What part did rivalry over trade play? How important a source of conflict was religion? Was national prestige ever a reason for a country to go to war? How about conflicting ideas on government? What other causes can you identify? Which of these may still lead to warfare in today's world?

The Geographic Setting

The Chapter Outline

1. The Era of Spanish Domination
2. Religious Wars
3. Absolute Monarchy in France
4. The Triumph of Parliament in England
5. States in Eastern Europe

Spain's defeat of the Ottoman navy at Lepanto increased the power and prestige of its empire and ended the Turkish threat to Europe from the sea.

1 The Era of Spanish Domination

Objectives

Focus Questions

★ ■ How did Spain become a world power? *(pages 385–387)*
● ■ Why did Spanish power fade in the 1600's? *(pages 388–389)*

Terms to Know

Invincible Armada
mystic

★ Note strategies for first objective on this page and p. 388.

During the Middle Ages, Spain had prospered under Muslim rule. The Christian kingdoms in northern Spain, however, were determined to regain the rest of the peninsula. Gradually their Reconquest succeeded (page 246). In the sixteenth century all of Spain was unified under a Roman Catholic monarch, and Spain became the leading state in Europe.

Isabella and Ferdinand

In 1469 the heirs to the two major kingdoms in Spain, Isabella of Castile and Ferdinand of Aragon, married. Though they continued to rule as separate monarchs, they took several steps to unify Spain.

Strong government. One step was to reduce the power of the Spanish nobility. The two rulers removed prominent nobles from important government positions, destroyed castles built without royal permission, and forbade private warfare. To win the support of other nobles, Isabella and Ferdinand allowed them to marry members of the Spanish royal family and gave them honorary positions in the government.

Sec. Rev.
ques. 2

Another step was to gain the support of the Church. An alliance with the papacy gave Isabella and Ferdinand the authority to appoint bishops both in Spain and in Spain's American colonies. The monarchs used this authority to reform the Church and to spend Church funds on national projects.

The most important of these projects was to complete the Reconquest of Spain from the Muslims. Granada, the last Muslim kingdom in Spain, fell to Catholic armies in 1492. Isabella and Ferdinand's triumphal entry into Granada reunified Spain after eight centuries of political division.

Religious persecution. Seeing religious unity as necessary if Spain were to thrive, Isabella and Ferdinand persecuted their religious opponents. They asked the Church to bring back the Inquisition (page 245), which harshly punished suspected heretics. Many Jews who had converted to Christianity were charged with practicing Judaism in secret. Thousands were tortured; some people were even burned at the stake. Finally, in 1492, Isabella and Ferdinand ordered all Jews who refused to be baptized to leave Spain.

The Muslims who remained after the fall of Granada were at first told they could keep their religion and customs. Then in 1502 the Catholic rulers insisted that the Muslims convert to Christianity. Many Muslims did just that, though they continued to follow some Islamic customs. Muslims who did not convert were forced to leave Spain.

The price of intolerance. The policies of Isabella and Ferdinand had serious consequences for Spain. Both Jews and Muslims had enriched Spanish arts, culture, and intellectual life. The Jews had also played a key role as business leaders and merchants. The Muslims had developed advanced farming methods, which had improved Spain's agricultural output. The religious policies of Spain's rulers thus hurt the economy.

385

★ RETEACHING. Have students identify three steps taken by Isabella and Ferdinand to strengthen their rule. *(Comprehension) Observing for Detail*
Biography Isabella was 18 years old when she married 17-year-old Ferdinand. One of their five children, Catherine of Aragon, married Henry VIII of England in 1509.
Vocabulary Note that the word *Inquisition* is from the Latin verb *inquiro*, which means "to inquire into."

★ REINFORCEMENT. Have students explain how Isabella and Ferdinand viewed religion, what part religion played in their policies, and the effects of these policies on Spain. (They believed that religious unity was necessary for Spain's growth. Their policies included the persecution of Muslims and Jews. The results included a loss of important artists, thinkers, and economic leaders.) *(Comprehension) Summarizing Information*

The Reign of Charles V

Sec. Rev.
ques. 3

Charles V, the grandson of Isabella and Ferdinand, was born in 1500. A member of the influential Hapsburg family of Austria, he was heir to Hapsburg lands as well as the Spanish empire. At the age of six Charles inherited the Netherlands from his father. Nine years later he was proclaimed King of Spain. By 1520 he had inherited the eastern Hapsburg lands—Austria, Hungary, and Bohemia. He also was crowned Holy Roman Emperor.

The Spanish at first regarded Charles as a foreigner, but he slowly won their loyalty and continued his grandparents' efforts to unify and strengthen Spain. As king of Spain, Charles V ruled a country brimming with vitality. During his reign, Spanish adventurers in the Americas conquered Mexico and Peru and explored much of what is now the southern United States. Silver and gold from the colonies began to pour into Spain.

In Europe, however, Charles faced problems that seemed impossible to solve. He constantly struggled with the Lutheran princes in the German states, who refused to accept his authority as Holy Roman Emperor. Charles's attempts to bring Italy under Spanish control were blocked by the French. The Ottoman Turks invaded Central Europe during the 1500's, threatening Hapsburg lands (page 278). The struggle with the Ottoman Empire continued to drain Hapsburg energies and wealth for more than a century.

Exhausted by these challenges, Charles gave up his throne in 1556 and retired to a Spanish monastery. His brother Ferdinand I inherited the eastern Hapsburg lands and the title of Holy Roman Emperor. Spain, the Netherlands, and Spain's lands in America and Italy went to Charles's son, Philip II.

Philip II's Rule of Spain

King of Spain from 1556 to 1598, Philip II was a serious, hardworking ruler. His goals were to build the power of both Spain and the Roman Catholic Church. Though Philip never controlled as much territory as his father had, he was even more set on reaching his goals.

Religious intolerance. Like earlier rulers, Philip wanted Spain to be entirely Catholic. He ordered Protestants to convert to Catholicism or leave Spain. Many were tried by the Inquisition. Those who refused to give up their beliefs were sent to prison. Some were tortured and executed. Since Protestantism had not taken deep root in Spain, it soon disappeared.

Philip also lashed out at Moriscos—Muslims who had converted to Christianity. The Moriscos had held on to much of their ancient culture. Some continued to practice Islam in secret. When Philip banned the use of Arabic and passed other restrictions in 1569, the Moriscos of Granada rebelled. After a hard-fought struggle, they were subdued and sent to other parts of Spain. Their children were taken from them and put in Christian homes. In 1609 Philip's son (Philip III) forced the 300,000 remaining Moriscos to leave Spain.

Battling the Ottomans. Philip also confronted the Ottoman pirates who were attacking ships in the Mediterranean Sea. Frightened by Ottoman expansion in the eastern Mediterranean, Philip joined forces with the Pope and the Republic of Venice against the Ottoman Empire. In 1571 the combined Christian fleets fought the Ottomans in a great naval battle near the port of Lepanto (lih-PAHN-toh) in Greece. The Christian forces overpowered the Turks and freed some 10,000 Christians held as slaves on the Ottoman ships. The Ottomans rebuilt their fleet, however, and remained a power in the Mediterranean for another 300 years.

The conquest of Portugal. Philip was more successful in his effort to conquer Portugal. The death of the Portuguese king in 1580 put Philip next in line to the throne. The Portuguese had no wish to be ruled by Spain, but Philip sent troops into Portugal and easily crushed all resistance. Portugal came under the Spanish Crown, and Philip gained that country's huge overseas empire.

Politics Although Philip II imposed Catholicism on non-Catholics in Spain and was considered a champion of the Church, Pope Sixtus V, a contemporary of Philip, judged the Spanish monarch to be "anxious above all to safeguard and increase his dominions. The preservation of the Catholic religion is only a pretext for his Majesty whose principal aim is the security and aggrandizement of his dominions."

Background Among those who fought and were wounded in the battle of Lepanto was Miguel de Cervantes, author of the novel *Don Quixote* (p. 332). Cervantes lost the use of his left hand as a result of wounds suffered in this battle.

Europe About 1560

In 1556 Emperor Charles V divided his vast empire between his brother Ferdinand, ruler of Austria, and his son Philip, king of Spain. Find the lands that each ruler received. Why might France have feared Hapsburg power? Note that the map shows the route taken by the Spanish Armada.

Map Answer: Hapsburgs now ruled much of central and southern Europe.

Rebellion in the Netherlands. Believing that Spain should profit from its holdings in the Netherlands, Philip raised Dutch taxes and passed trade laws that favored Spanish merchants. In 1566 the Dutch began a rebellion that lasted many years. Its leader was William, Prince of Orange, known as William the Silent. In time, the northern provinces, which were Protestant and Dutch-speaking, became the United Netherlands. They declared themselves a republic in 1581, but it was many years before Spain recognized their independence. The southern provinces, which were mostly Catholic, joined the rebellion but later returned to Spanish rule as the Spanish Netherlands.

Trouble with England. The war in the Netherlands brought Spain into open conflict with England. Rivalry between England and Spain had heated up because of the raids of English privateers who plundered Spanish treasure ships around the world.

When the Dutch revolt broke out, Elizabeth I, England's Protestant queen (page 341), sent troops to aid the Protestant rebels. English support for the Dutch enraged Philip.

Sec. Rev. ques. 4

Invincible Armada. In 1588 Philip sent a fleet, called the **Invincible Armada**, to invade England. About 130 ships, carrying over 3,000 cannons, set sail for England. Instead of the glorious victory Philip expected, however, his fleet met with disaster.

387

Biography William, the Prince of Orange, was called "the Silent" because he seldom revealed his inner thoughts, although he was considered an eloquent speaker.

Diego Velázquez was court painter to Philip IV of Spain. In *Las Meninas* (*The Maids*, 1656), the artist shows himself painting a portrait of the king and queen, who appear in the mirror behind him.

Standing between the Armada and England was the English navy. The English ships were smaller and quicker, and their captains and crews were more skillful sailors. In a sea battle in the English Channel, the English outfought the Armada and sank several ships. Storms blew many of the remaining Spanish ships into the North Sea. To return home, the commander of the Armada took his crippled fleet around Scotland and Ireland. More ships were wrecked, and only about half of the original Armada finally limped home to Spain. The defeat of the Armada was a terrible blow to Spanish pride.

Spain's Golden Age

★ See below.

In spite of its defeat by England, Spain remained a powerful nation. In fact, the greatest period of Spanish culture was still to come. That period, which lasted from Philip's reign until the middle of the 1600's, is known as the Golden Age.

388

The best known literary work of Spain's Golden Age is Cervantes' *Don Quixote* (page 332). Poets and playwrights also created important works. Some of the most beautiful writings came from Spanish **mystics**—people who believed they could contact God through meditation. Ignatius Loyola (page 342) and Saint John of the Cross wrote movingly of the relationship between God and humanity.

The religious devotion of the mystics also appeared in the works of El Greco, one of Spain's greatest painters. Often using saints and martyrs as subjects, El Greco combined strong colors with distorted shapes to produce a feeling of deep spirituality. Another famous Spanish painter of the Golden Age was Diego Velázquez. His portraits of members of the Spanish court showed the wealth, pride, and power of Spain at its height.

Spain's Decline

● Note strategies for second objective on this page and p. 389.

In the mid-1500's, Spain was regarded as the leading state in Europe. Within a century, however, Spain lost most of its power, and in 1700 the Spanish Hapsburg line came to an end. What caused the decline?

1. The cost of war. The wars fought by Charles V and Philip II placed a terrible strain on Spain's resources. Spain did not have an economy strong enough to support these wars.

2. The neglect of trade and industry. Unlike other Western European countries, Spain lacked a middle class of merchants and business leaders. When Jews and Muslims were driven out of the country, economic life began to decline. Spanish society placed a low value on trade and industry. Young men were encouraged to become soldiers or to enter the clergy or government service—fields that contributed little to production or trade. Many ambitious young Spaniards left the country to seek wealth and adventure in the Americas.

Sec. Rev. ques. 5

3. Changes in agriculture. Because trade in wool was profitable, the Spanish gov-

★ ENRICHMENT. Have students research one of the important achievements of Spain's Golden Age and explain how it expressed the values of Spanish society as described on pages 386–388. Students might find information on the Spanish mystics or El Greco and describe how they represent the religious concerns of the period, or research the painter Diego Velázquez and explain how his portraits represented Spain's wealth. (Synthesis) *Locating Information*

● RETEACHING. Have students review "Spain's Decline" (pp. 388–389) and outline the information that explains why Spanish power declined. (Comprehension) *Organizing Ideas in Written Form*

● REINFORCEMENT. Have students work in groups to discuss the problems faced by Spanish leaders during the late 1500's. Students should suggest ways in which the problems could have been resolved. (Synthesis) *Problem Solving* ernment granted special privileges to sheep raisers. Land that could have been used for farming was set aside for grazing sheep. As flocks grew larger, they ate so much of the shrubs and grasses on hillsides that the soil eroded. Many farmers grew discouraged and gave up farming. The resulting food shortages forced Spain to spend more and more on food imports.

4. The dependence on colonial wealth. Much of Spain's prosperity in the 1500's rested on Aztec and Inca treasure and on gold and silver from the newly discovered American mines. Instead of investing this wealth, the Spanish used it to pay for wars and imports of food and manufactured goods. This policy caused prices to skyrocket and left Spain dependent on its colonies.

● See below.

Raids on treasure ships by English and Dutch pirates soon cut down the flow of wealth to Spain. Moreover, the amount of silver mined in Spain's colonies gradually fell. Spanish rulers, however, continued to behave (and spend) as though nothing had

See lesson plans, pp. T383A–T383C.

changed. By the middle of the 1600's, Hapsburg Spain was poor and weak. It was never again in a position to dominate Europe.

See Sec. 1 *Closing the Lesson,* p. T383A.

Section Review

Answers to Section Review questions are in brackets on pages indicated.

1. **Define or identify:** Invincible Armada, mystic. (pp. 387, 388)
2. How did Isabella and Ferdinand unify Spain? (p. 385)
3. How did Charles V gain such a huge empire? (p. 386)
4. Why did Philip II send the Invincible Armada to attack England? What was the outcome? (pp. 387–388)
5. What caused Spain's decline as a world power? (pp. 388–389)
6. **Critical thinking:** Spain's leaders wanted both religious unity and national power. How did their pursuit of religious unity weaken Spain?

(See answer below.)

6. Students might suggest that lack of religious tolerance cost Spain many of its most productive citizens, and thus hurt the economy.

2 Religious Wars

Objectives

Focus Questions

★ ■ How did French leaders deal with religious conflicts? *(pages 389–390)*

● ■ What were the effects of religious conflicts in Germany? *(pages 390–391)*

Terms to Know

Edict of Nantes	Thirty Years' War
balance of power	Peace of Westphalia

★ Note strategies for first objective on this page and p. 390.

During the 1500's and 1600's, the Reformation spread throughout Europe. In some countries, such as Spain, emerging Protestant

groups were quickly stamped out. In France and Germany, however, Protestantism took deeper root, and the clash between Protestants and Catholics led to war.

France in the late 1500's

Religious warfare. During the 1500's the French monarchs remained Catholic. Many French nobles, however, became Protestants. They did so partly for religious reasons and partly to weaken the French monarchy. Rival Protestant and Catholic nobles competed for control of France.

In 1562 a full-scale civil war erupted between the Huguenots (French Protestants) and the Catholics. For more than 30 years, France was swept by bloody struggles.

389

● ENRICHMENT. Have students research one of the four reasons for Spain's decline and present the information to the class. When all reports have been given, students should evaluate the information, decide which factor they think was most significant, and explain their choices. *(Evaluation) Making Judgments*

★ RETEACHING. Have students list and explain the actions taken by Henry IV and Cardinal Richelieu to end religious conflict in France. *(Comprehension) Observing for Detail*

★ REINFORCEMENT. Have students review "The rule of Henry IV" (p. 390) and find information to support the following generalization: *A strong and united France mattered more to Henry than religion.* (He converted to Catholicism because France would not accept a Huguenot king, and he issued the Edict of Nantes.) *(Comprehension) Supporting Generalizations*

The most famous of the clashes between Catholics and Protestants took place in Paris in 1572. The date was August 24. Many Protestant nobles had gathered for the wedding of Henry of Navarre, one of their leaders. Perhaps encouraged by the royal family, a group of Parisians began to massacre the Huguenots. The violence spread, and more than 10,000 Huguenots died in what came to be called the St. Bartholomew's Day Massacre.

The rule of Henry IV. In 1589 Henry of Navarre inherited the French throne. As King Henry IV, he tried to restore peace after the years of violence. A strong and united France mattered more to Henry than his religious beliefs. Since the French would not accept a Huguenot king, he converted to Catholicism. "Paris is well worth a Mass," he reportedly explained.

Henry was the first ruler of the Bourbon dynasty. Brave and intelligent, he became one of the best-loved rulers in French history. To protect the Huguenots and end religious conflict in France, Henry issued the **Edict of Nantes** (NAHNT) in 1598. This document gave the Huguenots equal treatment under the law, equal opportunity to hold positions in the government, and freedom to practice their faith. Such religious toleration was unusual for the time. The Edict of Nantes helped bring order to France after decades of civil war.

Sec. Rev. ques. 2

Henry also brought prosperity to his kingdom. He began programs to build up the royal treasury and reduce waste and dishonesty in the government. He also encouraged trade by building roads and canals and by improving ports.

Richelieu's France

In 1610 Henry was murdered by a religious fanatic, and the throne went to his nine-year-old son, Louis XIII. Henry's second wife, Marie de Médicis (MAY-dee-sees), ruled France until Louis took on responsibility as king in 1615. Nine years later a remarkable statesman, Cardinal Richelieu (ree-shuh-LYOO), became Louis's chief minister.

390

Cool-headed, clear-sighted, and ruthless, Richelieu is seen as one of the great leaders in French history. His main goals were to strengthen both the king's authority at home and France's position in European affairs.

Suspecting the Huguenots of plotting with foreign countries against the French Crown, Richelieu sent troops to capture the main Protestant towns and destroy the Huguenots' armies. He did not, however, cancel the Edict of Nantes or forbid Huguenots to practice their religion.

Sec. Rev. ques. 3

Richelieu's biggest task in foreign policy was to preserve Europe's **balance of power**. That is, he wanted to keep any one country from dominating the others. Because the Hapsburg family posed the greatest threat to the balance of power (through its control of the monarchies of Austria, Spain, and the Holy Roman Empire), Richelieu set out to limit Hapsburg power. Richelieu soon led France into the bloody conflict known as the **Thirty Years' War** (1618–1648).

★ See below, left.

The Thirty Years' War

● Note strategies for second objective on this page and p. 391.

The trouble began in Bohemia, one of the German states, where the Holy Roman Emperor tried to impose Catholicism on the Protestants. The Protestants rebelled, and a full-scale war between Catholics and Protestants soon erupted throughout the German states.

Expansion of the war. The princes on each side in the war appealed to other European monarchs for help. The Protestant princes turned to the Protestant kings of Denmark, Sweden, and the United Netherlands. The Catholics turned to Spain. However, when Catholic France entered the war on the side of the Protestants, the war became more a struggle against Hapsburg ambitions than a religious conflict.

The war took place mostly on German soil. The armies of both sides were ruthless, slaughtering civilians and destroying farms and towns. More than a third of the German population died from war, disease, or famine. Thousands more fled the country.

Europe About 1648

The Thirty Years' War brought important changes to Europe. Compare this map with the map on page 387. What changes took place in the Netherlands between 1560 and 1648? How and why did the southern boundary of the Holy Roman Empire change?

Map Answers: (1) It was divided into independent United Netherlands and Spanish Netherlands. (2) Holy Roman Empire no longer included Savoy and Switzerland.

The Peace of Westphalia. In 1648 delegates met in the province of Westphalia to work out a peace agreement. Although the Peace of Westphalia caused few territorial changes, it had important effects on Europe.

Sec. Rev. ques. 4

(1) The Hapsburgs had failed in their attempt to unite the German states under the Holy Roman Emperor. The German states became virtually independent; the Holy Roman Empire now existed in name only.

(2) Unable to expand their power in Germany, the ambitious Hapsburgs turned their energies to the east. In time, they built a large and powerful empire in Central and Eastern Europe.

(3) Two republics, the United Netherlands and Switzerland, were recognized as independent of the Holy Roman Empire.

(4) For more than a century Hapsburg Austria and Hapsburg Spain had threatened France. After the Thirty Years' War, this threat faded. France became the leading power in Europe.

The Thirty Years' War was the last of the religious wars brought about by the Reformation. After the mid-1600's monarchs no longer went to war or made alliances purely for religious reasons. Instead they were guided more by a concern for state security and by a desire for land and economic power.

● See below.

391

See Sec. 2 *Closing the Lesson,* p. T383B.

● REINFORCEMENT. Have students analyze the following trend apparent in Europe after the mid-1600's: "Monarchs no longer went to war or made alliances purely for religious reasons. Instead they were guided more by a concern for state security and by a desire for land and economic power." In their analyses students might consider possible reasons for the emergence of the trend and its effects. *(Analysis) Analyzing Trends*

Check for Understanding. Ask: What two republics were recognized by the Peace of Westphalia? (United Netherlands, Switzerland.)
● ENRICHMENT. Have students research the Thirty Years' War and present oral reports on the war's major battles, their locations, and outcomes. *(Application) Locating Information*

1. **Define or identify:** Edict of Nantes, balance of power, Thirty Years' War, Peace of Westphalia. (pp. 390, 391)
2. What effect did the Edict of Nantes have on France? (p. 390)
3. What were Cardinal Richelieu's two main goals for France? What methods did he use to achieve these goals? (p. 390)
4. How did the Peace of Westphalia affect the German states? (p. 391)
5. **Critical thinking:** In Chapter 11 you read about Charlemagne's dream of a united Christian Europe. In what way did the Peace of Westphalia signal the end of that dream? (See answer below.)

See lesson plans, pp. T383A–T383C.

3 Absolute Monarchy in France

Objectives

Focus Questions

★ ■ Why did the reign of Louis XIV mark the height of absolute monarchy in France? *(pages 392–393)*
● ■ What problems resulted from the policies of Louis XIV? *(pages 393–395)*

Terms to Know

divine right
Versailles
Peace of Utrecht

War of the Spanish
Succession

★ Note strategies for first objective on this page and p. 393.

Like the German states, France had been torn by religious strife in the decades following the Reformation. The civil war between Catholics and Protestants in France was ended by the policies of Henry IV. Henry's successors followed his example, placing the interests of France and the strengthening of royal power above all else. The long reign of Louis XIV (1643–1715) marked the full flowering of absolute monarchy in France.

When Louis XIII died in 1643, the new king, Louis XIV, was not quite five years old.

His mother, Anne of Austria, ruled for her son along with the new chief minister, Cardinal Mazarin (MAZ-uh-rin), who had been trained by Richelieu.

Mazarin's overbearing manner and his attempts to raise taxes made him unpopular with many. In the late 1640's some nobles, with the backing of peasants and city dwellers, led a series of rebellions against the Crown. Though the revolts failed, they did alarm the young king. He grew convinced that only rule by a monarch with absolute power could prevent civil war.

Like other monarchs of the day, Louis believed that kings "are born to possess all and command all." Louis claimed that the ruler's power came from God and that no one should question it. This theory is known as **divine right**. A French bishop expressed the theory in the following words: "It is God Who establishes kings. . . . It is through them that He rules. . . . That is why the royal throne is not the throne of a man but the throne of God Himself."

After Mazarin's death in 1661, Louis XIV ruled as an absolute monarch, keeping the power of the state in his own hands. His famous description of this power was *"L'état, c'est moi"* (lay-TAH, SAY MWAH), a French phrase meaning "I am the state." No minister, however capable, set policy for the king.

392

The Court of the "Sun King"

Louis worked tirelessly to build the glory of France and the monarchy. Because of the splendor of his reign, he was called the "Sun King." The early years of Louis's personal rule gave France greater unity and a stronger central government than it had ever had. Louis chose many of his officials from the newer nobles and the middle class. Therefore, the old noble families lost much of their independence and power.

Sec. Rev. ques. 2

The beauty of Versailles. Louis's government spent lavishly on palaces and public buildings. The most magnificent was the royal family's home at Versailles (vayr-SY), near Paris. It took thousands of workers more than 20 years to complete this showplace. The palace contained hundreds of rooms, including a 240-foot hall with walls paneled in mirrors. Other rooms were decorated with tapestries, marble statues, and ceiling paintings showing Louis's achievements. The palace was surrounded by formal gardens with statues and fountains.

The royal court moved to Versailles in 1682, and social life revolved around the "Sun King." Louis ordered many nobles to live with him in the palace. Those who otherwise might have plotted against the king spent their time giving Louis his shirt in the morning, holding his candle at night, or watching him eat. The nobles were eager to please Louis in hopes that he would grant them pensions or appointments as bishops, ambassadors, or generals.

★ See below, left.

The capital of European culture. Louis XIV was king for 72 years. During his long reign, art, literature, drama, music, and ballet flourished in France, for Louis was the patron of many artists and writers. Two of France's greatest playwrights, Jean Racine (rah-SEEN) and Molière (mohl-YAYR), both lived at this time. In architecture, furniture, and dress, France set the style for Europe. French replaced Latin as the language of diplomacy. Other monarchs copied the fashions and manners of Louis's court.

Royal Policies

● Note strategies for second objective on this page and p. 395.

Realizing that a strong monarchy depended on a healthy economy, Louis XIV in 1665 named Jean Baptiste Colbert (kohl-BAYR) to

The magnificent Hall of Mirrors at Louis XIV's palace at Versailles symbolizes the wealth of the Sun King's court and the power of absolute monarchy.

★ ENRICHMENT. Have students work in groups to report on palace life at Versailles. Students might study palace architecture, fashions, or important ceremonies and celebrations, and present their findings in the form of charts, posters, skits, or oral reports. (Application) Locating Information

Cultural History Louis XIV believed he could avoid conspiracies if he moved his court to Versailles, where it was easier to keep track of the activities of the nobles.

● RETEACHING. Have students review "Royal Policies" (pp. 393–395) and find information to support the following statements: (a) Louis XIV's programs and policies bankrupted France. (b) The Huguenots were valuable to France. (Comprehension) Observing for Detail

● REINFORCEMENT. Have students make a chart showing the causes and effects of the War of the Spanish Succession. (Comprehension) Understanding Cause and Effect

Europe About 1721

Major territorial changes came about in Europe between 1648 and 1721. Compare this map with the one on page 391. How did Poland's territory change?

Map Answers: Poland lost eastern lands to the Russian Empire.

be his minister of finance. Colbert was a strong believer in mercantilism (page 367). He urged the establishment of French colonies and trading companies to compete with the Dutch and the English. He also improved methods of taxation, supported shipbuilding and a new navy, and had canals and roads built. The government encouraged new industries by inviting foreign artisans to teach their skills to French workers. The French silk, tapestry, and furniture industries benefited from this help.

Prosperous times did not last, however. Although Louis wished to strengthen the state, his luxurious court life and grand building programs took huge amounts of money.

394

Frequent wars also drained the French treasury. Unlike England, where Parliament limited the power of the monarch, France had no lawmaking body that could call a halt to the king's spending. The French assembly, the Estates-General, had not met since 1614.

Another reason for the decline in French prosperity was Louis's religious intolerance. Louis was convinced that the Huguenots might bring on civil war. Determined to create a France with "one king, one law, and one faith," he opposed the religious toleration that the Edict of Nantes had granted the French Protestants.

Huguenots had served France well in the armed forces and as government officials.

Sec. Rev.
ques. 3

Background Note that the original silver furniture in the Palace of Versailles was melted down and the precious metal used to help defray some of Louis XIV's war costs.

They were also important to French business and industry. Louis XIV nevertheless demanded that the Huguenots convert to Catholicism. When they refused, he turned to persecution. Finally, in 1685, he simply canceled the Edict of Nantes and barred the Huguenots from practicing their religion. Tens of thousands of Huguenots fled to Protestant countries in Europe. Others made their way to the English colonies in North America. France lost many of its most promising business leaders and artisans.

Louis's Ambitions in Europe

Sec. Rev. ques. 4

The Thirty Years' War had not only ended Hapsburg dominance in Europe, it also had given Bourbon France the chance to control the continent. Louis wanted to extend French lands to the north and east to give France a border that was easier to defend. Louis also planned to put a Bourbon prince on the Spanish throne, in hopes of gaining control of Spain and its huge empire.

To put these plans into action, Louis reorganized the French army. Other European states, fearful of Louis's ambitions, formed alliances to resist him. Between 1667 and 1714 France went to war four times. The most destructive of these conflicts was the War of the Spanish Succession (1701–1713).

Battle for control of Spain. The succession to the Spanish throne was in doubt because the Hapsburg king of Spain had no heirs. In 1700 he named as his successor Philip of Anjou, the grandson of Louis XIV. France rejoiced that a Bourbon prince had been named to the Spanish throne. The other major European powers, however, did not accept this turn of events. They knew that a Bourbon-controlled Spain would upset the balance of power in Europe. England, Hapsburg Austria, the German state of Brandenburg-Prussia, and the United Netherlands joined forces to block Philip.

The Peace of Utrecht. The war went badly for France, but disagreements among its enemies ended the fighting before France suffered great losses. The **Peace of Utrecht** (YOO-trekt), made up of several treaties signed in 1713 and 1714, restored the balance of power in Europe by preventing the union of the French and Spanish Crowns.

Philip of Anjou was allowed to keep the Spanish throne and Spain's colonial empire, on the condition that the same king would never rule both Spain and France. The Spanish Netherlands and Spanish lands in Italy went to the Austrian Hapsburgs. (The Spanish Netherlands was renamed the Austrian Netherlands.) Britain took Gibraltar from Spain (map, page 394) and gained some French possessions in North America and the West Indies. Like Hapsburg Austria and Hapsburg Spain before it, Bourbon France had failed in its attempt to dominate Europe.

● See below.

An empty treasury. At the time of Louis XIV's death in 1715, France was nearly penniless. Wars and careless spending had emptied the royal treasury and left the country in debt. The French system of taxation placed the burden of taxes on the peasants, who could least afford to pay. These money troubles were made worse by wars during the reign (1715–1774) of Louis XV, Louis's great-grandson and successor. Financial problems helped to weaken the monarchy and bring on the French Revolution in 1789.

See Sec. 3 *Closing the Lesson,* p. T383B.

Section Review

Answers to Section Review questions are in brackets on pages indicated.

1. **Define or identify:** divine right, Versailles, War of the Spanish Succession, Peace of Utrecht. (pp. 392, 393, 395)
2. Describe Louis XIV's court and his relations with the French nobles. (p. 393)
3. How did Louis XIV's religious policies hurt the economy? (pp. 394–395)
4. What caused the War of the Spanish Succession? What was its outcome? (p. 395)
5. **Critical thinking:** How did the situation of Huguenots in France compare with the situation of Jews and Muslims in Spain (Section 1)? (See answer below.)

395

Background The Duc de Saint-Simon, a noble in Louis XIV's court, wrote that after the revocation of the edict "the kingdom was depopulated, and our commerce ruined; many were driven to seek refuge in foreign lands, where they took our arts and crafts, enriching other countries and causing their cities to flourish at the expense of France."

Check for Understanding. Ask: Why did the economy of France suffer during Louis XIV's reign? (Frequent wars, luxurious court life, grand building programs, and the loss of Huguenots.)

● ENRICHMENT. Have students write an essay describing how they would have used the absolute power of the French monarchy to avoid or solve the problems of Louis XIV's reign. (Synthesis) Making Decisions

5. Students might point out that religious intolerance in Spain led to persecution and expulsion of Jews and Muslims; Huguenots fled persecution in France. Both countries suffered losses of economic, cultural, and intellectual wealth.

See lesson plans, pp. T383A–T383C.

4 The Triumph of Parliament in England

Objectives

Focus Questions

- ★ ■ How did Queen Elizabeth bring prosperity to England? *(pages 396–397)*
- ● ■ Why did disagreements between kings and Parliament lead to civil war? *(pages 398–399)*
- ▲ ■ What was the aftermath of the English Civil War? *(pages 399–400)*

Terms to Know

Petition of Right	Restoration
habeas corpus	Glorious Revolution
English Civil War	English Bill of
Commonwealth	Rights

★ Note strategies for first objective on this page.

Monarchy followed a different course in England than in France. In France the king remained an absolute monarch well into the 1700's. In England, Parliament took steps to limit the monarch's power and protect citizens' rights.

The Reign of Elizabeth I

In 1558 the last Tudor monarch, Elizabeth I, came to the English throne. Intelligent and self-confident, Elizabeth was one of the great rulers in European history. She was devoted to her people and said, shortly before her death, "Though you have had, and may have, many wiser Princes . . . you never had or shall have any that will love you better."

Peace and prosperity. Elizabeth's 45-year reign was a golden age for England. Despite challenges to her rule, the queen kept

396

peace within her kingdom. She showed respect for tradition, chose excellent advisers, and persuaded Parliament to approve her policies. The spirit of the Renaissance also made Elizabethan England a time of remarkable creativity in the arts. It was during this period that Shakespeare began writing his brilliant plays (page 333).

England grew prosperous and powerful under Elizabeth. English merchants, searching for new markets and raw materials, traded around the world. England gained its first trading post in India, and London became a busy center of commerce. By increasing overseas trade, expanding the English navy, and sponsoring voyages of discovery, Elizabeth laid the foundations of an empire.

Sec. Rev. ques. 2

The strengthening of Protestantism. During Elizabeth's reign, England aided the Protestant Dutch in their successful revolt against Spain, and stunned the world by defeating the Spanish Armada (page 388). These events showed that England was becoming one of the leading Protestant states in Europe.

Elizabeth also promoted Protestantism within England. While she was tolerant toward Catholics and Puritans (page 341), Elizabeth firmly established the Church of England as the country's official church.

However, several groups of Roman Catholics challenged the queen's right to the throne. They supported the claim of Mary, Queen of Scots (Mary Stuart), who was Elizabeth's cousin and a Roman Catholic. Mary was forced to give up the throne of Scotland in 1567. She took refuge in England, where she was kept under close watch for nearly 20 years. Backed by agents of France and Spain, Mary continued to be the center of plots against Elizabeth. Eventually Elizabeth's advisers convinced her that the Scottish queen was a danger. She reluctantly ordered Mary's beheading in 1587.

★ RETEACHING. Have students use the following words in a paragraph describing how Queen Elizabeth brought prosperity to England: peace, tradition, Parliament, merchants, India, London, overseas, navy, discovery. *(Comprehension)* ***Expressing Ideas in Written Form***
Background Remind students that the Tudors ascended the English throne in 1485 after defeating the family of York in the Wars of the Roses (p. 264).

★ REINFORCEMENT. Have students identify and rank in order of importance the actions of Queen Elizabeth that led to peace and prosperity. Then have students explain their order of ranking. *(Evaluation)* ***Making Judgments***
★ ENRICHMENT. Have students write a newspaper article about Queen Elizabeth I that might have appeared at the time of her death in 1603. *(Synthesis)* ***Synthesizing Information***

ⒻSee below.

Biography

Queen Elizabeth I

Elizabeth I was 25 years old when she became England's queen in 1558. Tall and red-haired, she was a graceful dancer and a skilled musician. Her education was in the finest Renaissance tradition. When Elizabeth was 16 her tutor wrote, "She talks French and Italian as well as she does English, and has often talked to me readily and well in Latin, moderately in Greek." Having spent her girlhood surrounded by the planners and schemers at the royal court, she had also become a shrewd and experienced politician.

The great question at the beginning of Elizabeth's reign was, whom would she marry? All her advisers assumed that she must marry someone, either an English noble or a foreign prince. From courts all over Europe came proposals. Elizabeth was charming to all her suitors but accepted none of them. For years she used marriage as bait to achieve her diplomatic goals. Eventually it became clear that she would never marry.

Above all, Elizabeth wanted peace and security for England. While religious strife raged in Europe, she pursued a moderate course. As long as her subjects were loyal, she cared little about their beliefs. She had no wish, she said, "to pry windows into men's souls." She sought peace abroad as well as at home, partly because war was too expensive for

This portrait of Queen Elizabeth I was painted in commemoration of her navy's defeat of the Spanish Armada. The Tudor queen's right hand covers a globe, thus symbolizing England's newly established position as a world power.

England, which was a much poorer country than France or Spain.

Elizabeth ruled from 1558 until 1603. These years marked the beginning of England's rise to greatness as a sea power (page 396). It was also a glorious age in English literature. Elizabeth was a favorite subject of poets, who referred to her as Gloriana. The common people called her Good Queen Bess. When she died, the throne passed to a new dynasty, the Stuarts. Elizabeth was both the last and the greatest of the Tudors.

397

Ⓕ FEATURE ACTIVITY. Have students identify the features of Queen Elizabeth I's rule that marked her as an effective leader. (Elizabeth was skilled in diplomacy; established peace and security as political goals; and pursued a moderate course of action. Also, her reign witnessed England's growth as a sea power; she was called "Good Queen Bess" by the common people.) (Evaluation) *Making Judgments*

Parliament and the Stuart Kings

● Note strategies for second objective on this page and p. 399.

James I. Because Elizabeth had no children, she was succeeded in 1603 by Mary Stuart's son, James I. James, however, failed to win the support of either the politicians or the people. James claimed to rule by divine right and resisted any interference in his decisions. His attitude caused friction with Parliament, which was determined to take a greater role in governing England.

James's ideas about religion also sparked controversy. He did not share Elizabeth's tolerance of Puritans. James feared that those who did not respect the authority of the Church of England would not accept the king's authority either. Therefore, he turned down Puritan demands for reforms in Church practices. He did, though, agree to a Puritan request for a new translation of the Bible. The new translation, commonly called the King James Version, is still widely used today.

Sec. Rev. ques. 3

Charles I. When James died in 1625, the throne passed to his son, Charles I. Tensions between Parliament and the monarch soon heated up. The conflict centered on two issues—taxes and religion.

Because of heavy spending and wars with France and Spain, both James I and Charles I were constantly short of funds. When Charles asked Parliament for more money in 1628, Parliament refused to provide it unless the king signed the **Petition of Right**.

Like the Magna Carta (page 238), the Petition of Right is one of the fundamental documents of English liberty. It limited the power of the king and set forth specific rights: (1) The monarch could not collect taxes without Parliament's consent. (2) Civilians could not be forced to provide food and shelter for soldiers. (3) Military law could not be imposed in time of peace. (4) No person could be kept in prison unless charged with a specific crime. This was the principle of **habeas corpus** (HAY-bee-us KOR-pus).

Although Charles signed the Petition of Right, he continued to impose taxes that Parliament considered illegal. When Parliament

398

James I refused to cooperate with Parliament. Parliament did, however, force the king's successors to give up some of their power.

protested, Charles disbanded it. For the next 11 years, until 1640, the king ruled without Parliament. This heavy-handed tactic aroused bitter opposition.

Religious strife. Charles's troubles with Parliament were made worse by his religious policies. Charles had many English Puritans imprisoned or fined. The Puritans continued to gain supporters, however, particularly among middle-class townspeople.

In 1637 Charles I tried to force Scottish churches to use an Anglican (Church of England) prayer book. The Lowland Scots, who were Calvinist Presbyterians (page 339), rose in revolt. Needing funds to fight in Scotland, Charles was forced to call a meeting of Parliament in April 1640. Because Parliament refused to vote Charles money unless its complaints were settled, the king disbanded it after three weeks. It is thus known as the Short Parliament.

The Long Parliament. Desperate for money, Charles called for new elections to Parliament in November 1640. The new Parliament met until 1653 (but was not dissolved until 1660) and is called the Long Parliament. This body, like the Short Parliament, tried to trim the monarch's powers. It passed laws calling for regular meetings of Parliament. It did away with the special court called the Star Chamber, where royal officials had held secret trials. New laws also limited the monarch's ability to raise money without Parliament's consent. The laws passed by the Long Parliament were landmarks in the growth of English liberty.

England Under Cromwell

Sec. Rev. ques. 4
In June 1642, Parliament moved to weaken the king's control over the army. Many Puritan members also called for reforms in the Church of England. Charles rejected Parliament's proposals and brought in soldiers to arrest its leaders. Outraged, the people of London rioted, and in August a civil war began.

The king's supporters, called Cavaliers or royalists, included Anglicans and Catholics. Most members of the House of Lords, who were aristocrats, also backed the king, along with some members of the House of Commons. Parliament had the support of Puritans and other middle-class townspeople, who resented the king's arrogance and high spending. They were known as Roundheads because many Puritans cropped their hair short instead of wearing the long, curly wigs fashionable at the royal court. The struggle between these two groups became known as the English Civil War. It was, in fact, several wars fought throughout England and southern Scotland between 1642 and 1651.

● See below.

A Puritan general named Oliver Cromwell organized the parliamentary forces into the New Model Army. After losing early battles to the Cavaliers, the New Model Army won important victories in 1644 and 1645 and took King Charles prisoner. Though the king escaped to Scotland and raised an army, his troops were again defeated in 1648.

Cromwell used his control of the army to seize power from moderate Puritans who wanted to negotiate with the king. In 1648 Cromwell forced his opponents out of Parliament. The remaining members abolished the House of Lords and brought the king to trial for treason. Charles I was beheaded early in 1649. Most people were shocked by the execution of the monarch.

With the backing of the army, Cromwell formed a republican government known as the **Commonwealth**. He was unable, however, to set up a smoothly working government that had the support of the English people. After disputes with Parliament, Cromwell tore up a new constitution written in 1653 and dismissed Parliament. Taking the title "Lord Protector," he ruled with the army's support until his death in 1658.

Cromwell succeeded in bringing order to the country, but at great cost. His army brutally crushed an uprising among Catholic royalists in Ireland. Cromwell then forced Catholic landholders to turn over their estates to Protestant English settlers. The Irish said that the "curse of Cromwell" had doomed their land.

Despite his harsh treatment of the Irish Catholics, Cromwell was generally tolerant in religious matters. He promised protection of all English Protestants. He also reopened England's doors to Jews, who had been banned for almost four centuries.

The Restoration

▲ Note strategies for third objective on this page and p. 400.
Cromwell's government was never popular with the English. They disliked military rule and wanted a return to monarchy. In 1660 Parliament invited the son of the executed king to take the throne as Charles II. His reign (1660–1685) is called the **Restoration** period. Charles II was known as the "Merry Monarch." He was popular with his subjects but often at odds with Parliament.

Religious issues lay at the heart of Charles II's problems with Parliament. England was still troubled by serious divisions among Catholics, Anglicans, and other Protestants. Charles urged more tolerant policies than Parliament was willing to grant. He particularly wanted to be sure that his brother James, a Roman Catholic, would inherit the throne. For the last four years of his reign, therefore, Charles did not call a meeting of Parliament.

399

Check for Understanding. Ask: Who were the Cavaliers and the Roundheads? (Cavaliers were supporters of the English king; Roundheads were supporters of Parliament.)
● ENRICHMENT. Have students work in groups to present a panel discussion that might have occurred between Roundheads and Cavaliers. Students might research these groups to find more information about their views. (Application) Understanding Point of View

▲ RETEACHING. Have students identify the following: Restoration; Glorious Revolution; Bill of Rights. (Comprehension) Observing for Detail
▲ REINFORCEMENT. Have students work in groups to discuss the issues that faced Mary and William in 1688. Students should decide which policies might have best resolved problems faced by England. Then have groups share their conclusions with the class. (Synthesis) Problem Solving

The English Bill of Rights

In 1689 Parliament drew up and presented to William and Mary the English Bill of Rights, "an act declaring the rights and liberties" of their subjects, that is, the English people. Adapted below are some of the rights listed in this document. Note that they aim at preventing monarchs from abusing their power.

> 1. The suspending of laws or the execution of laws by regal authority without consent of Parliament is illegal. . . .
>
> 4. Levying money [taxation] for the use of the Crown without grant of Parliament is illegal.
>
> 5. It is the right of the subjects to petition the king, and all arrests and prosecutions for such petitioning are illegal.
>
> 6. The raising or keeping of a standing army within the kingdom in time of peace, unless it be with consent of Parliament, is against the law.
>
> 7. Subjects who are Protestants may have arms for their defense as allowed by law. . . .
>
> 9. Freedom of speech, and debates or proceedings in Parliament, ought not to be questioned in any court or place out of Parliament.

1. How does the Bill of Rights limit the monarch's power to make laws and tax subjects?
2. How does the Bill of Rights protect freedom of speech and a person's right to petition the king?
3. **Critical thinking:** Why, do you think, were William and Mary willing to sign a document that limited their power as monarchs?

Ⓕ See answers below.

400

The Glorious Revolution

James II became king in 1685. He lacked his brother's charm and his policies angered many people. The English made allowances, however, because they thought that James's Protestant daughter Mary would succeed him. Then James's Catholic wife gave birth to a son. People feared that the child would be raised as a Catholic and would, as king, try to restore Catholicism to England. In 1689, therefore, Parliament offered the crown jointly to Mary and her husband William.

The English people cheered at this change of monarchs and thereafter called it the **Glorious Revolution**. James fled to France, where he found supporters. For many years afterward, he and his followers tried unsuccessfully to reclaim the throne for members of the Stuart family.

▲ See below.

Sec. Rev. ques. 5

The Glorious Revolution was a major step in establishing Parliament's supremacy over the English monarch. In 1689 Parliament presented the new rulers, Mary and William III, with the **English Bill of Rights**. The Bill of Rights listed Parliament's complaints against James II and set out rules that future monarchs would have to follow.

These rules made the Crown dependent on Parliament's support. Without the approval of Parliament, the monarch could not make or cancel laws, set taxes, or raise an army during peacetime. The monarch was forbidden to interfere with freedom of speech in the houses of Parliament. The Bill of Rights also strengthened the rights of the individual, outlawing excessive fines and cruel and unusual punishment for crimes.

England was still far from democratic. Because nobles continued to dominate Parliament, the new limitations on the ruler helped the wealthy more than the common people. Yet by reinforcing the principles of parliamentary government and individual liberties, the Bill of Rights gave more freedom to all of England's people. In addition, the Bill of Rights, like the Magna Carta and the Petition of Right, served as an example for reformers everywhere.

See Sec. 4 *Closing the Lesson*, p. T383C.

▲ **ENRICHMENT. Have students research the attempts by James II to reclaim the English throne for the Stuart family. Students might find out when the attempts were made, what they involved, and why they failed.** *(Application)* **Locating Information**

Ⓕ **Primary Source Answers** 1. The monarch cannot make laws or tax subjects without Parliament's approval. 2. Free speech is protected in any court or place outside of Parliament, and subjects are allowed to petition the king without being arrested or prosecuted. 3. Answers will vary. Students may suggest that William and Mary realized that Parliament would not have allowed them to rule otherwise.

Section Review

Answers to Section Review questions are in brackets on pages indicated.

1. **Define or identify:** Petition of Right, habeas corpus, English Civil War, Commonwealth, Restoration, Glorious Revolution, English Bill of Rights.
2. In what ways did England benefit from Elizabeth I's rule? (p. 396)
3. How did the policies of James I and Charles I lead to disagreements be-

tween the monarchy and Parliament? (p. 398)
4. What caused civil war to break out in England? (p. 399)
5. In what way was the Glorious Revolution a victory for Parliament? (p. 400)
6. **Critical thinking:** Why was control of tax collection such an important power for Parliament to have?
(See answer below.)

6. Students might suggest that control of taxation enabled Parliament to prevent monarchs from accruing huge debts or from waging unnecessary wars.

See lesson plans, pp. T383A–T383C.

5 States in Eastern Europe

Objectives

Focus Questions

★ ■ How did Hungary and Poland grow into strong states, then lose their independence? *(pages 401–403)*
● ■ How did Russia become a major European power? *(pages 403–406)*

Terms to Know

autocrat
Time of Troubles
westernize

★ Note strategies for first objective on this page and p. 403.

By the 1500's most of Western Europe had been settled for centuries. The frontier of settlement lay in the region east of the Elbe River, which had thick forests, many rivers, and vast marshlands. Farther east, broad grassy plains—the steppes—stretched from the Carpathian Mountains into Asia.

Since ancient times it had been easy for Asian nomads to cross the steppes and invade Europe. Frequent invasions slowed the formation of states in Eastern Europe. The variety of languages, peoples, and religions also made state-building difficult. Despite these obstacles, several strong states grew up.

The Slavic Peoples

The majority of the people living in Eastern Europe were Slavs, who came from the area near the Pripyat River (map, page 402). After the Germanic tribes moved west and south into Roman territory during the 300's (page 120), Slavic peoples began to move into the lands the Germans had left.

By the time of Charlemagne, the Slavs had split into three major groups. The Western Slavs—mainly Poles, Czechs (CHEKS), and Slovaks—became Roman Catholics and had ties with states in Western Europe. The Eastern Slavs, mostly Russians and Ukrainians, joined the Eastern Orthodox Church. The South Slavs included Roman Catholic Croatians (kroh-AY-shuns) and the Serbians and Bulgarians, who were Eastern Orthodox.

Late in the 800's, an invasion of the Danube River plain by Magyars cut the South Slavs off from the rest of the Slavic peoples. The Magyars were not Slavic. Their language was not even related to the Indo-European languages spoken by most Europeans.

401

★ RETEACHING. Have students review pp. 402–403 and then write a paragraph comparing the reasons for the decline of Hungary and Poland as states. (Hungary had strong rulers but was weakened by repeated Ottoman attacks. Polish rulers were unable to contain the power of nobles. Without a strong central government Poland was unable to protect itself from invaders and partition.) *(Comprehension)* ***Drawing Conclusions***

★ REINFORCEMENT. Have students explain how Poland's 1791 constitution might have strengthened the central government. (The establishment of a hereditary monarchy would have eliminated the election of a king by nobles, thus reducing their power.) *(Comprehension)* ***Drawing Inferences***

Geography The Carpathian Mountains are a crescent-shaped range extending about 900 miles through Czechoslovakia, Poland, Hungary, and Romania.

Formation of the Hungarian State

The Magyars were horseback-riding nomads originally from lands near the Volga River. Led by a chief named Arpád, they migrated into Europe at the end of the ninth century. Their raids westward were stopped by Otto I of Germany (page 241), and they settled down on the Danube River plain, in what is now Hungary.

About the year 1000, Stephen, a descendant of Arpád, was crowned king. During Stephen's long reign, the Hungarians converted to Christianity. Stephen unified Hungary and set up a feudal system that gave power to a few landowning nobles.

A number of strong rulers followed Stephen, gaining territory for Hungary and building its power. In 1241, however, Hungary, like the rest of Eastern Europe, was overrun by Mongol invaders (page 191). Half the population was killed, and the country was devastated. The Arpád line of rulers died out, and in 1308 the Hungarian nobles gave the crown to Charles Robert, a man of French descent. Charles introduced Western feudal practices and the ideals of chivalry. He also encouraged trade and the growth of towns.

Charles's son Louis I ruled Hungary for 40 years (1342–1382). Known as Louis the Great, he continued his father's attempts to limit the nobles' power. The rulers of territories to the east became vassals of the Hungarian king. To the south, however, Hungary had to defend itself against the Ottoman Turks, who were moving into Eastern Europe. The Ottomans threatened Hungary all through the 1300's and 1400's.

Sec. Rev. ques. 2

In 1526, at the Battle of Mohács (page 278), the Turks defeated the Hungarians and killed the Hungarian king. Hapsburg armies then marched in from Austria and claimed the crown of Hungary. Still the Ottomans advanced. By 1540 most of Hungary was under Ottoman rule.

Poland's Struggles for Unity

To the north of Hungary, the foundations of a Polish state were laid late in the 900's. Powerful nobles resisted the creation of strong central rule, however. Not until the 1300's did a powerful leader emerge. This was Casimir III, Poland's king from 1333 to 1370.

Early prosperity. Casimir ruled both wisely and humanely, bringing peace and prosperity to his people. In appreciation, they called him the "Peasants' King." Casimir encouraged the settlement of Polish lands by Western Europeans and also by Jews, who were being driven out of other European countries. In Poland, Jews were permitted to practice their religion freely.

Disunity and partition. During the 1500's Poland enjoyed a golden age of culture and prosperity. This golden age was short-lived, for feudal nobles soon regained the

KEY
— Poland before partitions
To Russia
To Prussia
To Austria

RUSSIA
BALTIC SEA
PRUSSIA
1793 Danzig
E. PRUSSIA
1772
1795 1795
1793 Warsaw
1795
Krakow 1772
AUSTRIA
Vienna
Buda Pest
OTTOMAN EMPIRE
Riga
W. Dvina R.
Niemen R.
1772
1793
Pripyat R.
Dnieper R.
Bug R.
Vistula R.
Kiev
Oder R.
Danube R.
Dniester R.

SCALE
0 — 150 mi
0 — 150 km

Partitions of Poland

Weakened by wars and lack of strong central government, Poland fell prey to three powerful neighbors. Which country gained most?

402

Map Answer: Russia.

Linking Past and Present The present-day Magyar population is about 15 million. Approximately 10.5 million Magyars live in Hungary; 4 million live in the countries of Romania, Czechoslovakia, Yugoslavia, Ukraine, Russia, and Austria. About 1 million people of Magyar descent live in the United States.

Biography Stephen, who was immensely loved and respected during his reign, was declared a saint in the Roman Catholic Church in 1083.

power they had lost to the monarchy. In 1572 the nobles began electing the monarch. To gain support, each new ruler gave the nobles more privileges. Polish nobles prided themselves on their many rights and their control over the parliament. Each noble had the right to halt meetings by a veto and even to dissolve the parliament. This prevented effective government and kept central rule weak.

Poland's weakness and lack of natural barriers (such as mountains) made it easy prey for foreign conquerors. By 1772 Russian influence was strong, particularly in eastern Poland. Poland's neighbors—Russia, Prussia, and Austria—all decided to take slices of Polish land. In this partition—the first of three—Poland lost about a third of its land and half its population.

Sec. Rev. ques. 3

The humiliation of the partition sparked a reform movement in Poland. The Polish parliament tried to strengthen the central government by passing a new constitution in 1791. The constitution called for a hereditary monarchy and an end to most feudal practices. Russia, fearing that a stronger Poland would be more difficult to dominate, crushed the reform movement. More Polish territory went to Russia and Prussia in 1793.

In 1794 Polish patriots raised a volunteer army. Although they were brilliantly led by Thaddeus Kosciusko (kahs-ee-US-koh), they could not stop the forces of Prussia and Russia. What was left of Poland was divided between Russia, Prussia, and Austria in 1795. With this third partition, Poland ceased to exist as an independent nation.

★ See below.

Russia as a Major Power

● Note strategies for second objective on this page and p. 405.

Czars against the boyars. During the late 1400's, as you read in Chapter 9, Czar Ivan the Great freed Russia from Mongol rule and expanded his territory. He also strengthened central rule by ending the self-government of towns, ignoring the council of boyars, and turning over the nobles' estates to his supporters.

Ivan's grandson, Ivan IV, continued policies of strong rule and expansionism.

Ivan IV built St. Basil's Cathedral in Moscow after a Russian victory over the Mongols. St. Basil's consists of eight separate churches, each capped by an onion-shaped dome.

These policies earned him the nickname "Ivan the Terrible." Like his grandfather, Ivan the Terrible was an **autocrat**—a ruler with unlimited power. His harsh treatment of the boyar class turned into a bloodbath in 1560. Suspecting that the leading boyars had murdered his wife, Ivan had them massacred. A group of soldiers, dressed in black and riding black horses, was sent to kill the boyars and their families and servants.

The Time of Troubles. Ivan's death in 1584 plunged Russia into turmoil. The murder of thousands of boyars had left Russia with few trained officials. Attempts to restore order limited the freedom of the peasants, **403**

Biography Kosciusko sailed to the American colonies in August 1776, and was appointed colonel of engineers in the Continental Army. In 1783 Congress awarded him citizenship and the rank of brigadier general.

★ **ENRICHMENT.** Have students write a letter that Kosciusko might have written to one of his friends who had fought during the American Revolution. In his letter, Kosciusko should discuss why the American colonies won independence and Poland did not. *(Synthesis) Connecting Historical Events*

● **RETEACHING.** Have students review "Great Russian Rulers" (pp. 404–406) and find information to support the following statements: (a) The focus of Peter's rule was westernization. (b) Catherine sought to stabilize society and expand Russian territory. *(Comprehension) Supporting Generalizations*

● **REINFORCEMENT.** Have students outline the information explaining how Peter strengthened central rule. *(Comprehension) Organizing Information in Written Form*

Growth of Russia, 1462–1796

Russian czars like Peter the Great (shown here disguised as a peasant) vigorously pursued territorial expansion. Which inland sea did Russia have access to in 1584? What other seas were accessible by 1796?

Map Answers: (1) Caspian Sea. (2) Black Sea, Baltic Sea.

who were now forbidden to move from one estate to another. Landowners needed the peasants' labor, while the government depended on their taxes. Gradually, the peasants became serfs, falling completely under the control of the landowners.

Adding to the unrest were armed bands of runaway serfs, farmers, and adventurers. Disorder was so widespread that the period from about 1598 to 1613 in Russia is known as the **Time of Troubles**. Moscow was threatened by civil war, peasant revolts, and invasion by Swedish and Polish armies. Several groups tried to seize power. In 1613 an assembly of townspeople and landholders elected a new czar, Michael Romanov, who began a new dynasty. The Romanov family ruled Russia until 1917 and transformed it into a powerful empire.

404

Great Russian Rulers

The leader most responsible for making Russia a European power was Peter I. Called Peter the Great, he ruled Russia from 1682 to 1725.

A leader of vision. Among the monarchs of the age, Peter stood out as a giant. Nearly seven feet tall, he had immense physical strength, vitality, and curiosity. As a boy, he began to admire the Western customs of the foreign traders he knew in Moscow. He also learned military skills, shipbuilding, and sailing.

In 1697 and 1698, disguised as an ordinary traveler, Peter became the first czar to visit Western Europe. What he learned in France, England, and the Netherlands con-

Biography During his journey through Western Europe, Peter used the name "Bombardier Peter Mikhailov." During his travels he visited many shipyards, hoping to increase his knowledge of shipbuilding.

vinced him that if Russia wanted to compete with other countries, it had to **westernize**—adopt technology and customs from the West.

"Window on the West." Peter saw that Russia needed better seaports to end its isolation from the West. Russia's Arctic ports were blocked by ice for much of the year. Peter resolved, therefore, to gain access to the Baltic Sea, then dominated by Sweden.

With the kings of Poland and Denmark as allies, Peter began the Great Northern War (1700–1721). Sweden's King Charles XII, only 18 when the war began, proved to be a brilliant military leader. He quickly halted the Russian advance. Peter, however, reorganized Russia's army and navy and defeated Sweden. Victory gave Peter the territory along the Baltic Sea that he wanted.

Strengthening central rule. Peter's reforms of the government, like his reforms of the army and navy, adapted Western ideas to Russian conditions. Peter replaced the old council of boyars with appointed officials. He also divided Russia into separate provinces and set up a more efficient bureaucracy to govern them. New industries were begun and supported with state money. Even the Russian Orthodox Church (a branch of the Eastern Orthodox Church) came under state control.

Sec. Rev. ques. 4

To make these changes work, Peter required all classes of society to serve the state in some way. Landowners acted as government officials or army officers; peasants became soldiers or worked on public building projects. Peter made especially heavy demands on peasants. These people were treated little better than slaves under Peter.

New customs and styles. Peter's admiration for the West went beyond its military and political ideas. Peter wanted to transform completely the old Russian way of life. He declared that the Russian nobles must wear Western styles of clothing. He also started schools for the children of the nobility, modernized the Russian calendar, and simplified the alphabet. He stopped excluding women from social life and tried to train his bureaucrats in the Western manner.

As a symbol of Russia's turn toward the West, Peter in 1703 built a new capital, St. Petersburg, near the Baltic coast. The new city was far removed from the old capital in Moscow. Peter's efforts to change Russia, however, created a deep cultural and social gulf between the westernized nobles and the rest of the people, who still followed traditional ways.

Catherine the Great. The most outstanding ruler to follow Peter was Czarina (empress) Catherine II, known as Catherine the Great. A German princess, Catherine had come to Russia at age 15 to marry Peter's grandson, the future Peter III. Catherine converted to the Russian Orthodox Church, educated herself by reading Western literature, and gained self-confidence and charm. She soon won the favor of the court.

Catherine's husband came to the throne early in 1762. When he was murdered a few months later, Catherine took his place. Catherine had a weak claim to the throne, yet her reign (1762–1796) was the most glorious in the history of Russia. The famous French writers of the day hailed her as the most forward-looking of European monarchs.

● See below.

Although she too wished to westernize Russia, Catherine ruled differently from Peter the Great. She freed the nobles from having to follow careers in the civil or military service, and she encouraged them to develop and manage their estates. She also gave merchants and townspeople more freedom, and she supported trade, education, and the arts and sciences. Catherine's rule, however,

Linking Past and Present

In 1764 Catherine the Great established the Hermitage museum, a collection of paintings she kept in a small building in St. Petersburg. The collection has grown over the years, and today the Hermitage is one of the finest art museums in the world.

● ENRICHMENT. Have students find out how Peter the Great and Catherine were viewed in the Soviet Union during the years under Communist rule. Students might do research on Soviet education to find out how Russian history under those rulers was taught. (Synthesis) *Locating Information* brought benefits mainly to the educated upper classes. She did next to nothing for the serfs. A rebellion by serfs in 1773 led to even harsher rule by the government.

Expansion. Like Peter the Great, Catherine wanted better seaports for Russia. The Baltic ports seized by Peter, though more useful than Arctic ports, were still closed by ice each winter. In two wars with the Ottoman Turks, Catherine finally won control of the northern shore of the Black Sea. Russia also gained rich farmlands in the west and much territory from the partitions of Poland (page 403). By the end of Catherine's reign, Russian society and culture were more stable, and Russia was a major European power.

See Sec. 5 *Closing the Lesson,* p. T383C.

Chapter 20   Summary and Timeline

1. Spain's rulers united their country in the late 1400's and made it the leading European power for a century. Then, under Charles V, Spain and its empire came into the hands of the powerful Hapsburgs of Austria. Involvement in many wars helped drive Spain from wealth to bankruptcy.

2. Religious conflicts dominated Europe in the sixteenth and seventeenth centuries. In France these conflicts led to greater tolerance. In Germany they led to the destructive Thirty Years' War.

3. The reign of Louis XIV marked the height of absolute monarchy in France. Louis used his power to promote French culture.

With no one to restrain him, however, Louis led France into unwise wars and serious economic trouble.

4. England prospered in the reign of Elizabeth I, but the Stuart kings who followed her tried to rule with absolute power. The English Parliament rebelled in the 1640's and set up a short-lived republic known as the Commonwealth. Monarchy was restored in 1660, but Parliament continued to limit royal power.

5. Foreign invasions cut short the development of strong states in Hungary and Poland. Russia, however, became a major power under czars Peter and Catherine.

1492 Muslim rule ends in Spain

1558 Elizabeth I begins rule of England

1588 Spanish Armada defeated

1598 Edict of Nantes

1618 Thirty Years' War begins

1628 Petition of Right

1643 Louis XIV becomes king of France

1682 Peter I begins rule of Russia

1689 English Bill of Rights

1762 Catherine II begins rule of Russia

1795 Partition of Poland completed

1500   1550   1600   1650   1700   1750   1800

406

5. Students might note that both rulers sought to westernize Russia and to expand its territory. Whereas Peter required all classes to serve the state, Catherine freed the nobles from civil and military service. She also gave merchants and townspeople—but not serfs—more freedom.

CHAPTER 20 REVIEW

See p. T383C for answers to Chapter Review.

Vocabulary Review

1. Match each of the following terms with its correct definition: *divine right, Edict of Nantes, habeas corpus, Time of Troubles, westernize.*
   a. theory that a ruler's power comes from God
   b. order that was issued by Henry IV in 1598, giving the Huguenots religious freedom
   c. period of widespread disorder in Russia from 1598 to 1613
   d. adopt the technology and customs of the West
   e. principle that no one should be kept in prison unless charged with a specific crime
2. Identify the terms in the following pairs.
   a. Petition of Right; English Bill of Rights
   b. English Civil War; Commonwealth
   c. Restoration; Glorious Revolution

People to Identify

Use the following names to complete the sentences below: *Casimir III, Charles I, Charles V, Ivan IV, Louis XIV, Philip II, Richelieu, Stephen.*

1. Versailles is an example of France's splendor during the reign of king ___?___.
2. King ___?___ of England agreed reluctantly to sign the Petition of Right.
3. During the reign of ___?___, the Hungarians converted to Christianity.
4. ___?___ sent the Invincible Armada to England.
5. Known as the "Peasants' King," ___?___ brought peace and prosperity to Poland.
6. France's chief minister during the reign of Louis XIII was ___?___.
7. As King of Spain and Holy Roman Emperor, ___?___ ruled a huge empire in the 1500's.
8. ___?___ was an autocrat who treated the boyars harshly and worked to expand Russia.

Places to Know

Match the letters on this map of Europe about 1648 with the places listed below. You may want to refer to the map on page 391.

1. Hapsburg Austria
2. Baltic Sea
3. Black Sea
4. England
5. France
6. Poland
7. Russia
8. Spain
9. Sweden

Recalling the Facts

1. What steps did Isabella and Ferdinand take to unify Spain?
2. How did Philip II strengthen the power of Spain and the Roman Catholic Church?
3. What factors led to Spain's decline?
4. What was the Thirty Years' War?

407

5. How did the Peace of Westphalia change the balance of power in Europe?
6. How did Jean Baptiste Colbert try to build up the French economy? Why did the economy decline nonetheless?
7. Why was the War of the Spanish Succession fought? How did the Peace of Utrecht restore the balance of power in Europe?
8. How did Elizabeth I lay the foundations for an English empire? How did she support Protestantism?
9. What did James I and Parliament disagree about?
10. What two issues led to conflict between Charles I and Parliament? How did civil war break out?
11. Why was Oliver Cromwell's rule unpopular with the English people?
12. What was the Glorious Revolution? How did it strengthen Parliament?
13. How did the nation of Hungary lose its independence?
14. What factors made Poland weak? What three countries partitioned Poland?
15. How did Peter the Great westernize Russian culture? How did Catherine the Great expand Russian territory?

Critical Thinking Skills

1. **Understanding chronology.** Use the information in the timeline on page 406 to start a timetable of important events. Add at least *(Comp.)* five more dates and events from the chapter.

2. **Supporting a main idea.** Explain and give evidence to support the following statement: "The English Parliament used the power of the purse to limit the power of the monarchy and protect citizens' rights." *(Comp.)*

3. **Drawing conclusions.** Both Peter I and Catherine II have the title "the Great" attached to their names. What did each monarch do to earn this title? What people in Russian society might not have agreed with this description of those rulers? What guidelines or criteria do you think should be used **408** to decide whether or not a ruler is great? *(Syn.)*

Thinking About Geography

Interpreting a map. Study the map of Russia on page 404. Note the locations of mountains, rivers, and seas. Then explain why Russia wanted a southern water route for trade with Europe. How did the Baltic Sea give Russia access to Europe? How did the Black Sea give access to Europe? *(Comp.)*

Enrichment: Primary Sources

The following statements are adapted from the advice Louis XIV of France gave to his 17-year-old grandson Philip when Philip became king of Spain.

66 1. Never omit any of your duties, especially toward God. . . .

7. Love the Spaniards. Do not give preference to those who flatter you most. Esteem those who for a good cause are not afraid to displease you; these are your real friends. . . .

9. Live in close union with France, since there is nothing so advantageous to our two powers as this union. . . .

33. I will end with one of the most important pieces of advice: Never allow yourself to be ruled; be the master; have no favorites or prime minister. Listen to, and consult your Council, but you decide yourself. 99

1. Which advisers does Louis say are the real friends of the king?
2. Which suggestion would help Philip maintain power as a ruler?
3. **Critical thinking:** Which piece of advice do you think was most valuable to Philip when he became king of Spain? Give reasons for your answer. *(Eval.)*

WORLD HISTORY
Checklist

UNIT 5

Try to identify the following key people, places, and terms from the unit. If you need help, refer to the pages listed.

Key People

Francesco Petrarch *(328)*
Niccolo Machiavelli *(329)*
Isabella d'Este *(329)*
Johann Gutenberg *(329)*
Desiderius Erasmus *(331)*
Sir Thomas More *(331)*
Miguel de Cervantes
   Saavedra *(332)*
William Shakespeare *(333)*
Michelangelo *(334)*
Leonardo da Vinci *(334)*
Martin Luther *(338)*
John Calvin *(339)*
Henry VIII *(339)*
Ignatius Loyola *(342)*
Prince Henry the Navigator
   (348)
Bartholomeu Dias *(348)*
Christopher Columbus *(349)*
Queen Isabella *(349, 385)*
Ferdinand Magellan *(353)*

Michelangelo's *David*.

Hernando Cortés *(355)*
Montezuma *(355)*
Francisco Pizarro *(355)*
Samuel de Champlain *(360)*
Francis Drake *(368)*
Charles V *(386)*
Philip II *(386)*
Henry IV *(390)*
Cardinal Richelieu *(390)*
Louis XIV *(392)*
Elizabeth I *(396)*
Charles I *(398)*
Oliver Cromwell *(399)*
Casimir III *(402)*
Ivan IV, "the Terrible" *(403)*
Peter I, "the Great" *(404)*
Catherine II, "the Great"
   (405)

Key Places

Wittenberg *(338)*
Trent *(341)*
Cape of Good Hope *(349)*
Strait of Magellan *(353)*
Tenochtitlán *(355)*
Jamestown *(359)*
Quebec *(360)*
Slave Coast *(379)*

Key Terms

Renaissance *(327)*
Vatican *(335)*
Protestant *(337)*
Reformation *(337)*
Peace of Augsburg *(339)*
Calvinism *(339)*
Act of Supremacy *(340)*
Counter-Reformation *(341)*
Age of Exploration *(347)*
monopoly *(348)*
Line of Demarcation *(351)*
Northwest Passage *(358)*
Puritan *(359)*
French and Indian War
   (363)
Commercial Revolution
   (367)
mercantilism *(367)*
capitalism *(371)*
free-enterprise system
   (371)
Middle Passage *(378)*
Invincible Armada *(387)*
Edict of Nantes *(390)*
balance of power *(390)*
Thirty Years' War *(390)*
Peace of Westphalia *(391)*
divine right *(392)*
Versailles *(393)*
War of the Spanish Succession *(395)*
Peace of Utrecht *(395)*
Petition of Right *(398)*
English Civil War *(399)*
Commonwealth *(399)*
Restoration *(399)*
Glorious Revolution *(400)*
English Bill of Rights *(400)*
Time of Troubles *(404)*

REVIEW ACTIVITIES. *Key People:* For each person listed, identify the European state that was his or her homeland and name the person's most important achievement or action. ***Key Places:*** Identify the continent and country for each place listed; then explain the significance of each place. ***Key Terms:*** Define or identify each term listed.

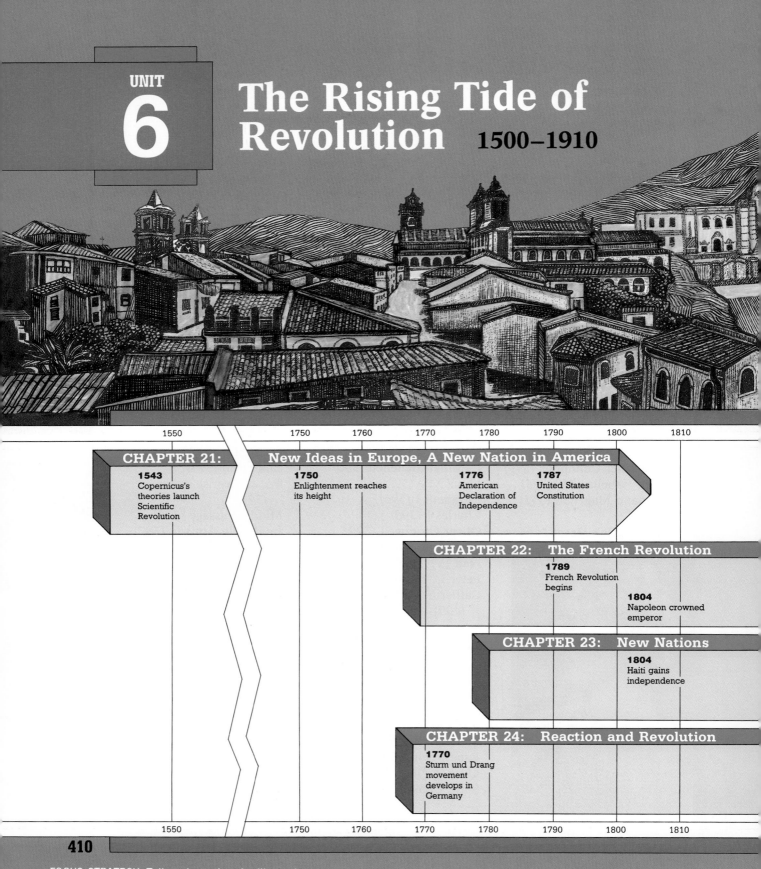

UNIT 6

The Rising Tide of Revolution 1500–1910

| | 1550 | 1750 | 1760 | 1770 | 1780 | 1790 | 1800 | 1810 |

CHAPTER 21: New Ideas in Europe, A New Nation in America

1543
Copernicus's theories launch Scientific Revolution

1750
Enlightenment reaches its height

1776
American Declaration of Independence

1787
United States Constitution

CHAPTER 22: The French Revolution

1789
French Revolution begins

1804
Napoleon crowned emperor

CHAPTER 23: New Nations

1804
Haiti gains independence

CHAPTER 24: Reaction and Revolution

1770
Sturm und Drang movement develops in Germany

| | 1550 | 1750 | 1760 | 1770 | 1780 | 1790 | 1800 | 1810 |

410

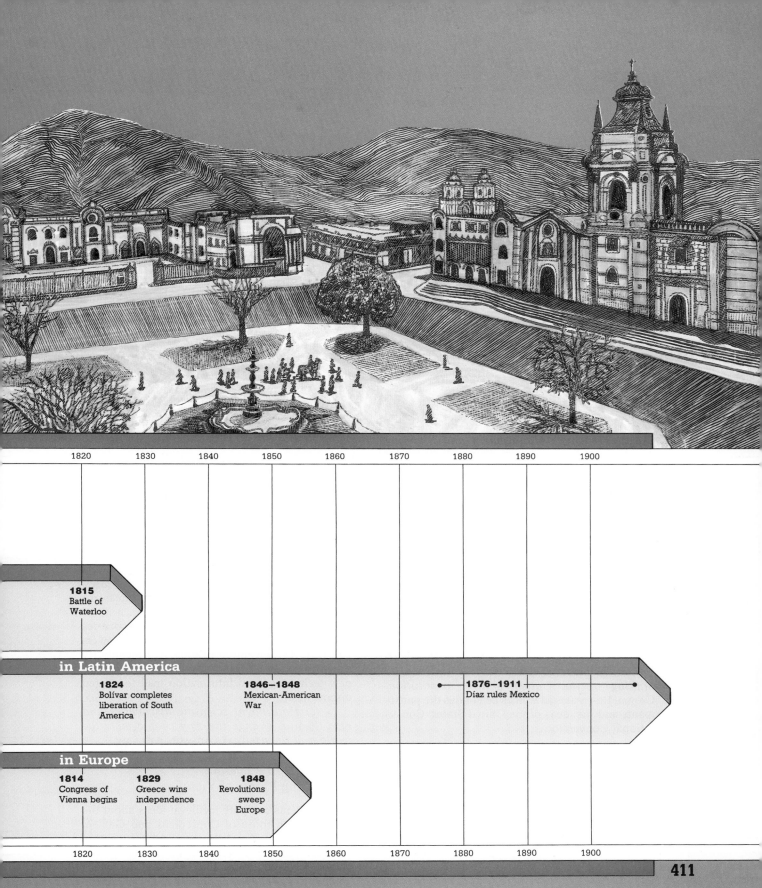

1820　1830　1840　1850　1860　1870　1880　1890　1900

1815
Battle of
Waterloo

in Latin America

1824
Bolívar completes
liberation of South
America

1846–1848
Mexican-American
War

1876–1911
Díaz rules Mexico

in Europe

1814
Congress of
Vienna begins

1829
Greece wins
independence

1848
Revolutions
sweep
Europe

1820　1830　1840　1850　1860　1870　1880　1890　1900

Have students refer to the unit timeline to answer the following question: **Which nations gained independence in the period shown
here?** (The United States, Haiti, nations in South America, and
Greece.)

New Ideas in Europe, A New Nation in America   1500–1800   (pp. 412–433)

Chapter Preview

Section 1 of this chapter examines scientific advances that led to a rejection of the medieval view of the universe and established the foundations of modern scientific thinking. Section 2 describes the Age of Reason—the Enlightenment—and explains how political thinkers applied reason and the scientific approach to the study of social and political life. The rebellion of American colonists against British rule and the founding of the United States are discussed in Section 3.

Bibliography

See the *Teacher's Management and Planning Guide* for additional listings. Starred titles are for both students and teachers.

Burke, James. *The Day the Universe Changed.* Little, Brown. Examines the critical periods since the Middle Ages when people's basic ideas about the world changed.

Cunningham, Noble, Jr. *In Pursuit of Reason: The Life of Thomas Jefferson.* Louisiana State University Press. A one-volume biography of the United States' leading personification of Enlightenment ideals.

Norton, Mary B. *Liberty's Daughters.* Little, Brown. Women's roles in the American Revolution.

*Peters, William. *A More Perfect Union: The Making of the United States Constitution.* Crown. Re-creates as well as celebrates the participants and the ideas of the United States' Constitutional Convention.

Redondi, Pietro. *Galileo: Heretic.* Princeton University Press. Much acclaimed account of Galileo's clash with the Inquisition.

Section Lesson Plans

SECTION 1   (pp. 413–418)
New Scientific Views

Objectives

After completing this section, students will be able to:
1. Explain how scientific discoveries led to new theories about the universe.
2. Describe advances that were made in the study of living things.

Introducing the Lesson

Remind students that scientific thinking during the Middle Ages was limited by belief in magic and superstition and by the use of astrology and alchemy. In the sixteenth and seventeenth centuries, however, new theories and discoveries about the universe began to change the way people thought about the world and themselves.

Then ask: *(a) What might account for the development of new scientific theory?* (Answers will vary. As knowledge about the world increases, scientific thinkers develop unproven ideas, or theories, about the unknown.)

(b) Why might many scientific discoveries occur during a particular time period? (Answers will vary. The invention of tools and technology often precedes scientific discoveries. Sometimes new technology and information lead to related discoveries.)

(c) How might scientific discoveries and new theories change the way people view the world and themselves? (Answers will vary.)

Developing the Lesson: Comparing Points of View

Have students compare medieval ideas about the universe with those of Copernicus and Galileo. (During the Middle Ages, people believed that God designed the universe for human beings, the planets revolved around the earth, and the dwelling place of God was beyond the planets and the stars. Copernicus developed a heliocentric theory, claiming that the sun was fixed at the center of the universe with all other planets revolving around it. Galileo agreed with Copernicus, and realized that knowledge of nature came from observation.) *(Comprehension)*

Developing the Lesson: Synthesizing Information

Have students work in groups to present a panel discussion explaining the relationships between the Renaissance (pp. 327–336), the Reformation (pp. 337–342), the Age of Exploration (pp. 346–363), and the Scientific Revolution. Students might explain the fundamental ideas of each period, show how they might have influenced one another, and speculate about why these developments occurred. *(Synthesis)*

Closing the Lesson: Drawing Inferences

Have students write an essay explaining how the scientific developments described in this chapter can be regarded as a "revolution" in the field of science. Students should define the word *revolution*, describe how a scientific revolution might affect people, and then explain whether or not the scientific changes between 1500 and 1800 were revolutionary. *(Synthesis)*

See *Section Review* questions, p. 418.

SECTION 2 (pp. 419–423)
Enlightenment Ideas and Reforms

Objectives

After completing this section, students will be able to:
1. Identify the leading philosophers of the Enlightenment.
2. Explain how Enlightenment ideas spread throughout society.

Introducing the Lesson

Remind students that during the Scientific Revolution, ideas and methods of the Middle Ages were abandoned for new ways of looking at the universe. During the period called the Enlightenment, political thinkers and other philosophers rejected medieval views of society and looked to nature and reason to explain social relationships.

Then ask: *(a) How might the Scientific Revolution have influenced the views of political thinkers and philosophers?* (Answers will vary. The discovery of natural laws that appeared to explain phenomena of the universe led some to look for natural laws to explain human behavior. As more people learned about the discoveries of natural scientists, the application of reason to social relationships became more acceptable.)

(b) How might an explanation of social relationships based on nature and reason differ from those based on medieval views? (Answers will vary. During the Middle Ages, people accepted the Biblical view of human nature and relationships: human beings were born sinful, but were offered salvation by Jesus Christ (pp. 126–127). An explanation of society and human nature based on nature and reason might reject the idea of salvation through religion and focus on the importance of human action.)

(c) How do you think future historians will describe present-day ideas about the nature of society? (Answers will vary.)

Developing the Lesson: Forming a Hypothesis

Have students develop a hypothesis about how Thomas Hobbes, John Locke, Montesquieu, and Jean Jacques Rousseau might feel about present-day society and government. Students might stage a panel discussion of Enlightenment views, create a newspaper in which students represent the views of the thinkers, or create a display in which various aspects of present-day society and government are evaluated by the Enlightenment philosophers. *(Synthesis)*

Developing the Lesson: Contrasting Historical Periods

Have students work in groups to contrast medieval ideas of human behavior, society, government, and religion with those of the Enlightenment. Students might present a debate between representatives of both periods or stage a court of Inquisition (p. 245) at which an Enlightenment philosopher is tried by the Church court for his or her views. *(Comprehension)*

Closing the Lesson: Making Judgments

Have students write an essay explaining their opinions about Enlightenment ideas. Students might explain which Enlightenment thinker best represents their personal views or summarize and evaluate the ideas expressed by the philosophers. *(Evaluation)*

See *Section Review* questions, p. 423.

SECTION 3   (pp. 424–431)
The American Revolution

Objectives

After completing this section, students will be able to:

1. Explain what led American colonists to rebel against Britain.
2. Discuss how the colonies won their freedom.
3. Describe the kind of government Americans formed.

Introducing the Lesson

Remind students that the British colonists in America were influenced by the ideas of the Enlightenment thinkers. The political philosophy of John Locke, Montesquieu, and Rousseau provided the intellectual framework for the American Revolution.

Then ask: *(a) What might lead members of a society to use force against their government?* (Answers will vary. A revolution is usually a result of government abuse and its violation of rights, and from the perception that change can only occur with the use of force.)

(b) How might a government protect itself from the rebellion of its citizens? (Answers will vary. Governments based on effective popular consensus are unlikely to experience revolutions. A government can attempt to protect itself by maintaining absolute control.)

(c) When, if ever, do you think revolutions are justified? (Answers will vary.)

Developing the Lesson:
Dramatizing Historical Events

Have students prepare a speech that might have been given by a supporter of American independence after the Boston Massacre. Students should refer to Enlightenment ideas, the mercantile policies of the British government (p. 367), and actions taken against American colonists by the British. Have students present their speeches to the class. *(Application)* (4A, 4G, AVS1, AVS3)

Developing the Lesson:
Making Decisions

Have students work in groups to stage a debate that might have occurred in the Second Continental Congress between those who wanted independence and those who wanted to remain loyal to Britain. After the debate, have the class judge the strength of the arguments as a basis for a vote on the issue. *(Synthesis)*

Closing the Lesson: Making Judgments

Have students compare the goals of the American Revolution and the Constitution with characteristics of present-day American society and then answer the following:

(a) Does the United States today reflect the political values of Americans in 1787?

(b) If the authors of the Constitution could have predicted how the nation and the world would change over the last two centuries, do you think they would have written the Constitution differently? (Synthesis)

See *Section Review* questions, p. 431.

Chapter 21 Review Answers
(pp. 432–433)

Vocabulary Review

1. (a) social contract (b) scientific method (c) Declaration of Independence (d) natural rights (e) federal system (f) philosophes
2. (a) Geocentric theory—earth-centered view of the universe; heliocentric theory—sun-centered view of the universe. (b) Atheist—person who denies the existence of God; deist—person who believes in God as the creator, but rejects Church rituals and the authority of the clergy. (c) Baroque—ornate artistic style popular from the 1500's to the early 1700's; Classical—simple, elegant artistic style of the late 1700's that reflected the style of ancient Greece and Rome. (d) Scientific Revolution—period during the 1500's and 1600's when new scientific theories and discoveries led to new ways of thinking about the world; Enlightenment—period during the 1600's and 1700's when thinkers began to apply reason and the scientific method to the study of society. (e) Constitution—plan of government created by the leaders of the United States in 1787; Bill of Rights—10 amendments to the Constitution proposed in 1789 to guarantee Americans certain basic liberties.

People to Identify

1. German composer who wrote music in the baroque style.
2. Aristocrat who translated Newton's work into French.
3. Polish scientist whose heliocentric theory marked the beginnings of modern scientific thinking.
4. Chief editor of the *Encyclopedia*.
5. American who helped convince the French to aid the colonists against Britain.
6. German astronomer who mathematically proved that planets revolve around the sun.
7. Philosophe who supported separation of powers to protect people's liberties.
8. Flemish doctor known as the father of modern anatomy.

Places to Know

1. B   2. D   3. A   4. C

Recalling the Facts

1. Galileo supported the heliocentric theory, an idea that contradicted Church teachings and thus challenged the authority of the Church and the Pope.
2. Newton's discoveries made it possible to explain the movements of planets and objects on earth.
3. Descartes favored using mathematics and logic rather than observation and experimentation.
4. Locke's belief that a government's power comes from the consent of the people is the basis of modern democratic government.
5. The philosophes criticized the special privileges given to the nobility and the clergy. Both groups paid few taxes.
6. Most philosophes believed that progress in the arts and sciences would improve life for all people; Rousseau believed that arts and sciences corrupted people's natural goodness.
7. At times they practiced religious toleration, ended censorship, discouraged serfdom, simplified laws, and widened opportunities for education. They did not want to take too many privileges away from the nobility for fear of losing the nobles' support.
8. They argued that both acts were examples of taxation without representation.
9. The Congress could not impose taxes to raise money, nor did it have any way to enforce its decisions.

10. They followed the principle of separation of powers by creating three separate branches of government—the executive, legislative, and judicial. They set up a system of checks and balances by giving each of the three branches some control over the others.

Critical Thinking Skills

1. Microbe—tiny life form; microfilm—film containing reduced-size photographs; micron—one millionth of a meter; microsurgery—surgery on tiny living structures or cells.
2–3. Answers will vary.
4. Answers will vary. Students might suggest that the philosophes would be pleased by the freedoms guaranteed by the Bill of Rights, such as freedom of the press and freedom of speech. The democratic political system in the United States, especially universal suffrage, would probably disappoint them.

Thinking About Geography

Answers will vary. Students might note the difficulty of enforcing British law in the colonies from a distance, and the time lag in communication between Britain and the colonies.

Enrichment: Primary Sources

1. 10,000 times smaller.
2. They sometimes stuck out two moving horns.
3. "These little animals were the most wretched creatures that I have ever seen."
4. Answers will vary. Students might suggest that many people would have had trouble believing in the existence of living creatures that could not be seen with the naked eye.

New Ideas in Europe, A New Nation in America

1500–1800

See chapter timeline, p. 431.

Before You Read This Chapter

What does the word *progress* mean to you? Do you believe that people, working together, can gradually make the world a better place to live? If so, you share the views of Europeans in a time known as the Enlightenment. Between 1500 and 1800, people gained new confidence in the power of the human mind to understand nature and to improve society. As you read, ask yourself what progress meant to these scientists, thinkers, and political leaders. How did each one hope to make people wiser, happier, or freer?

The Geographic Setting

The Chapter Outline

1. New Scientific Views
2. Enlightenment Ideas and Reforms
3. The American Revolution

The first balloon flight took place in France in 1783. Some peasants who saw the balloon thought the moon had fallen from the sky.

1 New Scientific Views

Objectives

Focus Questions

★ ■ How did scientific discoveries lead to new theories about the universe? *(pages 413–415)*

● ■ What advances were made in the study of living things? *(pages 416–418)*

Terms to Know

Scientific Revolution
scientific method
geocentric theory
heliocentric theory

★ Note strategies for first objective on this page and p. 415.

The Renaissance inspired a spirit of curiosity in many fields. In science, as in the arts and the humanities, people began to question ideas that had been accepted for hundreds of years. New scientific theories and discoveries led to changes so great that historians speak of a **Scientific Revolution** during the 1500's and 1600's.

The Scientific Method

The many discoveries of the Scientific Revolution were made possible by a new method of looking at nature. As early as the 1200's, the English thinker Roger Bacon (page 257) had argued that scientists should use experiments to learn about the natural world. At the time, Bacon's idea fell on deaf ears. In the 1500's, however, many scientists were following his advice. They used what has come to be called the **scientific method**—a logical procedure for gathering information and testing ideas.

The scientific method involves stating a problem or question, forming a hypothesis (an unproved theory), making observations and experiments, and drawing conclusions. Using the scientific method, scientists of the 1500's and 1600's revolutionized the way we think of the universe.

Changing Views of the Universe

The medieval view. In medieval times people believed that the sun, moon, and planets revolved around the earth. This idea had begun with the Greek philosopher Aristotle in the fourth century B.C. It had been re-stated by the Greek astronomer Ptolemy in the second century A.D. and supported by the Christian Church during the Middle Ages. The Church taught that God had designed the universe especially for human beings. He had placed the earth at its center, ringed by the planets. Beyond the planets lay the stars, and beyond the stars was the dwelling place of God.

This earth-centered view of the universe, called the **geocentric theory**, made sense to people of the Middle Ages. They observed the sun traveling across the sky every day, and they noted the changing patterns of stars at night. Yet, the earth did not appear to move. It seemed logical to think that the earth was the fixed center of the universe.

Copernicus. In the early 1500's, the geocentric view of the universe was questioned by Nicolaus Copernicus (koh-PUR-nih-kus), a Polish churchman, doctor, and astronomer. Copernicus thought that the sun was in a fixed position at the center of the universe and that the earth was one of the planets circling around it.

Sec. Rev. ques. 2

Copernicus's **heliocentric theory**—the idea that the sun was at the center of the universe—marked the beginnings of modern astronomy and modern scientific thinking. **413**

Copernicus knew, however, that most scholars and clergy of the time would reject his theory because it went against their religious views. Fearing persecution, he did not publish his work until 1543, the last year of his life. Not until the next century did Copernicus's ideas become widely accepted.

The Achievements of Galileo

One of the first people to agree with Copernicus was Galileo Galilei (1564–1642). An Italian scientist and mathematician, Galileo was a firm believer in the scientific method. Knowledge of nature, he thought, came from making "sensible experiments and necessary demonstrations."

Early in his career, Galileo caused a great stir with an experiment on the laws of motion. Galileo is said to have climbed the Leaning Tower of Pisa and dropped objects of different weight to the ground. To the sur-

414 Galileo made telescopes that helped him see the moon as no one had seen it before.

prise of many people, he found that light objects fall at the same speed as heavy objects. This discovery sparked controversy, as did Galileo's later work in astronomy.

Galileo's study of the skies. When Galileo heard about a recent Dutch invention—the telescope—he turned his attention to studying the stars. He made a telescope for himself, with which he could even see the moon's craters. He described his discovery enthusiastically:

66 It is a most beautiful and delightful sight to behold the moon. Anyone may know that the moon certainly does not possess a smooth and polished surface, but one that is rough and uneven, and, just like the face of the earth itself, it is everywhere full of vast bulges and deep chasms. 99

Galileo's observations seemed to disprove the medieval belief that objects in the heavens were smooth and perfectly shaped, and thus purer than the earth. Other scientists challenged his findings, but soon they used their own telescopes to confirm his reports. Galileo also discovered that Jupiter has moons circling around it. This finding challenged the view that all heavenly bodies moved around the earth.

A clash with the Church. Early in the 1620's Galileo asked the Pope's permission to write a book comparing Ptolemy's and Copernicus's ideas. The Pope agreed because Galileo had promised to uphold the Church's teachings. When the book was published in 1632, however, it shocked and angered the Pope. Galileo had kept his promise by making a final statement supporting Ptolemy's views. Yet the rest of the book clearly showed that he agreed with Copernicus. In 1633 he was brought before the Inquisition and accused in these words:

Sec. Rev. ques. 3

66 You, Galileo, were denounced to this Holy Office for holding as true the false doctrine taught by some that the sun is the center of the world and immovable and that the earth moves. 99

Biography Copernicus explained the heliocentric theory in his book, *Commentariolus*, where he added, "In the center rests the sun. For who would place this lamp of a very beautiful temple in another or better place than this where it can illuminate everything at the same time?"
Biography When Galileo died, one of his students described the scientist's "eagerness and impatience" for an afterlife where he could "enjoy and watch from a closer vantage point those eternal and immutable marvels that a telescope had brought closer to our mortal eyes."

Background The Leaning Tower of Pisa is a bell tower 177 feet tall (about eight stories high) with walls 13 feet thick at the base and 6 feet thick at the top. The tower was begun in 1173 and completed in 1372. After the first three stories were finished, the ground beneath the tower began to sink. Today the tower is about 17 feet out of line and its slant increases approximately 1/20 of an inch each year.

Threatened with torture, the 70-year-old Galileo was forced to retract what he had said. In addition he had to promise not to teach the heliocentric theory and had to remain under arrest in his own house, where he was closely watched. Still, these actions did not prevent the spread of Galileo's ideas. He continued to write, and with the aid of friends, he smuggled out new manuscripts.

Further Discoveries

Galileo was not alone in looking for new theories to explain what he saw in the skies. Other astronomers of the time included Tycho Brahe (BRAH-eh) of Denmark and Johannes Kepler in Germany.

Brahe. Like Renaissance artists, scientists of the early 1600's often depended on royal or wealthy patrons. With money from the Danish king, Brahe built one of the earliest modern observatories, Uraniborg, which means "castle of the skies." There he watched the stars for evidence to support his ideas. Brahe agreed with Copernicus that planets move around the sun, but he still thought that the sun circled the earth once a year.

Kepler. After Brahe's death in 1601, Johannes Kepler continued the Danish astronomer's work. Using Brahe's observations and measurements, Kepler showed that a mathematical order exists in the planetary system. More important, he took Copernicus's ideas from theory to fact: he proved mathematically that the planets revolve ★ See around the sun. Kepler's work made an enormous contribution to astronomy.

★ See below.

The Genius of Newton

The ideas of Copernicus, Galileo, Brahe, and Kepler changed the way people looked at the world. Isaac Newton (1642–1727), an English mathematician and scientist, came up with even more startling ideas.

Sec. Rev. ques. 4

Newton showed that all objects in the universe—things on earth, as well as moons, stars, and planets—obey the same laws of

motion. He explained this by demonstrating the actions of gravity and inertia (in-UR-shuh). Gravity is the attraction that draws all objects toward each other. This force, Newton found, increases with the mass of the objects. In addition, the closer together objects are, the greater the pull of gravity.

Inertia is resistance to change. According to the law of inertia, an object at rest will remain at rest unless a force causes it to move. Similarly, a moving object will keep moving in a straight line unless another force causes it to halt or change direction.

Newton's discoveries made it possible to explain the movements of planets. According to the law of inertia, the planets would move in a straight line endlessly into space. However, the gravitational pull from the sun forces the planets into oval-shaped orbits. With the same reasoning, Newton could explain the movements of objects on earth. Apples, for example, fall to the ground instead of flying upward because of gravity.

Newton's achievement was remarkable. Building on earlier discoveries, he had explained laws that operate everywhere in nature. In 1687 he published his ideas in a work known as the *Principia* (prin-SIP-ee-ah). The universe Newton described was like a giant clock, whose parts all worked together perfectly according to strict scientific laws. Newton believed that God was the creator of this orderly universe, the clockmaker who had set everything in motion.

415

Ⓕ See below, right.

The Geography Connection

Scientific Travelers

During the Age of Discovery, European explorers traveled to new lands to open trade routes, establish overseas empires, or search for gold and other riches. Through their efforts, the main landmasses of the earth were discovered. By the 1700's, however, a new kind of exploration had emerged—one that was primarily interested in scientifically examining what had already been found. The new explorers, armed with the latest navigational devices and a reliance on careful observation, added greatly to the expansion of knowledge that occurred during the Enlightenment.

James Cook, a British navigator and sea captain, was one of the new scientific travelers. Cook and a team of scientists set sail for Tahiti, an island in the Pacific Ocean, in 1768 (see map). There they conducted astronomical studies. From Tahiti, Cook's expedition headed south to search for a continent that was thought to lie in the southern Pacific Ocean or the southern Indian Ocean. Cook never found this continent, but in the course of his travels he charted much of the Pacific. He also collected detailed information about the plants, animals, and inhabitants he found along the way.

Alexander von Humboldt and Mungo Park were also scientific travelers. Humboldt, a German geographer, studied the vegetation and wildlife of South America. Park, a Scottish explorer, led an expedition to Africa that investigated the course of the Niger River.

The gains made by the scientific travelers were measured not in territory or wealth but in knowledge. These explorers gathered vast amounts of information about the geography, people, and resources of the world.

Making the connection. How did scientific travelers contribute to the advances made during the Enlightenment?

The Study of Living Things

● Note strategies for second objective on this page and p. 418.

Careful observation and use of the scientific method became important in many different fields. At the same time that astronomers began to explore the secrets of the universe, other scientists began to study the structure of living things.

Vesalius. In 1543, the year Copernicus published his theories, a Flemish doctor named Andreas Vesalius (vuh-SAY-lee-us) published a beautifully illustrated textbook on anatomy. Recognized as a pioneer in the field, Vesalius is often considered the father of modern anatomy.

416 As a child, Vesalius was so curious about the structure of living things that he dissected the bodies of mice, rats, dogs, and cats. As he grew older, he studied the writings of ancient doctors such as Galen (page 114). However, Vesalius did not accept many of the long-held ideas about human anatomy because they were based on studies of animals. He began to dissect human corpses, despite a Church ban against this practice. To find bodies, Vesalius had to search cemeteries in the middle of the night. Once he even climbed a gallows to remove a decaying corpse for study.

⌉ Sec. Rev.
⌋ ques. 5

Although his work caused great controversy, Vesalius knew more about anatomy than any other doctor in Europe. Teaching at the University of Padua in Italy, Vesalius urged his students not to rely on the theories of earlier scientists but to learn by investigating for themselves:

● RETEACHING. Have students review "The Study of Living Things" (pp. 416–418) and outline the information on the scientists. (Outline should include information on Vesalius, Harvey, Leeuwenhoek, and Linnaeus.) (Comprehension) *Organizing Information in Written Form*

● REINFORCEMENT. Have students explain how the microscope, the classification system, and Bacon and Descartes changed the study of science. (Evaluation) *Interpreting History*

Ⓕ GEOGRAPHY CONNECTION. Have students work in groups to plan a voyage of scientific investigation that might have occurred during the Enlightenment. Students might refer to the Atlas at the back of the book, choose a territory first explored during the Age of Discovery, and then outline specific questions and interests. (Synthesis) *Synthesizing Information*

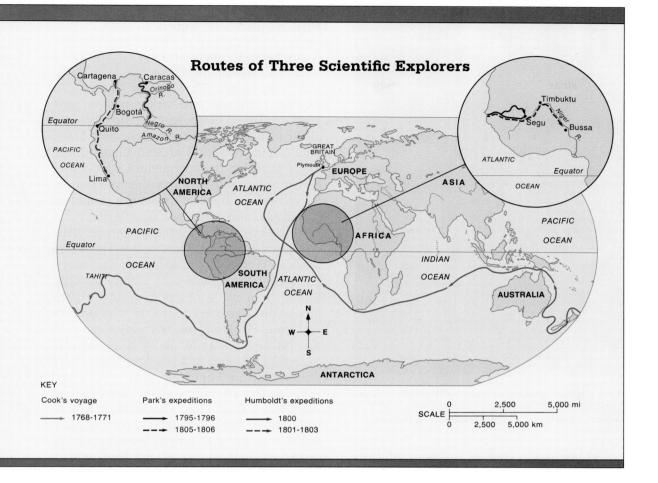

Routes of Three Scientific Explorers

Cartagena
Caracas
Orinoco R.
Bogotá
Equator
Quito
Negro R.
PACIFIC
OCEAN
Amazon R.
Lima

Timbuktu
Segu
Niger R.
Bussa
ATLANTIC
OCEAN
Equator

GREAT
BRITAIN
Plymouth
EUROPE
ASIA
NORTH
AMERICA
ATLANTIC
OCEAN
AFRICA
PACIFIC
OCEAN
Equator
PACIFIC
OCEAN
SOUTH
AMERICA
ATLANTIC
OCEAN
INDIAN
OCEAN
TAHITI
AUSTRALIA

N
W · E
S

ANTARCTICA

KEY

Cook's voyage
→ 1768-1771

Park's expeditions
→ 1795-1796
---→ 1805-1806

Humboldt's expeditions
→ 1800
---→ 1801-1803

SCALE
0   2,500   5,000 mi
0   2,500   5,000 km

66 How many things have been accepted on the word of Galen and often contrary to reason? Indeed, I myself am wholly astonished at my former stupidity and too-great trust in the writings of Galen and other anatomists. 99

Harvey.   One of the graduates of the University of Padua, an English doctor named William Harvey (1578–1657), discovered that blood circulates in the body and is pumped through vessels by the heart. As part of his research, Harvey examined the hearts of many animals. "I found the task so full of difficulties," he wrote, "that I was almost tempted to think that the motion of the heart was only to be understood by God." Harvey's careful work was another triumph for the experimental method.

Leeuwenhoek.   Scientists' investigations in many fields were made easier by the invention of the microscope. Anton van Leeuwenhoek (LAY-vun-hook), a Dutch shopkeeper and amateur scientist who lived from 1632 to 1723, was one of the first people to build and use a microscope. With this instrument, Leeuwenhoek studied the eye of an ox, the brain of a fly, wool fibers, and the seeds of plants. He even watched the blood racing through a tadpole's body.

One day Leeuwenhoek put some water under the lens of his microscope and saw "living creatures, little animals," swimming quickly about. Soon he was looking with "wonder at a thousand living creatures in one drop of water." Leeuwenhoek was peering into a mysterious new world—the world of one-celled living things.

417

Science Leeuwenhoek made more than 400 microscopes.

This engraving shows French philosopher René Descartes with Sweden's Queen Christina, whom he tutored in the last years of his life.

Linnaeus. One of the aims of early scientists was to find laws or systems that would reveal a logical order in nature. The Swedish biologist Carolus Linnaeus (lih-NEE-us) came up with such a system in the 1700's. Linnaeus started his work by studying plants and animals and writing careful descriptions of them. Linnaeus walked nearly 1,000 miles through the lonely, freezing areas of northern Europe to collect samples. From his observations Linnaeus developed a system for naming and classifying plants, and he published his research in 1753. Five years later, he published a system for classifying more than 4,000 animals.

Linnaeus's system, which gave a two-word Latin name to each kind of living thing, put similar animals into groups. For example, the group *Felis* (cat) included both *Felis domesticus* (the house cat) and *Felis leo* (the lion). Today's system of classifying living things is based on Linnaeus's model.

418

Philosophers of Science

A number of thinkers who were not working scientists played important roles in the Scientific Revolution. Sir Francis Bacon, an English politician and writer of the early 1600's, believed that science could help people live more comfortable lives and better understand the world around them. Bacon urged scientists to experiment. Like Galileo, he wanted scientists to free themselves from the cobwebs of the past—from ignorance and prejudice—and make new discoveries.

In France at about the same time, René Descartes (day-KART) took a keen interest in science. However, his approach to gaining knowledge was different from Bacon's. Rather than using observation and experimentation, Descartes relied on mathematics and logic. For Descartes, the only clear truth was his own mind and ability to reason. He expressed this idea in a few simple words: "I think, therefore I am."

Modern scientific methods are based on the ideas of Bacon and Descartes. Scientists have shown that observation and experimentation, together with general laws that can be expressed mathematically, can lead us to a better understanding of the natural world.

● See below.

See Sec. 1 *Closing the Lesson*, p. T411B.

Section Review

Answers to Section Review questions are in brackets on pages indicated.

1. **Define or identify:** Scientific Revolution, scientific method, geocentric theory, heliocentric theory. (p. 413)
2. How did Copernicus's view of the universe differ from the medieval view? (p. 413)
3. What brought Galileo into conflict with the Church? (p. 414)
4. What was new about Newton's description of the universe? (p. 415)
5. How did Vesalius, Harvey, and Leeuwenhoek make their discoveries? (pp. 416–417)
6. **Critical thinking:** What role did new technology play in the discoveries of the Scientific Revolution?

(See answer below.)

Background Note that the word *leviathan* refers to the image of a monstrous sea creature used by Old Testament writers to symbolize evil.

2 Enlightenment Ideas and Reforms

Objectives

Focus Questions

★ ■ Who were the leading philosophers of the Enlightenment? *(pages 419–421)*

● ■ How did Enlightenment ideas spread throughout society? *(pages 421–423)*

Terms to Know

Enlightenment	separation of
social contract	powers
natural rights	enlightened despot
philosophe	salon
atheist	baroque
deist	Classical

★ Note strategies for first objective on this page and p. 421.

The influence of the Scientific Revolution soon spread beyond the world of science. Philosophers admired Newton because he had used reason to explain the laws governing nature. People began to look for laws governing human behavior as well. They hoped to apply reason and the scientific method to all aspects of society—government, economics, religion, and education.

In this way, the ideas of the Scientific Revolution paved the way for a new period called the **Enlightenment** or the Age of Reason. This period reached its height in the mid-1700's. It began, however, with some key ideas put forth by English political thinkers in the mid-1600's.

Two Views on Government

Hobbes. Thomas Hobbes, an English philosopher of the 1600's, tried to create a science of politics. After witnessing the horrors of the English Civil War (page 398), Hobbes decided that conflict was part of human nature. Without governments to keep order, Hobbes said, there would be "war of everyone against everyone." In this state of nature, life would be "nasty, brutish, and short."

In his book *Leviathan* (1651), Hobbes argued that to escape such a bleak life, people gave up their rights to a strong ruler. In exchange, they gained law and order. Hobbes called this agreement, by which people created government, the **social contract**.

Because people act in their own self-interest, Hobbes said, the ruler needed total power to keep citizens under control. No matter how cruel or unfair the ruler might become, all citizens were bound to obey the government. Rebellion would only reopen the way to a lawless society.

Locke. The most influential ideas on government during the Enlightenment were those of John Locke (1632–1704). Locke viewed human nature very differently from Hobbes. While Hobbes saw people as naturally selfish and violent, Locke believed that a person is not born good or evil. Rather, he said, people's characters are shaped by their experiences. Locke felt that people could learn from experience and improve themselves. Therefore, he favored the idea of self-government.

According to Locke, all people are born free and equal, with three **natural rights**—life, liberty, and property. The purpose of government, said Locke, is to protect these rights. If a government fails to do so, he argued, citizens have a right to overthrow it.

Locke's theory had a deep influence on modern political thinking. His statement that a government's power comes from the consent of the people is the foundation of modern democracy. The ideas of government by popular consent and the right to rebel against unjust rulers later helped inspire struggles for liberty in Europe and the Americas.

419

★ RETEACHING. Have students identify the sources of the following ideas: (a) Without government, life would be "nasty, brutish, and short." (Hobbes) (b) An ideal society is a direct democracy. (Rousseau) (c) Government must protect the natural rights of citizens. (Locke) (d) Separation of powers would keep any individual or group from gaining too much power. (Montesquieu) *(Comprehension) Observing for Detail*

★ REINFORCEMENT. Have students write an essay explaining how Enlightenment views of human nature and society influenced new ideas about the purposes and forms of government. *(Comprehension) Understanding Cause and Effect*

Check for Understanding. Ask: What was Thomas Hobbes's definition of the "social contract"? (The social contract was the agreement by which people created government and exchanged their individual rights for law and order.)

Thomas Hobbes (1588–1679)
Social contract between people
and strong ruler.

John Locke (1632–1704)
Government by popular consent;
natural rights—life, liberty,
and property.

Voltaire (1694–1778)
Free speech; "enlightened" monarch.

Montesquieu (1689–1755)
Separation of powers.

Jean Jacques Rousseau (1712–1778)
Harmony with nature; new social
contract—direct democracy.

Denis Diderot (1713–1784)
Encyclopedia.

The Philosophes

The Enlightenment reached its height in France in the mid-1700's. Paris became the meeting place for the greatest thinkers of the day. The social critics of this period in France were known as **philosophes** (FIL-uh-sahfs), the French word for "philosophers."

The philosophes tried to apply reason to all aspects of life. They felt that if accepted ways of doing things did not make sense, those ways should be changed. The philosophes particularly opposed the traditions of absolute monarchy and divine right. They also objected to the special privileges enjoyed by the nobility and clergy. These two groups owned most of France's wealth, yet paid little or nothing in taxes.

Sec. Rev. ques. 2

Most of the philosophes turned away from traditional religious beliefs. They placed their faith in reason rather than in the Church. Some philosophes were **atheists**—

420

people who deny the existence of God. Most, however, were **deists**. That is, they believed in God as the creator of the universe, but they rejected Church rituals and the authority of the clergy. Deists accepted only those teachings that fit with scientific understanding. For example, they looked upon Jesus as a great moral teacher rather than as the son of God.

Voltaire. Probably the most brilliant and influential of the philosophes was François Marie Arouet (1694–1778). Using the pen name of Voltaire, he published more than 70 books of political essays, philosophy, history, and drama.

Voltaire often used humor against his opponents. He made frequent targets of the clergy, the aristocracy, and the government. Though he was sent to prison twice for insulting nobles, Voltaire never stopped fighting for tolerance, reason, and limited government. He also championed free speech and is remembered for the famous line, "I disapprove of what you say, but I will defend to the death your right to say it."

Montesquieu. Like Voltaire, the Baron de Montesquieu (MAHN-tus-kyoo), a lawyer and aristocrat, admired the English system of government. After studying the English model, Montesquieu outlined practices that he believed would protect people's rights and lead to good government.

In *The Spirit of the Laws* (1748) Montesquieu urged **separation of powers**—the division of authority among different branches of government. One branch, the legislature, would make laws. A second branch, the executive, would see that the laws were carried out. The third branch, the judiciary, would interpret the laws. Separation of powers, Montesquieu believed, would keep any individual or group from gaining total control of the government. This would, he said, safeguard the liberty of the people against corrupt leaders.

Sec. Rev. ques. 3

Rousseau. One of the greatest of the philosophes was Jean Jacques Rousseau (roo-SOH). Rousseau violently disagreed with other Enlightenment thinkers on many matters. Most philosophes believed that progress in the arts and the sciences would

Vocabulary The word *atheism* is from the Greek word *a-theos* which means "no god."

Check for Understanding. Ask: What is the difference between atheism and deism? (Atheism rejects the existence of God; deism accepts the existence of God as creator but rejects Church rituals and the authority of the clergy.)

improve life for all people. Rousseau, however, argued that arts and sciences corrupted people's natural goodness. "Man is born free, and everywhere he is in chains," he wrote.

Rousseau drew a sharp distinction between "civilized people" and what he called "natural man," or the "noble savage." People who live in a civilized society, said Rousseau, are unhappy, insecure, and selfish. He argued that if people lived outdoors, in harmony with nature, they would be better off.

In 1762 Rousseau explained his political philosophy in a book called *The Social Contract*. He proposed an ideal society based on a new kind of social contract. Under this contract, the people would not give a ruler or representative the power to make laws for them. Instead, they would have a form of direct democracy. Each member of the community would vote on issues, and the will of the majority would become law.

Political Reforms

The key thinkers of the Enlightenment had very definite views on the ideal government. They all admired the English system, with its limitations on royal power. However, only a few of them—notably Locke and Rousseau—believed that people were capable of governing themselves.

Sec. Rev. ques. 4

For this reason, most of the philosophes opposed democracy. "Once the common people begin to reason," Voltaire wrote, "then everything is lost. I hate the idea of government by the masses." According to Voltaire, the best form of government was a monarchy in which the ruler shared the ideas of the philosophes and respected the people's rights. Such an "enlightened" monarch would rule justly and introduce reforms.

Although the philosophes were a small group, they had great influence. In the late 1700's several monarchs—Holy Roman Emperor Joseph II of Austria, Frederick II of Prussia, and Catherine the Great of Russia—made reforms that reflected the Enlightenment spirit. These leaders became known as **enlightened despots**.

Catherine the Great, ruler of Russia, was hailed by French writers as the most forward-looking of European monarchs.

The enlightened despots supported the philosophes' ideas but did not succeed in bringing lasting political changes. At times the monarchs practiced religious toleration and ended censorship. They also discouraged serfdom, simplified laws, and widened opportunities for education. However, because their own power depended on support from the nobles, they did not want to take too many privileges away from the nobility.

★ See below, left.

The Spread of Ideas

● Note strategies for second objective on this page and p. 423.

The philosophes' views often got them into trouble. In France it was illegal to criticize either the Church or the government; many philosophes landed in jail or were exiled. Nevertheless, Enlightenment ideas spread throughout Europe. Organizations like the Royal Society of London, founded in 1660, held lectures on science and other subjects. Although the Enlightenment had begun among the educated upper classes, its ideas **421**

★ ENRICHMENT. Have students research one enlightened despot and explain how he or she made reforms that reflected Enlightenment ideas. (Application) Locating Information

● RETEACHING. Have students review "The Spread of Ideas" (pp. 421–423) and then answer the following: How did Enlightenment ideas spread? (Through organizations like the Royal Society of London; newspapers, pamphlets, and songs; salons; and the Encyclopedia.) (Comprehension) Observing for Detail

Check for Understanding. Ask: What was Rousseau's idea of the "social contract"? (People would not give a ruler the power to make laws; instead they would have a form of direct democracy.)

● REINFORCEMENT. Have students work in groups to dramatize a salon that might be held for present-day writers, philosophers, and artists. Current ideas about society, government, music, art, or literature should be expressed. (Application) Linking Past and Present

At the salon of Marie-Thérèse Geoffrin (front row, third from the right), a famous actor reads to a group of philosophes and aristocrats. French philosophes, including Voltaire (inset), often gathered at the homes of aristocrats to debate their ideas.

eventually reached middle-class people through newspapers, pamphlets, and even political songs.

The *Encyclopedia*. In their enthusiasm for learning, a number of the philosophes cooperated in publishing the *Encyclopedia*. Their purpose in writing this 28-volume work was to collect information on many topics, especially science and technology. The chief editor was the French writer Denis Diderot (dee-DROH). Many other philosophes, including Voltaire and Montesquieu, also contributed articles.

Diderot began publishing the first volumes in 1751. Censors of both the French government and the Church banned the work. They said it undermined royal authority, encouraged a spirit of revolt, and fostered "moral corruption, irreligion, and unbelief." Diderot finally won permission to continue publishing the *Encyclopedia*, and new volumes came out regularly until 1772.

The *Encyclopedia* gave the philosophes a chance to attack the injustices they saw in society. For instance, one article described war as a "violent sickness," a madness unworthy of civilized people. Another article condemned slavery, insisting that no one had the right to deprive people of their freedom.

Women's contributions to the Enlightenment. In the 1700's few women could gain the education to participate actively in science and philosophy. Still, women played an important role in spreading the ideas of the period. Some took part in the correspondence among the philosophes and wrote lively descriptions of European life.

In Paris, several wealthy women held salons—social gatherings where writers, philosophers, and artists met regularly. There they played music, read poetry, and discussed ideas. Contributors to the *Encyclopedia* often met at the salon of Marie-Thérèse Geoffrin (juh-FRAN), a self-educated widow who

422

corresponded with the king of Sweden and Catherine the Great of Russia. Geoffrin also gave financial backing to the *Encyclopedia*.

One woman fortunate enough to receive education in the sciences was Émilie du Châtelet (shah-tuh-LAY). Du Châtelet was an aristocrat trained as a mathematician and physicist. By translating Newton's work from Latin into French, she helped stimulate interest in science in France.

Grace and Balance in the Arts

The Enlightenment's admiration for order and reason was reflected in all the arts—music, literature, painting, and architecture. European art of the 1500's and 1600's had been dominated by the **baroque**—a grand, ornate style. Monarchs had built elaborate palaces such as Versailles (page 393). Musicians like the German composer Johann Sebastian Bach (BAHK) had written dramatic organ and choral music. Artists had created paintings rich in color and detail.

Under the influence of the Enlightenment, styles began to change. The arts began to reflect the new emphasis on order and balance. Artists and architects worked in a simple and elegant style that borrowed ideas from classical Greece and Rome. The style of the late 1700's is therefore called **Classical**.

Sec. Rev. ques. 5

Three composers in Vienna, Austria, rank among the greatest figures of the Classical period. They were Franz Josef Haydn (HY-dun), Wolfgang Amadeus Mozart (MOHT-sahrt), and Ludwig van Beethoven (BAY-toh-vun). Haydn was particularly important in developing new musical forms, such as the sonata and the symphony. Mozart wrote more than 600 works, although he only lived to be 35 years old. His operas, such as *Don Giovanni* and *The Marriage of Figaro*, set a new standard of elegance. Beethoven showed enormous range in his work. He wrote beautiful piano music, string quartets, and stirring symphonies. The music of these three men is still very much alive today—a lasting legacy of the Enlightenment.

● See below. See Sec. 2 *Closing the Lesson*, p. T411B.

● ENRICHMENT. Have students find information on representatives of the Classical period and explain how their works express Enlightenment ideas. Students might research the life and works of Classical architects, artists, or musicians such as Haydn, Mozart, or Beethoven. *(Application) Locating Information*

Section Review

Answers to Section Review questions are in brackets on pages indicated.

1. **Define or identify:** Enlightenment, social contract, natural rights, philosophe, atheist, deist, separation of powers, enlightened despot, salon, baroque, Classical. (pp. 419, 420, 421, 422, 423)
2. What traditions and privileges of monarchs, nobles, and clergy did the philosophes challenge? (p. 420)
3. Why did Montesquieu urge separation of powers in government? (p. 420)
4. What was the attitude of most philosophes toward democracy? (p. 421)
5. How did the ideas of the Enlightenment affect the arts? (p. 423)
6. **Critical thinking:** Compare the views of Hobbes, Locke, and Rousseau on government. (See answer below.)

At an early age Mozart gave concerts throughout Europe with his sister and father. His graceful yet powerful music reflected the artistic achievements of the Enlightenment. **423**

Biography In a letter to Mozart's father, Haydn wrote that the young composer was "the greatest composer" he knew. Mozart began writing music when he was five years old and has been called the greatest musical genius of all time.

6. Students might analyze the philosophers' understanding of human behavior to explain their ideas about government and society.

3 The American Revolution

Objectives

Focus Questions

★ ■ What led American colonists to rebel against Britain? *(pages 424–426)*
● ■ How did the colonies win their freedom? *(pages 426–428)*
▲ ■ What kind of government did Americans form? *(pages 428–430)*

Terms to Know

American Revolution	Constitution federal system
Declaration of Independence	checks and balances Bill of Rights

★ Note strategies for first objective on this page and p. 426.

Although Europe was the heart of the Enlightenment, the ideas of the philosophes spread across the Atlantic Ocean. In America, British colonists were growing unhappy with British rule. Many people began to respond warmly to the philosophes' ideas about limiting the power of government.

The Restless American Colonies

By the mid-1700's, British colonists had been living in America for more than 100 years. Each of the 13 colonies had its own government, and people had grown used to a good deal of independence. The colonists were still British subjects and were expected to obey British law, but many colonists had other ideas.

Trade restrictions. In the 1660's, Parliament had passed the Navigation Acts—laws that regulated colonial trade to Britain's **424** advantage. However, colonists found ways to get around these laws. Some people smuggled in goods to avoid paying British taxes. The many harbors along the Atlantic coast of North America made it easy for smugglers' boats to slip past the customs officials. In addition, the distance between Britain and the colonies made it hard to enforce the laws strictly.

For many years, Britain felt no need to tighten its hold on the colonies. Britain's mercantilist policies (page 367), had made colonial trade very profitable. Britain bought American raw materials at low prices, and sold manufactured goods back to the colonists. However, after the French and Indian War (page 363), Britain began to want more from America.

Unpopular taxes. The French and Indian War had been expensive, and Britain needed money to pay its war debts. Because the American colonies had benefited from the war, King George III and the British Parliament believed the colonists should help pay those debts.

Sec. Rev. ques. 2

Beginning in 1764, Britain took steps to toughen the earlier trade laws. Parliament also passed several new acts to tax the colonies. The colonists were outraged, believing that the new taxes violated their rights.

Colonists were especially opposed to the Stamp Act (1765). This act placed a tax on printed matter—newspapers, playing cards, licenses, legal documents, and advertisements. The colonists admitted that Parliament had the right to regulate their trade, but they argued that only their own legislatures had the right to tax them. "Taxation without representation," they declared, was against the principles of English law.

The Stamp Act roused people to action. Colonists wrote angry newspaper articles against it and boycotted British goods. Merchants in Britain began to complain about the

★ RETEACHING. Have students review "The Restless American Colonies" (pp. 424–426) and explain the causes of the conflict between Britain and its American colonies. (Trade restrictions, unpopular taxes, the Boston Massacre, the Intolerable Acts.) *(Comprehension)* **Identifying Causes**

Politics The colonists organized the Stamp Act Congress in October 1765; it was attended by 28 delegates from 9 colonies. The Congress issued the Declaration of Rights and Grievances opposing the British tax.

★ REINFORCEMENT. Have students write two editorials that might have appeared in British and American newspapers in 1767. One editorial should support British interests and defend British mercantile policy and the other should represent the views of American colonists. *(Application)* **Understanding Point of View**

The Thirteen Colonies

Between 1607 and 1733, England established 13 colonies along the Atlantic seaboard. Which were the middle colonies? What country claimed the region west of the Mississippi River?

Map Answers: (1) New York, Pennsylvania, New Jersey, Delaware. (2) Spain.

business they were losing. In 1766 Parliament reluctantly repealed the Stamp Act. Yet Parliament still insisted it had every right to tax the colonists. In 1767 it passed the Townshend (TOWN-zend) Acts, which placed taxes on many everyday items. The colonists claimed that the new laws were another case of taxation without representation.

The outbreak of violence. Anger over British policies was particularly great in Bos-

ton. In March 1770, a group of British soldiers fired into a crowd that had been making fun of them and throwing sticks and snowballs at them. Five colonists were killed and several more were wounded. This incident, which American patriots called the Boston Massacre, deepened tensions.

Fearing more revolts in the colonies, Parliament soon repealed the Townshend Acts, except for a tax on tea. The situation

425

Economics Note that the Townshend Acts imposed taxes on glass, lead, paint, paper, and tea. All of the taxes were repealed in 1770 except for the tea tax.

Background British soldiers had been assigned to Boston to keep peace but were viewed by colonists as intruders. After the Boston Massacre, all troops were withdrawn from the town and the soldiers accused of murder were put on trial. John Adams acted as the defense lawyer for the accused, five of whom were acquitted. Two soldiers convicted of manslaughter were released but were branded on the hand as punishment.

grew calmer, but the basic disagreement between Britain and the colonies remained.

Resentment in the colonies boiled over when Parliament again put restrictions on the tea trade. In 1773 a group of colonists disguised as American Indians dumped several hundred chests of tea into Boston's harbor. Some colonists cheered this form of protest. Others viewed the "Boston Tea Party" as a criminal act, since the colonists had destroyed valuable property and defied British law.

Sec. Rev. ques. 2, cont.

Toward independence. To punish the Bostonians, an angry Parliament passed a series of laws that colonists called the Intolerable Acts (1774). One of these laws, for example, closed the port of Boston to all ships until Massachusetts paid for the lost tea. Another law ended self-government in Massachusetts.

Upset at the harshness of the Intolerable Acts, leaders throughout the colonies met to discuss a plan of action. The meeting, called the First Continental Congress, was held in Philadelphia in 1774. Delegates from 12 colonies attended, demanding that Parliament repeal the Intolerable Acts and calling for a boycott of British goods. The British government refused to listen. As tension mounted, people in the colonies began to collect military supplies and train for armed conflict.

★ See below, left.

The Break from Britain

● Note strategies for second objective on this page and p. 427.

Battles at Lexington and Concord. In April 1775, British soldiers began marching from Boston to the nearby towns of Concord and Lexington. Their aim was to destroy weapons and gunpowder that the colonists had stored there. Warned that the British were on the way, the colonial militia gathered to stop them. Violence erupted, and before the dust settled, about 350 people had been killed or wounded.

The battles at Lexington and Concord marked a turning point in the relationship between Britain and the colonies. As the poet Ralph Waldo Emerson said, the first shot that rang out was a "shot heard round the world." It launched what would later be called the **American Revolution**.

Protesting colonists, disguised as Indians, dumped East India Company tea into Boston's harbor. Judging from the picture of the cheering crowd, what do you think was the artist's opinion of the Boston Tea Party? (See answer below.)

★ ENRICHMENT. Have students compare British actions in the American colonies with the colonial policies of Spain in the Americas (p. 356). Then have students form a hypothesis about why British colonists rebelled and Spain's colonists did not. (Synthesis) *Making Judgments*

Caption Answer: This artist seems to approve of the action since the crowd is shown cheering.

● RETEACHING. Have students make a timeline of important events of the American Revolution. (Comprehension) *Sequencing Information*

● REINFORCEMENT. Have students explain how the colonists used the Declaration of Independence to justify their revolution. (The document asserts that when a government threatens basic human rights, people have a right to abolish it and establish a new one.) (Comprehension) *Observing for Detail*

In the spring of 1775, though, few colonists favored separation from Britain. Angry as they were, they still hoped to reach a peaceful understanding with their home country. Yet colonial leaders knew they had to be prepared for trouble. In May they met at the Second Continental Congress in Philadelphia. There they created an army and named George Washington, a much-admired Virginian, to lead it.

The Declaration of Independence. Support for independence grew steadily over the next year. On July 4, 1776, the Second Continental Congress formally broke ties with Britain by adopting the Declaration of Independence. This document, written largely by the brilliant Thomas Jefferson, explained Americans' reasons for such a drastic move. It began with a stirring restatement of John Locke's theory of natural rights: "We hold these truths to be self-evident, that all men are created equal, that they are endowed by their Creator with certain unalienable Rights, that among these are Life, Liberty and the pursuit of Happiness."

The Declaration further said that if a government rules without the consent of the people, the people have the right to abolish it and establish a new one. In signing the Declaration, the members of the Second Continental Congress proclaimed that "these United Colonies are, and of Right ought to be, Free and Independent States."

● See below.

The War for Independence

Sec. Rev. ques. 3

The opposing sides. As commander of the Continental Army, George Washington faced two major problems. First, he could not count on a steady flow of money and supplies because the Continental Congress did not have the power to tax. Second, General Washington could never accurately predict how large his army would be from month to month, because soldiers often deserted or refused to fight outside their home states. Both these problems were made worse by the fact that only one third of the colonists actively supported the rebellion.

Thomas Jefferson, chief author of the Declaration of Independence, put basic ideas of freedom into memorable words. Jefferson continued to be a forceful leader after independence was won.

Nevertheless, the colonial forces had certain advantages over the British. Washington was a leader who gained the confidence and respect of his men. Also, the Patriots, as the soldiers were called, were fighting on their own territory. Their knowledge of the land helped them in battles. Finally, Continental soldiers were strongly motivated— they were fighting for their families, their homes, and their freedom.

The British, like the Americans, faced certain problems. About 3,000 miles lay between the British troops and the source of their supplies. In addition, the American colonies were so large that the British could bring only scattered areas under control. Although Britain's soldiers were more numerous and better trained in traditional warfare than the Continental Army, they were often surprised by the hit-and-run fighting style of the Patriots.

Victory. For two and a half years after the battles at Lexington and Concord, the war continued with neither side gaining a clear edge. Britain had captured New York City in the spring of 1776, but General Washington had led his troops to surprise victories **427**

Cultural History Thomas Jefferson stated that his aim was to "place before mankind the common sense of the subject in terms so plain and firm as to command their assent, and to justify ourselves in the independent stand we are compelled to take."

● **ENRICHMENT. Have students work in groups to decide which issue most influenced America's rebellion, high taxes or the desire for independence.** *(Analysis) Analyzing Historical Motives*

Cultural History The Declaration of Independence was read publicly for the first time on July 9, 1776. Patriots, elated by the prospect of freedom, pulled down a 4,000-pound statue of King George III. After the Revolutionary War began, lead from the statue was used to make muskets for the Continental Army.

in New Jersey. Then in the fall of 1777 the Americans won a decisive victory at Saratoga, New York. The surrender of British soldiers there became the turning point of the war.

The American victory impressed Britain's enemies in Europe. Since the start of the war, the American writer and scientist Benjamin Franklin had been in Paris asking for French help. In 1778 France decided to aid the Americans in the struggle against Britain. Later, Spain and the Netherlands also backed the American cause. These countries provided much-needed weapons, money, and troops. With this aid, the Americans forced the British to surrender at Yorktown, Virginia, in October 1781. For all practical purposes, the war was over.

The Treaty of Paris. Peace negotiations among the United States, Britain, France, the Netherlands, and Spain took almost two years. The Treaty of Paris, signed in September 1783, officially ended the war. By this treaty, Britain recognized the independence of its former colonies. A new nation, the United States, had been born.

The Making of a New Government

▲ Note strategies for third objective on this page and p. 430.

The Articles of Confederation. Having won their independence, the 13 states had to decide what form of government to use. Each state wrote its own constitution. To bring the states together, the Second Continental Congress set forth a plan of union in 1777. This plan, the Articles of Confederation, called for a "league of friendship" among the states.

The Articles of Confederation (approved by all the states in 1781) set up a Congress in which each state had one vote. The Congress was to handle foreign relations, settle disputes between the states, and deal with certain matters of common concern, such as relations with the Indians and the fixing of weights and measures. The Congress, however, could not impose taxes to raise money, nor did it have any way to enforce its decisions.

The states deliberately kept the Confederation government weak. Their experiences

Sec. Rev. ques. 4

428 After British forces captured Philadelphia in 1777, George Washington's ill-equipped troops camped at nearby Valley Forge. By the following spring, Prussian drill instructors had molded the ragged band into effective fighters.

Ⓕ See
below.

Biography

Benjamin Franklin

To European thinkers in the 1770's and 1780's, Benjamin Franklin was the greatest American of his time, more famous than George Washington. Though Franklin was known to Americans as a printer, publisher, author, civic leader, diplomat, and politician, his international fame came first from his scientific achievements.

Born in Boston in 1706, Franklin was the tenth son in a family of seventeen children. At the age of 12, he became an apprentice to his older brother James, a printer. Franklin liked the work and began to write pieces for his brother's newspaper. When he was 16, Franklin left for Philadelphia, where he prospered as a publisher.

Over the years, Franklin educated himself. His greatest interest was in the newly discovered phenomenon of electricity. Like other amateur scientists of his day, Franklin experimented with glass tubes, iron rods, silk, and other simple objects to create electric currents. At the time, many scientists believed that electricity consisted of two opposing forces. Franklin set up experiments that showed there was only one electrical force, which flowed from one object to another without being changed. Experimenting with the little-known force of electricity was risky. Twice Franklin was knocked unconscious while using electrical apparatus.

In 1752 Franklin performed his most famous—and most dangerous—experiment. He proved that lightning is a form of electricity by flying a silk kite in a thunderstorm. This experiment, coupled with his writings, won him many honors both at home and abroad.

---

with Britain had taught them to distrust centralized government. To make sure that the Congress would never have too much control over them, the states kept the most important powers for themselves.

Yet a weak central government created problems of its own. After the war Britain closed its Canadian and Caribbean ports to American ships and refused to leave the forts it still held on American soil. In the Mediterranean, North African pirates interfered with American shipping and captured American sailors. The Confederation government was too weak to fight the pirates and too poor to bribe them (as other countries did).

The worst problems facing the Confederation government came from its lack of authority at home. With no power to collect taxes, it could not raise enough money to pay its war debts or meet other expenses. With no real power over the states, it could not stop quarrels over trade and land. As these problems grew, many Americans realized that the Articles of Confederation had to be changed. **429**

Ⓕ FEATURE ACTIVITY. Have students write a brief essay explaining why Benjamin Franklin has been one of the most honored people in American history. Students should consider his background and his achievements. *(Synthesis)* *Drawing Conclusions*

The Constitution of the United States

The Preamble—or introduction—to the United States Constitution tells why the American people chose to adopt a new form of government.

66 We the people of the United States, in order to form a more perfect union, establish justice, insure domestic tranquility, provide for the common defense, promote the general welfare, and secure the blessings of liberty to ourselves and our posterity, do ordain and establish this Constitution for the United States of America. 99

1. Restate, in your own words, each of the following phrases from the Preamble: *form a more perfect union; insure domestic tranquility; promote the general welfare.*
2. According to the Preamble, who established the Constitution?
3. **Critical thinking:** How are Locke's ideas on government (page 419) reflected in the Preamble?

Ⓕ See answers below.

430

The Constitutional Convention. In May 1787, leaders from all the states began to gather in Philadelphia. Their goal was to find ways of strengthening the government. The delegates soon agreed that simply revising the Articles of Confederation would not solve the country's problems. They decided, instead, to write a new plan of government. This plan came to be called the **Constitution**.

The writers of the Constitution wanted to make the central government strong. At the same time, they wanted to keep any one person or group from gaining too much power. They decided to set up a **federal system** of government—one in which power is shared between the central government and the state governments.

The federal system was one safeguard against tyranny. In addition, the writers of the Constitution adopted Montesquieu's principle of the separation of powers (page 420). They created three separate branches of government: (1) the executive, headed by the President, (2) the legislative, consisting of a two-house Congress, and (3) the judicial, headed by the Supreme Court.

To prevent any one branch from gaining too much power, the founders set up a system of **checks and balances**. Under this system each branch of government exercises some control over the others. For example, the executive branch can refuse to approve laws passed by the legislature, and the legislative branch can reject treaties made by the executive branch.

The Bill of Rights. In 1789 the newly elected Congress met in New York City, then the nation's capital. One of its first acts was to draw up 10 amendments to the Constitution. These are known as the **Bill of Rights**, guaranteeing Americans freedom of religion, of speech, of assembly, and of the press. The Bill of Rights also assures citizens of other basic liberties, such as trial by jury.

With the Constitution and the Bill of Rights, Americans created a government that reflected the Enlightenment ideals of individual freedom. Their success inspired people around the world to work—and even to fight—for liberty in their own countries.

See Sec. 3 *Closing the Lesson,* p. T411C.

Sec. Rev. ques. 5

▲ See below.

Ⓕ **Primary Source Answers** 1. Possible answers: make a better government than the one under the Articles of Confederation and form a union of states that will benefit all; maintain peace within the country; ensure people's general well-being and help them lead happy and useful lives. 2. The people. 3. The government's power comes from the consent of the people, and people's natural right to life, liberty, and property are protected.

Cultural Background Fifty-five delegates representing 12 states attended the Constitutional Convention. Thirty-four delegates were lawyers and most of the others were planters or merchants; most representatives were under 40 years of age.

▲ **ENRICHMENT.** Have students write an essay predicting what might have happened if the United States had not abandoned the Articles of Confederation and adopted the Constitution. *(Evaluation) Predicting Events*

1. **Define or identify:** American Revolution, Declaration of Independence, Constitution, federal system, checks and balances, Bill of Rights. (pp. 426, 427, 430)
2. What steps led Americans to declare independence? (pp. 424–427)
3. What advantages and disadvantages did each side have at the beginning of the Revolution? (p. 427)
4. What problems did the newly formed Congress face under the Articles of Confederation? (pp. 428–429)
5. How did the government set up by the Constitution make use of the principle of separation of powers? (p. 430)
6. **Critical thinking:** How did Enlightenment ideas contribute to the American Revolution? (See answer below.)

6. Students might trace the sources of the following ideals: the social contract; unalienable rights; freedom and responsibility; democracy; and the separation of powers.

Chapter 21   Summary and Timeline

1. During the Scientific Revolution, Europeans rejected the medieval earth-centered view of the universe. Scientists such as Copernicus, Galileo, Brahe, and Kepler offered new theories based on observation, experimentation, and mathematics. Building on their work, the English scientist Isaac Newton described a universe governed by mathematical laws of motion. In the life sciences, Vesalius, Harvey, Leeuwenhoek, and Linnaeus used the scientific method to find order in living things.

2. The Enlightenment grew out of the achievements of the Scientific Revolution. Enlightenment thinkers such as Hobbes and Locke tried to understand and improve human society through the use of reason. The philosophes, including Voltaire, Montesqiueu, and Rousseau, attacked religious persecution and limits on freedom of thought. Enlightenment ideas spread throughout Europe, affecting all aspects of society.

3. Angry about taxes and inspired by Enlightenment ideals, American colonists declared their independence from Britain in 1776. After winning their freedom in the American Revolution, Americans formed a new government under the Constitution. The Bill of Rights guaranteed citizens certain rights.

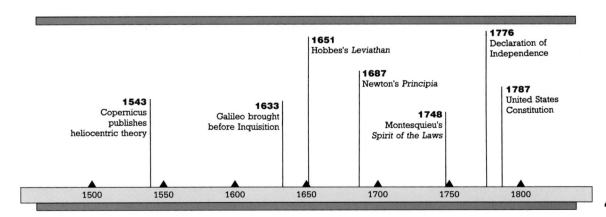

1651 Hobbes's *Leviathan*

1687 Newton's *Principia*

1776 Declaration of Independence

1787 United States Constitution

1543 Copernicus publishes heliocentric theory

1633 Galileo brought before Inquisition

1748 Montesquieu's *Spirit of the Laws*

1500 1550 1600 1650 1700 1750 1800

See p. T411C for answers to Chapter Review.

Vocabulary Review

1. Use the following terms to complete the sentences below: *Declaration of Independence, federal system, natural rights, philosophes, scientific method, social contract.*
   a. Hobbes called the agreement by which people create government the ___?___.
   b. The ___?___ uses experimentation and observation.
   c. The ___?___ broke ties between Britain and its American colonies.
   d. According to Locke, all citizens are born with ___?___.
   e. In a ___?___, power is shared between a central government and state governments.
   f. Social critics of the Enlightenment were known as ___?___.
2. Define or identify the terms in the following pairs.
   a. geocentric theory; heliocentric theory
   b. atheist; deist
   c. baroque; Classical
   d. Scientific Revolution; Enlightenment
   e. Constitution; Bill of Rights

People to Identify

Identify the following people and tell why each was important.
1. Johann Sebastian Bach
2. Émilie du Châtelet
3. Nicolaus Copernicus
4. Denis Diderot
5. Benjamin Franklin
6. Johannes Kepler
7. Baron de Montesquieu
432 8. Andreas Vesalius

Places to Know

Match the letters on this map with the places listed below. You may want to refer to the map on page 425.
1. Philadelphia   3. Saratoga
2. Yorktown   4. Boston

ATLANTIC OCEAN

Recalling the Facts

1. Why was the Church angered by Galileo's theories about the universe?
2. What was the significance of Newton's findings regarding gravity and inertia?
3. How was Descartes's approach to gaining knowledge different from Bacon's?
4. How have Locke's ideas influenced modern political thought?
5. What criticisms did the philosophes make of the nobility and the clergy?
6. On what issue did Rousseau disagree with most philosophes?

7. What sorts of reforms did enlightened despots make? Why did these monarchs fail to make lasting political changes?
8. What was the American colonists' main objection to the Stamp Act and the Townshend Acts?
9. What limitations were put on the national government under the Articles of Confederation?
10. How did the framers of the Constitution put into practice the idea of separation of powers? How did they establish a system of checks and balances?

Critical Thinking Skills

1. **Building vocabulary.** Leeuwenhoek's microscope introduced the world to microorganisms—living things too small to be seen with the naked eye. *Micro* comes from the Greek word *mikros*, meaning "little." Use a dictionary to define the following words: *microbe, microfilm, micron, microsurgery.* *(App.)*

2. **Locating and gathering information.** Use your library to find information on one of the scientists discussed in this chapter. Then write a biographical sketch describing the individual's early life, education, and contribution to the Scientific Revolution. *(App.)*

3. **Stating both sides of an issue.** Many people in Britain believed that the American colonists should help Britain reduce the cost of running and defending the colonies. Write a script for a debate between British supporters of this view and American colonists who opposed the idea. *(App.)*

✔ 4. **Drawing conclusions.** Most philosophes supported political liberty, yet did not favor democracy. What would please the philosophes about American society today? What would disappoint them? *(Syn.)*

Thinking About Geography

Inferring. How did the distance that existed between Great Britain and the American colonies contribute to the colonists' spirit of independence? *(Comp.)*

Enrichment: Primary Sources

In the following adapted passage, scientist Anton van Leeuwenhoek describes some of the tiny animals that he saw through his microscope.

66 In the year 1675, I discovered living creatures in rain, which had stood but a few days in a new tub. These little animals were to my eye more than 10,000 times smaller than the water-flea or water-louse, which you can see alive and moving in water with the bare eye.

I saw that the bodies consisted of five, six, seven, or eight very clear globules. When these animalcules bestirred themselves, they sometimes stuck out two little horns, which continually moved, after the fashion of horses' ears. The part between these little horns was flat, their body otherwise being roundish, except that it ran somewhat to a point at the end. At this pointed end it had a tail almost four times as long as the whole body, and looking as thick, when viewed through my microscope, as a spider's web. These little animals were the most wretched creatures that I have ever seen. 99

1. How small were the animalcules compared with the water-flea?
2. How did the animalcules change when they moved?
3. Which sentence gives Leeuwenhoek's personal opinion of the animalcules' appearance?
4. **Critical thinking:** Would everyone in 1675 have believed Leeuwenhoek's discovery of such little animals? Explain your answer. *(Syn.)*

✔

433

✔ A checkmark identifies questions and exercises calling for the three higher-order levels of thinking at the top of the Bloom taxonomy: Analysis, Synthesis, and Evaluation.

The French Revolution 1774–1815

(pp. 434–455)

Chapter Preview

Section 1 of this chapter examines the problems in French society that led to the French Revolution and the overthrow of Louis XVI. The aims of the moderates and the radicals who led the revolutionary government are explored in Section 2 and the effects of the revolution on France and other European countries are described. In Section 3, students learn about Napoleon's rise to power, his achievements, and the events that led to his defeat and eventual exile.

Bibliography

See the *Teacher's Management and Planning Guide* for additional listings. Starred titles are for both students and teachers.

Carr, John Laurence. *Robespierre: The Force of Circumstance*. St. Martin's. Brief biography.

*Castelot, Andre. *Queen of France*. Harper. Highly readable biography of Marie Antoinette.

Cronin, Vincent J. *Napoleon: An Intimate Biography*. Morrow. Emphasizes Napoleon's diplomatic and political goals.

*Pocock, Tom. *Nelson and His World*. Thames and Hudson. Well-illustrated biography of the English naval hero. Good on Nelson's youth.

Seward, Desmond. *Napoleon's Family*. Viking. Story of a family's rapid rise and fall.

Section Lesson Plans

SECTION 1   (pp. 435–440)
The Outbreak of Revolution

Objectives

After completing this section, students will be able to:
1. Describe the problems faced by France in the late 1700's.
2. Explain how the people of France pushed for reforms.

Introducing the Lesson

Remind students that a revolution is the overthrow of a government by its citizens. The revolution that occurred in France was similar to the American Revolution in that members of both societies rejected a government they believed to be oppressive.

Then ask: *(a) Which members of a society might be likely to support a revolution?* (Generally, people who see their government as oppressive and who believe that a change in leadership and structure would improve their opportunities are more likely than others to support a revolutionary cause. When revolutionary movements erupt, it is usually after a long period of government abuse and social unrest.)

(b) Why might a government threatened by revolution refuse to meet demands for change? (People who have power usually hold on to it despite threats of violence. Rather than relinquish control, rulers seek ways to repress rebellion.)

(c) Why does conflict between citizens and their government sometimes lead to revolution rather than a peaceful resolution of tension? (Answers will vary.)

Developing the Lesson: Comparing Historical Events

Have students compare the political, economic, and social problems of prerevolutionary France with those faced by the American colonies before they rebelled against Britain (pp. 424–426). (*France:* inequities in the class system, unfair tax system, high food prices, inefficient government, unfair laws, national debt. *American colonies:* trade restrictions, unfair taxes, conflict over political representation.) *(Comprehension)*

Developing the Lesson:
Solving Problems

Have students work in groups to dramatize a meeting of the Estates-General in the late 1700's. Representatives of each Estate should define the nation's social, political, and economic problems from their class's viewpoint and suggest ways to resolve the issues. *(Synthesis)*

Closing the Lesson: Making Judgments

Have students list the actions taken by the Third Estate to reform French government and society. Then have students evaluate which actions were probably necessary for reform and which might have been unnecessary. (The Third Estate established the National Assembly; ended feudalism and serfdom; banned or restricted tax privileges; opened Church, government, and army positions to all citizens; issued the Declaration of the Rights of Man; seized land belonging to Church and nobles; tried to bring the Church under state control; and established constitutional government.) *(Evaluation)*

See *Section Review* questions, p. 440.

SECTION 2   (pp. 440–445)
The Radical Stage of the Revolution

Objectives

After completing this section, students will be able to:
1. Describe how the French Revolution moved into a more extreme phase.
2. Discuss the aftermath of the Revolution.

Introducing the Lesson

Remind students that the goal of a revolution is to remove what is thought to be a bad government and replace it with one that better meets the needs of society. Strategies that are effective in removing a repressive government, however, may not be useful or appropriate in establishing a new political system.
     Then ask: *(a) What problems might face people whose goal is to establish a new government after a successful revolution?* (Answers will vary. The transition from revolution to government is not an easy one: revolutionary leaders may

not be effective government officials; people who have used violence to achieve political goals are sometimes reluctant to abandon its use; a society that has undergone revolution may experience severe economic problems.)
     (b) What circumstances might make the transition from revolution to effective government a peaceful one? (Answers will vary, but students might use as an example the American experience from the Revolution and the establishment of the United States government.)

Developing the Lesson:
Summarizing Information

Have students summarize events that led to war between Austria and Prussia. (After the arrest of Louis XVI, other monarchs feared that the French Revolution would spread to the rest of Europe. The revolutionaries were afraid that the family of the queen might help émigré nobles restore the Old Regime. France declared war on Austria; Prussia joined Austria in an invasion of France.) *(Comprehension)*

Developing the Lesson:
Organizing Information in Written Form

Have students outline the problems faced by the French government after the creation of the Constitution of 1791. Students should identify the problems as political or economic. (*Political:* resistance by the monarch; divisions among the revolutionaries; war with European nations; counterrevolution. *Economic:* widespread hunger in Paris). *(Comprehension)*

Closing the Lesson:
Evaluating Historical Events

Have students evaluate the effects of the French Revolution and answer the following questions:
     (a) What might account for the violence that followed the adoption of the Constitution of 1791?
     (b) How might the Reign of Terror have been avoided?
     (c) Did French society benefit from the Revolution? Why or why not?
(Evaluation)

See *Section Review* questions, p. 445.

SECTION 3   (pp. 446–453)
Napoleon's Conquest of Europe

Objectives

After completing this section, students will be able to:
1. Describe how Napoleon brought reforms to France.
2. Explain how Napoleon's wars of conquest led to his downfall.

Introducing the Lesson

Remind students that history provides many examples of strong leaders who rose to power after a period of national disorder. Within ten years of the storming of the Bastille, Napoleon Bonaparte overthrew the French government and became dictator. In 1804 he declared himself emperor.

Then ask: *(a) What might account for the rise of strong leaders in societies that have experienced unrest or revolution?* (Answers will vary. Sometimes people support a strong authority figure because of their need for peace and stability.)

(b) How else besides giving power to a strong leader might a society establish peace and stability after a period of disorder? (Answers will vary. If a society is based on strong political institutions and respected laws, turning over extensive power to a single individual might not be viewed as an appropriate or desirable way to establish stability and peace.)

(c) Who are some other leaders in history who rose to power as a result of social instability and disorder? (Answers might include Solon, Julius Caesar, Oliver Cromwell, Lenin, Adolf Hitler, Charles de Gaulle, Mao Zedong.)

Developing the Lesson:
Organizing Information in Written Form

Have students outline steps taken by Napoleon to win the support of each of the following groups:

(a) Bourgeoisie (Promised them government and army jobs; restored order; promoted trade and industry; placed taxes on imports; set up a national bank to provide credit.)

(b) Workers and peasants (Created new jobs, lowered food prices; allowed peasants to keep land they had gained during the Revolution.)

(c) Nobles (Offered pardons for those who had fled during the Revolution.)

(d) The Church (An agreement called the Concordat of 1801 balanced the rights of Church and state.) *(Comprehension)*

Developing the Lesson:
Making Judgments

Have students write an essay evaluating Napoleon's role in history. Students might consider the following questions:

(a) Did Napoleon defend or betray the best principles of the Revolution?

(b) Was Napoleon a great leader or a ruthless dictator? (Evaluation)

Answers to *Map Skill Practice*, p. 450.

1. Northeast Spain, United Netherlands, Austrian Netherlands, parts of Italy, the Illyrian Provinces, Corsica.
2. Spain, Kingdom of Naples, Kingdom of Italy, Switzerland, Confederation of the Rhine, Grand Duchy of Warsaw.
3. Norway, Denmark, Prussia, Austrian Empire.
4. Solid black line with arrows. About 600 miles (to Moscow).
5. Answers might include weather, terrain, access to supply lines, strength of Russia's armed forces.

Closing the Lesson: Debating an Issue

Have students work in groups to debate the following: *Napoleon's downfall was inevitable.* Students should choose their position for or against the statement. *(Synthesis)*

See *Section Review* questions, p. 453.

Chapter 22 Review Answers
(pp. 454–455)

Vocabulary Review

1. (a) guerrilla warfare (b) abdicate
(c) coup d'état (d) Old Regime (e) bourgeoisie
(f) Girondist (g) radical (h) suffrage (i) nationalism
2. (a) Napoleonic Code (b) Quadruple Alliance
(c) Napoleonic Wars

People to Identify

1. Duke of Wellington 2. Maximilien Robespierre 3. Lord Nelson 4. Marie Antoinette 5. Mary Wollstonecraft

Places to Know

1. B 2. E 3. A 4. D 5. C

Recalling the Facts

1. First Estate—clergy. Second Estate—nobility. Third Estate—peasants, city workers, middle class.
2. Many of the lower clergy felt concern for the poor in France, while many nobles were jealous of the king's power. Peasants were angry about poverty and unfair taxes, workers objected to high food prices, and middle-class people were dissatisfied with their lack of influence.
3. France faced enormous debts, worsened by later wars and by the king's inability to tax the wealthy.
4. Traditionally the three Estates met separately and each group had one vote. The Third Estate was nearly always outvoted two to one. Its members thus wanted to meet as one body, with each delegate having one vote. Under this method they felt they would have a better chance of bringing about reform.
5. It made changes in government administration, redistributed land, placed restrictions on the Church, and introduced constitutional government.
6. Monarchs welcomed the Revolution at first because they expected it to weaken France's power. However, the arrest of Louis XVI made them fear that their own people might turn against them.
7. Robespierre began the Reign of Terror, which led to imprisonment or death for anyone disagreeing with the Jacobins. Opposition to Robespierre's harsh tactics finally led to his execution.
8. The Revolution ended absolute monarchy in France, reduced the privileges of the Church and the nobility, aided the rise of the bourgeoisie, inspired reformers elsewhere, led to a new style of warfare, and promoted nationalist feelings.
9. He advanced within the army and then took part in a coup d'état that overthrew the Directory.
10. Napoleon did not favor political liberty or free elections. His police shut down newspapers that opposed him. His spies imprisoned people suspected of disloyalty.
11. The goal was to ruin Britain economically by cutting off its trade with other European nations. It was unsuccessful because Britain got around it and retaliated by blockading France and its allies. Additionally, middle-class European merchants whose businesses were hurt by the cutoff of British trade turned against Napoleon.
12. Napoleon lost many soldiers in Russia because of disease, exhaustion, supply shortages, desertion, and battle casualties. The retreat from Moscow, made during the cold Russian winter, only compounded these problems.
13. Napoleon's brief return to power between March and June 1815. It ended with Napoleon's defeat at the Battle of Waterloo and his exile to St. Helena.

Critical Thinking Skills

1. Answers will vary.
2. Napoleon's military successes increased the pride of French citizens in their country and helped make Napoleon a hero. This new nationalism helped Napoleon gain and maintain power within France. Nationalism in nations overrun by France hurt Napoleon because it eventually inspired conquered peoples to rebel against his rule.
3. Answers will vary but should note that the French document outlines many of the same ideas included in the American document. Both documents reflect some of John Locke's ideas: government power is based on the consent of the governed, and political leaders are responsible to the people.
4. Napoleon as an enlightened ruler and liberator: ended the privileges of the nobility and clergy, instituted the Napoleonic Code, ended serfdom, and promoted public education. Napoleon as a tyrant and dictator: conquered nations were forced to provide soldiers and taxes to support his armies, as well as raw materials for French industries. Opposition to Napoleonic rule was smashed.

Thinking About Geography

Charts will vary.

Enrichment: Primary Sources

1. The commander had put out a flag of peace.
2. He was captured and dragged through the crowd.
3. He describes the commander as "treacherous," the person who cut down the post as "brave," and the Bastille as "this house of horrors." He also calls the storming of the Bastille the introduction of "blessed liberty."

The French Revolution

1774–1815

See chapter timeline, p. 453.

Before You Read This Chapter

Who are the history-makers of today? Presidents and prime ministers? Religious leaders? Generals? It is often difficult to tell whether a single person has actually changed the course of history. This chapter describes how centuries of royal rule in France came to a violent end. As you read, ask yourself these questions: When did the actions of one person make a difference? When did people join forces to produce change? (Remember, even when people acted as a group, each member of the group made an individual decision to take part.)

The Geographic Setting

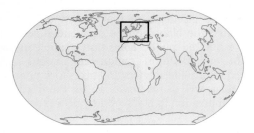

The Chapter Outline

1. The Outbreak of Revolution
2. The Radical Stage of the Revolution
3. Napoleon's Conquest of Europe

Napoleon Bonaparte had unlimited ambition for himself and for France. In 1812, at the height of his power, he posed for this portrait by his court painter, Jacques Louis David.

1 The Outbreak of Revolution

Objectives

Focus Questions

★ ■ What problems did France face in the late 1700's? *(pages 435–436)*

● ■ How did the people of France push for reforms? *(pages 436–440)*

Terms to Know

Old Regime
First Estate
Second Estate
Third Estate
bourgeoisie

French Revolution
émigré
Declaration of the
   Rights of Man

★ Note strategies for first objective on this page and p. 436.

Though American revolutionaries freed themselves from British rule, they kept many British ways of government. The revolutionaries in France, in contrast, wanted to create a new French society. Widespread unhappiness with the **Old Regime** (ray-ZHEEM)—the French political and social system in the years before 1789—produced a revolution that shook the continent.

The Three Estates

French society in the Old Regime was divided into three classes, called Estates. The **First Estate** was the clergy; the **Second Estate** was the nobility. The First and Second Estates together included only about 2 percent of the total population of 24 million. Everyone else belonged to the **Third Estate**.

The First Estate. The First Estate was divided into two groups, higher clergy and lower clergy. The higher clergy came from wealthy noble families. Like other aristocrats,

the higher clergy usually lived in luxury. The Church itself had enormous wealth, owning much land but paying no taxes.

The lower clergy were parish priests who came from the middle and lower classes. Many of these priests lived in poverty, and even helped peasants in the fields. They resented the pampered lives of the higher clergy and felt concern for France's poor people.

Sec. Rev. ques. 2

The Second Estate. Members of the Second Estate also were highly privileged. The nobility owned about a quarter of the land in France. They held the highest offices in the government and the army. Many nobles received generous gifts and pensions from the king, as well as food, labor, and payments from the peasants on their land. Some nobles owned large estates but paid almost no taxes. Despite their comfortable lives, nobles were often jealous of the king's power.

The Third Estate. The three groups that made up the Third Estate—peasants, city workers, and the middle class—included both rich and poor. The peasants, the largest group, had to struggle to make a living. Even though peasants owned about half the land in France, often their farms were too small to support their families. Many peasants owned no land at all and worked as day laborers on nearby farms.

Old-fashioned ways of farming were one reason for the poverty of the French peasant. Another reason was taxation. Because the clergy and the nobles paid almost no taxes, the heaviest burden fell on the peasants. Moreover, the peasants paid taxes to both the Church and the king. In some regions of France, taxes took more than half of a peasant family's income.

By 1789, French peasants were in an angry mood. They wanted a fairer tax system and an end to the payment of fees to the manor lords. A poor harvest in 1788, followed by a hard winter, added to their distress and misery.

435

★ RETEACHING. Have students make a diagram illustrating the class structure in France in 1789. The diagram should include a summary of the rights and responsibilities of each class. (First Estate: higher and lower clergy. Second Estate: nobility. Third Estate: peasants, city workers, and middle class.) *(Comprehension) Translating Information into Another Form*
Vocabulary Note that the word *estate* comes from a word meaning "status" or "standing."

★ REINFORCEMENT. Have students explain how inefficient government and debt contributed to France's problems in the 1700's. (Taxes and laws differed in the provinces, leading to confusion and injustice; Louis XIV left large debts, draining the treasury; and the wealthy would not accept a tax leading to a financial crisis.) *(Comprehension) Analyzing Information*
Check for Understanding. Ask: Which groups were included in the Third Estate? (Peasants, city workers, and the middle class.)

Sec. Rev. ques. 2, cont.

The other members of the Third Estate, the working class and the middle class, also felt dissatisfied with the Old Regime. The working class was hard hit by the bad harvest of 1788, which caused a grain shortage that drove up food prices in the city markets.

The middle class, or **bourgeoisie** (boor-zhwah-ZEE), consisted of merchants, bankers, lawyers, doctors, intellectuals, and government bureaucrats. Unlike the rest of the Third Estate, the bourgeoisie had money and education. They did not, however, have the prestige or influence that came with noble birth.

Many of the bourgeoisie took a keen interest in the reforms suggested by Enlightenment thinkers (Chapter 21). The philosophes (who came chiefly from the middle class) challenged the basic assumption of the Old Regime—that monarchs, clergy, and nobles were the natural leaders of society. From Locke onward, Enlightenment thinkers had stressed ideas of equality and liberty. Such ideas soon became a powerful force in France.

★ See below.

A cartoon from 1789 shows the relationship among the three Estates: A weary peasant bends under the weight of an aristocrat and a clergyman.

436

France's Slide into Chaos

Social inequality was only one problem facing France in the 1700's. The country also suffered from an inefficient government. Taxes and laws differed from province to province, causing confusion and injustice. Louis XVI, who took the throne in 1774, did little to make the government work better.

Of all France's problems, however, the most dangerous was debt. The French government was nearly bankrupt in the 1700's. Louis XIV, who died in 1715, had left enormous debts. Later European wars further drained the royal treasury.

Though the government was poor, France's clergy and nobility were not. Yet the king had no authority to tax the wealthy. Louis XVI asked the First and Second Estates to accept a tax on their lands, but they refused. The financial crisis that followed touched off the **French Revolution** in 1789.

Sec. Rev. ques. 3

Crisis and Revolt

● Note strategies for second objective on this page and p. 439.

The Estates-General. Since the nobles refused to be taxed, Louis XVI decided to call a meeting of the Estates-General (page 240). This assembly of delegates from the three Estates had not met since 1614. The king hoped for approval of a plan to tax the First and Second Estates.

The Estates-General met at Versailles in May 1789. Action stalled, though, because the delegates could not agree on a method of voting. Traditionally, each of the three Estates had met separately and each had voted as a group. For an issue to be decided, two of the three Estates had to agree. Because the nobility and clergy usually voted the same way, the Third Estate was nearly always outvoted two to one.

At the May meeting, the delegates of the Third Estate were mostly from the bourgeoisie. They wanted the three Estates to meet together, with each delegate having one vote. Because about half of the 1,200 delegates were from the Third Estate, they thought they

★ ENRICHMENT. Have students work in groups to prepare a dialogue that might have occurred between a member of the bourgeoisie and a noble over who should lead France. *(Synthesis)* *Understanding Point of View*

● RETEACHING. Have students list the following events in chronological order: women's march on Versailles; abolition of serfdom; the Constitution; Declaration of the Rights of Man. *(Comprehension)* *Sequencing Information*

● REINFORCEMENT. Have students predict how the reforms brought about by the French Revolution might have affected French society. *(Synthesis)* *Predicting Effects*

The storming of the Bastille by citizens of Paris in search of arms is the event that came to symbolize the French Revolution. July 14, "Bastille Day," is the most important national holiday in France.

would then have a better chance to bring about reform.

The National Assembly. The Third Estate's delegates decided to force the Estates to meet as one body. On June 17, 1789, they declared themselves the National Assembly and invited the other Estates to join them.

On the advice of the nobles, Louis XVI ordered the three Estates to continue to meet separately. Locked out of their meeting place at Versailles, the delegates of the Third Estate moved to the palace's indoor tennis court. Many of the clergy and some nobles joined them. Defying the king, they demanded a constitution for France and swore not to leave until they had achieved this goal. The oath they took came to be called the Tennis Court Oath.

Faced with this solid opposition, Louis gave in. After a week, he ordered all nobility and clergy to join the Third Estate in the National Assembly. The king's recognition of the National Assembly was the first victory for the bourgeoisie. Yet Louis, not wanting to seem weak, soon sent about 18,000 soldiers to Versailles.

The Storming of the Bastille

At this point, the people of Paris took matters into their own hands. They were already angry because of food shortages, unemployment, and high prices. Now they feared that the king's soldiers would crush the National Assembly and plunder the city.

On July 14, 1789, the people of Paris massed outside the Bastille (bas-TEEL). This

Sec. Rev. ques. 4

Linking Past and Present

In the chamber of the French National Assembly, the radicals were seated on the left, the conservative nobles on the right, and the moderates in the center. By the late 1800's the terms *left, right,* and *center* had become a shorthand way of describing political points of view. These terms are still in use today.

437

Check for Understanding. Ask: What was the Tennis Court Oath? (The promise made by members of the National Assembly to remain at the palace's tennis court until they had a constitution.)

Declaration of the Rights of Man

The Declaration of the Rights of Man set forth the ideals of the French Revolution. This document, portions of which are adapted below, reflected people's hopes for individual rights and freedom.

> 66 1. Men are born and remain free and equal in rights. . . .
>
> 2. The aim of every political group is the preservation of the natural rights of man. These rights are liberty, property, safety, and resistance to oppression. . . .
>
> 6. The law is the expression of the general will. All citizens have the right to take part in its making. . . .
>
> 10. No one may be disturbed on account of his opinions, even religious ones, as long as the expression of such opinions does not interfere with the established law and order. . . .
>
> 17. No one may be deprived of property, unless a legally established public necessity requires it, and just and prior payment has been made. 99

1. According to the Declaration, what are people's natural rights?
2. How does the Declaration define law?
3. How does the Declaration protect property rights?
4. **Critical thinking:** In what ways are the English Bill of Rights (page 400) and the Preamble to the Constitution of the United States (page 430) similar to this Declaration?

Ⓕ See answers below.

438

stone prison had become a hated symbol of oppression to the Parisians. Seeking guns and gunpowder, the crowds charged into the courtyard of the Bastille. The prison commander panicked and ordered the guards to open fire. Nearly 100 people were shot dead before the crowd overwhelmed the defenders and killed the commander. His head and the head of the mayor of Paris were stuck on poles and paraded through the streets of Paris.

The attack on the Bastille frightened the king into calling back his troops. The people of Paris had won another victory; their bold action had saved the National Assembly. Today the French people mark July 14 as Bastille Day—their day of national celebration.

The spirit of rebellion quickly moved from Paris to the French countryside. Rumors spread that the nobles were organizing armed bands to kill peasants and seize their property. A feeling of fear and desperation, called the Great Fear, took hold of the people. Peasants began to let loose centuries of stored-up hatred against the nobles. They burned the lords' manors and destroyed records of payments due. Middle-class landowners and well-to-do farmers also lost their homes and property as violence raged.

Major Reforms

The peasant uprisings convinced many nobles that they were in danger. A large number fled to other parts of Europe, becoming known as **émigrés** (EM-ih-grayz). The nobles who stayed in France realized that the Old Regime was coming to an end. One after another they rose in the National Assembly and reluctantly agreed to give up privileges their families had held for centuries.

On August 4, 1789, the National Assembly announced the end of feudalism in France. Serfdom was banned. The Church could no longer collect taxes, nor could the nobility demand fees, taxes, and labor from the peasants. All positions in Church, government, and army were opened to all citizens regardless of birth.

Sec. Rev. ques. 5

Background The Bastille, originally a fortress built in the late fourteenth century, had been turned into a prison by Cardinal Richelieu (p. 390). Prisoners held at the Bastille were usually there on political charges and had been arrested by order of the king. On July 14, 1789, there were only seven prisoners at the Bastille.

Vocabulary Note that the word *émigré* comes from a Latin word meaning "to move away."

This print depicts Parisian women marching on Versailles. The aristocratic woman on the left seems reluctant to join the revolutionaries.

A historic declaration. Inspired by Enlightenment ideals and the example of the American Revolution, the National Assembly decided to set forth the rights of French citizens. On August 27 it issued the **Declaration of the Rights of Man** (page 438). The Declaration stated that government belonged to the people as a whole. The aim of government, it said, was to preserve the "natural rights" of liberty and equality.

● See below.

The women's march on Versailles. The actions of the National Assembly could not prevent unrest among the city's poor. Many Parisian women had earned a living by making hats and dresses for noblewomen. As aristocratic families fled France, however, hatmakers and seamstresses found less and less work. Unemployment worsened, as did hunger.

On October 5, 1789, Parisian women rallied to protest the shortage of bread and the soaring food prices. Soon the streets echoed with shouts of "To Versailles!" Thousands of women and a crowd of supporters marched 12 miles in the rain, armed with sticks and farm tools. They stormed the palace and forced the royal family to return to Paris at knifepoint.

Further reforms. Deserted by many nobles and a virtual prisoner of his own peo-ple, Louis had no choice but to cooperate with the National Assembly. Over the next two years this body, controlled by the bourgeoisie, continued the work of reform. It made sweeping changes in several areas:

1. Government administration. To make the country easier to run, the reformers divided the country into departments governed by elected officials. Throughout the country, the metric system became the standard system of weights and measures.

In addition, the Assembly made changes in land ownership. The government took land from the Church and seized the estates of nobles who had fled. Much of this land was then sold to peasants.

2. Church influence. The National Assembly not only seized Church lands but tried to bring the Church and the clergy under state control. In 1790 it passed the Civil Constitution of the Clergy. This law stated that bishops and priests were to be elected by popular vote and paid by the government.

3. Constitutional government. Perhaps the most important act of the National Assembly was the adoption of the Constitution of 1791. This document limited the power of the king and set up an elected lawmaking body, the Legislative Assembly. To vote for representatives to the assembly, one had to be

Sec. Rev. ques. 5, cont.

439

Background The full title of the French document is *The Declaration of the Rights of Man and of the Citizen*. Louis XVI's refusal to sign the declaration resulted in increased revolutionary activity.

● ENRICHMENT. Have students write their own *Declaration of the Rights of Man* and broaden the statement to include the rights of all people. Declarations might focus on the responsibility of government to protect basic human rights and on the limits of government. *(Synthesis) Linking Past and Present* a male taxpayer. This qualification barred all women and about 30 percent of adult men. For its time, however, the Constitution of 1791 was generous in granting the vote.

Women in the Revolution

Many women had taken part in the events of the Revolution, and some hoped for a share in the promise of "equality." These women wanted better education for girls, fair laws dealing with marriage and divorce, and the right to sit on juries.

Women outside France also hoped for reform. Mary Wollstonecraft, an English writer who supported the French Revolution, published *A Vindication of the Rights of Woman* in 1792. In it she stated that it was natural for the "rights of man" to be extended to women. She urged better education for women as a way of achieving this goal.

See Sec. 1 *Closing the Lesson,* p. T433B.

See lesson plans, pp. T433A–T433C.

2 The Radical Stage of the Revolution

Objectives

★ Note strategies for first objective on this page and p. 443.

Focus Questions

★ ■ How did the French Revolution move into a more extreme phase? *(pages 440–445)*

● ■ What was the aftermath of the Revolution? *(page 445)*

Terms to Know

radical
counterrevolution
suffrage
Jacobin
Girondist

Reign of Terror
nationalism

440

The Constitution of 1791 marked the end of the first stage of the French Revolution. The bourgeoisie had made many gains—an end to special privileges, a limitation on the king's powers, and a chance to take part in government. The peasants, too, had benefited. Yet powerful groups were unhappy with the events of 1789–1791. Some felt that the reforms had gone too far; others felt that they had not gone far enough. The Revolution entered a second stage marked by violence that rocked much of Europe.

The Flight of the Royal Family

The people who felt that the Revolution had gone too far included the nobles, the king, and the queen, Marie Antoinette (an-twah-

Sec. Rev. ques. 2

Biography Mary Wollstonecraft, an English woman, lived in Paris from 1792 to 1795 because she was interested in the French Revolution. Her ideas, considered radical at the time, included equal educational opportunities for women. She argued that marriage could never be a real companionship if women were not as well educated as men. Wollstonecraft's daughter, Mary Shelley, wrote the novel *Frankenstein.*

★ **RETEACHING.** Have students use the following phrases in a paragraph summarizing the radical phase of the French Revolution: the attempted escape of the king; the Commune; Jacobins and Girondists; the Reign of Terror. *(Comprehension)* **Summarizing Information**

★ **REINFORCEMENT.** Have students develop a hypothesis explaining why events in France after the Revolution resulted in the Reign of Terror. *(Synthesis)* **Forming a Hypothesis**

NET). A member of the Hapsburg family of Austria, Marie Antoinette made plans for the royal family's escape to the Austrian Netherlands. There Louis could work with other European monarchs on plans to crush the Revolution.

Louis and his family slipped out of the palace on the night of June 20, 1791. As they headed toward the border, local townspeople recognized the royal family. Guards arrested them and forced them to return to Paris. When they reached the city, they were greeted by stony silence. Parisians refused to remove their hats, and soldiers refused to salute the king.

The attempted flight of the royal family cost Louis his subjects' support. Many now suspected the king and queen of plotting to overturn the recent reforms. In public meetings, the people of Paris called for changes in government.

Deepening Divisions

As doubts about the king increased, the most extreme revolutionaries grew stronger. These radicals—people favoring drastic change—wanted no king, not even one with limited power. They wanted France to become a republic. Among the radicals were many wage earners and small shopkeepers of Paris. They became known as the sans-culottes (sanz-kyoo-LOTS), meaning "without knee breeches," because the men wore long pants instead of the knee-length pants of the upper classes.

Though they had helped cause the Revolution by storming the Bastille and marching on Versailles, the Parisian working people had gained fewer benefits than the bourgeoisie and the peasants. They wanted a greater voice in the government, higher wages, lower food prices, and an end to food shortages.

Some of the bourgeoisie viewed the demands of the radicals as a threat to private property and to bourgeois control of the government. Other members of the bourgeoisie, however, became leaders of the radicals and

Marie Antoinette was a target for those who criticized the extravagance of the French court.

of the Revolution itself. They steered the Revolution in a more violent direction, bringing bloodshed to much of Europe.

War with Austria and Prussia

The events of the early years of the Revolution caused a stir throughout Europe. At first other monarchs had welcomed the Revolution because they expected it to weaken France's power. The arrest of Louis XVI, however, made monarchs fear that their own people might turn against them.

The French revolutionaries, too, had worries. They feared that Austria, ruled by the family of Marie Antoinette, might help the émigré nobles in a counterrevolution—a movement to restore the old way of government. Some radicals wanted France to strike first. War with Austria, they thought, might shake up other monarchs and advance the

441

Sec. Rev. ques. 3

Check for Understanding. Ask: Why did the attempted flight of the royal family cost the king his subjects' support? (Many subjects suspected the king and queen of plotting to overturn the reforms of the Revolution.)

cause of liberty everywhere. "Ten million Frenchmen, kindled by the fire of liberty, will make the tyrants tremble on their thrones," wrote one revolutionary.

On April 20, 1792, France declared war on Austria. Prussia backed Austria, and the two countries invaded France. They threatened to destroy Paris if the king or queen were harmed. Enraged, the Parisians rioted. A mob attacked the palace on August 10, killing hundreds of guards and servants. A radical government, the Commune, seized power and imprisoned the king. The Commune ordered elections to choose representatives for a new assembly, to be called the National Convention. For the first time, all adult males were granted **suffrage**—the right to vote.

The sans-culottes were armed men and women of the working class who volunteered to join France's revolutionary army. They wore red caps that symbolized liberty.

442

The Revolution in Crisis

The declaration of war on Austria showed that the French Revolution had moved into a radical stage. Its leaders were willing to take drastic action against all enemies.

Execution of the king and queen. The newly elected National Convention met for the first time in September 1792. Its first act was to end the monarchy and declare France a republic. The radical members then decided that the royal family was a danger to the republic. They accused Louis of working with the nobles and foreign agents. The Convention, by one vote, sentenced Louis to death. He was sent to the guillotine (GHEE-yuh-teen) and beheaded on January 21, 1793. Marie Antoinette met the same end later that year.

Expansion of the war. Events on the battlefield raised tensions inside and outside France. French armies recovered from early defeats, forced the invading Austrians and Prussians to retreat, and marched into the Austrian Netherlands. Alarmed by the surprising strength of the French armies, European monarchs and aristocrats pulled together. Britain and Spain became allies of Austria and Prussia. The once-confident French revolutionaries now found themselves at war with nearly all of Europe.

By the spring of 1793, the new French republic was in a state of crisis. Foreign troops had invaded France and were marching toward Paris. Food prices soared, and hungry Parisians looted stores. In western France, clergy and nobles led a counterrevolutionary movement.

Sec. Rev. ques. 4

Disputes among the revolutionaries. Violent disagreements also emerged within the National Convention. The most radical groups of revolutionaries were centered in Paris and included a political club called the **Jacobins**. Two of the most prominent Jacobins were Georges Danton (dahn-TAHN) and Maximilien Robespierre (ROHBZ-pih-yayr), both lawyers. The more moderate members of the Convention were known as

Background The guillotine was adopted by the French government in 1792 to provide a more humane and egalitarian method of execution. The machine was named for Joseph Guillotin, a physician and member of the National Assembly, who argued that all criminals condemned to death should be killed in the same way, and as painlessly and quickly as possible.

Social History The Jacobins were named after a Dominican monastery in Paris, where Jacobin meetings were held. *Jacobin* was the Parisian name for "Dominican."

Bourbon king Louis XVI was guillotined after a trial before the National Convention. His death was a victory for the radicals. Monarchs and conservatives throughout Europe were horrified.

Girondists (jih-RAHN-dists). They drew most of their support from people in the provinces outside of Paris. Leaders of both the Jacobin and Girondist groups came mainly ★ See from the bourgeoisie.
below.

The Jacobins took advantage of France's crisis to get rid of their opponents. Joining forces with poor Parisians, the Jacobins arrested Girondist leaders and set up the Committee of Public Safety. This group of about a dozen men held in its hands nearly unlimited power to deal with France's desperate situation.

Dictatorial Government

One of the most pressing problems for the Committee of Public Safety was to feed the hungry in Paris. The government fixed the price of certain foods and rationed bread.

Two other main tasks faced the Committee: pushing back enemy troops and protecting the government from its opponents within France.

A people's army. In August 1793 the Committee appealed to the whole nation to help in the war effort. For the first time in European history, a national draft called all able-bodied men for army service. The government said that everyone had a duty:

66 The young men shall go to battle and the married men shall forge arms. The women shall make tents and clothes, and shall serve in the hospitals; children shall tear rags [for bandages]. The old men will be guided to the public places of the cities to kindle the courage of the young warriors and to preach the unity of the Republic and the hatred of kings. 99

443

Social History The Girondists were members of the National Convention from the Gironde, a district in France.

★ ENRICHMENT. Have students work in groups to stage a session of the National Convention that might have been held in 1793. Students should represent Jacobins and Girondists and decide what strategies might effectively resolve the conflicts faced by the nation and protect France from further violence. *(Synthesis)* **Making Decisions**

Timetable

Revolutionary France

1789	Third Estate declares itself a National Assembly. Parisians storm the Bastille.
1789–1791	National Assembly issues Declaration of the Rights of Man and establishes constitution.
1792	France declares war on Austria.
1792–1793	National Convention abolishes monarchy, declares France a republic, and executes Louis XVI.
1793–1794	Committee of Public Safety makes reforms, organizes national army, and executes many opponents during Reign of Terror.
1795	New constitution establishes the Directory.

UNITÉ
INDIVISIBILITÉ
DE LA
RÉPUBLIQUE
LIBERTÉ
ÉGALITÉ
FRATERNITÉ
OU LA
MORT

444

The new French army, one million strong, was the largest army in the history of the world. It was united by loyalty to the republic and led by ambitious young generals. Soldiers marched off to war chanting the slogan "Liberty, equality, fraternity." They proudly sang the "Marseillaise" (mahr-say-YEZ), the rallying song of the Revolution (and now the French national anthem).

The Reign of Terror. The government's campaign against its opponents within France began one of the most notorious episodes of the French Revolution. Robespierre, the leading member of the Committee of Public Safety, was certain that everything he did was for the good of France. He hated the Old Regime and wanted to create a new and better society in which all people would be free, equal, and educated. Ruthless in his pursuit of this goal, Robespierre became a tyrant.

In an attempt to preserve the republic, Robespierre began what was referred to as the Reign of Terror—a brutal program to silence critics of the government. Robespierre set up a court to arrest and hear the cases of accused enemies of the republic. Between September 1793 and July 1794, at least 20,000 people (perhaps as many as 40,000) were found guilty and executed. Many other people were imprisoned.

The victims included clergy, aristocrats, and common people—anyone who disagreed with the Jacobins. Those taken before the court had no chance to defend themselves, and most trials were a mockery of justice. Mass executions took place in the countryside. In Paris, carts filled with condemned prisoners rolled through the streets to the public square where the guillotine was set up.

Huge crowds came to see these executions and to shout insults at the victims. When a famous person was to be guillotined,

A Jacobin poster called for the "unity and indivisibility of the republic" of France. It also made the now-famous demand for "liberty, equality, and fraternity—or death."

Background During the Reign of Terror, thousands of surveillance committees gathered information on citizens and arrested anyone considered suspect. As many as 120,000 people may have been arrested and held without trial.

Biography Before the Reign of Terror, Robespierre had been concerned with the rights of citizens and worked for such reforms as the abolition of capital punishment.

men and women left their jobs to watch the spectacle. Women wore silver and gold guillotines as jewelry; children even played with toy guillotines.

As the Terror claimed more and more victims, people questioned whether it had spiraled out of control. Not even Robespierre's fellow leaders felt safe: Danton and other politicians were executed early in 1794 for trying to stop the Terror. Feeling the cold chill of the guillotine blade at their necks, several members of the National Convention arranged for Robespierre's arrest on July 27, 1794. The next day it was Robespierre's turn to suffer the fate of his victims: he and his followers were sent to the guillotine.

Return to Moderation

● Note strategies for second objective on this page.

Sec. Rev. ques. 5

The fall of Robespierre put the reins of government back into the hands of moderates. Although their desires for reform had helped bring on the Revolution in 1789, these moderate leaders wanted no more of the Jacobins. Mostly members of the bourgeoisie, they did not want the monarchy restored, but neither did they want the common people to have political power. The moderates sought to undo some of the more radical reforms of the Revolution. They lifted price controls, for example, and once again limited voting rights to taxpayers only.

A new constitution, adopted in 1795, set up a republic headed by a group of five men, called the Directory. Once again, only prop-erty owners were allowed to vote, and the five directors put down uprisings by both the radical sans-culottes and those who supported monarchy. The Directory proved to be a weak government. It made no attempt to halt the growing inflation in France, and rumblings of discontent among the people grew louder and louder. The Directory's fall from power in 1799 (page 446) marked the end of the French Revolution.

Results of the French Revolution

The French Revolution radically changed French society. The Old Regime was completely overturned. Absolute monarchy came to an end, and the Church and the nobility lost their special privileges. The decline of the nobles aided the steady rise of the bourgeoisie, who soon came to dominate the government bureaucracy.

The effects of the Revolution were felt outside France as well. The ideals of liberty and individual rights, expressed in the Declaration of the Rights of Man, were echoed by reformers in Latin America and other lands. The Revolution also introduced a new style of warfare. Other European countries followed France's example by bringing together the people and resources of the entire nation to help in later war efforts. Finally, the Revolution promoted the spirit of **nationalism**—deep devotion to one's country. In time, nationalism spread throughout Europe and beyond.

See Sec. 2 *Closing the Lesson*, p. T433B.

Section Review

Answers to Section Review questions are in brackets on pages indicated.

(pp. 441, 442, 443, 444, 445)

1. **Define or identify:** radical, counterrevolution, suffrage, Jacobin, Girondist, Reign of Terror, nationalism.
2. Why did the royal family try to leave France? (pp. 440–441)
3. What were the aims of the sans-culottes and other radical revolutionaries? (p. 441)
4. What problems within France threatened the republic by 1793? (p. 442)
5. How did the government of France change after Robespierre's death? (p. 445)
6. **Critical thinking:** How did the Reign of Terror conflict with the slogan "Liberty, equality, fraternity"? (See answer below.)

445

● RETEACHING. Have students review "Return to Moderation" (above) and list the policies that restored order in France. (Price controls lifted, voting rights limited to taxpayers, and a new constitution adopted.) (Comprehension) Observing for Detail
● REINFORCEMENT. Have students summarize the results of the French Revolution. (Absolute monarchy ended, the Church and nobility lost privileges, and the bourgeoisie came to dominate government bureaucracy.) (Comprehension) Summarizing Information

● ENRICHMENT. Have students develop a hypothesis explaining why a violent period sometimes occurs after a successful revolution and sometimes does not. Students might contrast events after the French Revolution and the Communist revolutions in the Soviet Union or China with events after the American Revolution. (Synthesis) Forming a Hypothesis
6. Students might suggest that the brutal campaign was intended to wipe out dissent and allowed no defense for the accused.

See lesson plans, pp. T433A–T433C.

3 Napoleon's Conquest of Europe

Objectives

Focus Questions

★ ■ How did Napoleon bring reforms to France? *(pages 446–448)*
● ■ How did Napoleon's wars of conquest lead to his downfall? *(pages 448–452)*

Terms to Know

coup d'état
Napoleonic Code
Napoleonic Wars
Continental System

abdicate
guerrilla warfare
Quadruple Alliance
Battle of Waterloo

★ Note strategies for first objective on this page and p. 447.

By the end of the 1790's the people of France were tired of war, revolution, and violence. They were impatient, too, with the weak government of the Directory. In November 1799 a group of politicians carried out a **coup d'état** (koo day-TAH), or "strike against the state." They overthrew the Directory and placed a popular general at the head of the government.

Within a decade this leader, Napoleon Bonaparte, made France the dominant power of Europe. The reforms of the Revolution spread across Europe, and Napoleon proved himself to be one of the greatest military geniuses of all time.

Napoleon's Early Career

Born on the island of Corsica in 1769, Napoleon went to military school in France and became an officer. In 1793 he joined the French revolutionary forces and showed great talent for planning and leadership.

In 1796 Napoleon took command of the
446 French armies fighting the Austrians in Italy.

His brilliant tactics won key battles, forcing the Austrians to seek peace. Napoleon was now a hero, bursting with ambition. Not content to be a general—even a great one—Napoleon wanted to rule France.

A more immediate concern, however, was France's war with Britain. In an effort to weaken British power in the Mediterranean, Napoleon invaded Egypt in 1798. The campaign was a military failure, but it did spark French interest in ancient Egypt. In fact, it was one of Napoleon's officers who found the Rosetta Stone—the key to reading Egyptian hieroglyphics (page 40).

The Consulate

On his return to France, Napoleon joined in a plot to replace the Directory. In November 1799 Napoleon's soldiers surrounded the French legislature while he tried to speak to the lawmakers inside. The lawmakers, rightly sensing that his goal was to seize power for himself, drowned him out with cries of "Down with the tyrant!"

Napoleon left the building in a fury and called upon his troops to drive out the legislature. Bayonets raised, the soldiers marched into the hall, and the lawmakers fled. The Consulate, a new government headed by Napoleon, replaced the Directory.

Napoleon's Rule of France

Napoleon was a remarkable politician as well as an outstanding general. He knew that to stay in power, he had to preserve the reforms begun during the Revolution and solve the problems facing his country. To a great extent, he managed to gain the approval of every major group in France.

Winning political support. Napoleon pleased the bourgeoisie by promising them

Sec. Rev. ques. 2

★ RETEACHING. Have students review pp. 446–447 and identify the events in Napoleon's rise to power that occurred in the following years: **1793** (Joined revolutionary forces and displayed leadership.) **1796** (Took command of French armies fighting in Italy.) **1799** (Seized French legislature and replaced Directory with Consulate.) **1804** (Took title of emperor) *(Comprehension)* **Observing for Detail**

★ REINFORCEMENT. Have students evaluate Napoleon's political, social, and economic changes and draw conclusions about whether his policies worked for or against the revolutionary reforms. (Students should consider Napoleon's policies toward the bourgeoisie, peasants and workers, nobles, and the church; his educational reform; and the Napoleonic Code.) *(Evaluation)* **Drawing Conclusions** jobs in government and the army and by restoring order. He promoted trade and industry, and placed taxes on imports to protect French businesses from foreign competition. He also set up a national bank to provide credit for businesses and help keep the economy stable.

At the same time, Napoleon won the support of workers and peasants. The expansion of trade created many new jobs. To help poor city dwellers, Napoleon made food available at low prices. The French peasants backed Napoleon because he allowed them to keep the land that they had gained during the Revolution.

Napoleon even pleased the nobles. Though he did not restore their feudal privileges, Napoleon did offer pardons to the nobles who had fled during the Revolution. Most of the émigrés returned to France and promised loyalty to Napoleon. Many soon held high government posts.

A compromise with the Church. Napoleon reached an agreement with the Pope, called the Concordat of 1801, that balanced

At his coronation ceremony in 1804, Napoleon took the crown out of the Pope's hands to show his independence of Church authority.

the rights of Church and state. The Concordat gave the French government the authority to appoint members of the French clergy and to pay their salaries. The Church gained the right to confirm or refuse these appointments, but it gave up its claims to land taken from it during the Revolution.

The Napoleonic Code. As part of a reorganization of the government, Napoleon in 1800 appointed a staff of lawyers to draw up a code of laws for all of France. This was the first attempt in modern times to make such a code. Still in use in France today, the Napoleonic Code reflected some of the ideals of the Enlightenment and the Revolution. Under the Code, all French men were treated as equals, no matter what their birth or wealth. Feudalism and class privileges were abolished. The Code allowed people to practice the religion of their choice and protected their property rights.

On the other hand, some laws of the Napoleonic Code worked against equality. Workers were considered inferior to employers. Men received almost complete power over their families and family property, while women lost some rights. For example, a woman could acquire property only with her husband's written consent.

Government support for education. Napoleon's government needed trained army officers and educated public officials. To provide them, Napoleon started a national military academy and created a board of education to take full charge of schools and colleges. In time, this board set up a standard course of study for all teachers and schoolchildren. It also supervised schools and colleges throughout France.

From dictator to emperor. While Napoleon kept many of the social reforms of the French Revolution, he ignored some of the individual freedoms the French had won. Napoleon did not favor political liberty or free elections. His police shut down newspapers that dared oppose his rule. His spies hunted down and imprisoned people thought to be disloyal.

To symbolize his control of France, Napoleon took the title of emperor in 1804. The

Sec. Rev. ques. 3

★ See below.

447

Background Note that the Napoleonic Code became the basis of the legal system in areas controlled by France, including the present-day state of Louisiana and the province of Quebec in Canada.

★ **ENRICHMENT. Have students evaluate the influence of Enlightenment ideas about society and government (pp. 419–423) on Napoleon's policies.** (Synthesis) **Making Judgments**

Ⓕ See above.

Historic Places

The Louvre

Few buildings have reflected the changing trends of history more clearly than the Louvre (LOO-vruh) in Paris. In 1200 France's King Philip Augustus (page 240) built a castle on the banks of the Seine River to strengthen the city's defenses. It was a typical medieval fortress, with massive walls and a great stone tower. In the 1360's, Charles V replaced that castle with a fine palace, complete with paneled halls for state dinners and gilded weathervanes atop its many spires.

Even this building was not impressive enough for Francis I, however. In 1546 he ordered a new palace, to be designed in the latest fashion of the Renaissance. This classical building was the beginning of the present Louvre, although later rulers added wings and courtyards.

The kings of France were Europe's leading patrons of art, and many of their most beautiful possessions decorated the Louvre. In 1793, after the French monarchy was overthrown, the revolutionary government declared the Louvre a public museum. Napoleon enlarged both the building and its art collections. He filled the Louvre with great works of art from all the countries he conquered. After his defeat, however, France was forced to return most of those treasures.

Today the Louvre is one of the most famous art museums in the world. Its eight miles of galleries hold masterpieces ranging from the Greek sculpture *Winged Victory of Samothrace* (page 70) to Leonardo da Vinci's painting *Mona Lisa* (page 335).

event was marked by an elaborate ceremony in Paris. As the Pope reached out to crown Napoleon, the haughty emperor took the crown and put it on with his own hands. This act sent a message to France, and indeed to all the world—Napoleon recognized no authority higher than himself.

The Napoleonic Wars

• Note strategies for second objective on this page and p. 452.

Just as he had become master of France, Napoleon wanted to become master of Europe. Using both diplomacy and military skill, he broke up the alliance between Russia, Austria, and Britain and signed peace treaties with these countries.

Peace could not last long, however, for French expansion threatened British trade

448 and sea power. By 1803 Britain and France

were again at war. In 1805 Russia, Austria, and Sweden formed an alliance against Napoleon, which Prussia joined the next year. The wars that followed are referred to as the **Napoleonic Wars**.

Early victories. Between 1805 and 1807 Napoleon's armies rolled over the forces of Austria, Prussia, and Russia. France's stunning victory at Austerlitz in 1805 knocked Austria out of the war. Within two years Prussia and Russia were also forced to seek peace. Suddenly France was the leading power throughout Europe (map, page 450). Napoleon added some of the conquered lands to France. Others he gave to his relatives or loyal generals to rule.

In some ways, Napoleon brought the reforms of the Revolution to other parts of Europe. His administrators in conquered lands reduced the privileges of the nobles and

Sec. Rev. ques. 4

• RETEACHING. Have students review "The Napoleonic Wars" (pp. 448–449) and answer the following questions: (a) Why did Napoleon go to war against Britain, Russia, Austria, Sweden, and Prussia? (To become master of Europe.) (b) What was the Continental System? (Napoleon's effort to defeat Britain by forbidding France, its allies, and its territories to trade with Britain.) (Comprehension) Observing for Detail

• REINFORCEMENT. Have students work in groups to outline the reasons Napoleon's campaigns failed against Britain, Spain, and Russia. (Britain: Napoleon was unable to defeat British naval forces and the Continental System was generally ineffective. Spain: guerrilla warfare defeated Napoleon. Russia: Napoleon's army suffered from inadequate supplies and the harsh winter.) (Comprehension) Understanding Causes the clergy. They set up the Napoleonic Code and fairer systems of taxation. They put an end to serfdom, promoted public education, put qualified people in important jobs, and supported religious toleration. These reforms speeded up the social and political modernization of Europe.

There was, however, another side to Napoleon's rule. Conquered peoples were forced to provide soldiers for his army, taxes to pay for it, and raw materials for French industries. Opposition to Napoleonic rule was ruthlessly smashed. Those who had at first welcomed Napoleon as a "liberator" soon grew to hate him.

The Continental System. Napoleon's most determined enemy was Britain. Britain seized French ships and kept neutral ships from reaching French ports. In 1805 the French fleet left the Mediterranean Sea on its way to invade England. Near Trafalgar (truh-FAL-gur), a point of land on the southwest coast of Spain, the French met the British fleet, led by Lord Nelson. The British sank half of Napoleon's ships without losing any of their own.

After Trafalgar, Napoleon gave up his dream of invading England. He decided instead to defeat Britain by striking at its trade. Napoleon's plan was called the Continental System. It forbade France's allies and all countries under French control to import British goods. Napoleon hoped the Continental System would ruin Britain. Instead, backed by its powerful navy, Britain nearly ruined France.

Britain got around the Continental System by increasing its trade with the United States and by smuggling goods into Europe. The British navy, meanwhile, blockaded France and its allies. Middle-class merchants in Europe, whose businesses were weakened by the cutoff of British trade, turned against Napoleon.

A defeat in Spain. When Portugal refused to go along with the Continental System, Napoleon invaded that country and then decided to take Spain as well. In 1808 Napoleon sent in a large army and forced the Spanish king to abdicate—give up the throne. He then made his own brother, Joseph Bonaparte, king of Spain.

Sec. Rev. ques. 5

Bitterly resenting the French occupation, the Portuguese and Spaniards fought back with guerrilla warfare—surprise attacks by small bands of soldiers. The French troops, trained for regular warfare and hampered by the rugged Spanish terrain, could not overpower the rebels. In addition, Britain sent an army to help the guerrillas in what was called the Peninsular War. After five years of fierce battles, the French were driven out of Spain, and the British invaded France.

The Peninsular War was a costly defeat for Napoleon. It had tied up hundreds of thousands of French troops and given the British a base for their attack on France. Moreover, the Spanish success inspired patriots in other lands to resist Napoleon.

449

Check for Understanding. Ask: How did Napoleon spread the reforms of the French Revolution? (He appointed administrators in conquered lands who put these reforms into practice.)

Economics The Continental System was Napoleon's economic war against Britain; it successfully disrupted the English economy between 1808 and 1809. Britain established other markets, however, and Napoleon was forced to open French ports to enemy trade, imposing a high tariff on imported goods.

Biography Joseph Bonaparte, Napoleon's brother, was appointed king of Naples in 1806 and king of Spain in 1808, but he was never able to exercise much power. He came to the United States in 1815 and lived in Bordentown, New Jersey.

Background Spanish guerrilla attacks against Napoleon's forces were the first modern large-scale use of this kind of warfare. The term guerrilla comes from the Spanish word for war—guerra.

Map Skill Practice

See p. T433C for answers to *Map Skill Practice*.

Napoleon's Empire, 1812

1. This map shows Napoleon's empire, which covered almost the entire continent of Europe. What areas of the French Empire had not been part of France in 1789?

2. Which states came under the direct control of Napoleon?

3. Which states had formed alliances with Napoleon?

4. How is the route of Napoleon's march into Russia shown? How far did his army advance?

5. **Decision-making.** What should Napoleon have taken into consideration in planning his military campaign against Russia?

SCALE

0   300 mi

0   300 km

SWEDEN

NORWAY

AND

DENMARK

Baltic Sea

Moscow

Borodino ✕

Napoleon's route (1812)

North Sea

GREAT BRITAIN

PRUSSIA

RUSSIAN EMPIRE

London

UNITED NETHERLANDS

Berlin

GRAND DUCHY OF WARSAW (POLAND)

ATLANTIC OCEAN

AUSTRIAN

CONFEDERATION

Waterloo ✕

NETH.

OF

✕ Leipzig

✕ Jena

Varennes

THE

Versailles ● Paris

Rhine R.

RHINE

✕ Austerlitz

FRANCE

Vienna ●

SWITZERLAND

AUSTRIAN EMPIRE

ILLYRIAN PROVINCES

Black Sea

KINGDOM

Danube R.

PORTUGAL

ELBA

OF

ITALY

Adriatic Sea

OTTOMAN

Constantinople ●

Madrid ●

CORSICA

Rome ●

SPAIN

SARDINIA

KINGDOM

OF

NAPLES

EMPIRE

✕ Trafalgar

Mediterranean

SICILY

N

W   E

S

Sea

KEY

✕ Trafalgar

☐ French Empire

☐ States under Napoleon's control

☐ States allied with Napoleon

—·— Boundary of France, 1789

✕ Battle

450

The Invasion of Russia

By 1812 Napoleon's empire in Eastern Europe reached to the edge of the Russian Empire (map, page 450). Though Russia and France were allies, relations between the two countries were strained. Czar Alexander I had angered Napoleon by trading with Britain in violation of the Continental System. Napoleon feared that Russia would make an alliance with Britain. He decided to end the threat by invading Russia.

The Grand Army. Napoleon gathered troops from France and the conquered countries, creating an army of about 614,000 soldiers. In June 1812 the Grand Army, as it was called, invaded Russia. Realizing they could not beat the French in battle, the Russians slowly retreated eastward. They set fire to farms and crops along the way, thus depriving the huge French army of food.

Lured deeper into the vast Russian steppes, the Grand Army ran short of supplies. Disease, hunger, exhaustion, and desertion thinned the ranks. Battle losses claimed many lives. In September the Russians made a stand at Borodino, some 70 miles west of Moscow, but were again forced to retreat.

The Russian retreat allowed Napoleon to reach Moscow, but the victory was useless. The city was deserted and the Russians had set fires that destroyed nearly all of it. Realizing that his army could not survive a Russian winter in the devastated city, Napoleon ordered a retreat. Only about 100,000 soldiers remained in his army. On October 19, 1812, they began the long march westward.

Withdrawal from Moscow. The retreat became one of the worst disasters in military history. The soldiers had little food and not enough warm clothing. Russian peasants and horsemen attacked soldiers who fell behind. The temperature dropped to 30 degrees below zero. "The road is littered with men frozen to death," wrote one of Napoleon's generals. "The soldiers throw away their guns because they cannot hold them; both officers and soldiers think only of protecting themselves from the terrible cold." Fewer than 40,000 soldiers survived the march from Moscow.

In the winter of 1812, a grim Napoleon led the battered and half-frozen remnants of his Grand Army in retreat from Moscow.

Britain's Duke of Wellington began his military training in India. He fought the French in Spain and Portugal and headed the allied army that crushed Napoleon at Waterloo.

The Fall of Napoleon

No sooner had Napoleon's army staggered out of Russia than it met new dangers. In the German state of Prussia, anti-French leaders had been stirring people's feelings of nationalism. Elsewhere in Europe, other patriots urged rebellion against Napoleon.

In 1813, after Napoleon's retreat from Russia, Prussia declared war on France. Other states soon joined Prussia. In October 1813, allied forces from Prussia, Austria, Russia, and Sweden defeated Napoleon in the "Battle of the Nations" at Leipzig (LYP-sig), Germany.

The victorious allies then invaded France. When they reached Paris in March 1814, Napoleon abdicated. Louis XVIII, younger brother of the executed Louis XVI, was crowned king of France. The allies exiled Napoleon to the small island of Elba, off the western coast of Italy.

To keep France in line, Prussia, Austria, **452** Russia, and Great Britain agreed to form the Quadruple Alliance. They pledged to remain united against any future attempt by France to dominate Europe.

Napoleon's Final Defeat

At the time of his exile, Napoleon was only 44 years old. He still longed for the excitement of battle, the cheers of his soldiers, and the glory of victory. Moreover, he knew that many French people disliked their new king.

The Hundred Days. Escaping from Elba, Napoleon landed on the southern French coast on March 1, 1815, with about 1,000 soldiers. King Louis XVIII sent his army to arrest Napoleon. Sure of his ability to win back the soldiers' loyalty, Napoleon walked up to the royal troops. "If there is one soldier among you who wishes to kill his emperor," he said, "here I am." The king's troops shouted, "Long live the emperor!" and joined Napoleon. On March 20, 1815, Napoleon swept into Paris and received a hero's welcome. Thus began the period known as the Hundred Days.

● See below.

With Napoleon's return, the European allies once again took up arms against the French. In June 1815 forces of the two sides met in the Austrian Netherlands. There, at the **Battle of Waterloo**, Napoleon was decisively defeated. His army crumbled under the attack of troops led by the British Duke of Wellington and the Prussian field marshal, Gebhard von Blücher (BLOO-kur).

Napoleon surrendered to the British, who sent him to St. Helena, a lonely island a thousand miles from the Atlantic coast of Africa (map, page 603). On this rocky island Napoleon Bonaparte, emperor of the French, spent the last six years of his life.

Napoleon's mark on history. Napoleon's conquests radically changed Europe by spreading many of the French Revolution's reforms and ideals. Governments were reorganized, feudal ideas were rejected, and ideas of freedom and equality took root. In reaction to Napoleon, nationalist feelings grew. As a result, many European peoples took steps to create independent nations.

See Sec. 3 *Closing the Lesson*, p. T433C.

Background The Battle of Leipzig resulted in the death, injury, or imprisonment of approximately 75,000 French soldiers and 50,000 allied forces.

Geography The island of Elba lies about six miles off the west coast of Italy and has an area of approximately 86 square miles.

Biography Napoleon, nicknamed "the Little Corporal" because of his short stature, had an untiring capacity for work, a memory for details, and a personal magnetism that drew fierce loyalty from his supporters.

● ENRICHMENT. Have students develop a hypothesis to explain why the people of France accepted Napoleon's return as leader during the Hundred Days. When developing their hypotheses, students should consider the revolutionary period that preceded Napoleon's rule, the effects of Napoleon's policies on French society, and the results of the Napoleonic Wars. *(Synthesis)* **Forming a Hypothesis**

Section Review

Answers to Section Review questions are in brackets on pages indicated.

1. **Define or identify:** coup d'état, Napoleonic Code, Napoleonic Wars, Continental System, abdicate, guerrilla warfare, Quadruple Alliance, Battle of Waterloo. (pp. 446, 447, 448, 449, 452)
2. How did Napoleon gain the support of various groups within France? (pp. 446–447)
3. What reforms in law and education did Napoleon introduce? (p. 447)
4. How did occupied areas benefit and suffer under French rule? (p. 448)
5. What aggressive actions did Napoleon take against Britain, Spain, and Russia? How did each action contribute to Napoleon's defeat? (pp. 449, 451)
6. **Critical thinking:** Did Napoleon betray or carry forward the ideals of the French Revolution? Explain.

(See answer below.)

Chapter 22 Summary and Timeline

1. The Old Regime in France was based on absolute monarchy and on a nobility and clergy with special privileges. Unfair taxation and unequal opportunities caused widespread discontent among the Third Estate—the middle class, peasants, and city workers. In 1789 a financial crisis forced Louis XVI to call a meeting of the Estates-General. The bourgeoisie took over the meeting. Aided by uprisings of peasants and Parisian workers, they ended feudal privileges and limited the king's power.

2. In 1792, radicals who wanted to end monarchy altogether took control of the French Revolution. They established a republic, executed the king, and killed thousands of French people in what was called the Reign of Terror. Other European monarchs went to war against the French republic. In 1795 a moderate government called the Directory took power.

3. The Directory was easily overthrown in 1799 by a popular general, Napoleon Bonaparte. By 1804 he had made himself emperor. Napoleon's military genius enabled him to conquer much of Europe, bringing some of the reforms of the Revolution to other countries. However, his absolute rule, combined with growing feelings of nationalism, aroused opposition to French occupation. An alliance of European nations finally defeated Napoleon in 1815.

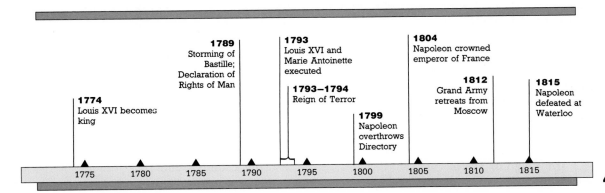

1774 Louis XVI becomes king

1789 Storming of Bastille; Declaration of Rights of Man

1793 Louis XVI and Marie Antoinette executed

1793–1794 Reign of Terror

1799 Napoleon overthrows Directory

1804 Napoleon crowned emperor of France

1812 Grand Army retreats from Moscow

1815 Napoleon defeated at Waterloo

1775   1780   1785   1790   1795   1800   1805   1810   1815

6. Students might point to Napoleon's reforms as furthering the ideals of the Revolution, but they should also note that his absolute rule and unwillingness to extend reforms throughout conquered lands betrayed those ideals.

See p. T433C for answers to Chapter Review.

Vocabulary Review

1. Match each of the following terms with its correct definition: *abdicate, bourgeoisie, coup d'etat, Girondist, guerrilla warfare, nationalism, Old Regime, radical, suffrage.*
   a. surprise attacks by small bands of fighters
   b. give up a throne
   c. overthrow of a state
   d. French political and social system before 1789
   e. middle class in France
   f. moderate member of the National Convention
   g. person who favors drastic change
   h. right to vote
   i. devotion to one's country
2. Use the following terms to complete the sentences below: *Napoleonic Code, Napoleonic Wars, Quadruple Alliance.*
   a. The ___?___ was a set of laws for all of France.
   b. Prussia, Austria, Russia, and Britain formed the ___?___ in 1814 to keep France from dominating Europe.
   c. The ___?___ resulted from Napoleon's desire to rule Europe.

People to Identify

Match each of the following people with the correct description: *Marie Antoinette, Lord Nelson, Maximilien Robespierre, Duke of Wellington, Mary Wollstonecraft.*
1. British leader of the forces that defeated Napoleon at the Battle of Waterloo
2. Jacobin who was mainly responsible for the Reign of Terror
3. leader of the British fleet that defeated Napoleon at Trafalgar
4. French queen married to Louis XVI and beheaded in 1793
5. English writer who said the "rights of man" should be extended to women

Places to Know

Match the letters on this map of Europe with the places listed below. You may want to refer to the map on page 450.
1. Waterloo
2. Elba
3. Trafalgar
4. Paris
5. Leipzig

Recalling the Facts

1. Who belonged to the First Estate? The Second Estate? The Third Estate?
2. Why were many people in France unhappy under the Old Regime?
3. What caused France's financial crisis in the late 1700's?
4. Why did the delegates of the Third Estate want to change the method of voting in the Estates General?

5. What broad reforms did the National Assembly make between 1789 and 1791?

6. Why did many European monarchs first support and then oppose the French Revolution?

7. How did Robespierre deal with opponents of his government? How did his actions backfire?

8. What were the eventual results of the French Revolution?

9. How did Napoleon come to power in France?

10. In what ways did Napoleon ignore individual freedoms the French had won?

11. What was the goal of the Continental System? Did it succeed? Explain.

12. Why was Napoleon's invasion of Russia a disaster?

13. What was the period known as the Hundred Days? How did it end?

Critical Thinking Skills

1. **Researching historical figures.** Prepare a list entitled "Who's Who in the French Revolution." Then choose five to ten people and write a few sentences describing each person's role in the Revolution. Your list might include Abbé Sieyès, Louis XVI, Marie Antoinette, Maximilien Robespierre, Georges Danton, Charlotte Corday, and Jean Paul Marat. *(Comp.)*

 2. **Drawing conclusions.** Historians have observed that nationalism was both an ally and an enemy of Napoleon. Explain this statement and give evidence to support it. *(Syn.)*

3. **Comparing primary sources.** Write a short essay comparing the American Declaration of Independence with the Declaration of the Rights of Man. Note ways in which the American document influenced the French document. *(Anal.)*

4. **Evaluating points of view.** To some people in the nations Napoleon conquered, the emperor was an enlightened ruler and a liberator of the people. Others considered him a tyrant and a ruthless dictator. List some arguments supporting each point of view. In your opinion, which view is most accurate? *(Eval.)*

Thinking About Geography

Making a chart. Make a chart showing information about the battles at Austerlitz, Trafalgar, Leipzig, and Waterloo. For each battle, give the date, the location, the forces that were involved, and the outcome. *(Comp.)*

Enrichment: Primary Sources

The following adapted passage appeared in a Parisian newspaper on July 14, 1789. It describes the storming of the Bastille.

❝ First the people tried to enter this fortress by the Rue St. Antoine [a street]. The treacherous commander of the Bastille had put out a flag of peace. So a confident advance was made, but artillery fire mowed down several French guards and some soldiers. The people took fright, but then they rallied and took shelter from the fire.

Some brave individual cut through a post that locked the drawbridge. It immediately fell and they came to a ditch and from there made an orderly attack. The commander was captured and dragged through the crowd.

Peaceful and blessed liberty, for the first time, has at last been introduced into this house of horrors. ❞

1. Why did the people storming the Bastille believe it was safe to enter the prison?

2. What happened to the commander of the Bastille?

3. **Critical thinking:** What words and phrases indicate that the author of this account supported the storming of the Bastille? *(Anal.)*

T455A

New Nations in Latin America   1780–1911
(pp. 456–469)

Chapter Preview

Section 1 of this chapter identifies the effects of colonial rule on Latin America and describes the development of independence movements and the establishment of independent countries. In Section 2 the problems these newly independent Latin American countries faced in building unified nations are discussed.

Bibliography

See the *Teacher's Management and Planning Guide* for additional listings. Starred titles are for both students and teachers.

Lavrin, Asuncion, ed. *Latin American Women: Historical Perspectives.* Greenwood Press. Individuals in the colonial period and later.

*Link, Paul. *Soldier of the Andes.* Messner. The life of José de San Martín.

Stein, Stanley J., and Barbara H. *The Colonial Heritage of Latin America.* Oxford University Press. Effects of the colonial background on the republics of Latin America.

Section Lesson Plans

SECTION 1   (pp. 457–461)
Latin American Independence

Objectives

After completing this section, students will be able to·
1. Explain why Latin Americans rebelled against foreign rule.
2. Describe how Latin Americans gained independence.

Introducing the Lesson

Remind students that Latin America had been colonized by the Spanish and the Portuguese in the fifteenth century. During the next three hundred years, colonial rule in Latin America created a system of economic and social inequality that resulted in the desire for independence and the eruption of revolutionary movements in the late 1700's.

   Then ask: *(a) What influences might have encouraged Latin Americans to revolt against colonial rule in the late eighteenth century?* (Answers will vary, but might include the impact of successful revolutionary movements in the English colonies and in France, the influence of Enlightenment ideals, and the decline of Spanish power in the 1600's.)

   (b) What advantages might Latin Americans have had in their efforts to overthrow colonial rule? (The distance between Spain and Portugal and their colonies might have worked to the Latin Americans' advantage. Also, the number of Latin American people who wanted independence probably was greater than the number who sought to maintain colonial rule.)

   (c) What disadvantages might Latin Americans have faced in their struggle for independence? (Answers will vary. People who are ruled by foreign powers usually have limited access to wealth and weapons. Spain and Portugal probably had more advanced technology, better political organization, and greater military strength than those opposing colonial rule.)

Developing the Lesson:
Comparing Historical Developments

Have students compare the causes of the revolutions in Latin America with the causes of the American Revolution (pp. 424–426). (Both the American and the Latin American wars of independence sought to end harmful economic policies. The Latin Americans, however, also fought to end a social system that favored Europeans and privileged certain classes at the expense of others.) *(Comprehension)*

Developing the Lesson:
Understanding Cause and Effect

Have students identify events in Europe that influenced independence movements in Latin America. (The adoption of the Declaration of the Rights of Man in France; confusion resulting from Napoleon's invasion of Spain in 1808; restoration of the Spanish constitution; Napoleon's invasion of Portugal.) *(Comprehension)*

Closing the Lesson: Observing for Detail

Have students identify the territory and events with which each of the following is associated:
    Tupac Amaru (Peru; led an Indian rebellion against forced labor and sales taxes.)
    Vincent Ogé (St. Domingue; called for citizen rights for free mulattos.)
    Pierre Toussaint L'Ouverture (St. Domingue; drove the French from the land and set up a new government.)
    Simon Bolívar (Great Colombia; the "Latin American George Washington" freed Great Colombia from Spanish rule.)
    José de San Martín (Peru and Chile; with Bolívar completed the independence movement in South America.)
    Miguel Hidalgo (Mexico; Creole priest who organized the Mexican revolt against the Spanish.)
    José María Morelos (Mexico; continued Mexican revolt against the Spanish; declared independence from Spain.)
    Agustín de Itúrbide (Mexico; captured Morélos; crowned himself emperor of Mexico in 1822; exiled within a year.)
    Pedro (Brazil; son of Portugal's king who declared Brazil's independence and became Emperor Pedro I.) *(Comprehension)*

See *Section Review* questions, p. 461.

SECTION 2   (pp. 462–467)
Challenges Facing the New Nations

Objectives

After completing this section, students will be able to:
1. Discuss the causes and results of Latin American disunity.
2. Describe how foreign countries influenced Latin America.
3. Explain what problems Mexico faced in the 1800's.

Introducing the Lesson

Remind students that Latin Americans fought to free themselves from foreign control and to end social inequality. After independence, however, Mexico and countries in Latin America were unable to overcome many forces working against national unity and democratic reform.
     Then ask: *(a) What factors might work against the development of national unity in a newly independent country?* (Answers will vary. National unity develops when members of a society share values, goals, and a sense of identity. A newly independent country faced with the problem of forming a new government and meeting the conflicting needs of many groups might have difficulty establishing national unity.)
     (b) How might the colonial period in Latin America have made democratic reform and social equality difficult to establish after independence? (Answers will vary. Latin Americans had no experience with self-government; democratic ideas, although attractive, had never been part of the colonial system. The colonial social system had existed in Latin America for hundreds of years and might have been difficult to eliminate.)

Developing the Lesson:
Forming a Hypothesis

Have students develop a hypothesis to answer the following question: *What actions might have been taken to establish an effective democratic system in Latin America?* (Answers will vary.) *(Synthesis)*

Developing the Lesson:
Predicting Events

Have students work in groups to predict how the following circumstances might affect the development of democracy in a newly independent state: geographic barriers, rise of dictators, neocolonialism, civil war. *(Synthesis)*

Closing the Lesson:
Making Generalizations

Have students write an essay explaining how events in Mexico in the nineteenth century represented problems faced by most Latin American nations after independence. (As in other Latin American countries, Mexico faced the following difficulties: *conflict with foreign countries* [Mexican-American War, French intervention]; *political and social unrest* [constitutional reform in 1857, War of the Reform]; *rule by dictators; problems arising from foreign investment and trade.*) *(Comprehension)*

See *Section Review* questions, p. 467.

Chapter 23 Review Answers
(pp. 468–469)

Vocabulary Review

1. (a) caudillo (b) puppet government (c) annex (d) neocolonialism
2. (a) *peninsulares*—people born on the Iberian peninsula and belonging to the highest social class in colonial society; Creoles—persons of Spanish or Portuguese descent born in the Americas, who were often wealthy but were considered socially inferior to the *peninsulares.* (b) Mexican-American War—war (1846–1848) between Mexico and the United States over American annexation of Texas; War of the Reform—Mexico's bloodiest civil war (1858–1860), pitting the army, Church, and upper classes against reformers and the poor.

People to Identify

1. Mestizo leader of an Indian rebellion in Peru in 1780.
2. Creole priest known as the "father of Mexican independence" for his leadership of an early revolt against Spain.
3. Indian lawyer who fought for reforms in Mexico during the 1850's and 1860's.
4. Austrian who became emperor of Mexico.

5. Caudillo who, between 1830 and 1837, helped Chile develop stable government.
6. Caudillo who harshly ruled Argentina from 1835 to 1852.
7. Ex-slave who led the rebellion in 1791 that drove the French from St. Domingue.

Places to Know

1. D   2. C   3. A   4. E   5. B

Recalling the Facts

1. They disliked heavy taxes and restrictions on trade, exposure to Enlightenment ideas had created a desire for reform, and many Latin Americans resented the rigid class system that favored Europeans over native peoples and resulted in social inequalities.
2. The Spanish raised colonial taxes. Both rebellions were crushed.
3. Haiti.
4. Bolívar put together a Latin American army to fight against Spain. He became president of Great Colombia in 1819 and in 1824 dealt the Spanish their final defeat, thus liberating South America from Spanish rule. San Martín led troops in the southern part of the continent and helped drive the Spanish from Chile and Peru.
5. In Mexico, Creoles joined forces with the rebels, and together they defeated the Spanish in 1821. In response to the demands of the people, the Portuguese ruler Pedro I declared Mexican independence in 1822.
6. Geographic barriers hindered communication and trade; racial barriers and the rigid colonial class system remained a source of conflict; political disagreements often pitted landowners and clergy against reformers.
7. Latin Americans had little experience in self-government; in addition, the army and wealthy landowners held the real power. These factors led to rule by caudillos.
8. The United States sympathized with the plight of the Latin American nations and feared a strong European presence nearby. Britain disagreed with Spain's anti-reform policies and wanted to protect its own Latin American trade.
9. His reforms separated Church and state, ended Church ownership of land, and allowed freedom of speech, press, and assembly. They also required that cases involving clergy and military officers be tried in the regular courts.

10. Benefits—foreign businesses invested heavily in industry and agriculture; railroads, mines, and oil fields were built; the treasury gained a surplus. Costs—investors in the United States and Europe took much of the profits from the new industries and mines; Creoles looked down on Mexican culture and traditions, causing a decline in Mexican national pride.

Critical Thinking Skills

1. Answers will vary.
2. Answers will vary, but students should note that foreign investors provided the money Latin American nations needed to invest in transportation, banking, and manufacturing, which speeded economic development. A major problem was that foreign involvement encouraged the development of single-export economies rather than diversified economies. When world demand for these exports dropped, the entire economy suffered. Another problem was the great influence foreign governments and investors gained over local governments.
3. The cartoon shows Díaz placing a crown on his own head. The cartoonist was saying that Díaz held absolute power.
4. Answers will vary. Some similarities are that both the American and the Latin American colonies were ruled by European powers, who established very favorable trading relationships with their colonies. In the American colonies, the Stamp Act and Townshend Acts sparked rebellion against the British; in the Latin American colonies, tax increases led to revolts against the Spanish in Peru and Colombia. Some differences are that the United States successfully instituted democratic government, while many Latin American nations came to be ruled by dictators. The American Revolution was against only one power, Britain. In Latin America, revolutions took place against Spain, Portugal, and France.

Thinking About Geography

Viceroyalty of La Plata: Argentina, Paraguay, Uruguay, part of Bolivia. *Viceroyalty of New Granada:* Great Colombia. *Viceroyalty of Peru:* Chile, Peru, part of Bolivia.

Enrichment: Primary Sources

1. To make people as happy and secure as possible and to ensure the political stability of the society.
2. Ultimate political power rests with the people, not the government.
3. National unity.
4. Answers will vary, but students should note that lack of experience, class conflict, and other barriers made democratic government and national unity extremely difficult.

New Nations in Latin America 1780–1911

See chapter timeline, p. 467.

Before You Read This Chapter

When you see the word *revolution*, what do you think of? Usually, it means the violent overthrow of a government. Yet most revolutionaries hope for more than a change of leadership. Often they want sweeping changes in society. As you read this chapter, try to develop your own definition of a revolution. If a new set of leaders simply replaces the old set, is that change a revolution? In your opinion, which events in the chapter were truly revolutionary?

The Geographic Setting

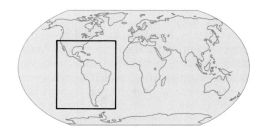

The Chapter Outline

1. Latin American Independence
2. Challenges Facing the New Nations

Artist Juan O'Gorman painted this dramatic mural of events in Mexican history.

Vocabulary The world *Creole* is from the Spanish *criollo*, meaning "native to the place."

1 Latin American Independence

Objectives

Focus Questions

★ ■ Why did Latin Americans rebel against foreign rule? *(pages 457–458)*

● ■ How did Latin Americans gain independence? *(pages 458–461)*

Terms to Know

peninsulares
Creole

★ Note strategies for first objective on this page.

In the late 1700's, tensions were high in the Latin American colonies. People were divided along racial, economic, and social lines. Heavy taxes and restrictions on trade aroused the anger of Latin Americans. Members of the educated classes, having learned of Enlightenment ideas, wanted reforms. Inspired by revolutions in France and the United States, Latin Americans launched their own revolts. By 1824 Spain and Portugal had lost all their mainland colonies in the Americas.

Inequalities in Colonial Society

One of the Latin Americans' chief complaints against colonial rule was social inequality. The Spanish and Portuguese had set up a rigid class system that favored Europeans over native peoples.

At the top of the social ladder were the *peninsulares* (peh-nin-soo-LAHR-ehs). These were people born on the Iberian (eye-BEER-ee-un) peninsula of Europe, where Spain and Portugal are located. The *peninsulares* dominated colonial life. They owned enormous estates, controlled mines and trade, and held the vast majority of high offices in the government, the army, and the Church.

Ranking below the *peninsulares* were the Creoles (KREE-ohlz)—persons of Spanish or Portuguese descent who had been born in the Americas. Creoles were legally equal to the *peninsulares* and often had great wealth. However, they were considered socially inferior and could not hold high office.

Below those of pure European descent were people of mixed heritage: mestizos and mulattos (page 375). Both groups were barred from the highest positions in Latin American society. They did, however, hold a wide range of jobs, becoming soldiers, farmers, laborers, lawyers, and merchants.

At the bottom of the class structure were Indians and African slaves. Most people of these groups led harsh lives, working in mines and on plantations. Although they formed the majority of the population, Indians and Africans had no real power.

The First Upheavals

The rebellion of Tupac Amaru. In the late 1700's the Spanish government raised colonial taxes to refill its empty treasury. Colonists responded with violence. In 1780 Tupac Amaru (too-PAHK ah-MAH-roo), a mestizo descendant of the Inca kings, led an Indian rebellion in Peru. The rebels demanded an end to forced labor and sales taxes. They also called for the appointment of Indian, rather than Spanish, governors. In the fighting that followed, thousands died and much property was destroyed. Finally, the Spanish forces crushed the rebellion and executed its leaders.

A revolt in Colombia. On the heels of the violence in Peru came a revolt in Colombia. There, too, the Spanish had raised taxes. **457**

★ RETEACHING. Have students review "Inequalities in Colonial Society" (above) and diagram the Spanish and Portuguese class system. (Classes included *peninsulares*, Creoles, mestizos, mulattos, and Indians and African slaves.) *(Comprehension)* **Translating Information into Another Form**

★ ENRICHMENT. Have students research the lasting effects of the Spanish and Portuguese colonial period on Latin America. *Application) Linking Past and Present*

★ REINFORCEMENT. Have students explain how the class system in Latin America reinforced Spanish and Portuguese control and social inequality. (The *peninsulares* had enormous wealth and controlled the government, army, and Church. This monopoly of resources made it difficult for others to change the social structure.) *(Comprehension) Identifying Cause and Effect*

Vocabulary "Iberian" was the name given by Greeks to an ancient people who lived along the Ebro (Iberian) River in northeastern Spain.

In 1781, Indian and mestizo peasants, led by Creoles, formed an army of 20,000 and marched on the capital city of Bogotá (boh-guh-TAH). The government first agreed to the people's demands, then broke its word and crushed the trusting rebels. To discourage future revolts, the Spanish court ordered that the last of the rebel leaders be hanged, and

> 66 that his head be removed from his dead body, that the rest of his body be quartered, that his torso be committed to flames. All his property shall be seized by the royal treasury, his home shall be burnt, and the ground salted, so that in this fashion his disgraceful name may be forgotten. 99

Horrible as this punishment was, it failed to stop further uprisings.

Toussaint L'Ouverture led the only successful slave revolt in history. He helped make Haiti the second independent nation in the Americas.

458

Revolution in Haiti

● Note strategies for second objective on this page and p. 461.

The first successful Latin American revolt was fought not against Spain or Portugal but France. The French colony of St. Domingue, located on the island of Hispaniola (map, page 460), was one of the most profitable European colonies in the Americas. About 400,000 black slaves worked on St. Domingue's sugar plantations. About 22,000 mulattos also lived in the colony. Most of these people were free and many owned land. They were barred, however, from practicing law, medicine, and other professions.

A mulatto named Vincent Ogé (oh-ZHAY) was in Paris when the Declaration of the Rights of Man was adopted in 1789. He returned to St. Domingue and called for similar rights of citizenship for the free mulattos there. Outraged by his demands, the French government had him tortured to death.

The execution of Ogé stirred unrest among the colony's mulattos. When the slaves rebelled in 1791, the mulattos joined them. Led by an ex-slave named Pierre Toussaint L'Ouverture (too-SAN loo-vayr-TOOR), the rebels drove the French from St. Domingue.

Sec. Rev. ques. 2

Toussaint had barely set up a new government when Napoleon came to power in France and sent troops to regain the colony. The French lost many battles to the rebels, however, and most of the French soldiers died of yellow fever. In 1804, after 13 years of war, the revolutionaries declared the colony of St. Domingue to be the independent nation of Haiti.

Revolution in South America

Events in Europe also contributed to a movement for independence in the northern part of South America. In 1808 Napoleon invaded Spain and put his brother on the throne. Taking advantage of the confusion in Spain, Creole leaders seized control of several South American cities. These uprisings sparked a widespread revolt against Spanish rule.

● RETEACHING. Have students make a chart showing the locations, dates, and outcomes of Latin American independence movements. (Charts should include information on the following: Peru, Colombia, Haiti, Chile, Mexico, Central America, and Brazil.) *(Comprehension) Sequencing Information*

Background Vincent Ogé served as Haiti's representative in the French National Assembly in 1789. Discouraged when the French refused to issue citizenship rights for mulattos, Ogé led a revolt in Haiti.

● REINFORCEMENT. Have students outline grievances against Spanish and Portuguese rule and identify the reforms sought by Latin Americans. (Grievances: forced labor, slavery, high taxes, job restrictions, loss of lands, social inequality. Reforms: appointment or election of Indian government officials, citizenship rights, return of lands, social equality.) *(Comprehension) Observing for Detail*

Check for Understanding. Ask: Where was the first successful Latin American revolt fought? (Haiti.)

Simon Bolívar. The greatest of the revolutionary leaders was Simon Bolívar (boh-LEE-vahr), sometimes called the "Latin American George Washington." Born in Venezuela to a wealthy Creole family, Bolívar studied in Spain. The French and American revolutions inspired him to put together a Latin American army to fight against Spain.

Bolívar's battle against the Spanish lasted several years. In 1819 he led thousands of soldiers west from the Orinoco River valley through the Andes. More than 100 of his followers died in the mountain crossing, but the remaining troops defeated the Spanish army. Later that year Bolívar became president of Great Colombia. This new nation included what are now Panama, Colombia, Venezuela, and Ecuador (map, page 460).

San Martín. While Bolívar was liberating northern South America, José de San Martín (SAHN mar-TEEN) was leading an army north from Argentina. Argentina had been free of Spanish rule since 1810. San Martín realized, however, that Argentina could remain free only if the Spaniards were driven from Chile and Peru.

Sec. Rev. ques. 3
In 1817 San Martín's well-trained troops crossed the Andes and captured Santiago, Chile. In 1821 they captured Lima, the capital of Peru and the center of Spanish power in South America. Still, the Spanish forces in the countryside remained strong. The following year, San Martín met secretly with Bolívar to talk about the liberation of South America. Bolívar's forces then took over the fight for Peru's independence.

Spain's defeat. The final battle was on December 9, 1824. In the thin, cold mountain air, Bolívar's troops crushed the Spanish army near the village of Ayacucho. This battle marked the triumph of the independence movement in South America.

Mexican Independence

As in South America, the independence movement in New Spain (modern Mexico) began as a reaction to Napoleon's invasion of

Inspired by the French Revolution, Bolívar and his troops liberated half of South America.

Spain. Events in New Spain, however, took a different course.

Hidalgo. In 1810 Miguel Hidalgo (ee-DAHL-goh), a Creole priest in a Mexican town named Dolores, organized a revolt of Indians and mestizos against Spanish rule. On a September day in 1810 Father Hidalgo rang the bell in the plaza of Dolores and then spoke to the townspeople. He called for independence, the return of lands that had been taken from Indians, and an end to slavery. His revolutionary call became known as the "Cry of Dolores" or *El Grito de Dolores.* Hidalgo's followers were untrained and armed only with knives and slings. As they began to march south toward Mexico City, their numbers grew. Sec. Rev. ques. 4

By the time they neared Mexico City, Father Hidalgo headed an army of more than 50,000. Afraid he might lose control of this undisciplined force, Hidalgo turned back. The Spaniards pursued and defeated the rebels and executed Hidalgo. Though the **459**

Biography Simon Bolivar was a skilled horseman who enjoyed performing for an audience. He liked expensive clothes and jewelry and was once arrested in Spain for wearing lace shirt cuffs and diamond links, adornments forbidden to colonial people.

Biography San Martin, the son of a Spanish military officer, was born in Argentina but moved to Spain with his family at the age of eight. Although he served as a Spanish officer against Napoleon's forces, he objected to Spain's colonial policies and joined the revolutionary effort in South America.
Check for Understanding. Ask: Where was the center of Spanish power in South America? (Lima, the capital city of Peru.)

UNITED STATES

MEXICO

Gulf of Mexico

Havana ★

•Dolores
Mexico
City ★ •Veracruz
•Oaxaca

BR. HONDURAS

GUATEMALA HONDURAS
EL SALVADOR
UNITED
PROVINCES
OF CENTRAL
AMERICA
NICARAGUA
COSTA
RICA
PANAMA

PACIFIC
OCEAN

CUBA

BAHAMA ISLANDS

JAMAICA HAITI HISPANIOLA PUERTO RICO
SANTO
DOMINGO

Caribbean Sea

LESSER ANTILLES

•Coro
★ Caracas TRINIDAD
VENEZUELA
R.
Boyacá
×
Bogotá
COLOMBIA
Orinoco
GREAT
COLOMBIA
GUIANAS

ATLANTIC
OCEAN

×Quito
Guayaquil•
ECUADOR

Amazon R.

Independent Latin America About 1830

Between Haiti's winning of independence in 1804 and the Battle of Ayacucho in 1824, most of Latin America gained independence. Which colonies did Spain still hold after 1830? What other European colonies remained at that time?

KEY
Independent states
Spanish colonies
French colonies
British colonies
Dutch colonies
× Battle

GALÁPAGOS IS.

A
N
D
E
S

Lima ★ PERU
Ayacucho ★

EMPIRE
OF
BRAZIL

BOLIVIA

ATACAMA
DESERT

PARAGUAY

Rio de Janeiro ★

CHILE

Tucumán•

Valparaíso•
★Santiago
Buenos Aires ★

URUGUAY

CENTRAL VALLEY

ARGENTINA

Río de la Plata

PATAGONIA
(unexplored)

SCALE
0 — 1,000 mi
0 — 1,000 km

FALKLAND IS.

Latin America About 1800

VICEROYALTY
OF
NEW
SPAIN

Mexico•

UNITED
STATES

ATLANTIC
OCEAN

Havana ★

VICEROYALTY OF SANTO DOMINGO
ST. DOMINGUE

Caribbean Sea

VICEROYALTY OF
NEW GRANADA
★Bogotá
GUIANAS

PACIFIC
OCEAN

N
W — E
S

Lima•

VICEROYALTY OF PERU

VICEROYALTY
OF
BRAZIL

VICEROYALTY
OF
LA PLATA

Rio de Janeiro
★

Buenos Aires ★

KEY
Spanish rule
Portuguese rule
French rule
British rule
Dutch rule

SCALE
0 — 500 mi
0 — 500 km

460

Map Answers: (1) Cuba, Santo Domingo, Puerto Rico. (2) British Honduras, Jamaica, the Guianas (British, Dutch, French).

rebellion failed, Hidalgo is remembered as the "father of Mexican independence." Mexicans celebrate September 16, the day the revolt began, as their Independence Day.

Morelos. A mestizo priest named José María Morelos (moh-RAY-lohs) took over leadership of the Mexican revolution. Unlike Father Hidalgo, Morelos set out to train an army. By 1813, with his small army in control of much of southern Mexico, Morelos declared independence from Spain.

The rebels drew up a new constitution promising equality for all people, the end of special privileges for the Church and the army, and the breakup of large estates. These ideas cost Morelos the support of many Creoles, who feared the loss of their wealth. After a series of defeats by the Spanish army, Morelos was captured and killed in 1815.

Rebel success. With the death of Morelos, hopes of independence for Mexico seemed to vanish. Guerrilla fighting continued off and on until 1820, however, when unrest in Europe again triggered revolt in Latin America. In that year soldiers in Spain rebelled and made the king restore the constitution of 1812, which favored social reform. Fearful that Spanish reform would spread to Mexico, Creoles joined forces with the rebels. They defeated the Spanish and declared Mexico's independence in 1821.

The Creoles hoped to establish an antireform government in Mexico. They supported Agustín de Iturbide (ee-toor-BEE-day), the officer who had captured Morelos. Iturbide took control of the government and in 1822 crowned himself emperor of Mexico. Within a year, his tyrannical rule had turned the whole country against him, and he was forced into exile. Mexico declared itself a republic in 1823.

Independence Throughout Latin America

Central America. The Central American states followed Mexico's example, declaring their independence from Spain in 1821.

The modern nations of Costa Rica, El Salvador, Guatemala, Honduras, and Nicaragua joined together in a league called the United Provinces of Central America. The league, which had a republican form of government, was crippled by disputes among its members. After 1838 it broke up, with each nation governing itself alone.

Brazil. Unlike most of Latin America, the Portuguese colony of Brazil gained independence peacefully. When Napoleon's armies invaded Portugal in 1807, Portugal's king moved the royal court to Brazil.

Sec. Rev. ques. 5

As the center of the empire, Brazil prospered, and demands for independence grew. In 1821 the king returned to Portugal and left his son Pedro to rule Brazil. A year later, on his father's advice, Pedro declared Brazil's independence and became Emperor Pedro I.

The collapse of European control. In only 20 years—from Haiti's independence in 1804 to the Battle of Ayacucho in 1824—Europe's 300-year dominance of Latin America came to an end. France lost Haiti and Portugal lost Brazil. Spain's great empire in the Americas also crumbled. Only Cuba, Santo Domingo, and Puerto Rico remained in Spanish hands.

● See below, left.

See Sec. 1 *Closing the Lesson*, p. T455B.

Section Review

Answers to Section Review questions are in brackets on pages indicated.
1. **Define:** *peninsulares*, Creole. (p. 457)
2. What developments led to Haiti's independence? (p. 458)
3. How did Bolívar and San Martín help to free South America from Spanish rule? (p. 459)
4. How did Mexico win its independence? (pp. 459–461)
5. What made Brazil's route to independence different from that of the other Latin American countries? (p. 461)
6. **Critical thinking:** Give examples of how events in Europe contributed to the independence movements in Latin America. (See answer below.)

Religion Note that Morelos was tried by the Inquisition court of the Catholic Church (p. 245) and was convicted of heresy and treason. The Church then turned Morelos over to the state, which ordered his execution by a firing squad.

● ENRICHMENT. Have students trace the political, economic, and social development of one of the Latin American nations that achieved independence during the nineteenth century. (Application) *Linking Past and Present*

6. Answers will vary. Students might explain how the French Declaration of the Rights of Man, Napoleon's invasion of Spain, and the restoration of the Spanish constitution provided opportunities for independence movements in Latin America.

2 Challenges Facing the New Nations

Objectives

Focus Questions

★ ■ What were the causes and results of Latin American disunity? *(pages 462–464)*

● ■ How did foreign countries influence Latin America? *(pages 464–465)*

▲ ■ What problems did Mexico face in the 1800's? *(pages 465–467)*

Terms to Know

caudillo
Monroe Doctrine
neocolonialism
annex

Mexican-American War
War of the Reform
puppet government

★ Note strategies for first objective on this page and p. 463.

Nation-building was a slow process in Latin America. It was hampered by geographical barriers, class conflict, and political disagreements. Even after strong leaders took power, there was little political freedom and a great deal of foreign influence. By 1900, however, several Latin American nations had made progress toward political and economic stability.

Obstacles to Unity

In the decades after independence, Latin America lacked feelings of nationalism. A number of problems stood in the way of unity.

Sec. Rev. ques. 2

1. Rugged mountains, dense forests, and large deserts covered much of the land, making travel and trade difficult. People in one area had little contact and little sense of solidarity with people elsewhere. Most Latin Americans continued to live, as their families had for years, in isolated communities. Their loyalties were to their villages rather than their country.

2. Racial barriers were another source of division. The rigid class system of colonial times survived long after independence. Creoles took for themselves the privileges once held by the Spaniards. They became leaders in the government, the Church, and the army. They also seized the plantations and cattle-raising lands that had been owned by the Spaniards. Few Creoles were willing to share any of their political or economic power with other groups in Latin American society.

Latin Americans of African descent benefited from the abolition of slavery. Yet the blacks, like mulattos, mestizos, and Indians, still had few rights. These people lived in poverty, with little hope of advancement for themselves or their children.

3. Political disagreements created still another barrier to national unity in Latin America. Some groups, including wealthy landowners and the clergy, wanted to keep existing traditions and institutions. Other Latin Americans pressed for change in the old order.

The Church's place in society was perhaps the most bitterly fought issue. During colonial times, the Roman Catholic Church had owned huge amounts of property. It also controlled education and aid to the poor. After independence, some people wanted the Church to keep its wealth and power. Other Latin Americans, however, believed that the Church was serving the interests of the well-to-do rather than the poor and should be made less powerful.

The fact that many clergy supported the Spaniards during the wars of independence further angered many Latin Americans. They believed that the government should take over Church lands and responsibility for education and aid to the poor.

462

★ RETEACHING. Have students review "Obstacles to Unity" (above) and outline problems that made Latin American unity difficult. (The rugged geography made trade, travel, and a sense of solidarity difficult; the rigid class system survived after independence; conflict arose between traditional institutions and new ways.) *(Comprehension)* *Translating Information into Another Form*

★ REINFORCEMENT. Have students review "The Rise of Dictators" (pp. 463–464) and find evidence to support the following generalization: *The end of colonial rule in Latin America did not result in real political change for most people.* (Power remained in the hands of the army and wealthy landowners, and leadership was exercised by dictators.) *(Comprehension)* *Supporting Generalizations*

Daily Life

Cowhands of the Americas

Raising livestock has been important in the Americas ever since the Spaniards introduced horses, cattle, and sheep in their colonies. Throughout the Americas, cowhands developed methods for managing large herds of cattle on unfenced prairies and rangeland. In Argentina, these cowhands are called *gauchos.* Elsewhere in Latin America, they are called *llaneros* (yah-NEH-rohs).

In North America, the original cowhands of the Southwest were the Mexican *vaqueros* (vah-KAYR-ohs). They learned to herd cattle from horseback, roping them with a lariat or lasso. The *vaqueros* wore practical working clothes—a wide-brimmed sombrero to keep off the sun and rain, high-heeled riding boots with spurs, and leather chaps to protect their legs from thorny brush. Easterners who moved to the frontier adopted the customs of the *vaqueros,* creating the traditional picture of the American cowhand.

★ See
below.

The Rise of Dictators

Unlike the British colonists to the north, Latin Americans had gained little experience in governing themselves during the colonial period. Thus the early years of Latin American independence were violent and unstable. Leaders drew up constitutions that called for regular elections and representative government, but were unable to put them into practice. Real power remained in the hands of the army and wealthy landowners. Slowly, though, stable central governments arose under leaders known as **caudillos** (kow-DEE-yohs), a Spanish word meaning "chiefs."

A caudillo was a dictator who came to power with the backing of the army and the rich landowners. To stay in power, the caudillos gave their supporters gifts of land and government jobs. Many of those appointed by the caudillos were unqualified and corrupt. While some caudillos did act for the good of their countries, each was a dictator who

Sec. Rev.
ques. 3

463

Background Portales was abducted and murdered during an attempt to overthrow his government.

Background The Monroe Doctrine was actually part of an annual message from President Monroe to Congress.

stayed in power through force. Rule by caudillos became so common in Latin America during the 1800's that the period is often called the Age of Caudillos.

Chile. Chile was the first Latin American country to develop a stable central government. It did so under the leadership of the caudillo Diego Portales (por-TAH-les), a Creole businessman. Portales controlled Chile from 1830 to 1837, although he never actually became its president. Portales stressed economic growth and ordered the building of railroads, ships, and telegraph lines.

Like most caudillos, Portales believed in the need for strong rule. The constitution he drew up for Chile in 1833 gave the president veto power over laws passed by the legislature, control of elections, and the right to appoint a successor.

Argentina. An even harsher leader brought unity to Argentina. Juan Manuel de Rosas, a Creole landowner and businessman, ruled the country from 1835 to 1852. With the help of the militia, spies, and secret police, Rosas stamped out all opposition. Like Portales, Rosas favored the interests of the well-to-do landowners. His policies did strengthen Argentina's central government, however, allowing the leaders who followed him to begin programs of economic development.

Foreign Interest in Latin America

● Note strategies for second objective on this page and p. 465.

The Monroe Doctrine. While the Latin American nations were struggling to bring order and prosperity to their lands, several European countries were plotting to restore colonial rule to Latin America. At the urging of the Spanish king, many other European monarchs, eager to stamp out nationalism, considered overthrowing the Latin American republics.

Britain and the United States opposed this idea. Britain disagreed with the anti-reform policies of Spain and its allies. The British also had been building a profitable trade with Latin America and were determined not to lose it. The United States, like Britain, sympathized with the Latin Ameri-

cans. Furthermore, the United States feared a strong European presence so close to home.

In 1823 Britain asked the United States to make a joint statement against Spain's plan. The United States decided to make its own declaration—a statement that became known as the **Monroe Doctrine**. The Monroe Doctrine said that the Americas would no longer be open to colonization by any European power. Any country that tried to interfere in the affairs of an American nation would be considered an enemy of the United States.

This was a forceful message. Yet the United States—still a young nation—lacked the military power to back up its words. The British navy, however, ruled the seas, and the British were prepared to enforce the Doctrine to protect their trade with Latin America. The new Latin American nations expected no further trouble with Spain.

Trade and investment. Years of revolution had weakened Latin American economies. Trade and farming had been severely disrupted. Warfare had claimed the lives of up to half the population in some areas.

In order to modernize, Latin American countries needed money to invest in transportation, banking, and manufacturing. The leaders of independence movements had hoped that their nations would attract European and North American investors, but this help was slow in coming. The rise of caudillos, however, brought order to the region. In the late 1800's trade picked up and foreign money began to flow into Latin America.

Neocolonialism. While trade and investment sped economic development, they also created problems for Latin American countries. Because raw materials were in great demand overseas, many of the countries concentrated on exporting only one or two products instead of building a broad-based economy. For example, Brazil relied heavily on coffee, and Argentina exported mainly beef. When world demand for such products dropped, the entire economy suffered.

Furthermore, foreigners who invested in Latin America gained tremendous influence over local governments. Though Latin Amer-

464

● RETEACHING. Have students review "The Monroe Doctrine" (above) and explain how American and British interests in Latin America resulted in the Monroe Doctrine. (Britain had built a profitable trade with Latin America, and the United States, which sympathized with Latin Americans, feared a strong European presence close to home.) (Comprehension) *Understanding Causes*

● REINFORCEMENT. Have students outline the ways foreign countries influenced Latin America after independence. (Europeans and North Americans invested money in Latin American transportation, banking, and manufacturing; foreign investment resulted in influence over local governments. Industrialization drew Europeans and Asian laborers.) (Comprehension) *Observing for Detail*

Background The Monroe Doctrine also stated that the United States would not interfere in European affairs.

ican nations were independent, they often had to bow to the demands of foreign governments and foreign business owners. This kind of domination is called **neocolonialism**.

● See below.

Immigration. Industrialization in Latin America led to heavy immigration from Europe. Latin American governments welcomed newcomers in order to fill the need for skilled labor. During the late 1800's Spanish, Portuguese, and Italian immigrants poured into Latin America. They were joined by smaller numbers of French, Irish, Chinese, Japanese, and Central Europeans. This mix of people gave the rapidly growing cities an international flavor. In addition, the immigrants' skills and their will to succeed boosted the Latin American economy.

Mexico in the Nineteenth Century

▲ Note strategies for third objective on this page and p. 467.

The Mexican-American War. Even before Mexico had gained its independence from Spain, American citizens had begun to settle in Texas, which was then part of Mexico. At first the Mexican government encouraged this settlement. Conflicts between the settlers and the government soon arose over such issues as the settlers' attempts to bring slaves to Texas. These conflicts led to fighting in 1835.

Despite a Mexican victory at the Alamo, a mission in San Antonio, (map, page 559), the settlers defeated the Mexican forces and declared their independence in 1836. In 1845 the United States decided to **annex** Texas—that is, make Texas a part of the United States. Mexico, which had never accepted the loss of Texas, objected to annexation, and in 1846 war broke out between Mexico and the United States.

The **Mexican-American War** was disastrous for Mexico. Forced to surrender in 1848, it lost vast territories to the United States. The land Mexico gave up included the present-day states of California, Nevada, and Utah as well as parts of Arizona, Colorado, New Mexico, and Wyoming. Less than 30 years after gaining independence, Mexico had shrunk to half its size.

Juárez. Humiliated by their defeat and angry at government corruption, the Mexican people looked for change. In 1855 a reform-minded government set out to strip the clergy and high-ranking army officers of many of their privileges.

In the late 1800's European settlers joined the Americans already living in Texas. This farm near La Grange, Texas, was built by a German family.

465

● ENRICHMENT. Have students work in groups to develop arguments for the following statement: *Foreign trade and investment both helped and hurt Latin American economies.* Students should present their arguments to the class and then evaluate the overall effects of foreign investment and trade on Latin America. *(Evaluation)* **Making Judgments**

▲ RETEACHING. Have students review "Mexico in the Nineteenth Century" (pp. 465–467) and identify the causes of the following problems faced by Mexico: the Mexican-American War; government reform by Juárez; War of the Reform; French intervention in Mexico; dictatorship of Díaz. *(Comprehension)* **Identifying Cause and Effect**

Indian leader Juárez tried to free Mexico from the domination of the Church and foreign bankers.

Sec. Rev. ques. 4

A key figure in this push for change was Benito Juárez (HWAH-res), an Indian lawyer and the minister of justice in the Mexican government. Juárez wrote many reforms into a new constitution drawn up in 1857. These reforms separated Church and state, ended Church ownership of land, and declared freedom of speech, press, and assembly. They also required that cases involving clergy or military officers be tried in the regular courts.

Opponents of the new constitution took up arms to overthrow the government. Juárez

Linking Past and Present

Today the president of Mexico is directly elected by the people for one six-year term. A Chamber of Deputies and a Senate make the nation's laws, and the Supreme Court of Justice upholds them. Each of the 31 Mexican states has its own governor, legislature, and judges, which gives the states some powers independent of the national government.

466

and his followers fled to Veracruz, where they set up their own government with Juárez as president. Thus began a bloody civil war in Mexico.

In the **War of the Reform** (1858–1860), the army, the Church, and the upper classes stood against the poor and those who wanted reform. In the end the reformers won the war. They regained Mexico City and made Juárez president. He became the first Indian to serve as head of state anywhere in the Americas after the European conquest.

French intervention in Mexico. The War of the Reform increased the already huge debts that Mexico owed to several European countries. In 1862 President Juárez declared that Mexico would have to delay payment on its debts. Determined to get their money back, Britain, Spain, and France sent troops to invade Mexico.

The British and Spaniards withdrew after Mexico promised to repay its debts. Emperor Napoleon III of France, however, saw an opportunity to replace Juárez with a **puppet government**—one controlled by an outside power. Thinking that Mexicans would welcome a return to monarchy, Napoleon III persuaded Archduke Maximilian of Austria to take control of Mexico. In 1864 Maximilian became emperor of Mexico.

Juárez refused to acknowledge Maximilian as Mexico's ruler and raised an army to drive out the French. The United States also objected to the French action, seeing it as a violation of the Monroe Doctrine. Yet Americans could do nothing because their own civil war was raging at the time (page 560). In 1866, however, the tide turned in Juárez's favor. The American civil war had ended, and the United States began to pressure France to leave Mexico. Faced with troubles at home as well, Napoleon III removed his troops. Juárez returned to power, and Maximilian's brief rule of Mexico ended before a firing squad.

Díaz. Juárez served as Mexico's president until his death in 1872. Mexico's next strong leader, General Porfirio Díaz (DEE-ahs), came to power in 1876. A ruthless dictator, he ruled Mexico almost continuously until 1911.

Biography Benito Juárez was a Zapotec Indian who used his legal skills to improve the status of Indians and to end their political exploitation.

Background The French army was repelled near the city of Puebla by a force of Mexican peasants on May 5, 1862. This victory, called the battle of *Cinco de Mayo* (Fifth of May), is celebrated as a national holiday in Mexico today.

Sec. Rev. ques. 4, cont.

Díaz worked to build up the economy as vigorously as Juárez had worked for reform. Under Díaz, foreign businesses invested heavily in Mexican industry and agriculture. Aided by foreign funds and advisers, Mexico built railroads and tapped mines and oil fields. The government soon boasted the first treasury surplus in the history of the Mexican republic.

These advances came at a tremendous cost, however. The major share of the profits in the new industries and mines went to investors in Europe and the United States. The newly rich Creoles adopted European ways and looked down on Mexican culture. Mexican national pride suffered as a result. Thus, while Mexico benefited from the economic policies of Díaz, beneath the surface were rumblings of discontent that would erupt in the years to come.

▲ See below.

See Sec. 2 *Closing the Lesson*, p. T455C.

Section Review

Answers to Section Review questions are in brackets on pages indicated.

1. **Define or identify:** caudillo, Monroe Doctrine, neocolonialism, annex, Mexican-American War, War of the Reform, puppet government. (pp. 463, 464, 465, 466)
2. What hindered the Latin American republics in building national unity? (p. 462)
3. How did caudillos like Portales and Rosas stay in power? (p. 463)
4. What reforms did Juárez bring to Mexico? How did the policies of Díaz both help and hurt Mexico? (pp. 466–467)
5. **Critical thinking:** What were the benefits and dangers of Latin America's involvement with other countries? (See answer below)

5. Students should note how foreign trade, investors, and immigrants helped Latin American economies. Students should also explain how foreign presence paved the way for neocolonialism and limited economic development in Latin America.

Chapter 23   Summary and Timeline

1. In the beginning of the nineteenth century, independence movements spread quickly through Latin America. Between 1804 and 1824, many Latin American colonies successfully revolted against European rule.

2. Nation-building progressed slowly in Latin America. Natural barriers and social and political conflict hampered efforts to unify countries. However, in the mid-1800's dictators (called caudillos) brought order and stability to these lands. This stability prompted a surge in trade and investment in Latin America, but the overall effects on Latin American societies were mixed. Mexico, which faced internal problems as well as threats from abroad, demonstrated the kinds of challenges confronting Latin America.

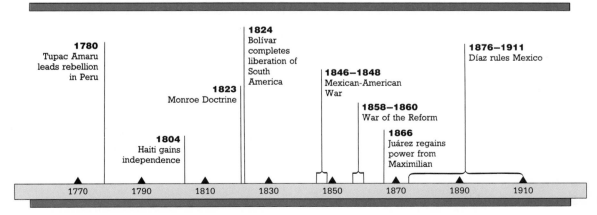

1780 Tupac Amaru leads rebellion in Peru

1823 Monroe Doctrine

1824 Bolívar completes liberation of South America

1846–1848 Mexican-American War

1858–1860 War of the Reform

1876–1911 Díaz rules Mexico

1804 Haiti gains independence

1866 Juárez regains power from Maximilian

1770   1790   1810   1830   1850   1870   1890   1910

▲ **REINFORCEMENT.** Have students make a chart titled *Problems Faced by Mexico in the 1800's* and classify problems as political, social, economic, or foreign relations. (Mexican-American War: foreign relations. Government reform by Juárez: political and social. War of the Reform: political and social. French intervention: foreign relations and economic. Dictatorship of Díaz: political and economic.) *(Analysis)* ***Analyzing Information***

▲ **ENRICHMENT.** Have students work in groups to stage a meeting that might have occurred among Mexican government officials in the mid-1800's. Students should outline the economic, political, and social problems facing the country and devise policies to resolve the issues. Have students present their policy decisions in class. *(Synthesis)* ***Making Decisions***

See p. T455C for answers to Chapter Review.

Vocabulary Review

1. Match each of the following terms with its correct definition: *annex, caudillo, neo-colonialism, puppet government.*
   a. Latin American dictator backed by the army and wealthy landowners
   b. regime controlled by an outside power
   c. add land to an existing country
   d. informal domination by one nation over another
2. Define or identify the terms in the following pairs:
   a. *peninsulares;* Creoles
   b. Mexican-American War; War of the Reform

People to Identify

Identify the following people and tell why each was important.
1. Tupac Amaru
2. Miguel Hidalgo
3. Benito Juárez
4. Archduke Maximilian
5. Diego Portales
6. Juan Manuel de Rosas
7. Pierre Toussaint L'Ouverture

Places to Know

Match the letters on this map of South America with the places listed below. You may want to refer to the map on page 460.
1. Brazil
2. Chile
3. Peru
4. Argentina
5. Great Colombia

Recalling the Facts

1. Why were Latin Americans unhappy with colonial rule in the late 1700's?
2. What action by the Spanish government led to rebellions in Peru and Colombia? What was the outcome of those revolts?
3. Which Latin American nation was the first to win independence?
4. What part did Simon Bolívar and José de San Martín play in the liberation of South America?
5. How did Mexico and Brazil each win independence?
6. What problems faced the newly independent Latin American countries?

7. What conditions in Latin American countries made it difficult for democratic governments to succeed? What type of rule did this lead to?

8. Why did the United States issue the Monroe Doctrine? Why did Britain support it?

9. What reforms did Benito Juárez make in Mexico's government?

10. What were the benefits and costs of Porfirio Díaz's economic policies?

Critical Thinking Skills

1. **Writing a biography.** Research and write a short biography of one of the leaders of the independence movements in Latin America. Include information on the leader's early life, his contributions to the independence movement, and his role following independence. *(App.)*

2. **Evaluating evidence.** How did Latin American nations benefit from European and North American involvement in their economic affairs? What problems did this involvement create? *(Syn.)*

3. **Interpreting a cartoon.** This cartoon appeared in a Mexican newspaper in 1897. How does the cartoon show President Díaz? What do you think the cartoonist was saying about Díaz? *(Anal.)*

4. **Comparing and contrasting.** Compare the Latin American independence movements with the American Revolution. How were they similar? Different? *(Syn.)*

Thinking About Geography

Comparing maps. Use the maps on page 460 to answer the following questions: What independent nations were made from the Viceroyalty of La Plata? From the Viceroyalty of New Granada? From the Viceroyalty of Peru? *(Comp.)*

Enrichment: Primary Sources

In 1819 Simon Bolívar spoke to a group preparing a new constitution for Venezuela. The following passage is adapted from his speech.

66 The most perfect system of government is that which produces the greatest possible sum of happiness, social security, and political stability. It must be republican, based on the sovereignty of the people, including the division of power, civil liberty, the outlawing of slavery, and the abolition of monarchy and privilege.

In order to form a stable government, you must have the foundation of a national spirit. We must mold all the people into one whole, our laws into one whole, and the national spirit into one whole. Unity must be our motto. 99

1. According to Bolívar, what should be the goals of good government?
2. What does Bolívar mean when he says that government should be "based on the sovereignty of the people"?
3. What does Bolívar consider the foundation of stable government?
4. **Critical thinking:** Did most Latin American nations in the 1800's follow Bolívar's guidelines for good government? Explain. *(Eval.)*

469

A checkmark identifies questions and exercises calling for the three higher-order levels of thinking at the top of the Bloom taxonomy: Analysis, Synthesis, and Evaluation.

T469A

Reaction and Revolution in Europe   1770–1850
(pp. 470–486)

Chapter Preview

Section 1 of this chapter describes the concerns of European leaders after the defeat of Napoleon, the decisions made at the Congress of Vienna, and the reasons for the formation of the Concert of Europe. The largely unsuccessful movements for independence and reform that occurred throughout Europe from 1820 to 1830 are also described. Section 2 discusses the Romantic movement and the growing nationalism of the nineteenth century. Section 3 describes the wave of revolutions that swept Europe in 1848.

Bibliography

See the *Teacher's Management and Planning Guide* for additional listings. Starred titles are for both students and teachers.

Kissinger, Henry. *A World Restored: Metternich, Castlereagh, and the Problem of Peace, 1812–1822*. Houghton Mifflin. A look at the balance of power.

*Postgate, Raymond. *Story of a Year: 1848*. Greenwood. Colorful account of the tumultuous year of revolutions.

Robertson, Priscilla. *Revolutions of 1848*. Princeton University Press. Examines social aspects and political events.

Rude, George. *The Crowd in History, 1730–1884*. Humanities Press. Examines crucial years in the development of democracy.

Weiner, Margery. *The Sovereign Remedy*. St. Martin's. Focuses on European congresses and the people who dominated them.

Section Lesson Plans

SECTION 1   (pp. 471–476)
Europe After Napoleon

Objectives

After completing this section, students will be able to:
1. Describe how order was restored to Europe after Napoleon's defeat.
2. Discuss the revolts that threatened this order.

Introducing the Lesson

Remind students that the Napoleonic Wars spread the ideals of the Enlightenment and the French Revolution throughout Europe. After Napoleon's loss of power, European leaders sought ways to repress political reform and to reinstate traditional patterns of authority.

Then ask: *(a) How did the ideals of the Enlightenment and the French Revolution differ from traditional patterns of authority?* (The Enlightenment and the French Revolution represented belief in individual freedom, the right of citizens to participate in government, and government's responsibility to society. The traditional system of authority supported the absolute power of monarchs.)

(b) What actions might European leaders have taken to repress movements for political reform? (Answers will vary. Government leaders might have used military power, limited freedom of speech, or imprisoned or executed those who sought political reform.)

(c) How might democratic ideals survive a period of repression? (Answers will vary.)

Developing the Lesson:
Understanding Point of View

Have students work in groups to stage a dialogue that might have occurred after the Napoleonic Wars between representatives of conservatism and liberalism. The supporters of each philosophy might explain why their viewpoints should guide the formation of government, or they might seek a compromise solution to problems faced by European nations. *(Synthesis)*

Developing the Lesson:
Understanding Cause and Effect

Have students write an essay explaining the following:

(a) How conservatism influenced the participants and outcomes of the Congress of Vienna. (European leaders blamed political upheaval on changes brought about by the French Revolution and were determined to restore order. They believed a return to traditional ways of rule was the solution.)

(b) How the causes of revolts in Europe can be traced to the policies of the Congress of Vienna. (Liberals and nationalists in many European countries rebelled against the policies of repression resulting from the Congress of Vienna.) *(Comprehension)*

Closing the Lesson:
Analyzing Information

Have students analyze the relationship between nationalism and liberalism after the Congress of Vienna and explain why many conservatives viewed the movements as a threat to peace and order. (Nationalist feelings and liberal beliefs resulted in movements for independence and reform. These campaigns challenged the political order established by the Congress of Vienna.) *(Comprehension)*

See *Section Review* questions, p. 476.

SECTION 2   (pp. 476–479)
The Romantic Movement

Objectives

After completing the section, students will be able to:
1. Explain how the Romantic movement changed styles in the arts.
2. Describe how Romantics helped to inspire nationalist feelings.

Introducing the Lesson

Remind students that historical events sometimes produce a reaction against ideas previously considered important. During the late eighteenth century, European artists and thinkers abandoned Enlightenment ideals that stressed the importance of human reason and drew inspiration from a Romantic view of nature and individuals.

Then ask: *(a) How did the Enlightenment influence events in eighteenth-century Europe?* (Enlightenment thinkers and artists expressed confidence in human reason, valued the rights of individuals, and worked for political reform. These ideals led to a rejection of absolute monarchy.)

(b) What late eighteenth-century events in Europe might have resulted in a change in artistic and intellectual values? (Answers will vary. The violence and upheaval brought on by the French Revolution and the Napoleonic Wars probably affected people's ideas and values.)

(c) What kinds of issues or events today might affect values held by people? (Answers will vary. Family and religious concerns, economic factors, relationships with foreign countries, and social issues influence the ways people think.)

Developing the Lesson:
Comparing Ideas

Have students work in groups to present a dialogue that might have occurred between a representative of Romantic ideals and an Enlightenment thinker. Students might include a discussion of Romantic and Enlightenment values and describe the similarities and differences between them. *(Synthesis)*

Developing the Lesson:
Forming a Hypothesis

Have students develop a hypothesis explaining the relationship between liberalism (p. 471), nationalism (p. 445), and Romanticism. Students might identify characteristics shared by the movements and then evaluate the differences among them. *(Synthesis)*

Closing the Lesson: Making Judgments

Have students work in groups to present a panel discussion titled *The Influence of Political and Social Events on Art and Literature.* Students might refer to historical periods already studied or identify political and social influences on contemporary artistic expression. *(Synthesis)*

See *Section Review* questions, p. 479.

SECTION 3   (pp. 479–484)
The Revolutions of 1848

Objectives

After completing this section, students will be able to:
1. Describe how poverty and corruption caused revolts in France.
2. Discuss the rebellions that rocked the Austrian Empire.
3. Explain why nationalist movements failed in Italy and Germany.

Introducing the Lesson

Remind students that nationalism is deep devotion to one's country and is marked by strong feelings of cultural pride. During 1848, nationalism motivated independence and reform movements in Europe.

Then ask: *(a) What might account for the strength of nationalism during certain periods of history?* (Answers will vary. Sometimes strong nationalist feelings develop when people believe they are being treated unfairly. Since history, culture, and national background are important sources of identity, national pride often encourages feelings of unity.)

(b) Why might nationalist feelings sometimes result in movements for independence and reform? (Answers will vary. People who have strong feelings of cultural pride often want their country to be a place where they are free to express their heritage.)

(c) What groups of people in the world today might be viewed as expressing nationalist aspirations? (Answers will vary, but students might suggest the Irish Republican Army in Northern Ireland, the Palestinians in the Middle East, the Tamils in Sri Lanka, and the Armenians in the Soviet Union.)

Developing the Lesson: Identifying Cause and Effect

Have students make a chart of the revolutions that occurred in Europe in 1848, identify their causes, and classify the causes as economic or political. (*France:* workers wanted jobs; property owners opposed working-class demands. *Austria:* aimed to establish a constitution and to end feudalism. *Bohemia:* goals included a constitution, an end to German control, and use of the Czech language in schools and by government offices. *Hungary:* desired a constitution and self-government. *Lombardy and Venetia:* goal was to unify Italy as an independent republic. *Germany:* aimed to unite the German states and establish liberal reform.) *(Comprehension)*

Developing the Lesson: Translating Information into Another Form

Have students work in groups to write a series of newspaper articles that might have appeared in Europe in 1848. Students should include articles that may have been written by reporters covering the political revolts in Europe, feature articles describing the economic crisis and the effects of the revolts on the lives of Europeans, and articles analyzing the events in Europe. Have students present their articles in class. *(Comprehension)*

Closing the Lesson: Analyzing a Statement

Have students write an essay explaining what Prince Metternich might have meant by the following statement: "When Paris sneezes, Europe catches cold." Students should relate the statement to events in Europe during 1848 and use examples from the text in support of their analyses. *(Analysis)*

See *Section Review* questions, p. 484.

Chapter 24 Review Answers
(pp. 485–486)

Vocabulary Review

1. romanticism 2. Frankfurt Assembly 3. legitimacy 4. socialism 5. Sturm und Drang

People to Identify

1. Charlotte Brontë   2. Victor Hugo
3. Louis Kossuth   4. William Wordsworth
5. Lord Byron   6. Eugène Delacroix
7. Louis Philippe   8. Sir Walter Scott
9. Giuseppe Mazzini

Places to Know

1. C 2. G 3. B 4. A 5. F 6. D 7. E

Recalling the Facts

1. Conservatives were mainly members of the upper class (aristocrats, clergy, wealthy business owners). Liberalism appealed to members of the rising middle class (bankers, merchants, lawyers, journalists, university students, intellectuals). Nationalism flourished among people who had strong ties to a homeland and who shared a common language, history, and set of beliefs.

2. To restore the balance of power, take away the freedoms people had gained, place former rulers back on their thrones, and build lasting peace.

3. They had hoped for a united homeland. Instead, the German states were made into an alliance of independent states dominated by Austria.

4. After coming to power, Charles X tried to give special privileges back to the nobility and clergy. In July 1830 he disbanded the legislature, limited voting rights, and censored the press, which prompted the people of Paris to revolt.

5. They found nature beautiful, mysterious, and a source of emotion and inspiration.

6. Some writers studied the histories and traditions of their countries, some collected folktales and songs, and others told colorful legends about their countries' past. Some musicians used folk melodies in their works. Wagner created operas based on German myths and legends.

7. A potato famine in Ireland and a drought in Europe resulted in high food prices, riots, and thousands of deaths. Failing businesses put many people out of work.

8. Those who owned property—peasants, members of the middle class, and aristocrats—were angered by the workers' revolt. Most French people feared socialism and wanted a stable society with few changes in the old system.

9. In Vienna, protestors wanted a constitution and an end to feudal practices. In Bohemia, Czech nationalists called for a constitution and demanded that the Czech language be used along with German in the schools and by government offices.

10. The revolutionaries planned to impose the Magyar language and culture on other ethnic groups. These groups opposed Magyar domination.

11. In Italy, the rebellion failed. Austria regained control of its territories and France defeated the Roman Republic and restored the Pope to power. In Germany, the uprising led the king of Prussia to give the people a constitution and an assembly. These measures lasted only until 1849.

Critical Thinking Skills

1. Answers will vary.

2. Answers will vary. The quotation suggests that the actions of France in the early 1800's greatly affected other European nations. These actions included the spread of liberal and nationalist ideas arising from the French Revolution and the conquests of Napoleon.

3. Answers will vary.

4. The Decembrist revolt took place in Russia in December 1825, because young Russian army officers had learned liberal ideas from the French and hoped to westernize Russia and establish a constitution. The other events took place in France. The "June Days" occurred in June 1848 after the government ended the workshop program. The Second Empire was created in 1852 when voters gave the president, Louis Napoleon, the title of Emperor Napoleon III.

Thinking About Geography

Austria, Prussia, and Russia gained territory as a result of the Congress of Vienna. France lost territory.

Enrichment: Primary Sources

1. Louis Philippe's abdication and the proclamation of the Second Republic in France.

2. The students felt they had more important things to do.

3. *Liberal:* "The word *democracy* was on all tongues." The emphasis on the "liberties and rights of the German people" to be won from monarchs. *Nationalist:* "Now had arrived the day for the establishment of 'German unity.'"

Reaction and Revolution in Europe   1770–1850

See chapter timeline, p. 484.

Before You Read This Chapter

Have you ever watched a pendulum swinging? The farther it goes in one direction, the farther it swings back in the other. Sometimes history seems to act like a pendulum. During the French Revolution, the pendulum swung toward radical change, away from monarchy and aristocracy. It swung so far that many people became alarmed. In this chapter, you will read how the pendulum seemed to swing back toward monarchy again, away from democracy and other new ideas. As you read, look for hints of further changes in Europe. Were these signs of a new swing of the pendulum?

The Geographic Setting

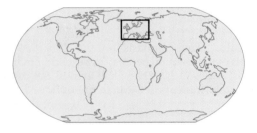

The Chapter Outline

1. Europe After Napoleon
2. The Romantic Movement
3. The Revolutions of 1848

1848 was a year of uprisings in Europe. Throughout the continent, revolutionary liberals and nationalists made monarchs tremble.

See lesson plans, pp. T469A–T469C.

1 Europe After Napoleon

Objectives

Focus Questions

★ ■ How was order restored to Europe after Napoleon's defeat? *(pages 471–474)*

● ■ What revolts threatened this order? *(pages 474–475)*

Terms to Know

Congress of Vienna   liberalism
conservatism   legitimacy

★ Note strategies for first objective on this page and p. 473.

Napoleon's conquests had made dramatic changes in the map of Europe, unseating established rulers and threatening the balance of power. After Napoleon's abdication in 1814 (page 452), European leaders were determined to return the continent to stability. Between September 1814 and June 1815, delegates from many European countries met in Vienna, Austria. The great powers—Britain, Austria, Prussia, and Russia—were represented, as well as France and smaller states.

The purpose of the Congress of Vienna was to work out a peace settlement. European leaders hoped to undo the changes brought by the French Revolution and restore former rulers to their thrones.

Forces in European Politics

Conservatism. The mood at the Congress of Vienna was one of conservatism—a philosophy based on the desire to preserve traditional ways of doing things. Nineteenth-century conservatism was a reaction against the ideas of the Enlightenment and the sweeping changes of the French Revolution.

Sec. Rev. ques. 2

It had its strongest support among upper-class Europeans. These people—aristocrats, high clergy, and wealthy business owners—stood to lose the most from changes in the social order.

Conservatives such as the English statesman Edmund Burke were alarmed that people in France had revolted. In their eyes the monarchy and the nobility were needed for a stable, well-run country. Conservatives felt that the French revolutionaries had come close to destroying civilization.

Liberalism. Conservatism was at odds with liberalism—another philosophy that grew out of the Enlightenment and the French Revolution. Liberalism stressed individual freedom, equality under law, and freedom of thought and religion. Both the French Declaration of the Rights of Man (page 439) and the American Bill of Rights (page 430) expressed these ideals.

In the 1800's, liberals were mainly members of the rising middle class. They included bankers, merchants, lawyers, journalists, university students, and intellectuals. They called for written constitutions, parliamentary government, and the protection of natural rights (page 419). Some liberals favored a republic in which all citizens, rich and poor, would vote and hold office. Other liberals worried about sharing power with the large mass of common people. They believed that governing was best left to those who were educated or owned property.

Nationalism. Nationalism was also growing in Europe in the 1800's. Nationalist feelings had taken hold in France during the Revolution (page 445). When foreign monarchs had threatened to conquer France, the French people—men and women, young and old—had united to defend their homeland. Never in the history of Europe had there been such an army. The soldiers of the Revolution fought not for money or a popular leader but for the French nation.

471

★ RETEACHING. Have students review "Forces in European Politics" (pp. 471–472) and explain the differences between conservatism and liberalism. (Conservatism is based on the desire to preserve traditional ways; liberalism stresses individual freedom, equality under the law, freedom of thought and religion.) *(Comprehension) Observing for Detail*

★ REINFORCEMENT. Have students outline the results of the Congress of Vienna. (New European borders, German Confederation, restoration of monarchies, Concert of Europe, Metternich System.) *(Comprehension) Translating Information into Another Form*

Biography Edmund Burke wrote that "all direction of [the public] must originate in a few" and that "God and nature never meant the people to think or act without guidance and direction."

Nationalism flourished even among people who did not live in a united or independent country. In many parts of Europe, such people still had strong ties to their homeland. They shared a common language, history, and set of beliefs, and they took great pride in their own culture. Nationalist movements—campaigns for independence and reform—became common in these lands.

The Congress of Vienna

Delegates to the Congress of Vienna made up their minds to bring back conservatism and block liberal and nationalist ideas. They had four major aims: restoring the balance of power, taking away the freedoms people had gained, placing former ruling families back on their thrones, and building a lasting peace.

The role of Metternich. There were nine ruling monarchs at the Congress of Vienna, including Czar Alexander I of Russia, King Frederick William III of Prussia, and the host, Emperor Francis I of Austria. Most of the other delegates were aristocrats.

Sec. Rev. ques. 3

One man in particular stood out at the Congress. This was Prince Klemens von Metternich (MET-ur-nik), a shrewd Austrian diplomat. Metternich hated the liberal ideas that had sparked the French Revolution. The belief that society could be reshaped according to the ideals of liberty and equality, said Metternich, had brought 25 years of war and upheaval (1789–1814).

Metternich also despised nationalism, fearing the changes it might make in the old order. Nationalism posed a special threat in the Austrian Empire, where many different peoples lived under Austrian rule. If they demanded self-rule, Metternich feared, the empire would collapse.

Potential conflict. Though they all wanted to protect the old order, the delegates to the Congress of Vienna disagreed on many matters. Both Prussia and Russia hoped to gain new lands in Europe. Prussia wanted to take over the German kingdom of Saxony. Russia wanted complete control of Poland, which had been divided among Russia, Prus-

472

sia, and Austria in 1795 (page 403). Britain and Austria, however, felt that these plans threatened the balance of power in Europe. Metternich was determined to keep any one state from dominating the continent. Most of the other delegates agreed that peace depended on a balance of power.

The dispute gave Prince Talleyrand of France a chance to regain some influence for his country. He joined Metternich and the British delegate, Lord Castlereagh (KAS-ul-ray), in a pledge to go to war with Prussia and Russia if necessary. Faced with this threat, the two empires backed down and reduced their demands for land. Prince Talleyrand's action also restored France to the status of a great power.

New European borders. Early in 1815, the delegates at Vienna finished drawing up a peace settlement. They hoped to restore a balance of power by changing many borders in Europe (map, next page).

To keep the French in check, the allies strengthened France's neighbors. Switzerland, directly to the east, regained its independence. The Netherlands, to the northeast, became a kingdom that included Belgium (the former Austrian Netherlands). The northern Italian state of Piedmont was taken from France and given to the Kingdom of Sardinia. Austria gained the Italian states of Lombardy and Venetia, as well as other territory on the Adriatic Sea. Finally, Prussia received land on France's eastern border, though not as much as it had wanted.

Sec. Rev. ques. 4

The other allies were also rewarded for having opposed Napoleon. Russia was allowed to keep Finland and a large part of Poland. Sweden received Norway. Britain kept the overseas possessions it had claimed during the Napoleonic Wars, including the Dutch Cape Colony in South Africa.

The German Confederation. In one of the major acts of the Congress, Metternich and the great powers organized the 39 German states into the German Confederation. This was an alliance of independent states, dominated by Austria. The establishment of the Confederation upset German nationalists, who had wanted one united homeland.

Biography Prince Talleyrand was ordained a priest in 1775 and appointed bishop in 1788. Elected to the French Estates-General, he was eager to eliminate the Old Regime, supported constitutional monarchy, and signed the Declaration of the Rights of Man. Talleyrand was excommunicated in 1791 for his role in giving control of the French Catholic Church to the state and for taking an oath to support the constitution.

Geography Note that Piedmont is a region in northwest Italy bordering France and Switzerland. Piedmont is almost completely surrounded by mountains.
Geography Sardinia is an island in the Mediterranean Sea, west of the Italian peninsula.

Europe in 1815

Hoping to restore the balance of power upset by Napoleon, the Congress of Vienna changed national borders in Europe and restored former monarchs to their thrones. Which two leading powers had territories within the boundaries of the German Confederation?

Map Answer: Kingdom of Prussia, Austrian Empire.

Restoration of monarchs. A guiding principle of the Congress was **legitimacy**. This was the idea that the monarchs who had been forced out of power during the French Revolution and the Napoleonic Wars were their nations' rightful rulers. Earlier, the Bourbon dynasty had been restored in France. Now the Congress put other "legitimate" rulers back on their thrones. Monarchy returned to Spain, Portugal, and Sardinia. The Pope regained the Papal States.

The settlement arranged at Vienna kept peace in Europe for many years. No one country was strong enough to dominate the continent. No power was so unhappy that it turned to war to undo the settlement.

★ See below.

Further Agreements

In March 1815 the rule of the Bourbon kings in France was suddenly interrupted by Napoleon's return. The Hundred Days (page 452) rekindled the great powers' fears of war. In 1815 Russia, Austria, Prussia, and Great Britain agreed to continue the Quadruple

473

Check for Understanding. Ask: What is the principle of legitimacy? (The idea that the monarchs who had been forced out of power during the French Revolution and the Napoleonic Wars were their nations' rightful rulers.)

★ ENRICHMENT. Have students work in groups to debate the following: The policies established by the Congress of Vienna were the most effective ways to ensure peace in Europe. (Synthesis) Debating an Issue

Cultural History The Decembrist revolt involved approximately 3,000 troops led by officers of the imperial guard.

Politics The Greek national revolution was supported by wealthy merchants who had been influenced by the ideals of the French Revolution.

Alliance they had formed a year earlier. They also decided to hold future meetings to keep peace in Europe and to protect the border changes made at the Congress of Vienna. This system of meeting to discuss problems and prevent war became known as the Concert of Europe.

Earlier in 1815, European monarchs had reached another agreement, called the Holy Alliance. This was a pledge by the monarchs to follow Christian principles of charity and peace in ruling their subjects and in dealing with each other. Most European monarchs signed the pact. Britain, however, doubted its usefulness and refused to join.

The Metternich System

In addition to the agreement at Vienna, Metternich looked for other ways to block the spread of liberal and nationalist ideas. He encouraged the rulers of Europe to resist any threats to the established order. This effort came to be called the Metternich system.

Under the Metternich system, conservative rulers censored books and newspapers and put many liberals in prison. Such attacks on liberalism were particularly strong in the German Confederation. Students in German universities had formed political clubs calling for national unity and liberal reforms. To crush such demands, Metternich persuaded the German Confederation to pass the Carlsbad Decrees in 1819. These laws set up a spy system to report on liberal groups. They also ordered censorship of newspapers.

Challenges to Conservatism

● Note strategies for second objective on this page and p. 475.

Despite the efforts of Metternich, the spirit of revolution grew. Liberals and nationalists in many countries continued to organize secret societies, print revolutionary newspapers, collect weapons, and plan revolts.

Spain. One of the first major challenges to the Metternich system took place in Spain. King Ferdinand VII, restored to the throne in 1814, was a harsh ruler who jailed

474

or exiled many reformers. In 1820, Spanish army officers rose against the king and forced him to restore an earlier, more liberal constitution. Afraid that the rebellion would spread, the great powers sent in a French army in 1823. The leaders of the Spanish revolt were brutally punished, and Ferdinand stayed in power.

Sec. Rev. ques. 5

Italy. Revolts also broke out in 1820 in Italy. There, reformers hoped to unite the many Italian states under one government. In addition, they hoped for freedom from the foreign powers that controlled the Italian states. Austrian armies quickly put down the revolts, first in Naples and then in Piedmont. Rulers in other Italian states jailed and executed leaders of the reform movements, and several thousand Italians fled to other lands.

Russia. Secret revolutionary groups also formed in Russia, led by young army officers who had learned liberal ideas from the French. They hoped to westernize Russia and establish a constitution. The officers had no support from the people, however. Their uprising in December 1825—the Decembrist revolt—was easily smashed by the new czar, Nicholas I. Five leaders of the revolt were hanged, and many more were exiled to the freezing wasteland of Siberia. To halt the further spread of liberal ideas, Nicholas began rigid censorship of the press. The czar also set up a secret police force to spy on potential troublemakers.

Greece. The first successful national revolution took place in Greece. In 1821 Greek patriots rebelled against rule by the Ottoman Turks. Sympathy for the Greeks was strong in other countries. Europeans and Americans admired ancient Greek culture. Russians viewed the Greeks' struggle as a holy war—a battle of Christians against the Muslim Turks. Many adventurous Europeans volunteered their help. In 1827 Britain, France, and Russia entered the war, and Greece won its independence in 1829.

France. The spirit of liberalism lived on in France as well. When Louis XVIII became king in 1814, he saw that the French people would not accept a return to absolute

Vocabulary Note that a concert, in a phrase like Concert of Europe, means an agreement based on the exchange of views and a consensus of opinion.

● RETEACHING. Have students review "Challenges to Conservatism" (pp. 474–475) and then draw a map of Europe indicating the countries in which revolts erupted after the Congress of Vienna. (Comprehension) Translating Information into Another Form

Politics The Holy Alliance, proposed by Russian Czar Alexander I, aimed to promote a "Holy Alliance of justice, Christian charity and peace." The agreement reasserted the divine right of kings.

● REINFORCEMENT. Have students make a chart indicating where, when, and why revolts broke out in Europe after the Congress of Vienna. Students should also indicate the results of each revolt. (Comprehension) Summarizing Information

Greece won its independence from Ottoman rule in 1829. In this picture the artist showed Greek patriots in traditional clothing fighting among the ruins of ancient Greece.

movement of government soldiers, they built barricades with paving stones, furniture, tree trunks, and wagons. Behind these barriers, guns in hand, they sang the "Marseillaise," the rallying song of the French Revolution. Many soldiers refused to fire on the rebels. The king, fearing for his life, fled to Britain.

Many of the French revolutionaries had hoped to set up a democratic republic. The middle-class liberals who controlled the rebellion, however, preferred to keep the monarchy. They named a new king, Louis Philippe (fih-LEEP), to replace Charles X.

Louis Philippe was known as the "Citizen King." Rather than kingly robes, he wore the clothes of a businessman. Instead of flying the royal family's flag, he flew the tricolor—the red, white, and blue flag of the Revolution. Yet Louis Philippe's policies generally favored well-to-do business owners and bankers. This satisfied neither the conservative nobles nor the liberals and radicals who had fought in the July Revolution. Voting power was still largely in the hands of the aristocracy, who made up less than 3 percent of the adult male population.

Belgium. The 1830 revolution in France touched off similar uprisings in other parts of Europe. In Belgium, a Catholic country ruled by Dutch Protestants, religious and cultural differences led to a revolt. Stirred by the events in Paris, Belgian patriots proclaimed their independence from the Netherlands. In 1831 the European powers recognized Belgium as an independent nation.

Poland. Soon after the Belgian crisis began, a rebellion broke out in Poland. The Congress of Vienna had set up a new kingdom of Poland ruled by the Russian czar, but Poles had not given up their hopes for independence.

Polish students and army officers were inspired by events in France and Belgium. When the czar threatened to send Polish soldiers to crush those revolutions, the Poles rose up against Russian rule. Russian armies put a quick end to the fighting, however, and Czar Nicholas I imposed even stricter rule on Poland. Other Polish rebellions continued through the 1800's, but none succeeded.

● See below.

475

monarchy. Louis issued a special charter that protected many of the rights gained during the French Revolution. The charter provided for an elected legislature, although only wealthy property owners could vote. It also guaranteed freedom of speech, press, and religion. Many nobles, led by the king's brother Charles, found the charter too liberal. They wanted a return to the Old Regime.

When Louis died in 1824, his brother became king. Charles X tried to bring back special privileges for the nobility and the clergy. In July 1830 he broke up the legislature, began censoring the press, and limited the voting rights of the bourgeoisie.

The people of Paris, led by students and middle-class liberals, rose in revolt. Workers and students stormed into the streets in what is known as the July Revolution. To halt the

See Sec. 1 Closing the Lesson, p. T469B.

Cultural History Louis XVIII was called "King Voltaire" by many conservative nobles who were unhappy with the monarch's liberal policies.

● ENRICHMENT. Have students write an essay analyzing the conflict between conservatism and liberalism in Europe after the Congress of Vienna. Students might consider the following questions: (a) In what ways did conservatives maintain power? (b) What might account for the persistence of liberalism despite conservative efforts to repress reform? *(Synthesis)* **Synthesizing Information**

(pp. 471, 473)

1. **Define or identify:** Congress of Vienna, conservatism, liberalism, legitimacy.
2. How did conservatism, liberalism, and nationalism all grow out of the French Revolution and the Enlightenment? (p. 471)
3. Who was the dominant leader at the Congress of Vienna? Why did he despise liberalism and nationalism? (p. 472)
4. What measures did the Congress take to limit France's power? (p. 472)
5. Which of the revolts of the 1820's succeeded? Which failed? (p. 474)
6. **Critical thinking:** Why did many members of the upper and middle classes in Europe oppose liberal reforms? (See answer below.)

6. Students might suggest that members of the upper and middle classes were trying to protect their property and privileges.

See lesson plans, pp. T469A–T469C.

2 The Romantic Movement

Objectives

Focus Questions

★ ■ How did the Romantic movement change styles in the arts? *(pages 476–478)*
● ■ How did the Romantics help to inspire nationalist feelings? *(pages 478–479)*

Terms to Know

romanticism
Sturm und Drang

★ Note strategies for first objective on this page and p. 477.

Along with liberalism and nationalism, another new movement—**romanticism**—swept over Europe during the late 1700's and 1800's. Romanticism was mainly an artistic and intellectual movement. It was partly shaped, however, by social and political events, especially the Enlightenment and the French Revolution. The Romantic movement also helped inspire the nationalist uprisings that sent shock waves through Europe after **476** the Napoleonic Wars.

New Directions in the Arts

In the mid-1700's, European arts and literature had followed Enlightenment ideals of order, reason, and restraint. Toward the end of the 1700's, European writers, painters, and musicians reacted against these ideals. The Romantic movement stressed the free expression of emotion. The greatest art, the Romantics felt, came from unleashing the human imagination rather than following strict formulas.

Sec. Rev. ques. 2

A new view of nature. The writers of the Romantic period shared some of the ideas put forth by the French thinker Rousseau (page 420). Like him, they saw nature as beautiful and mysterious, a source of inspiration and emotion. Enlightenment writers, in contrast, had not shown much interest in nature.

Romantic poets tried to paint memorable images with their words, hoping to create a sense of wonder and delight. The first important book of the Romantic movement was *Lyrical Ballads* (1798), by the English poets William Wordsworth and Samuel Taylor Coleridge. The Romantics' love for nature is shown in the following lines by Wordsworth:

Sec. Rev. ques. 3

★ RETEACHING. Have students review "New Directions in the Arts" (pp. 476–478) and identify the ideals of the Romantic movement. (Romantics valued the free expression of emotion and viewed nature as beautiful, mysterious, and a source of inspiration and emotion.) *(Comprehension) Observing for Detail*

★ REINFORCEMENT. Have students make a chart listing Romantic artists and explaining how their works represented Romantic ideals. (Charts should include information on Wordsworth and Coleridge, Goethe, Mary Shelley, Turner, Constable, Delacroix.) *(Comprehension) Translating Information into Another Form*

Cultural History Sturm und Drang stressed the importance of action and rebellion in contrast to the Enlightenment focus on reason and order.

Cultural History The novel *Jane Eyre* introduced a new kind of heroine: a middle-class woman who is forced to work for a living.

> ❝ My heart leaps up when I behold
>   A rainbow in the sky:
> So was it when my life began;
> So is it now I am a man;
> So be it when I grow old,
>   Or let me die! ❞

Inner experiences. Romantic writers drew inspiration from their own feelings and fantasies as well as from nature. In the 1770's a group of German writers formed what was called the Sturm und Drang (SHTOORM oont DRAHNG) movement, meaning "storm and stress." Their works described people struggling against society and trying to deal with their own powerful emotions. Johann Wolfgang von Goethe (GER-tuh), a member of this group, became one of Germany's most influential writers.

John Keats, one of England's best-known Romantic poets, led the sort of dramatic life the Sturm und Drang writers described. Beset by money troubles and ill health, he died at the age of 25. Yet Keats pro-duced some of the finest, most vivid poems in the English language.

Other Romantic writers wove tales of mystery and terror. Because many of these stories were set in Gothic castles and churches (page 261), they came to be called gothic novels. Mary Shelley wrote one of the earliest gothic novels, *Frankenstein*, in 1818. Charlotte Brontë's *Jane Eyre* and Emily Brontë's *Wuthering Heights*, both written in 1847, also used the gothic style.

New styles of painting. Like Romantic writers, the artists of this period freely expressed their emotions. Reacting against the balanced and ordered style of the Enlightenment, they used dramatic colors and bold brushstrokes to show their feelings.

Two of England's most noted Romantic painters were Joseph M. W. Turner and John Constable. Like Romantic writers, they found inspiration in nature. Constable painted the gentle landscapes of rural England. Turner showed nature's power and force by painting wild storm scenes.

★ See below.

John Constable painted many landscapes of the English countryside. In this painting, *Wivenhough Park* (1817), Constable displays a romantic view of nature.

477

Biography John Keats was interested in exploring the relationship between experiences that appeared contradictory, such as sorrow and happiness, actual events and dreams, and death and immortality.

Check for Understanding. Ask: Why were some stories written during the Romantic period called "gothic novels"? (They were set in Gothic castles or churches.)

Cultural History Gothic literature emphasizes mystery, vice, darkness, and death; some characters may represent both villain and victim.

★ ENRICHMENT. Have students work in groups to prepare a display on the writers and painters who represented Romantic ideals. Students might write biographical sketches of the artists, write synopses of Romantic novels, give examples of Romantic poetry, or provide examples of Romantic paintings. *(Application)* **Locating Information**

Eugène Delacroix, the most famous of the French Romantic painters, featured exotic locations and events in his work. His *Jewish Wedding in Morocco* (1839) is an example of the use of imagination and fantasy that characterized the art of the Romantic movement.

Sec. Rev. ques. 3, cont.

Eugène Delacroix (del-uh-KWAH) became France's leading Romantic painter. He was a master at creating dramatic, tragic scenes. He also had a love for exotic places and unusual events. A trip to Morocco in 1832 inspired him to paint lion hunts and the colorful wedding scene pictured above.

Nationalism and the Arts

● Note strategies for second objective on this page.

Literature. Romanticism influenced European nationalist movements by encouraging cultural pride. Many Romantics believed that every culture had its own character. Writers such as Madame de Staël (STAHL) in France studied the histories and traditions of their countries in order to understand this "national character." Some Romantic scholars, such as the Grimm brothers in Germany, collected folktales and songs. *Grimm's Fairy Tales,* printed in 1812, is still popular today.

Sec. Rev. ques. 4

Other Romantic writers tried to recapture their countries' past by inventing or retelling colorful legends. One of the most influential Romantic novelists was Sir Walter Scott, who made English and Scottish history come alive in such books as *Ivanhoe* and *Rob Roy.* In France, Victor Hugo's *Hunchback of Notre Dame* captured the flavor of Paris in the 1400's. Alexandre Dumas (doo-MAH) wrote *The Three Musketeers*, which described the adventures of three swashbuckling Frenchmen in the 1600's.

One Romantic who was deeply stirred by the nationalist spirit was the English poet Lord Byron. Byron became passionately interested in the Greek struggle for independence. In his poem *Don Juan,* he wrote:

66 The mountains look on Marathon,
And Marathon looks on the sea;
And musing there an hour alone,
I dreamed that Greece might still be
free. 99

478

Byron never finished *Don Juan.* In 1823 he decided to join the Greeks in their fight against the Turks. He died in Greece the next year.

Music. The music of the Romantic period also drew upon nationalist themes. Frédéric Chopin (shoh-PAN) of Poland and Franz Liszt (LIST) of Hungary expressed national pride by using folk melodies in their musical works. Many Austrian and German composers, such as Ludwig van Beethoven, Franz Schubert, and Robert Schumann, also found inspiration in folk songs. Richard Wagner (VAHG-nur) in Germany based his powerful operas on Germanic myths and legends.

Music had the power to move people deeply. In Italy, the beautiful operas of Giuseppe Verdi (VAYR-dee) helped stir nationalist feelings among those who wanted to unite that country's divided states. Russian audiences celebrated Russia's victory over Napoleon by listening to the *1812 Overture* by Peter Tchaikovsky (chy-KAWF-skee). The music of the Romantic period did more than just bring joy to its listeners. It helped launch the nationalist movements that were gathering force all over Europe.

See Sec. 2 Closing the Lesson, p. T469B.

See lesson plans, pp. T469A–T469C.

Section Review

Answers to Section Review questions are in brackets on pages indicated.

1. **Define or identify:** romanticism, Sturm und Drang. (pp. 476, 477)
2. How were Romantic ideas a reaction against the Enlightenment? (p. 476)
3. Who were some of the leading Romantic writers and artists? (pp. 476–478)
4. In what ways did Romantic writers and musicians contribute to nationalist movements? (pp. 478–479)
5. **Critical thinking:** Why would the French Revolution have been a source of inspiration to Romantics? (See answer below.)

5. Students might suggest that the Romantics were inspired by the passion, determination, hope, and strong sense of nationalism that characterized the French Revolution.

3 The Revolutions of 1848

Objectives

★ Note strategies for first objective on this page and p. 480.

Focus Questions

★ ■ How did poverty and corruption cause revolts in France? *(pages 479–480)*

● ■ What rebellions rocked the Austrian Empire? *(pages 481–482)*

▲ ■ Why did nationalist movements fail in Italy and Germany? *(pages 482–484)*

Terms to Know

socialism
Frankfurt Assembly

The revolutions of the 1820's and 1830's had challenged the conservatism of the Congress of Vienna. In the 1840's, movements for reform and independence continued in many parts of Europe. Economic misery and lack of political freedom set the stage for another wave of revolutions in 1848.

Economic Crisis in Europe

Between 1846 and 1848 Europe suffered an economic crisis. Ireland was especially hard hit. For many years, Irish peasants had depended on potatoes as their main food source. In 1845 and 1846 disease ruined nearly all of Ireland's potato crop. Close to **479**

★ RETEACHING. Have students review "Rebellion in France" (p. 480) and outline the problems that led to the 1848 uprising. (Working class discontent, restricted voting rights, government corruption, property owners' resentment of the working class.) (Comprehension) *Translating Information into Another Form*

★ REINFORCEMENT. Have students work in groups to prepare a dialogue that might have occurred between supporters and opponents of socialism. Students might represent members of the French working class and members of the middle class who owned property. Dialogues should explain socialism and give both groups' points of view. (Application) *Understanding Point of View*

500,000 people died from starvation and disease in one of the worst famines in modern history.

While the potato famine was devastating Ireland, a severe drought hurt the grain harvest in Europe. The resulting food shortages caused high prices, food riots, and widespread suffering. At the same time, businesses across Europe failed, which led to severe unemployment. In anger and frustration, many common people turned against their governments and demanded reforms.

Rebellion in France

Increasing discontent. Louis Philippe's rule (page 475) had never satisfied a large part of the French population. Resentment was strongest among members of the working class, who suffered from unemployment and low wages. Laws prevented French workers from striking, and few of them could meet the property requirements for voting. They also objected to the corruption common among government officials. Noting the workers' angry mood, the political writer Alexis de Tocqueville (TOHK-vil) warned, "I believe that we are at this moment sleeping on a volcano."

Sec. Rev. ques. 2

Many working-class men and women decided that radical changes were necessary. They turned to socialism—a philosophy that called for public ownership of factories, banks, and other businesses. Some socialists said that workers should own the businesses they worked for; others thought that all businesses should be owned by the government. Socialists agreed, however, that the country's wealth should be divided more evenly among all the people.

A workers' revolt. Tired of government corruption and delays in reform, angry mobs rioted in Paris on the night of February 22, 1848. Louis Philippe gave up his throne and left France in disguise three days later. In this way the Second French Republic was born.

The new government was headed by a committee of 10 people. Some of these leaders wanted political liberty but not social reform. Other committee members, led by the socialist Louis Blanc (BLAHNK), urged the new government to make changes that would help workers. As a result of Blanc's demands, the government set up a national workshop program to provide jobs. Nearly 200,000 people, desperate for work, poured into the city of Paris to sign up. Of this number about 120,000 found jobs—usually digging roads for very low pay.

The cost of the workshop program upset many taxpayers, including peasants and the middle class. When elections were held, these voters chose more conservative delegates to the assembly. In June 1848 the government closed the workshops, and Paris workers rose in protest over the loss of jobs. Men, women, and children again set up barricades in the streets of the city.

Three days of fierce street fighting followed between the workers and government soldiers. More than 10,000 people were killed or injured. Thousands more were thrown into prison.

A divided nation. The bloody "June Days" split France in two. In the words of one Frenchwoman, the country fell "prey to a feeling of terror unlike anything since the invasion of Rome by the barbarians." The working class now faced opposition, bordering on hatred, from all those who owned property—peasants, middle class, and aristocrats. Most French people feared socialism and wanted order and stability, not extreme changes in the old system.

Sec. Rev. ques. 3

In response to the June uprising, the French assembly changed the constitution to give the government stronger controls. At the same time, though, it gave voting rights to all adult males.

French voters then elected Louis Napoleon president of France. Nephew of the emperor Napoleon, Louis Napoleon ruled conservatively and became very popular. When the legislature opposed him, he disbanded it and set up a dictatorship. In 1852 the voters gave him a new title, Emperor Napoleon III. The Second Empire now replaced the republic created in 1848.

★ See below, left.

480

Background Note that the British government was supplying soup and flour to more than 2,000,000 Irish famine victims by August 1848. It has been estimated that more than a million people migrated overseas between 1846 and 1855 as a result of the potato famine.

★ **ENRICHMENT. Have students make a timeline showing political conflict in France between 1789 and 1848. Students should indicate the causes of the conflicts and their outcomes.** (Comprehension) Sequencing Information

Biography Alexis de Tocqueville, best known for his study Democracy in America, was impressed with the United States and helped to establish its reputation as a land of unlimited opportunity and equality. De Tocqueville was concerned, however, that the "tyranny of the majority" would threaten such values as tradition, taste, creativity, and honor.

Biography Note that Louis Blanc is credited with a statement that has become the classic description of socialism: "From each according to his abilities, to each according to his needs."

During the brief and bloody civil war known as the June Days, workers and students barricaded the streets of Paris. The government crushed the rebellion with cannons and created lasting divisions within French society.

The Austrian Empire

● Note strategies for second objective on this page and p. 482.

In 1848, as in 1830, the revolutionary spirit spread from France through the rest of Europe. In the Austrian Empire, several nationalist uprisings took place. Germans were the strongest nationality in the Austrian Empire, making up about 25 percent of the population. In Hungary, which was the eastern part of the empire, Magyars (Hungarians) were the largest nationality group. Some of the Slavic peoples, such as the Czechs and Poles, complained of mistreatment by both the Germans and the Magyars. Still other groups in the empire, including Italians, wanted self-government.

Austria's Hapsburg rulers used the army and the bureaucracy to hold their empire together. This task became more and more difficult, however, as the spirit of nationalism grew. With new pride in their cultures, Czechs and Hungarians protested against German domination of the empire. Writers began to write in their own language instead of the Latin, German, and French they had been taught to use in school.

Revolts in Vienna and Bohemia. Less than a month after the February 1848 revolution in France, students and workers in the Austrian capital of Vienna revolted. They demanded a constitution and an end to feudal practices. Students and workers took control of parts of the city, and peasants rebelled in the countryside.

Sec. Rev. ques. 4

The frightened emperor, Ferdinand I, gave in to the rebels' demands. He abolished serfdom and promised a constitution. He also dismissed Metternich, the aging white-haired prince who had come to be hated by the Austrian people.

A few weeks after the trouble in Vienna, an uprising broke out in the city of Prague (PRAHG), the Bohemian capital. At the same time, Czech nationalists in Bohemia met at an all-Slav congress. In an effort to rid themselves of German dominance, they called for a constitution for Bohemia. They also demanded that the Czech language be used along with German in the schools and by government offices.

Temporary reforms in Hungary. The most serious threat to Austrian rule occurred in Hungary. In March 1848 Louis Kossuth (KAHS-ooth), a Hungarian patriot, urged Hungarians to demand more self-government. The Austrian ruler, facing rebellion throughout his empire, agreed to these demands. Two weeks later, Hungary adopted a constitution that left it within the Austrian

481

● RETEACHING. Have students review "The Austrian Empire" (pp. 481–482) and find evidence to support the following generalization: *Nationalism caused uprisings in the Austrian Empire.* (The Austrian Empire was composed of many nationalities who were proud of their culture. Some groups complained of mistreatment and agitated for reform; others wanted self-government.) *(Comprehension) Observing for Detail*

● REINFORCEMENT. Have students make a chart organizing the information on the rebellions in the Austrian Empire. The chart should include the locations, dates, causes, and effects of the uprising. *(Comprehension) Translating Information into Another Form*

⑤ FEATURE ACTIVITY. Have students write a response to Kossuth's farewell statement that might have been written by representa- tives of the Hungarian people. (Application) *Understanding Point of View*

⑤ See above.

Biography

Louis Kossuth

Louis Kossuth was born in 1802 into a family with an aristocratic background but little money. He studied law and later began publishing a political journal. His fiery articles calling for Hungarian independence angered Austrian officials, and he was imprisoned from 1837 to 1840. Kossuth's defiance of Austria made him a national hero in Hungary. When he was released, crowds lined the roads chanting "Long live Kossuth!" He continued to speak and write for independence until the revolution of 1848 brought him briefly to power.

After Austria reconquered Hungary, Kossuth made a daring escape through the mountains. As he reached the border, he said farewell to Hungary: "Forgive me, my country, forgive the man now fated to roam the world. Forgive him if he caused so many of your sons to shed their blood. His aim was to help the birth of a free nation. The principles he sought to follow were those of George Washington."

Kossuth was indeed fated to roam the world. He traveled widely, seeking support for Hungary, until he died in 1894. He was buried in Hungary's capital, Budapest. After 45 years of exile, Louis Kossuth was home.

482

Empire but otherwise in charge of its own affairs. The constitution ended feudal privileges and guaranteed freedom of religion and freedom of the press. It also gave voting rights to all men who owned property.

The plan of the Hungarian revolutionaries, however, was to form a Hungarian state based on the Magyar language and culture. It became clear that the other ethnic groups in Hungary—Croats, Serbs, Romanians, and Germans—would not enjoy equal benefits. These peoples, who made up more than half the population of Hungary, strongly opposed Magyar domination.

Defeat of the rebels. Hapsburg Austria took advantage of both its military strength and the conflicts among the people of Hungary. In June 1848, imperial troops bombarded Prague and crushed the Czech rebellion. In October, Austrian soldiers attacked students and workers in Vienna. Thousands were killed as the army retook the city.

In Hungary, civil war had erupted. Serbo-Croatian troops, supported by the whole non-Magyar population and Austria, fought Magyar troops led by Kossuth. Unable to overcome Kossuth's fighters, Austria decided to pull the Serbo-Croatian soldiers back to Vienna. The Magyars then proclaimed Hungary an independent republic in April 1849.

Their independence was short-lived, however. The new Austrian emperor, 18-year-old Francis Joseph, had no intention of losing Hungary. He called for help from Czar Nicholas I of Russia. In June a Russian army attacked Hungary from the east, and by August the rebels had been defeated. The Hapsburgs had now silenced Magyars in Hungary, Czech nationalists in Prague, and liberals in Vienna.

● See below, left.

Failed Attempts at Unification

▲ Note strategies for third objective on this page and p. 483.

Italy. The Italians' desire for a united, independent Italy had been growing since the Congress of Vienna. Resentment was especially strong in the Austrian-held states of

● ENRICHMENT. Have students work in groups to analyze the sources of conflict between nationalist groups and the Austrian government. Then have students suggest political and social changes that might have prevented these revolts. (Synthesis) *Synthesizing Information*

▲ RETEACHING. Have students identify the following: Giuseppe Mazzini (Leader of Young Italy whose aim was to establish a republic.) Frankfurt Assembly (A national assembly elected by middle-class liberals who planned to establish a united Germany.) (Comprehension) *Observing for Detail*

Lombardy and Venetia. In 1831, Giuseppe Mazzini (juh-SEP-ee maht-SEE-nee) had started a secret society called Young Italy. Its members wanted to set up a republic, with Rome as the capital.

▲ See below, right.

In 1848 unrest gave way to rebellion in many parts of Italy. Several rulers of Italian states made liberal reforms, but the revolutionaries wanted more drastic change. In March 1848, revolts broke out in Venice and Milan. The king of Sardinia, the only state under Italian rule, declared war on Austria. Near the end of the year, the Pope fled Rome, and in February 1849, Italians proclaimed the Roman Republic.

Sec. Rev. ques. 5

By mid-1849, however, the Austrians had regained control. They defeated the Sardinians, recaptured Milan, and bombarded Venice into submission. France sent an army that defeated the Roman Republic and restored the Pope to power. The revolutionaries' dream of a united Italy had been shattered.

Germany. Many Germans still dreamed of a unified nation. The revolutions in France and the Austrian Empire gave hope to workers and middle-class German liberals. In March 1848 they took to the streets of Ber-

Meanwhile . . .
IN THE UNITED STATES

After the failure of the revolutions of 1848, thousands of Germans emigrated to the United States. Some were revolutionaries seeking political safety, and others were farmers eager for cheap land. They often settled in groups, many of them in the northern cities, though a significant number made their way as far south as Texas.

lin and other cities. Terrified by the resulting bloodshed, the king of Prussia, Frederick William IV, gave his subjects a constitution and an assembly. Other German rulers followed his example. This encouraged middle-class liberals to elect delegates to a national assembly in Frankfurt, which met from May 1848 to May 1849.

The **Frankfurt Assembly** drew up plans for a united Germany that would include all the German states except Austria. They asked Frederick William to be emperor of the new

Ⓕ See below, right.

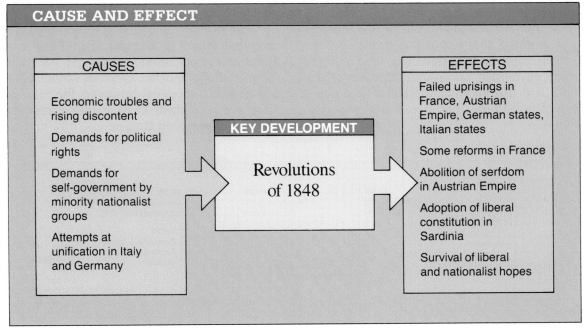

CAUSE AND EFFECT

CAUSES

Economic troubles and rising discontent

Demands for political rights

Demands for self-government by minority nationalist groups

Attempts at unification in Italy and Germany

KEY DEVELOPMENT

Revolutions of 1848

EFFECTS

Failed uprisings in France, Austrian Empire, German states, Italian states

Some reforms in France

Abolition of serfdom in Austrian Empire

Adoption of liberal constitution in Sardinia

Survival of liberal and nationalist hopes

483

nation, but he refused. He bluntly said he would never accept a crown from commoners, or as he put it, "pick up a crown from the gutter." Frederick William then restored a more conservative constitution. The Prussian king also disbanded the Frankfurt Assembly, dealing a death blow to this attempt at German unification.

Sec. Rev. ques. 5, cont.

Hopes for the future. The failure of unification movements in Italy and Germany was only temporary. Later in the 1800's, forceful action by Prussia would bring the German states under a single ruler. Italy too would achieve unity, largely through the efforts of the Kingdom of Sardinia. You will read about the triumph of nationalism in Germany and Italy in Chapter 26.

See Sec. 3 *Closing the Lesson*, p. T469C.

Section Review

Answers to Section Review questions are in brackets on pages indicated.

1. **Define or identify:** socialism, Frankfurt Assembly. (pp. 480, 483)
2. Why did socialism appeal to workers in France? (p. 480)
3. Why did the "June Days" lead to division among the French people? (p. 480)
4. What led different groups in the Austrian Empire to revolt? (p. 481)
5. What was the outcome of the Italian and German attempts at unification? (pp. 483–484)
6. **Critical thinking:** How successful were the rebellions of 1848? Explain. (See answer below.)

Chapter 24   Summary and Timeline

1. After the fall of Napoleon, the Congress of Vienna in 1815 returned conservatives to power throughout Europe. The conservatives fought to restore the authority of monarchs, the aristocracy, and the clergy. They were challenged by liberals, who wanted to extend individual rights and continue the reforms made during the French Revolution. Other opposition to the conservatives came from nationalists, who wanted free and unified homelands. Between 1820 and 1848, liberals and nationalists led a number of revolutions that threatened conservative rule.

2. The Romantic movement of the late 1700's and early 1800's reflected the liberal and nationalist movements. Romantic writers and painters stressed creativity and imagination, often using nature as a subject. Romantic writers and musicians used nationalist themes in their works.

3. In 1848, as in 1830, a revolt in France triggered others in Europe. Liberal and nationalist revolts broke out in the Austrian Empire, Italy, and the German states. After some early successes, however, the revolutions were crushed. Conservative rulers remained in power in Europe.

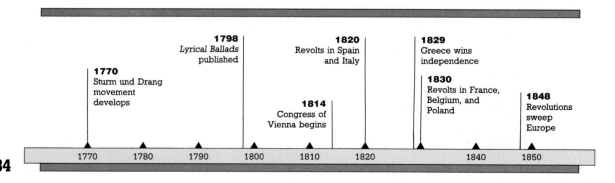

1770 Sturm und Drang movement develops

1798 *Lyrical Ballads* published

1814 Congress of Vienna begins

1820 Revolts in Spain and Italy

1829 Greece wins independence

1830 Revolts in France, Belgium, and Poland

1848 Revolutions sweep Europe

1770   1780   1790   1800   1810   1820   1840   1850

6. Students might note that although some liberal reforms were made, conservatives continued to dominate Europe. Though the rebellions failed to establish permanent republics, or in the case of Italy and Germany, unified states, they strengthened nationalism and encouraged calls for independence.

CHAPTER 24 REVIEW

See p. T469C for answers to Chapter Review.

Vocabulary Review

Match each of the following terms with its correct definition: *Frankfurt Assembly, legitimacy, romanticism, socialism, Sturm und Drang.*

1. artistic and intellectual movement emphasizing imagination and emotion
2. German national assembly that met in 1848 and 1849
3. principle that rulers who lost their thrones during the French Revolution and the Napoleonic Wars should be restored to power
4. philosophy that supports public ownership of business
5. German literary movement that emphasized people's struggles against society and their own emotions

People to Identify

Choose the name that best completes each sentence.
1. [Charlotte Brontë/Mary Shelley] and her sister Emily both wrote gothic novels.
2. *The Hunchback of Notre Dame* was written by [Alexandre Dumas/Victor Hugo].
3. [Louis Kossuth/Joseph M. W. Turner] was a leading Hungarian patriot.
4. [William Wordsworth/John Keats] wrote *Lyrical Ballads* with Samuel Taylor Coleridge.
5. The English poet [Ludwig van Beethoven/Lord Byron] fought with the Greeks.
6. [John Constable/Eugène Delacroix] became France's leading Romantic painter.
7. [Louis Napoleon/Louis Philippe] was known as the "Citizen King."

8. [Sir Walter Scott/Madame de Staël] wrote *Ivanhoe* and other books about English and Scottish history.
9. [Giuseppe Verdi/Giuseppe Mazzini] started the secret society called Young Italy.

Places to Know

Match the letters on this map of Europe with the places listed below. You may want to refer to the map on page 473.

1. Papal States
2. Frankfurt
3. Austrian Empire
4. Kingdom of Sardinia
5. Vienna
6. Greece
7. France

Recalling the Facts

1. Which groups in European society strongly supported conservatism? Liberalism? Nationalism?
2. What were the aims of the Congress of Vienna?
3. Why did the reorganization of Germany upset German nationalists?
4. What factors led to the uprising in France known as the July Revolution?

485

5. How did Romantic writers and painters view nature?

6. How did Romantic writers and musicians express cultural pride in their works?

7. How did an economic crisis between 1846 and 1848 cause widespread suffering in Europe?

8. Why did the bloody "June Days" of 1848 split France in two?

9. What did the rebels demand in Vienna? In Bohemia?

10. Why did civil war erupt in Hungary?

11. What were the results of the 1848 rebellions in Italy and Germany?

Critical Thinking Skills

1. **Using the library.** Research and prepare a short biography on one of the following delegates to the Congress of Vienna: Czar Alexander I, Lord Castlereagh, Prince Metternich, Prince Talleyrand. *(App.)*

2. **Analyzing a quotation.** Metternich is often quoted as having said, "When France sneezes, all Europe catches cold." What did Metternich mean by this remark? *(Anal.)*

3. **Giving an oral report.** Prepare an oral report on a Romantic composer. You might choose Franz Liszt, Anton Dvořák, Clara or Robert Schumann, or one of the composers mentioned in this chapter. You may want to accompany your report with a selection of the composer's music. *(App.)*

4. **Determining cause and effect.** Tell when and where the following events took place and describe the causes of each: the Decembrist revolt, the "June Days," creation of the Second Empire. *(Comp.)*

Thinking About Geography

Comparing maps. Compare the maps on pages 450 and 473, showing Europe during Napoleon's reign and after the Congress of Vienna. How did Austria change in size? Prussia? France? Russia? *(Comp.)*

486

Enrichment: Primary Sources

Carl Schurz was a German student who fought in the revolution of 1848. He later emigrated to the United States. In the following adapted passage, Schurz describes German students' reactions to the French rebellion in February 1848.

66 One morning, toward the end of February 1848, I sat quietly in my attic chamber, working, when suddenly a friend rushed into the room, exclaiming: "Do you not know what has happened? The French have driven out Louis Philippe and proclaimed the republic."

We tore to the market-square, the meeting place for all the students. What did we want there? Probably no one knew. But, since the French had proclaimed a republic, something of course must happen here, too.

The next morning there were the usual lectures to be attended. But what the professor had to say did not seem to concern us. Now had arrived the day for the establishment of "German unity." The word *democracy* was on all tongues.

On the 18th of March we too had our mass demonstration. At the head of the procession Professor Kinkel bore the revolutionary flag. He spoke about the liberties and rights of the German people, which now must be granted by the princes or won by force by the people. 99

1. What were the events that so excited the German students?
2. Why were the students no longer interested in the lectures?
3. **Critical thinking:** What words in the passage reveal the liberal views of the students? Their nationalist views? *(Anal.)*

✔ A checkmark identifies questions and exercises calling for the three higher-order levels of thinking at the top of the Bloom taxonomy: Analysis, Synthesis, and Evaluation.

WORLD HISTORY
Checklist

UNIT 6

Try to identify the following key people, places, and terms from the unit. If you need help, refer to the pages listed.

Key People

Nicolaus Copernicus (413)
Galileo Galilei (414)
Johannes Kepler (415)
Isaac Newton (415)
Francis Bacon (418)
René Descartes (418)
Thomas Hobbes (419)
John Locke (419)
Voltaire (420)
Baron de Montesquieu (420)
Jean Jacques Rousseau (420)
Johann Sebastian Bach (423)
Wolfgang Amadeus Mozart (423)
Ludwig van Beethoven (423)
George Washington (427)
Thomas Jefferson (427)
Benjamin Franklin (428)
Louis XVI (436)
Marie Antoinette (440)
Maximilien Robespierre (442)
Napoleon Bonaparte (446)
Pierre Toussaint L'Ouverture (458)
Simon Bolívar (459)
Miguel Hidalgo (459)
Benito Juárez (466)
Porfirio Díaz (466)
Klemens von Metternich (472)
Louis Philippe (475)
William Wordsworth (476)
John Keats (477)
Mary Shelley (477)
Charlotte Brontë (477)
Emily Brontë (477)
Eugène Delacroix (478)
Madame de Staël (478)
Sir Walter Scott (478)
Lord Byron (478)
Richard Wagner (479)
Giuseppe Verdi (479)
Louis Napoleon (480)
Louis Kossuth (481)
Giuseppe Mazzini (483)

Key Places

Yorktown (428)
Trafalgar (449)
Elba (452)
St. Helena (452)

The Spirit of '76 represents the American Revolution.

Key Terms

Scientific Revolution (413)
scientific method (413)
Enlightenment (419)
social contract (419)
natural rights (419)
philosophe (420)
separation of powers (420)
American Revolution (426)
Declaration of Independence (427)
Constitution (430)
federal system (430)
checks and balances (430)
Bill of Rights (430)
Old Regime (435)
bourgeoisie (436)
French Revolution (436)
Declaration of the Rights of Man (439)
radical (441)
suffrage (442)
Jacobin (442)
Girondist (443)
Reign of Terror (444)
nationalism (445)
coup d'état (446)
Napoleonic Code (447)
Napoleonic Wars (448)
Continental System (449)
Quadruple Alliance (452)
Battle of Waterloo (452)
Monroe Doctrine (464)
neocolonialism (465)
Mexican-American War (465)
War of the Reform (466)
Congress of Vienna (471)
conservatism (471)
liberalism (471)
romanticism (476)
Sturm und Drang (477)
socialism (480)
Frankfurt Assembly (483)

REVIEW ACTIVITIES: *Key People:* Make a chart identifying each key person as a leader in one of the following fields: government and politics, science, philosophy, music, literature, or painting. *Key Places:* Explain the significance of each listed place. *Key Terms:* Define or identify each term listed.

Industrialization and Its Impact 1750–1914

| 1760 | 1770 | 1780 | 1790 | 1800 | 1810 | 1820 | 1830 |

CHAPTER 25: The West in the Industrial Age

1769
Watt develops practical steam engine

1793
Whitney invents cotton gin

1830
Stephenson develops practical locomotive

CHAPTER 26:

1815
Italian nationalist groups begin to form

| 1760 | 1770 | 1780 | 1790 | 1800 | 1810 | 1820 | 1830 |

FOCUS STRATEGY. Tell students that the illustration presents a view, from inside a factory, of a typical British industrial town in the nineteenth century. Then ask: (a) What are some ways that industrialization appears to have influenced life in the town shown here? (Factories were built, railroads were laid, smoke from the factory filled the air, and women and children became factory workers.) (b) What advantage do you think the river offered this town? The river probably provided a way to ship manufactured goods to markets.)

1840   1850   1860   1870   1880   1890   1900   1910

1848
Marx and Engels' *Communist Manifesto*

1906
Sinclair's
The Jungle

1829–1884
British Parliament
makes democratic reforms

Nationalism in Europe

1853–1856
Crimean War

1871
Franco-Prussian War
ends; Germany unified

1912
Balkan Wars begin

1870
Italy unified

CHAPTER 27:   Europe in the Late 1800's

1860
Impressionist
movement begins

1896
Herzl calls for
Jewish homeland

1866
Tolstoy's
War and Peace

1905
Einstein publishes
theory of relativity

1840   1850   1860   1870   1880   1890   1900   1910

Have students refer to the unit timeline to answer the following questions: **(a)** What are three items listed on the timeline that indicate important industrial development? (Practical steam engine, 1769; cotton gin, 1793; practical locomotive, 1830.) **(b)** What events on the timeline indicate that nationalism continued to be a force in Europe? (Italian nationalist forces formed, 1815; Italy unified, 1870; Germany unified, 1871.)

T489A

The West in the Industrial Age 1750–1914

(pp. 490–511)

Chapter Preview

Section 1 of this chapter describes the factors that led to the start of the Industrial Revolution in Britain and outlines the discoveries and inventions that spurred industrial growth. The effects of industrialization on working and living conditions are also examined. In Section 2 new economic theories offered by laissez-faire capitalists and socialists are explained. In Section 3, students learn about social and political reforms undertaken by Britain, the United States, and other European nations.

Bibliography

See the *Teacher's Management and Planning Guide* for additional listings. Starred titles are for both students and teachers.

Ashton, Thomas S. *The Industrial Revolution, 1760–1830.* Oxford University Press. British economic forces that led to new system.

Bowditch, John, and Clement Ramsland, editors. *Voices of the Industrial Revolution.* University of Michigan Press. Source readings.

Cipolla, Carlo M. *The Economic History of World Population,* sixth edition. Barnes and Noble Imports. Modern civilization and energy sources.

Landes, David S. *The Unbound Prometheus: Technological Change and Industrial Development in Western Europe from 1750 to the Present.* Cambridge University Press.

*Rooke, Patrick. *The Industrial Revolution.* John Day. A readable overview.

Section Lesson Plans

SECTION 1 (pp. 491–497)
The Industrial Revolution

Objectives

After completing this section, students will be able to:
1. Explain why the Industrial Revolution began in Great Britain.
2. Describe new inventions and methods of production that helped to transform industry.
3. Describe how living and working conditions changed.

Introducing the Lesson

Remind students that throughout history new technological developments have brought about significant economic and social changes. New forms of transportation, new sources of energy, and advances in the way food and other goods are produced influence the way people work and live.

Then ask: *(a) What are some examples of technological changes that affected the way human beings worked and lived?* (Answers will vary, but might include the invention of tools, the taming of fire, the development of agriculture, domestication of animals, and the development of navigational aids, firearms, and the printing press.)

(b) What might account for the impact of technology on the way people work and live? (Answers will vary. Because food, clothing, and shelter represent basic survival needs, technological changes that affect these needs influence where people live, what they do for a living, and how well they live.)

(c) How have modern technological changes affected the lives of people? (Answers will vary, but might include a discussion of computer technology, high-speed transportation, nuclear power as a source of energy, and home-entertainment technology such as video cassette recorders and compact discs.)

Developing the Lesson: Forming a Hypothesis

Have students develop a hypothesis explaining why the Industrial Revolution began in Great Britain. In their hypotheses, students should note the difference between conditions and causes.

(Answers will vary, but students might explain that existing social, economic, and political conditions in Great Britain led to the development of agricultural and industrial inventions and innovations.) *(Synthesis)*

Developing the Lesson:
Analyzing Information

Have students explain the relationship between the seven conditions that made the Industrial Revolution possible in Great Britain and the inventions and innovations described in this section. Students might make a chart listing the conditions in one column, inventions and innovations in another column, and then draw lines to indicate relationships. (For example, Britain's labor supply helped the growth of the factory system, as did the availability of investment capital and entrepreneurs; the development of the Bessemer process was related to Britain's access to coal and iron ore.) *(Analysis)*

Closing the Lesson:
Linking Past and Present

Have students work in groups to present a panel discussion on how industrial societies have worked to solve many of the problems resulting from industrialization and urbanization. Students might examine the problems mentioned in the chapter and then cite examples of programs and policies that have been developed to remedy the problems. *(Synthesis)*

See *Section Review* questions, p. 497.

SECTION 2   (pp. 498–501)
New Economic Theories

Objectives

After completing this section, students will be able to:
1. Discuss new economic theories that arose after the Industrial Revolution.
2. Describe how socialists proposed to deal with changes in society.

Introducing the Lesson

Remind students that a theory is an unproven idea that attempts to explain some aspect of reality. After the Industrial Revolution, theories were developed to explain the changes in society brought about by industrialization and urbanization.

Then ask: *(a) During what other period in history were discoveries followed by the development of new theories?* (Students might mention the Scientific Revolution.)

(b) How might the development of new economic theories affect society? (Answers will vary. If a theory appears to accurately explain something that has occurred, then it might be used as a guide for economic planning.)

(c) How might economic theories that developed after the Industrial Revolution compare with theories that explain present-day society? (Answers will vary. Because modern society is highly industrial and urban, many theories that developed after the Industrial Revolution would be relevant today. However, thinkers today have the advantage of being able to base their theories on the observable results of over two hundred years of industrialization.)

Developing the Lesson:
Comparing Ideas

Have students compare the societies designed or predicted by Fourier, Owen, and Marx. (Fourier planned small societies where people would enjoy their work, have pleasant living conditions, perform jobs for which they were best suited, and share in what was produced. Owen's societies included higher wages, improved working conditions, reduced work hours, schools, comfortable housing, and food and clothing at fair prices. He urged the formation of communities where profits would be shared by all. Marx predicted a classless society where workers would own the means of production.) *(Comprehension)*

Developing the Lesson:
Observing for Detail

Have students outline Marx's scientific analysis of history, noting the failure of his predictions in the following areas: *economic forces; social classes; role of government; destruction of capitalism.* (Marx believed that history is shaped by economic forces and that throughout history, exploitation of the "have nots" by the "haves" has always caused a class struggle. Marx also believed that government has acted as a tool of the controlling economic class. Marx predicted that capitalism would lead to the expansion of the working class, which would rise in revolt and destroy the capitalist system.) *(Comprehension)*

Closing the Lesson: Predicting Events

Have students work in groups to predict how Karl Marx might have adapted his economic theory if he could have foreseen the enormous gains made by workers in the years following the Industrial Revolution. *(Synthesis)*

See *Section Review* questions, p. 501.

SECTION 3   (pp. 502–509)
Political, Economic, and Social Reforms

Objectives

After completing this section, students will be able to:
1. Explain how democracy gradually expanded in Britain.
2. Describe the economic and social reforms that took place in Britain, the United States, and Europe.

Introducing the Lesson

Remind students that political, economic, and social changes often result in unexpected problems and inequities. Societies resolve social problems in many different ways and often over long periods of time.

Then ask: *(a) What might explain the emergence of problems and inequities after significant political, economic, and social changes?* (Answers will vary. Any significant change that affects a great number of people creates new circumstances. Until problems are identified and efforts made to solve them, some people might suffer great hardships.)

(b) What are some ways that problems resulting from political, economic, and social changes might be resolved? (Answers will vary. Government reform, citizens' groups, special-interest groups, or electoral action are some ways in which social reform occurs in democratic societies. In some societies violent courses of action are resorted to as a way of resolving problems.)

(c) What are examples from recent history of efforts to address social problems or unfair policies? (Answers will vary, but students might mention equal rights movements, women's efforts for equality in the workplace, or compensation for individuals who have been injured through no fault of their own.)

Developing the Lesson: Observing for Details

Have students explain how the Industrial Revolution led to a demand for political reform in Great Britain. (Urbanization created inequities because membership in the House of Commons did not reflect the increase in urban population; British political life, dominated by aristocratic landowners, did not fairly represent the growing middle class. Industrialization created a class of workers who lacked representation, since property ownership was required of members of Parliament.) *(Comprehension)*

Developing the Lesson: Understanding Point of View

Have students work in groups to stage a rally for political, economic, and social reform that might have occurred in Great Britain or the United States after the Industrial Revolution. Students should represent individuals and groups seeking expansion of democratic rights; better working conditions; and improvements in health, education, and the standard of living for workers. Students might prepare and give speeches, draw posters, or circulate mock petitions demanding reform. *(Application)*

Closing the Lesson: Making Judgments

Have students write an essay evaluating the results of the Industrial Revolution. Students might explain problems caused by industrialization, describe efforts at political, economic, and social reform, and then evaluate how society today benefits from industrialization and urbanization. *(Evaluation)*

See *Section Review* questions, p. 509.

Chapter 25 Review Answers
(pp. 510–511)

Vocabulary Review

1. (a) entrepreneur (b) standard of living (c) Chartist movement (d) utopia (e) Bessemer process (f) communism (g) labor union
2. (a) Domestic system—production method in which workers labored at home; factory system—production method in which large numbers of

workers operated machines in one place. (b) *Communist Manifesto*—1848 book by Karl Marx and Friedrich Engels that expressed Marx's economic and political theories; proletariat—wage-earning laborers.

People to Identify

1. James Watt 2. Susan B. Anthony
3. William Gladstone 4. Henry Cort
5. Jethro Tull 6. Jane Addams 7. Eli Whitney

Recalling the Facts

1. Britain had many workers, abundant natural resources, investment capital, entrepreneurs, an efficient transportation system, good markets, and the support of the government.
2. Farm production increased because the wealthy landowners who bought out small farmers used more efficient farming methods. Many poor villagers who lost their lands became beggars or moved into the cities to look for work.
3. The steam engine replaced water power in coal mines, ironworks, and textile plants; it also led to the development of the locomotive and triggered an age of railway-building worldwide. Advances in electricity led to the invention of the electric generator, which allowed factories to run on electrical power.
4. Wages were low and employment was not secure, especially for the sick and the elderly. During business slumps many people lost jobs. Women and children were paid very little. No laws prevented or restricted child labor. Accidents were frequent and there were numerous health risks.
5. Entrepreneurs should run their businesses in the most profitable way; more profit is good for everyone; free competition allows people to do what they do best; government should not interfere with business.
6. Malthus believed that population growth kept humanity in a state of near-starvation and that it led to unemployment, low wages, and poverty. Ricardo said that the work force would always increase, which would keep wages low.
7. Owen raised wages, improved working conditions, reduced hours of work, and provided schools, housing, food, and clothing at reasonable prices.
8. Marx believed that the workers, made desperate by their poverty, would seize control of the government, take over the means of production, and destroy the capitalist system and the ruling class. The class struggle would then end and a classless society would emerge. *Flaws:* Marx failed to include the role of noneconomic forces in his theories, and he did not foresee the great gains workers

have made. He also failed to see the societal benefits that governments can effect, and he was wrong in predicting the occurrence of working-class revolutions and worker-ruled states.
9. It passed legislation that opened government positions to Catholics, gave the industrial cities more representation in Parliament, extended voting rights to more men, and provided for a secret ballot.
10. Its members disrupted politicians' speeches, marched on Parliament, bombed buildings, and burned railway stations.
11. City governments regulated housing, public recreation areas were set up, state governments regulated the workplace, and the federal government regulated big business.

Critical Thinking Skills

1. Fact—something done; artifact—object made by human workmanship; facsimile—exact copy, from the Latin "to make similar"; manufacture—to make into a finished product.
2. Charts will vary.
3. Answers will vary. Students might note that cooperative living can often be difficult due to differences in people's personalities and opinions. Some people might also have worked harder and produced more than others; they might have resented sharing the fruits of their labor equally.
4. Housing, sanitation, and hospital facilities were not adequate. Crime rates were high and police forces were small. Fire protection was minimal and the poor lived in crowded, poorly built houses. Open sewers, polluted rivers, factory smoke, and filthy streets allowed disease to spread.
5. The buildings were probably warehouses, used in the shipping and receiving of goods. The barges would probably travel through canals. Shipping by water was cheaper because transporting goods by railway was not yet a reality. Any other form of land transportation was slow and expensive.

Thinking About Geography

Maps will vary.

Enrichment: Primary Sources

1. To push the corves in and out of the mine.
2. It led to some loss of hair, swollen legs, and probably extreme fatigue.
3. Answers will vary. It is likely that many people were appalled to hear of such conditions. Many members of Parliament who heard children testify probably worked hard for reforms.

The West in the Industrial Age 1750–1914

See chapter timeline, p. 509.

Before You Read This Chapter

What kind of job do you expect to get when you finish school? For most people today, working means getting up at a regular time, leaving home, and going to a particular place—an office, a factory, a store. However, such jobs are a recent development historically. Before 1800, most people worked near their homes as farmers or as artisans. As you read this chapter, try to imagine how work changed between 1750 and 1900. What were the advantages and disadvantages of the new ways of working?

The Geographic Setting

The Chapter Outline

1. The Industrial Revolution
2. New Economic Theories
3. Political, Economic, and Social Reforms

Machines, like these for printing designs on cloth, revolutionized industry, agriculture, and the way people lived and thought.

See lesson plans, pp. T489A–T489C.

1 The Industrial Revolution

Objectives

Focus Questions

★ ■ Why did the Industrial Revolution begin in Great Britain? *(pages 491–492)*
● ■ What new inventions and methods of production helped to transform industry? *(pages 492–495)*
▲ ■ How did living and working conditions change? *(pages 495–497)*

Terms to Know

Industrial Revolution	factory system
entrepreneur	Bessemer process
enclosure movement	standard of living
domestic system	urbanization

★ Note strategies for first objective on this page.

During the 1700's, people in Western countries began producing goods in a wholly new way. Inventors built remarkable machines. New forms of power, such as steam, replaced animal strength and human muscle. The factory system of making goods came into use. All of these advances affected patterns of living as well as working. Because society was so transformed, this time of great change is known as the Industrial Revolution

Great Britain's Advantages

The Industrial Revolution began in Great Britain in the mid-1700's. Several factors made Britain ripe for industrial growth.

Sec. Rev. ques. 2

1. **Labor supply.** Britain had a large number of able workers. This was because its birth rate was increasing and its death rate was declining. Also, many small farmers had been forced to leave their lands (page 370) and were looking for work.

2. **Natural resources.** Britain was rich in coal and iron ore. From its colonies Britain imported other resources, particularly cotton, to use in making textiles.

3. **Investment capital.** Britain had capital—money and goods—ready to invest in new industries. The money came from wealthy landowners and from merchants who had grown rich through trade.

4. **Entrepreneurs.** Britain was home to energetic and daring entrepreneurs (ahn-truh-pruh-NURZ)—people who organized and managed businesses. The opportunity to make great profits spurred these entrepreneurs to build factories, work out efficient ways of producing goods, and search for new markets.

5. **Transportation.** As an island nation, Britain had many fine harbors as well as an extensive canal system. It was much cheaper to transport heavy goods by water than by land. The nation's large fleet of merchant ships made it easy to carry raw materials to factories and goods to markets. Britain also had a strong navy that could protect its merchant fleet.

6. **Markets.** Britain and its colonies overseas provided a good market for the sale of manufactured goods. As businesses expanded and new jobs were created, more people had money to spend on factory-made products.

7. **Government support.** The British government did much to boost the entrepreneurial spirit. It passed laws that protected businesses and helped them to expand.

The Agricultural Revolution

New farming methods. A revolution in agriculture had paved the way for the Industrial Revolution. New farming methods **491**

★ RETEACHING. Have students list the seven conditions that made the Industrial Revolution possible in England. Then have students write one sentence for each condition, explaining how it helped to create the necessary environment for the Industrial Revolution. *(Comprehension)* **Observing for Detail**

★ REINFORCEMENT. Have students describe the causes of each condition that made Britain ready for industrial growth. *(Comprehension)* **Understanding Cause and Effect**

★ ENRICHMENT. Have students write an essay explaining how the Age of Exploration (pp. 347–348) and the Commercial Revolution (pp. 367–372) might have helped to create the conditions that led to the Industrial Revolution in Great Britain. *(Synthesis)* **Understanding Cause and Effect** resulted in better harvests, and Britain found it easier to feed its growing population. Money that had once been used to import supplies of food could instead flow into British industries.

The agricultural revolution began about 1701, when Jethro Tull invented a mechanical drill for planting. The drill made straight rows of holes in the soil and dropped seeds into them. This was a great improvement over the old method of scattering seeds by hand. Tull also invented a horse-drawn hoe, which broke up and loosened the soil so that plants could grow better.

In the early 1700's Charles Townshend experimented with mixing lime and clay into the soil. This practice helped keep the soil fertile. Townshend also taught farmers to grow turnips, which could be stored to feed livestock during the winter. Before this time, farmers slaughtered much of their livestock in the fall, because there was not enough food to keep the animals alive through the winter.

The enclosure movement. The new farming methods spread slowly at first. Most small farmers had neither the money nor the desire to experiment with them. As time went on, however, wealthy landowners tried the new methods and had great success. They began buying out small farmers, who found it hard to compete. The landowners also began enclosing, or fencing in, public lands that villagers had once shared with each other. After 1760, Parliament encouraged the enclosure movement, as it was called.

As estates grew larger, farm production soared. Poor villagers, however, who had depended upon village lands for raising crops and livestock, lost their means of making a living. Forced out of their cottages, they became beggars or farm hands. Many flocked to the growing cities in search of work.

Revolution in the Textile Industry

● Note strategies for second objective on this page and p. 494.

New inventions. Textile-making was the first British industry to be drastically changed by the Industrial Revolution. Until **492** the 1700's, merchants bought wool or cotton

Factories sprang up all over the English countryside in the industrial age. This illustration of the ironworks at Coalbrookdale, England, is from 1805.

for workers to spin into yarn or thread and then weave into cloth. Since the workers did their work in their homes, this method of production was called the **domestic system**, or cottage industry.

In the eighteenth century a number of inventions helped workers make textiles faster. In 1733 John Kay invented a flying shuttle that speeded up the weaving of cloth. James Hargreaves's spinning jenny, perfected in the 1760's, made it possible for spinners to turn out thread more quickly.

Both the flying shuttle and the spinning jenny had to be run by hand. Soon, however, inventors found ways to use water power to run textile machines. Richard Arkwright's water frame, invented in 1769, used water power to run a spinning machine. In 1785 Edmund Cartwright invented a loom that was run by water power.

Sec. Rev. ques. 3

The new textile machines could turn out such quantities of thread and cloth that manufacturers now needed more raw materials than ever. Cotton fiber was most in demand. In 1793 an American named Eli Whitney found a way to help. He invented a device called the cotton gin, which mechanically tore the fibers from the seeds. Cotton production shot up and by 1820 cotton cloth accounted for almost half of Britain's exports.

The factory system. The new machines not only speeded up the output of thread and cloth but also changed the basic system of production. The machines were too expensive to be owned by individual workers and too large to be set up in farmhouses and cottages. Also, they had to be run by water power.

For these reasons, the factory system developed. Factories were built near rivers that could supply water power to run the machines. Large numbers of workers were brought together under one roof. Managers began to use division of labor, having workers perform only one task in making a product. All these changes allowed the factory system to produce goods more quickly, efficiently, and cheaply than was possible using the domestic system.

New Iron-Making Processes

As more machines were used in factories, more iron was needed to build them. In the early 1700's, however, the British iron-making industry faced serious problems. The iron ore mined in Britain had impurities that spoiled the quality of the finished product. The iron was brittle and thus hard to shape.

New methods of production soon revolutionized the iron industry. A breakthrough came in the 1780's when Henry Cort patented a puddling furnace. Iron was reheated in the furnace until the impurities were burned away. The iron was then passed through rollers to form sheets. Cort's process produced iron of better quality and was 15 times faster than the old system.

In the 1850's industry made another leap forward. Working independently, both William Kelly, an American inventor, and Sir Henry Bessemer, an English engineer, discovered what came to be called the **Bessemer process.** This was a quick and cheap method of making steel from iron. Because steel is more durable than iron, it was soon used in most heavy equipment.

The Miraculous Steam Engine

James Watt's improvement. As the Industrial Revolution gained speed, inventors looked for new sources of power. In 1769 James Watt, a Scottish engineer, developed a practical steam engine that burned coal. Steam had been used as a source of power since the early 1700's, but Watt's engine was the first to use steam efficiently.

In time, all industries came to depend on steam engines. Steam power replaced water power in coal mines, ironworks, and textile plants. Watt's engine was one of the most important technological breakthroughs of the Industrial Revolution.

Effect on the transportation industry. In the early 1800's inventors raced to find a way of using steam power for land transportation. George Stephenson, an English engineer, was the first to develop a practical locomotive. In 1830 Stephenson's *Rocket* sped over a railway line connecting the English cities of Manchester and Liverpool. The *Rocket* zoomed along at 16 miles per hour—an astonishing speed for the times.

Stephenson's success triggered an age of railway-building all over the world. Railways

493

Daily Life

Working by the Clock

Before the Industrial Revolution, most workers determined their own workday. Cottage workers, for example, began and ended their day's work, or stopped for a meal, whenever they pleased. After the Industrial Revolution, however, the working day was ruled by the clock.

For industrial workers, the day began when the factory whistle blew. Everyone had to be there at the same time to keep the system running smoothly. All day, people worked at a grueling pace, the pace set by the ma-

chines. Cottage workers might take breaks when they wanted, slow down, or speed up as fast as they wished. Factory workers could not stop until the clock said it was noon and the dinner whistle blew. After a brief meal, they went back to work until the closing whistle.

Not surprisingly, most cottage workers hated the new factory system. Its work schedules were like the ones in English prisons. Indeed, the earliest factory workers came from local poorhouses; many were orphaned children or homeless adults. They were forced to work in factories or lose their food and shelter. As the factory system spread, however, more and more workers had to adjust to life by the clock.

Sec. Rev. ques. 3, cont.

494

provided a fast, cheap means of carrying raw materials to factories and shipping manufactured goods to market. As transportation costs fell, manufacturers were able to lower the prices of their goods. This allowed more people to buy them.

Discoveries in Electricity

Technology in the nineteenth century moved from triumph to triumph. Many advances came from the findings of scientists working

● See below.

F **FEATURE ACTIVITY.** Have students write an essay expressing the viewpoints of cottage workers who gave up their work at home and took factory jobs. Essays should describe how daily life for the workers changed when their working day was determined by the clock. *(Application)* **Understanding Point of View**

● **ENRICHMENT.** Have students choose one invention or innovation of the industrial age and trace its development into modern times. Students should research the changes that have occurred in agricultural tools, sources of power, railroads, the factory system, or steel production. *(Synthesis)* **Linking Past and Present** in research laboratories. One area of widespread scientific interest was the mysterious force called electricity.

About 1800 Alessandro Volta, an Italian professor of physics, invented the first electric battery. This enabled scientists to make electricity and study it in laboratories. In 1831 Michael Faraday, an English physicist and chemist, produced electricity by moving a magnet through a coil of copper wire. Faraday's discovery led to the invention of the electric generator, which produced a current that could run machines. The generator allowed factories to use electricity as a source of power.

Effects of Industrialization

▲ Note strategies for third objective on this page and p. 497.

In the early years of the Industrial Revolution, Great Britain had tried to keep other countries from learning about its new technology. This effort failed. The Industrial Revolution soon spread throughout the West.

Advances in technology, combined with a boom in the production of coal and iron ore, spurred industrial growth in the United States and Germany. In both countries a rapid rise in population meant that the work force was growing all the time. Expanding industries found plenty of workers to take new jobs. By the late 1800's the United States and Germany had joined Great Britain as the world's industrial leaders.

The Industrial Revolution transformed Western society forever. It created new job opportunities for more and more people. It also helped raise the standard of living—a general measure of quality of life. In the early years, however, rapid industrialization caused severe problems. These were most serious for workers in the new factories and for the growing numbers of poor city dwellers.

Hardships for factory workers. The factory system produced goods efficiently, but workers led hard lives. Wages were generally low, and employment was never secure. During business slumps, employers lowered wages and laid off workers. Sick workers received no pay and were often fired.

Sec. Rev. ques. 4

Elderly workers faced cuts in pay and loss of jobs. Women earned less than men, and children had the lowest wages of all.

Many parents, needing every bit of income possible, had no choice but to put their children to work. No laws restricted child labor and factories hired children as young as six. Children also toiled in mines, crawling through narrow tunnels to haul heavy loads of coal. Some supervisors beat child workers to keep them awake and alert.

Because many factory owners did not consider safety an important concern, accidents were common. Workers sometimes lost fingers or suffered other injuries because of unsafe machines. Poor lighting, dirt, high noise levels, and smoke and fumes caused other health risks.

Factory work was often dull and repetitive. Workers might perform the same task over and over, up to 14 hours a day. The clock, the machine, and the production schedule ruled life on the job. If workers failed to keep up, they were fined or fired.

Grim life in cities. The Industrial Revolution led to rapid urbanization—growth of cities. Farm families that could no longer make a living in the countryside moved to the city to find jobs. Others left rural areas in search of higher pay and the excitement of city life. Between 1801 and 1851, for example, the population of the English city of Birmingham grew from 73,000 to 250,000. Liverpool, England, soared from 77,000 to 400,000.

Nineteenth-century cities were not prepared for such a population explosion. Housing, sanitation, and hospital facilities could not keep pace with the growing numbers of people. The crime rate was high, police forces were small, and there was little fire protection. The poor lived in crowded, ramshackle houses. Sometimes a whole family huddled together in one room or even shared a room with another family. Many people had no homes and lived in the streets. Open sewers, polluted rivers, factory smoke, and filthy streets allowed disease to spread. In Britain, about 26 out of every 100 children died before the age of five.

Sec. Rev. ques. 5

495

▲ RETEACHING. Have students review "Hardships for factory workers" and "Grim life in cities" (pp. 495–497) and outline the difficulties faced by workers in the early factories. Then have students explain how rapid urbanization created problems for those who lived in cities. (Comprehension) Observing for Detail

▲ REINFORCEMENT. Have students develop a hypothesis explaining why industrialization and urbanization affected social values. Students might explain how values based on a rural lifestyle might differ from values influenced by urban life and factory work. (Synthesis) Making Judgments

Check for Understanding. Ask: What factors caused rapid urbanization? (Farm families unable to make a living moved to cities for jobs. Others left rural areas in search of higher pay and exciting city life.)

The Geography Connection

Effects of Industrialization in Britain

Britain's richest coal fields are in the central and northern regions of the country. This geographic fact led to a major shift in Britain's centers of population between 1750 and 1850.

Before the 1700's, people used coal mainly as fuel for open fireplaces and forges. When the steam engine was invented, coal was found to be an efficient fuel for producing steam. Coal soon became the energy resource on which industrialization depended.

Many new industries and factories moved from the population centers in the south of Britain to be near the sources of coal. Soon coal-fired steam engines powered the iron foundries, textile factories, and railroads of northern Britain.

Industrialization required a large labor force. Britain had many unemployed workers as a result of the enclosure movement and the increased use of machinery in the textile industry. The masses of unemployed people moved north and west to find work in the coal fields and in the factories. One result of their migration is illustrated by the population maps below. As you can see, the areas of greatest population density—number of people per square mile—shifted dramatically. By 1850, northern Britain had become the most densely populated region outside of London. It had also become the world hub of the Industrial Revolution.

Making the connection. How did the location of a natural resource change the lives of people in Britain between 1750 and 1850?

Population Density in Britain

 GEOGRAPHY CONNECTION. Have students work in groups to list
the possible effects of the following on Britain's physical environment: increase in use of coal, increased industrialization, expansion of railroads, and shifts in population centers. *(Comprehension)*
Drawing Inferences

The writer Charles Dickens painted a dreary picture of a typical English city in his novel *Hard Times* (1854). He wrote:

66 It was a town of machinery and tall chimneys, out of which [endless] serpents of smoke trailed themselves for ever and ever, and never got uncoiled. It had a black canal in it, and a river that ran purple with ill-smelling dye, and vast piles of buildings full of windows where there was a rattling and trembling all day long. 99

Changing values. In preindustrial England, most people had lived in small villages and farmed the land worked by their families for years. Relatives, friends, and the village church gave them a sense of belonging. This feeling began to disappear as people left their hometowns to move to cities.

The factory system, with its long hours and irregular work schedules, weakened family life. Children and parents often worked in different parts of a factory and on different shifts. Parents thus found it hard to supervise their children. Runaways and abandoned youngsters wandered the streets of every city in Britain. Church attendance dropped in urban areas. To escape from their dreary lives, many men and women turned to alcohol.

The status of older people also changed. In rural areas, older people had much to offer the community. They taught young people about nature and farming; they showed them how to build and repair. In the industrial cities, older people lost some of the authority and respect they had enjoyed. Their experience simply did not apply to city life.

▲ See below.

Benefits of industrialization. While the Industrial Revolution disrupted the lives of many people, it also created new opportunities. Factory-made goods were plentiful and priced within the reach of most people. The growing cities offered many chances for advancement, and workers who acquired special skills and education had hopes of entering the growing middle class. You will read more in Chapter 27 about the benefits industrialization brought to society.

Sec. Rev. ques. 6

See Sec. 1 *Closing the Lesson*, p. T489B.

▲ ENRICHMENT. Have students write a letter that a woman who moved with her family from a rural community to a nearby city might have written to a friend back home. The letter should describe the family's new home, their jobs in a local textile factory, and the difference between urban and rural life. Have students read their letters in class. *(Application)* **Understanding Point of View**

This illustration of a slum neighborhood in London by French artist Gustave Doré shows the poverty, overcrowding, and depression that characterized the lives of the urban poor.

Section Review

Answers to Section Review questions are in brackets on pages indicated.

1. **Define or identify:** Industrial Revolution, entrepreneur, enclosure movement, domestic system, factory system, Bessemer process, standard of living, urbanization. (pp. 491, 492, 493, 495)
2. What conditions paved the way for industrialization in Britain? (p. 491)
3. What important inventions and new methods of production revolutionized industry? (pp. 492–495)
4. What hardships did factory workers face during the Industrial Revolution? (p. 495)
5. How did city life change? (p. 495)
6. What benefits did industrialization bring? (p. 497)
7. **Critical thinking:** Why can the period of industrialization that took place in the late 1700's and 1800's be called a "revolution"? (See answer below.)

497

7. Students might emphasize the transformation of society resulting from new production methods and the impact on people's lives.

See lesson plans, pp. T489A–T489C.

2 New Economic Theories

Objectives

Focus Questions

★ ■ What new economic theories arose after the Industrial Revolution?
    (pages 498–501)

● ■ How did socialists propose to deal with changes in society? *(pages 499–501)*

Terms to Know

laissez faire   proletariat
utopia   *Communist*
communism   *Manifesto*

★ Note strategies for first objective on this page.

Nineteenth-century thinkers spent a great deal of time analyzing the Industrial Revolution and looking for ways to correct the problems it created. Their solutions were based on theories that tried to explain the roles of workers, business owners, and government in an industrialized society.

The Economics of Industrialization

The principle of laissez faire. Some thinkers believed that government should not interfere with business. They based their views on the theory of **laissez faire** (LES-ay fayr), French words meaning "leave [business] alone." This idea was first stated by a Scottish philosopher and economist, Adam Smith.

Smith felt that society would run best under a free-enterprise system (page 371). In his book, *The Wealth of Nations* (1776), Smith set forth the principles of a laissez-faire economy. (1) Entrepreneurs should be free to run their businesses in the way that will bring

Sec. Rev. ques. 2

498

them the most profit. (2) What is good for the entrepreneur is good for everyone. More profit leads to business expansion, which creates more jobs and more goods. (3) Free competition gives people the chance to do the jobs they do best. (4) Government should not meddle in business. Its only duty is to keep peace and order.

Effects of population growth. A new theory about population supported the idea of laissez faire. In *An Essay on the Principle of Population* (1798), the English minister and economist Thomas Malthus declared that population always grows faster than the food supply. As a result, he said, humanity is never far from starvation.

Another effect of population growth, continued Malthus, is that the supply of workers becomes greater than the demand. This results, he said, in unemployment, low wages, and unending poverty. Malthus argued against government aid to the poor, saying that such help would only encourage larger families and increase population. Malthus concluded that lowering the birth rate was the only effective way of fighting poverty.

Sec. Rev. ques. 3

An English economist, David Ricardo, painted as gloomy a picture as Malthus. In a book published in 1817, Ricardo put forward his idea about the "iron law of wages." This theory said that workers will never earn much more than the minimum they need to survive. Ricardo's reasoning was that population growth, which constantly increases the work force, will always keep wages low.

Role of government. Some thinkers found the idea of laissez faire unacceptable. It seemed to them that the problems created by the Industrial Revolution could be solved only with the help of government. Early in the 1800's, these thinkers urged the passage of laws that would improve working conditions. They also wanted to expand voting rights and give greater educational opportunities to the poor.

★ RETEACHING. Have students review "The Economics of Industrialization" (above) and summarize the ideas of Smith, Malthus, and Ricardo. *(Comprehension) Observing for Detail*

★ REINFORCEMENT. Have students identify the source of the following ideas: (a) What is good for the entrepreneur is good for everyone. (Smith) (b) Population growth is always faster than the food supply. (Malthus) (c) Population growth keeps wages low. (Ricardo) *(Comprehension) Observing for Detail*

Check for Understanding. Ask: On what aspect of society did Malthus and Ricardo base their predictions about poverty? (Population growth.)

★ ENRICHMENT. Have students work in groups to debate the economic ideas of Smith, Malthus, and Ricardo. Students might find more information on these theories and cite events since the late eighteenth century to argue for or against the economists' views. *(Synthesis) Making Judgments*

Vocabulary Note that the word *phalansteries* is a combination of the two words *phalanx* and *monastery*.

Socialist Ideas

● Note strategies for second objective on this page and p. 501.

Many thinkers were disturbed by the fact that a few people had become very rich from industrialization, while most had remained poor. Some reformers thought that wealth should be more equally distributed. Under the capitalist system, the chief means of production, such as factories, mines, and railroads, were privately owned. Reformers favored socialism (page 480) as a way to lessen the gap between rich and poor. Under socialism, the means of production would be publicly owned and operated for the good of all the people.

Cooperative communities. Some socialists dreamed of creating a utopia—an ideal society. This could be done, they believed, if communities were owned by the people who lived and worked there.

One of the leading utopian socialists was Charles Fourier (foo-ree-AY), a French thinker. Fourier wanted to set up small communities where people would enjoy their work and have pleasant living conditions. Fourier called his communities phalansteries (FAL-un-stayr-eez). Each one was to have about 1,600 people. All members would do the job they were best suited for and would share in everything that was produced.

Fourier's ideas were popular for a few years. A number of communities based on his ideas were started, in Europe and in the United States, but all eventually failed.

A model town. Another utopian socialist who put his ideas into practice was Robert Owen. Born in poverty, Owen was managing a cotton mill in Manchester, England, by the age of 19. In 1799 he became manager and part owner of the New Lanark mills in Scotland.

Concerned about the poverty of the workers, Owen tried to turn New Lanark into a model community. He raised wages, improved working conditions, and reduced hours of work. Schools were set up for children. Owen made sure his workers lived in comfortable housing and he sold them food and clothing at fair prices. By 1815 his model town was drawing thousands of visitors from around the world.

Owen later urged the formation of socialist communities where profits would be shared by all and members would cooperate with one another for the good of the community. Coming to the United States in 1825, he set up such a community at New Harmony, Indiana. The residents of New Harmony could not live together without arguing, however, and some people even refused to work. The experiment ended in failure.

Sec. Rev. ques. 4

Pioneer socialist Robert Owen's model community at the New Lanark textile mills included dormitories and schools for mill workers.

499

● RETEACHING. Have students review "Socialist Ideas" (above) and make a chart listing the *Problems* of industrialization and their *Solutions* as defined by socialist theory. *(Comprehension) Translating Information into Another Form*

● REINFORCEMENT. Have students draw a diagram illustrating the sequence of historical events leading to the "classless society" predicted by Marx. *(Comprehension) Sequencing Information*

Social History Robert Owen suggested that each socialist community should include about 1,200 people living on 1,000 to 1,500 acres of land. Everyone would live in one large building with a public kitchen and eating hall, but each family would have its own private apartment. Children were to be raised by their parents until the age of three, after which the community would assume responsibility for them.

Cultural History Note that the town of New Harmony, Indiana, was declared a national historic landmark in 1965.

Karl Marx predicted that the negative effects of industrialization would cause the working class to revolt. His theories became the basis for modern communism. He is shown at his home in London with his wife, Jenny.

The Theories of Karl Marx

The most influential socialist thinker was Karl Marx (1818–1883). Marx worked as a newspaper editor in Prussia until government authorities, angry about his writings, forced him out of the country. He then settled in England. Marx did not believe that the problems of industrialization could be solved by simply reforming capitalist society. Those who wanted to set up utopian communities were, he said, misguided dreamers.

Marx insisted that capitalism had to be replaced by a different economic and social system. In his writings with his friend Friedrich Engels, Marx called this new system **communism**. He described communism as a form of complete socialism, in which all property and the means of production would be owned by the people. All goods and services would be shared equally.

Marx claimed that his theories were based on a scientific analysis of history. He said that history follows scientific law just as nature does. To understand the inner meaning of history, said Marx, one must realize that people's first concern has always been to obtain food and possessions. Therefore, he said, it is economic forces—such as the way goods are produced and distributed—that shape history.

The "class struggle." All through history, said Marx, there have been two classes in society—the "haves" and the "have nots." The "haves" control the production of goods and own most of the wealth. The "have nots" do the labor but get no rewards for it.

Marx claimed that the exploitation of the "have nots" by the "haves" has always caused a class struggle. In ancient Greece and Rome, the struggle was between master and slave; in medieval Europe, it was between lord and serf. In modern industrial society, said Marx, economic power is held by the bourgeoisie—the middle-class capitalists who own the factories, mines, banks, and businesses. According to Marx, these capitalists dominate and exploit the **proletariat** (proh-luh-TAYR-ee-ut)—the wage-earning laborers.

Marx's ideas about government were based on his economic thought. He claimed that the class that holds economic power also controls the government for its own advantage. For example, Marx said that in a capitalist society the lawmakers pass laws to help capitalists increase their profits. Similarly, the police protect the property of capitalists.

A working-class revolution. According to Marx, owners and managers in a capitalist system do not care about workers as human beings. While the capitalists reap large profits, said Marx, workers slave away in factories under miserable conditions and for low wages. Once workers are no longer needed, Marx said, they are fired, regardless of the hardship that unemployment brings.

The heart of Marx's doctrine was the belief that the capitalist system would disappear. Marx declared that shopkeepers and the owners of small businesses would be ruined by competition with powerful capitalists. They would be forced to become ordinary workers, and in this way the ranks of the working class would steadily grow larger. Soon, he said, there would be only a few rich people and the proletarian masses.

Sec. Rev. ques. 5

Biography Karl Marx earned a doctorate in philosophy in 1841. The Prussian government would not allow him a university position because he was Jewish, and Marx became a journalist. After his articles on economic issues caused the government to close the paper that employed him, Marx moved to Paris. There he ran into trouble for political activity and was expelled. After a period of time in Belgium, Marx moved to London with his wife and children.

Check for Understanding. Ask: What did Marx identify as the most significant forces in history? (Economic forces.)

At this stage, Marx predicted, a great upheaval in society would take place. Made desperate by their poverty, he claimed, the workers would seize control of the government, take over the means of production, and destroy the capitalist system and the ruling class. This would create a "dictatorship of the proletariat"—a society run by the working class. Marx believed violent revolution was necessary. The *Communist Manifesto*, published by Marx and Engels in 1848, sounded the call for a working-class revolution:

66 The Communists . . . openly declare that their ends can be attained only by the forcible overthrow of all existing social conditions. Let the ruling classes tremble at a communistic revolution. The proletarians have nothing to lose but their chains. They have a world to win. Workers of the world, unite! 99

With the destruction of capitalism, Marx said, the class struggle would end and a "classless society" would emerge. All people would share fairly in the wealth of the new society. With the exploiters gone, Marx declared, there would no longer be a need for a state, and it would eventually "wither away."

The failure of Marx's predictions. Marx gained a good deal of support for his theories. Scholars, however, point out basic flaws in his philosophy of history. Marx looked only at the role of economic forces; yet economics alone cannot explain important historical developments. Political, religious, and psychological forces affect events as well.

Scholars also point out that several of Marx's predictions were wrong. Marx did not foresee the enormous gains workers have made—higher wages, shorter hours, and better working conditions. Nor was he correct in thinking that the middle class would be pushed down into the ranks of the lower class. Instead, most industrialized countries now have a very large middle class.

Marx also argued that governments are run only to keep the "capitalist oppressors" in power. In democratic industrialized nations, however, the state serves workers as well as capitalists. Old-age benefits, help for the unemployed, and minimum-wage laws are examples of state support for workers.

Marx expected the workers of all nations to join forces against "capitalist oppressors." That did not happen. The great wars of the twentieth century have been waged between nations, not classes. Marx also predicted that working-class revolutions would break out in the industrialized nations. These revolutions never occurred. Rather, it was in largely agricultural nations—such as Russia, China, and Cuba—that Communist revolutions took place. In these countries, the Communists failed to create the kind of socialist society that Marx envisioned. Instead of the state withering away in those countries, it became more powerful. ● See below.

See Sec. 2 *Closing the Lesson*, p. T489C.

Section Review

Answers to Section Review questions are in brackets on pages indicated.

1. **Define or identify:** laissez faire, utopia, communism, proletariat, *Communist Manifesto.* (pp. 498, 499, 500, 501)
2. What was Adam Smith's philosophy of laissez faire? (p. 498)
3. What did Thomas Malthus and David Ricardo say about the effects of population growth? (p. 498)
4. What solutions did Charles Fourier and Robert Owen offer to improve the lives of working people? Were their experiments successful? (p. 499)
5. In Marx's view, how would the capitalist system disappear? (pp. 500–501)
6. **Critical thinking:** Compare the views of Adam Smith and Karl Marx on the capitalist system. (See answer below.)

501

Contemporary History Have students research the revolutions that toppled the Soviet-dominated Communist governments in Eastern Europe in 1989–1990 as well as the collapse of the Soviet Union itself in 1991, and consider Marx's forecasts in light of those upheavals.

6. Students might focus on the two theorists' ideas about the consequences of free enterprise.
● ENRICHMENT. Have students research economic conditions in present-day China and North Korea and evaluate the effects of Marxist theory and practice in those countries. (Evaluation) Locating Information

See lesson plans, pp. T489A–T489C.

3 Political, Economic, and Social Reforms

Objectives

Focus Questions

★ ■ How did democracy gradually expand in Britain? *(pages 502–505)*

● ■ What economic and social reforms took place in Britain, the United States, and Europe? *(pages 505–508)*

Terms to Know

Chartist movement
Factory Act
labor union

★ Note strategies for first objective on this page.

Urbanization and industrialization brought sweeping changes to Western nations. People looking for solutions to the problems created by these developments began to demand reforms. They wanted to improve conditions for workers and the poor, and to stop unfair business practices. Many people also began to call for political reforms. They demanded that ordinary people be given a greater voice in government.

Political Reforms in Britain

Government structure. Unlike the United States, Britain has never developed a written constitution. Its system of government grew out of the tradition of common law (page 237) and documents such as the Magna Carta and the Petition of Right (pages 238, 398).

Even today Britain has a monarch. Yet since the late 1600's, Parliament has held the real power. The monarch kept the right to veto, or reject, an act of Parliament, but no king or queen has done so since 1707.

The structure of the British Parliament has remained the same for more than 600 years. Parliament consists of a House of Lords and a House of Commons. Members of the House of Lords either inherit their seats or are appointed. Members of the House of Commons are elected by the British people. For several centuries the House of Lords dominated Parliament, but during the 1700's power shifted to the House of Commons. This shift made it easier for democracy to expand in Great Britain.

The office of prime minister also gained importance during the eighteenth century. Today the prime minister is usually the leader of the political party that holds the most seats in the House of Commons. The prime minister and other high-ranking government officials determine Britain's foreign and domestic policies.

Political parties have played a role in Britain since the late 1600's. The first two parties were the Whigs and the Tories. In the mid-1800's, the Whigs became the Liberal Party and the Tories became the Conservative Party. Both these parties remain active today.

A limited democracy. In the early 1800's political democracy in Britain was still limited. Women could not vote at all, and property requirements kept many men from voting or holding most public offices. Religious restrictions prevented Catholics, Jews, and other non-Anglicans from being elected to the House of Commons.

Representation in the House of Commons was unfair because it did not reflect the population increase in cities. Manchester, for example, had grown to a city of more than 100,000. Yet it had no representatives in the House of Commons.

Removal of religious restrictions. The removal of legal restrictions based on religion was an important step toward political democracy in Britain. In 1829 Parliament passed the Catholic Emancipation Act,

502

★ RETEACHING. Have students review "Political Reforms in Britain" (pp. 502–505) and outline the organization, power, and responsibilities of Britain's government. *(Comprehension) Translating Information into Another Form*

★ REINFORCEMENT. Have students make a time chart of British democratic reforms in the nineteenth century. (Catholic Emancipation Act, 1829; Reform Bills of 1832, 1867, and 1884; Ballot Act of 1872) *(Comprehension) Sequencing Information*

Politics The House of Lords includes approximately 1,150 members, the majority of whom take no active part in the proceedings. The House of Commons has 635 popularly elected members.

★ ENRICHMENT. Have students compare the British parliamentary system with the American congressional system. Students might draw diagrams of the structure of both governments, pointing out the differences and similarities. *(Analysis) Analyzing Information* which opened nearly all government jobs to Catholics. Jews and others still lacked full rights, since government officials, lawyers, and university students were required to swear by "the true faith of a Christian" in order to obtain their positions. Gradually restrictions were lifted so that Jews could hold office, serve on juries, and practice law.

Pressure for democratic reforms. In 1830 Parliament was still dominated by aristocratic landowners. The middle class—industrialists, bankers, merchants—pressed for a greater voice in British political life. The Revolution of 1830 in France (page 475) frightened parliamentary leaders, who feared that revolutionary violence would spread to Britain. Parliament soon passed the Reform Bill of 1832, which gave the new industrial cities more representation in Parliament. A change in property requirements extended voting rights to well-to-do men in the middle class.

Sec. Rev. ques. 2

Many workers, however, were still denied suffrage. The Reform Bill spurred them to organize the Chartist movement, which achieved great popularity. The People's Charter of 1838 demanded voting rights for all men, a secret ballot, an end to property requirements for serving in Parliament, pay for members of Parliament, and annual elections. Although the Chartists failed to win these demands, their protests convinced many people that workers had sound complaints. Eventually all the demands of the Chartists, except for annual elections, became law.

The right to vote. Over the years, workers in industry continued to press for political reform. The Reform Bill of 1867 gave the vote to working-class men, thus doubling the number of voters in Britain. Benjamin Disraeli (diz-RAY-lee), a novelist and politician (and future prime minister), played the leading role in this reform. Some of his fellow Conservative Party members feared that expanded voting rights would ruin Britain. Disraeli, however, claimed that this democratic advance would strengthen the bond between the state and its citizens.

The work of electoral reform was continued by the Liberal Party under the leadership of William Gladstone, who served as prime minister four times between 1868 and 1894. The Liberals sponsored the Ballot Act of 1872, which provided for the secret ballot. Before the passage of this act, employers sometimes threatened to fire workers if they failed to vote a certain way. Another new law, the Reform Bill of 1884, greatly increased the number of voters by giving suffrage to rural workers. Almost all men in Britain now had the right to vote.

The status of women. While working-class men in Britain were gaining more rights, women of all classes faced political and social inequality. Most people believed that a woman's place was in the home. Women should be concerned with their husbands and children, people said, not with politics or business.

Disraeli was a good friend of Queen Victoria, with whom he is pictured here. The social and political reforms he introduced were designed to improve conditions among Britain's farm and factory workers. Disraeli did not favor radical solutions, however, and tried to remain within the boundaries of traditional conservative policies.

503

English suffragists used dramatic and imaginative methods to publicize their cause. This picture shows them campaigning disguised as firemen on a fire truck.

As more men gained the right to vote, however, more women began to demand the same. Women also wanted the right to hold office and the right to inherit, buy, and sell property. In 1867 John Stuart Mill, a philosopher, economist, and member of Parliament, proposed that the vote be extended to women. Parliament rejected the idea, but more than one quarter of the members voted in favor.

As women became more vocal, resistance to their demands grew. Many people, both men and women, thought that women's suffrage was too radical a break with tradition. Some believed that women were already well represented in government because their husbands or male relatives could vote. Others claimed that women lacked the ability to take part effectively in political life. Queen Victoria, though she supported many other reforms, called women's suffrage "that mad, wicked folly."

Organization and protest. Many British women realized that to achieve other rights, they first had to get the vote. They organized reform societies, drew up petitions, and protested unfair laws and customs.

When these protests were ignored, some women took more drastic steps. In 1903 Emmeline Pankhurst organized the Women's Social and Political Union (WSPU). Pankhurst was assisted by her daughters Christabel and Sylvia. The WSPU campaigned against political candidates who opposed women's suffrage. To call attention to their cause, WSPU members disrupted the speeches of politicians, marched on Parliament, bombed buildings, and burned railway stations. One suffragist, Emily Davison, even gave up her life for the women's movement.

Sec. Rev. ques. 3

504

Social History In addition to the WSPU, Emmeline Pankhurst had started the Women's Franchise League in 1889, which secured for married women the right to vote in local elections. The slogan of the Women's Social and Political Union was "Deeds, Not Words."

⌈ She killed herself by running in front of the
⌊ king's racehorse at the Royal Derby.

Many citizens were outraged by these tactics. The police reacted with harshness. Protestors were arrested and given jail sentences. When some women went on hunger strikes, the authorities tied the women down and force-fed them through tubes placed down their throats. This measure was taken to make sure that the women did not die from starvation. The authorities did not want to give a martyr to the women's movement. Although these setbacks were crushing to women reformers, Parliament was beginning to take notice.

Economic and Social Reforms in Britain

● Note strategies for second objective on this page and p. 506.

Factory-reform laws. Faced with the problems of the Industrial Revolution, British reformers began to campaign for change. One of their first concerns was the plight of children who worked in mines and factories. They held meetings, wrote pamphlets, and drew up petitions calling for laws to limit child labor.

As a result of this pressure, Parliament passed the **Factory Act** in 1833. It forbade the employment of children under the age of nine. Children aged nine to thirteen could not work more than eight hours a day, and young people aged thirteen to eighteen could not work more than twelve hours a day.

Children were still subject to dangerous and unhealthy conditions. However, the Factory Act was an important law. It established the idea that the state could act to protect workers. Later laws further reduced the hours children and young people could work and also regulated hours for women. By the early 1900's the ten-hour day was established in England for all workers who were over the age of fourteen.

Improvements in education. British leaders and reformers also began to understand the value of education. They believed that education would help do away with poverty, crime, and superstitious beliefs. Starting

in 1833, Parliament began to vote small sums of money for elementary education. The Education Act of 1870 gave local governments the power to set up elementary schools. By 1891 these schools were free and attendance was required.

Sec. Rev. ques. 4

Worker responses to industrialization. In the early 1800's many weavers and other skilled handicraft workers were being replaced by machines. Upset about this situation, workers began organizing groups to prevent the loss of more jobs. Factory owners feared one group in particular. This was the Luddites—a gang of masked workers named after their legendary leader, Ned Ludd.

The Luddites showed their anger by attacking textile factories and smashing to bits the machines they blamed for putting them out of work. One writer noted how terrifying the group had become: "The dread name Ludd was . . . mentioned with fear and apprehension at the dinner tables of the rich. Men said that to disobey an order given on its authority was to risk immediate death."

The beginning of labor unions. Despite the actions of the Luddites, workers continued to find themselves replaced by machines in many industries. The loss of jobs meant poverty for them and their families. Because an individual worker could not stand up to a large company, workers in some crafts came together to form **labor unions**—organizations designed to represent workers' interests. To spur change, union members sometimes called strikes, refusing to work until management agreed to raise wages and improve conditions.

Linking Past and Present

Today most industrialized nations of the world strictly regulate child labor. For example, United States federal law sets minimum age requirements for certain kinds of jobs. It prohibits the employment of anyone under the age of 16 during school hours. No one under 18 can work at a hazardous job.

505

● RETEACHING. Have students review "Economic and Social Reforms in Britain" (pp. 505–506) and summarize advances in child labor laws, health, and workers' rights. (Factory Act of 1833 established minimum working age and restricted hours for children, Education Act of 1870 gave local governments power to start schools, various laws established legality of labor unions.) *(Comprehension) Observing for Detail*

● REINFORCEMENT. Have students work in groups to prepare a dialogue that might have occurred in 1900 between representatives of an American labor union and big business. Students should explain the conflict between the groups and suggest a solution. *(Synthesis) Understanding Point of View*

Parliament opposed the early unions. In 1799 and 1800 it had passed the Combination Acts, which banned unions. In spite of these laws, workers kept right on organizing. Parliament repealed the Combination Acts in 1824, and trade unions became legal in Britain. An outbreak of strikes frightened the government, however. In 1825 Parliament passed a law that allowed workers to form unions but not to strike. Not until 1871 were restrictions on trade unions removed, allowing workers to organize and strike.

Unions and politics. As the British trade union movement grew stronger, unions became involved in politics. In 1900, representatives of the various trade unions voted to start a political party that would represent workers' interests. In 1906, twenty-nine members of the new Labour Party were elected to Parliament.

Another party, the Liberal Party, won control of Parliament in the 1906 elections. Yet it saw a clear message in the Labour victories: unless the poor were helped, more and more workers would support the Labour Party. To keep this from happening, Parliament passed a number of reform laws between 1906 and 1914.

These laws set up new social services for British citizens. Meals were provided for needy schoolchildren, and medical clinics were started in the schools. Parents who neglected their children's health could be punished. The government gave pensions, or regular payments, to people over 70.

Sec. Rev. ques. 4, cont.

Other British laws protected workers and required factory owners to make working conditions safer. Employees won the right to payment for injuries received on the job. Employment centers were set up to help workers find jobs. The National Insurance Act of 1911 provided unemployment insurance and free medical treatment for workers.

Reforms in the United States

Sec. Rev. ques. 5

The formation of labor unions. In the United States, as in Britain, industrialization and urbanization caused serious problems.

Labor union movements began to develop at the same time as American businesses were growing larger.

The most successful of the early unions was the American Federation of Labor (AFL), started in 1881. The AFL organized skilled workers according to their craft or trade. For example, plumbers, electricians, and carpenters each had their own union. Under the leadership of Samuel Gompers, AFL membership grew to about one and a half million by 1904.

Unions tried to help workers gain higher wages and better working conditions. When management failed to meet workers' demands, union leaders sometimes called strikes. At times strikes led to violence, and government troops were often called in to keep order.

● See below, left.

Expansion of big business. Businesses grew rapidly in the United States in the late 1800's. American capitalists were firm believers in the laissez-faire principle (page 498). They did not want the government setting limits on the prices at which businesses sold goods, on the wages they paid workers, or on the profits they made. Prices, wages, and profits, they said, should be determined by the free market.

Some business organizations grew extremely powerful. Business leaders formed monopolies, bringing most of the companies in one industry under the control of a single management. By 1898, for example, Standard Oil refined more than 80 percent of all the oil produced in the United States.

Several other industries, including sugar refining, were under the control of monopolies. Many smaller firms could not compete. They were at the mercy of the monopolies, which could push up prices or lower them at will. Americans began to fear that these huge companies would destroy competition.

Reform efforts. In the United States, just as in Britain, reformers tried to find remedies for the problems caused by industrialization and urbanization. Among those calling for reforms were several writers who became known as "muckrakers." They investigated conditions in slums and factories, and

● ENRICHMENT. Have students find information on present-day labor unions in the United States. Students might research the types of labor unions, their internal organization, and how they exert political influence or work for social reform. (Application) *Locating Information*

Social History Note that the American Federation of Labor did not enroll individual members. A worker could join the union only by being a member of a craft union affiliated with the AFL.

Social History The name "muckraker" was first applied to reformers by Theodore Roosevelt in 1906. He compared them to "the man with the muck-rake," a character in John Bunyan's *Pilgrim's Progress* who was so intent on raking muck that he didn't notice a heavenly halo placed over his head.

Biography Ida Tarbell had a personal interest in the oil industry, since her father had been forced out of business by more powerful oil interests.

Biography Jane Addams was co-winner of the Nobel Peace Prize in 1931.

their books and articles revealed the unfair practices of some business leaders.

Ida Tarbell wrote about the oil industry, while Ray Stannard Baker took on the railroads. Lincoln Steffens exposed corruption in city politics. The most famous of the muckrakers, novelist Upton Sinclair, vividly described unsanitary and dangerous conditions in the meat-packing industry in his book *The Jungle* (1906).

Other people dedicated their lives to helping the poor, particularly immigrants. The reformers called for better housing and improved health care. Jacob Riis (REES), a Danish-born reporter in New York City, wrote articles describing slum conditions. In Chicago, Jane Addams founded Hull House in 1889. At this settlement house, immigrants

could learn English and get advice on health problems. Addams also worked for other social reforms, including voting rights for women, payments for injured workers, and laws regulating working hours for women.

Through the efforts of such people, many reforms were made in the United States during the early 1900's. City governments passed laws regulating housing conditions. Public parks, beaches, and playgrounds were set up. State governments prohibited child labor and limited the number of hours that women could work each week (generally no more than 60). Laws said that workers who were hurt on the job had the right to payment from their employers while recovering from their injuries.

During the same period, the federal government began to regulate big business. It broke up some monopolies and took legal action against companies that used unfair business practices. The government also supervised railroads to keep them from charging unfair rates.

Women and the reform movement. As in Britain, women in America began to press for changes in society during the mid-1800's. Some reformers, such as Carry Nation, wanted to prohibit the drinking of alcohol. Some called for better treatment of

Photographs such as this one, which appeared in a New York City newspaper, helped publicize the harsh life of child laborers.

507

Social History Note that Jacob Riis made use of the newly invented flashbulb to photograph the inside of tenement buildings. His stark photographs helped dramatize his writings.
Social History Hull House, named after the previous owner of the building, eventually became a settlement that included 13 buildings, a playground, and a camp near Lake Geneva, Wisconsin.

Social History Carry Nation was famous for the way she marched into saloons, singing and shouting and smashing bar fixtures with a hatchet. Her supporters sold souvenir hatchets, sometimes earning as much as $300 a week.

This painting shows miners on strike in France in 1911. By refusing to work, strikers forced some employers to recognize unions and were also able to negotiate for better wages and working conditions.

prisoners, orphans, the blind, and the mentally ill. Other women demanded the abolition of slavery.

Many also fought for the right to vote. In 1869 Susan B. Anthony, a powerful organizer, helped form the National American Woman Suffrage Association. During the 1890's four western states—Wyoming, Colorado, Utah, and Idaho—became the first states to extend the vote to women.

Changes on the European Continent

Labor reform. A large urban working class with special problems also developed on the European continent. As in Britain and the United States, workers organized labor unions to secure higher wages, shorter hours, and better working conditions. Most European trade unions were concerned mainly with gaining economic benefits and did not **508** become active in politics.

Some European labor leaders and reformers wanted sweeping changes. Among them were the socialists, who believed that the government should take over the banks, railroads, factories, and natural resources. They argued that this was the only way workers could share in the benefits of industrialization. Socialists organized political parties that tried to gain working-class support. Some of these parties favored peaceful reform through gradual changes in the law. Others claimed, as Karl Marx had, that only revolution would bring the changes they desired.

In response to the demands of workers, some European governments made social reforms. By 1914 Germany had taken the lead in passing social legislation. The German chancellor, Otto von Bismarck (page 517), provided workers with sickness and accident insurance and old-age benefits. New laws improved working conditions and eliminated child labor in mines and factories. In time, other European countries followed Germany's example.

See Sec. 3 *Closing the Lesson*, p. T489C.

Answers to Section Review questions are in brackets on pages indicated.

1. **Define or identify:** Chartist movement, Factory Act, labor union. (pp. 503, 505)
2. What political reforms had the effect of expanding democracy for men in Britain? (p. 503)
3. What steps did women in Great Britain take in their efforts to win the right to vote? (pp. 504–505)

4. What steps did British cities take to improve public health and education? (pp. 505, 506)
5. Why were labor unions formed in the United States? (p. 506)
6. **Critical thinking:** How were reform movements in the United States similar to those that were taking place in Great Britain? (See answer below.)

Chapter 25   Summary and Timeline

1. The Industrial Revolution, which began in Great Britain about 1750, was the result of rapid changes in agriculture and technology. Machines began to replace human labor, and the factory system replaced the domestic system of producing goods. New sources of energy, such as steam and electricity, also spurred industrialization. Workers flocked to cities to take factory jobs and found that urban conditions were often crowded and unhealthy. Strained by the hectic pace of industrial life, society was no longer as tightly knit as it once had been.

2. In response to the problems caused by the Industrial Revolution, nineteenth-century thinkers proposed changes in society. Some called for a laissez-faire economy, free from government interference. Others urged socialist reforms. Karl Marx predicted a struggle between workers and owners that, he said, would one day destroy capitalism and pave the way for a classless society where all people would share in the wealth.

3. Reformers worked for laws to improve factory conditions, public health, and education. Some workers organized labor unions that also demanded reforms in politics and society. More men gained the right to vote, while women in several countries worked to win political equality.

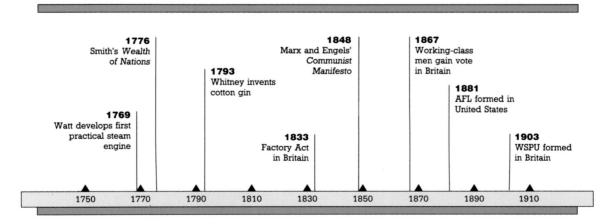

1776
Smith's *Wealth of Nations*

1793
Whitney invents cotton gin

1848
Marx and Engels' *Communist Manifesto*

1867
Working-class men gain vote in Britain

1769
Watt develops first practical steam engine

1833
Factory Act in Britain

1881
AFL formed in United States

1903
WSPU formed in Britain

1750   1770   1790   1810   1830   1850   1870   1890   1910

509

6. Students might point out that in both countries, unions spearheaded movements for labor reform, reformers addressed problems associated with industrialization and urbanization, and women's rights activists called for suffrage and social reforms.

See p. T489C for answers to Chapter Review.

Vocabulary Review

1. Use the following terms to complete the sentences below: *Bessemer process, Chartist movement, communism, entrepreneur, standard of living, labor union, utopia.*
   a. A person who organizes and manages a business is called an ___?___.
   b. The ___?___ is a general measure of the quality of life.
   c. The ___?___ pushed for political change in Britain.
   d. A ___?___ is an ideal society.
   e. The ___?___ was a fast, inexpensive method of turning iron into steel.
   f. Marx felt that ___?___, or complete socialism, would eventually replace capitalism.
   g. A ___?___ is an organization designed to represent workers' interests.
2. Define or identify the terms in the following pairs.
   a. domestic system; factory system
   b. *Communist Manifesto;* proletariat

People to Identify

Choose the name that best completes each sentence.
1. [James Watt/George Stephenson] invented the first efficient steam engine.
2. A leader in the women's suffrage movement in the United States was [Emmeline Pankhurst/Susan B. Anthony].
3. [William Gladstone/Benjamin Disraeli] served four terms as prime minister of Britain.
4. A puddling furnace invented by [Carry Nation/Henry Cort] produced high-quality iron.

5. [Friedrich Engels/Jethro Tull] invented a better way to plant seeds.
6. [Samuel Gompers/Jane Addams] established Hull House in 1889.
7. The cotton gin was invented by [Eli Whitney/Upton Sinclair].

Recalling the Facts

1. Why did the Industrial Revolution begin in Britain?
2. What changes in society were brought about by the enclosure movement?
3. How did new sources of power affect industry?
4. What problems did the Industrial Revolution create for British workers?
5. What were the principles of the laissez-faire economy described by Adam Smith?
6. What did Thomas Malthus and David Ricardo say about population growth?
7. How did Robert Owen attempt to make New Lanark a model community?
8. How did Marx think a classless society would be achieved? What flaws have scholars found in Marx's theories?
9. What steps did Parliament take between 1829 and 1884 to expand democracy in Britain?
10. How did the Women's Social and Political Union call attention to its cause?
11. What reforms were made in the United States in the early 1900's?

Critical Thinking Skills

1. **Building vocabulary.** The Industrial Revolution shifted the making of goods from homes to factories. The word *factory* comes

510

from the Latin verb *facere,* meaning "to make, to do." Using a dictionary, find the meanings of these words with the same root: *fact, artifact, facsimile, manufacture.* (App.)

2. **Making a chart.** Make a chart with the following headings: *Inventor, Invention, Significance.* In addition to the inventors mentioned in this chapter, find out how each of the following individuals made contributions to the Industrial Revolution: Samuel Crompton, Alexander Darby, Robert Fulton, John McAdam, Thomas Newcomen, Richard Trevithick. (App.)

✔ 3. **Hypothesizing.** The ideas of Charles Fourier were the basis for the phalansteries that arose in the United States and Europe in the early 1800's. All these communities eventually failed. Develop a hypothesis to explain why they did not succeed. (Syn.)

4. **Supporting a generalization.** Using your textbook, find evidence to support the following statement: "Rapid urbanization in the early 1800's caused serious problems for city dwellers." (Comp.)

5. **Analyzing visual information.** The engraving below, made in 1828, shows British barges loaded with cargo. What do you think the buildings near the water were used for? What transportation system would these barges have used to travel inland? Why was it less expensive in the early 1800's to deliver goods by water routes rather than by overland routes? (Comp.)

✔ A checkmark identifies questions and exercises calling for the three higher-order levels of thinking at the top of the Bloom taxonomy: Analysis, Synthesis, and Evaluation.

Thinking About Geography

Making a map. Use an encyclopedia or other reference books to locate the canals and railroads built in Britain between 1750 and 1850. Then draw a map, using symbols to show the major canals and railroads. Be sure to include a key. (App.)

Enrichment: Primary Sources

The following passage is adapted from testimony given by 17-year-old Patience Kershaw before a British parliamentary committee in 1842. The committee was investigating conditions in the coal mines.

❝ I go to the mine at five o'clock in the morning and come out at five in the evening. I get my breakfast of porridge and milk first. I take my midday meal with me, a cake, and eat it as I go. I get nothing else until I get home, and then have potatoes and meat, but not meat every day. The bald place on my head was made by pushing the corves [baskets used to carry coal to the mouth of a coal mine]. My legs have never swelled, but my sisters' did. I push the corves a mile and more under ground and back, eleven times a day. The men I work for beat me if I am not quick enough. ❞

1. What was Patience Kershaw's job in the mine?
2. In what ways did work in the mines affect Patience Kershaw and her sisters physically?
3. **Critical thinking:** What impression might testimony such as this have made on the British public? What effects might this testimony have had on the passage of child-labor laws? (Syn.)   ✔

511

Nationalism in Europe   1815–1914
(pp. 512–529)

Chapter Preview

Section 1 of this chapter examines the steps that led to the unification of the Italian states in 1870. In Section 2 the growth of Prussian power under Bismarck and the unification of Germany are described. Section 3 explains the impact of nationalism on the Hapsburg Empire in Austria, the Ottoman Empire, and imperial Russia.

Bibliography

See the *Teacher's Management and Planning Guide* for additional listings. Starred titles are for both students and teachers.

Beales, D. *The Risorgimento and the Unification of Italy.* Barnes and Noble. The rise of Italian nationalism surveyed.

Hibbert, Christopher. *Garibaldi and His Enemies.* Little, Brown. Exciting biography shows why Garibaldi became a hero.

*Kohn, Hans. *Nationalism: Its Meaning and History,* revised edition. Krieger. Summary of nationalism's origins and impact.

Pflanze, O. *Bismarck and the Development of Germany.* Princeton University Press. Bismarck's role interpreted.

Section Lesson Plans

SECTION 1   (pp. 513–516)
The Unification of Italy

Objectives

After completing this section, students will be able to:
1. Explain how Sardinia unified northern Italy.
2. Describe how all of Italy came under a single ruler.

Introducing the Lesson

Remind students that in 1848 the forces of nationalism and liberalism resulted in largely unsuccessful movements for independence and reform in Europe. In the late nineteenth century, a desire for unification, fueled by nationalism, led the Italian states to fight foreign domination.

Then ask: *(a) How important is nationalism to the success of independence movements?* (Answers will vary. Some might suggest that nationalist fervor is the most important element because it provides motivation and helps people to endure the struggle. Others might argue that strategic concerns play a larger role.)

(b) What besides nationalism is needed for a successful independence movement? (Answers will vary. Military strength, organization, and leadership are important factors.)

Developing the Lesson: Translating Information into Another Form

Have students work in groups to stage a meeting that might have occurred between Mazzini, Cavour, and Garibaldi. Students might include a discussion of each person's goals, strategies, and how best to use the strengths of each participant. *(Application)*

Developing the Lesson:
Organizing Information in Written Form

Have students refer to the map on p. 516 to make a chart illustrating the division of Italian states among foreign powers. The chart should include each *Italian State* and its *Controlling Power.* (*Hapsburg control:* Lombardy, Venetia, Parma, Modena, Tuscany. *Papal control:* Romagna, Republic of San Marino, Umbria, the Marches, Rome. *Bourbon control:* Kingdom of the Two Sicilies.) *(Comprehension)*

Answers to *Map Skill Practice,* p. 516.

1. Piedmont, Sardinia.
2. Lombardy.
3. Lombardy, Venetia, Parma, Modena, Tuscany.
4. Bourbons.
5. Venetia, Rome.
6. Answers might include: difficulty of organizing a united nationalist movement in areas under different government; difficulty of gathering an army capable of matching Austrian or French troops; effects of alliances that worked for or against unification.

Closing the Lesson:
Sequencing Information

Have students make a time chart of events leading to the unification of the Italian states. Students should include events from 1831 (p. 483) to the unification of Italy in 1870. (*1831*—Mazzini organized Young Italy; *1848*—revolts in Venice and Milan; *1849*—Italians proclaimed the Roman Republic; *mid-1849*—Austrians regained control; *1859*—Austria declared war on Sardinia; *1860*—Red Shirts liberated Sicily and captured Naples; Umbria, the Marches, Naples, and Sicily united with Sardinia; *1861*—Victor Emmanuel proclaimed king of Italy; *1866*—Venetia joined Italy; *1870*—Rome joined kingdom of Italy.) *(Comprehension)*

See *Section Review* questions, p. 516.

SECTION 2   (pp. 517–521)
The Unification of Germany

Objectives

After completing this section, students will be able to:
1. Explain how the German states combined to form an empire.
2. Describe the features of the new German Empire.

Introducing the Lesson

Remind students that nationalism motivated Italians and Germans to strive for the unification of their people under one government. Freedom from foreign control and national unity have continued to serve as powerful influences in more recent times.

Then ask: *(a) When did national unification become an important factor in world history?* (Although many peoples have had national identities for hundreds of years, the concept of a unified, self-governed nation which controls its own territory is a relatively modern one, dating from about the eighteenth century.)

(b) What might account for the importance of national unification? (Answers will vary. In modern times, a nation's security is influenced by its size, its strength, and by the loyalty of its people. A nation can also be an important source of a people's identity.)

Developing the Lesson:
Analyzing a Statement

Have students write an essay analyzing Bismarck's statement quoted on p. 517. Essays should draw conclusions about Bismarck's opinion of democratic governments and the role he assigned to war. Then have students comment on Bismark's choice of words. *(Analysis)*

Developing the Lesson:
Making Judgments

Have students compare Bismarck's mastery of realpolitik with the political techniques recommended by Machiavelli in his book, *The Prince* (p. 329). Students might compare and contrast Machiavelli's approach to politics and Bismarck's use of power. *(Synthesis)*

Closing the Lesson:
Organizing Information in Written Form

Have students make a chart comparing Italy's and Germany's unification efforts. The chart should include important events and their dates, the names of leaders, methods of unification, and the government formed when national unity was achieved. *(Comprehension)*

See *Section Review* questions, p. 521.

SECTION 3   (pp. 522–527)
Decline of the Eastern European Empires

Objectives

After completing this section, students will be able to:
1. Explain why nationalism became a strong force in the Austrian Empire.
2. List the factors that led to the decline of the Ottoman Empire.
3. Discuss why Russia failed to modernize as quickly as Western Europe.

Introducing the Lesson

Remind students that nationalism, liberalism, and democracy were forces of change unleashed in Western Europe in the eighteenth century. Eastern Europe, dominated by three large empires, also faced unrest and the threat of revolt.

Then ask: *(a) What is the difference between an empire and a nation?* (An empire is an expanse of territory, some of which may have been acquired by conquest, in which people with different cultural backgrounds live, and which has a powerful ruler. A nation is a people who share a common heritage and who usually inhabit a self-governing territory.)

(b) What problems faced by nations in Western Europe might have been expected to develop in Eastern Europe? (Answers will vary, but nationalist movements and demand for political reform might have been expected to arise.)

(c) What are some examples of political, economic, or social issues today that have given rise to political movements in many nations? (Answers will vary, but might include human rights concerns; nuclear disarmament; dishonesty in government; elimination of poverty, hunger, and disease; and environmental issues.)

Developing the Lesson:
Organizing Information in Written Form

Have students develop a chart comparing the problems faced by each of the Eastern European empires. (*Austria-Hungary:* weakened by two wars; territorial loss; Magyar independence movement; Serbia's efforts to cause unrest among the South Slavs. *Ottoman Empire:* territorial loss; Russian invasion; nationalist uprisings. *Russia:* economic problems including weak industry and inefficient agriculture; serfdom; political tensions caused by stern rulers; government corruption; poor education.) *(Comprehension)*

Developing the Lesson:
Making Judgments

Have students work in groups to summarize the efforts made by Austrian, Ottoman, and Russian rulers to prevent the decline of their empires. Then have students evaluate which efforts were more likely to have succeeded, which efforts were probably inadequate from the start, and why all these efforts eventually failed. Students should present their summaries and evaluations to the class. *(Synthesis)*

Closing the Lesson:
Understanding Cause and Effect

Have students work in groups to present a panel discussion explaining why and in what ways Russia lagged behind the West in political, economic, and social development. (Answers will vary. The Industrial Revolution made little impact on nineteenth-century Russia until Alexander II's rule, and his reforms ended after eight years; even after the abolition of serfdom, most peasants were not free to leave the land; although the establishment of zemstvos introduced some local self-rule, there is little evidence to suggest any real democratic reform.) *(Comprehension)*

See *Section Review* questions, p. 527.

Chapter 26 Review Answers
(pp. 528–529)

Vocabulary Review

1. Red Shirts 2. Pan-Slavism 3. tariff 4. Franco-Prussian War 5. Risorgimento 6. kaiser 7. realpolitik

People to Identify

1. Austrian emperor who created the Dual Monarchy of Austria-Hungary.
2. Russian czar who suppressed the Decembrist revolt and began Russification of Poland.
3. Sardinian king who became king of Italy on March 17, 1861.
4. Prussian king who became kaiser of the Second Reich.
5. German kaiser who presided over the transformation of Germany into a leading industrial power.

Places to Know

1. Sardinia   2. Balkan   3. Prussia

Recalling the Facts

1. Mazzini used fiery speeches to stir up patriotism; he favored a mass uprising to achieve independence. Cavour was practical and cautious; he built up Sardinia's economy and its army so it could take the lead in driving Austria out of northern Italy.
2. He feared a strong unified Italy.
3. Rome voted to join the kingdom of Italy in 1870.
4. The Zollverein took measures to improve the German economy and industry grew rapidly. Many Germans were pleased with economic unity and began to support political unity as well.
5. He felt that only through war could Germany become unified. Prussia defeated Austria because of superior training and arms, careful planning, and a good railway system.
6. The German kaiser, Prussian generals and aristocrats, and wealthy bankers and industrialists.
7. People began to learn how much better off Western Europeans were. They became aware of liberal, democractic, and nationalist ideals. They also heard about the rebellions in France and other parts of Western Europe.
8. Serbian leaders were seeking to expand by uniting their newly independent nation with the South Slavs in Austria-Hungary. Serbs thus encouraged nationalist movements among the South Slavs, which threatened the empire.
9. Russia sent forces into Ottoman territory, hoping to gain control of the Bosporus and the Dardanelles. Russia was defeated by the Turks with the aid of Britain, France, and Sardinia.
10. He abolished serfdom and undertook a land reform program that included the creation of village collectives. He also permitted local self-government, opened more schools, modernized the court system, reformed the army, and encouraged economic development.
11. He turned Russia into a police state, reinstituted programs of Russification, and persecuted Jews.

Critical Thinking Skills

1. His point of view was that Italy had a great heritage due to its Roman ancestors, the Church of Rome, and its Renaissance artists and writers. Mazzini was probably biased because he was an Italian patriot and nationalist leader who was using these examples to encourage nationalist pride among the Italian people.
2. Russia—the bear. Turkey—the turkey. Students might suggest that from the cartoonist's point of view, the bear's "protective" hug could crush the turkey.
3. Reports will vary.

Thinking About Geography

1. Answers will vary.
2. A warm water port would give Russia access to the Middle East, improve trade, and help with the defense of the country. Russia's attempts to gain access to the Mediterranean alarmed leaders in Britain, France, and Sardinia, who feared Russia's growing strength.

Enrichment: Primary Sources

1. The Sicilians.
2. He wants them to give money and weapons and to volunteer to fight.
3. A "pure conscience"—the satisfaction of knowing they have done what is right.
4. The battle cry is "Italy and Victor Emmanuel!" Victor Emmanuel was the king of Sardinia and a leader in the unification movement.

Nationalism in Europe

1815–1914

See chapter timeline, p. 527.

Before You Read This Chapter

A world map shows nations as patches of color, with boundary lines clearly marked. Yet if you saw the world from space, you could not tell where one nation ends and another begins. Nations are not natural features like oceans or mountains. Nations are built by people, and people often reshape national boundaries. As you read this chapter, notice how nationalism changed the map of Europe. Could events have taken a different course and produced a different map?

Garibaldi and other Italian nationalists, bearing the flag of a united Italy, land on the island of Sicily.

The Geographic Setting

The Chapter Outline

1. The Unification of Italy
2. The Unification of Germany
3. Decline of the Eastern European Empires

See lesson plans, pp. T511A–T511C.

1 The Unification of Italy

Objectives

Focus Questions

★ ■ How did Sardinia unify northern Italy? (pages 513–514)

● ■ How did all of Italy come under a single ruler? (pages 514–516)

Terms to Know

Risorgimento
Red Shirts

★ Note strategies for first objective on this page and p. 514.

As you read in Chapter 24, the Congress of Vienna divided Italy into many small kingdoms, states, and duchies. Italian nationalists had tried to unify the country in 1848, but they were no match for the foreign powers that ruled their land. Still, the forces of nationalism and liberalism remained strong. Italy moved slowly toward unification during the 1850's.

The Rise of Nationalism

During the Napoleonic Era, Italy had been dominated by the French. Even after Napoleon's defeat, most of Italy remained under foreign rule. Austria controlled the north, and the Spanish Bourbon family ruled the Kingdom of the Two Sicilies in the south (map, page 516).

After 1815, Italian leaders formed secret societies to keep alive their dream of independence. The movement for Italian unity became known as the Risorgimento (ree-sohr-jee-MEN-toh), or resurgence. Leaders of the Risorgimento organized a number of revolts during the 1820's and 1830's. None of the revolts had any lasting success.

One of the most important of the Italian nationalists during this period was Giuseppe Mazzini, creator of the group called Young Italy (page 483). Mazzini reminded the Italians that their Roman ancestors had ruled the greatest empire of the ancient world. In the Middle Ages the Church of Rome had carried its beliefs to all of Western Europe. During the Renaissance, Italian artists, writers, and artisans were the envy of the rest of Europe. "All is now changed," said Mazzini. "We have no flag of our own, no voice among the nations of Europe."

Sec. Rev. ques. 2

Sardinia: Leader of the Unification Movement

The unsuccessful revolutions of 1848 had shown that fiery words, noble thoughts, and brave patriots were not enough to bring independence. Italy needed trained soldiers and powerful allies to fight the Austrians. The man who best understood this was Count Camillo di Cavour (kuh-VOOR), prime minister of the Kingdom of Sardinia.

Unlike the emotional Mazzini, Cavour was cautious and practical. Mazzini had called for a mass uprising, but Cavour knew that Young Italy and other nationalist groups could not take on the Austrian army. He wanted the Kingdom of Sardinia to take the lead in driving Austria out of northern Italy.

Strengthening Sardinia. With the approval of Sardinia's king, Victor Emmanuel II, Cavour worked to boost the kingdom's economy and enlarge its army. He built railways, improved agriculture, and developed industry. These policies gave Sardinia the strong economic base it needed to lead the movement for unification.

Cavour next began to build alliances with other countries. In the mid-1850's Sardinia became an ally of Britain and France, joining them in the war against Russia in the **513**

★ RETEACHING. Have students summarize contributions made to Italian unification by Mazzini and Cavour. (Mazzini inspired the Italians by reminding them of the great Roman Empire, the importance of the Church of Rome, and the Italian Renaissance. Cavour implemented policies to strengthen Italy's chances of defeating Austria.) (Comprehension) Observing for Detail
Check for Understanding. Ask: What was the Risorgimento? (The movement for Italian unity.)

★ REINFORCEMENT. Have students list the ways Cavour sought to unify Italy and then evaluate the strengths and weaknesses of his strategies. (He worked to improve its economy, enlarge its army, build alliances.) (Evaluation) Making Judgments
Background Cavour started Il Risorgimento, a newspaper that championed unification. Cavour expanded the goals of Risorgimento to include the creation of a modern political system based on a constitutional monarchy, secularization, and economic development.

Crimea (page 524). Cavour had no quarrel with Russia, but he knew that friendship with Britain and France might prove useful. Also, fighting beside these great powers gave Sardinia new prestige.

Sec. Rev. ques. 3

In 1858 Cavour signed a secret treaty with Napoleon III of France. By the terms of this treaty, if Austria threatened Sardinia, France would help to drive Austria from Lombardy and Venetia. In return, Sardinia would give two small border territories, Nice (NEES) and Savoy, to France.

War with Austria. With France as an ally, Cavour was ready for trouble with Austria. He provoked Austria into declaring war against Sardinia in April 1859. Napoleon III kept his promise, and French troops rushed to the defense of Sardinia. The French and Sardinian forces won quick victories. Then, to Cavour's surprise and anger, the French emperor made a complete turnaround. Fearing the power of a unified Italy, Napoleon

The cool diplomatic style of Cavour (shown here) contrasted with Garibaldi's flamboyance. Cavour's statesmanship was the key to uniting Italy under Sardinia's Victor Emmanuel.

514

signed a truce with Austria that gave Lombardy, but not Venetia, to Sardinia.

New Sardinian states. Cavour tried to persuade Victor Emmanuel II to continue the war until all of northern Italy was freed, but the king accepted the peace terms. Besides gaining Lombardy, Sardinia got an unexpected bonus: the people of Parma, Modena, and Tuscany drove out their ruling Hapsburg princes and voted to join Sardinia. Romagna (roh-MAHN-yah), one of the regions of the Papal States, also voted to join Sardinia. France approved this plan, obtaining Nice and Savoy in return.

★ See below, left.

Unification Achieved

● Note strategies for second objective on this page.

While northern Italy was making progress toward unification, a new movement was rising in the south. In the spring of 1860, a thousand red-shirted Italian patriots sailed from Genoa and landed on the island of Sicily. This army was determined to free the Kingdom of the Two Sicilies from its Bourbon king.

The commander of the **Red Shirts**, as they were called, was Giuseppe Garibaldi, who had fought in the revolution of 1848. Garibaldi's patriotism and love of liberty made him a hero to all Italy. His stirring call for soldiers went like this: "I offer neither pay nor provisions; I offer hunger, thirst, forced marches, battles and death. Let him who loves his country in his heart, and not with his lips only, follow me."

● See below.

Thousands of Sicilian patriots joined Garibaldi in 1860. In little more than two months, his troops freed the island of Sicily and crossed over to the Italian mainland. Garibaldi's forces then swept into Naples, and the Bourbon king fled.

Garibaldi planned to march on Rome next. This alarmed Cavour, who feared that such a move would force Napoleon III to defend the Pope. Cavour knew that war with France would be a disaster for Italy. He also felt that Garibaldi was too hotheaded to lead the drive for unification. For these reasons, Cavour sent Sardinian troops to join Garibaldi and keep him from attacking Rome.

Sec. Rev. ques. 4

★ ENRICHMENT. Have students write an essay comparing the leadership styles of Mazzini and Cavour and evaluating which was more effective. (Evaluation) *Making Judgments*

● RETEACHING. Have students make a timeline of events resulting in the 1870 unification of Italy. Timelines should begin with 1860. (Timelines should include information for the following dates: Spring 1860; November 1860; March 17, 1861; 1866; 1870.) (Comprehension) *Sequencing Events*

● REINFORCEMENT. Have students analyze Garibaldi's statement quoted above. Students should explain its meaning and tell why it might have motivated thousands of soldiers to join the unification effort. (Analysis) *Analyzing Information*

● ENRICHMENT. Have students find information on Garibaldi and the Red Shirts and prepare a report on that army's beginnings, tactics, leaders, and sources of support. (Application) *Locating Information*

Historic Places

Vatican City

For centuries, Roman Catholic popes have dwelt in a complex of palaces and churches known as the Vatican. Surrounded by medieval and Renaissance walls, the Vatican stands on the west bank of Rome's famed Tiber River. The heart of the Vatican is St. Peter's Church, first built during the Roman Empire and rebuilt in the 1500's.

Before Italy was united, the Vatican was just one of many Italian territories ruled by the Pope. These lands were known as the Papal States. Like other parts of Italy, the Papal States were caught up in the drive for national unity during the 1850's and 1860's. Early Ital-

ian nationalists hoped that the Pope would help them unite Italy. Pope Pius IX turned against nationalism, however, and insisted on keeping his political power over the Papal States.

By 1870 most of the Papal States had become part of Italy, but the Pope still held Rome. On September 20, 1870, Italian troops marched on the city. A few hours of artillery fire ended centuries of papal rule. Pope Pius IX withdrew to the Vatican.

Vatican City became an independent state within Rome and was recognized as such by Italy in 1929. The Pope remains the head of its government. With an area of just 108.7 acres (see its borders outlined above), Vatican City is the smallest independent state in the world.

515

Map Skill Practice

See p. T511B for answers to *Map Skill Practice*.

Unification of Italy, 1870

1. On the map at the right, find the two regions that made up the Kingdom of Sardinia.
2. Which was the first state to unite with the Kingdom of Sardinia?
3. Which five states were ruled by the Hapsburgs?
4. Who controlled the Kingdom of the Two Sicilies?
5. By 1861, when Victor Emmanuel II was proclaimed king of Italy, which two states had not yet joined Italy?
6. **Drawing conclusions.** How do you think rule by three different powers might have affected Italy's quest for independence?

KEY

Kingdom of Italy, 1870

Under Hapsburg control

Under Pope's control

Under Bourbon control

Even without Rome, the union of states headed by Sardinia continued to grow. Early in November 1860, the papal provinces of Umbria and the Marches voted for union with Sardinia. Soon after, the people of Naples and Sicily also voted to join the lands ruled by Sardinia. On March 17, 1861, Victor Emmanuel was proclaimed king of Italy. Cavour died three months later, having nearly fulfilled his dream of a unified Italy.

Two important regions, papal Rome and Austrian-held Venetia, became part of Italy later in the decade. Italy received Venetia when Austria was defeated by Prussia in 1866 (page 518). In 1870 Rome's citizens voted to join the kingdom of Italy. The goal of Italian unification had at last been achieved.

516

See Sec. 1 *Closing the Lesson*, p. T511B.

Section Review

Answers to Section Review questions are in brackets on pages indicated.

1. **Identify:** Risorgimento, Red Shirts. (pp. 513, 514)
2. What examples did Mazzini use to remind Italians of their great heritage? (p. 513)
3. Why did Cavour provoke Austria into war in 1859? (p. 514)
4. For what reasons did Cavour want to stop Garibaldi from marching on Rome? (p. 514)
5. **Critical thinking:** Mazzini, Cavour, and Garibaldi all fought for Italian independence. How did their methods differ? (See answer below.)

5. Students might point out that Mazzini's and Garibaldi's efforts made strong appeals to emotion, while Cavour took a more cautious, strategic, and diplomatic approach to unifying Italy.

2 The Unification of Germany

Objectives

Focus Questions

★ ■ How did the German states combine to form an empire? *(pages 517–520)*

● ■ What were the features of the new German Empire? *(pages 520–521)*

Terms to Know

tariff	Franco-Prussian War
Zollverein	kaiser
realpolitik	

★ Note strategies for first objective on this page and p. 519.

The Germans, like the Italians, faced many obstacles in their efforts to unify their country. The German Confederation, formed in 1815, was not a true state, and the Frankfurt Assembly's attempt at unification in 1848 had failed. The steady growth of German nationalism, however, eventually made possible a united Germany.

The Push for Economic Unity

In Germany, just as in Italy, the first step toward unity was an economic one. In the 1830's a group of aristocratic Prussian landowners—the Junkers (YUNG-kurz)—persuaded Prussia's leaders to do away with all **tariffs**—taxes on imported goods.

In 1834, under the leadership of Prussia, German states formed the **Zollverein** (ZOHL-fuh-ryn), an organization that reduced tariffs among its members. The Zollverein also started a standard money system so that states could trade with each other more easily. By the mid-1840's the Zollverein included most of the German states. (Austria was not a member.)

The German economy improved greatly under the Zollverein, and industry boomed. Pleased with the new economic unity, many Germans began to support political unity as well. The movement for unity was led by Prussia, which was becoming the region's leading power.

Bismarck's Leadership

German unification came about largely through the efforts of Otto von Bismarck, who became Prussia's prime minister in 1862 under King William I. A highly controversial figure, Bismarck was known to be against Prussia's bureaucracy and liberal parliament.

Bismarck opposed democracy and wanted to strengthen the power of the king. He argued that duty to the state was more important than individual freedom. A cunning, practical thinker, he was a master of **realpolitik**—politics in which success matters more than legality or idealism. Bismarck let nothing stand in the way of his efforts to build up the Prussian military machine.

When Bismarck talked of a united Germany, he really meant that Prussia should dominate the other German states. Bismarck was convinced that the country could be united only through war. Germany's future, he said, would be settled "not by speeches . . . but by blood and iron." Austria was Prussia's major rival for power in the German Confederation. Bismarck's plan was to drive Austria from the Confederation and bring the other German states under Prussian control.

Sec. Rev. ques. 2

Wars of Unification

Victory over Denmark. Bismarck's first move was against Denmark. When Denmark claimed two coastal regions, Schleswig and Holstein (map, page 519), both Prussia **517**

★ RETEACHING. Have students use the following words in a paragraph summarizing Bismarck's strategies for unifying the German states: Junkers, Zollverein, realpolitik, "blood and iron." *(Comprehension)* **Observing for Detail**

Biography Bismarck was a man with a strong physical build and a healthy appetite for food and drink. He earned the respect and envy of many for his swordsmanship and had a long dueling scar which extended from his nose to his right ear.

★ REINFORCEMENT. Have students outline Bismarck's strategies to drive Austria from the German Confederation and to bring the German states under Prussian control. (Bismarck went to war with Austria, annexed a number of German states, organized the North German Confederation, and took control of the south German states.) *(Comprehension)* **Translating Information into Another Form**

Bismarck's "Blood and Iron" Speech

On September 29, 1862, shortly after he became Prussia's prime minister, Otto von Bismarck met with other German officials. Discussing the unification of Germany, Bismarck delivered a powerful speech, which is adapted below.

❝ Germany does not look to Prussia's liberalism, but to her power. The South German States would like to indulge in liberalism, and therefore no one will assign Prussia's role to them! Prussia must collect her forces and hold them in reserve for a favorable moment. Since the treaties of Vienna, our frontiers have been ill-designed for a healthy national state. The great questions of the time will be decided, not by speeches and resolutions of majorities, but by blood and iron. ❞

1. According to Bismarck, what was Prussia's role?
2. **Critical thinking:** What did Bismarck mean when he said that the great questions will be decided by "blood and iron"?

Ⓕ See answers below.

518

and Austria declared war on Denmark. Their combined forces quickly defeated the Danes and moved into Schleswig and Holstein. The two countries, however, disagreed over how their new territories should be run. Bismarck used this quarrel to push Austria into war.

Victory over Austria. Prussian soldiers crushed the Austrian army in the Seven Weeks' War of 1866. Austria had a large population from which to draw its troops, but the smaller Prussian army was so well trained that it was almost unbeatable. Careful planning, a good railway system, and new guns that could fire five rounds per minute also helped give Prussia the victory. Austria's defeat allowed Prussia to take over Schleswig and Holstein and a number of smaller German states.

After the war, Prussia organized a new union of states called the North German Confederation. Austria was not included in the new confederation, and it thus lost its influence in German affairs. Bismarck's goal of making Prussia the dominant German power had been achieved.

Bismarck's work was not yet complete, however. The south German states remained outside Prussia's control. The Catholic population of these states had little desire to be dominated by Protestant Prussia. France, wary of German expansion, also opposed Prussian control of these states.

Once again, Bismarck decided to use war as his strategy for uniting Germany. He was confident that if Prussia went to war with France, the south German states would side with Prussia.

Victory over France. A cause for conflict with France developed unexpectedly in 1868. That year, the Spanish throne was offered to a prince of the Hohenzollern (hoh-un-TSOHL-urn) family, the ruling family in Prussia. The thought of Hohenzollern Prussia to the east and a Hohenzollern king of Spain to the south alarmed France. The prince eased tensions by turning down the throne. However, France made this demand: King William I of Prussia should promise that no member of the Hohenzollern family would ever accept the Spanish throne.

Unification of Germany, 1871

A series of annexations and unions over a six-year period brought about a unified Germany. What regions made up the North German Confederation? What territory did France give to Prussia at the conclusion of the Franco-Prussian War?

Map Answers: (1) Westphalia, Saxony, Brandenburg, Silesia, West Prussia, East Prussia, Schleswig-Holstein. (2) Alsace-Lorraine.

Sec. Rev. ques. 3

★ See below.

King William I sent a telegram reporting the demand to Bismarck, who seized the chance to lure France into war. Bismarck changed the telegram to make it seem as if the French ambassador and the German king had insulted each other. He then gave the telegram to the newspapers to publish. Soon people in both countries demanded war.

In July 1870 France declared war, and the **Franco-Prussian War** began. The French believed that their army would sweep across Germany just as Napoleon's troops had done in the early 1800's. Yet the French forces were no match for Prussia's powerful army. Moreover, as Bismarck had expected, the south German states came to Prussia's aid.

519

★ **ENRICHMENT.** Have students compare the goals, values, and leadership style of Italian unification leader Cavour (pp. 513–514) with those of Bismarck. Students might find additional information to illustrate similarities or differences between the two national leaders. *(Comprehension) Observing for Detail*

Background The Franco-Prussian War was the first European conflict in which both antagonists used railroads, electric telegraphs, rifles, and breech-loading artillery—technological developments that revolutionized warfare in the 19th century.

Vocabulary The word *kaiser* is derived from the Roman title *Caesar*.

Check for Understanding. Ask: What were the two houses in the Second Reich's parliament? (The Reichstag and the Bundesrat.)

In only six weeks the French armies were defeated and Napoleon III was taken prisoner. Moreover, Paris was placed under siege by the Germans. Late in January 1871, with its people suffering from bitter cold and lack of food, Paris surrendered.

In February 1871, peace talks began at Versailles. France signed a treaty agreeing to pay Germany $1 billion. The treaty also forced France to surrender the border province of Alsace-Lorraine to Germany. France never forgot this humiliation.

The Birth of the Second Reich

● Note strategies for second objective on this page.

The Franco-Prussian War marked the final step in Bismarck's plan for unifying Germany under Prussian leadership. At Versailles on January 18, 1871, Prussia's King William I was crowned as Germany's **kaiser** (KY-zur)—emperor. Soon after, Bismarck became the nation's chancellor—its highest official below the kaiser. The new German Empire consisted of 25 states united under a strong central government. It became known as the Second Reich (RYK). (The Holy Roman Empire was considered the First Reich.)

Strict government. The constitution of the Second Reich set up a parliament for all of Germany. Adult male citizens voted to elect members of the Reichstag (RYK-shtahg), the lower house of parliament. Members of the Bundesrat (BOON-dus-raht), the upper house, were appointed by the different states. The Bundesrat had more power than the lower house, and its members usually opposed attempts to make Germany more democratic.

● See below.

Real power in the German Reich lay in the hands of the new German kaiser, the Prussian generals, the Prussian aristocracy, and a growing number of rich bankers and industrialists. Unlike the British monarch, the kaiser had a great deal of control over lawmaking. Through his chancellor he also controlled foreign affairs.

The rulers of Germany opposed democratic ideas and Western-style parliamentary government. The failure of democracy to take root in Germany had important consequences for the future.

Ⓕ See below.

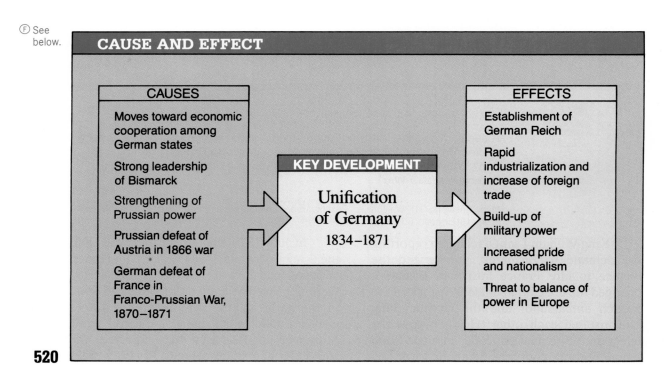

CAUSE AND EFFECT

CAUSES	KEY DEVELOPMENT	EFFECTS
Moves toward economic cooperation among German states		Establishment of German Reich
Strong leadership of Bismarck	Unification of Germany 1834–1871	Rapid industrialization and increase of foreign trade
Strengthening of Prussian power		Build-up of military power
Prussian defeat of Austria in 1866 war		Increased pride and nationalism
German defeat of France in Franco-Prussian War, 1870–1871		Threat to balance of power in Europe

520

● RETEACHING. Have students explain the following statement: *Under the leadership of William II, the German nation grew stronger and more nationalist.* (Comprehension) *Observing for Detail*

Ⓕ CAUSE AND EFFECT CHART ACTIVITY. Have students decide which cause of unification was the most significant and which effect was most important to Germany's strength. Have students explain their decisions. (Synthesis) *Making Judgments*

● REINFORCEMENT. Have students develop a hypothesis explaining why democratic ideas that influenced other European nations did not take root in Germany. (Synthesis) *Making Judgments*

● ENRICHMENT. Have students compare and contrast the German parliamentary system with that of Great Britain (pp. 398–400). (Synthesis) *Analyzing Information*
Vocabulary *Reich* is a German word meaning "empire" or "state."

The graphs show three of the factors that contributed to Germany's rapid economic and political development. Why was each factor important? What relationships can you see among those factors?

The Rise of Germany

Population

Millions

Steel Production

Millions of tons

Railroad Building

Thousands of miles of track

Source: B. R. Mitchell, *European Historical Statistics; The New Cambridge Modern History*

Growing power. William II, the grandson of William I, became kaiser of Germany in 1888. He supported Bismarck's "blood and iron" policies, but he was jealous of the chancellor's power. The young kaiser dismissed the aging Bismarck in 1890. Bismarck, one of the greatest statesmen of the century, had served for nearly three decades.

Under William II, Germany was transformed from a basically agricultural country into one of the world's leading industrial powers. The population grew from about 41 million in 1871 to 56 million in 1900 and close to 70 million by 1914. Coal, iron, and steel production shot up.

Aided by the skill of its scientists and inventors, Germany became a leader in the chemical and electrical industries. It built a large network of railroads, a merchant marine that rivaled Britain's, and a weapons industry second to none. This industrial expansion led to a large increase in Germany's foreign trade.

Most Germans took great pride in the growing power of their nation. Germany, once weak and fragmented, was now tightly united and intensely nationalistic. The new Germany threatened the balance of power in Europe and helped to create fears and rivalries that would one day lead to war.

See Sec. 2 *Closing the Lesson,* p. T511C.

Sec. Rev. ques. 4

Section Review

Answers to Section Review questions are in brackets on pages indicated.

1. **Define or identify:** tariff, Zollverein, realpolitik, Franco-Prussian War, kaiser. (pp. 517, 519, 520)
2. What was Bismarck's strategy for unifying Germany? (p. 517)
3. How did Bismarck lure France into war? (p. 519)
4. What factors helped Germany become one of the most powerful nations in the world? (p. 521)
5. **Critical thinking:** Bismarck has been called a later-day Machiavelli. Explain this comparison. You may want to re-read the discussion of Machiavelli on page 329. (See answer below.)

521

Graph Answers: (1) Population growth helped to fill industrial jobs and expand the military. Increased steel production resulted in the growth of the transportation industry and the build-up of armaments. Expansion of railways contributed to a growth in trade and improved military strategy. (2) The need for jobs created by population growth was met by rapid industrial expansion; increased steel output promoted the railroad industry.

5. Students might point how Bismarck's ideas—particularly his concern for strengthening the monarch's power and his belief that success mattered more than legality or idealism—were similar to those of Machiavelli.

3 Decline of the Eastern European Empires

Objectives

Focus Questions

★ ■ Why did nationalism become a strong force in the Austrian Empire? *(pages 522–523)*

● ■ What factors led to the decline of the Ottoman Empire? *(pages 523–524)*

▲ ■ Why did Russia fail to modernize as quickly as Western Europe? *(pages 524–527)*

Terms to Know

Pan-Slavism
Russification

★ Note strategies for first objective on this page and p. 523.

During most of the nineteenth century Eastern Europe was made up of three large empires: the Austrian Empire of the Hapsburgs, the Ottoman Empire, and imperial Russia. Compared to Western Europe, these Eastern European empires were backward, with a low rate of literacy and little industry. They were ruled by autocrats and so lacked representative forms of government.

Nationalism in Eastern Europe

Three multinational empires. The Ottoman Empire, though ruled by Turks, included many other nationalities as well. The European part of the empire included Greeks, Bulgarians, Macedonians, Serbs, and Romanians. The Ottoman Turks also ruled over Arabs in Asia and North Africa.

The Hapsburg Empire was ruled by German-speaking people in Austria. The empire also included Hungarians, Romanians,

522

and various Slavic groups—Czechs, Poles, Slovenes, Croats, and Slovaks.

Imperial Russia also contained many nationalities. It ruled most of Poland, which had a large Jewish population. Russia also controlled the lands of the Finns, the Baltic peoples, and the peoples living north of the Black Sea. Farther east, Russia ruled the descendants of the Mongols as well as Georgians and Armenians.

Western influences. As Western influences filtered into Eastern European societies, townspeople and villagers began to learn how much better off people were in Western Europe. They became aware of the ideals of liberalism, democracy, and nationalism. They also heard about the rebellions in many parts of Western Europe, especially the reforms that the French people had made. All this made Eastern Europeans take a closer look at their own situations.

Nationalism was the most powerful of the new influences to reach Eastern Europe. Because the Austrian, Ottoman, and Russian empires each contained dozens of peoples, nationalism threatened the very existence of those empires. Nationalism encouraged the peoples under Austrian, Ottoman, and Russian rule to take pride in their heritage and to seek independence.

Austria

The unification of Italy and of Germany weakened the Austrian Empire. Austria lost two wars and gave up control of important territories. Nationalist movements continued to chip away at Austrian power.

Sharing power. In Hungary, the Magyars had long been demanding independence (page 481). After Austria's defeat by Prussia in 1866, Emperor Francis Joseph decided that it would be wise to make a deal with the Magyars. In 1867 the empire became the Dual

★ RETEACHING. Have students review "Nationalism in Eastern Europe" (above) and explain what threatened the Eastern European empires. (All three empires contained many nationalities that sought independence.) *(Comprehension)* **Observing for Detail**
Check for Understanding. Ask: What Western influences gradually spread to Eastern European societies? (Ideals of liberalism, democracy, and nationalism.)

★ REINFORCEMENT. Have students write a paragraph explaining why Emperor Francis Joseph made concessions to the Magyars, what concessions were made, and what effect they had. (He created a dual monarchy, granted a constitution and a parliament, and gave Magyars control over their internal affairs.) *(Comprehension)* **Observing for Detail**

Austria's Emperor Francis Joseph heads a throng of royal guests at a banquet. Europe's ruling houses formed an interrelated group. Despite national rivalries, they supported one another against the threat of liberalism.

Monarchy of Austria-Hungary. The emperor kept his title in Austria and was also crowned King of Hungary. The Magyar nation of Hungary gained its own constitution, its own parliament, and complete control over its internal affairs. Decisions on foreign policy were made by the two governments together. Some Magyar nationalists rejected this arrangement, however. They wanted complete independence for Hungary.

Sec. Rev. ques. 2

Serbia and the South Slavs. Perhaps the most dangerous nationality problem in Austria-Hungary involved the South Slavs, who included Bosnians, Croats, and Slovenes. Serbia, independent since 1878, was seeking to expand by uniting with the South Slavs in Austria-Hungary. Serbia therefore encouraged nationalist movements among these peoples. The Austrians viewed the Serbian actions as a threat to the empire. The quarrel with Serbia would one day ignite the flames of World War I (Chapter 31).

★ See below.

The Ottoman Empire

● Note strategies for second objective on this page and p. 524.

"The sick man of Europe." By the nineteenth century, the once-powerful Ottoman Empire was losing control of its territories. In 1805 the Egyptian leader Mohammed Ali made Egypt virtually independent within the empire. In 1829 Greece won its independence, and Serbia gained self-rule. A year later, the empire lost another of its territories when France took over Algeria.

Sec. Rev. ques. 3

Called "the sick man of Europe" because of its fading powers, the Ottoman Empire was an easy target for its neighbors. Russia, eager to gain access to the Mediterranean Sea, hungrily eyed the straits controlled by the Ottomans—the Bosporus and the Dardanelles. Austria, too, hoped to gain former Ottoman territory, particularly in the Balkans (the mountainous peninsula in southeastern Europe).

523

★ **ENRICHMENT.** Have students research South Slav nationalist movements to find out how Serbians were involved. Students might report on the demands of the South Slavs and the results of their efforts. *(Application) Locating Information*
● **RETEACHING.** Have students make a timeline of events leading to the fall of the Ottoman Empire. (Timeline should include events for the following dates: 1805; 1829; 1830; early 1850's; 1853; 1877; 1878; 1908; 1912.) *(Comprehension) Sequencing Events*

● **REINFORCEMENT.** Have students work in groups to debate the following: *The fall of the Ottoman Empire could have been prevented.* Students should support their views by referring to events discussed in the text. *(Synthesis) Making Judgments*
Biography Mohammed Ali led Egypt from traditional to modern ways. He improved farming and industry, reorganized the government, took strict control over the economy, and created Western-style schools to train doctors, engineers, and other specialists.

In the early 1850's Russia invaded Ottoman territory in an attempt to gain control of the Bosporus and the Dardanelles. This led to war in 1853 in the area known as the Crimea (map, page 525). Fearing Russian expansion, Britain, France, and Sardinia sent troops to aid the Turks. Together these armies defeated the Russians in 1856.

Attempted reforms. Despite the victory over Russia, the Ottoman Empire remained dangerously weak. Beginning in the late 1700's, some Ottoman sultans had made reforms to strengthen the central government and to modernize the army.

These reforms were encouraged by Britain and France. At the end of the Crimean War, the British and French urged that the Ottomans speed up reforms, especially those that would help Ottoman Christians. In 1856 the Turks promised more liberal rule and guaranteed religious freedom. Yet these changes came too late to save the empire. Powerful groups within the empire slowed the pace of reform, and nationalist uprisings steadily drained Ottoman energies.

Revolt in the Balkans. Internal unrest had long plagued the Ottomans, particularly in the Balkans. In the 1870's the Slavic people of this region revolted. Russia joined the Balkan rebels in 1877, still looking for access to the Mediterranean.

The combined Balkan and Russian forces defeated the Ottoman Turks, and the Treaty of San Stefano (1878) forced the Turks to grant independence to Serbia, Montenegro, and Romania. The treaty also called for Bulgaria to become a self-governing state with territory along the Aegean Sea.

Foreign powers, especially Britain, worried that Russia would dominate Bulgaria and gain access to the Mediterranean. Many people in Britain began calling for war with Russia. One popular verse of the day described British feelings:

66 We don't want to fight,
But, by jingo, if we do,
We've got the ships,
We've got the men,
We've got the money too. 99

Later in 1878, the European powers met at the Congress of Berlin to change the San Stefano agreements. Russia was forced to accept a treaty returning Bulgaria to Ottoman rule. Russia's hopes for a port on the Aegean Sea had been dashed.

Breakup of the empire. By 1900 the collapse of the Ottoman Empire seemed inevitable. A 1908 revolt by a group of patriots called the Young Turks, who wanted to rebuild the empire, failed to halt the decline. In that same year, Bulgaria declared its independence and Austria took over Bosnia and Herzegovina.

● See below, left.

In 1912 Greece, Bulgaria, Montenegro, and Serbia declared war on the Ottomans. In the first of two Balkan Wars, the allied Balkan forces succeeded in driving the Turks from Europe, except for the area around Constantinople. Disputes among the victors, however, led to the second Balkan War in 1913. The Ottoman Turks joined Greece, Serbia, and Romania in defeating Bulgaria. The Ottomans regained some of their lost lands. For the most part, however, nationalism had broken up the once-vast Ottoman Empire.

Imperial Russia

▲ Note strategies for third objective on this page and p. 526.

A troubled empire. In the nineteenth century, Russia's huge empire had serious weaknesses. There was very little industry, and agriculture remained inefficient. Tens of millions of serfs were still tied to the land—uneducated, poor, and with no real incentive to work harder or develop more efficient methods of farming.

Serfs were little more than slaves to their lords. Their owners could force them to work in the fields, sell or rent them, and even take their wages if they worked in factories. In addition, the stern rule of the czars increased political tensions, particularly among minorities such as Poles and Ukrainians.

The czars of the 1800's followed a policy of expansion. Russia moved eastward across Siberia and southward beyond the Caspian Sea. Though the Crimean War had blocked Russia's longed-for route to the Mediterra-

524

● ENRICHMENT. Have students research the Young Turks and compare them with Young Italy (p. 483). Students might prepare a chart listing the groups' similarities and differences or present an oral report. (Application) *Locating Information*
▲ RETEACHING. Have students summarize the weaknesses that plagued Russia in the nineteenth century. (Little industry; inefficient agriculture; uneducated, poor serfs with little incentive; political tensions.) (Comprehension) *Observing for Detail*

▲ REINFORCEMENT. Have students work in groups to stage a meeting that might have occurred among advisers of Nicholas I. The advisers' task is to define Russia's problems and plan strategies to resolve the issues. (Problems include serfdom, an inefficient agricultural system, corrupt government officials, and poorly educated subjects.) (Synthesis) *Solving Problems* nean Sea, Russia continued to support Balkan independence. That support reflected not only the desire for a port on the Mediterranean, but also a belief in **Pan-Slavism**—the unity of all Slavic peoples.

Repression under Nicholas I. Like earlier czars, Nicholas I was quick to block any opposition to his rule. He began his reign in 1825 by suppressing the Decembrist revolt (page 474). Five years later, he put down a revolution among his Polish subjects. To prevent further uprisings, Nicholas adopted a policy called Russification—the attempt to force the Russian language and culture upon a subject nation. The use of Russification against the Poles, Nicholas hoped, would destroy Polish nationalism.

Nicholas wanted to turn Russia into a powerful state like the nations of Western Europe. Yet he was aware of his empire's weaknesses. Serfdom held back the modernization of agriculture, but Nicholas did not dare free the serfs. Many government officials were corrupt, but he could not do without them. He needed educated subjects, but education seemed to stir up disloyalty. His efforts to expand in the Black Sea region led to defeat in the Crimean War. When Nicholas died in 1855, Russia was still weaker than the Western powers.

The reforms of Alexander II. The new czar, Alexander II, believed that Russia had to follow the model of the Western countries in order to grow strong. Alexander, who

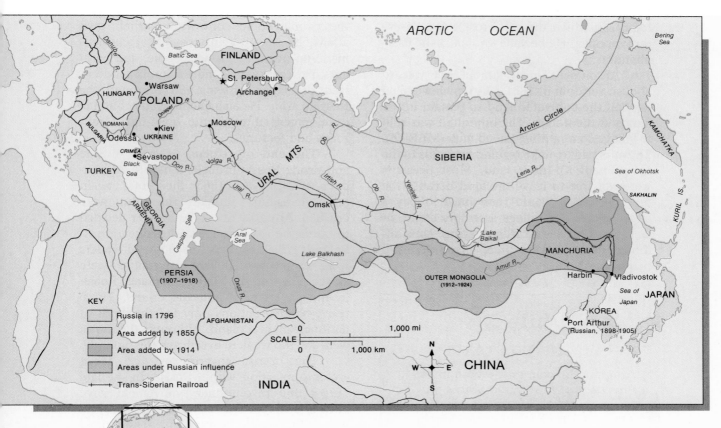

Russia, 1796–1914

The territorial growth that was begun by the early czars continued for several centuries. What transportation system linked Moscow with the Pacific coast? What non-Russian regions were under Russian influence?

525

The Volga Bargemen, painted in the 1870's, makes clear both the wretched condition of Russia's peasantry and the slow pace of industrialization.

ruled from 1855 to 1881, began an era of reform in which the gates to the West were thrown open. He became known as the czar-liberator.

Sec. Rev. ques. 4

Alexander's most famous act was to abolish serfdom in 1861. His new law called for half the cultivated land to remain in the hands of the nobles. The other half was sold to village communities called mirs (MEERZ). The mirs had to make regular payments to the government for their land. Most peasants were not free to leave the land because the other peasants would then have to pay a larger share. The village assembly could, in fact, block a peasant from leaving. Thus, although peasants were "free," many were still tied to the land.

Meanwhile . . .

IN THE UNITED STATES

Abraham Lincoln was sworn in as President of the United States on March 4, 1861, less than a month after Alexander II had ended serfdom in Russia. In 1862 Lincoln issued the Emancipation Proclamation, declaring the freedom of slaves in the rebellious states of the South.

526

Alexander made other changes. To give the people some control over their own affairs, he set up zemstvos—local councils made up of nobles, townspeople, and peasants. The czar opened more schools, modernized the court system, and reformed the Russian army. He also encouraged economic development through the building of railroads and factories.

The end of reform. Events outside and inside Russia brought a halt to Alexander's reforms. In 1863 the Poles again rebelled against Russian rule, but were crushed. After the revolt, Alexander decided to strengthen the policy of Russification in Poland. Polish soldiers and political leaders were exiled and Polish universities were closed. The Russian language replaced Polish in the government and the courts. These heavy-handed actions only fed the spirit of nationalism in Poland, although the Poles were still too weak to overthrow Russian rule.

The czarist government also faced armed opposition within Russia. In the late 1870's one revolutionary movement gave birth to a violent organization known as The Will of the People. A wave of assassinations swept the country, taking the lives of many prominent officials. In 1881, after a number of near misses, Alexander himself was killed when revolutionaries threw a bomb under his carriage.

▲ See below.

Cultural History Other reforms made by Alexander II included the release of political prisoners and Siberian exiles, the lifting of restrictions on religious minorities and foreign travel, and the abolition of medieval punishments. Despite these reforms, Alexander believed that his authority was God-given and that Russia was not ready for constitutional or representative government.

▲ ENRICHMENT. Have students write an essay evaluating the accuracy of Czar Alexander II's title—czar-liberator. Students should use evidence in the text to support their views. *(Synthesis) Making Judgments*

Return to repression. Alexander III replaced his father as czar. Determined to end revolutionary activity once and for all, he turned Russia into a police state teeming with spies and informers. The powers of the zemstvos were reduced. Programs of Russification began once again, and the government persecuted Russian Jews. Despite the repression, however, dissent and revolutionary violence continued.

Hopes of building a strong Russia on the model of the West seemed destined to fail. Alexander III did continue his father's policy of industrialization and railroad-building, but progress was slow. At the time of his death in 1894, Russia—and all of Eastern Europe— still lagged far behind Western Europe.

See Sec. 3 *Closing the Lesson*, p. T511C.

Chapter 26   Summary and Timeline

1. In spite of their defeat in the 1848 revolts, Italian nationalists continued to work for independence. The Sardinian leader Camillo di Cavour used shrewd political moves and strategic wars to bring northern Italian states together, while the inspiring leader Giuseppe Garibaldi helped unify the south. By 1870 all of Italy was united.

2. Otto von Bismarck steered a strong Prussian state toward dominance of a unified Germany. Expanding its territories and weakening its rivals, Prussia succeeded in uniting Germany. William II continued Bismarck's "blood and iron" policies. By the late 1800's, Germany was one of the most powerful nations in the world.

3. Nationalism weakened the multinational empires of Eastern Europe. The Austrian Empire, already threatened by Italian and German expansion, became the Dual Monarchy of Austria-Hungary to satisfy the Magyars. Pressures on the empire intensified as Southern Slavs began to demand independence. The crumbling Ottoman Empire fell prey to the ambitions of its neighbors. Even the support of Britain and France could not halt the Ottoman decline, and the Balkan Wars all but finished the empire. Nationalism in the Russian Empire came into conflict with the autocratic rule of the czars. As repression increased, tensions heightened, bringing Russia to the brink of revolution.

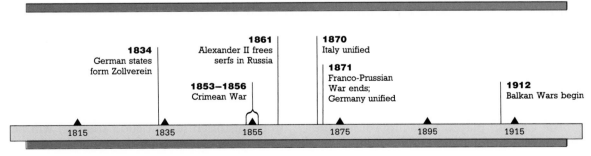

1834
German states form Zollverein

1853–1856
Crimean War

1861
Alexander II frees serfs in Russia

1870
Italy unified

1871
Franco-Prussian War ends; Germany unified

1912
Balkan Wars begin

| 1815 | 1835 | 1855 | 1875 | 1895 | 1915 |

527

5. Students might point out that in all three empires, one national group dominated many others. Nationalism encouraged subject peoples to seek independence, and the success of any one group inspired others.

See p. T511C for answers to Chapter Review.

Vocabulary Review

Use the following terms to complete the sentences below: *Franco-Prussian War, kaiser, Pan-Slavism, realpolitik, Red Shirts, Risorgimento, tariff.*

1. The ___?___, led by Giuseppe Garibaldi, freed Sicily and Naples in 1860.
2. Russia supported ___?___, the unity of all Slavic peoples.
3. A tax on imported goods is called a ___?___.
4. Napoleon III was taken prisoner during the ___?___.
5. The ___?___, or resurgence, was a movement for Italian unity.
6. Germany's emperor was known as the ___?___.
7. Otto von Bismarck practiced ___?___, taking a tough-minded approach to Prussian politics.

People to Identify

Identify the following people and tell why each was important.
1. Francis Joseph
2. Nicholas I
3. Victor Emmanuel II
4. William I
5. William II

Places to Know

Use the following place names to complete the sentences below and in the next column: *Balkan, Prussia, Sardinia.*
1. The Kingdom of ___?___, led by Camillo de Cavour, played a leading role in the movement for Italian unification.

2. By 1913 the ___?___ states of Greece, Serbia, Albania, Bulgaria, and Rumania had become independent.
3. Bismarck, as the leader of ___?___, took charge of the drive to unify Germany.

Recalling the Facts

1. How did Mazzini and Cavour differ in their approaches to unifying Italy?
2. Why did Napoleon III sign a truce with Austria and break his promise to Cavour?
3. What event marked the completion of Italian unification?
4. How did the Zollverein encourage German unity?
5. What did Bismarck believe was the only way to unite Germany? Why did Prussia win the Seven Weeks' War?
6. Who held real power in Germany's Second Reich?
7. How did Western influence encourage the growth of nationalism in Eastern Europe?
8. What problem did Serbia present for the leaders of the Dual Monarchy?
9. What were the causes of the Crimean War? What was its outcome?
10. Why was Alexander II of Russia known as the czar-liberator?
11. How did repression in Russia worsen under Alexander III?

Critical Thinking Skills

1. **Recognizing points of view.** All people have points of view on certain subjects. A good historian (and a good student) will be able to recognize when someone's point of

528

A checkmark identifies questions and exercises calling for the three higher-order levels of thinking at the top of the Bloom taxonomy: Analysis, Synthesis, and Evaluation.

view reflects bias—personal preference. Re-read the examples Mazzini used to remind Italians of their heritage (page 513). What was his point of view? Does it reveal any bias? Explain. *(Anal.)*

2. **Interpreting cartoons.** The cartoon below, from a British journal in 1853, comments on Russia's supposed "protection" of Turkey. Which figure in the cartoon is Russia? Which is Turkey? How does the cartoonist view the situation? *(Anal.)*

3. **Preparing a report.** The Crimean War marked the beginning of the modern nursing profession. Concerned over the lack of supplies for soldiers, Britain sent Florence Nightingale and a group of nurses to the Crimea. Prepare a report on Florence Nightingale's work in the Crimea and her contributions to the nursing profession. *(App.)*

Thinking About Geography

1. **Planning a trip.** Plan a tour of Italy, for which you will act as tour guide. The purpose of your trip is to visit places that were important in the unification of Italy. Prepare a short speech telling why each town or area was important. Include a map to use with your presentation. *(Comp.)*

2. **Relating geography and history.** Why did Russia want access to the Mediterranean Sea? How was the balance of power in Europe affected by Russia's attempts to gain access to the Mediterranean? *(Comp.)*

529

T529A

Europe in the Late 1800's   1850–1914
(pp. 530–548)

Chapter Preview

Section 1 of this chapter describes the technological and social changes that occurred in Europe after the Industrial Revolution. In Section 2 scientific discoveries, new theories, and the development of the social sciences are discussed. The influence of industrialism on the arts is described in Section 3, and the rise of extreme nationalism is discussed in Section 4.

Bibliography

See the *Teacher's Management and Planning Guide* for additional listings. Starred titles are for both students and teachers.

Eiseley, Loren. *Darwin's Century: Evolution and the Men Who Discovered It.* Doubleday. An account of the development of the theory of evolution.

*Longford, Elizabeth. *Queen Victoria: Born to Succeed.* Harper & Row. A highly readable popular biography of the woman who dominated European society in the late 1800's.

*Reynal, M. *The Nineteenth Century.* Skira. A beautifully illustrated study of European art in the 1800's.

*Sheehan, Vincent, translator. *Madame Curie: A Biography by Eve Curie.* The story of the celebrated scientist.

Sulzberger, C. L. *The Fall of Eagles.* Crown. Looks at the final flowering of the Hapsburg, Hohenzollern, and Romanov dynasties before their fall.

Tuchman, Barbara. *The Proud Tower.* Bantam. Tellingly selected details illuminate broad social and political trends in European society between 1890 and 1914.

Section Lesson Plans

SECTION 1   (pp. 531–534)
An Industrial Society

Objectives

After completing this section, students will be able to:
1. Describe how European society changed in the late 1800's.
2. Explain the class divisions that existed in Europe.

Introducing the Lesson

Remind students that the Industrial Revolution resulted in dramatic social changes. Economic opportunities and a higher standard of living developed as did unforeseen problems for city-dwellers and factory workers.

 Then ask: *(a) How does an industrial society differ from an agricultural society?* (They differ in very basic ways, such as where people live, the kind of work people do, the type of goods produced, and how people spend their leisure time.)

 (b) What elements of the Industrial Revolution caused great social changes? (Answers will vary, but might include urbanization, the factory system, and the mass production of goods.)

Developing the Lesson:
Comparing Historical Development

Have students compare the new European social structure that developed after the Industrial Revolution with the one that existed during the feudal period (pp. 218–225). Students should base their comparisons on the following: the bases of wealth and status, occupations and size of each class, and individual opportunity. *(Synthesis)*

Developing the Lesson:
Observing for Detail

Have students explain the economic and social consequences of rapid urbanization. Students might consider the following questions:
 (a) What impact might rapid urbanization have had on agricultural production? (Answers will vary.)

(b) How was society affected by rapid urbanization? (Demand for employment, housing, and sanitation grew.) (Comprehension)

Closing the Lesson:
Understanding Point of View

Have students write an essay describing life in Europe in the late 1800's, from the viewpoint of either an entrepreneur, a landowning aristocrat, a member of the middle class, or a factory worker. (Application)

See Section Review questions, p. 534.

SECTION 2   (pp. 535–539)
New Scientific Ideas

Objectives

After completing this section, students will be able to:
1. Describe the scientific advances that were made in Europe.
2. Explain how the modern social sciences developed.

Introducing the Lesson

Remind students that the Industrial Revolution produced radical technological changes in the production of goods. At the same time, important scientific advances were made that increased knowledge about the universe.

Then ask: (a) What is the difference between science and technology? (Science is the study of natural occurrences; technology results from the application of scientific principles.)

(b) How do changes in scientific understanding and technology affect each other? (Answers will vary. Sometimes new scientific understanding leads to the development of new technology; new technology often results in greater understanding of scientific principles.)

Developing the Lesson:
Comparing Historical Developments

Have students compare the influence of new scientific ideas in the 1700's (pp. 419–421) with the influence of scientific advances during the 1800's. (During the 1700's, scientists used reason to explain laws governing nature and thinkers looked for laws governing human behavior. The scientific theories of the 1800's also prompted scholars to study human society and behavior in a scientific way.) (Comprehension)

Developing the Lesson:
Organizing Information in Written Form

Have students make a chart listing the major scientists and the advances they made during the 1800's. (Comprehension)

Closing the Lesson: Making Judgments

Have students write an essay explaining which of the advances made in either the natural or the social sciences they consider to be the most significant. (Comprehension)

See Section Review questions, p. 539.

SECTION 3   (pp. 540–543)
New Trends in the Arts

Objectives

After completing this section, students will be able to:
1. Describe new styles that emerged in painting after 1860.
2. Explain how forms in music and literature changed.

Introducing the Lesson

Remind students that art, literature, and music are individual expressions that usually reflect the values and concerns of a particular period of time.

Then ask: (a) How might the Industrial Revolution have influenced art and literature? (Answers will vary. The Industrial Revolution resulted in important social changes, which are often reflected in the art of the times. Artists and writers might have used factories and cities as settings for their art; the growing middle class and factory workers might have served as subjects for artists.)

(b) How are present-day artists influenced by modern society? (Answers will vary.)

Developing the Lesson:
Analyzing a Primary Source

Have students analyze the statement by an impressionist artist on p. 540. In their analyses, students might consider the following questions:

(a) What seems to be the most important consideration to impressionists?

(b) Why might the impressionist artist have thought it important to forget "everything that has been seen before our time"? (Answers will vary, but might suggest the artist's need to see things in a new light.) (Analysis)

Developing the Lesson:
Forming a Hypothesis

Have students develop a hypothesis explaining why the Romantic movement gave way to realism. When writing their hypotheses, students should consider the impact of the Industrial Revolution on European society. *(Synthesis)*

Closing the Lesson:
Organizing Information in Written Form

Have students make a chart titled *Trends in the Arts After the Industrial Revolution.* Charts should summarize the changes that occurred in subject matter, goals, and methods of artistic expression in painting, music, literature, and drama. *(Comprehension)*

See *Section Review* questions, p. 543.

SECTION 4   (pp. 543–546)
Threats to Europe's Stability

Objectives

After completing this section, students will be able to:
1. Explain why extreme nationalism was a dangerous force.
2. Explain why anti-Semitism was widespread in Europe in the late 1800's.

Introducing the Lesson

Remind students that nationalism led many people in Europe to struggle against oppression and to work for unification and democratic reform. In the nineteenth century, however, extreme nationalism led to hatred and unfair treatment of certain groups.

Then ask: *(a) What might be some characteristics of extreme nationalism?* (Extreme nationalism might include a feeling of national superiority, abuse of different groups, and the subordination of social needs to military strength.)

(b) How might extreme nationalism result in hatred and unfair treatment? (Answers will vary.)

(c) What might be seen as present-day examples of extreme nationalism? (Answers will vary, but students might suggest South African apartheid or actions of the government of Iran.)

Developing the Lesson:
Distinguishing Fact from Opinion

Have students identify each of the following statements from the text as fact or opinion. Then have students explain the danger of accepting personal opinions as facts.

(a) "One's own racial or national group is superior to all others." (Opinion.)

(b) "Some struggling workers, feeling threatened by the many economic changes of the time, blamed other ethnic groups for their problems." (Fact.)

(c) "Extreme nationalists worried that minority groups would break down national unity." (Fact.)

(d) "[Spencer] claimed that those who were fittest for survival would become rich and successful." (Fact.)

(e) "The poor would remain poor because they were unable to compete." (Opinion.) *(Comprehension)*

Developing the Lesson:
Analyzing Information

Have students write an editorial that might have appeared in a nineteenth-century newspaper analyzing the errors of Spencer's theory of Social Darwinism. Editorials should explain the theory and then point out the mistakes in Spencer's thinking. (Answers will vary, but students might note that human society develops differently from living things; it would be difficult to provide "unmistakable proof" of "ceaseless devouring of the weak by the strong"; equating survival with wealth and success ignores other elements of human life; and the inability to compete is not the only reason for poverty.) *(Analysis)*

Closing the Lesson:
Synthesizing Information

Have students work in groups to prepare an argument that might have been given by defenders of Alfred Dreyfus in 1894. Students should identify the political and social issues involved in the Dreyfus Affair, define the French government's role, and predict the consequences for French society if the honor of the army were allowed to prevail over justice. *(Synthesis)*

See *Section Review* questions, p. 546.

Chapter 27 Review Answers
(pp. 547–548)

Vocabulary Review

1. (a) racism (b) ghetto (c) Social Darwinism (d) pogrom
2. (a) vaccination (b) Zionism

People to Identify

1. Louis Pasteur 2. Leo Tolstoy 3. Claude Monet 4. George Bernard Shaw 5. Gregor Mendel 6. Thomas Alva Edison 7. Charles Dickens 8. Pablo Picasso 9. Igor Stravinsky

Recalling the Facts

1. The amount of food available for consumption increased due to improvements in agriculture, new methods of refrigeration and canning, and better transportation. Improvements in medicine and sanitation also contributed to population growth.
2. Upper class—large landowners, wealthy businesspeople. Middle class—business owners, managers, lawyers, engineers, small shopkeepers, government workers, clerks. Working class—peasants, city workers.
3. Factory inspection laws were passed, governments began to provide social programs, workers could afford goods more easily, working hours were reduced, and leisure time was increased. Workers also gained more political power.
4. Dalton theorized that all matter is made up of tiny particles called atoms. Mendeleev helped make chemistry more systematic and mathematical by creating a table that classified elements according to their atomic structure. The Curies found that certain other minerals besides uranium give off radiation. Einstein published a theory of relativity that contradicted traditional ideas of an orderly universe. He also formulated a relationship between energy and matter.
5. The members of a species that are smarter, faster, stronger, or in other ways better fitted to survive than other members of the same species will survive. Religious thinkers saw Darwin's theory as a contradiction of Biblical teachings about creation.
6. After conditioning a dog's reflexes, Pavlov concluded that human actions were not always determined consciously. Freud worked to understand how the mind blocks out unpleasant events and how these events can be brought to the surface.
7. The impressionists tried to show their impression of an object rather than a realistic representation of it. They also chose new subject matter, such as the lives of people in an urban, industrialized setting. The post-impressionists showed objects as patterns of forms and flat surfaces and used vivid colors and distorted images. The expressionists used their works to express intense emotion. The cubists painted natural shapes as geometrical forms.
8. The works of writers reflected social problems and dealt with the everyday lives of ordinary people. Writers also explored complex psychological relationships between people, and portrayed characters with depth and honesty. Dramatists also wrote about ordinary people and used everyday language, not poetry, in their dialogues.
9. They put the prestige of their nation above democratic rights and individual freedoms, and viewed concern for those as signs of weakness and decay. They argued that war brought out the greatness of a nation.
10. In the Middle Ages, Jews were accused of poisoning wells to kill Christians. Through the years they were humiliated, tortured, massacred, or forced to convert to Christianity. Jews were often barred from owning land and belonging to craft guilds. In some countries Jews were forced to live in ghettos. In the 1800's extreme nationalists viewed Jews as a threat to their nations and anti-Semitic parties sprang up. In France, the Dreyfus Affair was partially caused by anti-Semitism. In Eastern Europe, Rumania and Russia persecuted Jews, and Russian officials encouraged pogroms. In Germany, racists spread myths about Jews.

Critical Thinking Skills

1–2. Answers will vary.
3. London. Moscow. The population of all the cities rose over this time period. Reasons might include urbanization and improvements in agriculture, medicine, and sanitation.

Thinking About Geography

Answers will vary, but should point out Darwin's idea that the isolation of the Galápagos Islands contributed to the emergence of new species there.

Enrichment: Primary Sources

1. Lying to the public about the case in order to cover up their mistake in convicting Dreyfus.
2. Condemning an accused man on the basis of a secret document and then acquitting a guilty man to help cover up that violation of the law.
3. His passion for "light," or truth and justice.

Europe in the Late 1800's

1850–1914

See chapter timeline, p. 546.

Before You Read This Chapter

Have you ever sat beside a river, watching the water race along? What is happening below the surface? The current may be slower, but there is still movement. As you read this chapter about late nineteenth-century Europe, you might keep the image of a river in mind. A current of change and discovery was flowing through Europe. What medical and scientific advances were causing a big splash? What new artistic ideas were flowing into the mainstream? What dangerous currents of thought were surfacing and gathering force?

The Geographic Setting

The Chapter Outline

1. An Industrial Society
2. New Scientific Ideas
3. New Trends in the Arts
4. Threats to Europe's Stability

The mechanical wonders displayed at London's Crystal Palace drew millions of visitors and marked Britain as the world's leading industrial nation.

1 An Industrial Society

Objectives

Focus Questions

★ ■ How did European society change in the late 1800's? *(pages 531–533)*

● ■ What class divisions existed in Europe? *(pages 533–534)*

Terms to Know

vaccination
pasteurization

★ Note strategies for first objective on this page and p. 532.

By the late 1800's, industrialization had taken hold in much of Western Europe. Along with the enormous economic changes of this period came important social changes. In little more than a century, Europe became the world's first industrial society.

An Era of Rapid Change

Sec. Rev. ques. 2

Areas of growth. In the late 1800's, advances in industry began happening faster than ever before. Steel, chemical, and electrical industries were the pacesetters. The increase in steel production was spectacular. In 1870 Britain, Germany, France, and Belgium produced about 385,000 tons of steel. By 1913 output was 32,000,000 tons—nearly 90 times as great. Chemists spurred industry and agriculture by developing such products as synthetic dyes and chemical fertilizers.

The growing use of electricity changed daily life forever. Thomas Alva Edison, an American inventor, found hundreds of uses for electricity. Among his inventions were the light bulb and the phonograph. In 1882, power stations designed by Edison were built in London and New York. Electric lights soon replaced gas globes and kerosene lanterns on city streets and in buildings. Electric streetcars and subways provided quick and cheap transportation.

Great Britain, the first country to industrialize, was still the leader in banking, shipping, and textile production. The United States and Germany, however, began to challenge Britain's position as the world's leading industrial nation. Germany was turning out more steel than Britain and leading in the chemical industry. The United States had surpassed Britain in the production of steel, iron, and coal.

The movement to cities. The rapid growth of industry led to a huge increase in the size of some cities. Eastern and southern Europe remained largely agricultural, but in northwestern Europe people were flocking to urban centers. Between 1880 and 1914, the population of Paris rose from two million to three million. In 1866 Berlin had 500,000 inhabitants; in 1914 it had more than two million. Large cities also grew up in the coal-mining regions of northern France and eastern Germany.

As Russia began to build factories in the late nineteenth century, its cities grew too. In 1863 only three Russian cities had a population of more than 100,000. Forty years later Russia had 15 cities of this size.

The cities of Europe were centers of culture as well as business. They could boast of universities, museums, concert halls, and theaters. Many had wide streets, beautiful parks, and fine houses. Yet the early problems caused by urbanization (page 495) had not vanished. Most European cities also had overcrowded, crime-ridden slums.

A population explosion. In 1800 the total population of Europe was about 190 million. By 1914 it had soared to 480 million. This population boom was partly due to the availability of more food. Improvements in **531**

★ RETEACHING. Have students review "Areas of growth" and "The movement to cities" (above) and then work in groups to list possible benefits of advances in industry, increased use of electricity, and rapid urban growth. Have each group compare its list with the others. *(Comprehension) Drawing Inferences*

Biography Thomas Edison received only three months of formal education, after which he was expelled for having limited ability. During his lifetime, Edison took out patents on almost 1,100 inventions.

★ REINFORCEMENT. Have students write an essay describing the economic and social trends that developed as a result of the Industrial Revolution and evaluating the relevance of those trends to society today. (Trends include increased production, growth of cities, population growth, and increased literacy.) *(Synthesis) Analyzing Information*

A scene in London from the 1880's reveals details of city life. Note that horse-drawn vehicles were the major form of transportation.

Sec. Rev. ques. 3

farming led to bigger harvests. Railways and steamships brought tons of grain to Western Europe from the farms of Russia and the United States. New methods of refrigeration and canning made it possible to ship beef from Argentina and the United States.

Advances in medicine and sanitation. Another reason for the population explosion was progress made against disease. In the late 1700's, an English country doctor named Edward Jenner made a breakthrough discovery. He found a way to prevent smallpox, a disease that killed many people and left others with badly scarred skin.

Jenner noticed that dairy workers who had a mild illness called cowpox rarely got smallpox. To test an idea, Jenner decided to make a solution that contained cowpox germs. He then injected it into the arm of a young boy. A few weeks later the boy was exposed to smallpox and did not catch it. Jenner's method of vaccination—injecting a person with a solution of weakened germs to

532

Biography Louis Pasteur also showed that the disease rabies was transmitted by agents too small to be seen with a microscope.

prevent disease—was soon being used all over Europe.

Jenner knew how to prevent smallpox, but he never learned the cause of the disease. Not until 50 years later did a French chemist, Louis Pasteur (pas-TUR), discover the tiny organisms, called bacteria, that cause many diseases. Realizing that bacteria could be killed by heat, he invented pasteurization—a way of using heat to sterilize milk. At about the same time, a German doctor, Robert Koch, also began to study bacteria. In 1882 he found the cause of tuberculosis, a common illness at that time.

Alerted to the danger of bacteria, scientists worked on ways to fight them. In the 1860's Joseph Lister, an English surgeon, began to use antiseptics to kill bacteria in hospital operating rooms. Patients having surgery were now less likely to die of infections caused by dirty instruments or the doctor's unwashed hands.

Public officials, too, began to understand that cleanliness helped prevent the spread of disease. European cities took steps to improve public health. They paved streets, built sewer systems, began regular garbage collections, and piped clean running water into homes. Such measures cut down the number of deaths caused by disease.

Public education. The general level of education rose sharply at the end of the ★ See below.

Louis Pasteur's discoveries helped eliminate deadly diseases like tuberculosis and rabies.

Check for Understanding. Ask: What improvements in food production and transportation contributed to a population explosion in Western Europe? (Improvements in farming led to greater harvests; railways and steamships increased the availability of food; new methods of refrigeration and canning made shipments of beef from Argentina and the United States possible.)

Science Note that Joseph Lister introduced his antiseptic methods at the Glasgow Royal Infirmary. Between 1865 and 1869 the surgical mortality rate in the Male Accident Ward fell from 45% to 15%.
★ ENRICHMENT. Have students research the expansion of public education in Europe during the late 1800's and develop a hypothesis explaining why it occurred and how it might have affected society. (Synthesis) Locating Information

Average Life Expectancy in Industrialized Nations, 1850–1910

Years of Age / Year

Source: E. A. Wrigley, *Population and History*

Average life expectancy is the number of years a person born in a given year can expect to live. What is the average life expectancy of someone born in an industrialized nation in 1900? What trend do you see in the graph? Graph Answers: (1) 50.5 (2) The increase of the average life expectancy.

nineteenth century. By 1900 most European countries required children to attend elementary school. Literacy had become common in most countries of northern Europe. In other parts of Europe, however, many people still could not read or write.

Even with the spread of public schooling, opportunities for education beyond elementary school remained severely limited. Formal education for most people ended at age 11 or 12, when they left school to take jobs. In Germany, for example, 92 percent of the youth attended primary school, but only 8 percent went on to secondary school. Even fewer people—and almost no women—went to universities. Higher education was usually possible only for boys in the middle and upper classes.

The Importance of Class

● Note strategies for second objective on this page and p. 534.

Inequalities in education point out the importance of class in nineteenth-century Europe. The Industrial Revolution transformed the European social structure, bringing new classes into prominence.

A new social structure. Before the Industrial Revolution, large landowners had stood at the top of society, controlling most of the wealth and power. Now a group of successful businesspeople, such as bankers and industrialists, rose to challenge them. These businesspeople gained power because of their wealth, not noble birth. Unlike the landowning aristocrats, who looked down on moneymaking, the bankers and industrialists were proud of their standing in the world of business.

Below the upper class came the middle class, which grew tremendously during the 1800's. The wealthy business and professional families of the upper middle class owned banks, stores, and factories or worked as managers, lawyers, or engineers. The lower middle class included small shopkeepers, government workers, and clerks.

The vast majority of the population still belonged to the the working class. This group included not only peasants but also the countless new city workers who had jobs in factories. They were generally uneducated and had few skills.

While workers remained on the bottom rung of society, they did make many gains during the late 1800's. The earliest factories were nightmares in terms of safety—poorly heated and cooled, and full of dangerous chemicals, such as lead, arsenic, mercury, and zinc. Factory inspection laws reduced the number of industrial accidents. In the 1880's the German government began to provide benefits for sick, injured, and elderly workers. By 1914 Austria, Italy, Denmark, Switzerland, France, and Britain had started similar social programs.

Sec. Rev. ques. 4

In a number of other ways, the lives of ordinary people improved. Many workers could afford to buy meat and eggs more regu-

533

● RETEACHING. Have students make a diagram of the social structure in Europe after the Industrial Revolution and indicate the members of each class. (*Upper class:* large landowners and successful business people. *Middle class:* wealthy business and professional families, small shopkeepers, government workers, and clerks. *Working class:* peasants and factory workers.) (*Comprehension*) *Translating Information into Another Form*

● REINFORCEMENT. Have students explain the following statement: *The Industrial Revolution created greater economic and social opportunities for many people.* (After the Industrial Revolution, social and economic standing depended less on heredity and more on wealth that could be acquired.) (*Comprehension*) *Understanding Cause and Effect*

Factory work in the late 1800's offered laborers a steady income, but unsafe conditions also brought health and safety risks. This painting shows the inside of a German ironworks in 1875.

larly and also clothes, shoes, and other mass-produced goods. The work week had been reduced to 55 or 60 hours. Workers now had leisure time that they could spend at sports, music halls, vaudeville theaters, and other popular recreations.

● See below.

Workers also gained more political power as the right to vote was broadened. By 1912 almost all adult males could vote in France, Britain, Belgium, Spain, Norway, Sweden, Italy, and Austria. New political parties gained support among workers. The Labour Party in Great Britain and the Social Democratic Party in Germany began to challenge the established leadership. Socialist and Socialist Democratic candidates won seats in the French and Austrian parliaments.

534

See Sec. 1 *Closing the Lesson,* p. T529B.

Check for Understanding. Ask: **How did life for ordinary people improve in the late 1800's?** (Many people could afford better food, clothing, and other goods. The number of work hours was reduced and people had more leisure time.)

● ENRICHMENT. Have students write an essay explaining how the transformation of the European social structure and gains made by workers might have affected the social values of the time. *(Synthesis) Analyzing Information*

5. Students might respond that advances in agriculture and transportation increased the amount and availability of food, encouraging population growth. Also, advances in medicine helped people live longer.

2 New Scientific Ideas

Objectives

Focus Questions

★ ■ What scientific advances were made in Europe? *(pages 535–539)*

● ■ How did the modern social sciences develop? *(page 539)*

Terms to Know

radiation   sociology
evolution   psychology
genetics

★ Note strategies for first objective on this page and p. 538.

Scientific discoveries during the 1800's brought better health care and better living conditions to many people. At the same time, a surge of scientific curiosity led to startling theories about the physical world. The findings in science influenced the study of human society and behavior as well.

Chemistry and Physics

New discoveries in chemistry. The Scientific Revolution of the 1500's and 1600's laid the foundation of modern physics and astronomy. Modern chemistry, on the other hand, did not begin to take shape until the late 1700's.

Since ancient times, people had believed that all matter was made of four "elements"—fire, air, water, and earth. In the 1700's, scientists disproved this theory by breaking down these substances into smaller elements. Joseph Priestley, an English scientist, began to experiment with air. He found that air was not a single substance but a mixture of gases. One gas in particular interested

him, because of its remarkable qualities. Priestley shared his discovery with a French chemist, Antoine Lavoisier (lah-vwah-zee-AY), who named this gas "oxygen."

In his own experiments, Lavoisier proved that fire is not a substance but a chemical reaction involving oxygen. He named many other elements as well, becoming known as the founder of modern chemistry. (Lavoisier also was active in French revolutionary politics and was sent to the guillotine in 1794, during the Reign of Terror.)

Sec. Rev. ques. 2

In the early 1800's, John Dalton, an English chemist, came up with the theory that all matter is made up of tiny, indestructible particles called atoms. According to his theory, the atoms of the various elements combine to create different substances. For example, one atom of carbon and two of oxygen always combine to form carbon dioxide. Though parts of Dalton's atomic theory were later proved wrong, his ideas were a forward step for modern chemistry and physics.

Dmitri Mendeleev (men-duh-LAY-uf), a Russian chemist, helped make chemistry more systematic and mathematical. In 1868 he worked out a table that classified elements according to their atomic structure. He left gaps in this table, predicting that elements not yet discovered would later fill them in. All the elements found since Mendeleev's time have fit into those gaps.

Advances in physics. In the late 1800's and early 1900's, scientists looked further into the structure of matter. In 1864 James Clerk Maxwell, an English physicist, predicted the existence of electromagnetic waves. Heinrich Hertz of Germany proved Maxwell's theory right in 1887. In 1895 a German physicist, Wilhelm Roentgen (RENT-gun), discovered a new form of electromagnetic waves. These very short waves could penetrate solid matter. At first Roentgen was not sure what the waves were, and he named them X-rays—*X* meaning

535

★ RETEACHING. Have students identify the person associated with each of the following scientific developments: atomic theory (Dalton); X-rays (Roentgen); radiation theory (Marie and Pierre Curie); theory of relativity (Einstein); theory of evolution and principle of natural selection (Darwin). *(Comprehension) Observing for Detail*

★ REINFORCEMENT. Have students make a chart identifying the scientific advances made during the 1800's. *(Comprehension) Translating Information into Another Form*

Biography After Lavoisier's execution, Joseph Louis Lagrange, one of the most important mathematical and physical scientists of the late 18th century, said "It took only an instant to cut off that head, and a hundred years may not produce another like it."

Biography

Marie Curie

When Marie Curie discovered a new radioactive element in 1898, she named it polonium in honor of Poland, her native land. At that time, there was no country called Poland. It had been divided and swallowed up by Austria, Prussia, and Russia (page 403). By choosing the name polonium, Marie Curie was reminding the world that Poles wanted a country of their own.

Marie Curie was born in the city of Warsaw in 1867. When she was 18, she took a job as a governess to help pay her older sister's way through medical school in Paris. Six years later Marie herself went to Paris to study science. There she met and married Pierre Curie.

Together Marie and Pierre Curie began the research on radioactivity for which they shared the Nobel Prize in physics in 1903. After Pierre died in a traffic accident in 1906, Marie Curie continued their work. In 1911 she won the Nobel Prize in chemistry for isolating pure radium. No one had ever won two Nobel Prizes before.

Over the following years, Marie Curie worked to establish centers for the study of radioactivity. She trained a new generation of physicists and chemists, many of whom made significant discoveries. In 1934 she died of leukemia brought on by years of working unprotected with radioactive material.

"unknown." He soon showed that X-rays could be useful in several scientific fields.

In 1897 the French scientist A. H. Becquerel (bek-uh-REL) found that uranium gives off high-speed rays, or **radiation**, similar to X-rays. He shared his discovery with a Polish-born chemist, Marie Curie, and her husband, Pierre Curie, a physicist. In their work, the Curies found that certain other minerals also give off radiation. Such minerals are said to be radioactive. The Curies theorized that the atoms in minerals such as radium were constantly breaking down and giving off energy in the form of radiation.

These ideas contradicted Dalton's theory that atoms, as the smallest unit of matter, could not be split. Physicists now began to investigate the makeup of the atom.

In 1911 Ernest Rutherford suggested a model for the structure of the atom. In this model, the atom looked something like the solar system. A heavy central core, or nucleus (NOO-klee-us), was surrounded by orbiting electrons. Rutherford's model was later

Biography Note that for his discovery of X-rays, Roentgen was awarded the first Nobel Prize in physics in 1901.

Ⓕ **FEATURE ACTIVITY. Ask: What might Marie Curie have included on a list titled "Difficulties and Accomplishments of My Life"?** (*Difficulties:* postponing her education to help her sister; working in an academic discipline dominated by men; her husband's death. *Accomplishments:* discovered a new radioactive element; isolated pure radium; won two Nobel Prizes; established study centers.) *(Evaluation)* **Making Judgments** changed as scientists found other particles within the atom.

Old ideas questioned. Not all scientists in the early 1900's agreed with these findings. Traditional (or classical) physics had been based on the theories of Isaac Newton (page 415). In the universe as Newton saw it, all the parts followed strict mathematical laws and worked in perfect harmony, like a smooth-running machine. The new discoveries in science, however, caused many scientists to doubt Newton's views.

Einstein's theory of relativity. The greatest challenge to Newtonian physics came from Albert Einstein (1879–1955), a brilliant, German-born scientist. In 1905, while working as a clerk in the Swiss patent office, Einstein published a scientific theory that forced people to reconsider the orderly universe described by Newton. Einstein's theory of relativity stated that, while Newton's laws apply in the ordinary world, they do not work for objects moving at speeds near the speed of light.

Sec. Rev. ques. 2, cont.

According to Einstein's theory, as things travel faster—approaching the speed of light—the everyday rules for time, space, and motion change. The only way to describe the motion of a moving object is to compare it with another moving object. Therefore, all motion is relative to some other motion and to the observer. Einstein's theory affected thinking about time and space as well; these too were seen as relative, not absolute.

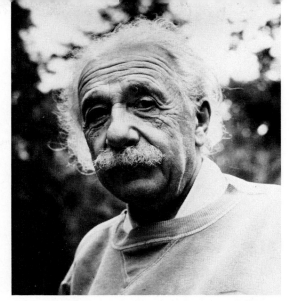

Albert Einstein, one of the greatest scientists in history, believed "the most beautiful thing we can experience is the mysterious. It is the source of all art and science."

Matter and energy. Einstein's 1905 paper also contained his formula for showing the relationship between matter and energy. This question had puzzled scientists like Marie Curie, who worked with substances that gave off energy in the form of radiation. In simple terms, Einstein's formula $E = mc^2$ means that mass and energy can be converted into each other. The tiny amount of matter in an atom can be changed into huge amounts of energy. In the 1940's, scientists used this knowledge to make the atomic bomb.

Evolution and Genetics

Just as new ideas revolutionized physics and chemistry in the 1800's, new theories changed other areas of science. Observing the many different kinds of plants and animals, naturalists asked themselves what caused living creatures to take such a great variety of forms. Many believed that each species had been created separately. Others, however, believed in evolution—the idea that living things change over time and that one species might slowly evolve into another. They tried to explain how this might happen.

Darwin's theory of evolution. One explanation was provided by a young English scientist named Charles Darwin. From 1831 **537**

Meanwhile . . .

IN THE NORTH ATLANTIC

As science and technology advanced, shipbuilders competed to build faster ocean liners. In 1912 the *Titanic* was not only the largest and fastest liner ever built but was hailed as an "unsinkable" ship. Tragically, on its first voyage the *Titanic* struck an iceberg in the North Atlantic and sank. About 1,500 of its passengers drowned.

Biography Charles Darwin was a poor student and was criticized by his father in 1825, who claimed that he cared "for nothing but shooting, dogs, and rat-catching," and would be "a disgrace" to himself and his family.

Charles Darwin's theories had a tremendous, far-reaching effect on the natural sciences. He formed those theories after a voyage to the Galápagos Islands aboard the *Beagle,* the ship shown here.

to 1836, Darwin worked aboard the *Beagle,* a ship making a scientific voyage to South America. Darwin carefully observed the unusual birds, plants, and animals living on the coast of South America and the Galápagos (gah-LAH-pah-gus) Islands. He concluded that many species of animals had died out, that new species had emerged in isolated places (such as the Galápagos), and that there were links between past and present species.

After he returned from the voyage, Darwin began to organize his findings. He came to believe that all living forms, including human beings, evolved from earlier forms of life that had existed millions of years ago. In 1859 Darwin published his theory in a book called *The Origin of Species.*

The principle of natural selection. Darwin based his theory partly on Malthus's idea (page 498) that populations tend to grow faster than the food supply. Because of competition for food, said Darwin, certain living things will survive and others will die before they have offspring. The advantage, he suggested, is with those members of a species that are smarter, faster, stronger, or in other ways better able to survive than other members of the same species. Darwin called this the principle of natural selection.

According to Darwin's theory, the fittest members of a species have offspring that share their special advantages. Little by little, over many generations, the species may change. In this way a new species can evolve.

Darwin's theory of evolution had a great impact on many fields of science, bringing about what is sometimes called the Darwinian Revolution. His theory also sparked a controversy that has raged ever since. Many religious thinkers denied Darwin's views. They pointed out that Darwin's ideas contradicted the Bible's account of the creation of life. Other people rejected the view that human beings are part of the animal kingdom.

Mendel's experiments. Darwin's theory did not explain how living things pass on characteristics to their offspring. Gregor Mendel, an Austrian monk, began to work out such an explanation in the 1860's.

Mendel carried out many experiments with pea plants, crossing yellow peas with green ones, tall plants with short ones, and so on. He found that in each new generation of pea plants, parental characteristics had not

Sec. Rev. ques. 3

★ See below.

538

Check for Understanding. Ask: Why did some people object to Darwin's idea of evolution? (Many religious thinkers claimed that the theory of evolution contradicted the biblical account of creation. Others rejected the notion that human beings are part of the animal kingdom.)

★ ENRICHMENT. Have students trace the development of one of the scientific advances made during the 1800's to modern times. Students might research the uses of X-rays and radiation in medicine, how Einstein's formula was used to make the atomic bomb, or how the science of genetics is used in the study of disease. (Application) *Linking Past and Present* smoothly blended. For example, crossing tall plants and short ones did not produce medium-size plants. Instead, individual plants inherited certain traits of each "parent" plant—some were short, some tall.

Later work by biologists led to the discovery of genes, which carry traits from parent to offspring. Mendel's work laid the foundation of the science of **genetics**—the study of inherited traits.

The Social Sciences

● Note strategies for second objective on this page.

The scientific theories of the 1800's prompted scholars to study human society and behavior in a scientific way. As thinkers examined society, politics, history, and economic life, the modern social sciences developed.

Sociology. The term sociology—the scientific study of human society—was invented by a French philosopher, Auguste Comte (KAWNT), in the mid-1800's. Comte believed that society, like nature, operated under a certain set of laws. He tried to discover these laws so that they could be used to help leaders make decisions. Most sociologists today do not believe that such laws exist. Instead, they carry out careful research and analyze their findings in order to find out how individuals and groups interact.

The study of the past. Nineteenth-century historians, particularly in Germany, also began to use the methods of science to make the study of history more accurate. Leopold von Ranke (RAHNG-kuh) said that historical writers should study primary sources as the best way to find out what actually happened.

Curiosity about the past encouraged scholars to look deeper into folklore, primitive societies, and ancient civilizations. From this interest the fields of archeology and anthropology developed. Both used historical research and scientific methods of investigation. On expeditions to ancient sites in Greece and the Middle East, archeologists uncovered the ruins of past civilizations.

Psychology. Another new social science was **psychology**—the study of the mind and behavior. Ivan Pavlov (1849–1936), a Russian biologist, broke new ground in psychology with a famous experiment. Ordinarily, a dog's mouth waters at the smell of food. Pavlov began ringing a bell each time he gave food to a dog. Eventually the dog learned to associate the bell with food. Each time the bell rang, the dog salivated, even if no food was present. Pavlov concluded that an animal's reflexes could be changed, or conditioned, through training. Pavlov applied these findings to humans. He believed that human actions were not always determined by conscious thought.

Sigmund Freud (FROYD), an Austrian doctor who lived from 1856 to 1939, came up with startling theories about how the mind works. In treating patients with psychological problems, Freud found that some of these problems could be traced back to childhood experiences. He concluded that his patients had blocked out unpleasant events, and that the patients would be helped if these hidden memories were brought to the surface. Freud encouraged his patients to talk about whatever came to mind. He also studied their dreams, looking for clues to their problems. Freud's theories, though hotly disputed by many people, have influenced psychologists to this day.

Sec. Rev. ques. 4

See Sec. 2 *Closing the Lesson,* p. T529B.

● Note strategies for second objective on this page.

Section Review

Answers to Section Review questions are in brackets on pages indicated.

1. **Define:** radiation, evolution, genetics, sociology, psychology. (pp. 536, 537, 539)
2. How did Lavoisier, the Curies, and Einstein contribute to scientific knowledge? (pp. 535, 536, 537)
3. Describe Darwin's principle of natural selection. (p. 538)
4. How did Freud try to uncover the sources of human behavior? (p. 539)
5. **Critical thinking:** Why were many of the scientific discoveries that were made in the late 1800's considered to be revolutionary? (See answer below.)

539

● RETEACHING. Have students identify the subject of the following: **sociology** (human society); **psychology** (the mind and behavior). *(Comprehension) Observing for Detail*
● REINFORCEMENT. Have students write an essay explaining how the social sciences might contribute to the development of society. (Answers will vary. Understanding social, historical, and psychological patterns might help those responsible for public policy plan better.) *(Synthesis) Making Judgments*

● ENRICHMENT. Have students find information on social science courses offered in local colleges or universities. Students might interview a social science professor and attend some classes. Have students describe the results of their research to the class. *(Application) Locating Information*
5. Students might suggest that the discoveries in this period caused many scientists to question long-held assumptions that had influenced physical, natural, and social sciences.

3 New Trends in the Arts

Objectives

Focus Questions

★ ■ What new styles emerged in painting after 1860? *(pages 540–542)*
● ■ How did forms in music and literature change? *(pages 542–543)*

Terms to Know

impressionism	cubism
post-impressionism	realism

★ Note strategies for first objective on this page and p. 541.

The arts in Europe during the late 1800's reflected the fresh ideas and creative energies of the times. Artists experimented with brand new forms and structures in their works. Many were influenced by the changes taking place in society, especially the impact of industrialization. Painters and writers began to explore the lives of ordinary people. By the early 1900's, the arts, like the sciences, were entering the modern age.

Painting

Sec. Rev. ques. 2

Impressionism.   Until the mid-1800's, most painters tried to show exactly what people or objects looked like. About 1860 a group of painters in Paris began to try giving their impression of a subject, rather than a realistic representation. Fascinated by light, they used pure, shimmering colors to capture a scene as it might look at a glance. This style of art became known as impressionism.

The leaders of the impressionist group were Édouard Manet (mah-NAY), Claude Monet (moh-NAY), Edgar Degas (deh-GAH), and Pierre-Auguste Renoir (ren-

540

WAHR). One artist described impressionism this way:

66 Right now a moment of time is fleeting by! Capture its reality in paint! To do that we must put all else out of our minds. We must become that moment and give the image of what we actually see, forgetting everything that has been seen before our time. 99

In addition to a new style, the impressionists found new subject matter. They painted the lives of ordinary people in an urban, industrialized world. They showed shop clerks and dock workers in dance halls and cafés. They painted performers in theaters and circuses. They also created city scenes—bridges, railroad stations, streets filled with traffic.

Post-impressionism.   In the 1880's painting took a new turn with the work of Paul Cézanne (say-ZAHN), a French artist who began as an impressionist. As the years passed, Cézanne moved even further from realistic painting. He showed objects as patterns of forms and flat surfaces, in a style that came to be called post-impressionism.

Post-impressionist painters experimented with vivid colors and distorted images. Paul Gauguin (goh-GAN), a Parisian stockbroker, gave up his business career to paint the landscape and people of the Pacific island of Tahiti. The paintings of Vincent van Gogh (van GOH), a Dutch-born artist, changed everyday scenes into patterns of swirling color and movement.

Expressionism and cubism.   Post-impressionism influenced other developments in art. Some painters became known as expressionists, because they tried to express intense emotion in their works. About 1907 in Paris, Georges Braque (BRAHK) and the Spanish-born Pablo Picasso began a movement that came to be called cubism. The

★ RETEACHING. Have students review "Painting" (pp. 540–542) and describe the following styles of art: impressionism (Gives an impression of a subject rather than a realistic representation.) post-impressionism (Shows objects as patterns of form and flat surfaces.) cubism (Shows natural shapes as geometrical forms.) *(Comprehension) Observing for Detail*

★ REINFORCEMENT. Have students examine the art by Renoir, van Gogh, and Braque shown on p. 541 and describe the characteristics that identify each work as impressionist, post-impressionist, or cubist. (Renoir used a soft, muted style and vibrant colors; van Gogh used distortion; Braque illustrated geometric form.) *(Evaluation) Analyzing a Primary Source*

Van Gogh, Vincent. *The Starry Night* (1889). Oil on canvas, 29×36¼. Collection, The Museum of Modern Art, New York. Acquired through the Lillie P. Bliss Bequest.

Van Gogh's *The Starry Night* (1889) sees the night sky as an explosion of light and movement. Why might this painting be called post-impressionist?

Renoir's impressionist painting *Girl with Watering Can* (1876) uses bright colors and hazy light to capture an instant of beauty.

Cubist paintings like Braque's *Head of a Woman* (1909) use geometric shapes to show familiar forms in a new, abstract way.

541

George Bernard Shaw's sharp-witted plays focused on social problems. He won the Nobel Prize for literature in 1925.

cubists looked at natural shapes and tried to paint them as geometrical forms. A human body, for example, might be shown as a series of triangles or boxes.

All these developments made art more abstract and less related to real objects. By the early 1900's it was not necessary for a painting to be of *something*. It could be pure color, shape, or pattern. Picasso expressed the viewpoint of the modern artist: "I paint forms as I think them, not as I see them."

Music

● Note strategies for second objective on this page.

Traditional forms. Music in the 1800's developed mainly along the lines set by the Romantics and the nationalistic composers (page 479). The most influential composer was Johannes Brahms, who used the forms of the German Classical tradition but added a sense of deep emotion to his works. Johann Strauss the younger, called "the waltz king," created the popular Viennese style of dance music in the 1870's and 1880's.

Sec. Rev. ques. 3

The first sign of a change in music appeared in the 1850's, with the "music dramas" of Richard Wagner (page 479). His long and powerful operas were an inspiration to later composers. He particularly influenced the symphonies of Gustav Mahler and the operas and other works of Richard Strauss in Vienna.

542

New harmonies. In the early 1900's a number of composers began to try out harmonies that sounded strange to their listeners. In France, Claude Debussy (deh-byoo-SEE) tried to create in music what the impressionist painters were attempting on canvas. Perhaps the most influential composer of the period was the Russian-born Igor Stravinsky. Some audiences, however, found his music hard to accept. When Stravinsky's ballet *The Rite of Spring* opened in Paris in 1913, a riot broke out in the theater.

Literature and Drama

Realism in literature. Many writers in the late 1800's rejected the Romantics' stress on personal emotions. Instead they wrote about social problems and the everyday lives of ordinary people. This new trend in literature was called **realism** because it tried to be true to life. Novels were set in villages, in city slums, and even in prisons.

In England particularly, there was a new audience for popular fiction because more people were able to read. They eagerly made their way through novels that came out in installments in weekly magazines. Charles Dickens published most of his novels in this way. Dickens's books, rich in both humor and tragedy, showed the harsh conditions in the factories and cities of England (page 495). In contrast, Thomas Hardy wrote of life in rural England. Both authors explored people's complex psychological relationships.

In France, Gustave Flaubert (floh-BAYR) described the life of a middle-class French woman in his novel *Madame Bovary* (1857). Émile Zola wrote in grim detail of middle-class and working-class life.

Some of the greatest masters of realistic fiction were Russian. Anton Chekhov described middle-class country life in plays and short stories. Fyodor Dostoyevsky (dahs-tuh-YEF-skee) probed the inner feelings of his characters in novels such as *Crime and Punishment* (1866). Count Leo Tolstoy showed the rich background of Russian society in his novel *War and Peace* (1866).

● RETEACHING. Have students review "Literature and Drama" (pp. 542–543) and find sentences that point to the interest of writers in industrialization, urbanization, and the rise of the common person. (Comprehension) Observing for Detail

Check for Understanding. Ask: How did realists differ from the writers who had come before them? (Realists did not stress personal emotions, as did the Romantics. Instead, they wrote about social problems and the lives of ordinary people.)

● REINFORCEMENT. Have students define realism, identify some writers who were realists, and give examples that indicate their realism. (Comprehension) Summarizing Information

● ENRICHMENT. Have students choose one of the writers discussed in this section, find an example of his work, and report on how the work represents the new concerns and interests of the period. (Analysis) Analyzing a Primary Source

Realism in drama. During the late nineteenth century the new emphasis on human psychology and social problems led to a new kind of drama. The characters in these modern plays were ordinary people who spoke in everyday language, not poetry. The plays of the Norwegian dramatist Henrik Ibsen shocked audiences with their honest pictures of family tensions and social problems. George Bernard Shaw, who was born in Ireland, became a leading writer in Britain with his witty plays and criticism of society. Drama in Russia flourished at the Moscow Art Theater, which opened in 1898 with Chekhov's play *The Sea Gull.*

See Sec. 3 *Closing the Lesson*, p. T529C.

See lesson plans, pp. T529A–T529C.

Section Review

Answers to Section Review questions are in brackets on pages indicated.

1. **Define or identify:** impressionism, post-impressionism, cubism, realism. (pp. 540, 542)
2. What new styles of painting developed in the late 1800's? (p. 540)
3. What composers experimented with new ideas in music? (p. 542)
4. **Critical thinking:** Did writers and artists of the late 1800's share similar ideas about representing the external world? Explain. (See answer below.)

4. Students might point out that both writers and artists explored the lives of ordinary people. Many artists, however, experimented with abstract forms and structures.

4 Threats to Europe's Stability

Objectives

Focus Questions

★ ■ Why was extreme nationalism a dangerous force? *(pages 543–544)*

● ■ Why was anti-Semitism widespread in Europe in the late 1800's? *(pages 544–545)*

Terms to Know

racism	Dreyfus Affair
Social Darwinism	pogrom
anti-Semitism	Zionism
ghetto	

★ Note strategies for first objective on this page and p. 544.

For many Europeans, especially the well-to-do middle class, the late 1800's and early 1900's seemed a time of peace and security. People were certain that European society was an enlightened one, and they saw signs of progress on every side. They failed to notice that the forces of nationalism and racism were growing within Europe, threatening to upset the stability of the continent.

Extreme Nationalism

In the first half of the 1800's, nationalism had been linked with movements for freedom. It led oppressed regions to seek independence from foreign rule and nurtured a sense of community among people who shared similar traditions.

In the second half of the century, however, nationalism began to get out of hand. Extreme nationalists believed the prestige of their nation to be more important than democratic rights and individual freedoms. Some nationalist thinkers even came to view democracy and concern for individual rights as signs of weakness and decay.

Sec. Rev. ques. 2

Extreme nationalists glorified war and military might. They argued that war brought out the heroism and greatness of a nation. Many of these extremists also spoke of ruling over all lands and peoples that "rightfully belonged" to their nation. Pan-Germans, for instance, wanted to unite all the German-speaking peoples in Central Europe. Some spoke of uniting the Germans with the Dutch, the Swiss, and the Scandinavians, who also had German ancestors.

543

★ RETEACHING. Have students explain the difference between nationalists in the early 1800's and nationalists in the late 1800's. (Nationalists led independence movements and nurtured a sense of community. Extreme nationalists believed national prestige was more important than democracy and they glorified war.) *(Comprehension) Observing for Detail*

Check for Understanding. Ask: Why did extreme nationalists glorify war? (They felt it brought out the heroism and greatness of a nation.)

★ REINFORCEMENT. Have students define Social Darwinism and explain how the theory was used to support belief in racism. (Social Darwinism stated that the concept of natural selection could be applied to social and economic life and that some groups, more "fit" than others, were intended by nature to dominate others.) *(Comprehension) Observing for Detail*

Background Note that a Pan-German League was formed in Germany in the late 1800's, but its extremist views never attracted a large following.

Racism

One of the greatest threats posed by extreme nationalism was its acceptance of **racism**—the belief that one's own racial or national group is superior to all others. Racism had existed for thousands of years, but it grew especially dangerous during the 1800's. Some struggling workers, feeling threatened by the many economic changes of the time, blamed other ethnic groups for their problems. Extreme nationalists worried that minority groups would break down national unity. Some thinkers began trying to find scientific evidence to back up racist ideas.

Sec. Rev. ques. 3

Social Darwinism. Darwin's theory of evolution concerned the development of living things. Herbert Spencer, an English philosopher, tried to apply Darwin's theory to all fields of knowledge, including sociology and economics. Spencer's philosophy, called **Social Darwinism**, attracted many followers in Britain and the United States in the late 1800's.

Social Darwinists argued that the concept of natural selection worked in the world of social and economic life just as it did in nature. Spencer claimed that in both worlds, "We have unmistakable proof that throughout all past time, there has been a ceaseless devouring of the weak by the strong." He and his followers claimed that those who were fittest for survival would become rich and successful. The poor would remain poor because they were unable to compete.

Sec. Rev. ques. 4

Some Social Darwinists expanded these ideas into racist thinking. They claimed that certain groups of people were "fitter"—brighter, stronger, and more advanced—than others. These "superior races," they said, were intended by nature to dominate "lesser peoples."

The spread of racism. In the late 1800's, racism could be found throughout Europe. Racist arguments were sometimes made to justify unfair treatment of local minorities. Governments often used racist thinking to explain why they had the right to rule other peoples.

544

In Germany, racists claimed that the German people were descended from the Aryans (page 55) whom they called a "superior race." As these ideas became popular in Germany, some German nationalists insisted that they had the right to dominate "inferior races." German racism was strongest against the Slavic peoples to the east and Jews in Germany itself.

★ See below, left.

Prejudice Toward European Jews

● Note strategies for second objective on this page and p. 545.

Anti-Semitism. Prejudice against Jews, known as **anti-Semitism**, had a long history in many parts of Europe. During the Middle Ages, many people had believed and spread incredible tales about the Jews. At the time of the Black Death (page 262), Jews were accused of poisoning wells to kill Christians. Over the centuries, mobs humiliated, tortured, and massacred Jews. In some lands, rulers forced Jews to convert to Christianity. Barred from owning land and from belonging to craft guilds, many medieval Jews became merchants and moneylenders.

In some countries, Jews were forced by law to live in **ghettos**. Though today the word *ghetto* describes a city slum, a ghetto at that time was a part of town set aside for Jews. The ghetto was separated from the other parts of town by walls and gates. At night and during Christian celebrations, Jews were forbidden to leave the ghetto.

In the 1800's, the ideals of the Enlightenment and the French Revolution resulted in legal equality for Jews in most of Western Europe. They could move out of the ghettos and take part in many activities that had been closed to them. With this new freedom, some Jews became successful in business, science, the arts, and, in a few countries, government. Yet most Jews remained poor.

Despite legal changes, anti-Semitism remained widespread in nineteenth-century Europe. Small shopkeepers and artisans resented competition from Jewish merchants. Peasants did not like dealing with Jewish moneylenders. In some countries extreme nationalists charged that Jews were a threat to

Sec. Rev. ques. 5

★ ENRICHMENT. Have students work in groups to present a panel discussion explaining the dangers of extreme nationalism, racism, and acceptance of Social Darwinism. *(Synthesis) Making Judgments*

● RETEACHING. Have students review "Prejudice Toward European Jews" (pp. 544–546) and make a time chart indicating expressions of anti-Semitism from the Middle Ages through the late 1800's. *(Comprehension) Sequencing Information*

● REINFORCEMENT. Have students list the causes of anti-Semitism in nineteenth-century Europe and label them as economic, political, or social. (Resentment against competition from Jewish merchants—economic. Peasants did not like dealing with Jewish moneylenders—social. Extreme nationalists claimed that Jews were a threat to the nation—political.) *(Comprehension) Analyzing Information* the state. Anti-Semitic political parties sprang up, and slurs against Jews were common in newspapers, magazines, and books.

The Dreyfus Affair in France. Anti-Semitism played a part in a scandal that rocked France in the late 1800's. The unsteady Third Republic had been set up in France at the end of the Franco-Prussian War (page 519). During the 1880's and 1890's the Third Republic was threatened by monarchists, aristocrats, nationalists, clergy, and army leaders. These groups wanted to return France to a monarchy or to have military rule.

A controversy known as the **Dreyfus Affair** became the battleground for these opposing forces. In 1894 Alfred Dreyfus (DRAY-fus), a Jewish army captain, was accused by the French government of selling military secrets to Germany. A court found him guilty, largely on the basis of false evidence. Dreyfus was sentenced to solitary confinement on Devil's Island, a French prison colony off the South American coast. In a few years, new evidence showed that he had been framed by other army officers.

Many army leaders, nationalists, leaders in the clergy, and anti-Jewish groups refused to let the case be reopened because that would cast doubt on the honor of the army. Dreyfus's defenders insisted that justice was more important. If Dreyfus was not guilty, they said, he should be freed no matter whom it might embarrass. Though he was pardoned and released in 1899, Dreyfus was not officially declared innocent until 1906.

Jews in Eastern Europe. Persecution of Jews was most severe in Eastern Europe. Rumania barred most Jews from voting and holding office. Russia restricted their admission into universities and secondary schools. Russian officials permitted and even encouraged **pogroms** (POH-grums)—organized campaigns of violence against Jewish communities. Hundreds of villages were burned and their people murdered. From the 1880's on, thousands of Jews fled Russia, many going to the United States.

In 1896 Theodor Herzl (HAYRT-sul), a Hungarian Jewish writer, called for a separate homeland where Jews would be safe from

Thomas Nast's 1881 illustration shows a Russian peasant threatening an elderly Jew. Such attacks led many East European Jews to emigrate.

persecution. A movement known as **Zionism** developed to pursue this goal. It was many years, however, before the state of Israel was established, making the dream a reality (Chapter 37).

● See below.

German anti-Semitism. The small Jewish population of Germany had made many contributions to German economic and cultural life. German Jews were far better off than the Jews of Russia. Yet they became victims of a myth spread by German racists. That myth claimed that Jews had begun a worldwide plot to dominate Germany by taking over political parties, governments, banks, and the press. German racists tried to get the government to pass anti-Jewish laws but failed.

By the early 1900's, actively anti-Semitic groups had weakened. Much harm had been done, however, by the spread of racist ideas. Many Europeans still kept an image of Jews as a threat to the nation in which they lived. **545**

See Sec. 4 *Closing the Lesson*, p. T529C.

Geography Devil's Island, located off the coast of French Guiana, is a narrow strip of land approximately 1,300 yards long and 440 yards wide. The island has rocky terrain and is covered with palm trees. After the last prisoners left in 1953, the island became a winter resort for tourists.

Background Major Hubert Joseph Henry, who allegedly discovered the document that indicted Dreyfus, committed suicide in 1898 after confessing that he had forged the evidence.

Biography In 1949, 45 years after his death, Herzl's remains were reinterred in Jerusalem, capital of the new state of Israel.

Vocabulary The word *Zion* is a common Biblical term referring to the holy city, Jerusalem.

● **ENRICHMENT. Have students research the growth of Zionism in the nineteenth century. Students might locate information on its leaders, source of support, and strategies.** (Application) *Locating Information*

1. **Define or identify:** racism, Social Darwinism, anti-Semitism, ghetto, Dreyfus Affair, pogrom, Zionism. (pp. 544, 545)
2. How did extreme nationalism differ from the nationalism of the early nineteenth-century? (p. 543)
3. Why did racist ideas take hold in Europe in the 1800's? (p. 544)

4. How did Social Darwinism tie in with racist ideas? (p. 544)
5. How was anti-Semitism expressed in Europe during the late nineteenth century? (pp. 544–545)
6. **Critical thinking:** How did extreme nationalists use racism in seeking their goals? (See answer below.)

6. Students might point out that extreme nationalists used racism as an excuse for their persecution of minority groups, claiming that minorities were inferior and enemies of national unity.

Chapter 27 Summary and Timeline

1. The late nineteenth century in Europe was a time of rapid industrial growth and urbanization. Improvements in health and agriculture produced population increases. Industrialization gave rise to a new upper class, a powerful middle class, and a huge class of urban workers. While workers remained at the bottom of society, they did gain political power and a higher standard of living.

2. Startling new discoveries in chemistry and physics marked the beginning of the modern age of science. Scientists studied the structure of the atom, the nature of radioactivity, and the laws of physics. In biology, the theory of evolution offered one explanation for the development of living things. Sociologists and psychologists also began studying human society and behavior in a scientific way.

3. Painting in the late 1800's was marked by experimentation with light, form, and color, leading to movements such as impressionism and cubism. Music generally followed the Romantic style, though some composers began to experiment with structure. In plays and novels, writers began to portray contemporary life in a realistic way.

4. Meanwhile, Europe was troubled by dangerous political forces. Extreme nationalism rejected ideas of freedom and called for the domination of other lands and peoples. Some nationalists adopted racist ideas, and anti-Semitism was widespread.

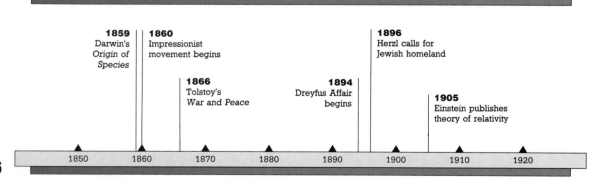

1859 Darwin's *Origin of Species*

1860 Impressionist movement begins

1866 Tolstoy's *War and Peace*

1894 Dreyfus Affair begins

1896 Herzl calls for Jewish homeland

1905 Einstein publishes theory of relativity

1850　1860　1870　1880　1890　1900　1910　1920

See p. T529D for answers to Chapter Review.

Vocabulary Review

1. Use the following terms to complete the sentences below: *ghetto, pogrom, racism, Social Darwinism.*
   a. The belief that one racial or national group is superior to others is called ___?___.
   b. A section of town where Jews were forced to live was called a ___?___.
   c. Those who believed in ___?___ claimed that the theory of natural selection could be applied to social and economic relations.
   d. A ___?___ is an organized campaign of violence aimed against Jews.
2. Choose the term that best completes each sentence.
   a. Edward Jenner's method of injecting a person with a solution of weakened germs to prevent disease is called [pasteurization/vaccination].
   b. The goal of [Zionism/sociology] was carried out with the founding of the state of Israel.

People to Identify

1. The French chemist [Louis Pasteur/Antoine Lavoisier] discovered bacteria.
2. [Leo Tolstoy/Thomas Hardy] wrote the novel *War and Peace*.
3. One of the leaders of the impressionist movement was [Claude Monet/Paul Cézanne].
4. [Henrik Ibsen/George Bernard Shaw], born in Ireland, became one of Britain's leading playwrights.
5. The work of [Gregor Mendel/Ernest Rutherford] laid the foundation for the science of genetics.
6. [Thomas Herzl/Thomas Alva Edison] designed electric power stations for London and New York.
7. The books of [Vincent van Gogh/Charles Dickens] described harsh living conditions in English cities of the 1800's.
8. [Pierre-Auguste Renoir/Pablo Picasso] painted natural shapes as geometrical forms.
9. One of the most influential composers of the early 1900's was [Igor Stravinsky/Johannes Brahms] of Russia.

Recalling the Facts

1. What changes contributed to population growth in Europe in the early 1900's?
2. Who made up the European upper class in the 1800's? Who made up the middle class? The working class?
3. How were the lives of workers improved in the late 1800's?
4. How did Dalton, Mendeleev, the Curies, and Einstein each contribute to scientific knowledge?
5. What was Darwin's principle of natural selection? Why did many people oppose his theory of evolution?
6. How did Pavlov and Freud contribute to the study of psychology?
7. How did the impressionists, post-impressionists, expressionists, and cubists change traditional ways of painting?
8. What were the characteristics of realism in literature and drama?
9. How did extreme nationalists view democratic rights and freedoms? How did they view war?
10. What forms did anti-Semitism take in Europe from the Middle Ages into the 1800's?

547

1. Giving a talk. Prepare a short talk on the life of one of the artists discussed on page 540. Try to locate two or three of the artist's works in a book to use as a visual aid. Explain why you think this artist made a significant contribution to artistic styles. *(Syn.)*

2. Using a graph. Use the graph below to answer the following questions: Which European city had the largest population during the period shown? Which city had the fewest people? What trend do you see in the graph? What might account for this? *(Comp.)*

Source: B. R. Mitchell, *European Historical Statistics*

3. Making judgments. In the early 1800's, nationalism was a positive force that contributed to the unification of Italy and Germany. In your opinion, was the extreme nationalism of the late 1800's a positive or a negative force in European affairs? Explain. *(Syn.)*

Thinking About Geography

Writing an essay. In an encyclopedia or other reference book, read more about Darwin's voyage to the Galápagos Islands. How, in his view, did the location of the Galápagos encourage the development of new species? *(App.)*

548

Enrichment: Primary Sources

On January 11, 1898, Major Esterhazy, the army officer who had actually committed the crimes of which Alfred Dreyfus was accused, was judged innocent by military court. Two days later Émile Zola wrote the president of France a letter about the Dreyfus Affair. Part of that letter appears below.

66 It is only now that the Affair is beginning, because only now are men assuming clear positions: on one hand, the guilty, who do not wish justice to be done; on the other, the followers of justice, who will give their lives so that justice may triumph.

I accuse the War Office of having carried on in the press an abominable campaign in order to screen their mistake and mislead the public.

I accuse the first Court Martial of having violated the law by condemning an accused man on the basis of a secret document and I accuse the second Court Martial of having, in obedience to orders, screened that illegal act by knowingly acquitting a guilty man.

As to the men I accuse, I do not know them. I have never seen them, I have no resentment or hatred toward them. I have but one passion—that of light. 99

1. Of what crimes did Zola accuse the French War Office?
2. What legal violations did Zola say were committed at the two Courts Martial?
3. **Critical thinking:** What did Zola claim to be his motive for making the accusations against the War Office and the Courts Martial? *(Comp.)*

WORLD HISTORY
Checklist

UNIT 7

Try to identify the following key people, places, and terms from the unit. If you need help, refer to the pages listed.

Key People

Jethro Tull *(492)*
Charles Townshend *(492)*
Eli Whitney *(492)*
Henry Cort *(493)*
Henry Bessemer *(493)*
James Watt *(493)*
George Stephenson *(493)*
Adam Smith *(498)*
Thomas Malthus *(498)*
David Ricardo *(498)*
Charles Fourier *(499)*
Robert Owen *(499)*
Karl Marx *(500)*
Friedrich Engels *(500)*
Benjamin Disraeli *(503)*
William Gladstone *(503)*
Emmeline Pankhurst *(504)*
Samuel Gompers *(506)*
Upton Sinclair *(507)*
Carry Nation *(507)*
Susan B. Anthony *(508)*
Giuseppe Mazzini *(513)*
Camillo di Cavour *(513)*
Victor Emmanuel II *(513)*
Giuseppe Garibaldi *(514)*
Otto von Bismarck *(517)*
William I *(517)*
William II *(521)*
Nicholas I *(525)*
Alexander II *(525)*
Alexander III *(527)*
Thomas Alva Edison *(531)*
Edward Jenner *(532)*
Louis Pasteur *(532)*
Robert Koch *(532)*
Joseph Lister *(532)*
Antoine Lavoisier *(535)*
John Dalton *(535)*
Dmitri Mendeleev *(535)*
Marie and Pierre Curie *(536)*
Ernest Rutherford *(536)*

Albert Einstein *(537)*
Charles Darwin *(537)*
Gregor Mendel *(538)*
Ivan Pavlov *(539)*
Sigmund Freud *(539)*
Claude Monet *(540)*
Pierre-Auguste Renoir *(540)*
Paul Cézanne *(540)*
Vincent van Gogh *(540)*
Pablo Picasso *(540)*
Johannes Brahms *(542)*
Igor Stravinsky *(542)*
Charles Dickens *(542)*
Thomas Hardy *(542)*
Leo Tolstoy *(542)*
Henrik Ibsen *(543)*
George Bernard Shaw *(543)*
Theodor Herzl *(545)*

Key Places

Kingdom of Sardinia *(513)*
Balkans *(523)*

Key Terms

Industrial Revolution *(491)*
entrepreneur *(491)*
standard of living *(495)*
urbanization *(495)*
laissez faire *(498)*
communism *(500)*
Communist Manifesto (501)
Chartist movement *(503)*
Factory Act (Britain) *(505)*
labor union *(505)*
Risorgimento *(513)*
Red Shirts *(514)*
tariff *(517)*
Zollverein *(517)*
realpolitik *(517)*
Franco-Prussian War *(519)*
Pan-Slavism *(525)*
Russification *(525)*
evolution *(537)*
racism *(544)*
Social Darwinism *(544)*
anti-Semitism *(544)*
Dreyfus Affair *(545)*
Zionism *(545)*

Steam engines gave rise to railroads and powered the Industrial Revolution.

549

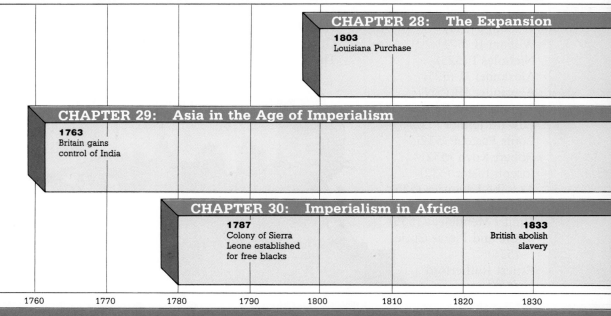

UNIT 8

Western Imperialism

1763–1914

	1760	1770	1780	1790	1800	1810	1820	1830

CHAPTER 28:   The Expansion

1803
Louisiana Purchase

CHAPTER 29:   Asia in the Age of Imperialism

1763
Britain gains
control of India

CHAPTER 30:   Imperialism in Africa

1787
Colony of Sierra
Leone established
for free blacks

1833
British abolish
slavery

	1760	1770	1780	1790	1800	1810	1820	1830

550

FOCUS STRATEGY. Tell students that the illustration represents a
city in India in the nineteenth century. Then ask: **(a) What religion
do you think is represented by the building shown on page 551?**
(Islam.) **(b) What architectural features shown here represent Muslim influence?** (The arches of the doors and windows; the onion-shaped
domes; and the minarets.) **(c) What religion might the temple on the
left page represent?** (Hinduism or Buddhism.)

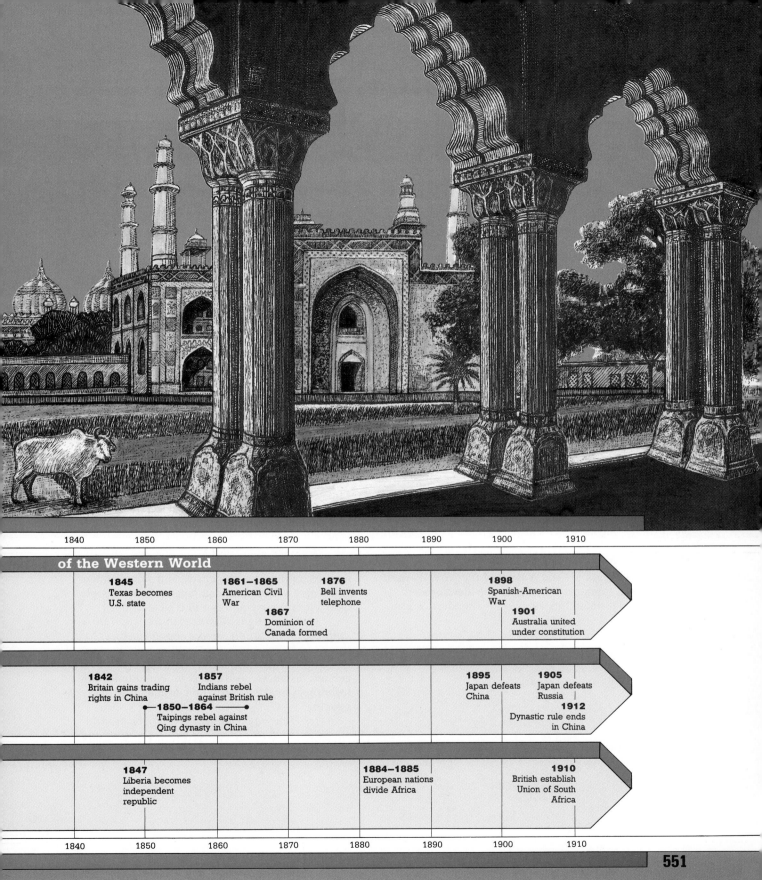

1840	1850	1860	1870	1880	1890	1900	1910

of the Western World

1845
Texas becomes
U.S. state

1861–1865
American Civil
War

1867
Dominion of
Canada formed

1876
Bell invents
telephone

1898
Spanish-American
War

1901
Australia united
under constitution

1842
Britain gains trading
rights in China

1857
Indians rebel
against British rule

1850–1864
Taipings rebel against
Qing dynasty in China

1895
Japan defeats
China

1905
Japan defeats
Russia

1912
Dynastic rule ends
in China

1847
Liberia becomes
independent
republic

1884–1885
European nations
divide Africa

1910
British establish
Union of South
Africa

1840	1850	1860	1870	1880	1890	1900	1910

Have students refer to the unit timeline to answer the following question: Which nation appears to have been the most active imperialist nation? (Britain.)

The Expansion of the Western World   1800–1914
(pp. 552–567)

Chapter Preview

Section 1 describes new developments in transportation and communication and explains how they helped to create a worldwide economy. Factors that led to migrations from Europe and Asia are discussed and causes of the Age of Imperialism are identified. Section 2 introduces the idea of Manifest Destiny and explains the causes and effects of the United States' expansion. The struggles for self-rule in Canada, Australia, New Zealand, and Ireland and the British response are described.

Bibliography

See the *Teacher's Management and Planning Guide* for additional listings. Starred titles are for both students and teachers.

Barratt-Brown, Michael. *The Economics of Imperialism*. Penguin. A good introduction to this complex issue.

Betts, Raymond F. *The False Dawn: European Imperialism in the Nineteenth Century*. University of Minnesota Press. Good survey.

*Dean, Vera M. *The Nature of the Non-Western World*. Mentor. Highlights the development of imperialism and its effect on the modern world.

Section Lesson Plans

SECTION 1   (pp. 553–558)
Worldwide Developments

Objectives

After completing this section, students will be able to:
1. Explain how technological achievements helped create a world economy.
2. Identify factors that caused the large-scale migrations of the late 1800's.
3. Describe how a new wave of European empire-building began.

Introducing the Lesson

Remind students that the Industrial Revolution caused significant social and economic changes in Europe. Although the standard of living improved for many people, some groups suffered hardships and sought opportunities made possible by advances in transportation and communication.

Then ask: *(a) What problems did industrialization cause for some farmers?* (Advanced farm technology was expensive and some farmers could not afford new equipment. Some people who left farming could not find factory jobs.)

(b) How might advances in transportation and communication create opportunities for some? (Advances in transportation usually make it easier and less expensive for people to travel greater distances. Advances in communication technology make information available to more people.)

(c) How has American society been influenced by modern systems of transportation and communication? (Answers will vary.)

Developing the Lesson:
Understanding Cause and Effect

Have students write an essay explaining the significance of transportation and communication developments in the late nineteenth and early twentieth centuries. Students might evaluate social and economic changes resulting from technological advances, or develop a hypothesis describing how life today would be different if changes in transportation and communication had not occurred. *(Synthesis)*

Developing the Lesson:
Synthesizing Information

Have students explain how the scientific and technological advances of the Industrial Revolution resulted in the migration of some people to distant lands. (Scientific and technological advances led to higher standards of living and better medical care. The resulting population growth caused overcrowding and fewer opportunities for young people. Many small farmers could not compete with those who could afford the latest equipment. Many artisans could not match the low prices of factory-made goods. Advances in transportation made travel faster, cheaper, and safer for people who sought greater opportunities in distant lands.) *(Comprehension)*

Closing the Lesson:
Observing for Detail

Have students summarize the economic, political, and social factors that helped to create a worldwide economy and led to the expansion of the Western world. (*Economic:* policies of free trade; adoption of the gold standard; network of banks; Western imperialism. *Political:* nationalism. *Social:* religious beliefs, concern for human welfare; Western belief that their institutions were superior.) *(Comprehension)*

See *Section Review* questions, p. 558.

SECTION 2   (pp. 558–565)
The United States and the British Empire

Objectives

After completing this section, students will be able to:
1. Describe how the United States expanded its territory and influence.
2. Explain how some of Britain's colonies moved toward self-rule.

Introducing the Lesson

Remind students that the economic and social needs of industrial nations resulted in the expansion of their territory and influence and the development of a world economy. This often caused conflict with people who were less powerful and unable to resist foreign control.

    Then ask: *(a) What conflicts might arise when powerful nations expand their territory and influence?* (Conflicts between different cultures and resistance to foreign rule might result in revolts by weaker peoples and repression by stronger countries.)

    (b) How might nations resolve these conflicts? (Since strong nations are usually reluctant to relinquish their power, they might seek political compromise.)

    (c) How do nations today try to resolve conflicts that arise between strong nations and weak ones? (Answers will vary. The United Nations was established to resolve international conflict. Regional alliances are often formed to protect member nations. Sometimes economic sanctions are imposed against nations that appear unwilling to resolve conflicts. Negotiation, arbitration, and war are other ways of dealing with international conflicts.)

Developing the Lesson: Analyzing Ideas

Have students analyze the idea of Manifest Destiny and answer the following questions: *(a) What did Manifest Destiny mean?* (The word *manifest* means "obvious" or "apparent," so *Manifest Destiny* implies the inevitability of territorial expansion.) *(b) How did the idea of Manifest Destiny support the economic and social needs of the United States?* (The United States needed land for its expanding population and raw materials for its growing industry.) *(c) How was Manifest Destiny similar to imperialism?* (Manifest Destiny involved the acquisition of territory owned and inhabited by other peoples.) *(Analysis)*

Developing the Lesson: Comparing Historical Developments

Have students make a chart comparing the situations in Canada, Australia and New Zealand, and Ireland. Students might identify the populations of each colony, the social or political problems that developed, and how the British resolved them before self-government was secured. (*Canada:* cultural and religious differences between French and English colonists led to conflict resolved by first separating the groups and then reuniting them and granting dominion status. *Australia and New Zealand:* initially populated by convicts, these colonies attracted settlers and immigrants. After a call for self-government, Britain granted parliamentary government and dominion status. *Ireland:* subjected to English control since the 1100's, the Irish grew to resent English presence. Over the centuries, restrictions on Catholics, the growth of English settlement, and imposition of the English language led to increased opposition to British rule. Ireland was formally joined to Britain in 1801. The British Parliament repealed some restrictions against Catholics, but did not grant home rule to southern Ireland until 1914.) *(Comprehension)*

Closing the Lesson: Solving Problems

Have students work in groups to discuss the following question: *How might industrial nations meet their economic and social needs without violating the territory and rights of less-powerful peoples? (Synthesis)*

See *Section Review* questions, p. 565.

Chapter 28 Review Answers
(pp. 566–567)

Vocabulary Review

1. genocide 2. segregate 3. gold standard 4. Manifest Destiny 5. secede

People to Identify

1. Samuel Morse 2. Abraham Lincoln 3. Lord Durham 4. Guglielmo Marconi 5. Alexander Graham Bell

Places to Know

1. A 2. E 3. C 4. G 5. B 6. F 7. D

Recalling the Facts

1. Railroads, steamships, the Suez and Panama canals, the telegraph, the telephone, and the radio all reduced communication or travel time, allowing merchants to get worldwide price information quickly and to buy and sell goods wherever it was most profitable. Policies of free trade and the adoption of the gold standard also helped international trade.
2. Population growth caused overcrowding and reduced economic opportunities, forcing people to leave Europe in search of better opportunities.
3. They expected to get new markets for manufactured goods, sources of raw materials, and places to invest capital. Nationalism led countries to seek new territory to add to their power and prestige. Military rivalries, religious beliefs, and concern for human welfare also spurred imperialism.
4. It sold land cheaply or gave it away to anyone who would work it.
5. The need for mass production of goods during the war sped industrialization. Immigrants provided labor to run the new factories.
6. The United States defeated Spain, gaining Puerto Rico, Guam, and eventually the Philippines. Cuba won its independence.

7. He announced the Roosevelt Corollary to the Monroe Doctrine, proclaiming that the United States would take over the affairs of any Latin American nation that could not keep order at home or pay its debts.

8. It passed the Quebec Act of 1774 to protect the rights of French Canadians, and in 1791 it created the provinces of Upper Canada, which was mainly English-speaking, and Lower Canada, which was mainly French-speaking.

9. They believed a central government could protect against American expansionism and build roads and railroads to unite Canada. The Dominion built a cross-country railroad, encouraged foreign investment, and encouraged immigration in order to build a labor force.

10. Britain was concerned about the Protestants in northern Ireland, a small minority who wanted Britain's protection.

Critical Thinking Skills

1. Reports will vary.

2. Canada faced conflicts between French and English settlers as well as demands by the colonists for self-rule. Alternative solutions will vary but may include the following: Upper and Lower Canada could have remained separate and each one given home rule; the two areas could have been reunited and given complete independence; British or French immigration could have been discouraged; the colonists' request for self-rule could have been denied altogether.

3. Essays will vary, but students should note that the "White Man's Burden" refers to colonization and that Kipling approved of colonists improving the lives of natives.

Thinking About Geography

1. Maps will vary.

2. The Suez Canal, which shortened the trip from London to Bombay by more than 4,000 miles, greatly encouraged international trade by revolutionizing world shipping. The Panama Canal, which shortened the travel time between New York and San Francisco by 60 percent, made trade between the east and west coasts of the United States easier. Answers will vary; students should note that these canals are not as important today as they once were because airplanes have replaced ships as the major means of global travel. Both canals continue to be important shipping routes for goods. Maps will vary.

Enrichment: Primary Sources

1. Before boarding the ship to America.

2. It described his travels and reported that the emigration committee was taking care of everyone, the weather was fine, and the ship was comfortable.

3. Like other immigrants of the late 1800's, he was probably seeking better opportunities and, like other Russian immigrants, freedom from repressive rule. Many immigrants today have similar hopes.

The Expansion of the Western World   1800–1914

See chapter timeline, p. 565.

Before You Read This Chapter

Have you ever heard the expression "It's a small world"? In the 1800's, people were discovering just that. New forms of transportation and communication were helping Westerners make new contacts. Masses of people were moving to distant lands. As you read this chapter, look for other developments of the 1800's. Why were some European countries reaching out for new colonies? What signs showed that the United States was maturing into a strong nation? How did some British colonies make a bid for greater independence?

The Geographic Setting

The Chapter Outline

1. Worldwide Developments
2. The United States and the British Empire

Sydney, Australia, was founded as a British prison colony in 1788. The city was celebrating its hundredth birthday when this picture was made.

1 Worldwide Developments

Objectives

Focus Questions

★ ■ How did technological achievements help create a world economy? *(pages 553–555)*

● ■ What caused the large-scale migrations of the late 1800's? *(pages 555–557)*

▲ ■ How did a new wave of European empire-building begin? *(page 557)*

Terms to Know

gold standard   imperialism
genocide

★ Note strategies for first objective on this page and p. 554.

The first contacts between Europe and most of the non-Western world came during the Age of Exploration (Chapter 18). With the Industrial Revolution, these contacts widened. Technological advances made travel and communication easier; population growth led many Europeans to move to new lands. Powerful European nations seeking wealth and prestige began to colonize vast territories.

Advances in Transportation

Sec. Rev. ques. 2

Railroads. In the late 1800's, railroads were built throughout the world. In Africa, Australia, and the Americas, railroads connected the populated coasts with the interiors. In Europe, railroads cut the travel time between cities.

Railroad travel was cheaper, as well as faster, than the kinds of transportation it replaced. It allowed the overland movement of people and goods on a much greater scale than ever before.

Steamships. The other major development in transportation in the 1800's was the invention of ocean-going steamships. For years steam had been used to power riverboats. It was not until mid-century, however, that technology allowed the building of ocean steamers. Like trains, steam-powered ships made the transportation of people and goods much faster and cheaper.

The Suez and Panama canals. The opening of the Suez Canal in 1869 revolutionized world shipping. In earlier times, the journey from Europe to Asia had required ships to go all the way around Africa. The canal allowed them to go through the eastern Mediterranean into the Red Sea (map, page 597). The trip from London to Bombay, India, was shortened by more than 4,000 miles.

The Panama Canal (page 561), completed in 1914, was just as important for travel in the Western Hemisphere. Ships sailing from the Atlantic to the Pacific Ocean could now pass through the Caribbean instead of going around South America.

Instant Communication

Along with advances in transportation came a number of improvements in communications. The telegraph, invented by Samuel F. B. Morse in 1837, sent messages by electrical impulse. Important information could now cross thousands of miles in seconds rather than days. In 1851 the first underwater telegraph line was laid across the English Channel, linking Britain with the rest of Europe. In 1866 the first transatlantic cable was laid, stretching undersea from Ireland to eastern Canada.

An offshoot of the telegraph was the telephone, invented by Alexander Graham Bell in 1876. The telephone was soon in common use for small areas; long-distance telephone service followed.

553

★ RETEACHING. Have students review "Advances in Transportation" and "Instant Communication" (pp. 553–554) and outline advances made in transportation and communication. (Railroads built; ocean-going steamships used; Suez and Panama canals opened; the telegraph, underwater telegraph cables, the telephone, and the "wireless" radio developed.) *(Comprehension)* **Observing for Detail**

★ REINFORCEMENT. Have students make a cause-and-effect chart illustrating the effects of technological advances on the world market. (Daily world price information created worldwide competition and level prices; policies of free trade established; the gold standard was adopted; network of world banks was started.) *(Comprehension)* **Understanding Cause and Effect**

The Geography Connection

The Suez Canal

The opening of the Suez Canal in 1869 dramatically changed patterns of trade. It gave ships a direct route from European ports to the Indian Ocean by connecting the Mediterranean Sea with the Red Sea (map, page 597).

Before the canal was opened, ships had to sail around the southern tip of Africa to reach Asia, a distance of about 10,000 miles. For most European nations, the Suez Canal cut that distance nearly in half. In the late 1800's this saved about two months on a one-way voyage.

Egyptian laborers under the direction of Ferdinand de Lesseps, a French canal builder, constructed the 100-mile-long canal. For part of the way, de Lesseps followed the general route of a canal dug by Egyptians some 12 centuries earlier. Nevertheless, the task was enormous. Nearly 100 million cubic yards of desert sand and sediments had to be removed. Plagued with difficulties, the construction took 10 years. Among other problems, a cholera epidemic in 1865 disabled many of the workers, and wind-blown sand continually filled the ditch.

The opening of the Suez Canal in November 1869 was a lavish international spectacle. Thousands lined the banks to witness the procession of vessels through the canal (shown here).

When it first opened to regular shipping, the Suez Canal consisted of a channel only 20 feet deep, 72 feet wide at the bottom, and 190 feet wide at the surface. It took a ship about 40 hours to pass through the canal. Later it was deepened and widened to accept larger vessels.

Ⓕ See below.

In 1895 Guglielmo Marconi, an Italian inventor, sent the first "wireless" radio message. Unlike the telegraph, the radio did not need wires because it used electromagnetic waves. The first successful transatlantic radio broadcast was made in 1901 from England to Newfoundland.

The World Market

Advances in transportation and communication affected the way goods were bought and sold. Dealers in a given product, such as wheat, cotton, or gold, were now able to get information about prices all over the world from day to day. They bought goods where prices were lowest and sold them where prices were highest. This competition caused prices to level out worldwide.

The development of a world market was also helped by new policies of free trade. During the last half of the nineteenth century, many governments removed barriers to international trade. The major European nations, for example, did away with high taxes on imports. Businesses could now sell their goods freely in Europe.

★ See below.

Sec. Rev. ques. 3

554

Ⓕ GEOGRAPHY CONNECTION. Have students develop a hypothesis explaining how the benefits for Europe resulting from the Suez Canal might have been drawbacks for others. *(Synthesis)* *Synthesizing Information*
Check for Understanding. Ask: What were some inventions that made communication easier? (Telegraph, telephone, and radio.)

★ ENRICHMENT. Have students examine current business magazines or the financial pages of newspapers to find evidence that today's economy is a world economy. Students might report on products, international businesses, or import-export activity. *(Application)* *Locating Information*

In 1875 the Suez Canal came under British control. Thus Great Britain's huge merchant fleet was assured speedy access to important markets in India and the Far East. Besides the commercial advantages, Britain's command of the Suez Canal also gave it important military advantages that would prove useful in later years.

Making the connection. How did the building of the Suez Canal benefit European nations?

In addition, all the leading industrialized nations went on the gold standard. That is, they guaranteed that anyone who held their currency could exchange it for an equal value of gold. The gold standard gave businesses throughout the Western world confidence in each other's currencies. This too encouraged international trade.

As trade grew during the late 1800's, European banks opened branches in many parts of the world. This network of banks made it easy to transfer funds and convert currencies, helping Europeans to do business far from home.

World Migrations

● Note strategies for second objective on this page and p. 556.

Sec. Rev. ques. 4

European population growth. The scientific and technological advances of the Industrial Revolution sparked a rapid population growth in Europe. Higher standards of living and better medical care meant that people were living longer than ever before. Between 1800 and 1900 the population of Europe more than doubled.

Unlike many other parts of the world, Europe had no frontier into which its growing population could spread. Population increases caused overcrowding, and opportunities for young people shrank.

These problems led tens of millions of Europeans to emigrate to distant lands. More than half of the emigrants went to the United States. Most of the rest headed for countries with plenty of land and few people. In places like Canada, South Africa, Australia, Argentina, and Brazil, the emigrants found better social and economic opportunities than were available in their native lands.

European emigrants. The European emigrants came from all walks of life. There were exiled princesses and wealthy business owners. There were scholars, artists, and working-class revolutionaries. Adventurous young men from noble families also set off to seek their fortunes.

The typical emigrant, however, was none of the above, but a farmer or artisan who was finding it harder and harder to make ends meet. Most were victims of the changing conditions brought about by the Industrial Revolution. Small farmers using traditional methods of planting and harvesting could not compete with farmers who used the latest technology. Artisans who made shoes or barrels by hand could not match the low prices of factory-made goods.

Many people went to a new land only temporarily. They stayed long enough to earn the money for more farmland or new machinery and then returned home. The transatlantic voyage, once too expensive and difficult to be made often, was now cheap, fairly comfortable, and safe.

555

● RETEACHING. Have students review "World Migrations" (pp. 555–557) and identify the reasons the following groups migrated to distant lands: **small farmers** (Could not compete with farmers using advanced technology.) **artisans** (Could not match low prices of factory-made goods.) **Armenians** (To escape genocide.) **other Asians** (To find a better life.). (Comprehension) *Observing for Detail*

● REINFORCEMENT. Have students write a paragraph explaining how scientific and technological advances of the Industrial Revolution contributed to the causes of world migrations. (Higher standards of living and better medical care meant that people were living longer; urban overcrowding reduced opportunities for young people.) (Comprehension) *Understanding Cause and Effect*

Background The Homestead Act of 1862 provided 160 acres of United States public land to any settler who would farm it for five years.

Some people even crossed the ocean for seasonal work. Many Italians, for example, made the crossing to Argentina each December to harvest wheat, and sailed home in time for spring planting. Historians estimate that half the Europeans who went to Argentina and a third of those who went to the United States during the 1800's eventually returned to their home countries.

Sec. Rev. ques. 4, cont.

Asian emigrants. The late 1800's and early 1900's witnessed a tremendous movement of people from Asia as well as Europe. The Japanese sent settlers to their own growing overseas empire (page 585), while other Japanese emigrated to the west coast of the United States. More than 12 million Chinese moved to Southeast Asia and to the United States. Millions of people from India settled in Southeast Asia and in southern and eastern Africa.

● See below.

Among the Asian emigrants were thousands of Armenians, a people living under

European Emigrants, 1820–1914

In the century preceding World War I, millions of European emigrants (such as those shown here entering New York harbor) left their home countries for other parts of the world. Where did the largest number of them settle? Why did so many poor people leave Europe during this time? (See answers below.)

2,3 million to Canada

33.6 million to the United States

3.6 million to South America

160,000 to South Africa*

2 million to Australia and New Zealand

North America · Europe · Asia · Africa · South America · Australia

Atlantic Ocean · Pacific Ocean · Pacific Ocean · Indian Ocean

*Figure for South Africa is for 1820–1888.
Source: *The Times Concise Atlas of World History*

556

Ottoman rule. Suspecting the Armenians of disloyalty, the Ottomans massacred many Armenians and deported others. Their campaign amounted to **genocide**—the systematic destruction of an entire people. Between 1894 and 1922, more than 1.5 million Armenians were killed. Many survivors fled to the United States or other countries.

Like European emigrants, people who left Asia hoped to find a better life abroad. Most of the Indians and Chinese moved to areas that had been colonized by the Western powers. There, some found work as traders, merchants, and clerks. Many others, however, wound up as poorly paid laborers, performing back-breaking work.

The Age of Imperialism

▲ Note strategies for third objective on this page.

As you read in Chapter 18, European powers had built overseas empires during the Age of Exploration. By the mid-1800's, however, most of these colonies had gained independence. Late in the 1800's, Western nations again competed for overseas territories. They began to practice **imperialism**—domination over other nations. Because of this burst of empire-building, the period from 1870 to 1914 is called the Age of Imperialism.

Economic motives. The most important cause of the Age of Imperialism was the search for profit. Western powers wanted three things: new markets, raw materials, and places to invest.

Sec. Rev. ques. 5

The Industrial Revolution had made it possible for Europeans to produce large surpluses of manufactured goods. Indeed, by the late 1800's, factories were turning out more than the Western world could use. Industrialists soon began to look elsewhere to sell their products. Among the peoples of Asia, Africa, and Latin America, there was great demand for manufactured goods, such as cotton cloth and farm tools.

In addition, industrialists looked to non-Western areas as sources of raw materials. No industrialized country had enough of all the raw materials—rubber, hemp, cotton, and so forth—to keep its factories busy.

Furthermore, Western bankers and entrepreneurs viewed the non-Western world as a promising place to invest their capital. They saw that enormous profits could be made by building mines, ports, and railroads. Yet developing countries were often politically unstable. Western investors believed that the best way to protect their investments was to have their government take over and run the areas where their money was invested. They, like the industrialists, quickly became strong supporters of empire-building.

Other forces. Nationalism, as well as the profit motive, encouraged imperialism. The late 1800's was a time of intense patriotic spirit in Europe. Nations tried to add to their power and prestige by adding to their territory. Military rivalries between the nations of Europe also fueled the scramble for empire. Sometimes countries would send troops or settlers into an area simply to prevent other powers from claiming it.

Religious beliefs and concerns for human welfare were an additional force behind the Age of Imperialism. Missionaries wanted their governments' help in spreading Christianity. Reformers wanted to stop the slave trade and other practices, such as suttee (page 58), that they considered cruel.

Many Westerners felt confident that their beliefs and institutions were superior to all others. They thought that imperialism would bring the benefits of civilization to the supposedly "backward" peoples of the non-Western world. In a famous poem, the English writer Rudyard Kipling suggested that Westerners were duty-bound to colonize. "Take up the White Man's burden," he wrote. "Send forth the best . . . to serve."

All these factors spurred Western nations to build overseas empires. Sure of their aims and armed with the latest technology, the Westerners usually overwhelmed the non-Western peoples they confronted. Of all the imperialist powers, none was more successful at empire-building than Great Britain. In addition to colonies in India (Chapter 29) and Africa (Chapter 30), Britain also controlled territory in North America, the Pacific region, and Ireland.

557

See Sec. 1 *Closing the Lesson*, p. T551B.

▲ RETEACHING. Have students identify the causes of the Age of Imperialism. (Economic: Western powers wanted new markets, new materials, and places to invest money. Nationalist: nations wanted to increase their power and prestige. Religious and humanitarian: missionaries and reformers wanted to spread Christianity and stop the slave trade.) (Comprehension) *Understanding Cause and Effect*

▲ REINFORCEMENT. Have students evaluate the similarities between the causes of the Age of Imperialism and the Age of Exploration (p. 347). (Imperialism: profit, nationalism, religion, technology. Exploration: wealth, power, religion, the Renaissance, technology.) (Comprehension) *Making Judgments*

▲ ENRICHMENT. Have students work in groups to develop a hypothesis about the effects of imperialism on societies dominated by Western powers. (Synthesis) *Making Judgments*

1. **Define or identify:** gold standard, genocide, imperialism. (pp. 555, 557)
2. What improvements in transportation and communication led to the creation of a world market? (pp. 553–554)
3. How did Western governments encourage the expansion of international trade? (pp. 554–555)
4. Why did the Industrial Revolution cause many Europeans to leave their homelands? What other peoples migrated during the late 1800's? (pp. 555–556)
5. What were the three main economic motives of European imperialists? What other factors prompted the spread of imperialism? (p. 557)
6. **Critical thinking:** How might people in non-Western countries have reacted to European imperialists? Explain your answer. (See answer below.)

See lesson plans, pp. T551A–T551C.

6. Answers will vary. They probably resented the economic, political, and cultural exploitation.

2 The United States and the British Empire

Objectives

Focus Questions

★ ■ How did the United States expand its territory and influence? *(pages 558–561)*
● ■ How did some of Britain's colonies move toward self-rule? *(pages 562–565)*

Terms to Know

Manifest Destiny   segregate
secede   Spanish-American War
Civil War   home rule

★ Note strategies for first objective on this page and p. 561.

The empire built by Britain outshone that of all other European powers during the 1800's. Because Britain held territory all over the globe, people said that "the sun never sets on the British Empire." As Britain prospered, so too did its colonies. Like the United States, which had already broken away from British rule, some of these colonies were becoming strong enough to stand on their own.

558

The Growth of American Power

The United States had won its independence from Britain in 1783 (page 428). During its first century as a self-governing nation, the United States rapidly grew in size, strength, and confidence.

Westward expansion. Not long after gaining independence, the United States began to expand its territory. In 1783 the United States' western boundary was set at the Mississippi River. Farther west lay the vast Louisiana Territory, owned first by Spain and later by France. In 1803 the French ruler, Napoleon Bonaparte, sold Louisiana to the United States. The Louisiana Purchase doubled the size of the United States, moving its western border to the Rocky Mountains.

Sec. Rev. ques. 2

As American settlers poured into the Louisiana Territory, some Americans argued that the United States should push even farther west, beyond the Rockies. These people believed in **Manifest Destiny**—the idea that the United States was meant to rule North America from the Atlantic Ocean to the Pacific. Many leaders in government eagerly took up the call for expansion.

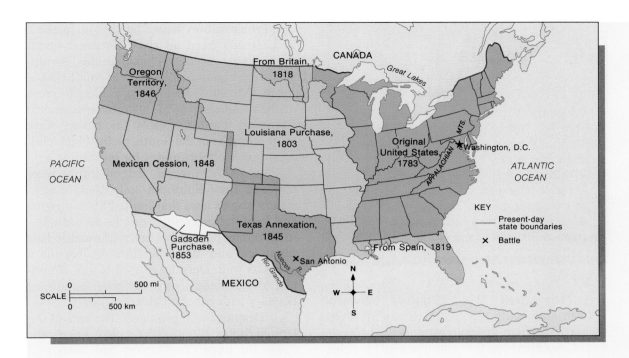

United States, 1783–1853

The United States gained vast territories in the first half of the nineteenth century. The nation acquired lands from Spain, Britain, France, and Mexico. By how much did the Louisiana Purchase of 1803 increase the size of the nation? What territory marked the northwestern border of the United States in 1846?

Map Answers: (1) The United States nearly doubled in size.
(2) Oregon Territory.

Piece by piece, new territory was added to the United States (map, this page). Spain gave up Florida to the United States in 1819. In 1845 Texas was annexed. Three years later, as part of the settlement of the Mexican-American War (page 465), the United States gained California and a huge amount of territory in the Southwest. In 1846 Britain and the United States divided the Oregon Territory. The Gadsden Purchase from Mexico in 1853 and the purchase of Alaska from Russia in 1867 brought the continental United States to its present boundaries.

The American government encouraged people to move west by selling the land cheaply or even giving it away to anyone who would work it. Once a territory had enough settlers, it asked to join the Union as a state. Between 1800 and 1848, the country grew from 16 states to 30.

American expansion west raised questions about the spread of slavery. States in the North, the more industrialized part of the country, had banned slavery. The South, however, still had a farm-based economy and relied heavily on slave labor. The two regions argued bitterly over whether new states should be free or slave.

Northerners and Southerners disagreed on a number of other issues as well. Northerners, for example, favored taxes on imports of manufactured goods. Southerners were against the idea, knowing it would mean higher prices on the many items they bought from Europe. Another matter of dispute was the division of power between the federal and state governments. Northerners argued that the federal government had final authority over the states, while many Southerners took the opposite view.

559

Geography The Oregon Territory included all of present-day Oregon, Idaho, Washington, and parts of Montana and Wyoming. The Gadsden Purchase added parts of present-day New Mexico and Arizona to the United States.

Social History Note that Secretary of State William H. Seward arranged the purchase of Alaska for $7.2 million. Opponents of the purchase believed that the United States had bought a cold wasteland and referred to Alaska as Seward's Folly, Seward's Ice Box, Walrussia, Frigidia, and the Polar Bear Garden.

Meanwhile . . .

IN EUROPE

While the United States was split by civil war, nationalists in Italy and Germany were struggling to unify their countries. The American Civil War broke out in 1861, the year that Victor Emmanuel was proclaimed king of Italy (page 516). The following year Otto von Bismarck became prime minister of Prussia (page 517).

The Civil War. Conflict between North and South reached a climax in 1860, when Abraham Lincoln was elected President. Southerners fiercely opposed Lincoln, who had promised to stop the spread of slavery. One by one, Southern states began to secede—withdraw—from the Union. These states formed a union called the Confederate States of America.

In April 1861 the **Civil War** erupted as Confederate and Union troops clashed in South Carolina. Four years of fighting followed, most of it on Southern soil. Although the South had superior military leadership, the North had a larger population, better transportation, greater resources, and more factories to turn out weapons and supplies. These advantages proved too much for the South to overcome. In April 1865 the South surrendered.

Reconstruction. As the Civil War was drawing to a close, President Lincoln announced that he would pursue a generous policy toward the South. He asked the nation to act "with malice toward none, with charity for all." Yet a great deal of bitterness remained on both sides. Lincoln's assassination less than a week after the end of the war only fueled tensions.

From 1865 to 1877, a period called Reconstruction, Union troops occupied the South. Though white Southerners resented this policy, blacks benefited. The Emancipa-

tion Proclamation, issued by Lincoln in 1863, had already freed all slaves in areas under Confederate control. Now, under Reconstruction, blacks could vote and run for office for the first time. Many were elected to serve in their state and local governments and in Congress. Public schools for blacks were built throughout the South, giving black children better opportunities for education.

In 1877, however, federal troops were removed from Southern soil. White Southerners passed laws that limited blacks' rights and kept the races segregated—separated—in all public places. Blacks continued to face prejudice and discrimination in Northern states as well. Decades passed before American blacks made significant progress toward equality with other citizens.

Despite these problems, the end of the United States' bloodiest war gave Americans cause for hope. The Union had been preserved. Americans could now dedicate their energies to building a great nation.

Economic modernization. Industrialization had begun in the United States in the early 1800's. The need for mass production and distribution of goods during the Civil War greatly speeded America's transformation into an industrialized nation. By 1914 the United States was the world's greatest producer of manufactured goods.

Industrialization could not have come so quickly without the tremendous contributions of immigrants. Between 1865 and 1914 more than 20 million immigrants moved to America from Europe and Asia. Immigration, combined with a high birth rate, nearly tripled the country's population during that period. The immigrants provided the labor needed to run the new factories that were springing up all over the Northeast and the Midwest. As people moved from farms to factories, cities grew rapidly. The population of Midwestern cities such as Detroit and Chicago grew by as much as 700 percent.

Overseas expansion. During the late 1800's the United States began to build its influence in world affairs. Americans felt concerned about Spain's imperialist policies, particularly in Cuba, just 90 miles south of

560

Background The first state to secede from the Union was South Carolina, followed by Mississippi, Alabama, Texas, Louisiana, Florida, and Georgia. In February 1861 these states joined together to form the Confederate States of America, with Jefferson Davis of Mississippi serving as president of the Confederacy.

Economics The South's economy suffered as the war progressed. By 1864, cigars sold for $10 each, butter was $25 a pound, flour cost $275 a barrel, and an officer's jacket cost $2,000.

Social History One of the greatest proponents of equality for blacks in the late 1800's was Frederick Douglass, who remarked in 1883, "While we recognize the color line as a hurtful force, a mountain barrier to our progress, wounding our bleeding feet with its flinty rocks at every step, we do not despair. We are a hopeful people."

Florida. When Cuban rebels declared their independence from Spain in 1895, many Americans wanted to come to their aid. For two years tensions between Spain and the United States rose steadily, leading to the **Spanish-American War** in 1898.

It took Americans only four months to win a clear victory. As part of the peace settlement, Spain granted independence to Cuba and gave two of its colonies—Puerto Rico and Guam—to the United States. Later in 1898, the United States gained another Spanish colony, the Philippines. That same year, in a separate move, Congress annexed the independent islands of Hawaii as well.

With new overseas possessions and new status as a mighty nation, the United States began playing a stronger role in Latin America. In 1903, when Colombia said it would not let the United States build a canal through its territory, the United States encouraged a revolt in northern Colombia. The revolutionaries declared their independence as the Republic of Panama, and the newly formed government quickly agreed to let the United States build a canal.

The United States was determined to protect the Panama Canal and other investments in Latin America. In 1904 President Theodore Roosevelt announced the Roosevelt Corollary to the Monroe Doctrine. This new policy stated that the United States would take over the affairs of any Latin American nation that could not keep order or pay its debts. During the next few years the United States sent troops to the Dominican Republic, Cuba, Haiti, and Nicaragua.

Many Latin Americans resented the growing influence and power of the United States. They felt that their neighbor to the north had turned from a protector to an aggressor. By taking a strong role in Latin America, however, the United States revealed its growth as a nation. In a little more than a century it had grown from an infant republic to a major power in international affairs. ★ See below.

Theodore Roosevelt became an American hero after leading his troops, the Rough Riders, against Spanish forces in Cuba. This picture shows the famous cavalry charge at the Battle of Santiago.

561

Background President Roosevelt stated that the Roosevelt Corollary was not designed to help the United States acquire colonies. Roosevelt claimed that he had "about the same desire to annex [the Dominican Republic] as a gorged boa constrictor might have to swallow a porcupine wrong-end-to."

★ ENRICHMENT. Have students find information on recent events involving the United States government and Latin American nations. Students might research the treaty that gives control of the Panama Canal to Panama by 1999 or American involvement in the Nicaraguan civil conflict. *(Application) Locating Information*

Growth of Canada

In 1791 the British Parliament established Upper Canada and Lower Canada (inset map). Canada has since grown to include ten provinces and two territories. (Years in parentheses indicate dates of formation.) Name the ten provinces.

Map Answer: British Columbia, Alberta, Saskatchewan, Manitoba, Ontario, Quebec, Newfoundland, Prince Edward Island, New Brunswick, Nova Scotia.

Canada's Struggles for Self-Rule

● Note strategies for second objective on this page and p. 565.

Canada was originally colonized by France, but it was ceded to Britain under the Treaty of Paris in 1763 (page 362). The French lived mostly in the lower St. Lawrence Valley. Many English-speaking colonists arrived in Canada after it came under British rule. Some were Scottish, some were English, and some were Americans who had stayed loyal to Britain during the American Revolution. They settled separately from the French— mostly along the Atlantic seaboard and north of the Great Lakes (map, this page).

Sec. Rev. ques. 3

562

A clash of cultures. Cultural and religious differences between French and En-glish colonists, along with the traditional rivalry of their homelands, caused conflict in Canada. The British Parliament therefore passed the Quebec Act of 1774 to protect the rights of French Canadians.

In 1791 Britain took another step to try to ensure peaceful relations. Parliament created two new provinces: Upper Canada, which was largely English-speaking, and Lower Canada, which was largely French-speaking. The Maritime Provinces—Nova Scotia, New Brunswick, Prince Edward Island, and Newfoundland—remained separate colonies.

Canadians were also brought closer together by the War of 1812, fought between the United States and Britain. The United

States wanted to halt British attacks on American ships. Many Americans also had hopes of seizing British territory in Canada. When the United States invaded Canada, French and British colonists fought side by side to throw back the American troops. At the war's end in 1814, Canada remained under British rule.

The Durham Report.   After the War of 1812, tensions between French and British colonists rose again. In the late 1830's, rebellions broke out in both Upper and Lower Canada. A British statesman, Lord Durham, went to Canada to review the colonists' demands for self-rule and make recommendations to Parliament.

Durham's report, issued in 1839, urged two major reforms. First, Upper and Lower Canada should be reunited as the Province of Canada, and British immigration should be encouraged. In this way, Durham said, the French would slowly become part of the dominant English culture. Second, colonists in both the Province of Canada and the Maritime Provinces should be allowed to govern themselves in domestic matters. Parliament should regulate only in matters of foreign policy. Within 10 years, both proposals had been carried out.

The Dominion of Canada.   By the mid-1800's, many Canadians believed that Canada needed a central government. A central government would be better able to protect the interests of Canadians against the expansionist aims of the United States. It could also plan the building of roads and railroads to link the northwest frontier with the rest of Canada.

In 1867 Nova Scotia and New Brunswick joined with the Province of Canada (divided into the provinces of Ontario and Quebec) to form the Dominion of Canada. (A Dominion was self-governing in domestic and foreign affairs, but remained a part of the British Empire.) During the next 30 years Manitoba, British Columbia, Prince Edward Island, Alberta, and Saskatchewan (sas-KACH-uh-wahn) entered the Dominion.

The Dominion government took several steps to strengthen Canada. It built a cross-country railroad to unite distant parts of the Dominion. It encouraged foreign investment to develop Canada's rich supply of natural resources. The government also encouraged immigration, to provide a labor force for Canada's farms and factories.

Australia and New Zealand

Australia was first colonized by Britain in 1788. Unlike the United States and Canada, it was not opened up to ordinary settlers. It was used instead as a prison colony, where British convicts were sent to serve their sentences. Sec. Rev. ques. 4 After their release, these people could buy land and settle as free men and women. Some of the convicts escaped, fleeing to the islands of New Zealand, which lay about 1,000 miles southeast of Australia.

In time, the former convicts in both Australia and New Zealand were joined by other British settlers who came of their own free will. Immigrants were attracted by open land and, in 1851 and 1892, by gold rushes. The population skyrocketed as scattered settlements multiplied and grew into separate colonies. By mid-century the free settlers had successfully pressured the British to stop sending convicts to Australia.

Like Canadians, the people of Australia and New Zealand wanted to rule themselves, yet remain in the British Empire. During the 1850's the colonies in both Australia and New Zealand became self-governing and created parliamentary forms of government. In 1901 the Australian colonies were united under a federal constitution as the Commonwealth of Australia. During the early 1900's both Australia and New Zealand became Dominions.

The people of Australia and New Zealand pioneered a number of social and political reforms. For example, the secret ballot, often called the Australian ballot, was first used in Australia in the 1850's. In 1893 New Zealand became the first nation in the world to give women full voting rights. Both countries also adopted social welfare policies much earlier than other English-speaking **563**

Check for Understanding. Ask: Why did many Canadians desire a central government? (They felt it would protect Canada's interests from United States' expansionist aims and help develop links to the northwest.)

Politics The Dominion of Canada was formed by the British North American Act, 1867. The act provided constitutions for Quebec and Ontario, confirmed the rights of French Canadians, and established a strong central government.

Cultural History Indigenous tribes opposed British settlement in both Australia and New Zealand. Aborigines and Tasmanians were defeated by superior British weapons in Australia, and the large Maori population in New Zealand lost much of their land.

Social History By 1830 approximately 58,000 convicts had been sent to Australia. Most were thieves, but many were Irish who had been arrested during political uprisings. Convicts either worked on government-run farms or were assigned to private employers.

Daily Life

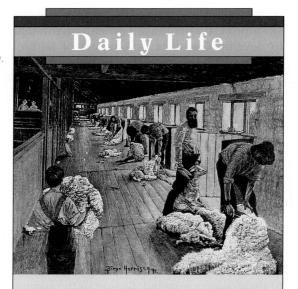

Sheep-Raising in Australia

Australians say that their country "rode to prosperity on the back of a sheep." The early settlers saw at once that the grassy plains would be good pastureland. However, breeds of sheep from the cool, rainy British Isles proved to be unsuited to Australia's warm, dry weather. The first sheep ranchers did not prosper.

The turning point came in 1796, when John MacArthur brought a new breed of sheep to Australia. MacArthur had come to Australia in 1790 as a young army officer on a convict ship. After a duel with his commanding officer, he left the army and settled down to ranching. He bought six Spanish merino sheep and found that this breed flourished on his lands. Their thick wool sold at high prices in London.

Sheep-raising became big business in Australia. The largest sheep ranches, called "stations," covered 1,000 square miles—bigger than some independent countries. Australia's population skyrocketed during a gold rush in 1851, but wool brought more wealth than gold in the long run. Australia remains the world's largest exporter of wool.

564

nations. These policies included old-age insurance, worker's compensation laws, and laws that helped labor unions.

Divided Ireland

English expansion into Ireland had begun in the 1100's, when the Pope granted control of Ireland to the English king. English knights invaded Ireland, and many settled there to form a new aristocracy. The Irish, who had a different ancestry, culture, and language, bitterly resented the English presence.

This resentment grew stronger after King Henry VIII (page 339) tried to tighten England's hold on Ireland. In hopes of planting a pro-English population in Ireland, Henry VIII and some later British leaders (such as Elizabeth I and Oliver Cromwell) encouraged English and Scottish subjects to move there. Large numbers did, mostly in the north. The native Irish, who were Catholic, opposed these Protestant settlers.

In the 1600's and 1700's, Irish Protestants passed laws limiting the rights of Catholics. For example, Catholics could no longer hold public office and they had to pay taxes to support the Church of Ireland, which was Protestant. In addition, English was made Ireland's official language.

Many Irish hated British rule. The British government, determined to preserve its control over Ireland, formally joined Ireland to Britain in 1801.* Though a setback for Irish nationalism, this move did give Ireland representation in the British Parliament. Under pressure from Irish Catholics, Parliament later repealed some of the laws discriminating against Catholics.

In the 1840's Ireland was devastated by a famine. A blight ruined the potato crop, and some 500,000 people died of starvation and disease (page 480). About one million more fled Ireland. Most went to the United States; others went to Britain, Australia, and Canada. Many people in Ireland blamed the

---

* Great Britain was renamed the United Kingdom at this time.

Social History By the late 1600's Ireland had a small upper class of Anglo-Irish Protestant landowners and a large Irish Catholic peasant class.

British for not doing more to help the victims of the famine.

During the second half of the 1800's, opposition to British rule over Ireland took two forms. Some people wanted Ireland to be completely independent. A greater number of the Irish preferred **home rule**—local control over internal matters only. The British refused, however, to consider home rule for many decades.

One reason for Britain's opposition to home rule was concern for Ireland's Protestants. A small minority of the population, who lived mainly in the north, the Protestants felt that they needed Britain's protection. Finally, in 1914, Parliament passed a home rule bill for southern Ireland only. Before the plan could really be tested, however, all of Europe was to be swept up in a worldwide war (Chapter 31).

● See below.

See Sec. 2 *Closing the Lesson*, p. T551C.

Section Review

Answers to Section Review questions are in brackets on pages indicated.

1. **Define or identify:** Manifest Destiny, secede, Civil War, segregate, Spanish-American War, home rule. (pp. 558, 560, 561, 565)
2. In what different ways did the United States gain territory in the 1800's? (pp. 558–559)
3. What cultural conflict caused problems for Canada? (p. 562)
4. How did Australia's early history differ from that of other British colonies? (p. 563)
5. What caused conflict between the British and the Irish in Ireland? (pp. 564–565)
6. **Critical thinking:** Compare the American idea of Manifest Destiny with the ideas that encouraged European imperialism in the late 1800's. (See answer below.)

Chapter 28   Summary and Timeline

1. In the 1800's, the Industrial Revolution helped bring about an expansion of European influence in the non-Western world. New technologies improved travel and communication, and international trade skyrocketed. Many Europeans, as well as Asians, moved to new lands in search of a better life. The nations of Europe also colonized large areas of the non-Western world.

2. Between 1803 and 1867, the United States stretched its borders all the way to the Pacific Ocean. By the end of the century it had become the dominant power in the Western Hemisphere. Meanwhile, British colonies such as Canada, Australia, and New Zealand moved gradually toward self-rule. Internal divisions and violence, however, continued to plague Ireland.

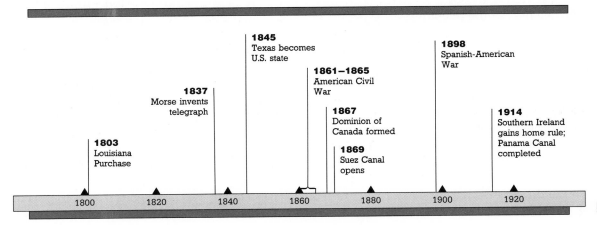

1845 Texas becomes U.S. state

1837 Morse invents telegraph

1861–1865 American Civil War

1898 Spanish-American War

1867 Dominion of Canada formed

1803 Louisiana Purchase

1869 Suez Canal opens

1914 Southern Ireland gains home rule; Panama Canal completed

1800   1820   1840   1860   1880   1900   1920

565

● **ENRICHMENT.** Have students make a time chart comparing the movement of Canada, Australia and New Zealand, and Ireland toward self-rule. Students might draw a chart for each territory and list events that moved it toward self-rule, or make one chart to include all territories. *(Comprehension)* **Understanding Chronology**

6. Students might suggest that both Manifest Destiny and the ideas supporting European imperialism were used to justify expansionist actions.

See p. T551C for answers to Chapter Review.

Vocabulary Review

Match each of the following terms with its correct definition: *genocide, gold standard, Manifest Destiny, secede, segregate.*

1. systematic destruction of a people
2. to separate, especially people of different races
3. money system in which a country's currency can be exchanged for gold
4. idea that the United States was meant to rule North America from the Atlantic to the Pacific Ocean
5. to withdraw from an organization

People to Identify

Match each of the following people with the correct description: *Alexander Graham Bell, Lord Durham, Abraham Lincoln, Guglielmo Marconi, Samuel Morse.*

1. inventor of the telegraph
2. President of the United States during the Civil War
3. British statesman who recommended that Canada be given self-government
4. Italian inventor who sent the first "wireless" radio message
5. inventor of the telephone

Places to Know

Match the letters on this map with the places listed below. You may want to refer to the map on page 559.

1. Canada
2. Gadsden Purchase
3. Louisiana Purchase
4. Mexico
5. Oregon Territory
6. Texas Annexation
7. United States in 1783

Recalling the Facts

1. How did new technology in the late 1800's and early 1900's lead to the development of worldwide markets? What other factors contributed to the growth of international trade?
2. What factors helped cause large-scale emigrations from Europe in the late 1800's?
3. How did European nations expect to profit from the empire-building of the late 1800's? How did nationalism promote empire-building? What other factors spurred imperialism?
4. How did the American government encourage the settling of the West?
5. How did the Civil War contribute to industrialization? What part did immigrants play in the industrial growth of the United States?
6. What was the outcome of the Spanish-American War?
7. What action did President Roosevelt take to protect the United States' interests in Latin America?
8. How did the British Parliament try to maintain peaceful relations between French and British settlers in Canada?

9. Why did many Canadians think Canada needed a central government? How did the Dominion government strengthen Canada?

10. Why did the British Parliament pass a home rule bill for southern Ireland only?

Critical Thinking Skills

1. **Preparing a report.** Research and write a report about one of the following topics: the Louisiana Purchase, the gold rush of 1849, the United States' acquisition of Alaska or Hawaii, the building of the Panama Canal, Canada's national holiday—Dominion Day, the early settlement of Australia. *(App.)*

2. **Problem-solving.** The Durham Report provided a set of recommendations for solving the problems Canada faced in the late 1830's. What were these problems? How else might they have been handled? *(Syn.)*

3. **Exploring literature.** Find a copy of Rudyard Kipling's poem "White Man's Burden." In a short essay, analyze the poem, answering the following questions: What is the burden Kipling speaks of? How did Kipling view colonists and natives in colonized lands? *(Anal.)*

Thinking About Geography

1. **Making maps.** Canada is the second largest country in the world. It has many different geographic and climatic regions and a wide variety of natural resources. Using an atlas or encyclopedia for reference, draw maps to show these features of Canada. *(App.)*

2. **Analyzing and drawing conclusions.** How did the Suez Canal affect world trade? What effect did the Panama Canal have on trade and travel? Are these canals as important today as they were in the early 1900's? Explain. Using an atlas for reference, label these canals on an outline map of the world and draw the routes of travel from Europe to Asia and from the Atlantic to the Pacific *(Comp.)* Ocean before and after their construction.

A checkmark identifies questions and exercises calling for the three higher-order levels of thinking at the top of the Bloom taxonomy: Analysis, Synthesis, and Evaluation.

Enrichment: Primary Sources

Mary Antin's father was a Russian Jew who moved to the United States in the late 1800's. Like many other immigrants, he came alone and sent for his family to join him later. In the adapted passage below, Antin describes her reaction to an early letter from her father.

❝ Mother brought us a thick letter from father, written just before boarding the ship. The letter was full of excitement. There was something in it besides the description of travel, something besides the pictures of crowds of people, of foreign cities, of a ship ready to put out to sea. My father was traveling without means of his own, without plans, to a strange world where he had no friends; and yet he wrote with the confidence of a well-equipped soldier going into battle. Father simply wrote that the emigration committee was taking good care of everybody, that the weather was fine, and the ship comfortable. But I heard something, as we read the letter, that was more than the words seemed to say. There was an elation, a hint of triumph, such as had never been in my father's letters before. My father was inspired by a vision. He saw something—he promised us something. It was this "America." And "America" became my dream. ❞

1. When had Mary Antin's father written the letter?
2. What did the letter actually say?
3. **Critical thinking:** What kind of vision of America did Mary Antin's father probably have? Do you think immigrants today have similar hopes? *(Syn.)*

567

T567A

Asia in the Age of Imperialism   1763–1914
(pp. 568–589)

Chapter Preview

Section 1 explains events that led to British colonial rule in India and discontent resulting in the formation of the Indian National Congress. Section 2 discusses the end of China's years of isolation and the impact of the West on China and Southeast Asia. Section 3 traces Japanese history from the arrival of Commodore Perry through the period of rapid modernization.

Bibliography

See the *Teacher's Management and Planning Guide* for additional listings. Starred titles are for both students and teachers.

Fairbank, John K. *The Great Chinese Revolution, Eighteen Hundred to Nineteen Eighty-Five.* Harper and Row. Changes in China.

*Kipling, Rudyard. *Kim.* Bantam. India under British rule. A literary classic.

O'Connor, Richard. *The Spirit Soldiers.* Putnam. Narrative history of the Boxer Rebellion.

*Roberts, John G. *Black Ships and Rising Sun.* Messner. Opening of Japan to the West.

Trevelyan, Raleigh. *The Golden Oriole: A 200-Year History of an English Family in India.* Viking. British rule in India.

Section Lesson Plans

SECTION 1   (pp. 569–572)
India Under British Rule

After completing this section, students will be able to:
1. Explain how India came under British rule.
2. Describe how British rule affected India.

Introducing the Lesson

Remind students that the Industrial Revolution created greater demand for raw materials and new markets. These economic factors, in addition to the rise of nationalism and the growth of nations, resulted in the expansion of empires.

Then ask: *(a) Besides creating new economic needs, how else might the Industrial Revolution have led to the Age of Imperialism?* (Advances in transportation made travel to distant lands faster and less expensive; improvements in communication and transportation made the control of foreign territory easier.)

(b) What advantages might industrialized nations have had over their colonies during the Age of Imperialism? (Industrialized nations usually possessed greater wealth and a stronger economy and enjoyed the benefits of technological advances.)

(c) How might a colonized nation be affected by foreign control? (Answers will vary. Since empires are built to benefit the stronger nation, the governments and economic systems of colonized nations would probably be affected. Industrial nations might also introduce technological improvements into the colony to increase profits.)

Developing the Lesson:
Sequencing Events

Have students make a timeline of events resulting in British control of India. Students should begin their timeline with the charter of the English East India Company in 1600. (Timeline should include information for the following dates: 1600, 1613, 1647, 1763, 1857, 1858, and 1876.) *(Comprehension)*

**Developing the Lesson:
Analyzing Cause and Effect**

Have students explain how changes resulting from British control led to the growth of Indian nationalism. (Better transportation and communication united the Indian people; colonial policies created resentment; British-educated Indians accepted Western political ideas.) *(Comprehension)*

**Closing the Lesson:
Comparing Historical Developments**

Have students work in groups to compare British colonial developments in India and North America (pp. 424–428). Then have students develop a hypothesis explaining why Americans were able to resist British policies more successfully than Indians. *(Synthesis)*

See *Section Review* questions, p. 572.

SECTION 2 (pp. 573–581)
Imperialism in China and Southeast Asia

After completing this section, students will be able to:
1. Explain how contact with the West affected China.
2. Discuss how the Chinese Empire fell.
3. Describe how imperialism affected Southeast Asia.

Introducing the Lesson

Remind students that in the sixteenth century, believing in the superiority of their traditions, the Chinese limited contact with outsiders and reorganized their government according to ancient principles.

Then ask: *(a) What advantages and disadvantages for China might its isolation have produced?* (China's isolation may have resulted in stability, but probably shielded it from the advances made during the Industrial Revolution.)

(b) What factors might have worked against China's policy of isolation during the eighteenth and nineteenth centuries? (Industrialized nations' need for raw materials and markets; European nationalism; faster, cheaper transportation and communication.)

**Developing the Lesson:
Evaluating Information**

Have students write an essay evaluating the effects of Western influence on China. In their essays students should address the following questions:

(a) Were conflicts in China caused by Western imperialism, or were they the result of China's years of isolation?

(b) In what ways might Western influence have been viewed as advantageous for China? *(Synthesis)*

**Developing the Lesson:
Synthesizing Information**

Have students describe the efforts at reform made by the Chinese in the "self-strengthening" movement (p. 577) and explain why the attempts at modernization failed to strengthen China or stop Western imperialism. (China established a foreign affairs office, reformed the tax system, built shipyards, railroads, and telegraph lines, and attempted to modernize schools, the army, and the civil service.) *(Comprehension)*

Answers to *Map Skill Practice*, p. 578.

1. India, Burma, Malaya, northern Borneo, southern New Guinea.
2. Portugal.
3. Japan.
4. French Indochina.
5. Russia held the largest sphere of influence. Students might suggest that because Russia was closer to China, it could claim and control larger regions than Britain could.

**Closing the Lesson:
Analyzing Information**

Have students compare the impact of Western imperialism on China, Southeast Asia, and India. Students should consider the history of each region, its attitude toward foreigners, and its internal strengths and weaknesses. (India and Southeast Asia were colonized by Western powers, while China never lost formal control over its government. European dominance of India and Southeast Asia stabilized political systems in those regions, despite the economic and social disadvantages of colonialism. Competition among Western powers in China created more problems for a nation already struggling with a corrupt and inefficient government. Rebellions against both foreign rule and the Chinese government resulted.) *(Synthesis)*

See *Section Review* questions, p. 581.

SECTION 3 (pp. 581–587)
The Modernization of Japan

Objectives

After completing this section, students will be able to:
1. Explain why Japan ended its isolation from the West.
2. Describe the effects of Japan's modernization.

Introducing the Lesson

Remind students that Japan, like China, closed itself off from foreign contacts in the seventeenth century and banned foreign travel and trade. When faced with Western imperialism, however, Japan responded with a program of modernization that rapidly made the nation a world power.

Then ask: *(a) What factors might influence the success or failure of a national program of modernization?* (Answers will vary, but government stability, national wealth, access to resources, and attitude toward change are important factors.)

(b) What advantages and disadvantages might result from rapid modernization? (Answers will vary. Advantages might include a higher standard of living, equality with other industrial nations, and political independence. Disadvantages might include social problems resulting from an abrupt break with traditional ways.)

Developing the Lesson:
Understanding Chronology

Have students make a timeline of events during Japan's era of modernization. (1853—Matthew C. Perry arrived in Japan; 1854—Treaty of Kanagawa; 1868—imperial government restored; Charter Oath; 1873—first draft law; 1882—delegation to Europe and the United States to study Western forms of government; 1889—the new constitution completed by Ito; 1894–1895—Sino-Japanese War; 1902—Great Britain and Japan sign 10-year treaty of alliance; 1904–1905—Russo-Japanese War; 1910—annexation of Korea.) *(Comprehension)*

Developing the Lesson:
Making Judgments

Have students evaluate the reasons for Japan's successful era of modernization (pp. 583–584) and explain which one might be considered most important. In their evaluations students might compare Japan's advantages with those enjoyed by Western nations during their process of industrialization. *(Synthesis)*

Closing the Lesson:
Observing for Detail

Have students outline the ways Japan was influenced by the West during its process of modernization. (Japan's modernization began in response to Western imperialism. The Charter Oath reflected Western democratic ideas; the Japanese army was reorganized using ideas from the French; the navy was remodeled after the British navy. Government leaders traveled widely in Western countries. The Japanese also borrowed Western ideas about modern factory, banking, taxation, communication, and transportation systems.) *(Comprehension)*

See *Section Review* questions, p. 583.

Chapter 29 Review Answers
(pages 588–589)

Vocabulary Review

1. (a) Open Door Policy (b) Nationalist Revolution (c) sphere of influence (d) Opium War
2. (a) Sino-Japanese War—(1894–1895) struggle for control of Korea, in which Japan's defeat of China illustrated China's inability to compete with westernized nations; Russo-Japanese War—(1904–1905) struggle won by the Japanese to get Russia to remove its troops from Manchuria. (b) Unequal treaty system—system imposed on China under the Treaty of Nanjing, in which conditions for trade were determined by Western nations; treaty ports—port cities where traders could live. (c) Sepoy Rebellion—(1857–1858) unsuccessful revolt by Indian soldiers against British rule sparked by British insensitivity to Hindu and Muslim beliefs; Boxer Rebellion—(1899–1900) unsuccessful revolt led by a Chinese secret society whose goal was to drive all foreigners, particularly Christian missionaries, out of China.

People to Identify

1. Robert Clive 2. Jahangir 3. Matthew Perry 4. Ito Hirobumi

Places to Know

1. B 2. H 3. G 4. I 5. D 6. A 7. F 8. C 9. E

Recalling the Facts

1. In 1613 the Mogul emperor Jahangir granted the East India Company permission to establish a trading post at Surat. The Mogul Empire weakened and the British defeated the French in India and elsewhere, forcing France to give Britain control over India in the Treaty of Paris (1763).

2. Britain extended its control over India and did not allow Indian states their independence; Indians were barred from high government jobs; suttee was outlawed; and the British were insensitive to Indian religions.

3. Educated Indians resented the racial discrimination they faced in seeking top government jobs. They were also barred from the finest clubs and hotels in India, and some railroad cars were reserved for the British. Many also objected to the lack of self-government in India.

4. Europeans wanted to trade with China, but until the introduction of opium, the Chinese had little interest in European goods; because the Chinese government forbade the import and sale of opium, it had to be smuggled in. Many Chinese became opium addicts and the Chinese treasury was drained.

5. The rules of trade were no longer made by China, but by the European powers, and European traders were allowed to set up ports.

6. They wanted to divide land equally among all peasants and give equal rights to women. Power struggles existed among its leaders; the Chinese, who opposed the reforms, and the Europeans, who wanted to protect their trade, aided the Manchus.

7. The efforts at modernization did not go very deep.

8. Conservatives at the Chinese court felt threatened by the emperor's reforms. With the aid of the Dowager Empress, the conservatives had the emperor overthrown and imprisoned for life.

9. Nationalism and the creation of a strong central government; democracy; and economic security for all Chinese. The Nationalist Party recognized that the government would need the backing of the military in order to survive, so Yuan Shikai, a powerful general, was made president.

10. They recognized that the Americans had superior technology, and that if they did not agree, the United States could easily defeat Japan.

11. It advocated rapid modernization through changes in the political and social system, marking a major change in Japan's attitude toward its relationship with the outside world.

12. The emperor was the head of state; a prime minister ran day-to-day activities; a parliament made laws and advised the emperor; the emperor could veto and issue laws. Western nations began to see Japan as an equal.

Critical Thinking Skills

1. China is a dragon. Germany, France, Russia, the United States, Japan, Italy, Austria, and Great Britain are represented. It is about to be dismembered by the other animals. The other nations are getting ready to "carve up" the parts or regions of China for their own purposes. Answers may vary; one interpretation is that the nations planning to carve up China were predatory and aggressive.

2. (a) The British Parliament abolished the East India Company and took direct control of India. (b) The unequal treaty system was established in China. Treaty ports were established. Britain gained the island of Hong Kong. (c) Foreign nations realized China's weakness and demanded further privileges from China. Japan became the dominant power in Korea and gained control of Formosa and the Liaodong Peninsula. (d) Foreign nations demanded compensation for the Boxers' actions. This compensation and other concessions weakened China further. (e) Four thousand years of dynastic rule ended.

Thinking About Geography

1. The Red and Mediterranean seas. The distance presented obstacles to efficient communication and trade as well as contributing to cultural misunderstandings; great differences in climate, culture, religion, and economic development led to further tensions between the governing country and the colony.

2. The mountainous islands of Japan offer little room for farming and few natural resources. The large population of Japan necessitated importing large amounts of food and other goods. Japan hoped to gain food supplies and raw materials for industry.

Enrichment: Primary Sources

1. In England opium smoking is forbidden because people know how harmful it is.

2. England has an obligation not to do harm abroad that it forbids at home. Moreover, China has never exported harmful products to foreign countries. Failure to stop the trade may lead China to stop the export of Chinese products that are essential to the economic welfare of foreign countries.

3. Other countries.

4. Answers will vary. The Queen may have thought it was China's responsibility to refuse to import opium, rather than Britain's responsibility to refuse to export it. She also may have not believed the minister's threat to end trade.

Asia in the Age of Imperialism 1763–1914

See chapter timeline, p. 587.

Before You Read This Chapter

Suppose you and your classmates decided to take over New York City. "Impossible!" you might say. "We would be outnumbered millions to one." In 1900, there were about 3,500 British administrators in India. The total population of India was 300 *million*. Yet the British were able to rule India. Similar situations existed in other Asian lands. As you read, ask yourself how Europeans came to control much of Asia. What advantages did the Europeans have? How did Asian countries respond?

The Geographic Setting

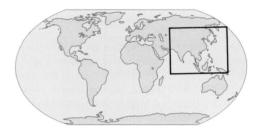

The Chapter Outline

1. India Under British Rule
2. Imperialism in China and Southeast Asia
3. The Modernization of Japan

Officials of the East India Company and the British government displayed their lofty status in India, traveling by elephant with an armed escort.

Economics Note that the Dutch were not interested in building an empire; they wanted to acquire a monopoly on trade, especially in spices.

1 India Under British Rule

Objectives

Focus Questions

★ ■ How did India come under British rule?
   (pages 569–571)

● ■ How did British rule affect India?
   (pages 571–572)

Terms to Know

sepoy
Sepoy Rebellion

★ Note strategies for first objective on this page and p. 570.

Europeans first came to India in search of trade. The desire to protect and expand this trade led Europeans to take political control of the country. Having forced France to give up its claims on India, Britain made India a prized part of its far-flung empire—the "jewel in the crown."

European Trade with India

Indian disunity. When the first Portuguese ships reached India in the early 1500's (page 349), the Indian subcontinent was not a single nation. Though its civilization was ancient and its cultural traditions strong, India had never been politically unified.

The Europeans who arrived in the 1500's traded mainly with southern India, which was divided among several rulers, both Hindu and Muslim. The Mogul Empire (page 275) had conquered much of the northern part of the peninsula. Many local rulers, especially in the Deccan and the south, continued to resist the Moguls, however.

European trading companies. During the 1600's the major European powers followed mercantilist policies, competing for colonies and trade (Chapter 19). The governments of England, France, and the Netherlands gave private joint-stock companies exclusive rights to represent their countries in trade with Asia. The Dutch East India Company was the first to break Portuguese control of the Indian trade, but the Dutch were more interested in the East Indies than in India.

On the last day of the year 1600, Queen Elizabeth I chartered the English East India Company, which was backed by 80 London merchants. In 1613 the Mogul emperor Jahangir (jah-HAHN-jeer) granted the East India Company permission to establish a trading post at Surat. By 1647 there were 27 English trading posts in India, mainly along the coast.

Agents of the English East India Company soon built up a thriving trade. They traveled all over India, setting up contracts with local weavers of cotton cloth. The English traded some of this cloth to the Dutch for spices and sent the rest back to England. Named calico after the port city of Calicut, it was widely used for tablecloths and, later, for clothing. By 1625 England was importing some three million yards of calico a year. England also bought sugar, silk, jewels, and tea. In return, Mogul India imported tin, lead, tapestries, and ivory.

France was late in joining the competition for trade with India. During the 1670's, however, the French East India Company was chartered. Like the English, the French made alliances with various Indian princes and set up trading posts on the Indian coast. The major French outpost in India was at Pondicherry, on the east coast.

British Rule of India

During the 1700's, a series of events led to British domination of India. First, the Mogul Empire weakened as local princes rebelled **569**

★ **RETEACHING.** Have students review "European Trade with India" (above) and explain how the East India Company contributed to the growth of English power in India. (It represented the government's interests in India, established a thriving trade, and brought great wealth to Britain.) *(Comprehension) Observing for Detail*

Critical Thinking. Ask: Why were most trading posts established along the coast? (Ships could dock conveniently and exchange goods without the extra costs and time it took to travel inland.)

★ **REINFORCEMENT.** Have students work in groups to stage a meeting that might have occurred between a British governor-general, his advisers, and representatives of Indian interests in 1857. Participants should identify and attempt to resolve the sources of conflict. *(Synthesis) Solving Problems*

Economics Unlike the Dutch East India Company, the English worked under competitive rather than monopoly conditions.

The British built 170-foot-long sailing ships called "East Indiamen" for trade with India and the Far East. They had large cargo holds and guns for use against pirates and enemy fleets. This East Indiaman from the 1790's is moored at the port of Calcutta at the mouth of the Ganges River.

against harsh Mogul rule. Second, Britain drove France out of its Indian outposts.

The conflicts between Britain and France over India, like those over North America (page 362), grew out of power struggles in Europe. The outbreak of the War of the Austrian Succession (1740–1748) in Europe sparked fighting between the French and British in India. For a time after this war, France was the leading power in India. Yet the British fought back, and the start of the Seven Years' War (1756–1763) in Europe set the stage for a British victory.

Sec. Rev. ques. 2

This showdown between France and Britain was fought by the two countries' trading companies, each with its own army. Led by a former East India Company employee named Robert Clive, a force of British and Indians defeated the French and their Indian supporters. Clive put a pro-British ruler on the throne of the state of Bengal, making it the base for East India Company expansion in India. In the Treaty of Paris of 1763, France accepted British control over India.

British government. India soon became an important source of wealth for Britain. The profits of the East India Company helped repay Britain's war debts and fund its emerging industries. To protect its interests, the British government began to take a more active part in governing India.

Laws passed in the late 1700's limited the powers of the East India Company and provided for a governor-general to rule India.

Like most of the British who came to India, the early governors were sure that the British way of life was superior. They felt they had a duty to reshape Indian life according to European standards. As one put it, "We are all British gentlemen engaged in the magnificent work of governing an inferior race." The British did not make much of an attempt to understand Indian customs. They did improve Indian life in some ways, but their real mission in India was to gain power and wealth for their homeland.

The British governors made many reforms in the system of government set up by the East India Company. They replaced East India Company employees with well-trained administrators, making the Indian government more efficient and less corrupt. The British also improved education and removed trade barriers among the Indian states.

Along with these reforms, however, came actions that angered many Indians. During the first half of the 1800's, the East India Company gradually took over more and more of India. Some Indian states were annexed entirely. Others were allowed to handle their internal affairs, but they did not have full independence. ★ See below.

570

Economics Initially, neither France nor Britain had any territorial design on India. The directors of the British and French trading companies simply wanted to make as much money as possible.

Background The War of the Austrian Succession and the Seven Years' War resulted from French and British competition for trade, colonies, and sea power and the duel between Austria and Prussia for supremacy in Europe.

★ **ENRICHMENT.** Have students research the East India Company to find information on its organization and its relationship to the British government. Students might explain how the trading company represented and earned profit for the British government. *(Application)* **Locating Information**

Politics The British promised to protect independent Indian states from attack in return for control of foreign relations. This arrangement often resulted in the Indian state giving up part of its territory to the company.

Vocabulary *Sepoy* comes from the Hindu word *sepahi,* meaning soldier.

Technology In 1858 there were barely 200 miles of track in India; by 1869 over 5,000 miles had been laid; in 1900 there were 25,000 miles.

Other British policies caused further discontent among Indians. Indians were barred from the highest jobs in the civil service. The British also outlawed suttee (page 58). Finally, Indian soldiers in British service, called **sepoys** (SEE-poyz), could be required to serve overseas even though Hindu custom taught that Hindus lost status by crossing open water.

The Sepoy Rebellion.   The sepoys' anger grew when the British introduced a new kind of rifle into the Indian army. In order to load the rifles, the sepoys had to bite off the tops of greased cartridges. Rumor spread that the cartridges were smeared with beef and pork grease. Hindus consider cows to be sacred, and the Koran forbids Muslims to eat pork. Indians of both religions were outraged at British insensitivity to their beliefs.

On a Sunday evening in May 1857, three sepoy units near Delhi rose in revolt. Thus began the **Sepoy Rebellion,** which soon spread to other areas. Fierce fighting went on for a year, but the British crushed the rebels in 1858.

Taking full control.   The Sepoy Rebellion convinced Britain of the need to tighten its hold over India. In 1858 Parliament closed the East India Company and annexed its Indian lands. The governor-general was replaced by a viceroy, whose power was

Sec. Rev. ques. 3

limited. The important decisions about India were now to be made in London. In 1876 Parliament declared Queen Victoria "Empress of India." In this way, all the Indian states became part of the British Empire.

India Within the Empire

● Note strategies for second objective on this page and p. 572.

Technological changes.   To govern a country as large as India, British officials needed better transportation and communication. They built the best road system in all of Asia, as well as a large network of railroads. Trains carried troops, hauled cotton and other goods to ports, delivered food to famine-stricken areas, and provided passenger service for travelers. Indian life changed as villagers visited other parts of the country or moved away to cities such as Bombay and Calcutta.

The British also set up a postal service, and in 1870 India and Britain were linked by telegraph. These improvements made Indians more aware of the rest of the world and allowed people from different regions to share experiences, news, and ideas. British technology was helping to unite India.

British technology harmed India as well, however. Indian cotton was quickly and cheaply woven into cloth in British mills. The

Sec. Rev. ques. 4

News of the rebellion of the sepoys near Delhi quickly spread to other parts of India under British rule, thus triggering further revolt. This engraving shows Indian cavalry attacking British footsoldiers.

571

● RETEACHING. Have students review "Technological changes" (pp. 571–572) and make a chart identifying the changes British rule brought to India and their effects. (The British built a road system and a network of railroads and set up postal and telegraph systems.) (Comprehension) *Identifying Cause and Effect*

● REINFORCEMENT. Have students write an editorial that might have appeared in an Indian newspaper in 1885. Editorials should represent the viewpoint of a member of the Indian National Congress who recognizes both the benefits and costs of British rule in India. (Application) *Understanding Point of View*

Economics Although the railway system helped spur the growth of trade and industry, it also put local artisans out of business by transporting cheap British manufactured goods throughout India.

machine-made cloth was shipped back to India, where it was sold at a lower price than domestic homespun cloth.

For centuries home spinning had been an important source of income for peasant families in India. By the late 1800's, however, the Indian textile industry had been nearly wiped out by British imports. Indian artisans now had no means of support but the already overburdened land. They could not turn to manufacturing because the market was already flooded with cheap British goods. High British tariffs barred the sale of Indian goods in Britain.

Sources of nationalism.   Many high-caste Indians were educated in Britain or in the British-style universities set up in India in the 1850's. As Indian students studied Western civilization, they read the works of English philosophers who wrote about nationalism and independence. These works helped fuel Indian discontent over British policies in India.

Sec. Rev. ques. 5

One of the Indians' major complaints about British rule was racial discrimination. British-educated Indians rejected the caste system, accepting the Western idea that a person's status should be based on his or her accomplishments. They were shocked, therefore, to realize that the British did not live up to their own ideals. The top jobs, the finest clubs and hotels, and the best railroad cars were reserved for the British. No matter how intelligent or educated, an Indian was not considered the equal of a European.

Many Indians also objected to the lack of self-government in their country. While colonies like Australia and Canada had been given much home rule, India was still ruled directly by a small group of British officials.

New Indian organizations.   In 1885 Indian nationalist leaders formed an organization called the Indian National Congress (later known as the Congress Party) to work for changes in British policy. Representing every province in British India, the delegates were mostly English-speaking Hindu professionals. They did not at first call for home rule or independence. They asked only that Indians be given better government positions.

572

The Congress also asked for lower taxes and free public education for all Indian children.

Indian Muslims did not feel comfortable with the Hindu-dominated Indian National Congress. They also worried that their rights would not be protected in an independent India. Seeing the British as defenders of Muslim rights against the Hindus, the Muslims were less eager than the Hindus to force the British out of India. In 1906 a group of Muslims formed the All-India Muslim League to look after Muslim interests in any talks about India's future.

British concessions.   Britain, eager to keep Indian nationalism in check, gave in to some Indian demands in the early 1900's. In 1905 the British viceroy had outraged both Hindus and Muslims by dividing the state of Bengal into two parts. In 1910 King George V announced that Bengal would be reunited. King George also declared that Calcutta, a city established by the British, would no longer be the capital of India. Instead the capital would be moved to Delhi, which lay in a region where Indian civilization had flourished for thousands of years. Yet even these moves were unpopular with some Indians, proof of the deepening divisions among the people of India.

See Sec. 1 *Closing the Lesson*, p. T567B.

● See below.

Answers to Section Review questions are in brackets on pages indicated.

1. **Define or identify:** sepoy, Sepoy Rebellion. (p. 571)
2. How did Britain end French rule in India? (p. 570)
3. How did Britain's policy toward India change following the events of the Sepoy Rebellion? (p. 571)
4. How was India helped by British technology? How was it harmed?
5. What factors led to the rise of Indian nationalism? (p. 572)
6. **Critical thinking:** In what ways did British reforms in India undermine British rule? (See answer below.)

(pp. 571–572)

Economics India cotton exports to Britain decreased after the American Civil War because British mills resumed their importation of cotton from the United States.

Politics Responding to British criticism that the Congress represented only an elite educated few, a Congress member responded that "the educated community represented the brain and conscience of the country, and was the legitimate spokesman of the illiterate masses."

● **ENRICHMENT. Have students work in groups to give a presentation on India during British rule. Students might research the Indian Civil Service, the railroad system, the structure of government under British rule, or why the British called India "the jewel in the crown."** (Application) *Locating Information*

6. Students might respond that many of the reforms outraged Indians and led to intensified opposition to British rule.

2 Imperialism in China and Southeast Asia

Objectives

Focus Questions

★ ■ How did contact with the West affect China? *(pages 573–575)*
● ■ How did the Chinese Empire fall? *(pages 575–579)*
▲ ■ How did imperialism affect Southeast Asia? *(pages 579–581)*

Terms to Know

Opium War
unequal treaty
  system
treaty port
Taiping Rebellion
sphere of influence

Sino-Japanese War
Open Door Policy
Boxer Rebellion
Nationalist
  Revolution

★ Note strategies for first objective on this page and p. 574.

As you read in Chapter 14, in the 1400's and 1500's the Ming rulers cut China off from the outside world. In 1644 the Manchus, a nomadic people from northern China, overthrew the Ming and established the Qing (CHING) dynasty. (*Qing* is sometimes spelled *Ch'ing.*) The Manchus tried to keep China in isolation, but Europe's growing power and interest in China made that task impossible.

China's Foreign Trade

For centuries, China's dealings with other Asian nations had been built on the Confucian principle of relationships between superiors and inferiors. China considered all foreign countries inferior and expected them to pay tribute to the emperor by sending lavish gifts. Of all China's neighbors, only Japan refused to send tribute.

The European nations that traded with China were not part of the tributary system, but they had to follow Chinese rules. The Chinese viewed trade as a privilege given to foreigners, not as a right. Foreign merchants were allowed in only one Chinese city—Guangzhou (GWONG-JOH), once known as Canton. Their contacts with the Chinese people were strictly limited by rules set down in the early 1700's:

66 1. No foreign warships may sail inside the inlet to the river.

2. Neither foreign women nor firearms may be brought into warehouses.

3. Foreign warehouses shall employ no maids and no more than eight Chinese male servants.

4. Foreigners living in the warehouses must not move in and out too frequently, although they may walk freely within a hundred yards of their warehouses.

Trade with the West encouraged Chinese artisans to manufacture luxury goods, like this ornate chess table, especially for Western markets.

573

★ RETEACHING. Have students review "The Opium War" (p. 575) and identify the following: **Opium War** (War fought between China and Britain over the selling of opium.) **unequal treaty system** (Pattern of trade established after the Opium War in which Western nations established trade conditions.) (*Comprehension*) **Observing for Detail**

★ REINFORCEMENT. Have students work in groups to analyze the rules established by the Chinese to limit foreign contact. Students should evaluate each rule and explain how it might have controlled foreign influence. (*Comprehension*) **Analyzing Information**

Religion One of the earliest Western contacts with China was through Jesuit missionaries, who attempted to balance their teaching of Christianity with Chinese culture and traditions.

In the new wave of empire-building in the 1800's, European and American traders set up warehouses throughout the world. The Chinese government limited foreign trade to the southern port city of Guangzhou. There the flags of European countries flew over the silk and tea businesses on the city's busy waterfront. Later Guangzhou became a center of the opium trade.

5. Foreigners may neither buy Chinese books nor learn Chinese.

6. Foreigners are not allowed to row boats freely in the river. They may, however, visit the flower gardens and the temple opposite the river in groups of ten or less three times a month, on the 8th, 18th, and 28th. They shall not visit other places.

7. Foreign traders must not remain in Guangzhou after the trading season; even during the trading season when the ship is laden, they should return home or go to Macau [a Portuguese colony]. 〞

For two centuries, European traders accepted the Chinese rules. The trade in Chinese tea and silk was so profitable that

Europeans would agree to any restrictions. They had to look hard, however, to find goods that the Chinese would take in return. China had "no need for the products of foreign barbarians," in the words of one emperor.

During the early 1800's, Europeans finally found something the Chinese wanted. This was opium, a narcotic drug made from the poppy plant. European traders could buy opium in India and sell it in China. Though the Chinese government forbade the sale of opium, many Chinese officials took bribes from British traders to smuggle in large amounts of the drug.

The opium trade was a threat to China in two ways. It harmed the Chinese people: by the 1830's, millions of Chinese had become addicts. It also drained the Chinese

★ See below.

574

★ ENRICHMENT. Have students find information on the effects of the opium trade in China. Students might research the effects of opium on individual users, the development of opium dens, the impact of opium use on China's economy, or how the sale and use of opium were eventually curtailed. (Application) *Locating Information* treasury. Silver had once flowed into Chinese banks as British traders paid for tea and silk. Now silver was leaving China as payment for opium. Concern over these problems finally prompted the Chinese government to crack down on the opium trade.

The Opium War

In 1839 the Chinese government began a campaign against opium use, arresting and executing opium dealers. Smuggling continued to increase, however. Aware that the British were hiding opium in their storehouses, the emperor sent soldiers to Guangzhou. The soldiers imprisoned British traders and government officials in their own warehouses and seized the opium.

The British viewed the Chinese action as an insult to their nation. They also saw the quarrel as a chance to get rid of Chinese restrictions on trade. The British struck back, and the **Opium War** began. The Chinese forces, badly organized and armed with old-fashioned weapons, lost battle after battle to the modern British army and navy. Finally, after three years, the Chinese government asked for peace and gave in to British demands.

Sec. Rev. ques. 2

The Treaty of Nanjing (1842) ended the war and established a new pattern for European trade with Asia: the **unequal treaty system**. The Chinese no longer made the rules, as they had done under the tributary system. Instead, Western nations laid out the conditions for trade.

The Treaty of Nanjing gave the British the right to trade in five **treaty ports**—port cities where traders could live. Foreigners accused of crimes would be tried under their own country's laws, not Chinese laws. Britain also gained the island of Hong Kong and a cash settlement for the destroyed opium.

In the next few years, other Western nations made similar treaties with China. These treaties forced China to give other countries the kinds of trading rights and privileges given to Britain.

China's Internal Problems

• Note strategies for second objective on this page and p. 579.

Conflicts with Western nations were not the only problems facing China and its Manchu rulers in the early 1800's. At this time, many Chinese still thought that their civilization was the greatest in the world. Beneath the surface, however, China was in the midst of crisis.

This crisis followed the general pattern of the dynastic cycle (page 142). The Qing government had become corrupt and inefficient. Public officials grew wealthy from bribes and high taxes, and they neglected duties such as flood control.

A disastrous flood of the Yellow River followed. China's food supply was already strained to the limit by population growth. When the flood destroyed crops, famine struck. Starving peasants left their lands in hopes of finding food. Often they were forced to sell their land at prices far below its value.

Sec. Rev. ques. 3

The Taiping Rebellion. As in earlier times, peasants reacted to these troubles by forming secret antigovernment societies. In 1850 one such society led an uprising against the Manchus. The rebels were led by a religious fanatic who claimed to be "the Heavenly Younger Brother" of Jesus. He called their movement *Taiping,* from the Chinese words for "great peace."

As one sign of rebellion, Taiping men cut off their pigtails, which the Manchu rulers had forced the Chinese to wear. The leaders

Linking Past and Present

In the decades after the Treaty of Nanjing, British influence spread in the Hong Kong region. In 1898 Britain obtained a 99-year lease on Hong Kong and nearby territories. In 1984 China and Britain issued a joint declaration returning Hong Kong to Chinese control as of 1997.

575

• **RETEACHING.** Have students list and describe the events resulting in the fall of the Chinese Empire. (Corrupt and inefficient government; Taiping Rebellion; threats from Western powers; Sino-Japanese War; overthrow of emperor; Boxer Rebellion; Nationalist Revolution.) *(Comprehension) Observing for Detail*

Biography Hung Hsiu-ch'uan, leader of the Taiping Rebellion, blamed the government for his inability to pass the civil service examination. He apparently suffered from an illness that caused delusions.

• **REINFORCEMENT.** Have students work in groups to prepare a panel discussion titled *Sources of Problems in China During the Age of Imperialism.* Participants should identify problems resulting from imperialism in China and those caused by China's internal weaknesses. *(Synthesis) Identifying Cause and Effect* of the **Taiping Rebellion** also called for changes in society. They proposed dividing land equally among all peasants. They wanted equal rights for women, including the right to take civil service examinations and become government officials. About one quarter of the rebel soldiers were women.

The Taipings built up a well-disciplined army of believers. After four years they had more than one million followers. Taiping forces easily defeated the imperial troops that were sent to fight them, and in the spring of 1853 the Taipings set up their capital in Nanjing. By this time, they controlled much of China.

The rebels' success frightened many Chinese, who opposed their reforms. Europeans, who wanted to protect their trade treaties, also became alarmed. Both groups aided the Manchus, who began to win military victories over the Taipings. The rebellion, weakened by power struggles among its leaders, finally collapsed in 1864. About 20 million people had died in the fighting, and parts of China had been devastated.

Threats from Western powers. The Taiping Rebellion was not the only revolt in the mid-1800's. The imperial government at the same time was resisting uprisings by peasants near the Yellow River and by the Muslims in northwest China.

Taking advantage of the confusion, the French and British made new trade demands. They also looked for reasons to begin a military conflict. A minor incident involving an "insult" to the British flag gave Britain the reason it needed. Similarly, Napoleon III's government claimed that Chinese authorities had murdered a French missionary.

With these excuses, Britain and France sent an army to invade China in 1856. The war went slowly, because many British troops were called away by the Sepoy Rebellion in India (page 571). Nevertheless, French and British soldiers captured the imperial capital at Beijing in 1860, forcing the emperor to flee.

Just as at the end of the Opium War, the Chinese government gave in to foreign demands for more trade. This time the Chinese also agreed to let British missionaries into China. Other Western nations claimed the same privileges.

Each of the major European powers now carved out a part of China as its **sphere of influence**—territory in which it had special authority. These areas were largely under European control, even though they still belonged formally to China. In them, Europeans had certain privileges, including the right to trade, to dig for minerals, to build railroads, and to set up military bases.

An American cartoon, printed in 1900, showed China at the center of imperialist competition in Asia.

Cultural History One of the Taiping reforms was the abolition of footbinding, a practice in which a young girl's toes were folded under the sole by tight bandages; eventually this painful treatment stunted growth of the feet. Tiny feet were considered attractive in China.

Attempts at Reform

The Opium War, the Taiping Rebellion, and the establishment of spheres of influence all rocked the foundation of the Qing dynasty. China's weakness and the power of the Western "barbarians" had become too obvious to ignore. If China was ever to free itself from foreign rule, it would have to modernize.

Yet the Chinese were slow to begin the process. Having boasted of their superiority for hundreds of years, the Chinese found it hard to turn to foreigners for help. Some still refused to believe in the need for change. Others hoped that Western technology could be blended with Chinese traditions.

"Self-strengthening." The desire to blend Western and Chinese ideas lay behind the government's "self-strengthening" movement, begun in the 1860's. In its attempt to modernize, China set up a foreign affairs office and reformed the tax system. It built shipyards, railroads, and telegraph lines. However, these efforts at modernization did not go very deep.

China's weakness was made clear by its defeat in the **Sino-Japanese War** of 1894–1895. (*Sino* is a prefix meaning "Chinese.") In this struggle for control of Korea, Japan's small but modern armies trounced the larger Chinese forces. The Chinese government realized that Japan's victory was due mainly to its use of Western technology and ideas. Once again China's defeat prompted foreign nations to demand further privileges in China.

The hundred days of reform. In 1898 the young emperor Guangxu (GWAHNG-SHOO) launched an ambitious program of reform to bring China quickly into the modern world. He called for great changes in traditional institutions, such as the schools, the army, and the civil service.

Conservatives at court felt threatened by the reforms. They turned to the Dowager Empress, the emperor's aunt, to help them. In September 1898—just 100 days after the first reforms were announced—she overthrew the emperor and sent him to prison for life. Many

Italian soldiers guard captured Boxers, whose nationalist rebellion steered popular resentment away from China's government and redirected it at the foreign presence.

of his advisers were put to death. The Dowager Empress then returned China to its earlier policy of slow change.

Demands from foreigners. At these signs of confusion in the Qing government, European nations began to demand still more influence in China. China seemed in danger of being completely carved up into colonies. Afraid of being shut out of Chinese trade, the United States stepped forward. In 1899 the American government called on other countries to follow an **Open Door Policy**—that is, to agree that all countries should have equal trading rights in China.

The Boxer Rebellion. Many Chinese saw the growing influence of foreign nations as the cause of China's problems. In 1899 another secret society sprang up. Known in English as the "Boxers," they were dedicated to driving all foreigners out of China. They particularly hated Christian missionaries and Chinese who had converted to Christianity. **577**

Economics There were two "self-strengthening" periods: the first (1861–1872) focused on production of weapons and machines; the second (1872–1894) tried to increase the variety of manufactured products.

Biography The Dowager Empress was nicknamed "Old Buddha." Although intelligent and able, she was intent on gaining as much personal power as possible and did little to improve conditions for the Chinese masses.

Cultural History The Boxers, known to the Chinese as the "Society of Harmonious Fists," practiced a traditional Chinese exercise that roughly resembled Western-style boxing.

Economics Economic troubles increased the popularity of the Boxers. In some regions flooding of the Yellow River resulted in famine, and northern China suffered from drought. The importation of foreign goods continued to put many Chinese merchants out of business.

Map Skill Practice

See p. T567B for answers to *Map Skill Practice*.

Spheres of Influence, 1911

The map below shows the extent of foreign control over Asian lands in 1911. Solid colors indicate lands that were independent nations or were colonies or territories held by other countries. Lands shown with diagonal lines were spheres of influence.

1. Which regions were part of the British Empire?
2. Foreign powers controlled a number of Asian cities through special treaties. Which country controlled the treaty ports of Goa and Macau?
3. Which country controlled the southern half of Sakhalin?
4. Which French colony bordered on a region of China that was dominated by France?
5. **Making inferences.** Which country held the largest sphere of influence? Why might that country's sphere have surpassed Britain's in size?

KEY

British
Russian
French
Japanese
German
Dutch
U.S.
Portuguese

578

Late in 1899, the Boxer Rebellion broke out in many parts of China. Mobs attacked missionaries and killed thousands of Chinese Christians. Many government officials and court nobles shared the Boxers' hatred of foreigners. Some of them simply looked the other way, while others actively helped the Boxers. The Empress herself showed sympathy for the Boxers.

The climax of the Boxer Rebellion came in 1900, when the rebels attacked the homes of foreign diplomats in Beijing. Nearly 1,000 foreigners, as well as about 3,000 Chinese Christians, had taken refuge there. After 55 days, an army of 20,000 British, American, Japanese, German, and Russian soldiers rescued them.

The foreign nations demanded payment for the Boxers' attacks on their citizens. A huge cash settlement and more concessions further weakened the Chinese government.

The last days of the Qing dynasty. In 1908 the Dowager Empress died at the age of 73. The imprisoned emperor had died the day before, and rumors spread that he had been poisoned. The heir to the throne was only two years old. Three years later, revolts broke out in much of China.

With the Nationalist Revolution, as this upheaval came to be called, 4,000 years of unbroken dynastic rule suddenly came to an end. The last Manchu emperor left the throne in February 1912.

The Nationalist Revolution

Sun Yat-sen. The leader of the Nationalist Revolution was a Western-educated Christian named Sun Yat-sen (SOON YAT-SEN). His political party, known as the Kuomintang, or Nationalist Party, supported a program called the "Three Principles of the People." These principles were: (1) nationalism and the creation of a strong central government, (2) democracy, and (3) economic security for all Chinese.

Yuan Shikai. The Nationalist Party knew that a revolutionary government would need the backing of the army to survive. For

Sec. Rev. ques. 4

Timetable

The Decline of Imperial China

1842	Treaty of Nanjing ends Opium War and gives special trading rights and Hong Kong to Britain.
1850–1864	Taiping Rebellion fails to bring about change in China.
1860	Britain and France claim spheres of influence.
1894–1895	Defeat in Sino-Japanese War awakens China to need for modernization.
1898	Guangxu's hundred days of reform fails.
1899–1900	Government is further weakened by Boxer Rebellion.
1911	Nationalist Revolution begins.
1912	Last Manchu emperor leaves throne.

this reason, Yuan Shikai (YOO-AHN SHUR-KY), a powerful general, was chosen as the president of the Nationalist Party. It soon became clear, however, that Yuan was not interested in democracy. Instead, he wanted to build his own power as a ruler and to bring back the Chinese Empire.

By 1913 Yuan had thrown his opponents out of the government and was ruling as a military dictator. His actions led to civil war in China. At the time of Yuan's death in 1916, the country was in chaos. As groups fought for control of the central government, warlords with private armies began to take over various parts of the country.

● See below, left.

Imperialism in Southeast Asia

▲ Note strategies for third objective on this page and p. 581.

Like China, Southeast Asia became the target of Western imperialism during the 1800's. Southeast Asia includes the present-day **579**

Politics Although Yuan was the most powerful leader in China, he never won the reverence the Chinese people traditionally held for emperors.
● ENRICHMENT. Have students research the Taiping Rebellion, the Boxer Rebellion, the Sino-Japanese War, or the Nationalist Revolution. Students might find information on individuals who played significant roles in these events, ideas and goals of important groups, or the backgrounds of the conflicts and their outcomes. *(Comprehension) Locating Information*

▲ RETEACHING. Have students identify the following countries as part of the British or French Empire: **Laos** (French), **Cambodia** (French), **Burma** (British), **Vietnam** (French), **Malaya** (British). *(Comprehension) Observing for Detail*
▲ REINFORCEMENT. Have students develop a hypothesis explaining why the lack of political, social, and cultural unity might make a region more vulnerable to imperialism. *(Synthesis) Forming a Hypothesis*

Biography

Sun Yat-sen

A traditional Chinese proverb says that knowing what to do is easier than doing it. Sun Yat-sen, a leader in the revolution against China's last emperor, disagreed. "Knowledge is difficult," said Sun Yat-sen. "Action is easy."

Sun's own life was filled with action as he traveled, organized, and plotted tirelessly to bring down the Qing dynasty and reform China's government. In the photo at the right, he is shown in a formal pose with his wife, Song Qingling.

Sun Yat-sen was born in 1866. His family were poor farmers in southern China. Sun's elder brother emigrated to Hawaii to find work, and Sun followed when he was 12. Later he studied medicine in China and the British colony of Hong Kong. Sun soon gave up his medical practice, however, and turned to political activities.

Sun organized secret revolutionary groups, both within China and among Chinese people living abroad. His work made him a hero to many Chinese in Britain and other Western countries. In 1912 Sun was elected temporary president of the new republic. Soon afterward, the last Manchu emperor left the throne.

Sun served only one day as president. He knew China needed a military leader to hold the country together, so he resigned in favor of a general. Unfortu-nately, the general soon tried to make himself ruler for life, and Sun was again forced into exile. From 1913 until his death in 1925, Sun continued to work for a united, democratic China.

Sun Yat-sen failed to unite China. Yet he became a symbol of China's efforts to build a strong, modern nation. Thus, despite many later changes in Chinese government, he is still known as the "father of modern China."

mainland nations of Burma, Thailand, Cambodia, Laos, and Vietnam, as well as the island nations of Indonesia, Malaysia, the Philippines, and Singapore (map, page 750).

This region, long a crossroads for world trade, was heavily influenced by other cultures. Vietnam was dominated by China for centuries. Many parts of Southeast Asia ab-sorbed Buddhism from India and Islam from Arabia. Powerful kingdoms, such as those of the Khmer (kuh-MAYR) and Thai (TY) peoples, developed as early as the 500's A.D. Southeast Asia was never politically united, however.

As in other parts of the world, the lack of unity among the peoples of Southeast Asia

580

Ⓕ **FEATURE ACTIVITY.** Ask: Why, do you think, did Sun Yat-sen come to be called the "father of modern China"? (He worked to eliminate dynastic control and for the reform of China's government; organized Chinese living at home and abroad; relinquished his political power to a military leader to secure national unity.) *(Synthesis)* **Drawing Conclusions**

Background The name Cambodia is used in this book. This is in agreement with official U.S. government policy, as stated by the U.S. Board of Geographic Names; it also reflects standard usage in U.S media.

made the region an easy target for Western imperialism. Traders from Europe began arriving in Southeast Asia in the 1500's. Lured by the area's rich natural resources, European nations took over much of Southeast Asia during the second half of the 1800's.

Great Britain and France were the most active imperialist powers. Britain, eager to protect and expand its holdings in India, moved into Burma and Malaya.

Sec. Rev. ques. 5

The French, meanwhile, were building up an empire in what are today the nations of Laos, Vietnam, and Cambodia (Kampuchea). Because the cultures of this region had been influenced by both China and India, the region as a whole was known as Indochina. French Indochina, which was larger than France itself, exported rice, tin, spices, and other products.

As you read in Chapter 28, the Philippines, once a Spanish colony, came under the control of the United States after the Spanish-American War in 1898. The only Southeast Asian nation that kept its independence during the Age of Imperialism was Siam (present-day Thailand). Located between British-run Burma and French Indo-china, Siam was modernized and open to Western trade. By playing off British against French interests, the Siamese monarchy managed to keep the nation free.

See Sec. 2 *Closing the Lesson*, p. T567B.

▲ See below, left.

Section Review

Answers to Section Review questions are in brackets on pages indicated.

1. **Define or identify:** Opium War, unequal treaty system, treaty port, Taiping Rebellion, sphere of influence, Sino-Japanese War, Open Door Policy, Boxer Rebellion, Nationalist Revolution. (pp. 575, 576, 577, 579)
2. How did the Treaty of Nanjing affect China's trade with the West? (p. 575)
3. What internal problems helped spark the Taiping Rebellion? (p. 575)
4. What were the "Three Principles of the People"? (p. 579)
5. How was Southeast Asia divided among the Western powers? (p. 581)
6. **Critical thinking:** How did China's isolation from the West contribute to its defeats by Western powers? (See answer below.)

6. Students might point out that China had lagged in adopting Western technology.

See lesson plans, pp. T567A–T567C.

3 The Modernization of Japan

Objectives

Focus Questions

★ ■ Why did Japan end its isolation from the West? *(pages 581–583)*
● ■ What were the effects of Japan's modernization? *(pages 583–587)*

Terms to Know

Charter Oath
Russo-Japanese War

★ Note strategies for first objective on this page and p. 582.

In the 1630's, the Tokugawa shoguns had begun a policy of isolation from the West (page 291). They forced Christian missionaries and many of their converts to leave the country. The shoguns also barred the Japanese people from foreign trade and travel, and they refused to let foreign ships enter Japanese ports. For more than two centuries, contacts with the West were limited to the visit of one Dutch trading ship per year. By 1850, however, Western nations dominated much of Asia. They were no longer willing to accept Japan's policy of isolation, and they had the power to force open its ports.

581

Check for Understanding. Ask: How did the Siamese nation avoid foreign control? (It pitted British interests against French interests.)

▲ ENRICHMENT. Have students work in groups to present a debate on imperialism from the viewpoints of British, French, and Southeast Asian leaders. (Synthesis) *Understanding Point of View*

★ RETEACHING. Have students outline the political, economic, and military changes resulting from Japan's modernization. (Political: restored imperial government; adopted Charter Oath. Economic: made trade concessions; ended feudalism. Military: modernized the army and navy.) (Comprehension) *Observing for Detail*

★ REINFORCEMENT. Have students explain why Japan's efforts to modernize were more successful than China's (pp. 577–579). (Synthesis) *Synthesizing Information*

U.S. Commodore Matthew Perry's warships caused a sensation when they appeared in Tokyo Bay in 1853. The military threat they posed forced Japan out of its long isolation and into a period of swift and determined modernization. Here curious Japanese inspect one of Perry's "black ships."

The Opening of Japan

Trade concessions. As the United States expanded westward toward the Pacific, American interest in trade with Pacific lands grew. In 1853, American warships under the command of Matthew C. Perry arrived in Tokyo. Perry brought a message to the shogun from the President. It asked for protection of shipwrecked sailors, the establishment of a refueling station, and a statement of friendship from Japan. The American fleet left, but Perry said he would return in a year for the Japanese reply.

The Japanese knew that they lacked the technology to win a war against the United States. The shogun therefore signed the Treaty of Kanagawa with the United States in March 1854. This treaty gave foreign traders only limited rights. Still, it was the first step

Sec. Rev. ques. 2

582

toward allowing foreign influence in Japan, and it weakened the Tokugawa government. Treaties with the British, Dutch, French, and Russians quickly followed. By the 1860's Japan, like China, had been forced to make many trade concessions to the West.

The Japanese debated how Western nations could be kept out of Japan. Some people argued that with a strong sense of tradition and national purpose, Japan could easily defeat the foreigners. Others felt that Japan would have to change. Through the Dutch, many educated Japanese had kept in touch with Western scientific advances. They argued that Japan should develop a blend of "Western science and Eastern ethics." They claimed that by learning Western ways and adapting them to Japanese culture, Japan could become superior to the West.

Meiji rule. The Tokugawa shoguns had held on to power partly by keeping the

★ See below.

Background Perry's request was granted after the Shogun's advisers warned, "If we try to drive them away, they will begin hostilities, and then we shall be obliged to fight . . . . Tens of thousands of men of war will come and surround our shores completely."

★ **ENRICHMENT.** Have students write an essay analyzing the idea that Japan should develop a blend of "Western science and Eastern ethics." Students should explain what supporters of the idea might have meant by the statement and then compare the results of Japan's modernization with the statement. *(Synthesis) Analyzing Information* daimyo (feudal lords) in competition with one another. Now the unpopularity of the foreign treaties gave these lords a chance to join together against the shogun. As a symbol of national unity, they wanted to give leadership back to the emperor. Japanese emperors had not had political power for several hundred years, but they were still respected by the people. Two slogans soon became popular: *"Sonno!"* ("Honor the emperor") and *"Joi!"* ("Expel the barbarian").

In 1866, two groups of feudal lords joined together to overthrow the shogun and restore imperial government. Two years later, the rebel forces seized the shogun's court in the name of the emperor. The last of the Tokugawa shoguns was forced to resign. The emperor, then only 15 years old, took the name *Meiji* (MAY-jee), meaning "enlightened government."

Japan's Turn to the West

● Note strategies for second objective on this page and p. 585.

Although the emperor was the formal ruler of Japan during the Meiji era (1868–1912), the important decisions were actually made by the group of young samurai who had led the rebellion. As military men, they were eager to close the gap in military power between Japan and the West. They believed that only through rapid modernization could their country hope to compete. Over the next 50 years, these men transformed Japan into a powerful modern state.

The Charter Oath. In April 1868 the Meiji emperor issued the Charter Oath, setting a new course for Japan. The Oath called for an assembly that would decide important matters by public debate. It also declared that feudalism would be ended and that commoners would be given the chance to hold many new jobs. The last of the Oath's five points clearly stated the direction that Japan would take: "Wisdom and knowledge shall be sought all over the world in order to promote the welfare of the empire."

Reasons for success. The Charter Oath marked a momentous change in Japan's attitude toward itself and the outside world.

PRIMARY SOURCE

The Charter Oath

On April 6, 1868, the Meiji emperor issued the Charter Oath. Prepared by the leaders of the revolt against the Tokugawa government, this important document stated guidelines for the new Japanese government.

  ❝ 1. Deliberative assemblies shall be established, and all matters shall be decided by public opinion.

    2. The whole nation shall unite so that the administration of affairs of state may be carried out.

    3. Every person shall be given the opportunity to pursue a calling of his choice.

    4. Unworthy customs and practices of the past shall be discarded, and justice shall be based on the principles of nature.

    5. Wisdom and knowledge shall be sought all over the world in order to promote the welfare of the empire. ❞

1. Which points showed that Japan's new rulers planned to end feudalism?
2. How did the Charter Oath reflect the aim of unifying and strengthening Japan?
3. **Critical thinking:** Do you think the Japanese government found these guidelines difficult to carry out? Why or why not?

Ⓕ See answers below.

In spite of protests by some Japanese, the plan for modernization went forward quickly. There were several reasons for its success.

1. Strong national feeling. Unlike many other Asian countries, Japan had a longstanding sense of its identity as a nation.

Sec. Rev. ques. 3

583

National loyalty was more important than loyalty to family or to a feudal lord.

2. *A prosperous and well-educated population.* When the Americans and Europeans first arrived, the Japanese people had a fairly high standard of living. About 40 percent of the Japanese people were literate, a large percentage for the time. During the years of Japan's isolation from the Western world, trade and agriculture had prospered, and the country had become urbanized.

3. *Acceptance of new ideas.* There was little resistance among the Japanese to borrowing useful ideas from other cultures. Unlike the Chinese, who did not trust modern ways, the Japanese saw that modernization could help them compete with the West.

The modernization process. The reforms of the Meiji era affected all parts of Japanese society. Large landowners had to give up direct control of their lands to the imperial government. Most did so volun-

Sec. Rev. ques. 4

Meiji Japan quickly adapted Western advances in science and industry to its own modernization effort. This print shows women in traditional dress using a telescope.

584

tarily. In return for their land, they were given cash and important government jobs.

Japan's military forces were completely overhauled. The samurai class lost its special privileges, as all classes were made equal before the law. The samurai were also ordered to throw away their swords, which had for centuries been a symbol of their position. In 1873 Japan's first draft law made all men subject to the draft. The new Japanese army was organized using ideas from the French, and the navy was remodeled after the British navy.

The Meiji government also relied on Western advice in industry, agriculture, and education. Government leaders traveled widely in Western countries. Japan's best students were sent to universities in Europe and the United States. There they studied modern banking methods, communications, military organization, and government.

While the Japanese freely accepted Western ideas, they carefully avoided borrowing money from foreign banks. The government did not want to give outsiders an excuse to meddle in Japan's affairs. To pay for modernization projects, the government set up a new system of taxation. Instead of paying taxes on their crops, peasants paid an annual tax based on the value of their land. This gave the government a steady source of income even when harvests were poor, but it was hard on peasant farmers.

Meiji advisers soon realized that the government itself would have to provide much of the capital needed for industrialization. The government gave its greatest support to industries such as shipyards and ironworks, which helped build military strength. It also built ports for foreign trade and developed the textile industry to make silk and cotton cloth for export. A government-financed factory turned out weapons for Japan's growing army and navy. Before long, private companies also began to build Western-style factories.

To speed up communications and transportation, the Meiji government introduced the telegraph and built a railroad linking

Cultural History A samurai's sword was considered a sacred symbol of his rank and honor and was an heirloom passed down through generations. The making of a sword was almost a religious ritual, and swordsmiths guarded their secrets. Today the Japanese government has designated many of these swords as national treasures.

Social History Many peasants were unhappy with the new draft law, which they called a "blood tax."
Check for Understanding. Ask: Why did Japan avoid borrowing money from Western banks? (The government did not want outsiders to have an excuse to meddle in Japanese affairs.)

Tokyo and a coastal port. The railroad helped cut travel time in Japan's hilly terrain, and by 1900 Japan had more than 15,000 miles of track.

Education, too, was part of the Meiji plan for modernization. The Meiji leaders set up a system of required schooling for men and women as well as for children. Along with reading and writing, all students were taught patriotism and loyalty to the emperor.

A new constitution. In 1882 Ito Hirobumi, one of the emperor's chief advisers, led a delegation to Europe and the United States to study Western forms of government. Their task was to recommend the form of government that would best fit Japanese society. A military man, Ito talked with Otto von Bismarck in Germany (page 517) and took many ideas from the organization of the German state. He headed the committee that wrote a new constitution for Japan. It was completed in 1889 and handed down to the people as a gift from the emperor.

Under the new constitution, the emperor remained the head of state and the highest authority in the country. A prime minister was appointed to take charge of the day-to-day running of the government. A parliament, called the Diet, was created to make laws and advise the emperor on government policy. In practice, the Diet had little power. The emperor could veto laws it passed and issue laws of his own.

The constitution gave the Japanese people a list of individual rights. Among them were freedom of speech, freedom of religion, and freedom from search and seizure. Every freedom, however, was qualified by the clause "except in cases provided in law." The interests of the state came before those of the citizen.

Western nations were impressed that Japan adopted a constitution less than 25 years after the end of feudalism. As a result, they agreed to end the unequal treaties of the 1850's and 1860's. By the turn of the century, the West had begun to view Japan as an equal. The Japanese, however, still mistrusted Western nations.

This woodblock print from 1883 shows a crowd gathered around the first electric streetlight in Tokyo.

Japanese Imperialism

A major handicap in Japan's drive for modernization was its lack of natural resources. Farmland was scarce, and growing enough food for the nation had always been a problem. During the Meiji period, scientific and medical advances caused a sudden population increase, further straining Japan's food supply. Japan was forced to import much of its food as well as most of the raw materials needed for industrialization.

Sec. Rev. ques. 5

Faced with this problem, Japanese leaders chose the same solution as the Western nations: empire-building. Overseas possessions would provide Japan with land, crops, and raw materials.

● See below.

Victory over China. By the 1890's Japan's modernized army and navy were as strong as many Western military forces. In the Sino-Japanese War of 1894–1895 (page 577), Japan defeated China. China's army failed to win a single battle; its navy was almost destroyed. The peace treaty gave Japan the **585**

Japan astounded the world with its 1905 victory in the Russo-Japanese War. A Japanese artist depicts one of the naval battles in which Japan's newly modernized navy crushed Russia's disorganized and outmoded fleet. The victory established Japan as a world power and led to a crisis in Russia that was to have revolutionary consequences.

island of Formosa (present-day Taiwan) and some small neighboring islands, as well as the Liaodong (lee-OW-DOONG) Peninsula in southern Manchuria. In addition, China recognized Korea's independence, leaving Japan to become the dominant foreign power in that country.

Western reaction to Japan's victory was mixed. Some European nations were worried that their spheres of influence in Asia might be endangered. They pressured Japan to give up its rights in Manchuria.

Britain, however, saw an advantage in Japan's victory. The British were concerned about Russian attempts to expand into Manchuria. They hoped that Japan's military strength would discourage Russia. In 1902, delegates from Great Britain and Japan signed a 10-year treaty of alliance. In this treaty, unlike the earlier trade agreements, Japan was treated as an equal partner. The alliance restored the Japanese pride lost when Western ships first entered Tokyo Bay.

Victory over Russia. The Japanese next tried to negotiate with Russia's Czar Nicholas II about his troops in Manchuria. Convinced that Japan was still a weak country, Russia delayed the discussions. This proved to be a fatal mistake.

On February 8, 1904, without warning, the Japanese navy attacked the Russian fleet anchored at Port Arthur on the Liaodong Peninsula. This was the start of what came to be called the **Russo-Japanese War**. Nearly a year later, after a bloody siege, Port Arthur fell to Japan. On land, Japanese troops steadily forced the Russians out of Manchuria.

In a desperate effort to hold Manchuria, the czar sent Russia's Baltic fleet to Japan. Britain, honoring its alliance with Japan, would not let Russian ships use the Suez Canal. The Russians were forced to sail all the way around Africa. When the fleet finally reached Japan, seven months and 10,000 miles later, it was wiped out by the Japanese navy.

Background The 10-year alliance between Great Britain and Japan was called the Anglo-Japanese Alliance and was the first military treaty that a Western nation signed on equal terms with a non-Western nation.

Thoroughly beaten and humiliated, and troubled by rebellion at home, Czar Nicholas called for peace. The treaty signed in 1905 confirmed Japan's claim to the Liaodong Peninsula (including Port Arthur) and to Russia's mines and industry in Manchuria. Russia also agreed to recognize Japan's interest in Korea and to allow Japan to take over the southern half of Sakhalin Island.

Japan as a world power. The Russo-Japanese War forced Western nations to admit that Japan was now an imperialist power. In 1910 the Meiji government annexed Korea with no interference from the West. Other Asian people were inspired by Japan's rapid growth. In countries still controlled by European powers, nationalist movements began.

In 1912 the Meiji emperor died, bringing to a close an era of dynamic progress. Japan was by this time the leading power in Asia. In the coming years, Japan would continue to flex its muscles in Asian affairs.

See Sec. 3 *Closing the Lesson*, p. T567C.

Section Review

Answers to Section Review questions are in brackets on pages indicated.

1. **Identify:** Charter Oath, Russo-Japanese War. (pp. 583, 586)
2. What events led to the opening of trade between Japan and the West after 1853? (p. 582)
3. What features of Japanese society enabled Japan to modernize quickly? (pp. 583–584)
4. What reforms did the Meiji government make? (pp. 584–585)
5. What conditions brought about Japanese imperialism? (p. 585)
6. **Critical thinking:** Compare Japan's leadership during the Meiji era with China's leadership during the late 1800's and early 1900's. What differences help explain Japan's greater success in modernizing? (See answer below.)

Chapter 29   Summary and Timeline

1. Merchants of the English East India Company arrived in India in the 1600's. Within 200 years, Britain took control of all India. In 1857, Indians rose up against the British in the Sepoy Rebellion. This led Britain to tighten control. In the early 1900's, Indian nationalists called for home rule.

2. In the 1800's the West ended China's isolation, forcing it to accept European trade. China was unwilling to adopt Western ideas, however, and modernization was slow. Angry at foreign domination and the weak Manchu government, the Chinese people launched a series of rebellions. A revolution finally toppled the empire in 1912, but the new government failed to unite the country.

3. Japan also was forced to open its ports because of Western pressure, but Japan did adopt many ideas from the West. A small ruling group led the government in modernizing Japan. By the early 1900's, Japan had begun its own empire in Asia.

1763 Treaty of Paris gives Britain control of India

1850–1864 Taiping Rebellion

1857 Sepoy Rebellion begins

1842 Opium War ends; Britain gains trading rights in China

1868 Charter Oath

1895 Japan wins Sino-Japanese War

1899 Boxer Rebellion begins

1905 Japan wins Russo-Japanese War

1911 Nationalist Revolution in China

1760   1780   1800   1820   1840   1860   1880   1900   1920

587

See p. T567C for answers to Chapter Review.

Vocabulary Review

1. Use the following terms to complete the sentences below: *Nationalist Revolution, Open Door Policy, Opium War, sphere of influence.*
   a. The American government called for an ___?___ in China, giving all countries equal trading rights.
   b. The ___?___ put an end to the Qing dynasty in China.
   c. Britain and the other major European powers each established its own ___?___ in China when China gave in to demands for more trade.
   d. A disagreement between China and Britain over British trading rights in China led to the ___?___.
2. Define or identify the terms in the following pairs.
   a. Sino-Japanese War; Russo-Japanese War
   b. unequal treaty system; treaty ports
   c. Sepoy Rebellion; Boxer Rebellion

People to Identify

Match each of the following people with the correct description: *Robert Clive, Ito Hirobumi, Jahangir, Matthew Perry.*
1. British commander whose military forces defeated the French in India
2. Mogul ruler who allowed the East India Company to establish its first trading post in India
3. naval officer who led an American fleet to Japan in 1853 to seek trading privileges for the United States
4. adviser to the Japanese emperor who studied Western governments and helped write a new constitution in 1889

Places to Know

Match the letters on this map of Asia with the places listed below. You may want to refer to the map on page 578.

1. Beijing		6. Manchuria
2. Calcutta		7. Nanjing
3. Delhi		8. Port Arthur
4. Guangzhou		9. Tokyo
5. Korea		

Recalling the Facts

1. How did the English first gain a foothold in India? What events in the 1700's enabled Britain to take control of India?
2. What British actions in the early 1800's angered Indians?
3. What criticisms did educated Indians have of British rule in India?
4. Why did Europeans smuggle opium into China? How did the opium trade hurt China?
5. How did trade with China change after the Treaty of Nanjing?
6. What changes did the leaders of the Taiping Rebellion call for? Why did the rebellion fail?
7. Why were China's efforts at "self-strengthening" unsuccessful?

8. What prevented Guangxu's program of reform from succeeding?

9. What were the goals of the Nationalist Party? Why was Yuan Shikai chosen to lead the revolutionary government?

10. Why did Japanese officials agree to the Treaty of Kanagawa?

11. Why was the issuing of the Charter Oath an important turning point for Japan?

12. How was Japan organized under the constitution issued in 1889? How did Western nations view Japan after the adoption of this constitution?

Critical Thinking Skills

✔ **1. Interpreting a political cartoon.** Examine the cartoon on page 576. What kind of animal is used to symbolize China? What other nations are represented? What appears to be happening to China in the cartoon? How might this cartoon reflect the "sphere of influence" concept? What view of the treatment of China did the cartoonist hold? *(Anal.)*

2. Identifying effects. Identify one or more effects of each of these conflicts: (a) Sepoy Rebellion, (b) Opium War, (c) Sino-Japanese War, (d) Boxer Rebellion, (e) Nationalist Revolution in China. *(Comp.)*

Thinking About Geography

1. Interpreting maps. Britain ruled India from a great distance. In 1869, the opening of the Suez Canal provided a much quicker sea route between Britain and India. Find the Suez Canal on the map on page 597. What two bodies of water does it link? How did the distance from Britain to India—even after the opening of the canal—affect relations be- *(Comp.)* tween the British and their Indian subjects?

2. Interpreting. How did the geography of Japan contribute to that country's decision to build an overseas empire? Consider land available for farming, population growth, and natural resources. What products did Japan hope to gain from overseas possessions? *(Comp.)*

Enrichment: Primary Sources

The passage below is adapted from a statement that the Chinese minister in Britain sent to Queen Victoria concerning the opium trade.

66 Where is your conscience? I have heard that the smoking of opium is very strictly forbidden by your country. That is because the harm caused by opium is clearly understood. Since it is not permitted to do harm to your own country, then even less should you let it be passed on to the harm of other countries.

Of all that China exports to foreign countries, there is not a single thing which is not beneficial to people. Foreign countries cannot get along for a single day without Chinese products. If China cuts off these benefits, then what can the barbarians rely upon to keep themselves alive?

On the other hand, articles coming from the outside to China can only be used as toys. We can take them or get along without them. Since they are not needed by China, what difficulty would there be if we stopped the trade? 99

1. What does the Chinese minister say he has heard about the attitude toward opium in England?

2. What reasons does he give for saying England should oppose the opium trade?

3. Who does he think would suffer most from an end to trade between China and other countries?

4. **Critical thinking:** How convincing to Queen Victoria were these arguments likely to be? Explain. *(Syn.)*

T589A

Imperialism in Africa 1780–1914
(pp. 590–608)

Chapter Preview

Section 1 of this chapter discusses changes on the African continent before European partition. The growth of African states and expansion of trade are described, and the development of black colonies and Dutch, English, and French settlements are traced. Section 2 examines the results of the 1884 Berlin Conference, the methods used by European nations to gain control of parts of Africa, and the resistance of African peoples to European imperialism. Section 3 describes the policies used by the various European nations in governing their African colonies and the effects of imperialism on the people of Africa.

Bibliography

See the *Teacher's Management and Planning Guide* for additional listings. Starred titles are for both students and teachers.

*Achebe, Chinua. *Things Fall Apart.* Fawcett. Classic novel about the impact of missionaries on traditional African society.

*Lee, Emanuel. *To the Bitter End: A Photographic History of the Boer War, 1899–1902.* Viking. Early snapshots with a concise narrative.

*Moorehead, Alan. *The White Nile.* Random House. The Nile's exploration and conquest from the 1850's to 1900.

Morris, Donald R. *The Washing of the Spears: The Rise and Fall of the Zulu Nation.* Simon and Schuster. Zulus encounter British forces.

Section Lesson Plans

SECTION 1   (pp. 591–595)
Africa Before Partition

Objectives

After completing this section, students will be able to:
1. Discuss the changes that took place in Africa in the late 1700's and early 1800's.
2. Explain how colonists, missionaries, and explorers increased European interest in Africa.
3. Describe how southern and northern Africa came under European rule.

Introducing the Lesson

Remind students that Europeans had been involved in Africa since the 1500's. Although explorers were motivated by a desire to penetrate the vast continent, most European interest was a result of the slave trade.

   Then ask: *(a) What conditions within a country might have made it difficult for a nation to resist colonization?* (Answers will vary. Lack of political unity and absence of modern technology might have hindered resistance to colonization.)

   (b) How might the slave trade have affected the ability of African nations to withstand imperialism? (Answers will vary. The growth of the slave trade expanded the European presence in Africa. The more advanced weaponry and technology of the Europeans would have made resistance very difficult.)

   (c) What might the African people have done to resist colonization successfully? (Answers will vary.)

Developing the Lesson:
Identifying Effects

Have students identify the effects of the development of new African states and stronger empires. (Sokoto Empire: jihad called; old ruling families toppled; largest empire in West Africa formed. Zulu kingdom: a unified and powerful nation formed. Egypt: state was modernized and strengthened.) *(Comprehension)*

Developing the Lesson: Evaluating Information

Have students work in groups to evaluate the positive and negative effects of the following: black colonies in Africa, mission stations, early exploration. (Answers will vary. Black colonies provided a refuge for former slaves and for slaves rescued from slave ships. Mission stations offered education and medical treatment. Early exploration triggered great interest in the African continent.) *(Comprehension)*

Closing the Lesson: Observing for Detail

Have students trace the early growth of Dutch, British, and French colonization in Africa. (1652—Dutch establish a supply post at Cape of Good Hope; 1658—Dutch overcome Khoisan; 1806—British gain control of Cape Colony; 1835–1845—Dutch settlers escape English rule through Great Trek; 1848—French gain control of Algeria; Tunisia and Morocco become French protectorates.) *(Comprehension)*

See *Section Review* questions, p. 595.

SECTION 2   (pp. 596–601)
The Conquest of Africa

Objectives

After completing this section, students will be able to:
1. Describe how the European nations divided Africa.
2. Explain what conflicts arose from European expansion.

Introducing the Lesson

Remind students that European interest in Africa increased with the growth of the slave trade and exploration. European conquest of Africa brought many changes to the people of that continent.

Then ask: *(a) What are some ways in which European conquest of other areas of the world affected people in other societies, for example, in the Americas?* (In North and South America, land and other resources were taken from the Indians. Europeans brought the Christian religion, a new social structure, and European customs and traditions. Many Indians died from exposure to new diseases.)

(b) How do you think ways of life in Africa were changed after European conquest? (Answers will vary.)

Developing the Lesson: Solving Problems

Have students write an essay explaining how they might have resolved the following issue: *If you had been the only native African representative at the Berlin Conference, how would you have tried to protect African interests and still have satisfied European interest in raw materials and new markets?* Have students read their essays in class. *(Synthesis)*

Developing the Lesson: Evaluating Information

Have students work in groups to present a panel discussion on the following question: *Which factor was most significant in the development of European imperialism in Africa: national rivalry, economic competition, or racism?* When discussing the issue, students should explain the relationships between the motives and support their conclusions with information from the text. *(Synthesis)*

Closing the Lesson: Observing for Detail

Have students identify the factors that contributed to Europe's ability to conquer Africa and Africa's failure to resist colonization. (European conquest: the Berlin Conference; superior military force and technology. African failure to resist colonization: inferior military force; lack of modern technology.) *(Comprehension)*

See *Section Review* questions, p. 601.

SECTION 3   (pp. 602–606)
European Rule of Africa

Objectives

After completing this section, students will be able to:
1. Describe how the imperialist powers ran their African colonies.
2. Identify the positive and negative effects of European rule.

Introducing the Lesson

Remind students that countries that fall under foreign control usually experience far-reaching changes. Sometimes these changes improve living conditions for people but sometimes these changes result in severe disadvantages.

Then ask: *(a) How might foreign control improve the standard of living for colonized people?* (Answers will vary. If the colonizing nation introduces new technology or advances in health and hygiene, the standard of living is likely to improve.)

(b) How might foreign control result in disadvantages for the colonized nation? (Answers will vary. Colonizing nations usually seek economic benefits and often impose policies which damage the economy of the subject state. Foreign powers impose their own political structure and seldom allow colonized people to exercise any real political power.)

(c) What changes resulting from foreign control might create resentment between the colonized people and the foreign power? (Answers will vary.)

Developing the Lesson: Drawing Conclusions

Have students work in groups to answer the following: *(a) Which colonial policy might better prepare a country for independence, direct rule or indirect rule? Why? (b) What effect might the paternalistic attitudes of some colonial officials have had on African peoples' nation-building skills?* Have students share their group's conclusions with the class. *(Synthesis)*

Developing the Lesson: Comparing Historical Developments

Have students make a chart comparing the patterns of colonization in Africa with those in Asia (Chapter 29). Students might note the reasons for colonization in both continents, the impact of colonization, and efforts made in both continents to improve the standard of living and local economies. (In both Africa and Asia, European nations viewed their colonies as sources of raw materials and markets for manufactured goods. In neither case was any attempt made to help the country to industrialize or to develop local economies.) *(Comprehension)*

Answers to *Map Skill Practice*, p. 603.

1. France.
2. Belgian Congo, German East Africa.
3. Guinea, Angola, Mozambique.
4. Liberia, Ethiopia.
5. Answers might include belief in their cultural and ethnic superiority; desire to convert people to Christianity; imperialistic goals of gaining economic and political advantages.

Closing the Lesson: Drawing Conclusions

Have students work in groups to discuss the following statement: *European empire-building in Africa did more harm than good.* Students should support their views with examples from the text. *(Comprehension)*

See *Section Review* questions, p. 606.

Chapter 30 Review Answers (pp. 607–608)

Vocabulary Review

1. mission station 2. South African War 3. assimilated 4. direct rule 5. indirect rule

People to Identify

1. The Mahdi 2. Henry M. Stanley 3. René Caillié 4. Cecil Rhodes 5. Menelik II 6. H. H. Kitchener

Places to Know

1. G   2. J   3. F   4. M   5. H   6. D   7. A   8. E 9. K   10. C   11. B   12. L   13. I

Recalling the Facts

1. Mohammed Ali reformed Egypt's army, education system, and economy. Improved irrigation raised the output of cotton, sugar, and grain. New buildings sprang up in Egypt's cities.
2. They kept detailed diaries and wrote vivid descriptions of unfamiliar places for people at home, sparking curiosity about Africa in the West. Westerners also explored Africa because they were eager to find new markets for Western goods.
3. Dutch farmers, wanting more land for farming, went to war with the Khoisan people. The Khoisan were forced to flee or work as laborers for the Dutch.
4. The Afrikaners were seeking a way to escape British rule.
5. France invaded Algeria in 1830 and gained control of Algeria in 1848.
6. Nearly all of Africa was divided among various European nations.

7. France wanted to control land from coast to coast across the continent.

8. The British conquered small trading states of the Niger Delta and defeated the Sokoto Empire. In 1914 Britain combined the conquered regions into the single colony of Nigeria.

9. British settlers conquered the Ndebele, who occupied territory named the Rhodesias.

10. Only white men could vote. Whites also owned most of the land and all of the mines and factories.

11. The British governed by indirect rule, which gave Africans some part in colonial government. Most other countries practiced direct rule.

12. European powers gained wealth from the export to Europe of raw materials and cash crops and from taxes levied on Africans.

13. Traditional life was undermined—African men were sent to work far from their villages; women had to work for Europeans to help meet tax payments; Africans no longer had time to make their own clothing, so they purchased goods on credit from European-owned stores and became indebted; disease spread rapidly when Africans moved to crowded towns; and urbanization led to increased crime and a breakdown of family and community bonds.

Critical Thinking Skills

1. Timetables will vary.

2. Answers will vary, but students should note that *racism* is defined as "the belief that one's own racial or national group is superior to others." European powers expressed these attitudes by dividing African lands among themselves without consulting the original inhabitants and by instituting policies of political and social inequality. Their actions were based on the belief that Africans were incapable of managing their own lives. The attempts of most colonial powers to encourage assimilation of Africans into colonial cultures was also based on a belief in the superiority of European culture.

3. (a) Students might point out that every attempt at conquest by Europeans met with African resistance. Examples include resistance by the following peoples: Khoisan, Ndebele, Zulu, Algerian, Ashanti, Mandinka, Egyptian, Sudanese, Ethiopian. (b) African rulers had to pay a "labor tax" by sending their people to work as forced laborers in mines or on rubber plantations. Africans were beaten, mutilated, or killed if they failed to meet unreasonable production quotas.

Thinking About Geography

Reports will vary.

Enrichment: Primary Sources

1. The whites destroyed the peaceful and quiet life the villagers had been leading, and the villagers feared they would be forced into slavery.

2. The white men had guns.

3. Students might suggest that the white men had no regard for the villagers as human beings and saw them only as a source of labor.

Imperialism in Africa

1780–1914

See chapter timeline, p. 606.

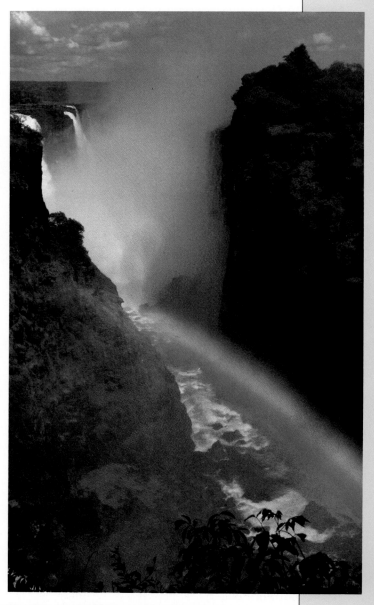

Before You Read This Chapter

If you have ever read a mystery story, you know that one of the problems is finding the motive. *Why* was the mysterious crime committed? Was it for money, for revenge, for self-defense? Some motives are easy to see, but others are less clear. As you read this chapter, think of yourself as a detective. Look for the motives that led Europeans to set up colonies in Africa. What did Europeans hope to gain or accomplish in Africa? How would Europeans have justified their actions? Consider the position of Africans as well. How did they respond to European colonization?

The Geographic Setting

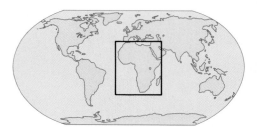

The Chapter Outline

1. Africa Before Partition
2. The Conquest of Africa
3. European Rule of Africa

Victoria Falls, on the Zambezi River in Africa, creates so much mist that local people call it "smoke that thunders."

1 Africa Before Partition

Objectives

Focus Questions

★ ■ What changes took place in Africa in the late 1700's and early 1800's? *(pages 591–592)*

● ■ How did colonists, missionaries, and explorers increase European interest in Africa? *(pages 592–594)*

▲ ■ How did southern and northern Africa come under European rule? *(pages 594–595)*

Terms to Know

mission station   protectorate
Great Trek

★ Note strategies for first objective on this page and p. 592.

Dramatic changes took place in Africa from the late 1700's to the early 1900's. New empires and states developed and many older states expanded. The Atlantic slave trade ended, but other kinds of trade grew. Missionaries and explorers, as well as traders, came to the continent. The first European colonies in Africa were also set up.

New States and Stronger Empires

In the late 1700's new states appeared in the Sudan of West Africa. Like earlier empires in the Sudan (Chapter 15), they depended heavily on trade across the Sahara. The new states were started by Muslim leaders who wanted to purify the practice of Islam and to spread Islam among non-Muslims.

The largest of the new Muslim states was the Sokoto Empire, in what is now northern Nigeria. Its leader was Usuman dan Fodio (OO-soo-mahn DAHN FOH-dih-oh),

a Muslim preacher and leader of the Fulani people. In 1804 he called for a jihad (page 199) to purify Islam among the Hausa and Fulani peoples. Within five years Usuman had toppled the old ruling families and combined their many small kingdoms into the largest empire in West Africa. The Sokoto Empire later became an important center of learning as well.

In southern Africa the powerful Zulu kingdom was started in the early 1800's by Shaka (SHAH-kah). Using new kinds of spears, Shaka's well-trained army won battle after battle. By 1819 Shaka ruled much of southeastern Africa.

Once in power, Shaka set about creating a new nation. All young men and women joined military units where they were taught to fight and to take pride in being Zulu. Although Shaka was killed in 1828, the Zulu remained a unified and powerful nation.

Under the leadership of Shaka and his nephew Cetewayo (shown above), the Zulu became the most powerful nation in southern Africa.

591

★ RETEACHING. Have students make a chart titled *Changes in African States* identifying new African states, reformed older states, and ways both became stronger. (New: Sokoto Empire: toppled old ruling families and combined many small kingdoms; Zulu kingdom— started by Shaka, strengthened by well-trained military; Reformed: Egypt—modernized and strengthened by Mohammed Ali.) *(Comprehension) Observing for Detail*

★ REINFORCEMENT. Have students answer the following questions: Why did Africans develop new products for industrial Europe? (When many European nations banned slave trading, Africans sought new sources of revenue.) What two products became important exports for Africans? (Palm oil and ivory.) *(Comprehension) Observing for Detail*

Cultural History Members of Shaka's army were instructed to return from war with their spear or not return at all.

Meanwhile, older states reformed and expanded during the early 1800's. Egypt had returned to Ottoman rule after the withdrawal of Napoleon's troops (page 446). Yet under Mohammed Ali, who ruled from 1805 to 1849, Egypt gained a large measure of independence. Mohammed Ali worked to modernize and strengthen Egypt. The army, education, and the economy were all reformed. Improved irrigation raised the output of cotton, sugar, and grain. New buildings sprang up in Cairo and other cities. Egypt extended its control southward into the eastern Sudan, which became an Egyptian colony. Under Ali's grandson, Ismail, the Suez Canal was built to connect the Mediterranean and Red seas.

★ See below.

New Trading Patterns

During the 1800's the African slave trade declined as more and more European countries banned slave trading. Replacing this lost trade, Africans offered new exports to meet the growing needs of industrial Europe.

Palm oil. In West Africa, palm oil had been an important export even before the slave trade declined. Slave traders bought palm oil to feed slaves during the Middle Passage (page 378). After 1800, Britain imported increasing amounts of palm oil for making candles, soap, and lubricating oil.

Other areas of West Africa later joined the palm oil trade. In return for their exports, Africans received cotton cloth, guns, salt, and other goods from European factories and mines. In 1850 the value of trade between Western Europe and West Africa was six or seven times what it had been in 1820.

Ivory. In eastern Africa an expansion of the ancient ivory trade attracted large numbers of European and American ships. Ivory was in great demand in middle-class homes for piano keys, billiard balls, and furniture. The center of the ivory trade was the island of Zanzibar, on Africa's eastern coast (map, page 597).

With the help of African traders, caravans from Zanzibar pushed inland to search for ivory. Some of the ivory was bought or stolen from local Africans, but the caravan traders also used powerful European rifles to hunt elephants for their tusks.

The Foreign Presence in Africa

● Note strategies for second objective on this page and p. 593.

Traders were not the only foreign travelers in Africa. Colonists, missionaries, and explorers also had a powerful effect on the continent, setting the stage for a European takeover in the late 1800's.

Black colonies in Africa. The colony of Sierra Leone was started in 1787 for free blacks returning to Africa from North America and Britain. Liberia was set up in 1820 for former American slaves. Neither colony attracted as many settlers as its sponsors had hoped. Sierra Leone, however, grew in importance after 1808, when Britain made it the base for its patrols against the slave trade. Over the next 60 years, 130,000 Africans were settled in Sierra Leone after being rescued from slave ships. European missionaries came to Sierra Leone to work with these settlers, some of whom became missionaries themselves.

Sec. Rev. ques. 2

Liberia, meanwhile, became Africa's first republic in 1847. Liberia's leaders created a government modeled after that of the United States. Though greatly outnumbered by native Africans, the American-born settlers held political and economic power in Liberia.

Mission stations. During the 1800's, Christian churches set up mission stations—self-sufficient religious communities headed by foreign missionaries. The mission stations offered Africans education and medical treatment, as well as instruction in Christianity. Many missionaries wrote vivid accounts of their experiences for people at home. Their descriptions of these unknown areas sparked great curiosity about Africa in the West.

Sec. Rev. ques. 3

Early exploration. This curiosity, as well as an eagerness to find new markets for Western goods, led to greater exploration of Africa. Daring men and women traveled to parts of the continent that no Westerner had

★ ENRICHMENT. Have students write a biography of Usuman dan Fodio, Shaka, Mohammed Ali, or Ismail. Students might compare the lives of these men with the lives of national leaders in Europe during the same time period, and compare their goals and leadership methods. (Synthesis) *Locating Information*

Background Because the ivory trade has caused a severe reduction of the elephant population, many African nations have banned the export of ivory. However, the illegal shooting of elephants remains a problem.

● RETEACHING. Have students identify the impact of foreign involvement in Africa. (Colonists started Sierra Leone and Liberia. Missionaries offered education, medical treatment, and religious instruction.) (Comprehension) *Identifying Effects*

● REINFORCEMENT. Have students draw a map of Africa and label the regions with the names of the Europeans who explored them. Students might refer to maps on pp. 151, 597, and 603. (Comprehension) *Connecting Geography and History* seen before, mapping and describing what they found. Africa's mighty rivers were of special interest since they offered trade routes to the interior of the continent.

In 1768 the Scotsman James Bruce reached the headwaters of the Blue Nile. The Niger River was charted by several British explorers—Mungo Park in 1796 and 1805–1806, and Richard and John Lander in the 1830's. In 1827–1828 René Caillié (ky-YAY) became the first European in modern times to reach the famous city of Timbuktu and live to tell the tale. The Englishmen Richard Burton and John Speke were the first Europeans to view the enormous lakes that form the source of the Nile. The Englishwoman Mary Kingsley studied coastal West Africa, reporting on its cultures and trade.

● See below.

Livingstone and Stanley. Popular interest in Africa reached a high point during the travels of a Scottish medical missionary named David Livingstone (1813–1873). Livingstone began his work in southern Africa, but soon moved northward. He traveled along the Zambezi and upper Congo rivers, writing accounts of his journeys for readers in England. Among Livingstone's discoveries were the giant waterfalls on the Zambezi River, which he named Victoria Falls after the British queen.

While on a journey in central Africa, Livingstone was out of touch with the outside world for about five years. In 1871 an American journalist, Henry M. Stanley, began to look for Livingstone. After nearly eight months of travel, Stanley found him at a trading town on Lake Tanganyika called Ujiji. Stanley's greeting—"Dr. Livingstone, I presume?"—is one of the most famous lines in the history of exploration.

This engraving records the famous meeting of Stanley and Livingstone near the shores of Lake Tanganyika in East Africa in 1871. Stanley (shown at center left) is raising his hat to greet the British missionary doctor.

593

Livingstone hoped that his work would expose the horrors of the slave trade and draw missionaries into new parts of Africa. Other missionaries did follow in Livingstone's footsteps and set up mission stations. Stanley, however, took another direction. He used guns to force his way down the Congo River to the Atlantic. Then he went to work for King Leopold II of Belgium, who used Stanley's explorations to lay claim to the Congo Basin (page 596).

Early Colonization of Africa

▲ Note strategies for third objective on this page and p. 595.

Before 1880 only a few small colonies were set up in Africa. Aside from some trading outposts and the black settler colonies of Sierra Leone and Liberia, only the southern and northern tips of the continent came under foreign rule.

Cape Colony. In 1652 the Dutch East India Company set up a supply post at the Cape of Good Hope (map, page 597). Dutch ships on their way to Asia stopped at the post for water and other supplies. A few Dutch farmers began to settle at the supply post, and it grew into a settlement called Cape Colony.

594 European and American church organizations established missions throughout Africa, such as the British medical station shown here.

As the Dutch farmers moved inland in search of more land, they came into conflict with the Khoisan (KOY-san) people, who kept herds of sheep and cattle. The Dutch demanded land and labor from the Khoisan, and by 1658 the two peoples were at war. The Khoisan were forced to flee into the harsh Kalahari Desert or work as laborers for the Dutch.

During the Napoleonic Wars, the Dutch lost Cape Colony to Britain. British rule, which began in 1806, affected the people of the colony in different ways. The British governor outlawed further expansion to prevent conflict with the powerful African states to the northeast. In 1833 the British government ended slavery in its possessions; this move freed the Dutch settlers' many slaves. Finally, the British made rules dealing with relations between the settlers and their African servants. These permitted Africans to file complaints against their masters and to speak in court.

Sec. Rev. ques. 4

The Great Trek. Resenting British rule, many Dutch settlers looked for ways to escape it. Between 1835 and 1845, about 14,000 Dutch farmers, in ox-drawn covered wagons, crossed the northeast Cape frontier at the Orange River. They took with them everything they owned, including slaves and African servants. This move came to be known as the **Great Trek** (*Trek* is a Dutch word meaning "migration.")

Before long the trekkers entered lands claimed by Africans. First they met and defeated the Ndebele (nn-day-BAY-lay). In 1838 a group of trekkers under Andreas Pretorius entered Zulu territory. At first King Dingane (din-GAHN), the half-brother of Shaka (page 591), treated the trekkers politely out of respect for their guns. Then a Zulu surprise attack killed Pretorius and others. The trekkers regrouped and near the end of 1838 defeated the Zulu at the Battle of Blood River (so named because the small river was said to have run red with Zulu blood).

To prevent the trekkers from expanding further, Britain annexed the nearby region of

---

▲ RETEACHING. Have students make a chart describing early European colonization in Africa. Charts should include the name of each territory, its colonizing nation and dates of settlements, and effects of early colonization. (Charts should include information on Cape Colony, Natal, Orange Free State, Transvaal Republic, Algeria, Tunisia, and Morocco.) *(Comprehension) Translating Information into Another Form*

▲ REINFORCEMENT. Have students make a timeline of events during the early colonization of Africa. (1652—Dutch post at Cape of Good Hope. 1658—Dutch at war with Khoisan. 1806—British in Cape Colony. 1834—Britain ends slavery in its possessions. 1835–1845—the Great Trek. 1838—trekkers defeat Zulu. 1848—France controls Algeria.) *(Comprehension) Sequencing Information*

Dutch settlers moved inland from the Cape Colony in the seventeenth and eighteenth centuries in search of more land to farm. By the early 1800's the countryside in southern Africa was dotted with isolated Dutch farmhouses.

Natal. Most of the trekkers then settled on an inland plateau, creating the Orange Free State and the Transvaal Republic (map, page 597).

The French in North Africa. The only other European colonization in Africa before 1850 took place along the coast of North Africa. The region, called the Barbary Coast (from the name "Berber"), was made up of Morocco, Algiers, Tunis, and Tripoli (the modern nations of Morocco, Algeria, Tunisia, and Libya). While Morocco was an independent kingdom, the other three were part of the Ottoman Empire. These lands had for centuries been inhabited by Muslim Berbers and Arabs.

France, which lay directly across the Mediterranean from the Barbary Coast, had a dispute over money with the ruler of Algiers. Using this as an excuse, France invaded Algeria in 1830. The French faced strong resistance to their invasion by the Algerian people. After a long and brutal war, however, France gained control of Algeria in 1848. Later, Tunisia and Morocco became French

Sec. Rev. ques. 5

protectorates—nations that are formally independent but whose policies are guided by an outside power.

▲ See below, left.

See Sec. 1 *Closing the Lesson,* p. T589B.

Section Review

Answers to Section Review questions are in brackets on pages indicated.

1. **Define or identify:** mission station, Great Trek, protectorate. (pp. 592, 594, 595)
2. What was so unusual about the West African colonies of Sierra Leone and Liberia? (p. 592)
3. What activities did missionaries and explorers undertake in Africa? (pp. 592–594)
4. How did the British acquire Cape Colony? What caused conflict between the British and the Afrikaners? (p. 594)
5. How did European colonization in North Africa come about? (p. 595)
6. **Critical thinking:** What different reactions might native-born Africans have had to the settlers of Sierra Leone and Liberia? (See answer below.)

595

▲ ENRICHMENT. Have students research the effects of European colonization on the Khoisan, the Zulu, the Ndebele, or Muslim Berbers and Arabs. *(Application) Locating Information*

6. Africans might have acknowledged kinship with the colonists; Africans might have regarded colonization as an intrusion, especially since the colonists and their sponsors maintained political power.

2 The Conquest of Africa

Objectives

Focus Questions

★ ■ How did the European nations divide Africa? *(page 596)*

● ■ What conflicts arose from European expansion? *(pages 596–601)*

Terms to Know

Berlin Conference
South African War

★ Note strategies for first objective on this page.

In the mid-1800's, 90 percent of Africa was still ruled by Africans. Yet European traders, missionaries, and explorers had already paved the way for foreign settlement and colonization. Several European nations had set up outposts and colonies along the coast, and they now claimed lands in the interior. By 1914, only two African nations—Ethiopia and Liberia—remained free of European rule.

The Berlin Conference

Until the early 1870's only France and Britain had taken a serious interest in Africa. In the next decade the entry of new powers led to increased competition. The first of the new-comers was the king of Belgium, Leopold II. Leopold claimed the huge basin of the Congo River as his personal possession in 1884. Then Germany declared protectorates over four African territories in 1884–1885.

To avoid serious conflict over this rapidly changing situation, Germany set up the **Berlin Conference** of 1884–1885. Twelve **596** European nations, plus the Ottoman Empire and the United States, took part. The peoples of Africa, whose future was to be decided, had no representatives.

The delegates decided that there should be free trade and travel on both the Niger and the Congo rivers. They also agreed that foreign powers had to establish control of any lands in Africa before claiming them as colonies, and that the imperialist nations would join forces if African peoples resisted. Thus the Berlin Conference made it easier for European powers to take over Africa without fighting among themselves.

Western Africa

● Note strategies for second objective on pages 597 and 600.

National rivalry, economic competition, and racism lay behind European imperialism in Africa. In western Africa, the desire to protect trade was the most important factor.

The French expansion across West Africa was part of a grand dream of controlling land from coast to coast across the continent. Citing Caillié's expedition to Timbuktu (page 593), the French government claimed all the land between Senegal and Algeria. After much African resistance, the French took Timbuktu in 1894. They also annexed parts of the coast, where French traders had long been active.

The strongest opponent of the French was the new empire created by Samori Touré (too-RAY). Samori had built a powerful state on the upper Niger River among the Mandinka people in the 1870's, using guns bought from European coastal traders. He proclaimed his empire a Muslim state and ordered all his subjects to adopt that religion.

Samori's armies were the best in West Africa. His blacksmiths were able to repair rifles and make new guns. Thus, Samori was able to fight effectively against the French. They battled him for almost 20 years before capturing him in 1898.

Sec. Rev. ques. 2

★ RETEACHING. Have students review "The Berlin Conference" (above) and identify the cause and effects of the Berlin Conference. (It was called to avoid conflict over African colonization and trade. Results included policies on trade, territorial control and colonization, and joint efforts against African resistance.) *(Comprehension) Identifying Cause and Effect*

★ REINFORCEMENT. Have students compare the policies of the Berlin Conference with the Open Door Policy for China (p. 577). (Both were established to prevent conflict among imperialist nations; neither involved input from non-Western peoples.) *(Application) Comparing Historical Developments*

★ ENRICHMENT. Have students research the Berlin Conference. Students might report on the delegates or evaluate the effects of the meeting. *(Application) Locating Information*

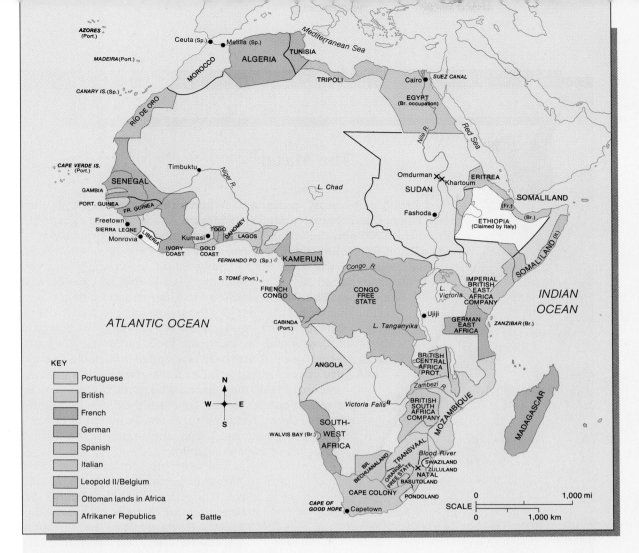

Imperialism in Africa, 1891

In the 1880's competing European governments began to stake out claims in Africa. What nations had made claims along the west coast of the continent by 1891? Which North African land did the Ottomans control?

Map Answers: (1) Spain, France, Britain, Portugal, Germany, Belgium. (2) Tripoli.

The defeat of Samori gave the French control over most of the interior of West Africa, but much of this land was dry and had few people. In contrast, the British took smaller but much more valuable lands in West Africa.

The British had taken control of a narrow strip of the Gold Coast early in the 1800's. The interior was ruled by the powerful Ashanti (page 380). The British fought four wars with the Ashanti between 1824 and 1874, twice burning Kumasi (koo-MAH-sih), the Ashanti capital. In 1896 the British took

Kumasi again and this time declared the kingdom a protectorate.

Ashanti resistance did not end, however. In 1900 the British governor demanded the surrender of the Golden Stool, the Ashanti royal symbol. The Ashanti rebelled and jailed the British governor, missionaries, and soldiers. British troops were sent in, and hundreds of people died in the year-long war. By superior force the British were able to regain control.

British military power also resulted in the conquest of their most important West **597**

● RETEACHING. Have students work in groups to present a meeting that might have occurred between African leaders who, faced with the conquest of their lands, sought ways to solve the problems facing their peoples. African representatives should identify the problems and suggest ways to negotiate with the imperialists. *(Synthesis) Solving Problems*

● REINFORCEMENT. Have students make a chart identifying imperialist goals in each African region, the dominant European nation in each region, and conflicts that arose. *(Comprehension) Translating Information into Another Form*

History The British believed that the Golden Stool was the throne of the Ashanti emperor. The Stool, however, was considered too sacred for the emperor to use as a royal chair; it symbolized the collected spirits of the Ashanti people and their ancestors.

Daily Life

The Masai

Throughout history, nomads have had a reputation as tough warriors. The nomadic Masai (mah-SY) of eastern Africa were no exception. From the 1700's to the late 1800's, they dominated the grasslands of the Great Rift Valley in present-day Kenya and Tanzania. When Arab merchants from the coast tried to move inland to expand their ivory trade, they faced Masai soldiers carrying 50-pound shields and 8-foot spears. The Arabs retreated to their coastal cities.

The Masai use the vast, dry grasslands as pasture for their herds of sheep, goats, and cattle. They value their cattle above all. Cow's milk is their main food, but cattle are more than a food source. A fine herd is a sign of high social status, and gifts of cattle help families make important alliances. When a Masai man marries, he gives his wife's family a gift of cattle. He also gives his new wife milking rights to several of his own cows. From these cows a woman raises a herd that she hands down to her sons when they are grown.

A person with no cattle cannot take part in these important aspects of Masai society. Thus the nomadic Masai look down on the Arusha, or farming Masai. However, the two groups trade regularly, exchanging grain for cowhides.

African colony, Nigeria. The small trading states of the Niger Delta were taken in the late 1800's. In 1902–1903, the British defeated the Sokoto Empire (page 591). In 1914 Britain combined the northern and southern peoples into the single colony of Nigeria.

Northeastern Africa

In northeastern Africa, the Europeans' main goal was to protect the sea route to British India. The opening of the Suez Canal in 1869, which gave a shortcut to India, made Egypt of great importance to Britain.

The building of the canal helped put Egypt deeply in debt to European banks. Things grew worse after the Civil War in the United States (page 560). Greater American cotton exports caused a drop in world cotton prices, hurting Egypt's cotton industry.

By 1875 the Egyptian government was near financial ruin. It accepted Britain's offer to buy its shares of stock in the Suez Canal Company. Egypt was also forced to accept British and French management of its finances. When Egyptian nationalists seized control of the government, Britain invaded. By 1882 Egypt was under British control.

Britain next looked to expand farther south. To protect Egypt, Britain decided to

ⓕ **FEATURE ACTIVITY. Have students describe the economic and social significance of cattle in Masai society.** (*Economic:* cow's milk is the main food; cowhides are used for trade. *Social:* size of a herd indicates social status; alliances made by gifts of cattle; when a Masai man marries, cattle are given to his wife's family; Masai with no cattle have low social status.) (*Comprehension*) *Observing for Detail*

When Europeans began to move into the Great Rift Valley in the 1880's, they found the Masai weakened by a bitter war. In 1890, a disease called rinderpest swept through the Masai herds, killing as many as 90 per cent of the cattle. The following year, drought struck the region. These disasters helped the British win control of the vast Masai homelands.

take control of lands around the source of the Nile. In an agreement signed in 1890, Germany let Britain take control of land along Lake Victoria. In return, Germany got territory that eventually became German East Africa (map, page 597).

Gaining control of the rest of the Nile Valley proved more difficult. Just a year before Britain occupied Egypt, a Muslim religious leader known as the Mahdi had led a revolt against Egyptian troops in the Sudan. The revolt went on after the British takeover of Egypt. In 1885 the British fort at Khartoum (kahr-TOOM) was overrun by the Mahdi's followers. The Sudan remained independent for the next 13 years.

In 1896, concerned about French and Belgian interest in the Sudan, the British decided to reconquer the region. They sent soldiers along the Nile, building a railroad as they went. At Omdurman in 1898, a British-Egyptian army led by General H. H. Kitchener met the Sudanese army. British machine guns cut down the attackers, killing more than 10,000 Sudanese at the cost of only 28 British soldiers.

As Kitchener's forces were driving toward the south, a French expedition was moving eastward to claim land west of the Nile. A few weeks after the Battle of Omdurman, these two groups met at Fashoda (map page 597). For a time, France and Britain seemed to be on the verge of war, but the Fashoda Incident was settled by diplomacy. The French government, already troubled at home by the Dreyfus Affair (page 545), gave up its claims to the lands along the Nile.

Southern Africa

In southern Africa, valuable minerals attracted European imperialism. Diamonds were found near the Orange River in 1867, and whites and blacks swarmed into the area in hopes of riches. Within a year the town of Kimberley on the edge of the diamond fields had become the second largest city in southern Africa. Despite protests from Afrikaners, as the descendants of the Dutch settlers now called themselves, Britain annexed the area. It now became part of the Cape Colony.

When gold was found in the Transvaal in 1886, large numbers of English-speaking miners flocked to the new city of Johannesburg. The Transvaal was too strong to be annexed easily by Britain. The British did, however, move to block the Afrikaners' route to the sea. They annexed Bechuanaland and set up the protectorate of Basutoland to prevent further Afrikaner expansion (map, page 597).

The Rhodesias. Cecil Rhodes, a British settler in the Cape who had made huge fortunes in the diamond and gold fields, urged Britain to claim the lands north of the **599**

Vocabulary The term *mahdi* ("rightly guided one") refers to a leader Moslems thought would bring about the final victory of Islam by divine power. Following Islam's triumph, a reign of righteousness would be established worldwide. Mahdi Mohammed Ahmed, who led the revolt, was one of several Islamic leaders who had claimed this title.

Check for Understanding. Ask: What was the result of the Fashoda Incident? (France gave up its claim to land along the Nile.)
Biography Rhodes came to South Africa because he had tuberculosis and hoped the climate would improve his health. Rhodes gained control of the Kimberley diamond mines and in 1890 became prime minister of Cape Colony. Part of his large fortune was left to Oxford University, which established the Rhodes Scholarships in his name.

Transvaal. Rhodes dreamed of extending his British South Africa Company's railroad from Capetown in the Cape to Cairo in Egypt. In 1890 he sponsored a "Pioneer Column" of white settlers into the fertile highlands later named the Rhodesias. This area was already occupied by the Ndebele (page 594), who had moved there to escape the Great Trek 50 years earlier.

The whites were almost defeated by a major rebellion of the Ndebele in 1896–1897. Armed with machine guns, the settlers kept control. The mild climate of Southern Rhodesia and the copper mines in Northern Rhodesia attracted more settlers from Britain.

Sec. Rev. ques. 4
Determined to break away from British influence, the Afrikaner republics finally went to war with Great Britain in 1899 in the **South African War**. (Because the British

Cecil Rhodes tried to extend British influence from Cairo, Egypt, to the Cape of Good Hope, as shown in this newspaper cartoon from 1892.

600

Meanwhile . . .

Meanwhile . . .

IN THE UNITED STATES

The Apache wars in the American southwest ended in 1886 with the surrender of Geronimo. In 1890, the last Indian war—the Ghost Dance War—came to a sad, bloody end. The Sioux chieftain Sitting Bull was killed while under arrest. Soon afterward, 200 Sioux were slaughtered at the Battle of Wounded Knee, in South Dakota.

called the Afrikaners Boers, this war is also known as the Boer War.) After losing several key battles, the Afrikaners turned to guerrilla war. The bloody struggle went on for three more years. Finally the Afrikaners surrendered in 1902.

The Union of South Africa. In 1910 the British government combined the British and Afrikaner colonies into a Dominion called the Union of South Africa. Racial inequality was built into the new state from its creation. Because of property qualifications and legal exclusions, mostly white men voted. Whites also owned most of the land and ran all of the mines and factories. Strong differences remained between the British and Afrikaner settlers, but they worked together to see that Africans were kept under white control.

● See below.

Ethiopian Independence

Ethiopia was the only African country that successfully resisted European imperialism. In 1873 Italy acquired a port on the Red Sea coast of Ethiopia and used it as a base to set up colonies (map, page 597).

Sec. Rev. ques. 5

In 1889 Ethiopia's emperor, Menelik II, signed a treaty with Italy granting some land in return for weapons and support. Italy immediately claimed the right to make Ethiopia

Check for Understanding. Ask: Why did the Afrikaner republics and Britain go to war in 1899? (The Afrikaners wanted to rid themselves of British influence.)
Vocabulary Note that *Boer* is a Dutch word meaning "farmer."

● ENRICHMENT. Have students draw political cartoons illustrating the division of Africa from African and European points of view. (Comprehension) *Translating Information into Another Form*

Social History Like other nations in Europe, Italy wanted a colonial empire. Their Red Sea port became the basis for the colony of Eritrea.

Ethiopian forces under King Menelik II defeated the Italian army at Aduwa and preserved their country's independence.

a protectorate. Britain supported Italy's claim, and the two nations agreed on how they would divide what was termed "Italian East Africa." Emperor Menelik, however, proclaimed Ethiopia's independence. With help from France, the Ethiopians prepared for an Italian invasion.

On March 1, 1896, the Italians attacked. At Aduwa they met an Ethiopian army carrying modern European arms. Outnumbered four to one, the Italians suffered a shattering defeat. The European nations, stunned by the Ethiopian victory, agreed to recognize the country's independence. Aside from Liberia, Ethiopia was the only part of Africa not under European control.

Even with so much of Africa divided among colonial powers, African resistance to foreign rule never really ended. It only changed form, as open warfare turned into guerrilla skirmishes and scattered rebellion.

See Sec. 2 *Closing the Lesson*, p. T589B.

Section Review

Answers to Section Review questions are in brackets on pages indicated.

1. **Identify:** Berlin Conference, South African War. (pp. 596, 600)
2. What ambitions did the French have in western Africa? What resistance did they encounter? (p. 596)
3. Why did Egypt become important to Great Britain? How did Britain gain control over the Suez Canal? (p. 598)
4. What led to war between the British and the Afrikaners? (p. 600)
5. Why did Ethiopia turn out to be an exception to European colonialism in Africa? (p. 600)
6. **Critical thinking:** Why were no African representatives present at the Berlin Conference? (See answer below.)

601

6. Students might point out that Europeans held little regard for African peoples' wishes and considered African lands open to colonization.

3 European Rule of Africa

Objectives

Focus Questions

★ ■ How did the imperialist powers run their African colonies? *(pages 602–605)*

● ■ What were the positive and negative effects of European rule? *(page 605)*

Terms to Know

direct rule   indirect rule
assimilate   paternalism

★ Note strategies for first objective on this page and p. 604.

By 1900 nearly all the African continent was in European hands. Treatment of Africans varied from colony to colony, depending on the policies of the ruling nation. Yet throughout Africa, European rule reshaped traditional societies. These changes both hurt and helped Africans.

Colonial Policies

Direct rule. The most common type of colonial government was **direct rule**—foreign control of all levels of government. France, Belgium, Germany, and Portugal followed this practice. They replaced African leaders with their own officials. They set up government institutions and passed laws based on European models.

Sec. Rev. ques. 2

The French believed that Africans could in time be **assimilated**—absorbed—into French culture. They would become full citizens, and their African culture would be replaced by French schooling, laws, language, and politics. Their lands would become overseas provinces of France, not colonies.

In Senegal, for example, a region with centuries of contact with France, some **602** coastal peoples were considered members of French society at birth. Other Africans became French citizens by meeting such requirements as learning the French language and working in the colonial civil service.

Indirect rule. Unlike other imperial powers, the British practiced **indirect rule**—the use of native officials to handle day-to-day tasks. Such a policy gave Africans some chance to take part in the colonial system. In British colonies the local chief remained the figure of authority and continued to handle community affairs in traditional ways. The resident, as the top British official was called, enforced British law and directed the chief to collect taxes and provide workers.

British colonial administrators explained indirect rule as a way of preparing Africans to govern themselves. Neither direct nor indirect rule, however, provided substantial responsibility or experience in political affairs for Africans.

Economic Domination

European powers expected their African colonies to be profitable. That is, each colony had to produce enough wealth to pay the costs of running it, with something left over as profit for the imperialist government and foreign investors.

Exports. The export of raw materials and cash crops to Europe accounted for most of Africa's wealth during the period of European rule. There were large rubber plantations in German East Africa and in the Congo. Mines dotted the map, from the Katanga copper belt in the Congo to the gold and diamond deposits in southern Africa. Great expanses of farmland produced cotton and other cash crops such as cacao (kuh-KAH-oh), used for making chocolate.

Sec. Rev. ques. 3

The colonial powers all followed the pattern set by the early Dutch settlers in the

★ RETEACHING. Have students identify ways in which imperialist nations maintained political and economic control over their colonies. (Direct rule and indirect rule were used to maintain political control; exports, white ownership of land, and taxation maintained economic control.) *(Comprehension) Observing for Detail*
Check for Understanding. Ask: What types of colonial rule did France and Britain practice in Africa? (France practiced direct rule; Britain practiced indirect rule.)

★ REINFORCEMENT. Have students work in groups to identify possible social and cultural effects of the following on the day-to-day life of African people: direct rule, indirect rule, export of raw materials and cash crops, white ownership of land, and taxation. *(Synthesis) Evaluating Information*

Map Skill Practice

See p. T589C for answers to *Map Skill Practice.*

Imperialism in Africa, 1914

1. The map below shows European claims in Africa by 1914. What nation controlled most of West Africa?
2. What two colonies separated Britain's largest claims in the north and south?
3. Portugal was the first European nation to explore Africa. What areas of mainland Africa did Portugal control by 1914?
4. Which two countries were independent of European rule?
5. **Drawing conclusions.** What attitudes and policies on the part of Europeans led them to carve up Africa?

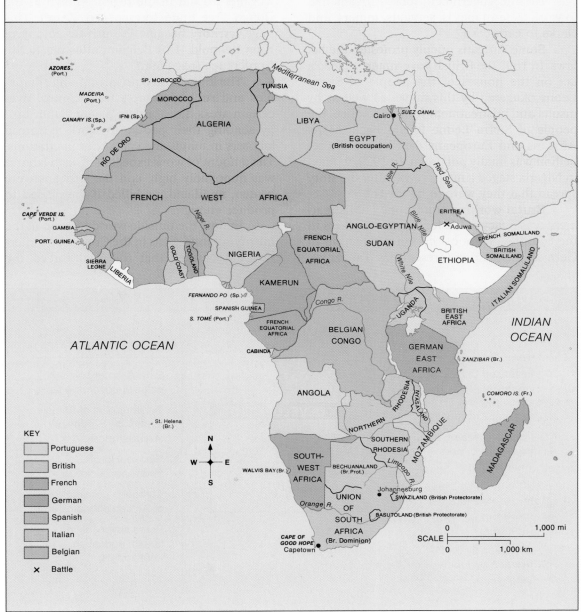

KEY

	Portuguese
	British
	French
	German
	Spanish
	Italian
	Belgian
✕	Battle

603

Cape Colony: white ownership of the land and black labor to work it. Because plantations often needed more workers than the local area could supply, recruiters brought in workers from all over Africa.

Taxes. Taxation was another source of wealth. Africans were expected to pay taxes in the currency issued by the colonial government. Africans who did not pay could be fined, arrested, or put on prison work gangs. Because Europeans controlled all the business and government jobs, Africans had to work as farm hands, servants, miners, and clerks to earn cash.

Some Africans openly protested the tax laws. In 1898 the British government placed a tax on the houses of the people of Sierra Leone. Angered by this move, as well as by insults and mistreatment from the police, the people of Sierra Leone fought back. Many Africans and Europeans died before the rebellion was finally put down. In 1929, women in Nigeria staged a major revolt after the story spread that they were to be taxed.

Brutal working conditions. Mistreatment was a fact of life for African workers in the colonies. To boost cotton production in German East Africa (present-day Tanzania),

Europeans forced Africans to work the fields in labor gangs. In 1905 many African plantation workers in this German colony rebelled in the Maji Maji uprising, named after a secret religious cult. Convinced that drinking a mixture of grain and water *(maji)* would protect them from European bullets, they confidently faced German machine guns. More than 100,000 Africans died in the fighting and in the famine that followed.

Probably the worst treatment of African workers existed in the region known as the Congo Free State (present-day Zaire). This huge territory became the private colony of King Leopold II of Belgium after the Berlin Conference (page 596).

The king granted private mining companies and rubber planters total control over certain areas. Local rulers paid a "labor tax" by sending their people to work as forced laborers in mines and on rubber plantations. The amount of work expected of each laborer was impossibly high, and the Africans were beaten, mutilated, or killed if they failed to produce enough.

Sec. Rev. ques. 4

★ See below.

In time the outside world learned of the horrifying conditions in the Congo. The international outrage that followed forced the

Ⓕ See below.

CAUSE AND EFFECT

CAUSES	KEY DEVELOPMENT	EFFECTS
Increased European interest in Africa stimulated by explorers' accounts		Establishment of colonial governments
Investors' search for new markets and sources of raw materials	Partition of Africa 1884–1914	Replacement of African leaders by European administrators
Mission stations established to spread Christianity		Weakening of traditional societies
European rivalry for overseas colonies		European domination of African economies
		Some advances in health, education, transportation

604

Ⓕ CAUSE AND EFFECT CHART ACTIVITY. Have students develop a hypothesis explaining which effects of the partition of Africa might have resulted in permanent changes in African societies and which effects were open to change. *(Synthesis) Evaluating Information*

★ ENRICHMENT. Have students research the economies of African nations since 1900 and identify long-term effects of European control. Students might find information on Africa's present-day mineral wealth, its dependence on cash crops, or current patterns of landownership and labor. *(Synthesis) Locating Information*

Belgian government to take over the colony from the king in 1908. Conditions in the Belgian Congo improved only slightly, however. The people of the Congo were still forced to do many kinds of labor.

The Impact on African Life

● Note strategies for second objective on this page.

Sec. Rev. ques. 5

Costs. European explorers, missionaries, and colonial officials usually considered the Africans to be childlike people, incapable of running their own lands or their own lives. This belief led Europeans to practice paternalism—the policy of trying to take care of people's needs without giving them any responsibility. White Europeans in Africa thought of darker-skinned peoples as social and cultural inferiors. Slavery had fed these prejudices, but the banning of the slave trade did not end them.

Though policies varied from colony to colony, there was racial discrimination everywhere. Most colonies had laws separating Africans from Europeans. In South Africa, for example, Africans could enter Afrikaner homes only as servants. Mission-educated Africans worked in colonial government offices, though only in low-level jobs.

Colonial policies weakened traditional African family and village life. African men were often sent to work far from their villages. Women, too, had to work for Europeans to help meet tax payments. Few Africans had time to make their own clothing, as they had in the past. They turned to manufactured goods bought on credit at stores owned by European companies. Whole families found themselves in debt to their employers.

In many areas, African workers who had left their villages moved to crowded towns hastily built close to work centers. Disease spread rapidly under these conditions. Rapid urbanization led to higher crime rates and the breakdown of family and community bonds.

Benefits. European rule did bring improvements to Africa, however. Once the wars of European conquest were over, the Europeans banned wars between African

Missionary schools, like this one in French-ruled Madagascar, provided a limited number of Africans with Western-style education.

peoples. The colonial powers built communication systems and railroads linking ports, mines, and plantations. These advances created jobs and brought Africans into contact with the outside world. Westerners also brought modern medicine and sanitation to Africa, which helped people live longer. New farming techniques introduced by Europeans increased food production.

Europeans also brought educational improvements to Africa. The literacy rate, which had been very low, rose as governments and missionaries built new schools. Some missionaries put together dictionaries for African languages that had never been written down. A small number of Africans studied to become ministers or teachers. The French and the British colonial administrations in particular gave Africans a chance to learn European-style government and law. A lucky few were even sent abroad to receive a university education.

The education brought by the Europeans led to calls for freedom from colonial rule. As in India, educated people began to question why the ideals the Europeans taught were not put into practice in their colonies. Africans saw that to win freedom, they had to meet the European colonials on equal terms. Education became a tool for Africans to regain independence.

605

See Sec. 3 *Closing the Lesson,* p. T589C.

● RETEACHING. Have students review "The Impact on African Life" (above) and write an essay on the costs and benefits of imperialism from the viewpoint of an African leader. Essays should evaluate the overall effects of imperialist policies. *(Evaluation) Evaluating Information*

Religion Christian missionaries often sacrificed comfortable lives to come to Africa, where many died from disease. They learned the local languages and became the interpreters of Africa to the world.

● REINFORCEMENT. Have students compare the effects of imperialism in Africa with those in India (pp. 569–572) and China (pp. 573–579). Then have students develop a hypothesis explaining similarities and differences. *(Synthesis) Comparing Historical Developments*

● ENRICHMENT. Have students work in groups to present a panel discussion on the long-term effects of imperialist rule in Africa. *(Synthesis) Linking Past and Present*

1. **Define:** direct rule, assimilate, indirect rule, paternalism. (pp. 602, 605)
2. What European powers practiced direct rule? What power practiced indirect rule? (p. 602)
3. By what means did European countries raise wealth from their African colonies? (pp. 602, 604)
4. What were the conditions in the Congo that led to a takeover by the Belgian government? (p. 604)
5. How did European rule affect traditional African ways of living? (p. 605)
6. **Critical thinking:** From the Africans' point of view, what were the advantages and disadvantages of direct rule? What were the advantages and disadvantages of indirect rule? (See answer below.)

Chapter 30   Summary and Timeline

1. When the international slave trade ended in the early 1800's, Europeans and Americans found new interests in Africa. Some blacks migrated to Africa and set up colonies there. Explorers and missionaries spread Christianity and western ways in Africa; they also brought information about Africa to people in Europe and the United States. Africa's resources attracted investors, and soon European nations began to claim African lands as part of their empires.

2. Conquest and colonization followed. The leading imperialist powers in Africa were France, Britain, and Belgium. Germany, Spain, Portugal, and Italy also had colonies. At the Berlin Conference of 1884–1885, Western nations divided the African continent among themselves. African peoples fought the takeover, but they could not withstand superior European armies and weapons.

3. Styles of colonial rule varied. All colonial powers imposed their own laws and institutions, however, and Africans had limited opportunities to take part in government. In general, Africans and European colonists lived separately. Colonialism brought the Africans hard work and few rewards, although some benefited from education and economic development. Wealth and power remained in European hands.

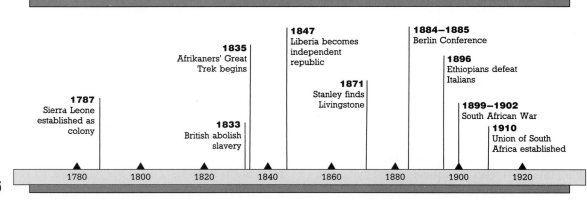

Timeline:

1787 Sierra Leone established as colony

1833 British abolish slavery

1835 Afrikaners' Great Trek begins

1847 Liberia becomes independent republic

1871 Stanley finds Livingstone

1884–1885 Berlin Conference

1896 Ethiopians defeat Italians

1899–1902 South African War

1910 Union of South Africa established

1780   1800   1820   1840   1860   1880   1900   1920

6. Students might point out that in both forms of government, European nations maintained economic and political power and imposed European laws and institutions on African society. Indirect rule, however, allowed for some local government.

See p. T589C for answers to Chapter Review.

Vocabulary Review

Use the following terms to complete the sentences below: *assimilated, direct rule, indirect rule, mission station, South African War.*

1. A __?__ was a self-sufficient community headed by foreign missionaries.
2. The Afrikaners' surrender to the British ended the __?__ and led to the creation of the Union of South Africa.
3. The French believed Africans would be __?__, or absorbed, into French culture.
4. Under __?__, colonial rulers controlled all levels of government.
5. Under __?__, imperial governments used native officials to handle day-to-day tasks of colonial government.

People to Identify

Choose the name that best completes each sentence. Write your answers on a separate sheet of paper.
1. [The Mahdi/Shaka] was the Muslim religious leader who led a revolt against Egyptian troops in the Sudan.
2. The American journalist who traveled down the Congo River was [Henry M. Stanley/David Livingstone].
3. [Usuman dan Fodio/René Caillié] was the French explorer who led an expedition to Timbuktu.
4. [James Bruce/Cecil Rhodes] sponsored a "Pioneer Column" of white settlers in the Rhodesias.
5. Ethiopian Emperor [Leopold II/Menelik II] resisted Italy's attempt to make his nation a protectorate.
6. [H. H. Kitchener/Andreas Pretorius] defeated the Sudanese at Omdurman.

Places to Know

Match the letters on this map of Africa in 1914 with the places listed below. You may want to refer to the map on page 603.

1. Aduwa
2. Bechuanaland
3. Blue Nile
4. Cape of Good Hope
5. Belgian Congo
6. Liberia
7. Morocco
8. Niger River
9. Orange River
10. Sierra Leone
11. Suez Canal
12. Union of South Africa
13. Zanzibar

Recalling the Facts

1. What reforms and improvements did Mohammed Ali bring to Egypt?
2. How did the work of missionaries create an interest in Africa among Westerners? Why else did Europeans explore Africa? **607**

3. How did Cape Colony expand during the 1650's?
4. Why did the Afrikaners make the Great Trek?
5. How did France gain control of Algeria?
6. What was the most important outcome of the Berlin Conference?
7. What was France's goal in Africa?
8. How did the British establish Nigeria?
9. How did the British gain control of the Rhodesias?
10. How was the Union of South Africa kept under white control?
11. How did British rule in Africa differ from that of other European powers?
12. How did the European powers obtain wealth from their African colonies?
13. What effects did colonial rule have on traditional African life?

Critical Thinking Skills

1. **Understanding chronology.** Use the information in the timeline on page 606 to start a timetable of important events. Add at least five more dates and events from the chapter. *(Comp.)*

2. **Making judgments.** Review the definition of racism on page 544. In what ways were the practices of European colonial powers in Africa racist? *(Eval.)*

3. **Observing for detail.** Give two or three details that support these statements. *(Comp.)*
   a. Many Africans did not passively accept colonization.
   b. The worst treatment of Africans existed in the Congo Free State.

Thinking About Geography

Researching a topic. Choose one of the African ethnic groups mentioned in the chapter. Write a short report about the region where the group lives and the group's way of life. Draw an outline map of Africa showing where the group lives. Indicate on the map other ethnic groups that live in the same region. *(App.)*

608

A checkmark identifies questions and exercises calling for the three higher-order levels of thinking at the top of the Bloom taxonomy: Analysis, Synthesis, and Evaluation.

Enrichment: Primary Sources

The passage below was adapted from the journal of a British missionary who toured the Congo Free State when it was the possession of the king of Belgium.

66 The people of a Congo village had been living in peace and quietness when the white men came with all sorts of requests to do this and to do that, and they thought it meant slavery. They attempted to keep the white men out of their country, but the rifles were too much for them. So they submitted, and made up their minds to do the best they could under the altered circumstances.

They were told to bring in rubber. This was quite a new thing for them to do. There was rubber in the forest several days away from their home, but that it was worth anything was news to them. A small reward was offered, and a rush was made for the rubber. They rejoiced in what they thought was their good fortune.

But soon the reward was reduced until they were told to bring in the rubber for nothing. This they tried to protest, but several were shot by the soldiers, and the rest were told, with many curses and blows, to go at once or more would be killed. 99

1. Why did the villagers want to keep the white men out of their country?
2. What made it impossible for the villagers to resist the whites effectively?
3. **Critical thinking:** How, do you think, did the whites view the villagers? Give examples that support your ideas.

(Anal.)

WORLD HISTORY
Checklist

UNIT 8

Try to identify the following key people, places, and terms from the unit. If you need help, refer to the pages listed.

Key People

Samuel Morse *(553)*
Alexander Graham Bell *(553)*
Guglielmo Marconi *(554)*
Abraham Lincoln *(560)*
Theodore Roosevelt *(561)*
Lord Durham *(563)*
Jahangir *(569)*
Robert Clive *(570)*
Guangxu *(577)*
Sun Yat-sen *(579)*
Yuan Shikai *(579)*
Matthew Perry *(582)*
Ito Hirobumi *(585)*
Usuman dan Fodio *(591)*
Shaka *(591)*
Mohammed Ali *(592)*
James Bruce *(593)*
René Caillié *(593)*
David Livingstone *(593)*
Henry Stanley *(593)*
Leopold II *(594)*
Andreas Pretorius *(594)*
Samori Touré *(596)*
the Mahdi *(599)*
H. H. Kitchener *(599)*
Cecil Rhodes *(599)*
Menelik II *(600)*

Key Places

Suez Canal *(553, 598)*
Panama Canal *(553, 561)*
Calcutta *(572)*
Delhi *(572)*
Guangzhou *(573)*
Nanjing *(575)*
Manchuria *(586)*
Port Arthur *(586)*
Egypt *(592)*
Zanzibar *(592)*
Sierra Leone *(592)*

Liberia *(592)*
Blue Nile *(593)*
Niger River *(593)*
Timbuktu *(593)*
Congo River *(593)*
Cape of Good Hope *(594)*
Cape Colony *(594)*
Morocco *(595)*
Algeria *(595)*
Senegal *(596)*
Nigeria *(598)*
Omdurman *(599)*
Orange River *(599)*
Bechuanaland *(599)*
Rhodesias *(600)*
Union of South Africa *(600)*
Ethiopia *(600)*
Aduwa *(601)*
Congo Free State *(604)*

Key Terms

imperialism *(557)*
Manifest Destiny *(558)*
Civil War *(560)*
Spanish-American War *(561)*
home rule *(565)*
Sepoy Rebellion *(571)*
Qing dynasty *(573)*
Opium War *(575)*
Taiping Rebellion *(576)*
Sino-Japanese War *(577)*
Open Door Policy *(577)*
Boxer Rebellion *(579)*
Nationalist Revolution *(579)*
Kuomintang *(579)*
Charter Oath *(583)*
Russo-Japanese War *(586)*
Zulu *(591)*
Great Trek *(594)*
Ndebele *(594)*
protectorate *(595)*
Berlin Conference *(596)*
Sudanese *(599)*
Afrikaners *(599)*
South African War *(600)*
direct rule *(602)*
indirect rule *(602)*
paternalism *(605)*

A British ship in Calcutta harbor.

609

THE SHAPING OF THE MODERN WORLD
1350–1914

UNIT 5: The Transition to Modern Times (1350–1807)

Chapter 17: Renaissance and Reformation

In the three centuries following the end of the Middle Ages, European society, politics, and culture underwent many changes. Two great movements—the Renaissance and the Reformation—began the transition from the medieval period to the modern era.

The Renaissance. The period known as the Renaissance began with a revival of interest in ancient Greece and Rome. Scholars who studied classical arts and literature—the humanities—came to be called humanists. They valued human achievements, and they rejected the medieval view that earthly existence was merely a preparation for life after death.

The Renaissance began about 1350 in the city-states of northern Italy. Wealthy Italians became patrons of the arts, encouraging the creation of literary and artistic masterpieces. The development of printing helped spread the ideas of the Renaissance.

610

Note to Teacher For suggested uses of the Survey, see introduction to this Teacher's Edition.

A Biblical scene by Michelangelo from the Sistine Chapel.

The Reformation. The Church had been powerful in the Middle Ages, but a number of its practices drew criticism. One critic was a German monk, Martin Luther. In 1517 he made public his differences with the Church. His greatest point was that faith was more important than works. Luther soon had a large number of followers in Germany.

The movement for Church reform, which came to be called the Protestant Reformation, spread to other countries. In Switzerland, John Calvin developed a form of Protestant belief based on the doctrine of predestination. John Knox carried many of Calvin's ideas to Scotland.

In England the Reformation became part of a struggle for political power. Wanting a male heir, King Henry VIII sought to divorce his wife and remarry. The Catholic Church opposed his plans, and the king withdrew England from the Pope's authority. In 1534 Parliament created the Church of England, headed by the monarch, not the Pope.

The Church's response to the spread of Protestantism was the Counter-Reformation. The Church reformed its administration and acted to suppress opponents of Catholicism. The Reformation ended religious unity in most of Europe and strengthened the state at the expense of the churches. It also spread literacy and encouraged the growth of the middle class.

Chapter 18: European Exploration and Colonization

In 1450, Europeans knew little of the world beyond their borders. They stood at the threshold, however, of the Age of Exploration. European adventurers began to explore and conquer other parts of the world.

New routes to Asia. One reason for the sudden burst of exploration was the desire for a sea route to Asia—the source of gold, silver, and spices. In addition, some European explorers sought land and adventures overseas; others hoped to spread Christianity. All the explorers were aided by advances in shipbuilding and navigation.

Portugal took the lead in exploration. In the late 1490's Vasco da Gama found a sea route around Africa to India. Portuguese traders soon set up trading posts and plantations on the coasts of Africa and Asia. While Portugal explored to the east, Spain searched for a westward passage to Asia. Christopher Columbus failed to reach Asia but landed on the islands of the Caribbean. Ferdinand Magellan's expedition (1519–1522) was the first to sail around the world.

The colonization of the Americas. In search of gold, the Spanish moved from the Caribbean islands onto the mainland of North America and South America. They conquered the Aztec and Inca empires. Almost all of Central America and South America became part of the huge Spanish colonial empire. Brazil was ruled by the Portuguese.

The English, French, and Dutch also sent explorers across the Atlantic. They claimed lands in eastern North America and in the

611

Caribbean. By the late 1700's, Britain had taken over the Dutch and French colonies in North America.

Chapter 19: A Changed and Changing World

The new wealth and lands of the Americas changed Europe's economy. The developments of the years 1450–1700 are known as the Commercial Revolution.

Worldwide economic changes. European rulers followed the theory of mercantilism, building up gold and silver and starting colonies. Growing world trade led to the development of capitalism. This was an economic system based on private property, the search for profit, and a market economy.

Population shifts. War, forced labor, and disease killed millions of Indians in the first decades after Europeans came to the Americas. To supply the labor they needed to run their mines and plantations, Europeans imported African slaves. The cultures of these peoples mixed to form new cultural groups.

In Africa local rulers sold slaves to European traders. These rulers raided each other, eager for prisoners of war who could be sold into slavery. During the 1800's abolitionists finally persuaded governments to end the international slave trade.

612

Chapter 20: Powerful States in Europe

The rise of Spain. In the late 1400's the Spanish rulers Ferdinand and Isabella unified Spain. They took power away from the nobles, conquered the last Muslim territory, and forced non-Catholics to leave Spain. Funded by the wealth of the Americas, for a time Spain was the strongest state in Europe. Warfare and poor economic management, however, led to its decline in the late 1500's. The defeat of the Armada in 1588 was a blow to Spanish power.

The growth of French power. In France conflict between Catholics and Protestants led to civil war during the 1500's. The war was ended by Henry IV, who granted religious toleration to the Huguenots. Henry was succeeded by his son, Louis XIII, but the power behind the throne was Louis's chief minister, Cardinal Richelieu. Richelieu took steps to strengthen the French monarchy and France's position in Europe. During the long reign of Louis XIV (1643–1715), absolute monarchy triumphed in France. Famed for his lavish court, Louis XIV did away with tolerance for the Huguenots.

The Thirty Years' War. The Thirty Years' War (1618–1648) began as a civil war between Catholics and Protes-

Louis XIV of France.

tants in the German states. It drew in most of the European powers. Protestant states went to war against the Catholic forces of Hapsburg Austria, Spain, and the Holy Roman Empire. To oppose the Hapsburgs, Richelieu's France joined the war on the side of the Protestants.

When the war ended in 1648, much of Germany was in ruins. France was the leading power in Europe, and the Holy Roman Empire was near collapse.

Limited monarchy in England. The reign of Queen Elizabeth I (1558–1603) was a golden age for England. Elizabeth, adored by her subjects, made England the leading Protestant state. The last Tudor, Elizabeth was followed by Stuart monarchs. These years were troubled by struggles between Parliament and the monarchy, as well as between English Protestants and Catholics.

Answers to Review Questions
1. Valued human achievement and rejected idea of existence as preparation for life after death.
2. Ended European religious unity, strengthened state at expense of churches, spread literacy, and encouraged the growth of the middle class.
3. Wanted sea route to Asia, land and adventures overseas, and spread of Christianity.

In 1642 the English Civil War broke out, as the forces of King Charles I fought the supporters of Parliament. Parliament wanted to limit the power of the monarchy. Oliver Cromwell, a Puritan, led the pro-Parliament army to victory and executed the king. Cromwell formed the Commonwealth, a republic he later ruled as dictator.

In 1660 Parliament restored the monarchy, but religious and political conflicts continued. In the "Glorious Revolution" of 1688, Parliament offered the throne to the Protestant rulers William and Mary. The new rulers agreed to the Bill of Rights, which gave the people of England basic rights and put the monarch under the power of Parliament.

Unified Russia. In late medieval times, strong states such as Hungary and Poland grew up in Eastern Europe. The strongest was Russia, unified by Ivan the Great in the late 1400's. Russia became more modern during the reign of Peter the Great (1682–1725). Peter introduced Western customs, reorganized the army, and built the first Russian navy. The most notable of Peter's successors was Catherine II (1762–1796). Under Catherine, Russia gained more territory and became one of the great powers in Europe.

Russia's Catherine the Great.

Review Questions

1. How did Renaissance humanist views differ from those of medieval people?

2. What were the effects of the Reformation?

3. What factors caused Europeans to embark on voyages of exploration during the late 1400's?

4. What European nations colonized Central and South America? North America?

5. What are the three basic features of capitalism?

6. How did European colonization of the Americas change the distribution of world population?

7. What were the most important results of the Thirty Years' War?

8. What was the outcome of the English Civil War? The Glorious Revolution?

9. What contributions did Peter and Catherine make to Russia?

UNIT 6: The Rising Tide of Revolution (1500–1910)

Chapter 21:
New Ideas in Europe,
A New Nation in America

Scientific advances. During the 1500's and 1600's, scientists began to use observation, reason, and mathematics to explain the natural universe. In the early sixteenth century the Polish astronomer Nicolaus Copernicus challenged the ancient belief that the moon, sun, and planets revolved around the earth. He claimed that the earth revolved around the sun. The Italian scientist Galileo Galilei backed Copernicus's theory. Galileo used mathematics to prove his observations of nature.

In England, Isaac Newton developed the first modern concept of the universe. Newton's work showed that all objects, whether on the earth or in the skies, behave according to unchanging natural laws.

Enlightenment philosophy. Enlightenment philosophers tried to uncover natural laws that govern

613

4. Spain and Portugal. England, France, Spain and the Netherlands.
5. Private property, the search for profit, and a market economy.
6. Europeans settled in the Americas and imported African slaves to replace the many Indians who died.
7. It made France the leading power in Europe and undermined the Holy Roman Empire.

8. Cromwell and Parliament won; they executed the king and set up the Commonwealth. William and Mary signed the Bill of Rights, which limited the power of the monarchy.
9. Peter introduced Western customs, reorganized the army, and built the first Russian navy. Catherine strengthened Russia and won more territory.

human behavior. In France Enlightenment thinkers challenged absolute monarchy and the doctrines of the Church. They looked to English political institutions as models of government.

The most influential political philosopher of the Enlightenment was John Locke. He wrote that government's power comes from the consent of the governed. He said that its purpose is to protect the people's natural rights to life, liberty, and property. Locke's ideas became the foundation of government in the United States of America.

The American Revolution. In the 1760's Parliament raised the taxes of the American colonists in order to pay for the French and Indian War. The colonists had no representatives in Parliament, and they protested that the new taxes violated the important principle of "no taxation without representation." Clashes between colonists and British troops led to war. The colonies declared their independence from Britain in 1776.

With economic and military aid from France, the colonists won the Revolutionary War at Yorktown, Virginia, in 1781.

The new United States were governed at first under the Articles of Confederation. This plan called for a weak central government. In 1787, delegates met at a Constitutional Convention to plan a stronger government.

614

The new Constitution set up a federal system, sharing power between national and state governments. It also called for separation of powers within the new national government.

Chapter 22: The French Revolution

The first stage. In 1789 the French nobility and clergy had special privileges left over from feudal times. The French Revolution began under the leadership of the bourgeoisie, who called for gradual reform. Their demands won popular support, but urban workers and peasants began to stage violent protests. In July 1789 the people of Paris stormed the Bastille.

Alarmed by the violence, the French National Assembly abolished feudalism and Church privileges. All offices were opened to members of the Third Estate.

George Washington.

In 1789 the National Assembly also adopted the Declaration of the Rights of Man. This document called for liberty, limited government, and equality before the law. The Constitution of 1791 set up a constitutional monarchy.

The second stage. In April 1792, Prussia and Austria went to war against France in an effort to stop the revolution. Fearful of invasion, the French elected radicals to the National Convention. The Convention abolished the monarchy, declared France a republic, and executed the king and queen.

In 1793 the Committee of Public Safety, led by the Jacobins, took over actual rule of France. During the Reign of Terror, the Committee sent thousands of people to the guillotine. The execution of the Jacobin leader Robespierre ended the Terror. From 1795 until 1799 France was ruled by the Directory.

Napoleon. The Directory was easily overthrown in 1799 by Napoleon Bonaparte, a popular general. In 1804 Napoleon took the title of emperor. He began a series of wars called the Napoleonic Wars, in which he conquered much of Europe.

Napoleon's control of the continent began to weaken when Spanish rebels drove the French out of Spain. In 1812 Napoleon invaded Russia and captured Moscow. The severe Russian

Napoleon's retreat from Moscow.

winter, however, forced his army to retreat.

The major powers of Europe then formed a coalition against Napoleon. After several defeats, he abdicated his throne and went into exile on the Mediterranean island of Elba. However, in 1815, Napoleon returned to France, reassembled his army, and entered Paris in triumph. Shortly afterward, British and Prussian forces decisively defeated him at the Battle of Waterloo.

Chapter 23:
New Nations in Latin America

Revolution. During the early 1800's, the nations of Latin America won independence from European colonial rule. The first successful revolution took place in the wealthy French island colony of St. Domingue. Inspired by the French Revolution, black slaves led by Pierre Toussaint L'Ouverture drove the French from the is-land and founded the nation of Haiti in 1804.

In the Spanish colonies (map, page 460), Simon Bolívar took up the struggle for independence. He and his army spent several years fighting the Spanish. In 1819 Bolívar became president of a new nation, called Great Colombia—present-day Panama, Colombia, Venezuela, and Ecuador—in northwest South America. Meanwhile, José de San Martín drove the Spanish out of Argentina and Chile. San Martín also captured Lima, Spain's stronghold in Peru. Bolívar then took over the fight for Peru's independence, defeating the Spanish in 1824.

A Creole priest, Miguel Hidalgo, began the movement for Mexican independence in 1810. The Spanish captured and executed Hidalgo. The revolution continued, however, and by 1821 Spain was forced to recognize Mexico's independence. In 1822 Brazil broke away from Portugal and set up an independent monarchy.

Independence. Geographical barriers, racial divisions, and political disagreements prevented the development of national unity in Latin America after independence was won. Leaders tried to set up representative governments, but many Latin American nations were soon controlled by caudillos. The caudillos ruled by force, bringing stability to the new governments. Some Latin American nations, such as Mexico, faced threats from abroad as well as problems at home. Mexico lost much land to the United States during the Mexican-American War (1846–1848).

Chapter 24:
Reaction and Revolution in Europe

The Congress of Vienna. After Napoleon abdicated in 1814, delegates from the nations of Europe met in Vienna to work out a peace settlement. The Congress of Vienna was dominated by Prince Klemens von Metternich, an Austrian diplomat. The peace settlement was a reaction against liberalism and nationalism. It restored the monarchies that had been toppled by the French Revolution and the Napoleonic Wars. Russia, Austria, Prussia, and Britain formed the Quadruple Alliance to settle future problems by diplomacy.

Rebellions in Europe. In the 1820's and 1830's, liberals and nationalists led rebellions in many countries. In Spain, Italy, Russia, and Poland, uprisings were suppressed by the monarchy. In 1830 the Parisians again rose in revolt. They named a new king, Louis Philippe.

The nationalist revolts of this period were in part inspired by the Romantic movement. Romantic artists and writers glorified the

615

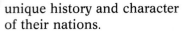

unique history and character of their nations.

In 1848 a new wave of revolutions swept Europe. The French overthrew Louis Philippe and set up a republic. In the Austrian Empire, Czechs, Hungarians, and some Austrians revolted against the conservative government. German nationalists tried to unite the German states. Nationalist revolts also broke out in several parts of Italy. All of these rebellions were suppressed, but the spirit of liberty did not die away.

Review Questions

1. What contributions to modern science were made by Copernicus? Galileo? Newton?

2. What issue led to war between Britain and its American colonies?

3. Distinguish between the first and second stages of the French Revolution.

4. What were the steps that led to Napoleon's fall from power?

5. How did L'Ouverture, Bolívar, San Martín, and Hidalgo contribute to Latin American independence?

6. What factors slowed the development of national unity in the new Latin American nations?

7. What happened at the Congress of Vienna?

8. How did the Romantic movement help inspire the revolts of the early 1800's?

UNIT 7: Industrialization and Its Impact (1750–1914)

Chapter 25: The West in the Industrial Age

The Industrial Revolution of the 1700's and 1800's transformed the economy and society of Western Europe and the United States. Inventors found new sources of energy and replaced human labor with machines. Manufacturing took the place of agriculture as the primary economic activity.

Industrialization. The Industrial Revolution began in Great Britain. Britain had a large labor supply, plentiful natural resources, capital for investment, and ambitious entrepreneurs. It also had a good transportation system,

overseas markets for manufactured goods, and a government that protected property rights. The textile industry was the first to adopt the factory system, in which large numbers of people worked together. Each worker was responsible for only one step in the making of a product. The new system produced goods faster and more cheaply than the domestic system, in which workers made goods at home.

The steam engine revolutionized industry as well as transportation, leading to the construction of the first railway lines during the 1830's. Machines also made farming more productive.

Other nations followed Britain's lead in industrial-

ization. The United States and Germany soon became leading industrial powers. Cities grew rapidly as rural people took factory jobs.

Some economists and political philosophers wrote about the problems of industrialization. In *The Wealth of Nations* (1776), Adam Smith

Textile printing machines.

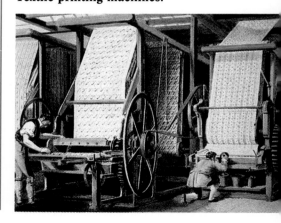

616

Answers to Review Questions
1. Copernicus said that the earth revolved around the sun. Galileo used mathematics to prove observations of nature. Newton showed that natural laws govern the motion of all objects.
2. Taxation without representation.
3. Began under the leadership of the bourgeoisie. Be-

came more violent under the Committee for Public Safety.
4. French driven out of Spain, failure of the Russian campaign, defeats by European coalition, defeat by British and Prussians at Waterloo.
5. L'Ouverture freed Haiti. Bolivar freed Peru and the nations of Great Colombia. San Martin freed Argentina

argued against government interference in business. In the mid-1800's, Karl Marx predicted that the workers would revolt against capitalism and set up a classless society.

Reforms. The standard of living of workers was very low in the early decades of the Industrial Revolution. It rose later in the 1800's, when governments and private persons made many reforms. Women and propertyless men began to gain political rights. Workers formed labor unions to win higher wages and better working conditions. Governments took steps to halt the misuse of power by large businesses. They also restricted child labor and gave aid to workers who were unable to support themselves.

Chapter 26: Nationalism in Europe

The Risorgimento. In 1815 the Congress of Vienna had divided Italy into a number of separate states, mostly held by foreign rulers. Only the Kingdom of Sardinia was ruled by an Italian family. Sardinia took the lead in the movement for unification known as the Risorgimento.

During the 1850's Sardinia's prime minister, Count Camillo di Cavour, won French aid in the effort to drive the Austrians from northern Italy. In southern Italy, the patriot forces of Giuseppe Garibaldi occupied the Kingdom of the Two Sicilies (Sicily and Naples). In 1860 these states came under the rule of the Sardinian king, Victor Emmanuel. He was proclaimed king of Italy in 1861. By 1870 Italy's unification was complete.

Garibaldi and the Red Shirts.

German unification. The unification of Germany was the work of the powerful state of Prussia and its prime minister, Otto von Bismarck. Since the Congress of Vienna, the German states had been linked in a loose union called the German Confederation. This confederation was dominated by Austria. Bismarck was determined to unite Germany under Prussian leadership.

Bismarck defeated Austria in the Seven Weeks' War of 1866. He then organized the North German Confederation, which excluded Austria. To win the loyalty of the other southern German states, Bismarck provoked a war with France in 1870. The Franco-Prussian War ended quickly with France's surrender in January 1871. The other German states agreed to join with Prussia in a German empire. The Prussian king William I was crowned kaiser of all Germany.

Trouble in the Austrian Empire. After its defeat by Prussia, the Austrian Empire faced problems at home. Non-German nationalities within the empire had begun to call for independence. In 1867 the Hungarians won a limited amount of self-rule. The empire became the Dual Monarchy of Austria-Hungary.

The sick man of Europe. During the 1800's the Ottoman Empire grew weaker. Nationalist movements succeeded in Greece and Egypt. Russia invaded Ottoman territory, touching off the Crimean War (1853–1856). The Turks won the war with British and French aid, but the empire continued to decline. Uprisings in the Balkans forced the Turks to recognize the independence of Serbia, Montenegro, and Rumania in 1878.

Imperial Russia. The czars exercised absolute rule over Russia during the 1800's. They harshly suppressed Polish nationalist movements. Czar Alexander II abolished serfdom in 1861, but his assassination ended the hope of other reforms in Russia. Some rulers tried to

617

and Chile. Hidalgo began the Mexican independence movement.
6. Geographical barriers, racial divisions, and political disagreements.
7. Peace settlement restoring toppled monarchies.
8. Romantics glorified their nations.

Renoir's *Girl with a Watering Can.*

modernize the Russian economy, but the country lagged behind Western Europe.

Chapter 27:
Europe in the Late 1800's

Social changes. During the late 1800's the population of Europe grew rapidly. The reasons for this growth were increased food production, medical and scientific advances, and higher standards of living. Class divisions changed as business leaders replaced landowners at the top of society. Harsh conditions for the working class led to the formation of socialist political parties.

Scientific advances. Advances in the physical sciences resulted in new technology. Darwin's theory of evolution revolutionized Western thinking about natural history. Social scientists sought universal laws governing human behavior.

Changes in European ways of life were reflected in painting, which became increasingly abstract. Literature often reflected the realistic concerns of the times.

Clouds on the horizon. In the late 1800's, European civilization was at the peak of its wealth and power. Its problems were growing, however. Extreme nationalism threatened democracy and glorified war. Social Darwinism encouraged exploitation of the weak by the strong. Anti-Semitism was so widespread that Jews began to seek a separate homeland where they would be safe from persecution.

Review Questions

1. Why did the Industrial Revolution begin in Britain?
2. What political and social reforms followed the Industrial Revolution?
3. Compare the unification of Germany with that of Italy.
4. What common problem plagued the Austrian, Ottoman, and Russian empires in the late 1800's?
5. What were the reasons for the rapid population growth in Europe in the late 1800's?
6. What problems threatened the peace of Europe during the late 1800's?

UNIT 8: Western Imperialism (1763–1914)

Chapter 28:
The Expansion of the Western World

Technological progress. During the 1800's, the development of railroads and ocean-going steamships made transportation faster and cheaper than ever before. The building of waterways such as the Suez and Panama canals made sea trips shorter. The telegraph, the telephone, and the "wireless" radio allowed rapid communication over long distances. All these inventions helped speed the development of an international economic system.

Migrations. Rapid population growth led to overcrowding in Europe in the 1800's. Europeans began to emigrate to frontier nations, such as the United States and Argentina. Millions of Asians also emigrated during this

618

period. They went to Japanese possessions, to European colonies in Asia and Africa, and to the Americas.

Imperialism. Western industrialists saw the undeveloped nations as markets for their surplus goods. They also hoped to use these nations as sources of raw materials. Western governments wanted to protect the investments of their citizens and to gain power and prestige. For these reasons, Western nations became caught up in a scramble for empire. Many Westerners favored imperialism. They thought that their beliefs and institutions were superior to all others.

Great Britain was the most successful of the Western empire-builders. Its English-speaking colonies rose in power and influence, and several of them eventually gained self-rule.

The United States. The United States had gained independence from British rule in 1783. During the nineteenth century, it expanded westward across North America. Tensions rose between the industrialized North and the agricultural South. In 1861 civil war broke out over slavery and other issues. The North won in 1865, and slavery was outlawed.

Mass immigration and a high birth rate tripled the United States population between 1865 and 1914. During the same period, the United States surpassed Britain as the world's top industrial power. By the turn of the century, it had joined in the competition for overseas territory. It began to dominate most of Latin America.

Canada. Canada's population was made up of French and English settlers whose cultural and religious differences caused conflict. By the mid-1800's, Canadians had won self-government in domestic matters. In 1867 the various provinces formed the Dominion of Canada, remaining within the British Empire but gaining full self-government. Hoping to develop the Canadian economy, the Dominion government encouraged immigration and investment by foreign nations.

Australia and New Zealand. Australia and New Zealand were first settled by British convicts sent to Australian penal colonies. Other British settlers later immigrated to these countries. They were attracted by free land and by gold rushes in 1851 and 1892. During the early 1900's, both countries became Dominions within the British Empire. The new nations pioneered political and social reforms such as the secret ballot, women's suffrage, and workers' compensation laws.

Ireland. In Ireland, the conflict between the Catholics and the Protestants continued. The British had dominated Ireland since medieval times, and in 1801 they joined Ireland to Great Britain.

The potato famine of the 1840's caused terrible suffering. A million people left Ireland in search of better economic conditions. During the second half of the nineteenth century, Irish opposition to British rule grew. The British were forced to change laws that discriminated against Catholics. The need to protect the Protestant minority, however, made Parliament hesitate to grant Irish home rule.

Chapter 29: Asia in the Age of Imperialism

British control of India. When European traders arrived in India during

A British official in colonial India.

the 1500's, they took advantage of religious and cultural rivalries to establish their influence. In the mid-1700's the British and French struggled for dominance in India. British forces defeated the French, and in 1763 Britain gained control.

The British East India Company was allowed to govern India until the late 1700's, when British public officials began to help run the colony. Indian discontent erupted in the Sepoy Rebellion of 1857, prompting the British government to assume direct control.

An Indian nationalist movement sprang up in the late 1800's. The Indian National Congress, founded in 1885, sought greater self-government.

Foreign influence in China and Southeast Asia. Since 1644, China had been under the rule of the Qing dynasty. The Manchus, who ran the Qing government, kept China isolated and discouraged foreign trade. Their attempt to halt the British trade in opium led to the Opium War (1839–1842). China was defeated and had to sign unequal trade treaties with Britain and with other Western nations.

The Qing dynasty grew weaker in the late 1800's. Western powers helped suppress the Taiping Rebellion (1850–1864), a peasant revolt. Defeat in the Sino-Japanese War of 1894–1895 was another blow to China. In the Boxer Rebellion of 1899, the Chinese made a final attempt to rid the country of Western influence. The rebellion failed, and Europeans gained still more control. Finally, in 1911–1912 Sun Yat-sen led the Nationalist Revolution. He overthrew the Qing dynasty and set up a Chinese republic.

In Southeast Asia, Great Britain and France were the two main colonial powers. Britain held Burma and the Malay Peninsula. France colonized Indochina. The Philippines, a Spanish

The World About 1900

Large empires still existed around 1900, but many nations had gained independence. Which empire possessed territories on six continents? (the British Empire)

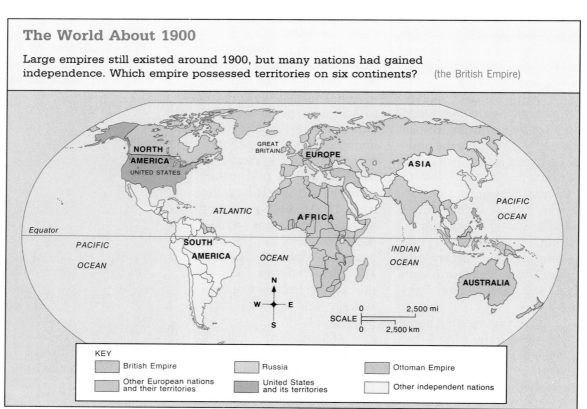

KEY
British Empire
Other European nations and their territories
Russia
United States and its territories
Ottoman Empire
Other independent nations

colony, came under the control of the United States in 1898, at the end of the Spanish-American War.

Japanese reaction to the West. Europeans first reached Japan in the 1500's, but for centuries Japan was closed to foreign contacts. In 1854 a show of American naval power forced Japan to accept Western trade.

The Meiji era, which began in 1868, was a time of rapid change. Unlike the Chinese, Japanese leaders set out to strengthen the country through Western methods. They ended feudalism, built a powerful army and navy, and laid the foundations of a modern industrial economy. In 1889 the emperor granted Japan a constitution that established a parliament, called the Diet.

Japan used its newfound power to revise its trade treaties and build an empire in Asia. By 1912 Japan had won wars against Russia and China, taken control of Korea, and become a major power in Asia.

Chapter 30: Imperialism in Africa

In the late 1700's and early 1800's, while several African states were beginning or expanding, European interest in Africa grew. New kinds of trade emerged to replace the slave trade. Europeans set up colonies, explored the interior, and claimed parts of the

The first electric streetlight in Tokyo.

continent. Soon the major European powers were competing for control of Africa.

Growing imperialism. Western nations held the Berlin Conference (1884–1885) to settle competing claims in Africa. They eventually divided almost all of Africa among themselves and agreed to back one another against African resistance.

The British dominated Southern Africa, defeating Afrikaners in the South African War (1899–1902). The British also held much of western Africa. The French ruled lands in central Africa. Only Liberia and Ethiopia remained free from European domination.

Government in Africa. Most African colonies were governed by direct rule—foreign control of all levels of government. British colonies, however, were governed by indirect rule. Local officials handled day-to-day tasks and

were allowed to manage community affairs in traditional ways.

Through taxation and the export of raw materials, African colonies provided income for European governments. Black Africans under colonial rule were often treated very harshly and had little or no political power. Traditional ways of life broke down in African regions under European domination.

European rule did benefit Africans in some ways. The Europeans reduced tribal warfare and built transportation and communication systems. Western medical and agricultural technology helped people live longer.

Review Questions

1. What nineteenth-century inventions speeded up the development of a world economy?

2. What were the causes of imperialism in the late 1800's?

3. Why did the British government take direct control of India?

4. Compare the responses of China and Japan to Western imperialism.

5. Which European powers controlled the most territory in Africa?

6. What were the disadvantages and advantages to the African people of European colonization?

621

Answers to Review Questions
1. Railroad, steamship, telegraph, telephone, radio.
2. Industrialists wanted markets for surplus goods and sources of raw materials. Western governments wanted to protect investments and gain power.
3. Sepoy Rebellion showed need for change.
4. China wanted to get rid of Western influence, while Japan used Western methods to grow stronger.
5. Britain and France.
6. Treated Africans harshly, denied them political power, destroyed traditions. Reduced tribal warfare, introduced modern technology, raised life expectancy.

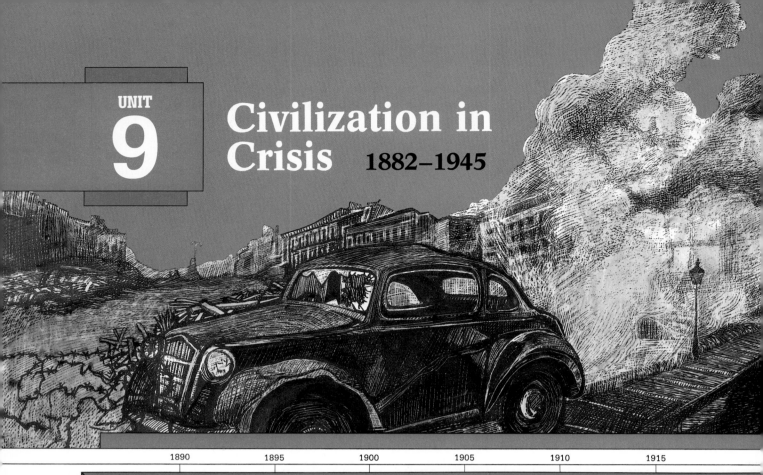

1890	1895	1900	1905	1910	1915

CHAPTER 31: The First World War

1882
Germany makes
alliance with
Austria-Hungary
and Italy

1907
France, Britain,
and Russia form
alliance

1914
World War I
begins

CHAPTER 32: Russia in Upheaval

1894
Nicholas II
becomes czar

1905
Workers revolt
in St. Petersburg

1890	1895	1900	1905	1910	1915

FOCUS STRATEGY. Tell students that the illustration depicts the terrible damage inflicted on many European cities during World War
I. Then ask: (a) Which time period do you think this illustration
represents: 1885–1900, 1901–1915, 1916–1930, or 1931–
1945? Explain your answer. (1931–1945. The car and the airplanes
point to this period of history.) (b) How might this picture represent a
"civilization in crisis" as suggested by the unit title? (Answers may
mention the extreme devastation shown in the picture.)

1920   1925   1930   1935   1940   1945

1918
Armistice ends
fighting

1917
Bolshevik
Revolution brings
Lenin to power

1929
Stalin takes control
of Soviet Union

1935–1939
Great Purge

CHAPTER 33: The World Between the Wars

1922
Mussolini takes
power in Italy

1929
Great Depression
begins

1936–39
Civil war in Spain

1933
Hitler forms Third
Reich in Germany

CHAPTER 34: World War II

1928
Kellogg-Briand
Pact

1939
World War II
begins

1945
Germany
and
Japan
surrender

1936
Germany and Italy
form military alliance

1920   1925   1930   1935   1940   1945

Have students refer to the timeline to answer the following questions: **(a) Which world war lasted longer, the first or the second?**
(World War II in Europe lasted from 1939 to 1945, two years longer than
the First World War.) **(b) Which two European nations shown on the
timeline experienced civil strife between 1905 and 1939?** (Russia
and Spain.)

The First World War   1882–1919

(pp. 624–643)

Section 1 examines the underlying causes of World War I and then traces the events that started the conflict. Section 2 follows the war on the major fronts and discusses the reasons for the allied victory. In Section 3, students learn about Wilson's Fourteen Points, the Versailles Treaty, and the political changes brought by the war.

Bibliography

See the *Teacher's Management and Planning Guide* for additional listings. Starred titles are for both students and teachers.

Macdonald, Lyn. *1914.* Atheneum. Examines the first months of World War I.

*Remarque, Erich Maria. *All Quiet on the Western Front.* Fawcett. Classic novel of a young man's experience of war.

Tuchman, Barbara. *The Guns of August.* Bantam. Pulitzer-Prize winning story of the outbreak of World War I.

Vaughan, Edwin Campion. *Some Desperate Glory.* Henry Holt. Journal of a British lieutenant on the Western Front; parts written under fire.

Section Lesson Plans

SECTION 1   (pp. 625–627)
The Outbreak of War

Objectives

After completing this section, students will be able to:
1. Discuss the underlying causes of World War I.
2. Describe how an assassination touched off the war.

Introducing the Lesson

Remind students that World War I was called "the war to end all wars." Advances in technology made possible conflict and destruction on a scale previously unknown to history.

Then ask: *(a) What factors in Europe might have contributed to the start of World War I?* (Colonial rivalry and extreme nationalism.)

(b) How might a world war differ from other wars? (Answers will vary. The term "world war" implies the involvement of many nations.)

(c) Why might war have often been seen as the most effective method of resolving international crises? (Answers will vary.)

Developing the Lesson:
Understanding Cause and Effect

Have students explain how each of the following contributed to the start of World War I: Triple Alliance and Triple Entente, militarism, imperialism, and nationalism. (The Triple Alliance and Triple Entente created rival groups of nations, each assured of military support. Militarism glorified war and readied the armed forces for conflict. Imperialism bred rivalry, jealousy, and mistrust. Nationalism increased tension among European nations.) *(Comprehension)*

Developing the Lesson:
Analyzing Information

Have students write an argument defending or refuting the following statement: *Austria could have prevented World War I, but it sought an opportunity to establish its superiority.* Students should support their views with information from the text. *(Synthesis)*

**Closing the Lesson:
Drawing Conclusions**

Have students work in groups to discuss the following: *If Gavrilo Princip had not assassinated Archduke Ferdinand, would World War I have occurred? Why or why not?* (Answers will vary. Tensions, rivalry, and power imbalances in Europe would still have existed. Austria might have found another excuse to invade Serbia, or some other nation might have provoked an incident.) *(Synthesis)*

See *Section Review* questions, p. 627.

SECTION 2   (pp. 628–634)
The Course of the War

Objectives

After completing this section, students will be able to:
1. Locate where the war's major battles were fought.
2. Explain why the United States became involved in World War I.

Introducing the Lesson

Remind students that World War I was the first war to involve all of Europe since the end of the Napoleonic Wars in 1815. Changes in Europe since Napoleon's times had a significant impact on the way the war was fought.

     Then ask: *(a) What changes had occurred in Europe after the Napoleonic Wars in 1815?* (The Industrial Revolution, population growth, urban growth, and the effects of the Age of Imperialism.)

     (b) What effect might these changes have had on warfare? (Answers will vary. Warfare probably involved more deadly weaponry, larger armies, greater damage to civilian populations, and conflicts in the colonial territories outside of Europe.)

     (c) How might a world war today be different from World War I? (Answers will vary.)

Developing the Lesson:
Organizing Ideas in Written Form

Have students write an essay explaining why the Allied Powers defeated the Central Powers in World War I. When writing their essays, students should consider preparedness, battle campaigns, members of the two different alliances, and unforeseen situations that arose during the course of the war. *(Synthesis)*

**Developing the Lesson:
Understanding Point of View**

Have students write one example of German propaganda aimed at persuading the United States to maintain neutrality and one example of British propaganda aimed at persuading the United States to join the Allies. Students should explain in a few sentences how the two examples are different and how they are the same. *(Analysis)*

**Closing the Lesson:
Drawing Conclusions**

Have students work in groups to identify the factors that brought the United States into World War I. Then have students answer the following questions:

     (a) How far should the United States go in defending democracy in other countries? (Answers will vary.)

     (b) Should the United States have continued to trade with the warring nations? (Answers will vary.)

     (c) Was the desire of the United States to protect its huge loans to Allied governments a valid reason for entering the war on the side of the Allies? If not, how should the matter of these debts have been handled by the United States government? (The United States decision to enter World War I was influenced not only by economic motives, but also by Allied propaganda, attacks on American shipping, the German U-boat attack on the *Lusitania*, and the Zimmermann telegram.) *(Synthesis)*

See *Section Review* questions, p. 634.

SECTION 3   (pp. 635–641)
The Peace Treaties

Objectives

After completing this section, students will be able to:
1. Describe how a peace settlement was reached.
2. Discuss the effects of World War I.

Introducing the Lesson

Remind students that an armistice is a treaty designed to end a war, establish peace and stability, and prevent further conflict. The Treaty of Versailles, which ended World War I, was an armistice written by European powers bent on revenge against Germany.

Then ask: *(a) If you had been a participant in the writing of the Treaty of Versailles, what provisions would you have included?* (Answers will vary.)

(b) Why might an armistice fail to prevent the development of future conflict? (Answers will vary. Changing international situations sometimes make earlier agreements irrelevant.)

Developing the Lesson: Evaluating Information

Have students evaluate the Treaty of Versailles and the Fourteen Points by answering the following questions: *(a) Which peace settlement would you have supported—the Treaty of Versailles or a settlement based strictly on the Fourteen Points? Why? (b) Which provisions of the Versailles Treaty do you think were justified? Unjustified? (Synthesis)*

Developing the Lesson: Comparing Historical Developments

Have students compare the isolationist policies of fourteenth-century China (pp. 284–285) and seventeenth-century Japan (pp. 292) with the isolationist sentiment in the United States after World War I. Students should compare the causes and effects of isolationism in China, Japan, and in the United States. *(Synthesis)*

Answers to *Map Skill Practice*, p. 637.

1. Russia.
2. German East Africa.
3. Ottoman Empire.
4. Japan.
5. Poland, Romania, and Italy gained new lands; nations of Czechoslovakia and Yugoslavia were formed; Austria and Hungary became separate nations.
6. The Polish Corridor was a strip of land that separated Germany from East Prussia and Poland. The corridor gave Poland access to the Baltic Sea.

Closing the Lesson: Understanding Effects

Have students work in groups to suggest which results of World War I improved the status of individuals, groups, and nations. (Suggestions might include the advancement of women's rights, the development of the principles of the Fourteen Points, the creation of the nations of Czechoslovakia and Yugoslavia.) *(Synthesis)*

See *Section Review* questions, p. 641.

Chapter 31 Review Answers (pp. 642–643)

Vocabulary Review

1. (a) propaganda (b) demilitarize (c) reparations (d) mandate (e) ultimatum (f) escalate (g) U-boat (h) militarism (i) isolationism (j) armistice (k) armaments (l) mobilize (m) total war
2. (a) Triple Alliance—agreement between Germany, Austria-Hungary, and Italy forged by Bismarck to isolate France and deprive it of allies; Triple Entente—treaty of friendship between France, Britain, and Russia, resulting from a shared fear of Germany. (b) Fourteen Points—Woodrow Wilson's plan for peace and a better world, resting on the five key ideas of self-determination, "peace without victory," disarmament, fair treatment of colonial peoples, and formation of the League of Nations; League of Nations—international organization that would help nations settle their quarrels and discourage war.

People to Identify

1. German chancellor who helped form alliances such as the Triple Alliance to strengthen Germany.
2. Archduke and heir to the throne of Austria-Hungary whose assassination set off the chain of events that started World War I.
3. Serbian nationalist who assassinated Archduke Ferdinand.
4. German kaiser who came to power in 1888, forced Bismarck out of office, and began a more aggressive foreign policy.
5. American President at the time of World War I who is remembered for his efforts to get the "Fourteen Points" peace plan accepted and to bring the United States into the League of Nations.
6. German diplomat whose telegram attempting to make an alliance with Mexico was made public, angering Americans and leading the United States to enter the war.

Places to Know

1. K 2. F 3. D 4. J 5. E 6. B 7. A 8. H
9. C 10. G 11. I

Recalling the Facts

1. The alliance system increased tensions, encouraged countries to act aggressively, and caused a chain reaction involving several nations when two countries came into conflict. Militarists' glorification of war and insistence on a constant arms buildup raised the level of tension in Europe and made it hard for civilian leaders to use diplomacy. The competition among imperialist nations for colonies, new markets, and new sources of raw materials created jealousy and mistrust among colonial powers. Nationalists' desires to strengthen their countries led to conflicting land claims and revolts, increasing tensions in Europe.

2. Germany entered the war to help its ally Austria because the alliance was important to German security, and because German generals believed they would win quickly. Russia entered the war to help the Slavs because if Austria took over Serbia, Austria would be close to controlling the Balkans. France joined its ally Russia in war when Germany declared war on France. Britain entered the war when Germany invaded Belgium because Britain had pledged to guarantee Belgium's neutrality and feared Germany would take control of Western Europe.

3. The plan failed because the Russian forces moved faster than expected, forcing Germany to withdraw troops from France and rush them eastward.

4. The Russian army suffered from low morale and was poorly trained, ill-equipped, and incompetently led. Allies could not ship supplies to Russia's ports because of German and Ottoman blockades. Heavy casualties at the front and food shortages at home led revolutionaries to overthrow the Russian government. The new leaders, realizing that Russia could not continue the war, signed a treaty with Germany.

5. Italy joined the Allies in return for the promise of territory in Austria and Africa. Japan joined the Allies in return for the promise of support in claiming China's Shandong Peninsula and German-held islands in the Pacific. The Arabs joined the British to help defeat the Ottoman Turks.

6. The Americans helped halt the German offensive at Château-Thierry in June 1918 and helped turn the tide in favor of the Allies.

7. France suffered great losses in the war, feared a future German attack, and was skeptical of Wilson's ideals. The French wanted an agreement that would punish Germany and destroy its ability to wage war, and that would give compensation for destroyed property.

8. Germany had to return Alsace-Lorraine and give France control of the coal mines of the Saar region for 15 years. Germany lost land to Poland. German territory on both sides of the Rhine River was demilitarized. The German army was reduced to only 100,000 men with no heavy artillery, tanks, or warplanes. The draft was abolished and the navy was limited to a small fleet with no submarines permitted. Germany lost its overseas territories in Africa, Asia, and the Pacific Ocean. Germany was required to pay reparations to other nations.

9. Many Americans supported the policy of isolationism and feared that membership in the League of Nations would drag the United States into future European wars.

10. Women took on many jobs formerly done by men and they gained greater political equality. By 1920 the United States, Russia, and many European countries had given women the right to vote.

11. Militarist ideas, imperialism, and national rivalries still existed after World War I.

Critical Thinking Skills

1. b, c, d, f, a, e.
2–3. Answers will vary.

Thinking About Geography

Answers will vary.

Enrichment: Primary Sources

1. Those who experienced a war will not want to enter into another war.

2. People of later generations, who have not experienced the horrors of war will not be as hesitant to start a war, and victorious countries often want an agreement that is very harsh to a defeated country, which causes the defeated country to seek retribution.

3. Wilson also expressed the idea of "peace without victory" because he feared that harsh punishment would cause Germany to seek revenge.

The First World War

1882–1919

See chapter timeline, p. 641.

Before You Read This Chapter

Suppose you had an amazing machine that could transport you back in time to June 1914. If you picked up a newspaper, you would read an account about the assassination of a European prince. Just one month later, the same newspaper would report the start of a war in Europe. That war would soon involve countries all over the globe. As you read this chapter, ask yourself how one event could have triggered a worldwide war. Why were the various nations fighting? What were the costs of the war? Could this war have been prevented?

The Geographic Setting

The Chapter Outline

1. The Outbreak of War
2. The Course of the War
3. The Peace Treaties

World War I changed the nature of warfare, as airplanes, tanks, submarines, and other weapons capable of terrible destruction were used for the first time.

1 The Outbreak of War

Objectives

Focus Questions

★ ■ What were the underlying causes of World War I? *(pages 625–626)*

● ■ How did an assassination touch off the war? *(pages 626–627)*

Terms to Know

World War I	armaments
Triple Alliance	ultimatum
Triple Entente	mobilize
militarism	escalate

★ Note strategies for first objective on this page.

When World War I broke out in Europe in the summer of 1914, few people were surprised. Dangerous political forces had been undermining the peace created a hundred years before at the Congress of Vienna (page 472). These forces included a rigid alliance system, militarism, imperialism, and extreme nationalism.

Entangling Alliances

One important cause of tension in Europe was the division of the continent into two rival groups of nations. Those groups formed when each of the leading countries of Europe sought allies to help it in case of war.

Sec. Rev. ques. 2

The Triple Alliance. After Germany won the Franco-Prussian War in 1871 (page 520), it took over the French border region of Alsace-Lorraine. The German chancellor, Otto von Bismarck, thought that France might seek help to regain this region. To block such a move, Bismarck began to make alliances with other European powers. The first, with Austria-Hungary and Italy in 1882, became known as the Triple Alliance. It provided that all members would help each other if any of them were attacked. Bismarck also made a pact with Russia in 1887. This alliance was weak, however, because Russia and Austria were potential enemies.

A new kaiser, William II, came to the German throne in 1888. Jealous of Bismarck's power, he forced Bismarck out of office. The kaiser then turned to a more aggressive foreign policy, built up the navy, and sought more colonial possessions. Germany abandoned its treaty with Russia and drew closer to Austria-Hungary, which it considered a more reliable ally.

The Triple Entente. The French had been humiliated by their defeat in 1871 and realized that France by itself was no match for Germany. Fearful of Germany's growing military and industrial strength, France began to look for allies of its own. In 1894, after the split between Germany and Russia, France made an alliance with Russia.

Next France approached its old colonial rival, Great Britain. The British had long avoided alliances, priding themselves on being strong enough to stand alone. Yet Germany had now become a serious rival for sea power and for colonies in Africa. Britain thus decided to cooperate with France. In 1904 they formed the Entente Cordiale (ahn-TAHNT cohr-DYAHL). The name, in French, means "friendly understanding."

France then tried to improve relations between its new partner and its older ally. Britain and Russia competed for colonies in western Asia, but they shared a distrust of Germany. In 1907 this mutual fear led Britain and Russia to sign an agreement. This created the Triple Entente—an understanding among France, Britain, and Russia. It was a treaty of friendship, not a firm military pact. The Germans, however, regarded the Triple Entente as a hostile alliance that threatened Germany from both the east and the west.

625

★ RETEACHING. Have students identify and explain the four causes of World War I. (The alliance system increased tension in Europe. Militarism glorified war and led to a constant military buildup. Imperialism increased competition among major powers. Nationalism created unrest.) *(Comprehension) Observing for Detail*

★ REINFORCEMENT. Have students evaluate and rank the causes of World War I in order of their importance. Students should explain their ranking. *(Evaluation) Evaluating Information*

★ ENRICHMENT. Have students find information to answer the following questions: Why did Bismarck think that France might seek help to regain Alsace-Lorraine? Why were Russia and Austria potential enemies? What were the terms of the Triple Entente? *(Application) Locating Information*

Check for Understanding. Ask: Who were the members of the Triple Alliance? (Germany, Austria-Hungary, and Italy.) The Triple Entente? (France, Russia, and Britain.)

By 1914 an armed and uneasy peace existed in Europe. What Bismarck had said in 1879 was still true: "The great powers of our time are like travelers, unknown to one another, whom chance has brought together in a carriage. They watch each other, and when one of them puts his hand into his pocket, his neighbor gets ready his own revolver in order to be able to fire the first shot."

The alliance system only heightened this tense situation. A country that knew it had allies was more likely to act aggressively in a crisis. In addition, the alliance system held the danger of a "chain reaction." A conflict between any two nations was likely to expand and involve those countries' allies.

Francis Ferdinand, archduke and heir to the Austrian throne, was photographed with his wife moments before their assassination.

Other Forces

Militarism. Another cause of mounting tension in Europe was **militarism**—a policy of glorifying war and readying the armed forces for conflict. Militarists urged a constant buildup of weapons and troops. They agreed with the Austrian historian who wrote that quarrels between nations "must be settled not at the conference table, but on the battlefield; not with the pen, but with the sword; not with ink, but with blood."

Sec. Rev. ques. 3

For some years the great powers of Europe had spent vast sums for **armaments**— weapons and military supplies. Except for Britain, which relied on its navy, they had also kept huge armies during peacetime. If one country enlarged its army or built new and mightier battleships, other countries did the same. These militarist policies had strong public support. Any signs of crisis brought loud cries for war, making it hard for civilian leaders to use diplomacy.

Imperialism. Disputes over colonies also pushed the powers of Europe toward the brink of war. These countries competed fiercely to gain colonies, new markets, and new sources of raw materials. Ambitious nations such as Germany and Italy, late in entering the race for colonies, wanted to catch up with Britain and France. Colonial rivalries thus bred jealousy and mistrust.

Nationalism. Extreme nationalism added to tensions in Europe. French nationalists were determined to regain Alsace-Lorraine, while German nationalists hoped to extend German power and territory. Russian Pan-Slavists (page 525) wanted Russia to rule over the Slavs of Eastern Europe.

Another Slavic nationalist movement took shape in Serbia. Serbia and other Balkan states had gained their independence from the Ottoman Empire in 1878 (page 524). The Slavs in Bosnia and Herzegovina, however, came under Austrian rule. The Serbs now wanted to create a "Greater Serbia" by uniting with other Slavic states and with the millions of South Slavs who lived in Austrian-controlled lands.

The dream of a Greater Serbia caused nightmares in Austria, where minority nationalities were a long-standing problem (page 523). Austrian leaders feared that a revolt by the South Slavs could break up the empire. Some Austrians urged the destruction of the small Serbian kingdom.

The Coming of War

● Note strategies for second objective on this page and p. 627.

Murder in Sarajevo. On June 28, 1914, in the Bosnian city of Sarajevo (sahr-ah-YAY-voh), a fateful shooting took place. A Serbian nationalist named Gavrilo Princip

626

● RETEACHING. Have students review "The Coming of War" (pp. 626–627) and make a timeline of the events in 1914 that led to World War I. (Timeline should include information for the following dates: June 28, July 23, July 28, July 30, August 1, August 3, August 4, August 6.) *(Comprehension)* **Sequencing Events**

● REINFORCEMENT. Have students identify which events leading to World War I were the results of the alliance system, militarism, imperialism, or nationalism. (Events include the assassination of Francis Ferdinand; Austria's ultimatum to Serbia and declaration of war; Germany's declaration of war against Russia and France; Britain's entry into the war; Austria's war against Russia.) *(Synthesis)* **Analyzing Information**

(PREEN-seep) assassinated Archduke Francis Ferdinand, heir to the throne of Austria-Hungary. By killing the archduke, Princip and other nationalists hoped to prepare the way for a Slavic revolution. The Austrian authorities, however, used the assassination as an excuse to take hostile actions against Serbia.

To carry out its plan against Serbia, Austria turned for support to its ally Germany. German leaders knew that an Austrian attack on Serbia would alarm Russia, which feared Austrian control of the Balkans. Russia and its ally France might join the conflict. Nevertheless, the Germans insisted that Germany must stand behind Austria, because the Austrian alliance was important to German security. Both countries wanted a quick attack that would defeat Serbia before other nations could come to its aid.

Sec. Rev. ques. 4

The ultimatum. Confident of German backing, Austria sent Serbia an **ultimatum** (ul-tuh-MAY-tum)—a final set of demands—on July 23, 1914. It ordered Serbia to end all anti-Austrian activities and to let Austrian officials handle the investigation of the murder of Francis Ferdinand. Austria gave Serbia 48 hours to meet these terms.

Austria had deliberately made its ultimatum too harsh for Serbia to accept. Yet the Serbs agreed to all the terms except the one dealing with the murder investigation. The Austrians, however, would not stop short of war.

The start of war. On July 28, 1914, Austria declared war on Serbia. Two days later, Russia ordered its armed forces to ready themselves for battle. When Russia ignored a German warning to stop **mobilizing**—organizing and preparing—its troops, Germany declared war against Russia on August 1. Two days later Germany also called for war on Russia's ally, France.

The war in Europe quickly **escalated**—grew more intense. The system of alliances trapped countries in a chain reaction. There seemed to be no way to escape.

Germany planned to get around the French armies along the French-German border by invading France through Belgium.

Background World War I eventually involved 30 nations in all six inhabited continents.

Linking Past and Present

After World War I ended in 1918, Serbia united with other Slavic states to form the Kingdom of Serbs, Croats, and Slovenes. In 1929 the kingdom changed its name to Yugoslavia.

When Belgium refused to let German troops cross its territory, Germany invaded that country on August 3. The British were now involved, for Britain had pledged to guarantee Belgium's neutrality. Moreover, the British realized that if Belgium and France fell, Germany would control Western Europe. On August 4, Britain joined the war on the side of its allies, Russia and France. Two days later, Austria declared war on Russia.

Less than six weeks after the shooting at Sarajevo, most of the great powers of Europe—and several smaller nations—had been drawn into World War I. On one side were Austria-Hungary and Germany. On the other side were Serbia, France, Russia, Britain, and Belgium. Before the war ended in 1918, many more countries would become involved.

See Sec. 1 *Closing the Lesson*, p. T623B.

● See below, left.

Section Review

Answers to Section Review questions are in brackets on pages indicated.

1. **Define or identify:** World War I, Triple Alliance, Triple Entente, militarism, armaments, ultimatum, mobilize, escalate. (pp. 625, 626, 627)
2. Why were the Triple Alliance and the Triple Entente formed? (p. 625)
3. How did militarism and nationalism add to tension in Europe? (p. 626)
4. Why did Austria make its ultimatum to Serbia so harsh? (p. 627)
5. **Critical thinking:** What role did fear of rival nations play in the creation of the European alliances? (See answer below.)

627

Background When the Serbian Minister of Public Information read Austria's ultimatum, he said, "There is nothing to do but die fighting."
● ENRICHMENT. Have students work in groups to stage a meeting that might have occurred between representatives of the Triple Alliance and the Triple Entente. Participants should discuss the following issues: *What are the potential risks and gains of war for each side? What are the alternatives to war?* (Application) Solving Problems

Background Gavrilo Princip was 19 years old and a member of "Black Hand," a secret society working for the independence of Serbia, when he assassinated the Archduke. Princip was spared the death penalty because of his age; in 1918 he died in prison of tuberculosis.
5. Students might note that Bismarck sought alliances out of fear that France would seek to regain Alsace-Lorraine from Germany. France sought alliances out of fear of Germany's growing strength.

See lesson plans, pp. T623A–T623C.

2 The Course of the War

Objectives

Focus Questions

★ ■ Where were the war's major battles fought? *(pages 628–633)*
● ■ Why did the United States become involved in World War I?
(pages 633–634)

Terms to Know

Allies	propaganda
Central Powers	U-boat
stalemate	armistice

★ Note strategies for first objective on this page and p. 633.

When war broke out in Europe in August 1914, most generals and political leaders felt sure the conflict would be short. The public shared this belief, and crowds gathered in city streets to show their loyalty to their homelands and their readiness to fight. Filled with dreams of adventure and glory, few people thought of the horrors of war. They expected their soldiers to return home in a few months.

Only a few leaders suspected that Europe was stumbling into a major war that would drastically change the world. "The lamps are going out all over Europe," said Britain's foreign secretary in 1914. "We shall not see them lit again in our lifetime."

The Allies and the Central Powers

As World War I unfolded, the Triple Entente countries—France, Britain, and Russia—came to be called the **Allies**. Germany and Austria-Hungary, members of the Triple Alliance, were now called the **Central Powers**. Italy, the other member of the Triple Alliance,

628

remained neutral at first. In 1915, it joined the Allies.

The war steadily widened (map, page 629). The Ottoman Empire and Bulgaria joined the Central Powers. In 1917 the United States entered the war alongside the Allies. Other countries in Europe, Asia, and Latin America also chose sides, though most did not send troops into battle.

The Western Front

The German attack. When the German army invaded Belgium in August 1914, it both expected and needed a quick victory. According to the German war plan, the bulk of the German army would roll through Belgium into France and capture Paris. German trains would then rush the victorious troops to the eastern front, where they would drive back the Russian forces. Everything depended on speed.

Germany's plan failed, however. The Russians moved faster than expected and invaded East Prussia late in August. Germany had to withdraw some troops from France and rush them eastward.

The remaining Germans on the western front advanced to within 40 miles of Paris. Then a French counterattack drove a wedge between the German armies. Instead of winning a quick victory, German troops now faced stubborn British and French resistance along the Marne River. The Germans then tried to reach the coast of the English Channel, capture the port cities, and swing back toward Paris. Again they were stopped, in heavy fighting near Ypres (EE-pruh), a town in Belgium.

Trench warfare. In the first four months of the war (August–November 1914), more than one and a half million soldiers were killed or wounded. As the winter of 1914–1915 began, both armies prepared for a

Sec. Rev. ques. 2

★ **RETEACHING. Have students identify the countries that joined the Allies and those that joined the Central Powers.** (Allies: France, Britain, Russia, Italy, United States, Japan, New Zealand, Australia. Central Powers: Germany, Austria-Hungary, Ottoman Empire, Bulgaria.) *(Comprehension) Observing for Detail*
★ **REINFORCEMENT. Have students make a chart summarizing the fighting on each of the war's fronts.** *(Comprehension) Summarizing Information*

Social History English novelist Sir Arthur Conan Doyle called August of 1914 "the most terrible August in the history of the world. One thought that God's curse hung heavy over a degenerate world."
Background The First Battle of Ypres lasted from October 20 to November 22, 1914. Germany lost at least 130,000 soldiers, Britain about 50,000, and France close to 70,000.

World War I Divides Europe

Rivalry for power and complex alliances drew most European nations into war by 1916. What major battles were fought in France? Through what countries did the western front extend?

Map Answers: (1) The battles at Argonne, Verdun, Château-Thierry. (2) Belgium, France, Germany, Austria-Hungary, Italy.

long fight. Soldiers dug a vast network of trenches for hundreds of miles across France. Between the opposing lines lay "no man's land," a wasteland of barbed wire, mud, torn earth, and shattered trees. Attacking soldiers had to climb out of their trenches and race across no man's land. An observer described the horrors of trench warfare:

66 The enemy sent down an enormous shower of concentrated machine-gun fire. It hummed and whirred through the air around the lines of steadily ad-

vancing troops. It thudded home into their sweating bodies, through equipment straps and khaki cloth. In a few minutes the first waves were wiped out. But wave upon wave came pouring out of the trenches. As they got entangled in the barbed wire, the enemy used rifle fire to kill them off one by one. Most, however, never got as far as the wire. They lay in no man's land as shells exploded among them, and bullets tore through the deadly air above their heads. 99

629

The Geography Connection

The Opening Campaign of World War I

Geography has often played an important role in the strategies and outcomes of battles. Geography was the main reason behind Germany's decision to invade France by advancing through Belgium in the opening campaign of World War I. Instead of attacking from Metz, the German city nearest the French border and only 180 miles from Paris, German forces marched an extra 70 miles to reach Paris by way of the Belgian plain.

German generals knew that a direct attack across the French-German border would involve great difficulties. The Ardennes Forest covered the northern end of the border, near Belgium (see map). The rugged Vosges (VOHZH) Mountains stretched along the southern end of the border, near Switzerland. A line of strong forts extended from Verdun to Belfort.

In contrast, an attack from the north through Belgium offered few obstacles. A 35-mile gap of clear, level land lay between the southern tip of the Netherlands and the northern edge of the Ardennes. This gap opened onto the broad Belgian plain. A ring of forts surrounding the city of Liège (lee-EZH) presented the only major obstacle.

As a result of the speed with which they swept through Belgium and France, German armies gained control of nearly all of Belgium and the industrial region of northeastern France. However, the Germans failed in their attempt to capture Paris and defeat the French.

Making the connection. Why did the Germans choose to take an indirect invasion route through Belgium rather than marching directly across the border into France?

German Invasion of France, 1914

630

The machine gun helped make World War I the deadliest war fought until then. Here American machine gunners crawl through a forest on the western front in 1918. The picture shows the devastation caused by the war.

New weapons. The frightful loss of life in trench warfare was partly the result of new kinds of weapons. The rapid fire of machine guns cut down thousands of soldiers trying to cross no man's land. Huge long-range guns sent explosive shells pouring into the trenches. Many soldiers were blinded or had their lungs scarred by poison gas. Tanks were first used in the war in 1916, and aerial battles between daring pilots took place for the first time late in the war.

Stalemate. Despite the heavy losses, little territory changed hands. Neither side could advance more than a few miles. In February 1916 the German army began a major offensive aimed at the French town of Verdun (vehr-DUN), which was protected by a ring of forts. In five months of siege, the Germans gained a little territory but failed to capture Verdun, and by December the French had regained their losses. The warring countries had reached a **stalemate**—a standoff that neither side could break. As the struggle for Verdun continued, more than 700,000 French and German soldiers were killed. Many more were wounded.

The stalemate dragged on through 1916 and 1917. While gains and losses of land were measured in yards, lives were being lost by the hundreds of thousands. Generals kept sending more troops to the front and ordering massive attacks.

The Eastern Front

There was more movement in the fighting on the eastern front than in France and Belgium. While the Germans were attacking France in 1914, the Russians won some early victories in eastern Germany. They were badly beaten at Tannenberg, however, by the armies of the German commander, Field Marshal Paul von Hindenburg. In the spring of 1915, another Austro-German attack forced the Russians into a retreat.

By late 1916 the Russian war effort was near collapse. The Russian army was poorly trained, ill equipped, and badly led. It had suffered staggering losses—more than two million soldiers were killed, wounded, or captured in 1915 alone. Moreover, Russia's allies could not ship supplies to its ports. A German fleet blocked the Baltic Sea, while the Ottomans still controlled the straits leading from the Mediterranean to the Black Sea.

The Russian army also suffered from poor morale. The heavy casualties at the front and food shortages at home increased the Russian people's discontent with czarist rule. In March 1917 the czar was forced to abdicate, and in November a new government took power (Chapter 32). Its leaders, realizing that Russia could not continue the war, signed a humiliating treaty with Germany in March 1918.

Other Fronts

The battles of World War I were not confined to the western and eastern fronts. As more nations became involved, fighting broke out elsewhere in Europe as well as in other parts of the world.

Italy. Although it remained neutral at first, in 1915 Italy made a secret agreement with France and Britain. In return for the promise of territory in Austria and Africa, Italy joined the war on the Allied side. Fighting soon raged on the Austrian-Italian border. In the fall of 1917, German and Austrian forces broke through the Italian lines at Caporetto and forced the Italian army to retreat.

Asia and the Pacific. Japan joined the Allies in August 1914, only a few weeks after the war started. In October, Japan moved to take over the German spheres of influence on China's Shandong Peninsula, as well as German-held islands in the Pacific Ocean. In

Sec. Rev. ques. 3

632

return for help from the Japanese navy, the Allies promised to support Japan's claim to these territories after the war. Meanwhile, the British Dominions of Australia and New Zealand seized other German islands in the Pacific.

The Ottoman Empire. Some of the fiercest fighting of the war took place along the coast of Turkey. The Ottomans had planted mines in the waters of the Dardanelles and put heavy artillery along the shores of these straits. These fortifications not only prevented Allied aid from reaching Russian ports but also kept the Russian fleet bottled up in the Black Sea.

A combined force of British, French, New Zealand, and Australian troops landed at Gallipoli (guh-LIP-uh-lee) in 1915. They hoped to reach Constantinople by land and gain control of the Dardanelles. With German help, the Ottomans resisted strongly, and the Allies withdrew after heavy losses.

The Allies fared better against the Ottomans in the Arab countries of the Middle

Much of World War I was fought in narrow trenches (right) designed to shield soldiers from enemy artillery. Troops from Australia and New Zealand (above) fight Turkish soldiers at Gallipoli. Ottoman forces were victorious in this battle, but by 1922 their empire would cease to exist.

Background Germany supplied money to the Russian revolutionary movement and arranged for the return of Lenin, the movement's leader. Germany hoped that Russia's internal problems would destroy its war effort.

Background Allied forces held Gallipoli for eight months, but withdrew after suffering approximately 100,000 casualties.

East. The Arabs in the Middle East had been part of the Ottoman Empire for more than 400 years. Eager to topple Ottoman rule, Arab nationalists aided the British forces that were protecting Britain's interests in the Middle East. By leading a series of raids on Ottoman-held towns and supply lines, the Arab and British forces succeeded in driving the Ottomans out of one area after another. The Ottomans withdrew from the war at the end of October 1918.

★ See below.

Africa. In West Africa, British and French troops seized the German coastal colonies of Togoland and Kamerun (later the Cameroons). At the same time, troops from the Union of South Africa took over the neighboring German colony of South-West Africa (map, page 603). In German East Africa (later Tanganyika), a small German army was never decisively defeated. Retreating into the African interior, the German soldiers did not surrender until they received news of the war's end.

The Role of the United States

● Note strategies for second objective on this page and p. 634.

American neutrality. When war broke out in 1914, President Woodrow Wilson announced a policy of neutrality for the United States. This policy proved hard to maintain, however. Britain and France made an effort to gain American support by spreading **propaganda**—information designed to influence people's beliefs or actions. Allied propaganda described the war as a struggle between democracy and authoritarian government. News stories from Britain pictured the Germans as arrogant and cruel. Some Americans, overcome by anti-German feelings, stopped using German words like *hamburger* and *sauerkraut*.

American neutrality was also undermined by attacks on American shipping. Both Britain and Germany interfered with shipping by neutral countries, including the United States. To keep war supplies from reaching Germany, Britain stopped merchant ships and seized their cargoes. Germany, in turn, tried to cut off Britain's sources of food and supplies by using submarines, called **U-boats**. (The *U* in "U-boat" was short for *Untersee*, the German word for "undersea.") Many sailors and passengers died when ships were sunk by U-boat attacks.

Sec. Rev. ques. 4

In May 1915 nearly 1,200 people died when a U-boat sank the British passenger ship *Lusitania*. Among the casualties were 128 Americans, most of whom were women and children. The German government defended the sinking, pointing out that the ship was carrying arms as well as passengers. Nevertheless, this tragedy shocked Americans and pushed them closer to war.

Economic motives also influenced the United States. American banks and businesses had loaned $1.5 billion to Allied governments. Much of this money was used to buy needed supplies from the United States.

633

★ ENRICHMENT. Have students research the effects of World War I on the civilian population of France, Germany, Austria-Hungary, Belgium, the Ottoman Empire, or Russia. Students might find information on how the civilian population supported the war effort, or describe how civilians were affected by the fighting. *(Application)* **Locating Information**

● RETEACHING. Have students identify the factors that brought the United States into World War I. (British and French propaganda, submarine attacks, economic motives, the Zimmermann telegram.) *(Comprehension)* **Identifying Causes**

● REINFORCEMENT. Have students work in groups to present a debate that might have occurred between Americans who wanted to maintain neutrality and those who believed the United States should join the Allies. *(Synthesis)* **Debating an Issue**

American bankers and manufacturers realized that they would probably lose their money if the Allies lost the war.

American entry into war. Early in 1917, a threatening incident provoked Americans further. In a secret telegram in code, a German diplomat named Arthur Zimmermann tried to make an alliance with Mexico. He promised that if Mexico helped Germany win the war, Germany would help Mexico regain Texas and other parts of the American Southwest. The British broke the German code and reported the message to the United States. Although Mexico remained neutral and did not join Germany, the "Zimmermann telegram" enraged Americans.

● See below.

In April 1917 the United States declared war on Germany. The American aim, President Wilson said, was to "make the world safe for democracy." Germany now tried to end the war quickly, before large numbers of American troops could be trained for combat and sent to France.

Russia's withdrawal from the war in the spring of 1918 released German troops from the eastern front. Rushed west to France, they joined other German soldiers in a massive march toward Paris. British and French soldiers could not hold back the German advance. A major German victory seemed at hand.

By early summer, however, American troops began to arrive in France. Under the command of General John J. Pershing, they joined with Allied forces. In June 1918 the Allies halted the German offensive at Château-Thierry (shah-TOH-tyeh-REE), on the Marne River. America's entry into the war proved to be a decisive factor, turning the tide in favor of the Allies.

The Armistice

Sec. Rev. ques. 5

Germany had thrown all its resources into this last, but unsuccessful, attack. Now it faced severe shortages of food, medicine, oil, and weapons. Allied troops swept eastward in a massive counterattack. It became clear to the German generals that the war was lost. In

634

late September they urged their government to ask for an **armistice**—a halt to the fighting.

Germany's position worsened steadily. In October and November 1918, the Ottoman Empire and Austria-Hungary surrendered, and rebellions in Germany forced the kaiser to give up the throne. The government of the newly established German republic quickly agreed to the armistice terms.

On November 11, 1918, the armistice was signed. Soldiers on both sides came out of the trenches and cheered. Enemies embraced in the midst of no man's land, rejoicing that the fighting was over. A newspaper correspondent with the British army in France wrote:

66 Last night for the first time since August in the first year of the war, there was no light of gunfire in the sky, no spreading glow above black trees where for four years of nights human beings were smashed to death. The fires of hell had been put out. 99

See Sec. 2 *Closing the Lesson*, p. T623B.

Section Review

Answers to Section Review questions are in brackets on pages indicated.

1. **Define or identify:** Allies, Central Powers, stalemate, propaganda, U-boat, armistice. (pp. 628, 631, 633, 634)
2. What was the German military plan at the beginning of the war? Why did German plans for a quick victory fail on both fronts? (p. 628)
3. In what ways did the war involve parts of Asia, the Pacific, and Africa? (pp. 632–633)
4. Why did the United States have trouble maintaining neutrality? (pp. 633–634)
5. What caused Germany to ask the Allies for an armistice? (p. 634)
6. **Critical thinking:** For what different reasons did Japan, Italy, and the United States enter the war? Why might these differences have made a peace agreement more difficult to reach? (See answer below.)

● ENRICHMENT. Have students work in groups to write news articles that might have appeared in American papers before the United States entered the war. Students might report on British, French, and German propaganda, describe submarine attacks on ships or the use of poison gas, or analyze the Zimmermann telegram. *(Analysis) Translating Information into Another Form*

Background The number of soldiers who died during World War I was staggering: Germany—1.8 million; France—1.4 million; Austria-Hungary—1.4 million; Russia—almost 2 million; Italy—700,000; Serbia—370,000; Britain and its Dominions—950,000; the United States—115,000.

6. Japan and Italy joined after being promised new lands. The United States joined after being provoked by Germany. Students might suggest that it would be difficult to satisfy all parties.

3 The Peace Treaties

Objectives

Focus Questions

★ ■ How was a peace settlement reached? *(pages 635–638)*

● ■ What were the effects of World War I? *(pages 638–640)*

Terms to Know

Fourteen Points
self-determination
League of Nations
Treaty of Versailles
demilitarize

mandate
reparations
isolationism
total war

★ Note strategies for first objective on this page and p. 638.

The armistice of November 1918 brought an end to the most terrible war the world had yet known. In January 1919, representatives of the victorious powers met in Paris to hammer out a peace agreement. Twenty-seven European and Asian nations took part in the peace talks. Most decisions, however, were made by the leaders of the four Allied nations. These men, called the "Big Four," were David Lloyd George of Great Britain, Georges Clemenceau (cleh-mahn-SOH) of France, Woodrow Wilson of the United States, and Vittorio Orlando of Italy.

The Paris Peace Conference

The Fourteen Points. In January 1918, President Wilson had offered a plan for peace in a speech to Congress. His proposal, known as the **Fourteen Points**, rested on five key ideas:

Sec. Rev.
ques. 2

1. Self-determination. Wilson claimed that nationalities should have the right to establish their own governments, free of foreign control. Under this principle, known as

self-determination, Austrian lands inhabited by Italians would belong to Italy. The South Slavs and the Czechs in Austria-Hungary would be free to form their own states.

2. "Peace without victory." Wilson declared that the end of the war should bring "a peace without victory." By this he meant that the Allies should treat their former enemies generously. Harsh punishment, Wilson believed, would only cause Germany to seek revenge. Wilson hoped that a just settlement would encourage the defeated nations to work with the victorious Allies for a new and better world. He wanted free trade and freedom of the seas for all countries.

3. Disarmament. Wilson believed there could be no lasting peace until militarism was ended. He wanted the nations of the world to disarm so that no country would fear its neighbors or try to invade them.

4. Fair treatment of colonial peoples. Wilson also called for imperialist nations to

In 1919 the "Big Four" Allied leaders met at Versailles to draw up a peace treaty. From left are Orlando of Italy, Britain's Lloyd George, Clemenceau of France, and U.S. President Wilson.

635

★ RETEACHING. Have students make a chart listing the territorial changes, military restrictions, and reparations agreed to in the Treaty of Versailles. *(Comprehension) Observing for Detail*

Check for Understanding. Ask: What was President Wilson's peace plan called? (The Fourteen Points.)

★ REINFORCEMENT. Have students work in groups to stage a meeting that might have occurred between representatives of the victorious Allied powers. Participants should discuss and evaluate Wilson's Fourteen Points. *(Synthesis) Synthesizing Information* look out for the welfare of people in their colonies. The interests of these people, he said, should have equal weight with the claims of the ruling government.

5. League of Nations. Wilson urged the formation of an international organization, to be called the **League of Nations**. He hoped that the League would help both large and small nations settle their quarrels. Wilson felt that open diplomacy, rather than secret treaties, could best preserve peace.

Obstacles to a settlement. Wilson pressed hard to get his ideas written into the peace treaties negotiated in 1919. His idealism, however, clashed with the outlook of the victorious European Allies. The war had caused great bitterness. Hatred between nations and peoples had not died when the guns fell silent.

The stiffest opposition to Wilson's ideas came from France. Most of the battles on the western front had been fought on French soil. Almost one and a half million French soldiers had died, and more than three million had been wounded. The French feared a future German attack and were skeptical of Wilson's ideals. They wanted to punish Germany and destroy its ability to wage war. The French also wanted payment for industries and farms that had been ruined.

Sec. Rev. ques. 3

Another problem was the difficulty of carrying out Wilson's principle of self-determination. Many different nationalities lived in Europe. No matter how the peacemakers juggled boundary lines, they could not find a solution that pleased everyone. Self-determination for one nationality was likely to violate the rights of another.

Self-determination for the Poles, for example, meant the creation of an independent Poland. For this new nation to build a sound economy and stand on its own, it needed access to the sea. However, the land between the new Poland and the Baltic Sea was inhabited mainly by Germans. Giving this land to Poland would violate the principle of self-determination for those Germans.

Secret treaties drawn up during the war acted as another barrier to self-determination. The European Allies had al-

636

ready agreed on how to share the spoils of war. Italy, for example, had been promised Austrian lands inhabited by Slavs, Germans, and Italians.

Separate peace treaties. The peace settlement made in Paris consisted of five separate treaties, one with each of the defeated states—Germany, Austria, Hungary, Bulgaria, and the Ottoman Empire. (The Dual Monarchy of Austria-Hungary had broken apart after it signed an armistice with the Allies.) The settlement with Germany, called the **Treaty of Versailles** (June 1919), was the most important of the agreements.

The Versailles Treaty

Territorial changes. The Treaty of Versailles granted France many of its demands. Germany had to return Alsace-Lorraine and give France control of the coal mines of the Saar region for 15 years. Germany also lost land to Poland. To give Poland access to the Baltic Sea, the Polish Corridor was created. This was a strip of land that separated East Prussia from the rest of Germany. The Baltic Sea port of Danzig became a free trading city, controlled by neither Poland nor Germany.

German territory on both sides of the Rhine River was **demilitarized**. That is, it was to remain free of military personnel and fortifications. To prevent Germany from again becoming a military threat, the treaty also reduced the German army to 100,000 men, with no heavy artillery, tanks, or warplanes. The draft was abolished; the new German army could consist only of volunteers. The navy was limited to a small fleet, and no submarines were permitted.

Sec. Rev. ques. 4

Mandates. Germany also lost its overseas territories in Africa, Asia, and the Pacific Ocean. Its African colonies were given to France and Britain as **mandates**. A mandate is a region that is administered by another country until it is ready for independence. Japan gained a mandate over some of the Pacific islands, but its claims on China's Shandong Peninsula were not settled.

Background Each nation that gained a mandate had to guarantee freedom of religion, ban slave trade, agree not to undertake military training of native inhabitants, and promise eventual self-government.

Map Skill Practice

See p. T623C for answers to *Map Skill Practice*.

Territorial Changes After World War I

1. Which country shown on the map below lost the most territory after World War I?

2. Compare the top inset map with the map on page 603. What had Tanganyika been called when Germany controlled it?

3. Which government lost Syria and Lebanon to France?

4. Which country received most of the Pacific islands lost by Germany?

5. Compare the main map with the map on page 629. How was the nation of Austria-Hungary split up after World War I?

6. **Making inferences.** What was the Polish Corridor and why was it a significant possession for Poland?

KEY
Territories lost by
- Germany
- Russia
- Austria-Hungary
- Ottoman Empire
- Bulgaria
- Postwar boundaries
- Rhineland

637

Reparations. The Versailles Treaty blamed the war on "the aggression of Germany and her allies." At the peace conference, the British prime minister had promised to punish Germany. The treaty thus required Germany to pay **reparations**—war damages—to other nations. Germany had to make up for the loss of property, factories, farms, ships, and other things destroyed in the war. The exact amount owed, $33 billion, was not determined until 1921.

Sec. Rev. ques. 4, cont.

The demand for reparations caused great bitterness among the German people. Many thought the amount was more than Germany could afford. They also said that all the warring powers, not just Germany, had been responsible for the war.

New states. The German losses of land were not the only territorial changes resulting from the war. The various nationalities in the former Austro-Hungarian Empire carved out their own states. The peacemakers recognized these as independent nations (map, page 637). Czechs and Slovaks formed the new country of Czechoslovakia (chek-uh-sloh-VAH-kee-uh). The Croats and Slovenes joined with Serbia to form Yugoslavia. Italy and Romania also gained land from the old empire, and Hungary became a separate nation. The new Austria, greatly reduced in size and power, was forbidden to unite with Germany.

Territorial changes reshaped the Middle East as well. The Ottoman Empire was stripped of all its lands outside Turkey. Some parts gained independence, while others came under the control of Britain, France, and Greece. Within Turkey, nationalists overthrew the Ottoman sultan (page 678).

The League of Nations. The Versailles Treaty included provisions to establish a League of Nations, as President Wilson had hoped. Members of the League agreed to respect the borders of fellow members and to take all disputes to the League for settlement. Eventually more than 60 countries joined the League of Nations.

Much to Wilson's disappointment, the United States did not join the League of Nations. **Isolationism**—the desire to stay out of **638** foreign entanglements—was strong in the United States after the war. Fearing that membership in the League of Nations would drag the United States into future European conflicts, the Senate refused to ratify the Treaty of Versailles.

★ See below, left.

Controversy over the Versailles Treaty. The fairness of the Versailles Treaty—particularly the treatment of Germany—was debated for many years. Critics pointed out that the kaiser's government had already been toppled. The burden of carrying out the treaty fell on a new democratic German government, making it very difficult for this new government to survive. Defenders of the treaty pointed out that the German economy had recovered quickly and that Germany was producing more iron, steel, and coal than before the war.

The Aftermath of War

● Note strategies for second objective on this page and p. 640.

World War I, called "the Great War" at the time, was a turning point in world history. The changes it brought and the problems it created continued long after the fighting ended.

Total war. World War I was the first **total war**—a war involving all the human and material resources of the countries taking part. At least 10 million soldiers died in the fighting and 21 million were wounded, nearly wiping out an entire generation of young men.

The war took a heavy toll on those far from the front, too. Some civilians, such as those aboard the *Lusitania*, were killed as a direct result of the conflict. Millions more died from hunger or from an influenza epidemic that swept through both neutral and warring countries.

Sec. Rev. ques. 5

People at home sacrificed whatever they could to make sure their armies had enough supplies. Americans, for example, did without meat every Tuesday and rationed such items as sugar and milk. Thousands of tons of steel and tin that might otherwise have been used for children's toys went instead to make airplanes, rifles, and ammunition. In order to

★ ENRICHMENT. Have students write two editorials that might have appeared in the United States during the debate about the League of Nations. One should represent the view of a supporter of League membership. One should represent the opposing view. (Application) *Understanding Points of View*

Background The German foreign minister said of the peace treaty's harshness, "The Allies could have expressed the [Versailles Treaty] in one clause—'Germany gives up her existence.'"

● RETEACHING. Have students make a chart listing the positive and negative results of World War I. (Positive: extension of women's political rights. Negative: wiped out entire generation of young men; militarism and imperialism persisted; extremist political parties developed; nationalist rivalries intensified.) (Comprehension) *Understanding Cause and Effects*

Ⓕ See
below.

Daily Life

The Influenza Outbreak of 1918

Wherever armies march, disease marches too. More than 8 million soldiers died on the battlefields of World War I, but the deadliest enemy of all struck when the battles were nearly over. In 1918 an outbreak of influenza swept through the American, European, and African troops in northern France. The illness spread rapidly through the trenches and barracks where everyone ate, slept, and fought in close quarters.

Homeward-bound soldiers carried the disease throughout Europe and to the Americas, Africa, Asia, and Australia. The "flu" spread like wildfire. In the city of Philadelphia, for example, 4,600 people died from influenza in a single week. In some cities (see picture) people were kept off public transportation unless they wore a face mask.

The flu of 1918 was more than an *epidemic,* or widespread disease. It was truly a *pandemic,* or worldwide outbreak. By the time the disease ran its course, it had killed more than 20 million people— far more than all the bullets, bombs, and artillery shells of World War I.

save fuel, daylight-saving time was invented in Europe.

To boost public support, governments on both sides of the war used propaganda. Posters and speeches urged civilians to give their all to the war effort. Newspapers were censored to avoid reporting defeats and thereby keep up morale at home. Governments steadily took more and more control over the economy, turning all the resources of production toward the war effort.

Women's rights. At the outbreak of the war, women suffragists in Britain and the United States (pages 503, 507) postponed their fight for equality so they could respond to their countries' wartime needs. To release men for military service, many women took jobs on farms and in offices, factories, and service industries. Women drove ambulances, mail trucks, and buses. They read gas meters and collected railway tickets. They worked as laboratory assistants, plumbers, and bank clerks. There were few jobs formerly held by men that women did not take on.

During the war, a number of political leaders argued that extending the right to vote to women would aid the war effort. By the **639**

Ⓕ **FEATURE ACTIVITY. Ask: (a) What factors contributed to the spread and virulence of influenza in 1918?** (Large numbers of soldiers living in close quarters; spread of the disease when soldiers returned home.) **(b) Do you think a flu pandemic could occur today?** (The existence of vaccines, improved hygiene, and better sanitation decreases the possibility of a flu pandemic today.) *(Synthesis)*
Drawing Conclusions

Women's contributions to the war effort included work in factories and at the scene of the fighting in Europe. American women's increased participation in the workforce helped win them the right to vote after the war.

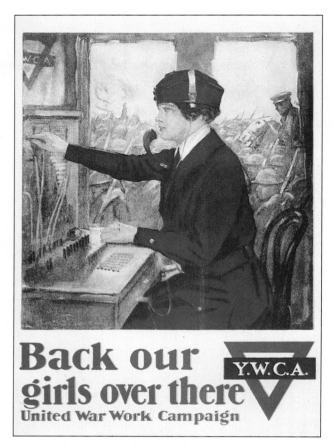

Back our girls over there
United War Work Campaign
Y.W.C.A.

end of the war, little opposition remained to granting women political rights. In 1918 British women over the age of 30 gained the vote. By 1928 Parliament lowered the voting age for British women to 21, the same as for men. In 1919, the United States Congress approved a constitutional amendment extending the right to vote to women. The Nineteenth Amendment became law in the United States in 1920. By 1920 women had the right to vote in most northern European countries and in Russia.

Unresolved problems. While World War I brought great political changes, it did not sweep aside the attitudes that had helped cause the war. Militarist ideas persisted, especially in those countries that felt cheated by the peace settlements. In the decade after the war, some extremists formed political parties that glorified war and violence. These parties paved the way for militarist leaders to take power in some countries.

Imperialism remained as well. Asians and Africans under European rule had been encouraged by Allied promises of independence and by Wilson's Fourteen Points. Their hopes sank as they realized that under the mandate system, they could only wait for independence at some future date.

Nationalist rivalries also intensified. Some Germans vowed that they would tear up the Versailles Treaty and regain lost lands. Italy claimed that it should have received more Austrian territory as well as a share of Germany's African colonies. The Japanese were disappointed by the territorial settlements in Asia.

Had the League of Nations been stronger, it might have been able to deal with these problems. However, conflicts among the League's members kept it from acting effectively. In the years ahead, peace would again break down and the world would be drawn into another devastating war.

● See below.

See Sec. 3 *Closing the Lesson*, p. T623C.

640

● REINFORCEMENT. Have students write an essay explaining how World War I might be considered a turning point in history. Students might consider the effects of the first total war, the wide-scale use of propaganda, and the expansion of political rights for women. (Synthesis) *Evaluating Information*

● ENRICHMENT. Have students find information on the League of Nations and how it worked in the years after World War I. Students might research how effective the League was in preventing or negotiating conflicts, or study the economic and cultural contributions made by the international organization. (Application) *Locating Information*

1. **Define or identify:** Fourteen Points, self-determination, League of Nations, Treaty of Versailles, demilitarize, mandate, reparations, isolationism, total war. (pp. 635, 636, 638)
2. What were the main points of President Wilson's plan for peace? (pp. 635–636)
3. What factors kept Wilson's plan from being accepted? (p. 636)

4. How was Germany punished for its part in the war? Why did some people think this was unfair? (pp. 636, 638)
5. What changes did World War I bring about? (pp. 638–640)
6. **Critical thinking:** How and why did the terms of the Treaty of Versailles differ from Wilson's Fourteen Points? (See answer below.)

6. The purpose of the Treaty of Versailles was to punish and demilitarize Germany, while Wilson sought ways to preserve peace with his Fourteen Points.

Chapter 31   Summary and Timeline

1. The forces that led to the outbreak of World War I had existed in Europe for decades. National rivalries and militarism brought about an arms race and the formation of opposing alliances. A nationalist movement among Serbian Slavs led to the assassination of the heir to the throne of Austria-Hungary in June 1914. With this excuse, Austria-Hungary began the war. Austria-Hungary and Germany were soon at war against Britain, France, and Russia.

2. Germany expected a quick victory in France, but by the winter of 1914–1915, it was clear that the war would be long. Trench warfare on the western front in France was made more brutal by new weaponry such as

machine guns, poison gas, and tanks. As other nations took sides, the conflict became truly a "world war." In April 1917 the United States entered the war on the Allied side. Combined Allied forces stopped the final German offensive in France, and the war came to an end in November 1918.

3. The peace settlements brought widespread political and territorial changes. Though President Wilson suggested generous peace terms in his Fourteen Points plan, the Treaty of Versailles punished Germany harshly. The League of Nations, proposed by Wilson, was formed to help ensure world peace, but bitter feelings and resentment lingered in many nations.

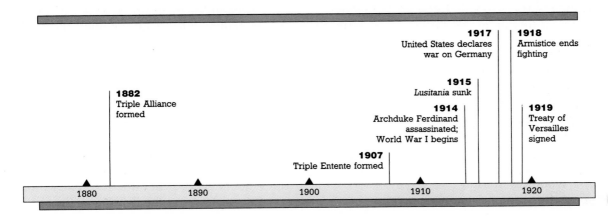

1882 Triple Alliance formed

1907 Triple Entente formed

1914 Archduke Ferdinand assassinated; World War I begins

1915 *Lusitania* sunk

1917 United States declares war on Germany

1918 Armistice ends fighting

1919 Treaty of Versailles signed

1880   1890   1900   1910   1920

641

See p. T623C for answers to Chapter Review.

Vocabulary Review

1. Match each of these terms with its correct definition: *armaments, armistice, demilitarize, escalate, isolationism, mandate, militarism, mobilize, propaganda, reparations, total war, U-boat, ultimatum.*
   a. information designed to influence people's beliefs or actions
   b. eliminate military personnel and fortifications
   c. payments made as compensation for property destroyed in war
   d. region administered by another country until it is ready for independence
   e. final demand
   f. grow more intense
   g. German submarine
   h. government policy that stresses readiness for war
   i. policy that calls for avoiding foreign entanglements
   j. halt to fighting
   k. weapons and military supplies
   l. organize and prepare
   m. war involving all the resources of the countries taking part
2. Identify the terms in the following pairs.
   a. Triple Alliance; Triple Entente
   b. Fourteen Points; League of Nations

People to Identify

Identify the following people and tell why each was important.
1. Otto von Bismarck
2. Francis Ferdinand
3. Gavrilo Princip
4. William II
5. Woodrow Wilson
6. Arthur Zimmermann

Places to Know

Match the letters on this map with the places and alliances listed below. You may want to refer to the map on page 629.

1. Allies
2. Austria-Hungary
3. Belgium
4. Central Powers
5. France
6. Germany
7. Great Britain (United Kingdom)
8. Italy
9. Russia
10. Sarajevo
11. Serbia

Recalling the Facts

1. Explain why the alliance system, militarism, imperialism, and nationalism were underlying causes of World War I.
2. Why did Germany, Russia, France, and Britain each become involved in World War I?
3. Why did the German war plan fail?
4. What factors led to the collapse of the Russian war effort?
5. What did Italy, Japan, and the Arabs each hope to gain by aiding the Allies?
6. What effect did the American entry into the war have on the fighting in Europe?

7. Why did France oppose Woodrow Wilson's peace plan?
8. What requirements were imposed on Germany by the Treaty of Versailles?
9. Why did the United States refuse to ratify the Versailles Treaty?
10. How did the war change women's position in society?
11. What problems remained unresolved after World War I? Why?

Critical Thinking Skills

1. **Sequencing events.** On a separate sheet of paper, list the following events in chronological order. *(Comp.)*
   a. Russia withdraws from war.
   b. Triple Entente signed.
   c. Archduke Ferdinand assassinated.
   d. Germany invades Belgium.
   e. Polish Corridor created.
   f. Battle of Verdun ends in stalemate.

2. **Analyzing quotations.** Explain the following statements quoted in this chapter. *(Comp.)*
   a. "When one of them puts his hand into his pocket, his neighbor gets ready his own revolver in order to be able to fire the first shot." (page 626)
   b. Quarrels between nations "must be settled not at the conference table, but on the battlefield; not with the pen, but with the sword; not with ink, but with blood." (page 626)
   c. "The lamps are going out all over Europe. We shall not see them lit again in our lifetime." (page 628)

3. **Hypothesizing.** Americans hoped that World War I would be "the war to end all wars." Do you think it might have been possible to work out a peace treaty that would have made this hope a reality? Explain. *(Syn.)*

Thinking About Geography

Recognizing geographic importance. Research the fighting that took place at Gallipoli, Château-Thierry, or another battle of World War I. Draw a map showing details of the battle. Include geographic features and explain how the shape and characteristics of the land influenced the battle. *(App.)*

Enrichment: Primary Sources

Adapted below is part of a memorandum that David Lloyd George sent to France before the victorious powers of World War I reached a peace agreement.

❝ When nations are exhausted by wars in which they have put forth all their strength and which leave them tired, bleeding and broken, it is not difficult to patch up a peace that may last until the generation which experienced the horrors of the war has passed away.

What is difficult, however, is to draw up a peace which will not provoke a fresh struggle when those who have had practical experience of war have passed away.

Those who say you can make Germany so feeble that she will never be able to hit back are utterly wrong. You may strip Germany of her colonies and reduce her armaments and her navy; all the same, in the end, if she feels that she has been unjustly treated, she will find the means of punishing her conquerors. ❞

1. Why, according to Lloyd George, is it easy to make a peace agreement that will last for a short period of time?
2. Why did he think it would be difficult to make a peace agreement that would last for a long time?
3. **Critical thinking:** How are Lloyd George's ideas similar to those of Wilson's Fourteen Points (pages 635–636)? *(Syn.)*

A checkmark identifies questions and exercises calling for the three higher-order levels of thinking at the top of the Bloom taxonomy: Analysis, Synthesis, and Evaluation.

Russia in Upheaval   1894–1939

(pp. 644–661)

Chapter Preview

Section 1 traces the developments in Russian society that led to the overthrow of Czar Nicholas II in March 1917 and to the Bolshevik Revolution of October 1917, which brought Lenin to power. Sections 2 and 3 examine the economic and political changes made by Lenin and then by Stalin to create the Soviet state.

Bibliography

See the *Teacher's Management and Planning Guide* for additional listings. Starred titles are for both students and teachers.

Carr, E. H. *The Russian Revolution: From Lenin to Stalin.* Free Press. Authoritative account by a leading scholar.

Conquest, Robert. *Harvest of Sorrow.* Oxford University Press. The grim story of Stalin's agricultural collectivization and state-inflicted famine of 1932.

Reed, John. *Ten Days That Shook the World.* Bantam. An account of the Russian Revolution.

*Solzhenitsyn, Alexander. *One Day in the Life of Ivan Denisovich.* Dutton. Life in a Stalinist work camp.

Section Lesson Plans

SECTION 1   (pp. 645–649)
The Overthrow of the Czar

Objectives

After completing this section, students will be able to:
1. Explain what caused the fall of the czarist regime.
2. Describe how the Bolsheviks came to power.

Introducing the Lesson

Remind students that, during World War I, Russia withdrew its support of the Allies as a result of civil and social unrest at home. Internal problems that had plagued Russia for decades finally erupted in revolution and ushered in history's first Communist government.

   Then ask: *(a) What problems created widespread civil and social unrest in Russia during the late 18th and early 19th centuries?* (The Russification of other national groups, refusal to respond to political discontent, social inequalities, severe oppression of the peasant class, and failure to industrialize as fast as the European countries and Japan.)

   (b) What characteristics of the Russian state would have made it hard for a revolution to succeed? (The power of the Russian autocrats, ruthless political repression, and the size of the nation.)

   (c) How might events in history have been different if the Communists had not won the revolution? (Answers will vary.)

Developing the Lesson:
Synthesizing Information

Have students work in groups to stage a meeting that might have occurred among representatives of Kerensky's Provisional Government, supporters of a military dictatorship, and the Petrograd Soviet. Participants should describe the form of government they represent and explain how their governments might resolve Russia's problems. *(Application)*

Developing the Lesson:
Forming a Hypothesis

Have students develop a hypothesis explaining why Japan's transformation into a modern constitutional state was successful and why Russian efforts failed. Students should consider the differences between Russia and Japan in society, history, geography, political institutions, and culture. *(Synthesis)*

Closing the Lesson:
Predicting Events

Have students work in groups to predict how the Bolsheviks would have dealt with problems that remained from the period of czarist rule. Students might review the principles of Marxism (pp. 500–501) and then decide how Marxist leadership would have tackled social, economic, and political problems. *(Synthesis)*

See *Section Review* questions, p. 649.

SECTION 2 (pp. 649–654)
State-Building Under Lenin

Objectives

After completing this section, students will be able to:
1. Describe how the Bolsheviks dealt with threats to their power.
2. Explain how the foundations of the Soviet state were laid.

Introducing the Lesson

Remind students that the Marxist government established in Russia after the Bolshevik Revolution replaced czarist autocracy with Communist control, destruction of all opposition, and religious and national persecution.

Then ask: *(a) Why might the Communists have believed it necessary to destroy all opposition?* (Answers will vary. The Bolshevik Revolution did not, in itself, solve the problems resulting in the czar's overthrow. The Communists might have thought that modernization was not possible unless those who opposed Marxist reforms were silenced.)

(b) How might the Communist leaders have answered the charge that Communist rule was no different from czarist rule? (Answers will vary. The Communists might claim that czarist rule benefited a small, wealthy class, while Communists ruled in the name of the workers and peasants.)

(c) When, if ever, might a government's suppression of opposition be considered legitimate? (Answers will vary.)

Developing the Lesson:
Summarizing Information

Have students make a chart identifying the problems faced by Russia after the Bolshevik Revolution. Then have the students describe the Communist policies designed to solve the problems. (*Problems after the Bolshevik Revolution:* famine, economic crises, nationalist movements, civil war, lawlessness. *Communist policies:* "dictatorship of proletariat," War Communism, New Economic Policy, formation of the Soviet Union, propaganda.) *(Comprehension)*

Developing the Lesson:
Drawing Conclusions

Have students work in groups to answer the following questions:
(a) What do you suppose was the reaction of governments around the world to Lenin's call for a worldwide revolution of the proletariat?
(b) Why might Lenin's call for revolution have evoked responses in countries where there was disorder or widespread poverty?
(c) Do you think that Lenin's call for revolution helped or harmed the cause of worldwide socialism in the long run?
Have students share their conclusions with the class. *(Synthesis)*

Closing the Lesson:
Analyzing Information

Have students develop a hypothesis explaining how Karl Marx might have evaluated the way Lenin applied Marxist principles in Russia. Students might refer to the discussion of Marxism in Chapter 25. *(Synthesis)*

See *Section Review* questions, p. 654.

SECTION 3 (pp. 654–659)
The Soviet Union Under Stalin

Objectives

After completing this section, students will be able to:
1. Explain how Stalin took power and made radical changes in the Soviet Union.
2. Describe the methods used by Stalin to terrorize and intimidate the Soviet people.

Introducing the Lesson

Tell students that under Stalin the Soviet Union continued to make use of repression and propaganda as political tools.

Then ask: *(a) Why did the Soviet Union view opposition to the Communist Party and its policies as a threat?* (Answers may indicate that since communism, based on Marxist principles, claimed to express the general will of the working class, any expression of opposition might have threatened communism's credibility.)

(b) How might opposition to Communist policies have affected the party's economic goals? (Opposition could have led to lack of cooperation and effort.)

(c) Why are democratic systems able to survive political dissent, while Communist governments feel threatened by opposition? (Answers will vary.)

Developing the Lesson: Observing for Detail

Have students answer the following questions:

(a) What were the Five-Year Plans? (Economic plans designed to direct industrialization.)

(b) How did they differ from Lenin's New Economic Policy? (Lenin's policy was a mixture of free enterprise and state control; Stalin's policies involved total state control.)

(c) What problems were created by the implementation of the first Five-Year Plan? (Shoddy goods were produced; working conditions were grim; workers received little pay, were poorly fed, and lived in overcrowded housing.)

(d) Why did the quality of goods decline? (Because the government concentrated on quantity, not quality.)

(e) How were people motivated to increase production? (Through "socialist competition," or the rewarding of those who produced more.)

(f) What methods did Stalin use to bring agriculture under state control? (Collectivization of farms and destruction of the kulaks.)

(g) What consequences did collectivization have in later years? (Farming output plummeted, loss of livestock, great loss of life.) *(Comprehension)*

Developing the Lesson: Synthesizing Information

Have students refer to the text to find evidence of totalitarian control in the Soviet government under Stalin. (State-managed economy, government control of writers, painters, and musicians, the Great Purge.) *(Comprehension)*

Closing the Lesson: Organizing Ideas in Written Form

Have students write an essay explaining what makes a totalitarian state different from a democratic government, why a totalitarian state could exist only in modern times, and what factors contributed to the formation of a totalitarian state in the Soviet Union. (In a totalitarian state, government controls all aspects of life and requires the tools of modern technology—especially such means of mass communication as the radio, television, and the telephone—to exploit and control people. Factors that contributed to the creation of a totalitarian state in the Soviet Union include Russia's long history as a police state, the difficulty rulers had in controlling the country's different classes and national groups, political turmoil that seemed to require totalitarian measures, and Stalin's ruthless campaign to destroy opposition.) *(Comprehension)*

See *Section Review* questions, p. 659.

Chapter 32 Review Answers (pp. 660–661)

Vocabulary Review

1. (a) Kremlin (b) nationalize (c) totalitarian state (d) Great Purge
2. (a) March Revolution (1917)—ended czarist rule; Bolshevik Revolution (November 1917)—ended the Provisional Government and put the Bolsheviks in power. (b) quota—numerical goal; collective farm—state-controlled farm made up of many smaller farms. (c) Treaty of Brest-Litovsk—1918 agreement between Russia and Germany under which Russia lost much of its western territory; Russian civil war—war between the Communists and a variety of forces opposed to the Communist takeover of the government. (d) ideology—set of beliefs; Marxism-Leninism—specific ideology that combined Marxism with Lenin's views on the role of the Communist Party in building socialism.

People to Identify

1. Nicholas II 2. Rasputin 3. Kerensky 4. Trotsky 5. Lenin 6. Joseph Stalin

Places to Know

1. C 2. B 3. D 4. A

Recalling the Facts

1. Many peasants who had traditionally been farmers were forced to work in factories. Their standard of living was low and they had little political power. The upper classes resented the influence of foreign companies in Russia.

2. Russia's defeat in the Russo-Japanese War, and the uprisings that occurred following this defeat, particularly the January 1905 uprising by workers in St. Petersburg. This incident led to widespread strikes and unrest.

3. The Provisional Government promised to restore order through democratic means. Military leaders offered a dictatorship that would restore order by armed force. The Bolsheviks offered rule by workers' and soldiers' soviets.

4. Industry, banks, and foreign trade were nationalized. Men under 50 were drafted for labor or the army. Women were called on to work in industry. Strikes were outlawed. Food was taken from peasants to feed the army and the people in the cities. The NEP replaced War Communism after widespread opposition arose to War Communism's harsh policies.

5. The Communists wanted the republics to appear independent, but in actuality all had identical constitutions and all were controlled by the Communist Party.

6. The Communists seized Church land and property, jailed or kept some clergy from earning a living, closed Church schools, and told state schools to teach that God did not exist.

7. Consumers suffered shortages, delays, and poor service. Factories produced shoddy goods. Working conditions were poor, and workers were poorly paid, fed, and housed. The government could force workers to work where they were needed.

8. He used armed force. Peasants who resisted, particularly the kulaks, were killed or sent to forced-labor camps. Collectivization led to a sharp drop in agricultural output and in the number of livestock. A severe famine struck many sections of the Soviet Union in 1932–1933. As many as 10 million people were thought to have died from collectivization.

9. In 1934 he likely ordered Sergei Kirov killed. Between 1935 and 1939, Stalin put many prominent Bolsheviks on trial, forced them to publicly confess to crimes they had not committed, and then had them executed. He had Trotsky murdered, and he launched attacks on the leaders of non-Russian nationalist movements, scientists, intellectuals, workers, and collective farmers. People were arrested and were often tortured until they confessed, whether innocent or not.

Critical Thinking Skills

1. Similarities: Both governments were highly centralized and non-democratic. Although the members of the Communist Party elected and controlled their leaders in theory, in practice all decisions were made at the top just as they had been under the czar. Fear and intimidation were used by both governments to force people to cooperate. Differences: The Communist government was much more intrusive in its citizens' lives. Also, no party played a role in the czarist government.

2. Answers will vary, but students might argue that a Russian victory would have enabled the czars to stay in power somewhat longer. However, it seems likely that discontent with the low standard of living, shortage of goods, and lack of democracy would have continued, causing organized opposition to increase, not cease.

3. History offers many examples of Stalin's failure to use power wisely. Students might cite Stalin's treatment of the kulaks, the 10 million deaths resulting from his agricultural policy, and the Great Purge of the 1930's.

4. Reports will vary.

Thinking About Geography

Charts should include: (1) Russian Soviet Federated Socialist Republic, Moscow, 6,593,391; (2) Kazakhstan, Alma-Ata, 1,064,092; (3) Ukraine, Kiev, 233,089; (4) Turkmenistan, Ashkhabad, 188,417; (5) Uzbekistan, Tashkent, 158,069; (6) Byelorussia, Minsk, 80,154; (7) Kirghizia, Frunze, 76,641; (8) Tadzhikistan, Duschanbe, 55,019; (9) Azerbaijan, Baku, 33,475; (10) Georgia, Tbilisi, 26,872; (11) Lithuania, Vilnius, 25,174; (12) Latvia, Riga, 24,595; (13) Estonia, Tallin, 17,413; (14) Moldavia, Kishinev, 13,012; (15) Armenia, Yerevan, 11,506. (Figures from *Information Please Almanac.*) The "Present political status" column should indicate independence gained by Latvia, Lithuania, and Estonia in 1991 and membership in the Commonwealth of Independent States for most of the other republics.

Enrichment: Primary Sources

1. He believed he was "God's anointed" and could do no wrong.

2. The people. They felt that the people had always supported them.

3. He meant that Nicholas could see only the dangers directly in front of him. He failed to see or understand long-term problems, especially once the immediate danger had passed.

Russia in Upheaval

1894–1939

See chapter timeline, p. 659.

Before You Read This Chapter

What country was the United States' rival as a superpower for many years after World War II? If you said "the Soviet Union," you are right. At the start of this century, however, there was no such thing as the Soviet Union. Instead there was Russia, a huge empire that lagged far behind the rest of Europe. As you read this chapter, see how Russia's lack of development caused upheaval in the early 1900's. How did Russia become the Soviet Union? What methods did its rulers use in governing that land?

The Geographic Setting

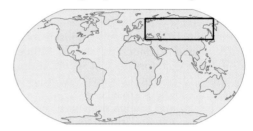

The Chapter Outline

1. The Overthrow of the Czar
2. State-Building Under Lenin
3. The Soviet Union Under Stalin

Lenin's speeches inspired support for the Russian Revolution. In 1917 the Bolsheviks took control of the government and began building a Communist state.

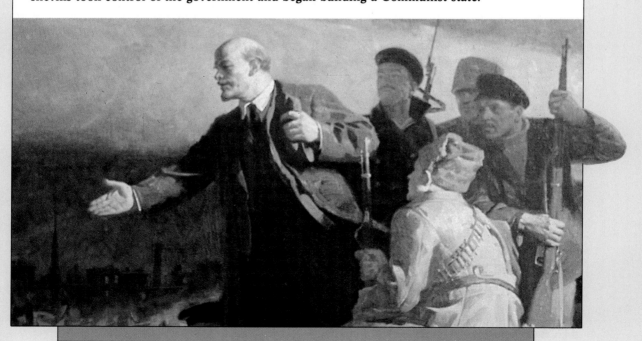

1 The Overthrow of the Czar

Objectives

Focus Questions

★ ■ What caused the fall of the czarist regime? *(pages 645–647)*

● ■ How did the Bolsheviks come to power? *(pages 647–649)*

Terms to Know

Bolshevik   March Revolution
soviet   Bolshevik
October Manifesto   Revolution

★ Note strategies for first objective on this page and p. 646.

For centuries the czars of Russia had tried to turn their backward country into a unified nation and world power. Many rulers made reforms, but they found that giving the people some freedom only brought demands for deeper changes. As a result, periods of tolerance and reform were followed by longer periods of harsh rule. At the end of the 1800's, Russia remained one of the most firmly autocratic states in the world. It was also one of the least developed, internally divided, and badly ruled states.

Russia Under Nicholas II

Nicholas II became czar in 1894. A member of the Romanov family, Nicholas had the same goal as his ancestors—to make Russia a respected world power. The 26-year-old czar was a devoted family man who led a simple, pious life. His trust in the tradition of Russian autocracy blinded him to the fact that times had changed. Unless he changed as well, the forces of history would sweep aside czarist rule.

Attempts at modernization. Compared with the industrial nations of Western Europe, Russia was weak and undeveloped. In 1900 Sergei Witte (VEET-yeh), the czar's ablest minister, began a program to move the country forward. Under Witte's direction, higher taxes and money borrowed from abroad were used to build up Russian industries. To speed industrialization, foreign experts were hired to run Russian factories, and many Russians were sent abroad to study. Witte pushed for the completion of the great Trans-Siberian Railroad (map, page 525) and the building of other railway lines. These steps boosted the growth of heavy industry, particularly iron and steel. For a while, Russia prospered.

Signs of unrest. Rapid industrialization, however, stirred discontent among the people of Russia. Farming had always been the mainstay of the Russian economy, but now many peasants worked in factories. The workers were unhappy with their low standard of living and their lack of political power. The upper classes resented the influence of foreign companies.

Critics of the government disagreed over what changes were needed. Some people called for a democratic republic like that of France. Others wanted a constitutional monarchy like that of Britain. A growing number wanted to bring socialism to Russia.

Sec. Rev. ques. 2

Linking Past and Present

Still in use today, the Trans-Siberian Railroad is the longest continuous rail line in the world. Much of the 5,750-mile line has been electrified, and it now joins with the Chinese Eastern Railway in Manchuria to form a railroad route across the whole of Asia.

645

★ RETEACHING. Have students identify the problems in Russian society in the late 1800's. (Rapid industrialization resulted in discontent over low standard of living and lack of political power; upper classes resented influence of foreign companies; disagreement over direction of reform.) *(Comprehension)* **Observing for Detail**

★ REINFORCEMENT. Have students summarize the disagreements resulting in the split between Russian Marxists. (Mensheviks decided that a socialist revolution would have to wait until the proletariat grew; Bolsheviks wanted to stage a revolution and rule Russia until the proletariat was ready to take power.) *(Comprehension)* **Summarizing Information**

An earlier socialist movement had failed because of lack of support from the Russian masses. During the reign of Alexander II (page 525), groups of idealistic young students traveled around the countryside. They hoped to rouse the peasants to rebel against the government. Proud of their way of life, the peasants did not want change. They handed the students over to the police.

Many later Russian revolutionaries accepted the view of history set forth by Karl Marx (page 500). They believed that revolution in Russia would come from the proletariat—that is, the working class—and not the peasantry. These revolutionaries promised to end exploitation of workers and to set up a state in which the workers would rule.

Lenin and the Bolsheviks. In the 1890's the Marxist revolutionaries found a leader in Vladimir Ilyich Ulyanov (ool-YAH-nof), better known as Lenin. Lenin had become a revolutionary while still in his teens, after his older brother was executed for plotting against the czar. As a university student, Lenin studied the works of Karl Marx and decided to devote his life to overthrowing czarist rule and setting up a socialist state.

In 1895 Lenin was arrested and sent to prison in Siberia for his political activities. ★ See below.

Five years later he left Russia for Western Europe. There, for most of the next 17 years, he worked against czarist rule.

In 1903 Russian Marxists split over revolutionary tactics. They all agreed that Russia had not yet become an industrialized, capitalist state. Russia was therefore not "ripe" for the sort of workers' revolution Marx had expected. Some Russian Marxists, who became known as Mensheviks, decided that a socialist revolution would have to wait until the proletariat had become larger and had grown more powerful.

Lenin and his followers, who became known as **Bolsheviks**, disagreed. Rather than wait for the proletariat to grow, they wanted to form a secret group that would help the workers stage a revolution. This group would then rule Russia until the proletariat was ready to take power.

The Revolution of 1905. In 1904–1905, two events dramatically revealed the weakness of the czarist government. First, Russia was badly beaten in a short war with Japan (page 586). Following this defeat, revolts broke out all over Russia, involving peasants, workers, sailors, non-Russians, and intellectuals. Each group had its own set of demands.

Nicholas II, the last czar of Russia's Romanov dynasty, posed with his family for this portrait shortly before the March Revolution. When he became czar, Russia's outdated economic and political systems required extensive reforms. Nicholas proved unequal to the task.

646

★ ENRICHMENT. Have students write a biography of one of the following people: Nicholas II, Alexandra, Lenin, Trotsky, or Rasputin. Students should conclude their biographies with an evaluation of the role their subject played in the fall of czarist rule. *(Evaluation) Evaluating Information*

Check for Understanding. Ask: Into what two groups did Russian Marxists split? (Mensheviks and Bolsheviks.)
Social History Lenin called the Revolution of 1905 a "dress rehearsal" for the later revolution that resulted in a Communist regime.

Sec. Rev. ques. 3

In January 1905 the workers of St. Petersburg marched unarmed to the royal palace to ask Nicholas II for reforms. The palace guards opened fire on the crowd, killing and wounding hundreds. The incident touched off widespread strikes and further unrest. Workers in St. Petersburg formed a **soviet**— representative council—to lead the strikers.

Nicholas still opposed reform, but he saw that things were getting out of hand. Reluctantly he issued the **October Manifesto**, which called for the formation of Russia's first parliament, the imperial Duma (DOO-mah). Nicholas promised that it would look after the interests of all the people.

Revolutionaries had harsh words for the October Manifesto. "A constitution is given, but the autocracy remains," charged Leon Trotsky, one of the Socialist leaders. Most Russians were satisfied with the reforms, however, and the Revolution of 1905 ran out of steam. Meanwhile, the Duma began meeting, but the czar kept the power to veto its decisions and to dismiss its members at will. Liberals and moderates who once had great hopes for the Duma were angry at the czar's high-handedness. At the outbreak of World War I in 1914, the regime had more enemies than ever before.

Wartime problems. Though Russia was not ready for battle, its interest in the Balkans dragged it into World War I. Russia was no match for imperial Germany, the most powerful country in Europe. As in the Russo-Japanese War, Russia's involvement in World War I exposed the weaknesses of its government.

Sec. Rev. ques. 4

In the summer of 1915, Nicholas II went to the front to rally his discouraged troops, leaving his wife, Alexandra, to run the government. Alexandra had no experience in ruling, but she was a firm believer in absolute monarchy. She ignored the czar's top advisers, trusting only a self-described "holy man" named Rasputin (ras-PYOO-tin).

Rasputin had gained the czarina's confidence by his control over the terrible disease (hemophilia) that threatened the life of her only son. While the best doctors in Europe stood by helpless, Rasputin was somehow able to ease the boy's suffering. People warned Alexandra that Rasputin was a greedy and corrupt man, but she refused to believe them. She allowed Rasputin to make more and more government decisions. Finally, in 1916, a group of nobles murdered Rasputin.

Meanwhile, the war was destroying the morale of the poorly organized and ill-equipped Russian armies. As early as 1915, soldiers were being sent into battle without rifles: they were told to pick up the weapons of the dead. By 1917, after two and a half years of defeats, the soldiers had little respect left for either their officers or the czar.

The March Revolution

● Note strategies for second objective on this page and p. 648.

In March 1917 came the final blow to the regime. A strike by women textile workers in Petrograd* led to a city-wide work stoppage, and soon riots broke out over shortages of food and fuel. When soldiers were ordered to shoot the rioters, they shot their officers instead and joined the rebellion.

Like the Revolution of 1905, the **March Revolution**, as it is called, was unplanned. The defeats of the war, the discontent of the people, and the weakness of the czarist autocracy had all fanned the flames of revolution. A week after rioting began, the czar abdicated in favor of the Provisional Government—a temporary body set up by the Duma.

The March Revolution brought down the czar, but it did not set up a strong government in his place. Several different political groups struggled for power. The Provisional Government was officially in charge. Led by Alexander Kerensky (kuh-REN-skee), it represented educated Russians who had adopted liberal, democratic ideas from the West. Kerensky wanted to continue the war against Germany and to set up a Western-style parliamentary government.

---

* St. Petersburg was renamed Petrograd in 1914 because the original name seemed too German. In 1924 the name was changed to Leningrad. In 1991 the name St. Petersburg was restored, in compliance with a citizens' vote.

647

Background Hemophilia, a hereditary disease, impairs blood's ability to clot. A hemophiliac who is cut or injured may bleed for hours or days.
● **RETEACHING.** Have students make a chart listing the three political groups that struggled for power in Russia, whom each group represented, and what policies each group supported. (Groups included the Provisional Government, the Petrograd Soviet, and the Russian people.) *(Comprehension) Translating Information into Another Form*

● **REINFORCEMENT.** Have students identify the three political forces that competed for power in Russia in 1917 and then explain why the victors were successful. (Parliamentary government, military dictatorship, and rule by workers' and soldiers' soviets vied for power. The Bolsheviks understood the demands of the various groups among the Russian people.) *(Comprehension) Drawing Conclusions*

This painting shows soldiers burning a portrait of Czar Nicholas II, symbol of the old Russia. Support for the Petrograd Soviet from army troops was a decisive factor in the outcome of the revolution.

Competing with the Provisional Government was the Petrograd Soviet, a powerful group of 2,000 to 3,000 soldiers, workers, and Socialist intellectuals. The Petrograd Soviet favored withdrawal from the war as well as radical social reforms to aid workers and peasants. It soon became clear that the Petrograd Soviet held most of the power in Russia.

By the summer of 1917, the Russian people had lost faith in both the Provisional Government and the moderate leaders of the Petrograd Soviet. They wanted real change— land reform, an end to hunger, and self-determination for non-Russians. Above all, they wanted to end the war.

The Bolsheviks knew that this was the moment to seize power. At the time of the czar's overthrow, the Bolshevik leaders had been either in jail or in exile. A month later, a German military train brought Lenin and his companions back to Petrograd from Western Europe. German leaders hoped that the return of the Bolsheviks would add to the turmoil within Russia and distract the Russians from the war against Germany.

By the end of the summer of 1917, three different forms of government were being offered to the bewildered people of Russia. One was a parliamentary government that promised to restore order through democratic methods. This was the course offered by Kerensky's Provisional Government.

Another choice, favored by some members of the old ruling classes, was a military dictatorship that promised to restore order by armed force. In September the army's commander-in-chief tried to overthrow Kerensky. The effort failed because the Petrograd Soviet won the support of most of the troops.

The third possibility was rule by the workers' and soldiers' soviets that had sprung up throughout the country. The leading soviet remained the Petrograd Soviet, now under the control of Lenin and the Bolsheviks. Alone among Russia's political leaders, Lenin understood the demands of the various groups among the Russian people. To the peasants he offered land that would be taken away from the landowners. To the workers he

Sec. Rev. ques. 5
● See below.

● ENRICHMENT. Have students develop a hypothesis explaining how events in Russia might have been different if Germany had not arranged for Lenin's return. *(Synthesis)* **Forming a Hypothesis** offered bread and control of the factories. To the non-Russian peoples he offered self-determination.

In addition to popular support, Lenin had a strong party organization, with able and energetic leaders and about 200,000 members. Unlike other groups that were seeking power, the Bolsheviks were disciplined and could act as a tightly knit unit. Lenin and his party soon gained control of the soviets in the major cities of Russia.

The Bolshevik Revolution

By the fall of 1917, people in the cities were rallying to the call, "All power to the soviets!" On November 7, Lenin's supporters, led by Leon Trotsky, seized government buildings in Petrograd and arrested the members of the Provisional Government. The **Bolshevik Revolution**, also called the Russian Revolution, was over in a matter of hours. Yet it would change the face of Russia forever.

Like the czars, Lenin dreamed of building up Russian power. He also believed that a

Soviet Republic dedicated to creating a Marxist society would serve as a model to the world. First, though, he had to deal with the problems left over from czarist rule.

See Sec. 1 *Closing the Lesson*, p. T643B.

Section Review

Answers to Section Review questions are in brackets on pages indicated.

1. **Define or identify:** Bolshevik, soviet, October Manifesto, March Revolution, Bolshevik Revolution. (pp. 646, 647, 649)
2. What effects did industrialization have on czarist rule? (p. 645)
3. What were the causes of the Revolution of 1905? What was its outcome? (p. 647)
4. How did World War I help to bring about the end of czarist rule? What kind of government was set up after the March Revolution? (p. 647)
5. What factors helped Lenin come to power in November 1917? (pp. 648–649)
6. **Critical thinking:** What steps could Nicholas II have taken to prevent the March Revolution? (See answer below.)

6. Students might suggest that the czar could have shared power with the Duma, better organized his armies, and negotiated with strikers.

See lesson plans, pp. T643A–T643C.

2 State-Building Under Lenin

Objectives

Focus Questions

★ ■ How did the Bolsheviks deal with threats to their power? *(pages 649–651)*
● ■ How were the foundations of the Soviet state laid? *(pages 651–653)*

Terms to Know

Treaty of Brest-Litovsk	Kremlin
nationalize	ideology

★ Note strategies for first objective on this page and p. 651.

The chaos in Russia worsened after the Bolshevik takeover. There was a huge gap between the Bolsheviks' plans for the future and the grim realities of Russian life. Russia was still plagued by the miseries that had brought down the Provisional Government—hunger, fear, and political disorder. People fled from the cities to the country, only to find war or famine there. Different nationalities—the Finns, the Ukrainians, and others—threatened to form their own states. There was no effective government or army. The chaos left Russia with no industry, no railway transport, and no commerce. Often there was no food.

649

Ⓕ See below.

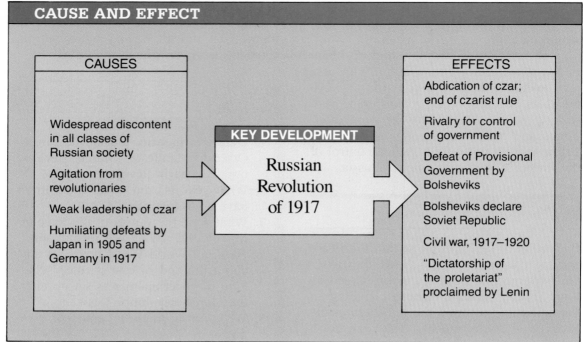

CAUSE AND EFFECT

CAUSES	KEY DEVELOPMENT	EFFECTS
Widespread discontent in all classes of Russian society	Russian Revolution of 1917	Abdication of czar; end of czarist rule
Agitation from revolutionaries		Rivalry for control of government
Weak leadership of czar		Defeat of Provisional Government by Bolsheviks
Humiliating defeats by Japan in 1905 and Germany in 1917		Bolsheviks declare Soviet Republic
		Civil war, 1917–1920
		"Dictatorship of the proletariat" proclaimed by Lenin

A Revolution Under Siege

A deal with Germany. Russia's internal conflicts crippled its fight against Germany in World War I. By the winter of 1917–1918, Russia lay defenseless before German troops. The Bolshevik leaders decided to accept the German terms for peace. In March 1918, the Russians signed the Treaty of Brest-Litovsk.

Under this treaty, Russia lost Finland, its possessions in Poland, and the Baltic provinces of Latvia, Lithuania, and Estonia. Lost too was the Ukraine, the region north of the Black Sea, which had the richest farmland in the empire. The Allied defeat of Germany in November 1918 canceled the Treaty of Brest-Litovsk. Yet Finland and the Baltic states were granted independence, and thus remained outside Russian rule.

The Bolsheviks, who now called themselves Communists, had learned a lesson from the war. The price of disunity was national humiliation. If the Communists wanted to stay in power, they would have to stamp out the opposition.

Civil war. Still smarting from their painful concessions to Germany, the Communists now faced a new challenge to their rule: civil war. The opponents of the Communists were known as "Whites." They included moderate Socialists and supporters of parliamentary government on one hand, and defenders of the czarist cause on the other. Though unable to cooperate, they offered strong resistance to the Communist "Reds." In the Ukraine, peasants called "Greens" fought both Whites and Reds in an attempt to gain Ukrainian independence.

Foreign armies also took part in the civil war. Western governments felt alarmed by Lenin's policies, especially his treaty with Germany. Troops from France, Britain, the United States, and Japan moved into Russia to help the Whites. The newly independent nation of Poland declared war on Russia too.

Communist Dictatorship

Terror tactics. To deal with the situation, Lenin proclaimed the "dictatorship of the proletariat" (page 501) and ordered that

Sec. Rev. ques. 2

Sec. Rev. ques. 3

650

Ⓕ **CAUSE AND EFFECT CHART ACTIVITY. Have students work either in groups or as a class group to add a third column headed "Long-Term Effects" to the chart. Allow students time to research recent developments as preparation for this activity.** *(Application) Locating Information*

Background By 1918 over a dozen nations or national groups had sent forces into Russia to fight the Bolshevik government, including the United States, Great Britain, France, Italy, Japan, Poland, Greece, Finland, Estonia, and Latvia.

force be used to smash all opposition. The Communist secret police soon began a campaign of terror. They executed tens of thousands of people thought to oppose Communist rule. Among the victims were Czar Nicholas, Czarina Alexandra, and all their children, who were shot to death in July 1918.

Economic policies. During these bloody years, the Communists made a bold effort to set up a Marxist society. One of their goals was to control all economic activity. Industry, banks, and foreign trade were **nationalized**—put under government control. Men under 50 were drafted for labor or for the army. The government also called upon women to work in factories and on construction projects. Strikes were forbidden. To feed the army and the people in the cities, soldiers seized food from the peasants.

These emergency measures, termed War Communism, only speeded Russia's decline. Commerce came to a standstill, and production fell disastrously. Many thousands of people died from hunger, cold, and disease.

By 1920 the Communists had gained the upper hand in the war. The Whites and Greens were crushed, and foreign troops soon left Russian soil. Yet the Communists could not stop to celebrate. The economic crisis was causing deep divisions even within the ruling group. Among peasants and factory workers, too, revolts were breaking out.

In March 1921, sailors at the Kronstadt (KROHN-shtaht) naval base near Petrograd rose in protest. It took weeks of bloody fighting to crush their revolt. Faced with such opposition, Lenin dropped the harsh tactics of War Communism and introduced the New Economic Policy, usually called NEP.

★ See below. Under NEP, Lenin temporarily put aside his plan for a state-controlled economy. Realizing how hard it was to build socialism in an undeveloped country like Russia, he let some small factories, businesses, and farms return to private ownership. The government kept control of major industries, banks, and means of communication.

Centralized government. Shortly after the Bolshevik takeover, the government was moved from Petrograd to the **Kremlin**, an old palace-fortress in Moscow. The new government was led by members of the Communist Party's Politburo (POHL-it-byoo-roh), or "political office." These men took drastic steps to protect the unity of the Party. Those who disagreed with them were thrown out of the Party and often imprisoned. All other political parties were banned.

The Politburo was backed by about half a million loyal Communist Party members, who made up less than one percent of the population. Almost all had been industrial workers. Members were watched carefully and were expected to show complete devotion to the Party.

In theory, the members of the Party elected leaders to represent their views. In practice, however, all decisions were made at the top, just as they had been in the days of the czar. Moreover, the Party leaders ran not just the government but also trade unions, youth leagues, and other organizations.

Sec. Rev. ques. 4

A recruitment poster for the Soviet Red Army asks "Have you volunteered yet?"

651

★ ENRICHMENT. Have students summarize the threats to power faced by the Bolsheviks after their take-over of Russia, and tell how they dealt with each. (Opposition of Whites and Greens; foreign assistance to Whites; internal revolts). *(Comprehension)* *Summarizing*

Background Once the chief support of the Bolshevik Revolution, sailors at Kronstadt demanded a representative assembly and free trade.

● RETEACHING. Have students review "Centralized government" (pp. 651–652) and describe the ways the Communist Party controlled Soviet society. (Government led by Party members; all other political parties banned; party leaders ran trade unions, youth leagues, women's groups, professional and cultural organizations.) *(Comprehension)* *Observing for Detail*

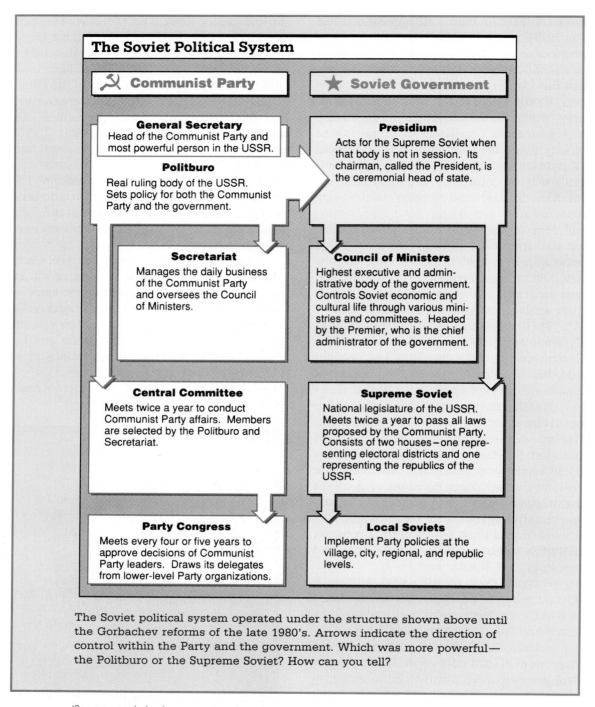

The Soviet Political System

☭ Communist Party

General Secretary
Head of the Communist Party and most powerful person in the USSR.

Politburo
Real ruling body of the USSR. Sets policy for both the Communist Party and the government.

Secretariat
Manages the daily business of the Communist Party and oversees the Council of Ministers.

Central Committee
Meets twice a year to conduct Communist Party affairs. Members are selected by the Politburo and Secretariat.

Party Congress
Meets every four or five years to approve decisions of Communist Party leaders. Draws its delegates from lower-level Party organizations.

★ Soviet Government

Presidium
Acts for the Supreme Soviet when that body is not in session. Its chairman, called the President, is the ceremonial head of state.

Council of Ministers
Highest executive and administrative body of the government. Controls Soviet economic and cultural life through various ministries and committees. Headed by the Premier, who is the chief administrator of the government.

Supreme Soviet
National legislature of the USSR. Meets twice a year to pass all laws proposed by the Communist Party. Consists of two houses—one representing electoral districts and one representing the republics of the USSR.

Local Soviets
Implement Party policies at the village, city, regional, and republic levels.

The Soviet political system operated under the structure shown above until the Gorbachev reforms of the late 1980's. Arrows indicate the direction of control within the Party and the government. Which was more powerful— the Politburo or the Supreme Soviet? How can you tell?

(See answers below.)

Though separate in organization, the state and the Communist Party were closely linked. (See the chart on this page.) Lenin made the soviets part of the government structure. Local government was run by soviets that were elected locally but guided by the Party. Above them were soviets at the district, regional, and republic level. The highest government authority in the country was called the Supreme Soviet. Its Council of Ministers, staffed with top Party members, formed the executive branch of the government.

652

Chart answers: The Politburo was more powerful than the Supreme Soviet. The arrows show that power flowed from the Politburo to the Presidium and from there to the Supreme Soviet.

Linking Past and Present. The political structure of the Soviet Union had undergone some change in 1990 as a result of Mikhail Gorbachev's reforms, but with the collapse of the Communist Party in 1991 the entire structure disappeared. You may want to have students look ahead and read about the disintegration of the Soviet Union and its Communist system in Chapter 35.

The Soviet Union. The many different nationalities within Russia had always been an obstacle to national unity, and the czars had tried to impose Russian culture on these peoples. The Communists tried a new approach in 1922, by forming the Union of Soviet Socialist Republics (called the USSR or Soviet Union, for short). Each of the 15 republics in the USSR represented a major nationality, such as the Georgians, Ukrainians, or Uzbeks (map, page 658). The republics had identical constitutions and all were controlled by the Communist Party. Smaller nationalities were given limited self-rule within the republics. In this way, the Communists paid lip service to the idea of self-determination without giving up any real power.

Religious persecution. From the beginning, the Communist Party opposed the Russian Orthodox Church and all other organized religions. According to Marxist teachings, religion was a tool that the ruling class used to exploit the workers. The Communist Party also saw the Russian Orthodox Church as a rival for the loyalties of the Russian people.

Sec. Rev. ques. 5

The Russian Orthodox Church and other religious groups suffered greatly under Communist rule. One of the first acts of the Bolsheviks was to seize Church land and property. Many of the clergy were jailed; others were simply kept from earning a living. Church schools were closed and state schools taught that God did not exist.

Propaganda. The Party kept its grip on the country by controlling information. To avoid unfavorable comparison with Western countries, Lenin deepened the isolation that had cut off Russia from the outside world since the start of World War I. The Party also used strict censorship to silence its critics at home.

The government then bombarded the public with its own ideology—set of beliefs. That ideology was Marxism-Leninism, a mixture of Marxism and Lenin's ideas on the role of the Party in building socialism. Lenin tried to give the Soviet people a faith in the Party and their nation. He taught them that the Soviet Union would lead the world away from the evils of capitalism and toward a bright socialist future.

● See below.

A Call for Revolt

Lenin hoped that Communist revolutions would soon break out around the world. He sent out a call for revolution to all who blamed their governments or employers for poverty, suffering, or injustice. In countries where there was disorder or widespread poverty, people began to listen. Communist parties sprang up in many Western countries as well as in India, China, Egypt, and Turkey.

In 1919 Lenin formed an organization to bring together these parties and to use them as a tool of Soviet foreign policy. This organization was the Communist Third International, often called the Comintern. The goal of world revolution, however, soon became secondary to that of strengthening Soviet Russia.

See Sec. 2 Closing the Lesson, p. T643B.

⧗ Timetable
Forming the Soviet State

1904–1905	Russia's defeat by Japan sparks revolt; Czar Nicholas II issues October Manifesto, establishing the Duma (parliament).
1914	Russia enters World War I.
1917	March Revolution forces czar to abdicate.
1917	Bolsheviks overthrow Provisional Government.
1918	Russia signs peace treaty (Brest-Litovsk) with Germany.
1920	Bolsheviks triumph in Russian civil war.
1921	New Economic Policy begins.
1922	Union of Soviet Socialist Republics is formed.

653

● REINFORCEMENT. Have students explain how the following is true: *The Communists paid lip service to the idea of self-determination without giving up any real power.* (Republics representing the major nationalities were created, but all had identical constitutions and were controlled by the Communist Party.) (Comprehension) *Observing for Detail*

Cultural History In June 1988 the Soviet Union celebrated the country's 1000th year of Christianity. Membership of the Russian Orthodox Church far outnumbered that of the Communist Party.

● ENRICHMENT. Have students write paragraphs suggesting why the Soviet system provided for a national legislature in which members voted on laws, even though the legislature held no actual power. (To provide the appearance of "democracy.") (Synthesis) *Hypothesizing*

3 The Soviet Union Under Stalin

Objectives

Focus Questions

★ ■ How did Stalin take power and make radical changes in the Soviet Union? *(pages 654–657)*

● ■ What methods did Stalin use to terrorize and intimidate the Soviet people? *(pages 657–659)*

Terms to Know

Five-Year Plan   gulag
quota   Great Purge
collective farm   totalitarian state

★ Note strategies for first objective on this page and p. 657.

Sec. Rev. ques. 2

Among those associated with Lenin in creating the Soviet state, the two men who stood out as leaders were Leon Trotsky and Joseph Stalin. When Lenin died in January 1924 after a series of strokes, these two men became bitter rivals for command of the Communist Party. The outcome of the power struggle would determine the future course of the **654** Soviet Union.

Stalin and Trotsky

Leon Trotsky was a widely traveled journalist, a forceful speaker, and a skilled organizer. Trotsky's planning was behind both the Bolshevik seizure of power in November 1917 and the strict discipline of the Red Army.

Joseph Stalin was of a rougher mold. A shoemaker's son, he was born in the province of Georgia, south of the Caucasus Mountains. When Lenin and Trotsky were living safely abroad, he stayed in Russia. His revolutionary activities earned him years in prison and a long exile in Siberia.

In 1922 Stalin was made general secretary of the Communist Party. Lenin soon came to distrust Stalin, and he wanted Trotsky, not Stalin, to succeed him as head of the Party. About a year before his death in 1924, Lenin wrote: "Comrade Stalin has concentrated boundless power in his hands, and I am not certain he can always use this power with sufficient caution."

Stalin used his position as general secretary to gain control of the Party. He began to give his own supporters important jobs at all levels of the Party. Trotsky and his supporters were driven out of the Party and, eventually, out of the Soviet Union.

In 1929, on his fiftieth birthday, Stalin was hailed as Lenin's successor and as the "great wise father" of the peoples of the Soviet Union. Stalin encouraged a "cult of personality" to grow up around him, in which he was glorified as an almost superhuman hero. Those who disagreed with him were branded as traitors. Stalin's rivals either gave in to his plans or were wiped out.

Stalin's Five-Year Plans

Stalin made great changes in the Soviet economy. In place of the New Economic Policy's mixture of free enterprise and state control, he began a program of rapid industrialization through total state control. In 1931 Stalin declared: "We are 50 or 100 years behind the advanced countries. We must make good this distance in 10 years or they will crush us."

Stalin set up a series of **Five-Year Plans** to direct industrialization. These plans set ambitious **quotas**—numerical goals—for the production of steel, coal, oil, and hydroelectric power, as well as for consumer goods. The planners also worked out detailed schedules for production and distribution of these goods. All economic activity, including agriculture, was now under state management.

The first and most drastic Five-Year Plan began in 1928 with the goal of increasing industrial output by 250 percent before 1933. To reach this target, the nation had to cut down on the production of consumer goods. For consumers, therefore, the Five-Year Plan meant shortages, delays, and poor service. The standard of living dropped sharply.

The attempt to make such widespread changes created staggering problems. Because the government concentrated on quantity and not quality, many shoddy goods were produced. Working conditions were grim. Workers received little pay, were poorly fed, and lived in overcrowded housing. The government could force workers to take any job for which they were needed, anywhere in the country. The system was intended to mold workers to obey "the single will of the leaders of the labor process."

Sec. Rev. ques. 3

The Communist Party tried to raise morale through "socialist competition." It rewarded workers who produced more than their fellow workers and held victory celebrations when production quotas were met. Young people were encouraged to believe that they were building a beautiful new world. Everyone was expected to make heroic sacrifices for the country, much as in wartime.

The government even tried to use literature and the arts to rally the workers. Writers, painters, and musicians were expected to produce works that backed government policies, a practice known as "socialist realism." These works were generally more socialist than realistic. Novelists described the joys of working for the state in simple tales: Boy

Joseph Stalin (front left) ruled the Soviet Union from 1929 until his death in 1953. Stalin used his dictatorial powers to attempt large-scale transformations of Soviet agriculture and industry.

655

Ⓕ See
below.

Historic Places

The Kremlin

Just as the White House stands for the American presidency, the Kremlin became a symbol of the Soviet government. American scholars and officials who study Russian and Soviet politics are often called "Kremlinologists." But what *is* the Kremlin?

During the Middle Ages, most Russian towns had central fortresses where people could take refuge in time of war. These fortresses were known as kremlins. Surrounded by wooden walls, kremlins were usually built near a river crossing or another strategic point.

Around 1150, one of Moscow's early princes built a kremlin beside the Moscow River, using logs from the nearby forest. Later princes and grand dukes

---

meets girl, and their love raises their factory's output to new heights. Painters, using a bold and direct style, showed people working cheerfully in fields or factories.

Collectivization of Agriculture

The problems caused by industrialization were enormous, but they paled in comparison with the chaos in the countryside. Stalin's demand for greater farm output turned into a war against his own people, in which millions died.

Higher food production was a big part of Stalin's plans for industrialization. By exporting food, the government could help pay for new factories. More food would also be needed to feed factory workers. Yet Stalin found that the peasants were not willing to produce the harvests required under the first Five-Year Plan. With the shops empty of goods, they had no reason to earn extra money. Stalin was determined, however, not

Sec. Rev.
ques. 4

656

Ⓕ **FEATURE ACTIVITY. Ask: How might the collapse of the Soviet Union affect the use of the Kremlin as a symbol?** (Since the Russian government has taken over the Kremlin, it will probably again become a symbol of Russia rather than of the Soviet Union.) *(Application)* **Synthesizing Information** rebuilt and enlarged Moscow's Kremlin. The massive brick wall that surrounds the Kremlin today was completed about 1500, during the reign of Ivan the Great. The domes of the buildings inside rise above the wall, as do the turrets of 20 towers. From near the back gate, a hidden passage runs down to the river.

Within the walls stand churches, palaces, museums, and government offices. While much of the Kremlin is off-limits to visitors, many buildings are open to the public. Some of Russia's finest cathedrals are here, including the Cathedral of the Assumption, where the czars were crowned, and St. Michael's Cathedral, where they were buried. Nearby is the Armory, now a museum housing the crowns, jewels, and gilded coaches of the czars. At the foot of Ivan the Great's Belfry, tourists can gaze at the Czar Bell (picture), the biggest bell in the world, cast in 1733. Equally impressive is the Czar Cannon, made in 1586.

The newest building in the Kremlin is the Palace of Congresses, built in 1961 as a site for Communist Party gatherings. The Soviet Communist Party collapsed in 1991, as did the Soviet government, but this building and the rest of the Kremlin still serve as a symbolic link between present-day Russia and its historic past.

to let the peasants stand in the way of his plan. He decided to bring agriculture forcibly under state control.

Stalin's plan called for **collective farms**, the combining of many small farms into large units. The collectives were expected to use modern machinery and scientific farming methods to produce more food than ever before. The Soviet peasants, however, had a long memory of serfdom, and they saw collectivization as the loss of their freedom. They resisted giving up their lands.

In the winter of 1929–1930, Stalin used armed force to collectivize the peasants' farms. Arguing that anyone "who is against collectivization is against the Soviet regime," he brought terror to much of the nation. The prime target was the kulaks, the more prosperous farmers. Stalin saw the kulaks as enemies of socialism, and he told Party workers to "liquidate the kulaks as a class." Thousands were shot or sent to **gulags** (GOO-lahgz)—forced-labor camps. Many of the remaining peasants killed their horses, cows, and pigs rather than turn them over to the collective.

Collectivization had terrible consequences for years to come. Farming output plummeted. The loss of livestock caused severe shortages of meat, dairy products, leather goods, and fertilizer. In 1932–1933 a severe famine hit many parts of the Soviet Union. Although his own people were starving, Stalin went on selling food abroad. As many as 10 million people died as a result of collectivization.

Sec. Rev. ques. 4, cont.

By the mid-1930's collective farms, each made up of hundreds of households, were the rule in the Soviet Union. Once collectivization had been completed, Stalin made one concession to the peasants. He allowed them to keep small plots of land for their private use. Food grown on these plots could be sold on the open market for whatever price it would bring. With this incentive, peasants worked much harder on these private plots. The tiny, privately held plots became the Soviet Union's most productive farmlands.

★ See below, left.

Political Terror

● Note strategies for second objective on this page and p. 659.

By 1930 Stalin's power was being threatened both inside and outside the Party. Many people blamed Stalin for the millions of lives lost in industrialization and collectivization. Criticisms came even from his own family. His wife, Nadezhda Alliluyeva (ah-lee-loo-YEH-vuh), urged her husband to moderate his policies. In 1932 she died, an apparent suicide.

Communist Party members voiced their complaints at the Party Congress of 1934. **657**

★ ENRICHMENT. Have students write an argument supporting this statement: *Economic systems that allow private ownership and encourage competition are more productive than those which do not.* Students should use examples from the text description of the Soviet economy to support their explanation. *(Synthesis) Drawing Conclusions*

● RETEACHING. Have students explain why Stalin initiated a campaign of political terror, identify the victims, and describe the methods used. (Stalin felt threatened by those who blamed him for the deaths of millions; some called for his resignation. His victims included real and imagined enemies in the Party and society, scientists, intellectuals, workers, farmers. He used interrogation and murder to intimidate people.) *(Comprehension) Observing for Detail*

The Soviet Union in 1939

The Soviet Union was the world's largest country, covering more than half of Europe and nearly two fifths of Asia. Under the Soviet system, the nation became a union of "republics," each one named for its major nationality group. Which of the Soviet republics was largest? What three republics located on the Baltic Sea did the Soviet Union annex in 1940?

Map Answer: (1) Russia. (2) Lithuania, Latvia, and Estonia.

They said that Stalin had gone too far. Some members even suggested that he step down in favor of the Party secretary in Leningrad, Sergei Kirov (KEE-rawf).

Stalin struck back at his critics with a campaign of terror. In December 1934, Kirov was murdered. Although Stalin had probably ordered the killing himself, he said that it was part of a plot against the Soviet leadership. Stalin used this claim to justify a purge, or removal, of real and imagined enemies in the Party and in the population at large.

Between 1935 and 1939, the period that became known as the **Great Purge**, some of the most important Communists were put on trial. They were forced to make public confessions of crimes that they could not possibly

have committed; then they were executed. In this fashion Stalin got rid of both the top Party members who had tried to promote Kirov and the "old Bolsheviks" who had joined the Party before 1917. In 1940, assassins sent by Stalin murdered Trotsky, who was in exile in Mexico. The Party members spared by the Purge were obedient bureaucrats who would not challenge Stalin.

Stalin used similar methods to intimidate the Soviet people as a whole. He launched attacks against scientists, intellectuals, workers, collective farmers, and leaders of non-Russian nationalist movements. The terror wiped out Stalin's supporters as well as his opponents, productive citizens as well as enemies of the state.

658

Background It has been estimated that approximately 8 million people were arrested and 800,000 executed during the Great Purge. Those arrested but not killed were sentenced to prison camps.

Contemporary History Have students find out how the three Baltic states won independence from the Soviet Union in 1991.

Like other workers, the secret police had quotas to fill. Whenever a new wave of arrests was due, the streets of Moscow and other cities emptied, and men and women fearfully awaited the midnight call of the police. Those arrested were subjected to days and nights of questioning, often under torture. The interrogations lasted until the prisoners—whether innocent or not—signed their "confessions."

Under Stalin, every person's total submission to the new order was required. The Soviet Union became a **totalitarian state**—a state in which the government controls every aspect of the lives of its citizens. Art, religion, and family relationships concerned the government as much as political activities. Free expression in any area could be punished as a crime against the state.

● See below, right.

See Sec. 3 *Closing the Lesson*, p. T643C.

Section Review

Answers to Section Review questions are in brackets on pages indicated.

1. **Define or identify:** Five-Year Plan, quota, collective farm, gulag, Great Purge, totalitarian state. (pp. 655, 657, 658, 659)
2. Who were the rivals for Soviet leadership when Lenin died? (p. 654)
3. How did the Five-Year Plans affect private business, consumers, and workers? (p. 655)
4. Why did Stalin collectivize Soviet agriculture? What effects did collectivization have on the economy? (pp. 656–657)
5. **Critical thinking:** How did the state created by Lenin and Stalin differ from that predicted by Karl Marx? (See answer below.)

5. Students might suggest that the state became increasingly repressive and showed no signs of "withering away," as Marx had predicted.

Chapter 32   Summary and Timeline

1. By the late 1800's, the czarist regime had lost touch with changes within Russia. Popular unrest, already widespread, only worsened under a government industrialization program. Weakened by wartime defeats, the regime finally collapsed in the March Revolution in 1917. By the end of the year, its democratic successor had fallen to Marxist revolutionaries known as Bolsheviks.

2. Lenin, the Bolshevik leader, kept the Bolsheviks in power despite challenges from outside and inside Russia. He also laid the foundation of a new state, the Union of Soviet Socialist Republics. Within the USSR, Lenin made the Communist Party the supreme authority.

3. Stalin succeeded Lenin in 1924. Determined to bring about rapid modernization, he ruthlessly enforced policies of industrialization and collectivization. Years of purges killed millions and made sure that Stalin would have no rivals for power.

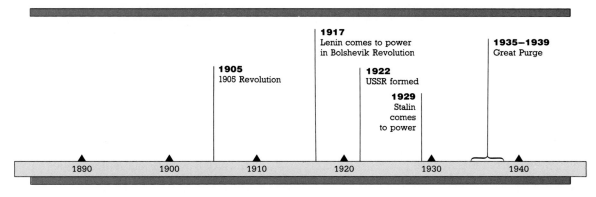

1917
Lenin comes to power
in Bolshevik Revolution

1935–1939
Great Purge

1905
1905 Revolution

1922
USSR formed

1929
Stalin comes to power

1890   1900   1910   1920   1930   1940

659

● REINFORCEMENT. Have students compare the causes and effects of the Great Purge with those of France's Reign of Terror during the French Revolution (pp. 444–445). Students should explain how the two periods were similar and different. *(Synthesis) Comparing Historical Developments*

● ENRICHMENT. Have students read and report on *Animal Farm* by George Orwell (tells the story of the Soviet revolution and the Stalinist period in parable form) or *Darkness at Noon* by Arthur Koestler (deals with the tactics of the police state). *(Application) Linking History and Literature*

CHAPTER 32 REVIEW

See p. T643C for answers to Chapter Review.

Vocabulary Review

1. Choose the term that best completes each sentence.
   a. Following the Communist takeover, the Soviet government moved to the [Bolshevik, Kremlin] in Moscow.
   b. The leaders of the Soviet Union took steps to [nationalize, purge] all industry, banks, and foreign trade in their country.
   c. In a [totalitarian state, gulag], the government controls every aspect of the lives of its citizens.
   d. During the [Great Purge, October Manifesto], many Bolsheviks were tried and put to death for crimes against the state.
2. Define the terms in the following pairs.
   a. March Revolution; Bolshevik Revolution
   b. quota; collective farm
   c. Treaty of Brest-Litovsk; Russian civil war
   d. ideology; Marxism-Leninism

People to Identify

Match each of the following people with the correct description: *Alexander Kerensky, Lenin, Nicholas II, Rasputin, Joseph Stalin, Leon Trotsky.*
   1. last czar of Russia
   2. "holy man" who influenced Alexandra
   3. head of the Provisional Government
   4. Communist rival assassinated on Stalin's order
   5. Bolshevik leader who proclaimed the "dictatorship of the proletariat"
   6. brutal Party chief whose purges resulted in millions of deaths

Places to Know

Match the letters on this map of the Soviet Union and bordering nations with the places listed below. You may want to refer to the map on page 658.
   1. Moscow   3. Leningrad
   2. Black Sea   4. Finland

Recalling the Facts

1. Why did industrialization in Russia lead to unrest?
2. What events of 1905 showed the weakness of Czar Nicholas's regime?
3. What were the differences between the three forms of government offered to the Russian people in 1917?
4. What measures were begun under War Communism? Why was it replaced by the New Economic Policy?
5. Did the Communists allow for independent republics within the newly formed Union of Soviet Socialist Republics? Explain your answer.

660

6. How did the Communists persecute religious groups?
7. What problems did Stalin's first Five-Year Plan create for the Russian people?
8. How did Stalin collectivize peasant farms? What were the results of his collectivization policy?
9. How did Stalin respond to criticisms of his regime?

Critical Thinking Skills

1. **Comparing.** In what ways was the Communist government similar to the czarist government? How was it different? *(Comp.)*

✔ 2. **Hypothesizing.** Russia's ill-equipped army suffered a humiliating defeat in World War I. Suppose Czar Nicholas II had managed the war effort more successfully and Russia had emerged victorious. Do you think the people would have still revolted in 1917 or would opposition to the czarist government have died out? Explain. *(Syn.)*

✔ 3. **Analyzing a quotation.** Lenin once expressed concern about Stalin's rule, noting that Stalin had "concentrated boundless power in his hands, and I am not certain he can always use this power with sufficient caution." Were Lenin's fears justified? Explain. *(Syn.)*

4. **Preparing an oral report.** Prepare a brief oral report on the treatment of the Russian Orthodox Church and other religious groups in the Soviet Union. How did they fare under Communist rule? Check the *Readers' Guide to Periodical Literature* to find sources of information. *(App.)*

Thinking About Geography

Making a chart. Using an atlas, locate each of the republics that were part of the Soviet Union from 1940 to 1991. Then make a chart, showing in separate columns the name of the republic, its capital city, its area, and its major nationality group. Also include a column titled "Present political status"; use almanacs or other current sources to find information for that column. *(App.)*

✔ A checkmark identifies questions and exercises calling for the three higher-order levels of thinking at the top of the Bloom taxonomy: Analysis, Synthesis, and Evaluation.

Enrichment: Primary Sources

Sergei Witte was Czar Nicholas's most capable minister. Unlike the czar, Witte realized that the Russian economy had to be modernized. Witte also had a keen sense of the weaknesses of czarist rule. In the following adapted excerpt from *The Memoirs of Count Witte*, he describes the czar's shortcomings.

66 His Majesty is afflicted with a strange nearsightedness, as far as time and space are concerned. He experiences fear only when the storm is actually upon him, but as soon as the immediate danger is over, his fear vanishes. Thus, even after the granting of the constitution, Nicholas considered himself an autocratic ruler in a sense which might be expressed as follows: "I do what I wish, and what I wish is good; if people do not see it, it is because they are plain mortals, while I am God's anointed."

The czar was made to believe that the people as a whole stood firmly with him. That was also Her Majesty's conviction. On one occasion, Prince Mirski remarked that in Russia everybody was against the existing regime. To this the czarina sharply replied that only the intellectuals were against the czar and his government, but that the people always had been and always would be for the czar. 99

1. Why did Nicholas believe that what he wished was good?
2. Who did the czar and czarina believe would always support them? Why did they believe this?
3. **Critical thinking:** Why did Sergei Witte call Nicholas nearsighted? *(Comp.)*

The World Between the Wars   1918–1939
(pp. 662–683)

Chapter Preview

Section 1 traces the rise to power of Mussolini in Italy and Hitler in Germany, examines the reasons for fascism's appeal in those countries, and explains the failure of democratic government in Eastern Europe. Section 2 describes the prosperity enjoyed by the United States after World War I, examines the causes and effects of the Great Depression, and identifies problems faced by Western democracies. In Section 3, efforts to modernize by the leaders of nations in Asia and the Middle East are described.

Bibliography

See the *Teacher's Management and Planning Guide* for additional listings. Starred titles are for both students and teachers.

*Allen, Frederick Lewis. *Only Yesterday.* Harper and Row. Highly readable account of the 1920's.

Friedrich, Otto. *Before the Deluge.* Harper and Row. The period before the rise of Nazism.

Galbraith, John Kenneth. *The Great Crash, 1929.* Avon. Combines economic study with a lively portrait of an era.

*Garraty, John A. *The Great Depression.* Harcourt Brace Jovanovich. A world-wide study.

Salisbury, Harrison K. *The Long March: The Untold Story.* Harper and Row. The 1934 march that forged Chinese communism.

Section Lesson Plans

SECTION 1   (pp. 663–670)
Dictatorships in Europe

Objectives

After completing this section, students will be able to:
1. Describe how fascism emerged in Italy and Germany.
2. Explain why democracy failed in Eastern Europe and in Spain.

Introducing the Lesson

Remind students that after World War I economic, political, and social crises plagued Europe. Some nations responded to the crises by giving their support to dictators.

Then ask: *(a) What types of economic problems might Europe have faced after World War I?* (Inflation, depression, unemployment, destruction of property and fields, trade disagreements.)

(b) What political conflicts might have arisen during this period? (Problems brought on by the Treaty of Versailles, unresolved nationalism, militarism, and imperialism.)

(c) Why might some societies have accepted the leadership of dictators as one way to solve their problems? (Answers will vary. Sometimes authoritarian leaders appear able to restore order, stability, and security.)

Developing the Lesson:
Analyzing Information

Have students compare Italian fascism and Nazism with Herbert Spencer's concept of Social Darwinism (p. 544) and the growth of extreme nationalism (p. 543). Then have students explain how the 19th-century ideas influenced the development of Fascist thought. (Italian fascism and Nazism reflected the Social Darwinist argument that the principal of natural selection worked in the social and economic world; that only the fittest of a species survives; and that certain groups of people, "superior races," were intended by nature to dominate "lesser peoples." Fascism was also influenced by extreme nationalism which subordinated democratic rights to the state; glorified war and military might; an accepted racism.) *(Comprehension)*

Developing the Lesson:
Forming a Hypothesis

Have students develop a hypothesis explaining the rise of authoritarian systems in Europe and totalitarianism in Russia during the period after World War I. Students should consider postwar economic, social, and political conditions. (Answers will vary. When European democracies seemed unable to solve many economic and social problems, people turned to authoritarian leaders to establish order. In Russia, the Communists saw totalitarian control as the only way to ensure their power.) *(Synthesis)*

Closing the Lesson:
Analyzing Information

Have students work in groups to discuss the following: *Why does the lack of democratic traditions make it more difficult for democracy to take root? How can societies without a democratic tradition increase their chances for a successful democracy?* Students should refer to the text discussion of failed democracies in Eastern Europe. *(Synthesis)*

See *Section Review* questions, p. 670.

SECTION 2   (pp. 670–675)
The Western Democracies

Objectives

After completing this section, students will be able to:
1. Explain what happened to the American economy in the 1920's.
2. Discuss the problems faced by European democracies after World War I.

Introducing the Lesson

Remind students that during the post-World War I period the Western democracies faced problems very similar to those encountered by Italy, Germany, the Eastern European nations, and Spain. Unlike those nations, however, Britain, France, and the United States did not replace democracy with authoritarian systems.

Then ask: *(a) What might account for the ability of Western democracies to preserve their government systems during times of economic and social turmoil?* (Answers will vary. The Western democracies had a longer history of national unity and stronger democratic traditions.)

(b) What might account for the ability of democratic institutions to survive difficult times in some nations, but fail in others? (Answers will vary. Institutions that have survived previous crises inspire confidence. Institutions that are untried or judged too weak to survive may be abandoned for a leader who seems able to restore order.)

(c) Are the United States democratic institutions strong enough to survive any threat, or are they vulnerable to social, economic, or political unrest? (Answers will vary.)

Developing the Lesson:
Understanding Cause and Effect

Have students make a cause-and-effect chart illustrating the relationships between the following: use of credit, inability to pay debts, production cutbacks; buying stock on credit, the "crash"; unemployment; the Great Depression. (Increased use of credit led to indebtedness that people could not repay. When people could not afford to buy goods, factories cut production. Many people bought stock on credit. After an economic boom, stock prices began to fall and panicky investors sold their stock causing a stock market crash. Because people who had lost their money could not afford new goods, production was cut, workers were laid off, and the Great Depression began.) *(Comprehension)*

Developing the Lesson:
Organizing Information

Have students make a chart describing each *Country,* its *Problems,* and the *Attempted Solutions* discussed in this section. (*United States:* the Great Depression was met with a program of economic reform called the New Deal. *Great Britain:* attempts to solve economic problems such as decreased exports and industry, and unemployment were unsuccessful. Britain also faced colonial conflict which was resolved by establishing the Commonwealth of Nations. *Ireland:* revolt over British rule was answered by the division of Ireland. *France:* economic problems caused by World War I led to political unrest, the formation of the Popular Front, and the election of a Socialist government.) *(Comprehension)*

Closing the Lesson: Solving Problems

Have students work in groups to suggest ways postwar problems might have been solved by international cooperation. (Answers will vary. Nations might have worked together for better coordination of markets, the loan of capital or the supplying of food, and the sharing of technology.) *(Synthesis)*

See *Section Review* questions, p. 675.

SECTION 3 (pp. 676–681)
Unrest in Asia and the Middle East

Objectives

After completing this section, students will be able to:
1. Identify the groups that struggled for control of China.
2. Explain why Japan adopted imperialist policies.
3. Describe how nationalism affected Middle Eastern nations.

Introducing the Lesson

Remind students that after the Industrial Revolution modernization was an important factor in the strength of a nation. Only industrialized nations could resist foreign control and compete in world affairs.

Then ask: *(a) After the Industrial Revolution, what did a policy of "modernization" mean?* (Modernization meant the development of industry, the expansion of communication and transportation systems, and the growth of world markets.)

(b) Why did the efforts of many nations to modernize include the adoption of Western ways? (Answers will vary. The Industrial Revolutions began in the West, and European nations and the United States represented the strongest powers. Some leaders, who believed traditional ways of life hindered modernization, might have felt that adopting Western customs was necessary and desirable.)

(c) Was the abandonment of traditional customs and the acceptance of Western clothing styles and social behavior necessary for the modernization of a nation? (Answers will vary.)

Developing the Lesson: Summarizing Information

Have students summarize actions taken by the Chinese and Japanese after World War I to establish internal order, stable government, and a strong economy. (In China, powerful warlords were defeated by the Nationalists, Soviet advisers were forced from China, and Chinese Communists were purged from the Kuomintang. Banking and trading systems were improved, and communication and transportation systems modernized. Japan strengthened its democracy and cooperated

with Western powers to reduce the risk of war in the Pacific. In 1931, Japan took control of Manchuria.) *(Comprehension)*

Developing the Lesson: Translating Information into Another Form

Have students make a chart comparing the ways leaders in Turkey and Persia modernized their countries. (*Turkey:* set up a one-party government; reduced the role of Islam; modernized social customs; provided government funds for industrialization. *Persia:* changed country's name to Iran; modernized the economy; brought in Western laws and customs.) *(Comprehension)*

Closing the Lesson: Drawing Inferences

Have students write an essay explaining why modernization was important for countries in Asia and the Middle East, and describing the advantages and disadvantages of modernization for Asian and Middle Eastern societies. Students should consider the impact of modernization on the economy, government, and traditions of the people involved. *(Comprehension)*

See *Section Review* questions, p. 681.

Chapter 33 Review Answers
(pp. 682–683)

Vocabulary Review

1. Temporary alliance.
2. Chinese protest of 1919 that began when university students and teachers demanded an end to foreign interference, limits on the power of the warlords, and extended democracy.
3. National Socialist German Workers Party, led by Adolf Hitler.
4. Franklin D. Roosevelt's program of economic reform and recovery from the Great Depression.
5. Conflict lasting from 1936 to 1939 in which the republican government of Spain fought against Francisco Franco's Falangists for control of that country.

People to Identify

1. Charles Lindbergh 2. Mao Zedong 3. Thomas Masaryk 4. Eamon De Valera 5. Franklin D. Roosevelt 6. Virginia Woolf

Places to Know

1. Northern Ireland 2. Bavaria 3. Manchukuo
4. Dublin 5. Shandong Peninsula 6. Saudi Arabia
7. Iran 8. Nanjing 9. Ruhr River

Recalling the Facts

1. Business owners, government officials, land-owners, the middle class, Italian soldiers, and war veterans supported Mussolini. Business owners, government officials, landowners, and the middle class wanted a strong government that would end strikes and curb working-class political power. Mussolini's dream of a new Italian empire appealed to nationalists and army officers, and veterans were drawn by the military-style organization of the new party. Veterans, many of whom were unemployed and poor, felt that Italy had forgotten their wartime sacrifices.

2. The Communists wanted to set up a state patterned after the new government in Soviet Russia. Military leaders, large landowners, and industrialists feared that the government would take over industry and break up large estates. Nationalists and militarists wanted to break the Treaty of Versailles, rebuild the German army, and restore Germany to a position of power in world affairs. They believed that these goals could be met if the Weimar Republic were destroyed.

3. Eastern Europe did not have a tradition of political democracy. When the new governments could not solve problems quickly, people blamed democracy. Democracy eventually gave way to authoritarianism.

4. Many Americans built up heavy debts through credit purchases. When they could not pay their debts, they stopped buying goods. Factories had to cut back production, and unemployment rose. In the 1920's it was possible for investors to pay a fraction of stock prices and use credit for the rest. Many Americans from all income groups were therefore lured into the stock market. As a result, stock prices rose.

5. The health of Britain's economy depended on foreign trade. However, Britain had lost many of its merchant ships in World War I and had lost markets to other trading nations. As exports dropped, British industry, mining, and shipbuilding declined, and unemployment soared.

6. Disputes among major parties stalled economic recovery after World War I. Unhappy with the government, many French voters turned either to the Communists or to one of the Fascist parties. Fear of fascism led a number of leftist political parties to unite to form the Popular Front.

7. Chiang lost support because he failed to make social reforms.

8. Japan's military leaders could now argue that expansion would restore prosperity.

9. To separate church and state, Kemal abolished religious courts, created a new legal system based on European law, and replaced religious schools with state-run schools. Kemal also took steps toward modernization that included extended political rights to women, changes in marital laws, and changes in dress. To develop the economy, Kemal provided government funding for education and worked to boost trade with the West. Unlike Kemal and Reza Shah, Ibn Saud had no wish to modernize his country.

10. The Balfour Declaration stated Britain's support of "the establishment in Palestine of a national homeland for Jewish people." The Arabs of Palestine did not wish to live as a minority in a Jewish state.

Critical Thinking Skills

1. 13 percent. It decreased steadily.

2. Answers will vary.

3. (a) Badly in need of money, American business leaders withdrew the capital they had invested in Europe. (b) Many countries raised tariffs on imports in order to protect their own industries.

4. Students might suggest that in periods of crisis, people often look to a person who appears to be a strong leader who will take charge and solve the country's problems. In addition, movements like Nazism often place blame on those seen as outsiders and offer simple solutions to complex problems.

Thinking About Geography

1. Newfoundland became a province of Canada in 1949.

2. Essays will vary.

Enrichment: Primary Sources

1. He says the Fascists deny both the possibility of peace and its usefulness.

2. Answers may include the description of pacifism as "an act of cowardice" and the sentence "War alone brings up to its highest tension all human energy and puts the stamp of nobility upon the people who have the courage to meet it."

3. Students may cite this sentence: "The Fascist accepts life and loves it and conceives of life as a duty of struggle and conquest."

The World Between the Wars 1918–1939

See chapter timeline, p. 681.

Before You Read This Chapter

Are you required to take a course in American government before you graduate from high school? Does your school also offer a course in economics? In school, politics and economics are separate subjects. In the world outside school, however, they are often closely linked. As you read this chapter, watch for connections between economic and political events. How did economic problems in the 1920's and 1930's undermine democracy in some countries? How did the economic crisis called the Great Depression change the role of government in many countries?

The Geographic Setting

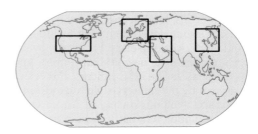

The Chapter Outline

1. Dictatorships in Europe
2. The Western Democracies
3. Unrest in Asia and the Middle East

Amid desperate economic troubles, fear of communism, and rapid social change, dictators came to power in Europe after World War I. In Germany, military spectacles like this one rallied support for Adolf Hitler's Nazi Party.

Vocabulary The word *fascist* comes from the Italian *fasces*, the word for an ancient Roman symbol of power and authority.

1 Dictatorships in Europe

Objectives

Focus Questions

★ ■ How did fascism emerge in Italy and Germany? *(pages 663–668)*

● ■ Why did democracy fail in Eastern Europe and in Spain? *(pages 668–669)*

Terms to Know

fascism   authoritarianism
Nazi Party   Spanish Civil War

★ Note strategies for first objective on this page and p. 667.

In the years after World War I, Europe was troubled by unemployment, inflation, and social unrest. Unhappiness over the peace settlements lingered, and many people feared the spread of Russian communism. Dictators took advantage of these conditions to seize power in many countries.

Fascist Italy

Postwar problems. Though Italy had been on the winning side in World War I, it seemed in some ways more like a defeated nation. Italy had suffered terrible casualties in the war, losing about one tenth of its young men. In addition, the peace settlement at Versailles gave Italy little of the German and Austrian territory.

Sec. Rev. ques. 2

After the war, there were food shortages, rising prices, unemployment, and business failures. Angered by the government's inaction, peasants seized lands from large estates and workers staged violent strikes. At the same time, Socialist and Communist political parties were gaining membership. The Bolshevik takeover in Russia (page 649) raised fears of a similar revolution in Italy.

Faced with these problems, many Italians turned to an ideology called **fascism**. Fascists stressed nationalism and placed the interests of the state above those of individuals. To strengthen the nation, fascists said, power must rest with a single strong leader and a small group of devoted party members. They claimed that political disagreements divided and weakened a nation.

Fascism was in part a reaction against the Communist victory in Russia. Fascists charged that communism stirred up class conflict and made people more loyal to their class than to their country.

The leading spokesperson for fascism in Italy was Benito Mussolini. Born in 1883, Mussolini was a Socialist for a time. He broke with the Socialists, however, when they opposed Italy's entry into World War I. In 1919 Mussolini and his followers organized the Fascist Party.

Mussolini drew support from a wide range of Italians. Business owners, government officials, and landowners wanted a strong government that would end strikes and curb working-class political power. For these same reasons, fascism also spread among Italy's middle class, including university students, shopkeepers, and professional people.

Italy's soldiers and war veterans were also attracted to fascism. Mussolini spoke of bringing back the glory and military strength of ancient Rome. His dream of a new Italian empire appealed to nationalists and army officers. Veterans, many of whom were unemployed and poor, felt that Italy had forgotten their sacrifices in the war. They liked the military-style organization of the new party: the Fascists wore black-shirted uniforms, carried weapons, and paraded in the streets.

The Fascists in power. By early 1922 the Fascist Party had more than 300,000 members and controlled several major Italian cities. In October 1922, Mussolini made his **663**

★ RETEACHING. Have students review pp. 663–667 and make a chart listing the causes of the rise of Italian and German fascism. (Italy: postwar economic problems, government inaction, social unrest, growth of Socialist and Communist parties. Germany: weak democratic government, defeat in World War I, effects of the Versailles Treaty, economic crises.) *(Comprehension)* **Comparing Information**

★ REINFORCEMENT. Have students outline the policies of Italian Fascists and German Nazis. (Italy: banned other parties; created secret police; imposed censorship, travel restrictions, and control of economy. Germany: banned unions and other political parties, conducted secret trials, persecuted enemies, made anti-Semitism official policy.) *(Comprehension)* **Observing for Detail**

Biography Mussolini was educated in a Catholic seminary and was expelled after stabbing a fellow student.

Italy's dictator, Benito Mussolini, is shown at the head of a military parade. Fascism appealed to people's sense of nationalism and glorified force and obedience to authority. The poster at left encourages Italians to increase grain harvests.

bid for power. Speaking at a giant rally of his followers, he said, "Either they will give us the government, or we shall take it by descending on Rome." A few days later, thousands of Fascists began a march on Rome. When key officials in the government, the army, and the police sided with the Fascists, King Victor Emmanuel III made Mussolini head of the Italian government.

Mussolini had often said that democracy was a weak and ineffective system. He set to work to establish a dictatorship in which the Fascist Party would have full control. He cracked down on all other parties, started a secret police force to spy on possible enemies, and had many of his opponents thrown into jail. The government also took over the press.

Mussolini's program to strengthen Italy included social and economic changes. To ensure a steady supply of soldiers, Mussolini made it hard for Italians to leave the country. He taxed single men, limited the number of jobs open to women, and encouraged Italian families to have more children.

The Fascists wanted Italy to become self-sufficient. Farmers were urged to use modern methods. To limit the power of workers and to control production, Mussolini reorganized the economy. All areas of production—farms, industries, transportation—were divided into 22 nationwide "syndicates," each organized like a corporation. Labor unions were banned, and each syndicate controlled wages, prices, and working hours in its own area.

Mussolini went to great lengths to win his people's enthusiastic loyalty. In the schools, children were taught to admire him as *Il Duce* (eel DOO-chay), meaning "the Leader," and to accept his ideas without question. University professors had to swear an oath of loyalty to the Fascist state. "Believe! Obey! Fight!" was the Fascist slogan. Government propaganda told the Italian people that the Fascists had done away with crime, poverty, and labor problems. Mussolini promised that his new Roman Empire would control the Mediterranean world.

Despite all this boasting, Mussolini and the Fascists never transformed Italy into a totalitarian state. Industrialists, landowners, the Catholic Church, and the army held on to much of their old influence.

The Rise of German Fascism

The Weimar Republic. Germany's defeat in World War I had disgraced the kaiser and left the country in shock. Early in November 1918, war-weary soldiers, sailors, and workers seized control of several German cities. They declared a republic, and Kaiser William II abdicated and fled to the Netherlands. A day later, Germany accepted the armistice (page 634).

An elected national assembly met in the city of Weimar (VY-mahr) in February 1919 and adopted a republican constitution. The new Germany, known as the Weimar Republic, was led by members of the Social Democratic Party. They were political moderates, eager for democracy to succeed.

The German people, however, had little experience with parliamentary democracy. Ruled by a kaiser since Germany's unification in 1871 (page 520), the Germans were used to strict rule. Some thought that democracy was a weak form of government unsuited to the German nation.

Extremists on both the left and the right shared a contempt for the Weimar government. On the left were the Communists, who wanted to set up a government like the one in Soviet Russia (page 649). In 1919, Communist uprisings broke out in several German cities. These uprisings failed, but they alarmed many Germans.

On the right, critics of the Weimar Republic included German nationalists, military leaders, large landowners, and industrialists. These groups disapproved of democracy and believed the Social Democrats to be little better than Communists. They feared that the government would take over industry and break up large estates.

Some people spread the rumor that Germany had not truly been defeated in the war. They claimed that the leaders of the Weimar Republic had betrayed Germany by urging peace. (It had, on the contrary, been the German army generals who had pushed for the armistice.) German nationalists and militarists wanted to break the Treaty of Versailles. They hoped to rebuild the German army (which the treaty forbade) and make Germany a world power once again.

Hitler and the Nazi Party. One of the harshest critics of the Weimar Republic was Adolf Hitler. Born in 1889 in a small town in Austria, Hitler quit school at age 16 and went to Vienna. He dreamed of becoming an artist, but he failed for lack of talent and spent five years drifting from job to job. Hitler welcomed the outbreak of World War I and volunteered to serve in the German army, where he was twice honored for bravery.

During his years in Vienna, Hitler adopted the extreme nationalist and racist ideas that were widespread in the late 1800's (page 544). After the war, he joined a small nationalist group in Munich. Its name was the National Socialist German Workers Party, but it was known as the **Nazi Party**. Hitler proved to be such a talented public speaker and organizer that he quickly became the party's leader.

With Hitler at its head, the Nazi Party began to grow. Parades and mass rallies drew excited crowds, who cheered Hitler's speeches attacking the Versailles Treaty and the Weimar government. In 1923 the Nazis tried to overthrow the government of the German state of Bavaria. The attempt failed, and Hitler was thrown into jail. While in jail, he wrote down his political views in a book titled *Mein Kampf* (MYN KAHMPF), or "My Struggle."

665

Social History The attempted takeover of Bavaria is often called the "Beer Hall *Putsch*" (overthrow) because it was launched in a Munich beer hall. Although sentenced to five years in prison, Hitler was released after serving only nine months.

Mein Kampf stressed two themes, racism and nationalism. Hitler claimed that the Germans were a "master race" descended from the Aryan people. He considered Jews, Slavs, and other peoples to be "inferior races" who weakened Germany. Hitler blamed the Jews for all of Germany's problems: its defeat in the war, high unemployment, and the spread of communism.

These racist ideas led to an extreme nationalism. Because Hitler believed that the Germans were a superior people, he felt they had the right to rule over other peoples. Hitler called on Germany to rebuild its strength, to win back lands lost in the Versailles Treaty, and to create a great German empire that would stretch across Europe.

Economic crises. Movements like Nazism (and leaders like Hitler) often succeed when times are hard and people are out of work, hungry, insecure, and restless. From 1919 to 1924 the Weimar Republic faced one crisis after another. Germany came near economic collapse in 1923, when inflation made

Sec. Rev. ques. 3

the currency almost worthless. Germans had to carry around large sacks of paper money just to buy a few groceries. The Nazis gained many followers in these years. Between 1924 and 1929, however, economic conditions improved and the Nazi Party's growth slowed.

In the fall of 1929 came a disastrous economic depression. In nearly every country, trade declined, banks collapsed, and factories closed down. Prices of stocks fell steeply, businesses went bankrupt, and unemployment soared. Germany was particularly hard hit. By 1932 more than six million people, nearly half the German labor force, were out of work.

Nazism's appeal. Hitler's political strategy was simple but effective. Over and over he repeated what he wanted people to believe. He gave them an enemy to hate and a cause to fight for. He played on their emotions with spellbinding speeches and used violence to impress them with the Nazi Party's power. Calling himself *Der Führer* (FYOO-rur)—"the Leader"—he said that he would bring Germany out of chaos.

As in Italy, many people in Germany were unhappy with democratic government and eager for strong leadership. Nazism had a powerful appeal for the less wealthy people of the middle class—shopkeepers, small farmers, office workers, teachers, and artisans. These people believed that Hitler would protect them from the large industrialists and from the Communists.

Many unemployed young men joined the "storm troopers" (or "Brown Shirts"), Hitler's private army. They were given food, shelter, uniforms, and a chance to devote themselves to a cause—the strengthening of Germany. "For us National Socialism is an idea, a faith, a religion," one of them wrote. Bands of storm troopers broke up rival political meetings, attacked Jews, and fought street battles with Communists.

By the end of 1932 the Nazis had become the strongest political party in Germany. They were still far, however, from having a majority in the Reichstag (the German parliament). At this point Hitler received much-needed help from a small group of

As runaway inflation gripped the German economy after World War I, paper money became more useful as fuel than as currency.

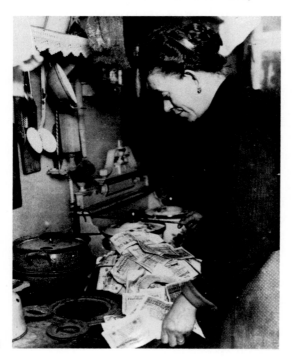

666

Check for Understanding. Ask: Why did Nazism become more appealing after 1929? (Many Germans, hurt by a disastrous depression, believed Hitler could lead them out of economic misery.)

Biography Hitler's view of democracy can be seen in this excerpt from *Mein Kampf:* "A majority can never replace a single man. Just as a hundred fools do not make one wise man, a heroic decision is not likely to come from a hundred cowards."

powerful industrialists, landowners, and bankers, as well as some generals. Most of these men did not share Hitler's extreme views, but they were impressed by his anti-communism and his promises to rebuild Germany. They felt they could use Hitler to advance their own interests. In January 1933 they persuaded Paul von Hindenburg, the 86-year-old war hero who had become president of the Weimar Republic, to make Hitler chancellor.

Elections to the Reichstag were set for March 1933. Shortly before the voting, a fire (probably set by the Nazis) swept through the Reichstag building. Hitler claimed that the fire was the beginning of a Communist takeover. He convinced Hindenburg to sign laws limiting freedom of speech and of the press. The Communist Party was also outlawed.

Hitler's Germany

★ See below.

The newly elected Reichstag gave Hitler absolute power. He quickly took steps to turn Germany into a totalitarian state. Thus was born the Third Reich (RYK), the successor to the Holy Roman Empire and to the German Empire under the kaisers (1871–1918).

New laws did away with trade unions, set up courts for secret trials, and banned all political parties except the Nazis. Hitler also took control of the army. Military leaders did nothing to stop the Nazi takeover. The generals still believed that they could keep Hitler in check.

Sec. Rev. ques. 3, cont.

Hitler, however, took orders from no one. He had enemies killed or tortured. In 1934 he ordered a purge of his own storm troopers. Hitler's personal guards, led by Heinrich Himmler, arrested and shot about 1,000 officers. The Nazi secret police, called the Gestapo (guh-STAH-poh), also made sure that the Führer's orders were obeyed.

The regime's heaviest blows were aimed at German Jews. Anti-Semitism became official government policy. Jews lost their citizenship and were forbidden to hold gov-

Hitler's emotional speeches appealed to many Germans who wanted a strong leader. The Nazi Party legally came to power in 1933.

ernment jobs, to own businesses, or to work at their professions. Stores refused to sell to them; landlords refused to rent them houses or apartments. Signs reading "Jews strictly forbidden in this town" or "Jews enter this place at their own risk" were posted in many places. Many Jews fled Germany, though they had to leave behind most of their belongings.

When a young Jew killed a German diplomat in Paris, the Nazis used the incident as an excuse for widespread terror. On November 10, 1938, gangs of Nazis set fire to synagogues throughout Germany and looted Jewish homes and stores. Many Jews were killed or wounded, and thousands were arrested during this *Kristallnacht* (kris-TAHL-nahkt), "the night of broken glass."

Despite events like these, most Germans were not alarmed by the first few years **667**

Background The mass murders ordered by Hitler are sometimes referred to as the "Blood Purge" or the "Night of the Long Knives."

★ **ENRICHMENT.** Have students research the lives and leadership styles of Mussolini and Hitler. Students might write a biographical sketch of the two fascist leaders, and then describe their use of propaganda and terror to create fascist states. *(Application)* **Analyzing Information**

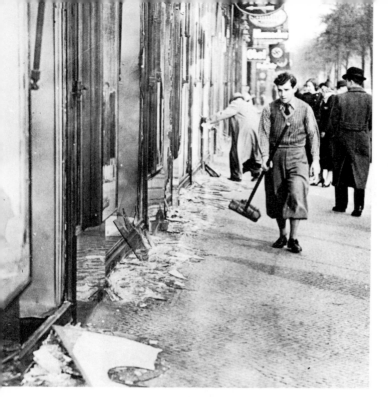

Jewish store owners inspect the damage done by Nazi thugs on *Kristallnacht*. Systematic persecution of Jews would follow.

of Nazi rule. The Nazi terror touched only a small percentage of the people. To most Germans, life still seemed normal. Moreover, the Nazi government took steps to rebuild the economy: it aided business, started a program of public works, and secretly revived the arms industry. In the first five years of Nazi rule, unemployment fell from six million to nearly zero, and workers' standards of living rose.

Meanwhile . . .

IN BERLIN

When the 1936 Olympics were held in Berlin, Hitler expected to see German athletes triumph and thus prove the "superiority" of the Aryan people. Yet the greatest hero of the 1936 Olympics was the black American runner Jesse Owens, who won four gold medals and set three Olympic records.

668

Germany's newfound prosperity brought Hitler the loyalty of both rich and poor.

Masters of propaganda, the Nazis worked hard to strengthen their hold on the German people. Radio, newspapers and magazines, films, books, art, and schools were all used to spread Nazi ideas. Children and young people were made to feel proud of joining the Hitler Youth, a Nazi training group. The Nazis burned books that praised democracy or argued against war, as well as those by Jewish authors. As in the Soviet Union, schoolbooks were rewritten to fit the views of the ruling party. Science books, for example, now proclaimed the superiority of the Aryan people.

By 1938 many German people felt pleased with the Nazi government. Businesses were thriving, workers had jobs, and the armed forces had been rebuilt. Hitler had made the world take note of the new Germany.

The Failed Democracies of Eastern Europe

● Note strategies for second objective on this page and p. 669.
The peace treaties that ended World War I had set up new governments in Eastern and Central Europe. Most of these governments had parliaments, like those in Western democracies. Eastern Europe did not, however, have a tradition of political democracy. Except for Czechoslovakia, the states of Eastern Europe lacked large numbers of business and professional people, who formed the backbone of democracy in Western Europe. When the new governments could not solve problems quickly, people blamed democracy. Democracy gave way to **authoritarianism**—a political system that stresses obedience to authority but does not try to control every aspect of life (as totalitarianism does).

Sec. Rev. ques. 4

In the first 15 years after the war, nearly all the new democracies in Eastern Europe fell. Hungary, Poland, Romania, Austria, Bulgaria, and Greece all moved toward authoritarian rule.

Only Czechoslovakia preserved the democratic government set up in 1918 under the leadership of Thomas Masaryk and Eduard Beneš (BEH-nesh). By the 1930's, however, conflict among different nationality groups within Czechoslovakia threatened the stability of the young republic. Nazi activities also caused unrest along the Czech-German border.

● See below.

Civil War in Spain

Though Spain stayed neutral in World War I, it could not escape instability. Strikes by factory workers, demands for local self-government, and arguments over the power of the Church combined to bring down the monarchy. In 1931 the king abdicated and a republic was declared.

The new republican government, run by liberals and socialists, began to make radical reforms. Opponents of these reforms, including army officers, landowners, and the Catholic Church, joined a Fascist party called the Falange (fuh-LANJ).

In July 1936, Falangist army officers in Spanish Morocco rebelled. Revolts quickly broke out all over Spain in what proved to be the start of the **Spanish Civil War**. By October the rebel soldiers had named their general, Francisco Franco, to be head of a Fascist Spanish state. For three years, bitter civil war raged in Spain between Franco's Falangists and the anti-Fascists. Hundreds of thousands of people were killed or wounded.

Events in Spain caught the attention of the outside world. The war, it seemed, was more than a struggle for control of Spain. It was a contest between rival ideologies. Both Hitler and Mussolini aided Franco because of his support of fascism. Stalin sent help to republican forces because Communists formed a strong group within their ranks. While the governments of Britain, France, and the United States stayed out of the war, thousands of volunteers from these countries flocked to Spain to join a republican force known as the International Brigade.

Sec. Rev. ques. 5

The republicans were no match for the Fascist forces, however. In 1939 Madrid fell to Franco. Spain came under a Fascist dictatorship that was to last until Franco's death in 1975. *See Sec. 1 Closing the Lesson, p. T661B.*

Pablo Picasso's *Guernica* commemorates the 1937 bombing of a town in northern Spain by Fascist forces in the Spanish Civil War—the first use of weapons of mass destruction against defenseless civilians. The Spanish-born artist's painting is one of history's most powerful antiwar statements.

669

1. **Define or identify:** fascism, Nazi Party, authoritarianism, Spanish Civil War. (pp. 663, 665, 668, 669)
2. How did conditions in Italy lead to the rise of fascism? What policies did the Fascists introduce? (pp. 663–664)
3. What problems led to the fall of the Weimar Republic? What changes did Hitler make once he gained power? (pp. 666–667)
4. Why did conditions in Eastern Europe make it hard for democratic governments to succeed? (p. 668)
5. What foreign nations participated in the Spanish Civil War? Why? (p. 669)
6. **Critical thinking:** The twentieth century has known two kinds of totalitarian states—Communist and Fascist. Using what you have learned in this section and in Chapter 32, compare and contrast the two. (See answer below.)

See lesson plans, pp. T661A–T661C.

6. Factors to consider: emphasis on state over individual rights; types of control exerted by the government; ideas about Marxism, private ownership, and nationalism; use of force in relations with other states.

2 The Western Democracies

Objectives

Focus Questions

★ ■ What happened to the American economy in the 1920's? *(pages 670–672)*
● ■ What problems did the European democracies face after World War I? *(pages 672–674)*

Terms to Know

Great Depression	Easter Rebellion
New Deal	coalition
Commonwealth of Nations	surrealism

★ Note strategies for first objective on this page and p. 672.

The older democracies—the United States, Britain, and France—had troubles of their own in the years after World War I. Unlike the countries discussed in Section 1, however, these democratic nations did not drift toward political extremism. Instead, they managed to control their problems without **670** changing their form of government.

The United States

After World War I, people in the United States had turned their backs on President Wilson's plan for peace. The Senate did not ratify the Treaty of Versailles, and the United States did not join the League of Nations (page 638). Americans wanted instead to enjoy prosperity at home and to avoid getting mixed up in European affairs.

The "Roaring Twenties." In the 1920's the American economy thrived, aided by new inventions and new methods of production. Just before the war, Henry Ford had come up with a moving assembly line. On it workers built automobiles out of interchangeable parts—parts of a uniform size and shape. The assembly line enabled companies to build cars more quickly and cheaply. Between 1919 and 1929, the number of American cars jumped by almost four times.

The same engine that made automobiles possible was also used in flying machines. In 1903 two Ohio brothers, Orville and Wilbur Wright, made the first successful motor-powered airplane flight, over the sand dunes of a North Carolina beach. Less than 25 years

★ RETEACHING. Have students identify the characteristics of the "Roaring Twenties." (New methods of production, like the assembly line, that increased production and decreased cost; new home products like vacuum cleaners, telephones, refrigerators, washing machines, and radios.) *(Comprehension) Observing for Detail*

★ REINFORCEMENT. Have students make a chart identifying the causes and effects of the Great Depression. (Causes: increased use of credit created debt; reduced spending led to decrease in production and unemployment; stock market crash. Effects: production fell and unemployment rose; people lost homes and savings; run on banks led to bank closings.) *(Comprehension) Understanding Cause and Effect*

Daily Life

New Consumer Goods in the 1920's

The booming prosperity of the 1920's brought a flood of new products for consumers to buy—and an intense effort to find new ways to sell them. Manufacturers all looked for methods to persuade buyers to choose their brand of cars, radios, toothpaste, or electric refrigerators.

Advertising artists and writers came up with techniques still in use today—colorful photographs, catchy slogans, testimonials by famous and glamorous people. Advertising dollars supported the fast-growing new medium of radio. Soap manufacturers sponsored daytime dramas (later called "soap operas"), while grocery stores paid for broadcasts of dance music. All this advertising paid off, as sales increased dramatically.

The most phenomenal success story of the 1920's was in the automobile industry. Car makers spent millions of dollars on magazine and newspaper advertising to introduce new models of sleekly styled cars in every color of the rainbow. The advertisements were so successful that by the end of the decade the number of cars on the American roads had nearly quadrupled.

later, in 1927, Charles Lindbergh made the first nonstop transatlantic flight. By the late 1930's, air travel was common. Cities built airports and airlines prospered.

Assembly lines were used for turning out a dazzling array of goods. Vacuum cleaners, telephones, refrigerators, washing machines, and radios became common in American homes. Profits of American businesses soared, and the standard of living rose for many people.

There were drawbacks to this prosperity, however. Not all Americans shared in their country's wealth. Farmers were hurt by falling prices for their crops, and industrial workers received low wages.

Another weakness in the economy of the 1920's was the great increase in the use of credit. Advertisements persuaded Americans to "buy now, pay later." They could pay a part of the cost at the time of the sale and pay the rest later in small installments. Credit allowed Americans to buy all the modern conveniences then coming into use, such as cars and household appliances. In time, many people owed thousands of dollars. When they could not pay their debts, they stopped buying. Factories had to cut back production, and unemployment rose.

A great many Americans were also buying stocks—shares in the ownership of corporations—on credit. Investors could pay

671

Sec. Rev. ques. 2

Check for Understanding. Ask: How did the increasing use of credit lead to problems? (When people could not pay their debts, they stopped buying. This led to cutbacks in production and unemployment.)

Ⓕ FEATURE ACTIVITY: Ask: (a) How do today's advertisements compare with the *Cole Aero-Eight* of the 1920's? (Automobile advertisements today usually include the same elements that appear on the 1920's poster: a picture and some promotional statements.) (b) How would you change the *Cole Aero-Eight* advertisement to reflect a present-day advertisement? (Answers will vary.) (Synthesis) *Synthesizing Information* only a fraction of the stock price and use credit for the rest. They then owned the stock and, if the price rose, they could sell it for a profit. The promise of quick and easy profits lured people from all income groups into the stock market.

This economic boom sent prices of stocks higher and higher. In October 1929, however, stock prices began to fall sharply. Panicky investors hurried to get rid of their stock while it was still worth something. The "crash" came on October 29, and stock prices continued to fall. By mid-November, stocks were selling for half (or less) of their September prices. Thousands of people saw their investments crumble.

The Great Depression. The collapse of the stock market set off a chain reaction that devastated the American economy. Americans who had lost their money in the stock market crash could no longer afford to buy new goods. Factories, already making more than they could sell, cut production and laid off more workers. Unemployed workers lost their savings, their homes, and even their trust in the country's future.

Banks had also been caught up in the boom of the 1920's and had made many bad investments. To stay in business, they began to demand that people repay loans. Few banks could collect anywhere near the amount that they had loaned. There was a "run" on the banks, as Americans tried to withdraw their money while they could still get it. By 1933 nearly one third of the country's banks had closed down, at least temporarily. The United States economy moved into the worst depression in its history, a time known as the Great Depression.

In 1932 Franklin D. Roosevelt, who had promised a "new deal" for the American people, was elected President by a landslide. He knew he needed to take drastic action. More than 13 million Americans—25 percent of the labor force—were out of work. Many people were hungry and homeless, and the nation was in despair. When Roosevelt took office in 1933, he began a vigorous program of economic reform that was known as the **672** New Deal.

This apple seller in New York City was one of millions of Americans left desperate and out of work by the Depression.

Under the New Deal, the federal government played a larger role in the economy than ever before. To restore public confidence in the financial community, the government laid down rules for banking and the sale of stocks. Such rules helped protect investors' money and guarded against future bank failures or stock market crashes. The government set up programs that created jobs for the unemployed. It encouraged farmers to cut back food production so that farm prices would rise. Laws were passed to protect the rights of unions. The Social Security Act provided income for the elderly as well as for the unemployed.

★ See below, left.

Troubles in Western Europe

● Note strategies for second objective on pp. 673 and 675.
The Great Depression sent shock waves through the world economy. Badly in need of money, American business leaders withdrew the capital they had invested in Europe. As sources of capital dried up, European banks and businesses failed. A number of countries raised tariffs on imports in order to protect their own industries. As more and more countries raised tariffs, however, world trade declined. This hurt industries that depended

Social History One woman described her daily visit to the Minneapolis unemployment office: "So we sit in this room like cattle waiting for a nonexistent job, willing to work to the farthest atom of energy, unable to work, unable to get food and lodging. Here we must sit in this shame looking at the floor, worse than beasts at a slaughter."

on trade. There was severe unemployment around the world, especially in industrial nations. (The graphs on page 674 show the agonizing impact of the Great Depression on the world economy.)

Great Britain. Even before the Great Depression, the British economy was in trouble. Britain depended on trade, but many of its merchant ships had been sunk in World War I, and it was losing markets to other trading nations. As exports dropped, British industry, mining, and shipbuilding declined, and unemployment soared.

The coal industry was hardest hit, since the development of water power and oil had recently reduced the demand for British coal. Mine owners called for wage cuts for the miners, and in 1926 the miners' union responded with a strike. The protest soon grew into a nationwide general strike as workers in other unions struck to support the miners. The general strike involved nearly three million workers—almost half the British labor force—but it lasted only 10 days.

British economic problems grew even worse during the Great Depression. Britain did not begin a broad program like the New Deal, however. The government gave aid to the poor, but it did little to revive industry or cut unemployment.

During the 1920's and 1930's, the British government also had to make major decisions about the territories of the British Empire. By World War I, several British colonies had become self-governing Dominions within the Empire. They had their own armies, tax systems, and currencies.

In 1931 Parliament passed the Statute of Westminster, which set up a new relationship between Britain and these Dominions. Canada, Newfoundland, Australia, New Zealand, and the Union of South Africa joined Britain in a **Commonwealth of Nations**. Member nations still saw the British monarch as their symbolic leader, but they were now fully independent countries.

Ireland. Another member of the new Commonwealth was the Irish Free State, or Eire. As you read in Chapter 28, a plan to give southern Ireland home rule was shelved when World War I broke out. Frustrated over the delay, Irish nationalists rebelled in Dublin in Easter week, 1916. British troops put down the **Easter Rebellion** and executed its leaders. Bitterness and violence between the Irish and the British continued.

In 1921 Britain tried to end the unrest by dividing Ireland. Northern Ireland, or Ulster, remained a part of Great Britain and was represented in the British Parliament. The rest of the country became a Dominion called the Irish Free State. However, many Irish nationalists, led by Eamon De Valera (deh vah-LAYR-uh), continued to seek total independence from Britain.

Sec. Rev. ques. 3

France. World War I had taken a heavy toll on France. Like other nations, it had suffered enormous casualties. It also had to deal with the devastation caused by four years of warfare on French soil. Mines, factories, and railroads lay in ruins. Villages, farms, forests, and orchards had been destroyed.

France had counted on Germany's payment of reparations (page 638) to help it rebuild. The Weimar government, faced with its own economic crises, announced in 1922 that it could pay no more. The French seized the German coal mines and steel mills along the Ruhr River to collect reparations, but the Germans refused to work under French control. Finally, in 1924, an international commission worked out a compromise known as the Dawes Plan. Germany agreed to make payments based on the health of its economy.

Partly because of economic troubles, France had been politically unstable ever since the Third Republic was formed in the early 1870's. Disputes among the major parties stalled economic recovery after World War I. Unhappy with the government, many French voters turned either to the Communists or to fascist parties.

Fear of fascism led a number of leftist political parties to unite in a **coalition**—temporary alliance—known as the Popular Front. The coalition pledged to defend the French republic against the nobles, the military, and the clergy. In 1936 the Popular Front, led by Socialist Léon Blum (BLOOM), won a majority in the French assembly.

Sec. Rev. ques. 4

673

● **RETEACHING. Have students identify the economic problems faced by Western Europe after World War I.** (Banks and businesses failed as Americans withdrew their European investments; higher tariffs resulted in a decline of trade; unemployment increased.) *(Comprehension) Understanding Cause and Effect*

Cultural History The Easter Rebellion lasted a week and was generally unpopular. However, the republicans gained much sympathy and support after Britain executed 15 of the rebellion's leaders.

● **REINFORCEMENT. Have students identify which of Western Europe's problems were a result of World War I and which resulted from the Great Depression.** (World War I: British merchant ships destroyed; rebellion in Ireland; French mines, factories, railroads, villages and farms destroyed. Depression: loss of capital; unemployment.) *(Comprehension) Identifying Cause and Effect*

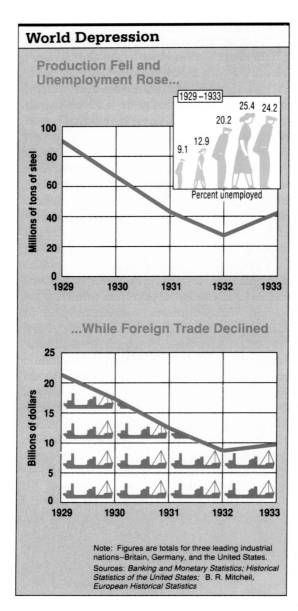

World Depression

Production Fell and Unemployment Rose...

1929–1933

9.1   12.9   20.2   25.4   24.2

Percent unemployed

Millions of tons of steel

100
80
60
40
20
0

1929   1930   1931   1932   1933

...While Foreign Trade Declined

Billions of dollars

25
20
15
10
5
0

1929   1930   1931   1932   1933

Note: Figures are totals for three leading industrial nations--Britain, Germany, and the United States.

Sources: *Banking and Monetary Statistics; Historical Statistics of the United States;* B. R. Mitchell, *European Historical Statistics*

These statistics for three leading industrial nations reflect the devastating effect the Great Depression had on the world economy. In what year did the economy reach its lowest point? Why did unemployment rise when production (represented here by steel output) and foreign trade declined?

(See answers below.)

Blum's government borrowed a number of ideas from the New Deal program in the United States. To end a wave of strikes that had backed up production, the government met some of the workers' demands. Workers

674

won a 40-hour week, paid holidays, and the right to form unions. Blum also nationalized the Bank of France and arranged for partial government control of the arms industry.

Despite these changes, the Popular Front failed to revitalize the French economy, and Blum stayed in office only a short time. The French remained bitterly split over reforms at home and the civil war in neighboring Spain. By the late 1930's, France was threatened both by internal problems and by the growing power of Germany and Italy.

Postwar Culture

The years after World War I were a time of artistic creativity. The war had upset the existing order in art as well as politics; artists felt free to try new themes. At the same time, the invention of radio and movies led to the growth of a new kind of popular culture.

Sec. Rev. ques. 5

Literature. Some writers developed new forms of expression. Novelists in the 1800's had often written from the point of view of an all-knowing narrator who stood outside the story. Some postwar writers, such as James Joyce in Ireland and Virginia Woolf in England, turned to a style known as "stream of consciousness." In their works, characters not only told the events of a story but also voiced their inner thoughts.

Other writers chose subjects that reflected the mood of the times. The American writer Ernest Hemingway used simple, direct language to describe the lives of people whose faith and optimism had been shattered by the war. Franz Kafka, a Czech author, wrote haunting stories of people alone and confused, who searched without success for meaning in life. The American writer T. S. Eliot, in his famous poem *The Waste Land*, suggested that Western society had lost its spiritual values.

Painting. Painters also developed new forms that reflected the anxieties of postwar life. A movement called **surrealism** began in Paris in the 1920's. Reacting against what they saw as the evils of European society, surrealists hoped to paint a different kind

Graph Answers: (1) 1932. (2) Large numbers of workers were laid off because demand for American products decreased both in America and abroad.

Literature Kafka's goal in writing can be partly understood in the following excerpt from one of his letters: "I think we ought to read only the kind of books that wound and stab us. We need the books that affect us like a disaster, that grieve us deeply, like the death of someone we loved more than ourselves, like being banished into forests far from everyone."

During the Depression, Americans found relief from their cares at the movies. Walt Disney broke new ground with full-length animated color films. *Fantasia* **(1940) united music and animation and featured Mickey Mouse.**

of reality. They tried to explore this reality by reaching into the unconscious mind. The works of such artists as Salvador Dali of Spain had a strange, dreamlike look.

Other influences on painting were African cultures, which Westerners had learned about through imperialism. The bold simplicity and abstract designs of African art appealed to many European painters looking for new styles.

Music. Like painting, music began moving in new directions after World War I. A number of composers experimented with atonal (ay-TOH-nul) music—music without recognizable harmony or pattern. Others were influenced by the jazz forms that started among blacks in the southern United States. The roots of jazz lay in black work songs, spirituals, and traditional African music. Jazz became immensely popular throughout the West in the 1920's.

Radio and movies. The coming of radio and motion pictures revolutionized popular entertainment after World War I. The first commercial radio stations began in the United States in the early 1920's. Within a few years, millions of Americans owned radios and listened every week to adventure shows, "soap operas," and music programs.

Silent movies had been popular before the war. After sound was added in 1927, many more people flocked to the theaters to see their favorite stars.
See Sec. 2 *Closing the Lesson,* p. T661B.

● See below, left.

Section Review

Answers to Section Review questions are in brackets on pages indicated.
1. **Define or identify:** Great Depression, New Deal, Commonwealth of Nations, Easter Rebellion, coalition, surrealism. (pp. 672, 673, 674)
2. What weaknesses in the economy of the United States contributed to the Great Depression? (pp. 671–672)
3. Why did some Irish nationalists oppose the creation of the Irish Free State? (p. 673)
4. What led to the formation of the Popular Front in France? (p. 673)
5. How did Western culture show the effects of World War I? (pp. 674–675)
6. **Critical thinking:** In what ways did the Great Depression demonstrate the connections among the world's economies? (See answer below.)

675

3 Unrest in Asia and the Middle East

Objectives

Focus Questions

★ ■ What groups struggled for control of China? *(pages 676–677)*

● ■ Why did Japan adopt imperialist policies? *(page 678)*

▲ ■ How did nationalism affect Middle Eastern nations? *(pages 678–680)*

Terms to Know

May Fourth Movement	Long March
	Balfour Declaration

★ Note strategies for first objective on this page and p. 677.

Both China and Japan had joined the Allies in World War I, but they had done so for different reasons. Japan had made secret treaties with the West that gave the Japanese a claim to German territories on China's Shandong Peninsula and in the Pacific. China, on the other hand, looked to the West for support against the Japanese.

During the peace conference at Versailles, the Western Allies made no decision about Shandong. They left the question to be settled between Japan and China. Angry at this lack of support, the Chinese delegation stormed out of the conference and refused to sign the Versailles Treaty. The Japanese also resented the behavior of the West, but they signed the treaty and strongly backed the new League of Nations.

Turmoil in China

The Chinese people felt that the West had once again taken advantage of their weaknesses. On May 4, 1919, university students **676** and teachers in Beijing took to the streets and demanded an end to foreign interference. They also wanted to limit the power of the warlords and to extend democracy. The **May Fourth Movement** grew as workers, manufacturers, shopkeepers, and professional people joined the protests.

Sun Yat-sen and the Kuomintang (page 579) shared the aims of the May Fourth Movement, but they could not strengthen central rule on their own. When Western governments failed to aid Sun, he accepted an offer from the Soviet Union's Comintern (page 653). In a 1923 agreement, Sun received military and political help in return for allowing Chinese Communists to join the Kuomintang.

When Sun died in 1925, Chiang Kai-shek (JYAHNG ky-SHEK), his hand-picked successor, became head of the Kuomintang. Chiang and other Nationalists distrusted the Chinese Communists and the advisers sent by the Soviets. Their first goal, however, was to defeat the warlords who controlled most of China. In 1926 Chiang led the Nationalist army in a successful drive against the warlords, and he moved China's capital to Nanjing. His troops eventually captured Beijing and took control of much of eastern China. Other nations recognized the Kuomintang as the official government of China.

Sec. Rev. ques. 2

Chiang then turned on his allies, the Communists. In 1927 he forced the Soviet advisers out of China. Chiang also purged the Chinese Communists in the Kuomintang, killing many of them.

Chiang's Nationalists next tried to strengthen and modernize China. The government made changes in the banking system to attract investment. The old "unequal treaties" with the West (page 575) were abolished. Communication and transportation were improved, and by the 1930's, China's coastal cities had become bustling centers of business and manufacturing.

★ RETEACHING. **Have students summarize the events leading to control of the Chinese government by the Nationalists.** (With Soviet military and political help, the Nationalists defeated the warlords who controlled most of China and moved the capital to Nanjing. Chiang forced Soviet advisers from China and purged Communists in the Kuomintang.) *(Comprehension)* **Observing for Detail**

★ REINFORCEMENT. **Have students trace the growth and influence of Chinese communism.** (When Western governments failed to help the Nationalists, the Soviet Union provided aid. After Chiang assumed power and gained control of the government, many Chinese became angry at his failure to make social reforms and joined the Communists.) *(Comprehension)* **Synthesizing Information**

Mao Zedong, a library worker at Peking University, adopted the ideas of the May Fourth Movement and helped found the Chinese Communist Party in 1921. Six years after their break with the Kuomintang, the Communists were nearly wiped out by Chiang Kai-shek's forces. Mao led the Red Army on the Long March to a safe camp in the remote hills of Yan'an (above). The Long March solidified Mao's leadership and forged the survivors into a tightly knit group.

The Kuomintang's power did not reach into the countryside, however. Warlords still ruled in distant regions. Sun had promised to distribute land among the peasants, but large landowners were in no mood for such a move. Chiang, who needed the support of the landowners and other wealthy Chinese, did not press the issue.

During the early 1930's many who had backed Chiang became angry at his failure to make social reforms. A large number left the Kuomintang and joined the Communists who had survived Chiang's purge of 1927. Driven into hiding in the hills of south-central China, the Communists were building up a base for revolution. Their leader was a young man named Mao Zedong (MOW dzuh-DOONG). (His name is sometimes spelled *Mao Tse-tung*.)

While Marxists and Soviet Communists viewed the proletariat as the major revolutionary class, Mao looked to the Chinese peasants for support. The peasants distrusted most outsiders, but Mao drew them into his Red Army, and trained them in methods of guerrilla warfare.

Chiang continued his attempts to destroy the Communists, using the warlords' armies as well as government troops. In 1934, Nationalist troops surrounded the Communists' main base. About 100,000 men, women, and children managed to break through Nationalist lines. They began a journey under Mao's leadership that became famous as the **Long March** (map, page 736).

The Long March began in October 1934 in southeastern China. It ended one year and nearly 6,000 miles later in the hills of northwestern China. The Communists trudged through mountains and deserts, fighting starvation, disease, and Nationalist bombings. Though fewer than 10,000 people survived the Long March, they would in time prove to be victorious.

★ See below.

677

Japanese Imperialism

● Note strategies for second objective on this page.

Japan watched power struggles in China with rising interest. If China grew weak, Japan might be able to gain control of its lands and natural resources.

In the 1920's, democracy seemed to be taking root in Japan. Industrialization had increased contacts with Europe, and many Japanese began to welcome Western political ideas. All Japanese men gained the right to vote in 1925. Political parties grew in power, workers and farmers formed unions, and women called for greater freedom. Along with reforms at home went a moderate foreign policy: Japan cooperated with Western efforts to reduce the risk of war in the Pacific.

The Great Depression threatened this moderation. Japan, an island nation, depended on trade for both markets and raw materials. Now trade declined, and many nations set high tariffs. Japan's profitable silk market in the United States fell by almost 70 percent and its rice market was cut in half. Soon many Japanese farmers and textile workers had lost their jobs. Short of cash, Japan felt trapped by the need to buy food, coal, oil, and iron ore from abroad.

Sec. Rev. ques. 3

All of these problems played into the hands of Japan's military leaders, who had long called for imperial expansion. They now argued that expansion would bring back prosperity. Japan already held territory in China and the Pacific, and it had annexed Korea. If the Nationalist government did not stand in the way, Japan could gain new resources through further expansion in China.

In September 1931, Japanese officers in Manchuria staged an explosion on a railway line. Blaming the incident on the Chinese, these troops defeated the local warlords' armies and quickly occupied all of Manchuria. Its rich deposits of coal and iron ore made Manchuria valuable to Japan. The Japanese set up a puppet state they called Manchukuo, and they built factories and military bases there.

678

In Japan itself, military leaders gained more and more control over the government during the 1930's. Like leaders in Germany and Italy, they charged that moderate policies weakened the nation. They also used threats, terror, and assassination to silence those who spoke against them.

● See below.

Nationalism in the Middle East

▲ Note strategies for third objective on this page and p. 679.

Nationalism became a major force in the Middle East after World War I, sparked by the breakup of the Ottoman Empire and by growing Western interest in the region. Several new states were formed, but this did not bring an end to conflict over the future of the Middle East.

Kemal's Turkey. After the Versailles conference, Turkey was all that remained of the Ottoman Empire. In 1919 Greece, hoping to take advantage of its neighbor's weakness, invaded Turkey. The sultan ordered his exhausted troops not to resist the Greeks, but a group of Turkish nationalists decided to fight back.

Led by a brilliant commander, Mustafa Kemal (keh-MAHL), the nationalists fought off the Greeks. In 1922 the Greeks withdrew and the last Ottoman sultan was deposed. The following year, Turkey became a republic and Kemal its first president.

Kemal's goal was to build a strong, modern Turkish state. Taking the name *Ataturk*, which means "father of the Turks," Kemal set up a one-party government and made a number of sweeping reforms:

1. Separation of church and state. Kemal wanted to reduce the role of Islam in Turkish life. Under the sultans, all activities had been regulated by Islamic law. Kemal put an end to religious courts and created a new legal system based on European law. He also replaced religious schools with state-run schools.

2. Modernization. During the rule of the sultans, Turkish women had lived by Islamic traditions, under the authority of their male relatives. Kemal extended political

● RETEACHING. Have students review "Japanese Imperialism" (above) and identify the causes. (Japan's need for food, coal, oil, and iron ore caused the nation to pursue expansionist policies.) *(Comprehension)* **Identifying Causes**
● REINFORCEMENT. Have students compare the move toward authoritarian government in Japan with Italy's and Germany's acceptance of fascism (pp. 663–668). *(Synthesis)* **Comparing Historical Developments**

● ENRICHMENT. Have students find information on the role of the military in Japan in the 1930's. Students should explain how military leaders were able to take greater control of the government. *(Comprehension)* **Drawing Conclusions**
▲ RETEACHING. Have students make a timeline of events in the Middle East, showing the growth of nationalism. (Students should include information for: 1902, 1919, 1923, 1928, 1932.) *(Comprehension)* **Understanding Chronology**

rights to women, including the right to vote and to hold public office. He also changed marriage laws. Men could no longer marry more than one woman; also, women could now divorce their husbands.

Kemal even set down rules for clothing. Governments workers were forced to wear Western business suits. All Turks were forbidden to wear the fez, a brimless hat that was part of their traditional clothing.

In 1935 Kemal required all Turkish citizens to take Western-style last names. Kemal also replaced Arabic script, which was difficult to write, with the Roman alphabet. This move was part of the government's massive literacy campaign to educate Turks throughout the country.

3. *Economic development.* Another of Kemal's programs was government funding for industrialization. He hoped in this way to raise the Turkish standard of living. To boost trade with the West, he adopted the Western calendar and the metric system of weights and measures.

Modernizing Persia. Before World War I, Persia had been carved up into British and Russian spheres of influence. After the war, when Russia's internal affairs were in chaos, the British tried to take over all of Persia. This action sparked a nationalist revolt in Persia, and in 1925 an army officer took the throne.

Persia's new leader, Reza Shah Pahlavi (PAH-luh-vee), followed policies much like those of Turkey's Kemal. In his effort to build a powerful Iran (Persia was renamed Iran in 1935), Reza Shah modernized the economy and brought in Western laws and customs. Reza Shah ran into heavy opposition from ethnic groups seeking self-rule as well as from religious leaders fearing the loss of their power. He responded with threats and with repression.

The unification of Arabia. As you read in Chapter 10, nomadic tribes had lived in Arabia for thousands of years. The loyalties of Arabians were to the tribe rather than to a nation, and only the faith of Islam united them. After the breakup of the Muslim Em-

Mustafa Kemal campaigned hard to westernize Turkey. Here he gives officials a lesson on the Roman alphabet. Note that he wears a modern, Western-style suit instead of traditional Turkish clothing.

pire in the 1200's, Arabia had returned to political disunity.

In 1902 Ibn Saud (sah-OOD), a member of a once-powerful Arabian family, began a successful campaign to unify Arabia. In 1932 he named the new kingdom after his family—Saudi Arabia.

Ibn Saud ruled for another 20 years. Unlike Kemal in Turkey or Reza Shah in Iran, he had no wish to modernize his country. A devout Muslim, he followed the teachings of the Koran (page 198) and governed as an absolute ruler. Laws required religious worship and banned alcohol. Women had to obey their male relatives and wear heavy veils

Sec. Rev. ques. 4

▲ See below.

679

▲ REINFORCEMENT. Have students evaluate the nationalist movements in Turkey, Persia, Arabia, and Palestine, and explain which changes were beneficial to their nations and which were not. *(Evaluation) Evaluating Information*

▲ ENRICHMENT. Have students work in groups to present biographical dramatizations of important Middle Eastern nationalist leaders. Students should find information on Kemal, Reza Shah Pahlavi, and Ibn Saud; stage interviews that might have occurred with these leaders; or present speeches that they may have given to raise nationalist fervor. *(Application) Translating Information into Another Form*

Middle East in the 1920's

After World War I, parts of the Ottoman Empire went to Britain and France as mandates. What countries went to France? What waterway connects the Mediterranean and Red seas?

Map Answers: (1) Lebanon, Syria. (2) Suez Canal.

if they went out in public. Such modern conveniences as telephones and automobiles were forbidden.

French and British mandates. Under the Versailles Treaty, France had received Syria and Lebanon as mandates. French troops occupied these areas and stayed despite local opposition. Britain had received mandates over Iraq, Transjordan (now Jordan), and Palestine. Jordan was made largely independent in 1928; Iraq was granted full independence in 1932. Palestine, however, posed special problems for the British.

Palestine is the ancient homeland of the Jews. Beginning about 2,000 years ago, Palestine was conquered over and over by a series of invaders. With each conquest, many Jews **680** fled their homeland and settled in other

countries. By the late 1800's, only a handful remained. Palestine had become part of the Ottoman Empire, and most of its people were Muslims. Like the Jews, these Muslims looked on Palestine as a homeland.

At that time, persecution of Jews in Europe and Russia led to the growth of Zionism (page 545). In the late 1800's and early 1900's, a small number of Jews began to immigrate to Palestine in hopes of building a Jewish homeland.

In 1917 the British government, which had won Palestine from the Ottomans, issued the **Balfour Declaration**. It said that Britain supported "the establishment in Palestine of a national home for the Jewish people," but added that the rights of non-Jews in Palestine would be respected. During the 1920's and 1930's, as political and economic upheavals rocked Europe, the trickle of Jewish immigration to Palestine became a steady stream. By the late 1930's, Jews made up 30 percent of the population of Palestine.

The growth of the Jewish population alarmed the Arabs of Palestine, who did not wish to live as a minority in a Jewish state. Tension rose between the two groups, leading to riots and many deaths. By the late 1930's Palestine was torn by civil war. The British wanted to satisfy both the Arabs and the Jews. They were beginning to discover, however, that this would be very hard to do.

Sec. Rev. ques. 5

The importance of oil. During the late 1800's and early 1900's, Western nations began to use petroleum products, such as oil and gasoline, for heating and transportation. In the early 1900's Western companies went to Middle Eastern rulers and asked for the right to drill oil there. The governments granted these requests in exchange for a share of the profits.

During the 1920's and 1930's, rising demand brought new oil exploration, and huge deposits were found in the Persian Gulf countries. With these discoveries, the Middle East's value to the West skyrocketed. Oil proved to be a mixed blessing for the region, however. It brought profits, but it also encouraged Western nations to try to dominate the Middle East.

See Sec. 3 *Closing the Lesson*, p. T661C.

Geography A reason for Palestine's interest to other nations throughout history is its location—it lies across the major land routes linking northern Africa with western Asia.

Politics The Balfour Declaration was actually stated in a November 2, 1917 letter from British Foreign Secretary Arthur Balfour to Lord Rothschild, the head of the British Zionist Federation.

1. **Identify:** May Fourth Movement, Long March, Balfour Declaration. (pp. 676, 677, 680)
2. Why did Sun Yat-sen allow Chinese Communists to join the Kuomintang? What was the eventual outcome of this alliance? (p. 676)
3. What factors allowed military leaders to come to power in Japan? (p. 678)
4. How did Ibn Saud's plans for Saudi Arabia differ from Kemal's plans for Turkey and Reza Shah's plans for Iran? (p. 679)
5. What brought Jews and Arabs into conflict in Palestine? (p. 680)
6. **Critical thinking:** A country's raw materials, or lack of them, can greatly affect its relations with the outside world. How was this true of both Japan and the Middle East after World War I? (See answer below.)

Chapter 33   Summary and Timeline

1. Fascism gained popularity in Italy and Germany after World War I. In 1922 the Italian Fascists, led by Benito Mussolini, took power. Mussolini then set out to destroy opposition to his rule and to build an Italian empire. The German Fascists, called Nazis, took power in 1933. Their leader, Adolf Hitler, used propaganda and violence to make Germany a totalitarian state. Another Fascist state was established in Spain, and several Eastern European countries moved away from democracy.

2. The Western democracies faced severe problems after World War I. A period of prosperity in the 1920's was cut short by the Great Depression, forcing Western governments to reform their economies. Western culture reflected the worries, but also the excitement, of these uncertain times.

3. Postwar crises affected Asia as well. The Chinese Nationalists established a government that united part of China. The Chinese Communists, however, remained a constant challenge. Militarists gained control of the Japanese government in the 1930's and began building an empire in Asia. In the Middle East nationalism gained strength, and oil discoveries enriched the region.

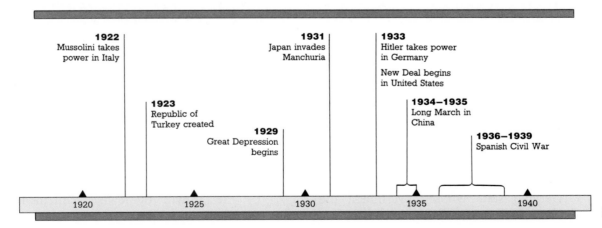

1922
Mussolini takes power in Italy

1923
Republic of Turkey created

1929
Great Depression begins

1931
Japan invades Manchuria

1933
Hitler takes power in Germany

New Deal begins in United States

1934–1935
Long March in China

1936–1939
Spanish Civil War

1920   1925   1930   1935   1940

681

6. Students might suggest that Japan's lack of raw materials prompted that country toward imperial expansion. In the Middle East, countries possessing rich oil resources had an upper hand in dealing with Western nations, but risked Western domination.

CHAPTER 33 REVIEW

See p. T661C for answers to Chapter Review.

Vocabulary Review

Define or identify each of the following terms.
1. coalition
2. May Fourth Movement
3. Nazi Party
4. New Deal
5. Spanish Civil War

People to Identify

Choose the name that best completes each sentence.
1. [Orville Wright/Charles Lindbergh] made the first nonstop transatlantic flight.
2. [Mao Zedong/Sun Yat-sen] was the leader of the Chinese Communists.
3. [Thomas Masaryk/T. S. Eliot] helped set up a democratic government in Czechoslovakia in 1918.
4. [Francisco Franco/Eamon De Valera] led the Irish independence movement in the 1920's.
5. During the Great Depression, [Franklin D. Roosevelt/Henry Ford] promised a "new deal" for the American people.
6. English writer [Ernest Hemingway/ Virginia Woolf] used a style known as "stream of consciousness."

Places to Know

Match each of the following places with the correct description: *Bavaria, Dublin, Iran, Manchukuo, Nanjing, Northern Ireland, Ruhr River, Saudi Arabia, Shandong Peninsula.*
1. region known as Ulster
2. German state whose government the Nazis tried to overthrow in 1923
3. puppet state set up in Manchuria
4. site of the Easter Rebellion of 1916
5. region involved in a territorial dispute between China and Japan
6. kingdom named by Ibn Saud in 1932
7. nation once called Persia
8. Chinese capital established by Chiang Kai-shek
9. body of water along which France seized German coal mines and steel mills to collect reparations

Recalling the Facts

1. From which groups did Mussolini's Fascist Party draw most of its support? Why were these people attracted to fascism?
2. What reasons did various groups have for opposing the Weimar government?
3. Why did most of the new democracies of Eastern Europe fail?
4. How did the use of credit in the United States lead to increased unemployment and high stock prices in the 1920's?
5. What economic problems did Britain face before the Great Depression?
6. Why did the Popular Front emerge in France?
7. Why did Chiang Kai-shek's government lose supporters in the 1930's?
8. How did the Great Depression help Japan's military leaders win support for imperial expansion?
9. What steps did Kemal take to modernize Turkey? How did Ibn Saud's government differ from those of Kemal and Reza Shah?
10. What was the Balfour Declaration? Why did the Arabs of Palestine feel threatened by the growth of Jewish settlement there?

Critical Thinking Skills

1. Reading a graph. The graph below shows the percentages of German workers who were unemployed from 1927 to 1937. What percentage of the work force was unemployed in 1929? What happened to unemployment from the year that Hitler came to power (1933) to 1937? *(Comp.)*

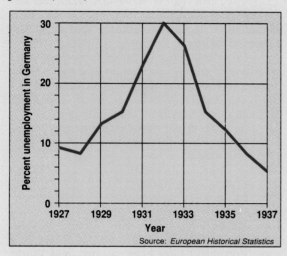

Source: *European Historical Statistics*

2. Outlining. Complete the first part of the outline below by filling in details under *A* and *B*. Then complete the second part.
  - I. Fascist Italy
    - A. Postwar problems
    - B. The Fascists in power
  - II. The rise of German fascism *(Comp.)*

3. Relating cause and effect. The Great Depression in the United States had a devastating impact on the world economy. List one cause for each of the following effects:
a. European banks and businesses failed.
b. International trade declined. *(Comp.)*

4. Drawing conclusions. Why do movements like Nazism and leaders like Hitler have a better chance of gaining power when *(Syn.)* times are hard and people are unemployed?

Thinking About Geography

1. Researching information. On the world map at the back of this book, locate these original members of the Commonwealth of Nations: Britain, Canada, Australia, New Zealand, Ireland, South Africa. Newfoundland was another original member of the Commonwealth. Use an encyclopedia or almanac to find out why Newfoundland is no longer a member of this organization. *(App.)*

2. Relating geography and history. Use your school or local library to find information on Mao Zedong's Long March (page 677). Study a map that shows the physical features of China. Then write an essay describing the march and the terrain the marchers covered. *(App.)*

683

 A checkmark identifies questions and exercises calling for the three higher-order levels of thinking at the top of the Bloom taxonomy: Analysis, Synthesis, and Evaluation.

World War II   1928–1945
(pp. 684–706)

Chapter Preview

Section 1 describes acts of Fascist aggression and British and French appeasement policies toward Hitler that led to World War II. Sections 2 and 3 trace the course of the war in Europe and Asia, the fall of Europe to the Axis Powers, and the war in the Pacific. The final section examines events that brought victory to the Allies in Europe and in Asia and the territorial and political results of the war.

Bibliography

See the *Teacher's Management and Planning Guide* for additional listings. Starred titles are for both students and teachers.

Engelmann, Bernt. *In Hitler's Germany: Everyday Life in the Third Reich.* Pantheon. Firsthand accounts of many Germans.

*Hersey, John. *Hiroshima.* Knopf. Classic account of the effects of the first atom bomb.

Lewin, Ronald. *Ultra Goes to War.* McGraw Hill. Breaking German codes help Allies win the war.

Orenstein, Henry. *I Shall Live: Surviving Against All Odds, 1939–1945.* Beaufort. A young Polish Jew's determination to "live to see Hitler destroyed."

*Ryan, Cornelius. *The Longest Day: June 6, 1944.* Crest. Allies invade Normandy.

Snyder, Louis L. *The War: A Concise History 1939–1945.* Simon and Schuster. Readable and fast-paced.

Section Lesson Plans

SECTION 1   (pp. 685–688)
The Path to War

Objectives

After completing this section, students will be able to:
1. Explain how Fascist aggression threatened peace during the 1930's.
2. Identify the events that led to the outbreak of war in Europe.

Introducing the Lesson

Remind students that the causes of World War II had their source in unresolved issues of World War I and the bitterness resulting from the Treaty of Versailles.

Then ask: *(a) What issues remained unsolved after World War I?* (Answers will vary. Nationalism, territorial conflicts, and militarism remained factors in European politics.)

(b) Why did the Treaty of Versailles create resentment among nations in Europe? (Many people, including President Wilson, believed that the Versailles Treaty was too harsh and made Germany's recovery from the war impossible.)

(c) How might these problems and others have set the stage for another world war? (Answers will vary.)

Developing the Lesson:
Solving Problems

Have students work in groups to develop a hypothesis describing how German aggression and expansion might have been stopped, and World War II avoided. In their hypotheses, students might consider the following: *Was there ever a point at which nonmilitary action might have been effective? (Synthesis)*

Developing the Lesson:
Organizing Ideas in Written Form

Have students write a series of newspaper articles that might have appeared in American papers after each of the following events: Hitler's 1935 decision to rearm Germany; Italy's invasion of Ethiopia; the formation of the Axis Powers; Hitler's claim to the Sudetenland; Germany's invasion of Czechoslovakia. In their articles, students should report and analyze the event and suggest possible repercussions. *(Application)*

Closing the Lesson: Discussing History

Have students work in groups to discuss the following:
(a) What might explain Britain's and France's appeasement policy toward Hitler's actions?
(b) Under what circumstances might appeasement have been effective?
(c) At what point should the appeasement policy probably have been abandoned?
(d) What measures other than appeasement might Britain and France have taken to help discourage Germany's aggressive actions? (Synthesis)

See *Section Review* questions, p. 688.

SECTION 2   (pp. 688–697)
The Conquest of Europe

Objectives

After completing this section, students will be able to:
1. Identify areas attacked by the Axis Powers.
2. Describe what life was like in occupied Europe.

Introducing the Lesson

Remind students that much of World War I had been fought in the trenches and was characterized by a lack of troop mobility. In World War II, German armies abandoned trench warfare and used a tactic of sudden, concentrated attack, resulting in rapid territorial gain.

Then ask: *(a) What tactical advantage might be gained by a campaign using fast-moving forces?* (Rapid military advances could catch the opposition off-guard, without sufficient time to prepare a defense.)

(b) What resources would a nation require to carry out a campaign of fast-moving attacks? (Answers will vary. A nation would need a well-developed plan of action, efficient systems of transportation, and support forces to maintain military control of conquered areas.)

(c) What might be some disadvantages of a campaign of fast-moving attacks? (Answers will vary. Such a campaign might exhaust military resources quickly. This tactic might be ineffective in a two-front war or in a situation where the enemy is able to respond effectively.)

Developing the Lesson:
Organizing Information

Have students make a chart of Axis military action. (Chart should include *Germany:* Poland—September 1939; Latvia, Lithuania, and Estonia—1939; Denmark and Norway—April 1940; Belgium, the Netherlands, Luxembourg—May 1940; France—June 1940; Leningrad—September 1941; Stalingrad—1942. *Italy:* invaded Egypt—1940.) *(Comprehension)*

Developing the Lesson:
Synthesizing Information

Have students write an essay explaining the following: *Resistance movements and the Allied war effort reflected the choice of civilized values as opposed to the values of Hitler and his Nazi supporters. (Comprehension)*

Closing the Lesson: Observing for Detail

Have students explain how Hitler's social policies in occupied countries reflected his beliefs about German superiority. (Hitler's policies were designed to have the peoples of occupied Europe serve the German "master race," and to enslave or eliminate "inferior" peoples. Racial "cousins" were to undergo re-education for a "Greater Germany." In Poland, programs of murder and terror resulted in the sentencing of over a million people to Soviet labor camps. Concentration camps were built and Hitler used food, weapons, oil, art, and labor from occupied areas to enrich Germany.) *(Comprehension)*

See *Section Review* questions, p. 697.

SECTION 3   (pp. 697–700)
War in the Pacific

Objectives

After completing this section, students will be able to:
1. Explain what led to war between the United States and Japan.
2. Describe how the United States halted the Japanese offensive in the Pacific.

Introducing the Lesson

Remind students that Japan was a member of the Allied Powers during World War I, but joined the Axis Powers in the years before World War II.

Then ask: *(a) What might cause a nation to change its alliances?* (Answers will vary. A country seeks alliances to promote its welfare and security and to meet national goals. If a nation perceives that a different ally might better meet national needs or goals, new alliances might be formed.)

(b) What might Japan's alliance with the Axis Powers have said about its foreign policy goals in the 1930's? (Answers will vary, but students might conclude that Japan's foreign policy included imperialist aims.)

Developing the Lesson:
Evaluating Information

Have students find evidence to support the following statement: *The United States was the only member of the Allies in a position to halt Japanese expansion.* (Britain was fighting the Axis

Powers in Europe and had inadequate resources to combat the Japanese as well. The United States was strong and held island bases in the Pacific.) *(Comprehension)*

Developing the Lesson:
Understanding Cause and Effect

Have students study the map on p. 699 and then answer the following: *Why did Japan's loss of naval superiority at Midway turn the tide of the war in Asia?* (Japan needed to control the sea lanes extending to the lands that supplied it with raw materials. An inadequate naval force would not have been able to protect shipping using these sea lanes.) *(Comprehension)*

Answers to *Map Skill Practice*, p. 699.

1. Japanese islands, half of the island north of Japan, Korea, Taiwan, smaller islands.
2. Manchuria, parts of eastern and southern China, Hong Kong, Burma, Thailand, French Indochina, Malaya.
3. About 7,500 miles.
4. 1945.
5. Students might suggest that since Japan controlled such a wide area, American forces island-hopped to secure areas before targeting Japan's mainland.

Closing the Lesson:
Analyzing Information

Have students work in groups to debate the following: *The Japanese attack on Pearl Harbor might have been avoided if the United States had joined the Allied war effort earlier than it did. (Synthesis)*

See *Section Review* questions, p. 700.

SECTION 4   (pp. 700–704)
Victory for the Allies

Objectives

After completing this section, students will be able to:
1. Explain how the Allies won the war in Europe and in the Pacific.
2. Describe the immediate aftermath of World War II.

Introducing the Lesson

Remind students that the territorial and political results of World War II continue to influence European affairs today. Lands occupied by the Soviet Union in 1945 remained Communist, and those occupied by the Allies are democracies.

Then ask: *(a) What might explain the stability of the territorial and political settlements of World War II?* (Answers will vary. The peace settlement might have been more fair than the Treaty of Versailles and, therefore, less likely to cause bitterness and resentment. Victorious powers may have worked more diligently to guarantee adherence to the peace terms.)

(b) Which factors do you think have contributed most to the avoidance of a third world war? (Answers will vary.)

Developing the Lesson:
Sequencing Events

Have students sequence the events that occurred in 1944 and 1945 leading to the end of World War II. (*1944:* Allies take Rome—June; D-Day—June 6; American victory at Leyte—fall. *1945:* Hitler commits suicide—April 30; European war ends—May 8; United States dropped atomic bomb on Hiroshima—August 6; United States dropped atomic bomb on Nagasaki—August 8; Pacific war ends—August 15.) *(Comprehension)*

Developing the Lesson:
Drawing Inferences

Have students consider the following statement made by Stalin about postwar free elections in Soviet-occupied countries: "A freely elected government in any of these Eastern European countries would be anti-Soviet, and that we cannot allow." (p. 703).

Then ask: *(a) Why, do you think, did Stalin fear that a free election would result in an anti-Soviet government?* (Stalin probably believed that citizens of these countries would choose democracy.)

(b) What does Stalin's statement reveal about the attitude of Europeans toward Soviet occupation of their country? (Europeans resented and feared Soviet occupation.)

(c) Why do you think pro-Soviet governments in Eastern Europe were viewed by Stalin as necessary for Soviet security? (Answers will vary.) *(Synthesis)*

Closing the Lesson: Making Judgments

Have students work in groups to discuss the following question: *In what ways might the world be different today if Hitler had not gained power and World War II had never been fought?* Have students share their group answers with the class. *(Synthesis)*

See *Section Review* questions, p. 704

Chapter 34 Review Answers
(pp. 705–706)

Vocabulary Review

1. (a) United Nations (b) Nazi-Soviet Pact (c) Battle of Midway (d) embargo (e) concentration camp
2. (a) Maginot Line (b) Axis Powers (c) Nuremberg Trials (d) Holocaust (e) blitzkrieg

People to Identify

1. British prime minister whose refusal to surrender to Germany led to the Battle of Britain.
2. Leader of the Free French forces.
3. American general who commanded Allied troops on D-Day.
4. Emperor of Ethiopia who protested Italy's invasion of his country to the League of Nations.
5. Fanatical believer in "Aryan superiority" who carried out Hitler's racial policies.
6. German leader of the Afrika Corps who was known as "The Desert Fox."
7. American President who decided to use the atomic bomb against the Japanese.

Places to Know

1. Sudetenland 2. Okinawa 3. Auschwitz
4. Stalingrad

Recalling the Facts

1. Hitler rebuilt Germany's military forces, moved troops into the Rhineland, and declared Austria a province of the Third Reich.
2. Italy. Japan.
3. They wanted peace, had economic problems, believed that the Versailles Treaty had been too harsh on Germany, and saw Hitler as an ally against the Communists.
4. September 1, 1939. April 1940.
5. As the Germans advanced, Soviet troops burned fields and destroyed equipment, leaving the German forces without food or supplies. German troops were eventually left to fight with clothing and equipment unsuitable for the harsh Russian winter.
6. The battles at Stalingrad and El Alamein.
7. Resistance fighters attacked German patrols, led strikes, and blew up factories. They printed underground newspapers and sent important information to the Allies over hidden radios. They rescued crews of downed planes, hid escaped prisoners, and helped them escape to Allied territory.
8. Japan had attacked Pearl Harbor, other American island bases in the Pacific, and British holdings in Malaya and Hong Kong.
9. The Japanese attack on Pearl Harbor had destroyed much of the United States' Pacific fleet and air force.
10. Advances into Italy, France (D-Day at Normandy), and Germany.
11. The Allied strategy was to "island-hop," with Allied forces seizing islands that were in strategic positions on the sea route to Japan. Japan announced defeat after atomic bombs were dropped on the cities of Hiroshima and Nagasaki.
12. Millions of people were dead or wounded. Often people were starving and homeless. Cities, farms, and factories were destroyed.

Critical Thinking Skills

1. Answers will vary, but students should choose from among the following: World War I—trench warfare, machine guns, long-range guns, poison gas, tanks, use of airplanes; World War II—blitzkrieg, aircraft carriers, radar, "island-hopping," atomic bombs.
2. About 6,115,000 Soviet military personnel were killed. About 3,250,000. 291,557. The Allies suffered the greatest losses.
3. Essays will vary.

Thinking About Geography

The Allies invaded Western Europe from Britain. Normandy was a short distance from Britain and was a good base from which to push toward Germany.

Enrichment: Primary Sources

1. They had posted scouts and had prepared for resistance by having grenades, dynamite bombs, and flaming bottles ready.
2. They first cut off the electricity and water supply and then came singly or in small groups rather than marching in a column.
3. Possible answer: The Jews had nothing to lose.

World War II 1928–1945

See chapter timeline, p. 704.

Before You Read This Chapter

What happens to a country that wins a war? To a country that loses? Britain was one of the victors in World War I, but it found itself weaker at the end of the war than at the start. France, too, was on the winning side, yet it suffered widespread destruction. As you read this chapter on World War II, keep track of the costs to both sides. Which countries suffered heavy bombings? High civilian casualties? Great economic losses? Military casualties? Can you predict which countries would recover quickly after the war, and which would not?

The Geographic Setting

The Chapter Outline

1. The Path to War
2. The Conquest of Europe
3. War in the Pacific
4. Victory for the Allies

German bombs exploding near St. Paul's Cathedral light up London's nighttime sky. Air raids forced Londoners to sleep in subways but did not destroy their will to fight.

See lesson plans, pp. T683A–T683C.

1 The Path to War

Objectives

Focus Questions

★ ■ How did Fascist aggression threaten peace during the 1930's? *(pages 685–686)*
● ■ What events led to the outbreak of war in Europe? *(pages 686–688)*

Terms to Know

Axis Powers   Nazi-Soviet Pact
appeasement   World War II

★ Note strategies for first objective on this page and p. 686.

In the years after World War I, many politicians wanted to make sure there would never be another world war. The leaders that took power in Germany, Italy, and Japan, however, were hungrier for power than for peace. Barely two decades after World War I had ended, another world war broke out—one that would become the bloodiest conflict in human history.

Peace Efforts

The Treaty of Versailles had established the League of Nations, which President Wilson hoped would keep world peace. Its members promised to bring their quarrels to the League for settlement, instead of going to war. The League also set up the mandate system to provide colonies with a stable way of moving toward independence. Though more than 60 nations were members of the League, it remained weak because it had no power to enforce its decisions.

Sec. Rev. ques. 2

During the 1920's, world leaders held several conferences to discuss disarmament and ways to keep peace. The most ambitious plan was the Kellogg-Briand Pact, drawn up in 1928. This treaty, which said that war would not be used "as an instrument of national policy," was signed by nearly every country in the world. Yet it did not include a plan to deal with countries that broke their pledge. The Pact was, therefore, only a small step toward peace.

Fascist Aggression

In postwar Germany, many people still had bitter feelings about the Treaty of Versailles (page 636). It had disarmed the country, taken away Germany's colonies, and ordered the payment of huge reparations. The Weimar government had tried to change the treaty by diplomacy. When Adolf Hitler gained power in the early 1930's, he vowed to destroy the treaty altogether.

German rearmament. Hitler's first step in restoring German power was to rebuild its military forces. In 1935 Hitler announced that Germany would build a peacetime army of 550,000 men. Britain and France condemned German rearmament as a violation of the Treaty of Versailles. Even so, neither government took action.

Italian expansion. Like Germany, Fascist Italy built up its army. In 1935 Benito Mussolini's troops invaded Ethiopia, the independent African kingdom that had resisted earlier Italian invasions (page 601). Haile Selassie (HY-lee suh-LAS-ee), Ethiopia's emperor, protested to the League of Nations, which denounced the invasion. The League also urged its members not to sell arms to Italy. Only a few nations went along, however, and the boycott failed. Ethiopia soon fell, becoming part of an Italian colony.

Sec. Rev. ques. 3

Civil war in Spain. Both the Fascist powers showed off their growing military strength during the Spanish Civil War of 1936–1939 (page 669). Hitler and Mussolini

685

★ RETEACHING. Have students make a chart identifying acts of Fascist aggression in the 1930's. (Germany: rebuilt military forces; supported Franco; occupied Rhineland, Austria, Sudetenland, and then all of Czechoslovakia. Italy: strengthened army; colonized Ethiopia; supported Franco. Germany and Italy formed Axis Powers.) (Comprehension) **Observing for Detail**

★ REINFORCEMENT. Have students make a timeline of Fascist aggressive actions in the 1930's. (1935—Germany rearmed, Italy invaded Ethiopia; 1936—Axis Powers formed, Germany and Italy backed Franco, Germany occupied Rhineland; 1938—Anschluss; Germany claimed Sudetenland; 1939—Germany invaded Czechoslovakia.) (Comprehension) **Understanding Chronology**

Background Selassie told the delegates to the League: "God and history will remember your judgment."

Check for Understanding. Ask: What was the Rhineland? (The demilitarized region between the Rhine River and the French border.)

Cultural History The popular film *The Sound of Music* (1965) told the story
of an Austrian family's courageous refusal to submit to the Nazis.

backed Franco's forces with soldiers and other aid. Franco's victory established another Fascist government in Western Europe. The war in Spain also brought Germany and Italy closer together. In 1936 they formed a military alliance, becoming known as the Axis Powers. (Japan later joined the Axis.)

German expansion. In March 1936, Hitler sent troops into the Rhineland, the demilitarized region between the Rhine River and the French border. This action violated the Versailles Treaty. German generals warned Hitler that this move was dangerous, since the German army was still weak. Hitler, however, felt certain that French and British leaders would take no action to stop him.

Appeasement. Hitler's gamble in the Rhineland paid off, thanks to the Western powers' policy of appeasement—giving in to others' demands in order to avoid conflict. Britain and France chose a policy of appeasement for a number of reasons.

1. After the horror of World War I, the people of Britain and France wanted peace at almost any price. Their hope for peace led them to ignore clear signs that Hitler was set on dominating Europe.

2. The desire for peace, combined with economic problems, had led Britain to make drastic cuts in its military spending. By the late 1930's Britain was not at all prepared for war. Without British support, France was not strong enough to challenge Germany.

3. Many people in Britain believed that the Treaty of Versailles had been much too hard on the Germans. As a result, they took a mild view of Hitler's treaty violations.

4. Many Europeans believed that Joseph Stalin was a worse threat to the West than Hitler. They welcomed Hitler's policy of anti-communism and hoped he would be an ally against the Soviet Union.

More German moves. Hitler, emboldened by British and French inaction, continued to enlarge German territory. Claiming that he was following the principle of self-determination, Hitler tried to bring all the German-speaking peoples into the Third Reich. The Treaty of Versailles had barred a union between Austria and Germany. Hitler

Sec. Rev. ques. 4

686

nevertheless proposed that the two states cooperate in certain areas. Most Austrians welcomed Hitler's plan. In March 1938, Hitler's troops entered Austria unopposed and carried out the Anschluss (AHN-shloos)—the union between Austria and Germany.

Hitler next turned to Czechoslovakia. While most of Czechoslovakia's 15 million people were Slavs, three million were German. Most of the German speakers lived in the Sudetenland (soo-DAYT-un-land), a region along the German border. When Hitler threatened to make war on Czechoslovakia, Mussolini and Prime Minister Neville Chamberlain of Britain stepped in.

In September 1938, these two leaders met in Munich with Hitler and Premier Edouard Daladier (dah-lah-DYAY) of France to decide Czechoslovakia's fate. No representative from Czechoslovakia, however, was invited to attend. Continuing the policy of appeasement, Chamberlain and Daladier agreed to let Hitler claim the Sudetenland. In return, Hitler promised to seek no more territory. Since it had no support from Britain or France, Czechoslovakia surrendered the Sudetenland to Germany without a fight.

Chamberlain returned to cheering crowds in Britain and told them that the Munich agreement had brought "peace with honor . . . peace for our time." Most of the British people supported Chamberlain.

Despite his promise at Munich, Hitler did not stop with the Sudetenland. In March 1939, German soldiers marched into Prague, the Czech capital. All of Czechoslovakia quickly came under German control.

★ See
below,
left.

The Coming of War

● Note strategies for second objective on this page and p. 688.

People began to wonder where Hitler would turn next. The answer came very soon: Poland. Hitler wanted to recover the Polish Corridor—the strip of land separating East Prussia from the rest of Germany. (The Polish Corridor had been given to Poland after World War I.) In March 1939, Hitler demanded that the Polish port of Danzig be returned to German rule and that Germany

Sec. Rev. ques. 5

Background Germany and Italy chose the term *axis* to express their idea
that all of Europe revolved around an imaginary line connecting their
two capitals.
★ **ENRICHMENT.** Have students work in groups to present a summit
meeting that might have occurred in March 1939 between European heads of state and the United States. Participants should
seek ways to prevent further territorial expansion by Germany
and Italy. (Synthesis) *Solving Problems*

● **RETEACHING.** Have students develop a hypothesis explaining why
Britain and France waited until the invasion of Poland before
agreeing to take action against Hitler. (Synthesis) *Forming a
Hypothesis*
● **REINFORCEMENT.** Have students develop a hypothesis explaining
Stalin's motives for signing the Nazi-Soviet Pact. Students might
refer to the discussion of the Soviet Union on pp. 654–659. (Syn-
thesis) *Forming a Hypothesis*

Aggression in Europe and Africa, 1935–1939

Attacks by Germany and Italy on weaker countries plunged Europe into war. What countries and other lands did the Axis Powers occupy? What lands did the Soviet Union take over?

687

Map Answers: (1) The Rhineland, Austria, the Sudetenland, Czechoslovakia, Albania, and Ethiopia.
(2) Estonia, Latvia, Lithuania, and eastern Poland.

See Sec. 1 Closing the Lesson, p. T683A.

be given a railroad and a highway through the Corridor. The Poles refused these demands, and Britain and France promised to help defend Poland's independence.

Sec. Rev. ques. 5, cont.

France and Britain tried to get the Soviets on their side as well, but mutual distrust stood in the way. Then Stalin and Hitler stunned the world by signing a pact of friendship in late August 1939. In this treaty, called the **Nazi-Soviet Pact**, the Soviet Union agreed to let Germany invade Poland. In return, Hitler promised Stalin territory in Eastern Europe.

● See below.

Early on the morning of September 1, German tanks rolled into Poland. Britain and France stood by their pledge to the Poles. On September 3, 1939, the British and French governments declared war on Germany. Thus began **World War II**, which would take millions of lives and cause frightful destruction before its closing days in 1945.

See lesson plans, pp. T683A–T683C.

Section Review

Answers to Section Review questions are in brackets on pages indicated.

1. **Define or identify:** Axis Powers, appeasement, Nazi-Soviet Pact, World War II. (pp. 686, 688)
2. What weakness crippled the League of Nations and the Kellogg-Briand Pact? (p. 685)
3. What aggressive actions did Italy take? (pp. 685–686)
4. What reason did Hitler give for the actions Germany took in Austria and Czechoslovakia? (p. 686)
5. Why did France and Britain declare war on Germany? (pp. 686, 688)
6. **Critical thinking:** How might different British and French policies have prevented war? (See answer below.)

6. Students might suggest that firm action to halt early German aggression could have averted war.

2 The Conquest of Europe

Objectives

Focus Questions

★ ■ What areas did the Axis Powers attack? *(pages 688–695)*
● ■ What was life like in occupied Europe? *(pages 695–697)*

Terms to Know

Allies
blitzkrieg
Maginot Line
concentration camp
Holocaust

★ Note strategies for first objective on this page and p. 693.

At the time of the invasion of Poland, Germany was far better prepared for war than Britain or France. Country after country fell **688** to the Axis armies. After the fall of France,

Britain stood alone until 1941, when first the Soviet Union and then the United States rallied to its support. By late 1942 the **Allies**—the nations fighting the Axis Powers—had begun to win the war.

Hitler's Conquests

Blitzkrieg in Eastern Europe. Germany's armies used a style of warfare that consisted of quick, concentrated attacks on land and in the air. It was called the **blitzkrieg** (BLITS-kreeg), or "lightning war." Less than a week after the September 1 invasion of Poland, a blitzkrieg by German tanks, bombers, and paratroopers opened the way to Warsaw. Soviet troops then invaded Poland from the east. On September 27, 1939, Poland surrendered. As they had agreed in the Nazi-Soviet Pact, Hitler and Stalin divided Poland. Hitler took over Danzig.

A sealift evacuated Allied troops from Dunkirk, France, just ahead of the invading German army. The collective effort rescued nearly 340,000 troops.

To gain access to the Baltic Sea, the Soviet government set up military bases in the countries of Latvia, Lithuania, and Estonia. It then demanded bases in Finland as well as a large piece of land on the border. When the Finns refused, Soviet troops invaded the country. All through the "winter war" of 1939, Finnish soldiers stubbornly battled the Soviet army. In March, however, Finland was forced to make peace and give up the disputed territory.

Blitzkrieg in Western Europe. Although Britain and France were officially at war with Germany, no fighting took place on the western front during the winter of 1939–1940. This time became known as the "phony war." Suddenly in April 1940, Germany struck with lightning speed at Denmark and Norway. The two Scandinavian countries fell quickly to invading German forces. In the next month, Belgium, the Netherlands, and Luxembourg also surrendered to Hitler.

Sec. Rev. ques. 2

France still felt secure behind the so-called **Maginot Line** (MAZH-ih-noh), a string of heavily defended forts along its border with Germany. As in World War I, however, German troops went around the French defenses by attacking through Belgium. Tanks and motorized infantry burst through the French lines and raced toward the English Channel. This German advance drove a wedge between the French army defending Paris and the British, Belgian, and French forces on the coast.

More than 300,000 Allied troops retreated to Dunkirk on the English Channel (map, page 694). To rescue the trapped soldiers, every available vessel set sail from England—fishing boats, tugboats, and private yachts, as well as merchant ships and navy destroyers. By June 4, 1940, about a week after the retreat, most of this strange rescue fleet had picked up the trapped soldiers and taken them to England. The "miracle of Dunkirk" inspired and united the British people in their resistance to Hitler.

The German armies moved steadily across northern France. Millions of French civilians fled south by train, car, bicycle, or even on foot. On June 10 Mussolini also declared war on France, and Italian troops invaded from the south. To save Paris from destruction the French did not try to defend the city, and German troops marched in on June 14. A few days later the French government asked for an armistice. Hitler arranged for it to be signed in the same railway car where Germany had agreed to the armistice ending World War I.

Under the terms of the armistice, Germany occupied northern France (including Paris) and the coast. In the south a puppet French government was set up at Vichy (VEE-shee).

689

Social History Although greatly outnumbered and poorly equipped, the Finns fought the Soviet army heroically, destroying whole divisions and cutting Russian supply lines. Ski patrols were a key to Finnish defense.

Check for Understanding. Ask: What five countries fell to Germany between April and May 1940? (Denmark, Norway, Belgium, the Netherlands, and Luxembourg.)

Background At Dunkirk, over 338,000 Allied troops (mostly British) escaped safely to Britain, but some 68,000 British troops were captured or killed.

BIOGRAPHY

Ⓕ See below.

Winston Churchill

When Winston Churchill became prime minister in May 1940, he told the British people, "I have nothing to offer but blood, toil, tears, and sweat." These were grim days for Britain, as Hitler's armies rolled across France, closer and closer to the English Channel.

All through the 1930's Churchill had spoken out in Parliament, warning of the growing danger from Hitler and urging that Britain's army be kept strong. Britain's leaders, however, had ignored him. When war came as he had predicted, Churchill was the obvious choice to lead the country.

Churchill was born in 1874 into an aristocratic family with a long military tradition. As a young man he traveled to India, Cuba, and South Africa as a war correspondent. In 1900 he entered politics and won election to Parliament. Thereafter, he held a variety of government offices.

In June 1940, a month after Churchill had become prime minister, France collapsed under the German attack. Churchill's ringing speeches and fearless

Britain holds out. With the defeat of France, Britain stood alone against the Axis Powers. Hitler had made plans for an invasion, but he hoped the British would agree to surrender beforehand. When Winston Churchill, Britain's new prime minister, refused, Hitler ordered his air force to start massive bombings of British factories, airfields, and seaports. On August 8, 1940, the Battle of Britain began. Almost every day that summer hundreds of planes battled in the skies over Britain as the Royal Air Force fought German aircraft. By late fall, German losses in the Battle of Britain caused Hitler to give up his invasion plans.

The British still had to face terrifying air raids, however. In what became known as "the blitz," German bombers struck at British cities, day and night. Through months of destructive air raids, the British held up well. Londoners were determined to keep the capital running in spite of the blitz.

In the Battle of Britain and also during the blitz, the pilots of the Royal Air Force were aided by radar, a new device developed by British scientists to spot enemy aircraft. In addition, the Allies had broken Germany's secret code. They now had much better infor-

690

Cultural History British citizens remained courageous throughout the bombing raids. One English writer noted that "the calm behavior of the average individual continues to be amazing. Commuting suburbanites placidly brag to fellow passengers on the morning trains about the size of bomb craters in their neighborhoods, as in a more peaceful summer they would have bragged about their roses and squash."

Social History Winston Churchill paid a tribute to the pilots of the Royal Air Force when he said "never in the field of human conflict was so much owed by so many to so few."
Ⓕ **FEATURE ACTIVITY. Ask:** What might Churchill have meant when he said, "It was the nation that had the lion's heart. I had the luck to be called upon to give the roar." (Comprehension) Interpreting Information

Reference Note See Franklin Roosevelt's *Four Freedoms Speech* urging passage of the Lend-Lease Act, p. 692.

sell, lease, or lend military equipment to nations whose defense was vital to American security.

The Invasion of the Soviet Union

Though he had failed to crush Britain, Hitler decided to attack the Soviet Union. Hitler despised communism, and he always knew that one day he would move against the Soviet Union. He wanted land for German settlers, grain to feed the German nation, and oil, coal, and iron ore to supply the German war machine.

Sec. Rev. ques. 3

By June 1941, German troops were massed along the Soviet border. On June 22 they swept into the Soviet Union along a front that stretched from the Baltic to the Black Sea. Hitler was confident of the result, saying "We need only break open the door and the whole rotten building will collapse."

Hitler's attack brought the Soviet Union immediate offers of help and support from Britain and the United States. The Lend-Lease agreement was extended to include the Soviet Union.

The German onslaught. The German invasion devastated the western part of the Soviet Union, and caused the Soviet people great hardship. In September 1941, for example, German soldiers surrounded the city of Leningrad, trapping about three million people. The siege of Leningrad lasted for more than two years. Nearly a million people died from starvation and disease.

The unprepared Soviet armies suffered terrible losses in the first months of the German offensive. By September, 2.5 million soldiers and tens of thousands of tanks and planes had been lost. Yet Soviet forces did not collapse completely. As the Soviets drew back from the advancing German armies, they burned crops in the fields and destroyed equipment. These "scorched-earth" tactics left no food or supplies for the German forces.

The arrival of autumn rains and winter snow also slowed the German offensive. Fresh Soviet troops arrived from Siberia with

spirit rallied the British people to fight on against Hitler. When it seemed that German armies would soon invade England, Churchill told the world,

> We shall go on to the end. We shall defend our island, whatever the cost may be. We shall fight on the beaches, we shall fight on the landing grounds, we shall fight in the fields and in the streets, we shall fight in the hills. We shall never surrender.

Churchill's distinguished career continued after the war. He served as prime minister again from 1951 to 1955. His writings won him the Nobel Prize for Literature. Queen Elizabeth II of Britain knighted him in 1953, and the American Congress made him an honorary citizen of the United States in 1963. He died in 1965.

On his eightieth birthday, when Churchill was being honored in Parliament, he said of his great war speeches, "It was the nation that had the lion's heart. I had the luck to be called upon to give the roar."

mation about Germany's plans for air strikes.

The blitz went on until the spring of 1941. Large areas of British cities were destroyed, and many thousands of civilians were killed. Moreover, German submarines blocked the shipment of food and supplies to Britain, causing severe shortages. The British government, lacking the money to buy supplies or military equipment, asked for American help. Because the United States was officially neutral, however, it could not lend money to a country at war. Then, in March 1941, Congress passed the Lend-Lease Act. It allowed President Franklin D. Roosevelt to

691

Background Two weeks after the Lend-Lease Act (above) was passed, Congress appropriated $7 billion for the Allied war effort. By the war's end, over $50 billion in aid would be sent to countries fighting the Axis Powers.

Roosevelt's Four Freedoms Speech

On January 6, 1941, President Franklin Roosevelt, in his annual message to Congress, urged passage of the Lend-Lease Act. In the same speech Roosevelt expressed his hopes about freedom for all peoples of the world. Part of his speech follows.

66 In the future days, which we seek to make secure, we look forward to a world founded upon four essential human freedoms.

The first is freedom of speech and expression everywhere in the world.

The second is freedom of every person to worship God in his own way everywhere in the world.

The third is freedom from want—which, translated into world terms, means economic understandings which will secure to every nation a healthy peacetime life for its inhabitants everywhere in the world.

The fourth is freedom from fear—which, translated into world terms, means a worldwide reduction of armaments to such a point and in such a thorough fashion that no nation will be in a position to commit an act of physical aggression against any neighbor—anywhere in the world. 99

1. What four freedoms did Roosevelt identify as essential?
2. According to Roosevelt, how could freedom from fear be achieved?
3. **Critical thinking:** Why did the President think it was appropriate to talk about Lend-Lease and the Four Freedoms in the same speech?

Ⓕ See answers below.

692

winter equipment, while the Germans shivered in summer uniforms as the temperature dropped to 30° below zero. German tanks and trucks would not start in the cold. The Russian winter stopped the German army much as it had defeated Napoleon's army more than a century before (page 451).

The Battle of Stalingrad. Even though their march into Russia had been halted, German forces held large areas of the Soviet Union. The spring and summer of 1942 brought a new German attack. The main target was Stalingrad, now called Volgograd (map, page 694). This city was a vital center for north-south transportation.

In late August, German troops reached the outskirts of Stalingrad. Six hundred German planes bombarded the city, enveloping it in flames and killing about 40,000 civilians. The people of Stalingrad would not, however, abandon their city. Soviet soldiers and civilians fought the Germans house by house and street by street. A German officer wrote in his diary:

66 Stalingrad is no longer a town. By day it is an enormous cloud of burning, blinding smoke. It is a vast furnace lit by the reflection of the flames. And when night arrives, the dogs plunge into the Volga and swim desperately to gain the other bank. The nights of Stalingrad are a terror for them. Animals flee this hell; the hardest stones cannot bear it for long; only men endure. 99

As the fighting dragged on, Soviet troops prepared for a massive attack to encircle the German army in Stalingrad. In late November, led by Soviet Marshal Georgi Zhukov, the Soviets struck. The German commander begged Hitler to let his freezing, exhausted army withdraw. Hitler refused. Finally, in February 1943, the last of the German troops in Stalingrad surrendered.

Sec. Rev. ques. 4

The Soviet victory marked the turning point in the war in Eastern Europe. Soviet troops had already begun to move westward. They would eventually make their way to Berlin, the heart of the Nazi empire.

Ⓕ **Primary Source Answers** 1. Freedom of speech and expression, freedom of religion, freedom from want, and freedom from fear. 2. Through worldwide arms reduction. 3. The purpose of Lend-Lease was to help a democratic nation, Britain, continue its fight against a totalitarian state.

Social History One British historian wrote that Hitler's refusal to withdraw German troops from Stalingrad "was perhaps the most monumental isolated example in military history of deliberate and wasteful sacrifice of human life." In the battle of Stalingrad, the Soviet Union lost more lives than the United States lost during the whole war.

In the ruins of Stalingrad a Soviet assault group hunts for German soldiers.
Most of the German war effort was concentrated against the Soviet Union.
This helps explain why the Soviet Union had the largest losses of any
warring nation—about 20 million Soviet citizens died as a result of the war.

The North African Campaign

In the first year of the war, while Hitler was expanding westward in Europe, Mussolini took steps to establish Italian control over the Mediterranean. In the fall of 1940, forces from the Italian colony of Libya invaded Egypt (map, page 694). Their aim was to capture the Suez Canal from Britain. Soldiers from Britain and the Commonwealth nations, however, forced an Italian retreat. To keep the British from taking Libya, Germany sent the Italians help—the trained desert fighters of the Afrika Corps, led by Field Marshal Erwin Rommel.

Rommel's troops and the British fought back and forth in the North African desert for more than a year. Rommel's skill and clever tactics earned him the nickname "The Desert Fox." In 1942 the British sent Field Marshal Bernard Montgomery to block Rommel's advance toward the Suez Canal. The armies of these two brilliant generals clashed at El Alamein (el ah-lah-MAYN), where the retreating British had taken a stand. Montgomery's forces turned and began a counterattack, and by November 1942, they had driven Rommel out of Egypt. El Alamein, the first major British victory of the war, made Montgomery a hero.

Meanwhile, American forces had joined the fighting against Germany in December 1941, after Hitler declared war on the United States. Early in November 1942, Allied troops under the American General Dwight D. Eisenhower landed in French Morocco and Algeria. Although the French colonies were under the pro-Nazi Vichy government, the French commander aided the Allies. The Afrika Corps was soon trapped between the two Allied armies.

★ See below.

693

Geography The Suez Canal was strategically important for the Allies, who depended on access to Middle Eastern oil. Hitler knew that the capture of the Canal could cut off Allied supplies.

★ **ENRICHMENT.** Have students work in groups to write newspaper articles reporting Fascist aggression in Europe and North Africa between 1939 and 1941. Students might draw maps to illustrate military campaigns and troop movements. *(Comprehension)*

World War II in Europe and Africa

Allied advances eventually put an end to Axis domination of Europe. What body of water did the Allies have to cross to reach Normandy? What countries remained neutral throughout World War II?

Map Answers: (1) English Channel. (2) Sweden, Portugal, Spain, Turkey, Ireland, Switzerland.

By May 1943 the Allies held all of North Africa. These victories ended the threat to the Suez Canal and made the Mediterranean safe for Allied ships. They also gave the Allies a base from which to invade southern Europe.

Europe Under Hitler

● Note strategies for second objective on this page and p. 696.

A policy of terror. At its height in 1942, Hitler's empire stretched from the Atlantic Ocean deep into the Soviet Union, and from Norway to North Africa (map, page 694). Hitler planned to have the peoples of occupied Europe serve the German "master race." Nazi racial policies were carried out by Heinrich Himmler, a fanatical believer in "Aryan superiority." The policies called for the enslaving or wiping out of all "inferior" peoples—Jews, Poles, Russians, and others.

The Nazis regarded peoples of Germanic descent, such as the Norwegians and Dutch, as racial "cousins." In the Nazi plan for Europe, they were to undergo re-education to make them valued citizens of a "Greater Germany." Ukrainian, Polish, and Czech children who "looked German"—blond and blue-eyed—were taken from their parents and sent to Germany. There they were to be brought up by German parents and trained in German schools.

When Poland fell in 1939, the Germans and Soviets both carried out sweeping programs of murder and terror against the Poles. The Soviet forces sent more than one million people from eastern Poland to labor camps in the USSR. Among those sent away were religious leaders, student leaders, business owners, government officials, and anyone else considered dangerous to Stalinist rule. The Soviets also imprisoned about 15,000 officers in the Polish army. Four years later, the bodies of 4,000 executed officers were found in the Katyn forest near the Dnieper River. The Nazis and Soviets accused each other of the massacre, but it was later proven that the Soviets were guilty.

In western Poland, the Nazis built several **concentration camps**—camps where political prisoners were held. University pro-fessors, government workers, and others were sent there. The Nazis also set up a resettlement program under which thousands of farm families from western Poland were moved to make room for German settlers.

Hitler used the resources of Europe to enrich Germany. German soldiers ate food harvested in France and the Soviet Union, and they fought with weapons made in Czech factories. German tanks ran on Rumanian oil. Nazi officials decorated their homes with works of art stolen from museums all over Europe.

The Nazis also demanded labor from the conquered peoples. Some seven million men and women were sent to forced labor camps in Germany. Hundreds of thousands died there of disease, hunger, mistreatment, and exhaustion. Prisoners of war and political prisoners were also sent to the camps. Of more than five million Russians taken prisoner by the Nazis, about three and a half million died in the camps.

The Holocaust. Himmler's deputy, Reinhard Heydrich (HY-drick), was the chief planner of the Nazi program to wipe out the Jews of Europe—always one of Hitler's main goals. Heydrich's plan was called "the Final Solution to the Jewish Problem." For the Nazis the "final solution" was genocide. Their systematic murder of European Jews has come to be called the **Holocaust**.

From all over Europe, Jews were rounded up, loaded into cattle cars, and shipped to death camps. Many were herded into gas chambers built for mass murder. Others were beaten, starved, and tortured to death by their guards. Some prisoners—Jews and others—were the victims of cruel medical experiments. About six million Jews, including one and a half million children, perished in the Holocaust.

The most notorious of the Nazi death camps was Auschwitz (OWSH-vitz), in Poland. Between three and four million people died in this one camp. After the war, the commandant at Auschwitz was tried for crimes against humanity and executed. His testimony during that trial included the following description of what happened to prisoners: **695**

● RETEACHING. Have students identify the causes and effects of Hitler's racial policies. (Causes: Hitler believed that the Germans were a "master race." Effects: "re-education of racial 'cousins,'" programs of murder and terror, concentration camps, the Holocaust.) (Comprehension) Observing for Detail

● REINFORCEMENT. Have students work in groups to organize a meeting of resistance fighters that might have occurred in a country occupied by Nazi Germany. Participants should identify their reasons for joining the movement and develop strategies for fighting Nazi aggression. (Application) Translating Information into Another Form

Vocabulary The word genocide is derived from the Greek genos (tribe or race) and the Latin cida (killer).

Nazi storm troopers round up Jewish women and children in the Polish city of Warsaw. Almost three million Polish Jews lost their lives in the Holocaust.

❝ The way we selected our victims was as follows: Those who were fit for work were sent into the camp. Others were sent immediately to the extermination plants. Young children were exterminated since they were unable to work. We tried to fool the victims into thinking they were to go through a process to rid them of lice. Of course, frequently they realized our true intentions, and we sometimes had riots and difficulties due to that fact. Women would hide their children under their clothes, but of course when we found them, we would send the children to be exterminated. ❞

● See below.

Resistance Movements

Nazi rule did not go unopposed in the countries Hitler's forces had overrun. In each occupied country, people banded together to form resistance movements. Resistance fighters in France and the Soviet Union made hit-and-run attacks on German forces. The Danish resistance protected almost all of Denmark's 8,000 Jews by smuggling them into neutral Sweden. Greek and Yugoslav resistance fighters, called partisans, waged guerrilla war against the Germans. At its height the Polish resistance numbered 300,000. Even some Italians and Germans opposed their government.

Resistance fighters attacked German patrols, led strikes, and blew up factories. They printed underground newspapers and sent information to the Allies over hidden radios. They rescued crews of downed planes, hid escaped prisoners, and helped them get away to Allied territory.

Resistance workers—men, women, and children—took great risks. The prison cell, the concentration camp, the torture room, and the firing squad awaited those captured

● **ENRICHMENT. Have students work in groups to present a panel discussion on Nazi programs of terror. Students might research concentration camps, death camps, the Holocaust, or medical experiments.** *(Application) Locating Information*

Literature and History *The Diary of Anne Frank* is the well-known autobiographical account of a young Jewish girl and her family, who were hidden by brave Dutch supporters in Amsterdam. For two years the Frank family and others lived in secret rooms above a spice factory until captured in 1944 by Nazis.

by the Nazis. For every German soldier killed by a resistance fighter, the Germans killed civilian hostages. For example, when Czech resistance fighters assassinated Reinhard Heydrich in 1942, the Czech village of Lidice (LEE-dit-shuh), containing about 500 people, was wiped out in revenge. Nazi forces killed the men of the village, shipped the women to labor camps, and sent the children to Germany.

Resistance took another form as government officials and rulers fled occupied countries and set up "governments in exile." Ordinary citizens who could escape to Britain joined army units that fought with the Allied troops. The Free French, led by General Charles de Gaulle (duh GAWL), included survivors of Dunkirk as well as others who escaped later. Poles, Czechs, Norwegians, Belgians, and Dutch also formed fighting units.

See Sec. 2 *Closing the Lesson*, p. T683B.

See lesson plans, pp. T683A–T683C.

Section Review

Answers to Section Review questions are in brackets on pages indicated.

1. **Define or identify:** Allies, blitzkrieg, Maginot Line, concentration camp, Holocaust. (pp. 688, 689, 695)
2. How did German troops conquer most of Western Europe? (p. 689)
3. What were Hitler's aims in invading the Soviet Union? (p. 691)
4. What was the turning point of the war in Eastern Europe? (p. 692)
5. Why was victory in North Africa important to the Allies? (p. 695)
6. **Critical thinking:** Why did the Allies move quickly to help Stalin when Hitler invaded the Soviet Union? Why might some people have objected to aiding the Soviets? (See answer below.)

6. Students might suggest that the Allies did not want Hitler to gain control of the Soviet Union's vast territory and resources. Some people might have objected to aiding a Communist country.

3 War in the Pacific

Objectives

Focus Questions

★ ■ What caused war between the United States and Japan? *(pages 697–698)*
● ■ How did the United States halt the Japanese offensive in the Pacific? *(pages 698–700)*

Terms to Know

embargo   Battle of Midway

★ Note strategies for first objective on this page and p. 698.

As you read in Chapter 33, Japan adopted imperialist policies in the 1930's, looking to become the leading power in Asia. Japan's bid to dominate the Pacific soon led to war with the United States.

Japanese Aggression

Japan's first moves were against the Asian mainland. Japan had annexed Korea in 1910. In 1931 Japanese troops occupied Manchuria, bringing that region's resources under Japanese control. Six years later Japan launched an all-out invasion of China, forcing Chiang Kai-shek's Nationalist forces to retreat into western China.

Hitler's moves against Britain, France, and the Netherlands gave Japan new chances to expand in the Pacific. These European countries had to leave their Pacific colonies undefended to fight against Hitler.

Japan planned to add these lands to its possessions on the mainland, to create the "Greater East Asia Co-Prosperity Sphere." This "sphere" would supply oil, rubber, and tin for Japanese industry, rice for the Japanese people, and markets for Japanese products.

Sec. Rev. ques. 2

697

★ RETEACHING. Have students identify the causes of increased Japanese aggression in the Pacific. (European colonies in the Pacific were undefended; Japan wanted raw materials, food, and markets.) *(Comprehension)* **Understanding Causes**

★ REINFORCEMENT. Have students compare the causes of Japanese and German aggression. (Japan needed raw materials, food, and markets, and wanted to create an "Asia for Asians." Germany wanted to overturn the Versailles Treaty, restore German power, bring all German-speaking peoples into the Third Reich, and have all of occupied Europe serve the "master race.") *(Comprehension)* **Synthesizing Information**

The surprise attack that crippled the U.S. fleet at Pearl Harbor was a stunning success for the Japanese military. In the long run, however, the decision to bomb Pearl Harbor proved disastrous for Japan, since it motivated outraged Americans to support an immediate declaration of war.

Pearl Harbor. Only the United States was strong enough to challenge Japanese expansion. It began by limiting trade with Japan and imposing an embargo—a ban—on the sale of vital raw materials to that country. Convinced that war with the United States was inevitable, Japan allied itself with the Axis Powers. Japanese leaders also began planning a massive surprise attack on the United States.

Sec. Rev. ques. 3

698 Early on the morning of December 7, 1941, Japanese planes took off from aircraft carriers to attack Pearl Harbor, the American naval base in the Hawaiian Islands. The warships in the harbor and the planes lined up along the runways were easy targets for the low-flying Japanese bombers. The attack destroyed much of the United States' Pacific fleet and air force.

★ See below, left.

At almost the same time, Japanese planes attacked other American island bases in the Pacific, as well as British holdings in Malaya and Hong Kong. Outraged, the United States and Britain declared war on Japan on December 8. A few days later, Germany and Italy declared war on the United States.

Japanese victories. The year following the attack on Pearl Harbor brought many Japanese victories. By early 1942, Japanese forces had taken the Philippines (an American possession) and Burma and Singapore (both British). The Japanese had also conquered the Dutch East Indies, French Indochina, and other territories in Southeast Asia and the Pacific (map, next page).

Japan claimed that it was creating an Asia for Asians. Yet the Japanese treated conquered peoples harshly. Under Japanese rule, thousands of Asian laborers and Dutch, Australian, and British prisoners of war were forced to build railways and roads through mountains and jungles. From the conquered lands Japan took rubber, tin, oil, and tons of food. Bitter about Japanese exploitation, the conquered peoples began to form resistance movements that carried on guerrilla warfare against the Japanese.

Sec. Rev. ques. 4

● Note strategies for second objective on this page and p. 700.

American victories. By the spring of 1942, the United States forces in the Pacific had begun to rebuild and were ready to fight back. Yet the Japanese pressed on, hoping to capture the island of New Guinea and then attack Australia. In May, American and Japanese ships and planes clashed in the Coral Sea off the east coast of Australia. Though neither side won a clear-cut victory, the Battle of the Coral Sea ended Japan's advance toward Australia.

Sec. Rev. ques. 5

Both sides then prepared for a showdown over Midway, an isolated island about 1,000 miles northwest of Pearl Harbor. Midway was valuable as an air base from which the Japanese could attack their next target—Hawaii.

★ **ENRICHMENT. Have students prepare a class report on the Japanese attack on Pearl Harbor. Students might find information on Japan's battle plan or the amount of destruction caused by the attack.** *(Application)* **Locating Information**

Politics In the United States Senate, the vote for the declaration of war on Japan was unanimous. In the House of Representatives, the only dissenting vote was that of pacifist Jeanette Rankin, who felt that a "good democracy" should not vote unanimously for war.

● **RETEACHING. Have students summarize how the United States halted Japan's Pacific offensive.** (The United States ended Japan's advance toward Australia, then defeated Japan at the Battle of Midway.) *(Comprehension)* **Observing for Detail**

● **REINFORCEMENT. Have students study the map on p. 699 and then work in groups to identify possible difficulties encountered by United States forces in Japan.** *(Comprehension)* **Drawing Conclusions**

Map Skill Practice

SOVIET UNION

1945

ASIA

MONGOLIA

MANCHURIA

Shenyang

Beijing
(Peking)

Yan'an

KOREA

JAPAN
Tokyo

CHINA

Nanjing

Hiroshima
Tokyo
Bay

Shanghai

Nagasaki

Chongqing
(Chungking)

OKINAWA
1945

TAIWAN

IWO JIMA
1945

BURMA

Hong
Kong

THAILAND

FRENCH
INDO-
CHINA

Manila

PHILIPPINES

MARIANA
ISLANDS

SAIPAN

GUAM
1944

MALAYA

Singapore

BORNEO

SUMATRA

DUTCH   EAST   INDIES

JAVA

LEYTE GULF
1944

CAROLINE   IS.

ALASKA

ATTU   KISKA   ALEUTIAN   ISLANDS
1943

PACIFIC   OCEAN

MIDWAY
1942

HAWAIIAN IS.
Pearl Harbor
Honolulu

WAKE I.

MARSHALL
ISLANDS

TARAWA
1943

GILBERT   IS.

NEW GUINEA

SOLOMON   IS.

GUADALCANAL
1942

INDIAN

OCEAN

Darwin

Coral

Sea

SCALE

0   1,000 mi

0   1,000 km

AUSTRALIA

Brisbane

Perth

Adelaide

Sydney
Canberra

Melbourne

N

W   E

S

NEW
ZEALAND

KEY

Japanese empire, 1931

Japanese gains by 1942

Extent of Japanese expansion

Allied advances

Burma Road

World War II in Asia and the Pacific

See p. T683C for answers to *Map Skill Practice.*

1. Using the map, identify areas that were part of the Japanese empire in 1931.
2. What areas of the Asian mainland did Japan gain by 1942?
3. What was the farthest east-west distance of Japanese expansion?
4. When did Allied forces advance into Manchuria?
5. **Decision-making.** How might the extent of Japan's control have influenced Allied strategy in the Pacific?

The **Battle of Midway** lasted from June 4 through June 7, 1942. Like the Battle of the Coral Sea, it was fought entirely by aircraft. A force of carrier-based American torpedo planes flew in low toward the Japanese ships. Nearly all of these American planes were shot down, but the attack scattered the Japanese ships and distracted the Japanese fighter pilots. Before the Japanese planes had time to react, high-flying American dive bombers roared down from the sky at the Japanese carriers. This timely bomber attack proved to be the deciding factor in the battle.

When the Battle of Midway ended, the Japanese had lost their four best aircraft carriers, along with the planes on deck and many skilled pilots. In this stunning victory, the United States had regained naval superiority in the Pacific. The tide of the war in Asia was beginning to turn.

● See below.

See Sec. 3 *Closing the Lesson,* p. T683C.

See lesson plans, pp. T683A–T683C.

6. Students might suggest that he regretted provoking the United States, a world power, into declaring war.

4 Victory for the Allies

Objectives

Focus Questions

★ ■ How did the Allies win the war in Europe and in the Pacific? *(pages 700–702)*

● ■ What was the immediate aftermath of World War II? *(pages 702–703)*

Terms to Know

D-Day   summit
Nuremberg Trials   United Nations

★ Note strategies for first objective on this page and p. 702.

By the end of 1942, the Allies had taken the offensive in both Europe and the Pacific.
700 During the next two and a half years, they

closed in on Hitler's empire. In the Pacific, the war moved from island to island, until the United States' use of the atomic bomb suddenly brought about Japan's surrender.

Axis Defeats in Europe

The surrender of Italy. The occupation of North Africa gave the Allies a base for the invasion of Italy. In July 1943, British and American troops landed on the island of Sicily. That same month Mussolini was overthrown, but German armies remained in Italy. Allied troops next landed on the Italian mainland. With the help of local Italian fighters, they fought their way north against stiff German resistance. The Allies took Rome in June 1944, but fighting did not end completely until the following year.

Sec. Rev. ques. 2

The invasion of France. The Allies were also planning an invasion of Western

Europe. After months of preparation, a huge Allied force led by General Dwight Eisenhower crossed the English Channel to invade Nazi-occupied France. **D-Day**, as the day of the landing in Normandy was called, came on June 6, 1944.

D-Day caught the Germans off guard. They had expected an Allied landing but had no way of knowing exactly when or where it would come. Some 120,000 Allied soldiers—mostly American, British, Canadian and Free French—landed on five beaches on the coast of Normandy. Many soldiers had to struggle ashore through four-foot waves in the face of fierce German gunfire. Yet less than a month later, one million Allied soldiers were in France. By the end of August, the Allies had freed Paris from German control and were pushing toward Germany.

The defeat of Germany. By the fall of 1944, Germany's position seemed hopeless. Soviet armies were nearing Germany from the east. In the west, American and British forces had reached the German border. Heavy bombing was devastating German cities.

Hitler made one last desperate attempt to stop the Allies. In mid-December 1944, German troops and tanks attacked American soldiers in the hilly forests near Germany's border with Belgium and Luxembourg. The attack took the Americans by surprise, and the Germans broke through their lines. Outnumbered five to one, the Americans stubbornly held key towns and roads in what became known as the Battle of the Bulge. Unable to crush this resistance, and short of gasoline for tanks and trucks, the German offensive halted. At the beginning of January, the Allies launched an attack that soon wiped out the German gains.

The Allies now could move into Germany from both east and west. Late in April 1945, American and Soviet troops met in eastern Germany. On April 30, with Soviet

On D-Day, Allied troops land on the beaches of Normandy in German-occupied France. The landing was the largest seaborne invasion in history and an essential step in the defeat of the Axis Powers in Europe.

Check for Understanding. Ask: What was D-Day? (The day Allied forces landed in Normandy.)

Sec. Rev. ques. 2, cont.

troops only blocks away from his underground headquarters in Berlin, Hitler committed suicide. A demoralized, devastated, and leaderless Germany surrendered unconditionally. The end of war in Europe was announced on May 8, 1945. That date became known as V-E Day, for "victory in Europe."

The Defeat of Japan

Island warfare. In the Pacific, the United States took the offensive against Japan after the Battle of Midway. The plan was to "island-hop." The Allied forces would seize only those islands that were in strategic positions on the sea route to Japan (map, page 699).

In August 1942, American soldiers attacked the Japanese base at Guadalcanal in the Solomon Islands, while Australians and other Allied troops fought in New Guinea. Although jungle warfare was slow and casualties were high, the Allies moved ever closer to Japan. In October 1944, American forces crushed the Japanese fleet at the Battle of Leyte (LAY-tee) Gulf. American troops, led by General Douglas MacArthur, were then able to reclaim the Philippines. MacArthur, who had left the Philippines in 1942 with the promise "I shall return," thus kept his word.

Sec. Rev. ques. 3

Casualties ran high in the Pacific because of the fierce determination of the Japanese. Infantry soldiers fought to the death rather than be taken prisoner. Kamikaze pilots, who took their name from the "divine wind" that had saved Japan from invasion in the 1200's (page 289), deliberately crashed their planes into American ships. In the battle for the island of Iwo Jima (EE-woh JEE-muh), it took American Marines three days to gain only 700 yards. In a month of fighting, more than 5,000 Americans were killed and another 15,000 were wounded. Casualties were even higher at Okinawa, the last battle in the Pacific war. The number killed there added up to about 12,500 Americans, 120,000 Japanese, and 42,000 Okinawans.

702

The atomic bomb. By mid-1945 Japan had been thoroughly beaten. Its armed forces were destroyed and its cities lay in ruins from American bombings. Still, Japan would not give up.

Harry Truman, who became President after Roosevelt died, hoped to avoid a costly invasion of Japan. He chose to use America's secret weapon: the atomic bomb. On July 26, 1945, Allied leaders warned Japan that if it did not surrender at once, it would suffer "complete and utter destruction." The Japanese sent no answer.

On August 6, 1945, a single atomic bomb was dropped on the Japanese city of Hiroshima (hee-roh-SHEE-muh). The world was stunned by the destructive power of the new weapon. The bomb completely demolished about 60 percent of Hiroshima. For four miles around the target point, almost no buildings were left standing. More than 80,000 people were killed and 37,000 more suffered severe injuries. Others later died from the effects of radiation released by the explosion.

On August 8, 1945, the Soviet Union declared war on Japan and invaded Manchuria. Still Japan did not surrender. The next day, an American plane dropped a second atomic bomb. This time the target was Nagasaki (nah-guh-SAH-kee), an important shipbuilding city. Again the effects were deadly.

★ See below, left.

Though the military leaders of Japan wanted to continue the war, Emperor Hirohito forced them to surrender for the good of the country. On August 15—called V-J Day for "victory over Japan"—the emperor announced the defeat to his people. On September 2, officials of the Japanese government signed the document of surrender on board the battleship *Missouri* in Tokyo Bay.

The War's Aftermath

● Note strategies for second objective on this page and p. 703.

Costs of the war. World War II was the most costly war in history. Perhaps 50 million people died, both soldiers and civilians. At least 10 million died in the Nazi

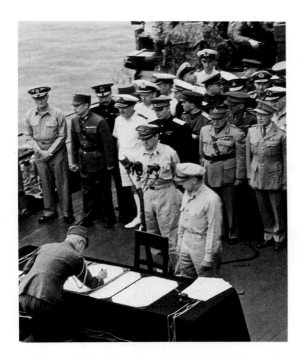

In September 1945, aboard the *USS Missouri*, a Japanese general signs a surrender document officially ending World War II. Japan had earlier refused the United States' demand for unconditional surrender. The Japanese did not give up until after atomic bombs had been dropped on Hiroshima and Nagasaki.

death camps, including six million Jews. Millions of others, made homeless, became refugees. The war also left vast areas of destruction, particularly in Europe and Asia. Cities, factories, and farms were in ruins. The world faced a gigantic task of rebuilding.

War crimes trials. Many people felt that those who had led the world into this destruction should be punished. A number of the surviving Nazi leaders were arrested and charged with "crimes against humanity." The

● See below.

Nuremberg Trials, held in Nuremberg, Germany, began in November 1945. Now, for the first time, most of the world learned the details of the horrors of the Holocaust and the Nazi death camps. About half of the officers tried at Nuremberg were sentenced to death; others were imprisoned. Several Japanese commanders who had ordered cruel treatment of prisoners of war were also tried by a military court.

Planning for a postwar Europe. During the course of the war, the Allies held three **summits**—meetings between top government leaders. In November 1943 Churchill, Stalin, and Roosevelt met at Tehran, Iran, to discuss strategy for the war in Europe. At that time, the Normandy invasion was planned.

The next meeting of the "Big Three" took place at Yalta, a Soviet city on the Black Sea, in February 1945. By that time, Soviet troops had occupied much of Eastern Europe and had begun to set up puppet governments there. At the urging of Churchill and Roosevelt, Stalin agreed to hold free elections in Eastern Europe after the war. He also promised to declare war on Japan after Germany's defeat. In return, Stalin gained some territory in Asia. All three leaders agreed to form the **United Nations** (UN), an international peacekeeping organization. They also agreed to divide defeated Germany into temporary occupation zones.

Sec. Rev. ques. 4

In July 1945, after Germany's surrender, Stalin, Churchill, and the new American President, Harry Truman, met at Potsdam, Germany. When Truman demanded that Stalin keep his promise to allow free elections in the occupied countries, Stalin refused. He said bluntly, "A freely elected government in any of these Eastern European countries would be anti-Soviet, and that we cannot allow." Disagreements over the future of Eastern Europe would soon split the Allies, raising fears of yet another world war.

See Sec. 4 Closing the Lesson, p. T683D.

Linking Past and Present

When Japan surrendered in 1945, many Japanese soldiers were fighting in remote jungles on Pacific islands. A few of these soldiers refused to give up when the war was over. As late as 1975, a Japanese soldier was found hiding in the jungle on the Indonesian island of Morotai. He explained, "My commander told me to fight it out."

● ENRICHMENT. Have students work in groups to write a script and dramatize a scene from the Nuremberg Trials. Students might find information on the trial of a particular individual or research background information on the trials. *(Application) Translating Information into Another Form*

Economics It has been estimated that the war cost Germany at least $272 billion.

Political History. Mention to students that a treaty signed in October 1990 by West and East Germany and the four allies that had divided defeated Germany into occupation zones formally ended the war that Germany had begun 51 years before. The treaty in effect restored full sovereignty to a reunited Germany.

Section Review

Answers to Section Review questions are in brackets on pages indicated.

1. **Define or identify:** D-Day, Nurem- (pp. 701, berg Trials, summit, United Nations. 703)
2. What events brought about the end of the war in Europe? (pp. 700–702)
3. How did the war come to an end in the Pacific? (p. 702)

4. What agreements did the Allied leaders make at Yalta? (p. 703)
5. **Critical thinking:** Give arguments for and against the dropping of atomic bombs on Hiroshima and Nagasaki in August 1945. (See answer below.)

5. Students in favor of the bomb might argue that the United States saved lives and money by ending the war. Students opposing the bomb might argue that the killing of civilians and the severity of destruction were not justified.

Chapter 34 Summary and Timeline

1. In the decade after World War I, many nations took part in efforts to preserve peace. The rise of dictators in Germany and Italy, however, led to aggression. Britain and France did little at first to halt Germany's violations of the Versailles treaty. At Munich in 1938 they continued the policy of appeasement. When Hitler moved against Poland in 1939, World War II broke out.

2. In 1940 German forces rapidly overran Western Europe, leaving Britain alone to face Hitler. The German invasion of the Soviet Union, however, brought that country into the war. A Soviet victory at Stalingrad in 1943 and victories in North Africa turned the tide of the war against Hitler. Meanwhile, the Nazis carried out cruel racial policies in occupied Europe, causing much opposition among the conquered peoples.

3. Japanese aggression against China in the 1930's led to war in Asia. In December 1941, a surprise Japanese attack on Hawaii drew the United States into the war. Japanese conquests in the Pacific came to an end with an important American victory in the Battle of Midway.

4. The Allied victory in Europe came in May 1945. War continued in Asia, but by dropping atomic bombs on two Japanese cities, the United States forced Japan to surrender in August 1945. At the war's end, world leaders were faced with the task of rebuilding shattered countries and creating a lasting peace.

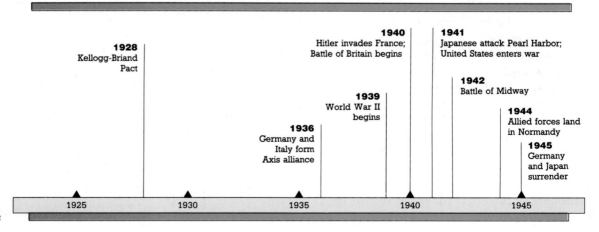

1928 Kellogg-Briand Pact

1936 Germany and Italy form Axis alliance

1939 World War II begins

1940 Hitler invades France; Battle of Britain begins

1941 Japanese attack Pearl Harbor; United States enters war

1942 Battle of Midway

1944 Allied forces land in Normandy

1945 Germany and Japan surrender

1925   1930   1935   1940   1945

See p. T683D for answers to Chapter Review.

Vocabulary Review

1. Match each of the following terms with its correct definition: *Battle of Midway, concentration camp, embargo, Nazi-Soviet Pact, United Nations.*
    a. international organization whose goal is to keep the peace
    b. arrangement by which Stalin agreed to Hitler's invasion of Poland
    c. Pacific air battle won by the United States in June 1942
    d. ban on trade
    e. area where the Nazis held political prisoners and other captives
2. Use the following terms to complete the sentences below: *Axis Powers, blitzkrieg, Holocaust, Maginot Line, Nuremberg Trials.*
    a. The _____ was a string of heavily defended forts along France's border with Germany.
    b. Germany, Italy, and Japan were known as the _____.
    c. The _____ exposed Nazi war crimes.
    d. The Nazis' systematic murder of European Jews is known as the _____.
    e. Germany's method of quick, concentrated attacks was called _____.

People to Identify

Identify the following people and tell why each was important.
1. Winston Churchill
2. Charles de Gaulle
3. Dwight D. Eisenhower
4. Haile Selassie
5. Heinrich Himmler
6. Erwin Rommel
7. Harry Truman

Places to Know

Choose the place name that best completes each sentence.
1. Hitler claimed a region of Czechoslovakia called the [Sudetenland/Rhineland].
2. The last island battle of the Pacific war took place at [Okinawa/Nagasaki].
3. Millions of people died in the Nazi death camp at [Auschwitz/Hiroshima].
4. The Soviet victory at [Pearl Harbor/Stalingrad] marked a turning point in the war.

Recalling the Facts

1. How did Hitler violate the Treaty of Versailles?
2. What nation invaded Ethiopia? China?
3. Why did Britain and France pursue a policy of appeasement with Germany?
4. When did Germany invade Poland? When did Italy invade France?
5. What stopped the German advance into Russia?
6. What were the first major Allied victories over Germany?
7. How did resistance movements aid the Allies?
8. Why did the United States and Britain declare war on Japan?
9. Why was the United States unable to hold back Japanese aggression until May 1942?
10. What Allied advances led to Germany's defeat in World War II?
11. Describe Allied strategy in the Pacific. What ended the war with Japan?
12. What were the postwar conditions like in the areas that had undergone wartime destruction?

✔ **1. Identifying trends.** New trends in weaponry, equipment, and tactics developed during both World War I (Chapter 31) and World War II. What do you think was the most significant new development in each war? Explain. *(Syn.)*

2. Using a graph. The graph below shows the number of battle deaths in selected countries during World War II. How many Soviet military personnel were killed? German? American? Which side suffered the greatest number of battle deaths, the Axis Powers or the Allies? *(Comp.)*

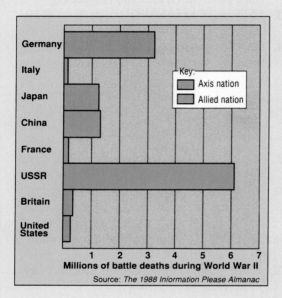

Germany
Italy
Japan
China
France
USSR
Britain
United States

Key:
■ Axis nation
■ Allied nation

1 2 3 4 5 6 7
Millions of battle deaths during World War II

Source: *The 1988 Information Please Almanac*

3. Reading an autobiography. Anne Frank, a 13-year-old Jewish girl, went into hiding with her family after German forces occupied the Netherlands. Read *The Diary of Anne Frank*. Then write an essay about the situation that European Jews faced during the Nazi era. *(App.)*

Interpreting a map. Look at the map on page 694. What base did the Allies use to invade Western Europe? Why, do you think, was Normandy chosen for the D-Day landing? *(Comp.)*

706

The following adapted passage describes an uprising in 1943 in which Jews in the Warsaw ghetto resisted Nazi troops.

❝ Every night scouts stood at their posts, ready to sound the alarm if the enemy should come.

At six o'clock the Nazis marched boldly into the ghetto in full battle array, with armored cars, machine guns, and tanks. The proud German column was met with fire from three sides. Grenades and flaming bottles cascaded down on them. Such strong resistance surprised the Germans. They quickly left the ghetto.

The next morning, after cutting off the electricity and the water supply, they were back. This time they did not parade down the center of the street. They came singly or in small groups, moving close to the walls. They moved under a hail of hand grenades, dynamite bombs, and flaming bottles thrown from windows, roofs, and attics. Our fighters battled for every building and for every floor of every building. The Germans usually set fire to the buildings.

After the wave of fire receded, small groups still held out without water, food, or ammunition. All hope of striking back at the enemy was gone. There was nothing left to do but try to escape. ❞

1. What suggests that the Jews were preparing for an attack?
2. How did the Nazis change tactics for their second attack?
3. **Critical thinking:** Why, do you think, did the Jews fight against seemingly hopeless odds? *(Syn.)*

✔ A checkmark identifies questions and exercises calling for the three higher-order levels of thinking at the top of the Bloom taxonomy: Analysis, Synthesis, and Evaluation.

WORLD HISTORY
Checklist

UNIT 9

Try to identify the following key people, places, and terms from the unit. If you need help, refer to the pages listed.

Key People

Francis Ferdinand *(627)*
Woodrow Wilson *(633)*
Nicholas II *(645)*
Lenin *(646)*
Rasputin *(647)*
Alexander Kerensky *(647)*
Leon Trotsky *(654)*
Joseph Stalin *(654)*
Benito Mussolini *(663)*
Adolf Hitler *(665)*
Heinrich Himmler *(667)*
Francisco Franco *(669)*
Henry Ford *(670)*
Orville and Wilbur Wright *(670)*
Charles Lindbergh *(671)*
Franklin D. Roosevelt *(672)*
James Joyce *(674)*
Virginia Woolf *(674)*
Ernest Hemingway *(674)*
Franz Kafka *(674)*
T. S. Eliot *(674)*
Salvador Dali *(675)*
Sun Yat-sen *(676)*
Chiang Kai-shek *(676)*
Mao Zedong *(677)*
Mustafa Kemal *(678)*
Reza Shah Pahlavi *(679)*
Ibn Saud *(679)*
Haile Selassie *(685)*
Neville Chamberlain *(686)*
Winston Churchill *(690)*
Dwight D. Eisenhower *(693)*
Charles de Gaulle *(697)*
Douglas MacArthur *(702)*
Harry Truman *(702)*

Key Places

Austria-Hungary *(625)*
Serbia *(626)*
St. Petersburg (Leningrad) *(647)*

Ireland *(673)*
Palestine *(680)*
Sudetenland *(686)*
Stalingrad (Volgograd) *(692)*
Auschwitz *(695)*
Pearl Harbor *(698)*
Normandy *(701)*
Iwo Jima *(702)*
Hiroshima *(702)*
Nagasaki *(702)*

Winston Churchill.

Key Terms

World War I *(625)*
Triple Alliance *(625)*
Triple Entente *(625)*
militarism *(626)*
Allies *(628)*
Central Powers *(628)*
U-boat *(633)*
Fourteen Points *(635)*
self-determination *(635)*
League of Nations *(636)*
Treaty of Versailles *(636)*
isolationism *(638)*
Bolshevik *(646)*
October Manifesto *(647)*
March Revolution *(647)*
Treaty of Brest-Litovsk *(650)*
Kremlin *(651)*
ideology *(653)*
Five-Year Plan *(655)*
Great Purge *(658)*
totalitarian state *(659)*
fascism *(663)*
Nazi Party *(665)*
authoritarianism *(668)*
Spanish Civil War *(669)*
Great Depression *(672)*
New Deal *(672)*
Commonwealth of Nations *(673)*
Easter Rebellion *(673)*
May Fourth Movement *(676)*
Long March *(677)*
Balfour Declaration *(680)*
Axis Powers *(686)*
appeasement *(686)*
Nazi-Soviet Pact *(688)*
World War II *(688)*
Allies *(688)*
concentration camp *(695)*
Holocaust *(695)*
D-Day *(701)*
Nuremberg Trials *(703)*
United Nations *(703)*

REVIEW ACTIVITIES. *Key People:* Identify each person listed and explain why each is considered a key person in history. *Key Places:* Show on a world outline map the location of each place. (See pages 74 and 162 of *Teacher's Resources: Geography* for world outline maps that can be copied.) *Key Terms:* Define or identify each term listed.

The Contemporary World 1945–2000

	1945	1950	1955	1960	1965	1970

CHAPTER 35: Postwar Europe and the Soviet Union

1945
United Nations
established

1948–1952
Europe receives
Marshall Plan aid

1957
Common Market
formed

1968
Soviet Union
invades
Czechoslovakia

CHAPTER 36: New Directions for Asia

1947
India and Pakistan
gain independence

1952
U.S. occupation
of Japan ends

1953
Korean War ends

1966
Cultural Revolution
begins in China

CHAPTER 37: Challenges for the Middle East

1948
State of Israel
established

1956
Suez Canal crisis

1967
Israel wins
Six-Day War

CHAPTER 38: Independent Africa

1951
Mau Mau
movement begins
in Kenya

1957
Ghana gains
independence

1967–1970
Nigerian Civil War

CHAPTER 39: The Changing Americas

1952
Puerto Rico
becomes
commonwealth

1962
Cuban Missile
Crisis

1965
Voting Rights Act
in United States

CHAPTER 40: Linking Past,

1962
Pope calls
Vatican II

1967
First successful human
heart transplant

1969
U.S. astronauts
land on moon

	1945	1950	1955	1960	1965	1970

FOCUS STRATEGY. Tell students that the illustration shows a
present-day cityscape, dominated by skyscrapers. Then ask:
(a) What elements in this drawing illustrate life in the contemporary world? (Skyscrapers and modern transportation.) (b) What, do
you think, might be the main occupation of people who live in this
city? (Students might suggest a variety of occupations—business, professions, construction, selling, etc.)

| 1975 | 1980 | 1985 | 1990 | 1995 | 2000 |

1979
Thatcher becomes
prime minister of Britain

1985
Gorbachev
comes to
power in
Soviet Union

1990
Germany
unified

1991
End of
Soviet
Union

1980
Solidarity formed
in Poland

1975
Vietnam united
under Communist
rule

1988
Soviets begin
withdrawal from
Afghanistan

1991
Cambodian
peace
agreement

1975
Civil war breaks
out in Lebanon

1980
Iran-Iraq
War begins

1987
Palestinians begin
protests in
occupied
territories

1991
Gulf War.
Arab-Israeli
talks
begin

1976
Soweto
uprisings in
South Africa

1980
Rhodesia
becomes
independent
Zimbabwe

1988
Agreements reached
on Namibian
independence

1990
Mandela
released
from
prison

1991
Democracy
movements

1979
Sandinistas take
power in
Nicaragua

1985
Guatemala and
Brazil elect civilian
governments

1989
Civilian
government
restored in Chile

Present, and Future

1981
First space shuttle
launched

1989–1991
End of communism in
Soviet Union/Eastern Europe

| 1975 | 1980 | 1985 | 1990 | 1995 | 2000 |

709

Have students look at the last events on the top and bottom bars of
the unit timeline and answer this question: What is the significance
of these events for people around the world? (Resulted in end of cold
war—and presumably reduced the threat of nuclear war.)

Europe Before and After the Cold War 1945–Present

(pp. 710–733)

Chapter Preview

Section 1 describes the goals of the United Nations and the duties of its six main branches. The section also traces the events that led to worsening relations between the United States and the Soviet Union. Section 2 discusses the economic recovery made by the nations of Western Europe after World War II, and then examines political and economic developments in Germany, France, Britain, and the countries of southern Europe in more recent years. Section 3 discusses the postwar foreign and domestic policies of the Soviet Union and the situation of the Eastern European nations that were dominated by Soviet power. The section concludes with an account of the extraordinary changes that turned the Soviet Union in new directions and liberated the satellite countries from Soviet rule.

Bibliography

See the *Teacher's Management and Planning Guide* for additional listings. Starred titles are for both students and teachers.

Timothy Garton Ash. *The Magic Lantern: The Revolution of '89*. Random House. An account of the collapse of the Communist regimes in Eastern Europe.

*Barzini, Luigi. *The Europeans*. Penguin. A brief, up-to-date overview.

Davison, W. P. *The Berlin Blockade*. Princeton University Press. Describes the Berlin crisis in the cold war.

Lewin, Moshe. *The Gorbachev Phenomenon: A Historical Interpretation*. University of California Press. Changing dynamics of Soviet leadership.

Mowat, R. C. *Creating the European Community*. Barnes and Noble. Europe's new economic institution.

Smith, Hedrick. *The New Russians*. Random House. An account of recent developments that have shaken the Soviet Union.

Zinner, Paul E. *Revolution in Hungary*. Columbia University Press. The Hungarian uprising of 1956 and its suppression.

Section Lesson Plans

SECTION 1 (pp. 711–718)
Cold War Tensions

Objectives

After completing this section, students will be able to:
1. Explain why the wartime alliance between the West and the Soviet Union collapsed.
2. Identify the main issues in Soviet-American relations during the 1940's and the 1950's.

Introducing the Lesson

Remind students that although the Western nations and the Soviet Union cooperated to defeat Fascist forces during World War II, fundamental differences existed between the democratic and Communist systems. After the war, those differences resulted in political realignments and the start of the "cold war."

Then ask: *(a) What were the differences between the democratic and Communist systems?* (Answers will vary, but should include beliefs about basic human, political, and civil rights; economic systems; and the role of government in society.)

(b) Why did these differences become more significant in international relations after World War II? (Answers will vary. Communism's stated goal of world revolution may have been seen as a serious threat, especially after the Soviet Union's refusal to allow free elections in occupied territories. The willingness of the United States to use atomic weapons against enemies perhaps posed a new threat to the Soviet Union.)

Developing the Lesson:
Drawing Conclusions

Have students draw conclusions about the following: *What organizational elements might have made it difficult for the United Nations to be an effective peace-keeping body?* (The power of the members of the Security Council to veto proposed actions; the lack of any real power in the General Assembly.) *Is the United Nations a valuable organization, or would its absence make any difference in international affairs?* (Answers will vary.) *(Evaluation)*

Developing the Lesson: Synthesizing Information

Have students make a chart identifying actions taken by the Western powers and the Soviet Union after World War II that added to the tension between the two powers. (*The West:* the United States announced the Truman Doctrine supporting containment policy; airlifted supplies to Berlin; established a democratic government in Germany; formed NATO; increased nuclear capability. *Soviet Union:* created puppet governments in occupied territories; ended contact between its satellites and the West; demanded that Turkey allow Soviet military bases; supported Communist forces in Greece; blockaded Berlin; established Communist government in Germany; formed the Warsaw Pact; increased its nuclear capability.) *(Comprehension)*

Closing the Lesson: Solving Problems

Have students work in groups to evaluate the foreign policy actions taken by Western nations and the Soviet Union in the decade following 1945. Then have students propose an alternate course of action that might have reduced rather than increased tensions between the West and the Soviet Union. *(Synthesis)*

See *Section Review* questions, p. 718.

SECTION 2　　　　　(pp. 718–723)
Western Europe

Objectives

After completing this section, students will be able to:
1. Explain how Western European nations cooperated on economic matters.
2. Discuss major postwar developments in Western Europe.

Introducing the Lesson

Remind students that after the First World War, unresolved social, economic, and political issues in Europe created problems that eventually resulted in World War II. Although the Second World War devastated Europe, international economic programs were designed to rebuild the nations.

　　Then ask: *(a) What problems probably faced European nations after World War II?* (Destruction of agricultural lands, industry, and cities; population loss; indebtedness.)

(b) Why might international economic programs for rebuilding have been more successful than national programs? (Because Western Europe suffered war damage, individual efforts would have been hindered by inadequate resources. Cooperative efforts to rebuild allowed the nations to pool their resources and to speed recovery.)

Developing the Lesson: Drawing Inferences

Have students work in groups to suggest possible long-term advantages and disadvantages of the EC for the nations of Europe. *(Possible advantages:* cooperation links nations and often creates cultural and social bonds. The greater the cooperation, the more willing nations become to negotiate and compromise on areas of conflict. *Possible disadvantages:* after the initial period of need has been met, the growth of individual national economies might be subordinated to the advantage of the group.) *(Evaluation)*

Developing the Lesson: Summarizing Information

Have students summarize important economic and political events in postwar West Germany, France, the United Kingdom, Italy, Portugal and Spain, and Greece. (*West Germany:* Marshall Plan funds allowed it to become the economic leader of Europe. Under *Ostpolitik*, tensions with the Soviet bloc eased, and in 1990 West and East Germany were reunited. *France:* nationalization of banks and industries allowed rapid economic growth. De Gaulle granted independence to Algeria and other colonies and pulled France out of NATO. In 1981, a Socialist government was elected. *The United Kingdom:* The Labor Party established a welfare state. In 1973 Britain joined the Common Market. India, Pakistan, Ceylon, and Burma were granted independence. Efforts to end unrest in Northern Ireland were unsuccessful. Under Margaret Thatcher, many nationalized businesses were sold by the British government to private stockholders. *Italy:* A republic was established and Italy's economy improved. *Portugal and Spain:* in 1986 Portugal elected its first civilian president in more than 50 years. Spain held democratic elections in 1975 and elected a socialist government in 1982. *Greece:* democratic forces won a civil war after World War II and began economic reform. A group of army officers seized control of the government in 1967, but constitutional government was restored in 1974. In 1981 Socialists gained power.) *(Comprehension)*

Closing the Lesson: Observing for Detail

Have students work in groups to debate the following issue: *If World War II had not occurred, Asian and African lands colonized by Great Britain and France would not have gained independence. (Synthesis)*

See *Section Review* questions, p. 723.

SECTION 3   (pp. 724–731)
The Soviet Bloc and Its Collapse

Objectives

After completing this lesson, students will be able to:
1. Discuss the Soviet Union's foreign and domestic policies in the postwar years.
2. Explain how the Gorbachev reform period ended in the collapse of the Soviet Union.
3. Tell how Soviet domination affected Eastern Europe.

Introducing the Lesson

Tell students that the Soviet Union used totalitarian control in its domination of Eastern Europe during the cold war. Beginning in the late 1980's , however, extraordinary changes took place.

Then ask: (a) *Given the nature of the Soviet political system through the cold war period, what kind of dissent would you have expected to develop?* (Answers may mention political, ethnic, or religious dissent.) (b) *Why did the Soviet government not take military action against the revolutions that broke out in Eastern Europe in 1989?* (Answers may mention Gorbachev's policies or the difficulty of maintaining a repressive system in the face of determined protest.)

Developing the Lesson:
Summarizing Information

Have students write a one-paragraph summary for each of the Soviet leaders since World War II, describing their approaches to national problems. (*Stalin:* used terror as a means of control; instituted new Five-Year-Plan. *Khrushchev:* launched de-Stalinization; introduced more liberal domestic policies and peaceful coexistence. *Brezhnev:* introduced re-Stalinization; encouraged industrial development; followed policy of détente; tried to expand Soviet influence. *Gorbachev:* began far-reaching reforms; built stronger ties with West; ended Soviet domination of Eastern Europe; was unable to halt economic deterioration and disintegration of political union. (*Comprehension*)

Developing the Lesson:
Organizing Information

Have students identify the factors that led to the 1989 revolutions in Eastern Europe and then to the rejection of communism in the Soviet Union itself. Students might then rank the factors in terms of which were most significant in these developments. (*Evaluation*)

Closing the Lesson:
Forming a Hypothesis

Have students develop a hypothesis explaining why repressive regimes attempt to crush opposition. In developing their hypotheses, students might consider the following: Why did the Soviet government, before the Gorbachev reforms, feel it necessary to prohibit any expression of dissent? How did the expression of criticism in 1989 affect the Soviet system? Have students share their hypotheses with the class. (*Synthesis*)

See *Section Review* questions, p. 731.

Chapter 35 Review Answers
(pp. 732–733)

Vocabulary Review

1. (a) nonaligned (b) Cuban Missile Crisis (c) Common Market (d) terrorism (e) martial law
2. (a) Cold war—atmosphere of tension and hostility that existed between the superpowers in the decades following World War II; détente—French word meaning "relaxation of tensions," used to describe Brezhnev's policy toward Western nations. (b) Containment—cold war policy of attempting to prevent communism from being imposed on other nations; deterrence—policy of discouraging an attack by making one's opponent fear a counterattack. (c) Truman Doctrine—foreign policy committing the United States to aid any country that requested help in resisting a Communist takeover; Marshall Plan—American aid program to spur Western Europe's economic recovery. (d) Dissident—opponent of an existing political system; human rights—basic rights and freedoms to which all humans are entitled. (e) NATO—mutual-defense pact formed by the Western powers; Warsaw Pact—mutual defense pact among certain Eastern European nations. The pact was formed in response to the NATO alliance.

People to Identify

1. John F. Kennedy 2. Lech Walesa 3. Willy Brandt 4. Margaret Thatcher 5. Mikhail Gorbachev 6. Alexander Solzhenitsyn 7. François Mitterrand

Places to Know

1. K   2. D   3. G.   4. J   5. F   6. B   7. A   8. H   9. E   10. C   11. I

Recalling the Facts

1. The Soviets were determined to protect their western frontier from invasion. Stalin used the threat of military force to put Communist puppet governments into the lands his army occupied. By the late 1940's, Communists controlled the governments of Poland, Czechoslovakia, Hungary, Romania, Yugoslavia, Bulgaria, and Albania.
2. The Soviets feared a revival of the German economy and opposed a unified Germany. The Western powers felt that a strong Germany was essential to Europe's stability. In response to plans for a German state, the Soviets blockaded Berlin, cutting off food and other supplies from the people of West Berlin. American and British cargo planes flew in supplies. The Berlin airlift prevented the Soviet blockade from succeeding, and the blockade was called off. West Germany, a parliamentary government, was created by the Western allies. The Soviet Union installed a Communist regime in East Germany.
3. Through summit conferences, the Antarctic Treaty, and a resolution calling for peaceful uses of outer space.
4. The parts of Germany that became West Germany included the country's heavily industrialized regions, along with its supplies of coal and iron ore. West Germany still had many skilled workers and trained managers available. The country also benefited from the knowledge and skills of thousands of East German refugees and from the labor of over three million workers from southern and southeastern Europe. In addition, under the Marshall Plan, the Germans were able to rebuild their industries and transportation networks with the most modern equipment.
5. Colonial wars in Vietnam and Algeria.
6. The losses of India, Ceylon, and Burma reduced Britain's expenses but cost Britain valuable markets for British goods.
7. Italy established a republic, and its northern region became more industrialized. Dictators in Portugal, Spain, and Greece were replaced by more democratic governments.
8. Khrushchev made it official policy to denounce Stalin and expose the crimes of the Stalin years.

He also devoted a larger percentage of the Soviet budget to housing and consumer goods, curbed the power of the secret police, and ended large-scale purges. He gave local officials more control over economic affairs and recruited work teams to bring parts of the steppes under cultivation.
9. Under Brezhnev, personal freedoms were once again restricted, full central planning was restored, and military spending was emphasized at the expense of consumer goods. Like Stalin, Brezhnev stressed industrial development.
10. *Glasnost* was Gorbachev's policy of openness about problems facing the Soviet Union. *Perestroika,* or "restructuring," was Gorbachev's program of economic and political reforms. Gorbachev planned to make the Communist Party more democratic by using the secret ballot and by giving voters a choice of candidates for Party offices. Gorbachev's economic reforms aimed at reviving the Soviet economy.
11. Gorbachev's reforms in the Soviet Union encouraged the peoples of the satellite states to demand changes in their own countries. Without Soviet aid, their governments yielded to protest actions, and new governments were formed.

Critical Thinking Skills

1. Some students might argue that the policy forced nations to stockpile weapons and increased hostility. Others might argue the threat of massive destruction lessened the chance of any nation making a first strike.
2. Biographies will vary.
3. Causes might include Brandt's *Ostpolitik,* West Germany's acceptance of existing boundaries in Eastern Europe, Gorbachev's reforms in the Soviet Union and the easing of tensions in Soviet relations with the West, the opening of the Berlin Wall, and the collapse of East Germany's Communist government. Effects should be based on supportable predictions.

Thinking About Geography

Charts will vary.

Enrichment: Primary Source

1. Army officers and soldiers refused to "go against the people," meaning they refused to use violence to put down public demonstrations.
2. Even though the people wanted law and stability and economic improvement, they didn't want change to come through the use of force.
3. Answers may suggest that the coup leaders assumed the armed forces would obey the generals who took part in the plot and may have misgauged the reaction of the people.

Europe Before and After the Cold War **1945–Present**

See chapter timeline, p. 731.

Before You Read This Chapter

Suppose you have a set of blank world maps. Your job is to color the two or three most powerful countries at certain times in history. Think back over what you have read. What countries were world powers in the 1700's and 1800's? One was certainly Great Britain. By the late 1800's, Germany was powerful as well. As you read this chapter, notice what has happened to Europe's power. After 1945, what two countries were the world's leading powers? What effects did their rivalry have? What countries will be world leaders in years to come?

The Geographic Setting

The Chapter Outline

1. Cold War Tensions
2. Western Europe
3. The Soviet Bloc and Its Collapse

A war-blasted church in Berlin, Germany, was left standing as a reminder of World War II. A new, memorial church stands alongside the old building.

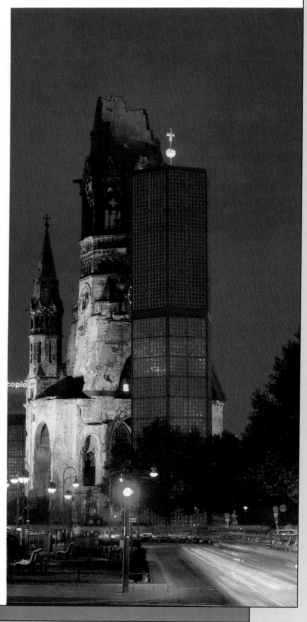

1 Cold War Tensions

Objectives

Focus Questions

★ ■ Why did the wartime alliance between the West and the Soviet Union collapse? *(pages 711–715)*

● ■ What were the main issues in Soviet-American relations during the 1940's and 1950's? *(pages 715–718)*

Terms to Know

cold war	nonaligned
bloc	NATO
Truman Doctrine	Warsaw Pact
containment	deterrence
Marshall Plan	Cuban Missile Crisis

★ Note strategies for first objective on this page and p. 714.

Allied cooperation had made it possible to defeat the Axis countries. Hoping to build a lasting peace, Allied leaders planned to go on working together after the war. Yet relations between the Soviet Union and the Western Allies soon turned sour, and a new era of world tensions began.

The United Nations

At their wartime meeting at Yalta (page 703), the leaders of the United States, Britain, and the Soviet Union had agreed to create the United Nations. In April 1945, delegates from 50 countries gathered in San Francisco. They drew up and signed the Charter of the United Nations. According to the Charter, the UN's main purpose was to "save succeeding generations from war." The UN would also promote national self-determination and respect for individual human rights, and it would help nations work together to solve their problems. By the fall of 1945, the Charter had been approved by a majority of the members. The UN soon established its headquarters in New York City.

The Charter set up six main bodies within the UN. The most important are the General Assembly and the Security Council. Every UN member nation has one vote in the General Assembly. The Assembly has the power to discuss any matter within the scope of the UN Charter and to suggest solutions. Also, the Assembly chooses the people or nations that serve in other bodies of the UN.

Sec. Rev. ques. 2

The Security Council deals with international conflicts. To stop aggressive acts by any one country, the Security Council may bar trade with that country or even send troops to keep the peace.

The victorious Allies of World War II—the United States, France, Britain, China, and the Soviet Union—became permanent members of the Security Council. Ten other members are elected by the General Assembly for two-year terms. Security Council actions must be approved by all permanent members. Each permanent member can veto actions it opposes. (In late 1991, after the Soviet Union came to an end, Russia took over the Soviet seat in the Security Council.)

The Division of Europe

The new superpowers. When World War II ended, the center of world power was no longer Western Europe. The United States and the Soviet Union had become the world's two strongest nations. In spite of their alliance against Hitler, relations between the two governments had been cool during the war. In the years afterward, the relationship worsened. The atmosphere of hostility between the superpowers in the postwar period is known as the **cold war**.

711

★ RETEACHING. Have students explain the goals of the following: **United Nations** (To avoid war and help settle international problems.) **Truman Doctrine** (To assist countries resisting communism.) **Containment** (To stop spread of communism.) **Marshall Plan** (To help Europe rebuild.) **NATO** (To maintain mutual security.) *(Comprehension) Observing for Detail*

★ REINFORCEMENT. Have students explain why the wartime alliance between East and West broke down. (Stalin used the threat of force to set up Communist puppet states; the Soviet Union cut off most contact between its satellites and Western nations.) *(Synthesis) Analyzing Information*

Check for Understanding. Ask: What was the cold war? (The atmosphere of hostility that existed between the United States and the Soviet Union following World War II.)

ICELAND

ATLANTIC

OCEAN

NORWAY

SWEDEN

FINLAND

SOVIET

Helsinki ★

Oslo ★

Stockholm ★

Baltic
Sea

ESTONIA

Moscow ★

UNION

North Sea

Copenhagen ★
DENMARK

LATVIA

LITHUANIA

EAST
PRUSSIA
Gdańsk •

UNITED
KINGDOM

IRELAND

Lubeck •

Stettin •

Poznan •

Warsaw ★

The
Hague • NETH. ★
London ★   Amsterdam

Berlin •

Potsdam •

POLAND

Brussels ★
BELG. ★ Bonn
LUX.

WEST
GERMANY

EAST
GERMANY

Prague ★

★ Paris

GERMANY

CZECHOSLOVAKIA

FRANCE

Bern ★

Vienna ★

Budapest ★

Geneva • SWITZ.

AUSTRIA

HUNGARY

ROMANIA

Trieste •

ANDORRA

ITALY

Adriatic Sea

Belgrade ★

Bucharest ★

Black Sea

YUGOSLAVIA

BULGARIA

PORTUGAL

Madrid ★

SPAIN

Lisbon ★

Rome ★

Tirana ★
ALBANIA

Sofia •

Istanbul •

Ankara ★

GREECE

TURKEY

N
W   E
S

Athens ★

M e d i t e r r a n e a n

KEY

Soviet Union

NATO members, 1955

Soviet gains, 1939–1945

Nonaligned nations

Other Communist countries

Prewar boundary

S e a

SCALE

0   300 mi

0   300 km

Postwar Europe

The Soviet Union dominated Eastern Europe after World War II.
Which Western European nations joined NATO? For Europe today
see the Atlas at the back of this book.

031
032
033

712

Map Answers: Iceland, Norway, United Kingdom, Denmark, the Netherlands, Belgium, Luxembourg, West Germany, France, Italy, Portugal.

The two countries came out of World War II in very different conditions. The United States had escaped the destruction of the war. It was rich in natural resources, and it led the world in farming and industry. Although the United States cut the size of its army at the end of the war, it kept the powerful military threat of atomic weapons.

Of all the nations that took part in the war, the Soviet Union had suffered the greatest losses. Four years of savage fighting had killed millions of the Soviet people and torn apart the western regions of the country. Now the Soviets were determined to protect their western frontier from invasion.

Stalin used the threat of military force to set up Communist puppet governments in the lands his army occupied—Poland, Czechoslovakia, Hungary, Romania, and Bulgaria. These countries were known as "satellites" of the Soviet Union. In Albania and Yugoslavia, Communists also gained power after the war. All these nations became part of the Soviet **bloc**—a group linked by a common interest.

To strengthen its hold over the rest of Eastern Europe, the Soviet Union cut off most contacts between its satellites and Western nations. Trade with the West was halted, and travel in either direction was limited. Western newspapers, magazines, books, and radio programs were banned.

The United States and the Western European countries viewed these changes with growing concern. Their fears were expressed in 1946 by Winston Churchill:

66 From Stettin in the Baltic to Trieste in the Adriatic, an iron curtain has descended across the Continent. Behind that line lie all the capitals of the ancient states of Central and Eastern Europe. Warsaw, Berlin, Prague, Vienna, Budapest, Belgrade, Bucharest, and Sofia—all these famous cities and the populations around them lie in what I must call the Soviet sphere. This is certainly not the liberated Europe we fought to build up. Nor is the new Europe one which contains the essentials of permanent peace. 99

Westerners quickly picked up the term *Iron Curtain* to describe the political barrier between the Soviet bloc and the West.

Western fears of Soviet expansion in Europe grew as a result of Communist moves in Turkey and Greece. In 1945 Stalin demanded that Turkey allow the Soviet Union to build military bases along the straits between the Black Sea and the Aegean. At the same time, the people of Greece were fighting a bloody civil war, and Communist-backed forces were gaining the upper hand.

New American policies. In response to Soviet expansionist activities, President Harry Truman announced a new American foreign policy, which came to be known as the **Truman Doctrine**. Speaking to Congress in March 1947, he asked that military and economic aid be sent to Greece and Turkey. He also called for the United States to aid any country that asked for help in resisting communism. Truman made his case with these words:

66 Our way of life is based on the will of the majority, and is distinguished by free institutions, representative government, and free elections. The Soviet way of life is based upon the will of a minority forcibly imposed upon the majority. It relies upon terror and oppression. The free peoples of the world look to us for support in maintaining their freedom. If we falter in our leadership, we may endanger the peace of the world—and we shall surely endanger the welfare of our nation. 99

The Truman Doctrine became the basis of the cold war policy known as **containment**—the drive to keep communism from spreading to other nations.

All the European countries needed help to rebuild after World War II. In June 1947, Secretary of State George C. Marshall announced an ambitious program to meet that need. "Our policy," said Marshall, "is directed not against any country or doctrine but against hunger, poverty, desperation, and chaos."

713

Check for Understanding. Ask: What did the term *Iron Curtain* describe? (The political barrier between the Soviet bloc and the West.)

Vocabulary The term *containment* was first used to describe Truman's cold war policy in a 1947 *Foreign Affairs* article written by George F. Kennan, then chief of policy planning for the U.S. State Department.

Marshall's proposal was put into effect as the European Recovery Program, commonly called the **Marshall Plan**. Between 1948 and 1952, the United States gave Western Europe more than $12 billion in aid. The results were striking. By 1952, industrial production in the Marshall Plan countries had exceeded prewar levels, living standards had risen considerably, and a new age of prosperity had come to Western Europe.

The Marshall Plan had been offered to all the European countries, but Stalin would not let the Soviet satellites take part. In 1949 the Soviet Union set up a plan of cooperation among the Iron Curtain countries. It was called Comecon (Council for Mutual Economic Assistance). Yet the economies of Eastern Europe did not grow as quickly as those in Western Europe.

Yugoslavia's separate path. In 1948 the first crack appeared in the Soviet bloc. Marshal Tito, the Yugoslav ruler, was a strong-willed nationalist with a mind of his own. When Tito refused to follow Stalin's orders, the Soviet dictator kicked Yugoslavia out of the Soviet bloc. Yugoslavia became **nonaligned**—neutral—in the cold war.

Crisis in Germany. In 1948, East and West came into direct conflict in Germany. After World War II, France, Britain, the United States, and the Soviet Union had each occupied an area of Germany (map, page 715). The four powers did not see eye to eye, however, on how Germany should be ruled. Giving up hope of Soviet cooperation, France, Britain, and the United States agreed in the spring of 1948 to combine their occupation zones into a West German state.

Sec. Rev. ques. 3

The Soviet Union bitterly opposed this idea. It feared that a rebuilt, reunified Germany might threaten Soviet security. To wreck the Western plan, the Soviets decided to blockade Berlin. Although the city lay in Soviet-occupied territory, it too had been divided into different occupation zones. France, Britain, and the United States held West Berlin, while the Soviets held East Berlin (map, page 715).

On June 24, 1948, Soviet troops blocked all roads, railroads, and waterways linking West Berlin to the Western zones. This cut off food and other supplies for the two million West Berliners. Within two days, however, American and British cargo planes were flying in supplies to West Berlin. Working around the clock, even in rough weather, the Berlin airlift flew more than two million tons of food, fuel, medicine, and machinery into West Berlin. Stalin saw that the blockade had failed, and he ended it in May 1949.

A divided Germany. Germany remained a center of cold war tensions. Shortly after the Berlin blockade was lifted, the Western countries carried out their plan to create a West German state. The Federal Republic of Germany (or West Germany) was to be a parliamentary democracy. A few months later, the Soviets set up a Communist regime in their zone, creating the German Democratic Republic (or East Germany).

New alliances. The crisis in Berlin convinced the Western powers of the need for military cooperation. In April 1949 they formed a mutual-defense pact called the North Atlantic Treaty Organization—**NATO**. The original NATO members were Belgium, Britain, Canada, Denmark, France, Iceland, Italy, Luxembourg, the Netherlands, Norway, Portugal, and the United States. In 1952 Greece and Turkey became members. In 1955 West Germany joined the alliance, and in 1982 Spain also joined.

Sec. Rev. ques. 4

The NATO agreement said that "an armed attack against one or more of its members in Europe and America shall be considered an attack against them all." To ward off aggressors, American forces and nuclear weapons were to be kept in Western Europe.

In 1955, after Germany joined the NATO alliance, the Soviet Union signed a mutual-defense pact with seven Eastern European countries—Albania, Bulgaria, Czechoslovakia, East Germany, Hungary, Poland, and Romania. (Yugoslavia did not join.) This alliance, called the Warsaw Treaty Organization, or **Warsaw Pact**, provided for Soviet troops to be kept in each member country. All Warsaw Pact armies were under the leadership of a Soviet commander in Moscow.

★ See below.

714

Biography Marshall was army chief of staff in 1939 and became a five-star general in 1944. He was Secretary of State from 1947 to 1949 and Secretary of Defense from 1950 to 1951. Marshall received the 1953 Nobel Peace Prize for his European economic recovery plan.

Background Britain and the United States had merged their occupation zones in 1946 and named the region Bizonia. France, fearing the growth of a powerful German state, decided against joining the British and American merger.

★ **ENRICHMENT.** Have students work in groups to find information on the economic, social, and political situations in Europe after World War II. Each student might select one nation to research and then present a group display or panel discussion. (Application) *Locating Information*

Contemporary History Both Comecon and the Warsaw Pact were disbanded in 1991 as a result of the collapse of Soviet control over Eastern Europe.

Divided Germany and Berlin

After World War II, each Allied nation occupied an area of Germany.
Where was Berlin located? Which nations occupied West Berlin?

Map Answers: (1) Near the center of East Germany. (2) France, Britain, United States.

Conflicts in Asia. Events in Asia also added to East-West tensions. In 1949 the Communists defeated the Nationalists and took over mainland China. One year later, the Communist government of North Korea invaded South Korea. These two events led many in the West to suspect the Soviet Union of seeking world domination. (You will read about the conflicts in China and Korea in Chapter 36.)

The Arms Race and the Space Race

● Note strategies for second objective on this page and p. 717.

Most members of the United States government had assumed that it would take the Soviets many years to build an atomic bomb. They were shocked to hear in the fall of 1949 that the Soviet Union had successfully tested an atomic bomb. During the 1950's both the **715**

● RETEACHING. Have students make a chart listing sources of *Conflict* and *Cooperation* between the United States and the Soviet Union after 1945. (Conflict: containment policy; space race; U-2 spy plane incident; Berlin Wall; Cuban Missile Crisis. Cooperation: "peaceful coexistence"; 1955 summit meeting; Antarctic Treaty) *(Comprehension)* *Synthesizing Information*

● REINFORCEMENT. Have students draw a political cartoon illustrating an event in Soviet-American relations during the postwar period. Students should include a written explanation of the event and their cartoon. *(Comprehension)* *Translating Information into Another Form*

Historic Places

The Berlin Wall

Nowhere in Europe were the tensions of the cold war clearer than in Berlin. In 1945 Berlin became a divided city in a divided country. After August 1961 the most striking symbol of these divisions was the Berlin Wall. The western side of the wall was covered with anti-Communist graffiti, but the eastern side was blank. East German guards patrolled the wall and kept watch from machine-gun towers. More than 75 people were killed trying to escape across the wall from East Berlin.

On June 26, 1963, United States President John F. Kennedy used Berlin to symbolize the divisions of the cold-war world. In a speech at Berlin's City Hall he said, "All free men, wherever they may live, are citizens of Berlin. And therefore, as a free man, I take pride in the words *Ich bin ein Berliner* [I am a Berliner]."

For many Berliners any hope that their city might some day be reunited—and the wall torn down—seemed remote. In 1989, however, astonishing changes came to the countries under Soviet domination, and with those changes came the crumbling of the Berlin Wall. It started with an announcement by the East German government that East Germans would be free to cross the wall into West Berlin without special permission. A flood of people eager to see the West followed. Soon Berliners were sitting on the wall and hammering holes in it with no interference from the border guards. With the fall of East Germany's Communist government, demolition of the wall began. The wall had become a different kind of symbol—a symbol of the human refusal to accept barriers to freedom.

USSR and the United States built more and more nuclear weapons. Each nation tried to develop weapons so powerful that the other would not dare to attack. This policy of discouraging an attack by making one's opponent fear an overpowering counterattack is called **deterrence**

As the arms race went on, the superpowers invented new types of weapons. In 1952 the United States exploded the first hydrogen bomb, a weapon much more powerful **716** than the atomic bomb. A year later, the Soviet Union also tested a hydrogen bomb. Both countries developed rockets that carried nuclear warheads. By 1957 Soviet engineers had build intercontinental ballistic missiles (ICBM's)—rockets that could reach targets in any part of the world.

Closely related to the arms race was the space race. The Soviet-American rivalry in space began in 1957, when the Soviets launched *Sputnik,* the first human-made craft to orbit the earth. Alarmed to find the Soviets so far ahead in space technology, the

F **FEATURE ACTIVITY Ask students why the East German government abandoned the effort to maintain the Berlin Wall as a barrier.** (Answers may suggest that the political upheavals in East Germany may have made officials aware of the impossibility of maintaining such a hated barrier.)

Vocabulary *Sputnik,* meaning "traveler," was the name of a number of Soviet space satellites.

one small step for a man, one giant leap for mankind," said Armstrong on that historic day.

Cooperation and Confrontation

Peaceful coexistence. In 1953 Stalin died. After a power struggle within the Communist Party, Nikita Khrushchev (kroosh-CHAWF) took over. Khrushchev broke with Stalin's position that war between capitalist and socialist states was inevitable. The Soviet Union, said Khrushchev, would follow a policy of "peaceful coexistence" with the West.

Sec. Rev. ques. 5

Peaceful coexistence eased some of the tensions between the superpowers. In 1955, Western and Soviet officials held the first postwar summit. Although they made no agreements, the leaders discussed such important topics as arms control.

Within a few years, the Soviet Union, the United States, and other countries had signed the Antarctic Treaty, banning military activity in that southernmost continent. Soviet and American leaders also called for the peaceful use of outer space. In 1959 Vice President Richard M. Nixon met with Khrushchev in Moscow, and later that year Khrushchev became the first Soviet leader to visit the United States. Plans were made for a summit conference between Khrushchev and President Eisenhower in Paris in 1960.

● See below.

New conflicts. In May 1960, just before the summit meeting was to have taken place, it was canceled. An angry Khrushchev explained that Soviet missiles had shot down an American U-2 spy plane. The plane had been taking photographs near a major industrial area in the Soviet Union.

Soon afterward, a development in Germany raised tensions still more. Since 1945, thousands of East Germans had fled to West Berlin as a way to enter West Germany. In August 1961, the East German government built a wall dividing East Berlin and West Berlin. Made of barbed wire and blocks of concrete, the wall stood 12 feet high and stretched for 28 miles. Guards limited traffic in and out, and mines were planted near the

United States government began pouring millions of dollars into its space program.

In 1959 the Soviets launched the first spaceship to land on the moon. Two years later, Soviet cosmonaut Yuri Gagarin became the first person to orbit the earth. Less than a month after Gagarin's flight, Alan Shepard became the first American astronaut to go into space. Before the end of the decade, on July 20, 1969, American astronauts Neil Armstrong and Edwin Aldrin became the first persons to land on the moon. "That's

717

Science and Technology Gagarin's flight circled the earth at a speed of more than 17,000 miles per hour. The total time of the trip was 1 hour 48 minutes.

Biography Yuri Gagarin became an international hero after his successful flight. He was training director for the Soviet women-cosmonaut program until 1963, then resumed training to enter space again. He died in 1968 when his jet crashed on a training mission. His ashes were buried in the Kremlin Wall.

● ENRICHMENT. Ask students to identify developments that affected the course of the cold war during the Khrushchev years. (Peaceful-coexistence policy, arms control discussions, U-2 crisis, building of Berlin Wall, Cuban Missile Crisis.) *(Comprehension)* **Organizing Ideas** base of the wall to discourage escape attempts. The Berlin Wall came to symbolize the contrast between the freedom in West Berlin and the repression in the East.

The greatest threat of a war between the superpowers came during the **Cuban Missile Crisis** of October 1962. After the Communist revolution in Cuba in 1959 (page 799), the Soviet Union had secretly shipped nuclear-armed missiles to Cuba. United States intelligence flights over Cuba soon turned up evidence of launching sites for these missiles. Alarmed at the presence of Soviet rockets only 90 miles from the United States, President John F. Kennedy demanded that they be removed. To prove he was serious, he also began a blockade of Cuba. After a tense few days, Khrushchev agreed to remove the weapons. Americans breathed a sigh of relief when the Soviets backed down. "It's eyeball to eyeball, and I think the other fellow just blinked," said one American official.

See Sec. 1 *Closing the Lesson*, p. T709B.

See lesson plans, pp. T709A–T709C.

6. Students might suggest that Stalin did not want the Soviet satellites to become dependent upon Western aid or to have them exposed to capitalist ideas.

2 Western Europe

Objectives

Focus Questions

★ ■ How did Western European nations cooperate on economic matters? *(pages 718–719)*

● ■ What were major postwar developments in Western Europe? *(pages 719–723)*

Terms to Know

Common Market   terrorism
welfare state

★ Note strategies for first objective on this page and p. 719.

In 1945 many people believed that Western Europe would never recover from World War

718 II. Cities, factories, ports, roads, and railroads had been bombed. Many farms had been destroyed. Governments were forced to ration bread and meat, and millions of people lived in fear of starvation. These conditions, plus the bitterness bred during the war, made many countries unstable. With American support, however, Western Europe recovered quickly.

European Unity

Through the Marshall Plan, the United States gave crucial help to Western Europe. Yet more than foreign aid was needed for Europe's long-range development. To stretch their limited resources of money, raw materials, and people, some Western European nations decided to work together.

Sec. Rev. ques. 2

In 1950 the French foreign minister, Robert Schuman, proposed a partnership

★ RETEACHING. Have students identify the postwar European organizations and their goals. (ECSC: pooled resources to speed reconstruction and development. Common Market: eliminated tariffs and improved transportation. European Community combined the other two; EC joined with seven other nations in 1991 to form European Economic Area.) (Comprehension) *Observing for Detail*

★ REINFORCEMENT. Have students identify the effects of the economic organizations formed in Europe after World War II. (Iron and steel production rose rapidly; produced an economic boom.) (Comprehension) *Identifying Effects* among France, West Germany, Italy, Belgium, Luxembourg, and the Netherlands. He suggested that the six countries pool their supplies of such goods as coal, iron, and steel, with the aim of speeding reconstruction and development. The Schuman plan was adopted in 1951 as the European Coal and Steel Community. Iron and steel production rose rapidly, and its members agreed in 1957 to join together in the European Economic Community, also called the **Common Market**. Its members planned to boost economic growth by getting rid of tariffs and improving transportation. The Common Market brought an economic boom to Europe in the 1960's.

In 1967 the Coal and Steel Community and the Common Market were combined in a single body known as the European Community (EC). In the 1970's and 1980's Britain, Denmark, Ireland, Greece, Portugal, and Spain also became members of the organization. In 1991 the European Community agreed to join with seven other nations to form the European Economic Area, the world's largest trading bloc.

★ See below.

West Germany

● Note strategies for second objective on this page and p. 723.
As the center of the Nazi empire, Germany had suffered tremendous damage during the final years of the war. Its cities and industries were in a shambles as a result of Allied bombings. Millions of refugees from Eastern Europe poured into West Germany just after the war, making food and housing shortages more severe. Humiliated, divided, and occupied, Germany reached its lowest point during the bitterly cold winter of 1946–1947, when many people died of hunger and cold.

The man who led Germany's revival was 73-year-old Konrad Adenauer (AHD-un-ow-ur), a long-time foe of both Nazism and communism. Adenauer became the Federal Republic's first chancellor in 1949.

Economic recovery. Several factors made economic recovery possible. The parts of Germany that became the Federal Republic included the most industrialized regions and areas rich in coal and iron ore. West Germany still had many skilled workers and trained managers, both among its own people

Sec. Rev. ques. 3

Refugees flooded back into Germany's cities after World War II. These Berliners carry their few belongings on small carts and even in baby carriages. Many found nothing but rubble where their homes had been.

and among the many East German refugees who crossed over the border. In addition, more than three million workers from southern and southeastern Europe had come to Germany in search of higher wages.

In the years after the war, West Germans even managed to turn the wartime destruction of their country to their advantage. Using Marshall Plan funds, they rebuilt factories, roads, and railroads with the most modern equipment. The economic growth rate skyrocketed under Adenauer and continued to flourish in years to come. From a defeated nation, West Germany became Europe's economic leader.

New leadership. In 1969 Willy Brandt became chancellor of West Germany and continued programs that spurred prosperity. At the same time he made great changes in foreign policy. Under Brandt's *Ostpolitik* (German for "eastern policy"), the country took steps to ease tensions with the Soviet bloc. West Germany agreed to recognize East Germany and to accept existing boundaries in Eastern Europe.

In 1982 Helmut Kohl became chancellor in a government formed by a coalition of political parties. Kohl worked to build closer ties with the United States and to reduce government involvement in the economy. In 1990 Kohl led the planning that brought about the reunification of the two Germanies. Consolidating East Germany's outmoded and inefficient industries into West Germany's high-powered economic system presents a major challenge for German leaders in the 1990's.

France

The Fourth Republic. Just as before the war, the many political parties in France were deeply divided on how to govern. In 1946 a coalition government drew on different parties to establish the Fourth Republic.

Although France had suffered less wartime bombing than Germany, the Nazis had stripped the country of machinery, vehicles, and farm products for the German war effort.

To rebuild, the Fourth Republic nationalized major banks, insurance companies, electrical companies, and the coal and steel industries. It also encouraged development by private industry. During the 1950's the economy grew rapidly. France also made social reforms, including the extension of voting rights to women.

Colonial wars. During the late 1940's the French colony of Indochina was torn by war. The Vietminh, a Communist-led nationalist movement in Vietnam (one part of Indochina), fought to drive out French colonial forces. Guerrilla warfare raged for years. Then in 1954, after a disastrous defeat at Dien Bien Phu, the French left Indochina (page 750).

That same year, a revolt broke out in Algeria, which was governed as part of France rather than as a colony. Many Algerian Muslims wanted independence, while French settlers in Algeria preferred to remain under French rule. An Algerian nationalist group known as the FLN (National Liberation Front) began to attack French military posts and French settlers' property.

Sec. Rev. ques. 4

The French government sent soldiers to keep order, but by 1957 a rebel victory seemed at hand. To prevent this, members of the French military took over the Algerian government. France itself was deeply split over the Algerian question, and it became clear that the Fourth Republic was too weak to outlast the crisis. French soldiers called on the wartime hero Charles de Gaulle to form a new government.

The Fifth Republic. President de Gaulle took steps to make his government, the Fifth Republic, stronger than the Fourth Republic. He began with the establishment of a new constitution that gave the French president more power and made the National Assembly weaker. Then, to end the Algerian crisis, de Gaulle granted Algeria its independence in 1962. Some other French colonies gained self-government but cooperated in foreign and economic policy.

De Gaulle's aim was to make France the dominant power in Europe once again. He built up economic ties with other European

Biography Helmut Kohl, born in 1930, has a Ph.D in political science from Heidelberg University. From 1959 to 1976, he held offices in the state of Rhineland-Palatinate and then became a member of the Bundestag. In late 1990 Kohl led his party—the Christian Democratic Union—to victory in the first free elections held in a united Germany in almost 60 years.

Politics Some of the political division in France was due to the animosity between those who had supported the pro-Nazi Vichy government and those who fought in the French resistance movement. Armed conflict erupted after the war and over 5,000 collaborators were killed before the new provisional government restored order.

nations and with former French colonies. By offering jobs in French industry to immigrants, France increased its work force.

De Gaulle's foreign policy was strongly, even defiantly, independent. Above all, he wanted to show clearly that France would not be influenced by the United States. He opposed Britain's entry into the Common Market, and in 1966 he pulled French forces out of NATO. Finally, de Gaulle ordered that France build up its own supply of nuclear weapons.

De Gaulle left office in 1969. For about 10 years, de Gaulle's successors followed the course he had charted. In 1981 French voters chose a Socialist president and gave the Socialists a majority in the French National Assembly. The new president, François Mitterrand (mee-tur-AHN), nationalized several industries and raised taxes on the rich. When these policies contributed to an economic downturn, Mitterrand began to move toward the political center by cutting taxes. Mitterrand also worked more closely with the United States and other NATO members.

The United Kingdom

Economic problems. Unlike most of continental Europe, Great Britain had not been conquered during World War II. Even so, the country's cities and industries had been severely damaged by bombing. Soon after the war ended, the Labour Party began calling for a welfare state—extensive government aid to citizens.

The Labour Party won an overwhelming victory in the 1945 elections, and in 1946 Parliament passed the National Insurance Act and the National Health Service Act. These acts greatly expanded earlier programs of unemployment insurance, health care, housing allowances, aid to the elderly, and benefits for children. In the next year, Britain also nationalized the Bank of England and some basic industries.

Unhappy with nagging economic problems, British voters put the Conservatives back in office in 1951. Conservative leaders

As president of France, war hero Charles de Gaulle saw his country's position in the world change as it lost its colonies and forged closer ties within Europe.

did not undo the welfare state, but they did lower taxes and return some industries to private ownership. Government leadership changed several times in the 1960's and 1970's, but neither Labour nor the Conservatives could handle such problems as outdated industrial machinery, low productivity, high unemployment, and labor unrest. In 1973 Britain joined the Common Market.

In 1979 a Conservative government was elected, headed by Margaret Thatcher, the first woman to become prime minister. Thatcher tried to breathe new life into the British economy by encouraging private en-

721

In 1979 British Conservative Party leader Margaret Thatcher became the first woman prime minister in European history.

terprise and cutting government spending. As part of her program for privatization, businesses that had been nationalized by the Labour government were sold off to private stockholders. In the 1980's many of these companies raised productivity, but unemployment in Britain remained high, especially in the depressed areas of the north. To reduce government spending, Thatcher also cut social-service programs, leading to charges that her government lacked compassion. In 1990 rising opposition to her dominant style of leadership led to a challenge from members of the Conservative Party. John Major, a Cabinet minister and Thatcher's own choice for her replacement, became prime minister.

Sec. Rev. ques. 5

Foreign policy. Exhausted by its struggle against Nazi Germany, Britain was in no position to hold on to its colonies after World War II. In 1947 Britain agreed to Indian demands for self-rule, creating an independent India and Pakistan (Chapter 36). Most of the former colonies joined the Commonwealth of Nations (page 673), although some later withdrew. The loss of these colonies lowered Britain's expenses, but it also cost Britain valuable sources of raw materials and markets.

Britain did not, however, give up all its **722** interests overseas. On April 2, 1982, the gov-ernment of Argentina invaded the Falklands, a small group of British-held islands off the Argentine coast. (Both Britain and Argentina had claimed the Falklands in the 1800's.) After Prime Minister Thatcher sent a British fleet to retake the islands, the Argentine troops were forced to surrender. The British public strongly supported Thatcher's handling of the Falklands war.

A far thornier problem for Britain was Northern Ireland. When Ireland was divided in 1921 (page 673), the Irish Free State (later called the Republic of Ireland) had received self-rule. Northern Ireland had remained part of Britain. The government of Northern Ireland was dominated by Protestants, and the large Catholic minority had little power. Many Catholics hoped that all Ireland would one day be independent and reunited. In 1968 violence broke out between Catholics and Protestants in Northern Ireland. As the fighting spread, the British government sent in soldiers to keep order.

Among those calling for Irish reunification was the Irish Republican Army (IRA). This was a nationalist organization that had been formed after the Easter Rebellion of 1916. Within the IRA there emerged a group dedicated to **terrorism**—the use of force and threats against civilians. IRA members carried out terrorist acts against Protestant Irish and guerrilla attacks against British forces. Several armed Protestant groups fought back with equal violence. Bombings and gun battles killed both soldiers and civilians.

In 1985 Britain and the Republic of Ireland signed an agreement that gave the Republic of Ireland a voice in the affairs of Northern Ireland. The two governments hoped that this agreement, known as the Anglo-Irish Pact, would help in the search for a way of restoring order and ending violence.

Nations of Southern Europe

Italy. In 1946 the Italian people decided not to restore the monarchy but to establish a republic. A coalition government was formed by the major political parties.

Political History In office for eleven and a half years, Thatcher had been the longest-serving British prime minister in more than 160 years—and so far Britain's only woman prime minister. A notable part of Thatcher's legacy was her early recognition of Mikhail Gorbachev's sincere interest in improving Soviet relations with Western leaders.

Geography The Falklands (called the *Islas Malvinas* by Argentina) lie about 310 miles east of the South American coast. Most of the island's 2,000 residents are British in origin.

Social History British troops were sent to Northern Ireland in 1969 to protect the Catholic minority. However, when it appeared to the Catholics that these forces were siding with the Protestants, the IRA initiated a guerrilla campaign that resulted in civil war.

As in France, conflicts were common among several parties, and Italy's leadership changed often. Still, the country made a quick recovery from the war, in part because of Marshall Plan aid. The government built up industry in the triangle formed by the cities of Milan, Turin, and Genoa. Soon Italy's economic growth was second only to West Germany's. The breakup of large estates in southern Italy and the redistribution of land made Italian farming more productive. Nevertheless, many southern Italians moved to the north or took jobs in other European countries to improve their standard of living.

Sec. Rev. ques. 6

In the 1980's, Italy faced labor problems and unrest. Some extreme Communist groups turned to terrorism. The result was the weakening of moderate coalition governments.

Portugal. Portugal had been ruled by a dictator since the 1930's and had stayed neutral in World War II. In the 1960's the Portuguese colonies in Africa rebelled against dictator Antonio Salazar. In 1974, four years after Salazar's death, the army overthrew his successor (page 783). The government remained unstable, but it began to move toward democracy. In 1976 the Portuguese people elected their first civilian president in more than 50 years.

Spain. In the years just after World War II the Western allies had little to do with Spain. That country was ruled by the Fascist dictator Francisco Franco (page 669). By the 1950's, however, the Western nations wanted to improve their defenses against the Soviet bloc, and they were attracted by Spain's strategic position. In exchange for military bases on Spanish soil, the United States gave loans and grants to Spain. The Spanish government used this money to expand industry and modernize agriculture.

Franco ruled as dictator until his death in 1975. He was succeeded by Juan Carlos I, the grandson of the last Spanish king. Juan Carlos took a giant step toward democracy by calling for elections that were held in 1977. In 1982 Felipe González of the Socialist Workers' Party became prime minister.

Greece. Civil war had broken out in Greece at the end of World War II. Communist guerrillas fought against Greece's pro-Western government, leading the United States to issue the Truman Doctrine (page 713). With American aid, the Greek government defeated the rebels in 1949. A series of moderate governments followed. In 1967, after disputes among Greece's leaders, a group of army officers known as "the colonels" seized power. They suspended the constitution and jailed many opponents.

In 1974 a dispute with Turkey over the island of Cyprus caused the collapse of the military government. A new constitution was adopted, and the army's role in politics declined. Elections in 1981 brought Socialists to power in the Greek government. Charges of corruption and economic problems enabled a conservative party to win elections in 1990. Constantine Mitsotakis took office as prime minister of Greece.

● See below.

See Sec. 2 *Closing the Lesson,* p. T709C.

Answers to Section Review questions are in brackets on pages indicated.

Section Review

1. **Define or identify:** Common Market, welfare state, terrorism. (pp. 719, 721, 722)
2. Why did Western European nations decide to work together on economic matters? (p. 718)
3. What factors helped to make West Germany an economic power in Europe during the period after World War II? (pp. 719–720)
4. What events in Asia and Africa contributed to the weakening of the Fourth Republic in France? (p. 720)
5. Why did Britain grant independence to some of its colonies after World War II? (p. 722)
6. Describe a major postwar development in each of the following countries: Italy, Spain, Portugal, Greece. (p. 723)
7. **Critical thinking:** How might the history of postwar Europe have been different if the United States had not offered the Marshall Plan? (See answer below.)

723

7. Students might respond that the economies of many European nations could have collapsed and that more countries might have become Communist.

● ENRICHMENT. Have students evaluate the role played by the United States in European recovery after World War II. Students might find information on the impact of the Truman Doctrine, the Marshall Plan, and NATO. (Evaluation) *Evaluating Historical Developments*

3 The Soviet Bloc and Its Collapse

Objectives

Focus Questions

★ ■ What were the Soviet Union's foreign and domestic policies in the postwar years? *(pages 724–725)*

● ■ How did the Gorbachev period of reform end in the collapse of the Soviet Union? *(pages 725–728)*

▲ ■ How did Soviet domination affect Eastern Europe? *(pages 729–730)*

Terms to Know

détente   *perestroika*
dissident   *glasnost*
human rights   martial law

★ Note strategies for first objective on this page and 725.

Like Western Europe after 1945, the people of the Soviet Union worked hard to recover from the wounds of war. The Soviet Union reshaped the governments and economies of Eastern Europe while strengthening its own military and industrial resources. It soon rose to the position of a superpower, matched only by the United States.

The Soviet Union

The aftermath of the war. In 1945 the Soviet Union faced the gigantic task of rebuilding. Over 20 million Soviet citizens had lost their lives in World War II. In the regions occupied by the German army, farming and industry had been devastated.

In dealing with the challenge, Joseph Stalin fell back on his policies of the 1930's. During the war (which the Russian people call "the Great Fatherland War") he had

724

acted more like a nationalist leader than a totalitarian dictator. The government had allowed more freedom to the people. Now central planning was restored and Stalin's orders were enforced by terror.

In order to counter any possible Western influence, Stalin isolated his country from the world. His fear of disloyalty hit hardest Russian prisoners of war returned from abroad; they had seen too much of the better life elsewhere. Together with writers and artists suspected of Western tendencies, they were imprisoned in the gulags (page 657), where many died. Stalin retightened the Communist Party's control over every aspect of Soviet life.

To speed economic recovery, Stalin launched a new Five-Year Plan, rebuilding industries with resources taken from Eastern Europe—machinery, raw materials, railroads, factories, and even skilled workers and technical experts. By 1949 Stalin's scientists exploded the first Soviet atomic bomb; by the time of his death they had produced a hydrogen bomb. Stalin, in short, laid the foundations for transforming his vast but poor country into a superpower.

Sec. Rev. ques. 2

Khrushchev. After Stalin's death in 1953 the emerging Soviet leader Nikita Khrushchev (page 717) relaxed the reins of dictatorship. Many victims of Stalin's terror were released from imprisonment. The loosening of political controls—the "thaw" as it was called—allowed a first glimpse of the gulags' horrors. In 1956 Khrushchev himself denounced Stalin in a secret speech that soon became known worldwide, revealing Stalin's brutality in stark detail. As a result, statues and pictures of Stalin were torn down. Even the city of Stalingrad on the Volga River, where the German army had been defeated, was renamed Volgograd.

This new policy of denouncing Stalin was called "de-Stalinization." Following Khrushchev's speech, anti-Soviet uprisings

★ RETEACHING. Ask students to identify the focus of Stalin's postwar Five-Year Plan and to explain how he planned to meet the aims of the plan. (Heavy industry and defense. He took resources from Eastern Europe for rebuilding industries.) *(Comprehension) Locating Information*

★ REINFORCEMENT. Have students make a chart identifying the economic and political policies of Stalin, Khruschchev, and Brezhnev. *(Comprehension) Observing for Detail* broke out in two satellite countries. In Poland Khrushchev arranged a peaceful compromise. In Hungary, however, a revolt was bloodily suppressed. In the following year (1957) Khrushchev's confidence and the Soviet Union's prestige as a superpower soared, as *Sputnik* I, the world's first manufactured satellite (page 716), circled the earth. Soviet space triumphs continued, until in 1969 the Americans landed a man on the moon.

Sec. Rev. ques. 3

Although committed to "peaceful coexistence," Khrushchev overconfidently challenged the United States in the Cuban Missile Crisis (page 718). Rebuffed by President Kennedy and beset by administrative and economic confusion at home, Khrushchev's prestige sank. In 1964 his closest associates in the Politburo fired him for what they called his "harebrained schemes."

Brezhnev. The man who followed Khrushchev was Leonid Brezhnev. Afraid that the "thaw" had weakened the hold of the Communist Party over the people, Brezhnev restricted personal freedoms, restored centralized planning, and built up Soviet military power. Under his rule the Soviet Union achieved equality with the United States in nuclear weapons.

Reassured by his country's new power, Brezhnev worked for peaceful relations with Western Europe and the United States, following a policy of **détente** (day-TAHNT), a French word meaning "relaxation of tensions." Détente promoted trade with the more technologically advanced Western countries; it also earned international respectability for the Soviet Union.

Détente did not, however, stop demonstrations of Soviet power. In 1968, together with its chief Eastern European satellites, the Soviet Union crushed a liberal socialist government in Czechoslovakia. Under the "Brezhnev Doctrine" the Soviet government was determined to prevent the overthrow of any Communist regime. With this aim, the Soviet Union in 1979 invaded Afghanistan to prop up a pro-Soviet government.

Sec. Rev. ques. 4

Meanwhile, in the mid-1970's Soviet living standards improved; never before had the Soviet peoples lived so well. The new sense of security and well-being, however, had dangerous consequences. The heroic Communist dedication to patriotic service faded. Moreover, the Soviet economy became stagnant.

In addition, the increased contact with the outside world intensified envious comparison between Soviet poverty and Western affluence, between Soviet totalitarianism and Western freedom. Such comparisons had been a source of disloyalty throughout Russian and Soviet history. Now, in the age of intense worldwide communication, it turned into a massive political force discrediting the entire Soviet system. Opposition to that system spread, and it became more open.

The dissidents. Even in the periods of greatest repression some people had raised their voices in opposition. These people were called **dissidents**—opponents of the government. Some dissidents were Jews, who faced severe discrimination. Many dissidents urged the government to respect **human rights**—the basic rights and freedoms to which all people are entitled. Soviet dissidents sometimes staged public protests. They used an underground press network to share ideas and information. Many dissidents were imprisoned or sent to mental hospitals.

One famous dissident was Alexander Solzhenitsyn (sohl-zhuh-NEET-sin), who spent years in a gulag for criticizing Stalin. His books about life in the gulags were read secretly in the Soviet Union and smuggled out of the country. In 1974 he was deported and went to live in the United States.

Another distinguished dissident was Andrei Sakharov (page 727). A physicist who helped the USSR develop the hydrogen bomb, he later took a stand in favor of human rights. In 1980 the government exiled him to the city of Gorki. Under the new policy of *glasnost* (next page), Sakharov was allowed to return to Moscow, where he urged Mikhail Gorbachev (gor-buh-CHAWF) to free dissidents still held. When Sakharov died in 1989, Gorbachev delivered a eulogy, calling him "a man of conviction and sincerity."

The Gorbachev reforms. Brezhnev died in 1982. The next two Soviet leaders **725**

Politics Many conservatives and pro-Stalinists objected to Khrushchev's reforms. In a heated exchange during a secret debate in 1957, Khrushchev is said to have yelled at two of his opponents, "Your hands are stained with the blood of our party leaders and of innumerable innocent Bolsheviks!" "So are yours," they replied. "Yes, so are mine," Khrushchev said, "I admit this. But during the purges I was merely carrying out your order. I was not responsible. You were."

were old men who died after short periods of power. In 1985 party officials chose an ambitious younger man, Mikhail Gorbachev, to head the Soviet Union. Unlike earlier Soviet leaders, Gorbachev had not fought in World War II; nor had he risen to power under Stalin's brutal regime. He had traveled in Western Europe, was well informed about the United States, and was aware of the pace of progress around the world. In contrast to former leaders, he publicly admitted that the Soviet system lagged "behind the demands of the times and of life itself." In order to overcome his country's backwardness, Gorbachev introduced drastic changes that struck at the very roots of the Soviet system.

Sec. Rev. ques. 5

Taking advantage of his country's unprecedented external security, the new leader dramatically abandoned the Soviet pretense of superiority over other countries. Gorbachev pulled the Soviet army out of Afghanistan, pressed for the reduction of nuclear weapons, surrendered Soviet control over the satellite nations of Eastern Europe, and permitted the reunification of Germany. He thus ended the 45-year-long cold war. For these extraordinary moves Gorbachev was awarded the Nobel Peace Prize in 1990.

While opening his country to the outside world, Mikhail Gorbachev proceeded with the far-reaching domestic reforms he called **perestroika** (payr-es-TROY-kuh), or "restructuring." Perestroika aimed at a "gen-

726

uine revolutionary transformation of Soviet life and institutions" by means of democratic government. For this purpose Gorbachev introduced the secret ballot in multi-candidate elections. A new legislature, called the Congress of Peoples' Deputies, elected him president and cut down the power of the Communist Party. Gorbachev also promised more self-government to the 15 Soviet republics.

At the same time his policy of **glasnost** (GLAHS-nuhst)—"openness"—lifted all restrictions on freedom of speech and self-expression. Glasnost took the lid off government secrecy, revealing the corrupt inefficiency of the Soviet system and the damage that had been inflicted on the environment.

Gorbachev's reforms eventually called for a market economy to replace the numbing rigidity of central planning. The Soviet economy was to be stimulated by individual enterprise based on private property and with the help of foreign investments. Yet Gorbachev avoided the term "capitalism." He stuck to socialism, emphasizing the need for protection against selfish greed. All along Gorbachev advertised his reforms as the only way to satisfy hopes for a higher standard of living, and for a while his popularity ran high.

Yet, having loosened the traditional Soviet controls, Gorbachev was unprepared for the consequences. As troubles mounted, his popularity faded. A devastating blow was an explosion at the nuclear power station at Chernobyl (chair-NOH-bil) in the Ukraine in 1986. This disaster sprayed poisonous radiation into the sky, killing 31 people outright, damaging the health of thousands of others, and ruining vital crops. Then, in 1988 an earthquake devastated parts of Armenia. Both disasters drained Soviet resources.

Even more serious were the economic consequences of Gorbachev's reforms. Despite all promises, the Soviet economy deteriorated, lowering the standard of living and slowing the progress of perestroika.

Worst of all, Gorbachev's reforms revealed the underlying lack of cohesion in Soviet society. Now that the artificial unity imposed by the Communist Party was fading, confusion and disillusion spread. The slogans

● Note strategies for second objective on pp. 726–727.

● RETEACHING. Ask students to identify the reasons why Communist hardliners took action to try to force Gorbachev out of power. (They were alarmed over public discontent and the Soviet Union's loss of status as a superpower.) *(Comprehension) Identifying Reasons*

● REINFORCEMENT. Have students explain why the events following the failed coup (page 728) could be called "the Russian Revolution of 1991." (Boris Yeltsin, the Russian president, took the lead in defying the coup's plotters; and it resulted in the fall of the Communist Soviet government.) *(Application) Applying a Concept*

Sakharov's Nobel Acceptance Speech

In 1975, Andrei Sakharov was awarded the Nobel Peace Prize for his work promoting nuclear disarmament. Denied permission to leave the Soviet Union, Sakharov was unable to accept the award personally. Yelena Bonner, Sakharov's wife, delivered his acceptance speech, part of which appears below.

66 For all those who went through the experience of the most terrible war in history, World War II, conception of war as the worst catastrophe for all mankind has become not only an abstract idea but a deep personal feeling, the basis for one's entire outlook on the world. To keep one's self-respect one must therefore act in accordance with the general human longing for peace, for genuine disarmament. . . .

I would like to end my speech expressing the hope in final victory of the principles of peace and human rights. The best sign that such hopes can come true would be a general political amnesty [pardon] in all the world, liberation of all prisoners of conscience everywhere. The struggle for a general political amnesty is the struggle for the future of mankind. 99

1. What effect did World War II have on Sakharov?
2. According to Sakharov, what action would show that the nations of the world were moving toward peace and the recognition of human rights?
3. **Critical thinking:** Why, do you think, did Sakharov work so hard for nuclear disarmament?

Ⓕ See answers below.

---

of freedom and democracy provoked widespread dissatisfaction. Now that all citizens had a chance openly to voice their views, ethnic and national minorities clamored for self-determination. Lithuania, Latvia, and Estonia demanded outright independence. The Russian republic, by far the largest in the Soviet Union, declared its independence under the leadership of Boris Yeltsin. Obviously, Gorbachev's "revolutionary transformation of Soviet life and institutions" had taken a dangerous turn.

The Collapse of Communism

The coup. In the face of growing division, Gorbachev as Secretary General of the Communist Party attempted a policy of reconciling differences between the warring factions. Sometimes he sided with the promoters of radical democratization led by Boris Yeltsin and at other times with the Communist hardliners, who were growing alarmed over the public discontent and the Soviet Union's disintegration as a superpower. After leaning

727

Ⓕ **Primary Source Answers** 1. It caused him to devote his life to seeking peace. 2. Granting general political amnesty for prisoners of conscience. 3. Answers will vary. Sakharov probably believed that disarmament would be a step toward peace.

Biography Gorbachev was born in 1931 near the city of Stavropol. He became a Communist Party member in 1952 and, after holding a number of local posts, rose to become the First Secretary of his local party committee in 1970. Gorbachev became a member of the Central Committee in 1971, a Politburo member in 1980, and General Secretary in 1985.

in their direction in early 1991, Gorbachev again sided with Yeltsin.

On August 19 the hardliners suddenly struck, while Gorbachev was vacationing on the Black Sea. They tried to pull off a coup, or take-over, by deposing him as president, taking him into custody, and declaring a state of emergency. The world wondered: Was the Soviet Union going to have a new dictatorship of the Communist Party, the secret police, and the army?

The threat of dictatorship mobilized a massive turnout of protesters in Moscow and Leningrad. In Moscow, Yeltsin emerged as a popular hero who was cheered for his bold defiance of the plotters; the city vibrated in fury, as tens of thousands rushed to his defense. Within two days it was obvious that the plotters had misjudged their own resources and the response of the people. Their coup had failed, with unexpected results.

When Gorbachev returned to Moscow, he faced, as he said, "a different country." The key pillars of Soviet strength had collapsed. Gorbachev resigned as Secretary General, and the Communist Party was officially disbanded.

Even more astonishingly, the Union of Soviet Socialist Republics started to fall apart. The demands of the three Baltic republics for independence were accepted and they became fully separate nations. Ten other republics declared their independence (though without making a full and final break with the other republics). The plotters of the coup had achieved what above all they had wanted to prevent: the collapse of the Soviet Union.

The end of the Soviet Union. After the failed coup the leaders of most of the Soviet republics formed a state council, with Boris Yeltsin, Russia's leader, as the most powerful member and with Gorbachev—but now a Gorbachev with little real power—as president. This state council had the task of finding a way to replace the former Communist-run government with a looser confederation; it also faced the immediate challenge of preventing the collapse of the economy.

The council's work—and Gorbachev's **728** efforts to form a new union of the republics

—soon broke down. After the people of Ukraine voted overwhelmingly in favor of independence, that republic and two other republics—Russia and Byelorussia (with the latter renamed Belarus)—bypassed Gorbachev and formed a looser federation called the Commonwealth of Independent States. Eleven of the twelve remaining republics also joined the new Commonwealth. In December 1991 Mikhail Gorbachev resigned as president of the Soviet Union.

A new era for the republics. With the collapse of the Soviet Union, the compulsory unity imposed by czars and then by Communists on Russians and neighboring peoples had come to an end. Yet the call for freedom, self-determination, and democracy seemed to inspire little incentive for rebuilding the republics by voluntary cooperation. The lack of democratic experience and the size of this vast area make the future of the members of the new Commonwealth uncertain. Among the basic questions to be resolved are these:

(1) Will the separate republics recognize that they are dependent on each other for their economic well-being? All the republics need oil and industrial equipment produced in the Russian republic; the Russians need food and raw materials from the surrounding republics. None of the republics, large or small, is economically self-sufficient.

(2) Will the republics be able to carry out a common foreign policy and will the four republics with nuclear weapons (Russia, Ukraine, Belarus, and Kazakhstan) be able to maintain secure control over those weapons?

(3) Will the leaders of the republics be able to preserve law and order? Or will the liberation from the hated Soviet yoke result in endless ethnic and nationalist strife as peoples compete for land and resources?

During the course of Gorbachev's reforms the heady ideals of freedom and democracy had set off explosive forces among the Soviet peoples. Now the former superpower has had to beg the rich countries for help. It will take years of deprivation and disorganization before the problems of the failed Soviet system can be resolved.

Eastern Europe

▲ Note strategies for third objective on pp. 729–730.

Soviet control. For the countries of Eastern Europe the years of Soviet domination after World War II brought many changes. Stalin imposed the same policies he used in the Soviet Union. Farms were collectivized and five-year plans favoring mining and industry over consumer goods were adopted. Moscow directed the economies of its satellites in ways designed to help the Soviet Union.

Rebellions in the 1950's and 1960's. Many people in Eastern Europe deeply resented the Stalinist governments that were forced on them. Khrushchev's "thaw" raised hopes that Soviet control was waning. In Poland and Hungary people took to the streets. When Polish workers rioted in June 1956 to demand "bread and liberty," Khrushchev put a new leader named Wladislaw Gomulka (goh-MOOL-kah) in power. Gomulka broke up collective farms and relaxed government controls over industry.

The events in Poland inspired a revolt in Hungary. In October 1956 many Hungarians joined in an uprising that began in Budapest. The rebels took over radio stations and even demanded that Soviet soldiers leave Hungary. Imre Nagy (NAZH), a Communist leader who had fallen from grace because of his liberal ideas, was brought back to power. Nagy promised an end to one-party government. The Soviet response was swift and brutal. On November 4, more than 2,000 Soviet tanks headed for Budapest. For two weeks the Hungarian rebels held off the Soviet forces, hoping for help from the West. But Western powers did not want to risk war with the Soviet Union. Thousands of Hungarians were killed in the revolution, and many fled the country. Nagy was replaced by János Kádár, who ruled Hungary until 1988.

Twelve years after the Hungarian uprising, a new leader in Czechoslovakia, Alexander Dubček (DOOB-chek), loosened government controls and allowed greater freedom of expression. These changes were part of what Dubček called "socialism with a human

Boris Yeltsin, president of the Russian republic (right), became the dominant figure in the Commonwealth of Independent States after Mikhail Gorbachev's resignation as Soviet president signaled the end of the Soviet Union.

face." Determined to keep a tight grip on its empire, the Soviet Union invaded Czechoslovakia in 1968 and crushed all dissent.

Solidarity in Poland. As trade expanded in the Soviet bloc, Eastern Europe in time developed some trade with the West. In the 1970's Eastern European standards of living gradually rose. They did not reach Western European levels, however, and by the 1980's several Eastern European countries, especially Poland, faced severe problems.

Shortages of food and clothing in Poland had led to riots in 1980. Workers took over the shipyard in Gdańsk (guh-DANSK), the port city formerly called Danzig. Strikes spread through the country. Unable to halt the unrest, the government gave workers the right to strike and to form unions.

The Polish workers formed Solidarity, the first labor union in the Soviet bloc not under government control. Lech Walesa (wah-LEN-sah), leader of the strike at Gdańsk, became head of the new union. Solidarity demanded more rights for workers, an end to censorship, more freedom for the **729**

▲ RETEACHING. Have students review pp. 729–730 and identify the causes and effects of rebellions in Eastern European countries. (Causes: resentment of Soviet control and Stalinist policies. Effects: uprisings and new governments.) *(Comprehension)* **Identifying Cause and Effect**

Catholic church, and the release of political prisoners. Polish workers held strikes and demonstrations throughout 1981.

In late 1981 Poland's leader, Wojciech Jaruzelski (yah-roo-SEL-skee), issued a decree establishing **martial law**—strict military rule. Jaruzelski also banned Solidarity. Throughout Poland its leaders, including Walesa, were imprisoned. But as Gorbachev's reforms made headway in the late 1980's, people in Poland and Eastern Europe generally dared to dream again of liberation from Soviet rule. They took action in 1989.

Peaceful revolutions. Liberation began in Poland under mounting popular pressure. Jaruzelski ended his military dictatorship in 1988, and in January 1989 Solidarity was legalized. In September it won an open election and then set up a government dedicated to democracy. Walesa was elected president of Poland in 1990 and vowed to bring a free market economy to Poland.

Hungary, which had enjoyed the most relaxed Communist regime in the 1980's, soon followed the Polish lead. Kádár was ousted in 1988. In May 1989 the Communist dictatorship in Hungary ended. The next year Hungarians voted a conservative government into power.

A dramatic change also took place in East Germany. In October 1989 the Communist leadership lost faith in its mission when confronted with huge demonstrations and a mass flight of people to the West. On November 9 anti-Communist German patriotism exploded. The Berlin Wall (page 716) was smashed and communism was overthrown in East Germany. The way lay open for German reunification in October 1990 (page 720).

The anti-Communist floodtide spread to Bulgaria. One day after the Berlin Wall crumbled, Todor Zhivkov, the longest-serving Communist dictator in the Soviet bloc, resigned. In mid-December a multi-party government took over. The change in Bulgaria left its mark on Romania. Here Nicolae Ceausescu (chuh-SHES-koo), the Communist dictator, defied all calls for reform. But on December 21, 1989, a mass demonstration organized in his support turned against him.

Sec. Rev. ques. 6

730

Four days later Ceausescu and his wife were shot to death. Thus ended the most ruthless of the Communist dictatorships.

A gentler transition took place on the same day in Czechoslovakia. After the peaceful resignation of the Communist leaders in November 1989, the leading advocate of democratic government, the playwright Vaclav Havel (HAH-vel), was elected president.

The final event of that momentous "year of revolution" came on December 26 in Yugoslavia, which had been the least regimented Communist state. On that day its Communist leaders suggested the formation of a multi-party system, which was duly approved by their party. At the beginning of 1990 only secluded Albania remained under Communist control, and that regime crumbled in 1991. Within a single year, Eastern Europe had joyously cast off 44 years of Soviet Communist domination.

What future for Eastern Europe? The joy over liberation soon vanished as political and economic problems mounted. As in the Soviet Union, the desire for freedom led to agitation for ethnic self-determination. The Yugoslav federal state fell apart, as Slovenes, Croats, and Macedonians voted for separate statehood. A bitter civil war broke out between Serbs and Croats.

Introducing Western-style democracy among inexperienced peoples posed an additional challenge. In Bulgaria and Romania the new governments were run by former Communists, causing civil unrest. Even in Poland and Czechoslovakia the democratically elected new presidents were accused of authoritarian tendencies.

The way to the future will not be easy for these nations. The profitable trade with the Soviet Union has ended and the transition to a market economy has at least for the short term lowered rather than raised living standards. In addition, industrial backwardness and environmental pollution hamper economic productivity. Over the long run, however, the release from Communist domination, together with new associations with democratic nations in other parts of the world, offers hope for a better future.

▲ REINFORCEMENT. Have students explain what Alexander Dubček might have meant by "socialism with a human face." (Comprehension) Drawing Inferences

See Sec. 3 Closing the Lesson, pp. T709C.

▲ ENRICHMENT. Have students work in groups to prepare reports on the current economic and political situation of the nations that were formerly satellites of the Soviet Union. (Comprehension) Locating Information

Section Review

Answers to Section Review questions are in brackets on pages indicated.

1. **Define or identify:** détente, dissident, *perestroika, glasnost,* human rights, martial law. (pp. 725, 726, 730)
2. How did Stalin's policies change after World War II? (p. 724)
3. Why was Khrushchev eventually forced out of office? (p. 725)
4. What was the Brezhnev Doctrine? How did it affect détente? (p. 726)

5. What changes came about in the Soviet Union under Gorbachev's leadership? (pp. 726–728)
6. How did the Gorbachev changes affect the countries of Eastern Europe? (pp. 730)
7. **Critical thinking:** How did Gorbachev's policies lead to the collapse of communism in the Soviet Union? (See answer below.)

7. The lifting of government secrecy and censorship led to open opposition and full revelation of the failures of the Communist system. The hardliners' attempted coup ended in the discrediting of Communist leaders and the abandonment of communism.

Chapter 35   Summary and Timeline

1. Allied leaders' hopes for a lasting peace after World War II led to the creation of the United Nations in 1945. The United States and the Soviet Union dominated postwar politics, and rivalry between the superpowers created an atmosphere of tension known as the cold war.

2. Much of Western Europe made a remarkable recovery after World War II, due to American aid and European economic cooperation. West Germany grew into one of the world's leading industrial powers. France, despite setbacks in Indochina and Algeria, followed an independent foreign policy under de Gaulle. Britain gave up its colonies, and

struggled with economic problems. Dictators in Spain, Portugal, and Greece gave way to more democratic governments. Italy established a republic, and its northern regions became more industrialized.

3. The Soviet Union faced a huge task of rebuilding in the postwar period. Stalin terrorized his people until his death in 1953. Khrushchev moved away from Stalinism, but Brezhnev tried to expand Soviet power. In the Gorbachev years, the cold war came to a close as the peoples of Eastern Europe broke away from Soviet control and political and economic upheaval brought an end to the Soviet Union itself.

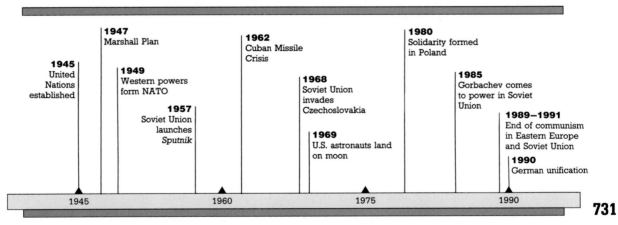

1945
United Nations established

1947
Marshall Plan

1949
Western powers form NATO

1957
Soviet Union launches *Sputnik*

1962
Cuban Missile Crisis

1968
Soviet Union invades Czechoslovakia

1969
U.S. astronauts land on moon

1980
Solidarity formed in Poland

1985
Gorbachev comes to power in Soviet Union

1989–1991
End of communism in Eastern Europe and Soviet Union

1990
German unification

1945   1960   1975   1990

See p. T709C for answers to Chapter Review.

Vocabulary Review

1. Use the following terms to complete the sentences below: *Common Market, Cuban Missile Crisis, martial law, nonaligned, terrorism.*
   a. Yugoslavia was __?__, or neutral, during the cold war.
   b. The __?__ brought the superpowers to the brink of war.
   c. The __?__ encouraged trade in Europe.
   d. The use of force and threats against civilians is called __?__.
   e. Poland's leader in 1981 declared __?__, or strict military rule.
2. Define or identify the terms in each of the following pairs.
   a. cold war; détente
   b. containment; deterrence
   c. Truman Doctrine; Marshall Plan
   d. dissident; human rights
   e. NATO; Warsaw Pact

People to Identify

Match each of the following people with the correct description: *Willy Brandt, John F. Kennedy, François Mitterrand, Mikhail Gorbachev, Alexander Solzhenitsyn, Margaret Thatcher, Lech Walesa.*

1. American President who demanded that Khrushchev remove nuclear-armed missiles from Cuba
2. leader of Solidarity, the Polish union
3. West German chancellor who agreed to recognize East Germany and to accept existing boundaries in Eastern Europe
4. prime minister of Britain, who encouraged private enterprise and greatly reduced government spending
5. Soviet leader who launched a program of drastic reforms
6. Soviet dissident and writer who was punished for criticizing Stalin
7. Socialist president of France who nationalized several industries and raised taxes on the rich

Places to Know

Match the letters on this map of postwar Europe with the places listed below. You may want to refer to the map on page 712.

1. Albania
2. Berlin
3. Budapest
4. Bulgaria
5. Czechoslovakia
6. Gdańsk
7. Moscow
8. Romania
9. Warsaw
10. West Germany
11. Yugoslavia

Recalling the Facts

1. How and why did Eastern European lands become part of the Soviet bloc?

732

2. What conflict developed between the occupying powers in Germany? How was this conflict resolved?

3. How did the Soviet Union and Western nations pursue peaceful coexistence?

4. What factors helped make West Germany an economic power in Europe?

5. What events in Asia and Africa led to the creation of a new French government?

6. How did Britain's loss of colonial possessions affect its economy?

7. What were major postwar developments in Italy, Portugal, Spain, and Greece?

8. Describe Khrushchev's domestic reform policies.

9. Why were Brezhnev's policies called "re-Stalinization"?

10. Describe Gorbachev's policies of *glasnost* and *perestroika*.

11. How did nations in Eastern Europe win freedom from Soviet domination?

Critical Thinking Skills

1. **Drawing conclusions.** Do you think the policy of deterrence increased or reduced the possibility of nuclear war? Explain. *(Syn.)*

2. **Writing a biography.** Write a biography of one of the following Nobel Peace Prize winners: George C. Marshall, Willy Brandt, Andrei Sakharov, Lech Walesa, Mikhail Gorbachev. *(App.)*

✔ 3. **Predicting.** Look at the chart showing causes and effects of the unification of Germany in the 1800's (page 520). Make a similar chart for the 1990 reuniting of Germany. To list effects, think about Germany's future and do some predicting. *(Syn.)*

Thinking About Geography

Making a chart. Make a chart of the nations in the European Community. In separate columns, list the name of each country; the year it joined the Community; its major exports; and its major imports. Use an encyclopedia or almanac to find this information. *(App.)*

Enrichment: Primary Sources

In a book he wrote about the attempt to force him out of office in 1991, Mikhail Gorbachev said the coup failed because of the drastic changes that had taken place in Soviet society.

66 The whole of society had changed, including the Army that was part of it. Officers and privates refused to go against their own people despite the threat of court martial. The forces of law and order and even the special commando troops behaved similarly. That was where the plotters went wrong: they did not realize that society was now not at all what it had been a few years back.

[People] had breathed the air of freedom and no one could now take that away from [them]. Certainly the people want the rule of law and stability, but not by means of dictatorship and not by states of emergency. The people were certainly tired of waiting for the standard of living to improve. But the people wanted a way out of the crisis to be found within the framework of democracy and not at the expense of freedom and human rights, not through the use of force. 99

1. How did the actions of the army during the attempted coup reflect the changes that had taken place in the Soviet Union?

2. Why, according to Gorbachev, did the Soviet people refuse to support the coup?

3. **Critical thinking:** Why might the coup leaders have believed they could succeed in forcing Gorbachev out of office? *(Syn.)* ✔

New Directions for Asia   1945-Present
(pp. 734–757)

Chapter Preview

Section 1 examines the changes that have taken place in China since the establishment of the People's Republic in 1949. Section 2 tells how India became independent and describes the present nations of South Asia. Section 3 focuses on Japan's remarkable postwar economic recovery and its democratic reforms and also deals with the two Koreas and the dynamic expansion of trade of the Pacific Rim nations. The final section traces changes that occurred in Southeast Asia since 1945, including the Vietnam War.

Bibliography

See the *Teacher's Management and Planning Guide* for additional listings. Starred titles are for both students and teachers.

*Cheng, Nien. *Life and Death in Shanghai.* Grove. The story of one woman's gallant struggle to survive with integrity during the Chinese Cultural Revolution.

Ching, Frank. *Ancestors: 900 Years in the Life of a Chinese Family.* Morrow. A compelling account of a family's roots in China and how modern events affected members of that family.

Erikson, Eric H. *Gandhi's Truth: On the Origins of Militant Nonviolence.* Norton. A study of Gandhi by a leader of the psychohistorical movement.

Karnow, Stanley. *Vietnam.* Viking. A comprehensive history of the Vietnam war, beginning long before American involvement.

Reischauer, Edwin O. *The Japanese Today: Change and Continuity.* Harvard University Press. A newly revised study.

*Shen Tong. *Almost a Revolution.* Houghton. A first-hand account of growing up in China, and the 1989 pro-democracy demonstrations.

Section Lesson Plans

SECTION 1   (pp. 735–739)
Communist Rule in China

Objectives

After completing this section, students will be able to:
1. Explain how the Communists took power and ruled China.
2. Describe Communist China's relations with other nations.

Introducing the Lesson

Remind students that the Communist Revolution in China established a Communist government in the world's most populous country. Although great economic strides have improved the standard of living for millions, Chinese society and traditions have been radically affected.

Then ask: *(a) What aspects of Communist rule might have resulted in social and cultural change?* (Answers will vary. Totalitarian control, rejection of old ways, and collectivization.)

(b) In what ways might a Communist revolution in any non-Communist country affect that country? (Totalitarian institutions would probably be established and the economic system would change.)

Developing the Lesson:
Comparing Information

Have students outline policies of the Chinese Communists that were similar to those implemented by the Soviet Communists. (Like the Soviets, the Chinese placed political power in the Communist Party, destroyed all opposition, used propaganda, organized Five-Year Plans and collective farms.) *(Comprehension)*

Developing the Lesson:
Forming a Hypothesis

Have students develop a hypothesis explaining the possible effects of the Cultural Revolution. Students should identify how old ways were attacked, and then develop a hypothesis explaining how the Cultural Revolution might have affected Chinese society. *(Synthesis)*

**Closing the Lesson:
Drawing Conclusions**

Have students compare China's rejection of Western ways during the Cultural Revolution with its policy of isolation from the West during the fifteenth century (p. 284), and then draw conclusions about the following: *(a) Were the motives behind the two periods of isolation similar or different? (b) What attitude about the West did China's isolationist policies reveal?* (Answers will vary.) *(Synthesis)*

See *Section Review* questions, p. 739.

SECTION 2　　　　　(pp. 739–744)
Turmoil in South Asia

Objectives

After completing this section, students will be able to:
1. Explain how India gained independence.
2. Identify challenges faced by the government of India.
3. Discuss other important developments in postwar South Asia.

Introducing the Lesson

Remind students that India faced many of the same problems that plagued China after World War II. Newly independent India struggled with social unrest, poverty, undeveloped industry, and a burgeoning population. Unlike China, however, India established a democratic system.

　　Then ask: *(a) What might account for two nations approaching similar problems so differently?* (Answers will vary. The strength of existing political institutions, traditions, ideas about government, and foreign support all may affect the policies chosen by countries as they face new situations.)

　　(b) Which system, Communist or democratic, offers the most effective solutions to the kinds of problems faced by China and India? (Answers will vary.)

Developing the Lesson:
Drawing Conclusions

Have students write an essay supporting or refuting the following statement: *The creation of the Muslim state of Pakistan produced more conflict than it resolved.* When writing their essays, students should cite examples from the text to support their arguments. *(Synthesis)*

**Developing the Lesson:
Solving Problems**

Have students work in groups to identify the problems that India faced after independence and suggest practical ways of dealing with the problems in a democratic system. (Problems include lowered harvests; hunger; refugees from Pakistan; food riots and strikes; government corruption; a staggering population increase; unemployment; illiteracy; and poor health, housing, and sanitation.) *(Synthesis)*

**Closing the Lesson:
Drawing Conclusions**

Have students answer the following questions: *(a) How would India's colonial experiences have affected its ties to the West? (b) Why might India have wanted friendly relations with the Soviets?* (Answers will vary.) *(Comprehension)*

See *Section Review* questions, p. 744.

SECTION 3　　　　　(pp. 744–748)
New Economic Powers in the Pacific

Objectives

After completing this section, students will be able to:
1. Explain how Japan rose from defeat to become an economic giant.
2. Identify other nations in the Pacific region that became prosperous.

Introducing the Lesson

Remind students that both Japan and South Korea received strong American support after World War II. Japan's and South Korea's democratic systems, however, took different paths.

　　Then ask: *(a) What factors might influence the strength of a democracy?* (A nation secure from threats would be more likely to develop a strong democracy than one whose security appears threatened.)

　　(b) Why might a nation threatened by revolution or foreign takeover restrict democratic rights? (The government might claim that forces working against democracy have the opportunity to organize in an open society.)

　　(c) How important to young democracies is the support of a nation like the United States? (Answers will vary.)

Developing the Lesson:
Observing for Detail

Have students find evidence to support each of the following statements:

(a) *The Japanese constitution of 1947 showed considerable American influence.*

(b) *Reform of land and industrial ownership led to wider distribution of wealth.*

(c) *Japan made a remarkable recovery in the postwar period.* (Comprehension)

Developing the Lesson:
Understanding Point of View

Have students write two editorials that might appear in a current Japanese newspaper supporting or opposing the remilitarization of Japan. (*For:* Japan's economic growth was linked to its low military spending; now that Japan is a rich nation, it should assume responsibility for its own defense. *Against:* Japan's need for defense is limited; heavy remilitarization could upset the balance of power in the region; and there has been a growing, strong domestic opposition to remilitarization.) (Application)

Closing the Lesson:
Evaluating Information

Have students work in groups to discuss the following: *Did the threat from North Korea justify South Korea's restriction of democratic rights, or should unrestricted democracy be established in South Korea?* (Synthesis)

See *Section Review* questions, p. 748.

SECTION 4 (pp. 749–755)
Conflict in Southeast Asia

Objectives

After completing this section, students will be able to:
1. Identify the challenges faced by the Philippines after independence.
2. Explain how Communists unified Vietnam.
3. Describe how the war in Vietnam affected the rest of Southeast Asia.

Introducing the Lesson

Remind students that Southeast Asia was important as a gateway to Asia. Regional conflict between democratic and Communist forces erupted after World War II and resulted in the Communist take-over of Vietnam.

Then ask: (a) *What factors might have contributed to the struggle between democracy and communism?* (The existence of Communist regimes in China and North Korea and the persistence of Western colonialism.)

(b) *Why might Southeast Asia's geographic location have contributed to the conflict?* (Answers will vary. Southeast Asia's coastline provides easy access to China.)

Developing the Lesson:
Evaluating Information

Have students evaluate the following statements: (a) *The conflict in Vietnam was an important test of the strength of both communism and democracy. (b) The conflict in Vietnam was essentially a civil war that grew in importance because of American involvement.* Students should explain how each statement might be accurate or inaccurate. Have students share their views in class. (Synthesis)

Developing the Lesson:
Making Decisions

Have students work in groups to write position papers recommending a course of action that the United States ought to have taken in each of the following situations: the French departure from Vietnam in 1954; the Gulf of Tonkin incident. (Synthesis)

Closing the Lesson: Making Judgments

Have the class discuss the following question: *What might explain the pattern of social reorganization and brutality that appears to follow the establishment of Communist governments?* (Evaluation)

See *Section Review* questions, p. 755.

Chapter 36 Review Answers
(pp. 756–757)

Vocabulary Review

1. (a) commune (b) civil disobedience (c) nuclear proliferation (d) gross national product
2. (a) Great Leap Forward—Five-Year Plan launched by Mao Zedong in 1958, with the aim of increasing China's industrial and agricultural production rapidly and transferring some of the country's wealth from the cities to the countryside; Cultural Revolution—Mao Zedong's campaign for purging China of old thoughts, old culture, old

ideas, old customs, and old habits. (b) Chinese Revolution—conflict between Chinese Communists and Nationalist Chinese that ended in 1949 with the Communist takeover of mainland China; Korean War—conflict from 1950 to 1953 that started when North Korea attempted to bring South Korea under Communist rule. (c) Vietcong—South Vietnamese who sympathized with and aided the efforts of the North Vietnamese to gain control of South Vietnam; Vietnam War—conflict from 1956 to 1975 involving a Communist struggle to take over South Vietnam.

People to Identify

1. Indira Gandhi 2. Ho Chi Minh 3. Mohandas K. Gandhi 4. Chiang Kai-shek

Places to Know

1. Amur River 2. Gulf of Tonkin 3. Bangladesh 4. North Korea 5. Manila 6. South Korea 7. Dien Bien Phu 8. Saigon

Recalling the Facts

1. Many Chinese were angered by the widespread corruption in Chiang Kai-shek's government.
2. Mao's first program, known as the Five-Year Plan, aimed at raising farm production through collectivization. His program also increased industrial production, particularly steel production.
3. Premier Khrushchev's policies of peaceful coexistence with the West and de-Stalinization angered Chinese Communists. In 1966 the Chinese and Soviets were involved in a border dispute over territory along the Amur River.
4. The Chinese realized that American technology could speed China's modernization. They also wanted American aid in case of a Soviet attack.
5. Members of India's Muslim community responded to the calls of nationalist leader Mohammed Ali Jinnah for protests against a united India. Some of these protests resulted in rioting and deaths. The protests convinced the British that a united India was impossible. The British Parliament and Indian leaders agreed in 1947 that India would be divided into two nations—a Hindu India and a Muslim Pakistan. India and Pakistan clashed over Kashmir, which both countries wanted for its water and other resources. In 1949 the two nations divided the region.
6. Many Afghans opposed the regime because its policies conflicted with their Islamic beliefs.
7. The industrial and business community of prewar Japan provided the nation with a basis for rebuilding after the war; the Japanese government gave loans for the expansion of important industries; Western nations allowed Japan to protect its

growing industries with high tariffs on imports; the Japanese people were an educated and cooperative workforce. Taiwan, Hong Kong, Singapore, South Korea, Malaysia, Indonesia, Thailand.
8. Problems faced by Aquino included outbreaks of violence, civil war with Communist guerrillas, opposition from political enemies, and charges of corruption and inefficiency.
9. North Vietnam and Vietcong troops used Cambodian territory as an escape route and for supply bases. In 1969 the United States bombed Cambodian bases and later invaded the country.
10. After Vietnam's invasion of Cambodia in 1978, refugees flooded into Thailand. Vietnamese and Cambodian troops clashed with Cambodian rebels in the refugee camps on the border between Thailand and Cambodia.

Critical Thinking Skills

1. India has modernized its industry and improved its agriculture, with a consequent increase in exports. Yet economic difficulties still plague India, and poverty remains an enormous problem. Also, India remains democratic despite recurring political and ethnic crises.
2. China. Taiwan. China.
3. Students might point out that the goal of the Versailles Treaty was to punish Germany for its part in the war, while Americans did not seek revenge on Japan. Although both countries were forbidden to rearm, Japan was not asked to pay reparations or to give up industrial resources. The United States worked in partnership with the existing Japanese government structure to bring about reforms.
4. Reports will vary.

Thinking About Geography

Burma, Thailand, Laos, Vietnam, Cambodia (Kampuchea). Malaysia, Burma, Laos, Vietnam.

Enrichment: Primary Sources

1. Mao's teachings left no room for other belief systems. Consequently, his followers practiced religious persecution against those who did not share their beliefs.
2. They had lost faith in Mao, who had been like a god to them. Some turned to their families, others to materialistic pleasures, but many turned to organized religion.
3. Students might suggest that Liang had been cut off from his own culture. He probably developed a distrust for political movements, especially those that forced people to change their beliefs, disregarded how the movement affected people's lives, or exploited youth.

New Directions for Asia

1945–Present

See chapter timeline, p. 755.

Before You Read This Chapter

Which is the largest continent? Which continent has the most people? Which includes both the largest democracy and the largest Communist country, in terms of population? The answer to all these questions is Asia. (The largest democracy is India, the largest Communist country, China.) Yet both democracy and communism originated outside Asia, in the West. Industrialization and nationalism also reached Asia from the West. As you read, look for ways in which these forces are changing Asia today. How have Asians put their cultural stamp on each?

The Geographic Setting

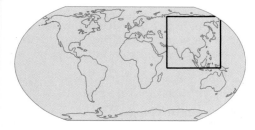

The Chapter Outline

1. Communist Rule in China
2. Turmoil in South Asia
3. New Economic Powers in the Pacific
4. Conflict in Southeast Asia

Modern skyscrapers loom over Hong Kong harbor, as a traditional Chinese boat sets sail.

1 Communist Rule in China

Objectives

Focus Questions

★ ■ How did the Communists take power and rule China? *(pages 735–737)*

● ■ What were Communist China's relations with the outside world? *(page 738)*

Terms to Know

Chinese Revolution   commune
Great Leap Forward   Cultural Revolution

★ Note strategies for first objective on this page and p. 737.

The struggle between the Nationalist and Communist forces in China began in the 1920's (page 677), and it continued on and off for more than two decades. Mao Zedong's Communists finally won the fight for mainland China, and they began to make radical changes in Chinese society and government.

The Chinese Revolution

China in World War II. In China the Second World War led to a three-way struggle among the Chinese Nationalists, the Chinese Communists, and the Japanese. Western powers supported Chiang Kai-shek's Nationalist government against the invading Japanese. The United States gave the Nationalists millions of dollars' worth of military aid, medical supplies, and food. Chiang, however, considered the Communists the real enemy. Chiang depended on the Allies to oppose the Japanese, while he kept his best troops to fight Mao Zedong's Red Army.

Throughout the war the Communists made guerrilla attacks on the Japanese to gain supplies and weapons. Mao Zedong also pre-

pared for a showdown with the Nationalists. The success of Mao's Red Army had earned it much popular support. Mao knew, too, that many Chinese were angry at the widespread corruption in Chiang's government. He tried to ensure that his troops treated civilians with fairness.

Communist victory. At the end of the war against Japan, full-scale fighting broke out between Mao's troops and the Nationalists. By 1949 the Chinese Revolution was over, and the Communists had taken control of mainland China. Chiang Kai-shek and his followers fled to the island of Taiwan (ty-WAHN). There they set up what they declared to be the government of China. On the mainland, Mao proclaimed the birth of the People's Republic of China on October 1, 1949.

Communist Rule in China

Mao and his followers set up the National People's Congress, which was made up of several thousand elected members. In theory this Congress ran the country, but the real power was in the hands of top officials in the Communist Party.

To protect its power, the Party destroyed all opposition in China. The new government killed more than one million people. Many others were sent to forced-labor camps. As in Stalin's Soviet Union, the public was bombarded with government propaganda. Books, billboards, and movies all urged people to be loyal to the new government in China.

Economic development. China's new government faced huge problems. Industries were producing at less than half of their prewar level. Railroads, bridges, ports, and roads needed repair. Trade had come to a halt, and inflation was so high that paper money was almost worthless.

735

★ RETEACHING. Have students review "Communist Rule in China" (pp. 735–737) and outline Mao's political and economic policies. (Political: elimination of opposition; propaganda program; Cultural Revolution. Economic: Five-Year Plans; collective farms; communes.) *(Comprehension) Observing for Detail*
Cultural History In 1927 Mao said that if a revolution was to succeed, it would be "necessary to bring about a brief reign of terror; otherwise one could never suppress the activities of the counterrevolutionaries."

★ REINFORCEMENT. Have students compare Deng Xiaoping's reforms with those made in the Soviet Union after Stalin (p. 725). (Deng broke up communes, encouraged small businesses, gave local officials a freer hand in economic matters, sought Japanese and Western help in improving technology and management, and tried to limit population growth.) *(Synthesis) Synthesizing Information*

Reference Note *Mao Zedong* is the Pinyin spelling of *Mao Tse-tung.*

East Asia

In 1949 Chinese Communists proclaimed the People's Republic of China, while Chinese Nationalists fled to Taiwan. In what direction from mainland China does the island of Taiwan lie?

Map Answer: Southeast (or east).

Sec. Rev. ques. 2

In 1953 Mao came up with the first of his Five-Year Plans, which were aimed at raising production in farms and industries. This strict economic plan set up large state-owned farms, much like those Stalin had formed in Russia (page 657). Within four years, all of China's farms had been collectivized. China was still not growing enough to feed all its people, but rationing and price controls brought a fairer distribution of food. Industrial production, especially steel production, increased, but China was still a mainly agricultural nation.

The Great Leap Forward. Mao was not satisfied with the modest gains of the first Five-Year Plan. In 1958 he launched a second, more ambitious Five-Year Plan called

736

the **Great Leap Forward**. Its goals were to increase industrial and agricultural production rapidly, and to transfer some of China's wealth from the cities to the countryside.

Since China lacked the capital and technology to build many large industrial plants, the government called on people to build small factories in the countryside. These rural factories were not well planned, however, and the goods they made were often of poor quality. The production goals of the Great Leap Forward could not be met.

The government also fell short of its goals for agriculture. Under the Great Leap Forward, collective farms were combined into even larger units called **communes**. In this way, the government hoped, food could

Cultural History The Chinese term for "Communist Party," *Kungch'antang,* is itself a propaganda slogan. *Kung* means "share," *Ch'an* means "production," and *tang* means "party." As leader of the "Share Production Party," Mao promised the people of China that production would be properly shared.

Check for Understanding. Ask: What were communes? (Large units of combined collective farms.)

be produced more efficiently. Yet many peasants were unhappy living on the huge farms, where they were housed in barracks, with many families broken up. Also, farm machinery was scarce, and natural disasters led to poor harvests. To avoid famine, China had to buy grain from abroad.

The Cultural Revolution. By the mid-1960's, the Communists had broken with many Chinese traditions, expanding education and women's rights and giving higher status to workers and peasants. Mao feared, however, that the original spirit of the revolution was being lost. In 1966, he launched the Cultural Revolution to purge China of "The Four Olds"—old thoughts, old culture, old customs, and old habits.

During this upheaval many long-time Party members were ousted. People who were thought to be corrupted by class privilege or Western ideas were sent to work on the communes or in factories. Others were jailed or killed. Artists were forced to glorify the common people. Paintings, poems, and songs were "beautiful" only if they were politically correct.

The most eager supporters of the Cultural Revolution were the millions of young Communists who joined military-style units known as the Red Guard. The government closed schools so that these young people could travel through China attacking anyone with traditional ideas. Their guidebook, called "the little red book," was *The Sayings of Chairman Mao*, a collection of short quotations from Mao Zedong.

The Red Guard ran wild in China's cities. Its members bullied and sometimes killed managers, teachers, and others who did not show enough revolutionary spirit. The Red Guard even turned against the army and against government and Party officials. Realizing that the Red Guard had gone too far, Mao put a stop to the Cultural Revolution in 1968.

China's new leadership. Mao died in 1976. Deng Xiaoping (DUNG SHAOW-PING), a veteran of the Long March (page 677), became the new leader of China. Deng decided that Mao's economic policies had set back China's development. In Mao's time all economic activity was under strict government control. During the 1980's, Deng and his followers decided to make sweeping economic changes.

Deng's reforms were aimed at giving people greater incentives to work. The communes were broken up, people were encouraged to start small businesses, and local officials were given a freer hand in economic matters. The government turned to Japan and the West for help in improving technology and management. To cope with soaring population growth, the government tried to persuade couples to have only one child.

Sec. Rev. ques. 3

★ See below.

Despite efforts at modernization, by the early 1990's China was in the middle of a serious economic slowdown. Many millions of people had no jobs; in fact, unemployment was said to be at its highest level since the Communist takeover in 1949.

A crackdown on hopes for democracy. By 1986 the apparent loosening of government controls could be seen at Chinese universities. Students were allowed to criticize some government policies in newspapers and in speeches. In June 1989 a peaceful gathering of university students in Beijing attracted worldwide attention. Hundreds of thousands of students and workers filled a large open area called Tienanmen Square. The demonstrators called for democratic reforms and meetings with government leaders.

Instead of talking with the students, however, the government declared martial law and sent in units of the Chinese army. Hundreds of unarmed students were killed and student leaders were arrested and executed as part of a brutal government crackdown that shocked the world. The military reaction, moreover, deepened the resentment felt by many Chinese people toward their government and its officials.

Martial law was lifted in early 1990, and Tienanmen Square was reopened to the public, but China's government leaders showed little willingness to consider democratic changes.

737

Cultural History One of Mao's sayings from "the little red book" showed how strongly he felt about those who did not support his government: "Not to have a correct political point of view is like having no soul."

Background After ending the Cultural Revolution, Mao disbanded the Red Guard and sentenced approximately 18 million Guards to hard labor for "re-education."

Background Note that in 1981 the Chinese government officially declared the Cultural Revolution a catastrophe.

Background In 1982 a new Chinese constitution was adopted, giving the people more freedom in their personal lives and putting more emphasis on initiative and individual reward in the workplace.

★ **ENRICHMENT. Have students work in groups to discuss this question: *Based on your study of the Soviet Union and China, are the economic and social goals of Communist governments attainable?* Then have each group report its conclusions to the class.** *(Synthesis) Evaluating Information*

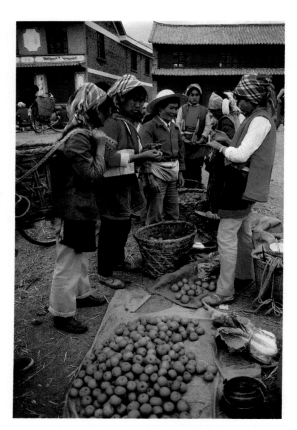

Deng's economic reforms in the 1980's boosted agricultural production by allowing Chinese farmers to sell surplus crops on the open market.

China and the World

● Note strategies for second objective on this page.

In the years just after the Communist victory in 1949, the People's Republic of China had few contacts with non-Communist countries. The nations of the West and China's neighbors in Asia all viewed the new regime with suspicion.

The United States in particular was alarmed at the idea of a Communist-controlled China. Many Americans feared that Chinese Communists would take over Asia, just as the Soviets had taken over Eastern Europe.

Another source of conflict between China and the West was Taiwan. The United States and the United Nations recognized Chiang Kai-Shek's government on Taiwan as **738** the only government of China. In the early

1950's the United States signed a mutual-defense treaty with Chiang and gave Taiwan economic and military aid.

The Sino-Soviet split. For several years after the Chinese Revolution, the People's Republic and the Soviet Union were close allies. After 1956, however, relations between the two governments grew strained. The Chinese saw Khrushchev's policies of de-Stalinization and peaceful coexistence with the West as signs of weakness. Soon Soviet and Chinese leaders were publicly denouncing each other.

In 1966 the war of words heated up over a border dispute. The Chinese claimed 750,000 square miles of Soviet land along the Amur River (map, page 736). In March 1969 fighting broke out in this area. The fighting did not grow into full-scale war, but the two Communist giants kept large armies on either side of the border. Sec. Rev. ques. 4

Détente. While Sino-Soviet relations worsened, the climate between China and the United States improved. With the end of the Cultural Revolution, China took a friendlier view toward the West. The Chinese realized that American technology would speed modernization. They also hoped for American help in case of a Soviet attack. The United States, for its part, hoped to end the Vietnam War (page 750) and establish détente with both Communist powers.

In 1971 President Richard M. Nixon accepted an invitation to visit mainland China the following year. With this shift in American policy, the General Assembly of the United Nations voted in November 1971 to make the People's Republic, and not Taiwan, the official representative of China. By 1979, China and the United States had formally established diplomatic relations.

China's relations with the West were damaged by the crackdown on the 1989 pro-democracy movement. Nevertheless, Chinese and U.S. officials continued to meet. In relations with Gorbachev's Soviet Union, China's leaders followed a cautious course. When the Soviet Union vanished in 1991, China was left as the only Communist country of major importance in the world.

See Sec. 1 *Closing the Lesson*, p. T733B.

● See below.

● RETEACHING. Have students make a chart identifying the causes and effects of Chinese-Soviet conflict. *(Comprehension) Identifying Causes*

● REINFORCEMENT. Have students write an essay explaining how the reform movements started by Gorbachev and Deng probably helped ease ideological conflict between the Soviet Union and China. *(Synthesis) Identifying Effects*

Background In 1960 Moscow stopped economic and military aid to China and withdrew the teams of technicians that had been helping to modernize the country.

● ENRICHMENT. Have students look for information on changes in China's foreign policy that resulted from the collapse of the Soviet Union. *(Comprehension) Locating Information*

1. **Define or identify:** Chinese Revolution, Great Leap Forward, commune, Cultural Revolution. (pp. 735, 736, 737)
2. Describe Mao Zedong's first Five-Year Plan. (p. 736)
3. What economic reforms did Deng Xiaoping make? (p. 737)
4. What led to the split between China and the Soviet Union? (p. 738)
5. **Critical thinking:** How might the Sino-Soviet split have encouraged both Chinese and American leaders to improve relations between their two countries? (See answer below.)

5. Students might suggest that the split encouraged the United States to seek greater influence on Chinese leaders. Facing a hostile Soviet Union, the Chinese needed an ally, and the United States had resources useful to China.

See lesson plans, pp. T733A–T733C.

2 Turmoil in South Asia

Objectives

Focus Questions

★ ■ How did India gain independence? *(pages 739–740)*
● ■ What challenges did the newly established government of India face? *(pages 740–742)*
▲ ■ What were other important developments in postwar South Asia? *(pages 742–744)*

Terms to Know

civil disobedience
nuclear proliferation

★ Note strategies for first objective on this page and p. 740.

Indian opposition to British domination had its beginnings in the early nineteenth century (Chapter 29) and grew during the first half of the 1900's. Britain finally gave India self-rule, but violence threatened the new governments of South Asia. Pakistan broke up into two countries, while Afghanistan fell victim to Soviet aggression.

The Indian Independence Movement

Gandhi. The most admired of India's independence leaders was Mohandas K. Gandhi (GAHN-dee). Trained as a lawyer, Gandhi was a deeply religious Hindu who gave up Western ways and renounced worldly goods. He attracted millions of followers, who called him Mahatma (mah-HAHT-mah), or "Great Soul." Gandhi rejected violence in any form. During his 30-year campaign for Indian independence, he urged the use of civil disobedience—nonviolent resistance to laws and acts that are thought unjust.

Nonviolent protests in India often took the form of boycotts in which Indians refused to work and spent the day in prayer and fasting. Gandhi also led a march to the sea in protest of the tax on salt. The British jailed him a number of times, but the protests he led and the life-threatening fasts that Gandhi himself carried on won worldwide sympathy for Indian independence.

Divisions among the nationalists. In the 1930's another leader emerged in the nationalist movement. This was Jawaharlal Nehru (jah-WAH-har-lahl NAY-roo). Nehru **739**

Mohandas Gandhi used nonviolent tactics in his campaign to free India from British rule. Einstein said of him: "Generations to come will scarcely believe that such a one as this walked the earth in flesh and blood."

Sec. Rev. ques. 2

and Gandhi had different dreams for India's future. Nehru wanted India to become more industrialized. Gandhi hoped that India would return to a simple and traditional way of life. The two men did agree, however, that their main goal should be an independent, united India in which Hindus and Muslims could live together in peace.

Sec. Rev. ques. 3

Events in the 1930's undermined that hope. Indian Muslims, outnumbered by Hindus, feared that Hindus would control India if it won independence. Tensions began to grow between the Hindu-dominated Congress Party and the Muslim League (page 572). Mohammed Ali Jinnah, head of the Muslim League, began to call for the formation of a separate state in northwestern India, to be named Pakistan, from words meaning "Land of the Pure."

World War II. During World War II, India provided the Allies with troops, supplies, and military bases. The Congress Party said, however, that it would stop this aid unless Britain agreed to immediate independence for India. Britain responded by jailing Gandhi, Nehru, and thousands of other nationalists who were disrupting the war effort.

After the Labour Party took power in Britain in 1945, the government offered to grant India its independence. The British at first planned for India to be united. Many Muslims, however, were outraged at the idea and called for protests. In most of the country, the protests were peaceful, but in Calcutta rioting left 5,000 people dead.

The British Parliament quickly realized that a united India was impossible. In 1947, British and Indian leaders agreed that when the British left India, the subcontinent would be divided into two nations—a largely Hindu India and a Muslim Pakistan.

Partition. The boundaries for partition were drawn along religious lines. The Muslim country of Pakistan was created out of two separate regions—West Pakistan in the Punjab and East Pakistan in part of Bengal. The rest of the subcontinent became the country of India. Within the new India and Pakistan, however, lived millions of Hindus and Muslims who suddenly found themselves in the "wrong" country. In the largest human migration in history, five to six million people moved between India and Pakistan. About 500,000 died during the fights and riots that the partition sparked.

Gandhi spoke out against the violence and fasted for peace. His concern for all Indian people eventually cost him his life. In January 1948, Gandhi was shot and killed by an extremist Hindu who believed him to be a traitor to his own religion.

★ See below, left.

Independent India

● Note strategies for second objective on this page and p. 742.

The new government. Indians celebrated their independence on August 15, 1947. The nation soon drew up its first constitution, modeled on the American and British democracies. The Congress Party dominated Indian politics. Nehru, the party's leader, became India's first prime minister and held that office until his death in 1964.

★ ENRICHMENT. Have students compare the ideas and methods of Martin Luther King, Jr., with those of Gandhi. Students might write a report on the similarity between King and Gandhi, or work with others to present a panel discussion on the American civil rights movement led by King during the 1960's. (Synthesis) *Synthesizing Information*

● RETEACHING. Have students make a timeline of events that created problems for India after independence in 1947. (Comprehension) *Sequencing Events*
● REINFORCEMENT. Have students develop a hypothesis explaining why it might be difficult to maintain a democratic system of government in a nation like India with its social, economic, and political problems. (Synthesis) *Making Judgments*

India's new constitution gave women greater voting and property rights. It also outlawed discrimination against untouchables (page 56). Jobs, schools, political offices, and public buildings had to be opened up to India's 60 million outcastes. Enforcing this order was hard, however, particularly in the countryside, where people still clung to their Hindu traditions.

One of Nehru's toughest tasks as prime minister was to give the new nation a sense of unity. Never in India's long history had the subcontinent been united; each region had its own religion, language, and customs. After independence, the people of India were still divided by their loyalties to various Hindu groups or to the Muslim minority.

Territorial disputes. The ongoing hostility between India and Pakistan included a dispute over Kashmir (see map), a region that both countries wanted for its water and other resources. Indian and Pakistani troops fought in Kashmir until the UN arranged a truce in 1949. The territory was divided between India and Pakistan, but control of Kashmir remains hotly disputed. A nationalist movement has even demanded independence for Kashmir.

India also had a dispute with its neighbor to the northeast—China. In 1962, Chinese soldiers crossed the border into Indian territory. The Chinese government quickly recalled its troops, but the invasion prompted Nehru to set aside more money for national defense.

South Asia

In 1947 the Indian subcontinent was divided into two nations—India and Pakistan. Which nation was made up of two separate regions? What is the capital of India?

Map Answers: (1) Pakistan. (2) New Delhi.

Indira and Rajiv Gandhi. Two years after Nehru's death in 1964, the Congress Party elected his daughter, Indira Gandhi, to be prime minister of India. During her first five years in office, Gandhi won admiration for her strong economic policies.

The next few years, however, brought a number of serious problems to India. Severe drought lowered harvests, and hunger spread. The high price of oil on the world market put a severe strain on the Indian economy. At the same time, thousands of refugees were pouring into the country, fleeing a civil war in East Pakistan. The United States and other countries sent millions of tons of grain to India. Even so, food riots and strikes broke out across the country.

Meanwhile . . .

IN THE HIMALAYAS

In 1953 Edmund Hillary of New Zealand and Tenzing Norgay of Nepal became the first people to climb Mount Everest, the world's highest mountain. Located in the eastern Himalayas between Nepal and Tibet, Mount Everest rises 29,028 feet above sea level.

741

Biography Before her election as prime minister, Indira Gandhi had been active in India's government. After serving as an adviser to her father during his term of office, she was elected to Parliament in 1964 and became minister of information and broadcasting the same year.

Biography Indira Gandhi was not related to Mohandas Gandhi; she took the name of her husband, Feroze Gandhi (no relation to Mohandas Gandhi), whom she married in 1942.

During these troubled times, some Congress Party leaders blamed Indira Gandhi for corruption in her government. In June 1975, a court found her guilty of campaign fraud and barred her from holding office for the next six years. Two weeks later, however, the prime minister declared a state of emergency. Over the next two years, Gandhi jailed thousands of her opponents, censored the press, and limited civil liberties. In 1977 Gandhi ended the state of emergency and called for elections. She was voted out of office, but three years later won re-election.

In 1984 Indira Gandhi sent troops to the Punjab, to crush a rebellion among Sikh extremists demanding self-rule. This move outraged Sikhs throughout India. Four months later, Indira Gandhi was assassinated by three of her own Sikh bodyguards.

Rajiv (rah-JEEV) Gandhi, the son of Indira Gandhi, succeeded his mother as prime minister. He continued her policies, such as trying to contain unrest among the Sikhs. In 1989, however, Rajiv Gandhi lost office in

parliamentary elections that focused on charges of widespread national corruption and runaway inflation. In 1991 Rajiv Gandhi seemed to be on the way to regaining the office of prime minister when he was killed by a bomb blast at an election rally. The Congress Party returned to power, but without leadership from the family that had dominated Indian politics since 1947.

A land of contradictions. Beginning in the 1960's, modern technology and new farming methods greatly increased India's agricultural output. India also became a leading industrial producer. It continued to make traditional products such as sugar and textiles, but steel and engineering products became more important as exports.

This success, however, did not solve India's economic problems. The country's steadily rising population severely strained its resources. Unemployment remained high, and poverty continued to be a massive problem. Less than half of India's people were literate. Most cities lacked adequate health care, housing, and sanitation. Recently, moreover, a wave of Hindu fundamentalism has led to growing Hindu-Muslim hostility and outbreaks of violence. In its first decades of independence India had built the foundations of a working democracy. By the early 1990's, however, India faced the possibility that economic problems and religious intolerance could shake those foundations.

Indian Prime Minister Nehru takes a stroll with his daughter, Indira Gandhi. Nehru, his daughter, and his grandson Rajiv Gandhi held the office of prime minister over much of the period since India gained independence.

742

Conflicts Elsewhere in South Asia

▲ Note strategies for third objective on this page and p. 744.

Divided Pakistan. From its beginnings in 1947, Pakistan was a divided country. A thousand miles of Indian land lay between East and West Pakistan, and the two regions were widely different. West Pakistan was dry, hilly, and moderately populated. Its main language was Urdu (OOR-doo), and its people had a higher standard of living than people in East Pakistan. East Pakistan was hot, rainy, and densely populated. Floods and famine were common. The East Pakistanis

Sec. Rev. ques. 4

Background After Indira Gandhi was voted out of office, she formed the Congress I (for Indira) Party. In 1980, when the Congress I Party gained control of Parliament, Indira Gandhi again became prime minister.

● **ENRICHMENT. Have students choose one of the problems faced by India after independence and research India's efforts to deal with it.** Students might focus on Hindu-Muslim relations, Kashmir, or population growth. (*Application*) **Locating Information**

▲ **RETEACHING. Have students make a chart identifying the economic, social, and political causes of the conflict between East and West Pakistan.** (*Comprehension*) **Identifying Causes**

▲ **REINFORCEMENT. Have students identify and suggest solutions for the problems faced by Bangladesh and Pakistan after 1971.** (Bangladesh: overcrowded; suffered from food shortage, war damage, and political instability. Pakistan: political instability, unrest, and conflict with India.) (*Synthesis*) **Solving Problems**

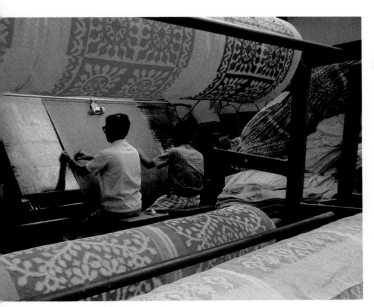

Textile manufacturing is a major industry in India.

spoke Bengali (ben-GAH-lee) and were closer in their traditions to their Hindu neighbors in India than to the West Pakistanis.

For the first 20 years of Pakistan's existence, West Pakistanis dominated the government. West Pakistan also experienced an economic boom in the 1960's. East Pakistan, overcrowded and impoverished, looked with envy at the other half of the country.

This growing inequality increased tension between East and West Pakistan. In the 1970 elections, the East Pakistanis won enough votes to gain control of the government. The West Pakistani dictator, however, refused to step down. When riots broke out in East Pakistan, he declared martial law. In the violence that followed, hundreds of thousands of East Pakistanis were killed by the army. Millions fled to India.

Bangladesh. In 1971, East Pakistan declared its independence as Bangladesh, meaning "the Bengal nation." Pakistani forces invaded, but India gave help to the Bengalis, and the invasion was halted.

One of the world's most overcrowded nations, Bangladesh faced severe problems. It could not produce enough food for its growing population. Much of the country, includ-

ing its few industries, had been devastated in the civil war. Floods, famine, and plague caused widespread suffering.

Bangladesh has also been troubled by political instability. After a series of coups and assassinations, a military government took over the country in 1982. Eight years later, an opposition movement launched demonstrations and strikes and succeeded in carrying out a short revolution. The general who had ruled Bangladesh since 1982 was forced out of office.

Instability in Pakistan. Pakistan (former West Pakistan) had its own concerns. In 1970, Zulfikar Ali Bhutto (BOO-toh) became prime minister. Hoping to stabilize the country's economy, Bhutto nationalized several of Pakistan's industries. This action scared away foreign investors. Bhutto's reforms made him many enemies in Pakistan, and he was accused of corruption.

In 1977, for the third time in 30 years, the army seized control of the government. Bhutto was imprisoned and later executed. The new regime, headed by General Zia ul-Haq (ZEE-uh ool-HAHK), replaced Pakistani civil law with traditional Islamic law. After Zia's death in 1988, the party led by Bhutto's daughter, Benazir Bhutto, won nationwide elections. After 20 months in office, Bhutto was abruptly dismissed by a presidential order. In 1990 conservative members of the National Assembly chose Nawaz Sharif, an industrialist, to be prime minister.

A continuing worry for Pakistan is India. The two nations are suspicious of each other, and both have built modern armies to protect themselves. Pakistan became especially alarmed in 1974, when India tested an atomic bomb. There have been reports that Pakistan is building bombs. People concerned about **nuclear proliferation**—the spread of nuclear weapons to additional countries—have urged Pakistan not to build nuclear weapons.

Afghanistan. Pakistan's neighbor to the north, Afghanistan, had gained full independence from Britain in 1919. A number of Afghanistan's monarchs tried to modernize

743

the country, but the Muslim tribes that made up most of the population resisted change. In 1973, military officers overthrew the last of the monarchs and established a republic. Five years later a group of Soviet-backed Communists overthrew the military regime and set up a one-party Marxist state. Angry at interference with their Islamic beliefs, many Afghans rebelled against the Communist government.

Sec. Rev. ques. 5

Determined to protect communism around the world, the Soviets invaded Afghanistan in 1979. The Soviets had more soldiers and better weapons than the Afghans. They soon won control of the cities, but they were unable to wipe out resistance in the countryside. The United States gave the Afghan rebels military and economic aid.

More than four million Afghans fled their war-torn country, crossing the borders into Iran and Pakistan. Another million people were killed in the fighting. By the late 1980's, the Soviet invasion had cost Afghanistan one third of its population.

In 1989 the Soviet Union, having failed to crush the Muslim guerrillas, pulled its

See lesson plans, pp. T733A–T733C.

troops out of Afghanistan. Civil war continued as guerrilla factions attacked cities and towns controlled by the central government, but Afghanistan's conflict was no longer part of a superpower rivalry.

▲ See below, left.

See Sec. 2 Closing the Lesson, p. T733B.

Section Review

Answers to Section Review questions are in brackets on pages indicated.

1. **Define:** civil disobedience, nuclear proliferation. (pp. 739, 743)
2. How did Gandhi and Nehru differ in their hopes for India's future? (p. 740)
3. What were the causes and results of the partition of India? (p. 740)
4. How did East Pakistan become the independent state of Bangladesh? (pp. 742–743)
5. Why did the Soviet Union invade Afghanistan in 1979? (p. 744)
6. **Critical thinking:** Why might the use of civil disobedience often be more effective than violence in achieving political goals? (See answer below.)

6. Students might suggest that while violence usually begets further violence, civil disobedience draws attention to injustices and leaves open the possibility of negotiation and reform.

3 New Economic Powers in the Pacific

Objectives

★ Note strategies for first objective on this page and p. 746.

Focus Questions

★ ■ How did Japan rise from defeat to become an economic giant? (pages 744–747)

● ■ What other nations in the Pacific region became prosperous? (pages 747–748)

Terms to Know

gross national product
Korean War

744

When World War II ended, the United States was in control of much of the Pacific. In the decades that followed the war, however, Japan and other Pacific nations became more and more powerful. The Pacific region began to play a major role in world trade.

The Occupation of Japan

A new form of government. After the Allied victory in World War II, the United States army occupied Japan from 1945 to 1952. President Harry Truman named General Douglas MacArthur to head the Allied occupation forces. The long-range aim of the

▲ ENRICHMENT. Have students refer to periodicals and newspapers to research the current situation in Afghanistan. (Application) *Locating Information*

★ RETEACHING. Have students list the reforms in Japan after World War II that resulted in a democratic government and economic prosperity. (American occupation reduced the power of the Japanese armed forces and established a constitutional democracy. Economic reform included land redistribution and industrial reorganization.) *(Comprehension) Observing for Detail*

American occupation was to help Japan become a democratic country.

The first step toward this goal was to reduce the power of the Japanese armed forces. Military leaders were removed from the government and from all official posts, and some were tried for war crimes.

The next step in the occupation was to make basic political reforms. In 1947 the authoritarian Japanese constitution of the Meiji era (page 585) was replaced by a democratic constitution. The constitution set up a two-house Diet (legislature) elected by the people, with a prime minister responsible to the Diet. Until this time, Japanese emperors had been considered divine. Now the emperor was to serve only as the "symbol of the state." The constitution also said that the Japanese would "forever renounce war" and would not keep military forces.

The new constitution showed a good deal of American influence. A bill of rights guaranteed education, freedom of speech and religion, and other rights. A supreme court was set up with the authority to declare laws unconstitutional. Workers gained the right to bargain with employers. Women won equal political and economic rights, as well as legal equality in marriage and family matters. Long-standing Japanese traditions, however, often stood in the way of these new freedoms.

Sec. Rev. ques. 2

Other reforms. For hundreds of years, much of the land in Japan had been in the hands of large landowners. Most small farmers had rented the land they worked. After World War II, the government put a limit on the amount of land each farmer could own. The government bought up land and sold it at low prices to landless peasants.

Other reforms distributed wealth more fairly. The *zaibatsu* (ZY-baht-soo)—great Japanese industrial firms owned by a handful of powerful families—were ordered to disband and sell their stock on the open market. Industrial workers were encouraged to form unions.

The Japanese also made changes in education. The Japanese built more colleges and began to use modern methods of teaching. Schools in prewar Japan had stressed loyalty and obedience to the emperor and the nation. In the postwar years, schools taught democratic values.

In April 1952 Japan regained full independence when a peace treaty, signed by Japan, the United States, and 47 other countries, went into effect. Another treaty allowed American forces to use Japanese bases, giving the United States a firm ally in Asia. The United States guaranteed Japan's security against attack, while Japan put back together a "self-defense" force of its own.

This robot-artist is an example of how the Japanese have embraced modern technology. Many Japanese also retain a traditional reverence for nature.

745

Social History The effects of Japan's land redistribution policies can be seen in the following statistics: in 1931 about 31 percent of the farmers owned their own farms; by 1957 this figure had increased to nearly 70 percent. In 1931 about 42 percent of the farmers were large landowners; by 1957 this figure had decreased to about 27 percent.

Daily Life

Working in Japan

For young people in Japan, applying for a job can be a trying experience. They face long employment exams and investigations of their family and their private life. Companies take these special steps even for low-paying, entry-level jobs. Both the employee and the company are getting ready for a long-term relationship. To a Japanese company, hiring a new worker is almost like adopting a new member of the family.

Workers at the biggest Japanese companies know that they can keep their jobs as long as they live. They will never be laid off or fired. Only about one fourth of Japan's workers have such "lifetime jobs," but nearly all companies will go to great pains to avoid firing a full-time employee.

Working for a large, well-known company has many other benefits as well. It helps a person's children get into good schools. It makes getting a housing loan easier. Some companies even run their own vacation resorts for employees.

Japanese workers pay for their security by hard work. They spend long hours on the job during the week and often go in on Saturdays as well. Also, most Japanese companies do not pay workers if they stay home for a day because of illness. Nevertheless, nearly all Japanese workers feel a strong sense of loyalty to their companies.

A New Prosperity

Postwar Japan went through great political changes, but its economic recovery was even more remarkable. Between 1946 and 1967, Japan's **gross national product**—the total annual value of a nation's goods and services—grew at a rate of 10 percent a year. This was higher even than in West Germany, the fastest-growing European economy. Japan led the world in shipbuilding and its cars, steel, cameras, and electronic equipment were exported in record quantities. By the late 1960's, Japan had become the third largest economic power in the world. (The United States and the Soviet Union were first and second.)

The economic miracle in Japan can be traced to a number of causes. (1) The thriving industrial and business community of prewar Japan gave the nation a basis for rebuilding when the war was over. (2) The Japanese gov-

746

ernment made loans for the expansion of important industries. The government had plenty of capital for investment because it did not have to spend much on defense. Businesses could spend large amounts of money on research and development, particularly in high-technology fields such as electronics. (3) During Japan's economic recovery, Western nations allowed that country to protect its growing industries with high tariffs on imports. (4) The Japanese had an educated and cooperative work force. Japanese workers, unlike many in the West, put group effort and the success of their company ahead of individual achievement.

Despite the upturn in Japan's economy, problems remained. Japan was short of land and natural resources. Even with better postwar farming methods, Japan could not grow enough food for its people. It had to import almost all its soybeans, wheat, and sugar. It also depended on foreign countries for raw materials—crude oil, iron ore, and lumber.

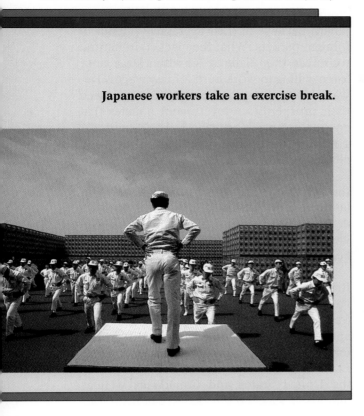

Japanese workers take an exercise break.

In addition, the Japanese government was so concerned with economic growth that it often failed to consider quality of life. As more people moved to overcrowded cities, housing became an acute problem. With tiny apartments now costing over half a million dollars, average Japanese families can no longer expect to live in homes of their own.

Japan's Foreign Affairs

The balance of trade. Unlike most countries, Japan enjoyed a trade surplus in the 1980's. That is, it exported a greater value of goods than it imported. Japan's trading partners began to demand that Japan cut back its exports and buy more foreign goods. This pressure came especially from the United States, where the automobile and electronics industries faced heavy competition from Japanese imports. In the late 1980's, the Japanese government promised to open markets to more foreign goods; yet Japan continued in the 1990's to have a huge trade surplus.

Defense. Close ties with the United States helped Japan recover and grow in the postwar decades. Under the terms of its constitution, Japan kept only a small self-defense force and depended on the United States to guarantee its military security. As Japan became an economic superpower, however, some of its people began to push for more military spending. Japan's military budget rose sharply in the 1980's, though it was still tiny by American standards. The United States government approved of Japan's efforts to take more responsibility for its own defense.

Relations with other nations. Like the United States, Japan did not recognize the Communist government in China for many years. After the death of Mao, Japan saw the more moderate policies of China's new leaders as a good sign and in 1972 the two countries established diplomatic relations. China's plans for modernization opened up a ready market for Japan's industrial products, and the two nations are now strong trading partners. As part of an effort to establish a new role in world affairs, Japan sought better relations with the Soviet Union as well. Japan also has greatly expanded its foreign aid to less developed nations in Asia, Latin America, and Africa.

The Two Koreas

● Note strategies for second objective on this page and p. 748.
Japan had annexed the country of Korea in 1911. When the Second World War ended, Korea was divided at the 38th parallel of latitude into Soviet and American occupation zones. With Soviet help, Communists set up a government in North Korea; the United States backed a non-Communist government in South Korea. Both governments claimed the right to rule the entire peninsula.

The Korean War. In June 1950, North Korea made a surprise attack on the south, hoping to bring all of Korea under Communist rule. The United Nations at once sent **747**

Economics Between 1960 and 1980 Japanese production of passenger cars increased more than 100 percent, as Japan supplied both domestic and foreign markets.
● RETEACHING. Have students explain how Korea was divided and how North and South Korea differ. (After World War II Korea was divided between American and Soviet forces; Communists set up government in North, United States backed government in South.) (Comprehension) Identifying Cause and Effect

Background The strain on public transportation in Japan is evidenced by the presence of "pushers" and "pullers" at commuter train platforms. Pushers help to pack people tightly into trains. Pullers remove passengers who are preventing the train doors from closing.
● REINFORCEMENT. Have students draw a map of the Pacific Rim countries, showing the natural resources and the goods produced in each country. (Comprehension) Translating Information into Another Form

troops to aid the south, and the **Korean War** began. By November the UN soldiers had driven the Communists deep into North Korean territory.

As the retreating Communists came near China, about 200,000 Chinese soldiers poured over the border into Korea, catching the UN forces by surprise. With Chinese help, the North Koreans pushed the UN troops back to the 38th parallel. Fighting continued until a truce was declared in 1953.

Separate paths. After the war, the two Koreas set out on different paths. North Korea became a totalitarian state on the Stalinist model. Industry was nationalized and farms were collectivized. Government economic plans favored heavy industry. The government wiped out dissent and tried to cut its citizens off from the outside world.

South Korea, on the other hand, was officially a democracy, though the people were often denied their rights. South Korean leaders silenced their political opponents, arguing that solidarity was important to avoid a takeover by the north. In 1987 mass protests forced the government to revise the constitution and hold elections. The government's commitment to democracy remained uncertain. Strong government support for private industry gave the South Korean economy spectacular success. As exports skyrocketed, South Korea's gross national product grew to four times the size of North Korea's.

Sec. Rev. ques. 4

With the end of the cold war, tension on the peninsula eased, and the two Koreas agreed to discuss issues of mutual concern. In 1991 the two countries even signed a non-aggression pact. Nevertheless, uncertainty about North Korea's nuclear weapons program delayed the withdrawal of United States forces from South Korea.

Trade in the Pacific

South Korea and Japan were not the only success stories in Asia during the 1970's and 1980's. Taiwan, Hong Kong, and Singapore also took an active part in world trade. Along with South Korea, they shared the nickname

748

"four little dragons" (the big dragon being Japan) because of their aggressive pursuit of foreign markets. What they lacked in natural resources, they made up for with a large labor force willing to work hard for low wages. Taiwan, Hong Kong, and Singapore also owed their prosperity to government policies that encouraged private business. Their major exports include textiles, small appliances, and electronic equipment.

Sec. Rev. ques. 5

Three other nations worked to follow the example of their stronger neighbors. Malaysia, Indonesia, and Thailand were less developed than the "four little dragons" but were richer in natural resources. Oil, tin, rubber, and rice are among their exports.

Economists predict that the Pacific Rim—the group of nations that border the Pacific Ocean—will be the focus of world trade in the next century. To promote trade and economic links, Pacific Rim nations have formed a group called APEC (Asia-Pacific Economic Cooperation). Members include the United States and Canada as well as nations of Asia and the Pacific. These nations already produce half the world's goods and services, and account for about 40 percent of total world trade.

● See below.

See Sec. 3 *Closing the Lesson*, p. T733C.

Section Review

Answers to Section Review questions are in brackets on pages indicated.

1. **Define or identify:** gross national product, Korean War. (pp. 746, 748)
2. How did the occupation of Japan by American forces in the postwar period change that country? (p. 745)
3. Why was Japan able to make such a rapid economic recovery after World War II? (p. 746)
4. What major differences exist between North and South Korea? (p. 748)
5. What factors helped many Pacific Rim countries to prosper? (p. 748)
6. **Critical thinking:** Why can Japan's recovery after World War II be considered an "economic miracle"? (See answer below.)

4 Conflict in Southeast Asia

Objectives

Focus Questions

★ ■ What challenges did the Philippines face after independence? *(pages 749–750)*

● ■ How did Communists unify Vietnam? *(pages 750–752)*

▲ ■ How did the war in Vietnam affect the rest of Southeast Asia? *(pages 752–754)*

Terms to Know

Vietcong   Tet offensive
Vietnam War   boat people
domino theory
Gulf of Tonkin Resolution

★ Note strategies for first objective on this page and p. 750.

When World War II began, much of Southeast Asia was still under European control. During the war, the Japanese occupied most of this territory and allowed local leaders to govern it. Many of these leaders later headed national liberation movements against both Japan and the Western colonial powers.

The Philippines

Because the United States did not try to keep control of the Philippines, independence came peacefully for that country. In 1946 a new constitution set up a democratic government for the young nation.

The Philippines had suffered much during the war. Filipinos were torn between their desire for economic independence and their desperate need for American aid. Moreover, the Philippine government was riddled with corruption and faced armed rebellion.

During the late 1960's and early 1970's, warfare broke out when Communist rebels set up strongholds in the countryside. At the same time, revolts started among the Muslim minority (most Filipinos are Roman Catholics), and students demonstrated against the government. In response, President Ferdinand Marcos declared martial law and jailed thousands of his opponents.

Many Filipinos were unhappy with Marcos's leadership, but there was no effective anti-Marcos movement until the 1980's. In August 1983 Benigno Aquino (ah-KEEN-oh), an outspoken opposition leader, was killed. Many believed that the Marcos government had ordered the assassination.

To satisfy his critics, Marcos agreed to allow an election. In the voting, held in February 1986, Marcos claimed victory over his opponent—Corazon Aquino, widow of the murdered politician. Aquino claimed that Marcos had rigged the election. A few weeks later, Marcos fled the country.

Sec. Rev. ques. 2

Corazon Aquino began her presidency with wide popularity. Yet she faced outbreaks of violence as well as civil war with Commu-

Corazon Aquino defeated Ferdinand Marcos in the 1986 Philippine presidential elections. Here she reviews cadets at a military academy. **749**

★ RETEACHING. Have students review "The Philippines" (pp. 749–750) and identify the problems faced by the Philippines after independence. (Government corruption; warfare between government and Communists; revolts among Muslim minority; student demonstrations; widespread poverty.) *(Comprehension) Observing for Detail*

★ REINFORCEMENT. Have students work in groups to explain which of the problems faced by the Philippines most threatened national security, and then suggest ways the problem might have been resolved. Have each group share its conclusions with the class. *(Synthesis) Solving Problems*

Southeast Asia

The region that makes up Southeast Asia includes a peninsula and several islands. What country includes the largest islands? What are the two main Philippine islands?

Map Answers: (1) Indonesia. (2) Luzon, Mindanao.

nist guerrillas in the countryside. Her government was also threatened by opposition from political enemies and by charges of corruption and inefficiency in her administration. For all these reasons, democracy in the Philippines remained fragile.

★ See below.

The Vietnam War

● Note strategies for second objective on pp. 751–752.

The collapse of French control. The French returned to Indochina after World War II to find much of it under the control of the Vietminh, a nationalist group begun in 1941 by Ho Chi Minh. Ho, a Communist, had set up a government in the northern part of **750** Vietnam.

Unwilling to part with Indochina, France sent troops to fight the Vietminh. Vietnamese peasants gave help and supplies to Ho's guerrilla forces. Communist China also aided the Vietminh, while the United States helped France. In 1954, the Vietminh defeated the French at Dien Bien Phu, and the French pulled out of Indochina.

Sec. Rev. ques. 3

Later in 1954, peace talks were held at Geneva, Switzerland. The resulting settlement, known as the Geneva Accords, temporarily divided Vietnam at the 17th parallel of latitude. Elections to unite the country were set for 1956. Until then, it was agreed, Ho Chi Minh's Communist government would control the north, and a non-Communist government would lead the south.

★ ENRICHMENT. Have students work in groups to present a panel discussion on one of the following: the 1986 election in the Philippines; the Philippine Senate's decision in 1991 not to renew the base-leasing treaty with the U.S.; the impact of the eruption of Mount Pinatubo on U.S.-Philippine relations; Corazon Aquino's administration. (Synthesis) *Locating Information*

● RETEACHING. Have students make a timeline of events resulting in Communist control of Vietnam. (Timeline should include the following dates: 1941, 1954, 1956, 1957, 1960, 1963, 1964, 1965–67, 1969, 1973, 1975.) (Comprehension) *Sequencing Events*

Unwilling to accept a divided nation, South Vietnam's leaders refused to sign the Geneva Accords. They did not want to lose the north, which had the greater share of Vietnam's industry, minerals, and farmland. They also feared that the Communists would win the 1956 elections.

Conflict between north and south. Ho Chi Minh was determined to bring all Vietnam under Communist rule. North Vietnamese soldiers crossed the 17th parallel to recruit and train South Vietnamese sympathetic to the north's cause. These southerners became known as the **Vietcong**. In 1957 the **Vietnam War** began, as Vietcong soldiers attacked villages in the south. By 1960 the Vietcong were strong enough to attack South Vietnamese army units.

Meanwhile, South Vietnamese President Ngo Dinh Diem (NO DIN dee-EM) tried to restore order. Yet his harsh treatment of the Buddhist community and charges of government corruption cost him popular support. Diem was overthrown and murdered late in 1963.

American involvement. The Vietcong successes alarmed the United States government, which had been aiding South Vietnam since the 1950's. Some Americans worried that the fall of South Vietnam would lead to Communist victories in other countries, a belief known as the **domino theory**. Under President John F. Kennedy, thousands of American military advisers were sent to South Vietnam.

American involvement in the war grew in 1964. In August of that year, President Lyndon B. Johnson reported that North Vietnamese patrol boats had attacked two American ships in the Gulf of Tonkin (map, page

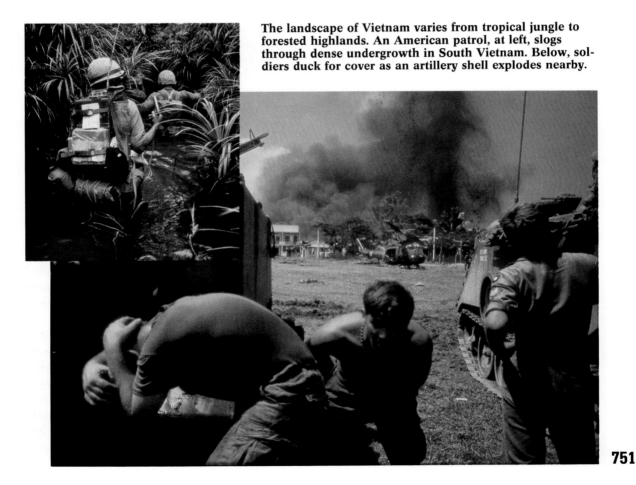

The landscape of Vietnam varies from tropical jungle to forested highlands. An American patrol, at left, slogs through dense undergrowth in South Vietnam. Below, soldiers duck for cover as an artillery shell explodes nearby.

751

● REINFORCEMENT. Have students use the following terms to explain events leading to Communist control in Vietnam: Vietminh, Dien Bien Phu, the Geneva Accords, Vietcong, the domino theory, the Gulf of Tonkin Resolution, the Tet offensive. (Comprehension) *Synthesizing Information*
Background By the time the French were defeated at Dien Bien Phu, the United States was paying four fifths of France's military costs in Indochina.

Background President Kennedy had increased the number of military advisers in Vietnam to about 16,000; the American presence grew dramatically after 1964. By August 1965 there were approximately 125,000 American troops in Vietnam.

750). A few days later, Congress passed the **Gulf of Tonkin Resolution**, giving the President the power to send United States forces to Vietnam. From 1965 through 1967, Johnson sent hundreds of thousands of soldiers to Vietnam. American planes began bombing raids against North Vietnamese bases.

The United States soon discovered, however, that soldiers and bombs alone could not win the war. Vietcong guerrillas would strike at villages and then fade into the jungle; they rarely fought large-scale open battles. Many South Vietnamese civilians, fed up with corruption in their government, aided the Vietcong. North Vietnamese supplies continued to flow down the Ho Chi Minh Trail to Vietcong hideouts in the south.

In January 1968, during the religious holiday of Tet, Vietcong and North Vietnamese forces made a massive attack on the south. Known as the **Tet offensive**, the attack ended in heavy losses for the Communists. Yet the Communists' ability to launch such a powerful strike led many people in the United States to question South Vietnam's chances of winning the war. The war had

sparked widespread protests in the United States, and American leaders now considered withdrawing from Vietnam.

Peace talks between the United States and North Vietnam began in Paris in 1968. In 1969 President Richard Nixon began calling troops home. Bombing raids and ground fighting continued until 1973, however, when the United States, South Vietnam, and North Vietnam signed the Paris Peace Accords. Under this agreement, all United States forces left Vietnam, and all sides pledged not to try to reunify Vietnam by force.

Sec. Rev. ques. 4

The truce quickly broke down. The Communists continued to attack South Vietnam, which could not hold out without American help. In April 1975, the South Vietnamese capital city of Saigon fell to the North Vietnamese. South Vietnam surrendered and Vietnam was united under Communist rule.

Vietnam's leaders made great changes in the south. Industries were nationalized. Teachers and former government officials were sent to "re-education camps" to be made loyal Communists; many city dwellers were sent into rural areas to work on farms. Heavy military spending and rigid state control stood in the way of prosperity. Hundreds of thousands of Vietnamese fled their country to escape persecution and poverty.

● See below, left.

Timetable

The Vietnam War

1954	Vietminh defeat French at Dien Bien Phu; Geneva Accords divide Vietnam.
1957	Vietcong attack villages in South Vietnam.
1964	Gulf of Tonkin Resolution leads to direct American involvement.
1968	Tet offensive.
1970	U.S. troops invade Cambodia.
1973	Paris Peace Accords; U.S. forces withdraw.
1975	South Vietnam falls to North Vietnam; Communists come to power in Cambodia and Laos.

752

Other Conflicts in Southeast Asia

▲ Note strategies for third objective on this page and p. 754.

Cambodia (Kampuchea). The turmoil of the Vietnam War spread to neighboring nations. Cambodia, once a part of French Indochina, had been independent since 1953 under Prince Norodom Sihanouk (SEE-uh-nuk). Sihanouk's government had hoped to stay neutral during the war in Vietnam, but North Vietnamese and Vietcong troops used Cambodian territory for supply bases. In 1969 United States planes began to bomb the country in an attempt to wipe out these bases. A year later, American troops invaded Cambodia, supporting the overthrow of Sihanouk by Lon Nol, a strong anti-Communist. Yet Vietnamese Communists penetrated even farther into Cambodia.

Biography President Johnson once said to the United States ambassador in South Vietnam, "I am not going to lose Vietnam. I am not going to be the President who saw Southeast Asia go the way China went."

● **ENRICHMENT. Have students find information on Vietnam today. Students might research the role of the Communist Party in the government, the economic situation, status of returning refugees, immigration, or relations with the U.S.** (Application) *Locating Information*

▲ **RETEACHING. Have students review "Other Conflicts in Southeast Asia" (pp. 752–754) and outline ways that the Vietnam War affected Cambodia, Laos, and Thailand.** (Cambodia: war spread to Cambodia and Communists gained power. Laos: Communists gained control in 1975. Thailand: remained independent, but thousands of refugees flooded the country.) (Comprehension) *Organizing Information*

Relief workers carry rice into a refugee camp in Thailand. The camps are filled with the families of Cambodians who fled their country's political turmoil in the late 1970's. Most in the camps have lived there all their lives.

Sec. Rev. ques. 5

With Vietnamese help, a group of Communists in Cambodia, the Khmer Rouge (kuh-MAYR ROOZH), overthrew Lon Nol in 1975. The new regime, led by Pol Pot, proved to be one of the most brutal of the 1900's. The government emptied the cities, sending former city dwellers under armed guard to work in the fields. Mass executions became common. As many as one million people, about a sixth of the total population, were killed outright by the Khmer Rouge. A million or more people died of disease and starvation as a result of government actions.

Relations were bad between the Khmer Rouge, which was backed by China, and Vietnam, which was supported by the Soviet Union. In 1978 a Vietnamese army invaded Cambodia. China responded by sending troops to Vietnam, but later withdrew them. In 1979 Pol Pot was replaced by a Communist leader friendly to Vietnam, and the Republic of Kampuchea was established.

The change in leadership did not end the conflict in Cambodia. The Vietnamese Communists and their Cambodian supporters fought a coalition of forces, representing various factions including Pol Pot supporters, anti-Communists, and backers of Prince Sihanouk. In 1989, however, Vietnamese troops left Cambodia. Two years later the four main factions signed a UN-arranged treaty and agreed to make peace.

Laos. Laos won full independence from France in 1954. Like Cambodia, it was torn by internal conflicts. Three factions—pro-Western forces, neutralists, and a Communist group known as the Pathet Lao fought for power. It was not until 1975 that the Pathet Lao gained complete control of the government. The Pathet Lao then asked Vietnam for help in defeating the anti-Communist forces, and thousands of Vietnamese troops moved into Laos.

The Communist victory in Laos added to the flood of Indochinese refugees. By 1985, **753** more than 250,000 people had fled from Laos, seeking to escape poor economic conditions and lack of individual freedom.

Thailand.   Thailand (which had been called Siam before 1939) was never colonized by Europeans. The kingdom was occupied by Japan during World War II, but it regained its independence after Japan's defeat. Pro-Western in its outlook, Thailand sent troops to fight in the Korean and Vietnam wars. During the Vietnam War, Thailand allowed the United States to set up military bases within its borders.

Sec. Rev. ques. 5, cont.

The upheavals throughout Indochina worried Thailand, which shares borders with Laos and Cambodia (map, page 750). After 1975, when Communists took over both of those countries, the Thai government tried to stay on good terms with its neighbors. The Thais hoped to combine economic cooperation with political neutrality.

Vietnam's invasion of Cambodia in 1978 created the sort of crisis Thailand had feared. Refugees flooded into Thailand, and Vietnamese leaders accused Thailand of protecting the Khmer Rouge. Vietnamese and Cambodian troops repeatedly clashed with Cambodian rebels in the refugee camps that straddled the border between Thailand and Cambodia. The Thai government, fearing Vietnam, channeled aid to anti-Vietnamese rebels in Cambodia.

Victims of war.   Oppressed by war, poverty, and Communist rule, hundreds of thousands of refugees fled Laos, Cambodia, and Vietnam in the 1970's and 1980's. As many as 200,000 sought shelter in Thailand. Other displaced persons, the **boat people,** simply sailed their boats out into the ocean, hoping to be rescued and given new homes. Many died at sea, but the largest number of those saved settled in the United States. By 1990 probably one and a half million people had fled Southeast Asia, victims of the upheavals that had shaken the region since the end of World War II.

▲ See below.

See Sec. 4 *Closing the Lesson,* p. T733C.

In the aftermath of war, many desperate Vietnamese fled their country by boat. Survivors of the sea voyage often ended up in refugee camps, from which they applied for admission to the United States and other countries.

▲ **REINFORCEMENT. Have students develop a hypothesis explaining why Thailand, unlike Cambodia and Laos, did not face civil war between Communist and non-Communist factions.** *(Synthesis) Evaluating Information*

Economics Thailand's policy of encouraging a free market rather than experimenting with collectivist, socialist planning has kept it in the lead among the nations of Southeast Asia. Some economists expect Thailand to become Asia's fifth industrialist "little dragon."

Background It has been estimated that over 250,000 people died at sea during their attempts to flee Communist rule in Southeast Asia.

▲ **ENRICHMENT. Have students evaluate the domino theory. Students should consider the recent history of China, Vietnam, Cambodia, and Laos.** *(Evaluation) Synthesizing Information*

1. **Define or identify:** Vietcong, Vietnam War, domino theory, Gulf of Tonkin Resolution, Tet offensive, boat people. (pp. 751, 752, 754)
2. How did Corazon Aquino come to power in the Philippines? (p. 749)
3. What event caused the French to withdraw from Vietnam? Why did the United States become interested in Vietnam? (pp. 750–751)
4. When and why did American forces leave Vietnam? What was the outcome of the struggle between North and South Vietnam? (p. 752)
5. What happened to Cambodia under the rule of Pol Pot? What caused tension between Thailand and Vietnam? (pp. 753–754)
6. **Critical thinking:** How was a small nation like North Vietnam able to fight effectively against South Vietnamese and American forces? (See answer below.)

6. Factors to consider: sympathetic guerrilla forces in South Vietnam, familiarity with terrain, determined leadership.

Chapter 36   Summary and Timeline

1. In China, World War II was followed by civil war. The Communists defeated the Kuomintang in 1949, and Mao Zedong formed a new government, known as the People's Republic of China. Mao made vast changes in Chinese agriculture and society. After the violence of the Cultural Revolution, China's leaders took a more moderate stance.

2. Guided by the nationalist leader Mohandas Gandhi, India won its independence from Britain in 1947. Though the country has had to struggle against poverty and political unrest, the government has remained democratic. Pakistan was also formed in 1947, amid violence and bloodshed. In a 1971 civil war, East Pakistan won its independence, taking the name of Bangladesh.

3. After World War II the United States occupied Japan and worked to rebuild it as a democratic nation. Japan's economy became one of the world's strongest. Other Pacific Rim countries achieved economic growth by encouraging trade and private enterprise.

4. Most of Southeast Asia became independent during or just after World War II. The Philippines gained independence peacefully in 1946, but internal conflicts threatened its democracy. North and South Vietnam clashed in the Vietnam War, which began in 1957. In 1975, Communist forces took over South Vietnam. Communist rebels also came to power in Cambodia and Laos in 1975. After a long civil war, a UN plan brought peace to Cambodia in 1991.

| 1947 India and Pakistan gain independence | 1949 Communists take power in China | 1953 Korean War ends | 1966 Cultural Revolution begins in China | 1975 Vietnam united under Communist rule | 1979 China and U.S. establish diplomatic relations | 1986 Aquino comes to power in Philippines | 1989 Pro-democracy demonstration in China | 1991 Cambodian peace pact |

1945   1960   1975   1990

755

See p. T733C for answers to Chapter Review.

Vocabulary Review

1. Match each of the following terms with its correct definition: *civil disobedience, commune, gross national product, nuclear proliferation.*
    a. agricultural unit in China made up of large, state-owned farms
    b. nonviolent resistance to laws and acts that are thought unjust
    c. international spread of nuclear arms
    d. total annual value of a nation's goods and services
2. Identify the terms in each pair:
    a. Great Leap Forward; Cultural Revolution
    b. Chinese Revolution; Korean War
    c. Vietcong; Vietnam War

People to Identify

Choose the name that best completes each sentence.
1. [Indira Gandhi/Mohammed Ali Jinnah] became India's prime minister in 1966.
2. [Ho Chi Minh/Ngo Dinh Diem] led the movement for Vietnam's independence.
3. The Indian leader who gave up Western ways was [Mohandas K. Gandhi/Jawaharlal Nehru].
4. In 1949 [Deng Xiaoping/Chiang Kaishek] and his followers fled to Taiwan.

Places to Know

Match each of the following places with the correct description: *Amur River, Bangladesh, Dien Bien Phu, Gulf of Tonkin, Manila, North Korea, Saigon, South Korea.*

756

1. body of water near territory claimed by the Soviet Union and China
2. body of water in which North Vietnamese patrol boats reportedly attacked American destroyers in 1964
3. name meaning "the Bengal nation," taken by East Pakistan in 1971
4. part of Korea that became Communist
5. capital city of the Philippines
6. part of Korea that adopted a non-Communist government
7. site of Vietminh victory over the French in 1954
8. capital city of South Vietnam, which fell to the North Vietnamese in 1975

Recalling the Facts

1. Why did the Chinese Communists gain popular support during World War II?
2. What was Mao Zedong's initial plan for economic development in China?
3. What caused the Sino-Soviet split?
4. Why did China seek better relations with the United States in the 1970's?
5. What events led to the partitioning of the Indian subcontinent? Why was Kashmir split up?
6. Why did many Afghans oppose the government that took over Afghanistan in 1978?
7. What factors encouraged Japan's postwar economic growth? What other Pacific nations experienced economic growth?
8. What problems did Corazon Aquino have to deal with in the Philippines?
9. How was Cambodia drawn into the Vietnam War?
10. How did Vietnam's invasion of Cambodia affect Thailand?

Critical Thinking Skills

1. Analyzing. What factors make it possible for India to be called "a land of contradictions"? *(Comp.)*

2. Using graphs. Study the circle graphs below, which show trade statistics for three Pacific Rim nations. Which of the three countries has depended most heavily on its trade with Japan? The United States? For which country is trade with other Pacific Rim countries most important? *(Comp.)*

China

15.7 11.6 48.2 24.5

□ Percent of trade with Pacific Rim nations (excluding Japan and the United States)

South Korea

27 18.8 22.2 32

□ Percent of trade with Japan

Taiwan

27.4 16.2 18.4 38

□ Percent of trade with the United States

□ Percent of trade outside of the Pacific Rim

Source: *Far East Economic Review*, 1985

✔ **3. Making a comparison.** Compare Germany's treatment by the Allies following World War I (pages 636–638) with Japan's treatment by the Allies following World War II. How were they different? Why was Japan's occupation successful? *(Syn.)*

4. Preparing a report. Research and write a report about one of the following topics: agriculture in China since 1949, Gandhi's teaching of civil disobedience, Southeast Asian refugees in the United States. *(App.)*

Thinking About Geography

Studying a map. Use the map of Southeast Asia on page 750 to answer the following questions. Which countries of Southeast Asia

✔ A checkmark identifies questions and exercises calling for the three higher-order levels of thinking at the top of the Bloom taxonomy: Analysis, Synthesis, and Evaluation.

Enrichment: Primary Sources

Liang Heng was a member of the Red Guard during the Cultural Revolution. The passage below was adapted from Liang's 1986 account of how China emerged from that time of turmoil.

❝ I had once been too young and too fanatical to understand what religious persecution was, and the vast suffering it had caused. Maoism had been China's all-encompassing religion, and it left no room for any other belief system.

Ironically, many of the young people who were once Mao's greatest worshipers were now most curious about religion. Mao had been like a god to our generation, and when we lost our faith in him, we began to look for something else to believe in. Some turned to their families, others to materialistic pleasures—but many others were attracted to organized religion, both Western and Chinese. I shared their curiosity about what we had once been cut off from, and now felt even more drawn to understand the complex world of China's religious life. ❞

1. According to Liang, how had Maoism affected religious life in China?
2. What caused many people of Liang's generation to seek new beliefs? Where did they search?
3. **Critical thinking.** How might Liang's experience have affected his life and his outlook on political movements? Explain your answer. *(Anal.)*

T757A

Challenges for the Middle East   1945–Present
(pp. 758–775)

Chapter Preview

Section 1 discusses the creation of the state of Israel and the resulting conflict between Arab states and Israel. Section 2 examines the changes that have taken place in the Middle East since World War II as the countries of the region gained independence and as some of these countries acquired both wealth and political influence through the control of oil resources.

Bibliography

See the *Teacher's Management and Planning Guide* for additional listings. Starred titles are for both students and teachers.

Antonius, George. *The Arab Awakening.* International Book Center. Story of Arab nationalism.

Elon, Amos. *The Israelis.* Holt, Rinehart, and Winston. History of the Zionist movement and state of Israel.

Miller, Judith, and Laurie Mylroie. *Saddam Hussein and the Crisis in the Gulf.* Times Books. An account of the rise of the Iraqi dictator and his attack on Kuwait.

*Sadat, Jehan. *A Woman of Egypt.* Simon and Schuster. Autobiography of Anwar Sadat's widow, with insights on Egyptian culture.

Shipler, David. *Arab and Jew: Wounded Spirits in a Promised Land.* Penguin. Social and cultural aspects of the Arab-Israeli conflict.

Section Lesson Plans

SECTION 1   (pp. 759–764)
A Region of Conflict

Objectives

After completing this section, students will be able to:
1. Describe how Israel was established.
2. Name the wars fought between the Arab states and Israel.
3. Discuss the major issue that divides Israelis and Palestinians.

Introducing the Lesson

Remind students that present-day Israel was created by the partition of Palestine in 1948. Conflict between Israel and the Arab states over this partition has resulted in bitterness and violence that continues to threaten peace in the Middle East.

Then ask: *(a) Why do you think the Jewish people wanted a state in Palestine?* (The Jewish people raised the issue of establishing a state in Palestine in the late 1800's when anti-Semitism increased in Europe. When Hitler took over Germany and launched his program of persecution of European Jews, many Jews believed that a separate homeland was their only hope for security.)

(b) What might explain the conflict resulting from the partition of Palestine? (The land from which Israel was created had been inhabited for centuries by Arabs, who felt that their claim on the territory was stronger than the Jewish claim.)

(c) How is it possible to meet what many believe to be the legitimate claims of both the Israelis and the Arabs? (Answers will vary.)

Developing the Lesson:
Understanding Cause and Effect

Have students identify the causes of each of the following:
(a) British abandonment of plans to create a Jewish state out of its mandate in Palestine. (The British were discouraged by Arab reaction to the plan.)
(b) Britain's decision to turn the issue over to the United Nations. (Britain was unable to find a solution acceptable to both sides.)

(c) The failure to reach a peace settlement after the 1948 war. (Arab states refused to meet with Israel to write up a peace settlement, and they vowed to drive the Israelis into the sea and restore Palestine to the Arabs.)

(d) Sadat's decision to attack Israel in the October War. (He believed that a successful attack would restore Arab honor, show that Israel could be beaten, and give Egypt a stronger bargaining position.) *(Comprehension)*

Developing the Lesson: Debating an Issue

Have students work in groups to discuss the problem of terrorism in the Middle East and then to debate the following: *The best way to combat terrorism is to refuse to negotiate with those who use it as a political tool. (Synthesis)*

Closing the Lesson: Solving Problems

Have students identify the factors that make settlement of the Arab-Israeli conflict difficult and suggest realistic solutions to the conflict. When making proposals, students should speculate about Arab and Israeli responses to each solution, and then describe the kinds of compromises required from both sides. *(Synthesis)*

See *Section Review* questions, p. 764.

SECTION 2   (pp. 765–773)
The Nations of the Middle East

Objectives

After completing this section, students will be able to:
1. Explain how nationalism grew in the Middle East after World War II.
2. Discuss developments that took place in the non-Arab states.
3. Describe the troubles that shook the Arab states.

Introducing the Lesson

Remind students that the Middle East is a geographic region that has been the focus of international attention for decades. The source of much conflict, the Middle East is also the source of most of the world's oil supply.

Then ask: *(a) What factors besides geography make the Middle East a region?* (Cultural factors such as language, religion, and customs.)

(b) How might these factors also be a source of conflict? (The Middle East is home to three major world religions—Judaism, Christianity, and Islam. Conflict in this region has often been caused by cultural and religious differences between supporters of these religions.)

(c) How might the presence of enormous oil reserves have heightened the tension in the Middle East? (Because oil is a vital resource for industrialized nations, political alliances and disagreements have influenced the availability and cost of oil and have led to the involvement of outside powers in regional conflicts.)

Developing the Lesson: Forming a Hypothesis

Have students develop a hypothesis explaining how Middle East affairs might be different today if the Pan-Arabism movement had been successful. When developing their hypotheses, students should consider the possible effects of Pan-Arabism on the Israeli-Arab conflict, OPEC, the civil war in Lebanon, and the Persian Gulf War. *(Synthesis)*

Answers to *Map Skill Practice*, p. 760.

1. Dead Sea, Jordan River.
2. Egypt (because the Sinai Peninsula is Egypt's territory), Lebanon, Syria, Jordan.
3. Gulf of Suez, Red Sea, Gulf of Aqaba, Mediterranean Sea.
4. Lebanon is on the northern border of Israel; Jordan is to the east.
5. Sinai Peninsula, Golan Heights, West Bank, Gaza Strip.
6. Sinai Peninsula.
7. Students might suggest that Egypt might close the canal to Israel, thus damaging Israeli trade.

Developing the Lesson: Drawing Conclusions

Have students answer the following questions:

(a) What role does Islam play in Middle Eastern affairs? (In Iran, Saudi Arabia, and Libya, Islamic law is strictly enforced.)

(b) What might be the long-range consequences of Iraq's attempted take-over of Kuwait and the resulting war? (Student answers might mention political and environmental developments and changes in relations among Middle Eastern states and their relations with the U.S.)

T757C

Closing the Lesson: Evaluating Information

Have students rank the following in order of their impact on Middle Eastern affairs: nationalism, oil, and the conflict between Arabs and Jews. After students have explained their ranking, have students predict how important each issue will be in the future. *(Synthesis)*

See *Section Review* questions, p. 773.

Chapter 37 Review Answers (pp. 774–775)

Vocabulary Review

1. (a) Iran-Iraq War (b) OPEC (c) Camp David Accords (d) Palestine Liberation Organization
2. (a) Secular—non-religious; fundamentalism—movement for strict observance of religious law. (b) Six-Day War—conflict of 1967 between Egypt and Israel in which Israel took over the Sinai Peninsula, the Golan Heights, and the West Bank; October War—conflict of 1973 in which Egypt and Syria invaded the Israeli-occupied Sinai Peninsula and Golan Heights. By the end of the war, the Israelis had crossed into Egypt and held more Syrian territory than before the war.

People to Identify

1. Saddam Hussein 2. Reza Shah 3. Ayatollah Ruhollah Khomeini 4. Faisal 5. Yasir Arafat 6. Jimmy Carter 7. Muammar al Qaddafi 8. Hosni Mubarak

Places to Know

1. G 2. D 3. J 4. F 5. B 6. I 7. H 8. C 9. A 10. E

Recalling the Facts

1. They sought to escape persecution by the Nazis in Germany and anti-Semitism that was common in other parts of Europe.

2. The Jews argued that they had ancient claims to Palestine; that they would be persecuted until they had a state of their own; and that they had developed Palestine. The Arabs argued that Palestine had been an Arab land and its population was mainly Arab, and that it would be unfair to settle the Jews at the expense of the Arabs of Palestine. The United Nations recommended dividing Palestine into two states—one Arab, the other Jewish. In 1948 the Jewish state of Israel was created. The Arabs in Palestine refused to set up an Arab state and to recognize Israel as a legitimate state.

3. At the end of the 1948 war, Israel occupied about half of the territory that the UN had assigned to the Palestinian Arabs. Transjordan took nearly all the rest. Egypt occupied the Gaza Strip. Hundreds of thousands of Palestinian Arabs fled to the Arab states to escape the rule of an Israeli government.

4. The PLO acted as a state within a state, and their raids on Israel brought counterattacks that threatened Jordan's security. When the PLO refused to leave Jordan, Jordan's army fired on them wherever they were found, and civil war broke out. Hussein's army won, but thousands of civilians died in this period known as "Black September."

5. Its goal was to unite the Arab world under a single government. Religious differences, particularly between Shiite and Sunni Muslims, economic differences, and political differences blocked Arab unity. Political differences arose because governments were secular, Islamic, conservative monarchies, or socialist republics. Some allied with the United States, others with the So-

6. Conservative Muslims condemned the shah's modernization program and his adoption of Western ways. They wanted a return to traditional Islamic customs. Liberals critized the shah's policy of spending billions on defense while many Iranians were still poor. They also attacked the shah for jailing, torturing, and killing his political opponents.

7. Saudi Arabia used its oil wealth to build hospitals, schools, and irrigation works. The government provided free education for all children and invested heavily in projects to improve agricultural production and develop modern industry.

8. Nasser wanted to end foreign influence in Egypt and strengthen the country's economy. To rid the country of foreign influences, Nasser seized control of the Suez Canal in 1956. To strengthen the economy, Nasser limited the amount of land one person could own, lowered rents, and set up farm cooperatives. He also began construction of the Aswan High Dam to provide hydroelectric power and irrigate new farmlands. He also cut Egypt's dependence on the export of cotton, put large businesses under government control, and encouraged the development of industry.

9. Israel hoped to drive out PLO guerrillas who had taken over southern Lebanon and were using it as a base to wage warfare on northern Israel.

10. President George Bush ordered U.S. forces sent to Saudi Arabia after Iraq's Saddam Hussein invaded and occupied Kuwait. These forces took part in the military action that in February 1991 drove the Iraqi forces out of Kuwait.

11. The Madrid Conference was a meeting organized by the U.S. to create an opportunity for representatives of Israel, Egypt, Syria, Lebanon, Jordan, and the Palestinians to meet face to face and take up the persistent problems of the Middle East. It was important because it was hoped it would be a first step in finding ways to resolve these problems.

Critical Thinking Skills

1. Fugitive—one who flees; refuge—shelter or protection; centrifugal—moving in a direction away from a center or axis; subterfuge—a strategy or trick used to conceal, evade, or escape.

2. Students may suggest that a single Arab government might have been more successful at controlling the oil industry. Also, wealth and economic development might have been more evenly distributed throughout Arab lands.

3. One trend has been that since 1948, most immigrants into Israel have been Sephardic Jews. By the 1980's, Sephardic Jews made up more than half of Israel's Jewish population. Sephardic Jews tend to be more conservative than Ashkenazi Jews. The growth of Israel's Sephardic population has been linked to a political shift to the right and a decrease in power for the Labor Party. Another trend is the immigration of Jews from the Soviet Union, with a likely impact in the near future on Israel's politics and need for housing, jobs, and resources.

4. (d) 1948 (e) 1956 (b) 1963 (c) 1967 (f) 1973 (g) 1978 (a) 1981

Thinking About Geography

The Middle East continues to have great strategic importance, both as a crossroads of three continents and as a region of vast oil resources.

Enrichment: Primary Sources

1. Balfour was speaking for the government of Great Britain.

2. The rights of the Palestinian Arabs were to be respected.

3. Their claim for support rested on the statement that Britain viewed with favor the establishment in Palestine of a national home for the Jewish people and would use its "best endeavors to make the achievement of this object easier."

Challenges for the Middle East 1945–Present

See chapter timeline, p. 773.

Before You Read This Chapter

Over the centuries, the Middle East has seen the rise and fall of many empires. At various times, the region has been united under the Assyrians, the Persians, the Romans, the Byzantines, the Arabs, and the Ottomans. Yet today the Middle East may well be the most fragmented, dis-united region in the world. As you read this chapter, try to identify the causes of conflict. What issues have led to wars? To unrest within countries? Are there any forces that might encourage peace?

The Geographic Setting

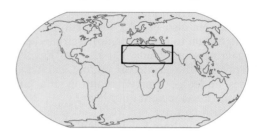

The Chapter Outline

1. A Region of Conflict
2. The Nations of the Middle East

The glass walls of the Kuwaiti stock exchange building—in a photo taken before the Iraqi invasion in 1990—reflected the more traditional form of the State Mosque.

See lesson plans, pp. T757A–T757C.

1 A Region of Conflict

Objectives

Focus Questions

★ ■ How was Israel established?
   (pages 759–760)
● ■ What wars were fought between the
   Arab states and Israel? *(pages 760–763)*
▲ ■ What major issue divides Israelis and Pal-
   estinians? *(pages 763–764)*

Terms to Know

Six-Day War   Palestine Liberation
October War   Organization
Camp David
   Accords

★ Note strategies for first objective on this page and p. 760.

Today, as in the past, the Middle East is home to a wide range of peoples. Followers of Judaism, Christianity, and Islam—the three great religions that began in this region—all live there. Muslims form the majority in the Arab nations of the Arabian Peninsula and North Africa and in non-Arab nations such as Turkey and Iran. Jews are the majority in Israel. Christian minorities exist in several Middle Eastern countries. The many differences among the peoples of the Middle East have often led to conflict.

The dispute between Arabs and Israelis in the Middle East has been one of the most bitter conflicts of modern times. The roots of this conflict reach back many hundreds of years. The Arab world suffered domination by foreign powers well into the 1900's, and Arabs had a strong desire to set up their own independent nations without outside interference. The Jews, on the other hand, believed that they had a historical right to reclaim their ancient homeland in the Middle East (page 44).

The Establishment of Israel

Early emigration.   The Zionist movement of the late 1890's (page 545) proposed the setting up of a state where Jews could escape the anti-Semitism that was common in Europe. Jews did not begin to move to Palestine in large numbers, however, until Hitler came to power in Germany in the 1930's. As the Nazis began to persecute the Jewish people, more and more Jews took refuge in Palestine. The Arabs saw the European Jews as foreign intruders. Violence between the two groups was an ongoing problem.

Discouraged by the Arab reaction, Britain gave up its plans to create a Jewish state out of its mandate in Palestine (page 680). In the British view, having one friendly, westernized state in the Middle East could not make up for the loss of good will among the Arab countries. The Arab population totaled 40 million, and Middle Eastern oil was vital to Britain's economy.

World War II, however, made the Zionists more determined than ever to build a Jewish state in Palestine. After the nightmare of the Holocaust (page 695), Jewish survivors in refugee camps all over Europe wanted to start new lives in Palestine.

The partition of Palestine.   By 1946, Jews made up more than one third of the population of Palestine. The conflict between Arabs and Jews had turned into open civil war. Unable to find a solution that both sides would accept, in 1947 Britain turned the problem over to the United Nations.

At the UN, the Jews made several arguments in support of their case: (1) Palestine had belonged to the Jews until the Romans drove them out during the first and second centuries A.D. The Jews had never given up hope of returning to Palestine. (2) The Jewish people had been persecuted for centuries, and they would not be safe until they had a

Sec. Rev. ques. 2

759

★ RETEACHING. Have students summarize arguments made in 1947 for and against the creation of a Jewish state in Israel. (For: Palestine once belonged to the Jews; Jewish people would not be safe without a state of their own; the Arabs had never developed Palestine. Against: Arabs had been in Palestine for centuries and it was unfair to take their land.) (Comprehension) Observing for Detail

★ REINFORCEMENT. Have students write two editorials that might have appeared in newspapers in 1947, one supporting the creation of a Jewish state in Palestine and one opposing the idea. Have students read their editorials in class. (Comprehension) Understanding Point of View

Check for Understanding. Ask: What world event led to the increased migration of Jews to Palestine? (Hitler's rise to power in Germany and his persecution of Jews.)

◆ Map Skill Practice

See p. T757B for answers to *Map Skill Practice*.

Arab-Israeli Wars

1. Using the map at right, name the natural features that mark Israel's present-day eastern border.
2. List the countries that share a border with Israel.
3. What bodies of water surround the Sinai Peninsula?
4. Where are Lebanon and Jordan in relation to Israel?
5. What areas did Israel occupy after the Six-Day War in 1967?
6. From what area had Israel withdrawn by 1982?
7. **Making inferences.** Why was Egypt's control of the Suez Canal seen as a threat to Israel?

KEY
- Israel before 1967 war
- Territories occupied by Israel after 1967 war
- Area from which Israel withdrew, 1975–1982

SCALE
0 — 100 mi
0 — 100 km

state of their own. (3) The Arabs had never developed Palestine. Jewish pioneers in Palestine, in contrast, had built cities, industries, and schools, and introduced modern medicine to help both Arabs and Jews.

The Arabs, for their part, argued that Palestine had been an Arab land for hundreds of years and its population was mainly Arab. While they sympathized with Jewish suffering, it was not they who had persecuted the Jews. It would be wholly unfair, they said, to solve the problems of the Jews at the expense of the Arab people who lived in Palestine.

After all arguments were heard, a UN committee decided that both sides had legitimate claims. Partition of Palestine, the UN felt, was the best answer to the problem. The

760

General Assembly recommended dividing Palestine into two states—one Arab, the other Jewish. In 1948 the Jewish state of Israel was created. The Arabs in Palestine refused, however, to accept the UN plan. They did not set up an Arab state, nor did they recognize Israel as a legitimate state.

★ See below, left.

Arab-Israeli Wars

● Note strategies for second objective on this page and p. 762.

The 1948 war. On May 14, 1948, when Israel became a state, British troops left Palestine. The next day, the armies of five Arab nations—Egypt, Iraq, Lebanon, Syria, and Jordan (called Transjordan at the time)—attacked Israel. UN diplomats ar-

Sec. Rev. ques. 3

★ ENRICHMENT. Have students research patterns of Jewish migration and settlement from the time of Roman occupation to modern times and draw a map of places where Jewish communities developed. *(Application) Locating Information*

● RETEACHING. Have students make a timeline of events in the Arab-Israeli conflict. (Timelines should include events for the following dates: 1948, 1956, 1967, 1973, 1977, 1978, 1981, 1982.) *(Comprehension) Sequencing Events*

● REINFORCEMENT. Have students work in groups to identify the causes of the following: **the 1948 war** (Arab states vowed to restore Palestine to Arabs); **the Suez Canal crisis** (Nasser seized the Canal); **Six-Day War** (Nasser blocked the Gulf of Aqaba); **the October War** (Egypt attacked Israeli forces). *(Comprehension) Understanding Causes*

Social History After the partition of Palestine, over 725,000 Arabs left Palestine and settled in surrounding countries.

ranged a truce, but the Arab states refused to meet with Israel to draw up a peace settlement. They vowed to drive the Israelis into the sea and restore Palestine to the Arabs.

The 1948 war had lasting effects on the region. At the end of the war, Israel held all of its own land, plus about half the territory that the United Nations had assigned to the Palestinian Arabs. Transjordan took nearly all the rest. Egypt occupied the Gaza Strip along the coast. Hundreds of thousands of Palestinian Arabs fled to the Arab states to escape the rule of an Israeli government.

The Suez Canal crisis. The 1948 war was only the start of fighting between Israel and its Arab neighbors. In 1956 the Egyptian leader, Colonel Gamal Abdel Nasser, seized control of the Suez Canal, which had been run by a British and French investment company. Hoping to regain the canal and knock Nasser from power, Britain and France joined with Israel to retake the waterway. The United States criticized this action, and the Soviet Union threatened to step in and help Egypt. Britain, France, and Israel agreed to call off the attack. United Nations peacekeeping troops were sent to the Egyptian-Israeli border to prevent further fighting.

Sec. Rev. ques. 3, cont.

During the years after the Suez Canal crisis, an uneasy peace existed between Israel and Egypt. Yet Arabs continued to make raids on Israel from Syria and Jordan, and the Israelis fought back. During the mid-1960's, these border clashes happened more and more often. In 1967 Nasser ordered UN forces to leave Egypt. Nasser made a military pact with Jordan, supported Syrian attacks on Israel, and built up Egyptian forces along the Israeli border.

The Six-Day War. In May 1967, Nasser ordered Egyptian forces to blockade the Gulf of Aqaba, a route used by Israeli ships to reach the Red Sea. In June 1967 the Israelis, expecting a full-scale Egyptian invasion, struck first. In only a few hours they destroyed the air forces of Egypt and Syria, catching hundreds of planes on the ground. Within six days Israeli forces had shattered the Egyptian army in the Sinai Peninsula. Israeli soldiers took over the Sinai, the Golan Heights of Syria, and the West Bank of the Jordan River, including the ancient city of Jerusalem.

After the Six-Day War, as the conflict came to be known, Arabs and Israelis still could not come to terms. Israel insisted that

The Israeli government has created permanent settlements, such as this one, on the occupied West Bank of the Jordan River.

761

Background After the Suez Canal crisis, a UN Emergency Force was organized to patrol the frontiers of Israel and Egypt.

Check for Understanding. Ask: Between what nations was the Six-Day War fought? (Egypt, Syria, and Israel.)

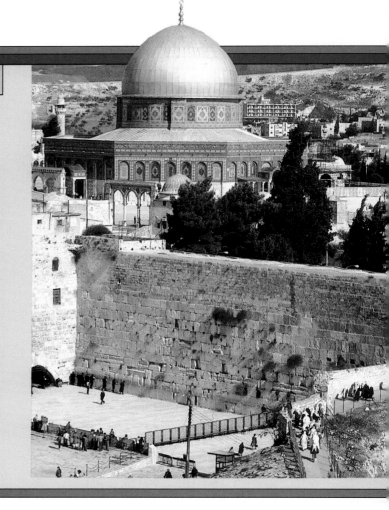

Historic Places

Jerusalem

Ⓕ See below.

The city of Jerusalem, which is nearly 4,000 years old, has played an important role in the history of three major world religions. Today it is a holy city to the believers of Judaism, Christianity, and Islam.

Around 1000 B.C., Jerusalem was captured by a Jewish army under King David, who made the city his capital. His son Solomon built a great temple there, and the place where that temple stood is sacred to Jews throughout the world. The temple was destroyed and rebuilt several times during Jerusalem's war-torn history. All that remains of the last temple, built in Roman times and destroyed by a Roman army in A.D. 70, is a single foundation wall, known as the Western Wall or Wailing Wall.

To Christians, Jerusalem is holy because of its links with Jesus' life. The

---

no territory would be given back unless Arabs recognized the Jewish state's right to exist. Arab leaders answered that the Jews, by taking land from the Palestinians, had committed a crime against the Arab people. They demanded that Palestinian independence be part of any peace agreement.

The October War. The Six-Day War humiliated the Soviet Union as well as the Arab states, since the Arabs had used Soviet arms against the Israelis. Hoping to improve its tarnished image in the Arab world, the Soviet Union gave more military aid to Egypt and Syria. Thousands of Soviet advisers trained the soldiers of the two Arab nations. Within a few years, the Egyptian army had better leaders, training, and equipment than before the Six-Day War. Anwar el-Sadat, who became president after Nasser, decided to attack Israeli forces in the Sinai Peninsula. He

reasoned that a successful attack would restore Arab honor, show that Israel could be beaten, and give Egypt a stronger bargaining position with Israel.

In October 1973, Egyptian troops and tanks crossed the Suez Canal and overwhelmed the Israeli outposts. At the same time Syrian soldiers moved into the Israeli-occupied Golan Heights.

Sec. Rev. ques. 3, cont.

Syria and Egypt made impressive gains in the opening days of the October War, as it was called. Their missiles wiped out many Israeli tanks and reduced the effectiveness of the Israeli air force. Israel's disciplined, American-equipped military forces, however, soon gained the upper hand. By the end of the October War, the Israelis had crossed to the west bank of the Suez Canal and into Egypt. They also held more Syrian territory than before the war.

● See below.

Background The October War was also called the *Yom Kippur War,* after the Jewish holy day on which it began.

Ⓕ **FEATURE ACTIVITY.** Have students write a brief essay describing how members of the Jewish, Islamic, and Christian religions might explain the importance of Jerusalem to their religious and cultural traditions. *(Application) Understanding Point of View*

● **ENRICHMENT.** Have students find information on current relations between Israel and Egypt. Students might research the effects of the Camp David Accords on Egyptian-Israeli relations, cite recent negotiations between the two nations, or find evidence of cultural and social exchanges. *(Application) Locating Information* city's greatest Christian monument is the Church of the Holy Sepulchre. It stands on the place where, according to tradition, Jesus was crucified and buried.

To Muslims, the holiest spot in the city is the rock where the altar of Solomon's temple stood. Islam teaches that Mohammed rose to heaven from this spot and spoke with the great religious figures before him, including Adam, Moses, and Jesus. Over this rock, about A.D. 690, a Muslim caliph built the Dome of the Rock. Its huge roof, covered with dazzling tiles of blue, white, and gold, towers above the Wailing Wall (see picture).

These sacred sites have drawn thousands of people to Jerusalem. Many were peaceful pilgrims, but others have come as crusading warriors. For nearly 20 centuries, Jews, Christians, and Muslims have battled to control the city, even though the name *Jerusalem* means "city of peace."

The Camp David Accords. In 1977 Anwar el-Sadat paid a historic visit to Israel, announcing that Egypt was ready to make peace. At the urging of President Jimmy Carter, Sadat agreed to come to the United States to meet with Israeli prime minister Menachem Begin (BAY-gin). In 1978 at Camp David, Maryland, Sadat and Begin reached an agreement that became known as the Camp David Accords. Israel agreed to give up the Sinai Peninsula in return for peace and diplomatic recognition. The Accords also called for a five-year period of self-government for the West Bank and Gaza Strip, to be followed by a final decision about the status of those areas.

Sec. Rev. ques. 4

Other Arab leaders blasted Sadat, saying that he had betrayed their cause by making a separate peace with Israel. In 1981 Sadat was assassinated by Muslim radicals who opposed peace with Israel and cooperation with the West. Sadat's successor, Hosni Mubarak (moo-BAHR-ahk), promised to honor the Camp David Accords. Israel withdrew from the Sinai Peninsula in 1982, but self-government for the occupied territories has not yet come to pass.

The Palestinian Question

▲ Note strategies for third objective on this page and p. 764.

The question of how to deal with Palestinians made homeless by the creation of Israel remained unsolved throughout the years of the Arab-Israeli wars. While the Camp David Accords marked a step toward peace in the region, there was little movement toward a settlement for the Palestinians.

The PLO. As a result of the Arab-Israeli wars, Palestinians became scattered throughout the Middle East. Some lived in Israel or in lands occupied by Israel; others lived in refugee camps in Arab countries. The Palestine Liberation Organization (PLO) was formed in 1964 to represent all Palestinians. The PLO charter called for the destruction of Israel and for the creation of a Palestinian state. PLO efforts to reach these goals led to conflict with Arab states as well as Israel.

"Black September." Jordan was the PLO's main base for attacks against Israel during the 1960's. PLO guerrilla groups in Jordan refused to recognize the authority of Jordan's King Hussein (hoo-SAYN). They acted as a state within a state, and their raids on Israel brought counterattacks from Israel that threatened Jordan's security.

Sec. Rev. ques. 5

In September 1970 Hussein ordered PLO guerrillas to leave his country. When they refused, the army was told to fire on them wherever they were found. Civil war then broke out in Jordan. Ten days later, Hussein's army triumphed over the PLO, but not before thousands of innocent civilians had died. Palestinians, who made up more than half of Jordan's population at the time, referred to the period as "Black September."

PLO terrorism. After being thrown out of Jordan, the PLO moved to southern **763**

▲ RETEACHING. Have students identify the following: **PLO** (Palestine Liberation Organization, formed to destroy Israel and create a Palestinian state.) **Black September** (September 1970, when civil war broke out in Jordan during Hussein's attempt to eliminate the PLO.) **Yasir Arafat** (PLO leader.) *(Comprehension)* *Observing for Detail*

▲ REINFORCEMENT. Have students work in groups to present a panel discussion on the following: *How might conflict between the PLO and Israel be resolved?* Students should identify the issues involved in the Palestinian-Israeli conflict and suggest solutions that would be fair to both sides. *(Synthesis)* *Solving Problems*

West Bank women joyfully welcomed home delegates who represented the Palestinians at meetings on Middle East issues held at Madrid, Spain, in 1991.

A meeting at Madrid. Taking advantage of the changed perspectives that followed the Gulf War, U.S. Secretary of State James Baker persuaded Israel and its Arab neighbors—Syria, Egypt, Lebanon, Jordan, and the Palestinians—to agree to meet at the royal palace in Madrid, Spain, in late 1991. The purpose was to create an occasion for representatives of the various countries to talk face to face about the issues that had for so long tormented the Middle East.

No great breakthrough came about at Madrid, but none had been expected. Instead, the plan was for the meeting to open the way for a series of Middle East peace talks. Along the way, it was hoped, rigid positions might ease and differences be resolved. Issues on the agenda for the meetings included the future status of occupied lands and various boundary questions, allocation of water resources, establishing a system for settling disputes, and planning for peaceful economic development. No easy solutions appeared but the fact that such meetings were held raised hopes that a Middle East peace process had started.

See Sec. 1 *Closing the Lesson*, p. T757B.

Lebanon. Headed by Yasir Arafat (AHR-uh-faht), the PLO launched raids on Israel to weaken Israeli morale. The PLO also used terrorism to draw world attention to the Palestinian cause. For example, PLO guerrillas seized and killed Israeli athletes at the 1972 Olympic Games. In response, Israel attacked PLO bases in Lebanon and elsewhere. Israel even invaded Lebanon in 1982, hoping to destroy PLO forces (page 771).

▲ See below, right.

Policy changes. A breakthrough in the Palestinian situation seemed possible in 1988 when Arafat declared that the PLO renounced terrorism and accepted Israel's right to exist. He also called for the creation of a Palestinian state in the occupied territories. United States officials opened a "dialogue" with the PLO, but these talks ended in 1990 when PLO leadership failed to condemn a PLO terrorist raid on Israeli beaches. PLO support for Iraq in the Gulf crisis (page 772) was seen by many as harming the Palestinian

764 cause in the eyes of the world.

Social History Note that the PLO had its roots in the *fedayeen*, Arab guerrilla fighters dedicated to Israel's destruction. The fedayeen, meaning "men of sacrifice," were Palestinian refugees committed to regaining their former territory from Israel.

6. Factors to consider: religious and political conflicts; unresolved territorial disputes; intervention by outside countries; problems of refugee populations; militarization.

▲ **ENRICHMENT. Have students find information on relationships between the PLO and Arab nations. Students might research the locations of PLO bases or the amount and kind of support given to the PLO by Arab nations. Have students present their information in class.** (Application) *Locating Information*

2 The Nations of the Middle East

Objectives

Focus Questions

★ ■ How did nationalism grow in the Middle East after World War II? *(pages 765–766)*

● ■ What developments took place in the non-Arab states? *(pages 766–769)*

▲ ■ What troubles shook the Arab states? *(pages 769–772)*

Terms to Know

Pan-Arabism   fundamentalism
secular   Iran-Iraq War
OPEC

★ Note strategies for first objective on this page and p. 766.

To the outside world, the Arab-Israeli conflict often seems the dominant issue in the Middle East. Yet that conflict rarely touches the lives of many people in the region. Within the Middle East, the issues of nationalism and economic development have been especially important. Middle Eastern leaders first pushed for independence for their nations. After independence, some nations used their natural resources (such as oil) to help themselves modernize. Other nations, which lacked such resources, found it hard to build stable economies.

The Rise of Nationalism

The road to independence. As you read in Chapter 33, nationalism gained strength among the Arab peoples of the Middle East during World War I. Arabs fought on the Allied side against the Ottomans, hoping that victory would bring them independence. At the war's end, however, the League of Nations divided Arab lands into mandates under European control.

In the 1920's, nationalist movements took hold in much of the Middle East. Several Arab nations gained independence during the 1930's. The remaining mandates became independent after World War II.

Arab unity. For many Arabs, freedom from colonial rule was only a first step in a larger plan. The next step was to erase the national boundaries drawn by foreigners. In 1945 the Arab League was formed to help organize Arab states. Some Arabs wanted to go even further. These Arabs believed in **Pan-Arabism**—a movement to reunite the Arab world under a single government.

The most popular Pan-Arabist leader was Egyptian president Gamal Abdel Nasser (page 761). During the late 1950's and 1960's, Nasser won many followers in the Arab world. In 1958 Syria and Egypt joined to form the United Arab Republic, which Nasser hoped would one day include all Arab lands.

National boundaries were hard to break down, however. Middle Eastern Arabs shared a common culture and language, but they were not all alike. One important difference was religion. The great majority of Arabs were Muslims, but some of these belonged to the Sunni branch of Islam and others belonged to the Shiite branch (page 200). In many areas of the Middle East there was great hostility between the two groups.

Other divisions among the Arab states were based on wealth. The average person in oil-rich Saudi Arabia, for example, made more than ten times as much money each year as the average Egyptian. Such great inequalities caused resentment among people in the poorer Arab countries.

Political differences, too, stood in the way of Arab unity. Some Arab states had governments that were **secular**, or non-religious. Others were governed under Islamic law. Some were conservative monarchies, while **765**

★ RETEACHING. Have students review "The Rise of Nationalism" (pp. 765–766) and make a chart identifying and explaining sources of *Arab Unity* and *Arab Differences.* (Unity: desire to erase national boundaries drawn by foreign powers; common culture and language; OPEC. Differences: division between Sunni and Shiite Islam; economic inequalities; government.) *(Comprehension) Synthesizing Information*

★ REINFORCEMENT. Have students explain how OPEC nations used the oil industry as a political weapon. (After the 1973 October War, Arab members of OPEC raised the price of oil and decreased production; they cut off supplies to the United States and the Netherlands.) *(Comprehension) Observing for Detail*

Background The United Arab Republic was formed at Syria's request because many Syrians were impressed with Nasser's reforms in Egypt, favored Arab unity, and feared the growth of Communist influence.

others were socialist republics. Some relied on the Soviet Union for military and economic aid; some relied on the United States.

Nasser's plan for Arab unity ended in failure. No other states joined the United Arab Republic, and Syria pulled away in 1961. Libyan leader Muammar al Qaddafi (kuh-DAHF-ee) made several pleas for Arab unity in the 1970's and 1980's, calling for unions with four different countries in the Middle East. Although these attempts, like those of Nasser, failed, the dream of unification lingered in the Arab world.

★ See below.

Oil production. Foreign control of the oil industry was an important issue to the leaders of many Middle Eastern countries. Since the early 1900's, the Middle East had been a major producer of oil, a fuel with a growing market in the industrialized world. By 1945, oil was the region's most important export. For many years, however, the lion's share of the profits from the oil business went to foreign companies. Troubled with unstable governments and weak economies, most Middle Eastern countries were not strong enough to stop this foreign exploitation.

As nationalist movements gained strength, Middle Eastern leaders began to claim a greater share of oil profits for their nations. In 1960 a group of major oil-exporting nations formed OPEC (Organization of Petroleum Exporting Countries). By the early 1970's OPEC included the eight largest oil producers of the Middle East— Algeria, Iran, Iraq, Kuwait (koo-WAYT), Libya, Qatar (KAH-tahr), Saudi Arabia, and the United Arab Emirates. The other members were the South American countries of Ecuador and Venezuela, the African countries of Gabon and Nigeria, and the Asian country of Indonesia.

OPEC members acted together to set oil prices and deal with the industrial nations. Because OPEC controlled such a large part of world oil production, its profits and power soared.

After the 1973 October War the Arab members of OPEC decided to make oil a "weapon." To remind the world that they saw support for Israel as an anti-Arab act, they raised the price of oil and decreased production. They also cut off supplies to the United States and the Netherlands, which were strong allies of Israel. The oil embargo caused severe shortages in the West. In response, industrialized nations cut their use of oil and increased their own production of the fuel. As a result, world oil prices fell sharply during the mid-1980's. OPEC members began fighting among themselves for markets.

The Non-Arab States

● Note strategies for second objective on this page and p. 768.

Turkey. Turkey remained neutral during most of the Second World War, joining the Allies only in 1945. After the war, Turkey became more friendly with the United States. In 1947 President Harry Truman sent aid to Turkey to keep it from falling under Soviet control (page 713).

During the 1950's, new Turkish leaders encouraged foreign investment and reduced the government's control over the economy. The economy worsened, however, and the government lost support. In 1960 a military coup brought a new government to power.

During the 1960's and 1970's, the Turkish government faced inflation and unemployment, both of which were made worse by

Wealth from oil revenues brought tremendous changes in Middle Eastern societies. Although some nations rejected Western ideas, most adopted Western technology, such as television.

766

Middle East and North Africa

The histories and cultures of Middle Eastern and North African nations are closely linked. What nations surround the Persian Gulf? What nations border Israel?

Map Answers: (1) Iran, Iraq, Kuwait, Saudi Arabia, United Arab Emirates. (2) Egypt, Jordan, Syria, Lebanon.

the rise in oil prices during the 1970's. Hundreds of people were killed each year in ethnic and religious violence. Military leaders once again took power in 1980 and restored order. In 1983 the Turkish people elected a new government. This government forged strong ties with the West and established a market-based economy in Turkey.

Iran. The Iranian leader Reza Shah (page 679) refused to side with the Allies in World War II. In 1941 he was forced from his throne by British and Soviet troops. Rule of Iran then fell to his son, Mohammed Reza Pahlavi, who supported the Allies.

In the 1950's the shah was challenged by nationalists who wanted Iran to have more control over its oil resources. Led by Iran's prime minister, Mohammed Mossadegh, the nationalists overthrew the shah and took over foreign-owned oil facilities. The nation-

alists were soon thrown out themselves, however, and the shah returned to power with strong Western support.

The shah made the creation of a modern, industrial Iran his top priority. His policies, however, broke with many ancient traditions. He divided up some large estates and gave land to the peasants. His government encouraged greater use of modern farming methods. In 1963 women won both the right to vote and the right to serve as members of the Iranian parliament.

Conservative Muslims condemned the shah's moves to modernize the country and bring in Western ways. They demanded a return to traditional Islamic customs. Liberals charged that the shah was spending billions on arms while many Iranians were still poor. They also criticized the shah for jailing, torturing, and killing his political opponents.

Sec. Rev. ques. 2

767

Background Turkey has sought membership in the European Community but faces the objections that its government continues authoritarian measures, including repression of the Kurdish minority.

Social History The Shah of Iran created a secret police force, SAVAK, to control resistance to his programs.

Ayatollah Khomeini, leader of Iran's Shiite Muslims, led a fundamentalist revolution that reversed the shah's pro-Western policies. Khomeini died in 1989.

Growing political violence forced the shah to leave Iran in 1979. The new government, headed by the Shiite religious leader Ayatollah Ruhollah Khomeini (koh-MAY-nee), turned Iran away from the West and toward Islam. Like the shah, however, Khomeini would not put up with any opposition. He had thousands of Iranians put in prison or executed.

Sec. Rev. ques. 2

In October 1979 the shah traveled to the United States for medical treatment. The following month a mob took over the American embassy in Iran's capital city, Tehran. They demanded that the shah be returned to Iran for trial, but the American government refused. For more than a year, the Khomeini government refused to return more than 50 Americans being held hostage in the embassy. Iran and the United States became enemies and tensions remained long after the hostages had been released.

Following the Islamic revolution in Iran, fundamentalism—a movement for strict observance of religious law—swept through many Muslim countries in the Mid-

768

dle East. Islamic fundamentalists believed that Western influence was harmful to Islam and should be wiped out. Fundamentalist movements sprang up in many Middle Eastern countries in the 1980's, threatening governments as different from each other as radical Iraq and moderate Saudi Arabia. Fundamentalist groups also carried out acts of terrorism against Israel and the West.

The Iran-Iraq War. In 1980 Saddam Hussein (hoo-SAYN), the ruler of Iraq, ordered an invasion of Iran. Hussein hoped to win disputed border regions and islands in the Persian Gulf.

The Iraqis made early victories but failed to follow up on them. Iranian leaders used the invasion to rally the people behind the Khomeini government. The invading Iraqi troops were thrown back, and Iranian forces captured Iraqi territory. Fearful of the spread of Islamic fundamentalism, most of the Arab states gave Iraq money and arms. The Iran-Iraq War continued into the late 1980's. Iraq used poison gas against attacking Iranian troops. Iraq and Iran hurled bombs and missiles at each other's capitals. Both sides also attacked ships heading to and from the other's ports. The United States and other nations sent warships to the Persian Gulf to protect the vital flow of oil.

In 1988 Iran and Iraq, exhausted by the savage fighting, agreed to a cease-fire arranged by the United Nations. The costs of the war were tremendous. More than a million people had been killed, and valuable oil facilities had been destroyed.

Israel. Since its creation in 1948, Israel has grown into a modern, advanced state. Its victories over the Arab states have also made it the dominant military power in the Middle East. Yet the years of high military spending have taken their toll on the Israeli economy, increasing the country's dependence on aid from the United States.

● See below.

There have been important changes in the Israeli population over the past four decades. About 85 percent of the people of Israel are Jews. The rest are mostly Muslim and Christian Arabs. Israel's Jews come from all parts of the world. In the first half of this

Background A new constitution approved in 1979 established Islamic law as the basis of Iran's legal system. Khomeini was made supreme ruler for life. After his death, Hashemi Rafsanjani became president, and Ali Khameini became supreme religious leader.

● ENRICHMENT. Have students work in groups to develop a hypothesis suggesting what effect the growing number of Soviet Jewish immigrants might have on Israel's future. Have students discuss their hypotheses in class. *(Synthesis) Understanding Cause and Effect* century, most immigrants were Ashkenazi, or European, Jews. After 1948 most were Sephardic, or African and Asian, Jews. By the 1980's Sephardic Jews made up more than half of Israel's Jewish population.

Sephardic Jews tended to be poorer, less educated, and more conservative than Ashkenazi Jews. As Israel's Sephardic population has grown, the Israeli government has moved toward the right. The Labor Party, which dominated Israeli politics in the years after independence, has lost ground to the conservative Likud Party.

Sec. Rev. ques. 3

A more recent trend is the arrival of thousands of Jews from the Soviet Union as the result of a freer Soviet policy on emigration. Israeli officials have forecast that a million Soviet immigrants, many of them highly educated professional people, may settle in Israel by the mid-1990's, swelling the population by 20 percent. Such growth will affect not only Israel's politics but its need for resources, housing, and jobs as well.

The Arab States

▲ Note strategies for third objective on pp. 770–772.

North Africa. In politics and culture, the North African countries of Libya, Tunisia, Algeria, and Morocco are considered a part of the Middle East. North Africa shares the Arabic language and the Islamic religion of the Arab nations.

After World War II, the countries of North Africa finally gained independence. Tunisia and Morocco began programs of development and formed close trade ties with Western Europe. Algeria, too, worked to modernize, funded by rich deposits of natural gas. It adopted some features of socialism, and most of its industry was taken over by the state.

Libya came under the rule of Muammar al Qaddafi (page 766) in 1969. Qaddafi ruled according to what he called "Islamic Socialism." He nationalized much of Libya's economy and made laws based on his own reading of the Koran. Determined to rid the country of Western influences, Qaddafi forged ties with the Soviet Union and supported terrorist groups.

Egypt. Egypt was made a British protectorate during World War I, and in 1922 it was given partial independence and in 1936, full independence. British troops later left Egypt, except for the region around the Suez Canal. Yet British influence over the Egyptian government remained strong.

Many Egyptians resented their corrupt leader, King Farouk. They were also angry at the great gaps between rich and poor in Egyptian society. In 1952 Egyptian army officers overthrew the king; a year later they declared Egypt a republic. A leading figure in the revolt was Colonel Gamal Abdel Nasser, who by 1954 was in effect the ruler of Egypt.

Nasser's first goal was to end foreign influence in Egypt. With that aim in mind, he seized the Suez Canal in 1956 (page 761). Nasser's next goal was to strengthen Egypt's economy. To help the peasants, he put a limit on the amount of land one person could own. He also lowered rents and set up cooperatives where farmers could get tools and seeds at low prices. In 1956 Egypt began to build the Aswan High Dam on the Nile River, with aid from the Soviet Union. The dam provided hydroelectric power and stored water to irrigate new farmlands.

Nasser also tried to boost Egypt's economy by cutting its dependence on the export of cotton, its major crop. He put large businesses under government control and encouraged the development of industry. Egypt's income grew, but not fast enough to meet the needs of the country's rising population. Economic growth was also held back by the conflict with Israel, which led Egypt to set aside huge sums for military spending.

After Nasser's death in 1970, his successor, Anwar el-Sadat, took a more pro-Western course. He reduced government controls on business and expelled Soviet advisers. Egyptian-American relations improved. In the late 1970's, Sadat surprised the world by making peace with Israel (page 763). After Sadat's assassination in 1981, the new Egyptian leader, Hosni Mubarak, promised to follow Sadat's policies. Like Sadat, Mubarak had to contend with Islamic fundamentalism and a weak economy.

Sec. Rev. ques. 4

769

Background Sadat expelled approximately 20,000 Soviet advisers and military personnel from Egypt.

(F) See
below.

The Geography Connection

Water for Desert Lands

In the dry lands that extend through much of the Middle East, water has always been a scarce and precious natural resource. Nomadic herders traveled from oasis to oasis to find water for themselves and their animals, and farming and trading centers grew up around these wells and springs.

The oil boom that began after World War II led to urbanization and an increase in water usage. To meet the rising demand, many nations of the Middle East have used their oil wealth to finance huge water projects. Strategically placed dams and advanced irrigation techniques have helped conserve available water. However, creating fresh water through desalinization—taking the salt out of sea water—has been the most common solution to the problem.

The first desalinization plant in the Middle East was built in Israel in 1965, to provide water for the desert town of Eilat. By the early 1990's desalinization plants dotted the coastlines of Middle Eastern countries, producing millions of gallons of fresh water a day. The only drawback of desalinization is the vulnerability of sea water to contamination from oil spills. This was shown in the Gulf War when a massive oil slick threatened desalinization plants along Saudi Arabia's Persian Gulf coast.

Making the connection. How have the people of the Middle East met the problem of a lack of fresh water?

Saudi Arabia. The discovery of vast oil reserves in the 1930's helped push Saudi Arabia into the twentieth century. Bedouin tribesmen gave up desert life and learned Western technology and ways of living.

Saudi leaders worked to make their country prosperous. In the 1950's Prince Faisal (FY-sul) used oil profits to build hospitals, schools, and irrigation systems. By the time Faisal became king in 1964, modern cities had sprung up in the country's vast deserts. The government provided free education for all children and spent heavily to improve agricultural production and develop industry.

By the 1970's Saudi Arabia was one of the richest nations in the world. The government earned billions of dollars each year from the sale of oil. The Saudis began to invest in real estate, banks, and companies in other countries. Islamic fundamentalists have criticized the Saudi government for its modernization programs and its friendship with the United States. Economic progress, however, has not deeply changed Saudi Arabian society. While many middle-class Saudis would like to see Western-style reforms, the country remains an absolute monarchy and Islamic law is strictly enforced.

Iraq. A British mandate until 1932, Iraq had rich oil resources that helped fund economic development. Under King Faisal II, the Iraqi government carried on a program of modernization during the 1940's and 1950's. With British help, the Iraqis built roads, railroads, and irrigation systems. They also laid a pipeline to carry oil to the Persian Gulf.

Many Iraqis, however, resented the British presence. In 1958 a group of leftist, Pan-Arabist army officers murdered Faisal, and after that, Iraq was troubled by growing political violence. Not until 1968 did a stable government emerge. Saddam Hussein (page 768) became president in 1979.

In the 1970's and 1980's the Iraqi government maintained ties with the Soviet Union, which supplied Iraq with arms. Iraq

770

▲ RETEACHING. Have students identify the effects of the profitable oil industry on Saudi Arabia. (It introduced Western technology and ways of living to Saudi Arabia and created economic resources for hospitals, schools, irrigation systems, agricultural and industrial improvements.) (Comprehension) *Observing for Detail*

Social History Note that Saudi Arabia's system of justice is based on the Islamic tradition of "an eye for an eye." Punishments are often considered harsh by Western standards.

(F) GEOGRAPHY CONNECTION. Have students explain how the oil industry has affected the availability of water in the Middle East. (The postwar oil boom resulted in urbanization and an increase in water usage; oil wealth was used to finance water projects.) (Comprehension) *Understanding Cause and Effect* spoke out against Egypt's move to make peace with Israel and continued to be hostile to the Jewish state. The Iraqi government also fought for years against the Kurds, a minority group seeking self-rule. Iraq's affairs were dominated in the 1980's by its war with Iran. In 1990 Iraq again went on the offensive when Saddam Hussein sent his forces to invade Kuwait (page 772).

Jordan. The nation of Jordan, a British mandate after World War I, won full independence in 1946. Lacking the wealth of the oil-rich nations, Jordan was a fairly poor, agricultural country. In the 1948 Arab-Israeli war, Jordan gained part of the West Bank of the Jordan River. The West Bank became the economic heartland of Jordan. When Israel took it over in 1967, Jordan's economy suffered. In 1988, however, Jordan's King Hussein announced that his country would not try to regain control of the West Bank.

Syria. Syria became a French mandate after World War I and gained independence during World War II. After a socialist government took control in 1971, Syria raised its oil production and built a vast dam on the Euphrates River to provide irrigation and hydroelectric power.

Economic growth was slowed by Syria's involvement in the stormy politics of the Middle East. Its wars with Israel cost Syria territory as well as soldiers and supplies. High spending on arms drained Syrian resources.

Lebanon. Like Syria, Lebanon was a French mandate after World War I. Lebanon was granted its independence in 1943, and three years later all French troops left the country. Lebanon prospered, becoming a center for banking and tourism, and was home to many different religious and political groups. Christians dominated the government and the economy, even though they were a minority. Muslims, who made up the majority, wanted more power and higher living standards. Also in Lebanon were thousands of Palestinians (most of them Muslims) who had fled to Lebanon after Israel was established in 1948.

In 1975 a bloody civil war broke out among Christians, Muslims, and Palestinians.

The following year Syrian soldiers entered Lebanon to try to stop the fighting, but did not succeed. By the 1980's, tens of thousands of people had died. The chaos in Lebanon opened the way for the PLO to set up bases in the southern part of that war-torn nation. Armed with Soviet tanks and heavy artillery and aided by Syrian troops, PLO forces made guerrilla attacks on northern Israel. To drive the PLO away, Israel invaded Lebanon in 1982 and kept soldiers there for three years.

Sec. Rev. ques. 5

In the end, the PLO was not destroyed, but it was driven out of southern Lebanon and the capital city of Beirut. Rival Christian and Muslim private armies continued to battle for control of the city, and a number of Westerners were taken hostage by extremist groups. In 1990 most of these militias agreed to pull out of Beirut and leave the city patrolled by Lebanese and Syrian troops. After fifteen years of fighting, peace returned to the war-ravaged city.

The Gulf War

By the end of the Iran-Iraq War, the Iraqi dictator Saddam Hussein had the largest army in the Arab world. In 1990 he used it in another bid for expanded power. Hussein accused oil-rich Kuwait, Iraq's neighbor on the Persian Gulf (map, page 767), of overproducing oil in violation of OPEC quotas, and demanded

Meanwhile . . .

IN THE UNITED STATES

Seeking to escape turmoil in the Middle East, many Muslims have come to America. Muslim immigrants in recent years have included Arabs, Iranians, Pakistanis, Lebanese, Indians, and others. It is expected that within 30 years Muslims will outnumber Jews in the United States, becoming the nation's second largest religious community, after Christians.

771

Political History In 1991 Jordan's King Hussein approved a charter establishing guidelines for democratizing reforms, including legalizing political parties and expanding women's rights.

▲ **REINFORCEMENT. Have students identify causes and effects of Lebanon's civil war.** (Causes: power struggle. Effects: Many killed, destruction, PLO bases, Israeli and Syrian involvement.) *(Comprehension) Identifying Cause and Effect*

Social History Although Christians dominated the Lebanese government, a "gentlemen's agreement" in Lebanon after World War II provided for an equal division of government positions among the Muslim and Christian sects in Lebanon. The civil war erupted after changes in the Shiite population increased conflict between Christians and Muslims.

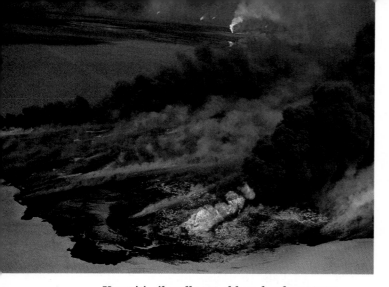

Kuwaiti oil wells set ablaze by the retreating Iraqi invaders were finally extinguished in late 1991.

Sec. Rev. ques. 6

that Kuwait make a favorable settlement of territorial disputes with Iraq.

When Kuwait did not comply, Iraqi forces invaded. Over the next few months the Iraqi forces established a harsh occupation in Kuwait; Saddam Hussein declared the emirate to be Iraq's "nineteenth province."

Iraq's aggression met with almost universal condemnation from the world's leaders, and the United Nations imposed a tough embargo on that nation's trade. As fear mounted that Saddam Hussein might order his soldiers into Saudi Arabia, the United States sent troops to defend that country in an action called Operation Desert Shield.

Joining in the multinational effort were some 33 allied nations, including the Islamic countries of Saudi Arabia, Egypt, Syria, and Turkey. UN members also pledged billions of dollars to help pay for the cost of the action.

In November 1990 the UN Security Council adopted a resolution authorizing the use of force against Iraq if that nation had not withdrawn from Kuwait by January 15, 1991. The United States government declared that the resolution had "established clearly that there is a peaceful way out of this conflict: the complete, immediate and unconditional withdrawal of Iraq from Kuwait, the restoration of the legitimate government of Kuwait, and the release of all hostages." Iraq had released a number of American and other hostages before the UN resolution was

adopted, and soon freed the rest. Saddam Hussein declared his intention, however, of holding on to Kuwait in defiance of the UN.

On January 17, 1991, Operation Desert Shield became Operation Desert Storm as American, British, and French airplanes and missiles struck at missile sites and other military targets in Iraq and Kuwait.

After a five-week air campaign, in which the allies' high-technology weaponry inflicted crippling damage on Iraq's military forces, the allied command launched a massive desert offensive. Allied forces moved rapidly into Kuwait and southern Iraq and overwhelmed Saddam Hussein's army. Only a hundred hours after the start of the land campaign, Kuwait was free of Iraqi control. The United States declared a cease-fire, and Iraq finally accepted the UN resolution.

The Gulf War had been short but its impact was far-ranging. Iraq suffered heavy loss of life and economic deprivation. The Iraqi Kurds rebelled against Saddam Hussein's repressive rule but failed to break free. On discovering that Iraq had a secret program to build nuclear weapons, the UN ordered the work stopped and told Iraq to give up its nuclear industry.

In Kuwait, Iraqi sabotage to oil wells left the environment devastated. The bitter experience of hostile occupation also changed the way Kuwaitis felt about their restored government. After liberation, they demanded a voice in the running of their country. The call for democratizing was even heard in Saudi Arabia.

The Gulf War also had an impact on power politics in the Middle East. The Arab countries that had supported the U.S.-led coalition continued their Western ties after the war as a way of maintaining their security and also for the economic advantages they hoped it would bring them.

Perhaps the most significant consequence of the Gulf Crisis was its paving the way for the Madrid Conference (page 764) and the meetings that followed as both Arabs and Israelis looked to the United States for help in finding solutions to the problems of the Middle East.

▲ ENRICHMENT. Have students make a chart of Middle Eastern nations, identify each country as Arab or non-Arab, and list its religion, type of government, economic characteristics, and important trends and developments. *(Comprehension) Translating Information into Another Form*

See Sec. 2 *Closing the Lesson,* p. T757C.

Background The diplomatic coalition that opposed the Iraqi take-over of Kuwait numbered 33 nations; some 16 nations contributed to the allied military forces in the Gulf, with the U.S. contributing by far the most.

Resource Material Use Houghton Mifflin's "Persian Gulf Worksheets" to extend your class's investigation of the Gulf War.

Answers to Section Review questions are in brackets on pages indicated.

1. **Define or identify:** Pan-Arabism, secular, OPEC, fundamentalism, Iran-Iraq War. (pp. 765, 766, 768)
2. What were the causes and effects of Iran's 1979 revolution? Why did Iraq invade Iran in 1980? (pp. 767–768)
3. What population trends play a part in Israel's politics and economy? (p. 769)
4. How did Sadat's policies for Egypt differ from those of Nasser? What problems did Mubarak face? (p. 770)
5. What groups fought each other in the Lebanon war? (p. 772)
6. What caused the Gulf War? What were the results of the war? (771–772)
7. **Critical thinking:** How might rapid modernization in the Middle East have contributed to the growth of Islamic fundamentalism? (See answer below.)

7. Students might suggest that conservative elements distrusted modernizing reforms. Fearful of losing traditional Islamic ways, they gained popularity by opposing dependence on Western aid and ideas.

Chapter 37 Summary and Timeline

1. The UN partitioned Palestine in 1948, dividing it between Arabs and Jews. The Arabs did not, however, set up an Arab state in Palestine, choosing instead to attack the newly founded state of Israel. When the war ended, the Palestinians had lost their lands. Many became refugees in Arab nations. War broke out between Arabs and Israelis again in 1956, in 1967, and in 1973. The leaders of Egypt and Israel signed a peace agreement in 1977. Disputes over the Palestinians stood in the way of peace for the region, however.

2. Nationalism became a powerful force in the Middle East as the region emerged from foreign domination after World War I. Using capital from oil production, some nationalist leaders were able to modernize their nations. The non-Arab countries of Turkey and Iran suffered political unrest in the postwar period. Iran went from the pro-Western rule of the shahs to the anti-Western rule of Islamic extremists. Saudi Arabia, Egypt, and Jordan were Arab nations that followed more moderate policies. Like Syria and Libya, Iraq was one of the more extreme Arab nations, hostile to the United States and Israel. In 1990 the Iraqi dictator's invasion of Kuwait provoked world-wide condemnation and the imposing of economic sanctions on Iraq. In the Gulf War of 1991, a U.S.-led alliance forced Iraq to give up Kuwait.

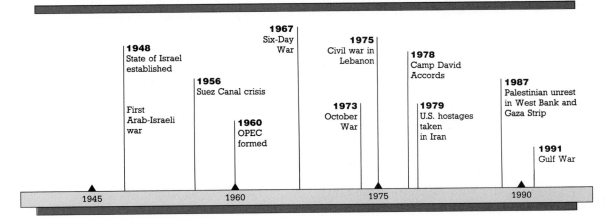

1948
State of Israel established

First Arab-Israeli war

1956
Suez Canal crisis

1960
OPEC formed

1967
Six-Day War

1973
October War

1975
Civil war in Lebanon

1978
Camp David Accords

1979
U.S. hostages taken in Iran

1987
Palestinian unrest in West Bank and Gaza Strip

1991
Gulf War

1945   1960   1975   1990

See p. T757C for answers to Chapter Review.

Vocabulary Review

1. Use the following terms to complete the sentences below: *Camp David Accords, Iran-Iraq War, OPEC, Palestine Liberation Organization.*
   a. The __?__ was fought in the 1980's between two neighboring Islamic states.
   b. __?__ members work together to set oil prices in international trade.
   c. The __?__ called for a five-year period of self-government for the West Bank and Gaza Strip.
   d. The __?__ sought to create a Palestinian state.
2. Define or identify the terms in the following pairs.
   a. secular; fundamentalism
   b. Six-Day War; October War

People to Identify

Match each of the following people with the correct description: *Yasir Arafat, Jimmy Carter, Faisal, Saddam Hussein, Ayatollah Ruhollah Khomeini, Hosni Mubarak, Muammar al Qaddafi, Reza Shah.*
   1. ruler of Iraq who ordered an invasion of Kuwait in 1990
   2. Iranian leader who refused to side with the Allies in World War II
   3. Shiite religious leader who headed Iran after the overthrow of the shah in 1979
   4. king of Saudi Arabia who began a modernization program in the 1950's
   5. head of the PLO
   6. American President who negotiated a meeting between Sadat and Begin
   7. Libyan leader who called for Arab unity
   8. Egyptian leader who followed Sadat

774

Places to Know

Match the letters on this map of the Middle East with the places listed below. You may want to refer to the maps on pages 760 and 767.

1. Gaza Strip
2. Golan Heights
3. Gulf of Aqaba
4. Jerusalem
5. Lebanon
6. Sinai Peninsula
7. Suez Canal
8. Syria
9. Turkey
10. West Bank

Recalling the Facts

1. Why did large numbers of Jewish people emigrate to Palestine in the 1930's?
2. What arguments were presented to the United Nations about the creation of a Jewish state in Palestine? What decision did the UN reach, and how did Arab nations react to the decision?
3. What was the outcome of the 1948 war?

4. What caused fighting between Jordan's King Hussein and the PLO in 1970?

5. What was the goal of Pan-Arabism? What were the obstacles to achieving this goal?

6. What led to the overthrow of the shah of Iran in 1979?

7. How did the discovery of oil affect economic development in Saudi Arabia?

8. What were Nasser's goals for Egypt? How did he work to achieve these goals?

9. Why did Israel invade Lebanon in 1982?

10. Why were United States forces sent to Saudi Arabia in 1990?

11. What was the Madrid Conference, and why was it important?

Critical Thinking Skills

1. **Building vocabulary.** The settlement of Palestinian refugees has been a major problem in the Middle East. The word *refugee* comes from the Latin *fugere*, meaning "to flee." Use a dictionary to define the following: *(App.) fugitive, refuge, centrifugal, subterfuge.*

2. **Inferring.** How might Arab unity have benefited the Arab states? *(Syn.)*

3. **Identifying trends.** What have been the most important trends in the population of Israel since the state's formation in 1948? *(Comp.)* What impact has each trend had on Israel?

4. **Placing events in time.** From the information in the chapter, find the year in which each of the following events occurred. Arrange these events in chronological order, writing the date next to each. *(Comp.)*

   a. Sadat is assassinated.

   b. Iranian women gain the right to vote.

   c. Egypt loses the Sinai Peninsula in the Six-Day War.

   d. The nation of Israel is created.

   e. Egypt seizes control of the Suez Canal from Britain.

   f. Arab OPEC members restrict oil shipments.

   g. The Camp David Accords are signed.

Drawing conclusions. During the cold war the oil of the Middle East made that region one of major interest to the superpowers. How are recent developments in world affairs likely to affect that interest? *(Syn.)*

Enrichment: Primary Sources

In November 1917 Arthur Balfour, the British foreign secretary, wrote to Baron Edmond de Rothschild, a Zionist leader in Britain. The letter is adapted below.

66 Dear Lord Rothschild,

I have much pleasure in conveying to you, on behalf of His Majesty's Government, the following declaration of sympathy with Jewish Zionist aspirations:

"His Majesty's Government views with favor the establishment in Palestine of a national home for the Jewish people, and will use their best endeavors to make the achievement of this object easier, it being clearly understood that nothing shall be done which may prejudice the civil and religious rights of existing non-Jewish communities in Palestine, or the rights and political status enjoyed by Jews in any other country."

I should be grateful if you would bring this declaration to the knowledge of the Zionist Federation.

Yours sincerely,

[Signed] Arthur James Balfour 99

1. For whom was Balfour speaking in this letter?

2. What does the declaration say about Palestinian Arabs' rights?

3. **Critical thinking:** On what part of this letter did Zionists base their claim of British support? *(Comp.)*

A checkmark identifies questions and exercises calling for the three higher-order levels of thinking at the top of the Bloom taxonomy: Analysis, Synthesis, and Evaluation.

Independent Africa　1945-Present
(pp. 776–793)

Chapter Preview

In Section 1, the growth of nationalist movements in Africa is described, and developments that led to independence for African nations are traced. Section 2 tells about South Africa's apartheid policies, the growth of opposition to the government's racist policies, and the dramatic changes in policy in recent years. Section 3 identifies some of the problems facing African nations and the role of foreign influence in African affairs.

Bibliography

See the *Teacher's Management and Planning Guide* for additional listings. Starred titles are for both students and teachers.

Legum, Colin, *et al. Africa in the 1980's: A Continent in Crisis.* McGraw Hill. Current issues facing African countries.

Lloyd, Peter C. *Africa in Social Change,* revised edition. Penguin. Impact of modern developments on village life.

Minter, William. *King Solomon's Mines Revisited.* Basic Books. The relationship between the West and southern Africa in this past century.

*Paton, Alan. *Cry, the Beloved Country.* Scribner's. A novel of apartheid in South Africa.

Section Lesson Plans

SECTION 1　　　　　(pp. 777–781)
National Independence

Objectives

After completing this section, students will be able to:
1. Explain the origins of the African nationalist movement.
2. Describe how African nations gained their independence.

Introducing the Lesson

Remind students that the Berlin Conference in 1885 divided most of Africa among colonial powers. After World War II, nearly all of Africa achieved independence.

Then ask: *(a) What might be viewed as political, social, and economic priorities for a newly independent nation?* (Answers will vary. Stable government and a strong economy would probably be priorities.)

(b) What advantages and disadvantages might a colonized nation have in its transition to independence? (Answers will vary. Some colonies gained independence with political institutions already developed and strong leaders ready to assume power. Other colonized nations gained independence with little political preparation.)

(c) What problems might African nations have faced after they gained independence? (Answers will vary.)

Developing the Lesson: Drawing Conclusions

Have students compare events during Ghana's and Zaire's transition to independence and draw conclusions about the following:

(a) What factors enabled Ghana to make a smooth transition to nationhood? (A healthy economy, a strong educational system, little rivalry among ethnic groups, and British efforts to prepare its colonies for self-rule.)

(b) Why was each of these factors important in easing the transition to self-rule? (Answers will vary.)

(c) What contrasting factors contributed to the violence and bloodshed that accompanied Zaire's independence? (Paternalistic policies of the Belgian government, lack of governmental experience among the Africans in the colony, limited educational opportunities for Africans.)

(d) How would each of these factors have made the transition more difficult? (Answers will vary.) *(Comprehension)*

Developing the Lesson: Analyzing Information

Have students evaluate the importance of *negritude* and nationalism for African peoples before independence. In their analyses, students should consider Africa's experience with the slave trade and the paternalistic attitude of many foreign powers. (Answers will vary, but students should consider the effects of slavery on national pride and culture and the effects of years of paternalism on a nation's ability to establish an effective government.) *(Synthesis)*

Closing the Lesson: Making Judgments

Have students work in groups to consider the alternatives France gave to its African colonies. Students should identify and evaluate the advantages and disadvantages of both choices, and then explain which alternative they would have chosen. *(Synthesis)*

See *Section Review* questions, p. 781.

SECTION 2   (pp. 781–786)
White Rule in Southern Africa

Objectives

After completing this section, students will be able to:
1. Explain how racist policies affected the peoples of South Africa.
2. Discuss how the peoples of southern Africa sought majority rule.
3. Describe events that spurred the growth of the South African protest movement.

Introducing the Lesson

Tell students that the apartheid policies of South Africa's white-minority government evoked outrage from the world community. In recent years, in response to economic, social, and cultural pressure from many nations, South Africa began to make changes in its apartheid system.

Then ask: *(a) What might have accounted for South Africa's long refusal to change racist policies?* (Answers may suggest that white South Africans felt they had a right to maintain their government and to refuse to submit to international pressure. They might also have feared that their own interests would be overwhelmed if the black majority were to gain political power.)

(b) What responsibility, if any, do other nations have to work for change in South Africa? (Answers will vary.)

Developing the Lesson: Drawing Conclusions

Have students identify examples of American and Soviet involvement in Africa after independence and then answer the following: *How might the involvement of the superpowers in the internal affairs of newly independent nations such as Mozambique have offered both advantages and disadvantages?* (Superpower involvement often included economic and military aid. Sometimes superpower involvement broadened a conflict to include issues that otherwise would not have affected individual countries; sometimes internal conflicts were fueled by resources supplied by the superpowers.) *(Comprehension)*

Developing the Lesson: Observing for Detail

Have students summarize developments relating to South Africa's apartheid system since the 1970's. (The collapse of white rule in the Portuguese colonies and in Zimbabwe led opponents of white rule in South Africa to step up their protests. The South African government responded with greater repression and violence. In 1990 a reform government adopted a more flexible policy, releasing Nelson Mandela and taking steps toward the dismantling of the apartheid system.) *(Comprehension)*

Closing the Lesson: Forming a Hypothesis

Have students develop a hypothesis explaining why the world community responded so strongly to the domestic policies of South Africa. When forming their hypotheses, students should answer the following question: *Do nations have a right to get involved in the domestic issues of another country? (Synthesis)*

See *Section Review* questions, p. 786.

SECTION 3 (pp. 787–791)
Challenges Facing Africa

Objectives

After completing this section, students will be able to:
1. Explain problems faced by the newly independent African nations.
2. Describe changes that occurred in African society.
3. Discuss the role played by outside powers in Africa.

Introducing the Lesson

Remind students that African nations worked to stabilize their governments and to improve the standard of living after independence. Many nations witnessed industrialization, rising literacy, and improved health conditions.

Then ask: *(a) What factors might have helped Africa in its drive for modernization?* (Answers will vary. Africa was rich in natural resources, which provided materials for industrialization.)

(b) What factors might have hindered Africa's modernization process? (Answers will vary. Years of colonialism had affected the development of Africa's economy and of its leadership.)

Developing the Lesson:
Understanding Cause and Effect

Have students describe how the colonial experience affected the political stability of many African nations in their early period of independence. (Sometimes ethnic conflict resulted from colonial boundaries originally drawn to suit foreign powers. Few Africans had government experience and often were unskilled in government management.) *(Comprehension)*

Developing the Lesson:
Synthesizing Information

Have students identify the major problems faced by African nations after independence and describe the methods adopted to deal with the problems. (Some national leaders established one-party systems by stifling opposition parties. Protests put pressure on leaders to allow new parties to form. Emphasis on industrialization led to debt and neglect of agriculture. To pay debts, many agricultural products were exported. When food shortages occurred, relief services were not always successful. Efforts made to increase food produc-

tion included the promise of higher market prices, and the use of better seed, improved livestock, irrigation, and fertilizer.) *(Comprehension)*

Closing the Lesson: Drawing Conclusions

Have students explain the advantages of international organizations like the Organization of African States. (Answers will vary. Organizations like the OAS help nations tackle common problems and share vital resources, and they try to mitigate the negative effects of nationalism. Such organizations also increase the benefits of cooperation and reduce international tension.) *(Comprehension)*

See *Section Review* questions, p. 791.

Chapter 38 Review Answers
(pp. 792–793)

Vocabulary Review

1. Pan-Africanist—movement to defend the rights of persons of African descent; Organization of African Unity—international body established to settle disputes and deal with social and economic issues that concern Africa.
2. African National Congress—organization opposed to the apartheid policies of the South African government; Mau Mau—secret guerrilla movement that attacked white-owned plantations in Kenya.
3. pass laws—laws keeping people from moving freely within a country; divest—to sell off.

People to Identify

1. (a) Desmond Tutu (b) Jomo Kenyatta (c) W. E. B. Du Bois
2. (a) South African leader of the "Black Consciousness" movement who was imprisoned and killed by police.
(b) South African president who took steps to end the apartheid system.
(c) Prime minister of the new Congo government who, faced with civil war, sought help from the UN and the Soviet Union.
(d) Head of the African National Congress who was convicted of planning to overthrow the South African government and sentenced to life in prison; he was released in 1990.
(e) Leader of ZANU who became prime minister of the new nation of Zimbabwe.

(f) Prime minister of the newly independent Gold Coast who renamed the country Ghana.

Places to Know

1. Ghana 2. Zaire 3. Zambia 4. Angola 5. Mozambique 6. Tanzania 7. Malawi 8. Soweto

Recalling the Facts

1. The Gold Coast was able to make a smooth transition to independence because of its healthy economy, strong educational system, and lack of rivalry among different ethnic groups.
2. French colonies were given the choice of having partial independence as members of a new French Community or choosing complete independence and losing economic aid from France. French colonies were allowed to gain full independence without losing aid.
3. The Belgian government had followed a paternalistic policy in governing its colony, leaving the new nations ill-prepared for independence. Few Congo Africans had advanced education, and none had held high government offices. Riots, an army mutiny, and an attempt at secession by the Katanga province were also a hindrance.
4. White control of the land around Mount Kenya caused a severe land shortage in that region, increasing the poverty of many Kikuyu.
5. Neither Africans nor persons of mixed race were allowed to live in white areas or even enter them except as employees. Africans were required to carry passes that showed where they lived and worked and if their taxes were paid. Rural Africans were forced to live on reservations called "homelands."
6. In 1974 military leaders overthrew Portugal's dictator and the new government granted independence to the African colonies.
7. After Portugal withdrew from Mozambique and Angola, rebels opposed to the Smith government gained bases from which to attack Rhodesia. Convinced that the Smith government could not last, South Africa cut off military aid to Rhodesia in 1976. Under mounting international pressure, Smith agreed to majority rule.
8. The South African president declared a state of emergency in July 1985, and the police were given broad powers.
9. South Africa extended apartheid policies to Namibia, a mandate of South Africa since World War I. In 1966 the UN canceled South Africa's mandate and recognized SWAPO as the legitimate Namibian government. For many years South Africa ignored the UN's decision, but Namibia became independent in 1990.
10. In 1966, Muslims in northern cities killed thousands of Ibo and other southerners. In May 1967 the Ibo declared independence for southeastern Nigeria as the Republic of Biafra. This act set off civil war.
11. In an attempt to industrialize, young African nations neglected agriculture. Also, most grew export crops at the expense of food crops for domestic use; the population was growing rapidly; and severe droughts struck much of the continent.
12. The involvement of large international corporations in parts of Africa has caused the profits of African labor to flow into Europe and America.
13. The United States was allowed to set up a military base in Ethiopia; Somalia, involved in a land dispute with Ethiopia, sought Soviet aid. When Marxists took over Ethiopia's government, they moved closer to the Soviet Union. Somalia then switched to the United States for aid. The Soviet Union, China, the United States, and other countries gave military aid to southern African liberation movements. After Angola won independence, the Soviet Union supported the Angolan government, while the United States helped South Africa arm the UNITA guerrillas.

Critical Thinking Skills

1. Exactitude—the quality of being exact; fortitude—strength of mind to meet adversity or bear pain with courage; gratitude—state of being grateful; magnitude—greatness of size, quantity, number, or position; solitude—state of being alone.
2. Answers will vary.
3. 57 years. 69 years. Angola. France.
4. Students might suggest that other countries refuse to recognize the independence of the "homelands" because they do not want to legitimize South Africa's apartheid policy.

Thinking About Geography

This activity can also be done in class with a wall map of Africa.

Enrichment: Primary Sources

1. He is referring to the collapse of Soviet rule in Eastern Europe.
2. One-party rule. His use of the words "dishonestly touted" shows he disagrees.
3. He says that shifts in the past—from multiparty government "to one party to no party (the military)" lead him to be cynical—though he nevertheless welcomes the democracy movement.

Independent Africa

1945–Present

See chapter timeline, p. 791.

Before You Read This Chapter

What does it take to make a nation? Land? People? What else? Since 1945, many new nations have been established in Africa. Like nation-builders on other continents, African nationalists found that many serious problems remained in their countries even after independence. As you read this chapter, try to decide what makes a nation. What caused the rise of nationalism in Africa after World War II? What sometimes happened to that feeling of nationalism after independence was won? What role does nationalism play in an increasingly interdependent world?

The Geographic Setting

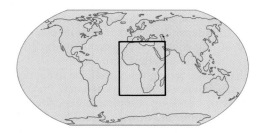

The Chapter Outline

1. National Independence
2. White Rule in Southern Africa
3. Challenges Facing Africa

Many African countries suffer from ethnic divisions. This government poster from the West African nation of Ghana promotes a sense of national identity.

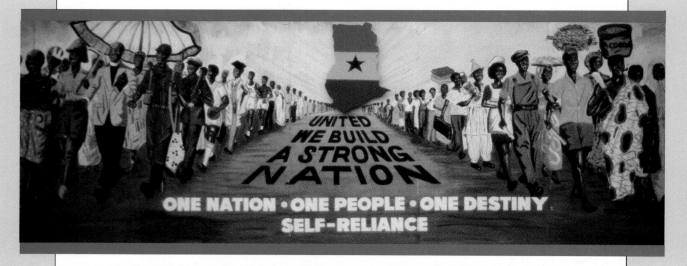

1 National Independence

Objectives

Focus Questions

★ ■ What were the origins of the African nationalist movement? *(pages 777–778)*

● ■ How did African nations gain independence? *(pages 778–780)*

Terms to Know

Pan-Africanist   Mau Mau
African National
  Congress

★ Note strategies for first objective on this page and p. 778.

As you read in Chapter 30, European nations took over most of Africa during the Age of Imperialism. For nearly a century the peoples of Africa lived under colonial rule. After World War I, movements for greater rights for Africans started to gain strength in black Africa. After World War II, African nationalists began to demand complete independence. Eventually the old colonies became independent countries.

African Nationalism

The post-World War II independence movements had their roots in the African past. Nationalists wanted to bring back the time when Africans ruled themselves. They did not, however, call for a return to the states of pre-colonial Africa. Instead they worked to strengthen national unity within the colonial boundaries.

Early nationalists. As early as the 1800's, blacks were organizing to protect their rights. In 1900 West Indian and American blacks formed the Pan-Africanist movement to defend the rights of persons of African descent. They held a series of Pan-African congresses, speaking against segregation and other forms of racial discrimination. A leader of this movement was W.E.B. Du Bois, a black American professor and writer.

In the early 1900's another movement began in the United States. A young Jamaican named Marcus Garvey started the Universal Negro Improvement Association (UNIA) in 1914. Garvey called for the independence of all blacks and urged black Americans to return to Africa.

The UNIA at its peak had hundreds of thousands of supporters. Its newspaper, *Negro World*, had readers around the globe. Because it encouraged black pride and independence from white rule, the paper was banned by colonial governments in Africa. Africans were aware of these Western struggles for racial equality, and some believed rumors that black Americans were coming to take part in an armed liberation of the African continent.

In Africa other movements to win equality were also taking shape. Some Africans described the value and distinctiveness of African culture. This was most notable among well-educated French-speaking Africans and black West Indians, who wrote poems and essays in praise of *negritude* (a French word meaning "blackness").

Other early leaders formed organizations that pushed for African political rights. One of the most well-known groups was the African National Congress, set up by two American-educated black South Africans in 1912. The ANC spoke out in favor of African interests and pushed for blacks to be represented in the South African Parliament. By the 1930's blacks in many parts of Africa had started to call for greater rights.

Among these Africans was Nnamdi Azikiwe (ah-ZEE-kee-way) of Nigeria. The son of an Ibo (EE-boh) clerk, Azikiwe—known

777

★ RETEACHING. Have students review "African Nationalism" (pp. 777–778) and make a timeline of events in the African nationalist movements. (1900—Pan-Africanist movement; 1912—African National Congress; 1914—Universal Negro Improvement Association; 1937—*West African Pilot*.) *(Comprehension)* **Sequencing Events**

★ REINFORCEMENT. Have students summarize the ideas on which African nationalism and independence movements were based. (Protection of political rights; an end to segregation and other forms of racial discrimination; independence from white rule; the return of black Americans to Africa; black pride; respect for African culture; self-determination; end to low pay.) *(Comprehension)* **Synthesizing Information**

Kwame Nkrumah led the independence movement in Ghana. Admired for his Pan-Africanist views, Nkrumah's popularity later declined because of corruption in his government and his increasingly harsh rule.

to many as "Zik"—was educated in America. When he returned to Africa in 1934, he edited a newspaper in the Gold Coast. In 1937 he moved to Nigeria and began to publish the *West African Pilot,* which helped spread ideas of self-determination throughout the colony.

★ See below.

Sec. Rev. ques. 2

Rising nationalist sentiment. Movements like Zik's made little progress until after World War II. The war weakened the will of European nations to hold on to their colonies. It also led to increased demands for equal rights. Africans who served in the armed forces during the war had the chance to exchange ideas with other Africans and Asians who wanted self-rule.

Nationalist movements got support from the rising numbers of Africans who earned wages in the rapidly growing towns and cities of colonial Africa. After the war these urban workers held a series of strikes to call for an end to low pay. They were among

778 the growing number of literate Africans who

read nationalist newspapers and joined the nationalist parties that sprang up everywhere.

African nationalists south of the Sahara drew encouragement from the successes of Asian nationalist movements and from the independence of most of North Africa by the early 1950's. They were also inspired by the gains made by American blacks after World War II (page 805).

African Independence

● Note strategies for second objective on this page and p. 780.

The Gold Coast. At the end of the Second World War, Britain began to give Africans a larger role in colonial government. The British assumed that such limited self-government might lead to independence at some future date. In 1957 the British colony of the Gold Coast won full independence. Most other African colonies then began calling for self-rule.

The Gold Coast was able to make a smooth transition to independence, aided by its healthy economy and strong educational system. Because there was little rivalry among the different peoples within its boundaries, the Gold Coast, soon to be known as Ghana, was more stable than many other African countries.

The leader of the Gold Coast's independence movement was Kwame Nkrumah (nn-KROO-mah). Nkrumah had worked his way through college in the United States, where he was influenced by the ideas of Marcus Garvey. In 1947 he founded the Convention People's Party in Africa. The party's election victory in 1951 made him prime minister, though his government was still under the authority of Britain.

On March 6, 1957, the Gold Coast gained full independence, and Nkrumah renamed the country Ghana in memory of the earlier empire (page 297). Over the next few years, the other British colonies in West Africa became independent—Nigeria in 1960, Sierra Leone in 1961, and Gambia in 1965.

French colonies. Britain's decision to grant independence to Ghana put pressure on France to do something about its own

West African colonies. France's president, Charles de Gaulle, gave the French colonies a choice: they could have partial independence as members of a new French Community, or they could choose complete independence and lose French aid. Only Guinea (GHIN-ee), under the leadership of Sékou Touré (SAY-koo too-RAY), chose independence in 1958. The following year, however, the constitution of the Community was changed to allow the French colonies to achieve full independence without losing aid. French West Africa was divided into seven independent nations.

Sec. Rev. ques. 3

From West Africa the call for independence spread into central and eastern Africa. France's other colonies in Africa south of the Sahara became independent as separate states in 1960. Only the small territory of French Somaliland chose to remain under French rule. In 1977 it became independent as Djibouti.

The Belgian Congo. The huge Belgian Congo gained independence in 1960. However, Belgian colonial policies had left the Congo unprepared for independence. The Belgian government had followed a paternalistic policy for many years (page 604). Congo Africans had never received advanced education or held high government posts.

Sec. Rev. ques. 4

In the late 1950's, when the French moved to grant independence to their colonies, riots broke out in the Belgian Congo. The Congolese protested unemployment and the lack of political rights. As violence grew and white settlers fled, the Belgian government decided to give the colony its independence in June 1960. The move to independence was marred by a mutiny in the army and an attempt by the mineral-rich Katanga province to secede.

Faced with civil war, Patrice Lumumba (loo-MOOM-bah), prime minister of the new Congo government, asked the United Nations and then the Soviet Union for help. Alarmed at this move, President Joseph Kasavubu fired Lumumba. UN troops moved into Katanga, and several years of unrest followed.

In 1965 the army, led by Joseph Mobutu, took control of the government. Under a new constitution, Mobutu gained great power as president. The new government restored African names for towns, mountains, and rivers, did away with Western personal names, and changed the name of the country to Zaire (zah-EER).

Kenya. The struggle for independence was also violent in Kenya, an important British colony in eastern Africa. There the white settlers, who formed less than one percent of the population, enjoyed a very privileged position. Not only did they have great influence in the colonial government, but they also owned vast tracts of land in the fertile highlands around Mount Kenya.

Sec. Rev. ques. 5

The earliest African opposition leaders were Kikuyu (kee-KOO-yoo), the largest ethnic group in Kenya, who also lived near Mount Kenya. In 1947 Jomo Kenyatta, a Kikuyu, became leader of a large nationalist organization. Like many other black leaders in Africa, Kenyatta had been educated abroad. An author and a gifted speaker, he became very popular among black Kenyans. However, the white settlers refused to listen to Kenyatta's call for reform, and the chance for peaceful change in Kenya was lost.

The land claims of the settlers caused a severe land shortage in the Mt. Kenya region, deepening the poverty of many Kikuyu. In 1951 some Kikuyu formed a secret guerrilla movement, known as **Mau Mau**, which began attacking white-owned plantations. They also

Linking Past and Present

Like the Gold Coast, many other newly independent African nations took names that were important in African history. For example, in 1960 French Sudan renamed itself Mali, after an ancient African kingdom (page 298). Southern Rhodesia chose the name Zimbabwe, for the great Bantu cultural center of the tenth century (page 301).

779

Background Sékou Touré said, "We prefer poverty in freedom to riches in slavery." Although Touré declared Guinea a neutral nation, his close cooperation with Eastern bloc countries angered many Western nations.
Geography Katanga province is one of the richest mining regions in all of Africa. Covering an area of over 191,000 square miles, it has deposits of gold, copper, cobalt, silver, coal, manganese, and tin.

Vocabulary Note that the word *Zaire* means "river."
Check for Understanding. Ask: How did actions of white settlers deepen the poverty of the Kikuyu? (They appropriated land in the Mount Kenya region, causing a severe land shortage.)

Biography

Jomo Kenyatta

On a fall day in 1952, Kenya's government police arrested Jomo Kenyatta and charged him with being a terrorist. Kenyatta was an African nationalist leader who demanded independence for Kenya, then a British colony. Though he strongly denied being a terrorist, he was tried and sentenced to seven years in prison.

Kenyatta was born about 1894, the son of a Kikuyu farmer. He had several names during his lifetime. His childhood name was Kamau wa Ngengi. As a young man, he added the name *Kenyatta,* a Kikuyu term for the fancy beaded belt he wore. In 1938, when he was leading the struggle to win greater rights for Africans, he took the new first name *Jomo,* which means "burning spear."

Kenyatta remained in prison and then under house arrest from 1952 until 1961. Meanwhile, in 1960, Kenyans won the right to vote and promptly chose Kenyatta to be their president. When he was finally released in 1961, he negotiated with Britain to make Kenya fully independent. Kenya celebrated its independence on December 12, 1963.

Kenyatta's goal was to create a peaceful, prosperous, united country. He said:

> Where there has been racial hatred, it must be ended. Where there has been tribal animosity, it will be finished. Let us not dwell upon the bitterness of the past. I would rather look to the future, to the good new Kenya, not to the bad old days.

Kenyatta remained president of Kenya until his death in 1978. All across Africa, flags were lowered in his honor. Kenyans gave him yet another name—*Mzee,* "the father of his people."

---

forced other Kikuyu to join the movement.

The British government cracked down on the Mau Mau movement. British officials declared a state of emergency and suspended many political rights. The government accused Kenyatta of leading the movement and imprisoned him, along with thousands of other Africans. Using arms and troops brought in from overseas, the British destroyed the last of the guerrilla bands in 1956. During the conflict fewer than 100 settlers were killed, but well over 10,000 Africans lost their lives.

Meanwhile, independence in the rest of British East Africa was moving forward. Tanganyika became independent under Julius Nyerere (ny-uh-RAY-ray) in 1961 and Uganda in 1962.* Continuing Kenyan demands for independence made it clear that the settlers could no longer stand in the way of majority rule. Kenya became independent in 1963; Jomo Kenyatta served as president until his death in 1978.

See Sec. 1 *Closing the Lesson,* p. T775B.

● See below.

* In 1964 Tanganyika merged with Zanzibar to become Tanzania.

● REINFORCEMENT. Have students identify factors that contributed to or worked against a smooth transition to independence in African nations. (Factors contributing to smooth transition: some previous self-rule; healthy economy; strong educational system; little internal rivalry. Against: paternalistic colonial policies; lack of advanced education; internal conflict.) (Comprehension) *Observing for Detail*

● ENRICHMENT. Have students work in groups to explain possible advantages and disadvantages resulting from so many African nations gaining independence in a ten-year time span. Students should identify possible benefits and problems for African nations. (Synthesis) *Making Inferences*

Ⓕ FEATURE ACTIVITY. Ask: What was the significance of Kenyatta's name changes? (Kenyatta's names reflected his identification with elements of traditional Africa.) (Synthesis) *Drawing Conclusions*

1. **Identify:** Pan-Africanist, African National Congress, Mau Mau. (pp. 777, 779)
2. What effect did the Second World War have on the African struggle for independence? (p. 778)
3. What choice did France initially give its African colonies? What did the colonies decide? (p. 779)
4. Why was the Belgian Congo unprepared for independence? (p. 779)
5. What were the main events in Kenya's struggle for independence? (pp. 779–780)
6. **Critical thinking:** Why did the newly independent government of the Congo replace Western names with African ones? (See answer below.)

2 White Rule in Southern Africa

Objectives

Focus Questions

★ ■ How did racist policies affect the peoples of South Africa? *(pages 781–782)*
● ■ How did the peoples of southern Africa seek majority rule? *(pages 782–784)*
▲ ■ What events spurred the growth of the South African protest movement? *(pages 784–786)*

Terms to Know

apartheid
pass laws
divest

★ Note strategies for first objective on this page and p. 782.

White settlers in the Belgian Congo and Kenya had tried and failed to prevent independence. Settlers in southern Africa were more successful in holding off African equality. In fact, in one part of southern Africa the struggle to eliminate discrimination is still going on.

South African Inequality

South Africa had become a Dominion in 1910 (page 600), and it remained a nation ruled by people of European descent. In 1960 about 19 percent of the country's population was white, the highest in Africa. The white population was divided between Afrikaners, speaking Afrikaans (a language derived from Dutch), and English speakers. The majority of the South Africans—68 percent—were African. In South African terms the rest were classified by law as Asian and "Coloreds" (people of mixed ancestry).

The South African economy was the most developed in Africa, leading the world in gold and diamond production. During the 1900's, South African manufacturing developed as well. Large numbers of Africans and persons of mixed race worked in the mines and factories, often in dangerous conditions.

Apartheid laws. In the 1948 elections, whites voted to give control of the country to the National Party, which was dominated by Afrikaners. The new government quickly began a policy called **apartheid** (ah-PART-hayt), an Afrikaans word meaning segregation or "apart-ness." This policy was later renamed "separate development."

781

Apartheid laws restricted the rights of nonwhites and spelled out policies for segregation. Neither Africans nor persons of mixed race were allowed to live in white areas or even to enter these areas except as employees. To keep track of the movement of Africans, the government established a system of **pass laws**—laws keeping people from moving freely within a country. Africans had to carry passes that showed where they lived and worked and if their taxes were paid.

Rural Africans were forced to live on reservations called "homelands," which in fact were little more than rural slums. In order to survive, the Africans who lived there had to travel into "white" South Africa to work. In 1976 South Africa began declaring these "homelands" to be independent African nations, but other countries continued to view them as part of South Africa.

Opposition to apartheid. During the 1950's, a coalition of African, Asian, and mixed-race groups held peaceful protests against segregation, the pass laws, and other apartheid policies. Some whites backed these protests. In 1955 a "Congress of the People," attended by some 3,000 South Africans of all colors, spoke out for nonracial democracy. The "Freedom Charter" approved at this meeting declared: "South Africa belongs to all who live in it, black and white. No government can justly claim authority unless it is based on the will of all the people."

The South African government used violence to repress the growing protest movement. In 1960 police in Sharpeville, a town near Johannesburg, fired on an unarmed crowd of Africans protesting the pass laws. Sixty-nine people were killed. The "Sharpeville Massacre" focused worldwide attention on South Africa's racist policies. When Africans, Coloreds, and Asians continued their peaceful protests in even greater numbers, the government declared a state of emergency and arrested thousands of the protest leaders. It also banned the African National Congress and the Pan-Africanist Congress, an extremist group founded in 1958.

Sec. Rev. ques. 2

No longer able to protest peacefully, the opposition movements turned to violence. With the help of police informers, however, the government destroyed these groups. In 1964, African protest leaders—including Nelson Mandela, head of the African National Congress—were convicted of planning to overthrow the government and were sentenced to life in prison. Mandela's wife, Winnie Mandela, remained free and became a leader in the protest movement.

★ See below, left.

This cartoon illustrates the explosive racial tensions in southern Africa in the 1970's. What is about to happen? Why? (A bomb is about to explode. Blacks are repressed; whites are ignoring the problem.)

from HERBLOCK ON ALL FRONTS (New American Library, 1980).

782　"WE'LL JUST SIT TIGHT"

Unrest in Southern Africa

● Note strategies for second objective on pp. 782–784.

White minority rule. After watching the South African government maintain white rule in the face of well-organized opposition, other white minorities in southern

---

Geography Most of the South African homelands are scattered areas of land that lack resources and are not suitable for farming.

★ **ENRICHMENT.** Have students work in groups to research anti-apartheid leaders in South Africa. Students might find information on leaders' backgrounds, policies and methods, and current situations. Have students present their findings in class. (Synthesis) *Locating Information*

Biography In 1991 Winnie Mandela was found guilty of kidnapping 4 youths and sentenced to six years in prison. She won a reprieve to allow her to appeal.

● **RETEACHING.** Have students make a timeline of events resulting in the independence of Southern Rhodesia. (Timeline should include information for the following dates: 1923, 1960, 1965, 1976, 1978, 1980.) (Comprehension) *Sequencing Events*

Africa began to believe that they could do the same. Some whites had settled in the British and Portuguese colonies in southern Africa before 1945, but their numbers increased after World War II. Yet whites remained a small minority in southern Africa. Outside South Africa, whites were less than five percent of the population of southern African states.

Southern Rhodesia. In 1923 Britain handed over the government of the colony of Southern Rhodesia to the white minority. Rhodesian whites were given half of the colony's farmland. Their farms had good roads and railroads, which African areas often lacked. Whites also got the best education and health care. In 1960 the white government proposed a new constitution, which would have guaranteed white control of Southern Rhodesia for another fifty years. African protests against the new constitution were soon banned by the government, and many African leaders were thrown in jail.

Zambia and Malawi. In neighboring Nyasaland and Northern Rhodesia, which were still under direct British control, Africans had greater political freedom. Black leaders there began to work for independence under majority rule. In 1963 Northern Rhodesia became independent, changing its name to Zambia. In 1964 Nyasaland gained independence, taking the name of Malawi.

Independence for Rhodesia. Great Britain refused to grant full independence to Southern Rhodesia unless its white-settler government agreed to majority rule. The white minority, led by Ian Smith, defiantly replied with a "unilateral declaration of independence" (UDI) in 1965. The constitution of this new government divided the country by race and provided for lasting white domination. South Africa was the only country to recognize the independence of Rhodesia.

The Portuguese colonies. Angola and Mozambique, the oldest colonies in Africa, were governed as overseas territories of Portugal. The Portuguese government claimed that it wanted colonists to be absorbed into Portuguese society and culture. Only 35,000 of the ten million Africans in the territories,

however, had become Portuguese citizens by 1960. Early in 1961, African uprisings broke out in Angola among workers in the towns and the countryside. The government and settlers struck back with violence that killed about 20,000 Africans. About 400,000 others fled for their lives.

Portugal's NATO allies gave it modern arms to fight the African rebels. The rebels were short of weapons, but they were helped by their newly independent African neighbors. By the late 1960's, guerrillas were active inside Angola and Mozambique, as well as in Portugal's West African colony of Guinea.

The wars with colonial rebels were a severe strain on Portugal's economy and population. Many Portuguese soldiers wondered why they were sacrificing so much to keep the colonies when they had so few political rights at home. In 1974 military leaders overthrew Portugal's longtime dictatorship. The new government decided to grant independence to all its African colonies.

Sec. Rev. ques. 3

The guerrilla movement known as FRELIMO (the Front for the Liberation of Mozambique) became the new government of Mozambique in June 1975. In Angola three guerrilla groups fought for control before independence day in November 1975. The Soviet Union and the United States aided different sides in the Angolan struggle. When South African troops invaded Angola in support of an American-backed group called UNITA (Union for the Total Independence of Angola), they were driven back by newly arrived Cuban troops. The Cubans and the Soviets backed the Movement for the Popular Liberation of Angola (MPLA). The MPLA was recognized by most of the world as the true government of Angola, although the United States continued to back UNITA.

In both Angola and Mozambique the new governments made reforms, ending forced labor and improving education and health care. They offered citizenship to all, but most Portuguese settlers chose to leave. The loss of skilled workers slowed efforts by both nations to modernize their economies. Angola was better off than Mozambique be-

783

- REINFORCEMENT. Have students make a chart identifying important events in the struggle for independence in the following countries: Southern Rhodesia, Zambia, Malawi, Angola, Mozambique. *(Comprehension)* *Synthesizing Information*

Social History Note that Angola is named for an early king named N'gola.
Check for Understanding. Ask: Why did many Portuguese soldiers question their country's colonial wars? (They wondered why they were sacrificing so much to keep their colonies when they had so few political rights at home.)
- ENRICHMENT. Have students find current information on the status of UNITA, the anti-government faction in Angola. *(Application)* *Locating Information*

cause it had extensive oil reserves under development by Western oil companies.

In 1991 the closing of the cold war brought superpower rivalry in Angola to an end. Leaders of the government and of UNITA signed a peace treaty concluding their country's long civil war.

Zimbabwe. Portugal's withdrawal from Angola and Mozambique meant that the rebels opposed to the Rhodesian government now had bases from which they could attack Rhodesia. Convinced that the Smith government could not last, South Africa cut off military aid to Rhodesia in 1976. Both South Africa and the United States urged Ian Smith to accept majority rule. Under mounting pressure, Smith agreed. In 1978, the African guerrillas also agreed to compromise, guaranteeing the white population 20 percent of the seats in the new parliament.

In the 1980 elections, white voters gave all 20 seats to Smith's Rhodesian Front Party, but 63 percent of the African votes went to the ZANU (Zimbabwe African National Union) party. ZANU's leader, Robert Mugabe (moo-GAH-bee), became prime minister of the new nation of Zimbabwe.

Sec. Rev. ques. 4

Whites in Zimbabwe accepted Mugabe's government, reassured by his moderate policies and by the deal that had given them extra voting power. There was no white flight from Zimbabwe as there had been from the Portuguese colonies. In the 1980's Mugabe consolidated his power and by 1990 Zimbabwe was virtually a one-party state.

Namibia. For years South Africa had defied world opinion by supporting racial inequality in neighboring Namibia. The former German colony of South-West Africa, Namibia had been made a mandate of South Africa after World War I. Though it contained few people, Namibia had valuable minerals, grazing lands, and fishing. South Africa was supposed to rule the colony in the interest of its native population. Instead, South Africa extended its apartheid policies to Namibia after 1948. In 1966 the United Nations canceled South Africa's mandate over the territory and recognized the South-West African People's Organization, called SWAPO, as the

784

legitimate government of Namibia.

The South African government ignored the UN decision and sent in soldiers to destroy SWAPO bases. SWAPO guerrillas attacked targets in Namibia from bases in Angola, on Namibia's northern border. Talks on the future of Namibia led to an agreement in 1988, in which South Africa promised to give up control of Namibia. In 1990 Namibia became the youngest independent nation on the African continent.

Changes in South Africa

▲ Note strategies for third objective on pp. 785–786.

South Africa's isolation. During the 1950's newly independent Asian and African nations began to condemn South Africa's racial policies. This criticism caused South Africa to withdraw from the British Commonwealth in 1961, declaring itself a republic. Over the next two decades, South African athletes were excluded from many sporting events, including the Olympics. The United Nations condemned apartheid and imposed an arms embargo on South Africa. In Western countries some churches, colleges, and unions began to **divest**—sell off—the stock they held in companies that did business in South Africa.

The collapse of white rule in the Portuguese colonies and in Zimbabwe deeply affected South Africa. Leftist governments in the new nations gave aid and support to South African and Namibian blacks fighting white rule.

Heavy military spending made South Africa the dominant military force in southern Africa. South African leaders used this power not only to maintain a grip on Namibia but to launch raids on neighboring black-ruled countries, which they said were harboring guerrilla fighters. In addition, South Africa used its economic muscle to undercut the economies of its African neighbors—the "Frontline States," as Angola, Botswana, Mozambique, Tanzania, Zambia, and Zimbabwe were called. These states sought ways to lessen their economic dependence while continuing to support opponents of apartheid.

Politics Note that the policy of reserved seats for whites in the Zimbabwean parliament ended in 1987.

Politics Independent Namibia's first president was Sam Nujoma. One of the founders of SWAPO, Nujoma spent 30 years in exile during the struggle for independence.

Continuing protests. Encouraged by black victories elsewhere, opponents of white rule within South Africa stepped up their activities. The South African government used a variety of tactics—from concessions to undercover agents and brute force—to silence the protesters. But these tactics were met with mass demonstrations, boycotts, and labor strikes. Anger ran high in black areas, especially among the young.

In 1976 riots broke out during a student protest march in Soweto (soh-WAY-toh), a black township outside Johannesburg. In the police crackdown that followed, more than 700 blacks were killed, and more than 5,000 were injured. These protests were in part the result of work by a young African named Steven Biko (BEE-koh). Biko promoted a "Black Consciousness" movement much like the "black power" movement in the United States (page 806). During the government crackdown on student protests, Biko was arrested. In 1977 he died after being severely beaten by police.

Limited reforms. During the 1980's South Africa's isolation grew deeper. Growing public sentiment in many Western countries caused governments to limit their investments and trade with the last of Africa's white-ruled nations. Foreign banks and corporations, under pressure from stockholders and fearful of future instability, pulled out of South Africa. Religious leaders in many nations spoke out against apartheid. In 1984, Anglican Archbishop Desmond Tutu, a black South African, received the Nobel Peace Prize for his efforts to bring about peaceful change.

In response to internal and external pressures, the South African government modified apartheid laws during the early 1980's. African labor unions were legalized, the hated pass laws were abolished, and segregation was ended in many public places. Nevertheless, the races continued to live apart, and blacks continued to be excluded from political life. The constitution of 1984 gave representation to Coloreds and Asians but not to the black majority.

In the fall of 1984, violence resumed. Street fighting between police and protesters left hundreds of blacks dead. In the townships, radicals hunted down and killed other blacks who they claimed had helped the government. South African President P. W. Botha (BOH-tah) responded by declaring a new state of emergency in July 1985. The police were given broad powers to jail protesters without trial, ban meetings, censor news, and set curfews.

Raised hopes. A new era for South Africa opened in 1989, when President Botha was forced out of office by another member of the National Party, F. W. de Klerk. De Klerk was committed to the abolition of apartheid. Under his leadership, the South African government repealed the law that required segregation in public places and the National Party opened its membership to blacks.

Perhaps most important, de Klerk opened a new era in relations between the government and black leaders. To defuse some of the tension between South Africa and its neighbors, de Klerk made good-will visits to black African nations. Within his own country, he legalized the banned African National Congress and other opposition groups, lifted the state of emergency, and freed political prisoners. Most symbolic of de Klerk's turn-around of government policy was the South African Parliament's abolition of the law that required all people to be classified by race (page 781).

Sec. Rev. ques. 5

One of the freed political prisoners was Nelson Mandela (page 782). Mandela and de Klerk began a series of meetings aimed at charting a course for the dismantling of apartheid and planning a new constitution. Mandela announced that the ANC was suspending its long "armed struggle" against the South African government. In return, the government promised to repeal security laws and allowed exiled black leaders to return to South Africa.

Obstacles. While de Klerk's policies offered hope, obstacles to a resolution of South Africa's conflicts remained. One problem was disagreement over the form of government South Africa should adopt. In general, the white minority supported a form

785

▲ RETEACHING. Have students explain the role played by each of the following in South Africa: Steven Biko; Desmond Tutu; Nelson Mandela; P. W. Botha; F. W. de Klerk. (Comprehension) *Observing for Detail*

▲ REINFORCEMENT. Have students identify the ways in which international pressure was brought on South Africa in the 1980's. (Condemnation of apartheid from other nations and from UN; South African athletes barred from Olympics; UN arms embargo; divestment policies and limitations on trade and investment.) (Comprehension) *Observing for Detail*

Nelson Mandela, seen here with President F. W. de Klerk of South Africa, re-entered the drive to end apartheid after his release from prison.

of power-sharing similar to that negotiated by Rhodesian whites (page 784). Black South Africans, who make up two thirds of the population, wanted simple majority rule.

Another problem was violence among rival black groups. In the province of Natal, heavy fighting had broken out in 1988 between supporters of the ANC and supporters of the conservative Inkatha movement, led by Zulu chief Mangosuthu Buthelezi (boo-tuh-LAY-zee). In 1990 this violence spread to the townships around Johannesburg, where the conflict was not only political but ethnic. Members of Nelson Mandela's Xhosa tribe tended to be ANC supporters, while ethnic Zulus supported Inkatha. Many hundreds of people were killed in savage fighting. While Mandela and Buthelezi reached agreement on a plan to stop the bloodshed, it proved impossible to enforce.

Violence in the townships strained relations between de Klerk and Mandela. The ANC charged that security forces favored Inkatha and had even encouraged that movement's violence. Newspaper disclosures eventually forced de Klerk to admit that secret government funds had indeed been channeled to Inkatha.

Meanwhile, both de Klerk and Mandela faced strong opposition from hard-liners in their own parties. White racist groups vowed to fight reforms. Radical blacks found the

pace of change too slow. Extremists on both sides continued to carry out terrorist acts. Despite such obstacles, a significant step was taken in late 1991 when black and white political leaders met near Johannesburg. At this Convention for a Democratic South Africa, called Codesa for short, representatives of nineteen political parties took the first steps toward drawing up a nonracial constitution for their country.

See Sec. 2 *Closing the Lesson*, p. T775B.

Section Review

Answers to questions are in brackets on pages indicated.

1. **Define:** apartheid, pass laws, divest. (pp. 781, 782, 784)
2. What was the Sharpeville Massacre? How did the South African government respond to protests that followed? (p. 782)
3. How did Portugal's African colonies win independence? (pp. 783-784)
4. What changes came to Zimbabwe and Namibia in the 1980's? (p. 784)
5. What changes have come about in South Africa since 1989? (pp. 784-786)
6. Why has resistance to majority rule lasted much longer in South Africa than it did in, for example, the former Portuguese colonies? (See answer below.)

Sec Rev. ques. 5 (cont.)

786

▲ ENRICHMENT. Have students work in groups to make predictions for South Africa. Students should describe events that might occur, identify a time frame for their occurrence, and predict what South Africa's situation in 20 years might be. *(Synthesis) Predicting Events*

6. Students might suggest that South Africa's government represents the white minority who actually live there, while Portugal ruled its colonies from Europe.

3 Challenges Facing Africa

Objectives

Focus Questions

★ ■ What problems did the newly independent African nations face? *(pages 787–788)*

● ■ What changes occurred in African society? *(pages 788–790)*

▲ ■ What role did outside powers play in Africa? *(page 790)*

Terms to Know

Nigerian Civil War
Organization of
   African Unity

★ Note strategies for first objective on this page and p. 788.

After they had won independence, the new nations of Africa had much to do. Africans had high hopes for progress, but change often came more slowly than expected. They also wanted to be nonaligned, yet many formed ties with the superpowers. For many African countries, the early years of independence were turbulent.

Political Instability

Cultural differences. Rivalry among the various African peoples was a source of disunity in some new nations. The boundaries of the new nations, based on old colonial boundaries, often brought together peoples that spoke different languages and followed different customs. For most Africans, ethnic loyalty was stronger than national loyalty. Sometimes bitter rivalries sprang up between ethnic groups.

The Nigerian Civil War of 1967–1970 showed how religious, ethnic, and other cul-

tural differences could lead to tragic conflict. Like many other African countries, Nigeria had boundaries that dated from the colonial period. The northern half of the country, dominated by the Hausa people, was largely Muslim. As a result of missionary work, the southern half of Nigeria was heavily Christian, and its people were better educated than the northerners. Nigerian leaders had to balance northern and southern interests. They also had to deal with an intense rivalry between the Yoruba people in the southwest and the Ibo of the southeast.

Sec. Rev. ques. 2

Hoping to end political conflict and corruption, a group of Nigerian military officers seized control of the government in January 1966. Most of these officers belonged to the Ibo. When word got out that Yoruba and nothern leaders had been killed, many people decided that it was an Ibo grab for power.

In July a second army revolt placed a northerner at the head of Nigeria's government. In September and October, Muslim mobs in northern cities killed some 20,000 Ibo and other southerners, causing thousands more to flee to their homes in the southeast. Unable to get help from the military government, in May 1967 the Ibo proclaimed the independence of southeastern Nigeria as the Republic of Biafra. This act set off a civil war. By 1970 Biafra had been defeated, but not before many civilians had died from the fighting and from famine.

Since the civil war Nigerian governments have precariously maintained peace by building a tradition of sharing power among the nation's ethnic groups.

The challenge of leadership. Another cause of instability was the inexperience of many African leaders. The colonial period had given few Africans the chance to learn how to run their own governments. Nationalist leaders were good at whipping up popular support, but many turned out to be less skilled at managing their nations. Once in

787

★ RETEACHING. Have students work in groups to identify and suggest solutions for problems faced by the newly independent African nations. (Problems included cultural differences that led to bitter rivalries and inexperienced leaders who suppressed opposition and permitted corruption.) *(Synthesis)* **Solving Problems**

★ REINFORCEMENT. Have students write an essay explaining how colonial rule contributed to the problems faced by newly independent African nations. (The boundaries of the new nations, based on colonial boundaries, often brought together people of different cultures. Ethnic loyalties sometimes caused rivalry. Colonial rule had given few Africans the chance to learn how to rule.) *(Comprehension)* **Understanding Cause and Effect** office, some refused to allow any opposition. Corruption, too, became a problem. Some officials took advantage of their position to build up personal fortunes.

Other African leaders, however, succeeded in changing their independence movements into national governments. Among the leaders who used their experience to build strong governments were Jomo Kenyatta of Kenya, Félix Houphouët-Boigny (oo-FWAY-bwahn-NYEE) of the Ivory Coast, and Julius Nyerere of Tanzania.

Demands for democracy. Still another problem was the tendency toward establishing one-party systems in the African states. Some national leaders tried to stifle opposition parties, claiming that a multiparty system encouraged ethnic conflict. In recent years, protests against one party-rule have surfaced throughout Africa. In at least 14 countries, African leaders have been forced to give opposition groups legal status. The push for democracy has brought new leadership to a number of countries.

African Society

● Note strategies for second objective on this page and p. 789.

Economic development. The new African nations developed their natural resources to build prosperity. Zambia and Zaire expanded mining operations. Nigeria, Angola, and other Atlantic coast nations developed thriving oil industries. Many countries built factories to process their farm products.

Prosperity was elusive, however, and ambitious development programs often led to setbacks rather than betterment. A major problem was paying for the new industrial projects. To secure the funds, many African states borrowed heavily. By the end of the

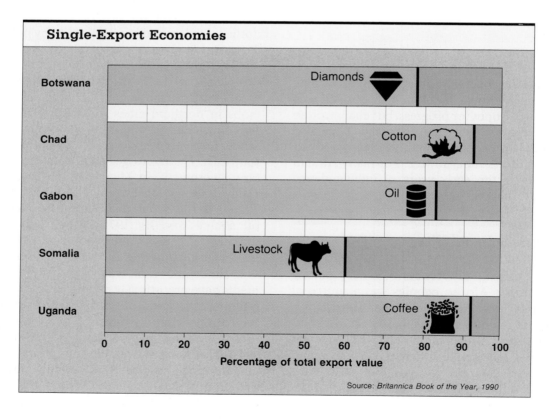

Single-Export Economies

Botswana — Diamonds

Chad — Cotton

Gabon — Oil

Somalia — Livestock

Uganda — Coffee

Percentage of total export value
0 10 20 30 40 50 60 70 80 90 100

Source: *Britannica Book of the Year, 1990*

Many African countries depend on one export for a majority of their income from trade. Which countries show the greatest dependency on one product? What might be the drawbacks to this type of economy? (See answers below.)

788

Graph Answers: (1) Chad and Uganda. (2) Any factor that causes a decrease in revenue for that product can have disastrous effects. Factors might include a drop in demand, a drop in supply, or a low world price for the product.

★ ENRICHMENT. Have students research the Nigerian Civil War or recent democracy movements in African countries. *(Application)* *Locating Information*

● RETEACHING. Have students review "African Society" (pp. 788–790) and identify economic and social changes made in African society. (Economic: developed natural resources; built factories; tried to increase food production with better seed, improved livestock, irrigation, fertilizer. Social: built schools; improved public health by building clinics, hospitals.) *(Comprehension)* Observing for Detail

Economics Inadequate development of food crops was also a legacy from the colonial period, when much land was used only for export crops.

1980's, African nations owed over 200 billion dollars to Western governments and international organizations. In many of Africa's debtor countries, huge interest payments made it impossible for governments to improve education, create jobs and train people for them, and establish basic health facilities. Severe poverty resulted.

Sec. Rev. ques. 3

Food shortages. The drive to industrialize often caused young African nations to neglect agriculture. Moreover, to pay back the funds they had borrowed to build factories, most had to depend on income from agricultural exports. This prompted them to grow export crops—peanuts in Senegal, for example—at the expense of food crops for domestic use. At the same time, the population was growing rapidly: from 200 million in 1950 to about 670 million in 1990. By the 1980's most countries south of the Sahara were unable to produce enough food to meet their needs.

Nature, too, was unkind. In the 1970's and twice in the 1980's, severe droughts struck much of the continent. Tens of millions of people faced starvation. Western countries sent huge shipments of food and medical supplies. Relief groups set up emergency camps where food was handed out to starving refugees. Despite these efforts, many thousands, especially in Ethiopia and Mozambique, died of starvation. In 1990 the UN Food and Agricultural Organization warned that continuing drought and crop failures indicated a worsening food shortage in many parts of Africa.

To lower the risk of future food shortages, African nations tried to increase food production. Farmers were promised higher market prices. They were taught to use better seeds and improved kinds of livestock. Irrigation and fertilizer made land more productive. Yet by spending more money on food production, these nations left themselves with less capital for industry.

Education. In spite of economic problems, the new African nations struggled to build more schools. It was often hard to find enough trained teachers in the years just after independence, but school enrollment

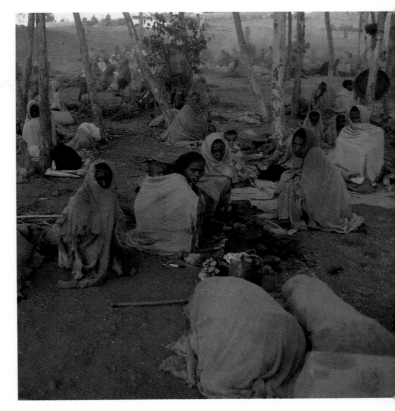

Ethiopian famine victims huddle on the parched earth of a refugee camp. Drought and warfare have caused millions in eastern Africa to flee their homes. The spreading desert continues to threaten many Africans with starvation.

steadily rose. Nigeria used its oil profits to provide primary education for all children and to build a dozen new universities. Tanzania, one of the poorest countries on the continent, raised its literacy rate from 31 percent in 1961 to 85 percent in 1990—one of Africa's highest rates.

Health. Improving public health was also a priority in Africa. Despite a severe shortage of doctors, more and more clinics and hospitals were built. Health workers tried to prevent the spread of disease, which had run unchecked in many parts of Africa. A UN-funded program for smallpox vaccination eliminated the world's last cases of that disease in Ethiopia and Somalia in 1978. During the first two years of its independence, Mozambique's new government pro-

Sec. Rev. ques. 4

● REINFORCEMENT. Have students describe problems that resulted from efforts to industrialize Africa. (The drive to industrialize resulted in the neglect of agriculture and in food shortages; to pay back funds borrowed to build factories, some nations developed export crops at the expense of food crops.) (Comprehension) **Identifying Cause and Effect**

● ENRICHMENT. Have students prepare a table of statistics on industrial production, agricultural output, and population levels for each of the African nations discussed in this section. Students might refer to Facts on File, The Atlas of African Affairs, current almanacs, or periodicals. (Application) **Locating Information**

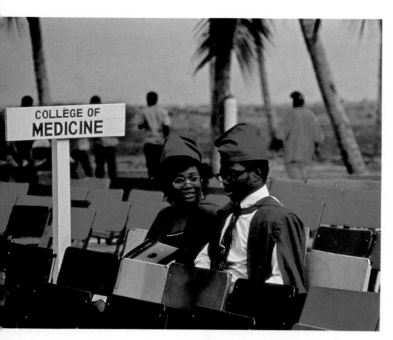

Education was one of the many challenges facing African nations after gaining independence. Few schools or universities had existed in colonial times. These medical school graduates studied for their degrees at the University of Lagos in Nigeria.

tected 4 million of its people against common diseases. However, diseases such as malaria, leprosy, sleeping sickness, tuberculosis, and AIDS (page 820) are serious problems.

Africa and the World

▲ Note strategies for third objective on this page.

International cooperation. The new African nations, remembering their Pan-Africanist roots, tried to work together. Most African states joined an international body called the Organization of African Unity (OAU), established in 1963. Members of the OAU promised to settle their disputes peacefully. They set up commissions to deal with social, economic, and health issues that concern all of Africa.

Another multi-nation organization in Africa is the Economic Community of West African States. In 1990 the sixteen nation-members of this organization sent a peace-

790

keeping force to Liberia to try to end a civil war in that country.

Africa's markets and resources continued to interest business leaders in the West. The involvement of large international corporations in some parts of Africa has been called neocolonialism (page 465) because the profits of African labor have flowed out of the continent and into Europe and America.

Superpower involvement. Africa's resources and strategic location attracted foreign governments as well as companies. One area of tension was the "horn" of Africa—Ethiopia, Djibouti, and Somalia—which commands the important sea route from the Mediterranean Sea through the Suez Canal and the Red Sea to the Indian Ocean. The United States began by setting up a military base in Ethiopia to watch these routes. In return it provided Ethiopia with military aid. *Sec. Rev. ques. 5* The American arms strengthened Ethiopia in a long-standing land dispute with Somalia, and Somalia responded by turning to the Soviet Union for aid. After the American-supported dictatorship of Emperor Haile Selassie (page 685) was overthrown in 1974, Ethiopia's new Marxist leaders moved closer to the Soviet Union. Somalia then switched to the United States for aid.

Another area with heavy outside involvement was southern Africa. The Soviet Union, China, the United States, and other Eastern and Western countries gave military aid to the southern African liberation movements in their struggle for majority rule. After Angola became independent, the Soviet Union supported the Angolan government with Cuban troops, while the United States helped South Africa arm the UNITA rebels fighting the Angolan government.

The startling changes in superpower *Sec. Rev. ques. 6* relations in recent years, however, have affected Africa. The Soviet Union, undergoing internal crises, stopped aiding Ethiopia's Marxist government and in 1991 that government collapsed. Moreover, Angola's civil war ended as U.S.-Soviet rivalry ceased to be a factor. Thus, with the close of the cold war, Africa no longer is seen as an arena for international rivalry. ▲ See below.

See Sec. 3 *Closing the Lesson*, p. T775C.

▲ RETEACHING. Have students make a chart of African countries in which foreign influence has been important, indicating foreign powers and nature of influence. (Charts should include information on Ethiopia, Somalia, Namibia, and Angola.) (Comprehension) *Synthesizing Information*

▲ REINFORCEMENT. Have students work in groups to suggest ways that international associations like the OAU might help to solve African problems. (Synthesis) *Solving Problems*

▲ ENRICHMENT. Have students present a panel discussion on the following: What role should nations of other parts of the world play in Africa today? What role should they *not* play? Students may support their conclusions by citing the effects of superpower influence during the cold-war era and citing useful kinds of foreign involvement. (Synthesis) *Evaluating Information*

Section Review

Answers to Section Review questions are in brackets on pages indicated.

1. **Identify:** Nigerian Civil War, Organization of African Unity. (pp. 787, 790)
2. What triggered the clash between ethnic and regional groups in Nigeria in 1966? (p. 787)
3. How did the drive for industrialization affect African agriculture? (p. 788)
4. What were some of the goals of the newly independent African nations? (pp. 789, 790)
5. Why did the United States and the Soviet Union consider the "horn" of Africa a strategic location? (p. 790)
6. How was Angola involved in the cold war? (p. 790)
7. **Critical thinking:** Why might some African leaders have found it harder to govern a nation than to lead an independence movement? (See answer below.)

7. Students might suggest that governing a nation required a broader knowledge of government and politics than did the leading of independence movements.

Chapter 38   Summary and Timeline

1. The African nationalist movements after 1945 were part of a global struggle for black equality. Independence came first in Ghana in 1957. The rest of British and French West Africa followed by 1960, along with the Belgian Congo, later known as Zaire. After a period of violence, Kenya gained independence from Britain in 1963.

2. In postwar southern Africa, settlers defending white rule faced rising opposition. Black protest movements grew larger in South Africa after 1950 in response to racist apartheid laws. Many leaders were jailed by the South African government. The whites in Southern Rhodesia declared their independence from Britain in 1965 in an effort to preserve white rule. However, they accepted majority rule in 1980. Armed nationalist movements in Angola and Mozambique forced Portugal to grant these areas independence in 1974. Shaken by growing protests, South Africa in 1990 finally took steps toward dismantling its apartheid system.

3. The nations of Africa faced serious difficulties in their efforts to build national unity. One-party rule became the pattern. Education and health care expanded and industrialization was pushed, but much money had to be spent on food programs. During the cold-war era outside powers played an active role in African politics, but more recent events have ended superpower rivalry on that continent.

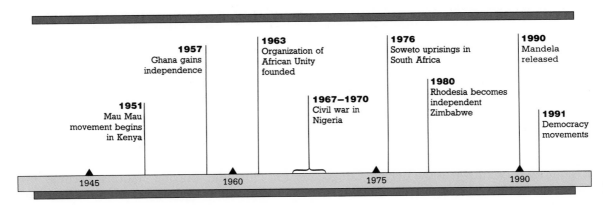

1951 Mau Mau movement begins in Kenya

1957 Ghana gains independence

1963 Organization of African Unity founded

1967–1970 Civil war in Nigeria

1976 Soweto uprisings in South Africa

1980 Rhodesia becomes independent Zimbabwe

1990 Mandela released

1991 Democracy movements

1945   1960   1975   1990

CHAPTER 38 REVIEW

See p. T775C for answers to Chapter Review.

Vocabulary Review

Define or identify the terms in each pair.
1. Pan-Africanist; Organization of African Unity
2. African National Congress; Mau Mau
3. pass laws; divest

People to Identify

1. Choose the name that best completes each sentence.
   a. Archbishop [P. W. Botha/Desmond Tutu] received the Nobel Peace Prize for his efforts to bring about peaceful change in South Africa.
   b. [Jomo Kenyatta/Félix Houphouët-Boigny] became Kenya's president.
   c. [W.E.B. Du Bois/Sékou Touré] was an American professor, writer, and Pan-Africanist leader.
2. Identify the following people.
   a. Steven Biko
   b. F. W. de Klerk
   c. Patrice Lumumba
   d. Nelson Mandela
   e. Robert Mugabe
   f. Kwame Nkrumah

Places to Know

Match each of the following places with the correct description: *Angola, Ghana, Malawi, Mozambique, Soweto, Tanzania, Zaire, Zambia.*
1. country once known as the Gold Coast
2. country once known as the Belgian Congo
3. Former British colony that was known as Northern Rhodesia
4. former Portuguese colony that UNITA and the MPLA sought to control
5. former Portuguese colony that was governed by FRELIMO after independence
6. country formed when Tanganyika merged with Zanzibar
7. country once known as Nyasaland
8. township of Johannesburg

Recalling the Facts

1. What enabled the Gold Coast to make a smooth transition to independence?
2. What choices did de Gaulle initially offer France's African colonies seeking independence? What change was made in this policy?
3. What made the transition to independence difficult for the Belgian Congo?
4. How did white settlement in Kenya affect the Kikuyu?
5. What restrictions were placed on Africans and people of mixed race by South Africa's apartheid policy?
6. Why did Portugal grant independence to its African colonies?
7. What events led Ian Smith's government to agree to majority rule in Rhodesia?
8. How did the South African government react to the 1980's protest movements?
9. Why was South Africa involved in conflict in Namibia?
10. What events triggered the Nigerian Civil War?
11. What factors caused food shortages in many new African nations?
12. Why has some foreign involvement in Africa been considered neocolonialism?
13. How did outside nations become involved in tensions on the horn of Africa?

Critical Thinking Skills

1. **Researching words.** Leopold Sédar Senghor, a poet and statesman from Senegal, referred to African cultural pride as *negritude. Negritude* comes from the French word meaning "blackness." The suffix *-tude* comes from the Latin *-tudo,* "a condition or state of being." Use a dictionary to find the meaning of each of the following words: *exactitude, fortitude, gratitude, magnitude, solitude.*   (App.)

2. **Hypothesizing.** If African countries were to unite, what do you think would be their prospects for dealing with some of the problems they face?   (Syn.)

3. **Using a graph.** "Life expectancy" is the average number of years newborn babies can expect to live if health conditions stay the same. Use the graph below to answer the following questions: What was the life expectancy in Zimbabwe in the late 1980's? What was the life expectancy in China? What country had the lowest life expectancy? What country had the highest life expectancy?   (Comp.)

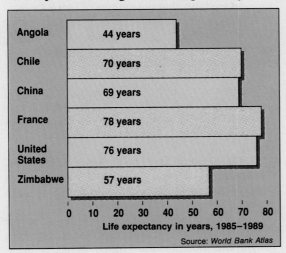

Country	Life expectancy
Angola	44 years
Chile	70 years
China	69 years
France	78 years
United States	76 years
Zimbabwe	57 years

0 10 20 30 40 50 60 70 80
Life expectancy in years, 1985–1989
Source: *World Bank Atlas*

4. **Inferring.** Why might other countries have refused to recognize the independence of the South African homelands?   (Comp.)

Thinking About Geography

Comparing maps. Compare the map of colonial Africa on page 603 with the Atlas map of present-day Africa at the back of the book. List the nations of modern Africa along with the names each one had as a colony.   (Comp.)

Enrichment: Primary Sources

A Nigerian journalist calls the move for democracy in Africa a "wind of change."

66 The . . . wind of change is not African but is blowing from Eastern Europe. . . . With it has come the demand for major political reforms: for multiparty democracy where once one-party rule was dishonestly touted as the indigenous African form of political administration and for elections where, only a short time ago, none dared question the right to the perpetual rule of one man. Democracy is the buzzword. We hear it shouted from the rooftops in Togo, Benin, Ethiopia, Zaire, Ivory Coast, and Algeria.

There is reason to be happy at this turn of events. Yet what is new? We have come full circle, multiparty to one party to no party (the military), back to one party . . . and now back to multiparty.

We are, perhaps, being cynical— which comes naturally to Africans who have watched events before. Still, let us welcome the wind of change. . . . The trick is to keep hope burning, like a candle protected from the wind. 99

1. Why does the writer say the wind of change came from Eastern Europe?
2. What kind of government does he say was once called typically African? What is his opinion of that belief?
3. **Critical thinking:** Why is the writer cautious in his expectations for the democracy movement?   (Analysis)

793

A checkmark identifies questions and exercises calling for the three higher-order levels of thinking at the top of the Bloom taxonomy: Analysis, Synthesis, and Evaluation.

The Changing Americas   1945-Present
(pp. 794–815)

Chapter Preview

Section 1 examines the various paths to economic development taken by Latin American nations and then looks at the causes of conflict in Central America. Section 2 deals with the United States from the 1950's to the present and discusses major foreign and domestic issues of this period. In the final section, Canadian history since 1945 is examined.

Bibliography

See the *Teacher's Management and Planning Guide* for additional listings. Starred titles are for both students and teachers.

Diggins, John Patrick. *The Proud Decades: America in War and Peace, 1941–1960.* Norton. The United States emerges as a superpower.

Garrow, David J. *Bearing the Cross: Martin Luther King, Jr. and the Southern Leadership Conference, 1955–1968.* Morrow. An account of King's role in the civil rights movement.

*Harrington, Michael. *The Other America.* Penguin. Problem of poverty in the midst of plenty.

Isaacson, Walter and Evan Thomas. *The Wise Men: Six Friends and the World They Made.* Simon and Schuster. The men who formed American foreign policy after World War II.

Lewis, A. *Portrait of a Decade: The Second American Revolution.* Random House. The civil rights movement.

Revkin, Andrew. *The Burning Season.* Houghton. The story of Chico Mendes, the Brazilian who was murdered for his efforts to save the Amazon rain forest.

Weintraub, Stanley. *A Marriage of Convenience: Relations Between Mexico and the United States.* Oxford University Press.

Section Lesson Plans

SECTION 1   (pp. 795–803)
Upheaval in Latin America

Objectives

After completing this section, students will be able to:
1. Describe how some Latin American nations have sought progress.
2. Identify conflicts that have caused hardship in Central America.
3. Identify challenges faced by Latin American nations.

Introducing the Lesson

Remind students that the nations of Latin America have faced political and economic problems since their independence. Social unrest, economic development, and political instability remain difficult issues in Latin America.

   Then ask: *(a) What in Latin America's history might account for the economic and political problems many nations in that region face today?* (Most of Latin America was colonized by European countries and greatly influenced by Europe.)

   (b) In what ways do foreign countries influence Latin America today? (Foreign nations influence political and economic issues in Latin America.)

   (c) What might account for foreign interest in Latin America? (Because of Latin America's geographic location, the United States is interested in maintaining good relations with the nations of that region. During the cold war the Soviet Union had close relations with Cuba and probably regarded the establishment of other Marxist governments in Latin America as an opportunity to extend its influence.)

Developing the Lesson:
Understanding Geography

Have students draw a map of Latin America and identify the type of political system in each nation. (Maps should include Mexico, Argentina, Chile, Puerto Rico, Cuba, Nicaragua, El Salvador, Guatemala, Panama, Honduras and Costa Rica.) *(Comprehension)*

Developing the Lesson:
Making Judgments

Have students work in groups to present a panel discussion on the following questions:

(a) *What national interests are most important to the United States in formulating its Latin American policies?*

(b) *How are those interests best served?*

(c) *What form of support should American aid to Latin America take—economic aid, military aid, moral support, or a combination of all three? (Evaluation)*

Closing the Lesson:
Drawing Conclusions

Have students work in groups to answer the following questions:

(a) *What might account for the political instability of many Latin American nations?* (Economic and social problems affect the political stability of Latin America.)

(b) *What are the similarities and differences between the nations of Latin America and other countries once colonized by European nations?* (Like other nations once under foreign control, Latin American countries have had difficulty making economic progress and have struggled with poverty and foreign debt. Latin American nations were also affected by the rivalry between the United States and the Soviet Union.) *(Synthesis)*

See *Section Review* questions, p. 803.

SECTION 2   (pp. 804–809)
Stability and Change in the United States

Objectives

After completing this section, students will be able to:
1. Describe what national issues faced Americans in the postwar years.
2. Identify issues that have dominated American foreign policy.

Introducing the Lesson

Remind students that after World War II, the United States emerged as the world's strongest economic and military power. Despite the many challenges of the cold-war era and more recent developments in international relations, the United States continues to have great influence in the world.

Then ask: (a) *What accounts for the growth of American power after World War II?* (Possession of atomic weapons gave the United States a military advantage over others. The United States was the only major Allied power whose territory had not been devastated by the war. A healthy economy, high living standard, and strong democratic institutions contributed to the United States' preeminent position.)

(b) *How has the United States influenced other nations since World War II?* (The United States played an instrumental role in the establishment of West Germany's and Japan's democratic systems. The strength of the American economy resulted in vast foreign investments. The United States supported many nations in their struggle against communism and led the multinational effort to halt Iraqi aggression in the Middle East.)

(c) *In what ways do you think the United States will continue to be a major influence in world affairs?* (Answers will vary.)

Developing the Lesson:
Evaluating Information

Have students identify and explain which events in domestic and foreign affairs have most influenced American society since World War II. Students might consider the following questions:

(a) *Which events evoked a significant response from American citizens?*

(b) *Which events produced the most change in American society?*

(c) *Which events still affect the values and concerns of American society?*

Have students share their conclusions with the class. *(Synthesis)*

Developing the Lesson:
Synthesizing Information

Have students work in groups to make a chart summarizing political, economic, and social developments in the United States during each decade since World War II. When developing their charts, students should assign to each decade a label that summarizes the general mood of the period. *(Comprehension)*

Closing the Lesson: Predicting Events

Have students work in groups to discuss the following questions:

(a) *What economic concerns face the United States in the future? How might they be resolved?*

(b) What important social concerns face the United States in the future? How might they be resolved?

(c) What issues in foreign affairs will be important in the future? How might they be resolved? (Synthesis)

See *Section Review* questions, p. 809.

SECTION 3   (pp. 810–813)
New Challenges for Canada

Objectives

After completing this section, students will be able to:
1. Discuss issues that have dominated postwar Canada.
2. Explain the role Canada has played in world affairs.

Introducing the Lesson

Remind students that Canada and the United States share the world's longest undefended border. Although the United States and Canada have not always agreed on political and economic issues, the relationship between these countries has been cordial and cooperative.

Then ask: *(a) What factors might contribute to friendly relations between Canada and the United States?* (Answers will vary. Their physical proximity makes cooperation important for the national security of both countries. The United States and Canada share common political and cultural values, which both countries inherited largely from Great Britain.)

(b) In what areas might Canada and the United States most benefit from cooperation? (Answers will vary, but cooperation in economic and defense areas might be especially advantageous for both countries.)

Developing the Lesson:
Drawing Conclusions

Have students discuss the following questions:

(a) How might the responsibility of Canada's central government for regulating trade among the provinces bring it into conflict with the provinces? (Answers will vary. Each province would probably be most interested in its own individual economic strength, while the central government would focus on national needs.)

(b) Which government might most effectively handle services such as health care, unemployment benefits, the needs of the disadvantaged, and education—Canada's federal government or the individual provincial governments? Why? (Opinions will vary.)

Developing the Lesson:
Debating an Issue

Have students work in groups to debate the following issue: *Canada has more to gain than the United States from a friendly and cooperative relationship between the two nations.* When debating the issue, students might consider the economic and military strengths of the two nations, and the possible effects on each nation of less friendly relations. *(Synthesis)*

Closing the Lesson:
Comparing Historical Developments

Have students compare the relationship between the United States and Canada with that between the United States and Latin America.

Then ask: *(a) How is the history of the two relationships different?* (The United States has taken a more active military and economic role in the development of Latin American nations. Relations with some Latin American nations have been hostile.)

(b) What might account for the differences between the two? (Canada has had a more stable political and economic system than most Latin American nations. Although once a British colony, Canada did not have the same economic problems that faced Latin American nations that were once European colonies. *(Synthesis)*

See *Section Review* questions, p. 813.

Chapter 39 Review Answers
(pp. 814–815)

Vocabulary Review

1. sunbelt 2. default 3. Watergate scandal 4. Organization of American States 5. separatist
6. referendum

People to Identify

1. Porfirio Díaz   2. Fernando Collor de Mello
3. Juan Péron 4. Henry Kissinger 5. Pierre Trudeau
6. Fulgencio Batista 7. Martin Luther King, Jr.
8. Omar Torrijos 9. Manuel Noriega 10. Anastasio Somoza 11. Joseph McCarthy

Places to Know

1. A   2. D   3. B   4. C

Recalling the Facts

1. The constitution gave the government power to organize farming collectives and take control of certain resources; allowed the formation of labor unions; established an eight-hour work day; provided for free, compulsory education; and limited the power and wealth of the Catholic Church.

2. In both countries the Depression and the political unrest that followed led to military takeovers.

3. Pinochet suspended the legislature, ordered severe censorship, and used violence against political opponents.

4. Castro nationalized foreign holdings; started campaigns against illiteracy and racial discrimination; allied himself with the Soviet Union; and set up a one-party Marxist state.

5. Discontent with the repressive and corrupt Somoza regime led to the formation of the Sandinistas. In 1979 the Sandinistas ousted the Somoza government. The American government supported the contras.

6. The treaty established that the United States would return the Canal Zone and transfer control of the canal to Panama by 1999.

7. Latin American leaders tried to make their nations less dependent on foreign markets for their products and to prevent foreigners from owning too many of their nations's resources.

8. The economy boomed; employment and wages rose; many people bought new homes; suburbs and shopping centers flourished; as the number of cars increased, more highways were built; and more people moved to the sunbelt. The population rose because of a high birth rate and increased immigration, especially from Latin America and Asia.

9. Democratic Presidents developed programs to exert greater government control over the economy and to promote economic equality and social change. Reagan believed the government had become too big and was interfering too much in citizens' lives.

10. Cold-war concerns dominated the foreign policies of all U.S. presidents of that era. Policy toward the Soviet Union affected policy toward all other regions and countries.

11. The two countries developed a much more cooperative relationship, as exemplified by important agreements on arms controls and the reduction of forces in Europe.

12. Increased output; growing population; reduced unemployment; expanded industry; discovery of oil and uranium; completion of the St.

Lawrence Seaway. Canada continued to export much of its rich supply of raw materials and to buy most of its manufactured goods from abroad.

13. They argued that Quebec was a nation within a nation, with its own culture and history.

Critical Thinking Skills

1. Timelines will vary.

2. Students might suggest that the oil boom did benefit the country and Mexican leaders could not have anticipated the drop in oil prices. However, the decision to neglect agriculture was a serious mistake, since it forced Mexico to increase its foreign debt, a key factor in the economy's near collapse.

3. Students might suggest that civil rights activists believed that few people would end discriminatory practices voluntarily and that change could best be achieved by making discrimination unlawful. Students might argue that without these laws and their strict enforcement, progress in this area would have been much slower.

4. Recommendations will vary.

Thinking About Geography

Answers may suggest that the U.S. takes a greater interest in Mexico and the Caribbean nations since they are geographically much closer than, for example, the nations of southern South America.

Enrichment: Primary Sources

1. The meeting between European (more specifically Spanish) and Native American peoples that took place as a result of Columbus's voyages to the Caribbean region.

2. Students' answers may cite the removal of military regimes in many Latin American nations and the return to democracy and restoration of regard for human rights. They may also cite efforts to reduce civil violence in some of the Central American countries.

The Changing Americas

1945–present

See chapter timeline, p. 813.

Before You Read This Chapter

Not so long ago, schoolbooks on history and geography often called North and South America "the New World." Of course, these continents were new only from a European point of view. To the many Indian peoples who lived in the Western Hemisphere before Columbus arrived, the Americas were not new at all. Therefore, most books stopped using the expression. However, as you read this chapter, ask yourself if the Americas are truly a new world in any way. What do the countries of the Western Hemisphere have in common? Are their problems and opportunities the same as those of Europe, Asia, and Africa—the "Old World"?

The Geographic Setting

The Chapter Outline

1. Upheaval in Latin America
2. Stability and Change in the United States
3. New Challenges for Canada

Cities throughout the Americas have grown tremendously since 1945. Below is the skyline of one such city—Dallas, Texas.

See lesson plans, pp. T793A–T793C.

1 Upheaval in Latin America

Objectives

Focus Questions

★ ■ How have some Latin American nations sought progress? *(pages 795–799)*

● ■ What conflicts have caused hardship in Central America? *(pages 800–802)*

▲ ■ What challenges face Latin American nations? *(pages 802–803)*

Terms to Know

default
Organization of
   American States

economic
   nationalism

★ Note strategies for first objective on this page and p. 799.

Although most of Latin America had become independent by 1824, its leaders still needed to unify their nations and rebuild war-torn economies (Chapter 23). As in colonial times, many of the new nations were dependent on the sale of plantation crops or minerals in the world market. Because little industry developed, Latin America's economic problems lasted into the late 1900's.

Mexico

The situation in Mexico at the beginning of the 1900's was typical of the experience of other Latin American countries. The caudillo Porfirio Díaz came to power in 1876 (page 466). Díaz was a harsh dictator, but his rule brought order and stability to Mexico. This encouraged foreign investment, and capital flowed into the nation's mines, plantations, and railroads.

The policies of Díaz created problems, however. He allowed his supporters and foreign investors to take over peasant lands and

Sec. Rev.
ques. 2

make them part of their plantations. By 1910 one percent of the population held 85 percent of Mexico's land. As more and more land was used to grow export crops, there was less land available to grow food for Mexicans. Many landless peasants had no place to work; some faced starvation.

Revolution. After more than 30 years in power, Díaz announced that he would allow free elections in 1910. As election day approached, Díaz became alarmed at the popularity of his challenger, a wealthy Creole named Francisco Madero (mah-DAY-roh). Díaz had Madero arrested and jailed and won the election through fraud. Madero escaped and called for revolution.

Violent revolt soon broke out among peasants demanding land reform. The peasants' leader, Emiliano Zapata (sah-PAH-tah), gave his support to Madero, and Díaz was overthrown. As president, however, Madero failed to keep the support of either the peasants or the landowners. After his overthrow in 1913, civil war swept the country. Peasants led by Zapata and Pancho Villa (VEE-yah) fought a guerrilla war against government troops.

A new constitution. Although fighting continued until 1920, a government established in 1917 drew up a new constitution. Combining ideas of nationalism and social reform, the constitution gave the Mexican government power to distribute land to the peasants and to regulate the exploitation of oil and other resources. It allowed workers to form unions, limited the work day to eight hours, and provided for free, compulsory education. Limits were set on the political power and wealth of the Catholic Church.

Economic expansion. The 1917 constitution provided a basis for modern Mexico. Lázaro Cárdenas (KAHR-day-nahs), president from 1934 to 1940, successfully carried out many of the aims of the constitution. Cárdenas encouraged Mexicans to start their **795**

★ RETEACHING. Have students make a chart identifying the sequence of governments and their dates for the following nations: Mexico, Brazil, Argentina, Chile, Puerto Rico, and Cuba. *(Comprehension) Translating Information into Another Form*

Linking Past and Present In 1991 the Mexican government gave official recognition to the Roman Catholic Church, ending the limitations imposed on the Church in the 1917 constitution.

★ REINFORCEMENT. Have students work in groups to discuss the following question: *What enabled authoritarian governments to take over in Latin American countries?* Students should consider the role played by economic and social issues. (Answers will vary, but might include the apparent ability of authoritarian regimes to repress social unrest and to strengthen national economies.) *(Comprehension) Analyzing Information*

The Arts

"Grand Tenochtitlán" by Diego Rivera.

Mexico's Revolutionary Murals

A visitor to Mexico City today can still see one of the most striking results of the Mexican Revolution. Sweeping murals in brilliant colors cover the walls of many government office buildings, libraries, museums, and schools.

For inspiration, the artists who painted these murals looked to Mexico's Indian heritage, to dramatic events in Mexican history, and to the life of the peasants. Some of the murals glorify great historic figures such as Montezuma and Father Hidalgo. Other scenes in the murals show the harsh dignity of peasant farmers or the determined armies of revolutionaries. Still others present myths and legends of the Mayas and Aztecs.

The style of art represented by these murals is sometimes referred to as social realism. The foremost pioneers of this style were Diego Rivera, José Clemente Orozco, and David Alfaro Siqueiros (see-KAY-rohs). All three were committed to revolutionary social change. In fact, Orozco was forced to flee the country several times because of his political views. Siqueiros was jailed or exiled seven times, partly for his efforts to organize unions. Despite the controversy surrounding these men, Mexico honors them for their powerful artistic vision.

F **FEATURE ACTIVITY. Have students develop a hypothesis explaining what the artist Diego Rivera might have wanted to communicate when he created his mural, "Grand Tenochtitlán," shown above. When forming their hypotheses, students should refer to specific elements of the mural.** (Synthesis) *Forming a Hypothesis*

Point out to students that they will find other works by Mexican artists on page 456 (Juan O'Gorman) and in the Portfolio of World Art Masterpieces at the back of the book (José Clemente Orozco).

own businesses, gave huge tracts of land to peasant villages, and built rural schools. In 1938 he ordered the government to take over the oil holdings of foreign companies.

During the next 30 years, new factories were built, agriculture and tourism grew, and the government built highways and railroads. Amid this progress, however, many Mexicans continued to live in poverty. As in most of Latin America, Mexico's population grew rapidly, putting a severe strain on the economy. Millions of people moved from the countryside to the cities in search of jobs. Housing shortages, overcrowding, and pollution resulted. As Mexico's population soared, thousands of Mexicans crossed the United States border illegally, hoping to find work.

By the 1970's Mexico faced inflation, unemployment, and food shortages. The nation was importing more goods than it was exporting. Under President José Lopez Portillo (por-TEE-yoh), the country began a search for oil within its own borders. Valuable oil reserves were found, and Mexico soon became a major oil exporter.

Sec. Rev. ques. 2, cont.

New issues. The oil boom created its own problems, however. Corruption by high officials cost the government millions of dollars. The government neglected agriculture, and was forced to buy food from abroad. Mexico took out huge loans from foreign banks to cover its expenses.

The drop in world oil prices during the 1980's crippled the Mexican economy. Inflation soared, and it appeared that the government would **default**—fail to pay—its enormous foreign debt. The government was forced to take out new loans to help pay its old ones. Desperately trying to prevent economic collapse, the government slashed domestic spending. Mexico began to balance its finances, but at great cost to the poor.

Economic hardship produced political unrest, as Mexicans looked for new leadership. The PRI, a party that had ruled for more than 50 years, found itself challenged by other parties; but the PRI candidate, Carlos Salinas de Gortari, won the 1988 presidential elections. Salinas was able to cut inflation and restore economic growth. Progress to-

ward establishing a system that gave Mexican voters a real choice, however, still seemed far in the future.

Brazil

During the worldwide depression of the 1930's (page 672), prices for Latin America's exports dropped sharply. High unemployment and widespread discontent followed. In Brazil, Getulio Vargas (VAHR-gus) took over the government in 1930 with the help of the army and became dictator.

While Vargas called himself the "Father of the Poor" and made many social reforms, he also imposed censorship and limited constitutional rights. Vargas increased government control of the economy and lowered Brazil's dependence on coffee exports.

Vargas was driven from office by military leaders in 1945. After a series of civilian presidents, the army took over the nation in 1964, and military leaders ruled for two decades. In 1985 the army agreed to give up power. Elections were held, and civilian rule returned to Brazil.

Brazil's new democracy was soon plagued by severe economic problems: high inflation and debt, and sluggish growth. In 1990 a new president, Fernando Collor de Mello (picture, next page), took office pledging to revive the economy. He carried out an economic "shock" program, even harsher than Mexico's in the 1980's, in an effort to halt severe inflation, but had little success.

Collor took steps to preserve Brazil's Amazon rain forest, the world's largest. The rapid destruction of the Amazon through farming, mining, and other projects has threatened thousands of biological species and endangered the global environment.

Argentina

In Argentina, as in Brazil, the crisis and unrest of the Great Depression led to a military takeover. In 1946 Juan Perón (pay-ROHN) was elected president. Perón's wife Eva, a

797

Economics Mexico's major trading partners are the United States, Japan, and western European countries.
Background Note that PRI is an abbreviation for *Partido Revolucionario Institucional,* or the Institutional Revolutionary Party. It was formed in 1929.

Critical Thinking. Ask: Why did the depression cause Latin American export prices to drop sharply? (People in other nations had less money to spend on imports. The drop in demand led to a drop in prices.)
Background Eva Perón was given the affectionate nickname "Evita."

Fernando Collor de Mello won office in Brazil's first direct presidential election since 1960. His goals for Brazil included revival of the economy, more efficiency in government, and protection of the Amazon.

former radio and movie star, became virtually co-president of Argentina. She began reforms in education, gained voting rights for Argentine women, and won immense popularity among the workers and the poor.

Juan Perón set up an authoritarian government, bringing the press and the unions under government control. Yet many of his policies earned him much popular support. A strong nationalist, he worked to make Argentina economically self-sufficient. He also improved workers' wages and benefits.

Despite Perón's efforts, the Argentine economy remained weak. Support for his policies faded, particularly after the death of his wife in 1952, and he was ousted by the military in 1955.

A series of unstable and harsh governments followed. Unemployment and inflation rose; the country faced strikes and protests. In 1973 Perón was again elected president. He died the next year and was succeeded by his third wife, Isabel Perón.

Argentina's problems continued, and in 1976 military leaders again took over the government. To control dissent they carried out acts of kidnapping, torture, and murder. Thousands of Argentines who came to be

called *los desaparecidos,* "the disappeared ones," were killed by government-sponsored death squads.

In 1982 Argentine troops invaded the Falkland Islands, a British colony several hundred miles off the coast. Argentina was defeated in a short war (page 722), and soon after the military rulers agreed to give up power.

Since then, Argentina has had civilian rule. In 1989 Carlos Menem was elected president. Menem faced serious economic problems, especially persistent inflation, but made progress in establishing Argentine confidence in civilian government. In 1990, however, Menem's pardoning of former army officers convicted of human-rights crimes during the years of military government touched off charges that he was appeasing Argentina's military establishment.

Chile

Chile had the strongest tradition of democracy in South America. Civilian governments ruled the country beginning in the 1920's.

In 1970 Chileans elected Salvador Allende (ah-YEN-day), a Marxist, as head of a coalition government. Allende nationalized mines and banks, began land reform, and raised wages. Inflation and the national debt rose sharply. Foreign investors, fearing their property would be seized by the Marxist government, began to pull their money out of Chile. At the same time, the United States put severe economic and political pressure on the Chilean government. The country was thrown into turmoil and, in 1973, Allende was overthrown and was killed in a military coup.

The new Chilean government, led by General Augusto Pinochet (peen-oh-CHET), struck quickly to put down the opposition. Pledging to wipe out communism in Chile, the government suspended the legislature, ordered severe censorship, and used violence against political opponents. Many Chileans left the country, and the government was criticized by the United Nations for its violations of human rights.

In 1988 Pinochet agreed to let the people of Chile vote on whether he should remain in power. Most Chileans voted against him, and he agreed to step down after elections the following year.

In 1990 a new civilian president, Patricio Aylwin, took office. Aylwin promised to heal the nation and appointed a commission to investigate the army's human-rights record. Pinochet remained head of Chile's military forces, however, and vowed to prevent any prosecution of officers for past abuses.

Different Paths in the Caribbean

As you read in Chapter 28, both Cuba and Puerto Rico were Spanish colonies until the Spanish-American War. Since that time, these two islands have followed very different paths of development.

Puerto Rico. As a result of the Spanish-American War, Puerto Rico fell under American control. The United States ruled the island directly until the 1940's, when Puerto Ricans were given the right to elect their own leaders. In 1952 Puerto Rico became a self-governing commonwealth.

Puerto Rico continues to have very strong ties to the United States. Puerto Ricans are American citizens. However, they pay no federal taxes, and cannot vote in national elections. Some Puerto Ricans have called for complete independence, and others want Puerto Rico to join the United States as the fifty-first state. Still others prefer to remain a commonwealth. The issue remained controversial into the 1990's.

Cuba. Cuba became formally independent after the Spanish-American War. However, the United States reserved the right to keep naval bases in Cuba and intervene in Cuban affairs to maintain peace. In addition, American businesses owned most of Cuba's industries and resources.

In 1952 Fulgencio Batista (bah-TEES-tah) took control of the Cuban government. Batista's dictatorship was harsh, and in 1956 rebels led by Fidel Castro took up arms against his rule. After three years of warfare, Batista was ousted, and Castro took power. In the first days of his regime, Castro nationalized foreign holdings, launched a campaign against illiteracy, and began a program to root out racial discrimination. He also allied himself with the Soviet Union, set up a one-party Marxist state, and executed or imprisoned his opponents.

Sec. Rev. ques. 3

In 1960 the United States stopped trading with Cuba. The following year it broke diplomatic ties and backed an unsuccessful invasion of Cuba's Bay of Pigs by Cuban exiles. Tensions between the two nations worsened in 1962 over the Cuban Missile Crisis (page 718).

In that same year the United States helped oust Cuba from membership in the **Organization of American States** (OAS)—a group of nations in the Americas, including the United States, that work together on common issues. It took this action because Cuba had declared itself a Marxist-Leninist state. The United States also criticized Cuba for backing revolutionary movements in Latin America and later in Africa.

★ See below.

Cuban-American relations have remained uneasy over the years. Cuba continued to accuse the United States of exploiting the peoples of Latin America. As Latin America's economic problems mounted, Castro's tough talk began to win him some support in the region. By the 1990's, however, Cuba was facing new problems. The Soviet Union, struggling with its own internal crises, ended its economic aid for Cuba and thus left Castro isolated and in desperate need of other sources of financial help.

Conflict In Central America

● Note strategies for second objective on pp. 800–801.

The small nations of Central America (map, page 801) shared many problems with the rest of Latin America—one-product economies, limited local industry, dependence on foreign capital, and extremes of poverty and wealth. Many groups looked for ways to change this situation, and in the 1970's and 1980's Central America became a battleground for these groups.

799

Politics Puerto Rico has one elected delegate to the United States House of Representatives who may take part in debate and serve on committees, but cannot vote on the floor of the House.

Economic history As one way of searching for economic help, Castro in 1991 opened up Cuba's socialist economy to private foreign investors.

★ ENRICHMENT. Have students research the Organization of American States and find information on its structure, goals, members, and the effectiveness of its programs and policies. (Comprehension) *Locating Information*

Nicaragua. Nicaragua's government and economy were dominated by the United States in the early 1900's. American troops occupied the country until 1933, and before leaving they set up a powerful National Guard to protect conservative interests. The leader of the National Guard, General Anastasio Somoza (soh-MOH-sah) set up a dictatorship during the 1930's. He was succeeded by his son Luis in 1956 and by his other son, Anastasio Somoza Debayle, in 1967. The Somozas built up the economy to enrich themselves and their friends, while most Nicaraguans suffered from great poverty and repression.

Sec. Rev.
ques. 4

Discontent with the Somoza regime led to the creation of the Sandinistas, a rebel group named after a popular anti-American rebel of the 1920's. Civil war broke out in 1978, and a year later the Sandinistas overthrew the Somoza government. After the revolution the Sandinistas cracked down on opposition and accepted aid from the Soviet Union. Meanwhile, the United States, fearful of the spread of communism in the region, began supporting the anti-Sandinista guerrillas known as contras. The contras launched attacks on Nicaragua from base camps in Honduras and El Salvador.

The war continued through much of the 1980's, causing enormous hardship for the people of Nicaragua. Finally, in 1988, a shaky truce was declared. Plans were then made for presidential elections in 1990.

The elections resulted in an upset victory for the American-backed candidate, Violeta Chamorro, the leader of a broad coalition of anti-Sandinista forces. Chamorro promised to work for national unity, but the Sandinistas, still the most powerful political party in Nicaragua, tried to block Chamorro's efforts to forge new policies, and Nicaragua remained unstable.

El Salvador. El Salvador had a long history of military dictatorship. During the late 1970's, demands for land and jobs for the nation's poor became widespread. In 1979 army leaders overthrew the dictator and began to redistribute land, but leftist groups did not think the changes went far enough, and

rightist groups opposed any reforms. In 1980 a bitter civil war erupted between the American-supported government and rebels aided by the Soviet bloc.

In 1984 elections were held in El Salvador, bringing a moderate civilian leader, José Napoleón Duarte (doo-AHR-tay), to power. Duarte tried to carry out political and economic reforms but was opposed by the rebels and by hard-line conservatives. The military organization remained the chief power in the country. During the 1980's government security forces and right-wing death squads tortured or killed thousands of suspected leftists.

By 1990 the civil war seemed to be at a stalemate. But a new civilian president, Alfredo Cristiani, held peace talks with rebel leaders, and in 1991 negotiations sponsored by the United Nations resulted in a cease-fire and the signing of a formal peace pact. Whether El Salvador's long civil war had truly come to an end remained to be seen.

Guatemala. Until 1944, Guatemala was ruled by a series of dictators who favored foreign investment as the way to economic development. Popular protest, however, brought on a 10-year period of reform. The government took over many large estates, including American-owned fruit plantations, and gave this land to small farmers. In 1954 an American-sponsored revolt toppled the reformist government. Military dictators took over, reversing many earlier reforms.

In the 1960's leftist rebels began to fight Guatemala's military government. The military leaders fought back in a ruthless campaign to restore order. By the early 1980's the government had crushed most of the rebel forces.

Under pressure from the United States, the Guatemalan government allowed free elections in 1985, and a civilian president was elected. In 1990 another civilian president won office—the first time in the country's history that one elected civilian had followed another in office. Nevertheless, Guatemala's army continued to be powerful, and serious economic and social troubles continued into the 1990's.

● RETEACHING. Have students review "Conflict in Central America" (starting on p. 799) and identify the causes and effects of the 1980's civil war in Nicaragua. (Discontent with the Somoza regime resulted in his removal by the Sandinistas; their move toward the Soviet Union resulted in American aid for the contras.) (Comprehension) Identifying Cause and Effect

● REINFORCEMENT. Have students work in groups to discuss the following issues: Why might Marxism be attractive to rebels like the Sandinistas in Nicaragua? Why might the United States perceive Marxist governments in Central America as a threat? (Synthesis) Evaluating Information

Background During the Nicaraguan revolution approximately 2 percent of the population was killed and $1.3 billion in material damage was done.

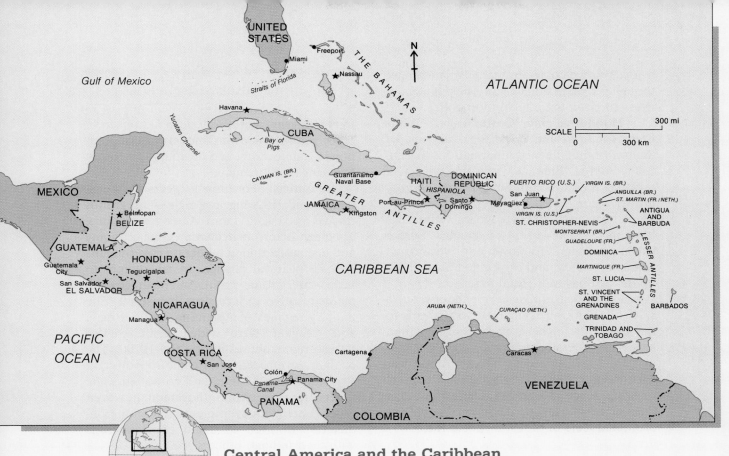

Central America and the Caribbean

At its closest point, how far is Cuba from Miami? What two nations are on the island of Hispaniola? What seven nations are in Central America?

Map Answers: (1) About 200 miles. (2) Haiti, Dominican Republic. (3) Belize, Guatemala, Honduras, El Salvador, Nicaragua, Costa Rica, Panama.

● See below.

Panama. After winning its independence from Colombia in 1903 with American help, Panama granted the United States the right to build the Panama Canal (page 561). The Canal Zone, a 10-mile-wide strip of land bordering both sides of the Canal, became American property and prospered while the rest of the country remained poor. During the 1950's people in Panama began to demand control of the Canal Zone and the canal.

In 1968 General Omar Torrijos (toh-REE-hohs), a staunch nationalist, became Panama's leader. Torrijos supported the movement for Panamanian control of the canal. In 1977 a new Panama Canal treaty was signed. In it, the United States agreed to return the Canal Zone and transfer control of the canal to Panama by 1999.

Two years after Torrijos's death in 1981, General Manuel Noriega became the new head of the Panamanian armed forces and the unofficial leader of the country. By 1988, rumors had spread that Noriega had secret ties to drug dealers and was using his office for personal gain. The United States cut off all aid, and some Panamanians took to the streets to call for Noriega's removal.

The Panamanian dictator was finally ousted from power after President George Bush sent United States forces into Panama in late 1989. General Noriega escaped capture for a number of days by taking refuge in the Vatican embassy in Panama City. The United States government wanted to gain custody of the fallen leader in order to have him face drug-trafficking charges in court. The Vatican released Noriega to United States officials in early 1990. He was then sent to a federal prison in Miami, Florida.

The presence of the United States **801**

● ENRICHMENT. Have students refer to newspaper articles and periodicals to find information on recent political developments in one of the Central American nations discussed in this section. Students might research recent events in Nicaragua, Guatemala, El Salvador, or Panama. *(Application)* **Locating Information**

Political History Noriega was indicted on 12 counts involving drug trafficking, money laundering, and racketeering, and went on trial in Miami's federal court in September 1991.

troops was welcomed by many Panamanians, though people in other Latin American countries criticized the intervention policy.

Honduras and Costa Rica. While both Honduras and Costa Rica were spared the unrest that plagued other nations in Central America, they did feel the effects of regional conflicts. Honduras, a poor country formerly dominated by American fruit companies, was used by Nicaraguan contras as a base for attacks inside Nicaragua. Border clashes between Honduran and Nicaraguan soldiers resulted, and the United States built up its own bases in Honduras.

Costa Rica, unlike its neighbors, set up a smoothly working democratic system early in the 1900's. Its higher standard of living and lack of a professional army brought it stability. In 1987 President Oscar Arias was awarded the Nobel Peace Prize for his efforts to bring peace to Central America. Despite this success, growing economic problems prompted fears of unrest in Costa Rica.

Relatives of "disappeared" victims of Argentina's military government demonstrated in Buenos Aires. Their protests helped restore civilian rule in 1983.

MIGUEL ANGEL
LABRADOR PEREZ

DESAPARECIDO
13-12-1976

802

Present and Future Challenges

▲ Note strategies for third objective on this page and p. 803.

In recent years, Latin American nations have taken giant steps toward modernization, economic stabilization, and democratic reforms. Challenges still remain.

Politics. For many years ruthless, well-armed left-wing and right-wing groups existed in several Latin American nations. Their acts of terrorism disrupted the economy and also undermined moderate governments seeking peaceful change. In an attempt to keep order, some Latin American governments resorted to terrorism themselves. The military regimes of Argentina, Chile, Brazil, and Uruguay were widely criticized for human-rights abuses during the 1970's. The civilian government that came to power in Argentina in 1983 tried and convicted some officers for their crimes. In general, however, Latin American governments emerging from dictatorship tried to avoid confrontations with their military officers.

The decade of the 1980's saw one Latin American country after another return to democracy. The most striking case was Paraguay, where in 1989 the 35-year rule of General Alfredo Stroessner came to an end. Many of the new governments have shown their determination to follow democratic principles. Still, the unrest that can be triggered by political extremism and poverty continued to challenge Latin American democracy in the 1990's.

Economic trends. Some of Latin America's economic problems date back to colonial days, while others have only recently appeared. Since the early years of independence, many Latin American countries have depended on the export of one or two products. During the Great Depression, the demand for Latin American exports dried up. This experience taught Latin Americans the need to build broad-based economies.

The result has been an increase in **economic nationalism**—the effort to bring about economic independence through local control and industrialization. Leaders such as Juan Perón of Argentina tried to make their

▲ **RETEACHING.** Have students review "Problems Facing Latin American Nations" (pp. 802–803) and outline the challenges that remain for Latin America. (Political extremism, economic weakness, social inequality, drug trafficking.) *(Comprehension) Observing for Detail*

▲ **REINFORCEMENT.** Have students work in groups to write policies or programs that might deal effectively with Latin America's problems. *(Synthesis) Solving Problems*

Cultural History A commission appointed to investigate military crimes in Argentina was headed by a well-known author, Ernesto Sábato. The commission's report, entitled *Nunca mas* ("Never Again") called the military's actions "the greatest and most savage tragedy in our history."

Political History One Latin American country where the move to democracy faced obstacles was Haiti, where the first democratically elected president, Jean-Bertrand Aristide, was ousted by a military coup in 1991.

nations less dependent on foreign markets for their products and to prevent foreign companies and investors from owning too many of their nations' resources.

Yet this strategy contributed to new problems, such as foreign debt. Nations often borrowed from foreign banks to pay for the building of new roads and factories. If their economies failed to grow as quickly as expected—a problem Mexico faced in the 1980's—they found themselves deeply in debt. To make their debt payments, they were often forced to impose harsh economic policies that hurt the poor and gave rise to social unrest. Some Latin Americans called on their governments to refuse to repay their loans, arguing that foreign debt was a new form of economic domination. In the 1990's, however, some countries—for example, Mexico and Chile—have been able to make payments on their foreign debts.

In recent years, economic nationalism has been giving way to free-market policies in much of Latin America. Many countries now stress private enterprise, greater foreign investment, and increased trade. Brazil and Argentina are working to create a free trade zone—one with no tariffs—that might eventually lead to the creation of a Latin American common market.

Social inequality. As you read in Chapter 23, Latin America's rigid class system stayed in place long after independence. A small group of people controlled almost all of the land and wealth, while the rest of the population lived in extreme poverty. Some people, including a few clergy of the Catholic Church, began to call for greater attention to the needs of the poor.

Many Latin American countries responded with programs of land reform, which gave poor people land of their own to farm. Yet, as the case of El Salvador shows, opponents of land reform can undermine change through terror and violence. Many rural people move to cities in search of better opportunities; there they live crammed into slums, with poor sanitation and little education or health care.

One way for poor farmers to make money has been to grow the plants from which illegal drugs like cocaine are made. Growing demand for such drugs has led to the rise of an underground industry—worth billions of dollars a year—in many Latin American nations, including Mexico, Bolivia, Peru, and Colombia. The United States, where large amounts of the illegal and dangerous drugs are sold, has joined with other governments to try to halt the drug traffic. This effort has been slowed by corruption and by the dependence of many Latin American nations on the drug trade. Bolivia, for example, earns more from cocaine exports than from all other exports combined. The Colombian economy also boomed from the drug traffic, though violence from drug gangs threatened the fabric of Colombian society. The need to build diverse, stable economies remains a pressing concern for all nations in the region.

Sec. Rev. ques. 5

See Sec. 1 *Closing the Lesson,* p. T793B.

Section Review

Answers to Section Review questions are in brackets on pages indicated.

1. **Define or identify:** default, Organization of American States, economic nationalism. (pp. 797, 799, 802)
2. How did Díaz's policies both help and harm Mexico? What problems did Mexico's oil boom cause? (pp. 795, 797)
3. Why did relations between the United States and Cuba become strained after Castro took power? (p. 799)
4. Who were the Sandinistas? The contras? Which group did the United States government support in Nicaragua's civil war? (p. 800)
5. What problems have slowed international efforts to halt the drug trade? (p. 803)
6. **Critical thinking:** Name some Latin American nations that have recently moved toward democracy. What forces threaten democracy throughout the region? (See answer below.)

803

▲ ENRICHMENT. Students might investigate (1) methods used by the U.S. government to stop the flow of drugs from Latin America or (2) the terrorist campaign carried out by drug cartels in Colombia and the reasons for the cartels' pledge to halt that violence in 1991 (the national assembly's banning of extradition, in opposition to U.S. government wishes). (Comprehension) Locating Information

6. Students may mention Brazil, Argentina, Chile, or Paraguay, or may base their answers on recent developments. Students might suggest that political instability, poverty and economic weakness, human rights violations, or social unrest may threaten democracy.

2 Stability and Change in the United States

Objectives

Focus Questions

★ ■ What national issues faced Americans in the postwar years?
(pages 804–806)

● ■ What issues have dominated postwar American foreign policy?
(pages 806–809)

Terms to Know

sunbelt
civil rights
Watergate scandal

★ Note strategies for first objective on this page and p. 805.

At the end of World War II the United States was prosperous, stable, and secure. Americans quickly brought their troops home from overseas and turned to "winning the peace." The future looked promising as Americans entered the last half of the 1900's. Nevertheless, critical problems lay ahead.

Challenges at Home

Peace and prosperity. For the United States, the period after the Second World War was one of growth and confidence. Americans went on a buying spree, spending wartime savings on goods and services that had not been available during the war years. As the economy boomed, millions of people found new jobs. Earnings were higher than ever before, and the nation enjoyed the highest standard of living in the world.

Peace and prosperity created changes in Americans' ways of living. Many people bought new homes, particularly in suburban

Sec. Rev. ques. 2

804

areas around major cities. As the number of cars in the nation increased, Congress approved the building of thousands of miles of new highways. These improvements in transportation made suburban shopping centers popular. More people began moving to the West, especially to California. This trend continued into the 1980's as Americans were attracted to the warm weather and expanding job opportunities of the sunbelt—the states stretching from the southeast Atlantic coast to southern California.

While American society was changing, the American people were changing as well. The population grew because of a high birth rate, medical advances that increased the average life span, and immigration. A law passed in 1965 allowed more Asians and Latin Americans to enter the country. These areas replaced Europe as the sources of most American immigrants.

The growth of the federal government. Franklin Roosevelt (President from 1933 to 1945) had responded to the Great Depression of the 1930's by greatly expanding the government's role in the economy (page 672). This trend toward "big government" continued under the postwar Presidents.

Democratic Presidents tended to expand government programs to promote social change and economic equality. Harry Truman (1945–1953) raised the minimum wage, built low-income housing, and expanded Social Security. John F. Kennedy (1961–1963) and his successor, Lyndon Johnson (1963–1969), began dozens of programs to increase opportunities for the poor and to provide economic security for the elderly and handicapped. Jimmy Carter (1977–1981) set up the Department of Energy and the Department of Education to conserve and develop energy resources and to improve education.

The first three Republican Presidents of the postwar era were Dwight Eisenhower (1953–1961), Richard Nixon (1969–1974),

Sec. Rev. ques. 3

★ RETEACHING. Have students review "Challenges at Home" (pp. 804–807) and identify social changes that occurred in the United States after World War II. (More home ownership; growth of suburban areas; more car ownership; anti-discrimination laws and policies.) (Comprehension) Observing for Detail

★ REINFORCEMENT. Have students make a comparison between the political trends after World War II and the policies of recent Presidents. (Political trends after World War II promoted social change, economic equality, energy conservation, and an expanded role for the federal government. Ronald Reagan halted the growth of the federal government.) (Synthesis) Observing for Detail and Gerald Ford (1974–1977). These Presidents preserved the Democrats' programs and, to a lesser degree, added programs of their own. Ronald Reagan, a Republican elected in 1980, was the first postwar President to push for a halt to the growth of the federal government. Reagan believed that the government was interfering too much in the lives of the citizens and doing tasks that could be done better by state and local governments. He also argued that high government spending held back economic growth.

Under Reagan, funding for many federal programs was cut back and some were eliminated. President George Bush continued these policies. The main body of social programs begun by earlier administrations, however, was not dismantled. Most Americans felt the federal government had an important role to play in society.

★ See below.

Economic ups and downs. One reason why the federal government became more active in society was to help the many Americans who had not shared in postwar prosperity. Yet higher spending for social programs, as well as for the Vietnam War (page 751), helped spark inflation in the early 1970's.

Under President Reagan, inflation was brought under control and unemployment fell. It appeared, however, that new problems had emerged to replace the old ones. The federal budget deficit (the amount by which government spending exceeds government earnings) skyrocketed during the 1980's, and continued to mount in the 1990's despite efforts to cut down spending. Unemployment resurfaced and became a severe problem during the recession that started in 1990.

Struggles for equality. An issue of increasing concern in the postwar years was civil rights—the right to be treated equally under law and have equality of opportunity. Several groups, most notably African Americans, sought equal treatment after years of discrimination. Black Americans had benefited from the nation's prosperity, and many enjoyed greater opportunities than their parents and grandparents. Yet racial discrimination continued to be a serious problem.

In the 1940's, civil rights leaders began a struggle against discrimination and segregation. Leaders of the movement turned to the federal courts, and, in a series of cases beginning in 1941, the Supreme Court banned various forms of segregation. A Supreme Court decision in 1954—*Brown v. Board of Education of Topeka*—ruled against the idea of "separate but equal" schooling. More American public schools became integrated.

Civil rights leaders used other means besides the federal courts to achieve their goals. Following the example set by Gandhi in India (page 739), black Americans began to seek justice through nonviolent direct action. A Baptist minister named Martin Luther King, Jr. emerged as a national leader in the drive for civil rights. Boycotts and "sit-ins" throughout the South forced businesses to give African Americans equal rights.

Martin Luther King, Jr. used nonviolence in the struggle for civil rights. King was inspired by Mohandas Gandhi (whose picture is on the wall).

805

★ ENRICHMENT. Have students develop a hypothesis explaining why Reagan's views of government and his effort to limit the growth of the federal government were acceptable to much of the American people. Students should base their hypotheses on the economic, political, and social issues discussed in the text. *(Synthesis) Drawing Conclusions*

Social History Chief Justice Earl Warren wrote in his opinion: "To separate [school children] from others of similar age and qualifications solely because of their race generates a feeling of inferiority as to their status in the community that may affect their hearts and minds in a way unlikely ever to be undone."

The federal government played an important role in civil rights matters. With the support of President Johnson, Congress passed the Civil Rights Act of 1964, banning several kinds of discrimination. A year later Congress passed the Voting Rights Act, which allowed federal workers to register voters who had been denied registration by the states. The Civil Rights Act of 1968 banned housing discrimination.

During the 1960's and 1970's other groups raised their voices against injustice. Hispanics began their own campaign for civil rights. American Indians criticized government policies that ignored treaties and destroyed tribal ties and customs. Handicapped persons demanded better opportunities and access to public buildings.

Women made up the largest group seeking full equality. Women led campaigns seeking access to jobs in fields usually reserved for men. For example, many women reached high-level positions in government and business for the first time. On the other hand, a constitutional amendment to forbid sex discrimination failed to win approval.

A time of unrest. Overall, the postwar period had been a time of optimism among the American people. During the late 1960's and 1970's, however, a number of problems caused many Americans to question whether the country was on the right course.

In the mid-1960's riots broke out in black areas of some major cities. In some cases the National Guard had to be called in to halt the looting and burning of buildings. In 1968 riots again broke out when Martin Luther King, Jr. was assassinated. After his death a number of more radical black leaders, frustrated by what they saw as the slow pace of social change, turned away from King's goals of nonviolence and racial integration. Instead they emphasized "black power" and called for the use of force to achieve their goals. Their activities created an atmosphere of tension and fear.

The growing antiwar movement also added to tensions during this period. As the war in Indochina dragged on, more and more

Americans demanded that the United States pull out from the conflict. Large antiwar demonstrations, some of which led to violence, were held in cities and on college campuses throughout the country.

Sec. Rev. ques. 4

By 1972 the war was winding down, but a new ordeal was beginning. In June 1972 there was an attempted burglary at Democratic Party headquarters. The investigation of this burglary revealed information about abuses of power by the Nixon administration. This **Watergate scandal** (named after the building in which the burglary occurred) led to the jailing of several of Nixon's top aides and finally to the resignation of the President himself. These events, coming at the same time as the American withdrawal from Vietnam, were serious blows to many Americans' faith in their government. On the other hand, the government's ability to deal efficiently with the crisis was a clear signal of its strength and stability.

World Leadership

● Note strategies for second objective on pp. 806–807, 809.

The tensions of the cold war (Chapter 35) dominated American foreign policy for many years after World War II. The two superpowers competed for power and prestige in a variety of ways. The American commitment to fight Soviet expansion led the United States into conflicts around the globe.

Anti-communism at home. Soviet postwar expansion in Europe, as well as the mood of the cold war, heightened Americans' fear of communism. Some Americans began to worry about the presence of Communist spies in the United States itself. In 1950 a little-known senator from Wisconsin, Joseph McCarthy, began his own search for Communist spies. McCarthy accused hundreds of government officials of disloyalty, destroying many people's careers on the basis of little or no evidence. McCarthy's campaign came to a halt in 1954 when it became obvious that he could not back up his charges.

Anti-communism abroad. Fear of the spread of communism throughout the world brought the United States into several con-

● RETEACHING. Have students review "World Leadership" (pp. 806–809) and make a chart titled *American Foreign Policy after 1945*. Students should identify the policy, its date, and the presidential administration in which it occurred. *(Comprehension) Translating Information into Another Form*

Political History McCarthy's methods finally caused the Senate to condemn him in December 1954. He died in 1957.

flicts during the 1950's and 1960's. From 1950 to 1953, American troops helped defend South Korea from invasion by the north (page 747). After Cuba's Communist revolution, the United States sponsored the Bay of Pigs invasion (page 799) and later forced the removal of Soviet nuclear missiles from the island (page 718). The Kennedy administration began a buildup of nuclear weapons to offset Soviet nuclear forces.

The Vietnam War. America's involvement in the war in Southeast Asia also stemmed from its commitment to fighting communism. As you read in Chapter 36, United States military advisers were sent to help anti-Communist forces in Southeast Asia after France's withdrawal from its former colonies there. By 1968, hundreds of thousands of American troops were in Vietnam, and the war was becoming more and more unpopular in the United States. In March 1968 President Lyndon Johnson announced that he would not seek re-election but would work to reach a cease-fire. Peace talks began in Paris in May.

In his campaign for the presidency in 1968, Richard Nixon pledged to end the war honorably. In October 1972 Henry Kissinger, one of Nixon's top advisers, worked out an agreement with North Vietnam. In 1973 the Paris Peace Accords were signed. Within a few months, American troops left Vietnam. The costs of the war to the United States had been great—more then 56,000 Americans killed and about 300,000 wounded. In addition, many American soldiers remained missing in action.

An East-West dialogue. As American involvement in Vietnam decreased, the United States concentrated on its policy of détente, trying to improve relations with China and the Soviet Union. In 1972 President Nixon's visit to China signaled a major shift in American policy and the start of a new relationship between the two nations.

Sec. Rev. ques. 5

Later in 1972, Nixon became the first American President to visit Moscow since World War II. During the visit he and Soviet leader Brezhnev signed the first Strategic Arms Limitation Treaty (SALT). This agreement limited the numbers and types of missiles each nation could have.

An oil crisis. In 1973, the October War broke out in the Middle East. Because the United States supported Israel, the oil-rich Arab countries placed an embargo on oil to the United States (page 766). This cutback in the nation's oil supply led to rising fuel prices and sharp increases in the cost of living. Even though imports were resumed in 1974, Nixon tried to cut American dependence on Arab oil.

Foreign policy under Carter. The election of Jimmy Carter as President in 1976 brought a new focus to foreign policy—human rights. Carter spoke out against apartheid in South Africa and Rhodesia (now Zimbabwe). He also urged Soviet leaders to release political prisoners and to allow Soviet Jews to leave the country.

President Carter made wide use of diplomacy to deal with world problems. In 1977, a long-lasting dispute with Panama over the Canal Zone was settled (page 801). In 1979 full diplomatic relations were established with the People's Republic of China. Carter's greatest triumph was achieved in 1978, when he sponsored the peace talks that led to the Camp David Accords (page 763).

Presidents Ford and Carter had continued the policy of détente begun under Nixon. Yet Soviet actions during Carter's presidency began to raise fears about Soviet expansion. In 1979, Soviet troops invaded Afghanistan

Linking Past and Present

In 1982 the United States dedicated the Vietnam Veterans Memorial in Washington, D.C. The monument consists of two black granite walls inscribed with the names of all American soldiers killed or missing in Vietnam. The simple memorial has become a place of pilgrimage for veterans and their families.

● REINFORCEMENT. Have students rank the major events that occurred in American foreign relations after 1945 in order of their importance and then explain their ranking. *(Synthesis)* *Evaluating Information*

Check for Understanding. Ask: What was the policy of détente? (The effort to improve relations with China and the Soviet Union.)

(page 725). Carter halted sales of American grain to the Soviet Union, called for a boycott of the 1980 Moscow Olympic Games, and delayed completion of SALT II, the arms limitation treaty he had signed earlier that year.

Reagan's foreign policy. Soviet policies drew sharper criticism from President Reagan. To fight Soviet expansion in the Americas, he pushed for aid to non-Communist governments in Central America and to the Nicaraguan contras. He also ordered an invasion of the island of Grenada after it had been taken over by Marxists.

Opposition to the Soviet Union affected United States policy toward Africa as well. The United States supported rebels seeking to overthrow the Marxist government of Angola (page 784). In its dealings with South Africa, the Reagan administration stressed that country's importance to American security. Reagan worried that punishing South Africa for its apartheid policy would permit a Communist takeover of South Africa.

President Reagan vowed to take a hard line against terrorism. It was revealed in 1986, however, that the United States had secretly sold weapons to Iran in hopes of gaining the release of hostages in Lebanon. The sale not only seemed to contradict a pledge never to make deals with terrorists but also may have violated American law.

The end of the cold war. By the late 1980's Gorbachev's leadership of the Soviet Union had brought about a dramatic improvement in relations between the superpowers. Arms control was the arena in which the improvement first appeared. During the presidency of George Bush, the two countries reached agreements banning intermediate-range nuclear weapons in Europe, limiting long-range nuclear weapons, and ending the production of chemical weapons.

As the cold war faded, both the United States and the Soviet Union made deep reductions in their military forces in Europe. The dismantling of the Soviet empire in Eastern Europe in 1989 was greeted with enthusiasm in the United States. After the attempted overthrow of Gorbachev in 1991 (page 728)

and the breakdown of the Soviet system that followed, President Bush announced huge reductions in the nuclear arsenal of the United States. Gorbachev said the Soviet Union would do the same.

By the end of 1991 Gorbachev had resigned and the Soviet Union had fallen apart (page 728). Led by Boris Yeltsin, leaders of most of the Soviet republics formed the Commonwealth of Independent States, an alliance rather than a union. The United States then began to develop diplomatic relations with the individual republics of the Commonwealth. A major concern of United States policy was the security of Soviet nuclear missiles, located in the individual states of Russia, Ukraine, Belarus, and Kazakhstan.

Whatever the future of the Commonwealth states may be, the cold war clearly ended with the collapse of the Soviet empire. The United States, as the winner, was left as the world's one superpower—a position of enormous responsibility.

A cooperative foreign policy. The new relationship with the Soviet Union, and then with the new Commonwealth states, fit well with the foreign policy pursued in general by the Bush administration. An experienced diplomat, Bush based his foreign policy more on consensus than confrontation. He sought to eliminate barriers to American trade with Japan, for example, through talks aimed at finding reforms that could be made by both countries. Also, though he publicly condemned the Chinese government's brutal crackdown on pro-democracy demonstrators, Bush used secret diplomacy to maintain communication with China's leaders.

To improve inter-American relations, Bush asked banks voluntarily to reduce massive Latin American debts. He also proposed the establishment of a hemispheric free-trade zone to encourage private investment in Latin America. Bush's sending of troops to overthrow Noriega's rule of Panama, however, opened old wounds. Latin American leaders condemned the action, saying it was a return to the days when United States presidents felt free to intervene in the affairs of Latin American nations (page 561).

Military Policy As President, Ronald Reagan launched an eight-year, $2.3 trillion budget for defense, including plans for a larger navy, expanded counterinsurgency forces, the MX missile, the B-1 bomber, and the Strategic Defense Initiative (Star Wars).

Foreign Policy The sale of weapons to Iran was popularly called the Iran-contra affair. It was reported that profits from the arms sales were used to support the contras in Nicaragua.

The 1980's were a decade of hostage-taking as terrorist groups seized individuals for political advantage. From 1984 to 1991 Islamic militants in Lebanon captured seventeen Americans and held them captive, killing three. Here Terry Anderson, last of the hostages to gain release, was welcomed home at a ceremony in Washington, D.C.

See Sec. 2 *Closing the Lesson*, p. T793B.

The focus on consensus was again shown in Bush's response to Iraq's invasion of Kuwait (page 772). The United States put together a coalition that included not only Western nations but also the Soviet Union and moderate Arab states. In a six-week war the coalition won a decisive victory.

For the United States the Gulf War had significant consequences. It had unified the American people and shown the nation's ability to assemble and lead a coalition of many different countries. One outcome of this multinational coalition was the opportunity for the United States and Soviet Union to arrange the Madrid Conference (page 764), at which Arabs and Israelis gathered in a single room to speak about divisive issues. Gorbachev, representing the Soviet Union at this

● See below.

conference, found himself on the sidelines, showing how that country, once America's most powerful enemy, had shrunk into insignificance.

● ENRICHMENT. Have students work in groups to predict the course of American foreign affairs for the 1990's. Students should identify areas of concern and predict what they think might be the most significant achievement of the decade. *(Synthesis)*

Section Review

Answers to Section Review questions are in brackets on pages indicated.

1. **Define or identify:** sunbelt, civil rights, Watergate scandal. (pp. 804, 805, 806)
2. How did American ways of living and population change after World War II? (p. 804)
3. How did postwar Democrats seek to expand the role of the federal government? How and why did President Reagan attempt to reverse this trend? (p. 805)
4. In what ways did the Vietnam War dominate U.S. concerns from the late 1960's to 1973? (p. 806)
5. How did the focus of foreign policy change under the presidents from Nixon to Bush? (pp. 807–809)
6. **Critical thinking:** How might the end of the cold war affect the foreign policy of future U.S. presidents? (See answer below.)

809

6. Answers might suggest the possibility of more emphasis on cooperative international problem-solving or on other activities consistent with U.S. superpower status.
Note: See Chapter 40 for additional discussion of current trends in international affairs.

See lesson plans, pp. T793A–T793C.

3 New Challenges for Canada

Objectives

Focus Questions

★ ■ What issues have dominated postwar Canada? *(pages 810–812)*
● ■ What role has Canada played in world affairs? *(page 812)*

Terms to Know

separatist
referendum

★ Note strategies for first objective on this page and p. 811.

Despite a relatively small population and a short history as an independent nation, Canada had become one of the world's leading industrial producers by the end of World War II. In the period of growth and prosperity that followed the war, Canadians had to face serious challenges to the unity of their nation.

Building a Modern Economy

Strengths. Canada's economic success, though spurred by World War II, was the result of earlier events. During the first part of the 1900's immigration into Canada increased, new railroads were built, and trade with the United States grew. Canada entered a period of economic growth that was interrupted only by the Great Depression of the 1930's. Rich mineral deposits were discovered, while lumbering and manufacturing made rapid gains. Capital for investment poured in from Great Britain and the United States.

During and after World War II, Canada's economic output rose, its population grew, and Depression-era unemployment

810

was greatly reduced. Established industries were expanded and new ones appeared. The discovery of oil in Alberta in 1947 made Canada an important oil-producing nation. After vast deposits of uranium were found in Saskatchewan and Ontario in the 1950's, Canada built nuclear power stations to generate electricity.

Sec. Rev. ques. 2

Between 1945 and 1956, Canada's growing prosperity attracted more than a million immigrants from war-torn Europe. Most settled in the large cities. These immigrants expanded the labor force and the country's market for consumer goods.

Canada's postwar growth was also helped by the completion in 1959 of the St. Lawrence Seaway. This was a joint project with the United States that opened the Great Lakes to Atlantic Ocean shipping. The seaway helped the economy on both sides of the border and provided some areas with hydroelectric power. Except during winter months, ships from distant countries could serve the heartland of North America. The seaway carried more shipping each year than the Suez and Panama canals combined.

Weaknesses. By the 1980's, Canada was among the world's leading economic powers. Yet its economy faced some major problems, especially in the area of foreign trade. As in colonial times, Canada's prosperity was based in large part on the export of raw materials, such as minerals, wheat, lumber, and fish. However, Canada continued to buy most of its manufactured goods from abroad. Many Canadians called for greater development of their own industries as a way to lower the country's dependence on imports and provide jobs for the nation's unemployed.

Many Canadians also had mixed feelings about their neighbor to the south, the United States. Almost three quarters of Canada's exports were sold in the United States, while well over half of Canada's imports

★ RETEACHING. **Have students identify the strengths and weaknesses of Canada's postwar economy.** (Strengths: greater economic output, less unemployment, industrialization, oil and uranium reserves, expanded labor force and market. Weaknesses: reliance on exports of raw materials, heavy imports of manufactured goods, American involvement in economy.) *(Comprehension)* **Observing for Detail**

★ REINFORCEMENT. **Have students work in groups to discuss the following issue:** *Canada's relationship with the United States is both harmful and beneficial to it.* **Students should cite evidence from the text to support their conclusions.** *(Synthesis)* **Evaluating Information**

Vancouver, Canada's third-largest city, is one of the busiest ports on the Pacific coast. Canadian products shipped from Vancouver include wheat, wood, and petroleum.

came from there. American stockholders and companies controlled more than half of Canada's major industries.

Sec. Rev. ques. 3

American involvement in the Canadian economy strained relations between the two countries. Some Canadians saw their reliance on American markets and capital as a threat to their independence and economic growth. They argued that profits from the sale of their raw materials did not fully benefit Canadians, and they feared the effects of American economic slowdowns.

Threats to National Unity

The role of the federal government. In the postwar years, disagreements arose over the division of power between Canada's central government and the provinces, particularly in economic matters. While provincial governments owned the resources, the central government was in charge of all trade. This led to disputes between the federal government and some provinces.

These disputes also moved into other areas. For instance, Canada's national leaders wanted to improve health care, unemployment benefits, pensions for the elderly, and education—even though these services were usually handled by the provinces. Some provincial leaders charged that there was already too much federal interference in their affairs. All the provinces sought a larger share of tax money to improve local government services and to stimulate the economy.

French separatism. The most serious threat to national unity was posed by the French-speaking majority in the province of Quebec. Eighty percent of Quebec's people were French-speaking or bilingual, yet most of its businesses were run by English-speaking Canadians. Moreover, English was used in business and government, creating hardships for those who spoke only French. In addition, living standards in Quebec were below the national average. As a result, Quebec's leaders began demanding major reforms in the 1960's.

Sec. Rev. ques. 4

Soon a "quiet revolution" was under way in Quebec. The provincial government, dominated by French Canadians, began to establish more self-government for Quebec. Some French-Canadian leaders wanted independence for Quebec. Quebec, they argued, was not a province but a nation within the nation, with its own culture and history. These people were separatists—people who favor withdrawing their group from a larger group.

★ See below.

The federal government opposed the separatists. Under Pierre Elliott Trudeau, a French Canadian who became prime minister in 1968, the federal government tried to improve relations with Quebec. English-speaking federal officials were encouraged to learn French. Provinces were asked to make both English and French their official languages and to set up schools for French-

811

★ ENRICHMENT. Have students research the separatist movement in Quebec and then answer the following question: *Would separation from Canada create more advantages or disadvantages for Quebec?* Have students share their research and conclusion with the class. (Evaluation) *Drawing Conclusions* speaking children. Moreover, English-Canadian schools were urged to teach French as a second language. More federal money was given to the province, and the two levels of government tried to find ways of working together. In the Official Languages Act, passed in 1969, the Canadian government recognized both English and French as national languages.

Not satisfied with these efforts, some separatists joined a political party dedicated to independence for Quebec. As tensions rose, a few people resorted to bombings and kidnappings to speed Quebec's independence. In 1980 a referendum—popular vote—was held in Quebec to decide the issue. A substantial majority of the people of Quebec voted to remain a part of Canada.

In 1982 Canada adopted a revised constitution which made important changes in Canada's relationship with Britain. No longer was British approval needed for constitutional amendments. The Constitution Act of 1982 also more clearly defined the powers of the federal and provincial governments and added a charter guaranteeing civil liberties for all Canadians.

The province of Quebec never endorsed the 1982 constitution, feeling that the document did not adequately recognize its distinct heritage. Consequently, in 1987, another effort to clarify Quebec's minority status was made in the form of a constitutional amendment called the Meech Lake Accord. Conceived by Prime Minister Brian Mulroney, the amendment would have granted special status to Quebec as a "distinct society" within the Canadian federation. But the Meech Lake Accord failed to win approval.

The Inuit land settlement. Canada has other groups in its population that feel they deserve special status as much as the people of Quebec. One such group is made up of the Inuit people—the Eskimos—who live in Canada's Arctic areas. In 1991 the Canadian government agreed to give the 17,000 Inuit self-government rights and ownership of a massive territory—equal in size to a fifth of Canada and stretching to the North Pole.

812

Canada in World Affairs

● Note strategies for second objective on this page.

World War II ended Canada's traditional policy of isolationism. Geography, trade, and cultural interests all forced Canada to take a more active role in international affairs. With the United States on its southern border and the Soviet Union lying across the polar ice cap, Canada would likely have been involved in any conflict between the two superpowers. Moreover, Canada's trade routes crisscrossed the Atlantic and Pacific, and the country had cultural ties with French-speaking and English-speaking countries all over the world. These factors shaped Canada's foreign policies in the postwar years.

Sec. Rev. ques. 5

From the beginning of the cold war, Canada sided with the nations of the West against the Soviet Union. In 1949 Canada played a major role in the creation of NATO (page 714), contributing troops, funds, and materials, and also took part in other international organizations. Canada helped create the United Nations in 1945 and remained a major supporter of that organization and its peace-keeping operations.

Relations with the United States. As in economic matters, Canada's closest ties in foreign affairs and defense were with the United States. The two countries together planned, built, and ran radar installations defending the continent. In 1957 the North American Air Defense Command (NORAD) was established to ward off a possible air attack on North America.

Despite its close relations with the United States, however, Canada often chose a separate path in foreign affairs. For example, Canada continued its trade with Cuba after the United States had cut off commerce with that nation. It also granted recognition to the People's Republic of China before the United States did.

An important step in U.S.-Canadian trade relations came in 1988 with the signing of a Free Trade Agreement. This agreement had as its aim the ending of almost all trade barriers between the United States and Canada by the end of the century.

● See below.

See Sec. 3 *Closing the Lesson,* p. T793C.

● RETEACHING. Have students answer the following: What factors contributed to the end of Canada's isolation? (Its proximity to the two superpowers, extensive trade routes, and its ties to French-speaking and English-speaking countries.) What was Canada's role in world affairs after World War II? (Canada helped create the UN and supported its peace-keeping efforts.) (Comprehension) Observing for Detail

● REINFORCEMENT. Have students summarize Canada's foreign relations with the United States. (Both countries help defend the continent. Canada continued trade with Cuba after the United States cut it off, and recognized China before the United States.) (Comprehension) Observing for Detail

● ENRICHMENT. Have students find information on the effect of the 1988 U.S.-Canada Free Trade Agreement. (Application) Locating Information

Section Review

Answers to Section Review questions are in brackets on pages indicated.

1. **Define:** separatist, referendum. (pp. 811, 812)
2. What natural resources spurred Canada's economic growth? (p. 810)
3. Why did many Canadians express concern over United States involvement in the Canadian economy? (p. 811)
4. What problems of Quebec's French-speaking people came to national attention in the 1960's? What changes did the government make? (pp. 811–812)
5. Why did geography force Canada to end isolationism after World War II? (p. 812)
6. **Critical thinking:** Review the description of Canadian history in Chapter 28. How does this help explain the separatist movement in Quebec? (See answer below.)

6. Students might respond that the separatist movement stemmed from cultural and political conflicts between Canada's original French settlers and British colonists.

Chapter 39   Summary and Timeline

1. The pursuit of economic development has been the main goal of Latin American nations in recent years. Poverty and dependence on foreign capital are still major concerns. Many nations have made progress toward democracy but still face problems resulting from inequality and extremism.

2. The United States emerged from World War II powerful and prosperous. The federal government grew steadily until the 1980's, when efforts were made to cut back. African Americans and other groups sought equal rights. In foreign affairs, the United States became involved in conflicts in several parts of the world. Cold-war tension with the Soviet Union continued into the 1980's. With the collapse of the Soviet Union in 1991, the cold war ended and the United States began shaping its foreign policy to fit its new role in world affairs.

3. In Canada, increased production during and after World War II spurred the economy. Economic and military dependence on the United States created concern, however. Conflicts between the provinces and the federal government endangered national unity as Quebec threatened to separate from Canada.

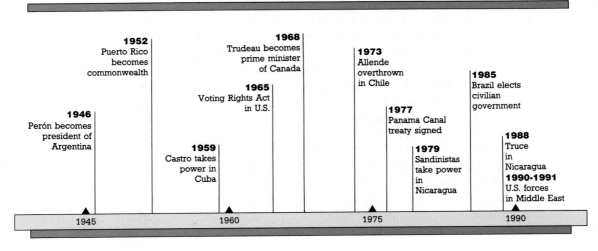

1946 Perón becomes president of Argentina

1952 Puerto Rico becomes commonwealth

1959 Castro takes power in Cuba

1965 Voting Rights Act in U.S.

1968 Trudeau becomes prime minister of Canada

1973 Allende overthrown in Chile

1977 Panama Canal treaty signed

1979 Sandinistas take power in Nicaragua

1985 Brazil elects civilian government

1988 Truce in Nicaragua

1990-1991 U.S. forces in Middle East

1945   1960   1975   1990

See p. T793C for answers to Chapter Review.

Vocabulary Review

Match each of the following terms with its correct definition: *default, Organization of American States, referendum, separatist, sunbelt, Watergate scandal.*

1. states stretching from the southeast Atlantic coast to southern California
2. fail to pay
3. incident that led to Nixon's resignation from the American presidency
4. group that involves Latin American nations and the United States in working on common issues
5. person who favors withdrawing his or her group from a larger group
6. popular vote

People to Identify

Match each of the following people with the correct description: *Fulgencio Batista, Porfirio Díaz, Fernando Collor de Mello, Martin Luther King, Jr., Henry Kissinger, Joseph McCarthy, Manuel Noriega, Juan Perón, Anastasio Somoza, Omar Torrijos, Pierre Trudeau.*

1. dictator who brought order to Mexico in the late 1800's
2. Brazilian president who pledged to revive the economy
3. Argentine president whose nationalist policies won popular support
4. Nixon adviser who negotiated American withdrawal from the Vietnam War
5. French Canadian who became prime minister of Canada in 1968
6. Cuban dictator ousted from power by Castro's forces
7. Baptist minister who led the civil rights movement in the United States

8. Panamanian general who supported his country's control of the Panama Canal
9. Panamian leader who was ousted from power by U.S. forces
10. Nicaraguan dictator from the 1930's to 1956
11. United States senator who started a hunt for Communist spies in the 1950's

Places to Know

Match the letters on this map of Central America and the Caribbean with the places listed below. You may want to refer to the map on page 799.

1. Bay of Pigs
2. Costa Rica
3. Guatemala
4. Honduras

Caribbean Sea

Recalling the Facts

1. What changes did Mexico's 1917 constitution provide for?
2. How did the Great Depression affect the governments of Brazil and Argentina?
3. What methods did Pinochet use in ruling Chile?

814

4. What changes did Castro make after coming to power in Cuba?

5. What led to the formation of the Sandinista government in Nicaragua? How did the United States show its opposition to the Sandinista government?

6. How did the 1977 Panama Canal Treaty change the status of the Canal Zone?

7. How did Latin American leaders try to achieve economic nationalism?

8. How did American society change after World War II? How did the population change?

9. How did Democratic Presidents try to expand the role of the federal government in the postwar years? Why did Reagan seek to reverse this trend?

10. How did the cold war affect U.S. foreign policy around the world?

11. How had U.S.-Soviet relations changed by 1990?

12. What factors contributed to Canada's postwar economic growth? What were Canada's economic weaknesses?

13. Why did some French-Canadian leaders call for Quebec's independence?

Critical Thinking Skills

1. **Making a timeline.** Make a timeline showing major events in the Americas during the 1900's. Use the chapter to find specific dates for events. (Comp.)

✔ 2. **Drawing conclusions.** Did the discovery of oil reserves in Mexico do more to hurt or help the country's economy? Explain your answer. (Syn.)

✔ 3. **Critical thinking.** Why did civil rights activists want the United States government to pass laws against racial discrimination? Do you think progress toward equal opportunity would have been made without government intervention? Explain your answer. (Syn.)

✔ 4. **Synthesizing.** Imagine that you are an adviser to the leaders of Puerto Rico. You have been asked to write a brief report on the political status of the commonwealth. The report should (1) describe the advantages and disadvantages of various options for changing the political status of Puerto Rico and (2) make recommendations for action by Puerto Rico's leaders. (Syn.)

Thinking About Geography

Analyzing. Review the geography concept of relative location (page GR11). How does relative location play a part in U.S. relations with different Latin American nations? (App.)

Enrichment: Primary Sources

In 1991 leaders of 19 Latin American nations and Spain and Portugal met in Guadalajara, Mexico. Below are excerpts from their joint declaration.

66 . . . We have met . . . to examine . . . the great challenges facing our countries. . . . We represent a vast set of nations sharing roots and the rich heritage of a culture based upon combinations of different peoples and bloodlines. Five hundred years after our first meeting, . . . we are determined to project the force of our community into the third millennium. . . .

We express the wish to build together a common future of peace, greater well-being and social equality. We are committed to our peoples' economic and social development, a full respect for human rights, the extension of democratic practices, . . . and respect for the norms of international law. 99

1. What was the meeting referred to in the first paragraph?
2. **Critical thinking:** How do recent developments in Latin America support the commitment expressed in the second paragraph? (Comp.)

✔ A checkmark identifies questions and exercises calling for the three higher-order levels of thinking at the top of the Bloom taxonomy: Analysis, Synthesis, and Evaluation.

Note—Thinking About Geography: Page GR11 is located in the Geographic Themes section preceding page 324.

Linking Past, Present, and Future   1960-2000 and beyond

(pp. 816–834)

Chapter Preview

Section 1 describes advances in space exploration since the beginning of the space age, and identifies other scientific developments in the fields of medicine and genetics. In Section 2, economic and environmental challenges are discussed and changes in world politics are examined. Section 3 identifies the effects of mass communication on the world and describes recent world trends.

Bibliography

See the *Teacher's Management and Planning Guide* for additional listings. Starred titles are for both students and teachers.

*Allen, Joseph P. and Russell Martin. *Entering Space: An Astronaut's Odyssey*. Stewart, Tabori & Chang. Everyday life while orbiting Earth at 17,000 miles per hour.

Critchfield, Richard. *The Golden Bowl Be Broken: Peasant Life in Four Cultures*. Indiana University Press. Peasant life in Iraq, Mauritius, India, and Indonesia.

Dyson, Freeman. *Weapons and Hope*. Harper and Row. Nuclear deterrence and disarmament.

Findley, Carter Vaughn, and John Alexander Murray Rothney. *Twentieth-Century World*. Houghton. Discusses such themes as global interrelatedness, rise of the mass society, technology and nature, and the search for values.

Kennedy, Paul. *The Rise and Fall of the Great Powers*. Random House. A 500-year look at the links between economics and military might.

Section Lesson Plans

SECTION 1   (pp. 817–821)
A New Scientific Revolution

Objectives

After completing this section, students will be able to:
1. Identify achievements human beings have made in space.
2. Describe how scientific advances have changed ways of living.

Introducing the Lesson

Remind students that human beings have studied and explored the world and the universe from the beginning of time. The rate of scientific discovery and technological change has increased during our time and human beings have used these developments to improve the quality of their lives.

Then ask: *(a) Why has the rate of scientific discovery increased in modern times?* (Answers will vary. People today have more and better technological tools which they use to expand their knowledge about the universe.)

(b) How do scientific advances improve our standard of living? (Answers will vary. Many scientific advances increase life expectancy, increase the ease and speed with which work can be done, and create new forms of leisure.)

(c) How might scientific advances create problems? (Answers will vary. Although scientific knowledge in itself cannot harm us, the choices human beings make about the use of scientific discoveries sometimes have harmful effects.)

Developing the Lesson:
Solving Problems

Have students work in groups to identify the most important problems facing the world community today and then suggest how future scientific research might help solve these problems. (Answers will vary, but students might suggest the following problems: world hunger, poorly developed agricultural areas, staggering population growth, nuclear and other military threats, and environmental concerns.) *(Synthesis)*

Developing the Lesson:
Discussing Issues

Have students work in groups to discuss the following questions:

(a) Should nations spend large amounts of money on space research?

(b) Should space research be used to design and build weapons?

(c) Should scientists be allowed to alter genetic codes? Why or why not?

(d) Should chemicals that permanently pollute the environment be used to control disease-transmitting insects? (Synthesis)

Closing the Lesson: Drawing Inferences

Have students outline ways in which the new scientific revolution has increased the interrelatedness of the world and then answer the following question: *How has this interrelatedness changed ways of living throughout the world?* (International interrelatedness has increased as a result of the following: communications satellites; competition in space exploration; environmental problems; sharing of technological and scientific information.) *(Comprehension)*

See *Section Review* questions, p. 821.

SECTION 2 (pp. 822–827)
The Reshaping of International Relations

Objectives

After completing this section, students will be able to:
1. Describe the economic challenges faced by the world's nations.
2. Identify recent developments in world politics.

Introducing the Lesson

Remind students that scientific advances have linked the nations of the world economically and politically. Because of this close international relationship, the foreign policies and actions of various nations affect the security and quality of life for all.

Then ask: *(a) How might international interdependence be an advantage to the nations of the world?* (Answers will vary. It is possible for all nations to benefit from technological and cultural advances and to see a common benefit in striving for peace.)

(b) How might international interdependence be a disadvantage to the nations of the world? (Answers will vary. Conflicts that arise between nations have greater repercussions. Economic and social problems that occur in one nation may well affect others.)

Developing the Lesson:
Making Judgments

Have students work in groups to debate the following issue: *Wealthy nations have an economic and social responsibility to help Third World nations improve the lives of their people.* When preparing the debate, students should consider specific policies that might be needed and how these would affect citizens of wealthy nations. *(Synthesis)*

Developing the Lesson:
Synthesizing Information

Have students write an essay explaining how international interdependence has resulted in economic crises for some nations and given rise to political conflict. (Economic interdependence has made nations more vulnerable to problems that occur elsewhere. Because nations depend on each other for vital supplies, any social, economic, or political disruption in one country might affect the economy of another. During the cold war many nations allied themselves with one of the superpowers; and tension between the superpowers affected those allies. Despite the closing of the cold war, international affairs remain unpredictable, with potential for new sources of conflict. Students may cite current developments. *(Synthesis)*

Closing the Lesson:
Predicting Events

Have students work in groups to predict the unfolding of events in Third World countries. Students should consider possible developments in Third World economies and political changes. *(Synthesis)*

See *Section Review* questions, p. 827.

SECTION 3   (pp. 828–832)
New Patterns of Living

Objectives

After completing this section, students will be able to:
1. Describe how mass communication has affected modern life.
2. Identify trends in religion and culture that have influenced the modern world.

Introducing the Lesson

Remind students that trends are patterns of events, attitudes, or behaviors that characterize a certain period of time and reveal important ideas and beliefs of a society.

Then ask: *(a) How do trends develop?* (Answers will vary. Trends reflect a pattern of choices made by people who are influenced by events during their time.)

(b) Why do trends change? (Because what people value, and the kinds of things they want, change over time.)

(c) What trends do you think will characterize the 1990's? (Answers will vary.)

Developing the Lesson:
Making Judgments

Have students work in groups to answer the following questions: *(a) What five items would you choose as artifacts to represent current **American culture** and society for future students of history? (b) What five items would you choose as artifacts to represent the **world** today for future students?* Have students explain their choices to the class. *(Analysis)*

Developing the Lesson:
Comparing Historical Developments

Have students write an essay explaining which period of history might be seen as most similar to our own. Students might consider the Renaissance, the Age of Discovery, the Enlightenment, the Romantic Era, the period before World War I, or any others. *(Synthesis)*

Closing the Lesson:
Making Judgments

Have students discuss this question: *What evidence is there that the world today is "a global village"? Is this trend likely to continue in the future or not?* Have students explain their answers. *(Synthesis)*

See *Section Review* questions, p. 832.

Chapter 40 Review Answers
(pp. 833–834)

Vocabulary Review

1. Coal, oil, or natural gas.
2. Large company that owns businesses in many different countries.
3. Style of art that represented familiar objects exactly and continued pop art's focus on mass-produced commercial goods.
4. Part of the earth's atmosphere that screens out harmful radiation from the sun.
5. Architectural style that uses such features as domes, arches, and columns from earlier styles.
6. Material that allows the transmission of electricity over vast distances with almost no energy loss.

People to Identify

1. Kawabata Yasunari 2. Walter Gropius 3. James D. Watson 4. Samuel Beckett 5. Andy Warhol 6. Jackson Pollock 7. Christiaan Barnard 8. John Paul II

Recalling the Facts

1. Satellites have been used to make scientific observations, facilitate worldwide communications, and provide military intelligence. Unmanned spacecraft that head deep into space have gathered information about other planets.
2. Space shuttles are reusable spaceships that take off like rockets and land like gliders. They will be used to carry cargo to space stations, place satellites in orbit, make experiments, and launch spacecraft.

3. They have been used to bring some diseases under control that used to kill millions every year.

4. Economic interdependence has raised standards of living. It has also made the world economy more vulnerable.

5. The developing nations of Africa, Asia, and Latin America have experienced the most rapid population growth.

6. Overgrazing stripped the land of plants that had anchored topsoil. Winds blew away the topsoil, turning vast areas into deserts.

7. Decreased demand led to an oversupply of oil and a drop in oil prices.

8. They argued that economic differences between developed and developing nations seemed more important than political differences between non-Communist and Communist countries.

9. Answers might mention closing of cold war, move away from communism in some countries, greater unpredictability in world affairs, rise of new economic powers and growth of trading blocs, greater importance of UN, move toward more unity in Europe.

10. Banks in industrialized nations faced collapse if Third World nations defaulted on past loans.

11. Mass communication has made people more familiar with the products of other cultures.

12. Church membership has grown rapidly in the United States.

13. The rise of Islamic fundamentalism in Asia and the Middle East indicates a reaction against Western influences.

Critical Thinking Skills

1. Reports will vary.
2. Diagrams will vary.
3. Answers will vary.
4. 86.4%. 1.6%. 15.8%. 13.6%. 62.5%. Among the generalizations that students might suggest are the following: since 1900 the movement of people from rural to urban areas has increased. The trend toward increased urbanization is expected to continue into the twenty-first century.

Thinking About Geography

Reports will vary.

Enrichment: Primary Sources

1. People with specialized occupations, such as pharmaceutical technicians, botanists, welders, journalists, and artists.
2. They will not be primarily "aviators" of space.
3. Answers will vary.

Linking Past, Present, and Future   1960–2000 and beyond

See chapter timeline, p. 832.

Before You Read This Chapter

One of the purposes of this book has been to show you the richness of our human past. It is natural, therefore, to end the book by connecting that past with the present and the future. As you read this chapter, ask yourself these questions: What has changed, and what has remained constant, over the course of human history? How will our future be connected with our past—and with what we know and do today?

Space exploration has given us a new way of looking at the planet Earth.

The Geographic Setting

The Chapter Outline

1. A New Scientific Revolution
2. The Reshaping of International Relations
3. New Patterns of Living

See lesson plans, pp. T815A–T815C.

1 A New Scientific Revolution

Objectives

Focus Questions

★ ■ What achievements have human beings made in space? *(pages 817–819)*
● ■ How have scientific advances changed ways of living? *(pages 819–821)*

Terms to Know

genetic engineering
superconductor

★ Note strategies for first objective on this page and p. 819.

You have read about several great revolutions of knowledge in the past. Today, however, the rate of scientific and technological change is faster than ever before. Almost every day, advances in knowledge and skills allow people to do things that people of the past could not have dreamed of doing. As a result, people today have great new powers—but we also have new problems to add to many of the old ones.

The Space Age

The space age began with the launching of the Soviet satellite *Sputnik* in October 1957. The first liquid-fueled rocket had been launched in 1926 by an American, Robert Goddard, but early rockets were not powerful enough to reach space. Several nations continued to work on rockets before and during World War II. Germany was the most successful, building rockets called the V-1 and V-2 that it used against Britain in the closing year of that war. By the 1950's, the development of stronger engines, plus the invention of computers to guide rockets, made space flight possible for the first time.

Most of the objects sent into space since *Sputnik* have been satellites. France, Italy, Japan, China, and Israel, as well as the United States and the Soviet Union, have all placed satellites in orbit around the planet.

Satellites allow scientists to see and study the whole earth in much greater detail than ever before. Satellites also relay telephone and television signals from places on opposite sides of the globe. Using military satellites, nations can keep watch over potential enemies, and in this way protect themselves against surprise attack. | Sec. Rev. ques. 2

Unlike satellites, which orbit the earth, other kinds of robot spacecraft head deep into space. By the early 1980's, spacecraft from earth had landed on Venus and Mars as well as on the moon. They were equipped to take photographs, collect soil samples, and send back information to earth. Other spacecraft flew by Mercury, Jupiter, and Saturn, passing close enough to take photographs and to gather information about the atmospheres of those planets. *Pioneer X,* launched in 1972, had traveled entirely out of our solar system by 1983. This tiny spacecraft is still sending information back to earth as it continues its long, lonely trek to the stars.

Human crews have piloted many missions as well. In 1969 the United States landed the first human beings on the moon (page 717). The first American space station, *Skylab,* was lifted into orbit in 1973. The Soviets launched several space stations beginning in 1971. Some Soviet cosmonauts have lived in a space station for a full year, performing experiments and gathering data. Huge space stations, large enough to hold hundreds of colonists, are now being planned. They will be a giant step toward a permanent human presence in space.

Also, in the 1970's the United States began to build a fleet of space shuttles—reusable spaceships that took off like rockets but landed like gliders. They are to be used for **817**

★ RETEACHING. Have students make a chart identifying important advances in space exploration made by the United States and by the Soviet Union. *(Comprehension) Translating Information Into Another Form*
★ REINFORCEMENT. Have students write an essay explaining the importance of space exploration. Students might explain how advances in space exploration can benefit nations and the world as a whole. *(Comprehension) Making Judgments*

Check for Understanding. Ask: Why do nations use military satellites? (To protect themselves against surprise attack by keeping watch over potential enemies.)
Science and Technology The goals of *Skylab* included the study of engineering and science technology in a space environment.
Check for Understanding. Ask: What is a space shuttle? (A reusable spaceship that takes off like a rocket but lands like a glider.)

Ⓕ See
below.

The Arts

Exploration Art

Among the settlers Sir Walter Raleigh sent to Virginia in 1585 was an artist, John White. When White returned to England from America, he carried with him a special vision of the "New World." White's drawings captured the mysterious beauty of the land and its people (pictures, pages 319 and 360). John White was an early exploration artist, and he helped persuade Europeans to invest both money and hope in a land they had never seen.

Artists of later centuries continued to send exciting images to the people back home. In the 1700's William Hodges, a member of Captain Cook's scientific expedition (page 416), created romantic landscapes of the South Sea Islands. Other artists joined in the scientific exploration of Africa, South America, and Antarctica in the 1800's and 1900's.

Today's exploration artists often carry cameras. They bring back striking pictures from the farthest frontiers of land and sea—and beyond. The latest romantic images come not from Earth, but from space. The *Voyager* spacecraft took close-up pictures of several planets. A photo of Saturn's rings, with color enhanced by computer, appears above. The inset shows Saturn and five of its moons artistically grouped together. Photographs of the planets provide today's special vision of new worlds.

818

Ⓕ **FEATURE ACTIVITY. Ask: (a) How does exploration art differ from artistic creations traditionally called fine art?** (Unlike fine art, exploration art aims to introduce unfamiliar places or things to a wide audience.) **(b) What do you think exploration art of the future will be like?** (Answers will vary.) *(Synthesis) Drawing Conclusions*

Science and Technology The *Voyager* "photos" were actually radio signals sent back to Earth and converted into pictures. The picture of Saturn and its moons is a composite of several such "photos."

Sec. Rev.
ques. 3

★ See
below.

carrying cargo to space stations, placing satellites in orbit, making experiments, and launching spacecraft. The shuttle *Columbia* made its first orbital flight in 1981. In 1986 the shuttle *Challenger* exploded, killing all aboard. In 1988 the shuttle program resumed with the successful flights of *Discovery* and *Atlantis*. Two years later shuttle launches sent an atomic-powered probe to explore the sun and telescopes to view distant objects in the universe. Meanwhile, planning continued on projects to build a settlement on the moon and to send astronauts to Mars.

The United States and the Soviet Union competed in space exploration after the launching of Sputnik. At times, however, they worked together in space. In 1975, American astronauts and Soviet cosmonauts met in space, linking their Apollo and Soyuz spacecraft in orbit, sharing a meal, and carrying out experiments.

By 1992 more countries were planning space programs. The break-up of the Soviet Union left the future of the Soviet space program in doubt. While the Russian government may continue some space projects, others were canceled or put up for sale. Meanwhile, Canada, Japan, and the European Community all have plans for space

exploration. It is likely, however, that new ventures into space will be internationally sponsored and that the days of superpower domination of space technology are over.

Other Scientific Frontiers

● Note strategies for second objective on this page and p. 821.
New science and technology have allowed humans to reach farther into the vastness of space. These advances have also made it possible for scientists to explore the tiny worlds inside living things.

Genetic engineering. In the 1950's James D. Watson, an American, and Francis H. Crick, a Briton, figured out the chemical processes that go on inside the gene. In 1953 Watson and Crick described the structure of a large molecule known as DNA, which is present in the nucleus of living cells. It was, they found, made up of thousands of atoms arranged like a twisted ladder. The different arrangements of the atoms in each DNA molecule spell out a "genetic code" that determines the biological traits of living things.

In the years that followed, scientists learned to change the arrangement of the atoms to make new traits. This process, called **genetic engineering** allowed scientists to

Ⓕ See
below.

CAUSE AND EFFECT

CAUSES	KEY DEVELOPMENT	EFFECTS
Scientific curiosity Advances in aviation and rocket technology during World War II Development of high-speed computers Rivalry between United States and Soviet Union	The Exploration of Space 1957–present	New knowledge about earth and its atmosphere Better understanding of solar system and universe beyond Development of new technologies for use on earth Plans for colonization of moon and planets

819

★ ENRICHMENT. Have students find information on recent developments in the American space program or on internationally sponsored space projects. (Application) *Locating Information*
Ⓕ CAUSE AND EFFECT CHART ACTIVITY. Have students explain how the effects of space exploration might be both beneficial and harmful to human societies. (Synthesis) *Drawing Conclusions*

● RETEACHING. Have students outline ways scientific advances have benefited human beings. (Genetic engineering has allowed scientists to make drought- and disease-resistant plants and study genetic diseases; medical advances have led to cures for illnesses and to new drugs, surgeries.) (Comprehension) *Observing for Detail*
● REINFORCEMENT. Have students work in groups to identify problems resulting from new scientific advances and to suggest ways of resolving them. (Synthesis) *Solving Problems*

make new kinds of plants that were more resistant to drought and disease. They also carried out research on human diseases that had genetic causes, implanting normal genes into the cells of patients born with defective genes.

The idea behind genetic engineering has been around for thousands of years. People have long bred animals for greater size or speed. Now that it is possible to create new forms of life, many people are asking whether this new knowledge is being misused. Some fear that newly made bacteria, for example, may harm the environment or even human beings in ways that can never be undone.

Medical advances. New knowledge about living things has helped researchers discover cures for many illnesses. The first of the "wonder drugs," penicillin, was discovered accidentally in 1928 by Alexander Fleming, but was not widely used until World War II. Since then, more and more antibiotics have been developed. Using these bacteria-killing drugs, medical science has brought under control some diseases—such as pneumonia and tuberculosis—that used to kill millions each year.

Though there has been progress against some diseases, a new and deadly disease appeared in the 1980's. First identified in 1981, Acquired Immune Deficiency Syndrome (AIDS) attacks the human body's defenses against disease. AIDS is spread through sexual activity with infected persons, the transfusion of contaminated blood, and the sharing of hypodermic needles. Thousands of people throughout the world have been infected with the AIDS virus. Many governments are working together in a race against time to halt the spread of AIDS.

The last few decades have witnessed remarkable advances in the field of surgery. Doctors have learned how to replace diseased or damaged parts of the body. A South African surgeon, Dr. Christiaan Barnard, performed the first successful human heart transplant in 1967. Other organs, such as the liver and kidney, have been transplanted as well. Microsurgery—surgery using microscopes—has made it possible to reattach severed

Sec. Rev. ques. 4

820

International health organizations often sponsor medical clinics in developing nations. This one in Thailand helps Cambodian refugee mothers and their babies.

limbs. Doctors are also using lasers to cut away diseased tissue without harming the healthy tissue around it.

Some of the new treatments remain very expensive. This raises new social and moral questions that society must deal with. Do all citizens have a right to advanced medical care? How might society deal with the rising costs of medical treatment? Issues related to health care will become increasingly important in the years ahead.

Computers. As you learned in Chapter 1, record-keeping is a basic part of civilization. The development of written language helped make civilization possible. In the 1400's the invention of the printing press revolutionized society by greatly speeding the spread of information. In the 1900's the first practical computers launched a similar revolution.

Computers have nearly unlimited uses. They can store huge amounts of information and can guide spacecraft and control military equipment. Scientists are trying to build computers that use artificial intelligence to think

Science Note that penicillin prevents the growth of cell walls, which are necessary for the survival of bacteria.

like human beings. Someday there might be computers that think, learn, and create at least as well as people can.

The "information revolution" made possible by computers also raises questions for the future. How should information—about *you*, for example—be handled? Do people have the right to withhold information about themselves? What does the government have the right to know about you? Knowledge in any form—a clay tablet, a book, a microchip—has always been power.

See Sec. 1 *Closing the Lesson* p. T815B.

Who should share in this power? Who should control it?

Superconductors. Another area of great promise lies in new ways of transmitting electricity. When electricity is sent through ordinary power lines, much energy is lost. Scientists in many countries are now trying to learn more about **superconductors**—materials that at low temperatures will allow electricity to be sent with almost no energy loss. This research has enormous implications for the future.

● See below.

Section Review

Answers to Section Review questions are in brackets on pages indicated.

1. **Define:** genetic engineering, superconductor. (pp. 819, 821)
2. What are some uses of satellites? (p. 817)
3. What are the achievements of the American space shuttle program? (p. 819)
4. How have advances in technology changed the field of medicine? (p. 820)
5. What goal do scientists have for computers of the future? (p. 821)
6. **Critical thinking:** If, through genetic engineering, scientists could create people with twice the intelligence of people now, should they be allowed to do so? Explain. (See answer below.)

6. Answers might focus on issues related to freedom of scientific pursuit or the possible misuse of such knowledge.

See lesson plans, pp. T815A–T815C.

2 The Reshaping of International Relations

Objectives

★ Note strategies for first objective on this page and p. 822.

Focus Questions

★ ■ What economic, political and environmental challenges face the nations of the world? *(pages 822–826)*
● ■ What are the special concerns of the Third World nations? *(pages 826–827)*

Terms to Know

interdependent
multinational
  corporation
fossil fuel

greenhouse effect
ozone layer
Third World

The key fact in contemporary life is the new globalism of human affairs. Never before in all human existence have events and developments had effects that are so world-wide in scope. People of widely different religions, languages, cultures, races—people rich and poor—are now interdependent in their everyday lives. The politics and economies of their countries are closely tied together, and so also are their relations to their natural environments. People of countries on all the continents and inhabited islands share the world news; they are linked by satellite telephone and FAX machines; they see and hear each other on their home television sets. The English language is their most widely used medium for communication.

821

● ENRICHMENT. Have students find information on superconductors. Students might research how they function and explain their possible impact on energy use. *(Application)* *Locating Information*

★ RETEACHING. Have students give brief identifications of the following: globalism; Pacific Rim; United Nations; unification of Germany; Charter of Paris; NATO. *(Comprehension)* *Observing for Detail*

Global Challenges

The new globalism creates both worldwide unity and disunity. On the one hand, people want the latest goods and technical achievements; all want a higher standard of living. On the other hand, all want to retain their traditional national or ethnic identities.

Whatever their differences, people everywhere now aspire to the ideals of freedom and democracy. But where people are not used to peaceful cooperation, freedom can lead to a breakdown of law and order. Moreover, where people are not used to governing themselves—as in the lands of the former Soviet Union—democracy may even lead to anarchy. The search for prosperity likewise has divided people. In their ever closer associations, the rich countries have become richer, the poor poorer.

In bringing sharply different peoples into closer connections, the new globalism has imposed creative challenges on people around the world. It offers new opportunities in a world wide open to human enterprise while also making life more difficult. As the twenty-first century comes closer, all of humanity has to adjust to the strenuous pace of inescapable worldwide interdependence.

The Population Explosion

Perhaps the most challenging result of the spread of knowledge around the world has been the phenomenal increase in the world's population. Advances in medicine, technology, and agriculture, and an overall rise in the traditional standard of living caused by worldwide trade, have led to a population explosion, especially in Asia, Africa, and Latin America.

Sec. Rev. ques. 2

For thousands of years the human population stayed about the same—at less than a million people. During the 1800's it increased, reaching one and a half billion by 1900. In the 1900's, despite two world wars, totalitarian terror, and countless natural catastrophes, the world's population has grown

822

to five and a third billion. If the current rate of growth continues, the figure will double within 50 years.

One result of the population explosion has been greater urbanization. In developing nations, most people have lived in rural areas, but that is changing quickly. Just as in the Western world during the 1800's, the population explosion in developing nations has led to rapid growth of cities. Rising population and urbanization put enormous pressure on the environment and on energy resources.

World Politics

Worldwide interaction and the population explosion have affected the character of politics around the world. All governments today, even those that are clearly dictatorships, claim to be democratic and to exist and act for the benefit of their peoples. In today's world, governments must guarantee food, employment, public services, and even contentment to ever more demanding citizens. That task is especially difficult in poor countries or in countries where religious or ethnic strife makes cooperative action impossible. In many parts of the world, governments continue to use force to maintain stability and order. Only countries that enjoy wealth, an orderly society, and international power are able to sustain a truly democratic system.

Shifting power. The preservation of peace and order in international relations is not easy. During the cold war, world politics were shaped by the rivalry between the United States and the Soviet Union. The smaller and weaker countries sided with one or the other superpower. What all had in common was the dread of the possibility of nuclear war.

The collapse of the Soviet Union as a superpower in 1990–1991 drastically changed this situation. The United States was left as the only superpower, determined to build a more peaceful world order. But the United States cannot do that alone. It needs the assistance of two other rapidly growing centers of global power: the countries of

Sec. Rev. ques. 3

World Population: Developed and Developing Nations

The world's population is increasing rapidly, largely as a result of improvements in medical care. Where is population increasing faster—in developed or developing nations? What might be some effects of rapid population growth? (The map above is based on a Peters projection of the world. The Peters projection emphasizes landmasses of developing nations.)
(See answers below.)

Map labels:
NORTH AMERICA
EUROPE
ASIA
AFRICA
SOUTH AMERICA
AUSTRALIA
ATLANTIC OCEAN
PACIFIC OCEAN
PACIFIC OCEAN
INDIAN OCEAN

◇ Developed (Australia, Canada, Europe, Japan, New Zealand, U.S., USSR)

◇ Developing (all other regions)

Peters projection

1950
1.7 billion (67%)
0.8 billion (33%)
Total population: 2.5 billion

1985
3.6 billion (75%)
1.2 billion (25%)
Total population: 4.8 billion

2020*
6.9 billion (84%)
1.3 billion (16%)
Total population: 8.2 billion
* Figures for this year are projections

◆ Developed (Australia, Canada, Europe, Japan, New Zealand, U.S., USSR)

◇ Developing (all other regions)

Source: U.S. Bureau of the Census; UNESCO; and *World Population Projections*

Western Europe and those of the Pacific Rim—above all, Japan. The commercial powers of East Asia for the first time in history play an equal role with Western nations.

Global organizations. The end of the cold war gave new importance to the United Nations (page 711). The UN and its political, economic, educational, and humanitarian agencies stand as symbols of the new globalism. More loosely organized international groupings like the Organization of American States (OAS) or the Organization for African Unity (OAU) aim at regional cooperation. Obviously, global interdependence requires that governments team up with each other across national boundaries.

Peaceful cooperation, however, re-quires a common willingness to change deeply rooted traditional ways and ambitions—a willingness that often is overwhelmed by nationalist emotion. Regions or areas where long-lasting hostilities block efforts to resolve problems have been the Middle East, Yugoslavia, and Kashmir. But troubles fester in many other parts of the world as well.

The future of Europe. With the end of cold-war rivalry, much of the world's attention focused on Europe. In 1990 East and West Germany were united, making Germany the strongest and most populous nation in Europe. Unification raised fears that Germany might overshadow its neighbors. But the new Germany is dedicated to demo-

Sec. Rev. ques. 4

823

Graph answers: (1) Developing. (2) Answers might mention the following: not enough food to support larger populations; fewer employment opportunities; increased pollution and other environmental damage; overcrowded cities; scarcity of energy resources.

cratic government and to mutually beneficial cooperation with its neighbors. Its location creates close ties to the states of Eastern Europe now liberated from Soviet control and to the lands of the former Soviet Union. All of them hope to benefit from German industrial skills and enterprise. At the same time, Germany is committed to its other neighbors through membership in the European Community.

Meanwhile, the nations of the European Community (page 719) are striving to complete their economic, financial, and political unity. Yet concerns about the need to yield certain kinds of sovereignty continue. Under pressure to expand its membership, the EC has agreed to extend its single-market benefits to more of Europe's nations in the European Economic Area formed in 1991. The countries of Eastern Europe will also seek membership when their economies are sufficiently advanced to merit EC membership.

A common concern of the EC countries is the influx of migrants from North Africa or Eastern Europe if borders are freely opened. In some EC countries resentment against these strangers seeking economic betterment has erupted in violence.

Europe's internal tensions, however, have been restrained by a new spirit of peace. At the end of the cold war the Warsaw Pact—the Soviet Union's military alliance with its Eastern European satellites—was dissolved; Soviet forces were called home. Strategic nuclear weapons have been reduced and nuclear arms for battlefield use withdrawn from Europe. NATO, the Western military alliance formed during the cold war (page 714), has heavily cut its forces. In the Charter of Paris, which officially ended the cold war (1990), leaders of 32 European nations and the United States and the Soviet Union, pledged to cooperate in building a new era of "democracy, peace, and unity" in Europe.

The Global Economy

The economies of the various parts of the world have been linked for centuries. After

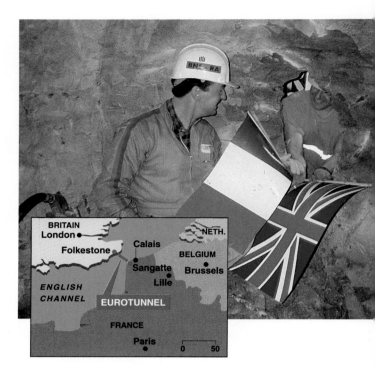

Construction of the tunnel under the English Channel symbolized a new era in European relations. Here tunnel workers displayed French and British flags after making a breakthrough in construction under the Channel. Inset map shows route of the tunnel.

European nations started establishing colonies in the Western Hemisphere, the resources of that part of the world were tied into the traditional trade among Europe, Asia, and Africa. In the 1800's, as empire-building and industrialization greatly intensified world trade, the economies of the world became interdependent—dependent on each other.

In the twentieth century, however, the world saw the creation of the even tighter economic interdependence that supports the new globalism. The new economic order rests on three main pillars: the United States, the Economic Community of Western Europe, and Japan, the economic superpower of East Asia, supplemented by "the little dragons" of the Pacific Rim (page 748).

These three blocs have many interconnections with the rest of the world. The

Sec. Rev. ques. 5

824

industrialized nations of these blocs rely on imported raw materials for their factories; poor countries need the cheap mass-produced goods plus the capital and know-how of the advanced countries for developing their own economies. All need oil, the most important item of trade in global interdependence. Either a shortage or a glut of oil sends shock waves around the world. Controlling the world's oil supply, the Organization of Oil Exporting Countries (OPEC, page 766) plays a key part in global politics and economics.

Other key players are the **multinational corporations,** world-spanning companies not tied to any particular country. These companies produce such things as computers, automobiles, chemicals, weapons—items of universal demand—and locate their factories where labor is cheap. Some multinationals are richer than many poor countries and are able to wield immense influence in global affairs. Bankers and investors also play an important role. They control the flow and supply of money around the world, with the help of international agencies like the International Bank for Reconstruction and Development (also called the World Bank) and the International Monetary Fund (IMF).

Global economics is more peaceful than global politics. But economic concerns produce their own tensions. In building up political power, governments need to promote their own economic interests. They also are under pressure to guard their own people against foreign competition. In theory, worldwide free trade serves everybody best. In the short run, however, people may lose jobs, industries may fail, and national economies may suffer as a result of competition in world trade. Protectionism in one form or another, therefore—the effort to protect a nation's own industries and trade from foreign competition—is a common practice among governments and is a source of international friction as well as of extensive international regulation.

As in world politics, international cooperation does play a part in global economics, often with the help of United Nations agencies or by direct negotiation. The leading industrial countries of the world, for instance, have formed the Organization for Economic Cooperation and Development (OECD) with the aim of promoting their interests. The global economy is alive with business enterprise linking peoples and countries, now reaching also into Eastern Europe and the lands of the former Soviet Union.

New Sources of Energy

Expanding economic productivity has led to a search for additional sources of energy. Industrialized nations need **fossil fuels**—coal, oil, and natural gas—to run their factories, offices, and means of transportation, as well as to light and heat their houses and other buildings. By the 1970's so much fossil fuel was being used that scientists warned of shortages within decades.

Concerned about limited fuel supplies, Western countries began to look for new oil fields. The result, in the 1980's, was a temporary oversupply. But known oil reserves are slowly being exhausted, except in the Arab states on the Persian Gulf and in Russian Siberia, where supplies are expected to last for a long time.

By the 1980's some countries were heavily dependent on nuclear power. France, Belgium, Sweden, and Taiwan produced more than half of their electricity this way. Yet while nuclear power is cheaper and more efficient than many other forms of energy, it is also more dangerous. In 1986 an accident at the Chernobyl nuclear power plant in the Soviet Union spread radioactivity over much of Europe (page 726). Nuclear power plants also produce dangerous radioactive wastes. Disposing of this waste safely is expensive and difficult.

The possibilities of wind, water, and solar power have been explored but as yet are not practical for use on a large scale. Many other new technologies are also being studied. The world's nations will need both conservation and alternate sources of energy to meet their future energy needs.

Environmental Concerns

The population explosion and expanding industrialization have imposed threats on the natural environment never before experienced. One threat is global air pollution. Fumes from fossil fuels make the air unhealthy to breathe. In the 1980's, scientists warned that carbon dioxide was gathering in the earth's atmosphere. Like the glass in a greenhouse, this gas was trapping the sun's heat around the earth. Over the next 60 years, scientists predicted, the greenhouse effect would raise the earth's temperature by 9 degrees Fahrenheit. This amount of warming, they said, would change climates in ways that might prove disastrous.

A different kind of pollution threatens the ozone layer—a part of the earth's atmosphere that screens out harmful radiation from the sun. Chemicals rising into the air have been eating away at the ozone layer. Scientists warn that unless this process is slowed, more people than ever before will suffer from skin cancer.

Other environmental problems have been caused by new agricultural techniques. Chemical fertilizers and pesticides, used to boost farm output, often drain into lakes, rivers, and oceans. There they may pollute supplies of drinking water and harm wildlife.

Meanwhile . . .

IN BRAZIL

Since the 1970's, millions of acres of Amazon rain forest have been burned to clear land for farms and ranches. Environmentalists warn that this destruction has altered the earth's climate, because smoke from the fires has added to the greenhouse effect. The Brazilian government has promised to protect what remains of the Amazon forest.

In developed nations, governments have banned the most dangerous pesticides and have tried to protect drinking water from pollution. Developing countries, eager to promote economic growth, sometimes take actions that cause long-term environmental damage. To get more farmland and firewood, governments in developing countries have cleared millions of acres of forests. This threatens to destroy the natural balance of the environment.

The destruction of forests in South Asia has been a factor in tragic floods in Bangladesh, where hundreds died, thousands lost their homes, and much of the nation's food was destroyed. In Africa south of the Sahara, overgrazing stripped the land of plants that had anchored valuable topsoil. Winds then blew away the topsoil, turning vast areas into desert. In the 1980's these conditions resulted in famines that killed tens of thousands of Africans.

Sec. Rev. ques. 6

The Third World

Note strategies for second objective on pp. 826–827.

During the cold-war era the term Third World came into use as a term applied to the majority of nations in Africa, Asia, and Latin America. In these Third World lands, mostly located south of the equator or near it (map, page 823), live the poorest and most rapidly increasing majority of the world's population. Many of these people barely survive in urban slums and shanty towns, with only polluted water to drink and inadequate food, with little access to education, medical care, and economic opportunities, and subject to devastating natural catastrophes.

The contrast with life in the "First World"—the developed countries mostly located in the Northern Hemisphere—is dramatic and stark. The First World countries have 21 percent of the world's population, yet they consume 85 percent of the world's energy. Americans are especially privileged, making up only 5 percent of the world's people but using one third of the world's resources.

● RETEACHING. Identify the problems faced by Third World nations. (Poverty; lack of education, medical care, economic opportunities; inability to deal with natural catastrophes; unequal access to world's resources; indebtedness to richer countries.) *(Comprehension)* **Identifying Factors**

● REINFORCEMENT. Have students explain how the end of the cold war affected the situation of Third World countries. (Some of these countries lost the aid they had received as allies of superpowers during the cold war. Also, they now have to compete for aid with countries of Eastern Europe and the Soviet Union.) *(Comprehension)* **Identifying a Trend**

Deposed statues of Communist heroes—now ex-heroes—were collected and abandoned in a park in Moscow in 1992, symbolizing the collapse of the regime that once controlled Russia and most of Eastern Europe.

Sec. Rev.
ques. 7

The inequality between North and South, between the developed and the developing countries, became a growing cause of concern in the later decades of the 1900's. The United Nations declared the 1970's the "development decade." Yet, despite all efforts, the gap between the rich and the poor has widened. Most developing countries are unable to escape their huge indebtedness to the rich countries.

Their economic dependence deprives the Third World countries of political power. For many years they were often drawn into the cold-war struggle. To get economic and military aid, they sided with one or the other of the superpowers. Now that the cold war is over, some of these countries have lost that aid. These countries continue to ask for more help, but now they compete with the "Second World"—Eastern Europe and the republics that were once part of the old Soviet Union—for the limited funds available from the rich First World countries. Thus they feel exploited. Yet they admire the developed countries. Some privileged citizens in these countries copy Western life styles while disregarding the needs of the people and supporting dictatorships.

Prospects for the Future

The population explosion and global interdependence have created a new age in human existence. This new age offers many opportunities for human talent. The whole world lies open to creative enterprise.

Optimists foresee a happier world guided by the ideals of freedom and democracy as exemplified by the United States. They rejoice in the collapse of Communist regimes and military dictatorships and expect to see wider prosperity based on free enterprise. Realists, on the other hand, call attention to the obstacles, asking whether unprepared peoples are ready to assume more demanding responsibilities. They point to continuing conflicts and violence, to terrorism and desperation born of hopelessness. An objective observer must note that the new globalism has not changed one long-time truth—both good and bad are still found in human history.

See Sec. 2 Closing the Lesson, p. T815B.

827

8. Some students might say that efforts to deal with environmental problems will require close international cooperation. Others might say that some nations will give priority to their own problems and goals.

3 New Patterns of Living

Objectives

Focus Questions

★ ■ How has mass communication affected modern life? *(page 828)*

● ■ What trends in religion and culture have influenced the modern world? *(pages 828–831)*

Terms to Know

abstract expressionism
pop art
new realism

International Style
post-modernism
existentialism

★ Note strategies for first objective on this page.

For most of the world's history, the vast majority of people knew little or nothing about the arts, literature, or music of other cultures. Travel was expensive and difficult. Learning, in the form of writing and reading, was available only to a few people. There was no radio or television, no film or record industry.

Mass Communication

Today almost everyone is familiar with the products of other cultures. Western music, television programs, fashion, and films are popular throughout much of the world. Western artists, in turn, have been influenced by the art of non-Western peoples. Western fashion designers use ideas from Asia and Africa. People in the West have taken an interest in the philosophies and religions of Asia and the Middle East.

Sec. Rev. ques. 2

This increased contact among cultures has done much to enrich the lives of all peoples. As a student, you know more about the world and its riches than did the pha-

828

raohs and emperors of bygone civilizations. Such increased knowledge has also caused new problems. Some people in developing countries charge that their traditions are being undermined by Western influences such as television. Others worry that too much contact among peoples will destroy the richness and variety of the world's cultures.

★ See below.

The Search for Meaning

● Note strategies for second objective on pp. 829 and 831.

From earliest times, human beings have held religious beliefs that gave meaning to their lives. The rapid social change that followed the Industrial Revolution led some people away from religion. Since the Second World War, however, there has been a great renewal of interest in religion.

In the United States, for example, church membership has grown rapidly, especially in fundamentalist Protestant churches. The Roman Catholic Church has also gained new members throughout the world. In 1962 the Pope called a special council, later known as Vatican II. It modernized the Catholic religious service and called for unity among all Christian churches. Other people turned to the religions of the Orient, such as Zen Buddhism (page 289).

Even through the cold-war years, faith lived on in the Communist-ruled countries of Eastern Europe. Pope John Paul II, a Pole, raised the hopes of Catholics and others behind the Iron Curtain for a return of religious and political freedom. In the Soviet Union, after Gorbachev came to power in 1985, freer practice of religion was allowed, and in 1990 the Soviet legislature officially ended state control of religious institutions.

Sec. Rev. ques. 3

Meanwhile, in Asia and the Middle East, a reaction against Western culture led to the rise of Islamic fundamentalism (page 768). Since that time, fundamentalism has spread to other Islamic countries.

★ **RETEACHING. Have students review "Mass Communication" (above) and explain how mass communication has influenced different cultures.** (Western culture is available to many more people, and the West has been influenced by the art and ideas of non-Western peoples.) *(Comprehension) Observing for Detail*

★ **REINFORCEMENT. Have students write an essay explaining how contact with different cultures can enrich our lives.** *(Synthesis) Drawing Conclusions*

★ **ENRICHMENT. Have students research the effects of Western culture on one of the developing nations of Africa, Asia, or Latin America.** *(Application) Locating Information*

Religion Vatican II, which was initiated by Pope John XXIII, ranks as one of the most important developments in the history of the Catholic Church. The special council encouraged greater Church participation by laypersons and recognized the spiritual values of non-Catholic religions.

Although people around the world hold different religious beliefs, they are all looking for a deeper understanding of life. The search for meaning, for the answers to questions people have asked since the earliest times, will go on. These questions—about the origins and purposes of life—are a deep-seated part of the human inheritance.

Cultural Change

From the Old Stone Age to the present day, human beings have used art to express their ideas about life and the world around them. Works of art thus tell us a great deal about the times in which they were made. As you have learned, art is sometimes all that remains from the civilizations of the past.

Painting. After World War II, painting was dominated by **abstract expressionism**. This style of painting featured bold colors and large canvases. Unlike earlier artistic movements, which had begun in Europe, this style was originally American. Some abstract expressionists applied paint in a random way. Jackson Pollock, for example, poured and splattered paint onto his canvases rather than applying it with a brush.

During the 1960's, some artists reacted against abstract expressionism in a movement known as **pop art**. Pop art took many of its images from American popular culture. Artists like Andy Warhol painted everyday objects such as soup cans and comic strips with photographic precision. They were trying to erase the boundaries between "high art" and "popular art."

Map Answers: (1) Christianity and Islam. (2) Sunni. (3) India.

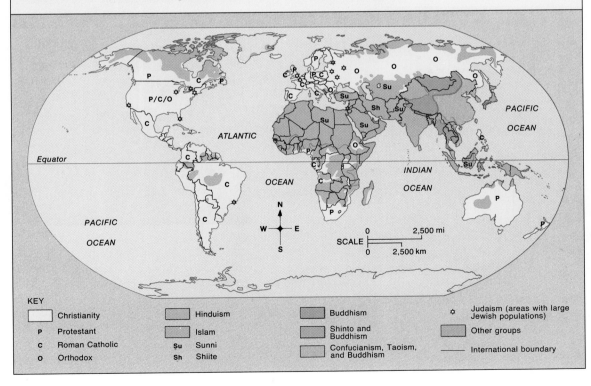

Major Religions of the World

This map shows where each of the major religions of the world is dominant today. Which two religions seem to be the most widespread? To which branch of Islam do the people of northern Africa belong? In what country is Hinduism the dominant religion? (You may want to refer to the Atlas.)

KEY

☐ Christianity	☐ Hinduism	☐ Buddhism	✧ Judaism (areas with large Jewish populations)
P Protestant	☐ Islam	☐ Shinto and Buddhism	☐ Other groups
c Roman Catholic	Su Sunni	☐ Confucianism, Taoism, and Buddhism	— International boundary
o Orthodox	Sh Shiite		

829

● RETEACHING. Have students explain the meaning of "global village" and identify the advantages and disadvantages of the concept for the peoples of the world. (Synthesis) *Drawing Conclusions*

Reference Note "Cultural Change" is a brief overview of contemporary cultural trends and is not intended to be a comprehensive survey.

● REINFORCEMENT. Have students write an essay explaining the recent trend of renewed interest in religion. (Synthesis) *Drawing Inferences*

Cultural History Note that Andy Warhol created most of his art with a process called silk-screen printing. He used this process to give his work an impersonal and mass-produced appearance.

Contemporary Architecture

The Seagram Building in New York City (1958), designed by Mies van der Rohe, was the first of many skyscrapers built in the International Style.

Mexican architect Luis Barragán used natural materials and graceful forms to give this housing development and stable (1968) a harmonious, peaceful look.

Architect Moshe Shafdie designed Habitat—these prefabricated apartments—for Montreal's 1967 world's fair.

The Pompidou Center in Paris (1976) playfully displays the pipes and airshafts that remain hidden in most buildings.

The Portland (Oregon) Building (1982) by Michael Graves is an example of a post-modernist use of ornamentation.

Beginning in the 1970's, a new generation of artists continued the trend that began with pop art. The **new realism**, as their style was called, represented familiar objects exactly. Their pictures were often hard to distinguish from photographs. The new realists painted scenes from everyday life and continued pop art's focus on mass-produced commercial goods.

● See
below.

Architecture. Since World War II, most architecture has been influenced by the **International Style**, which began in Germany during the 1920's. International Style architects such as Walter Gropius worked with geometric shapes, using industrial materials such as glass, steel, and concrete. Most of their buildings are simple and uncluttered. The skyscrapers that make up the skylines of many of the world's cities reflect this style.

Sec. Rev.
ques. 4

During the 1960's and 1970's, a new generation of architects rejected International Style buildings, saying they were simply "glass boxes." They and their successors are known as **post-modernists**. These architects have revived earlier styles by using such features as domes, arches, and columns in their buildings.

Literature. Postwar European literature was heavily influenced by **existentialist** philosophy. This was a way of thinking about life that developed in Europe during the 1940's and 1950's. To the existentialists, the universe has no meaning; each person is left alone to make decisions and to build his or her own life. Existentialist thinkers said that human beings must be held responsible for the choices they make.

Existentialist writers such as Jean-Paul Sartre (SAHR-truh) wrote about characters who were cut off from the people and the society around them. Some wrote books and plays that showed what they saw as the absurdity of modern life. In Samuel Beckett's play *Waiting for Godot*, for example, two men wait endlessly for a third who never appears and who may not even exist.

It has been argued that today, in the West, painting, literature, and music have entered a period of uncertainty. For many people, these arts no longer speak to what is deeply important about human life, and no longer both enrich and entertain as did the great novels or paintings or symphonies of the past. This subject remains a matter of great controversy.

People in the West now have access to the works of writers of many different regions. Latin American writers such as Gabriel García Márquez (gahr-SEE-uh MAHR-kays) of Colombia have written novels of fantasy and imagination. Chinua Achebe (uh-CHAY-bay), a Nigerian, has written of the impact of colonialism on his country and described life after independence. Japanese writers such as Kawabata Yasunari (yah-SOO-nah-ree) have become widely known for their attempts to blend Japanese and Western traditions in their works.

A global village. Today, people in nearly every country have a chance to see how people in other nations live. Television and radio can bring the same events to millions of people at the same time. A family in Japan can watch a soccer match being played in Buenos Aires or in Hamburg. Audiences throughout the world can watch Olympic athletes compete in France or Spain. They can see televised performances of rock, opera, dance, or jazz from Vienna, Tokyo, London, or New York. In a way, the world has become a "global village," in which the peoples of the world can know as much about each other as people in small towns know about their neighbors.

In all times and in all places, however, the common, ordinary human things have remained the same. People have needed in the past—and will need in the future—to laugh and to have fun. They need to feel that they belong to something larger and better than themselves. They need to feel useful. They need to have friends and heroes. They need to feel love and hope. They need to build things. They need to feel sheltered and cared for. They need to feel comforted in times of grief and fear. They need to learn and to create and to wonder. These things have not changed in thousands of years, and are not likely to change in the future.

831

See Sec. 3 *Closing the Lesson*, p. T815C.

● ENRICHMENT. Have students work in groups to answer this question: *When people in the future visit museums and view the works of today's artists, or when people in the future listen to music that is popular today, what will they learn about us? (Analysis)* **Making Judgments**

Cultural History In *Things Fall Apart*, Achebe's first novel, he describes how life in an Ibo village changed when missionaries and colonial administrators arrived. The main character in the novel has difficulty accepting European interference in the traditional ways of his society.

1. **Define or identify:** abstract expressionism, pop art, new realism, International Style, post-modernism, existentialism. (pp. 829, 831)
2. How has the development of mass communication changed the life of the average person? (p. 828)
3. What trends have developed in religion since World War II? (p. 828)

4. How has the International Style changed the appearance of many of the world's cities? (p. 831)
5. **Critical thinking:** What trends described in this section have had an influence on your life? In what way? (See answer below.)

5. Answers may refer to culture, commercial goods, travel, and international issues, among others.

Chapter 40   Summary and Timeline

1. In the post-1960 era the United States and the Soviet Union made great progress in space exploration. The first moonwalk took place in 1969, and by the 1980's spacecraft were traveling to the outer reaches of the solar system. Other scientific advances of recent decades included genetic engineering and improvements in medicine.

2. Governments around the world faced severe problems in the postwar era. Overpopulation, environmental pollution, and energy shortages all cried out for solutions. The superpowers engaged in cold-war rivalry until the abandonment of communism in Soviet-bloc nations launched a new era in international relations. Mean-

while, Third World nations faced difficult economic problems. Moves toward democracy in many lands raised hopes for the future.

3. Mass communication brought the cultures of the world closer together as the century passed. There was a revival of religious fundamentalism, both in Christianity and in Islam. Painters took part in movements such as abstract expressionism, pop art, and the new realism. Architecture was influenced first by the International Style and then by post-modernism. European literature was influenced by existentialist thought, and important new writers arose in the Third World as well as the West.

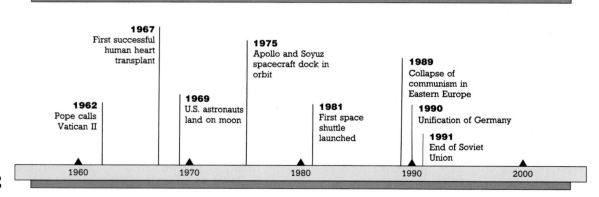

1967
First successful human heart transplant

1975
Apollo and Soyuz spacecraft dock in orbit

1989
Collapse of communism in Eastern Europe

1962
Pope calls Vatican II

1969
U.S. astronauts land on moon

1981
First space shuttle launched

1990
Unification of Germany

1991
End of Soviet Union

1960   1970   1980   1990   2000

CHAPTER **40** REVIEW

See p. T815C for answers to Chapter Review.

Vocabulary Review

Define each of the following terms.
1. fossil fuel
2. multinational corporation
3. new realism
4. ozone layer
5. post-modernism
6. superconductor

People to Identify

Match each of the following people with the correct description: *Christiaan Barnard, Samuel Beckett, Walter Gropius, John Paul II, Jackson Pollock, James D. Watson, Andy Warhol, Kawabata Yasunari.*

1. writer who blended Japanese and Western traditions
2. International Style architect
3. American scientist who teamed with Crick to describe the DNA molecule
4. author of *Waiting for Godot*
5. leader in the pop art movement
6. abstract expressionist painter
7. surgeon who carried out the first successful human heart transplant
8. Polish Pope who encouraged the struggle for religious and political freedom in Communist countries

Recalling the Facts

1. What uses have been found for space satellites and other unmanned spacecraft?
2. What are space shuttles? What uses will they serve?
3. How have antibiotics contributed to medical advances since World War II?
4. How have nations benefited from greater economic interdependence? What has been one drawback?
5. Where has population increased most rapidly in the twentieth century?
6. What caused vast lands in sub-Saharan Africa to turn into deserts?
7. What situation caused hardship in oil-producing regions in the 1980's?
8. Why did many Third World leaders object to taking part in the superpower rivalry?
9. What new trends developed in world affairs in the 1990's?
10. How did Third World debts threaten the economies of industrialized nations?
11. How has mass communication affected people's knowledge of other cultures?
12. What evidence shows that there is renewed interest in religion in the United States?
13. What religious trend in Asia and the Middle East has reflected a reaction against Western influences?

Critical Thinking Skills

1. **Preparing an oral report.** Research one of the following topics for an oral report: information yielded by space probes; the construction of the English Channel tunnel; ethical issues related to genetic engineering; environmental problems in Eastern Europe; the future of nuclear energy; the existentialist philosophy of Jean-Paul Sartre. *(App.)*

2. **Making a diagram.** Make a diagram that shows how the greenhouse effect has come about. Then write a paragraph explaining the possible dangers of this trend. *(Comp.)*

3. **Predicting.** In 1965 a Gallup Poll survey of Americans showed they were most concerned about the Vietnam War, civil rights, and the threat of war. Polls in recent years have shown that uncertainty about the na-

833

 A checkmark identifies questions and exercises calling for the three higher-order levels of thinking at the top of the Bloom taxonomy: Analysis, Synthesis, and Evaluation.

tion's economic future, drugs, the state of the environment, and international tensions were major concerns. Make one list of issues that you think concern Americans today and a second list predicting what people's concerns will be in the year 2000. Then write an essay offering evidence to support your predictions. *(Syn.)*

4. Interpreting graphs. The graphs below show patterns of world urbanization in 1900, 1985, and 2020 (projected). What percentage of the population lived in rural areas in 1900? What percentage of the population lived in cities of more than one million in 1900? In 1985? What percentage of the population lived in urban areas in 1900? What percentage of the population is expected to live in urban areas in 2020? Write two or three sentences describing the trends in urbanization shown on these graphs. *(Comp.)*

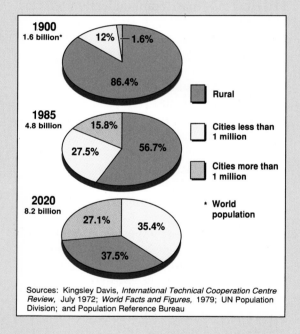

1900
1.6 billion*
12% — 1.6%
86.4%

■ Rural

1985
4.8 billion
15.8%
27.5%   56.7%

□ Cities less than 1 million

2020
8.2 billion
27.1%   35.4%
37.5%

▨ Cities more than 1 million

* World population

Sources: Kingsley Davis, *International Technical Cooperation Centre Review*, July 1972; *World Facts and Figures*, 1979; UN Population Division; and Population Reference Bureau

068

Thinking About Geography

Preparing a report. Research and write a report on the Amazon rain forest (page 826). In your report, describe the climate, plant life, and wildlife in the region. Include a discussion of how and why parts of the forest have

834

been destroyed and the environmental effects of this destruction. Conclude with an assessment of efforts to protect the forest. *(App.)*

Joseph P. Allen is one of the small but growing group of men and women who have gone beyond Earth's atmosphere into space. In this passage, adapted from his own account of life in space, Allen looks at the future of space travel.

66 In the shuttle era, so many people go into space to do so many kinds of jobs that the term *astronaut* alone no longer adequately describes the individuals or their duties. The principal positions on each shuttle flight are, of course, commander, pilot, and one or more mission specialists.

Yet it won't be long before pharmaceutical technicians, botanists, welders, journalists, and artists begin to ride the spaceships into orbit; and it will make no more sense to call them astronauts than it does to call someone who rides in the tourist class of a jetliner an aviator.

By the turn of the twenty-first century, the term *astronaut* will conjure up images only of the pioneers of space, and will relate not to the exciting and unknown future, but to the proudly remembered past. 99

1. What kinds of people does Allen say will soon go on space flights?
2. How would those people be different from the "astronauts" of recent years?
3. **Critical thinking:** Do you think space travel will become as common as airline travel? Why or why not? *(Syn.)*

WORLD HISTORY
Checklist

UNIT 10

Try to identify the following key people, places, and terms from the unit. If you need help, refer to the pages listed.

Key People

Nikita Khrushchev *(717, 724)*
John F. Kennedy *(718)*
Charles de Gaulle *(720)*
Margaret Thatcher *(721)*
Mikhail Gorbachev *(725)*
Andrei Sakharov *(725)*
Boris Yeltsin, *(727)*
Lech Walesa *(729)*
Mao Zedong *(735)*
Deng Xiaoping *(737)*
Richard Nixon *(738, 807)*
Mohandas K. Gandhi *(739)*
Indira Gandhi *(741)*
Corazon Aquino *(749)*
Ho Chi Minh *(750)*
Lyndon B. Johnson *(751)*
Gamal Abdel Nasser *(761)*
Anwar el-Sadat *(762)*
Jimmy Carter *(763)*
Menachem Begin *(763)*
Mohammed Reza Pahlavi *(767)*
Ayatollah Ruhollah Khomeini *(768)*
Saddam Hussein *(768)*
Marcus Garvey *(777)*
Kwame Nkrumah *(778)*
Patrice Lumumba *(779)*
Jomo Kenyatta *(779)*
Nelson Mandela *(782)*
Robert Mugabe *(784)*
Desmond Tutu *(785)*
F. W. de Klerk *(785)*
Porfirio Díaz *(795)*
Juan Perón *(797)*
Salvador Allende *(798)*
Augusto Pinochet *(798)*
Fidel Castro *(799)*
Ronald Reagan *(805)*
Martin Luther King, Jr. *(805)*
George Bush *(808)*

Christiaan Barnard *(820)*
Pope John Paul II *(828)*
Jean-Paul Sartre *(831)*
Gabriel García Márquez *(831)*
Chinua Achebe *(831)*

The earth as seen from space.

Key Places

Berlin *(714)*
Gdańsk *(729)*
Suez Canal *(761)*
Sinai Peninsula *(761)*
West Bank (Jordan River) *(761)*
Persian Gulf *(768)*
Saudi Arabia *(770, 772)*
South Africa *(781)*

Namibia *(784)*
Puerto Rico *(798)*
Bay of Pigs *(799)*
Nicaragua *(800)*
Panama *(801)*
Quebec *(811)*

Key Terms

cold war *(711)*
Truman Doctrine *(713)*
containment *(713)*
Marshall Plan *(714)*
NATO *(714)*
Warsaw Pact *(714)*
deterrence *(716)*
Cuban Missile Crisis *(718)*
Common Market *(719)*
terrorism *(722)*
détente *(725)*
dissident *(725)*
human rights *(725)*
perestroika (726)
glasnost (726)
Cultural Revolution *(737)*
civil disobedience *(739)*
gross national product *(746)*
Korean War *(748)*
Vietnam War *(751)*
domino theory *(751)*
October War *(762)*
Camp David Accords *(763)*
PLO *(763)*
OPEC *(766)*
Iran-Iraq War *(768)*
Gulf War *(772)*
African National Congress *(777)*
apartheid *(781)*
civil rights *(805)*
multinational corporation *(825)*
fossil fuel *(825)*
Third World *(826)*

835

THE TWENTIETH CENTURY
1900–The Present

UNIT 9: Civilization in Crisis (1882–1945)

Chapter 31:
The First World War

Causes of the war. In the late 1800's, tension between France and Germany led to the formation of a series of defensive alliances among European nations. Germany, Austria, and Italy formed the Triple Alliance. France, Britain, and Russia formed the Triple Entente. The alliance system made it difficult for a conflict in Europe to be resolved peacefully. A war between any two nations was likely to involve each country's allies.

In addition to the alliances, extreme nationalism, militarism, and conflicts over colonial territory heightened tensions in Europe in the early 1900's. The outbreak of war came in the summer of 1914, when a Serbian nationalist assassinated Archduke Francis Ferdinand, the heir to the throne of Austria-Hungary. Austrian leaders, backed by their German allies, used the assassination as an excuse to declare war on Serbia. Two days later, Russia started to mobilize; this led Germany to declare war on Russia. Within days, most of Europe was at war. The main members of the Allies were France, Britain, and Russia; the Central Powers were Germany and Austria.

The fighting of the war. The Germans were in the position of fighting a war on two fronts—against Russia on the east, and against the rest of the Allies on the west. The war strategy required a quick victory on the western front, but this proved impossible. By the winter of 1914–1915, fighting on the western front was at a stalemate. Both of the armies were dug into trenches and, despite heavy losses, neither was able to make significant gains.

On the eastern front there was more movement, with the ill-equipped and poorly led Russian army suffering devastating losses. New weaponry, including machine guns, poison gas, and tanks, made the fighting of World War I more deadly

836

World War I was the first war in which nations made use of modern technology in such weapons as airplanes, tanks, submarines, and machine guns.

than any previous war. Battles for small gains of territory often cost tens of thousands of lives. Europe's far-flung empires made this the first true world war, with fighting in the Middle East, Asia, and Africa as well as Europe.

In April 1917 the United States declared war on Germany and thus joined France and Britain as a member of the Allies. The fresh American troops helped to turn the tide of the war. In March 1918 Russia withdrew from the fighting, but the German troops who moved from the eastern to the western front could not change the outcome of the war. In the fall of that year Austria-Hungary and the Ottoman Empire surrendered, and Germany's kaiser was overthrown. The new German government signed an armistice in November 1918.

Legacy of the war. President Woodrow Wilson of the United States tried to shape a lasting peace with his Fourteen Points, which called for self-determination of nations, generous terms for defeated countries, disarmament, fair treatment of colonial peoples, and the creation of an international peacekeeping organization called the League of Nations.

The European Allies, however, rejected most of Wilson's plan. The Versailles Treaty (1919) limited the size of the German military forces, stripped Germany of its colonial possessions, took away German territory in Europe, and required the Germans to pay heavy reparations to the Allied nations.

Many people in Germany and elsewhere felt the peace settlement was too harsh. Many unresolved problems persisted in the 1920's, including militarist ideas and nationalist rivalries.

Chapter 32: Russia in Upheaval

The revolutions of 1917. At the turn of the twentieth century, Russia lagged far behind the modern European states, both politically and economically. The czars were absolute rulers who reigned over a nation of poor, uneducated peasants. The attempts of Nicholas II's government to bring Russia into the twentieth century through rapid industrialization stirred discontent, among upper and lower classes alike. Though many Russians were dissatisfied with their country's government, they did not agree on what changes ought to be made.

Russia's terrible suffering during World War I led to a rebellion that brought about the abdication of the czar in March 1917. The liberal reformers who headed the Provisional Government after the March Revolution wanted to continue to fight Germany and to create a Western-style democracy. They were opposed by the Bolsheviks, who controlled the powerful Petrograd So-

837

viet, and by aristocrats who hoped to restore order with a military dictatorship. In the fall of 1917, the Bolsheviks, led by Lenin, overthrew the Provisional Government; this was the Bolshevik Revolution.

Communists in power. In March 1918 Lenin made a humiliating peace agreement with Germany in the Treaty of Brest-Litovsk.

For the next two years Russia was torn by civil war. The Communists, or "Reds," fought the "Whites," a coalition of moderate Socialists, liberals, and czarists whose only common goal was the overthrow of Lenin. The Whites received aid and troops from Allied governments who were alarmed by the Communist takeover in Russia. The "Greens" fought both groups in an ill-fated attempt to win Ukrainian independence.

By 1920 the Reds were victorious. During the rest of the decade, they brought all of Russia under Communist Party control, imprisoning all opponents. Communist officials centralized government power, nationalized the economy, persecuted religious groups, and bombarded the people with propaganda.

In 1922 Communist leaders declared the Russian Empire to be the Union of Soviet Socialist Republics. Under this arrangement, the Communists paid lip service

to the idea of self-determination without giving up either power or territory. Each of the so-called republics within the Union was under the control of the Party rulers in Moscow.

Stalin's rule. After Lenin's death in 1924, Joseph Stalin gained control. Under his brutal rule, the Soviet Union became a totalitarian state.

Stalin was determined to modernize the Soviet Union. Beginning in 1928, a series of Five-Year Plans aimed at forcing on the Soviet people industrialization and the collectivization of agriculture. These plans set impossibly high goals and drove the Soviet people mercilessly. Citizens' property was confiscated, people faced severe shortages of essential goods, including housing, food and clothing, and they were forced to work wherever and under whatever conditions the Soviet government demanded. Those who resisted were shot or sent to forced-labor prison camps.

These policies caused millions of deaths and shattered the Soviet economy. Bent on eliminating all possible "enemies of the state," secret police terrorized the Russian people. This terror reached its height during the Great Purge of the late 1930's as Stalin held mock trials resulting in the conviction and execution of many Communist leaders.

Chapter 33:
The World Between the Wars

Fascism in Italy. In Italy and Germany, many people were bitter about the peace settlements that had followed World War I. This bitterness, combined with severe economic problems and fear that Communist revolutions would spread westward, enabled extremist political movements on the right to gain much support.

In 1922, Benito Mussolini seized power in Italy, promising to restore order and prosperity by cracking down on leftists and creating a new Italian empire overseas. Though the Italian Fascists followed many totalitarian policies, they were unable to bring the country entirely under their control. The Church, the army, and industrialists and landowners continued to have much influence in Italy.

Nazism in Germany. After the armistice, the moderate leaders of the Weimar Republic tried to bring democracy to Germany. They were opposed by extremists on both left and right. During the Great Depression, Germany was hard-hit by economic crises, and Adolf Hitler's Nazis made rapid gains. Hitler was a forceful leader who promised to restore German national pride as well as order and prosper-

838

ity. By 1932 the Nazis were the strongest political party in Germany.

In 1933 the newly elected Reichstag gave Hitler dictatorial power. Under his direction, the German government banned opposing political parties and independent labor unions, and illegally rebuilt Germany's armed forces. The Nazis also launched a campaign of persecution against Jews and used a barrage of propaganda to tighten their hold on the German people.

Eastern Europe and Spain. In most of Eastern Europe, the new democracies set up after the war quickly fell to authoritarian dictators in the 1920's and 1930's. Only Czechoslovakia managed to maintain democratic institutions.

In 1936 civil war broke out in Spain between a leftist coalition and forces led by Francisco Franco. Franco, who received aid from Italy and Germany, won the Spanish Civil War in 1939 and set up a fascist-type dictatorship.

The Western democracies. The established democracies faced serious problems during the Great Depression of the 1930's. In the United States, Franklin Roosevelt became President in 1933 and responded with the New Deal, a program of social and economic reform that greatly expanded the role of the federal government.

In Great Britain the government provided aid to the poor, but did not undertake a broad program of reform like the New Deal. In 1931, Britain established the Commonwealth of Nations, which gave Dominion status to such nations as Canada and Australia. These nations had full independence, but they recognized the British monarch as their symbolic leader.

Despite their difficulties, the United States and Great Britain remained politically stable. Although France was troubled by extremist movements, it remained democratic between the wars, unlike Germany and Italy. In 1936 fear of fascism in France led to the formation of a leftist coalition, the Popular Front, which made sweeping reforms intended to benefit the working class and centralize control of the economy.

Unrest in Asia. The years after World War I were unsettled ones for China. In 1925, Chiang Kai-shek became head of the Kuomintang (the Nationalist Party) and fought the warlords who controlled much of China and then the Chinese Communists. The Communists, led by Mao Zedong, eluded Nationalist troops and in the

mid-1930's established a base in northwestern China.

In Japan the budding democratic institutions of the 1920's gave way to military dictatorship during the depression years of the 1930's. Japanese militarists hoped to conquer an empire in Asia in order to gain control of the natural resources needed by Japan's growing industries. In 1931 a Japanese military force occupied Manchuria, a region of China, and set up a puppet state that was called Manchukuo.

The impassioned speeches of Adolf Hitler held strong appeal for many Germans who wanted forceful leadership for their country in the 1930's.

839

During the 1920's and 1930's, nationalist leaders modernized Turkey and Persia (present-day Iran), while Arabia was unified under a traditionalist monarchy. The Middle East became of much greater interest to industrialized countries because of the increasing consumption of oil and the discovery of huge deposits of that resource in the Persian Gulf countries.

Chapter 34: World War II

Fascist aggression. During the 1930's the Fascist leaders of Italy and Germany, driven by extreme nationalist and militaristic sentiments, pursued aggressive policies. In 1935 Italy invaded Ethiopia, and in the following year the leaders of Germany and Italy formed the Axis alliance. The Axis Powers jointly backed Franco's forces in the Spanish Civil War. In 1936 Hitler violated the terms of the Versailles Treaty by sending German forces into the Rhineland.

When France and Britain, eager to avoid war, took no action to stop Hitler's aggressions, the German ruler grew even bolder. French and British leaders met with Hitler at Munich in 1938 and agreed to allow him to take over Czechoslovakia's Sudetenland in return for a promise that he would seek no additional territory.

This policy of appeasement failed. Hitler took over all of Czechoslovakia and signed a treaty with Stalin that made the German dictator free to attack Poland. The German invasion of Poland in September 1939 finally caused France and Britain to take action by declaring war on Germany.

The war in Europe. In the first months of World War II, the action was in Eastern Europe. German and Soviet armies divided Poland and the Soviet Union invaded Finland. In the spring of 1940, the Germans turned their attention to Western Europe, conquering Denmark, Norway, Belgium, the Netherlands, Luxembourg, and France.

By June 1940, England stood alone. The following year, however, Hitler invaded the Soviet Union, forcing the German army to fight on two fronts. In 1943 the tide of the war turned against the Axis Powers with victories for the Soviet army at Stalingrad and for the British and American forces in North Africa.

Hitler's ruthless policies in German-occupied Europe reflected Nazi racial theories. The German dictator put into action plans designed to destroy the Jews of Europe; this plan for mass murder, called the Holocaust, brought about the death of six million Jews, two thirds of the Jewish popula-

tion of Europe. The Nazis also carried out brutal programs against millions of other enslaved workers, prisoners of war, and political prisoners. Courageous people in every occupied country risked their lives to resist Nazi policies and help the Allied cause.

War in the Pacific. Japan, whose militarist leaders were bent on conquering an empire, was allied with Nazi Germany. In 1937 Japan had invaded China. In the early years of World War II, Japan seized colonial possessions of the European powers in Asia.

The United States, which was not yet at war, was the only power capable of challenging the Japanese drive for expansion. Japanese leaders, believing that war between the two countries was inevitable, attacked the United States fleet at Pearl Harbor in December 1941. The United States responded by joining forces with the European Allies and China.

Japan made rapid advances in Asia and the Pacific over the next few months, taking Burma, Malaya, and the Philippines. The tide of the war in the Pacific began to turn in June 1942 with the American victory at Midway. The United States then pursued a policy of "island-hopping," striking at strategic Japanese holdings in the Pacific in a steady advance toward Japan's home islands.

840

4. He announced Five-Year Plans that set impossibly high goals, confiscated private property, forced people to do work demanded of them, and used terror tactics.

5. Hitler's promises to restore order, prosperity, and national pride won wide support in Germany. In 1933 his Nazi Party gained a majority in the Reichstag. As absolute ruler, Hitler crushed all opposition, persecuted Jews, and illegally rebuilt Germany's armed forces.

6. The United States launched the New Deal, a program of social and economic reforms. Britain aided the poor, but did not make major reforms. France experienced political instability, which led to the election of the Popular Front in 1936. The leftist Front made sweeping reforms that centralized control of the economy.

7. In 1936 Germany and Italy formed the Axis alliance and jointly backed Franco's forces in the Spanish Civil War.

Allied victory. In 1943 the Allies invaded Italy. The Italians overthrew Mussolini and surrendered, but German forces remained in the country, fighting the Allies' northward advance. On June 6, 1944 (called D-Day), the Allies landed forces in Normandy, thus launching an invasion of German-occupied France. By the end of the summer, Allied soldiers had liberated the city of Paris and were marching toward Germany. In December 1944 the Germans made an unsuccessful last-ditch effort to stop the Allied advance in the Battle of the Bulge. In the spring of 1945, Allied armies converged on Germany from west and east, and Germany surrendered unconditionally, with the announcement of the end of the war in Europe coming on May 8, 1945.

Meanwhile, the war in the Pacific continued with heavy casualties. To bring the war to a quick end, President Harry Truman of the United States decided in August 1945 to use newly developed

Japan's surprise attack on Pearl Harbor in December 1941 brought the United States into World War II. Japan made rapid advances early in the war but lacked the resources to hold its empire together.

atomic bombs. Single bombs were dropped on the Japanese cities of Hiroshima and Nagasaki. Faced with utter destruction, the Japanese government announced its surrender on August 15, 1945. World War II was finally over.

World leaders then faced the task of rebuilding shattered governments and economies and of finding ways to keep peace in the atomic age. Formation of the United Nations was part of that effort.

Answers start on page 839.

Review Questions

1. What were the causes of the First World War? Where did most of the fighting take place?

2. What proposals did President Wilson make in his Fourteen Points? What were the actual terms of the Versailles Treaty?

3. What was the sequence of events that led to the Bolsheviks' seizure of power in Russia in 1917?

4. What methods did Stalin use in trying to achieve rapid industrialization in the Soviet Union?

5. How did Hitler come to power in Germany and what policies did he pursue?

6. How did the democratic nations try to deal with the Great Depression?

7. What sequence of events, beginning in 1936, led to the outbreak of World War II in September 1939?

8. How and when did World War II end in Europe? in the Pacific?

841

That same year Hitler violated the Versailles Treaty by invading the Rhineland. In 1938 French and British leaders agreed to allow Hitler to take over Czechoslovakia's Sudetenland. He then took over all of Czechoslovakia and reached an agreement with Stalin that made him free to attack Poland. The invasion of Poland in September 1939 finally caused France and Britain to declare war on Germany.

8. The last stage of the European war began with the Allied landing in France in June 1944. Germany's unconditional surrender was announced on May 8, 1945. The dropping of atomic bombs on two Japanese cities brought about the end of the war in the Pacific. It ended on August 15, 1945, with the surrender of Japan.

UNIT 10: The Contemporary World (1945–2000)

Chapter 35:
Europe Before and After the Cold War

The cold war. At the end of World War II, Allied leaders created the United Nations, an organization designed to promote national self-determination, prevent war, build respect for human rights, and help nations work together to find solutions for their problems.

When the war ended, the United States and the Soviet Union were the most powerful nations in the world. They soon came into conflict when Stalin refused to let go of the Eastern European countries his armies had occupied in the closing months of World War II.

In response to Soviet expansionist activities, in 1947 the United States announced the Truman Doctrine, declaring that it would aid any country that was resisting Communist aggression. This doctrine became the basis for the United States' postwar policy of containment of communism.

The atmosphere of hostility that developed between the superpowers in the late 1940's became known as the cold war. During the 1950's and 1960's the superpowers competed for power and influence throughout the world and also carried on an arms race as well as a rivalry in developing the technology of space exploration.

Recovery in Western Europe. World War II had caused terrible destruction throughout Western Europe. In launching the Marshall Plan in 1947 the United States gave European nations massive financial aid to help with rebuilding. The West European countries also speeded their recovery by cooperating and pooling their resources through the Common Market, which became the basis of the European Community. In the 1990's the members of EC plan even closer economic integration.

Germany had been divided in the postwar era into West Germany, a parliamentary democracy, and East Germany, a Communist regime within the Soviet-controlled bloc. West Germany quickly became Europe's leading economic power. For the German people the reunification of West and East Germany in 1990 marked the end of the postwar period.

France pursued an independent foreign policy in the postwar years, but suffered political instability and lost the important colonies of Indochina and Algeria.

Its economy severely strained by the war, Britain gave up most of its overseas colonies and created a welfare state that provided extensive government services to citizens. This trend was partially reversed during Margaret Thatcher's years as prime minister. The issue of Northern Ireland's political status continued to cause serious problems.

Elsewhere in Western Europe, Italy established a republic, but political instability was a chronic problem. Land reform in the south and industrialization in the north, however, led to higher standards of living. Portugal and Spain, which had long been ruled by dictators, moved toward democracy during the 1970's and 1980's. Greece was troubled by political instability and conflict with neighboring Turkey over control of the island of Cyprus.

The Soviet Union. Stalin died in 1953. His successor as leader of the Soviet Union was Nikita Khrushchev. He attempted to make some reforms, including economic decentralization and greater production of consumer goods, and generally sought coexistence with the West. Khrushchev's policies met stiff resistance from other Kremlin leaders, and he lost power in 1964. His successors reversed his reforms, with disastrous results for the Soviet economy.

President Boris Yeltsin of Russia, shown here with Mikhail Gorbachev, led the formation of a new commonwealth of former Soviet republics.

While they continued to pursue expansionist policies, they also at times called for détente—the relaxation of cold-war tension.

The Gorbachev era. In 1985 Mikhail Gorbachev came to power. Determined to turn around the stagnant Soviet economy, Gorbachev made revolutionary changes, such as ending the Communist monopoly on power and making tentative moves toward starting free-market reforms. While Soviet citizens had greater personal freedom, their economic situation remained grim.

Even more striking was the turn-around in Soviet foreign relations. Gorbachev built stronger ties with the West, reaching important agreements on arms reduction with the United States and following a policy of close cooperation with the former cold-war enemy.

Eastern Europe. For Eastern Europe the period that followed World War II was one of tight Soviet control. Communist governments centralized their economies and planners directed economic activity in ways that would benefit the Soviet Union. Recovery from wartime destruction was slow. Rebellions against Communist rule, such as those in Poland and Hungary (1956) and Czechoslovakia (1968) met with brutal repression.

In the 1980's, the success of Poland's bold Solidarity movement and Gorbachev's dramatic reforms encouraged Eastern Europeans to overthrow their Communist governments. Some of these nations took steps to establish democracy and reform their economies.

The end of the Soviet Union came in 1991 after a failed attempt to overthrow Gorbachev. When Gorbachev failed to preserve the central government, most of the Soviet republics joined the new Commonwealth of Independent States.

Chapter 36: New Directions for Asia

Communism in China. During World War II China was torn by a three-way war among Nationalists, Communists, and Japanese invaders. In 1949 Communist forces took control of the country. Once in power, the Communists under Mao Zedong pursued goals of rapid industrialization and the collectivization of agriculture, using Stalinist tactics to establish totalitarian control.

In the late 1950's, Mao broke with his Soviet allies over Khruschchev's reforms. In the early 1970's, fearful of a Soviet attack and in need of modern technology, Chinese leaders began to seek detente with the West.

After Mao's death in 1976, the more moderate Deng Xiaoping came to power in China. During the 1980's, Deng made sweeping reforms designed to boost the economy through capitalist-style incentives. A popular movement for political liberalization was brutally suppressed in 1989.

Independent India. In 1947, Britain withdrew from India and the former colony became two independent nations—India and Pakistan. Pakistan consisted of the predominantly Muslim regions in the east and west of the subcontinent.

India adopted a democratic constitution, outlawed discrimination against untouchables, and gave women greater political and property rights. Despite progress in many areas, India faced per-

843

sistent problems, including illiteracy, rapid population growth, food shortages, political corruption, ethnic strife, and disputes with neighboring countries.

Pakistan and Bangladesh. The new Muslim nation of Pakistan was ethnically divided. The people of East and West Pakistan had different histories, languages, and cultures. In 1971 East Pakistan declared itself the independent nation of Bangladesh.

Pakistan has been troubled by political instability since independence. Muslim fundamentalism became a force in the country in the late 1970's. Relations between India and Pakistan remained tense.

Afghanistan. Afghanistan had gained independence from Britain in 1919, but remained rural and economically undeveloped. In 1978 Communists overthrew the military government. In the civil war that followed, the Soviet Union invaded Afghanistan in order to prevent the overthrow of the Marxists. The Soviet forces faced heavy resistance and withdrew in 1989.

Japan. After World War II American forces occupied a demilitarized Japan. Under occupation Japan set up a democratic government and adopted reforms in landowning, women's rights, and education. A spectacular economic recovery made Japan by the 1960's a leading industrial power.

Korea. After World War II Korea was divided in two—a Communist north and an anti-Communist south. In 1950 North Korea invaded South Korea. The United Nations sent troops to aid the South in a three-year war that ended inconclusively. South Korea has become an important industrial power, one of the "four little tigers"—Asian countries that aggressively pursue foreign trade.

The Philippines. The postwar era was one of political instability for the Philippines. In 1986 long-time dictator Ferdinand Marcos fled the country, and a democratic government led by Corazon Aquino came to power. Such problems as a guerrilla rebel movement, poverty, and political corruption continue to trouble the Philippines.

Southeast Asia. After World War II Southeast Asia became a cold-war battlefield. The United States fought unsuccessfully to defend anti-Communist South Vietnam against attack by Communist North Vietnam. Under a peace agreement signed in 1973, the United States withdrew its forces from Vietnam. In 1975 South Vietnam surrendered, and Vietnam was united under Communist rule. Laos and Cambodia also came under Communist rule in 1975.

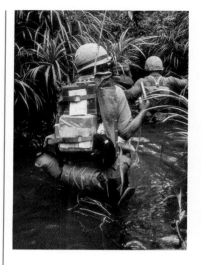

American involvement in Vietnam began in the early 1960's, grew heavy in the mid-1960's, and ended in 1973.

Chapter 37: Challenges for the Middle East

Arab-Israeli conflict. During the 1930's, large numbers of Jews emigrated to Palestine in order to escape Nazi persecution. Arabs resented the immigrants as intruders. After World War II, the United Nations ruled that both Arabs and Jews had rights to Palestine, and recommended that the region be divided into two states, one Arab and the other Jewish. Jews established the state of Israel in 1948, but Arabs rejected the compromise, vowing to destroy the Jewish state.

In three wars between Arab nations and Israel

(1948, 1967, and 1973), Israel emerged the victor. In the Camp David Accords of 1977 Egyptian president Anwar el-Sadat became the first Arab leader to make peace with Israel. In return, Israel withdrew from the Sinai Peninsula. Other Arab nations condemned Sadat.

The future of Palestinian Arabs, who were now scattered throughout the Middle East, remained a major point of difference in efforts to establish peace in the region. In the late 1980's Palestinians on the Israeli-occupied West Bank began a violent uprising to support their demand for the creation of an independent state.

Israel. Israel became the most advanced nation in the Middle East and also a leading military power. Important changes in Israel's population have been the growth of the Arab population and a great expansion in immigration from the Soviet Union.

Trends in the Middle East. Between 1920 and 1950, Arab nations gained independence from France and Britain. The Pan-Arabist movement, led by Gamal Abdel Nasser of Egypt, was a powerful force in the 1950's and 1960's, but political, religious, and economic divisions prevented the establishment of a single Arab state. Nonetheless, the dream of Arab unity continued to influence regional politics.

After World War II Arab nations sought greater control of the profits from oil. In 1960 they formed the Organization of Petroleum Exporting Countries (OPEC) to control prices and production. Because it controlled a large portion of the world's oil, OPEC became a powerful force in the international economy.

Iran and Turkey suffered from political unrest in the postwar period. Leaders in both countries allied with the United States and attempted to modernize. Conservative Shiite Muslims in Iran opposed modernization, demanding a return to Islamic ways. In 1979 Islamic fundamentalists led by the Ayatollah Khomeini overthrew the pro-Western shah. Iran became the center of a worldwide Islamic fundamentalist movement that threatened many governments and preached a message of hostility to the United States.

In 1980 Iraq invaded Iran, hoping to overthrow the fundamentalists and gain valuable territory. The two countries fought a bitter war that ended in a stalemate in 1988.

The cold war was an important factor in Middle East politics through the 1980's. Radical states, such as Libya, Syria, and Iraq, were aided by the Soviet Union and sponsored anti-Israeli and anti-Western terrorist move-

Saddam Hussein's aggression against neighboring Kuwait plunged the Middle East into crisis.

ments. The United States was a strong backer of Israel, the region's only democracy. The United States also maintained ties with moderate Arab states, such as Egypt, Saudi Arabia, and Jordan.

The Gulf crisis. In 1990 a confrontation between Iraq's dictator, Saddam Hussein, and a coalition of nations began when Iraq sent forces to invade and occupy neighboring Kuwait. Saddam Hussein declared Kuwait to be a part of Iraq. The international coalition, led by the United States, sent forces to the Persian Gulf area to deter further Iraqi aggression.

845

When Iraq refused to withdraw its forces from Kuwait, the U.S.-led allied forces began the Gulf War, first with heavy air strikes on Iraq and concluding with a hundred-hour land offensive that liberated Kuwait.

The impact of the war reached beyond the Gulf region. One outcome was the agreement of Arabs and Israelis to a U.S. proposal to hold face-to-face meetings on Middle Eastern problems.

Chapter 38: Independent Africa

African nationalism. After 1945, the nationalist movements that had begun in Africa during the early twentieth century gathered fresh momentum. Africans who had fought for colonial powers in World War II had a new perspective on their situation. Encouraged by the success of Asian independence movements and the civil-rights movement in the United States, African nationalists called for independence for their own countries. War-weary and economically strapped, European nations no longer had the will to administer unruly African colonies.

In 1957 Ghana became the first African nation to gain independence (from Britain). It was quickly followed by the rest of British and French West Africa and the Belgian Congo. After a violent struggle, Kenyans won independence in 1963.

In British and Portuguese southern Africa, white settlers put up stiffer resistance to black rule. In South Africa, Afrikaners had imposed strict racial segregation, called apartheid, in 1948. Black protests were put down by force. Zambia and Malawi gained independence in the early 1960's. In Southern Rhodesia, whites declared their independence from Britain in 1965 in an attempt to avert black rule. In 1980, however, Rhodesia became Zimbabwe after blacks and whites agreed on a power-sharing constitution.

Angola and Mozambique won independence in 1975 after the struggle to keep control of those lands brought down the government of Portugal.

By the late 1980's, after years of violence and resistance to change, the South African government began to yield in its adamant stand on apartheid laws. In 1990 new leadership in South Africa's white government released black leaders, such as Nelson Mandela, from prison and launched reforms aimed at preparing the nation for the dismantlement of the apartheid system. Many problems remained for South Africa, including hard-line opposition from extremists on both sides.

Challenges to development. The African nations faced a number of problems after gaining independence. Ethnic and religious differences within nations sometimes led to conflict, as in the Nigerian Civil War. Lack of experience in government was a persistent legacy of past foreign rule. Many new governments were corrupt or dictatorial. In recent years, protests against one-party rule have put pressure on long-time leaders to allow democratic reforms.

Troubles in Africa's underdeveloped economies led to serious food shortages and high foreign debts. African governments encouraged farmers to use modern technology in order to increase agricultural production, but emphasis on export crops reduced food supplies. Positive developments included the raising of literacy rates by spending large portions of revenues on education and on programs for the improvement of public health.

Africa and the world. Africa's resources and strategic location made it important in the cold war. Two important areas of superpower-backed conflict were the "horn," which commands the sea route to the Suez Canal, and southern Africa, in which blacks fought long battles for independence and majority rule. In the 1990's Africa is no longer the scene of superpower ri-

846

1. The cold war was the period when the United States and the Soviet Union competed for power and influence throughout the world. It began in the late 1940's when Stalin refused to relinquish control of Eastern Europe.

2. Gorbachev launched revolutionary reforms in the Soviet system. Eastern Europeans, encouraged by this liberalization, overthrew their Communist governments and moved toward democracy and free-market economies. Political and economic crises led to the break-up of the Soviet Union. Most of the republics joined a new confederation.

The release of Nelson Mandela and other ANC leaders from prison symbolized the move away from apartheid in South Africa.

valry, but its markets and resources continue to interest business leaders in the rest of the world. The involvement of large international corporations in Africa has been called neocolonialism because the profits of African labor flow out of the continent and benefit overseas investors.

Chapter 39: The Changing Americas

Latin America in the postwar era. In the twentieth century, Latin American countries continued to be troubled by corruption, social inequality, political extremism and instability, and slow economic development. Rapid population growth, rapid urbanization, and spiraling debt were also problems.

In the 1980's a number of nations made progress toward greater democracy—for example, Mexico, Brazil, Argentina, Chile, and Paraguay. Cuba, however, remained an isolated Marxist state under the rule of Fidel Castro.

For much of the postwar period Central America was a cold-war battleground as in Nicaragua, El Salvador, and Guatemala the superpowers backed rival groups in ongoing civil wars. With the end of the cold war, this situation changed; in Nicaragua, for example, a truce signed in 1988 allowed an elected president to take office in 1990, and a civilian-led government was elected in Guatemala.

In 1989 the United States sent forces to Panama to oust a corrupt dictator, Manuel Noriega. The invasion was part of a hemispheric war on the illegal drug trade, which had become an important source of income for many Latin American countries.

The United States. After World War II, the United States emerged as one of the world's two superpowers. The next decades were a period of growth and prosperity for most Americans. The role of the federal government was greatly expanded. American blacks waged a campaign to end racial discrimination. Their successes inspired women and members of other minor-ity groups also to seek full equality.

In foreign policy, the United States pursued a policy of containment of communism—a policy that led to involvement in the Korean and Vietnam wars and aid to anti-Communist groups and governments all over the world. In the early 1970's, cold-war tensions were relaxed as President Richard Nixon forged new relationships with China and the Soviet Union. Tension increased again after the Soviet invasion of Afghanistan in 1979 and remained high until Mikhail Gorbachev began to reverse Soviet expansionist policies. That change of direction made it possible for the United States and the Soviet Union to deal with international concerns more cooperatively.

The nation's first post-cold-war crisis was the stand taken against Iraq's aggression in Kuwait in 1990. The United States led the multinational effort to drive Iraqi occupation forces out of Kuwait.

Canada. After World War II Canadian industry grew and the country enjoyed a high rate of immigration. Rich mineral deposits, including oil and uranium, were discovered. With the United States, Canada built the St. Lawrence Seaway, linking the Great Lakes with the Atlantic Ocean. However, Canada's exports were

847

---

3. Mao pursued goals of rapid industrialization and collectivization of agriculture, and established totalitarian rule.
4. India and Pakistan gained independence from Britain in 1947. In 1971 East Pakistan declared itself independent as Bangladesh.

5. After the United Nations recommended division of Palestine into two states, Jews established the state of Israel in 1948.
6. Pan-Arabism was the movement to unite Arab countries into a single state. Islamic fundamentalism aimed at rejecting modernization and returning to traditional Islamic ways.

mostly raw materials, and Canadians bought most of their manufactured goods from abroad, especially from the United States. Many Canadians saw their continued dependence on the United States as a problem.

In Quebec, which was predominantly French, a separatist movement became powerful during the 1960's. Canada's federal government continues to face the problem of how to deal with French-Canadian separatism and the reactions to it of other peoples within the Canadian federation.

Chapter 40: Linking Past, Present, and Future

Exploring space. The space age began in 1957 with the launching of the Soviet satellite called Sputnik. In 1969 the first human beings—United States astronauts—walked on the moon. By the 1980's spacecraft were traveling to the planets of the solar system and sending back valuable information. In 1983 Pioneer X traveled out of the solar system and continues to head toward the stars. Meanwhile, space shuttles have placed satellites in orbit and made scientific experiments. Planning continues for space stations that will allow a permanent human presence in space.

Scientific advances. In the area of medicine, scientific advances of recent years include the discovery of DNA, genetic engineering, the development of antibiotics, and technology that allows organ transplants.

Computers have been a major breakthrough in modern technology. Computers have revolutionized the storage and processing of information for people in all walks of life. Looking ahead, superconductors hold out the promise of cheap and abundant energy. Many scientific advances raise new ethical questions.

A global economy. Economic issues are of major importance to the world as the nations' economies have become closely interdependent. While standards of living have been raised, people are also more vulnerable, since economic crises in one part of the world can have deep-felt effects on other regions. One feature of the late twentieth century is the continuing expansion of multinational corporations, huge companies that own businesses in many different countries.

Environmental issues. Advances in fields such as medicine, technology, and agriculture have led to a population explosion with most of the growth in developing countries. Rising population and urbanization put enormous pressure on the environment and on energy resources. Global air pollution threatens the health of all life on earth and may change the earth's climate in disastrous ways. Other forms of damage to the environment come from the use of pesticides and chemical fertilizers, overgrazing, and the destruction of forests. Concerned about limited supplies of fossil fuels, some countries have begun a search for other energy sources.

International relations. For more than four decades after World War II, world politics was dominated by the cold war between the United States and the Soviet Union. By the early 1990's the shift of Soviet-bloc nations away from communism had brought that era to a close. Other important recent developments have included the unification of Germany, the closer integration of the countries of Western Europe, and a greater reliance on the United Nations as a forum for discussion of world problems.

Many difficult issues remained in world politics, however. Third World nations, for example, had been drawn into the superpower struggle, taking sides in return for economic and military aid. Yet some Third World leaders argued that the most important differences among nations lay between North and South (rich and

7. Africans who had fought in the war had gained new confidence from their contacts with other colonial peoples seeking self-rule. They were encouraged by the success of Asian independence movements and by the American civil rights movement. European powers no longer had the resources or the will to hold onto colonial possessions.

8. Challenges have included ethnic and cultural divi-

sions, lack of experienced leaders, high foreign debts, economic underdevelopment, food shortages, inefficient agriculture, low literacy, and disease. African nations were also drawn into cold-war conflicts.

9. Problems included corruption, social inequality, political extremism and instability, economic underdevelopment, rapid population growth and urbanization, and foreign debts.

Space exploration has given us a new way of looking at our planet.

poor) and demanded a redistribution of the world's wealth. The issue of Third World debt continues in today's world. Another concern is the uncertain impact on the rest of the world of the instability resulting from the Soviet Union's economic and political crises.

Meanwhile, in many lands people remain trapped in poverty and repression, and regional conflicts still threaten peace and security. Yet the end of the cold war raised hopes for a world in which strides could be made toward a better life.

World cultural trends. Mass communication has greatly increased contact among the peoples of the world. Over the past few decades, there has been a widespread renewal of interest in religion. Christianity continued as a force behind the Iron Curtain despite government repression. Islamic fundamentalism was a reaction against rapid westernization.

New art forms, including abstract expressionism, pop art, and the new realism in painting, the International Style and post-modernism in architecture, and existentialism in literature, express the uncertainties of modern life.

People today know much more about different cultures and about world events than their ancestors. The technology that makes this possible creates new opportunities for human beings to know more about each other as inhabitants of the "global village."

ATLAS

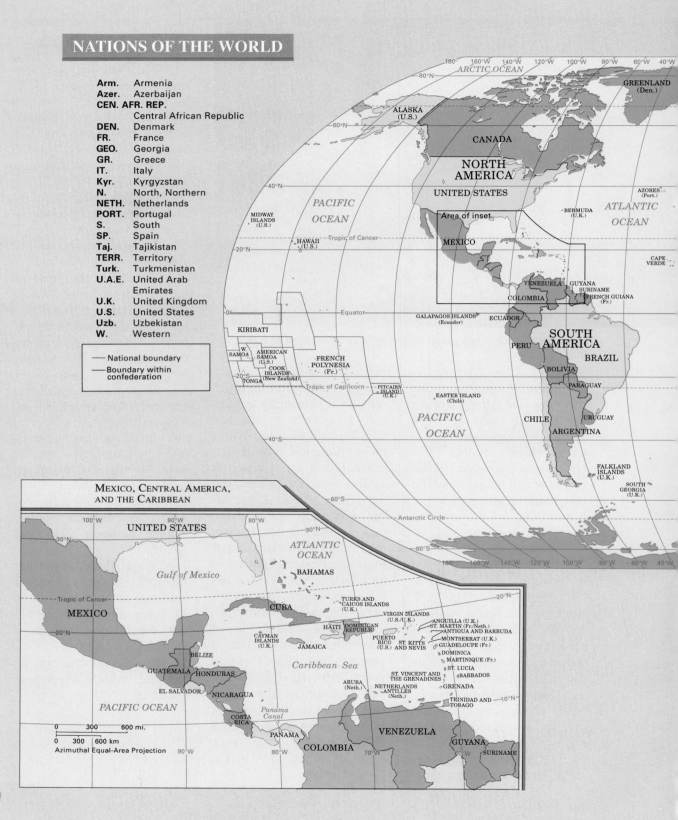

NATIONS OF THE WORLD

Arm.	Armenia
Azer.	Azerbaijan
CEN. AFR. REP.	
	Central African Republic
DEN.	Denmark
FR.	France
GEO.	Georgia
GR.	Greece
IT.	Italy
Kyr.	Kyrgyzstan
N.	North, Northern
NETH.	Netherlands
PORT.	Portugal
S.	South
SP.	Spain
Taj.	Tajikistan
TERR.	Territory
Turk.	Turkmenistan
U.A.E.	United Arab Emirates
U.K.	United Kingdom
U.S.	United States
Uzb.	Uzbekistan
W.	Western

— National boundary
— Boundary within confederation

ATLAS

ARCTIC OCEAN

GREENLAND (Den.)

ALASKA (U.S.)

CANADA

NORTH AMERICA

UNITED STATES

AZORES (Port.)

ATLANTIC OCEAN

BERMUDA (U.K.)

Area of inset

MEXICO

PACIFIC OCEAN

MIDWAY ISLANDS (U.S.)

HAWAII (U.S.)

Tropic of Cancer

CAPE VERDE

Equator

VENEZUELA

GUYANA

SURINAME

COLOMBIA

FRENCH GUIANA (Fr.)

GALAPAGOS ISLANDS (Ecuador)

ECUADOR

KIRIBATI

PERU

SOUTH AMERICA

BRAZIL

W. SAMOA

AMERICAN SAMOA (U.S.)

FRENCH POLYNESIA (Fr.)

COOK ISLANDS (New Zealand)

TONGA

BOLIVIA

PARAGUAY

Tropic of Capricorn

PITCAIRN ISLAND (U.K.)

EASTER ISLAND (Chile)

CHILE

URUGUAY

ARGENTINA

PACIFIC OCEAN

FALKLAND ISLANDS (U.K.)

SOUTH GEORGIA (U.K.)

Antarctic Circle

MEXICO, CENTRAL AMERICA, AND THE CARIBBEAN

UNITED STATES

ATLANTIC OCEAN

Gulf of Mexico

BAHAMAS

Tropic of Cancer

MEXICO

CUBA

TURKS AND CAICOS ISLANDS (U.K.)

VIRGIN ISLANDS (U.S./U.K.)

ANGUILLA (U.K.)

ST. MARTIN (Fr./Neth.)

ANTIGUA AND BARBUDA

HAITI

DOMINICAN REPUBLIC

MONTSERRAT (U.K.)

CAYMAN ISLANDS (U.K.)

PUERTO RICO (U.S.)

ST. KITTS AND NEVIS

GUADELOUPE (Fr.)

JAMAICA

DOMINICA

MARTINIQUE (Fr.)

BELIZE

Caribbean Sea

ST. LUCIA

GUATEMALA

HONDURAS

ST. VINCENT AND THE GRENADINES

BARBADOS

ARUBA (Neth.)

GRENADA

EL SALVADOR

NICARAGUA

NETHERLANDS ANTILLES (Neth.)

TRINIDAD AND TOBAGO

PACIFIC OCEAN

Panama Canal

0   300   600 mi.

0   300   600 km

Azimuthal Equal-Area Projection

COSTA RICA

PANAMA

COLOMBIA

VENEZUELA

GUYANA

SURINAME

850

The abbreviations below apply to the inset map of Europe.

ALB.	Albania
EST.	Estonia
LAT.	Latvia
LITH.	Lithuania
Bel.	Belarus
Mol.	Moldova
Sl.	Slovenia
Cr.	Croatia
Se.	Serbia
Mo.	Montenegro
Ma.	Macedonia
Bo.	Bosnia and Herzegovina

For maps of major regions of the world, see the pages that follow. For a physical map of the world, see the Geography Review at the front of the book.

EURASIA: *Political/Physical*

National capital ⊛

Major city •

National boundary —

800 mi.

400

0

800 km.

400

0

Robinson Projection

ARCTIC OCEAN

75°N

NORTH AMERICA

SIBERIA

60°N

Bering Sea

INDEPENDENT STATES

Lena River

STANOVOI RANGE

Sea of Okhotsk

SAKHALIN

Irkutsk

Lake Baikal

Amur River

DA HINGGAN LING

Harbin

KURIL ISLANDS

45°N

ALTAI MTS.

Ulan Bator

MONGOLIA

Vladivostok

Sapporo

180°

GOBI (DESERT)

Beijing

N. KOREA
Pyongyang
Seoul
S. KOREA

Sea of Japan

JAPAN

Tokyo

SHAN

Huang He

Yellow Sea

Osaka

PLATEAU OF TIBET

PEOPLE'S REPUBLIC OF CHINA

Jiang

Chang

Shanghai

30°N

Brahmaputra R.

Thimphu
BHUTAN

East China Sea

BANGLADESH
Dhaka

Xi Jiang

Taipei
TAIWAN

PACIFIC

Calcutta

MYANMAR (BURMA)

Irrawaddy R.

Guangzhou

MACAO (Port.)
HONG KONG (U.K.)

Hanoi

LAOS

HAINAN

OCEAN

Vientiane

Gulf of Tonkin

Philippine

Bay of Bengal

Mekong R.

Rangoon

THAILAND

Da Nang

Sea

ANDAMAN ISLANDS (India)

Bangkok

CAMBODIA

VIETNAM

Manila

15°N

Phnom Penh

Ho Chi Minh City (Saigon)

PHILIPPINES

NICOBAR ISLANDS (India)

South China Sea

Bandar Seri Begawan

MALAYSIA
Kuala Lumpur
MALAYSIA
Singapore
SINGAPORE

BRUNEI

BORNEO

0°

SUMATRA

CELEBES

INDONESIA

NEW GUINEA

Java Sea

Jakarta
JAVA

Arafura Sea

15°S

Timor Sea

AUSTRALIA

90°E   105°E   120°E   135°E   150°E   165°E

AFRICA: *Political/Physical*

EUROPE

ASIA

Strait of Gibraltar

MADEIRA ISLANDS (Port.)

CANARY ISLANDS (Sp.)

Tunis ✹

Algiers ✹

Casablanca • ✹Rabat
Marrakech • *ATLAS* MOUNTAINS

TUNISIA
Tripoli ✹

Mediterranean Sea

Suez Canal

MOROCCO

Alexandria •
✹Cairo

QATTARA DEPRESSION

WESTERN SAHARA (Morocco)

ALGERIA

LIBYA

S A H A R A

EGYPT

Nile River

Tropic of Cancer

Red Sea

AHAGGAR MOUNTAINS

TIBESTI MOUNTAINS

MAURITANIA

MALI

NIGER

CHAD

NUBIAN DESERT

NILE BASIN

Nouakchott ✹

Timbuktu •

S A H E L

Khartoum ✹

ERITREA

Bab el Mandeb

Cape Verde

Niamey ✹

Kano •

Lake Chad

S U D A N

DJIBOUTI
✹ Djibouti

Gulf of Aden

Dakar ✹ SENEGAL

Bamako •

BURKINA FASO

✹ N'Djamena

SUDAN

Banjul ✹ GAMBIA

Ouagadougou ✹

AMHARA PLATEAU

Bissau ✹ GUINEA-BISSAU

GUINEA

BENIN

NIGERIA

Addis Ababa ✹

Conakry ✹

TOGO

Abuja ✹

CENTRAL AFRICAN REPUBLIC

ETHIOPIA

SOMALIA

Freetown ✹
SIERRA LEONE

CÔTE D'IVOIRE GHANA

Porto-Novo ✹

Lagos •

Monrovia ✹
LIBERIA

Abidjan •

Accra ✹ Lomé ✹

CAMEROON

Bangui ✹

Mogadishu ✹

Malabo ✹

Yaoundé ✹

Gulf of Guinea

EQUATORIAL GUINEA

UGANDA

KENYA

SÃO TOMÉ AND PRINCIPE

✹Libreville

Zaire River

CONGO BASIN

Lake Albert

Kampala ✹

ANNOBÓN (Equatorial Guinea)

São Tomé •

GABON

CONGO

Kigali ✹

Nairobi •

RWANDA

Lake Victoria

Equator

ATLANTIC OCEAN

INDIAN OCEAN

Victoria ✹ SEYCHELLES

Kasai R.

Brazzaville ✹

✹ Kinshasa

Bujumbura ✹ BURUNDI

SERENGETI PLAIN

ASCENSION (U.K.)

CABINDA (Angola)

ZAIRE

L. Tanganyika

ZANZIBAR

TANZANIA

Dar es Salaam •

Luanda ✹

Cuanza R.

KATANGA PLATEAU

MITUMBA MTS.

GREAT RIFT VALLEY

ST. HELENA (U.K.)

Lubumbashi •

Moroni ✹ COMOROS

ANGOLA

MALAWI

MAYOTTE (Fr.)

ZAMBIA

Lilongwe ✹

Lusaka ✹

Lake Malawi

Harare ✹

Antananarivo ✹

NAMIBIA

L. Kariba

Zambezi R.

NAMIB DESERT

OKAVANGO BASIN

Victoria Falls

MOZAMBIQUE

Mozambique Channel

MADAGASCAR

Port Louis ✹
MAURITIUS

WALVIS BAY (S. Africa)

Windhoek ✹

ZIMBABWE

BOTSWANA

Limpopo River

RÉUNION (Fr.)

Tropic of Capricorn

KALAHARI DESERT

Gaborone ✹

Johannesburg • Pretoria ✹

✹Maputo

✹Mbabane
SWAZILAND

Orange River

Vaal R.

LESOTHO
Maseru ✹

SOUTH AFRICA

GREAT KAROO

DRAKENSBERG MTS.

Durban •

Cape Town ✹

Cape of Good Hope

Cape Agulhas

✹ National capital

• Major city

— National boundary

0   400   800 mi.

0   400   800 km

Azimuthal Equal-Area Projection

ATLAS

854

NORTH AMERICA: *Political/Physical*

ASIA

ARCTIC OCEAN

EUROPE

Bering Strait

Beaufort Sea

QUEEN ELIZABETH ISLANDS

ELLESMERE ISLAND

GREENLAND (Denmark)

Arctic Circle

BANKS ISLAND

BROOKS RANGE

Yukon River

ALASKA RANGE

Fairbanks

Anchorage

Gulf of Alaska

KODIAK ISLAND

ALEXANDER ARCHIPELAGO

QUEEN CHARLOTTE ISLANDS

VANCOUVER ISLAND

Puget Sound

Seattle

Portland

VICTORIA ISLAND

Great Bear Lake

Mackenzie River

Great Slave Lake

LAURENTIAN SHIELD

Baffin Bay

BAFFIN ISLAND

Labrador Sea

Hudson Bay

UNGAVA PENINSULA

LABRADOR

NEWFOUNDLAND

CANADA

Edmonton

Vancouver

Calgary

COAST MOUNTAINS

ROCKY MOUNTAINS

Lake Winnipeg

Winnipeg

Quebec

St. Lawrence River

PRINCE EDWARD ISLAND

CAPE BRETON ISLAND

Montreal

Ottawa

Bay of Fundy

ATLANTIC OCEAN

Lake Superior

Minneapolis

BLACK HILLS

Milwaukee

Lake Michigan

Lake Huron

Toronto

L. Ontario

Lake Erie

Boston

Cape Cod

Missouri River

Chicago

Detroit

Cleveland

New York

Philadelphia

SIERRA NEVADA

Great Salt Lake

Salt Lake City

San Francisco

COAST RANGES

Omaha

Snake R.

Denver

Colorado River

Kansas City

Indianapolis

St. Louis

Ohio River

Louisville

APPALACHIAN MTS.

Baltimore

Washington

UNITED STATES

Wichita

Nashville

Charlotte

Cape Hatteras

BERMUDA (U.K.)

Los Angeles

MOJAVE DESERT

San Diego

GRAND CANYON

Phoenix

Fort Worth

Red River

Atlanta

Birmingham

PACIFIC OCEAN

Ciudad Juárez

Chihuahua

Rio Grande

Austin

San Antonio

Houston

New Orleans

Mississippi River

Jacksonville

Cape Canaveral

Tropic of Cancer

BAJA CALIFORNIA

Monterrey

SIERRA MADRE ORIENTAL

Gulf of California

SIERRA MADRE OCCIDENTAL

Cabo San Lucas

MEXICO

PLATEAU OF MEXICO

Guadalajara

Mexico City

Veracruz

Puebla

Acapulco

ISTHMUS OF TEHUANTEPEC

YUCATÁN PENINSULA

Miami

Nassau

BAHAMAS

Gulf of Mexico

Havana

CUBA

Santiago de Cuba

CAYMAN ISLANDS (U.K.)

San Juan

PUERTO RICO (U.S.)

VIRGIN ISLANDS (U.S. U.K.)

ANGUILLA (U.K.)

ANTIGUA AND BARBUDA

DOMINICAN REPUBLIC

ST. KITTS-NEVIS

GUADELOUPE (Fr.)

Port-au-Prince

HAITI

Santo Domingo

DOMINICA

Roseau

MARTINIQUE (Fr.)

ST. LUCIA

Castries

BARBADOS

Bridgetown

JAMAICA

Kingston

Kingston

ST. VINCENT AND THE GRENADINES

St. George's

GRENADA

Port-of-Spain

TRINIDAD AND TOBAGO

Belmopan

BELIZE

Caribbean Sea

NETHERLANDS ANTILLES

ARUBA (Neth.)

GUATEMALA

Guatemala City

HONDURAS

Tegucigalpa

NICARAGUA

MOSQUITO COAST

San Salvador

EL SALVADOR

Managua

Lago de Nicaragua

San José

COSTA RICA

ISTHMUS OF PANAMA

Panama City

PANAMA

SOUTH AMERICA

Equator

Legend

- ⊛ National capital
- • Major city
- — National boundary

0 — 400 — 800 mi.

0 — 400 — 800 km

Azimuthal Equal-Area Projection

N W E S

SOUTH AMERICA: *Political/Physical*

CENTRAL AMERICA

Caribbean Sea

ATLANTIC OCEAN

Barranquilla
Cartagena
Maracaibo
Caracas

Gulf of Panama

LLANOS
VENEZUELA
Orinoco River
Angel Falls

Georgetown
Paramaribo

Medellín
Bogotá
COLOMBIA

GUYANA
GUIANA HIGHLANDS
SURINAME
FRENCH GUIANA (Fr.)
Cayenne

MALPELO (Colombia)

OCCIDENTAL MTS
Magdalena R.
Cauca R.

Equator
GALAPAGOS ISLANDS (Ecuador)

Quito
ECUADOR
Guayaquil
Gulf of Guayaquil
Iquitos

Rio Negro

AMAZON
BASIN
Manaus

Solimões River
Amazon River
Madeira River
Tapajós River
Xingu River

Belém

Fortaleza

Trujillo
PERU

A N D E S

Lima
Cuzco

PLATEAU OF MATO GROSSO

BRAZIL

São Francisco River
Tocantins River

Recife

Salvador

Arequipa

Lake Titicaca
La Paz
ALTIPLANO
BOLIVIA
Sucre

BRAZILIAN HIGHLANDS
Brasília

PACIFIC OCEAN

ATACAMA DESERT

Antofagasta

Tropic of Capricorn

SAN FELIX ISLAND (Chile)
SAN AMBROSIO ISLAND (Chile)

GRAN CHACO
PARAGUAY
Asunción

Paraguay River
Salado River
Paraná River

Belo Horizonte

São Paulo
Santos
Rio de Janeiro

Pôrto Alegre

Córdoba
Rosario

URUGUAY

CHILE
A N D E S

Valparaíso
Santiago
JUAN FERNANDEZ ISLANDS (Chile)

Buenos Aires
Montevideo
Rio de la Plata

ATLANTIC OCEAN

ARGENTINA
PAMPAS

Concepción
Colorado R.
Bahía Blanca

Valdivia

Gulf of San Matias

N
W   E
S

PATAGONIA
Comodoro Rivadavia
Gulf of San Jorge

| | 400 | | 800 mi. |
| 0 | 400 | 800 km | |

Azimuthal Equal-Area Projection

Strait of Magellan
FALKLAND ISLANDS (U.K.)
TIERRA DEL FUEGO

SOUTH GEORGIA (U.K.)

Cape Horn
Drake Passage

✷ National capital
• Major city
— National boundary

ATLAS

856

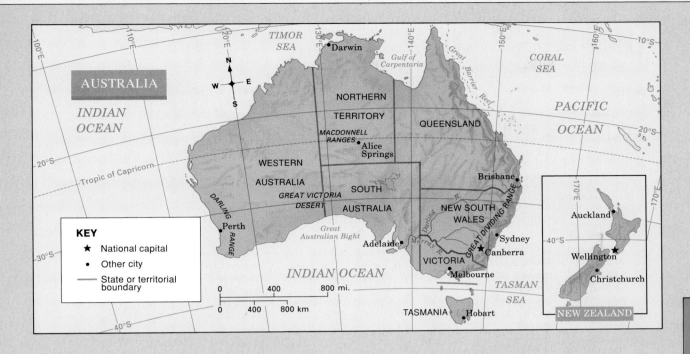

TABLE OF NATIONS

AFRICA

Nation	Capital	Area (sq. mi.)	Population	Nation	Capital	Area (sq. mi.)	Population
Algeria	Algiers	919,595	26,000,000	Guinea	Conakry	94,925	7,500,000
Angola	Luanda	481,350	8,500,000	Guinea-Bissau	Bissau	13,948	1,000,000
Benin	Porto-Novo	43,483	4,800,000	Kenya	Nairobi	224,960	25,200,000
Botswana	Gaborone	231,800	1,300,000	Lesotho	Maseru	11,720	1,800,000
Burkina Faso	Ouagadougou	105,870	9,400,000	Liberia	Monrovia	43,000	2,700,000
Burundi	Bujumbura	10,747	5,800,000	Libya	Tripoli	679,536	4,400,000
Cameroon	Yaoundé	183,569	11,400,000	Madagascar	Antananarivo	226,660	12,400,000
Cape Verde	Praia	1,557	400,000	Malawi	Lilongwe	45,747	9,400,000
Central				Mali	Bamako	478,819	8,300,000
Afr. Rep.	Bangui	241,313	3,000,000	Mauritania	Nouakchott	397,953	2,100,000
Chad	N'Djamena	495,752	5,700,000	Mauritius	Port Louis	787	1,100,000
Comoros	Moroni	690	500,000	Morocco	Rabat	172,413	26,200,000
Congo	Brazzaville	132,046	2,300,000	Mozambique	Maputo	303,073	16,100,000
Côte d'Ivoire	Abidjan	124,502	12,500,000	Namibia	Windhoek	318,261	1,500,000
(Ivory Coast)				Niger	Niamey	489,206	8,000,000
Djibouti	Djibouti	8,490	400,000	Nigeria	Abuja	356,700	122,500,000
Egypt	Cairo	386,900	54,500,000	Rwanda	Kigali	10,169	7,500,000
Equatorial				São Tomé			
Guinea	Malabo	10,830	400,000	and Principe	São Tomé	370	100,000
Ethiopia	Addis Ababa	472,432	53,200,000	Senegal	Dakar	75,954	7,500,000
Gabon	Libreville	103,346	1,200,000	Seychelles	Victoria	175	100,000
Gambia	Banjul	4,093	900,000	Sierra Leone	Freetown	27,700	4,300,000
Ghana	Accra	92,100	15,500,000	Somalia	Mogadishu	246,199	7,700,000

857

AFRICA

Nation	Capital	Area (sq. mi.)	Population	Nation	Capital	Area (sq. mi.)	Population
South Africa	Pretoria, Cape Town	471,440	40,600,000	Tunisia	Tunis	63,379	8,400,000
Sudan	Khartoum	967,491	25,900,000	Uganda	Kampala	91,343	18,700,000
Swaziland	Mbabane	6,704	800,000	Zaire	Kinshasa	905,365	37,800,000
Tanzania	Dar es Salaam	364,900	26,900,000	Zambia	Lusaka	290,586	8,400,000
Togo	Lomé	21,925	3,800,000	Zimbabwe	Harare	150,699	10,000,000

THE AMERICAS

Nation	Capital	Area (sq. mi.)	Population	Nation	Capital	Area (sq. mi.)	Population
Antigua and Barbuda	St. John's	170	100,000	Guyana	Georgetown	83,000	800,000
Argentina	Buenos Aires	1,072,067	32,700,000	Haiti	Port-au-Prince	10,714	6,300,000
Bahamas	Nassau	5,380	250,000	Honduras	Tegucigalpa	43,277	5,300,000
Barbados	Bridgetown	166	300,000	Jamaica	Kingston	4,411	2,500,000
Belize	Belmopan	8,867	200,000	Mexico	Mexico City	761,600	85,700,000
Bolivia	La Paz, Sucre	424,162	7,500,000	Nicaragua	Managua	50,180	3,900,000
Brazil	Brasília	3,286,470	153,300,000	Panama	Panama City	29,761	2,500,000
Canada	Ottawa	3,851,809	26,800,000	Paraguay	Asunción	157,047	4,400,000
Chile	Santiago	292,132	13,400,000	Peru	Lima	496,222	22,000,000
Colombia	Bogotá	455,355	33,600,000	St. Kitts	Basseterre	100	40,000
Costa Rica	San José	19,652	3,100,000	St. Lucia	Castries	238	150,000
Cuba	Havana	44,218	10,700,000	St. Vincent, Grenadines	Kingstown	150	100,000
Dominica	Roseau	290	88,000	Suriname	Paramaribo	63,251	400,000
Dominican Republic	Santo Domingo	18,704	7,300,000	Trinidad and Tobago	Port-of-Spain	1,980	1,300,000
Ecuador	Quito	109,484	10,800,000	United States	Washington, D.C.	3,540,939	252,800,000
El Salvador	San Salvador	8,260	5,400,000	Uruguay	Montevideo	68,040	3,200,000
Grenada	St. George's	133	100,000	Venezuela	Caracas	352,143	20,100,000
Guatemala	Guatemala City	42,042	9,500,000				

ASIA (and the Middle East)

Nation	Capital	Area (sq. mi.)	Population	Nation	Capital	Area (sq. mi.)	Population
Afghanistan	Kabul	250,000	16,600,000	Israel	Jerusalem	8,020	4,900,000
Armenia	Yerevan	11,500	3,300,000	Japan	Tokyo	243,574	123,800,000
Azerbaijan	Baku	33,400	7,300,000	Jordan	Amman	37,297	3,400,000
Bahrain	Manama	240	500,000	Kazakhstan	Alma-Ata	1,049,200	17,000,000
Bangladesh	Dhaka	55,598	116,600,000	Korea, North	Pyongyang	46,768	21,800,000
Bhutan	Thimphu	18,000	700,000	Korea, South	Seoul	38,031	43,200,000
Brunei	Bandar Seri Begawan	2,226	300,000	Kuwait	Kuwait	6,880	1,400,000
Burma (Myanmar)	Rangoon	261,220	42,100,000	Kyrgyzstan	Bishkek	76,600	4,500,000
Cambodia	Phnom Penh	69,884	7,100,000	Laos	Vientiane	91,429	4,000,100
China	Beijing	3,691,521	1,151,300,000	Lebanon	Beirut	4,015	3,400,000
Georgia	Tbilisi	26,900	5,500,000	Malaysia	Kuala Lumpur	128,328	18,300,000
India	New Delhi	1,229,737	859,200,000	Maldives	Male	115	213,215
Indonesia	Jakarta	735,268	181,400,000	Mongolia	Ulan Bator	604,250	2,200,000
Iran	Tehran	636,293	58,600,000	Nepal	Kathmandu	54,463	1,900,600
Iraq	Baghdad	167,920	17,100,000	Oman	Muscat	82,030	1,600,000
				Pakistan	Islamabad	310,400	117,500,000
				Philippines	Manila	115,830	62,300,000

ASIA (and the Middle East)

Nation	Capital	Area (sq. mi.)	Population	Nation	Capital	Area (sq. mi.)	Population
Qatar	Doha	4,000	500,000	Turkey	Ankara	300,947	58,500,000
Saudi Arabia	Riyadh	865,000	15,500,000	Turkmenistan	Ashkhabad	188,500	3,800,000
Singapore	Singapore	220	2,000,000	United Arab			
Sri Lanka	Colombo	25,332	17,400,000	Emirates	Abu Dhabi	32,000	2,400,000
Syria	Damascus	71,498	12,800,000	Uzbekistan	Tashkent	172,700	21,000,000
Taiwan	Taipei	13,895	20,500,000	Vietnam	Hanoi	127,246	67,600,000
Tajikistan	Dushanbe	55,300	5,500,000	Yemen	Sanaa	203,850	10,100,000
Thailand	Bangkok	198,455	58,800,000				

EUROPE

Nation	Capital	Area (sq. mi.)	Population	Nation	Capital	Area (sq. mi.)	Population
Albania	Tirana	11,100	3,300,000	Liechtenstein	Vaduz	61	30,000
Andorra	Andorra			Lithuania	Vilnius	25,174	3,800,000
	la Vella	175	50,000	Luxembourg	Luxembourg	999	400,000
Austria	Vienna	32,375	7,700,000	*Macedonia	Skopje	9,900	2,066,000
Belarus	Minsk	80,200	10,400,000	Malta	Valletta	122	400,000
Belgium	Brussels	11,781	9,900,000	Moldova	Kishinev	13,000	4,400,000
*Bosnia and				Monaco	Monaco-Ville	0.73	28,000
Herzegovina	Sarajevo	19,741	4,400,000	Netherlands	Amsterdam,		
Bulgaria	Sofia	42,823	9,000,000		The Hague	16,041	15,000,000
*Croatia	Zagreb	21,829	4,601,000	Norway	Oslo	125,049	4,300,000
Cyprus	Nicosia	3,572	700,000	Poland	Warsaw	120,727	38,200,000
Czechoslo-				Portugal	Lisbon	35,550	10,400,000
vakia	Prague	49,374	15,700,000	Romania	Bucharest	91,700	23,400,000
Denmark	Copenhagen	16,631	5,100,000	Russia	Moscow	6,592,800	148,900,000
Estonia	Tallinn	18,370	1,600,000	San Marino	San Marino	24	23,000
Finland	Helsinki	130,119	5,000,000	*Slovenia	Ljubljana	7,819	1,892,000
France	Paris	211,208	56,700,000	Spain	Madrid	194,885	39,000,000
Germany	Berlin	137,777	78,700,000	Sweden	Stockholm	173,800	8,600,000
Greece	Athens	50,961	10,100,000	Switzerland	Bern	15,941	6,800,000
Hungary	Budapest	35,919	10,375,000	Ukraine	Kiev	233,100	52,000,000
Iceland	Reykjavik	39,709	255,000	United			
Ireland	Dublin	26,600	3,600,000	Kingdom	London	94,247	57,500,000
Italy	Rome	116,500	57,700,000	Vatican City	Vatican City	0.17	800
Latvia	Riga	25,400	2,700,000	Yugoslavia	Belgrade	39,480	10,951,000

OCEANIA

Nation	Capital	Area (sq. mi.)	Population	Nation	Capital	Area (sq. mi.)	Population
Australia	Canberra	2,966,150	17,500,000	Solomon			
Fiji	Suva	7,078	700,000	Islands	Honiara	11,500	300,000
Kiribati	Tarawa	277	69,000	Tonga	Nuku'alofa	290	100,000
Nauru	Yaren	8.2	9,100	Tuvalu	Funafuti	10	9,000
New Zealand	Wellington	103,884	3,500,000	Vanuatu	Port Vila	5,700	200,000
Papua				Western			
New Guinea	Port Moresby	178,704	3,900,000	Samoa	Apia	1,093	200,000

*Has declared independence from the Yugoslav federation.
Sources: Population Reference Bureau; *Information Please Almanac.*

TIME CHART OF WORLD HISTORY

The Ancient World

	Prehistory	3000 B.C.	2500 B.C.	
The Middle East and North Africa	• **9000–6000** Farming begins. • **6000** Çatal Hüyük built. • **3200** Sumerians settle in Mesopotamia, develop cuneiform writing. • **3100** Menes unites Upper and Lower Egypt.	• **2686–2181** Old Kingdom in Egypt; Egyptians develop hieroglyphics. • **2600** Great Pyramid at Giza built.	• **2350** Sargon of Akkad conquers Sumer. • **2100** City-state of Ur. • **2040–1786** Middle Kingdom in Egypt.	
Asia and the Pacific	• **9000–6000** Farming begins.	• **3000** First use of bronze.	• **2500** Indus Valley civilization develops.	
Europe and Russia	• **25,000** Cro-Magnon cave paintings.	• **2600** Artisans on Crete work with gold and bronze.	• **2500–2000** Growth of Minoan civilization.	
Africa	• **10,000** Fishing communities develop. • **9000–6000** Farming begins. • **3100** Menes unites Upper and Lower Egypt.	• **3000–2500** Farming spreads in western Sudan. • **2686–2181** Old Kingdom in Egypt; Egyptians develop hieroglyphics. • **2600** Great Pyramid at Giza Built.	• **2500–2000** Growth of Sahara Desert forces cattle herders to migrate. • **2040–1786** Middle Kingdom in Egypt.	
The Americas	• **20,000** Last Ice Age allows humans to migrate from Asia to Americas. • **3500** Farming in Valley of Mexico.	• **3000–2500** Migrations continue throughout Western Hemisphere.	• **2500–2000** Farming spreads from Valley of Mexico.	
	Prehistory	3000 B.C.	2500 B.C.	

The Ancient World

2000 B.C.	1500 B.C.	1000 B.C.	500 B.C.	A.D. 1	A.D. 500
• **1792** Hammurabi of Babylon unites Mesopotamia. • **1600–1200** Hittite Empire; Hittites learn ironworking. • **1570–1090** New Kingdom in Egypt.	• **1304–1237** Rameses II rules Egypt. • **1290** Hebrew Exodus from Egypt. • **1200** Phoenicians begin settling Mediterranean colonies. • **1020** Kingdom of Israel established.	• **972–922** Hebrew kingdom peaks under Solomon. • **814** Phoenicians establish Carthage. • **660** Height of Assyrian Empire. • **605–562** Babylon flourishes under Nebuchadnezzar. • **547** Cyrus builds Persian Empire.	• **334–323** Growth of empire of Alexander the Great. • **146** Carthage destroyed by Rome.	• **29** Jesus crucified. • **66–73** Judaean revolt against Rome fails. • **354** Augustine born.	
• **2000** Yellow River Valley civilization develops. • **1600–1100** Shang dynasty in China.	• **1500** Aryans invade Indus Valley. • **1500–500** Vedic Age in India; caste system develops. • **1100–256** Zhou dynasty in China.	• **800–300** Upanishads recorded in India. • **563** Buddha born. • **551** Confucius born. • **518** Persians rule northern India.	• **400's** Magadha Empire in India. • **327** Alexander invades India. • **221–206** Qin dynasty; Great Wall completed. • **269–232** Mauryan Empire peaks under Asoka. • **202 B.C.–A.D. 220** Han dynasty in China.	• **100** Chinese invent paper. • **220–589** Age of Disunity in China. • **320–500** Gupta Empire in northern India. • **400's** Start of Yamato dynasty in Japan.	
• **1900** Greek-speaking tribes enter Greece, leading to creation of Mycenaean civilization. • **1700–1450** Height of Minoan civilization.	• **1300** Trojan War; Achaeans dominate Mediterranean.	• **800** Start of Hellenic Age. • **700's** Homer's *Iliad* and *Odyssey*. • **500's** Athens moves toward democratic rule. • **509** Roman Republic founded.	• **490–479** Persian Wars. • **460–429** Age of Pericles in Athens. • **431–404** Peloponnesian War. • **400's–300's** Height of Greek philosophy. • **300's** Start of Hellenistic Age. • **264–146** Punic Wars. • **27 B.C.–A.D. 180** Pax Romana.	• **300's** Roman Empire divided; Christianity becomes official religion of Roman Empire. • **370's** Germanic invasions begin. • **476** Fall of Western Roman Empire. • **481** Clovis unites Franks.	
• **1600** Kingdom of Kush established. • **1570–1090** New Kingdom in Egypt. • **1525** Egypt conquers Kush.	• **1500–1000** Kush influenced by Egyptian culture. • **1304–1237** Rameses II rules Egypt.	• **700's** Kush takes over Egypt. • **590** Kushites move capital to Meroë.	• **500** Nok culture emerges; Bantu migrations begin; Kushites develop ironworking. • **200** Peak of Kushite power. • **23** Rome attacks Kush.	• **350** Aksum conquers Kush; Aksum adopts Christianity.	
• **2000–1500** Emergence of villages in Valley of Mexico.	• **1200** Olmec civilization begins.	• **1000** Northwest Coast culture begins.	• **400's B.C.–A.D. 400's** Hopewell culture. • **100's** Olmec civilization vanishes.	• **100** Rise of Teotihuacán; rise of Anasazi culture in American Southwest. • **300–700** Maya civilization.	
2000 B.C.	1500 B.C.	1000 B.C.	500 B.C.	A.D. 1	A.D. 500

TIME CHART OF WORLD HISTORY

The Middle Ages

	A.D. 500	600	700	800	900	
The Middle East and North Africa	• **527–565** Justinian rules Byzantine Empire. • **537** Hagia Sophia completed. • **570** Mohammed born.	• **600's** Slavs and Avars invade Balkans. • **622** The Hegira. • **632–661** Muslim conquests. • **661** Umayyads take over caliphate.	• **717–718** Arab attack on Constantinople fails. • **750** Abbasids replace Umayyads.	• **800's** Islamic culture flourishes in Baghdad. • **809** Death of Harun al-Rashid.	• **980** Avicenna born. • **900's** Seljuk Turks convert to Islam.	
Asia and the Pacific	• **500's** Buddhism comes to Japan. • **589–618** Sui dynasty in China. • **592** Prince Shotoku takes power in Japan.	• **618–907** Tang dynasty in China. • **668** China controls Korea. • **600's** Taika Reforms in Japan.	• **712** First Muslim invasion of India. • **784** Japanese capital moved to Heian.	• **800's** Border attacks weaken Tang government; Tang persecute Buddhism in China.	• **907** Tang dynasty falls. • **960** Song dynasty established.	
Europe and Russia	• **511** Frankish lands divided among Clovis's sons. • **529** Benedictine monastery built at Monte Cassino. • **590–604** Gregory the Great is Pope.	• **631** Visigoths capture Spain. • **687–714** Pepin II reunites Franks.	• **700's** Spain and Portugal under Muslim rule. • **731** Venerable Bede writes history of Church in England. • **732** Franks halt Muslim invasion of Europe.	• **800** Charlemagne crowned Emperor of Romans. • **843** Charlemagne's empire divided among his sons. • **800's** Vikings raid Western Europe; Vikings conquer Slavs in Russia. • **800's–1100's** Romanesque architecture.	• **900's** Magyars settle in Hungary. • **962** Otto the Great becomes first Holy Roman Emperor. • **988** Great Prince Vladimir of Kiev converts to Christianity.	
Africa	• **500–700** Growth of Empire of Ghana.	• **600's** Arab conquest of North Africa spurs trade across Sahara.	• **700–1000** Ghana at height of its power.	• **869** Revolt by East African slaves in Middle East.	• **900–1000** Growth of trade results in spread of languages.	
The Americas	• **500** Height of Maya civilization.	• **600** Teotihuacán attacked and burned.	• **700** Beginnings of Mississippian culture.	• **850** Mayas begin abandoning cities.	• **950** End of Maya civilization. • **900's–1000's** Vikings explore northeast coast of North America.	
	A.D. 500	600	700	800	900	

862

The Middle Ages

	1000	1100	1200	1300	1400	1500
	• **1054** Christian Church splits into Roman Catholic Church and Eastern Orthodox Church. • **1071** Seljuks defeat Byzantines at Manzikert.	• **1100's** Crusader states established. • **1187** Saladin recaptures Jerusalem.	• **1204** Crusaders sack Constantinople. • **1258** Mongols destroy Baghdad, ending Abbasid caliphate. • **1200's** Osman establishes Ottoman state.	• **1300's** Ottomans conquer Byzantine lands.	• **1453** Constantinople falls to Ottomans.	
	• **1000** *The Tale of Genji.* • **1000's** Muslim attacks on India from Afghanistan; feudalism develops in Japan; Chinese print books from wooden blocks.	• **1127–1279** Southern Song dynasty in China. • **1185** Kamakura shogunate established in Japan; samurai dominate Japanese society.	• **1206** Delhi sultanate established. • **1215** Mongols control northern China. • **1260–1294** Kublai Khan rules Mongol Empire. • **1275** Marco Polo arrives in China. • **1281** Mongol invasion of Japan fails.	• **1333** Kamakura shogunate collapses. • **1368** Ming dynasty established. • **1398** Mongols under Tamerlane destroy Delhi.	• **1405–1433** Zheng He leads sea voyages for China. • **1497** Da Gama sails from Portugal for India. • **1400's–1500's** Age of the Country at War in Japan.	
	• **1000** Stephen unifies Hungary and converts it to Christianity. • **1054** Christian Church is divided. • **1066** Norman conquest of England. • **1096** First Crusade begins. • **1000's–1100's** Growth of towns; first universities.	• **1122** Concordat of Worms. • **1144** Second Crusade begins. • **1154–1189** Henry II establishes common law in England. • **1189** Third Crusade begins. • **1100's** First Gothic cathedrals built.	• **1202** Fourth Crusade begins. • **1215** Magna Carta. • **1232** Inquisition set up. • **1240** Mongols rule Kiev. • **1265–1321** Dante.	• **1309–1377** Babylonian Captivity. • **1330–1370** Casimir III rules Poland. • **1337–1453** Hundred Years' War. • **1348** Black Death reaches Europe. • **1378–1417** Great Schism.	• **1400's** Renaissance flourishes in Italy. • **1450–1700's** Age of Exploration; Commercial Revolution. • **1450's** Gutenberg invents printing press. • **1480** Ivan the Great declares Russia's independence. • **1492** Spain reunited.	
	• **1076** Muslims capture capital of Ghana. • **1000's** Rulers of Mali convert to Islam; Bantu kingdoms grow up in East Africa; Islam and northeastern Africa.	• **1100's–1200's** Islam spreads in East Africa.	• **1200–1230** King Lalibela builds stone churches in Ethiopia.	• **1300's** Abu Bakari leads Mali expedition into Atlantic Ocean; Kongo kingdom established. • **1312–1332** Mali reaches peak under Mansa Musa.	• **1468** Songhai capture Timbuktu. • **1488** Dias sails around tip of Africa. • **1400's** Luba state and Lunda Empire set up in central Africa; Great Zimbabwe in southeast Africa.	
	• **1000** Toltec empire emerges. • **1085** Anasazi complete Pueblo Bonito.	• **1150** Toltecs conquered.	• **1200** Peak of Mississippian culture. • **1200's** Drought destroys Anasazi culture.	• **1325** Aztecs build Tenochtitlán.	• **1438** Incas build empire in Andes. • **1492** Columbus reaches Caribbean. • **1494** Treaty of Tordesillas. • **1400's** Aztecs rule central Mexico.	
	1000	1100	1200	1300	1400	1500

TIME CHART OF WORLD HISTORY

The Modern Era

	1500	1550	1600	1650	1700	
The Middle East and North Africa	• **1500** Ismail establishes Safavid Empire. • **1520–1566** Suleiman I rules Ottoman Empire. • **1526** Ottomans defeat Hungarians at Mohács. • **1529** Ottomans besiege Vienna.	• **1571** Christians defeat Ottomans at naval battle of Lepanto. • **1588** Abbas the Great becomes Safavid leader.	• **1629** Abbas the Great dies, leading to Safavid decline.	• **1600's–1700's** Ottoman Empire loses strength.	• **1722** Safavid Empire falls.	
Asia and the Pacific	• **1526** Delhi sultanate falls, leading to creation of Mogul Empire. • **1542** Portuguese arrive in Japan. • **1500's** European traders begin arriving in Southeast Asia.	• **1556** Akbar inherits Mogul throne. • **1598** Tokugawa shogunate begins in Japan.	• **1600** English East India Company chartered. • **1630's** Japan limits foreign contacts. • **1644** Manchus overthrow Ming dynasty, beginning Qing dynasty. • **1630–1650** Taj Mahal built.	• **1658–1707** Aurangzeb expands Mogul Empire.	• **1700's** Arts and commerce thrive in Tokugawa Japan; Britain and France struggle over India.	
Europe and Russia	• **1517** Luther challenges Church. • **1519–1522** Magellan leads circumnavigation of globe. • **1508–1512** Michelangelo paints Sistine Chapel. • **1534** Act of Supremacy in England. • **1543** Copernicus publishes heliocentric theory.	• **1555** Peace of Augsburg. • **1558** Spanish Armada. • **1558–1603** Elizabeth I rules England. • **1563** End of Council of Trent. • **1564** Galileo, Shakespeare born. • **1598** Edict of Nantes.	• **1605** Cervantes's *Don Quixote*. • **1618–1648** Thirty Years' War. • **1642–1651** English Civil War. • **1643–1715** Louis XIV rules France.	• **1653–1658** Cromwell "Lord Protector" of England. • **1682–1725** Peter the Great rules Russia. • **1687** Newton publishes *Principia*. • **1688** Glorious Revolution in England. • **1600's** Palace at Versailles built.	• **1701–1713** War of the Spanish Succession. • **1700's** Height of Enlightenment; Industrial Revolution begins in England; baroque period in art and music.	
Africa	• **1505–1545** King Affonso rules Kongo. • **1518** Spain licenses slave trade to Americas. • **1528** End of Askia Mohammed's rule of Songhai.	• **1590** Songhai Empire collapses.	• **1600's** Dahomey becomes slave-trading center.	• **1652** Dutch East India Company sets up trading post at Cape of Good Hope. • **1665** Portuguese invade Kongo.	• **1700's** Transatlantic slave trade peaks. • **1700's–1800's** European explorers map Africa.	
The Americas	• **1513** Ponce de León discovers Florida. • **1518** First African slaves arrive in Americas. • **1521** Cortés conquers Aztecs. • **1532** Pizarro defeats Incas. • **1535** Cartier claims eastern Canada for France.	• **1560** Spain claims American Southwest. • **1580** Iroquois League formed.	• **1607** Jamestown colony started. • **1608** Champlain establishes Quebec. • **1600's** New England colonies formed.	• **1660's** Navigation Acts. • **1672** Joliet and Marquette explore Great Lakes. • **1682** La Salle explores Mississippi River and claims region for France.	• **1702–1713, 1744–1748** French and English struggle for control of North America.	
	1500	1550	1600	1650	1700	

The Modern Era

1750	1800	1850	1900	1950	2000
• **1768–1792** Ottomans lose territory along Black Sea to Russia. • **1798** France invades Egypt.	• **1805–1849** Mohammed Ali rules Egypt. • **1830–1848** France takes control of Algeria.	• **1853–1856** Crimean War. • **1869** Suez Canal opens. • **1878** Treaty of San Stephano. • **1882** Britain controls Egypt.	• **1908** Revolt by Young Turks. • **1923** Ataturk declares Turkish Republic. • **1925** Reza Shah takes throne in Persia. • **1932** Kingdom of Saudi Arabia declared. • **1948** State of Israel created; first Arab-Israeli war.	• **1967** Six-Day War. • **1973** October War. • **1975** Civil war begins in Lebanon. • **1978** Camp David Accords. • **1979** Iranian Revolution. • **1980–1988** Iran-Iraq War. • **1991** Gulf War.	
• **1763** Treaty of Paris gives Britain control over India.	• **1839–1842** Opium War. • **1800's** Britain tightens hold on India.	• **1850–1864** Taiping Rebellion. • **1850's** Australia and New Zealand gain self-government. • **1854** Commodore Perry arrives in Tokyo. • **1857** Sepoy Rebellion. • **1868** Meiji era begins in Japan. • **1899–1900** Boxer Rebellion.	• **1911–1912** Nationalist Revolution in China. • **1931** Japan invades Manchuria. • **1941** Japan attacks Pearl Harbor. • **1945** Japan surrenders. • **1947** India and Pakistan independent. • **1949** People's Republic of China established.	• **1950–1953** Korean War. • **1975** Communist victories in Vietnam, Cambodia, and Laos. • **1979** Soviet Union invades Afghanistan. • **1989** Student protest crushed in China. • **1991** Cambodia peace plan.	
• **1756–1763** Seven Years' War. • **1762–1796** Catherine the Great rules Russia. • **1772–1795** Partitions of Poland. • **1789–1799** French Revolution.	• **1804** Napoleon crowned emperor. • **1815** Battle of Waterloo; Congress of Vienna ends. • **1830** Locomotive invented. • **1833** Factory Act in Britain. • **1848** Revolutions in Europe; *Communist Manifesto.*	• **1856–1939** Freud. • **1859** Darwin's *Origin of Species.* • **1870** Italy unified. • **1870–1914** Age of Imperialism. • **1871** Franco-Prussian War ends; Germany unified.	• **1905** Einstein's theory of relativity. • **1914–1918** World War I. • **1917** Bolshevik Revolution. • **1933** Hitler takes power. • **1936–1939** Spanish Civil War. • **1939–1945** World War II in Europe.	• **1956** Revolutions in Poland and Hungary. • **1957** Common Market. • **1979** Thatcher elected British prime minister. • **1985** Gorbachev takes power in Soviet Union. • **1989** Revolutions in Eastern Europe. • **1990** Germany unified. • **1991** Collapse of Soviet Union.	
• **1787** Sierra Leone established. • **1795** Kingdom of Ashanti formed.	• **1806** Britain takes control of Cape Colony. • **1807** Britain and United States ban slave trade. • **1819** Zulu kingdom controls southeastern Africa. • **1820** Liberia established. • **1835–1845** Great Trek.	• **1870's** Samori Touré builds empire. • **1884–1885** Berlin Conference. • **1896** Ethiopia defeats Italy at Aduwa. • **1898** Britain and Egypt defeat Sudanese at Omdurman; Fashoda Incident. • **1899–1902** South African War.	• **1905** Maji Maji uprising in German East Africa. • **1910** Union of South Africa created. • **1912** African National Congress formed. • **1947** Kenyatta leads Kenyan independence movement. • **1948** South Africa begins apartheid policy.	• **1957–1970's** African colonies achieve independence. • **1980's** Civil war in Angola. • **1990** Namibia independent. Mandela released. • **1991** Negotiations on political reform in South Africa.	
• **1754–1763** French and Indian War. • **1763** Britain gains control of French lands in North America. • **1776** Declaration of Independence. • **1783** Treaty of Paris ends Revolutionary War. • **1787** U.S. Constitution drafted.	• **1803** Louisiana Purchase. • **1812** War of 1812. • **1821** Mexico and Central America become independent. • **1823** Monroe Doctrine. • **1824** Bolivar completes liberation of South America. • **1846–1848** Mexican-American War.	• **1858–1860** War of the Reform in Mexico. • **1861–1865** U. S. Civil War. • **1867** Dominion of Canada formed. • **1876** Bell invents telephone. • **1898** Spanish-American War.	• **1903** Wright brothers invent airplane. • **1910** Mexican Revolution. • **1914** Panama Canal completed. • **1929** Great Depression begins. • **1945** United Nations founded.	• **1959** Cuban Revolution. • **1969** Moon landing. • **1972** SALT I signed. • **1982** Constitution Act in Canada. • **1980's** Civilian rule restored in Argentina and Brazil; civil wars in Central America. • **1991** El Salvador truce.	
1750	1800	1850	1900	1950	2000

Skill Review

From Reading Through Critical Thinking

History of the World takes you on a journey from prehistory to today. Along the way you will encounter a great variety of people, cultures, and events. At times, the people and events may seem so remote in time and place that their significance may be hard to grasp. To help you get maximum comprehension and enjoyment from your study of world history, the following pages introduce you to valuable techniques and ways of thinking called skills. The skills are presented in three groups: **Study Skills, Critical Thinking Skills, and Participation Skills.**

Study Skills

Study skills can help you locate, gather, organize, and present information. Acquiring information through reading, building your vocabulary, locating and retrieving information from print and electronic systems, reading and interpreting graphic materials, organizing ideas in written form, understanding time and chronology, and taking tests are study skills that can help you learn more effectively and efficiently.

1. Acquiring Information Through Reading

Understanding and remembering what you read is essential for effective learning. Begin any reading assignment by getting a general idea of what the material is about. You can usually do this by reading the titles (chapter and section) and the main headings. Look, for example, at the title for Chapter 23 (page 456), "New Nations in Latin America." It tells you immediately what the main reading focus will be.

The titles of the sections in that chapter, "Latin American Independence" and "Challenges Facing the New Nations," show the subject organization. Within each section, major headings broaden this organization. Surveying the title and headings will prepare you for your study of a section. Look at Section 1 of Chapter 23 and list the major headings, which, in effect, form an outline of the section. Only the details are missing.

In this book, each section begins with focus questions to guide your reading. In Chapter 23, Section 1, two questions—(1) **Why did Latin Americans rebel against foreign rule?** and (2) **How did Latin Americans gain independence?**—help you focus on important details as you read (see page 457). If you read to find answers to these questions, you are more likely to look for and remember the significant information about Latin American countries and their struggle for independence.

Skimming. You *skim* a reading selection to get a general idea of its content. Follow these steps when skimming: (1) Read the title of the selection. (2) Read the first two or three paragraphs. Introductory paragraphs usually preview the content of a selection. (3) Read the first and last sentences of all other paragraphs. (4) Read headings, and notice the words that are being introduced. In this book, new words are printed in red.

Scanning. The purpose of *scanning* is different from that of skimming. You scan to find specific information. Scanning is often used to find answers to review questions.

Look for key words or phrases as you glance down the page of the reading selection. Use section titles, headings, words in red type, and first and last sentences of paragraphs to help you find the information you are looking for.

Finding the main ideas. History is the study of important events and concepts that have shaped the lives of people over time and in different places. These important events and concepts make up the *main ideas* on which the study of history is based and organized. When you have identified and remembered the main ideas, you have begun to gain an understanding of the why's of history.

Taking notes. Taking good notes will help you identify and remember the main ideas in a reading assignment or a lecture.

If you follow these suggestions, you will find you are taking better notes:

a. Read through each passage before you take notes. To be sure you understand what is important in each passage, read through it before writing anything down. You may find that the first sentence is merely introductory and not a main theme.

b. Write down only main ideas and the most important information. Taking notes is picking out main ideas from supporting details. Watch for words and phrases that signal main points. Examples are: *first, finally, most important,* and *the causes of.*

c. Use drawings or diagrams to show cause and effect or to show relationships. There are times when it might be more helpful to use drawings to remember a concept. Look at this example:

Nationalism	
Positive	*Negative*
Freedom	Racism
Independence from foreign rule	Restriction of rights/freedoms
Sense of community/ traditions	Glorification of aggression

d. Write notes in a shortened form, using abbreviations and symbols. Because you are taking notes for your own use, you need not use complete sentences or even complete words. In note-taking, you can eliminate such words as *the, a,* and *an.*

Symbols can simplify note-taking too. Some commonly used symbols are *&* (and), *w/* (with), and *w/o* (without).

e. Review your notes. Within a few days after you take notes on an assignment, review them to make sure you understand what they mean. If you find you have abbreviated too much, go back to your textbook, find the meaning for those notes you do not understand, and write them out more fully.

Observing for details. Finding the main ideas in a reading selection is a good way to get a general understanding of history. For a fuller understanding, however, you need to know more about the significant events that comprise these main ideas, and you need to learn the details that brought meaning to the events. When you observe, or look for details, keep the following key questions in mind: (1) *What* happened? (2) *Where* did it happen? (3) *When* did it happen? (4) *Why* did it happen? (5) *Who* was involved? (6) *How* did it happen?

You probably can answer some questions simply, particularly those beginning with *where, when,* and *who.* Others, such as *why* and *how* questions, may require a more careful reading to determine the answers.

2. Building Vocabulary

The more words you understand, the more effective your study will be. There are many ways to increase your vocabulary:

a. As you read, be aware of words that you do not understand or that are unfamiliar. Some may be words that you will find in other areas of reading. But many will be specialized words, used largely in history and social studies materials. Look up definitions for unfamiliar words in the Glossary (following this Skill Review) or in a dictionary and write them in a notebook.

b. From time to time, study these words and their definitions. If possible, work them into your assignments so that you become comfortable using them.

c. Look for these words as you read any other resources.

Context clues. When you come across a word in your reading you do not understand, you can often figure out its meaning from the *context*—the setting in which the word is used. For example, if you look at page 440 in Chapter 22, you will find the following:

> Mary Wollstonecraft, an English writer who supported the French Revolution, published *A Vindication of the Rights of Woman* in 1792.

Notice the word *vindication* in the title of the book. The two sentences that complete the paragraph about Wollstonecraft and her book are clues to the meaning of *vindication.* The two ending sentences indicate that she favored an extension of rights and opportunities for women. The context suggests, therefore, that *vindication* probably reflects a supporting attitude. If you look up the word, your inference would be confirmed by finding that one meaning of the word is "defense" or "justification."

Examples. An *example* can explain an unfamiliar word by showing what kinds of things the word refers to. In Chapter 29, page 583, under the heading "Japan's Turn to the West," you will read this passage:

> Although the emperor was the formal ruler of Japan during the Meiji era (1868–1912), the important decisions were actually made by the group of young samurai who had led the rebellion. As military men, they were eager to close the gap.

If the word *samurai* is unfamiliar, you could figure out from the phrase "As military men" that *samurai* refers to men in the military profession.

Synonyms. Sometimes, an unfamiliar word will appear in the same context with a similar word, or *synonym.* If you know the meaning of the synonym, you can often figure out the meaning of the unfamiliar word. In

868

Chapter 38, page 780, in the Biography feature on Jomo Kenyatta, you will find the following passage:

> Where there has been racial hatred, it must be ended. Where there has been tribal animosity, it will be finished. Let us not dwell upon the bitterness of the past.

The word *animosity* may be unfamiliar to you. But elsewhere in the passage, Kenyatta also uses the words *hatred* and *bitterness* in the same context. This suggests that *animosity* is an extreme ill-feeling against someone, the meaning of both *hatred* and *bitterness.*

3. Locating and Gathering Information

There may be times when you need more information about a given topic than you can find in the textbook. Knowing how to locate and gather additional information will save you considerable time when you are researching a topic.

Using the library. To make use of a library, there are basic things you need to know. Since most libraries are organized similarly, you can use your library skills in nearly any library.

Books can be either fiction or nonfiction. Books of fiction are usually alphabetized on library shelves, using the last names of authors.

The Dewey decimal system is used by some libraries to arrange books of nonfiction. Under this system, subjects are organized in ten categories that are numbered from 000 to 999. The groups are subdivided so that every subject within a category has its own number. History is indexed under the 900 numbers, for instance, while modern history begins at 909.

Some libraries use the Library of Congress system rather than the Dewey decimal system. The Library of Congress system uses 21 lettered classifications.

Using the card catalog in a library will enable you to find books quickly. Card catalogs list the books in a library in three ways: by author, title, and subject. If you need a specific book, look under the author's name or under the book's title. If you are looking for books on a particular subject, look at the subject card.

Any of the cards (author, title, or subject) will tell you where you can find a book in the library. In the upper left-hand corner of the card, you will find the book's call number. This number will be either under the Dewey decimal system or the Library of Congress system.

Computer systems are in use in most libraries today and in some cases have replaced card catalogs. However, computerized systems organize a library's holdings in much the same way as card catalogs do: books, records, videotapes, and other items can be found according to author, title, or subject. Computerized systems can give you more information than card catalogs can. For instance, once you have located a certain book, the screen entry will tell you whether your library's copy is available, checked out, on reserve, or missing. If your library has no copy, the computer will tell you what branch of the library system does have a copy.

Another important source for locating books and other items is the librarian. Librarians will help you understand the card catalog and learn the computer system, and will locate other sources that may be useful to you.

Using reference books. There are a number of basic reference books you should be familiar with if you are doing research for an assignment or if you want to find more information about a subject.

Dictionaries. Dictionaries are not new to you, but there are special dictionaries you may not be aware of in most libraries.

Many libraries have dictionaries on such specialized subjects as geography, biography, and jazz. Libraries also have dictionaries of foreign languages. In the reference section of this textbook, you will find a biographical dictionary on pages 900–906.

Encyclopedias. You probably know that in an *encyclopedia* you will find articles arranged alphabetically by subject. You should also become familiar with using the index (a separate volume) for a set of encyclopedias. The index will help you locate information more quickly.

Atlases and gazetteers. *Atlases* are books of maps. Not all atlases contain the same information. Some may concentrate on political maps, which are those that show political areas—countries, states, provinces, and cities. Other atlases may specialize in physical maps, which depict an area's geographical features. This book contains an atlas on pages 850–856.

Gazetteers are dictionaries that list names of physical geographical features as well as political place names—cities and countries. Gazetteers give pronunciations, locations, and other pertinent information about a place, such as population and area.

Almanacs and yearbooks. These references are published yearly and give up-to-date data on many subjects. Such *almanacs* as *Information Please Almanac* are loaded with statistics. For example, you can find a list of the world's largest islands, highest waterfalls, and greatest artificial lakes. Also, there is an article on every country of the world, giving information on population, exports and imports, capital, literacy rate, units of money, and a wealth of other information. Almanacs also list important events of recent years.

Yearbooks, such as *The Statesman's Year-Book,* contain material about current events, economics, and the latest developments in science and the arts. The *World Book Year-Book* is organized like an encyclopedia. It contains articles that report recent developments in many fields.

Periodical indexes. The *Readers' Guide to Periodical Literature* lists articles that have appeared in nearly 200 periodicals—magazines and newspapers. The *Read-*

ers' Guide is issued several times a year and is compiled into an annual single-volume edition. Here you will find references to articles that will give the most recent information on certain topics. If you are unsure how to request periodicals, consult the librarian.

Most libraries have *The New York Times Index,* which lists articles that have appeared in *The New York Times.* Articles are listed in this index by subject. Often, the newspaper you want will be on microfilm. If so, you must find the corresponding microfilm cartridge and use the projector in order to read your article on a screen. If you need to save the article for your research, you may copy it by inserting coins into the microfilm copier, much as you would with an ordinary copying machine.

4. Reading and Interpreting Graphic Materials

Graphs and charts are used throughout this textbook to present certain kinds of facts. Some information can be more memorable or make a greater impact when presented in a visual or graphic form.

Graphs. Comparing numerical data is a useful skill in studying history. Graphs present statistics in a form that makes understanding easier and emphasizes visually how numbers of different things change.

Line graphs and bar graphs can show changes over time on one graph. *Line graphs* use dots and lines to plot information. They are useful for showing trends. *Bar graphs* use bars, either vertical or horizontal, to represent quantities. *Circle graphs* (sometimes called pie graphs) always show 100 percent of something. To show changes over time, you would need two or more circle graphs, one for each of the selected years. Graphs can sometimes be used in combination to show different aspects of related subjects.

Look at the graphs on these pages. They all have something to do with corn. Notice that each graph has its own title, which tells what the graph depicts.

The bar graph and the line graph are constructed similarly in that they both have a horizontal axis and a vertical axis. The *horizontal axis* is the information shown along the bottom of the graph. On the bar graph, the horizontal axis shows years from 1981 to 1989. On the line graph, the horizontal axis shows certain days in June 1988. Notice that the intervals between the years and days are evenly spaced.

The *vertical axis* is the information shown along the side of the graph. On the bar graph the vertical axis is on the left while on the line graph the vertical axis is on the right. The vertical axis on the line graph shows the price of corn per bushel. What does the vertical axis on the bar graph show? Again, the intervals between the items shown on the vertical axes are evenly spaced.

870

Answer: Number of bushels.

Share of World Corn Production

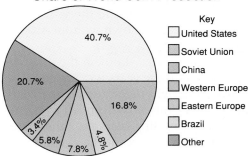

Key
- United States
- Soviet Union
- China
- Western Europe
- Eastern Europe
- Brazil
- Other

40.7%
20.7%
16.8%
3.4%
5.8%
7.8%
4.8%

Organization of the United Nations

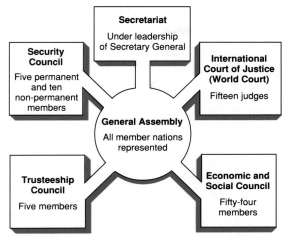

Notice the circle graph at the top of this page. The graph has been divided into segments that are each a percentage of a whole or 100 percent. The segments are colored to correspond with the colors in the key. That makes it possible for you to tell which color represents the corn production of a given area of the world.

Use the three graphs to answer the following questions:

1. In which year that information is given for did the United States have its greatest corn production? 1987

2. In which year did the United States produce about three and a half billion bushels of corn? 1983

3. On which date in 1988 was corn priced at its highest? Lowest? June 21. June 1 or 9.

4. What area of the world produces the most corn? What percentage of the total world corn production? United States, 40.7%

5. Which graph would you look at to find how many bushels of corn the United States produced in 1981? Bar graph

Charts. Charts are a good way to summarize information. Charts may take different forms, but they are organized to permit quick reading and easy comprehension. Since they are set up in rows and columns, some charts resemble tables. Others may be flow charts or diagrams that show how one thing causes something else to happen or how one thing leads to another. Organizational charts depict how certain organizations operate. What is the subject of the organizational chart shown above? Explain the information it presents.

5. Organizing Ideas in Written Form

As you study world history, you may be asked to write reports. Reports, such as term papers and essays, usually begin with an introduction that states your purpose and establishes your readers' interest. The body of the paper is your presentation of the material. Here you give and support the facts and your points of view. Be sure this material relates to the purpose stated in your introduction. End your report with a conclusion, which restates your paper's main points.

Outlining. An efficient way to organize ideas on a reading assignment is to outline what you read. An outline is also an important step in preparing a report. Making an outline helps you organize your thoughts. The outline then becomes a guide to follow when you write your report.

When you make an outline, you need to identify the main ideas and distinguish them from the supporting details. Main ideas become main headings in your outline and supporting details become subheadings. For example, the passage in the textbook that answers the question "What were the under-

871

lying causes of World War I?" (pages 625–626) could be outlined as follows:

Causes of World War I
  I. Entangling alliances
      A. Triple Alliance
           1. Germany, Austria-Hungary, Italy
           2. Basic mistrust of France
      B. Triple Entente
           1. France, Great Britain, Russia
           2. Basic mistrust of Germany
  II. Other forces
      A. Militarism
           1. Glorification of war
           2. Buildup of armaments
      B. Imperialism
      C. Nationalism

Notice that in this outline, main headings start with a Roman numeral. Subheadings start with a capital letter and additional supporting details with an Arabic numeral. A main heading should always have at least two subheadings.

Summarizing. Another way to organize information is to summarize. A summary is a brief statement of important ideas written in paragraph form, which records the main ideas as concisely as possible. Summarizing is useful for taking notes as you prepare to write a report.

The following guidelines will help when you are writing a summary: (a) Look for key words and use them in your summary. (b) Use as few words as possible but avoid changing the meaning of the passage you are summarizing. (c) Write the summary in paragraph form.

6. Understanding Time and Chronology

The calendar used in most countries of the Western world divides time into two periods: the years before the birth of Jesus (B.C.) and the years since then (A.D.). The letters A.D. stand for the words *anno Domini*, a Latin phrase meaning "in the year of the Lord." The letters B.C. follow the year, as in "227 B.C."

The letters A.D., however, position as they would in Latin; they precede the year, as in "A.D. 44." If a year is shown without A.D. or B.C., you can assume it is A.D.

Using timelines. Look at the timeline below. Notice that the years B.C. are counted backward (from right to left), while the years A.D. are counted forward (from left to right). When you are counting years B.C., the lower the number the more recent the event.

Counting the Centuries

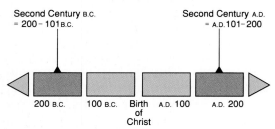

The timeline is marked off in centuries, or groups of 100 years. Notice the shaded centuries and the terms used to describe each one. The "second century B.C." refers to the years from 200 B.C. to 101 B.C. and *not* the 200's B.C. The "second century A.D." refers to the years A.D. 101–200. What years make up the first century B.C.? What will be the first year of the twenty-first century? See answers below.

You will find two kinds of timelines in this book. At the beginning of every unit, you will find a "multiple" timeline that will give you a preview of important events in all the chapters of the unit. At the end of each chapter in this book there is a timeline that places the chapter's major events in chronological order. Use this timeline to review the chapter contents.

Understanding the vocabulary of time. Besides knowing the difference between B.C. and A.D., it is important in the study of history to understand terms that place events in a certain time period. *Year, decade,* and *century* are concepts you are familiar with. They are terms that are definite periods of time, that is, a decade is always 10 years and a century is always 100 years.

Answers: 100 B.C.—1 B.C.; 2001.

SKILL REVIEW

Not all terms related to time periods are definite. Some may cover a wide span of time. *The Age of Enlightenment*, for example, is less specific than 1650–1800. Other terms that suggest time periods are *The Great Depression, at the time of the French Revolution, the period of the Romantic Movement, during the Industrial Revolution,* and *the years between the wars.* Although these phrases are not specific, they do give you an idea of a period of time.

There are other terms that are even less clear-cut. *Many years ago, in the future, soon, not so long ago,* and *in ancient times* are examples of indefinite time phrases that some writers may use instead of terms that put events into a definite context. When you are writing history papers or answering essay questions on tests, try to use definite time phrases. Place events in fixed time periods.

Sequencing events. *Sequencing* is putting events in the order in which they happened. Certain words give clues to the order of things: *first, last, just before, just after, later, soon,* and *in the meantime* are examples that help you understand in what order events occurred.

7. Taking Tests

If you have developed good study habits, your chances of doing well on tests are much better than if you leave your studying until just before a test is given. Preparation is the key to success on tests.

Reading your assignments carefully and taking notes as you read will reduce the amount of work required to prepare for a test. If you have kept up with daily assignments, getting ready for a test is merely reviewing material you already know.

On history tests you are likely to find both multiple-choice and essay questions.

Multiple-choice questions give four answers to choose from. Read the question to see if you can answer it without looking at the choices. If you think you know the answer and it is one of the choices, chances are you are right. If you are not sure what the answer is, read the choices, ruling out those you know to be incorrect. Select the one you think is right from the remaining choices.

Essay questions ask you to write a brief composition in a short amount of time. These questions usually have a limited focus. Read each question carefully. If you are asked to summarize the ideas of Voltaire, for example, concentrate on his philosophy, not on any other aspects of his life that do not relate directly to his ideas.

Answers to essay questions should be well organized and carefully written. You will be graded on grammar, spelling, and organization, as well as on content.

Be sure to follow the directions as printed on the test or as given by the teacher. Skim through the test quickly to see what it contains and how much time you feel you can spend on each section. If you do not know the answer to a question, leave it and go on. Once you have worked through the test, go back to questions you left, and spend the remaining time trying to determine the answers.

Critical Thinking Skills

Understanding history requires you not only to develop a memory for facts and dates but also to *think* effectively.

The critical thinking skills described here provide guidelines for effective thinking. They also show you how one critical thinking process is related to another. In order to make wise decisions, for example, you have to ask the right questions. Before you can judge the validity of a historical source, you need to be able to distinguish between statements of fact and opinion. You can draw a valid conclusion about a historical period only after you have practiced synthesizing about that period. Knowing *how* to study history will greatly increase your appreciation of *why* you study history.

1. Defining and Clarifying Problems

History is largely the account of problems and solutions. Often, a solution leads to another problem and the process continues. When you study history, learn to identify the central problem in any discussion. If you focus on this element, many other elements will fall into place.

The decision-making process. The identifying and solving of problems in your own life involves making choices, or making decisions. This can be something as simple as choosing what to eat in a restaurant or as complex as deciding what career to pursue. When you need to deal with difficult problems, there are steps you can take to help you make the right decision.

    a. Identify the problem clearly.
    b. Consider the various alternatives.
    c. Consider the merits and probable consequences of each of the alternatives.
    d. Make a decision.

Throughout history individuals have been faced with problems whose solutions have affected the lives of thousands or even millions of people. For instance, at the close of World War I, Allied leaders met in France to create a peace agreement. Their chief problem was to determine the treatment of Germany, which had lost the war. France, Great Britain, and Italy called for punitive treatment—reparations for destroyed land and industry, and demilitarization so that Germany could not threaten the rest of Europe again.

The United States called for a more generous treatment of Germany, believing that a Germany punished would become a Germany bent upon revenge. The United States was outvoted. When the peace treaty was complete, Germany was thoroughly humiliated in territorial, economic, and military terms. The results of this decision are well known—they eventually culminated in the outbreak of another war in Europe.

Consider the following situation: It is 1962, during the cold-war era of tension between the United States and the Soviet Union. United States aircraft flying over Cuba discover that Soviet nuclear missiles have been set up on launching sites on that island, just 90 miles from Florida. The United States President demands of the Soviet Union that the missiles be removed, but they are not.

What should the President's next step be? Put yourself in that position, and apply the decision-making steps: What is the problem? What are the possible alternatives? What are the merits and probable consequences of each? What course of action will you decide to take?

As you may know, President John F. Kennedy did face this very problem. To read about his choice of action, see page 718.

Asking questions. You can speed the process of learning how people have solved problems historically by asking questions as you read. As you answer these questions, you gather the information relevant to the problems at hand. Consider Chapter 26, under Section 3, entitled "Imperial Russia" (pages 524–527). If you quickly skim this section, you will see five headings: *A troubled empire, Repression under Nicholas I, The reforms of Alexander II, The end of reform,* and *Return to repression.*

If you made a list of questions to answer based upon these headings, you might start with these three: What major problems faced the Russian Empire in the nineteenth century? Was Nicholas I able to deal effectively with these problems? What reforms did Alexander II start?

What will be your questions for the last two headings in that section of Chapter 26?

Analyzing. The purpose of analyzing is to show you understand what you have read. Understanding helps you identify problems quickly and determine whether people were successful in solving them. When you analyze information, you do three things:

    a. Break down the information into its different parts.

b. Recognize the relationship of one part to another.

c. Understand why the material has been organized as it has.

Analysis can be applied to large reading selections, such as chapters, or to single paragraphs or even sentences.

Look at Chapter 25, pages 490–511. You can break down this chapter into its three parts: Section 1, "The Industrial Revolution"; Section 2, "New Economic Theories"; and Section 3, "Political, Economic, and Social Reforms." What is the relationship among these sections? Why has the author chosen to organize the chapter in this way?

If you look closely at each of the sections, you will notice that Section 1 mainly describes the technological developments of the Industrial Revolution and how these changes affected people. Section 2 describes the new economic theories that came about to explain the relationships among people in an industrial society, and Section 3 describes the ways in which people looked for solutions to the problems created by industrialization.

You can conclude from the way the chapter is organized that the author views the history of the industrializing period in this way: (1) Certain very basic changes in the ways people produced goods took place during the late 1700's and early 1800's and had drastic effects on the way people worked and on urban life. (2) Observation of those changes caused some people to formulate theories; they needed to explain the reasons for the changes and propose solutions to the problems they saw in the economic and social systems of the industrial age. (3) The search for improvements in life became more widespread as reformers, workers, labor leaders, and political leaders sought practical solutions.

2. Making Judgments

As you study history, you need to make judgments about what you are learning and reading. Sometimes, you need to judge the importance of several causes that led to a specific effect. Another time you may have to make a judgment about people's behavior when the reason is not directly stated. Furthermore, you will often have to judge whether you are reading statements of facts or opinion and decide in what ways each is valid.

Many of the judgments you will make will call for the use of interpretation skills. Interpreting is the identification of a relationship between two or more facts, ideas, or values. You may be asked to use interpretation skills in any of the ways described below.

Determining cause-and-effect relationships. Identifying cause-and-effect relationships is essential to understanding life both in the past and today. An action that produces an event is a **cause.** The event or development produced by an action is an **effect.** Why some things happened and others did not can be traced to causes. In other words, what made certain things happen and what kept others from happening?

During the Industrial Revolution, for example, new machines run by steam power made it possible to produce textiles more quickly than individuals could produce cloth by hand. The new machines were too big to be kept in workers' homes, so factories were built to house them. Textile workers moved from home production to factory production.

Look at the cause-and-effect relationship in the following diagram:

Invention of textile-producing machines   Increased production of cloth

(Cause) ——————————→ (Effect)

Sometimes, an effect becomes the cause of another effect. This kind of cause-and-effect relationship is shown below.

New inventions   Increased production   Growth of factories

(Cause) ——→ (Effect/Cause) ——→ (Effect)

Some cause-and-effect relationships may not be clear until many years after the **875** events have occurred. Historians may find after studying an event that several causes led to an effect or that one cause was responsible for multiple effects. Look at this diagram:

Multiple Causes		Multiple Effects	
Cause			→ Effect
Cause	→ Effect	Cause	→ Effect
Cause			→ Effect

Make it a habit to notice the various effects of certain causes, which of these effects became causes, and whether multiple causes or multiple effects were involved.

Distinguishing among facts, opinions, and values. **Facts** are those things that are known to be true or to have happened. Facts are based on information that can be checked for accuracy. **Opinions** express how people feel about something, what their beliefs are, and what attitudes they take. **Values** are opinions that often involve standards of right and wrong. All values are opinions, but not all opinions are values. You may express an opinion on a subject you know little about. You may also express an opinion about what you think will happen in a certain situation. In either example your opinion may prove to be fact. Values are never facts. They may be so much a part of the creed you live by that they seem like facts. If they cannot be proven to be true, however, they are not facts.

It is important that you distinguish among facts, opinions, and values. Even though opinions are not always based on fact and values cannot be proven to be true, you can still learn from them. You can learn how people felt at a certain time, what they considered important, and what they thought about. You cannot always learn what really happened or what the facts were.

Certain words give clues that opinions are being presented: "It is my belief" or "in my view" are clues to what somebody thinks. Not all opinions are easily recognized. You need to read carefully to identify what you read as fact or opinion.

Read the passage from the primary **876** source document for Chapter 26, page 529,

taken from a speech by Giuseppe Garibaldi.

See answers below, left.

What can you identify as fact? What can you identify as opinion? Do you recognize any value statements? When people write facts, they use little emotional language. When people express opinions and values, however, they may become emotional in their choice of words.

Recognizing points of view. A **point of view** reflects an individual's opinion, attitude, belief, or feeling. When you study history, you should try to recognize a point of view for what it is.

Favorable points of view are generally written in positive language, such as "this will benefit all people." Negative points of view take an opposite approach, such as "the election of this candidate will lead to mass unemployment."

Detecting bias. Look carefully for **bias**—personal preference—on the part of the person whose views are being presented. For a viewpoint to be effective in persuading people to act, the language used may appeal to people's emotions. Many famous historical figures had strong opinions that show up in their writings and speeches. Examine these views carefully. Just because a person is famous or highly regarded does not mean you must agree with his or her opinions. A good student will detect bias and opinion when examining historical documents or reading newspapers and magazine articles.

Interpreting political cartoons. An effective way to express opinions and points of view is through political cartoons.

Political cartoons often use symbols to represent certain things. The United States, for example, is often depicted as Uncle Sam while the Soviet Union is frequently shown as a bear. Knowing what the various symbols stand for is critical to understanding a political cartoon. How are the countries Japan, China, and Germany symbolized in the cartoon on page 576?

See answer below.

Cartoons in daily newspapers usually deal with contemporary people or events. The events and people depicted in the car-

Answers: *Facts:* The Sicilians were fighting against the enemies of Italy and for Italy. "Italy and Victor Emmanuel!" was their battle cry.
Opinions might include the statement that it was the duty of all Italians to help in the struggle and that rulers would lose power. *Value statements* include those that praise courage and selfless devotion.

Answer: The political cartoon on page 576 shows Japan as a tiger, China as a dragon, and Germany as an eagle.

toons used in this textbook were contemporary when the cartoons were first drawn.

Making and supporting generalizations. **Generalizations** are brief summaries or conclusions that are based on facts. You may not recognize them often as topic sentences, which express the main idea of a paragraph.

In Chapter 22, page 445, for example, notice the topic sentence, "The French Revolution radically changed French society." The paragraph gives facts that support this generalization. It tells you that the Old Regime was overturned and that absolute monarchy was ended. The Church and the nobility lost their special privileges. The power of the nobles declined as that of the bourgeoisie rose.

Keep in mind that generalizations are used to make broad statements, such as the example above. However, they do not take into account specific examples that fall outside the generalization, such as the fact that many French people still looked up to the clergy and the nobility, or that some French people hoped for a return to power of the monarchy.

Inferring. The skill of inferring asks you to read between the lines. Inferring is pulling more information from your reading than is actually and specifically stated. On page 563, for example, the discussion of the settlement of Australia tells you that the continent was originally used as a prison colony by Great Britain, starting in 1788. Very few free settlers went to Australia to live until later in the 1800's, when they discovered the vast land available and found gold. If you combine your knowledge of Great Britain's colonial activity in other parts of the world with the fact that it sent only prisoners to Australia, you can infer that Britain did not consider Australia worthy of colonization in the late 1700's and early 1800's. When you infer, you make an assumption based on what you have read.

Evaluating historical sources. Sometimes, different historical sources provide different views of the same event. When this happens, you need to evaluate the accuracy and fairness of these differing views.

When you evaluate historical documents, consider the following questions:

1. *Is the information from primary sources or secondary sources?* It is important to know whether the material is a primary source, written at the time an event happened, or a secondary source, written long after the event occurred. Primary sources are records from the past, such as newspapers, diaries, letters, and government documents. Secondary sources are written by people who were not witnesses to or participants in the events they write about. Sometimes, secondary sources may be more useful than primary sources even though they were written by people who had not witnessed the events. Secondary sources may be more accurate, more objective, and more complete. This textbook is a secondary source.

2. *Is the material fact or opinion?* As you know, historical evidence includes statements of both fact and opinion. You read on page 876 that facts can be checked, whereas opinions state feelings, attitudes, or values. When you choose between fact or opinion, remember that even if you agree with a statement, it must be proved, to be a fact.

3. *Is the information accurate?* A good way to check accuracy is to see how the information is presented in other sources. If you find that different sources give different data, you may wonder where your source got the information. You may also begin to question the accuracy. On the other hand, if you find that different sources give the same basic information, it is likely that the material is accurate. Determining a writer's credentials is another way to check accuracy. What makes that person qualified to write about the subject?

3. Drawing Conclusions

In the process of gathering information and judging its importance to your study of history, there are points at which you must stop and draw conclusions. For example, was World War I an inevitable outcome of the opposing forces at work in Europe, or was it a tragic overreaction to a relatively minor conflict? Or was it, perhaps, both? The skills of forming hypotheses, synthesizing, and predicting will help you pull together what you do know in order to draw conclusions about what you do not know.

Forming hypotheses. People often say that history is the study of facts, dates, and events. This is partly true, but there are things about the world that people do not have full knowledge about. Historians, archeologists, scientists, or other scholars try to find answers for these unknowns by piecing together bits of information they may acquire from different kinds of sources. When they think they may know what caused something or what occurred in a given situation, they will form a **hypothesis**—a theory based on a certain amount of evidence. Hypotheses are not proven facts but might be called "educated guesses."

Suppose that a historian has been thinking about the effect of the behavior of the winner of a war on the durability of the peace settlement. After studying many wars and their peace settlements, the historian hypothesizes that a generous policy on the part of the winner is more likely to ensure a lasting peace than a policy based on harsh treatment of the defeated side.

The historian cites as evidence supporting this hypothesis the peace settlement following World War I. Many historians believe that the demands made by the victorious Allies on a defeated Germany by the terms of that settlement played a part in the conditions that led to the outbreak of World War II a quarter-century later. In contrast, after World War II, the western Allies helped the defeated Axis countries rebuild their devastated countries, with very different results from the aftermath of World War I. It is possible that other historians might challenge this hypothesis, of course. A good historian would respond with additional evidence or by acknowledging the arguments against the hypothesis.

Synthesizing. Synthesizing allows you to demonstrate creative thinking when you explain events of history. Synthesis calls for putting material together in some way to form a new whole. When you synthesize, you create a new or different approach to a subject. In order to do this effectively, you need to use what knowledge you already have of a historical event.

Using the Revolutionary War as an example, you could synthesize in a variety of ways. You might write a play about the Boston Tea Party, focusing on the American colonists' decision to stage a major protest against British policy in the American colonies. Or you might prefer to create a diary for one of the soldiers in Washington's army, describing that person's daily life.

Another activity to consider is writing a newspaper article describing a major battle or campaign. In any type of synthesis, you should not alter known events. In writing your article, think of ways of making the information more meaningful or more understandable to your readers. Remember that a newspaper article is written for the readers of the time, not for people who might be reading it 200 years later. To make the article meaningful for your readers, try to put yourself in their place and think of what their feelings, views, or expectations about the war might be.

Predicting events. Another aspect of synthesizing is *predicting.* Predicting can be separated into two categories.

The first of these asks you to speculate about what might have happened if something else had not. Suppose, for example, that the colonial Americans had continued to lose battles and believed that they might lose the war. To whom might they have gone for help? You might want to consider these questions: What other nations were enemies of Britain at that time? What might these nations have gained by helping the colonists? How could they have allied with these na-

878

tions without becoming politically and financially indebted to them?

The other form of prediction asks you to suggest the outcome of a situation that is not yet resolved. Your prediction should be based on solid evidence, not guesswork. Take, for example, the question of a Palestinian state (pages 763–764). Might this be a possibility? What would be necessary on the part of the PLO? Of other Palestinians? Of Israel? Predict the outcome.

Participation Skills

Both study skills and critical thinking skills are necessary for success in the classroom and in the real world. A third group of skills, called **participation skills,** is also crucial for life in our society. The ability to work together for a common end—to share ideas and opinions, to give each participant a respectful hearing, and ultimately to decide upon a plan of action—is an important part of life in a democracy.

As a student of world history you are aware of how often the failure of people to compromise in the interests of all can lead to disastrous results. Learning to cooperate with others and participate in decision making will help you interact with your classmates. It will also benefit you later on when you serve as a leader in your labor union, sit on your city council, plan a community action to preserve the environment, or engage in any of the hundreds of other cooperative endeavors that make up life in our society.

1. Setting Goals

When you work as a group, as when you work independently, you want to work as efficiently as possible. Begin by **setting goals.** What is the group to accomplish—a letter to the editor? a campaign poster? a debate? Suppose, for example, that after class study of the chapter on the Russian Revolution, you are staging a meeting that might have been

held among representatives of Kerensky's Provisional Government, the supporters of a military dictatorship, and the Petrograd Soviet (pages 647–648).

Your goal is to present the debate, but you might also list the intermediate goals that must be met before you can reach your final goal. Your list might look something like this:

Intermediate Goals
1. Assign people to play representatives.
2. Research positions of each representative.
3. Rehearse the debate. (Decide whether the rehearsal will only be spoken or whether it will be acted out.)

Once you have clarified what you have to do, you can work more efficiently.

2. Setting Time Limits

You probably have had the experience of working in a group, and, just as you have completed your initial discussion, your teacher announces, "All right, time for the first debate on solar energy." What happened? You forgot to set a time limit.

Amount of time. In order to use your time wisely, look at the task your group must accomplish and the time you have been allotted. If you have only one class period in which to discuss, research, and create a chart showing the major ideas and accomplishments of the Age of Enlightenment, the time you have for each portion will be very limited.

Number of people. The number of people in your group is also important to the allocation of time. As a group leader or member, do not hesitate to say, "We have only ten minutes for the discussion. Since there are five of us, this means two minutes apiece." Then ask the group to agree to help enforce the time rule.

Personalities. The personalities of the people in any group are another good reason to limit speaking time. Some students

879

speak well in groups, while others are more comfortable expressing their ideas in writing or in some graphic form. Giving each speaker the same amount of discussion time prevents the domination of the group by practiced speakers.

3. Reaching Decisions

When you work in groups, you always reach a point at which you need to make a decision about something. How do you accomplish this? Some groups simply leave it up to the leader. This is fast but not very democratic.

A more democratic method is to call for a vote and then go along with the wishes of the majority. In this case it is important to listen to the members who are a minority to learn why they have voted in the way they have. If the minority feel strongly enough about their point of view, you need to consider more discussion and another vote.

The most democratic way of coming to a group decision is the use of consensus. **Consensus** means, literally, "to feel with." In practice it is the process of reaching a position or point of view that is acceptable to all members of the group. If this sounds familiar to you, it is; a jury in a criminal trial must reach a consensus decision before it can render a verdict. If all the jury members cannot agree, no verdict is rendered, and the judge will call for a retrial.

Consensus in practice can be both frustrating and exciting. And since it is usually time consuming, you should seek a consensus only if the project allows a lot of time.

Imagine, for example, that you are working with a group to support a particular candidate in a school election. You need to decide how to publicize your candidate. Some group members want to display flashy posters at popular school meeting places. Others want to write humorous, issue-based ads for use on the school radio station. Still others like the idea of sticking leaflets on school lockers with a discussion of the issues.

After a brief discussion you call for a straw vote to get a sense of the group; a majority favors the posters. But you decide to work for a consensus. "Let's take some time to come up with a campaign that satisfies everyone. First of all, why didn't the minority vote for the posters?"

One voter says she voted against the posters because they remind her of the last mayoral election, in which one candidate used flashy posters but refused to debate the issues. Another voter in the minority says he wants to use radio spots because they don't cost money; the school station has to provide a certain amount of free time to each of the candidates.

The discussion continues. One voter says he isn't necessarily against issues and content but he's an environmentalist, and he doesn't want to waste paper to print leaflets that many students will just throw away. The hallways will be full of litter too. "Why," he says, "couldn't we put the serious content on the posters?" Next, the student who voted against the posters says she didn't know the radio was free and, of course, they should use it. Furthermore, she's all for the posters as long as they deal with the issues.

At the end of the discussion, the group agrees to two approaches: radio spots and graphically interesting posters that deal with the issues. The decision has been reached in forty-five minutes, compared with the ten minutes taken before the initial vote; but look at what has been accomplished. Each member has expressed his or her values in the context of the discussion, group members have learned more than they knew before the initial vote, and everyone in the group is committed to the decision that has been made.

The skills described in these pages will not only benefit you in history courses but will also be helpful in other subjects you are taking now or will be taking. Many of these skills are also known as "life skills" because you will use them throughout your life.

Glossary

In this glossary you will find definitions for vocabulary words and key terms used in *History of the World*. These words and terms are printed in red the first time they are used in the book. The page number following each definition tells you on what page the word is first used in the text. Remember that many words have more than one meaning. The definitions given here are the ones that will be most helpful to you in reading this book.

Words that are difficult to pronounce are respelled where they first appear in the text. These words also have a special spelling in this glossary. You can find out the correct pronunciation of these words by using the abbreviated pronunciation key at the bottom of left-hand pages. The full pronunciation key below shows how to pronounce each letter. The key also shows the difference between primary and secondary stress marks.

Pronunciation Key

ă	pat	hw	which	ô	alter, caught, for, paw	ŭ	cut, rough
ā	aid, they, pay	ĭ	pit			û	circle, firm, heard, term, turn, word
â	air, care, wear	ī	by, guy, pie	oi	boy, noise, oil		
ä	father	î	dear, deer, fierce, mere	o͝o	took	v	cave, valve, vine
b	bib			o͞o	boot, fruit	w	with
ch	church	j	judge	ou	cow, out	y	yes
d	deed	k	cat, kick, pique	p	pop	yo͞o	abuse, use
ĕ	pet, pleasure	l	lid, needle	r	roar	z	rose, size, xylophone, zebra
ē	be, bee, easy	m	am, man, mum	s	miss, sauce, see		
f	fast, fife, off, phase, rough	n	no, sudden	sh	dish, ship	zh	garage, pleasure, vision
		ng	thing	t	tight		
g	gag	ŏ	pot	th	path, thin	ə	about, silent, pencil, lemon
h	hat	ō	go, row, toe	*th*	bathe, this	ər	butter

Primary stress ′ Secondary stress ′

A

abdicate: to give up a powerful position, especially a throne (page 449).

abolitionist: a reformer who opposed slavery (page 380).

absolute monarchy: a government in which a ruler has complete power (page 240).

abstract expressionism: an American artistic style characterized by the use of bold colors and large canvases (page 829).

acropolis (ə-krŏp′ə-lĭs): the highest ground in a Greek city, on which stood a fortress (page 76).

Act of Supremacy: an act of Parliament that declared the English monarch head of the Church of England (page 340).

adobe (ə-dō′bē): sun-baked clay bricks used by some North American Indians in the Southwest to build houses (page 316).

African National Congress: a nationalist group formed in 1912 to seek greater political rights for blacks in South Africa (page 777).

Age of Disunity: the period (A.D. 220–589) following the fall of the Han dynasty when China was beset by warfare and political unrest (page 145).

Age of Exploration: the period (about 1450–1700) when European sea captains made voyages of exploration and set the stage for an expansion of European power around the world (page 347).

agora (ăg′ər-ə): the marketplace of an ancient Greek city (page 76).

ahimsa (ə-hĭm′-sä′): a Buddhist doctrine of nonviolence that stresses the sacredness of human and animal life (page 137).

alchemy (ăl′kə-mē): an ancient field of study based on searching for ways to turn common metals into gold (page 257).

881

Allies: the countries that allied against the Central Powers during World War I, including France, Britain, and Russia (page 628); the countries that allied against the Axis Powers during World War II (page 688).

American Revolution: the war (1776–1783) in which Britain's American colonies won their independence (page 426).

annex: to add (territory) to an existing country (page 465).

anti-Semitism: prejudice against Jews (page 544).

apartheid (ə-pärt′hāt′): South Africa's government policy of racial segregation and white supremacy (page 781).

appeasement: the policy of giving in to the demands of an aggressor in order to maintain peace (page 686).

apprentice: a person bound by agreement to a master artisan for a specific amount of time in return for instruction in a craft (page 232).

aqueduct (ăk′wĭ-dŭkt′): a bridgelike structure supporting a channel through which water is transported over a distance (page 114).

archipelago (är′kə-pĕl′ə-gō′): a large group of islands (page 286).

archon (är′kŏn′): one of a group of officials, chosen from the nobility, who ruled Athens before Solon's political reforms (page 77).

armaments: weapons and military supplies (page 626).

armistice: a halt to fighting; a truce (page 634).

artifact: an object, made by a human being in the distant past, that has survived to the present (page 13).

artisan: a worker with skill in a specific craft (page 19).

assimilate: to absorb (page 602).

astrology: the study of stars and planets and their movements, with the aim of predicting events on earth (page 257).

atheist: one who denies the existence of God (page 420).

authoritarianism: a political system that stresses obedience to authority but exercises less control over the lives of its citizens than a totalitarian system does (page 668).

autocrat: a ruler with unlimited power (page 403).

Axis Powers: the alliance of Germany, Italy, and Japan in World War II (page 686).

B

Babylonian Captivity: a term used by Romans to describe the period (1309–1377) when all the Popes were French, ruled from Avignon, and supported policies favorable to France (page 265).

balance of power: the distribution of power among nations so that no one country dominates (page 390).

balance of trade: the difference in value between imports and exports (page 367).

Balfour Declaration: a statement issued in 1917 by the British government supporting the establishment of a Jewish state in Palestine (page 680).

baron: a feudal lord (page 236).

baroque: an ornate style of art and architecture popular in Europe between the 1500's and early 1700's, characterized by richness in color and detail; also, the style of music from the same period (page 423).

barter: trade in which people exchange goods without using money (page 19).

Battle of Hastings: the battle in 1066 in which the Normans, led by William the Conqueror, defeated the Saxon king and took control of England (page 236).

Battle of Midway: a World War II naval battle that allowed the United States to reestablish its naval superiority in the Pacific (page 700).

Battle of Waterloo: the 1815 battle in which Napoleon was decisively defeated by the European allies (page 452).

bazaar: marketplace (page 30).

Bedouin (bĕd′ōō-ĭn): a nomadic Arab (page 197).

Behistun Rock (bā′hĭs-tōōn′): a cliff in what is now western Iran, which provided the key to cuneiform (page 33).

Berlin Conference: an international conference held in Berlin (1884–1885) to discuss colonial claims in Africa (page 596).

Bessemer process: a quick, cheap method of making steel from iron (page 493).

Bill of Rights: the first ten amendments to the U.S. Constitution (page 430).

Black Death: also known as the bubonic plague; a contagious, usually fatal disease, transmitted by fleas from infected rats, that reached epidemic proportions in fourteenth-century Europe (page 262).

blitzkrieg: a German word meaning "lightning war"; a sudden, rapid military attack (page 688).

bloc: a group of nations, parties, or people united for a common purpose (page 713).

boat people: the name given to Southeast Asian refugees of the 1970's and 1980's who sailed out into the ocean, hoping to be rescued and given new homes (page 754).

Bolshevik: a follower of the Marxist movement led by Lenin (page 646).

Bolshevik Revolution: also called the Russian Revolution; the 1917 revolution that ended the leadership of the Provisional Government and put the Bolsheviks in power (page 649).

bourgeoisie (boor′zhwä-zē′): the middle class, especially in France (page 436).

Boxer Rebellion: a series of attacks led by a Chinese secret society, the "Boxers," against foreign missionaries, diplomats, and Chinese Christians (page 579).

boyar: a Russian noble (page 191).

882

Bronze Age: the period when bronze replaced copper and stone as the main material used in tools and weapons (page 21).

Buddhism: (bōō′ dĭz′əm): a religion founded in India and based on Siddhartha Gautama's teachings (page 133).

bullion: gold or silver measured in large quantities (page 349).

bureaucrat (byōōr′ə-krăt′): a trained public official who is appointed rather than elected (page 63).

Bushido (bōōsh′ĭ-dō′): the code of behavior followed by Japanese samurai (warriors), characterized by discipline and duty (page 288).

C

caliph (kā′lĭf): a Muslim political and religious leader (page 199).

calligraphy: the art of fine handwriting (page 283).

Calvinism: the Protestant belief developed in the sixteenth century by John Calvin, based on the concept of predestination (page 339).

Camp David Accords: an agreement reached in 1978 between Israel and Egypt that included Israel's agreement to give up the Sinai Peninsula in return for peace and diplomatic recognition (page 763).

capital: wealth or property that is used to produce more wealth (page 371).

capitalism: an economic system based on the private ownership and use of capital; also called the free-enterprise system (page 371).

carbon-14 dating: analysis of the amount of carbon-14 within a once-living material, used to determine approximate age (page 14).

cardinal: a high-ranking official of the Roman Catholic Church (page 243).

caste: in Hindu society, a fixed social grouping based on class, occupation, and tradition (page 56).

caudillo (kou-dē′yō): in Latin America, a dictator who came to power by gaining the support of the army and wealthy landowners (page 463).

Central Powers: a group of nations, led by Germany and Italy, that fought the Allies in World War I (page 628).

charter: a document granting a group of people certain rights and privileges (page 233).

Charter Oath: a five-point policy issued by Japan's Meiji emperor, which described Japan's plan for modernization (page 583).

Chartist movement: an English reform movement in the 1800's, led by workers who demanded increased political power (page 503).

checks and balances: a system in which each branch of government exercises some control over the others, thereby preventing any one branch from gaining too much power (page 430).

chinampa: an Aztec garden built of layers of dirt, vegetation, and mud in shallow waters to increase farmland (page 312).

Chinese Revolution: the struggle between Nationalist and Communist forces in China that began in the 1920's and ended in 1949 when the Communists, led by Mao Zedong, took over mainland China (page 735).

chivalry (shĭv′əl-rē): a code of behavior for feudal knights and nobles (page 220).

Christianity: a religion based on Jesus' teachings, developed in the eastern Mediterranean during the first century A.D. (page 125).

circumnavigate: to sail completely around something (page 354).

Circus Maximus: a Roman outdoor arena in which public games, such as chariot races, were held (page 110).

city-state: an independent, self-governing community consisting of a city and the surrounding territory (page 29).

civil disobedience: the use of nonviolent resistance to defy laws thought to be unjust (page 739).

civilization: an advanced level of culture, usually characterized by organized government and religion, division of labor, a class structure, and a system of writing (page 21).

civil rights: the right to be treated equally under the law and have equality of opportunity (page 805).

Civil War: the war (1861–1865) between the North and South in the United States over issues of slavery, commerce, and states' rights (page 560).

clan: a group of families or a small tribal community (page 286).

classical: a style of art and thought emphasizing order and simplicity (page 84).

Classical: a simple and elegant style of art, architecture, and music popular in Europe during the late 1700's, based on ideas from classical Greece and Rome (page 423).

classics: great literary works (page 283).

clergy (klûr′jē): the ordained officials of an organized religion (page 213).

coalition: a temporary alliance of different factions, parties, or nations (page 673).

Code of Hammurabi: the laws of Hammurabi (ruler of Babylon, 1792–1750 B.C.), which were carved on a block of stone and displayed as a lasting record (page 32).

cold war: the term applied to the period of extreme tension

ă pat ā pay â care ä father ě pet ē be ĭ pit ī pie î fierce ŏ pot ō go ô paw, for oi oil
ōō book ōō boot ou out ŭ cut û fur th thin *th* the hw which zh vision ə about

and hostility between the United States and the Soviet Union in the years following World War II (page 711).

collective farm: a large farm where the livestock, equipment, and machinery of many small farms are brought together under government control (page 657).

colony: a settlement of people in a territory outside their homeland that is bound to the parent country by government, trade, or culture (page 73).

Colosseum: a Roman outdoor arena in which public games were held (page 110).

Commercial Revolution: the period of Western history (1450–1700) when new resources and new business practices resulted in great changes (page 367).

common law: a system of law developed in England in medieval times, based on earlier royal court decisions and established customs (page 237).

Common Market: also called the European Economic Community; an organization formed in 1957 to stimulate economic growth by eliminating tariffs and improving transportation within the member nations (page 719).

Commonwealth: the republican government established in England by Cromwell after the English Civil War (page 399).

Commonwealth of Nations: an organization formed in 1931 of independent nations within the British empire united by allegiance to the British crown (page 673).

commune (kŏm′yōōn): an agricultural unit in China made up of large, state-owned farms (page 736).

communism: an economic and social system in which all property and means of production are owned by the people and all goods and services are shared (page 500).

Communist Manifesto: a work published in 1848 by Karl Marx and Friedrich Engels that describes the basic principles of communism and calls for a working-class revolution (page 501).

concentration camp: a camp where political prisoners are held (page 695).

Concordat of Worms (vôrms): an agreement reached in 1122 between the Church and the Holy Roman Emperor that recognized the Church as the supreme authority in spiritual matters and ruled that monarchs could have no authority over the Church (page 244).

confederacy: a loose alliance of several states, communities, or cultural groups (page 319).

Congress of Vienna: a meeting of European leaders that returned conservatives to power throughout Europe after the fall of Napoleon (page 471).

conquistador (kŏn-kē′stə-dôr′): a Spanish conqueror of American Indian civilizations (page 355).

conservatism: a political philosophy that emphasizes preserving of traditions and established institutions (page 471).

Constitution: the United States' plan of government, which calls for a federal system with separation of powers (page 430).

containment: the policy of limiting communism to those countries where it already exists (page 713).

Continental System: Napoleon's plan to ruin Britain's trade by forbidding France's allies and countries under French rule to import British products (page 449).

Counter-Reformation: also called the Catholic Reformation; the reform movement that began within the Roman Catholic Church in the 1500's as a reaction to the Reformation (page 341).

counterrevolution: a movement that opposes a revolution and attempts to restore the government previously in power (page 441).

coup d'etat (kōō′dä-tä′): the sudden overthrow of a government (page 446).

Creole (krē′ōl′): a person of Spanish or Portuguese descent born in the Americas (page 457).

crucify: to put to death by nailing to a cross (page 126).

Crusades: in the Middle Ages, a series of campaigns led by European Christians seeking to regain the Holy Land from the Muslim Turks (page 187).

Cuban Missile Crisis: the 1962 confrontation between the United States and the Soviet Union, when President Kennedy secured the removal of Soviet nuclear missiles from Cuba (page 718).

cubism: a style of painting characterized by depictions of natural shapes as geometric forms (page 540).

Cultural Revolution: Mao Zedong's campaign (1966–1968) to purge China of traditional cultures, ideas, and institutions (page 737).

culture: the unique way of life of a people (page 14).

cuneiform (kyōō′nē-ə-fôrm′): a system of writing used by Sumerians and later peoples in Mesopotamia, with wedge-shaped characters marked on clay tablets (page 30).

curriculum: a course of study (page 255).

czar: the title given to Russian emperors from the late 1400's to 1918 (page 193).

D

daimyo (dī′mē-ō′): a local lord in traditional Japanese society (page 289).

D-Day: June 6, 1944, the day Allied forces landed in Normandy and invaded Nazi-occupied France (page 701).

Declaration of Independence: the document signed on July 4, 1776, that broke ties between Britain and its American colonies (page 427).

Declaration of the Rights of Man: a document issued by the National Assembly during the French Revolution (page 439).

default: to fail to pay money owed (page 797).

deist: a person who believes in God but rejects organized religion (page 420).

deity: a god or goddess (page 273).

demilitarize: to free from military control by removing all military personnel and fortifications (page 636).

democracy: a form of government based on rule by the people (page 77).

depose: to remove a person from a throne or other high office (page 243).

détente (dā-tänt′): a relaxing of tensions between nations (page 725).

deterrence: a policy of discouraging an attack by making one's enemy fear an overpowering counterattack (page 716).

dharma (där′mə): the rights and duties of members of various classes in Indian society (page 56).

dhow (dou): an Arabian sailing ship (page 306).

dictator: a ruler with absolute power (page 103).

diplomacy: the art of managing relations between governments, especially in respect to making agreements, treaties, and alliances (page 187).

direct democracy: a form of government in which all citizens can participate first-hand (page 81).

direct rule: a type of colonial government in which foreigners control all levels of government (page 602).

disciple: a devoted follower (page 126).

dissident: one who openly disagrees with his or her nation's policies (page 725).

divest: to sell off stock, especially the stock of companies that do business in South Africa (page 784).

diviner: an African prophet believed to read signs from the spirit world and predict the future (page 304).

divine right: the theory that monarchs receive their power from God and consequently should not be questioned or disobeyed (page 392).

division of labor: dividing work within a community so people can specialize in particular skills (page 18).

domesticate: to tame wild animals, making them useful to human beings (page 18).

domestic system: production in which raw materials are distributed to employees who work in their homes to produce goods (page 492).

domino theory: the belief that if one nation comes under Communist control, its neighboring nations will also come under Communist control (page 751).

Dreyfus Affair (drā′fəs): the case in which Alfred Dreyfus, a Jewish captain in the French army, was wrongly accused (1894) and convicted of selling military secrets to Germany (page 545).

duchy (dŭch′ē): land ruled by a duke or duchess (page 241).

dynastic cycle: the rise and fall of dynasties in a regular pattern (page 142).

dynasty: a series of rulers from the same family (page 36).

E

Eastern Orthodox Church: the Eastern branch of the Christian Church, headed by the patriarch in Constantinople (page 184).

Easter Rebellion: an unsuccessful rebellion of Irish nationalists against the British during Easter week in 1916 (page 673).

economic nationalism: a nation's effort to achieve economic independence through local control of markets and production and industrialization (page 802).

Edict of Nantes (nänt): a 1598 document issued by Henry IV that gave French Protestants religious freedom (page 390).

embargo: a suspension of foreign trade, often limited to certain products and directed at specific nations (page 698).

émigré (ĕm′ĭ-grā′): a noble who fled France during the French Revolution (page 438).

empire: a state in which one ruler controls several kingdoms or territories (page 31).

enclosure movement: a widespread trend in England in the 1700's, involving (1) the buying up of small landholdings by large landowners and (2) the fencing in of lands previously open for public use (page 492).

encomienda: one of the grants given by the Spanish government to settlers in the Americas entitling them to demand labor and taxes from the Indians living there (page 356).

English Bill of Rights: the document signed by Mary and William III in 1689 that gave Parliament some power over the monarch and strengthened the rights of individuals (page 400).

English Civil War: the struggle (1642–1651) between the supporters of Charles I and the supporters of Parliament over proposed reforms of the military and the Church of England (page 399).

enlightened despot: a European ruler who introduced reforms reflecting the spirit of the Enlightenment (page 421).

Enlightenment: also called the Age of Reason; the period of Western history (in the 1700's) when thinkers called

GLOSSARY

for the use of reason in analyzing and improving society (page 419).

entrepreneur (än′trə-prə-**nûr**′): one who starts and operates a business (page 491).

epic: a long poem that describes the adventures of a hero or heroes (page 59).

Epicureanism (ĕp′ĭ-**kyōōr**′ē-ə-nĭz′əm): a Hellenistic school of philosophy that developed in Athens about 200 B.C. and stressed the importance of simple pleasures (page 92).

escalate: to grow or increase rapidly (page 627).

evolution: the idea that living things change over time and that one species might evolve into another (page 537).

excavate: to dig up an archeological site (page 19).

excommunicate: to expel a person from the Roman Catholic Church (page 243).

existentialism: a philosophy that stresses each person's responsibility for his or her choices in life (page 831).

Exodus: the flight of the Hebrews, led by Moses, from Egypt to Canaan in about 1290 B.C. (page 44).

extended family: a household that includes parents, children, and other close relatives, such as grandparents (page 63).

F

Factory Act: an 1833 act of Parliament that restricted employment of minors in Britain (page 505).

factory system: a method of production in which workers are brought together to produce goods with machines in factories (page 493).

fallow: referring to farmland that is unplanted (page 223).

fascism: an ideology that stresses nationalism and dictatorship and places the strength of the state above the welfare of individual citizens (page 663).

886 **federal system:** government

where power is shared by the central government and the states (p. 430).

feudalism: a political system in which a king granted the use of land to nobles in return for loyalty, military assistance, and services (page 61).

fief (fēf): land granted by a feudal lord to another noble (page 218).

filial piety: respect for and obedience to one's parents (page 64).

First Estate: under the Old Regime in France, the social class made up of the clergy (page 435).

First Triumvirate (trī-**ŭm**′vər-ĭt): the three Roman generals (Gnaeus Pompey, Marcus Licinius Crassus, and Julius Caesar) who ruled the Roman Republic from 60 to 46 B.C. (page 103).

Five Pillars of Islam: the five religious duties of Muslims, including prayer, fasting, and pilgrimages to the holy city of Mecca (page 198).

Five-Year Plan: one of a series of ambitious plans created by Stalin to direct the industrialization and economic reorganization of the Soviet Union (page 655).

fossil: traces of ancient animal and plant life preserved in rock (page 14).

fossil fuel: a fuel, such as coal, oil, or natural gas, derived from living matter of a previous geologic time (page 825).

Four Noble Truths: the major principles of Buddhism, which recognize the inevitability of suffering and encourage individuals to achieve a state of "not wanting" and practice moderation in order to reach enlightenment (page 133).

Fourteen Points: President Wilson's terms for peace after World War I (page 635).

Franco-Prussian War: a six-week war in which the French were defeated by Prussia in 1870 (page 519).

Frankfurt Assembly: a German

national assembly of elected delegates, which met (1848–1849) to draw up plans for a united Germany (page 483).

free-enterprise system: an economic system based on private ownership of capital and the idea that people are free to use their capital as they wish (page 371).

French and Indian War: the war between France and England, which began in 1754, over territory around the Great Lakes and the St. Lawrence River (page 363).

French Revolution: the rebellion of the French people, beginning in 1789, against the monarchy and the class structure of the Old Regime (page 436).

fresco: a watercolor painting on fresh plaster (page 335).

friar: a monk who lives among the people, preaching and doing good works (page 245).

fundamentalism: a movement calling for strict observance of religious law (page 768).

G

genetic engineering: a process that changes the arrangement of atoms in genes in such a way that new traits are developed (page 819).

genetics: the study of inherited traits (page 539).

genocide: the systematic destruction of an entire people (page 556).

geocentric theory: the belief that the earth is at the center of the universe (page 413).

ghana (gä′nə): a ruler of the Soninke empire in Africa (page 297).

ghetto: in Europe, a section of a town or city where Jews were required to live; today, a city slum (page 544).

Girondist (jə-**rŏn**′dĭst): one of the moderate members of the French National Convention (page 443).

glacier: a huge, slow-moving sheet of ice (page 16).

gladiator: a person, usually a

slave or condemned criminal, who fought other gladiators or wild animals as public entertainment in ancient Rome (page 110).

glasnost (**glăs′**nŏst): beginning under Gorbachev in the 1980's, a government policy of "openness" about problems within the Soviet Union (page 726).

Glorious Revolution: the change of monarchs in England in 1689, in which James II was removed from power and Parliament offered the throne to Mary and William of Orange (page 400).

Golden Horde: the Mongol army of nomadic tribesmen, led by Genghis Khan, that invaded Asia in the 1200's (page 191).

gold standard: the policy of backing a nation's currency with its full value in gold (page 555).

Gospels: the first four books of the New Testament in the Christian Bible, which describe Jesus' life and teachings (page 126).

Gothic: a style of architecture developed during the twelfth century, which featured pointed arches, flying buttresses, and large, stained-glass windows (page 261).

grand jury: a group of citizens authorized to determine whether evidence justifies charging a person with a crime (page 237).

Great Depression: the severe economic slump that followed the collapse of the stock market in 1929 (page 672).

Great Leap Forward: Mao Zedong's ambitious, but unsuccessful Five-Year Plan for China, launched in 1958 with the aim of increasing industrial and agricultural production and transferring some of China's wealth to the countryside (page 736).

Great Purge: the period of Soviet history (1935–1939) when Stalin had thousands of Party members and other citizens arrested and, in many cases, executed as enemies of the state (page 658).

Great Schism (**sĭz′**əm): the period (1378–1417) when two Popes held office at the same time (page 265).

Great Trek: the migration of Dutch settlers out of Cape Colony in southern Africa to escape British rule (page 594).

Great Wall: a 1,500-mile stone wall stretching across northern China (page 141).

Greco-Roman culture: the eastern Mediterranean culture that developed from the blending of Greek and Roman cultures (second century B.C.) (page 112).

greenhouse effect: the gradual warming of the earth's temperature caused by the buildup of carbon dioxide in the atmosphere (page 826).

gross national product (GNP): the total value of all goods and services produced in a nation over a specific period of time (page 746).

guerrilla warfare: a type of warfare in which small groups of fighters make surprise attacks (page 449).

guild: a medieval organization formed by merchants of the same trade or artisans of the same craft, to protect its members and set business policies (page 232).

gulag (**gōō′**lăg′): a forced-labor camp in the Soviet Union (page 657).

Gulf of Tonkin Resolution: the resolution passed in 1964 that gave the President the power to send United States forces to Vietnam (page 752).

Gulf War: the six-week war (January–February 1991), in which a U.S.-led multinational coalition forced Iraq to withdraw from Kuwait and give up its claim to that land.

H

habeas corpus (**hā′**bē-əs **kôr′**pəs): the principle stating that no person can be kept in prison unless charged with a specific crime (page 398).

Hagia Sophia (**hä′**jă sō-**fē′**ə): a cathedral built in Constantinople (532–537), featuring a dome over a rectangular building (page 186).

Hanseatic League (**hăn′**sē-ăt′ ĭk): alliance of German cities to promote and protect trade in the 1300's (page 250).

Hegira (hĭ-**jī′**rə): Mohammed's flight from Mecca to Medina in A.D. 622 (page 199).

heliocentric theory: the belief that the sun is at the center of the universe (page 413).

Hellenic Age: the period (about 800–323 B.C.) when the civilization of the ancient Greeks took shape and reached its height (page 73).

Hellenistic Age: the period (about 323–100 B.C.) following Alexander's conquests when Greek culture spread throughout the lands he had conquered (page 91).

helot (**hĕl′**ət): a farm laborer in ancient Sparta (page 76).

heresy (**hĕr′**ĭ-sē): the holding of beliefs considered wrong by the Church (page 244).

hieroglyphics (hī-ər-ə-**glĭf′**ĭks): ancient Egyptian writing (page 40).

Hinduism: the faith of most of India's people, characterized by the goal of returning to Brahman through reincarnation (page 57).

history: the study of the human past; a record of events and developments from the past (page GR1).

Holocaust: the Nazi plan for the systematic murder of European Jews (page 695).

home rule: the policy of giving one part of an empire local control over its internal matters (page 565).

ă pat ā pay â care ä father ĕ pet ē be ĭ pit ī pie î fierce ŏ pot ō go ô paw, for oi oil
ōō book ōō boot ou out ŭ cut û fur th thin *th* the hw which zh vision ə about

humanities: subjects, such as language, literature, history, and philosophy, that are concerned with humankind and culture (page 327).

human rights: basic rights and freedoms to which all people are entitled (page 725).

Hundred Years' War: a series of conflicts (1337–1453) between France and England over French lands held by the English king (page 263).

I

Ice Age: one of the extremely long periods during which temperatures in the Northern Hemisphere were cold enough to produce huge sheets of ice over much of the land (page 16).

icon (ī′kŏn): a religious image (page 186).

ideology: a set of beliefs reflecting the social needs and aspirations of an individual, group, class, or culture (page 653).

Iliad: one of the two epics written by Homer, which tells of the tragic quarrel between two heroes of the Trojan War (page 75).

illuminated manuscript: a book in which medieval monks copied, by hand, ancient manuscripts (page 214).

imperial: relating to an empire or emperor (page 119).

imperialism: the policy of empire-building, or extending a nation's control over other lands for economic and political advantages (page 557).

impressionism: a late nineteenth-century style of painting characterized by the attempt to show how movement, color, and light appear to the eye at a glance (page 540).

indentured servant: an individual who agreed to work a certain number of years in exchange for passage to a new land (page 374).

indirect rule: a type of colonial government that uses local officials to handle some tasks but reserves the highest power for the governing nation (page 602).

indulgence: a pardon for sinning, given by the Catholic Church, at first as a reward for some special service and later in return for a contribution of money (page 337).

Industrial Revolution: a period of change in the methods of producing goods and organizing labor, which began in Britain during the 1700's and resulted from the invention of new machines and the discovery of new forms of power (page 491).

inflation: a sharp, steady rise in prices caused by a scarcity of goods and excess demand (page 369).

Inquisition: in Europe, a thirteenth-century Church court that sought out and tried persons suspected of heresy (page 245).

interdependent: mutually dependent (page 824).

International Style: a style of architecture begun in Germany in the 1920's, characterized by the use of geometric shapes and industrial materials (page 831).

Invincible Armada: the Spanish fleet of ships sent by Philip II in 1588 to invade England (page 387).

Iran-Iraq War: a war fought between Iran and Iraq over disputed territories and religious differences (1980–1988) (page 768).

Iron Age: the period following the Bronze Age when knowledge of ironworking spread (page 43).

Islam (ĭs′läm): the monotheistic religion founded in Arabia by Mohammed during the seventh century A.D. (page 198).

isolationism: policy of avoiding involvement in the affairs of other nations (page 638).

isthmus: a narrow strip of land connecting two larger land masses (page 156).

J

Jacobin: a member of the most radical group in the French National Convention (page 442).

Janissary Corps: an elite infantry unit of the Ottoman army, considered the fiercest and most loyal of the sultan's soldiers (page 277).

jihad (jĭ-häd′): an Arab term for "holy war," applied to the effort to convert or conquer nonbelievers (page 199).

joint-stock company: a company financed by the selling of shares of stock that give the purchasers part ownership (page 368).

journeyman: a day laborer who has completed an apprenticeship and works for a master craftsman (page 232).

Judaism: the Hebrew religion (page 45).

Justinian's Code: a collection of the ancient laws of Rome (page 182).

K

kaiser (kī′zər): the title of the German emperor in the late 1800's and early 1900's (page 520).

karma: in Hinduism, the accumulated good and bad acts of all of one's previous lives (page 57).

kiva (kē′və): the central room in a pueblo, used for community ceremonies and religious rituals (page 317).

knight: a mounted warrior in medieval Europe (page 220).

Koran: the holy book of Islam (page 198).

Korean War: the conflict (1950–1953) between Communist North Korea and non-Communist South Korea, in which a UN army, largely made up of American forces, fought on the side of South Korea (page 748).

Kremlin: a palace-fortress in Moscow where Bolsheviks set up the government after their takeover (page 651).

L

labor union: an organization designed to represent workers' interests (page 505).

laissez faire (lĕs'ā fâr'): a doctrine based on the belief that government should not interfere with business (page 498).

Law of Nations: a branch of Roman law that was applied to citizens in all parts of the Empire regardless of nationality (page 115).

law of succession: a law stating how a government will replace leaders who die or resign before their terms end (page 106).

law of supply and demand: an economic principle based on the premise that increased demand for a product will drive the price up, while a surplus will force the price down (page 371).

layman: a person who is not a member of the clergy (page 245).

League of Nations: an organization of nations established in 1920 to promote world peace (page 636).

Legalism: a Chinese philosophy of the third century B.C. that assumed that people were evil and selfish and lived well only under strict rules (page 141).

legislature: a governmental body that has the responsibility for making laws (page 360).

legitimacy: the idea that European rulers forced out of power during the French Revolution and Napoleonic Wars were their nations' rightful rulers (page 473).

liberalism: a political philosophy that emphasizes progress and reform and stresses the importance of individual freedom, equality under the law, and freedom of thought and religion (page 471).

limited monarchy: a government in which the ruler's powers are limited by law or by a governing body, such as a parliament (page 239).

Line of Demarcation: a line drawn through the North and South poles, established by the Pope in 1493 to divide unsettled lands between Spain and Portugal (page 351).

literacy: the ability to read and write (page 304).

Long March: Mao Zedong's journey across China with 100,000 supporters to escape Nationalist forces (page 677).

M

Maginot Line (măzh'ĭ-nō'): a string of heavily defended forts built by France along its border with Germany in the 1930's (page 689).

Magna Carta (măg'nə kär'tə): meaning "Great Charter," a document agreed to by King John of England in 1215 that recognized the barons' rights and privileges (page 238).

mandate: a region administered by another country until it is judged ready for independence (page 636).

Mandate of Heaven: the early Chinese belief that rulers needed the gods' approval to stay in power (page 61).

Manifest Destiny: the nineteenth-century idea that the United States had the right and duty to expand westward to the Pacific Ocean (page 558).

manor: the self-sufficient estate of a medieval lord (page 222).

manorial system: the economic system in Europe during the Middle Ages, based on large estates owned by lords and worked by serfs (page 222).

March Revolution: a 1917 uprising of workers and soldiers in Petrograd that ended czarist rule in Russia (page 647).

market economy: an economic system based on the buying and selling of goods and services with little or no government intervention (page 371).

maroon: a member of a community of runaway slaves in the Americas (page 375).

Marshall Plan: the European Recovery Program through which the United States provided aid to Western Europe after World War II (page 714).

martial law: strict controls maintained over a nation by military forces (page 730).

martyr: a person who endures persecution or even death rather than give up his or her beliefs (page 128).

Mau Mau: a guerrilla movement that opposed British colonial rule in Kenya in the 1950's (page 779).

May Fourth Movement: in China, a 1919 uprising of university students and teachers who demanded an end to foreign interference and called for democracy (page 676).

medieval: relating to the Middle Ages (page 212).

mercantilism (mûr'kən-tē-lĭz'əm): an economic policy that stressed the accumulation of gold and silver, the founding of colonies and regulation of their trade, and profiting from foreign trade (page 367).

Messiah (mə-sī'ə): a savior, promised by Jewish prophets, who Jews believed would restore their kingdom's ancient greatness and bring an age of prosperity and peace (page 125).

mestizo: a person of mixed American Indian and European ancestry (page 375).

Mexican-American War: the war fought between Mexico and the United States in 1846–1848 (page 465).

GLOSSARY

ă pat ā pay â care ä father ĕ pet ē be ĭ pit ī pie î fierce ŏ pot ō go ô paw, for oi oil
ōō book ōō boot ou out ŭ cut û fur th thin *th* the hw which zh vision ə about

Middle Ages: the period from about A.D. 500 to 1500 that began with the decline of the Roman Empire (page 211).

middle class: in the Middle Ages, an urban social class that included merchants, artisans, their families, and others who did not have feudal obligations; later, those who were socially and economically between the working class and the nobility or very wealthy upper class (page 234).

Middle Passage: the route taken by slave ships that carried enslaved Africans to the Americas; part of the triangular trade route linking Europe, Africa, and the Americas (page 378).

migrate: to move from one region or country and settle in another (page 16).

militarism: the policy of glorifying war and readying armed forces for conflict (page 626).

millet: in the Ottoman empire, a separate community of Jews or Christians with its own religious leader (page 277).

minaret: the slender tower of a mosque from which Muslims are called to prayer (page 206).

mission station: one of the self-sufficient religious communities set up by American and European Christians in West Africa (page 592).

mobilize: to organize and prepare for war (page 627).

moneychanger: during the Middle Ages, a person who exchanged coins from one region for those of another and also loaned money for interest (page 231).

money economy: an economic system based on the use of money, first introduced by the Lydians (page 46).

monopoly: the control of all (or nearly all) trade and production of a certain good or service (page 348).

monotheism: the belief in one God (page 45).

Monroe Doctrine: the American foreign policy statement that declared the Americas closed to future colonization by European nations (page 464).

monsoon: seasonal winds that cross southern Asia, producing wet and dry seasons (page 53).

morality play: a type of medieval religious drama in which characters representing human virtues and vices acted out conflicts between good and evil (page 258).

mosque (mŏsk): a Muslim place of worship (page 206).

mulatto: a person of mixed European and African ancestry (page 375).

multinational corporation: a large company that owns businesses in many different countries (page 825).

Muslim: a follower of Islam (page 198).

mystic: one who believes he or she can contact God through meditation (page 388).

N

Napoleonic Code: the code of laws commissioned by Napoleon in 1800, which stated that all men should be treated as equals (page 447).

Napoleonic Wars: a series of wars between France and most of the major European powers that resulted from Napoleon's desire to rule Europe (page 448).

nationalism: a feeling of devotion to and pride in one's country (page 445).

Nationalist Revolution: the overthrow of the Qing dynasty in 1912 by republican revolutionaries, ending China's dynastic rule (page 579).

nationalize: to bring under government control a resource or economic operation that previously was privately owned (page 651).

NATO: the North Atlantic Treaty Organization; a mutual-defense pact formed in 1949 by the United States and major Western European countries, which operates under the premise that an attack against one member will be considered an attack against all (page 714).

natural laws: according to the ancient Greeks, the general rules that nature follows (page 86).

natural rights: rights that all human beings are entitled to (page 419).

Nazi Party: the common name for Hitler's National Socialist German Workers Party, which promoted state control of the economy, racist nationalism, and national expansion (page 665).

Nazi-Soviet Pact: a 1939 agreement between Hitler and Stalin that resulted in Germany's invasion of Poland and gave the Soviet Union territory in Eastern Europe (page 688).

neocolonialism: informal domination of a nation by a foreign government or foreign business owners (page 465).

New Deal: an economic reform program adopted by President Franklin D. Roosevelt to overcome the problems created by the Great Depression (page 672).

new realism: a style of painting that began in the 1970's, characterized by extremely realistic representations of familiar objects (page 831).

New Stone Age: the part of the Stone Age that began about 8000 B.C. with the development of farming; also called the Neolithic Age (page 13).

Nigerian Civil War: a conflict (1967–1970) that arose when the Ibo of southeastern Nigeria proclaimed the independence of Biafra (page 787).

nirvana: the Buddhist term for a state of enlightenment (page 133).

nomad: one of a group of people who have no fixed home and wander from place to place in search of food and water (page 15).

nonaligned: not committed to the goals and policies of either side in a competitive situation (page 714).

Northwest Passage: a waterway many explorers of the 1500's believed to exist through North America; it was expected to provide a route between Europe and Asia (page 358).

nuclear proliferation: the spread of nuclear weapons to countries that do not have them (page 743).

Nuremberg Trials: the trials, beginning in 1945, of surviving leaders of Nazi Germany (page 703).

O

oasis: (ō-ā′sĭs): a small, fertile area in a desert where water is available from a spring or well (page 197).

October War: the 1973 conflict between Arabs and Israelis that resulted in Israel gaining control of much Egyptian and Syrian territory (page 762).

October Manifesto: a statement issued by Nicholas II in 1905 calling for the formation of Russia's first parliament, the Duma (page 647).

Odyssey: one of Homer's two epics; it tells the adventures of Odysseus on his way home to Greece after the Trojan War (page 75).

Old Regime (rĭ-zhēm′): the French political and social system in the years before 1798 (page 435).

Old Stone Age: the earliest and longest part of the Stone Age, which began more than two million years ago; also called the Paleolithic Age (page 13).

OPEC: the Organization of Petroleum Exporting Countries; an organization of major oil-exporting nations formed in 1960 to set oil prices and production levels (page 766).

Open Door Policy: a plan, proposed by the United States in 1899, giving all countries equal trading rights in China (page 579).

Opium War: the struggle (1839–1842) between Britain and China over China's efforts to stop Britain's profitable opium trade (page 575).

oracle: a temple where priests and priestesses in ancient Greece gave prophecies; also the priest or priestess giving the prophecy (page 74).

oratory: the art of public speaking, taught to older boys as part of their education in ancient Rome (page 111).

order: a community of monks or nuns (page 213).

Organization of African Unity (OAU): an organization formed in 1963 by independent African nations for the purpose of settling disputes peacefully and addressing social, economic, and health issues that concern all of Africa (page 790).

Organization of American States (OAS): an organization formed by Latin American nations and the United States with the aim of working together on common issues (page 799).

ostracism (ŏs′trə-sĭz′əm): in ancient Athens, the practice of forcing a person believed dangerous to leave the city-state for ten years (page 78).

ozone layer: a part of the earth's atmosphere that screens out harmful radiation from the sun (page 824).

P

Palestine Liberation Organization (PLO): a group formed in 1964 by Palestinian Arabs to work toward the establishment of a Palestinian state (page 763).

Pan-Africanist: relating to the movement formed in 1900 by West Indian and American blacks to defend the rights of persons of African descent (page 777).

Pan-Arabism: a movement to reunite the Arab world under one government (page 765).

Pan-Slavism: a nineteenth-century movement calling for the unity of all Slavic peoples (page 525).

papacy: the office or authority of the Pope (page 214).

papyrus (pə-pī′rəs): a reedlike plant from which the ancient Egyptians made paper scrolls (page 40).

parliament: an assembly of representatives who make the laws of a nation; in England, consists of the House of Lords and House of Commons (page 239).

Parthenon: the temple of Athena, which stands on the Acropolis in Athens (page 84).

pass laws: laws preventing people from moving freely within a country (page 782).

pasteurization: a treatment that uses heat to sterilize milk (page 532).

paternalism: a policy of providing for peoples' needs without giving them any responsibility (page 605).

patriarch (pā′trē-ärk′): in the Byzantine Empire, the head of the Church in Constantinople; today, a title held by high-ranking bishops in certain churches (page 182).

patrician (pə-trĭsh′ən): one of the class of wealthy landowners to which the leaders of the Roman Republic belonged (page 98).

patron: a person who supports the arts (page 327).

Pax Romana (päks rō-män′ə): the period (27 B.C.–A.D. 180) when ancient Rome and the empire it ruled enjoyed long

---

ă pat ā pay â care ä father ĕ pet ē be ĭ pit ī pie î fierce ŏ pot ō go ô paw, for oi oil
ŏŏ book ōō boot ou out ŭ cut û fur th thin *th* the hw which zh vision ə about

periods of peace and prosperity (page 106).

Peace of Augsburg: a treaty signed in 1555 that ended religious wars in Germany and allowed the German princes to decide whether Catholicism or Lutheranism would be followed in their lands (page 339).

Peace of Utrecht (yōō′trĕkt′): a series of treaties signed in 1713 and 1714 that ended the War of the Spanish Succession and restored the balance of power in Europe by preventing the union of the French and Spanish Crowns (page 395).

Peace of Westphalia: the 1648 peace settlement that ended the Thirty Years' War, allowing the German states to become virtually independent and France to become the dominant power in Europe (page 391).

Peloponnesian War: the war between Athens and Sparta that began in 431 B.C. and eventually led to the weakening of the Greek city-states (page 89).

peninsulares (pə-nĭn-syə-lər′əs): people of Iberian descent who belonged to the upper class in Latin America's colonial society (page 457).

peon: a peasant, especially in the American lands conquered by Spain (page 356).

perestroika (păr-əs-troi′kə): Gorbachev's program of political and economic reforms for the Soviet Union (page 726).

persecution: systematic mistreatment (page 128).

Persian Wars: the long struggle of the Greek city-states against the Persian Empire's attempt at conquest (490–479 B.C.) (page 79).

perspective: the impression of depth and distance on the flat surface of a painting (page 333).

Petition of Right: a document signed in 1628 by Charles I

that limited the power of the English monarch and granted the people specific rights (page 398).

pharaoh (fâr′ō): a ruler of ancient Egypt (page 36).

philosophe (fĭl′ə-säf): any of the leading social critics of the eighteenth-century French Enlightenment (page 420).

pilgrimage: a trip with a special religious purpose (page 159).

plebeian (plĭ-bē′ən): a member of the class of common people in ancient Rome (page 98).

pogrom (pō′ grəm): an organized campaign of persecution against Jews, especially in Russia (page 545).

polis (pō′lĭs): a city-state of ancient Greece (page 76).

polytheism: the belief in many gods (page 32).

pop art: an artistic movement of the 1960's that tried to erase the boundaries between "high art" and "popular art" and took many of its images from American popular culture (page 829).

post-impressionism: a late nineteenth-century style of painting characterized by depictions of objects as patterns of form and flat surfaces (page 540).

post-modernism: an architectural movement begun in the 1960's that revived earlier styles and features, such as domes, arches, and columns (page 831).

predestination: the belief that certain people are chosen by God for salvation (page 339).

prehistory: the period of time before writing and other record-keeping systems were developed (page 13).

privateer: a ship that is privately owned but authorized by government to attack and capture enemy ships (page 359).

proletariat (prō′lĭ-târ′ē-ət): wage-earning laborers (page 500).

propaganda: news and information designed to influence people's beliefs or actions (page 633).

prophet: a person who is believed to have the ability to communicate messages from God (page 45).

protectorate: a nation that is formally independent but whose policies are guided by an outside power (page 595).

Protestant: any Christian not belonging to the Roman Catholic or Eastern Orthodox Church (page 337).

psychology: the scientific study of the mental processes and behavior of human beings (page 539).

pueblo (pwĕb′lō): meaning "town" in Spanish, one of the large community dwellings used by certain North American Indian tribes in the Southwest (page 316).

Punic Wars (pyōō′nĭk): a series of three wars fought between Rome and the North African city-state of Carthage between 264 and 146 B.C. (page 99).

puppet government: a government that is controlled by an outside power (page 466).

Puritan: in the sixteenth and seventeenth centuries, a Protestant who believed that the Church of England had not gone far enough in reforming its doctrines and ceremonies (page 359).

Q

Quadruple Alliance: an alliance formed in the early 1800's by Prussia, Austria, Russia, and Great Britain to prevent France from dominating Europe (page 452).

quipu (kē′pōō): an Inca system of record-keeping that used colored cords knotted at intervals to indicate different sums (page 315).

quota: a specific number set as a goal (page 655).

892

R

racism: the belief that one's own racial or national group is superior to others (page 544).

radiation: high-speed rays of energy given off by certain elements (page 536).

radical: a person who favors drastic change (page 441).

rajah: a chief in the early Aryan society of India; later, a ruler of a state in India (page 56).

realism: a late nineteenth-century literary movement characterized by depictions of reality, social problems, and the lives of ordinary people (page 542).

realpolitik: a German term meaning "realistic politics"; politics in which success matters more than legality or idealism (page 517).

Reconquest: the 500-year struggle by Spanish Christian kingdoms to recover Spain from the Muslims (page 246).

Red Shirts: in the 1860's, an army of Italian patriots led by Giuseppe Garibaldi (page 514).

referendum: the practice of letting people vote directly on an issue of law (page 812).

Reformation: the sixteenth-century European movement that rebelled against the authority of the Roman Catholic Church (page 337).

Reign of Terror: a period (1793–1794) when brutal measures were used to eliminate enemies and critics of the revolutionary republic set up in France (page 444).

reincarnation: a spiritual belief of Hindus that the soul is reborn over and over in different bodies until it is purified (page 57).

Renaissance (rĕn′ĭ-säns′): meaning "rebirth," the period of Western history, beginning in the 1300's, when far-reaching changes occurred in the arts, intellectual life, and ways of viewing the world (page 327).

reparations: payments made by one nation to another in compensation for property destroyed in war (page 638).

republic: in ancient Rome, a form of government that was not a monarchy; in modern times, a democratic government in which citizens choose representatives to govern them (page 97).

Restoration: the period (1660–1685) following the English Civil War, during which Charles II reigned in England (page 399).

Risorgimento (rē-sôr′jē-**mĕn′** tō): meaning "resurgence," a movement for Italian unity in the early 1800's (page 513).

ritual: a religious ceremony (page 15).

Roman Catholic Church: the branch of the Christian Church that is headed by the Pope (page 184).

Romanesque (rō′mən-**ĕsk′**): a style of architecture developed during the Middle Ages, characterized by rounded arches, thick walls, small windows, and little ornamentation (page 260).

romanticism: a nineteenth-century movement that stressed emotion and imagination over order and reason and that influenced European social and political thinking, art, and literature (page 476).

Rosetta Stone: a stone tablet carved in 196 B.C., containing inscriptions in three kinds of writing—hieroglyphics, a more recent Egyptian script, and Greek (page 40).

Russification: the policy of imposing Russian culture and language on cultural minorities under Russian rule (page 525).

Russo-Japanese War: the war between Russia and Japan that began in 1904 over territories on the Asian mainland and ended in 1905 with a Japanese victory (page 586).

S

sacrament: a special Christian ceremony, such as baptism, communion, or marriage (page 214).

salon: during the Enlightenment, a social gathering where writers, philosophers, and artists met regularly (page 422).

samurai (săm′oō-rī′): a class of noble-warriors in feudal Japan (page 288).

Sanskrit: an Indo-European language used in India for literature (page 138).

savanna: a flat, open grassland with scattered clumps of trees and shrubs (page 149).

Scholastics: a group of medieval philosophers who argued that reason could be used to explain Christian teachings (page 256).

scientific method: a logical procedure for gathering information and testing ideas that involves the use of hypotheses, experimentation, and observation (page 413).

Scientific Revolution: the great change in ways of thinking about the physical world that came about in the sixteenth and seventeenth centuries, when the foundations of modern science were laid with the development of new theories (page 413).

scribe: a record-keeper (page 30).

secede: to withdraw formally from an alliance, organization, or association (page 560).

Second Estate: under the Old Regime in France, the social class made up of the nobility (page 435).

Second Triumvirate: the three supporters of Julius Caesar (Mark Antony, Lepidus, and

GLOSSARY

ă pat ā pay â care ä father ĕ pet ē be ĭ pit ī pie î fierce ŏ pot ō go ô paw, for oi oil
oō book ōō boot ou out ŭ cut û fur th thin *th* the hw which zh vision ə about

Octavian) who controlled Rome after defeating Caesar's murderers (page 104).

secular: non-religious (page 765).

segregate: to separate, especially by race or nationality (page 560).

self-determination: the principle that national groups should have the right to establish their own governments, free of foreign control (page 635).

self-sufficient: able to produce everything that is needed (page 223).

separation of powers: the division of a government into several branches, each having its own powers (page 420).

separatist: a person who favors withdrawing his or her group from a larger group (page 811).

sepoy: a soldier in Britain's Indian army (page 571).

Sepoy Rebellion: a revolt by soldiers in Britain's Indian army (1857–1858) called by Indian nationalists "the first war for independence" (page 571).

serf: a medieval peasant legally bound to live and work on a lord's estate (page 222).

shah: a Muslim ruler (page 275).

Shiite (shē'īt'): one of the group of Muslims who broke away from the main body of Islam in the seventh century (page 200).

Shinto: an early Japanese religion based on respect for the forces of nature (page 286).

shogun: one of the military leaders who ruled Japan in the name of the emperor from the twelfth to the nineteenth century (page 288).

silent barter: in Africa, a method of trade in which goods were left at a prearranged place, without actual contact between individuals (page 154).

894 **Silk Road:** in ancient China, the route that silk merchants traveled as they headed westward through China to India, Persia, and Roman provinces along the Mediterranean (page 143).

Sino-Japanese War: the war (1894–1895) between China and Japan for control of Korea (page 577).

Six-Day War: the conflict between Arab and Israeli forces in 1967 that was prompted by Egypt's blockade of the Gulf of Aqaba; resulted in Israel's gaining control of territory that included the ancient city of Jerusalem (page 761).

social contract: a term created by Thomas Hobbes to describe an agreement where people give up their individual rights in exchange for the law and order provided by government (page 419).

Social Darwinism: the belief that the concept of natural selection works in social and economic relations just as it does in nature (page 544).

socialism: a philosophy that calls for government or worker ownership and operation of business and industry for the benefit of society (page 480).

sociology: the scientific study of human society (page 539).

Socratic method: a technique emphasized by Socrates that encouraged people to become aware of their own views and those of others by asking questions (page 87).

Sophist (sŏf'ĭst): the name for a Greek teacher who, in the decades after the Persian Wars, traveled from city to city teaching speech, grammar, gymnastics, mathematics, and music (page 87).

South African War: also called the Boer War; the conflict between the British and Afrikaners over territory in South Africa (1899–1902) (page 600).

soviet: a representative council of workers, peasants, or soldiers in the Soviet Union (page 647).

Spanish-American War: the 1898 war between Spain and the United States (page 561).

Spanish Civil War: the struggle in the 1930's between Franco's Falangists and anti-Fascist republican forces (page 669).

sphere of influence: a section of one country in which another country has special authority (page 576).

spoils: goods taken from the opposition during a war (page 119).

stalemate: a standoff or draw, making further action impossible for either side (page 631).

standard of living: a general measure of quality of life (page 495).

steppe: the prairie grassland area located south of the immense forests in northern Russia (page 188).

stoa (stō'ə): in ancient Greece, an open porch used as a meeting place (page 92).

Stoicism (stō'ĭ-sĭz'əm): an important Hellenistic school of philosophy that developed in Athens about 200 B.C.; emphasized dignity, self-control, and reason (page 92).

Stone Age: the name for the prehistoric period when tools and weapons were made of stone (page 13).

Sturm und Drang (shtŏŏrm' ōŏnt dräng'): meaning "storm and stress"; a literary movement formed in the 1770's by German writers whose works described people's struggles with their emotions and society (page 477).

subcontinent: a large land mass, such as India, that is geographically and culturally distinct from the rest of a continent (page 53).

suffrage: the right to vote (page 442).

sultan: the political ruler of a Muslim country (page 202).

sultanate: a Muslim kingdom (page 273).

summit: a meeting between top government officials from two or more nations (page 703).

sunbelt: the portion of the United States that stretches from the southeastern Atlantic coast to southern California (page 804).

Sunni (so͞on′ē): the group of Muslims who hold traditional Islamic beliefs (page 200).

superconductor: a material that allows the transmission of electricity over great distances with very little energy loss (page 821).

surplus: a supply greater than what is needed (page 41).

surrealism: a twentieth-century artistic movement character-ized by depictions of dreams and other products of the unconscious mind (page 674).

T

Taiping Rebellion: a movement against the Manchus in China (1850–1864) that proposed significant changes in Chinese society (page 576).

Taj Mahal: a tomb in Agra built by Shah Jahan for his wife; considered a masterpiece of Mogul architecture (page 275).

Taoism (dou′ĭz′əm): a Chinese philosophy based on discovering the Tao, or "way," of the universe and living in harmony with nature (page 140).

tariff: a tax on imported or exported goods (page 517).

technology: the development of methods, materials, and tools used in doing work (page 20).

Ten Commandments: according to Hebrew belief, the laws given to Moses by God (page 44).

terrace-farming: a method of farming that involves cutting into the sides of mountains and building step-like banks of soil (page 313).

terra cotta: hard ceramic clay (page 300).

terrorism: the use of violence, especially against random victims, in an effort to win demands or influence the policies of a government (page 722).

Tet offensive: a massive attack that was made by Vietcong and North Vietnamese forces in January 1968 against South Vietnam, which led many people to question South Vietnam's chances of winning the Vietnam War (page 752).

theocracy: a form of government in which the ruler is seen either as a god or as a chosen representative of the gods (page 24).

Third Estate: the largest social class under the Old Regime in France, made up of peasants, city workers, and the middle class (page 435).

Third World: the developing nations of Africa, Asia, and Latin America (page 826).

Thirty Years' War: a religious war (1618–1648) between Protestants and Catholics that involved most of the major European states in a struggle over the balance of power in Europe (page 390).

Time of Troubles: a period (1598–1613) in Russian history when disorder was widespread and Moscow was threatened by civil war, peasant revolts, and foreign invasions (page 404).

Torah: the Hebrew name for the first five books of the Bible (page 45).

totalitarian state: a state in which government leaders are given complete authority over the lives of citizens (page 659).

total war: a war that involves all of the human and material resources of the countries that are taking part (page 638).

totem (tō′təm): a clan or family symbol (page 318).

Treaty of Brest-Litovsk: the 1918 treaty that took Russia out of World War I and gave much of its western territory to Germany (page 650).

Treaty of Versailles: the settle-ment made with Germany at the end of World War I that called for territorial changes, reparations, and German demilitarization (page 636).

treaty port: a coastal trade center in China where Westerners were allowed to conduct business in the 1800's (page 575).

trial by ordeal: a medieval system of justice in which an accused person was given a physical test to prove his or her innocence (page 212).

trial jury: a group of citizens authorized to hand down a decision following a trial (page 237).

tribute: payment demanded from a conquered people as evidence of their submission (page 38).

Triple Alliance: an alliance between Germany, Austria-Hungary, and Italy formed in 1882; it guaranteed that all members would help if any were attacked (page 625).

Triple Entente: an agreement signed in 1907 among Russia, France, and Britain to aid one another in war (page 625).

troubadour (tro͞o′bə-dôr′): in medieval times, a noble who wrote songs and poems for noblewomen, usually praising their beauty and promising devotion (page 259).

Truman Doctrine: the Amer-ican foreign policy, as stated in 1947 by President Truman, of aiding any country that requested help in resisting communism (page 713).

Twelve Tables: the Roman laws, collected in 451 B.C.,

ă pat ā pay â care ä father ĕ pet ē be ĭ pit ī pie î fierce ŏ pot ō go ô paw, for oi oil
ōō book ōō boot ou out ŭ cut û fur th thin *th* the hw which zh vision ə about

895

that gave the common people some protection against unfair decisions by patrician judges (page 98).

tyrant: a ruler who held complete power in a Greek city-state; a dictator (page 78).

U

U-boat: the name given to German submarines in World War I (page 633).

ultimatum (ŭl′tə-mā′təm): a statement that threatens serious action if specified demands are not met (page 627).

unequal treaty system: a pattern of trade established by the Treaty of Nanjing (1842), which forced the Chinese to accept trade conditions dictated by foreigners (page 575).

United Nations: an international organization created in 1945 to promote national self-determination, human rights, and cooperation among nations (page 703).

urbanization: the movement of people from rural areas to cities (page 495).

utopia (yōō-tō′pē-ə): an ideal society (page 499).

V

vaccination: an injection of a solution of weakened germs with the object of providing immunity against a disease (page 532).

vassal: a medieval noble who pledged loyalty and services to a feudal lord in exchange for a grant of land and serfs (page 218).

Vatican: the palace of the Pope in Rome (page 335).

Vedas: four sacred Indian texts that include collections of hymns, prayers, explanations of religious rituals, and wise sayings (page 55).

vernacular (vər-năk′yə-lər): the language usually spoken in a region or country (page 258).

Versailles (vər-sī′): a palace in France built as the home for Louis XIV (page 393).

veto: to reject a proposal or act; in ancient Rome, a power held by consuls that enabled them to check one another's actions (page 98).

viceroy (vīs′roi′): a representative of the Spanish king in Spain's American colonies (page 356).

Vietcong: South Vietnamese people who were sympathetic to the Communist North Vietnamese government's efforts to gain control of South Vietnam (page 751).

Vietnam War: the war between Communist North Vietnam and non-Communist South Vietnam following the withdrawal of the French colonial government; resulted in the formation of a united Communist nation in 1975 (page 751).

W

War of the Reform: a civil war (1858–1860) fought between conservatives and liberals in Mexico (page 466).

War of the Spanish Succession: the conflict (1701–1713) between France and most of the leading European states over the accession of a Bourbon prince to the Spanish throne (page 395).

Wars of the Roses: a civil war (1455–1485) between two rival branches of the English royal family (page 264).

Warsaw Pact: a mutual-defense pact formed in 1955 by the Soviet Union and seven Eastern European countries (page 714).

Watergate scandal: the term applied to events surrounding a 1972 burglary at Democratic Party headquarters and the resulting exposure of abuses of power by the Nixon administration (page 806).

welfare state: a nation whose government provides extensive aid to its citizens (page 721).

westernize: to adopt technology and customs from the West (page 405).

World War I: the war fought in Europe from 1914 to 1918 over tensions caused by the alliance system, militarism, imperialism, and extreme nationalism (page 625).

World War II: the war that began in Europe with the German invasion of Poland (1939) and in Asia with Japan's invasion of China (1937); eventually involved most of the world's nations and ended in 1945 with the atomic bombing of Japanese cities (page 688).

Z

Zen Buddhism: a Buddhist sect that emphasizes enlightenment through meditation and stresses simplicity and discipline (page 289).

ziggurat (zĭg′ə-răt′): one of the large brick temples built by the people of ancient Mesopotamia (page 30).

Zionism: a movement begun in 1896 to create a separate homeland for Jews (page 545).

Zollverein (tsôl′fər-īn): an organization of German states formed in 1834 to reduce tariffs among its members (page 517).

Zoroastrianism (zôr′ō-ăs′trē-ə-nĭz′əm): a religion founded by the Persian teacher Zoroaster in the sixth century B.C.; it was based on the belief in the struggle between the forces of good and evil (page 48).

Dictionary of Ancient Places

This listing is provided as a quick-reference guide to important places in ancient history. It includes villages, cities, regions, kingdoms, battlesites, and natural locations. Page references at the end of each entry tell where the place is first mentioned and where it can be located on a map.

A

Adrianople (ā′drē-ə-**nō**′pəl): the town where in A.D. 378 the Visigoths defeated the Romans; now the city of Edirne in northwest Turkey (page 122; map, page 121).

Adulis (**ăd**′ū-lĭs): a port city of the ancient kingdom of Aksum, on the southwest coast of the Red Sea (page 154; map, page 152).

Akkad (**ăk**′äd′): a kingdom in northern Mesopotamia, in what is now Iraq. It conquered Sumer about 2350 B.C. and became an empire that stretched from the Persian Gulf to the Mediterranean Sea (page 31; map, page 30).

Aksum (**ăk**′sōōm): an ancient kingdom in what is now the northern highlands of Ethiopia; its capital, Aksum, survives in the modern town of the same name (page 153; map, page 152).

Alexandria: an Egyptian city founded in 332 B.C. by Alexander near a mouth of the Nile River; occupied continuously from that time (page 91; map, page 91).

Altamira (ăl′tə-**mĭr**′ə): a cave in which prehistoric wall paintings were discovered in 1879; located near Santander in northern Spain (page 16; map, page 22).

Anyang (**än**′**yäng**′): the location of a great city of the Shang Dynasty; now a town in eastern China (page 60; map, page 60).

Athens: a famous city-state of ancient Greece; occupied continuously from Stone Age times to the present (page 76; map, page 72).

Azania: a trading region of eastern Africa with many independent port cities, extending along the coast of what is now Tanzania, Kenya, and Somalia (page 154; map, page 152).

B

Babylon: a city on the Euphrates River ruled by Hammurabi when he conquered and united Mesopotamia in 1792 B.C.; its remains are near modern Hilla in central Iraq (page 31; map, page 30).

Bethlehem: the town in Judaea near Jerusalem, where Jesus was born; still known by its ancient name (or by the Arabic equivalent, Bayt Lahm), it is governed today by Israel (page 126; map, page 128).

Byzantium (bĭ-**zăn**′shē-əm): ancient Greek city on a peninsula in the Bosporous Strait; in A.D. 330, Constantinople was built on the same site (page 181; map, page 107). *See Constantinople.*

C

Canaan (**kā**′nən): the home of the ancient Israelites in Palestine; now the part of Palestine west of the Jordan River (page 44; map, page 45).

Cannae (**kăn**′ē): a battlefield where Hannibal defeated the Romans in 216 B.C., near present-day Barletta in southern Italy (page 100; map, page 100).

Carthage: an ancient city on the north coast of Africa, destroyed in 146 B.C.; it was not far from modern Tunis, the capital of Tunisia (page 99; map, page 100).

Çatal Hüyük (chä-**täl**′ hü-**yük**′): a village of the New Stone Age, located near what is now the city of Konya in south central Turkey (page 19; map, page 22).

Chaeronea (kĕr′ə-**nē**′ə): an ancient town, not far from the modern city of Levádhia in eastern Greece; Philip of Macedon defeated the Greek city-states here in 338 B.C. (page 90; map, page 91).

Chang'an: the capital of the Han Dynasty, located where the city of Xi'an stands today in central China (page 142; map, page 143).

Constantinople (kŏn′stăn-tə-**nō**′pəl): the capital of the eastern part of the Roman Empire, built by the emperor Constantine in A.D. 330, now the city of Istanbul in Turkey (page 120; map, page 121).

D

Delos: an island in the south Aegean Sea, center of the Delian League, which was founded in 478 B.C. to protect Greece from the Persians (page 80; map, page 72).

Delphi (**dĕl**′fī): an ancient town of central Greece, the home of one of the most famous of the Greek oracles; a town by that name is located in central Greece today (page 74; map, page 72).

897

E

Egypt: an ancient African kingdom centered on the Nile valley, covering about the area of modern Egypt, and parts of modern Sudan (page 34; map, page 35).

G

Gaul: a Roman province, roughly covering the same area as France today (page 107; map, page 102).

Ghana: a great empire of the Soninke people, in the west Sahara region of Africa, that grew with the expansion of the Saharan trade after A.D. 500; not to be confused with the modern African nation of that name (page 155; maps, pages 152, 298).

Giza (**gē′**zə): a city near the Great Pyramid; it keeps its ancient name today and is located near Cairo, Egypt (page 37; map, page 35).

H

Harappa (hə-**răp′**ə): a city of the early Indus Valley civilization; a town with the same name stands near its ruins in the Punjab region of Pakistan (page 53; map, page 54).

I

Israel: the kingdom of the Hebrews before its division into two parts about 933 B.C.; also, the northern part of the kingdom after it was divided. At different periods these kingdoms covered parts of what are now Israel, Jordan, Lebanon, and Syria (page 44; map, page 44).

J

Jerusalem: the capital of the ancient kingdom and the modern state of Israel (page 44; map, page 44).

898

Judaea (jo͞o-**dē′**ə): a province, formerly the kingdom of Judah, that revolted against Roman rule in A.D. 66; it corresponds to what is now southern Israel and southwestern Jordan (page 107; map, page 107).

Judah: the southernmost of the two kingdoms of the Hebrew people after the earlier kingdom was divided about 933 B.C.; it covered approximately the area that today is southern Israel (page 45; map, page 44).

K

Kalinga: a coastal province of the Mauryan Empire, corresponding roughly to the modern state of Orissa on the east coast of India (page 137; map, page 137).

Kerma: the capital of the ancient kings of Kush before about 590 B.C.; today a city on the Nile River in Sudan (page 152; map, page 152).

Knossos (**nŏs′**əs): an ancient city on the north coast of Crete, site of a palace inhabited by the royal family of the Minoan civilization (page 71; map, page 72).

Kush: a kingdom established by the Nubians around 1600 B.C. in part of the area now occupied by Egypt, Sudan, and Ethiopia (page 152; map, page 152).

L

Lascaux (läs-**kō′**): a famous cave near the town of Montignac, in central France, where wall paintings from the Old Stone Age were found in 1940 (page 16; map, page 22).

Luoyang (**lwō′**yäng′): the second capital of the Zhou Dynasty today the city of Honan in eastern China (page 62; map, page 60).

Lydia: a kingdom that flourished in the 500's B.C. in the area that is now western Turkey (page 46; map, page 47).

M

Macedonia (măs′ĭ-**dō′**nē-ə): a kingdom of northern Greece in ancient times, ruled by Philip and his son, Alexander the Great; its former territory is now divided among Yugoslavia, Bulgaria, and Greece in the area where they meet (page 90; map, page 91).

Magadha (**mä′**gə-də): an ancient kingdom in eastern India that expanded to rule the entire plain of the Ganges and all of northern India as far as the Punjab (page 136; map, page 137).

Marathon: a plain in eastern Greece where the Greeks defeated the Persians in 490 B.C. (page 79; map, page 78).

Masada (mə-**sä′**də): mountaintop fortress where Jewish rebels resisted Roman troops in A.D. 72-73; it now lies within Israel on the Dead Sea (page 107).

Memphis: the capital city of Egypt beginning about 2100 B.C. under the pharaoh Menes; its ruins are now partially covered by the village of Mit Rahina in northern Egypt near Cairo (page 36; map, page 35).

Meroë (**měr′**ō-ē): the capital of Kushite Egypt, built about 590 B.C., where the city of Kabushiyah, Sudan, is now (page 152; map, page 152).

Mesopotamia (měs′ə-pə-**tā′** mē-ə): a region between the Tigris and Euphrates rivers, home to the earliest of the great river valley civilizations; now part of Iraq (page 21; map, page 30).

Mohenjo-Daro (mō-**hěn′**jō-**dä′**rō): a city of the early Indus Valley civilization; now in ruins south of Larkana in southern Pakistan (page 53; map, page 54).

Mycenae (mī-**sē′**nē): the most important city of the Mycenaean civilization, now the site of excavated ruins in the Peloponnesus region of Greece near the city of Corinth (page 72; map, page 72).

N

Nineveh (nĭn′ə-və): a capital city of the Assyrian Empire; its remains are near present-day Mosul in northern Iraq (page 46; map, page 30).

Nubia: part of the kingdom of Kush from 1600 B.C. to A.D. 400; today much of it is covered by Lake Nasser in Egypt and Sudan (page 38; map, page 35).

O

Olympia: an ancient town in the northwest Peloponnesus region of Greece. Games honoring Zeus were held there every four years in ancient times, which were the forerunner of today's Olympic Games. Now in ruins near a modern town of the same name (page 74; map, page 72).

Olympus, Mount: a mountain in the Thessaly region of northern Greece, once believed to be home to the Greek gods (page 74; map, page 72).

Ophir (ō′fûr): a land mentioned in the Bible as a rich trading country, probably located on the Somali Peninsula (page 154).

P

Palestine: a region that was home to the Israelites and included the ancient kingdoms of Israel and Judah; it is the area covered by the present-day state of Israel and the region on the West Bank of the Jordan (page 38; maps, pages 44, 47).

Phoenicia (fĭ-nĭsh′ə): an ancient region ruled by numerous city-states along the shore of what is now Syria, Lebanon, and Israel (page 43; map, pages 2-3).

Plataea (plə-tē′ə): an ancient town near which the Greeks defeated the Persians in 479 B.C.; its ruins now are near Erithrai in eastern Greece (page 79; map, page 78).

R

Rome: a city, once the capital of the Roman Empire, that has existed at the same place in central Italy for more than 2,500 years (page 96; map, page 98).

S

Salamis (săl′ə-mĭs): an island near Athens where Greek forces defeated the Persians in a key sea battle in 480 B.C. (page 79; map, page 81).

Sardis: the capital of Lydia, one end of the Royal Road, captured by the Persians in 546 B.C.; its ruins now lie east of the city of Izmir in western Turkey (page 48; map, page 47).

Sidon: a trading port of ancient Phoenicia, on the site of modern-day Sayda in south Lebanon (page 45; map, page 44).

Sparta: a militaristic city-state of ancient Greece, now partly covered by a town of the same name in the southern Peloponnesus region of Greece (page 76; map, page 72).

Sumer: an area in southern Mesopotamia (now southern Iraq) where the world's first advanced civilization arose (page 29; map, page 30).

Susa: the capital city of the Persian Empire, now the village of Shūsh in southwest Iran (page 48; map, page 47).

Syria: an ancient land conquered by Egyptian pharaoh Thutmose III about 1490 B.C. and later became part of other empires; the territory it covered is now in Syria, Lebanon, Israel, and Jordan (page 38; map, page 44).

Syria Palestina: identical with Judaea, a province formed under Roman rule in A.D. 70 in what is now southwestern Jordan and southern Israel (page 108; map, page 107).

T

Tarsus: an ancient city, home of the missionary Paul; its ruins are near the modern city of the same name in south Turkey (page 127; map, page 128).

Teotihuacán (tĕ′ō-tē′wä-kän′): the first true city in the Americas, which flourished between A.D. 250 and 900; its ruins lie within Teotihuacán, a town in central Mexico (page 159; map, page 158).

Thebes (thēbz): the capital city of the Middle Kingdom of Egypt; today it lies in ruins south of Qena, Egypt (page 37; map, page 35).

Thebes: a town in central Greece from ancient times through the present, site of a Mycenaean palace (page 72; map, page 72).

Thermopylae (thər-mŏp′ə-lē): a narrow pass where a small Greek force fought a far larger army of Persians in 480 B.C., near the present-day town of Lamia in northern Greece (page 79; map, page 78).

Troy: a city, also called Ilium, that is the setting for Homer's *Iliad;* it exists as a ruin near Hissarlik on the Aegean coast (page 75; map, page 72).

Tyre: a great trading port of ancient Phoenicia, today surviving as Sur, a town in southern Lebanon (page 43; map, page 44).

U

Ur: a Sumerian city-state that took over Sumer and Akkad about 2100 B.C.; its remains lie near the town of An Nasiriya in southern Iraq (page 31; map, page 30).

Z

Zama: an ancient town, the site of the battle in which Scipio defeated Hannibal in 202 B.C., west of modern-day Tunis in Tunisia (page 101; map, page 100).

ANCIENT PLACES

899

Biographical Dictionary

This dictionary lists many of the important people you will encounter as you read *History of the World*. The page numbers at the end of each entry refer to the first time a person is mentioned in the book. Many of these significant people are discussed more than once. For complete page references, consult the Index.

A

Abbas I (1572?–1629). Safavid shah (page 279).

Abu Bakari II. Ruler of Mali in the early 1300's (page 298).

Achebe, Chinua (ə-**chä′**-bä) (1930–). Nigerian writer (page 831).

Akbar (1542–1605). Indian ruler who expanded the Mogul Empire (page 274).

Akhenaton (ä′kə-**nä′**tən). Egyptian pharaoh (1375–1358 B.C.) and religious reformer (page 38).

Alexander II (1818–1881). Russian czar who abolished serfdom (page 525).

Alexander III (1845–1894). Russian czar who tried to end revolutionary activity (page 527).

Alexander the Great (356–323 B.C.). Conqueror of Greece and the ancient Middle East (page 90).

Alfred the Great (849–899). West Saxon king (page 236).

Allende, Salvador (ä-**yĕn′**dä) (1908–1973). Chilean Marxist leader (page 798).

Aquinas, Thomas (ə-**kwī′**nəs) (1225?–1274). Dominican monk and Scholastic philosopher (page 256).

Aquino, Corazon (ä-**kēn′**ō) (1933–). President of the Philippines (page 749).

Aristotle (ăr′ĭ-**stŏt′**əl) (384–322 B.C.). Greek philosopher (page 88).

Ashurbanipal (ä′sho͞or-bä′nē-päl′). Ruler of the Assyrian Empire (669–626 B.C.) (page 46).

Askia Mohammed. Songhai ruler (1493–1528) who created an Islamic empire (page 299).

Asoka. Ruler of India (273–232 B.C.) who supported the Buddhist ideal of nonviolence (page 137).

Attila (ə-**tĭl′**ə) (406?–453). King of the Huns who attempted to conquer Rome (page 122).

Augustine (354–430). Early Christian thinker who wrote *The City of God* (page 128).

Augustus (63 B.C.–A.D. 14). First Roman emperor (page 105).

Aurangzeb (ôr′əng-zĕb′) (1618–1707). Mogul emperor (page 275).

Avicenna (ăv′ĭ-sĕn′ə) (980–1037). Muslim philosopher (page 204).

B

Bach, Johann Sebastian (bäk) (1685–1750). German composer (page 423).

Bacon, Francis (1561–1626). English politician and writer (page 418).

Bacon, Roger (1214–1294). English monk, philosopher, and scientist (page 257).

Barnard, Christiaan (1921–). South African surgeon who performed the first successful human heart transplant in 1967 (page 820).

Beethoven, Ludwig van (bā′tō-vən) (1770–1827). German composer (page 423).

Begin, Menachem (bā′gĭn) (1913–1992). Israeli prime minister who signed the Camp David Peace Accords (page 763).

Bismarck, Otto von (1815–1898). Prussian prime minister and Germany's first chancellor (page 517).

Bolívar, Simon (bō-**lē′**vär) (1783–1830). Venezuelan leader who drove the Spanish out of northern South America (page 459).

Brahms, Johannes (1833–1897). German composer (page 542).

Brontë, Charlotte (1816–1855). English author who wrote *Jane Eyre* (page 477).

Brontë, Emily (1818–1848). English author who wrote *Wuthering Heights* (page 477).

Bruce, James (1730–1794). Scottish explorer (page 593).

Bush, George (1924–). 41st U. S. President (page 808).

Byron, Lord (1788–1824). English Romantic poet who wrote *Don Juan* (page 478).

C

Caesar, Julius (100–44 B.C.). Roman general, statesman, and historian (page 103).

Caillié, René (kä′yä′) (1799–1838). French explorer of Africa (page 593).

Calvin, John (1509–1564). French-born Swiss Protestant reformer who developed Calvinism (page 339).

Carter, Jimmy (1924–). 39th U. S. President (page 763).

Casimir III (1309–1370). Polish king (page 402).

Castro, Fidel (1927–). Cuban Marxist leader (page 799).

Catherine the Great (1729–1796). Russian ruler (page 405).

Cavour, Camillo di (kə-vōōr′) (1810–1861). Prime minister of Sardinia (page 513).

Cervantes Saavedra, Miguel de (sər-vǎn′tēz) (1547–1616). Spanish author who wrote *Don Quixote* (page 332).

Cézanne, Paul (sā-zǎn′) (1839–1906). French post-impressionist painter (page 540).

Champlain, Samuel de (shǎm-plān′) (1567?–1635). French explorer of eastern Canada (page 360).

Chandragupta Maurya (mär′yä) (d. 286 B.C.). Founder of the Mauryan Empire (page 136).

Charlemagne (shär′lə-mān′) (742–814). Frankish king who was dedicated to spreading Christianity in Europe (page 215).

Charles I (1600–1649). English king who was beheaded for treason (page 398).

Charles V (1500–1558). Holy Roman Emperor and ruler of Spain, the Netherlands, and the eastern Hapsburg lands (page 386).

Chaucer, Geoffrey (1340?–1400). English author who wrote *The Canterbury Tales* (page 259).

Chiang Kai-shek (jyäng′kī′shěk′) (1887–1975). Leader of the Chinese Nationalists (page 676).

Churchill, Winston (1874–1965). British prime minister during World War II (page 690).

Clovis (klō′vĭs) (466–511). Frankish ruler (page 215).

Columbus, Christopher (1451?–1506). Italian navigator who discovered the Americas while searching for a westward route from Europe to Asia (page 349).

Confucius (kən-fyōō′shəs) (551–479 B.C.). Chinese philosopher (page 63).

Constantine (280?–337). Roman emperor who founded Constantinople (page 119).

Copernicus, Nicolaus (kō-pûr′nə-kəs) (1473–1543). Polish astronomer whose heliocentric theory claimed the sun was at the center of the universe (page 413).

Cortés, Hernando (1485–1547). Spanish conquistador who defeated the Aztecs in Mexico (page 355).

Cromwell, Oliver (1599–1658). Puritan general who overthrew the English monarchy and formed the Commonwealth (page 399).

Curie, Marie (1867–1934) and **Pierre** (1859–1906). Husband and wife scientists who studied radioactivity in minerals (page 536).

Cyrus the Great (600?–530 B.C.). Persian leader and founder of the Persian Empire (page 46).

D

Dante Alighieri (dän′tä ä-lē-gyä′rē) (1265–1321). Italian author who wrote *The Divine Comedy* (page 259).

Darwin, Charles (1809–1882). English scientist who developed the theory of evolution (page 537).

de Gaulle, Charles (də-gôl′) (1890–1970). Leader of the Free French and president of France's Fifth Republic (page 697).

Delacroix, Eugène (dəl-ä-krwä′) (1798–1863). French Romantic painter (page 478).

Deng Xiaoping (düng′ shou′pĭng) (1904–). Chinese leader who succeeded Mao Zedong and started economic reforms (page 737).

Descartes, René (dā-kärt′) (1596–1650). French mathematician (page 418).

d'Este, Isabella (děs′tä) (1474–1539). Italian Renaissance patron of the arts (page 329).

Dias, Bartholomeu (dē′-əs) (1450?–1500). Portuguese navigator who discovered the Cape of Good Hope (page 348).

Díaz, Porfirio (dē′äs) (1830–1915). Mexican dictator (page 466).

Dickens, Charles (1812–1870). English author (page 542).

Diocletian (dī′ə-klē′shən) (245–313). Roman emperor (page 119).

Disraeli, Benjamin (dĭz-rā′lē) (1804–1881). English prime minister and head of Conservative Party (page 503).

Drake, Francis (1540?–1596). English naval hero (page 368).

Durham, Lord (1792–1840). English statesman who reviewed Canadian demands for self-rule (page 563).

E

Edison, Thomas Alva (1847–1931). American inventor whose inventions included the electric light bulb and the phonograph (page 531).

Einstein, Albert (1879–1955). German-born scientist who developed the theory of relativity (page 537).

Eisenhower, Dwight D. (1890–1969). Leader of the Allied forces in World War II and 34th U. S. President (page 693).

Eleanor of Aquitaine (1122?–1204). Ruler of Aquitaine and the wife of Louis VII of France and later of Henry II of England (page 222).

Eliot, T. S. (1888–1965). American-born poet who wrote *The Waste Land* (page 674).

Elizabeth I (1533–1603). English queen of the Tudor dynasty (page 396).

Engels, Friedrich (1820–1895). German socialist who wrote the *Communist Manifesto* with Karl Marx (page 500).

Erasmus, Desiderius (ĭ-rǎz′məs) (1466–1536). Dutch Renaissance humanist who wrote *The Praise of Folly* (page 331).

BIOGRAPHICAL DICTIONARY

F

Ford, Henry (1863–1947) American automobile manufacturer who developed the moving assembly line (page 670).

Fourier, Charles (fŏŏ′rē-ā′) (1772–1837). French utopian socialist (page 499).

Francis Ferdinand (1863–1914). Heir to the Austrian-Hungarian throne whose assassination started World War I (page 627).

Franco, Francisco (1892–1975). Spanish Fascist dictator (page 669).

Freud, Sigmund (**froid**) (1856–1939). Austrian doctor who developed a number of psychological theories (page 539).

G

Galileo Galilei (1564–1642). Italian scientist and mathematician who supported Copernicus's heliocentric theory (page 414).

Gandhi, Indira (1917–1984). Prime minister of India (page 741).

Gandhi, Mohandas K. (**gän**′dē) (1869–1948). Indian leader who led a 30–year campaign for India's independence (page 739).

García Márquez, Gabriel (gär-**sē**′ə **mär**′kəs′) (1928–). Colombian writer (page 831).

Garibaldi, Giuseppe (1807–1882). Commander of the Red Shirts, a group of Italian patriots (page 514).

Gladstone, William (1809–1898). English prime minister and head of the Liberal Party (page 503).

Gompers, Samuel (1850–1924). Leader of the American Federation of Labor (AFL) (page 506).

Gorbachev, Mikhail (gôr-bə-**chäf**′) (1931–). Soviet leader who began far-reaching political and economic reforms and who resigned in 1991 (page 726).

902 **Gregory VII** (1020?–1085).

Pope who was involved in a struggle over authority with the Holy Roman Emperor (page 243).

Gutenberg, Johann (**gōōt**′ən-bûrg′) (1398–1468). German printer who produced the first printed book using movable type (page 329).

H

Haile Selassie (**hī**′lē sə-**läs**′ē) (1892–1975). Ethiopian emperor (page 685).

Hammurabi (hä′mə-**rä**′bē) (18th century B.C.). Babylonian ruler who developed a strict code of laws (page 31).

Hannibal (247–183? B.C.). Carthaginian general who led a successful attack against the Romans during the Second Punic War (page 100).

Hardy, Thomas (1840–1928). English novelist and poet (page 542).

Harun al-Rashid (hä-**rōōn**′ äl-rä-**shēd**′) (764?–809). Muslim caliph (page 204).

Hatshepsut (hăt-**shĕp**′-sōōt′) Egyptian queen (1504–1482 B.C.) (page 38).

Havel, Vaclav (**hä**′vel) (1936–). Playwright and activist; elected president of Czechoslovakia in 1989 (page 730).

Hemingway, Ernest (1899?–1961). American author (page 674).

Henry IV (1050–1106). Holy Roman Emperor (page 243).

Henry IV (1553–1610). French king; first ruler of the Bourbon dynasty (page 243).

Henry VII (1457–1509). English king and founder of the Tudor dynasty (page 264).

Henry VIII (1491–1547). English Tudor king (page 339).

Henry the Navigator (1394–1460). Portuguese prince who sponsored exploration of the West African coast (page 348).

Herodotus (484?–425? B.C.).

Greek historian, known as "the father of history" (page 84).

Herzl, Theodor (**hĕrt**′səl) (1860–1904). Hungarian Jewish writer who began the Zionist movement (page 545).

Hidalgo, Miguel (ē-**däl**′gō) (1753–1811). Priest who led an unsuccessful revolt against Spanish rule in Mexico (page 459).

Hitler, Adolf (1889–1945). German Nazi dictator who used propaganda and extreme violence to enforce his racist and nationalist ideas (page 665).

Hobbes, Thomas (1588–1679). English philosopher and author of *Leviathan* (page 419).

Ho Chi Minh (1890–1969). Vietnamese Communist leader (page 750).

Homer (8th century B.C.). Greek epic poet who wrote the *Iliad* and the *Odyssey* (page 75).

Huss, John (1374–1415). Bohemian religious reformer (page 265).

Hussein, Saddam (1937–). Dictator of Iraq; invaded Kuwait in 1990 (page 768).

I

Innocent III (1161–1216). Pope who claimed the right to intervene in the affairs of any European state (page 244).

Isabella (1451–1504). Spanish queen who sponsored Columbus's voyages (page 349).

Ito Hirobumi (1841–1909). Chief adviser to the Japanese emperor who used Western ideas to develop a new constitution (page 585).

Ivan III (1440–1505). Founder of unified Russia; known as "the Great" (page 192).

Ivan IV (1530–1584). Russian czar whose harsh rule earned him the nickname "the Terrible" (page 403).

J

Jahangir (jə-**hän′**gēr′) (1569–1627). Mogul emperor (page 569).

Jefferson, Thomas (1743–1826). 3rd U. S. President and author of the Declaration of Independence (page 427).

Jenner, Edward (1749–1823). English doctor who developed a vaccine for smallpox (page 532).

Jesus (4? B.C.–A.D. 29?). One of the world's great religious leaders; believed by most Christians to be the Son of God (page 126).

Joan of Arc (1412–1431). French military leader and heroine (page 263).

John (1167?–1216). Early English king who signed the Magna Carta (page 238).

John Paul II (1920–). Polish pope who encouraged the struggle for religious and political freedom in Communist countries (page 828).

Johnson, Lyndon B. (1908–1973). 36th U. S. President (page 751).

Juárez, Benito (**hwä′**reš) (1806–1872). Mexican reformer and president (page 466).

Justinian (jŭs-**tin′**ē-ən) (482–565). Byzantine ruler (page 182).

K

Kafka, Franz (1883–1924). Czech author (page 674).

Keats, John (1795–1821). English Romantic poet (page 477).

Kemal, Mustafa (kĕ-**mäl′**) (1881–1938). First president of the republic of Turkey (page 678).

Kennedy, John F. (1917–1963) 35th U. S. President (page 718).

Kenyatta, Jomo (1894?–1978). Leader of Kenya's independence movement and Kenya's first president (page 779).

Kerensky, Alexander (kə-**rĕn′**skē) (1881–1970). Leader of the Provisional Government set up in Russia in 1917 (page 647).

Kepler, Johannes (1571–1630). German astronomer (page 415).

Khomeini, Ayatollah Ruhollah (kō-**mä′**nē) (1900–1989). Shiite religious leader who headed Iran's government after the overthrow of the shah in 1979 (page 768).

Khrushchev, Nikita (krōōsh-**chôf′**) (1894–1971). Soviet leader (1953–1964) (page 717).

King, Martin Luther, Jr. (1929–1968). American civil rights leader (page 805).

Koch, Robert (1843–1910). German doctor who discovered the cause of tuberculosis (page 532).

Kohl, Helmut (1930–). West German chancellor who became chancellor of reunited Germany in 1990 (page 720).

Kossuth, Louis (kô-**sōōth′**) (1802–1894). Hungarian patriot (page 481).

Kublai Khan (**kōō′**blĭ **kän′**) (1215–1294). Mongol emperor (page 284).

L

Lalibela (lä′lĭ-bĕl-ə). Ethiopian king (1200–1230) (page 305).

Laozi (lou′dzŭ′) (604?–531? B.C.). The first great Chinese teacher of Taoism (page 140).

Lavoisier, Antoine (lä-vwä-zē-ā′) (1743–1794). French chemist who named oxygen (page 535).

Lenin, Vladimir Ilyich (1870–1924). Bolshevik leader who seized control of Russia in 1917 (page 646).

Leonardo da Vinci (də vĭn′chē) (1452–1519). Italian Renaissance painter, engineer, scientist, and inventor (page 334).

Leopold II (1835–1909). Belgian king who claimed the Congo Basin (page 594).

Lincoln, Abraham (1809–1865). 16th U. S. President, who held office during the Civil War (page 560).

Lindbergh, Charles (1902–1974). American aviator who made the first nonstop transatlantic flight (page 671).

Li Si (lē sē) (d. 208 B.C.). One of the founders of the Chinese philosophy Legalism (page 141).

Lister, Joseph (1827–1912). English surgeon who began the use of antiseptics in hospital operating rooms (page 532).

Locke, John (1632–1704). English political philosopher (page 419).

Louis XIV (1638–1715). French ruler who was called the "Sun King" (page 392).

Louis XVI (1754–1793). French king whose demand for higher taxes touched off the French Revolution (page 436).

Louis Napoleon (1808–1873). French president who became Emperor Napoleon III (page 480).

Louis Philippe (fĭ-**lēp′**) (1773–1850). French king known as the "Citizen King" (page 475).

Loyola, Ignatius (1491–1556). Spanish nobleman who founded the Society of Jesuits (page 342).

Luther, Martin (1483–1546). German monk and Protestant religious reformer (page 338).

M

MacArthur, Douglas (1880–1964). American general in World War II (page 702).

Machiavelli, Niccolo (mäk′ē-ə-vĕl′ē) (1469–1527). Florentine diplomat who wrote *The Prince* (page 329).

Magellan, Ferdinand (1480?–1521). Portuguese navigator whose fleet of ships were the first to circumnavigate the globe (page 353).

Malthus, Thomas (1766–1834). English economist and

minister who wrote *An Essay on the Principle of Population* (page 498).

Mandela, Nelson (1918–). Head of the African National Congress in South Africa; imprisoned from 1964 to 1990 (page 782).

Mansa Musa. Ruler of Mali (1312–1332) (page 299).

Mao Zedong (**mou′ dzŭ′ dōōng′**) (1893–1976). Chinese Communist leader who formed the People's Republic of China (page 677).

Marcos, Ferdinand (1917–1989) Philippine president who fled the country in 1986 after losing an election (page 749).

Marie Antoinette (ăn′twə-**nĕt′**) (1755–1793). French queen, wife of Louis XVI (page 440).

Marx, Karl (1818–1883). German political philosopher and economist whose theories laid the basis for the political-economic system called communism (page 500).

Mazzini, Giuseppe (mät-**tsē′**nē) (1805–1872). Italian revolutionary (page 483).

Mencius (**mĕn′**shē-əs) (372–289 B.C.). Chinese philosopher (page 140).

Mendel, Gregor (1822–1884). Austrian monk whose experiments laid the foundation for the science of genetics (page 538).

Mendeleev, Dmitri (mĕn′də-**lā′**əf) (1834–1907). Russian chemist who classified elements according to their atomic structure (page 535).

Menelik II (1844–1913). Ethiopian emperor who successfully fought off Italian domination (page 600).

Menes (**mē′**nēz) Egyptian pharaoh who established the first dynasty in the 3100's B.C. (page 36).

Metternich, Klemens von (**mĕt′**ər-nĭk) (1773–1859). Austrian prince and delegate at the Congress of Vienna (page 472).

Michelangelo (mĭ-kəl-**ăn′**jə-lō′) (1475–1564). Italian Renaissance sculptor, painter, architect, and poet (page 334).

Mitterrand, François (mē-tər-**än′**) (1916–). French socialist president (page 721).

Mohammed (570?–632). Founder of Islam (page 198).

Mohammed Ali (1769–1849). Egyptian ruler who worked to modernize and strengthen Egypt (page 592).

Monet, Claude (mō-**nā′**) (1840–1926). French impressionist painter (page 540).

Montesquieu, Baron de (**mŏn′**-tĕs-kyōō′) (1689–1755). French philosopher and author of *The Spirit of the Laws* (page 420).

Montezuma (mŏn′tə-**zōō′**mə) (1480?–1520). Aztec ruler who died in the Spanish conquest of Mexico (page 355).

More, Thomas (1478–1535). English statesman who wrote *Utopia* (page 331).

Moses (13th century B.C.). Hebrew prophet and lawgiver (page 44).

Mozart, Wolfgang Amadeus (**mōt′**särt) (1756–1791). Austrian composer (page 423).

Mugabe, Robert (1925–). First prime minister of Zimbabwe (page 784).

Murasaki Shikibu (11th century). Author of the Japanese court novel *The Tale of Genji* (page 288).

Mussolini, Benito (1883–1945). Italian Fascist leader; dictator of Italy from 1922 to 1945 (page 663).

Mwene Mutapa (**mwä′**nä mō-tä′pä) (15th century). Ruler of Great Zimbabwe (page 302).

N

Napoleon Bonaparte (1769–1821). French general who overthrew the Directory in 1799 and declared himself emperor in 1804; exiled to St. Helena in 1815 (page 446).

Nasser, Gamal Abdel (1918–1970). Egyptian leader (page 761).

Nebuchadnezzar (630?–562 B.C.). King of Babylon who conquered much of the Fertile Crescent (page 46).

Newton, Isaac (1642–1727). English mathematician and scientist who showed that all objects in the universe obey the same laws of motion (page 415).

Nicholas I (1796–1855). Russian czar who adopted a policy called Russification (page 525).

Nicholas II (1868–1918). Last Russian czar (page 645).

Nixon, Richard M. (1913–). 37th U. S. President and first to resign from office (page 738).

Nkrumah, Kwame (ən-**krōō′**mə) (1909–1972). Leader of the Gold Coast's independence movement (page 778).

O

Owen, Robert (1771–1858). English utopian socialist (page 499).

P

Pahlavi, Mohammed Reza (1919–1980). Iranian shah who was overthrown by Ayatollah Ruhollah Khomeini (page 767).

Pahlavi, Reza Shah (**pä′**-lä-vē) (1877–1944). Iranian leader (page 679).

Pankhurst, Emmeline (1858–1928). British reformer who organized the Woman's Social and Political Union (WSPU) (page 504).

Pasteur, Louis (păs-**tûr′**) (1822–1895). French chemist who discovered that bacteria caused many diseases (page 532).

Paul (A.D. 5?–67?). Early Christian missionary who developed many of the ideas that form the basis of Christianity (page 127).

Pavlov, Ivan (1849–1936). Russian scientist whose experiments with dogs led him to conclude that human actions are not always determined by conscious thought (page 539).

Pericles (pĕr'ĭ-klēz') (495?–429 B.C.). Leader of Athens during its "golden age" (page 80).

Peron, Juan (pĕ-rôn') (1895–1974). A former president of Argentina (page 797).

Perry, Matthew (1794–1858). American commodore who first opened Japan to foreign trade (page 582).

Peter the Great (1672–1725). Russian czar who began to westernize Russia (page 404).

Petrarch, Francesco (pē'trärk) (1304–1374). Italian poet (page 328).

Philip II (1527–1598). Spanish king who worked to expand the power of both Spain and the Roman Catholic Church (page 386).

Philip Augustus (1165–1223). French monarch who defeated the English and claimed English territories in northern France (page 240).

Picasso, Pablo (1881–1973). Spanish-born painter (page 540).

Pinochet, Augusto (pēn'ō-chĕt') (1915–). Chilean general who succeeded Allende (page 798).

Pizarro, Francisco (1470?–1541). Spanish explorer who defeated the Incas in Peru (page 355).

Plato (427–347 B.C.). Greek philosopher and author of *The Republic* (page 88).

Polo, Marco (1254?–1325?). Venetian trader whose account of his travels stimulated European interest in China (page 284).

Pretorius, Andreas (1799–1853). Dutch South African who was killed by Zulus while leading a group of trekkers out of British-ruled territory (page 594).

Ptolemy (tŏl'ə-mē) (367?–283 B.C.). Ruler of Egypt who established a dynasty centered in Alexandria (page 91).

R

Rameses II (răm'ĭ-sēz') Egyptian pharaoh (1304–1237 B.C.) who ruled during the Hebrews' exodus from Egypt (page 38).

Rasputin (răs-pyoo'tĭn) (1871?–1916). Self-described holy man who advised Russian czarina Alexandra (page 647).

Reagan, Ronald (1911–). 40th U. S. President (page 805).

Renoir, Pierre-Auguste (rĕn'wär') (1841–1919). French impressionist painter (page 540).

Rhodes, Cecil (1853–1902). Englishman who expanded British South African rule into the Rhodesias (page 599).

Ricardo, David (1772–1823). English economist (page 498).

Richelieu (rē-shə-loo') (1585–1642). Chief minister of France's Louis XIII (page 390).

Robespierre, Maximilien (rōbz'pē-âr') (1758–1794). French Jacobin responsible for the Reign of Terror (page 442).

Rommel, Erwin (1891–1944). German commander of the Nazi Afrika Corps in north Africa during World War II (page 693).

Roosevelt, Franklin D. (1882–1945). 32nd U. S. President, who held office during the Great Depression and World War II (page 672).

Roosevelt, Theodore (1858–1919). 26th U. S. President (page 561).

Rousseau, Jean Jacques (roo-sō') (1712–1778). French philosopher and writer (page 420).

Rutherford, Ernest (1871–1937). Scientist who developed a model for the structure of the atom (page 536).

S

Sadat, Anwar el- (1918–1981). Egyptian president who signed the Camp David Peace Accords (page 762).

Saint Benedict (480?–543). Italian monk who established the Benedictine order (page 213).

Saint Dominic (1170–1221). Founder of the Dominican order of friars (page 245).

Saint Francis of Assisi (1182–1226). Founder of the Franciscan order of friars (page 245).

Saint Patrick (389?–461?). Irish monk who converted the Irish to Christianity (page 214).

Sakharov, Andrei (1921–1989). Soviet physicist and dissident (page 726).

Sargon the Great. Ruler of Akkad in 2300's B.C., who created the world's first empire (page 31).

Sartre, Jean-Paul (sär'trə) (1905–1980). French existentialist writer (page 831).

Saud, Ibn (sä-ood') (1880–1953). Saudi Arabian king (page 679).

Shah Jahan (1592?–1666). Mogul ruler who built the Taj Mahal (page 275).

Shakespeare, William (1564–1616). English poet and playwright whose works include *Hamlet* (page 333).

Shaw, George Bernard (1856–1950). Irish-born English playwright (page 543).

Shelley, Mary (1797–1851). English author who wrote *Frankenstein* (page 477).

Shotoku. 6th-century Japanese prince and author of the Seventeen-Article Constitution (page 287).

Siddhartha Gautama (gä'tə-mə) (563?–483? B.C.). Founder of Buddhism (page 133).

Smith, Adam (1723–1790). Scottish economist who wrote *The Wealth of Nations* (page 498).

905

Socrates (sŏk′rə-tēz′) (470?–399 B.C.). Greek philosopher (page 87).

Sophocles (sŏf′ə-klēz′) (496?–406 B.C.). Greek dramatist who wrote *Antigone* and *Oedipus Rex* (page 86).

Staël, Madame de (stäl) (1766–1817). French Romantic writer (page 478).

Stalin, Joseph (1879–1953). Communist leader who followed Lenin as ruler of the Soviet Union; ruled as totalitarian dictator through the 1930's and World War II (page 654).

Stanley, Henry (1841–1904). American journalist and African explorer (page 593).

Stephenson, George (1781–1848). English engineer who developed the first practical locomotive (page 493).

Stravinsky, Igor (1882–1971). Russian-born composer (page 542).

Suleiman I (soo′lā-män) (1490?–1566). Sultan of the Ottoman Empire (page 278).

Sunni Ali (d. 1492). King of the Songhai people in Africa (page 299).

Sun Yat-sen (soon′ yät′sĕn′) (1866–1925). Leader of the Nationalist Revolution in China (page 579).

T

Thatcher, Margaret (1925–) First woman prime minister of Britain (page 721).

Thucydides (thoo-sĭd′ĭ-dēz) (471–400 B.C.). Greek historian (page 85).

Tokugawa Ieyasu (ē-ə-yä′-soo). 17th-century Japanese ruler who established the last shogunate to rule Japan (page 290).

Tolstoy, Leo (1828–1910). Russian author who wrote *War and Peace* (page 542).

Touré, Samori (tō-rä′). Late 19th-century Mandinka leader who resisted French forces in Western Africa for nearly twenty years (page 596).

Toussaint L'Ouverture, Pierre (too-săn′ loo-vĕr-tür′) (1743–1803). Haitian revolutionary and statesman (page 458).

Trotsky, Leon (1879–1940). Bolshevik leader (page 654).

Truman, Harry (1884–1972). 33rd U. S. President (page 702).

Tutu, Desmond (1931–). South African archbishop who won the Nobel Peace Prize in 1984 for his work against apartheid (page 785).

V

van Gogh, Vincent (văn gō′) (1853–1890). Dutch-born post-impressionist painter (page 540).

Venerable Bede (673–735). English monk who completed a history of the Church in England (page 212).

Verdi, Giuseppe (vär′de) (1813–1901). Italian composer (page 479).

Victor Emmanuel II (1820–1878). King of Sardinia and first king of a united Italy (page 513).

Virgil (70–19 B.C.). Roman who wrote the *Aeneid* (page 112).

Vladimir (965?–1015). Kievan prince who brought Christianity to Russia (page 191).

Voltaire (1694–1778). French philosopher and writer (page 420).

W

Wagner, Richard (väg′nər) (1813–1883). German composer (page 479).

Walesa, Lech (wä-lĕn′sä) (1943–). Polish labor leader and president (page 729).

Washington, George (1732–1799). Commander of the Continental Army and the first U. S. President (page 427).

Watt, James (1736–1819). Scottish inventor of a coal-burning steam engine (page 493).

Whitney, Eli (1765–1825). Inventor of the cotton gin (page 492).

William I (1797–1888). Prussian king who was Germany's first kaiser after Prussia's victory in the Franco-Prussian War (page 517).

William II (1859–1941). German kaiser who gave up his throne when Germany was defeated in World War I (page 521).

William the Conqueror (1027–1087). Duke of Normandy who defeated the Saxons at the Battle of Hastings and then became king of England (page 236).

Wilson, Woodrow (1856–1924). 28th U. S. President (page 633).

Woolf, Virginia (1882–1941). English author (page 674).

Wordsworth, William (1770–1850). English Romantic poet (page 476).

Wright, Orville (1871–1948) and **Wilbur** (1867–1912). American inventors who developed the first successful motor-powered airplane (page 670).

Wu Hou (woo′ hō′). Chinese empress (690–735) and the only woman in China to rule in her own right (page 281).

Wycliffe, John (wĭk′lĭf) (1320?–1384). Religious reformer who completed the first English translation of the Bible (page 265).

Y

Yoritomo Minamoto (1147–1199). Shogun and founder of the Kamakura shogunate (page 288).

Yuan Shikai (yü-än′ shĭr′kī′) (1859–1916). President of the Chinese Nationalist Party who set up a dictatorship (page 579).

Z

Zheng He (jŭng′ hŭ′). 15th-century Chinese admiral (page 285).

Text Credits and Sources

Grateful acknowledgment is made to authors, publishers, and other copyright holders for permission to reprint (and in some selections to adapt slightly) copyright material listed below. **27** From *Cro-Magnon Man* (*The Emergence of Man* series) by Tom Prideaux and the Editors of Time-Life Books, Inc. Time-Life Books, Inc., Publisher. Copyright © 1973 by Time, Inc. Used by permission. **33** From *Ancient Near Eastern Texts Relating to the Old Testament* (Third Edition with Supplement), edited by James B. Pritchard. Copyright © 1969 by Princeton University Press. Excerpts from "The Code of Hammurabi" adapted by permission of Princeton University Press. **36, 37** Quotations from two Egyptians reprinted in *The Ancient Egyptians*, edited by Adolph Ehrman. Copyright © 1966. Published by Methuen and Co. **51** From *Herodotus: History (Book I)*, translated by George Rawlinson. Published by John Murray, 1880. **66** Adapted from *The Laws of Manu with Extracts from the Seven Commentaries*, translated by Johann Georg Buhler. The Clarendon Press, 1886. **90** From *Thucydides: History of the Peloponnesian War*, translated by Rex Warner (Penguin Classics, 1954) pp. 117–119. Copyright © 1954 by Rex Warner. Reproduced by permission of Penguin Books, Ltd. **95** From *Thucydides: History of the Peloponnesian War*, translated by Rex Warner (Penguin Classics, 1954, 1972) p. 48. Copyright © Rex Warner, 1954. Reproduced by permission of Penguin Books, Ltd. **117** From *Roman Civilization: Selected Readings, Volume II, The Empire*, edited by Napthali Lewis and Meyer Reinhold. Copyright © 1951 Columbia University Press. Used by permission. **131** From *Tacitus: The Agricola and the Germania*, translated by H. Mattingley and revised by S. A. Hanford (Penguin Classics, 1948, 1970) pp. 105–106. Copyright © 1948, 1970 by the Estate of H. Mattingley. Copyright © 1970 by S. A. Hanford. Reproduced by permission of Penguin Books, Ltd. **138** From *The Edicts of Asoka*, edited and translated by N. A. Nikam and Richard McKeon. Copyright © 1959 by The University of Chicago Press. Reprinted by permission of The University of Chicago Press. **147** From *Sources of Chinese Tradition: Volume I*, compiled by Wm. Theodore de Bary, Wing-tsit Chan, and Burton Watson. Copyright © 1960 by Columbia University Press. Used by permission. **164** From *The Book of the Jaguar Priest*, translated by Maud Worcester Makemson. Copyright © 1951, Henry Schuman, Inc. Published by Harper & Row. **192** From writings of Archbishop Plano Carpini, reprinted in *A History of Russia*, by Nicholas V. Riasanovsky. Copyright © 1963 by Oxford University Press. **193** From a fifteenth-century Russian subject, reprinted in *Peasant Uprisings in Seventeenth-Century France, Russia, and China* by R. Mousnier. Copyright © 1970. Published by Harper & Row. **195** From *The Alexiad of the Princess Anna Comnena*, translated by Elizabeth A. S. Dawes. Copyright © 1967. Reprinted by permission of the publishers, Routledge and Kegan Paul, Ltd. **209** From *Avicenna on Theology* by Arthur J. Arberry. Copyright © 1951. Reprinted by permission of the publishers, John Murray, Ltd. **213** From *The Rule of St. Benedict*, edited and translated by Abbot Justin McCann. Copyright © 1952. Published by the Paulist Press. **227** From *Medieval Village, Manor, and Monastery* by G. G. Coulton. Copyright 1925, Cambridge University Press. Reprinted by permission of Cambridge University Press. **249** From a contemporary account of the Crusades, reprinted in *The Crusades* by Regine Pernoud. Published by G. P. Putnam's Sons. Copyright © 1962 by Martin Secker and Warburg Ltd. **253** From *Translations and Reprints from the Original Sources of European History*, edited by the Department of History of the University of Pennsylvania, University of Pennsylvania Press, 1895. **259** From *The Divine Comedy by Dante Alighieri*, translated by H. R. Huse. Copyright © 1954 by H. R. Huse. Reprinted by permission of Holt, Rinehart and Winston, Inc. **268** From *The Decameron* by Giovanni Boccaccio, translated by Richard Aldington. Doubleday and Company, Inc. Copyright © 1930 by Madame Catherine Guillaume. Reprinted by permission of Rosica Colin, Ltd. **285** From *Sources of Chinese Tradition*, compiled by Wm. Theodore de Bary, Wing-tsit Chan, and Burton Watson. Copyright © 1960 by Columbia University Press. Used by permission. **292** From *An Introduction to Haiku* by Harold G. Henderson. Copyright © 1958 by Harold G. Henderson. Reprinted by permission of Doubleday, a division of Bantam, Doubleday, Dell Publishing Group, Inc. **295** Adaptation from Prince Shotoku's Constitution, in "Nihongi: Chronicles of Japan from the Earliest Times to A.D. 697" by W. G. Aston in *The Transactions and Proceedings of the Japanese Society of London* (Supplement I). Published by Kegan Paul, Trench, Trubner and Co., Ltd., 1896. **299** From a fourteenth-century Arab scholar, reprinted in *The African Past* by Basil Davidson, published by Grosset and Dunlap. Copyright © 1967. **309** From *Ibn Battúta: Travels in Asia and Africa* by Ibn Battúta, translated and selected by H.A.R. Gibb. Copyright © 1929. Reprinted by permission of the publishers, Routledge and Kegan Paul Ltd. **322** From *Historia Del Nuevo Mundo* by Bernabe Cobo, translated by Benjamin Keen in *Latin American Civilization History and Society, 1492 to the Present.* Copyright © 1986. Reprinted by permission of Westview Press, Inc. **345** From Baldassare Castiglione *The Book of the Courtier*, translated by Leonard Eckstein Opdycke. Charles Scribner's Sons, 1903. **353–354** From a sailor's journal entry, reprinted in *The European Renaissance* by J. H. Parry. Copyright © 1968. Published by Harper & Row. **365** from *Readings in Latin-American Civilization 1492 to the Present*, edited by Benjamin Keen. Copyright © 1955. Reprinted by permission of Benjamin Keen. **377** From King Affonso, reprinted in *The African Past* by Basil Davidson. Copyright © 1964 by Little, Brown and Co. and Penguin Books Ltd. **383** From the autobiography of Olaudah Equiano, a former slave, in *Africa Remembered*, edited by Philip D. Curtin. Published by The University of Wisconsin Press. Copyright © 1967 by the Regents of the University of Wisconsin. **400** Adapted from the English Bill of Rights, 1689. **408** From *A King's Lessons in Statecraft: Louis XIV: Letters to His Heirs*, translated by Herbert Wilson. Published by T. Fisher Unwin, Ltd. Copyright © 1924. Extensive efforts to locate the rights holder were unsuccessful. If the rights holder sees this notice, he or she should contact the School Division Permissions Department, Houghton Mifflin Co., One Beacon Street, Boston, MA 02108. **430** From the Preamble to the Constitution of the United States. **433** From *Antony Van Leeuwenhoek and His "Little Animals,"* translated and edited by Clifford Dobell. Copyright © 1932 by Harcourt, Brace and Company. **438** From *The Declaration of the Rights of Man and Citizen*, 1789. **442** Quotation adapted from an eighteenth-century French revolutionary, reprinted in *The Era of the French Revolution, 1789–1799* by L. Gershoy. Published by Van Nostrand, 1957. **443** From the Decree of August 1793. **455** From a July 14, 1789, newspaper account of the storming of the Bastille, reprinted in *The Press in the French Revolution: A Selection of Documents Taken from the Press of the Revolution for the Years 1789–1794* by J. Gilchrist and W. Murray. Published by St. Martin's Press, 1971. **458** From *African Experience in Spanish America* by Leslie B. Rout. Copyright © 1977. Used by permission of the publisher, Cambridge University Press. **469** From a speech by Simón Bolívar, 1819. **478** Excerpt from *Don Juan* by Lord Byron from *English Romantic Writers* edited by David Perkins. Copyright © 1967, Harcourt, Brace and World. **486** From *The Reminiscences of Carl Schurz.* Copyright © 1907 by The McClure Company. **497** From *Hard Times* by Charles Dickens, published by Thomas Nelson and Sons, Ltd. **505** From *The English: A Social History 1066–1945* by Christopher Hibbert. Copyright © 1987 by Christopher Hibbert. Published by W. W. Norton and Company. **511**

908

Art Credits

Cover calligraphy: Jeffrey Broadkin.

Cover image (front and back): Cartonnage of Nespanetjerenpere. *(front)* Seth Joel, photographer. Reprinted from *Egyptian Treasures,* © 1978 by Harry N. Abrams, Inc. and The Brooklyn Museum. *(back)* Justin Kerr, photographer. The Brooklyn Museum, 35.1265, Charles Edwin Wilbour Fund.

Frontispiece: Michael Holford.

Illustrations on pages 31, 82, 85, 99, 109: Brian Delf. Page 27: Nancy Lambert-Brown. Pages 10–11, 68–69, 178–179, 270–271, 324–325, 410–411, 488–489, 550–551, 622–623, 708–709: Misuk Pak. Column art on pages 166–177 and 610–621: Quarasan. Column art on pages 323-1 through 323-12 and on 836–849: Chris Costello.

Maps on pages GR4, GR5, 26, 50, 65, 94, 116, 130, 163, 194, 208, 267, 294, 308, 321, 344, 364, 382, 407, 432, 454, 468, 485, 556, 566, 588, 607, 642, 660, 732, 774, 814: Precision Graphics. Map on page 823: Earth Surface Graphics. Maps on pages 23 and 825: Deborah Perugi.

All other maps by Donnelley Cartographic Services.

Charts and graphs on pages 23, 37, 114, 147, 227, 373, 521, 533, 548, 652, 674, 683, 706, 757, 788, 793, 823, 834: Earth Surface Graphics. Pages 260, 334: Timothy Jones. Pages 870–872: Graphics etcetera.

The following abbreviations are used for some sources from which several illustrations were obtained:

AL/AR—Alinari/Art Resource. AR—Art Resource. BA—Bettmann Archive. BBC/BA—BBC Hulton Picture Library/Bettmann Archive. BL—British Library. BM—British Museum. BN—Bibliothèque Nationale, Paris. BS—Black Star. GC—Granger Collection. GI/AR—Giraudon/Art Resource. HPS—Historical Pictures Service. IB—Image Bank. LB—Lee Boltin. MC—Mansell Collection. MFA—Museum of Fine Arts, Boston. MH—Michael Holford. MMA—Metropolitan Museum of Art. NGA—National Gallery of Art, Washington. NMM—National Maritime Museum, Greenwich. PML—Pierpont Morgan Library. PR—Photo Researchers. SC/AR—Scala/Art Resource. VAM—Victoria and Albert Museum, London. WC—Woodfin Camp. WW—Wide World.

v LB. **vi** Luis Villota/The Stock Market. **vii** *(top) Histoire d'Olivier de Castille* (detail) Ms. Fr. 12574, fol. 181 v, Flemish 15th century. Coll: BN. *(bottom)* Belt mask, ivory, Benin Tribe, Nigeria, c. A.D. 1550. Coll: MMA, Rockefeller Collection. Photo: LB. **viii** Louvre, SC/AR. **ix** *(top)* GI/AR. *(bottom)* Brown Brothers. **x** "Canton Factories" (detail), Chinese artist, oil on glass. Coll: Peabody Museum of Salem. Photo: Mark Sexton. **xi** AP/Wide World Photos. **xii** NASA. **xiv** *(left)* Coll: NMM. Photo: MH. *(right)* Lee Boltin. **xvi** NMM. **xvii** NMM. **xviii** "Geographer" (detail) by Jan Vermeer van Delft. Coll: Stadelsches Kunstinstitut, Frankfurt-am-Main. **xx–xxi** D & J Heaton/TSW/Click/Chicago. **12** Photo: Jean Vertut. **14** © Robert Frerck/Odyssey Productions. **17** "Frescoes of Tassili" (detail). Coll: Musée de L'Homme, Paris. Coll: Henri Lhote, Photo: Erich Lessing/Magnum. **19** L. Migdale/PR. **24** Arch. Photo/Vaga, New York/S.P.A.D.E.M. **28** LB. **30** BM. **32** MH. **37** Robert Caputo/Stock Boston. **39** LB. **40** AR. **41** MMA. **42** Hirmer Verlag, Munich. **45** AR. **52** Cartier-Bresson/Magnum. **55** MH. **57** (detail) Kula, Punjab Hills, early 18th century. Coll: © 1983, MFA, Ross-Coomaraswamy Collection. **58** Coll: MMA. Photo: LB. **61** Coll: MMA, Department of Far Eastern Art, "Great Bronze Age of China" exhibit, from Historical Museum, Beijing, People's Republic of China. **62** Erich Lessing/Magnum. **63** BN. **67** *(left)* Lascaux Cave (detail), France. FGTO. *(right)* "Laurel Leaf" Solutrean flint spear. MH.

70 Louvre-GI/AR. **73** AR. **75** BM. **77** Louvre, SC/AR. **79** Vatican Collection, SC/AR. **85** Robert Frerck/Odyssey Productions. **86** Gary Cralle/Image Bank. **88** MMA. **92** By Lysippus, marble, c. 6–4th century, B.C. Coll: Louvre. Photo: Erich Lessing/Magnum. **96** Relief of Roman Officers (detail), Coll: Louvre. **103** Vatican Collection, SC/AR. **104** Roman bas relief (detail), 1st century B.C. Coll: Staatliche Antikensammlung Muenchen/Studio Kopperman, Munich. **106** Vatican Collection, SC/AR. **110** Roger Wood, Kent. **111** Louis Renault/PR. *(inset)* J. Messerschmidt/Bruce Coleman. **113** Anthony King. **114** Anthony King. **118** Oliver Benn/TSW. **120** Erich Lessing/Magnum. **122** BM. **125** Vatican Collection, SC/AR. **127** Ronald Sheridan/The Ancient Art and Architecture Collection. **132** Werner Forman Archive. **134** Luis Villota/Stock Market. **138** Jagdish Agarwal/Dinodia Picture Agency. **141** An Keven/Picture Group. *(inset)* Yang Limen/Picture Group. **143** Robert Harding Associates. **144** "Ladies Preparing Newly Woven Silk" (detail) ink, colors, and gold on silk, by Emperor Hui Tseung, Northern Sung Dynasty, early 12th century. Coll: MFA, Chinese and Japanese Special Collection Fund. **148** From *Denkmaeler aus Aegypten und Aethiopien* by Richard Lepsius, Plate 136, Vol. 4. Courtesy of the Newberry Library, Chicago. **153** Dr. Timothy Kendall. **155** WC. **159** Werner Forman Archive. **161** Tony Morrison. **165** GC. **167** Field Museum, Chicago. **168** *(left)* c. 2350–2150 B.C. Coll: Baghdad, Iraq, Museum. Photo: Hirmer Verlag, Munich. *(right)* Robert Caputo/Stock Boston. **171** Robert Frerck/Odyssey Productions. **172** By Lysippus, marble, c. 6–4th century, B.C. Coll: Louvre. Photo: Erich Lessing/Magnum. **173** Relief of Roman Officers (detail). Coll: Louvre. **175** (detail) Kula, Punjab Hills, early 18th century. Coll: 1983, MFA, Ross-Coomaraswamy Collection. **176** Werner Forman Archive.

180 BM. **181** BL. **183** BM. *(inset)* GI/AR. **184** *Sinopsis Historiarum,* Juan Skylitzes, Biblioteca Nacional, Madrid/MAS. **186** D & J Heaton/TSW. **189** John Massey Stewart, London. **191** MH. **192** Interfoto MTI, Budapest. **196** Robert Frerck/Odyssey Productions. **198** New York Public Library, Spencer Collection. Astor, Lenox, and Tilden Foundations. **201** Alan Hutchison, Hutchison Library. **204** Ceramic wall title panel (detail), from pavilion of Shah Abbas the First, Isfahan, Islamic, late 16th or early 17th century. Coll: VAM. **205** From Traduction Litterale et Complete du Dr. J. C. Madrus, *Le Livre des Mille Nuits et une Nuit*/UCLA Special Collections. **206** M. Reichenthal/Stock Market. **210** MH. Carthage Mosaic. Coll: BM. **211** British Museum. **214** Moralized Bible (detail), Paris, Ms. 240, fol. 8, 1235. Coll: PML. **216** SC/AR. **219** Coll: Statens Historiske Museum, Stockholm. Photo: Werner Forman Archive. **220** *Histoire d'Olivier de Castille* (detail), Ms. Fr. 12574, fol. 181 v., Flemish, 15th century. Coll: BN. **221** Cary Wolinsky/Stock Boston. **224** *Hours of the Virgin* (detail), Ms. 399, fol. 12 v. Coll: PML. **228** BL. **231** SC/AR. **232** GC. **233** *Chronique de Hainout* (detail), Ms. 9242, fol. 274 v. Coll: Koninklijke Bibliotheek Albert Ier, Brussels. **237** MH. **239** M. Bertinetti/PR. **241** From *Vie et Miracles de Saint Louis,* Ms. S. 5716, fol. 16 and fol. 246/BN. **243** "Vita della Contessa Matilda di Canossa" (detail), A.D. 1115. Coll: Biblioteca Vaticana, Madeline Grimaldi Archives. **247** Fr. 22495f.43/BN. **250** Porterfield and Chickering/PR. **253** *Hours of the Virgin,* "July" (detail), Ms. 399, fol. 8 v. Coll: PML. **254** Sonia Halliday and Laura Lushington. **257** *Laurentius da Voltalina Kolleg des Henricus D'Allemania* (detail), Min 1233. Coll: Kupferstich Kabinett, Staatliche Museum Preussischer Kulturbesitz. **258** From *The Canterbury Tales,* EL26C9 fol. 153 v. Reproduced Courtesy of the Huntington Library, San Marino, California. **260** Sonia Halliday Photographs. **262** Ms. 13076.77 fol. 24/Koninklijke Bibliotheek Albert Ier, Brussels. **263** Froissart's *Chronicle,* miniature, "Battle of Crécy"/BN. **264** (detail) French-Flemish School, 15th Century. Coll: Archives Nationales. Photo: GI/AR. **269** (detail) Girandon/AR.

272 Georg Gerster/Comstock. **274** *(right)* Robert Harding Associates. *(left)* Khem Hara, gouache on paper. Coll: MMA,

ACKNOWLEDGMENTS

Rogers Fund, 1925. **276** Pete Turner/IB. **279** Sonia Halliday and Laura Lushington. **281** George Hulton/PR. **284** *(right)* Covered water jar, Ming Dynasty, c. 1522–1566. Coll: The Asia Society, New York, Mr. and Mrs. John D. Rockefeller 3rd Collection, 1979. Photo: Otto E. Nelson. *(left)* "Recumbent Water Buffalo," Chinese jade, possible Yuan Dynasty, A.D. 1280–1368 or Early Ming Dynasty, A.D. 1368–1644. Photo: MH. **287** MFA. **289** By Mitsuaki. Coll: BM. **292** Orion Press. **296** Georg Gerster/PR. **299** Georg Gerster/PR. **300** LB. **301** *(right)* Belt mask, ivory, Benin Tribe, Nigeria c. A.D. 1550. Coll: MMA, Rockefeller Collection. Photo: LB. *(left)* Mask of the Zaire Souge Tribe, wood. Coll: MMA, Rockefeller Collection. Photo: LB. **304** "Map of Catalane of 1375." Coll: BL. **305** Georg Gerster/ Comstock. **306** Marc and Evelyne Bernheim/WC. **310** Coll: BM. Photo: LB. **312** GC. **314** John Henebry, Jr. **319** John White, "Pomicoc"/BM. **323** Pete Turner/IB. **323-2** Dallas and John Heaton/TSW/Chicago, Ltd. **323-3** *(top)* MH. *(bottom)* AR. **323-4** Ceramic wall tile panel (detail), from pavilion of Shah Abbas the First, Isfahan, Islamic, late 16th or early 17th century. Coll: VAM. **323-5** SC/AR. **323-7** *Chronique de Hainout* (detail), Ms. 9242, fol. 274v. Coll: Koninklijke Bibliotheek Albert Ier, Brussels. **323-8** *(top)* From *The Canterbury Tales* EL26C9 fol. 153v. Reproduced Courtesy of the Huntington Library, San Marino, California. *(bottom)* Sonia Halliday and Laura Lushington. **323-9** (detail) French-Flemish School. 15th century. Coll: Archives Nationales. Photo: GI/AR. **323-10** *(top)* Pete Turner/IB. *(bottom)* C George Gerster/Comstock, Inc. Benin tribe, Nigeria c. A.D. 1550. coll: MMA, Rockefeller Collection. Photo: LB. **GR12** © Xavier Zimbardo/Gamma-Liaison.

326 AR. **328** Copy of "Map of Catena" (detail), Florence, 1490. Coll: Museum of Florence. Photo: SC/AR. **330** All rights reserved, Kunsthistorisches Museum, Vienna. **331** (detail) Coll: BM. **332** William Shakespeare (attributed to John Taylor)/The National Portrait Gallery, London. *(inset)* Drawing by Walter Hodges, Courtesy of the Folger Shakespeare Library. **334** "School of Athens" (detail) by Raphael. Coll: Vatican. Photo: SC/AR. **335** *(bottom)* Michelangelo, "Pièta." St. Peter's, Rome/ Robert Harding Associates. *(top)* Louvre, SC/AR. **336** *(bottom)* Isabella Stewart Gardner Museum, Boston/Art Resource. *(top)* All rights reserved, Kunsthistorisches Museum, Vienna. **338** SC/AR. **341** (detail) By Hans Holbein the Younger. Coll: Barberini Gallery, Rome. Photo: SC/AR. **346** *(left)* NMM. Photo: MH. *(right)* "Francesco Roselli," Florence, c. 1508. NMM. **349** Photo: AL-Brogli/AR. **352** NMM. **355** New York Historical Society. **357** Navajo pictograph of Spanish army/priest (detail), Canyon de Chelly. Photo: Robert Frerck/Odyssey Productions. **358** "Henry Hudson and Son Adrift in Hudson's Bay" (detail), anonymous. Coll: Tate Gallery/Art Resource. **360** BM. **362** "Chief of the Taensa Indians Receiving La Salle, March, 1682" (detail) by George Catlin. Coll: NGA, Paul Mellon Collection. **366** "Return from Brazil of the Dutch Fleet" (detail) by H. C. Vroom. A1361. Rijksmuseum-Stichting, Amsterdam. **369** "Geographer" (detail) by Jan Vermeer van Delft. Coll: Stadelsches Kunstinstitut, Frankfurt-am-Main. Photo: Jurgen Hinrichs. **374** 1786c.9, Plate v. BL. **377** Jean-Loup Charmet. **380** "Slave Deck of Albany Prize to HMS *Albatross.*" Coll: NMM. **384** A7861/NMM. **388** SC/AR. **393** (detail) Coll: Museum of Versailles. (photo) Réunion Des Musées Nationaux Paris, France. *(inset)* SC/AR. **397** Bridgeman Art Library/AR. **398** Scottish National Portrait Gallery. **403** George Holton/PR. **404** MH. **409** (detail) Coll: Galleria del Academia, Florence. Photo AL/AR.

412 BN. **414** Photo: D. E. Smith Collection, Columbia University. *(inset)* SC/AR. **418** GC. **421** (detail) by Torelli. Photo: GC. **422** "First Reading of 'L'Orphelin de Chine' at Home of Madame Geoffrin" (detail) by Lemonnier, 1725. Coll: Musées des Beaux Art, Rouen. *(inset)* GI/AR. **423** "Mozart as a Child with His Father and His Sister" (detail), by Louis Carmotelle. Coll: Musée Carnavalet, Paris. Photo: GI/AR. **426** Museum of the City of New York, The Harry T. Peters Collection. **427** (detail) By Rembrandt Peale, 1805. Coll: New York Historical Society. **428** "Washington Reviewing His Troops," by William Trego. Coll: The Valley Forge Historical Society. **429** (detail) by Joseph Siffred Duplessis. Coll: MMA Bequest of Michael Friedsam, 1931, The Friedsam Collection. **430** GC. **434** Jacques-Louis David, "Napoleon in His Study" (detail), dated 1812. National Gallery of Art, Washington, Samuel H. Kress Collection. **436** Jean-Loup Charmet. **437** MC. **439** Photographie Bulloz, Paris. **441** SC/AR. **442** Photographie Bulloz, Paris. **443** GI/AR. **444** MC. **447** SC/AR. **449** Adam Wolfitt/WC. **451** Ernest Meissonier, "Campagne de France 1814," RF 1862 Louvre/Art Pompier. **452** GC. **456** Robert Frerck/Odyssey Productions. **458** GC. **459** Photo: Courtesy of Geomundo, monthly magazine © Editorial America, S.A. **463** "Gauchos in a Horse Corral" by James Walker. Coll: Thomas Gilcrease Institute of American History and Art, Tulsa, Oklahoma. **465** "Louis Hoppe Meyenberg's Farm, Williams Creek Settlement by La Grange, Fayette County, Texas." Coll: Courtesy of the San Antonio Museum Association, San Antonio, Texas. **466** Vintage albumen print, c. 1860. Coll: Bancroft Library, University of California, Berkeley. **469** HPS. **470** GI/ARCRL21706. **475** "Greek War of Independence" (detail) by Peter Heinrich von Hess, 1828. Photo: Archives Photographique Larousse. **477** John Constable, "Wivenhoe Park, Essex," 1816. NGA, Widener Collection. **478** GI/AR. **481** HPS. **482** Interfoto/MTI, Budapest. **487** "The Spirit of '76" (detail) by Archibald M. Willard, Board of Selectmen, Abbot Hall, Marblehead, Ma.

490 BA. **492–493** MC. **494** HPS. **497** GC. **499** MC. **500** HPS. **503** BM. **504** MC. **507** Brown Brothers. **508** Jean-Loup Charmet. **511** MC. **512** Moro, Rome. **514** Coll: Museo Nazionale del Risorgimento, Turin. Photo: AR. **515** SC/AR. **518** HPS. **523** All rights reserved, Kunsthistorisches Museum, Vienna. **526** Tass/Sovfoto. **529** HPS. **530** GC. **532** *(top)* "St. Martins-in-the Fields" (detail) by William Logsdail, Tate Gallery/ Art Resource. *(bottom)* "Pasteur in His Laboratory" (detail) by Albert Edelfelt, 1885. Coll: Versailles Museum. Photo: Lauros-GI/AR. **534** "Iron Workers" (detail) by Adolph von Mensel, c. 1875. Coll: Nationalgalerie, East Berlin. **536** Brown Brothers. **537** BA. **538** GC. **541** *(bottom left)* Auguste Renoir, "A Girl with a Watering Can," 1876. NGA, Chester Dale Collection. *(top)* Vincent van Gogh, "The Starry Night," 1889, oil on canvas, 29 × 36¼". Coll: MOMA, New York. Acquired through the Lillie P. Bliss bequest. *(bottom right)* George Braques, "La Pêcheuse," 13 oeuvres du MAM, réparés pour l'art du XXième Siècle/AR © ARS, NY/S.P.A.D.E.M., 1989. **542** GC. **545** BA.

552 E. T. Archive. **554–555** "Passage of El-Guisr" by Edouard Rion from the book *Inauguration of the Suez Canal* by G. Nicloe, 1869. Coll: BL. **556** New York Public Library, Special Collections. **561** Library of Congress. **564** HPS. **568** "An English Dignitary Being Transported by Elephant with an Armed Escort" (detail), 18th century. Coll: VAM. Photo: MH. **570** "British East Indiaman at Calcutta" (detail) by Frans Balthezar Solvyens, 1794. Coll: Peabody Museum of Salem. Photo: Mark Sexton. **571** From *History of the Indian Mutiny* by Charles Ball, London, 1858–59. Coll: BL. **573** The Peabody Museum, Salem. Photo: Mark Sexton. **574** "Canton Factories" (detail), Chinese artist, oil on glass. Coll: Peabody Museum of Salem. Photo: Mark Sexton. **576** "The Real Trouble Will Come With the Wake," Puck, August 15, 1900. **577** California Museum of Photography, Keystone-Mast Collection, Neg. 73994 ku. University of California. **580** BBC/BA. **582** By Yoshitoshi, 1949-5-14-06, BM. **584** "Women Watching Stars," by Ota Chou, 1936. Coll: National Museum of Modern Art, Tokyo. Photo: Bradley Smith. Laurie Platt Winfrey, Inc. **585** Orion Press. **586** 1946-9-091(1-3), BM. **590** Larry Tackett/Tom Stack & Associates. **591** (detail) By Carl Sohn, 1882. By courtesy of the Royal Collection, London. **593** GC. **594** Dispensary at Msalabani, present-day Tanzania, c. 1890. Photo: The United Society for the Propagation

910

of the Gospel. **595** Print by Samuel Daniel. Coll: BM. Photo: Fotomas Index, London. **598** Roland Jacobs. **599** Roland Jacobs. **600** Mary Evans Picture Library. **601** Mary Evans Picture Library. **605** Normal School at Antananarivo, Madagascar, established by London Missionary Society, 1879. Photo: HPS. **611** AR. **612** Coll: Museum of Versailles. Photo: Service de Documentation Photographique de la Réunion des Musées Nationaux. **613** (detail) By Torelli. Photo: GC. **614** "George Washington at Verplanck's Point, N.Y., 1782 after Victory at Yorktown" (detail), 1790. Coll: The Henry Francis du Pont Winterthur Museum. **615** Ernest Meissonier, "Campagne de France 1814," RF 1862 Louvre/Art Pompier. **616** BA. **617** Moro, Rome. **618** Auguste Renoir, "A Girl with a Watering Can," 1876. NGA, Chester Dale Collection. **619** "An English Dignitary Being Transported by Elephant with an Armed Escort" (detail), 18th century. Coll: VAM. Photo: MH.

621 Orion Press. **624** Topham/The Image Works. **626** Keystone/Three Lions. **631** U.S. Army. **632–633** Brown Brothers. **633** Imperial War Museum. **635** Brown Brothers. **639** Culver Pictures. **640** (right) GC. (left) Roger-Viollet. **644** Tass/Sovfoto. **646** A La Vieille Russie, Inc. **648** Anne S. K. Brown Military Collection, Brown University Library. **651** Sovfoto/Eastfoto. **655** Sovfoto/Eastfoto. **656** Stuart Cohen/Comstock. **662** Culver Pictures. **664** WW. (inset) by Adolfo Busi, 1928. Civiche Raccolte d'Arte Applicata ed Incisioni. **666** BA. **667** Roger-Viollet. **668** WW. **669** AR/ARS, NY/S.P.A.D.E.M., 1989. **671** HPS. **672** Culver Pictures. **675** 1940, The Walt Disney Company. **677** Sovfoto/Eastfoto. **679** HPS. **684** FPG. **689** GC. **690** Karsh, Ottawa/WC. **693** Novosti from Sovfoto. **696** UPI/Bettmann Newsphotos. **698** National Archives. **701** UPI/Bettmann Newsphotos. **703** WW. **707** Culver Pictures, Inc.

710 David Pollock/The Stock Market. **716–717** Shostal/Superstock. **719** BS. **721** John Launois/BS. **722** Peter Jordan/Gamma Liaison. **727** Jasmin/Gamma Liaison. **729** Anthony Suau/ABC News/Black Star. **734** Andy Caulfield/Image Bank. **738** A. Jongen/BS. **740** Cartier-Bresson/Magnum. **742** © Brian Brake/Photo Researchers, Inc. **743** Johangir Gazdar/WC. **745** Chuck Fishman/WC. (inset) Ethan Hoffman/Archive Pictures **747** Diego Goldberg/Sygma. **749** Sygma. **751** © Philip Jones Griffith/Magnum Photos. (inset) © James Pickerall/Black Star. **753** Ian Berry/Magnum. **754** Magnus Bartlett/WC. **758** James Willis/Tony Stone Worldwide. **761** Alon Reininger/WC. **762** J. P. Laffont/Sygma. **764** Ricki Rosen/SABA. **766** Minosa-Scorpio/Sygma. **768** Karai/Sygma. **772** Philip Jones Griffiths/Magnum Photos. **776** Robert Frerck/Odyssey Productions. **778** UPI/Bettmann Archive. **780** David Moore/BS. **782** From *Herblock on All Fronts* (New American Library, 1980). **786** AP/Wide World Photos. **789** David Burnett/WC. **790** Bruno Barbey/Magnum. **794** Bob Daemmrich. **796** (detail) By Diego Rivera. Photo: Robert Frerck/TSW/Click/Chicago. **798** © Bob Strong/Sipa Press. **802** © Peter Menzel/Stock, Boston. **805** Bob Fitch/BS. **809** Robert Trippett/Sipa Press. **811** Donald E. Waite/Bruce Coleman, Inc. **812** Sygma. **816** NASA. **818** Jet Propulsion Laboratory. **820** David Cross/*Time* Magazine. **820** F. McConnaughey/PR. **824** © Sygma. **827** Peter Turnley/Black Star. **830** (center) Ezra Stoller/ESTO. (top left) René Burri/Magnum. (bottom left) Peter Aaron/ESTO. (bottom right) Francisco Hidalgo/Image Bank. (top right) Tibor Bognar/The Stock Market. **835** NASA. **837** Topham/The Image Works. **839** Roger-Viollet. **841** National Archives. **843** AP/Wide World Photos. **844** © James Pickerall/Black Star. **845** Setboun/Sipa Press [108.684]. **847** AP/Wide World Photos. **849** NASA.

This index includes references not only to the text but also to pictures (*p*), charts (*c*), graphs (*g*), and maps (*m*). Page numbers marked n refer to footnotes.

INDEX

INDEX

INDEX

INDEX

921

923

INDEX

INDEX

933

935

INDEX

INDEX

PORTFOLIO OF WORLD ART MASTERPIECES

THE ANCIENT WORLD

Art reveals the interests and values of societies and frequently gives intimate and unique glimpses of how people actually lived. In portraits and statues, whether of gods, ghanas, saints, samurai, maharanas, or merchants, it preserves the memory and fame of men and women who shaped societies. In paintings, drawings, and carvings it also shows how people worked, played, relaxed, suffered, and triumphed. Art, therefore, is extremely useful to the historian, especially for distant periods and remote cultures where written records are scarce or hard to understand. Every work of art has meaning and has something of its own to say.

The art of early societies, apart from public buildings such as temples, mosques, and shrines, was created for an aristocratic elite and reflected their tastes and values. Only a wealthy Greek could afford to buy a richly painted vase or wine cup. Only a wealthy Roman family could paint the walls of its house in dazzling fresco. And only affluent Chinese could support the luxurious lifestyles depicted in their court scenes. The Royal Standard of Ur, *below,* shows aspects of Sumerian society in peacetime. The upper band of the standard, a triangular box on a pole used on ceremonial occasions, illustrates a royal banquet. In the lower band herdsmen lead animals. *(By courtesy of the Trustees of the British Museum.)*

As the following Egyptian, Han, and Greek scenes reflect, however, competition and rigorous sport were frequent themes of ancient art. Treated in an exuberant and light-hearted manner by the Etruscan and Han artists, these subjects assumed an increasingly military character as the sphere and nature of conflict changed and the struggle for empire grew fundamental to political development.

Art shows the changes and continuity of life and the impact of societies and cultures on one another. The scenes of agricultural work and commerce common in ancient art remained popular in the Middle Ages. Inspired by the rise of Christianity and Islam, however, early medieval artists turned to the illustration of religious faith.

937

938

CAT
FOWL
FISH
THROW STICK
DECOY
PAPYRUS BOAT
PAPYRUS
LOTUS

Egyptian Tomb-Painting *(above)* Egyptian artists laid heavy emphasis on the physical enjoyment after death of the ordinary pleasures of life. The hunting of birds in the valley of the Nile was an economic necessity for the poor and a favorite sport of the rich. In this fresco the noble hunter and his family take a leisurely journey through a swamp, with the hunting of birds merely the excuse for the outing. *(Reproduced by permission of the Trustees of the British Museum)*

Queen Nefertari *(next page)* Egyptian art sought to maintain the dignity of the pharaoh and the royal family. Among the interesting artistic features of this fresco, which portrays Queen Ahmes-Nefertari (around 1100 B.C.), are those that would later influence Greek art, including such details as the pose of the queen, her clothing, and the vegetation in the background. *(Reproduced by permission of the Trustees of the British Museum)*

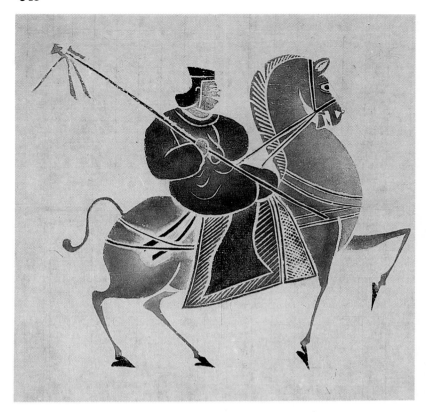

Prancing Horse *(left)* Cavalry was an important part of Chinese armies in the Han period (page 142). Here the artist has depicted both the strength and delicacy of the horse. The cavalryman carries a lance decorated with a ribbon, and the entire scene is more festive than military. *(E. T. Archive)*

Ladies of the Court *(below)* A gentle and elegant side of Chinese court life radiates from this illustration, painted in ink and color on silk, of court ladies being instructed by their teacher. Ladies of the court were expected to be graceful, well-bred, and stimulating. *(E. T. Archive)*

Buddhist Art in India Buddhist wall paintings from the Gupta period (page 138) survive at Ajanta, in south-central India. Though religious in inspiration, they show scenes of everyday life, like this detail of a royal servant holding a dog on a leash. *(Satish Pavashaw/Dinodia Picture Agency)*

Greeks at Work and at Play Athenian vase-painting was a form of art that often produced glimpses of daily life, especially in aristocratic households. The scene below represents how the women of the house produced woolen cloth, from the spinning of yarn to the completion of the cloth itself, held here by two women. *(The Metropolitan Museum of Art, Fletcher Fund, 1931)* On the right a hunter and his dog set off for a day of hunting. The artist has caught the excitement of the moment when the pair are about to depart. The first stop of the young man and his dog might be at the house of a friend or at a meeting place where several people would make up a party for a day of hunting, exercise, and fun. *(Courtesy, Museum of Fine Arts, Boston, The Francis Bartlett Fund)*

Etruscan Piper *(next page)* Much of Etruscan art, like that of Minoan Crete, depicts the lighter side of life. This young man plays the *aulos,* a Greek musical instrument. The *aulos,* which was musically highly versatile, was very popular, especially among those who liked to dance. Here the young piper dances forever in rhythm to his own playing. *(Scala/Art Resource)*

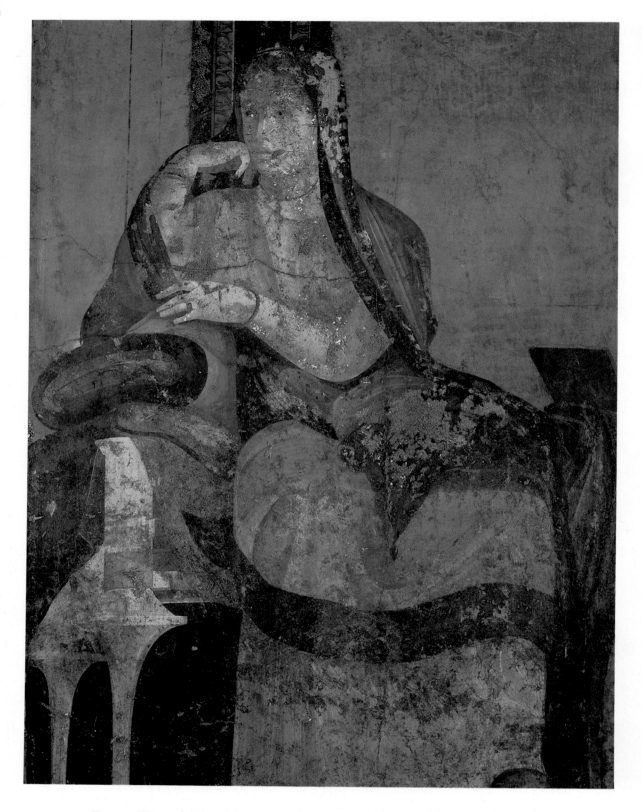

Roman Woman One of the best sources of knowledge about Roman painting is the city of Pompeii (page 113), from which this picture comes. The woman here demonstrates from her pose and dress some of the important values expected of Roman women: dignity, serenity, and modesty. *(Scala/Art Resource)*

MEDIEVAL TIMES

The art of early societies, apart from public buildings such as cathedrals, mosques, and temples, was created for an aristocratic elite and reflected the tastes and values of that high-born class. Only a rich Aztec warrior could afford the ornate necklace shown on page 947. Only a wealthy European nobleman could commission an illuminated manuscript as exquisite as *Les Très Riches Heures du Jean, Duc de Berry* (see page 951).

Nonetheless, one of the most impressive examples of early medieval art is the series of mosaics from San Vitale, Ravenna, Italy. In the scene *below,* the Empress Theodora (wife of Justinian) and her courtiers bring an offering to the sanctuary of Christ, just as the Three Kings had brought gifts to the Christ-Child (Matthew 2:8–10), an episode illustrated on the hem of Theodora's gown. The thousands of pieces of glass and stone that constitute this mosaic brilliantly reveal the portrait of Theodora (page 182) and the ritualistic character of the Byzantine court. *(Scala/Art Resource.)*

One of the primary functions of art during the Middle Ages was to teach. Books were considered especially valuable objects because of the skill, time, and precious materials needed to produce them. Copies of books of Christian psalms or of the Islamic Koran taught the reader the tenets of his or her faith and also represented the wealth of the possessor.

Art shows the changes and continuity of life and the impact of societies and cultures on one another. Just as the religious art of the early Middle Ages replaced the pagan art of antiquity, the art of the later Middle Ages increasingly displayed worldly rather than spiritual interests, a change in direction that echoed much of the art—also inspired by a wealthy urban class—of the Song Dynasty in China (see page 952).

946

Visigothic Eagle *(below, left)* Sixth century. The eagle was a standard symbol of nobility and power among the Germanic peoples. A fine example of Visigothic craftsmanship, this richly jewelled eagle—worn as a cloak clasp or as a brooch—could be afforded only by the wealthiest and most powerful members of the nobility. *(Walters Art Gallery, Baltimore)*

Ostrogothic Buckle and Clasp *(below, right)* Even before their migrations, Ostrogothic workmen had achieved a high degree of craftsmanship—as these jewels illustrate. Both are elaborately embossed with inset enameled stones. Men wore the clasp on the right shoulder, women on both shoulders. *(Walters Art Gallery, Baltimore)*

Aztec Jewelry *(next page, top)* Aztec men and women of the warrior class loved elaborate jewelry such as this rich necklace and earrings of cast gold, one of the few examples of Aztec artistry to escape the Spanish melting pot. *(Dumbarton Oaks Research Library and Collections, Washington)*

Gold Crown *(next page, bottom)* A crown worn as a sign of royalty, this intricately wrought gold diadem (about 900–1000) is a stunning example of South Asian craftsmanship. Indian or Pakistani in origin, it probably was created in Kashmir. *(Kronos Collection)*

Opening Pages of a Koran *(above)*, made in Egypt about 850 by Mohammed ibn al-Wahid. As these intricately designed pages reflect, classical Islamic tenets forbade the representation of human beings in art. To celebrate the teachings of Mohammed, Muslims instead developed an elaborate script that itself served as decoration. *(The Granger Collection)*

Arghan Khan with Two of His Wives and His Son, Ghazan *(next page)*, from the illuminated manuscript of Rashid-al-Din (Persia, about 1350–1400). Persian artists used vivid and glowing colors, giving their work an enameled appearance. This scene suggests the refined pleasures of the Persian court—conversation, poetry, chess, and music. *(Bibliothèque Nationale, Paris/Robert Harding)*

حکایت

اجکامی که اباقاخان بعد ازطوس دربان کلیات مصالح ملک فرمود

وبعد ازانک ازطوعها ازعترت فارغ شده بشبرشاه رلیغ را باطراف ملک روانه داشتند نمدن زبان سعادت دعیت اجان شهریف آرام یافت اکماه شاه زادگارد

Saint Nicholas and the Emperor Constantine *(above, left)* In the High Middle Ages, this fourth-century bishop enjoyed enormous popularity throughout the Christian world. His image appeared on Byzantine seals; artists represented him more frequently than any other saint except the Virgin; and nearly four hundred churches were dedicated to him in England alone. Because of Nicholas's reputation as the patron of youth and the custom in the Netherlands of giving children presents on his feast day (December 6), the institution of Santa Claus derives from him.

This scene illustrates the famous legend that Nicholas appeared before the emperor Constantine, enthroned at right with regal headband, and ordered him to release three prisoners. *(The Metropolitan Museum of Art, Gift of Glencairn Foundation, 1980)*

The Apostle Jude Thaddeus *(above, right)* Since stained glass (page 261) was produced in the cathedral or abbey workshop near the stone sculpture that it was to accompany, the glass often resembled the architectural sculpture. This mid-thirteenth-century portrait of the apostle Jude Thaddeus suggests the monumental strength of a statue. The artist pieced the stained glass together as we would a jigsaw puzzle. *(Walters Art Gallery, Baltimore)*

Les Très Riches Heures du Jean, Duc de Berry *(next page)* This illustrates March in a manuscript book of calendar miniatures produced for the duke of Berry, brother of the king of France. With exquisite detail the artists capture four scenes of agricultural life in the early fifteenth century. A shepherd with a dog guards a flock of sheep; three peasants prune vines while another works in a different field; and an aged farmer guides a wheeled plow and oxen. Symbolically, a vast castle dominates the landscape. *(Giraudon/Art Resource)*

Chinese Tapestry Attributed to the Emperor Hui-Tsung of the Song dynasty (1082–1135). This tapestry scene depicts women pounding silk. A talented painter, Hui-Tsung may have copied the scene from an eighth-century Tang work or his court artists may have done so. Although the hair styles and garments are inaccurate, the work is still one of the earliest and finest examples of Chinese art. *(Courtesy, Museum of Fine Arts, Boston, Chinese and Japanese Special Fund)*

LATER MIDDLE AGES AND THE RENAISSANCE

The art of the later Middle Ages, a time that saw the emergence of a rich urban middle class, increasingly displayed worldly rather than spiritual interests. In the Renaissance, portraiture became a common artistic form, a reflection of the new era's emphasis on individualism. Prominent patrons used art to display their wealth, power, and social status, as is evident in Gozzoli's *Journey of the Magi* (page 955). Europeans remained deeply religious but wished to reconcile Christian belief with classical art's emphasis on human dignity and their own worldly concerns.

These interests are evident as well in the works of the Mogul and Persian royal courts. As trade carried the techniques and media of cultures around the world, individual societies learned and adapted them to convey their own particular messages. The Muslim artist who painted the imaginary meeting between Emperor Jahangir and Shah Abbas, set amidst European and Chinese goods *(next page),* displays both his faith in the power of Islam and pleasure in the material world. In the remarkable Persian scene *below,* Chinese building tiles were used to depict a European merchant showing cloth to a lady. *(The Metropolitan Museum of Art, Rogers Fund, 1905.)*

Long before Portuguese explorers arrived in Africa, however, Benin sculptors had established a rich artistic tradition. Commemorative busts of royalty (page 960), though serving a religious purpose, glorified the king and his court. African rulers demanded that artists remain within palace confines, a practice later popular in Edo Japan and Louis XIV's France.

Jahangir and Abbas *(facing page)* In this imaginary scene the Mogul emperor Jahangir (left) entertains the Persian shah Abbas. Above, angels hold a semicircular row of golden orbs bearing the words, "Likeness of His Majesty Nur-ad-din Jahangir Padshah." At lower left is Asaf Khan, Jahangir's brother-in-law; at lower right, Khan Alam, Jahangir's ambassador to the court of Abbas. Scholars have identified the dark table and white pitcher as Italian, the brown porcelain cup as Chinese, and the glass vases as Venetian. Inscriptions at top and bottom hail Jahangir and Abbas as heroes and world conquerors united to bring peace to all peoples. *(Courtesy of the Freer Gallery of Art, Smithsonian Institution, Washington)*

Journey of the Magi *(below)* Benozzo Gozzoli (about 1459). Few Renaissance paintings better illustrate art in the service of aristocratic families, in this case the Medici family (page 327). Commissioned by Piero de' Medici to adorn his palace chapel, everything in this fresco painting—the large crowd, the feathers and diamonds worn by many of the riders, the African servant in front—serve to emphasize the power and wealth of the Medici. Although the painting has as its subject the Biblical story of the Magi (the three kings), there is nothing especially religious about it. *(Scala/Art Resource)*

Lo Sposalizio (Wedding) *(next page)* Raphael (about 1504). Younger than Michelangelo and Leonardo da Vinci but considered their equal as a Renaissance master painter, Raphael produced this painting of the marriage of Mary and Joseph when the artist was just 21 years old. It shows Raphael's superb grasp of symmetry and perspective (page 334). The temple in the background suggests his genius as an architect. *(Scala/Art Resource)*

Daimyo Residence *(below)* This stunningly elegant room with its lengthy walls, sliding screens, and precious objects—such as the Chinese ceramics, incense burners, and tea ceremony instruments—all illustrate the authority, power, and wealth of the Japanese lords (page 289). From the room's raised platform, the daimyo received his guests, issued orders to his servants, and carried out his administrative duties. *(The Tokugawa Art Museum, by permission of the International Society for Educational Information, Tokyo)*

Ginevra de Benci *(below)* Leonardo da Vinci (1452–1519). Da Vinci painted this Florentine lady early in his career, when he was about 22. Her pale face stands out against the dark juniper tree—*ginepra* in Italian, a reference to her name—in the background. Its expression of a deep inner life led the writer Vasari to say of the painting, "it looked like Ginevra herself and not like a picture." Work on this portrait perhaps prepared da Vinci for the *Mona Lisa* (page 335), which he started soon afterward. *(National Gallery of Art, Washington; Ailsa Mellon Bruce Fund)*

A Woman Peeling Apples Pieter de Hooch (HOHK) (1629–1677). Stability, seriousness, and thrift are idealized in this Dutch scene. Like other Dutch master painters, this artist emphasized realistic detail and excelled in the depiction of light filtering through a window. *(Reproduced by permission of the Trustees of the Wallace Collection)*

Portrait of a Merchant Jan Gossaert (GOSS-art) (about 1530). The banker sits at his desk with quills and inkstand; business letters hang on racks behind him. The skeptical expression on his face probably reflects the cautious nature of someone whose business is lending money. Gossaert did much of his work at Antwerp, then the commercial capital of Europe. *(National Gallery of Art, Washington; Ailsa Mellon Bruce Fund)*

Colombian Figure Pendant *(above)* about 1400–1600. The Tairona, who lived on the Caribbean side of Colombia, successfully resisted imperialism for almost one hundred years, succumbing to the Spanish only at the end of the sixteenth century. This male figure, with a headdress that intricately combines bird and animal heads with spiral elements, has a decidedly fierce air, its eyes glaring from beneath the visor. Warrior or not, the bejeweled figure was certainly intended to depict someone rich and powerful. *(The Metropolitan Museum of Art, Gift of H. L. Bache Foundation, 1969)*

Head of Queen Mother, Benin, about sixteenth century *(right)*. West African craftsmen from the kingdom of Benin produced works in bronze of great technical sophistication. This head probably memorialized the mother of a king and served a religious purpose. Note the choker of gold links, symbolic of her rank and wealth. *(British Museum/Werner Forman Archive)*

THE EARLY MODERN PERIOD

As values changed, so did major artistic themes. Europeans of the sixteenth and seventeenth centuries remained deeply religious and showed a new interest in the world around them. Their middle-class attitudes and experiences and their appreciation of agricultural life replaced the activities and interests of a small, wealthy aristocratic class as the subject matter of art. The scenes of everyday life presented in seventeenth-century painting were considered interesting in themselves and worthy of high art.

In the later seventeenth century, the court baroque style, inspired by the rise of absolute rulers, spread throughout Europe. Art in Manchu China and Tokugawa Japan also reflected the power of emperors and the social distinction of nobles. Japanese samurai displayed their wealth through elegant paintings and silk screens decorated with scenes from varied aspects of life, while all arts of the Qing Dynasty were organized to exalt and glorify the Chinese emperor and state. As page 965 illustrates, the Qing dealt harshly with art perceived as heretical; hence Chinese artists of that period, discouraged from innovation, rarely displayed the brilliance of their predecessors.

Nonetheless, the Western enthusiasm for Chinese art inspired its abundant production, particularly in the medium of porcelain. The *famille verte* style of pottery, characterized by foliated edges and elegant court scenes and beautiful landscapes, was especially popular; the 4¼-inch bowl pictured below is an impressive example. *(Ashmolean Museum, Oxford.)* Its reception in Europe is just one instance of the impact of cultures on one another, as shown through art.

Saint Mark's Square: Looking South-East Canaletto (1697–1768). The Venetian Canaletto worked primarily for wealthy aristocrats. His most enthusiastic patrons were English nobles, who bought many of his magnificent views of historic Venice while making the continental "grand tour" that topped off the education of the English upper class. This lively scene *(above)* features Saint Mark's on the left, the Ducal Palace, ships in the lagoon, and market stalls. *(National Gallery of Art, Washington, Gift of Mrs. Barbara Hutton)*

A Woman Weighing Gold *(facing page)* Vermeer (about 1657). Vermeer painted pictures of middle-class women involved in ordinary activities in the quiet interiors of their homes. Unrivaled among Dutch masters for his superb control of light, in this painting Vermeer shows the woman weighing gold on her scales. *(National Gallery of Art, Washington, Widener Collection)*

Japanese Combat Scene In the late eighteenth century, during the long Tokugawa peace (pages 290–292), Japanese artists drew inspiration from the many legends of samurai warfare in earlier centuries. This six-leaf screen *(above),* probably from the home of a lord or wealthy merchant, provides useful information about armor and weapons. The shortage of iron in Japan meant that most armor consisted of layers of heavily padded cloth. *(Courtesy of Christie's, London/The Bridgeman Art Library)*

Burning of the Books (about 1780). The vivid scene on the next page illustrates the royal absolutism of the Qing rulers in China (page 573), a period which witnessed both the compilation of the great imperial manuscript collection, *The Four Treasuries,* and a literary inquisition that lasted for more than 15 years. In this painting the emperor displays his domination of the Chinese learned world by ordering the burning of books considered anti-Qing, a judgment that was applied to a great range of works, from rebellious tracts to writing that was merely judged unliterary. *(Bibliothèque Nationale, Paris/E. T. Archive)*

Ashanti Staff Top *(left)* In the early eighteenth century, the Ashanti of central Ghana expanded northward, subdued various peoples, and established a powerful successor state to the medieval African kingdoms of Ghana and Mali. The gold trade was the basis for its economic and political power. A splendid example of the Ashanti's superb skill in gold-working, this staff top reflects the region's great wealth. *(Lee Boltin)*

The Spinners *(below)* Diego Velázquez (1599–1660). In the foreground of this masterpiece, five servant women perform the menial task of transforming bundles of wool into yarn for weaving, while in the studio behind, elegant ladies watch a mythological figure weave a tapestry (from a story in Ovid's *Metamorphoses*). Velázquez intended to suggest the distinction between craft and art, between the worlds of myth and reality, and between the humble and aristocratic. *(Museo del Prado, Madrid)*

Woman with a Parrot (seventeenth century). Birds and animals were favorite subjects of Islamic painters in Mogul India (also see page 274). This painting dates from the seventeenth century, during the reign of Aurangzeb (page 275). *(By courtesy of the Board of Trustees of the Victoria & Albert Museum/E. T. Archive)*

Self-Portrait Judith Leyster (about 1609–1660). The Dutch artist Judith Leyster painted portraits and scenes from daily life in the city of Haarlem in Holland. While still in her early twenties, Leyster became the only female member of the Haarlem painters' guild. In this self-portrait, she turns from her easel to look at the viewer with calm self-possession. The painting before her shows the figure of a musician holding his violin and bow, while Leyster holds the tools of her own trade—a palette and brush. *(National Gallery of Art, Washington; Gift of Mr. and Mrs. Robert Woods Bliss)*

EIGHTEENTH AND NINETEENTH CENTURIES

In the eighteenth century some European artists recalled the Renaissance by choosing to focus on aristocratic lifestyles and interests. The Romantic artists of the eighteenth and nineteenth centuries, however, rejected worldly interests and sought to reach new levels of emotional expression. Their art reflected a turbulent Europe caught up in revolutionary change. For painters such as John Constable (page 971), nature replaced reason as the proper source of inspiration.

Art shows the impact of societies and cultures on one another. The graceful Mogul painting below combines Indian, Persian, Turkish, and Arabic elements, a fusion that reflects the various sources of culture in eighteenth-century India. Typical of the best works of the Mogul period, which rested solidly on the Hindu caste system, this formalized scene of a spring festival portrays a court activity. *(By courtesy of the Board of Trustees of the Victoria & Albert Museum)*

The Hall of Mirrors by Candlelight *(above)* The splendor of Louis XIV's palace at Versailles (page 393) long served as a model of royal elegance for European monarchs. Ludwig II of Bavaria built his version of the palace of Versailles and its famous Hall of Mirrors on a large lake in southern Germany in the nineteenth century. *(Werner Neumeister/George Rainbird/Robert Harding Picture Library)*

The Haywain *(above)* John Constable (1776–1837). Even as the Industrial Revolution was transforming the land, the beauties of the English countryside were displayed in the landscapes of John Constable (page 477). In sharp contrast to Joseph Turner, England's other great Romantic painter, Constable revealed a nature that was harmonious and rich in spiritual values. The first artist of importance to paint outdoors, he strongly influenced young French painters like Eugène Delacroix (page 478). *(Reproduced by courtesy of the Trustees, The National Gallery, London)*

Japanese Tea Ceremony This delicate painting by the Japanese master Kitagawa Toshikata (about 1890) shows women preparing a tea ceremony, a custom that provides deep insights into Japanese culture. Gracious but ritualized with strict rules of dress and behavior, the ceremonial serving of tea to honored guests displays the highly prized values of courtesy, loyalty, and self-discipline. The elegant simplicity of traditional Japanese interiors is also apparent. *(E. T. Archive)*

Summer in Peking Wang Da Quang (about 1900). A neighborhood of the Chinese capital in the early twentieth century bustles with energy in this lively scene. Traditional pushcarts and rickshaws coexist with a fancy carriage and a Western bicycle as children play their games and shoppers go about their business. Despite all the activity and hard work, a certain tranquility seems to reign. *(E. T. Archive)*

Le Moulin de la Galette à Montmartre Auguste Renoir (1841–1919). The French impressionist painters (page 540) generally affirmed the beauty and value of modern life, reflecting Western Europe's nineteenth-century faith in science, progress, and democracy. In this 1876 masterpiece, Renoir transformed a popular outdoor dance hall into an enchanted land. Impressionist painters applied colors directly to the canvas without first mixing them, a revolutionary technique that let the eye participate (by itself "mixing" the colors) in creating a realistic scene. *(Cliché des Musées Nationaux-Paris)*

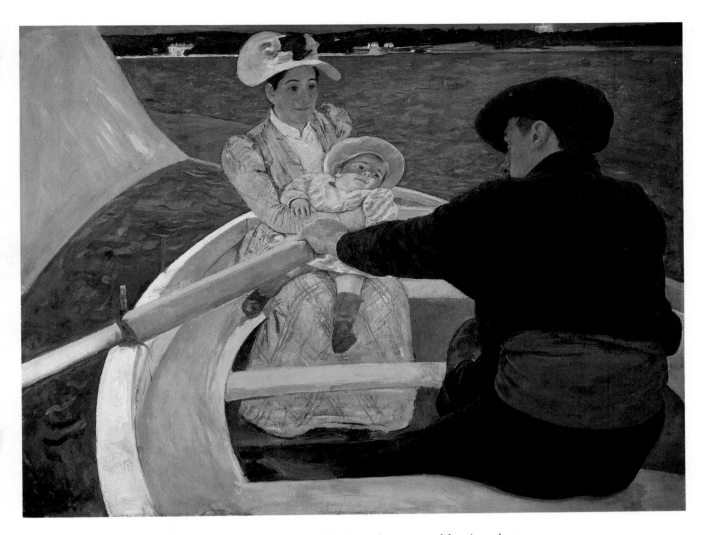

The Boating Party Mary Cassatt (1844–1926). Born into a wealthy American family, Mary Cassatt moved to Paris, where she painted mothers and their children with a sensitivity unequaled in recent times. Here she captures with tender realism an attentive mother and her squirming child on a hot afternoon outing. Cassatt helped many French impressionists by successfully encouraging American collectors to buy their paintings. (*National Gallery of Art, Washington, Chester Dale Collection*)

Young Girl from a Carved Sceptre *(below, left)* As this nineteenth-century wooden figurine from the Belgian Congo (modern Zaire) suggests, African colonies were not passive objects of European conquest. Many native rulers used diplomacy and trade to increase their own power. Warfare, though generally unsuccessful against European technological superiority, was also widespread. *(Private collection/Werner Forman Archive)*

Helmet Mask of Kuba Tribe *(below, right)* The Kuba, a Bantu-speaking people who settled in the Congo region, believed their king ruled by divine right. This ferocious mask, made of cloth, shells, beads and hemp, was a symbol of his authority. *(Lee Boltin Picture Library)*

NINETEENTH AND TWENTIETH CENTURIES

Latin American and African artists of the nineteenth and twentieth centuries emphasized nationalist themes in their work, turning against Western styles and techniques. The artifacts shown on page 979 purposefully used ancient styles to show their intent of preserving the African heritage. Similarly, in opposition to foreign control, a genuine folk culture, reflected in *Haitian Landscape* (page 978), throve in rural areas throughout Latin America.

Artists of the twentieth century in Europe anticipated and then gave expression to the anxieties and terrors that have characterized modern times.

Some continued the impressionists' experimentation with abstract design, a process that led to the cubist movement (pages 540, 542). Cubist works of art reflect the viewpoints of a society that was not as sure of its values and aims as was Europe in the nineteenth century. Other artists took part in the movement known as expressionism, which emphasized the portrayal of inner experience. In *The Dance of Life* (below), the Norwegian artist Edvard Munch showed solitary figures struggling with terror and uncertainty—a favorite theme of twentieth-century art. *(Nasjonalgalleriet, Oslo)*

Old Man with Medicine Horn *(next page, above)* This sculpture from Kenya is another example of African artists' efforts to reclaim their precolonial past. Such a man as this, empowered by his medicine horn to heal, held a revered role in the social order that preceded foreign domination. *(African Heritage Collection, Nairobi, Kenya/Werner Forman Archive)*

Multiple-Mask Headdress *(next page, below)* This ornate headdress is the work of the great Nigerian carver, Ochai of Otobi (died 1949). A committed nationalist, Ochai specialized in carvings that preserved Africa's rich heritage. *(Department of Antiquities, Lagos, Nigeria/Werner Forman Archive)*

Haitian Landscape *(detail) (below)* Jean-Gilles (born 1943). The folk art of Latin America has achieved wide popularity in recent times. The oil paintings of the young Haitian Joseph Jean-Gilles convey a fresh, unaffected view of the world. In this outstanding example hundreds of multicolored trees dot the green landscape as farmers cultivate the fields below. *(Art Museum of the Americas, Washington)*

Birthday (*above*) Marc Chagall (1889–1985). No modern artist has expressed more joyfully the enduring mystery of love than the Russian-born Jewish painter Chagall. In this 1915 painting the prospect of a birthday bouquet from his beloved Bella sends the young husband soaring in bliss. Love and fantasy go hand in hand, Chagall seems to say. (*Copyright 1991 ARS, New York/ADAGP; Photo: Carmelo Guadagno*)

The Grand Constructors (*next page*) Fernand Léger (1881–1955). The twentieth-century fascination with urban life, the machine, and workers dominates the work of this French artist. Yet the robot-like action of the workers in this 1950 picture also suggests that dehumanization may accompany our modern marvels. (*Musée National Fernand Léger, Bot/S.P.A.D.E.M., Paris/V.A.G.A., New York*)

Water Splashing Festival—Song of Life Yuan Yunshen, Lian Weiyun, and Fei Zheng (1979). Chinese artists created dozens of huge murals for the decoration of the Capital International Airport in Beijing. Though reflecting the techniques of Western as well as traditional Chinese painting, the murals were seen as an overwhelming and distinctly Chinese achievement. In this detail, people of the Dai minority group in China celebrate, with appropriately flowing gestures, their Water Splashing Festival. *(Eastfoto)*

Zapatistas *(below)* José Clemente Orozco (1931). "It is better to die on your feet than to live on your knees," rebel leader Emiliano Zapata (page 795) told the peasants who fought with him in the Mexican Revolution. The strength and unity of the "Zapatistas" are suggested by the symmetrical composition in this painting by Orozco, one of Mexico's foremost artists. *(Collection, The Museum of Modern Art, New York. Given anonymously. Oil on canvas, 45 × 55")*

Nuit de Noël *(left)* Henri Matisse (1869–1954). In his youth Matisse led avant-garde artists who delighted in breaking with tradition. This design for a church stained-glass window, however, glows with a beauty inspired by that of medieval masterpieces. *(Collection, The Museum of Modern Art, New York. Gift of Time, Inc. 1952. Gouache on cut-and pasted paper, 10′7″ × 53½″.)*